W9-AKC-292

Managing Human Resources

Fourth Edition

Luis R. Gómez-Mejía
Arizona State University

David B. Balkin
University of Colorado, Boulder

Robert L. Cardy
Arizona State University

Upper Saddle River, Ne... ersey 0745...

Library of Congress Cataloguing-in-Publication Data

Gomez-Mejia, Luis R.
Managing human resources / Luis R. Gómez-Mejia, David B. Balkin, Robert L. Cardy.—4th ed.
p. cm.
Includes bibliographical references and index.
ISBN 0-13-100943-5
1. Personnel management. I. Balkin, David B. Cardy, Robert L. Title.

HF5549 .G64 2003
658.3—dc21

Acquisitions Editor: David Parker
Editor-in-Chief: Jeff Shelstad
Assistant Editor: Ashley Keim
Editorial Assistant: Melissa Yu
Media Project Manager: Anthony Palmiotto
Executive Marketing Manager: Shannon Moore
Marketing Assistant: Amanda Fisher
Senior Managing Editor (Production): Judy Leale
Production Editor: Blake Cooper
Production Assistant: Joe DeProspero
Permissions Supervisor: Suzanne Grappi
Associate Director, Manufacturing: Vincent Scelta
Manufacturing Buyer: Diane Peirano
Design Manager: Maria Lange
Art Director: Kevin Kall
Interior Design: Karen Quigley
Cover Design: Karen Quigley
Illustrator (Interior): Rainbow Graphics
Photo Researcher: Debbie Hewitson
Image Permission Coordinator: Zina Arabia
Manager, Print Production: Christy Mahon
Composition/Full-Service Project Management: Rainbow Graphics
Printer/Binder: R.R. Donnelley

Credits and acknowledgments borrowed from other sources and reproduced, with permission, in this textbook appear throughout the text and on page 659.

Pearson Education LTD.
Pearson Education Singapore, Pte. Ltd
Pearson Education, Canada, Ltd
Pearson Education–Japan
Pearson Education Australia PTY, Limited
Pearson Education North Asia Ltd
Pearson Educación de Mexico, S.A. de C.V.
Pearson Education Malaysia, Pte. Ltd

10 9 8 7 6 5 4
ISBN 0-13-100943-5

To my two sons, Vince and Alex
—L.G.M.

To my parents, Daniel and Jeanne
—D.B.B.

To my parents, Ralph and Dorothy; my wife, Laurel;
and my two daughters, Lara and Emery

—R.L.C.

Brief Contents

Contents

Thematic Examples

Technology TOC

Global/Diversity TOC

Emerging Trends TOC

Customer-Driven HR TOC

The Plan of the Fourth Edition

How do businesses succeed in today's competitive environment? The factor that can set an organization apart is its people. The quality of the organization's employees, their enthusiasm and satisfaction with their jobs, their experience, and their sense of fair treatment all affect the firm's productivity, customer service, reputation, and survival. In short, people make the difference.

Although relatively few students in human resource management (HRM) courses will become HR specialists, virtually all will have to work with other people. Dealing with other people is a fact of organizational life, regardless of whether you are in accounting, finance, operations management, or some other area. Because we believe that every manager is a human resource manager, we've written our book for students who plan to manage others at some time in their career.

The idea that all future managers need to understand HRM issues is at the heart of *Managing Human Resources*. We cover all the core HRM topics, but our managerial perspective makes the topics meaningful to students in any area of business. Our emphasis is on how to manage human resources and how to successfully implement HRM programs. Because managers in all departments and functions confront HR issues daily, we believe this approach is better than one that looks at HRM primarily from the perspective of the HR department.

Since the first edition of *Managing Human Resources* was published, the general management perspective has become much more prevalent among practicing managers. Recent environmental and organizational forces have contributed greatly to this trend. Organizations are becoming flatter. Technology such as the Internet fosters communication between all levels of personnel, and managers are expected to be generalists with a broad set of skills, including HRM skills. At the same time, fewer firms have a highly centralized, powerful HR department that acts as monitor, decision maker, and controller of HR practices throughout the organization.

Organizations need to be more flexible than ever before to deal with a rapidly changing competitive landscape where global forces play a key role. Many traditional HR programs designed for a stable, predictable context (for instance, carefully defined jobs, which were often used as the basis for setting pay and selecting workers) may actually become a hindrance in contemporary volatile business environments. Discretion in decision making has become critical (witness the recent scandals at Andersen Consulting, WorldCom, Enron, and others), not only at the top executive ranks but also at all levels within the organization.

Information technology also encourages a managerial approach to human resources. Why? The technology has permeated most traditional HR functions, decentralizing decisions and increasing the participation of managers and employees in all aspects of HR practice. Managers and employees have greater access to human resource information, both inside and outside the company through both formal (Web pages) and informal (chat rooms and e-mail messages) means. An effect of the Internet, then, has been to democratize the turf of the traditional HR department.

The growing importance of a general management perspective to HRM has not lessened the importance of HR specialists, however. Many tools and techniques for selection, training, compensation, performance appraisal, and other traditional HR functions can greatly enhance the quality of hires, the skills of the workforce, job satisfaction, and employee motivation. But HR specialists' focus has shifted from one of control to one of advice and support to line managers. The forces reinforcing this trend include downsizing, outsourcing of the HR function, information technology, and the inclusion of HR courses in undergraduate, graduate, and executive education programs designed for the general manager (rather than the HR specialist).

Our goal for the fourth edition of *Managing Human Resources* is to emphasize a general management approach even more than we did in the three previous editions. Because of our increased emphasis on managing people, rather than on the designed HRM tools and techniques or the activities of the HRM department, this book should be relevant to every business student. We believe that no matter what area of management students aspire to, they will have to work with the most important resource—people. For instance, whom should we hire? How much should we pay the new hire? How do we handle conflict between people of different backgrounds? How do we decide who should be laid off in the case of downsizing? How do we provide performance feedback to capitalize on employees' strengths? How can ethical decisions be made when the interests of the organization (reducing cost), the manager (having a harmoniously working team), and the employee (keeping a job) may not coincide under difficult economic conditions? What should the supervisor do when a long-standing employee is accused of sexual harassment? How students manage these and other similar HR issues in the future will be a critical determinant of their effectiveness as managers and the effectiveness of their organization. Although students taking a "survey" HRM course should learn how to use HR tools or techniques that may help in addressing HR concerns, they will seldom be involved in the actual design of those tools and techniques.

Each chapter of this text takes the managerial perspective and examines issues relevant to today's managers. HRM from the managerial perspective is the overriding key to engaging the students and promoting their appreciation and learning the effective management of people. This fourth edition offers an updated and more applied content with an even clearer emphasis on the managerial perspective.

1. New chapter vignettes based on recent events are used to illustrate why the chapter content is relevant to managers.
2. Most chapters include at least one new feature titled "Manager's Notebook: Emerging Trends," which addresses the management of contemporary HR issues that have become salient since the previous edition of the text.
3. Most chapters include at least one new feature title "Manager's Notebook: Customer-Driven HR." Consistent with the general management perspective of the text, this feature provides an example of how line managers and employees act as customers that utilize HR programs to become more effective in their jobs. Furthermore, the customer-driven perspective views employees as customers of the organization's management practices. This perspective encourages students to consider the impact of management decisions on outcomes such as employee loyalty and retention. This new feature reinforces the theme that "every manager is an HR manager."
4. Based on feedback received from instructors and students using the text, we have extended the cases at the back of each chapter. At least half of the cases have been replaced in this new edition. They all include a team exercise in addition to discussion questions.
5. Two new end-of-chapter features have been added that present managerial situations that parallel the "emerging trends" and "customer-driven HR" themes discussed in the body of the text. These new features conclude with analytical questions and issues, experiential exercise, and group projects such as role-plays and debates.
6. We have greatly expanded coverage of international HR issues, which are now covered in most chapters. For instance, the management of diversity has become a major issue in western Europe where foreign workers (mostly from northern Africa and eastern Europe) now represent 10 to 20 percent of the population.
7. Over 600 new references have been added to summarize and integrate the most recent HR research.

The text is organized as follows:

- ***Chapter 1, "Meeting Present and Emerging Strategic Human Resource Challenges,"*** has been substantially revised, focusing on emerging environmental and organizational trends affecting HR practices. Some of the themes receiving special attention in the new edition include employment and compensation risk, coping with information overflow, globalization, corporate corruption, security issues, and the need to establish work/life balance to help attract and retain employees.

- ***Chapter 2, "Managing Work Flows and Conducting Job Analysis,"*** examines use of teams, including virtual teams, and problem-solving teams. The chapter has expanded coverage of outsourcing human resource management activities and examines both its costs and benefits.
- ***Chapter 3, "Understanding Equal Opportunity and the Legal Environment,"*** contains new court decisions in several areas including racial, gender, and disability forms of employment discrimination. Expanded text content is provided on pregnancy discrimination and information on how to handle a sexual harassment investigation.
- ***Chapter 4, "Managing Diversity,"*** provides numerous new examples of how firms deal with diversity issues at work. It also provides new coverage of employees with mixed identities, the special concerns of various employee groups, and how the management of diversity has become an international phenomenon as many countries around the world face unprecedented immigration and women enter the workforce in large numbers.
- ***Chapter 5, "Recruiting and Selecting Employees,"*** includes expanded coverage of the use of technology in recruitment and selection. A customer-driven focus is presented by considering job candidates as customers of the organization's selection process and by considering customers of the organization's products or services as potential employees. Background checks and security issues are given heightened consideration.
- ***Chapter 6, "Managing Employee Separations, Downsizing, and Outplacement,"*** includes expanded consideration of layoffs and how they should be handled. The costs of turnover, the use of contingent workers, and how to avoid being a layoff victim are new or expanded topics.
- ***Chapter 7, "Appraising and Managing Performance,"*** initiates new or expanded coverage of coaching, self-management, the balanced scorecard, and the use of performance review software. Coverage also includes business strategy in addition to job analysis as a source of performance criteria.
- ***Chapter 8, "Training the Workforce,"*** includes new content in e-learning and preemployment training. Coverage is expanded on the topic of reducing training costs and determining the return on investment in training.
- ***Chapter 9, "Developing Careers,"*** presents new content on the effect of telecommuting on careers and the option of switching industries more easily than careers. Coverage of career self-advancement is expanded through consideration of desirable and undesirable characteristics in today's workplace, virtual career advice, and mentoring.
- ***Chapter 10, "Managing Compensation,"*** offers expanded coverage of new trends in compensation such as use of variable pay to minimize layoffs, employees' exposure to stock market risks, application of information technology to make compensation decisions, the design of global compensation programs, and the passage of "living wage" legislation in several metropolitan areas.
- ***Chapter 11, "Rewarding Performance,"*** offers expanded treatment of the positive and negative effects of incentive programs. New coverage includes nonmonetary incentives, educating employees on pay-related risks, the use of compensation systems worldwide, contemporary trends in executive pay, and incentive management on the Web.
- ***Chapter 12, "Designing and Administering Benefits,"*** includes expanded coverage of 401(k) retirement plans with a discussion of the investment risk associated with keeping a large percentage of retirement plan funds invested in an employer's stock. An international comparison of unemployment insurance benefits coverage in the United States has been provided. Finally, new content on health insurance plans for small businesses and self-employed individuals has been added to the text.
- ***Chapter 13, "Developing Employee Relations,"*** has increased emphasis on developing employee relations through technology, such as the use of Web sites for grievances that can be rapidly addressed by managers and the use of Internet-based job satisfaction surveys that provide immediate employee feedback on various company policies and initiatives. Expanded coverage is also provided on public recognition programs designed to improve employee morale.

- ***Chapter 14, "Respecting Employee Rights and Managing Discipline,"*** includes new content on employer restrictions on office romance between employees and the debate over the use of no-dating policies within companies. New information on employee drug-testing policies has been added including coverage on preemployment and probable cause drug-testing procedures.
- ***Chapter 15, "Working with Organized Labor,"*** has updated information on emerging trends in labor union growth, labor contracts, strike activities, and labor relations in other countries. Expanded content has been added on the Railway Labor Act and the Weingarten right of a union employee, which is derived from a court case that gave unionized employees the right to have a union representative present during a disciplinary investigation.
- ***Chapter 16, "Managing Workplace Safety and Health,"*** includes new content on depression and hearing loss. Online approaches to increasing fitness are a new consideration as are managing threats from bioterrorism and desk rage.
- ***Chapter 17, "International HR Challenge,"*** has been thoroughly updated, including new material on worldwide recruiting, women expatriates, balancing the need for global integration with tailor-made HR policies to fit particular cultures, and the use of information technology to access skilled labor in different countries around the world.

Themes

In addition to the managerial perspective, we thread several themes throughout this book, including:

- The need to provide customer-driven HR programs and services to managers and employees
- The need to analyze emerging trends impacting HRM practices and develop proactive responses to deal with them
- The need to foster cooperation between line managers and the HR department
- The importance of operating within a legal framework and acting ethically
- The effects of reorganizing, outsourcing, and quality management on HRM
- Workforce diversity as a source of competitive advantage in the global economy
- The changing forces of technology and their implications for HRM

Features

Managing Human Resources contains a number of innovative pedagogical features. Every chapter contains *learning objectives* phrased as management challenges, an *opening vignette* that draws students into the chapter, a *running marginal glossary of key terms*, a *summary*, a *list of key terms* with page references, *discussion and review* questions, and *end-of chapter notes* and *references*. In addition, each chapter contains these features:

The Managerial Perspective

This chapter introductory section previews what's to come in the chapter and how the HR material is relevant to managers.

Question of Ethics

Several of these segments raise ethical questions that relate to the chapter's content. They are designed to provoke thought and debate on issues that are not easily resolved.

Manager's Notebooks

Approximately two thirds of the Manager's Notebooks are new in this fourth edition. They are divided into three categories. These notebooks provide management advice on a variety of issues that managers confront daily, from providing feedback during an appraisal session to preparing employees for a layoff. A second type of notebook is new to this fourth edition, which we call "emerging trends." These Manager's Notebooks discuss issues that are becoming important to HRM practice and that are likely to require increased attention in the future. For instance, many countries around the world have recently enacted legislation to facilitate or actively encourage the use of stock-based incentive plans. This means that multinational firms need to reconsider their incentive plans to adapt to this new trend. The third type of Manager's Notebooks is also new to this fourth edition, which we call "customer-driven HR." These Manager's Notebooks examine HR practices illustrating how managers and employees can benefit by approaching employees as internal customers. For instance, one of these Manager's Notebooks illustrates how line managers and employees can instantly access salary data on their own for hundreds of positions, analyzed to meet their needs (e.g., by location, by experience).

Issues and Applications

To give extended applications that relate to HR topics, we have Issues and Applications features in every chapter that showcase HR practices (both good and bad) around the globe. For instance, Chapter 9 spotlights the glass ceiling in Asia and a feature in Chapter 11 addresses the surge in piecework due to the Internet. Over 35 percent of these features are new.

"You Manage It!" Discussion Cases

Each chapter concludes with four cases based on scenarios from actual companies. Approximately two thirds of these cases are new. Based on feedback received from the prior edition, we have lengthened the cases to provide more in-depth coverage, and for each we have included critical thinking questions and team exercises. The "You Manage It!" cases are now divided into three categories, two of which are new. The first category, which we call "discussion case," is similar to the concept successfully used in previous editions. The detail and length of the case study offer a challenging student assignment for individual analysis and group work. The second category, which we call "emerging trends," is new to this fourth edition. It provides an example that illustrates an HR-related issue that is likely to require increased attention in the future. Students are asked to analyze the situation by responding to critical thinking questions and engaging in team-based exercises. The third category, which we call "customer-driven HR," is also new to this fourth edition. It provides an example that illustrates how managers and employees can be effectively serviced by HR programs or how to overcome the roadblocks that make it difficult for particular HR programs to be helpful to the end users. Students are also asked to analyze the situation by responding to critical thinking questions and engaging in team-based exercises.

Managerial Challenge: Discussion Questions

Approximately half of the discussion questions at the end of each chapter have been replaced. This section has been reworked by expanding the length of the coverage for the issues at hand and focusing the question on the managerial challenges involved.

New Part-Ending On Location! Videos

There are 6 new videos each with discussion questions throughout this book. These cases have an applied focus that helps students build their HR management skills. Parts 2 through 6 close with a new video case and discussion questions. These cases have an applied focus that helps students build their HR management skills.

In addition, each chapter includes numerous examples of HRM practices at a wide variety of companies, from small, service-providing organizations to huge megacorporations. A concise dictionary of HRM terminology is provided at the end of the book, along with a subject index and a name, company, and product index.

The Teaching and Learning Package

Each component of the teaching and learning package has been carefully crafted to ensure that the HRM course is rewarding for both instructors and students.

Instructor's Manual

- A chapter overview/lecture launcher
- Annotated outline (including all text features)
- Answers to all end-of-chapter discussion questions and end-of-chapter "You Manage It!" critical thinking questions
- Sample syllabi
- Key to PowerPoints

Text Web Site www.prenhall.com/gomez

The text Web site features cases and articles designed to support student research. Level-one cases include cases from previous editions as well as cases not included in the text that the authors want to make available to students. The authors will update level-one cases twice yearly to coincide with the beginning of each semester.

Level-two cases and readings are drawn from the Xanedu/Proquest database and are thematically organized to correspond with the table of contents. Level-two cases and readings include selections from scholarly journals, business media, and popular press. These cases and readings will also be updated twice yearly to coincide with the beginning of each semester.

For Instructors

Text-specific faculty resources include downloadable supplements (Instructor's Manual, PowerPoint presentations, and test item file).

For Students—Student Version of PowerPoint Package

The Student PowerPoints (available on the Web only) are black and white, contain no teaching notes, and do not have graphics. These Student PowerPoints allow a student to print the slides at home, bring them to class, follow along with the instructor's PowerPoints, and take notes.

Test Item File

The *Test Item File* contains 17 chapters of 140+ questions per chapter, all of which have been carefully checked for accuracy and quality. This comprehensive set consists of multiple-choice, case, true/false, short answer, and essay questions. Each test question is ranked by level of difficulty (easy, moderate, or difficult), type of question (recall, integration, or application), and contains page references to give the instructor a quick and easy way to balance the level of exams or quizzes.

PH Custom Test

The test item file is designed as a computerized package that allows users to custom design, save, and generate classroom tests. Available on CD-ROM, PH Custom Test gives instructors the ability to edit, add, or delete questions from the test item file and to export files to various word processing programs including Word and WordPerfect.

PowerPoint Package

There are more than 300 slides on the PowerPoint CD that accompanies the fourth edition of *Managing Human Resources*. The majority of these slides also contain useful teaching notes. The final slide for each chapter is entitled "Case" and contains an exercise based on chapter material. This case can be discussed by the entire class or by dividing the class into small groups that report back and compare notes. Each case applies its corresponding chapter material to a real-world setting.

On Location! Human Resource Management Video

Six videos offer students the opportunity to view real-life HR executives from companies like BMG and Hotjobs, who discuss current human resource issues such as sexual harassment and discrimination, recruiting, the complexities of restructuring, incentives and benefits, labor relations, and the successes and failures of expatriate employees.

Acknowledgments

The contributions of many people made this book possible. The support and contributions of David Parker, Jeff Shelstad, Melissa Yu, Ashley Keim, and Jessica Sabloff also made a tremendous difference.

The production and manufacturing teams at Prentice Hall also deserve special mention. Production Editor Blake Cooper handled the details, scheduling, and management of this project with grace and aplomb. Many thanks, also, to Judy Leale, Arnold Vila, and Vincent Scelta. Kudos to Permissions Supervisor Suzanne Grappi and Photo Researcher Elaine Soares. Without their assistance many visuals and text items would never have made their way into this book.

Our experience in working with everyone at Prentice Hall has been superb. Everyone at PH approached this book with commitment and enthusiasm. We were partners with the PH staff and feel that we are part of a high-performance work team. We appreciate the commitment they displayed and would like to thank them for the experience.

We would also like to thank the many colleagues who reviewed the manuscript and offered valuable feedback. Their comments were pivotal in the development of the text:

Uzo Anakwe	Pace University
Kamala Arogyaswamy	University of South Dakota
Kristen Backhaus	SUNY New Paltz
Trevor Bain	University of Alabama
Murray Barrick	University of Iowa
Richard Bartlett	Muskingum Tech College
Deborah Bishop	Saginaw Valley State
Larry Brandt	Nova Southeastern University
Mark Butler	San Diego State University
Steve Childers	East Carolina University
Denise Daniels	Seattle Pacific University
Kermit Davis	Auburn University
Kerry Davis	Auburn University
Michelle Dean	University of North Texas
Rebby Diehl	Salt Lake Community College
Cathy DuBois	Kent State University
Rebecca Ellis	California Polytechnic State University
Anne Fiedler	Barry University
Hugh Findley	Troy State University
David Foote	Middle Tennessee State University
David A. Hofmann	Michigan State University
David Kaplan	James Madison University
Anachai Kongchan	Chulalongkor University
Lewis Lash	Barry University
Stan Malos	San Jose State
Joe Mosca	Monmouth University
Paul Muchinsky	University of North Carolina/Greensboro
Elaine Potoker	Maine Maritime Academy
Jim Sethi	University of Montana-Western
Janice Smith	North Carolina A&T
Howard Stager	Buff State
Cynthia Sutton	Indiana University

Thomas Tang	Middle Tennessee State University
Edward Ward	St. Cloud State
Sandy Wayne	University of Illinois at Chicago
Les Wiletzky	Hawaii Pacific University
Carol Young	Wittenberg University

Finally, this book would not have been possible without the indulgence of family and friends. We sincerely appreciate the patience and tolerance that were extended to us as we wrote the fourth edition.

Luis R. Gómez-Mejía
David B. Balkin
Robert L. Cardy

About The Authors

Luis R. Gómez-Mejía holds the Horace Steel chair in the W. P. Carey College of Business at Arizona State University. He received his Ph.D. and M.A. in industrial relations from the University of Minnesota and a B.A. in economics from the University of Minnesota. Prior to entering academia, Professor Gómez-Mejía worked for eight years in human resources for the City of Minneapolis and Control Data Corporation. He has served as consultant to numerous organizations since then. Prior to joining ASU, he taught at the University of Colorado and the University of Florida. He has served two terms on the editorial board of the Academy of Management Journal and is editor and cofounder of the Journal of High Technology Management Research. He has published over 120 articles appearing in the most prestigious management journals including the Academy of Management Journal, Administrative Science Quarterly, Strategic Management Journal, Industrial Relations, and Personnel Psychology. He has also written and edited a dozen management books published by Prentice Hall, Southwestern Press, JAI Press, and Grid. He was ranked one of the top nine in research productivity based on the number of publications in the Academy of Management Journal. He has received numerous awards including "best article" in the Academy of Management Journal (1992) and Council of 100 Distinguished Scholars at Arizona State University (1994). Professor Gómez-Mejía's research focuses on macro HR issues, international HR practices, and compensation.

David B. Balkin Is Professor of Management in the College of Business Administration at the University of Colorado at Boulder. He received his Ph.D. in industrial relations from the University of Minnesota. Prior to joining the University of Colorado, he served on the faculties of Louisiana State University and Northeastern University. He has published over 35 articles appearing in such journals as the Academy of Management Journal, Strategic Management Journal, Industrial Relations, Personnel Psychology, Journal of Labor Research, and Academy of Management Executive. One of his publications (coauthored with Luis R. Gómez-Mejía) was selected as the best article published in 1992 in the Academy of Management Journal. Professor Balkin has written or edited three books on HRM topics. He has consulted for a number of organizations, including U.S. West, Baxter Healthcare, Hydro Quebec, and The Commonwealth of Massachusetts. Professor Balkin's research focuses on the interaction between business strategy and HR policies, and the design and implementation of reward systems.

Robert L. Cardy Is Professor of Management in the W. P. Carey College of Business at Arizona State University. He received his Ph.D. in industrial/organizational psychology from Virginia Tech in 1982. He is an ad hoc reviewer for a variety of journals, including the Academy of Management Journal and the Academy of Management Review. He is editor and cofounder of the Journal of Quality Management. Professor Cardy has been recognized for his research, teaching, and service. He was ranked in the top 20 in research productivity for the decade 1980–89 based on the number of publications in the Journal of Applied Psychology. He was doctoral coordinator in ASU's management department for five years and received a University Mentor Award in 1993 for his work with doctoral students. He authors a regular column on current issues in HRM and received an Academy of Management certificate for outstanding service as a columnist for the HR division newsletter. Professor Cardy was a 1992 recipient of a certificate for significant contributions to the quality of life for students at ASU. His research focuses on performance appraisal and effective HRM practices in a quality-oriented organizational environment.

Part I: Introduction

Meeting Present and Emerging Strategic Human Resource Challenges

Challenges

After reading this chapter, you should be able to deal more effectively with the following challenges:

1. **Explain** how a firm's human resources influence its performance.
2. **Describe** how firms can use HR initiatives to cope with workplace changes and trends such as a more diverse workforce, the global economy, downsizing, and new legislation.
3. **Distinguish** between the role of the HR department and the role of the firm's managers in utilizing human resources effectively.
4. **Indicate** how members of the HR department and managers within a company can establish a strong partnership.
5. **Formulate** and implement HR strategies that can help the firm achieve a sustained competitive advantage.
6. **Identify** HR strategies that fit corporate and business unit strategies.

According to business experts, "Most Americans have had no choice but to become more risk tolerant."[1] This is because most American workers face some form of employment and compensation risk, and this risk continues to increase unabatedly over the years. Corporate America has rescinded its tacit promise of long-term employment security. In 1999, one of the most prosperous years in U.S. history, U.S. companies laid off more workers than in times of recession. Four years later, as the economy slowed down, layoffs increased even more, to approximately 2 million job cuts.[2] At the same time, the use of temporary workers has become a standard practice.[3] The use of variable incentive pay has increased to the extent that, as a percentage of total compensation, it is now triple what it was about a decade ago. The result is many workers cannot predict exactly how much they will get paid. And the recent cases of Enron, Global Crossing, Polaroid, WorldCom, and Xerox, among many other companies, have vividly shown that pay risk is very real, with large numbers of workers losing much of their wealth almost overnight as stock prices plummeted.

There is a positive side to these trends. By sharing employment and compensation risk with workers, companies can get the work done without hiring more people. They can also shift resources from salary expenses to other investments such as information technology. As productivity stayed strong during the past decade and companies did not have to commit to high fixed salaries, real compensation rose faster than at almost any time in history. Despite a huge influx of immigrants, expected to depress earnings at the bottom of the wage structure, real earnings for less skilled labor rose by 120 percent in the 1990s versus a decline of 35 percent from 1982 to 1991.[4] In other words, employees bear more risk with their pay in exchange for the potential to earn more. And greater reliance on temporary employees also means that it is easier for workers to find new jobs when they become unemployed.[5] For many employees who are dissatisfied with a corporate setting or face the possibility of being laid off, entrepreneurship represents a way out. Seventy percent of *Inc. Magazine*'s 500 firms were started by entrepreneurs who got their original idea while working for other employers.[6] And contrary to conventional wisdom that jobs would move overseas as globalization increased, foreign firms invested $1.3 trillion in U.S. factories and businesses during the past decade, surpassing U.S. investments abroad and, thereby providing the resources for much of the improvements made in information technology equipment and software and creating a large number of jobs.

This book deals with the managerial challenges firms face as they try to use human resources effectively. This book is for all future managers, not just those who plan to work in a human resources department, because we believe that each manager is a human resources manager. We offer helpful guidelines and information that managers—from supervisors to top executives—can apply to everyday situations. For instance, we examine how to hire and retain the best people, reward employees fairly, train and develop employees, and use a diverse workforce to gain a competitive advantage.

THE MANAGERIAL PERSPECTIVE

This book is about the people who work in an organization and their relationship with that organization. Different terms are used to describe these people: *employees, associates* (at Wal-Mart, for instance), *personnel, human resources*. None of these terms is better than the others, and they often are used interchangeably. The term we have chosen for the title of this text, and which we will use throughout, is **human resources (HR).*** It has gained widespread acceptance over the last decade because it expresses the belief that workers are a valuable and sometimes irreplaceable resource. Effective human resource management (HRM) is a major component of any manager's job.

Human resources (HR) People who work in an organization. Also called *personnel.*

Human resource strategy A firm's deliberate use of human resources to help it gain or maintain an edge against its competitors in the marketplace. The grand plan or general approach an organization adopts to ensure that it effectively uses its people to accomplish its mission.

Human resource tactic A particular HR policy or program that helps to advance a firm's strategic goal.

A **human resource strategy** refers to a firm's deliberate use of human resources to help it gain or maintain an edge against its competitors in the marketplace.[7] It is the grand plan or general approach an organization adopts to ensure that it effectively uses its people to accomplish its mission. A **human resource tactic** is a particular policy or program that helps to advance a firm's strategic goal. Strategy precedes and is more important than tactics. The opening examples illustrate how companies are using HR strategies, such as sharing compensation risk with employees, to remain competitive in rapidly changing markets.

In this chapter, we focus on the general framework within which specific HR activities and programs fit. With the help of the company's human resources department (HR department, for short), managers implement the chosen HR strategies.[8] In subsequent chapters, we move from the general to the specific and examine in detail the spectrum of HR strategies (for example, those regarding work design, staffing, performance appraisal, career planning, and compensation).[9]

---

*All terms in boldface also appear in the Key Terms list at the end of the chapter.

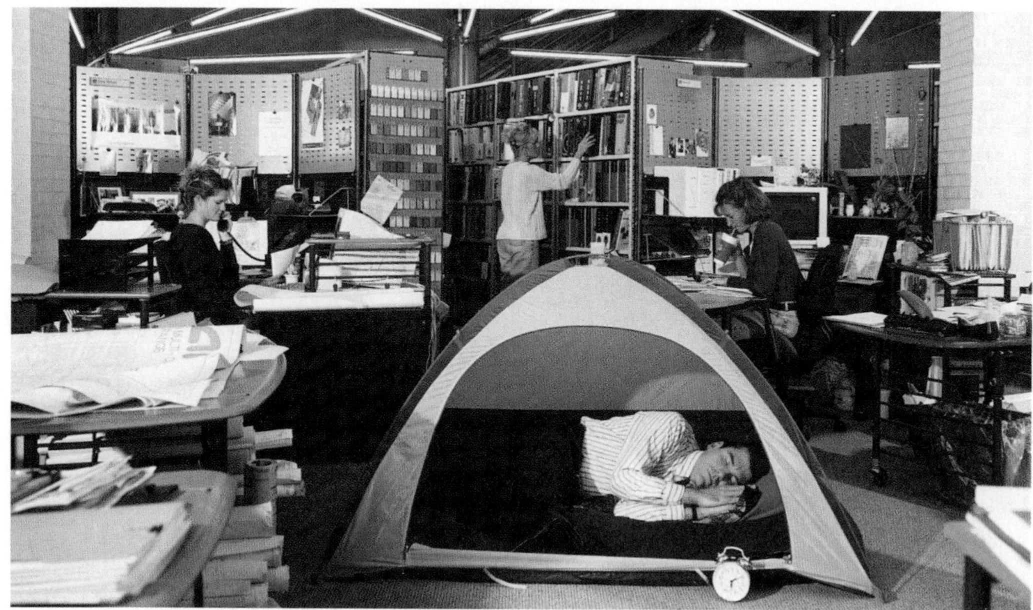

Businesses are finding innovative ways to retain employees who must work harder than ever to keep their firms competitive. Architectural firm Gould Evans Goodman has a "nap tent" for workers to use whenever they need to catch up on sleep. Other businesses offer employees benefits such as on-site yoga classes, sculpting lessons, and concierge services.

Human Resource Management: The Challenges

Before we take up the HR challenges that face managers, we need to define *manager* and say a word about where human resources fit into the organization. **Managers** are people who are in charge of others and are responsible for the timely and correct execution of actions that promote their units' successful performance. In this book, we use the term *unit* broadly; it may refer to a work team, department, business unit, division, or corporation.

Manager
A person who is in charge of others and is responsible for the timely and correct execution of actions that promote his or her unit's success.

All employees (including managers) can be differentiated as line or staff. **Line employees** are directly involved in producing the company's good(s) or delivering the service(s). A *line manager* manages line employees. **Staff employees** are those who support the line function. For example, people who work in the HR department are considered staff employees because their job is to provide supporting services for line employees. Employees may also be differentiated according to how much responsibility they have. *Senior employees* are those who have been with the company longer and have more responsibility than *junior employees*. *Exempt employees* (sometimes called *salaried employees*) are those who do not receive extra pay for overtime work (beyond 40 hours per week). *Nonexempt employees* do receive overtime compensation. This text is written primarily to help students who intend to be managers deal effectively with the challenges of managing people.

Line employee
An employee involved directly in producing the company's good(s) or delivering the service(s).

Staff employee
An employee who supports line employees.

Figure 1.1 on page 4 summarizes the major HR challenges facing today's managers. Firms that deal with these challenges effectively are likely to outperform those that do not. These challenges may be categorized according to their primary focus: the environment, the organization, or the individual.

Environmental Challenges

Environmental challenges are the forces external to the firm. They influence organizational performance but are largely beyond management's control. Managers, therefore, need to monitor the external environment constantly for opportunities and threats. They must also maintain the flexibility to react quickly to challenges. One common and effective method for monitoring the environment is to read the business press, including *BusinessWeek*, *Fortune*, and the *Wall Street Journal*. (The Appendix at the end of this book provides an annotated listing of both general business publications and more specialized publications on HR management and related topics.)

Environmental challenges
Forces external to a firm that affect the firm's performance but are beyond the control of management.

Seven important environmental challenges today are rapid change, the rise of the Internet, workforce diversity, globalization, legislation, evolving work and family roles, and skill shortages and the rise of the service sector.

Key HR Challenges for Today's Managers

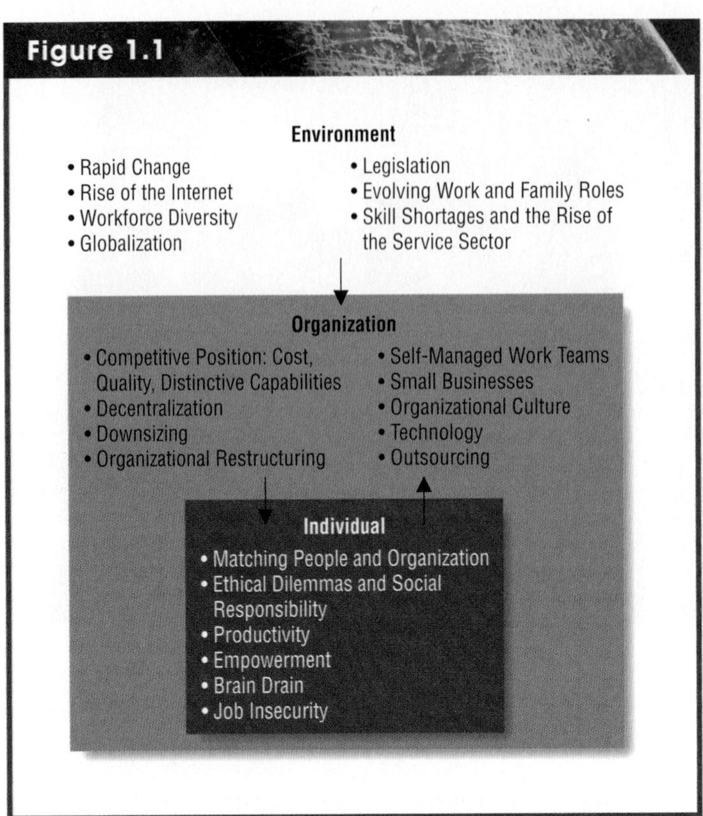

Figure 1.1
Environment
• Rapid Change
• Rise of the Internet
• Workforce Diversity
• Globalization
• Legislation
• Evolving Work and Family Roles
• Skill Shortages and the Rise of the Service Sector
Organization
• Competitive Position: Cost, Quality, Distinctive Capabilities
• Decentralization
• Downsizing
• Organizational Restructuring
• Self-Managed Work Teams
• Small Businesses
• Organizational Culture
• Technology
• Outsourcing
Individual
• Matching People and Organization
• Ethical Dilemmas and Social Responsibility
• Productivity
• Empowerment
• Brain Drain
• Job Insecurity

A Question of Ethics

How much responsibility does an organization have to shield its employees from the effects of rapid change in the environment? What risks does this type of "shock absorber" approach to management entail?

Rapid Change

Many organizations face a volatile environment in which change is nearly constant.[10] For this reason IBM's new CEO, Sam Palmisano, tells his managers that he doesn't believe in forecasts longer than one week.[11] If they are to survive and prosper, they need to adapt to change quickly and effectively. Human resources are almost always at the heart of an effective response system. Here are a few examples of how HR policies can help or hinder a firm grappling with external change:

- **New company town** As firms experience high pressure to become more productive and deal with very short product life cycles (often measured in months), Americans are working longer, harder, and faster. As a result, the line between home and work is blurred for many employees. To deal with this phenomenon, observes sociologist Helen Mederer at University of Rhode Island, "companies are taking the best aspects of home and incorporating them into work."[12]

  For instance, BMC Software in Boston (one of *Fortune's* 100 best companies to work for), implements this policy:

  > [W]ithin the compound's high walls, people laze on hammocks strung between pine trees. Others pump iron in the gym, practice their jump shot on the gleaming basketball court, or hang around the putting green, horseshoe pits, or beach volleyball court. Cooks harvest oregano from the herb garden for the day's meal. Free bananas are everywhere. And an array of services—bank, store, dry cleaner, hairdresser, nail salon—complete the self-contained community.

  As 30-year-old Christine Choi notes: "You never have to leave the place."[13]

- **Dealing with stress** Rapid change and work overload can put employees under a great deal of stress. In 2003, the Bureau of Labor Statistics reported that 50 percent of the 19.8 million Americans who say they work at home at least once a week aren't compensated for it. In other words, millions of employees must work at home just in order to catch up.[14]

  Unless the organization develops support mechanisms to keep stress manageable, both the firm and employees may pay a heavy price. In some extreme cases, workplace violence may result. Typically, however, the observed results of poorly handled stress are more subtle yet still highly destructive, costing the company money. "As microchip power has doubled every 18 months, workloads and stress levels have ballooned, too. More and more executives are fizzling from the pressure, developing blowout tempers, micromanaging down to the paper clips, and firing off foul-mouthed flame mail."[15] To deal with this, firms facing very rapid change—such as Sun Microsystems and Intel—pay the Growth and Leadership Center (GLC) in Mountain View, California, an average of $12,000 a head for weekly coaching sessions lasting 10 weeks for key employees on the border of burnout due to stress. Most of these "coached" employees were "prodigies on meteoric tears through their companies" before their career derailed because they could not handle the stress.[16]

Throughout this book we emphasize how HR practices can enable a firm to respond quickly and effectively to external changes.

The Internet Revolution

The dramatic growth of the Internet in recent years probably represents the single most important environmental trend affecting organizations and their human resource practices. In the mid-1990s, the term *Web economy* had not yet been coined; it is now a common phrase in business circles.[17] The statistics also indicate that the "Web economy" is not just a hyperbole. U.S. corporations' spending on Internet technology quintupled between 1998 and 2003. According to the Commerce Department, 54 percent of Americans were using the Internet in 2002—over twice as many as only three years earlier.[18] The percentage of firms using the Internet as part of their normal business practices has quadrupled since early 1998, reaching the astonishing figure of 80 percent at the start of the millennium.[19] The Internet is having pervasive impact on how organizations manage their human resources, as the following examples show:

- **Necessitating greater written communication skills** Companies have discovered that Internet technology creates a high demand for workers who can deal effectively with e-mail messages.[20] This skill is key if companies want to keep fickle Internet customers loyal, making them less likely to go to a competitor by simply tapping a few keystrokes.

  E-mail writing may also involve legal issues. For instance, an employee's e-mail response to a customer complaint may be legally binding on the firm, and there is the "written" record to prove it. This means that this new "faceless" technology is pushing organizations to pay much greater attention to literary skills among employees than ever before.

  And, although English is the main language of the Internet, almost half of Internet communication takes place in foreign languages and only 7 percent of users on a global basis are native English speakers.[21] Major multimillion-dollar blunders due to language problems have already been documented, such as the case of Juan Pablo Davila, a commodity trader in Chile. He typed the word "buy" on the computer by mistake instead of "sell." To rectify his mistake, he started a frenzy of buying and selling, losing 0.5 percent of his country's GNP. His name became [an Internet-related] verb, "davilar," meaning "to screw up royally."[22] In addition, Internet and e-mail technology demands greater cross-cultural sensitivity on the part of employees who must deal with an increasingly diverse customer base, often with limited English skills.[23]
- **Dealing with information overflow** The use of e-mail has grown by more than 600 percent since the late 1990s, with approximately 1.4 trillion messages sent from business alone in North America during 2002.[24] Although executives spend on average four hours a day receiving, checking, preparing, and sending e-mails, they are still spending 130 minutes a day in formal and informal face-to-face meetings. According to Neil Flett, CEO of a large communication consulting firm, "While some have seen e-mail as a time-saving device, e-mail appears to be adding to the time spent communicating in business, not reducing time."[25]

  According to some estimates, almost a third of e-mails received by employees were not directly relevant to their jobs, and considering that employees are now receiving an average of 30 e-mails each day, this may translate into as much as one hour a day of lost productivity.[26]
- **Redefining jobs** The Internet is raising a surprisingly complex question: What constitutes a core business? Is it a set of related products? A body of knowledge or intellectual property? A process for providing services? Or is it a means for putting together orders that can be deployed across multiple industries, as exemplified by online retailer Amazon.com? As noted

by the *Wall Street Journal*, "Companies today have much more freedom to choose what they want to be."[27] As a result, jobs are becoming more ambiguous and the old paradigm of matching people's current skills to jobs is being rendered obsolete in many organizations. In the Internet age, adaptability has become a key trait needed to succeed.[28]

- **Breaking down labor market barriers** More than ever before, the Internet is creating an open labor market where information about prospective employees and firms is available on a global basis and may be obtained quickly and inexpensively.[29] There are at least 2,500 job sites that promise to match job seekers and employers. For instance, Monster.com receives some 2.5 million unduplicated visitors a month; its extensive listings are gathered by 200 salespeople who call on corporations.[30] The job sites help workers obtain direct access to many job opportunities that were difficult to spot before the Internet was used. In addition, the ease of sending résumés to multiple Web recruiters means that companies must respond quickly to attractive candidates' résumés. If companies delay, they will lose the chance to woo applicants because other companies will have done so first, says Neil Fox, chief information officer of Management Recruiters International, Cleveland.[31] One added benefit of Internet recruitment is that non-job-related factors such as race, gender, ethnic origin, sexual preference, disabilities, and the like are less likely to play a role in hiring decisions unless the applicant wishes to divulge this information.
- **Keeping workers from leaving** A more efficient labor market is probably fueling turnover of workers who are unhappy with their current employer, forcing firms to treat employees better or risk losing talent to competitors.[32] For instance, at WRQ in Seattle, a software company, besides high financial incentives, 95 percent of its employees have flexible work hours, most offices have magnificent mountain views, and facilities include a nap room with futons, on-site massages, and dock space for kayaking commuters.[33]
- **Using online learning** Corporate training has always been dominated by in-house traditional "paper-and-pencil" training programs. Over the last five to eight years, however, there has been a tremendous migration from classroom learning to online learning.[34] For example, General Motors and the U.S. Army have launched major Internet training programs, as highlighted in the Issues and Applications feature titled "E-Learning Reaches Employees Everywhere." From 2003 to 2005, corporate spending on online training and education is likely to increase from $9 billion to $18 billion.[35]

Issues and Applications

E-Learning Reaches Employees Everywhere

Talk about a headache. General Motors Corp. (GM) has 175,000 employees at thousands of dealerships located across the United States. Training employees in how to sell and service new car models takes months and costs a small fortune. "It can take three to four months to reach everyone," notes Jacques Pasquier, the person in charge of training for GM's dealerships.

Enter new technology. GM is installing interactive distance learning (IDL) technology in all its U.S. dealerships. The technology means that GM trainers can reach employees at the dealerships and teach a live course beamed in by satellite. Those who take the courses can ask the instructor questions and see the instructor's every move. Pasquier asserts that through IDL he will be able to reach his workforce in less than a week—without the cost of sending employees to hotels or trainers to locations all over the country.

The U.S. Army is taking a different approach to e-learning. It now offers more than 1,000 information technology courses to its 479,000 enlisted personnel. SmartForce, an Internet educational company, provides the courses for the Army via the Internet.

E-learning via satellite or the Internet is taking off in the corporate world. International Data Corp. estimates that 1998 revenue in the corporate e-learning market was $550 million, compared to projected revenues of $9.1 million in 2004. E-learning cannot completely replace classroom-based courses, but it is fast becoming an accepted, cost-effective alternative.

Source: *BusinessWeek* (2000, January 10). Log on for company training, 140. See also Symmonds, W. C. (2002, Dec. 3). Giving it the old online try. *BusinessWeek*, 76–80; and Boyle, M. (2002, March 18). They are counting your hours. *Fortune*, 184.

- **Enabling HR to focus on management** The Internet allows firms to handle many operational HR details much more quickly and efficiently. Freedom from many bureaucratic "paper shuffling" chores allows HR personnel to devote more attention to solving managerial problems and supporting line managers in dealing with human resource issues. According to Philip Fauver, president and CEO of Employease Inc., the Internet is "the enabler."[36] For a flat fee of about $5 to $6 per employee, Employease manages HR information for 700 small to mid-size companies. One of its clients is Amerisure Insurance Cos., in Farmington Hills, Michigan. According to Derick Adams, Amerisure's HR vice president, the Internet allowed his 14-member HR department to devote more attention to important managerial challenges. For instance, Adams notes that his department was able to "develop a variable pay plan after handing off the department's data entry work to Employease."[37]

Workforce Diversity

Managers across the United States are confronted daily with the increasing diversity of the workforce. Approximately one third of the U.S. workforce is now made up of African Americans, Asian Americans, Latinos, and other minorities.[38] In many large urban centers, such as Miami, Los Angeles, and New York, the workforce is already at least half composed of minorities. The influx of women workers is another major change in the composition of the U.S. workforce. Women with children under age 6 are now the fastest-growing segment of the workforce. Currently, more than 75 percent of employed men have employed wives. This compares with 54 percent in 1980.[39]

These trends are likely to accelerate in the future. By 2050, the U.S. population is expected to increase by 50 percent, with nearly half of the population consisting of minority groups. Nonwhite immigrants, mostly Hispanics, will account for 60 percent of the population growth. Despite fears that immigrants are not assimilating (a concern voiced about the offspring of Italian, Irish, and Jewish immigrants a few generations ago), children of immigrants actually do better than children of natives in the same socioeconomic class.[40] This finding about assimilation helps explain why 48,000 Hispanic households in the United States boasted an income of $100,000 or more in 2003, double what it was in 1993.[41] Similarly, the percentage of Hispanics in managerial and professional jobs, although still about half that of whites, has more than doubled during the past 15 years.[42] And for blacks, a large number are reaching positions of power "in which credentials have little to do with color"; these include, for instance, Richard Parsons (CEO of AOL), Kenneth Chenault (CEO of AmEx), and Stanley O'Neal (CEO of Merril).[43]

Furthermore, never before in history has such a large-scale mixing of the races occurred, due to a sharp rise in the rate of intermarriage.[44] This increase means that traditional groupings are being redefined as many children share multiple identities. "One day race will not be needed because it will be obsolete," notes Candy Mills, a magazine editor in Los Angeles, who is black. Candy is married to a French-Hungarian with whom she has a child. Speaking of her family, she says, "We are what America will look like in maybe 100 years."[45] The U.S. Census Bureau has acknowledged this reality, incorporating "mixed" categories for future population censuses.

All these trends present both a significant challenge and a real opportunity for managers.[46] Firms that formulate and implement HR strategies that capitalize on employee diversity are more likely to survive and prosper. Chapter 4 is devoted exclusively to the topic of managing employee diversity. This issue is also discussed in several other chapters throughout this book.

Globalization

One of the most dramatic challenges facing U.S. firms as they enter the twenty-first century is how to compete against foreign firms, both domestically and abroad. Many U.S. companies are already being compelled to think globally, something that does not come easily to firms long accustomed to doing business in a large and expanding domestic market with minimal foreign competition. The Internet is fueling globalization, and most large firms are actively involved in manufacturing overseas, international joint ventures, or collaboration with foreign firms on specific projects. Trade barriers for developed countries are down 90 percent. For instance, the North American Free Trade Agreement allows countries such as Mexico to export $153 billion worth of goods annually to the United States without facing traditional import-export duties and regulations. In addition, U.S. firms employ about a million Mexicans in *maquiladoras* (U.S.-owned firms operating in Mexico), allowing these companies to produce goods at a lower cost for the global market.[47] Over time, however, increasing wages have been putting a squeeze on these companies. The average maquiladora wage in 2003 stood at $3.52 an hour, up from $2.29 in 1997. Unless maquiladora workers learn to use more advanced technology to justify the higher wage, Mexico's loss is likely to become China's, Vietnam's, or Guatemala's gain.[48] During 2001–2002, a total of 350 maquiladora plants picked up their tents and moved to lower-wage countries, leaving 240,000 Mexicans out of work.[49]

The implications of a global economy on human resource management are many. Here are a few examples:

- **Worldwide company culture** Some firms try to develop a global company identity to smooth over cultural differences between domestic employees and those in international operations. Minimizing these differences increases cooperation and can have a strong impact on the bottom line. For instance, the head of human resources at the European division of Colgate Palmolive notes, "We try to build a common corporate culture. We want them all to be Colgaters."[50]
- **Worldwide recruiting** Some firms recruit workers globally, particularly in the high-technology area, where specialized knowledge and expertise are not limited by national boundaries. For instance, Unisys (an e-business solutions company whose 37,000 employees help customers in 100 countries apply information technology) recruits between 5,000 and 7,000 people a year, 50 percent of whom are information technology (IT) professionals. At any given time, there are approximately 100 recruiters working to fill jobs across various countries. In the words of one Unisys executive: "If we were looking for someone to run a practice in Europe, we would not hold the search to a single country. We would be looking across borders to try to find the best person."[51]
- **Global alliances** Some firms actively engage in international alliances with foreign firms or acquire companies overseas to take advantage of global markets. Making such alliances work requires a highly trained and devoted staff. For instance, Philips (a Dutch lighting and electronics firm) became the largest lighting manufacturer in the world by establishing a joint venture with AT&T and making several key acquisitions, including Magnavox, parts of GE Sylvania (which had been the lighting division of Westinghouse), and the largest lighting company in France.[52]
- **A virtual workforce** Because of restrictive U.S. immigration quotas,[53] U.S. firms are tapping skilled foreign labor but not moving those workers to the United States. The Internet is making this possible with little additional expense. For example, Microsoft Corp. and Real Networks Inc. use a Bangalore, India, company, Adite Corp., to handle customer e-mails.[54] In addition, many "virtual" expatriates work abroad but live at home. "Virtual expatriation arises when someone takes an assignment to manage an operation or area abroad without being located permanently in that country. . . . Communications technology [allows them] to stay in touch with far-flung troops. . . . The virtual expat is a new breed of manager that is multiplying."[55]

These illustrations show how firms can use HR strategies to gain a worldwide competitive advantage. An entire chapter of this book (Chapter 17) is devoted to the HR issues firms face as they expand overseas. In addition, most chapters address international concerns as they relate to the topic being discussed. We also include international examples throughout the book to illustrate how firms in other countries manage their human resources.

Legislation

Much of the growth in the HR function over the past three decades may be attributed to its crucial role in keeping the company out of trouble with the law.[56] Most firms are deeply concerned with potential liability resulting from personnel decisions that may violate laws enacted by the U.S. Congress, state legislatures, or local governments.[57] These laws are constantly interpreted in thousands of cases brought before government agencies, federal courts, state courts, and the U.S. Supreme Court.[58]

How successfully a firm manages its human resources depends to a large extent on its ability to deal effectively with government regulations. Operating within the legal framework requires keeping track of the external legal environment and developing internal systems (for example, supervisory training and grievance procedures) to ensure compliance and minimize complaints. Many firms are now developing formal policies on sexual harrassment and establishing internal administrative channels to deal with alleged incidents before employees feel the need to file a lawsuit. In a country where mass litigation is on the rise,[59] these efforts may well be worth the time and money.

Legislation may differentiate between public- and private-sector organizations. (*Public sector* is another term for governmental agencies; *private sector* refers to all other types of organizations.) Some legislation applies only to public-sector organizations. For instance, affirmative action requirements (see Chapter 3) are typically limited to public organizations and to organizations that do contract work for them. However, much legislation applies to both public- and private-sector organizations. In fact, it is difficult to think of any HR practices that are *not* influenced by government regulations. For this reason, each chapter of this book addresses pertinent legal issues, and an entire chapter (Chapter 3) provides an overall framework that consolidates the main legal issues and concerns facing employers today.

Evolving Work and Family Roles

The proportion of *dual-career* families, in which both wife and husband (or both members of a couple) work, is increasing every year. Unfortunately, women face the double burden of working at home and on the job, devoting 42 hours per week on average to the office and an additional 30 hours at home to children. This compares to 43 hours spent working in the office and only 12 hours at home for men.[60]

More companies are introducing "family-friendly" programs that give them a competitive advantage in the labor market.[61] These programs are HR tactics that companies use to hire and retain the best-qualified employees, male or female, and they often pay off. For instance, among the Big Six accounting firms, half of all recruits are women, but only 5 percent of partners are women. Major talent is wasted as many women drop out after lengthy training because they have decided that the 10- to 12-year partner track requires a total sacrifice of family life. These firms have started to change their policies and are seeing gains as a result. KPMG and Ernst & Young, for example, have recently begun offering child-care and elder-care referral services. Since average monthly day care costs in 2003 reached $516, this type of support can make a major difference in whether or not an employee with young children decides to stay with a firm.[62] Ernst & Young and Coopers & Lybrand have introduced alternative scheduling to allow employees flexibility in their work hours. The 50 percent increase in the number of women partners in Big Six firms in the 1990s is credited to such programs.[63] One program growing rapidly in popularity is the so-called PTO, which stands for "paid time off." Unlike traditional sick time (which is often used for reasons other than illness), PTO allows employees to take time off for any reason and for varied lengths of time (a few hours, a day, a week, etc.) as long as the supervisor is informed ahead of time. In 2002, approximately two thirds of companies had PTO programs, about double the number in 1997.[64]

Family-friendly policies are discussed in detail in Chapter 12 under the heading "Employee Services." Special issues that women confront in the workplace are discussed in Chapter 4.

Skill Shortages and the Rise of the Service Sector

The U.S. service sector has experienced much faster growth than the manufacturing sector over the past 40 years. According to the Bureau of Labor Statistics, that trend is expected to accelerate during the next decade. Employment in the service sector is expected to increase 32 percent from 2003 through 2012, whereas in manufacturing the percentage of growth is close to zero. The categories with the fastest growth are expected to be professional specialties (27 percent) and technical occupations (22 percent). The fastest-growing occupations demand at least two years of college training.[65] Expansion of service-sector employment is linked to a number of factors, including changes in consumer tastes and preferences, legal and regulatory changes, advances in science and technology that have eliminated many manufacturing jobs, and changes in the way businesses are organized and managed.

A Question of Ethics

What is the ethical responsibility of an employer to employees who lack basic literacy and numeracy skills? Should companies be required by law to provide training opportunities for such employees, as some have proposed?

Unfortunately, many available workers will be too unskilled to fill those jobs. Even now, many companies complain that the supply of skilled labor is dwindling and that they must provide their employees with basic training to make up for the shortcomings of the public education system. For example, 84 percent of the 23,000 people applying for entry-level jobs at Bell Atlantic Telephone (formerly NYNEX) failed the qualifying test.[66] Chemical Bank reported that it had to interview 40 applicants to find one proficient teller.[67] David Hearns, former chairman and CEO of Xerox, laments that "the American workforce is running out of qualified people."[68]

To rectify these shortcomings, companies spend at least $55 billion a year on a wide variety of training programs. This is in addition to the $24 billion spent on training programs by the federal government each year.[69] Nonetheless, the skill shortage is likely to remain a major challenge for U.S. firms. Chapter 8 focuses directly on training; Chapters 5 (staffing), 7 (appraising employee performance), and 9 (career development) discuss issues related to the skills and knowledge required to succeed on the job.

Organizational Challenges

Organizational challenges Concerns or problems internal to a firm; often a by-product of environmental forces.

Organizational challenges are concerns or problems internal to a firm. They are often a by-product of environmental forces because no firm operates in a vacuum. Still, managers can usually exert much more control over organizational challenges than over environmental challenges. Effective managers spot organizational issues and deal with them before they become major problems. One of the themes of this text is *proactivity*: the need for firms to take action before problems get out of hand. This can be done only by managers who are well informed about important HR issues and organizational challenges. These challenges include the need for a competitive position and flexibility, the problems of downsizing and organizational restructuring, the use of self-managed work teams, the rise of small businesses, the need to create a strong organizational culture, the role of technology, and the rise of outsourcing.

Competitive Position: Cost, Quality, or Distinctive Capabilities

Human resources represent the single most important cost in many organizations. Organizational labor costs range from 36 percent in capital-intensive firms like commercial airlines to 80 percent in labor-intensive firms like the U.S. Postal Service. How effectively a company uses its human resources can have a dramatic effect on its ability to compete (or survive) in an increasingly competitive environment.

An organization will outperform its competitors if it effectively uses its workforce's unique combination of skills and abilities to exploit environmental opportunities and neutralize threats. HR policies can influence an organization's competitive position by controlling costs, improving quality, and creating distinctive capabilities.

- **Controlling costs** One way for a firm to gain a competitive advantage is to maintain low costs and a strong cash flow. A compensation system that uses innovative reward strategies to control labor costs can help the organization grow, as we discuss in Chapters 10 and 11. A well-designed compensation system rewards employees for behaviors that benefit the company.

  Other factors besides compensation policies can enhance a firm's competitiveness by keeping labor costs under control. These include better employee selection so that workers are more likely to stay with the company and to perform better while they are there (Chapter 5); training employees to make them more efficient and productive (Chapter 8); attaining harmonious labor relations (Chapter 15); effectively managing health and safety issues in the workplace (Chapter 16); and structuring work to reduce the time and resources needed to design, produce, and deliver quality products or services (Chapter 2).

Total quality management (TQM) An organizationwide approach to improving the quality of all the processes that lead to a final product or service.

- **Improving quality** The second way to gain a competitive advantage is to engage in continuous quality improvement. Many companies have implemented **total quality management (TQM)** initiatives, which are programs designed to improve the quality of all the processes that lead to a final product or service. In a TQM program, every aspect of the organization is oriented toward providing a quality product or service. For many people, TQM became another passing fad, partly because of zealous overuse of the term in the 1990s and partly because it may have been oversold as a cure-all for organizational problems. Nevertheless, continuing evidence shows that firms that effectively implement quality programs tend to outperform those that don't.[70] And it is still sadly true that despite improvements *Consumer Reports* pegs the present quality of American vehicles at Japanese levels in 1985.[71]
- **Creating distinctive capabilities** The third way to gain a competitive advantage is to use people with distinctive capabilities to create unsurpassed competence in a particular area (for example, 3M's competence in adhesives, Carlson Corporation's leading presence in the travel business, and Xerox's dominance of the photocopier market). Chapter 5 (which discusses the recruitment and selection of employees), Chapter 8 (training), and Chapter 9 (the long-term

grooming of employees within the firm) are particularly relevant to managers seeking to establish distinctive capabilities through the effective use of human resources.

Decentralization

In the traditional organizational structure, most major decisions are made at the top and implemented at lower levels. It is not uncommon for these organizations to centralize major functions, such as HR, marketing, and production, in a single location (typically corporate headquarters) that serves as the firm's command center. Multiple layers of management are generally used to execute orders issued at the top and to control the lower ranks from above. Employees who are committed to the firm tend to move up the ranks over time in what some have called the *internal labor market*.[72] However, the traditional topdown form of organization is quickly becoming obsolete, both because it is costly to operate and because it is too inflexible to compete effectively. It is being replaced by **decentralization,** which transfers responsibility and decision-making authority from a central office to people and locations closer to the situation that demands attention. The Internet helps companies to decentralize even faster by improving the communication flow among the workforce, reducing the need to rely on the traditional organizational pyramid.[73]

Decentralization
Transferring responsibility and decision-making authority from a central office to people and locations closer to the situation that demands attention.

HR strategies can play a crucial role in enhancing organizational flexibility by improving decision-making processes within the firm. The need for maintaining or creating organizational flexibility in HR strategies is addressed in several chapters of this book, including those dealing with work flows (Chapter 2), compensation (Chapters 10 and 11), training (Chapter 8), staffing (Chapter 5), and globalization (Chapter 17).

Downsizing

Periodic reductions in a company's workforce to improve its bottom line—often called **downsizing**—are becoming standard business practice, even among firms that were once legendary for their "no layoff" policies, such as AT&T, IBM, Kodak, and Xerox.[74] Although U.S. firms traditionally were far more willing to resort to layoffs as a cost-cutting measure vis-à-vis companies in other industrialized nations, globalization is quickly closing the gap. During 2002–2003, for instance, Japanese firms once legendary for their tight job security (such as Sony and Hitachi) have eliminated thousands of jobs.[75] In countries that on paper have strong anti-layoff regulations, such as Germany and Italy, the government often looks the other way. At the time of this writing, German companies, ranging from electronic giant Siemens to chip maker Infineron Technologies to Commerzbank, have announced thousands of layoffs. Countries such as France, where authorities have repeatedly blocked management efforts to cut costs via layoffs, often find that these well-intentioned efforts are counterproductive, leading to a wave of bankruptcies. This was the fate of appliance maker Moulinex, once considered an icon of French industry, which shut its doors in 2002, with almost 9,000 employees losing their jobs as a result.[76]

Downsizing
A reduction in a company's workforce to improve its bottom line.

In addition to fostering a lack of emotional commitment,[77] transient employment relationships create a new set of challenges for firms and people competing in the labor market, as well as for government agencies that must deal with the social problems associated with employment insecurity (including loss of health insurance and mental illness). However, the good news for laid-off employees is that the poor-performance stigma traditionally attached to being fired or laid off is fading.[78] For instance, during the most recent recession, half of those who were laid off had found a new job within weeks. This same survey also shows that attachment to a particular organization is quickly fading, with one in five workers changing employment status during a single quarter.[79]

In spite of these trends, some argue that those relatively few companies that remain committed to job security earn a higher return to shareholders.[80] Two companies often used as examples of this no-layoff policy include Southwest Airlines (which hasn't had layoffs in 30 years) and Nucor Steel (which hasn't laid off employees since its inception in the 1960s).[81]

Chapter 6 of this book is devoted to downsizing and how to manage the process effectively. Other chapters of this book also shed light on this important issue, including the chapters on benefits (Chapter 12), the legal environment (Chapter 3), labor relations (Chapter 15), and employee relations and communications (Chapter 13).

Organizational Restructuring

The past two decades have witnessed a dramatic transformation in how firms are structured. Tall organizations that had many management levels are becoming flatter as companies reduce the number of people between the chief executive officer (CEO) and the lowest-ranking employee in an effort to become more competitive.

Mergers and acquisitions have been going on for decades, reaching a new peak of close to $1.7 trillion in 2002.[82] Often mergers fail because the cultures and HR systems of the firms involved do not coalesce.[83] A newer and rapidly growing form of interorganizational bonding comes in the form of joint ventures, alliances, and collaborations among firms that remain independent, yet work together on specific products to spread costs and risks. For instance, Coca-Cola and Schweppes run a huge soft-drink bottling plant that has brought both companies tremendous cost savings. Ford and Nissan successfully designed a minivan together, and Ford has had a successful strategic alliance with Mazda for almost 25 years.

To be successful, organizational restructuring requires effective management of human resources. For instance, flattening the organization requires careful examination of staffing demands, work flows, communication channels, training needs, and so on. Likewise, mergers and other forms of interorganizational relations require the successful blending of dissimilar organizational structures, management practices, technical expertise, and so forth. Chapter 2 deals specifically with these issues. Other chapters that focus on related issues are Chapter 5 (staffing), Chapter 8 (training), Chapter 9 (career development), and Chapter 17 (international management).

Self-Managed Work Teams

Another sweeping organizational change has been in the supervisor–worker relationship. The traditional system, in which individual employees report to a single boss (who oversees a group of three to seven subordinates), is being replaced in some organizations by the self-managed team system. In this system employees are assigned to a group of peers and, together, they are responsible for a particular area or task. It has been estimated that 40 percent of U.S. workers are operating in some kind of team environment.[84]

According to two experts on self-managed work teams, "Today's competitive environment demands intense improvement in productivity, quality, and response time. Teams can deliver this improvement. Bosses can't. . . . Just as dinosaurs once ruled the earth and later faded into extinction, the days of bosses may be numbered."[85] Michael H. Walsh, former CEO of Tenneco Inc., is even more blunt about the redundancy of bosses: "In a hierarchical organization, bosses don't do much. . . . They just preside and take all the credit. It's criminal. A lot of good people are buried down there, and their bosses are happy to keep them buried."[86]

Very few rigorous scientific studies have been done on the effectiveness of self-managed work teams. However, case studies do suggest that many firms that use teams enjoy impressive payoffs. For example, company officials at General Motors' Fitzgerald Battery Plant, which is organized in teams, report cost savings of 30 to 40 percent over traditionally organized plants. At FedEx, a thousand clerical workers, divided into teams of 5 to 10 people, helped the company reduce service problems by 13 percent.[87]

HR issues concerning self-managed work teams are discussed in detail in Chapter 2 (work flows), Chapter 10 (compensation), and Chapter 11 (rewarding performance).

The Growth of Small Businesses

According to the U.S. Small Business Administration (SBA), the precise definition of a small business depends on the industry in which it operates. For instance, to be considered "small" by the SBA, a manufacturing company may have a maximum of 500 to 1,500 employees (depending on the type of manufacturing). In wholesaling, a company is considered small if the number of its employees does not exceed 100.[88]

An increasing percentage of the 14 million businesses in the United States can be considered small. One study using tax returns as its source of data found that 99.8 percent of U.S. businesses have fewer than 100 employees and approximately 90 percent have fewer than 20 employees.[89] Another study reports that approximately 85 percent of these firms are family owned.[90]

Unfortunately, small businesses face a high risk of failure. Although 1.3 million new businesses start every year, 40 percent of them fail in the first year, 60 percent of them fail before the

Female entrepreneurs such as Juanita Powell Baranco are increasing in number. As the owner of a multimillion-dollar auto business, she's her own boss in a field that is typically dominated by men.

start of the third year, and only 10 percent survive a decade.[91] To survive and prosper, a small business must manage its human resources effectively; the firm does not have the slack enjoyed by more mature, established firms. For instance, a mediocre performance by one person in a 10-employee firm can mean the difference between making a profit and losing money. In a company with 1,000 employees, one mediocre performance is so diluted that it is unlikely to exert much influence on the bottom line.

Most chapters in this book incorporate small-business examples to show how the HR practices discussed in that chapter relate to the special needs of small firms.

Organizational Culture

The term **organizational culture** refers to the basic assumptions and beliefs shared by members of an organization. These beliefs operate unconsciously and define in a basic "taken for granted" fashion an organization's view of itself and its environment.[92] The key elements of organizational culture are:[93]

Organizational culture
The basic assumptions and beliefs shared by members of an organization. These beliefs operate unconsciously and define in a basic taken-for-granted fashion an organization's view of itself and its environment.

1. *Observed behavioral regularities* when people interact, such as the language used and the rituals surrounding deference and demeanor.
2. The *norms* that evolve in working groups, such as the norm of a fair day's work for a fair day's pay.
3. The *dominant values espoused* by an organization, such as product quality or low prices.
4. The *philosophy* that guides an organization's policy toward employees and customers.
5. The *rules of the game* for getting along in the organization—"the ropes" that a newcomer must learn to become an accepted member.
6. The *feeling* or *climate* that is conveyed in an organization by the physical layout and the way in which members of the organization interact with one another, customers, and outsiders.

Firms that make cultural adjustments to keep up with environmental changes are likely to outperform those whose culture is rigid and unresponsive to external jolts. IBM's bureaucratic culture—with its emphasis on hierarchy, centralization of decisions, permanent employment, and strict promotion-from-within policy—played a large role in its difficulties earlier in the 1990s.[94] Similarly, Campbell's Soup Co.'s problems in the 2000s are often attributed to norms and values that have not kept up with rapidly changing consumer tastes. "It's definitely a risk-averse, control-oriented culture. It's all about two things: financial control and how much they can squeeze out of a tomato. Campbell needs to reward risk-taking, remove organizational roadblocks, and summon up the courage to move bold initiatives from proposal to execution quickly and regularly."[95] In contrast, Hewlett-Packard, named one of the best-managed new companies more than a decade ago, retained its strong position through the 2000s. Many attribute Hewlett-Packard's continued success to the fact that the corporation divided into smaller sections in the mid-1980s, making it more nimble and able to bring new products to market quickly.[96]

Given its pervasiveness, we refer to organizational culture throughout this book—for instance, in discussing work design, performance appraisal, pay for performance, labor relations, and worker safety.

Technology

Technological advances are being introduced to organizations at an ever-increasing pace. At least half of all U.S. workers have experienced dramatic changes in their job duties as a result of this trend.[97] Although technology is rapidly changing in many areas, such as robotics, one area in particular is revolutionizing human resources: information technology.[98] Computer systems that were state of the art three years ago are now obsolete and being replaced by faster, cheaper, more versatile systems.[99] The *telematics technologies*—a broad array of tools including personal computers (PCs), networking programs, telecommunications, and fax machines—are now available and affordable to businesses of every size, even one-person companies. These technologies, coupled with the rise of the Internet, have had many effects on the management of human resources in organizations, specifically:

- **The rise of telecommuting** Because technology makes information easy to store, retrieve, and analyze, the number of company employees working at home (*telecommuters*) at least part-time has been increasing by 15 percent annually. According to one survey, approximately one in five workers participated in some form of telecommuting in 2002—at home, on the road, in telework centers, or in satellite offices. Most telecommuters earn $40,000 or more annually.[100] Because telecommuting arrangements are expected to continue growing in the future, they raise many important questions concerning issues such as performance monitoring and career planning.
- **The ethics of proper data use** Questions concerning data control, accuracy, right to privacy, and ethics are at the core of a growing controversy brought about by the new information technologies, particularly the Internet.[101] Personal computers now make it possible to access huge databases containing information on credit files, work history, driving records, health reports, criminal convictions, and family makeup. One Web site, for example, promises that in exchange for a $7 fee, it will scan "over two million records to create a single report on an individual."[102] It is tempting to access these types of data for personnel decisions such as hiring, promotions, international assignments, and the like. A critical observer notes: "The worst thing about this information blitzkrieg is that even though errors abound, what's said about us by computers is usually considered accurate, and significant decisions are made based on this information. Often those affected are unaware of the process and are given no chance to offer explanations."[103]
- **The boss knows where you are clicking** Many companies are using sophisticated software that monitors when, how, and why workers are using the Internet (see Manager's Notebook titled "Workers, Surf at Your Own Risk"). This software provides employers with amazing electronic-eavesdropping capabilities to every office that uses the Internet. For instance, "Telemate. Net can also report Web site visits by individual employees and rank them by roughly two dozen categories, including some that most employers would not be happy about, from games, humor, and pornography to cults, shopping, and job hunting. And it can instantly generate logs naming precisely who went to what sites at what times."[104]

MANAGER'S NOTEBOOK

Emerging Trends

Workers, Surf at Your Own Risk

Cyberslackers, Beware! E-mail and Internet monitoring by employers is on the rise now that employees who are found to be Internet abusers can be replaced from the plentiful soft-labor market.

And that means that terminations on such grounds—mainly viewing porn sites, trading stocks, or posting to chat rooms—are up, too. Websense, a maker of Internet monitoring systems, found one out of three companies surveyed reported terminating someone for Net abuse, a 10 percent increase over last year. "Employers cannot overlook the impact on productivity," says report co-author David Greenfield, noting that 70 percent of Net surfing is done at work. Since the downturn, companies including E*Trade and JDS Uniphase have become converts to monitoring software, says Websense's Ted Ladd. Many companies that had relied on managers to check monitors are now users. "We're trying to ensure a healthy workplace," says Frank Gillman of Los Angeles law firm Allen Matkins, which recently upgraded its system.

E-monitors scan for keywords and note when something questionable is sent or viewed. Says Rob Spence of Ireland's Baltimore Technologies: "If I want to screen every outgoing e-mail that has the word 'résumé,' . . . I can do that." So think about who's watching before hitting "send."

Source: Reprinted with permission. Palmer, A. T. (2001, June 15). Workers: Surf at your own risk. *BusinessWeek*, 14 (Up Front section). See also Armour, S. (2002, June 19). Security checks worry workers. *USA Today*, A-1.

Some blue-chip clients using this software include Phillip Morris Co., Maytag Corp., and Sears, Roebuck and Co.[105] In addition, by 2003 almost a third of large U.S. firms had begun checking employee e-mail, doubling the number from three years earlier. These practices are becoming increasingly controversial, and they are ripe for abuses in the hands of unscrupulous supervisors and managers.[106] Because only a handful of firms have "zero tolerance policies" that prohibit any personal use of computer equipment, there is much room for interpretation and arbitrary judgment when managers are given discretion to examine these data. For instance, one manager may consider some language obscene, whereas another manager may consider the same language to be normal slang. One could also envision situations where interpersonal likes and dislikes may influence "how hard" supervisors look for cybernetic offenses.

- **An increase in egalitarianism** Because information is now available both instantaneously and broadly, organizational structures are becoming more *egalitarian,* meaning that power and authority are spread more evenly among all employees. This means that the levels of management between top and first-line management become less important—especially because technology allows high-level management to communicate directly with first-line management. In addition, groupware networks, which enable hundreds of workers to share information simultaneously, can give office workers intelligence previously available only to their bosses.[107] They also enable the rank-and-file to join in online discussions with senior executives. In these kinds of interactions people are judged more by what they say than by their rank on the corporate ladder.[108]

The challenges and implications of rapidly changing technologies—especially information technologies—for human resources are discussed in every chapter of this book.

Internal Security

The September 11, 2001, terrorist attacks have engendered a U.S. collective obsession with security. This has dramatically increased demand for employee monitoring and screening of applicants. Many consulting firms are now focusing their attention on how to detect potential security problems. Two well-known firms specializing in these issues include Visionics Corp., a maker of facial-recognition software, and Kroll Inc., which provides a wide range of services, from background checks to the detection of potential security problems in the employee population. Fueling this push is the belief that the occurrence of new terrorist attacks is only a matter of time and that airplanes may no longer be the target. This means a wide range of firms and industry groups, from trucking associations to sporting-event organizers, have made security screening a top priority.[109] For example, the National Football League had the Super Bowl designated a "national security special event" for the first time so it could run names of concession workers and stadium employees through the FBI lists.[110]

Apart from potential terrorist attacks, other security concerns also loom large these days. One concern is violence at work, which seems to have been rising over the years. Another in this cyberage is the possibility of computer sabotage by hackers or by disgruntled employees and ex-workers. The FBI estimates the cost of the average attack at $2.7 million. Consider the following cases under investigation.

> An axed systems administrator hacked back into his former company's computers, then published user I.D.'s, passwords, and secret company information in public chat rooms. Another pink-slipped worker sent bawdy e-mails, complete with a pornographic picture attached, to everyone at the high-tech company where he had worked. And at an import–export outfit, the CEO can't access any of his old e-mail: A former employee wiped it all out.[111]

Although few would question that security checks are necessary, one concern from a human resource perspective is to ensure that applicants' and employers' rights are not violated and that due process is followed whenever suspected problems are identified. This can become a slippery slope when the data may be interpreted in different ways. For example, should a person convicted of a drunken driving violation 15 years ago be denied a job as a flight attendant? Should a person arrested for shoplifting as a teenager be denied a job as a cashier years later? Should a student expelled from college for smoking marijuana in a dorm 10 years ago be automatically excluded from serving as a police officer? How about people whose past reveals some facts that may be potentially interpreted as warning signals, depending on the bias of the evaluator (for instance, graduation from a Middle Eastern university, frequent job changes, multiple divorces, and the like)? Health sites offer tools used by medical pros and companies to track data, including test results from HIV and cancer exams.[112] Should firms use this type of information as part of their selection process?

Greater scrutiny of people through magnifying lenses is unearthing all sorts of data, so how this information is used has become one of the major human resource challenges facing organizations today. For example, according to a 2002 study conducted by a computer-based, security-service firm, Automatic Data Accessing, more than 40 percent of résumés misrepresent education or employment history. But "how employers respond when they find an employee has fibbed varies depending on company policies, the worker's value, and the organizational culture. Many companies say they are willing to overlook some degree of inaccuracy."[113] In other words, how security-related information is used is a matter of interpretation, perhaps except in the most grievous cases. Chapter 14, "Respecting Employee Rights and Managing Discipline," deals with these and other related issues.

Outsourcing

Outsourcing
Subcontracting work to an outside company that specializes in and is more efficient at doing that kind of work.

There is an ongoing movement at many large firms to shift work once performed internally to outside suppliers and contractors, a process called **outsourcing.** Their motivation is simple: Outsourcing saves money. The *Wall Street Journal* reports that more than 40 percent of *Fortune* 500 companies have outsourced some department or service—everything from HR administration to computer systems.[114] For example, American Airlines hires outsourced labor to work in its operations at 28 smaller airports. The savings are considerable. American pays its veteran agents up to $19 an hour, plus benefits. Subcontracted employees performing the same job earn only $7 to $9 an hour and receive minimal benefits.[115]

Outsourcing creates several HR challenges for firms. Although it often helps companies slash costs, employees may face layoffs when their jobs are farmed out to the lowest bidder. For instance, United Parcel Service (UPS) subcontracted 5,000 jobs at its 65 customer service centers.[116] In addition, the firm remains accountable for the actions of its subcontractors. Customer dissatisfaction can result if subcontractors are not carefully watched and evaluated. For instance, a group of former employees at now-liquidated Skillset Software Inc. filed suit in 2002 against its outside HR provider, TriNet Group Inc., for negligence in handling their claim. Part of the problem is that these HR providers often don't provide enough access and human interaction (many rely extensively on the Web) to handle employee concerns and complaints.[117] Finally, many believe that subcontractors tend to take on more work than they can handle.[118] When subcontractors are overloaded, small businesses may not receive the best available service and support from subcontractors.

We discuss outsourcing and its challenges for HRM throughout this book. Chapter 2 discusses subcontracting within the context of downsizing, and Chapter 15, on labor relations, discusses how outsourcing affects unions.

Individual Challenges

Human resource issues at the individual level address the decisions most pertinent to specific employees. These **individual challenges** almost always reflect what is happening in the larger organization. For instance, technology affects individual productivity; it also has ethical ramifications in terms of how information is used to make HR decisions (for example, use of credit or medical history data to decide whom to hire). How the company treats its individual employees is also likely to affect the organizational challenges we discussed earlier. For example, if many key employees leave the firm to join competitors, the organization's competitive position is likely to be affected. In other words, there is a two-way relationship between organizational and individual challenges. This is unlike the relationship between environmental and organizational challenges, in which the relationship goes only one way (see Figure 1.1); few organizations can have much impact on the environment. The most important individual challenges today involve matching people and organizations, ethics and social responsibility, productivity, empowerment, brain drain, and job security.

Individual challenges Human resource issues that address the decisions most pertinent to individual employees.

Matching People and Organizations

Research suggests that HR strategies contribute to firm performance most when the firm uses these strategies to attract and retain the type of employee who best fits the firm's culture and overall business objectives. For example, one study showed that the competencies and personality characteristics of top executives can hamper or improve firm performance, depending on what the firm's business strategies are. Fast-growth firms perform better with managers who have a strong marketing and sales background, who are willing to take risks, and who have a high tolerance for ambiguity. However, these managerial traits actually reduce the performance of mature firms that have an established product and are more interested in maintaining (rather than expanding) their market share.[119] Other research has shown that small high-tech firms benefit by hiring employees who are willing to work in an atmosphere of high uncertainty, low pay, and rapid change in exchange for greater intrinsic satisfaction and the financial opportunities associated with a risky but potentially very lucrative product launch.[120]

Chapter 5 deals specifically with the attempt to achieve the right fit between employees and the organization to enhance performance.

Ethics and Social Responsibility

Recent well-publicized scandals at Enron, WorldCom, Tyco, and Global Crossings, in which corruption apparently became a way of life at the top, have brought ethics to the forefront of many employees' concern.[121] The fact that prestigious accounting and consulting firms apparently were coconspirators in many of these actions has reinforced a public perception that integrity in business often takes a back seat to plain greed.[122] Unfortunately, many of those being trained for these types of positions seem to share the view that it is okay to act unethically as long as you don't get caught. A recent survey of 443 M.B.A. students reported in *USA Today* revealed that 52 percent would buy stock on inside information received from a friend, 26 percent would let a gift sway a company purchasing decision, and 13 percent would pay off someone to help close a business deal.[123]

In response to these concerns, people's fears that their employers will behave unethically are increasing,[124] so much so that many firms and professional organizations have created codes of ethics outlining principles and standards of personal conduct for their members. Unfortunately, these codes often do not meet employees' expectations of ethical employer behavior. These negative perceptions have worsened over the years.[125] In a poll of *Harvard Business Review* readers, almost half the respondents indicated their belief that managers do not consistently make ethical decisions.[126]

The widespread perceptions of unethical behavior may be attributed to the fact that managerial decisions are rarely clear-cut. In fact, most of the aggressive "revenue enhancing" decisions made by executives at Enron and other firms listed previously were not technically illegal and did not violate accounting standards.[127] Furthermore, close working relationships between accounting firms and the companies they are supposed to monitor are fairly common, often justified on the grounds that "the quality of [auditing] is improved when auditors know more about their clients."[128] Except in a few blatant cases (such as willful misrepresentation), what is ethical or unethical is open to debate. Even the most detailed codes of ethics are still general enough to allow much room for managerial discretion. Perhaps even more so than in other business areas, many specific decisions related to the management of human resources are subject to judgment calls. Often these judgment calls constitute a Catch-22 because none of the alternatives is desirable.[129]

Although some companies are using the Web to monitor employees' cybernetic behavior, as discussed earlier, others are using the Web to infuse employees and managers with ethical values. For instance, many of Lockheed Martin's 160,000 employees are required to take a step-by-step online training program on ethics. "The system records each time an employee completes one of the sessions, which range from sexual harassment and insider trading to kickbacks and gratuities."[130] The Web-based ethics program alerts Lockheed Martin managers when employees fall behind schedule in completing the required sessions.

In recent years, the concept of social responsibility has been frequently discussed as a counterpart to ethics. A company that exercises *social responsibility* attempts to balance its commitments—not only to its investors but also to its employees, its customers, other businesses, and the community or communities in which it operates. For example, McDonald's established Ronald McDonald houses years ago to provide lodging for families of sick children hospitalized away from home. Sears and General Electric support artists and performers, and many local merchants support local children's sports teams.

An entire chapter of this book is devoted to employee rights and responsibilities (Chapter 13); it addresses important ethical issues in employer–employee relations. However, because most of the topics discussed in this book have ethical implications, each chapter includes (at selected points) pertinent ethical questions for which there are no absolute answers.

Productivity

From the early 1970s until the mid-1990s, U.S. productivity was rising, but at a lower rate than that of most other industrialized nations. Most experts agree that productivity gains from technology have altered the economic playing field since the mid-1990s, allowing for continued economic growth, low unemployment, and low inflation. **Productivity** is a measure of how much value individual employees add to the goods or services that the organization produces. The greater the output per individual, the higher the organization's productivity. For instance, U.S. workers produce a pair of shoes in 24 minutes, whereas Chinese workers take three hours.[131] In a "knowledge-based economy" driven by technology, the success of organizations will depend more and more on the value of intangible human capital. This capital may be "the creativity of their designers (Intel Corp. comes to mind), the proficiency of their software architects (as at Sun Microsystems Inc.), the knowledge of marketers (Procter & Gamble Co., for instance), and even the strength of the internal culture (as in the case of Southwest Airlines)."[132] As noted in the Manager's Notebook "Keeping Track of Productivity," companies are increasingly using computer technology to give managers and employees instant access to productivity data. Two important factors that affect individual productivity are ability and motivation.

Productivity
A measure of how much value individual employees add to the goods or services that the organization produces.

MANAGER'S NOTEBOOK

Customer-Driven HR

Keeping Track of Productivity

Like beauty, productivity is sometimes in the eye of the beholder. An employee may think she's a real go-getter, only to learn months later, when the annual bonus and performance review are discussed, that she's nothing special.

Replicon's new ProMax software tool hopes to change that. Alberta-based Replicon, maker of time-sheet management software for companies like Kraft and Hewlett-Packard, launched ProMax as an add-on to its time-sheet product in 2002 to give managers—and employees—instant access not only to billable hours across multiple projects but also productivity rates for individuals and entire departments.

When employees load the Web-based time-sheet manager to enter or check their hours worked, two small barometers display their productivity (expressed as a percentage of a predetermined bonus target) and that of their team or department. A green barometer means the employees (or teams) are above the target, yellow indicates they are doing okay, and red means they are not pulling their weight. Jeremy Simon, senior project director at IT security firm Reminton Associates based in Schumberg, Illinois, has used ProMax and says the productivity information has allowed him to do reviews of his 20 engineers at frequent intervals rather than annually. "It's the best thing we've ever done for the company," he says. And compared with similar software packages that cost anywhere from $50,000 to $150,000, Simon says, ProMax was a steal at $6,360.

One of Simon's engineers, Dah Samaan, says that although ProMax hasn't made him more productive, he does like knowing where he stands—for better or worse. When we spoke to him, he was in the red at 23 percent. "It's been a bad week," he admits. Which reminds us: ProMax can also be used to determine who gets the ax come layoff time. But at least now no one can say he didn't see it coming.

Source: Adapted with permission from Boyle, M. (2002, March 18). They are counting your hours. *Fortune*, 184.

Employee **ability,** competence in performing a job, can be improved through a hiring and placement process that selects the best individuals for the job;[133] Chapter 5 specifically deals with this process. It can also be improved through training and career development programs designed to sharpen employees' skills and prepare them for additional responsibilities; Chapters 8 and 9 discuss these issues.

Ability
Competence in performing a job.

Motivation refers to a person's desire to do the best possible job or to exert the maximum effort to perform assigned tasks. Motivation energizes, directs, and sustains human behavior. Several key factors affecting employee motivation are discussed in this book, including work design (Chapter 2), matching of employee and job requirements (Chapter 5), rewards (Chapters 11 and 13), and due process (Chapter 14).

Motivation
A person's desire to do the best possible job or to exert the maximum effort to perform assigned tasks.

A growing number of companies recognize that employees are more likely to choose a firm and stay there if they believe that it offers a high **quality of work life.** A high quality of work life is related to job satisfaction, which in turn is a strong predictor of absenteeism and turnover.[134] A firm's investments in improving the quality of work life also pay off in the form of better customer service.[135] We discuss issues covering job design and their effects on employee attitudes and behavior in Chapter 2.

Quality of work life
A measure of how safe and satisfied employees feel with their jobs.

Empowerment

Many firms have reduced employee dependence on superiors and placed more emphasis on individual control over (and responsibility for) the work that needs to be done. This process has been labeled **empowerment** because it transfers direction from an external source (normally the immediate supervisor) to an internal source (the individual's own desire to do well). In essence, the process of empowerment entails providing workers with the skills and authority to make decisions that would traditionally be made by managers. The goal of empowerment is an organization consisting of enthusiastic, committed people who perform their work ably because they believe in it and enjoy doing it (*internal control*). This situation is in stark contrast to an organization that gets people to work as an act of compliance to avoid punishment (for example, being fired) or to qualify for a paycheck (*external control*).

Empowerment
Providing workers with the skills and authority to make decisions that would traditionally be made by managers.

Empowerment can encourage employees to be creative and to take risks, which are key components that can give a firm a competitive edge in a fast-changing environment. Empowering employees is "the hardest thing to do because it means giving up control," says Lee Fielder, retired president of Kelly Springfield Tire Co., a unit of Goodyear. "But [according to Fielder], managers who try to tell employees what and how to do every little thing will end up with only mediocre people, because the talented ones won't submit to control."[136] To encourage risk taking, General Electric past CEO Jack Welch exhorted his managers and employees to "shake it, shake it, break it."[137]

HR issues related to internal and external control of behavior are explicitly discussed in Chapter 2 (work flows).

Brain Drain

Brain drain
The loss of high-talent key personnel to competitors or start-up ventures.

With organizational success more and more dependent on knowledge held by specific employees, companies are becoming more susceptible to **brain drain**—the loss of intellectual property that results when competitors lure away key employees. High-tech firms are particularly vulnerable to this problem. Important industries such as semiconductors and electronics suffer from high employee turnover as key employees, inspired by the potential for huge profits, leave established firms to start their own businesses. This brain drain can negatively affect innovation and cause major delays in the introduction of new products.[138] To make matters worse, departing employees, particularly those in upper management, can wreak considerable havoc by taking other talent with them when they leave.

To combat the problem of defection to competitors, some firms are crafting elaborate anti-defection devices. For example, Compaq Computer introduced a policy that revokes bonuses and other benefits to key executives if they take other employees with them when they quit. Micron Technology staggers key employees' bonuses; they lose unawarded portions when they leave.

Issues concerning brain drain and measures for dealing with it effectively are discussed in several chapters of this book, particularly in Chapter 3 (equal opportunity and the legal environment), Chapter 4 (managing diversity), Chapter 6 (employee separations and outplacement), and Chapter 11 (rewarding performance).

Job Insecurity

Most workers cannot count on a steady job and regular promotions. Close to half a million U.S. jobs are being eliminated each year. Even the most profitable companies (including Procter & Gamble, American Home Products, AT&T, Sara Lee, and Xerox) have laid off workers. Job insecurity is not just a U.S. phenomenon. For instance, an increasing number of Japanese firms have dropped their traditional lifetime employment policies in recent years.[139]

Companies argue that regardless of how well the firm is doing, layoffs have become essential in an age of cutthroat competition. In addition, the stock market sometimes looks favorably on layoffs. For employees, however, chronic job insecurity is a major source of stress and can lead to lower performance and productivity. Reed Moskowitz, founder of a stress disorder center at New York University, notes that workers' mental health has taken a turn for the worse because "nobody feels secure any more."[140]

Although union membership has been declining in recent years, many workers still belong to unions, and job security is now a top union priority. In return for job security, though, many union leaders have had to make major concessions regarding pay and benefits.

We discuss the challenges of laying off employees and making the remaining employees feel secure and valued in Chapter 6. We discuss employee stress (and ways to relieve it) in Chapter 16. We explore union–management relations in Chapter 15.

Planning and Implementing Strategic HR Policies

To be successful, firms must closely align their HR strategies and programs (tactics) with environmental opportunities, business strategies, and the organization's unique characteristics and distinctive competence. A firm with a poorly defined HR strategy or a business strategy that does not explicitly incorporate human resources is likely to lose ground to its competitors. Similarly, a firm may have a well-articulated HR strategy, yet fail if its HR tactics do not help it implement its HR strategy effectively.

The Benefits of Strategic HR Planning

Strategic human resource (HR) planning
The process of formulating HR strategies and establishing programs or tactics to implement them.

The process of formulating HR strategies and establishing programs or tactics to implement them is called **strategic human resource (HR) planning.** When done correctly, strategic HR planning provides many direct and indirect benefits for the company.

Encouragement of Proactive Rather Than Reactive Behavior

Being *proactive* means looking ahead and developing a vision of where the company wants to be and how it can use human resources to get there. In contrast, being *reactive* means responding to problems as they come up. Companies that are reactive may lose sight of the long-term direction of their business; proactive companies are better prepared for the future. For instance, as bankruptcies have soared in the 2000s, companies need to hold their key talent tightly, and this may involve offering special inducements for star performers to persevere through hard times "even though it may seem counterintuitive to continue spending money on employee compensation when the firm can't pay its bills."[141]

Explicit Communication of Company Goals

Strategic HR planning can help a firm develop a focused set of strategic objectives that capitalizes on its special talents and know-how.

For instance, 3M has had an explicit strategy of competing through innovation, with the goal of having at least 25 percent of revenues generated from products introduced during the past five years. To achieve this goal, 3M's human resource strategy may be summarized as "Hire top-notch scientists in every field, give each an ample endowment, then stand back and let them do their thing. The anything goes approach has yielded thousands of new products over the decades, from sand-paper and magnetic audio tape to Post-it notes and thinsulate insulation."[142]

In 2002, 3M's new CEO, Jim McNerney fine-tuned this decades-long HR strategy with the objective of doubling the rate of growth for the next decade. While trying to avoid stifling 3M's hallmark creativity, top management has begun to specify where R&D money should be spent and to establish uniform performance standards across 3M. McNerney presents this fine-tuning as a "balancing act": "My job is to add scale in a fast-moving, entrepreneurial environment. If I end up killing that entrepreneurial spirit, I will have failed."[143]

Stimulation of Critical Thinking and Ongoing Examination of Assumptions

Managers often depend on their personal views and experiences to solve problems and make business decisions. The assumptions on which they make their decisions can lead to success if they are appropriate to the environment in which the business operates. However, serious problems can arise when these assumptions no longer hold. For instance, in the 1980s IBM deemphasized sales of its personal computer because IBM managers were afraid that PC growth would decrease the profitability of the firm's highly profitable mainframe products. This decision allowed competitors to move aggressively into the PC market, eventually devastating IBM.[144]

The strategic HR planning process can help a company critically reexamine its assumptions and determine whether the programs that follow from these assumptions should be modified or discontinued. However, strategic HR planning can stimulate critical thinking and the development of new initiatives only if it is a continuing and flexible process rather than a rigid procedure with a discrete beginning and a specific deadline for completion. This is why many firms have formed an executive committee, which includes an HR professional and the CEO, to discuss strategic issues on an ongoing basis and periodically modify the company's overall HR strategies and programs.

Identification of Gaps Between Current Situation and Future Vision

Strategic HR planning can help a firm identify the difference between "where we are today" and "where we want to be." By forcing managers to think ahead, strategic planning can serve as a catalyst for change and mobilize the firm's resources to achieve or enhance a competitive edge in the future. Going back to the 3M example, despite a $1 billion budget and a staff of 7,000, 3M's vaunted laboratory was not able in recent years to deliver fast growth, partly because some of the R&D lacked focus and money wasn't always wisely spent. To speed up growth, 3M announced a series of performance objectives in 2002 for individual business chiefs who had before enjoyed much free rein. In addition, 3M introduced specially trained "black belts" in 2002 to root out inefficiencies in departments from R&D to sales.[145]

Encouragement of Line Managers' Participation

Like most HR activities, strategic HR planning will be of little value unless line managers are actively involved. Unfortunately, top management (including HR professionals) sometimes tends to see strategic planning as its domain, with line managers merely responsible for implementation. For HR strategy to be effective, line managers at all levels must buy into it. If they do not, it is likely to fail. For example, a large cosmetics manufacturing plant decided to introduce a reward program in which work teams would receive a large bonus for turning out high-quality products. The bonus was part of a strategic plan to foster greater cooperation among employees. But the plan, which had been developed by top executives in consultation with the HR department, backfired when managers and supervisors began hunting for individual employees responsible for errors. This created divisiveness within teams and conflict with supervisors. The plan was eventually dropped.

Identification of HR Constraints and Opportunities

Human resources play a major role in the eventual success or failure of any strategic business plan. When overall business strategy planning is done in combination with HR strategic planning, firms can identify the potential problems and opportunities with respect to the people expected to implement the business strategy.

Motorola is a good illustration of a highly successful firm that formulates HR strategies in tandem with its business strategies. A cornerstone of Motorola's business strategy is to identify, encourage, and financially support new-product ventures. To implement this strategy, Motorola relies on in-house venture teams, normally composed of five to six employees, one each from research and development (R&D), marketing, sales, manufacturing, engineering, and finance. Positions are broadly defined to allow all employees to use their creativity and to serve as champions of new ideas.

Creation of Common Bonds

A well-developed strategic HR plan with involvement at all levels can help the firm create a sense of shared values and expectations. This is important because a substantial amount of research shows that, in the long run, organizations that have a strong sense of "who we are" tend to outperform those that do not. A strategic HR plan that reinforces, adjusts, or redirects the organization's present culture can foster values such as a customer focus, innovation, fast growth, and cooperation.

The Challenges of Strategic HR Planning

In developing an effective HR strategy, the organization faces several important challenges.

Maintaining a Competitive Advantage

Any competitive advantage enjoyed by an organization tends to be short-lived because other companies are likely to imitate it. This is as true for HR advantages as for technological and marketing advantages. For example, many high-tech firms have "borrowed" reward programs for key scientists and engineers from other successful high-tech firms.

The challenge from an HR perspective is to develop strategies that offer the firm a sustained competitive advantage. For instance, a company may develop programs that maximize present employees' potential through carefully developed career ladders (see Chapter 9) while at the same time rewarding them generously with company stock with strings attached (for example, a provision that they will forfeit the stock if they quit before a certain date).

Reinforcing Overall Business Strategy

Developing HR strategies to support the firm's overall business strategy is a challenge for several reasons. First, top management may not always be able to enunciate clearly the firm's overall business strategy. Second, there may be much uncertainty or disagreement concerning which HR strategies should be used to support the overall business strategy. In other words, it is seldom obvious how particular HR strategies will contribute to the achievement of organizational strategies. Third, large corporations may have different business units, each with its own business strategies. Ideally, each unit should be able to formulate the HR strategy that fits its business strategy best. For instance, a division that produces high-tech equipment may decide to pay its engineering staff well above average to attract and retain the best people, while the consumer products division may decide to pay its engineers an average wage. Such differentials may cause problems if the engineers from the two divisions have contact with each other. Thus, diverse HR strategies may spur feelings of inequity and resentment.

Avoiding Excessive Concentration on Day-to-Day Problems

Some managers devote most of their attention to urgent problems. They are so busy putting out fires that they have no time to focus on the long term. Nonetheless, a successful HR strategy demands a vision tied to the long-term direction of the business. Thus, a major challenge of strategic HR planning is prodding people into stepping back and considering the big picture.

It takes considerable effort to detach oneself from current events and past history and trace a master plan for the organization's future direction. This is particularly true in many small companies, whose staffs are often so absorbed in growing the business today that they seldom pause to look at the big picture for tomorrow. Also, strategic HR planning in small companies is often synonymous with the whims of the company owner or founder, who may not take the time to formalize his or her plans.

Developing HR Strategies Suited to Unique Organizational Features

No two firms are exactly alike. Firms differ in history, culture, leadership style, technology, and so on. The chances are high that any ambitious HR strategy or program that is not molded to organizational characteristics will fail.[146] And therein lies one of the central challenges in formulating HR strategies: creating a vision of the organization of the future that does not provoke a destructive clash with the organization of the present.

Coping with the Environment

Just as no two firms are exactly alike, no two firms operate in an identical environment. Some must deal with rapid change, as in the computer industry; others operate in a relatively stable market, as in the market for food processors. Some face a virtually guaranteed demand for their products or services (for example, medical providers); others must deal with turbulent demand (for example, fashion designers). Even within a very narrowly defined industry, some firms may be competing in a market where customer service is the key (IBM's traditional competitive

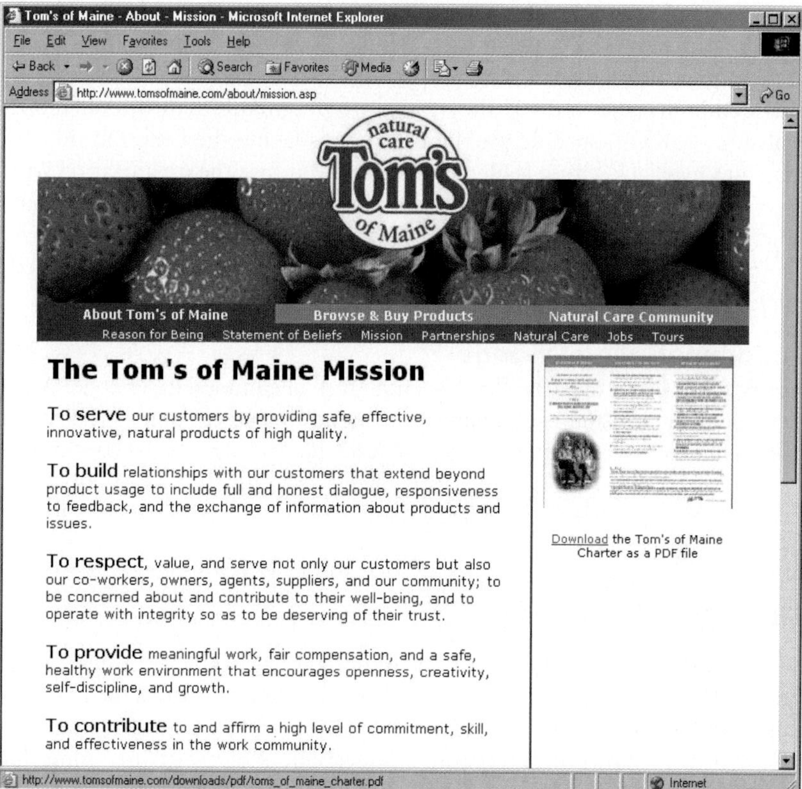

Natural products supplier Tom's of Maine needs to have a mission that is flexible enough to move the company toward the future without conflicting with its current goals. Tom's of Maine's mission statement outlines a forward-thinking company vision.

advantage), while others are competing in a market driven by cost considerations (the competitive advantage offered by the many firms producing IBM clones). A major challenge in developing HR strategies is crafting strategies that will work in the firm's unique environment to give it a sustainable competitive advantage.

Securing Management Commitment

HR strategies that originate in the HR department will have little chance of succeeding unless managers at all levels—including top executives—support them completely. To ensure managers' commitment, HR professionals must work closely with them when formulating policies. This is a point we emphasize again and again throughout this book.

Translating the Strategic Plan into Action

Often a strategic plan that looks great on paper fails because of poor implementation. The acid test of any strategic plan is whether or not it makes a difference in practice. If the plan does not affect practice, employees and managers will regard it as all talk and no action.

Cynicism regarding the strategic plan is practically guaranteed when a firm experiences frequent turnover at the top, with each new wave of high-level managers introducing their own freshly minted strategic plan. Perhaps the greatest challenge in strategic HR planning lies not in the formulation of strategy, but rather in the development of an appropriate set of programs that will make the strategy work.

Combining Intended and Emergent Strategies

There is a continuing debate over whether strategies are *intended* or *emergent*—that is, whether they are proactive, rational, deliberate plans designed to attain predetermined objectives (intended) or general "fuzzy" patterns collectively molded by the interplay of power, politics, improvisation, negotiation, and personalities within the organization (emergent).[147] Most people agree that organizations have intended *and* emergent strategies, that both are necessary, and that the challenge is to combine the best aspects of the two.

When based on a rigorous analysis of where the organization is and where it wishes to go, intended strategies can provide a sense of purpose and a guide for the allocation of resources. Intended strategies are also useful for recognizing environmental opportunities and threats and mobilizing top management to respond appropriately. On the downside, intended strategies may lead to a top-down strategic approach that squashes creativity and widespread involvement.

Emergent strategies also have their advantages and disadvantages. Among their benefits: (1) They involve everyone in the organization, which fosters grass-roots support; (2) they develop gradually out of the organization's experiences and, thus, can be less upsetting than intended strategies; and (3) they are more pragmatic than intended strategies because they evolve to deal with specific problems or issues facing the firm. On the negative side, emergent strategies may lack strong leadership and fail to infuse the organization with a creative vision.[148]

Combining intended and emergent strategies effectively requires that managers blend the benefits of formal planning (to provide strong guidance and direction in setting priorities) with the untidy realities of dispersed employees who, through their unplanned activities, formulate emergent strategies throughout the firm.

Accommodating Change

Strategic HR plans must be flexible enough to accommodate change. A firm with an inflexible strategic plan may find itself unable to respond to changes quickly because it is so committed to a particular course of action. This may lead the organization to continue devoting resources to an activity of questionable value simply because so much has been invested in it already.[149] The challenge is to create a strategic vision and develop the plans to achieve it while staying flexible enough to adapt to change.

Strategic HR Choices

Strategic HR choices
The options available to a firm in designing its human resources system.

A firm's **strategic HR choices** are the options it has available in designing its human resources system. Choices are strategic to the extent that they affect the firm's performance either favorably or unfavorably in the long run.

Figure 1.2 shows a sampling of strategic HR choices. At this point, it is important to keep three things in mind. First, the list of strategic HR choices in Figure 1.2 is not exhaustive.

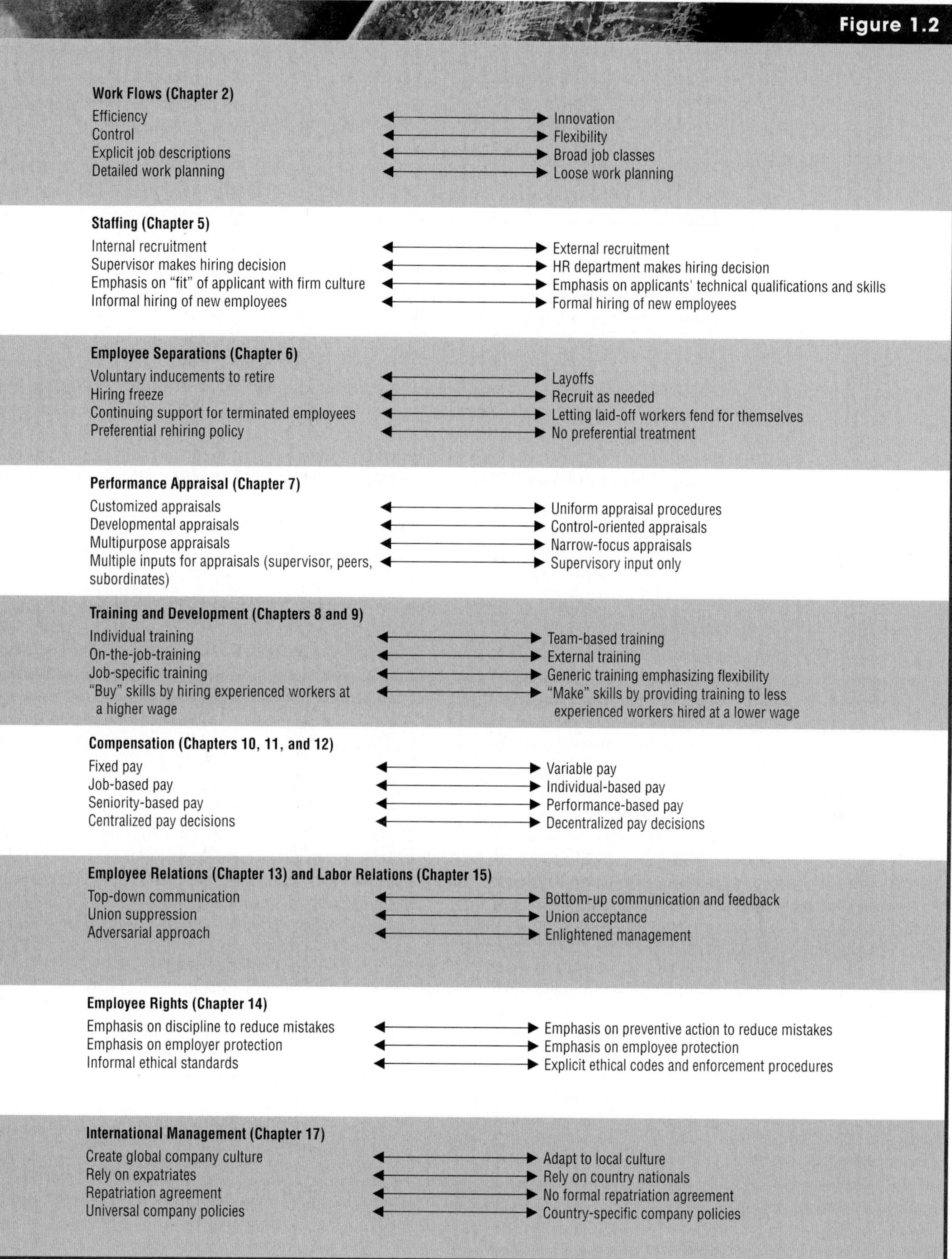

Figure 1.2

Work Flows (Chapter 2)
Efficiency ↔ Innovation
Control ↔ Flexibility
Explicit job descriptions ↔ Broad job classes
Detailed work planning ↔ Loose work planning

Staffing (Chapter 5)
Internal recruitment ↔ External recruitment
Supervisor makes hiring decision ↔ HR department makes hiring decision
Emphasis on "fit" of applicant with firm culture ↔ Emphasis on applicants' technical qualifications and skills
Informal hiring of new employees ↔ Formal hiring of new employees

Employee Separations (Chapter 6)
Voluntary inducements to retire ↔ Layoffs
Hiring freeze ↔ Recruit as needed
Continuing support for terminated employees ↔ Letting laid-off workers fend for themselves
Preferential rehiring policy ↔ No preferential treatment

Performance Appraisal (Chapter 7)
Customized appraisals ↔ Uniform appraisal procedures
Developmental appraisals ↔ Control-oriented appraisals
Multipurpose appraisals ↔ Narrow-focus appraisals
Multiple inputs for appraisals (supervisor, peers, subordinates) ↔ Supervisory input only

Training and Development (Chapters 8 and 9)
Individual training ↔ Team-based training
On-the-job-training ↔ External training
Job-specific training ↔ Generic training emphasizing flexibility
"Buy" skills by hiring experienced workers at a higher wage ↔ "Make" skills by providing training to less experienced workers hired at a lower wage

Compensation (Chapters 10, 11, and 12)
Fixed pay ↔ Variable pay
Job-based pay ↔ Individual-based pay
Seniority-based pay ↔ Performance-based pay
Centralized pay decisions ↔ Decentralized pay decisions

Employee Relations (Chapter 13) and Labor Relations (Chapter 15)
Top-down communication ↔ Bottom-up communication and feedback
Union suppression ↔ Union acceptance
Adversarial approach ↔ Enlightened management

Employee Rights (Chapter 14)
Emphasis on discipline to reduce mistakes ↔ Emphasis on preventive action to reduce mistakes
Emphasis on employer protection ↔ Emphasis on employee protection
Informal ethical standards ↔ Explicit ethical codes and enforcement procedures

International Management (Chapter 17)
Create global company culture ↔ Adapt to local culture
Rely on expatriates ↔ Rely on country nationals
Repatriation agreement ↔ No formal repatriation agreement
Universal company policies ↔ Country-specific company policies

Strategic HR Choices

Second, many different HR programs or practices may be used separately or together to implement each of these choices. For example, if a firm chooses to base pay on performance, it can use many different programs to implement this decision, including cash awards, lump-sum annual bonuses, raises based on supervisory appraisals, and an employee-of-the-month award. Third, the strategic HR choices listed in Figure 1.2 represent two opposite poles on a continuum. Very few organizations fall at these extremes. Some organizations will be closer to the right end, some closer to the left end, and others closer to the middle.

A brief description of the strategic HR choices shown in Figure 1.2 follows. We will examine these choices and provide examples of companies' strategic decisions in these areas in later chapters.

Work Flows

Work flows refer to the ways tasks are organized to meet production or service goals. Organizations face several choices in what they emphasize as they structure work flows (Chapter 2). They can emphasize:

- efficiency (getting work done at minimum cost) or innovation (encouraging creativity, exploration, and new ways of doing things, even though this may increase production costs)
- control (establishing predetermined procedures) or flexibility (allowing room for exceptions and personal judgment)
- explicit job descriptions (in which each job's duties and requirements are carefully spelled out) or broad job classes (in which employees perform multiple tasks and are expected to fill different jobs as needed)
- detailed work planning (in which processes, objectives, and schedules are laid out well in advance) or loose work planning (in which activities and schedules may be modified on relatively short notice, depending on changing needs)

Staffing

Staffing encompasses the HR activities designed to secure the right employees at the right place at the right time (Chapter 5). Organizations face several strategic HR choices in recruiting, selecting, and socializing employees—all part of the staffing process. These include:

- promoting from within (*internal* recruitment) versus hiring from the outside (*external* recruitment)
- empowering immediate supervisors to make hiring decisions versus centralizing these decisions in the HR department
- emphasizing a good fit between the applicant and the firm versus hiring the most knowledgeable individual regardless of interpersonal considerations
- hiring new workers informally or choosing a more formal and systematic approach to hiring

Employee Separations

Employee separations occur when employees leave the firm, either voluntarily or involuntarily (Chapter 6). Some strategic HR choices available to the firm for handling employee separations are:

- use of voluntary inducements (such as early retirement packages) to downsize a work force versus use of layoffs
- imposing a hiring freeze to avoid laying off current employees versus recruiting employees as needed, even if doing so means laying off current employees
- providing continuing support to terminated employees (perhaps by offering them assistance in securing another job) versus leaving laid-off employees to fend for themselves
- making a commitment to rehire terminated employees if conditions improve versus avoiding any type of preferential hiring treatment for ex-employees

Performance Appraisal

Managers assess how well employees are carrying out their assigned duties by conducting performance appraisals (Chapter 7). Some strategic HR choices concerning employee appraisals are:

- developing an appraisal system that is customized to the needs of various employee groups (for example, by designing a different appraisal form for each job family) versus using a standardized appraisal system throughout the organization
- using the appraisal data as a developmental tool to help employees improve their performance versus using appraisals as a control mechanism to weed out low producers
- designing the appraisal system with multiple objectives in mind (such as training, promotion, and selection decisions) versus designing it for a narrow purpose (such as pay decisions only)
- developing an appraisal system that encourages the active participation of multiple employee groups (for example, supervisor, peers, and subordinates) versus developing one that asks solely for the input of each employee's supervisor.

A Question of Ethics

Experts in career development note that in today's increasingly chaotic business and economic environment, individual employees need to prepare themselves for job and career changes. Does an employer have an ethical duty to help employees prepare for the change that is almost certain to come?

Training and Career Development

Training and career development activities are designed to help an organization meet its skill requirements and to help its employees realize their maximum potential (Chapters 8 and 9). Some of the strategic HR choices pertaining to these activities are:

- choosing whether to provide training to individuals or to teams of employees who may come from diverse areas of the firm
- deciding whether to teach required skills on the job or rely on external sources for training
- choosing whether to emphasize job-specific training or generic training
- deciding whether to hire at a high wage people from outside the firm who already have the required talents ("buy skills") or to invest resources in training the firm's own lower-wage employees in the necessary skills ("make skills")

Compensation

Compensation is the payment that employees receive in exchange for their labor. U.S. organizations vary widely in how they choose to compensate their employees (Chapters 10, 11, and 12). Some of the strategic HR choices related to pay are:

- providing employees with a fixed salary and benefits package that changes little from year to year (and, therefore, involves minimal risk) versus paying employees a variable amount subject to change
- paying employees on the basis of the job they hold versus paying them for their individual contributions to the firm
- rewarding employees for the time they have spent with the firm versus rewarding them for performance
- centralizing pay decisions in a single location (such as the HR department) versus empowering the supervisor or work team to make pay decisions

Employee Rights

Employee rights concern the relationship between the organization and individual employees (Chapter 14). Some of the strategic choices that the firm needs to make in this area are:

- emphasizing discipline as the mechanism for controlling employee behavior versus proactively encouraging appropriate behavior in the first place
- developing policies that emphasize protecting the employer's interests versus policies that emphasize protecting the employees' interests
- relying on informal ethical standards versus developing explicit standards and procedures to enforce those standards

Employee and Labor Relations

Employee and labor relations (Chapters 13 and 15) refer to the interaction between workers (either as individuals or as represented by a union) and management. Some of the strategic HR choices facing the firm in these areas are:

- relying on "top-down" communication channels from managers to subordinates versus encouraging "bottom-up" feedback from employees to managers
- actively trying to avoid or suppress union-organizing activity versus accepting unions as representatives of employees' interests
- adopting an adversarial approach to dealing with employees versus responding to employees' needs so that the incentive for unionization is removed (enlightened management)

International Management

Firms that operate outside domestic boundaries face a set of strategic HR options regarding how to manage human resources on a global basis (Chapter 17). Some of the key strategic HR choices involved in international management are:

- creating a common company culture to reduce intercountry cultural differences versus allowing foreign subsidiaries to adapt to the local culture
- sending expatriates (domestic employees) abroad to manage foreign subsidiaries versus hiring local people to manage them
- establishing a repatriation agreement with each employee going abroad (carefully stipulating what the expatriate can expect upon return in terms of career advancement, compensation, and the like) versus avoiding any type of commitment to expatriates
- establishing company policies that must be followed in all subsidiaries versus decentralizing policy formulation so that each local office can develop its own policies.

Selecting HR Strategies to Increase Firm Performance

No HR strategy is "good" or "bad" in and of itself. Rather, the success of HR strategies depends on the situation or context in which they are used. In other words, an HR strategy's effect on firm performance is always dependent on how well it fits with other factors. This fact leads to a simple yet powerful prediction for HR strategies that has been widely supported by research: Fit leads to better performance, and lack of fit creates inconsistencies that reduce performance.[150] *Fit* refers to the consistency or compatibility between HR strategies and other important aspects of the organization.

Figure 1.3 depicts the key factors that firms should consider in determining which HR strategies will have a positive impact on firm performance: organizational strategies, environment, organizational characteristics, and organizational capabilities. As the figure shows, the relative contribution of an HR strategy to firm performance increases:

1. The greater the match between the HR strategy and the firm's overall organizational strategies.
2. The greater the extent to which the HR strategy is attuned to the environment in which the firm is operating.
3. The more the HR strategy is molded to unique organizational features.
4. The more the HR strategy enables the firm to capitalize on its distinctive competencies.
5. The more the HR strategies are mutually consistent or reinforce one another.

Corporate strategy
The mix of businesses a corporation decides to hold and the flow of resources among those businesses.

Business unit strategy
The formulation and implementation of strategies by a firm that is relatively autonomous, even if it is part of a larger corporation.

Fit with Organizational Strategies

Depending on the firm's size and complexity, organizational strategies may be examined at two levels: corporate or business. A corporation may have multiple businesses that are very similar to or completely different from one another. **Corporate strategy** refers to the mix of businesses a corporation decides to hold and the flow of resources among those businesses. The main strategic business decisions at the corporate level concern acquisition, divestment, diversification, and growth. **Business unit strategies** refer to the formulation and implementation of strategies by firms that are relatively autonomous, even if they are part of a larger corporation. For instance, until fairly recently, AT&T as a corporate entity owned hundreds of largely inde-

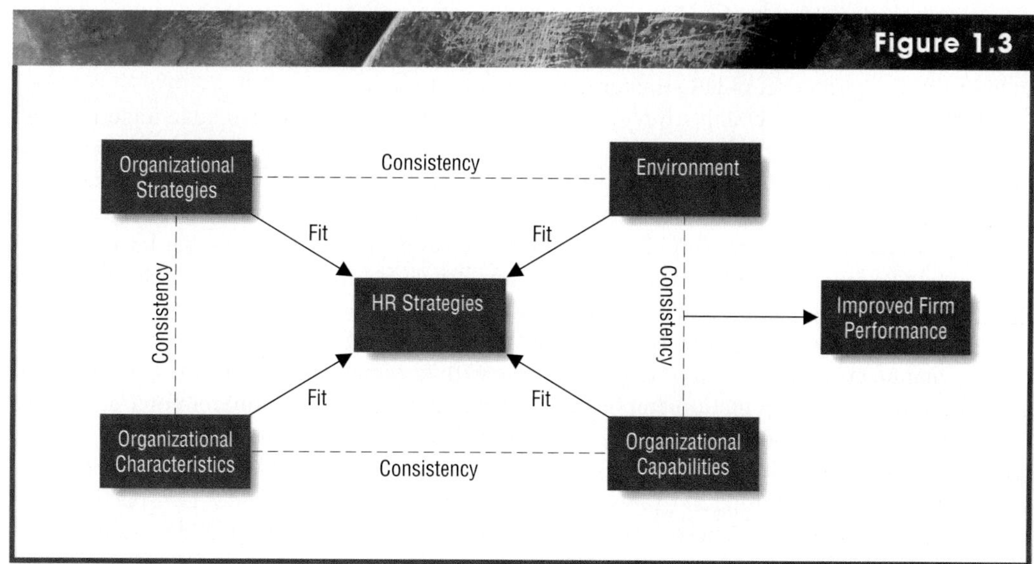

Effective HR Strategy Formulation and Implementation

pendent firms, including perfume makers and Hostess Twinkies, each with its own business strategy.[151] Similarly, diversified giant DuPont combines businesses such as drugs, agriculture, and chemicals under one roof.[152] In the case of firms that produce a single product or highly related products or services, the business and corporate strategies are identical. For companies that have distinct corporate and business unit strategies, it is important to examine each in terms of its fit with HR strategies.

Corporate Strategies

There are two major types of corporate strategies and matching HR strategies. Corporations adopting an *evolutionary business strategy* engage in aggressive acquisitions of new businesses, even if these are totally unrelated to one another.[153]

In evolutionary firms, the management of change is crucial to survival. Entrepreneurship is encouraged and control is deemphasized because each unit is relatively autonomous. Certain HR strategies fit best with an evolutionary strategy. HR strategies that foster flexibility, quick response, entrepreneurship, risk sharing, and decentralization are particularly appropriate. Because the evolutionary corporation is not committed to a particular business or industry, it may hire workers from the external market as needed and lay them off to reduce costs if necessary, with no promise of rehiring them. These HR strategies are appropriate because they "fit" with the organizational reality that change is the only constant.

A Question of Ethics

The dark side of strategic planning is that workers are sometimes thought of as numbers on a page or dollars in a budget rather than as flesh-and-blood human beings. When divisions are spun off or merged, individual employees are dramatically affected. What responsibility does the employer have toward its employees in situations like these?

At the other end of the spectrum, corporations adopting a *steady-state strategy* are very choosy about how they grow. They avoid acquiring firms outside their industry or even companies within the industry that are very different from them. Firms with a steady-state strategy have an inward focus. Top managers exercise a great deal of direct control over the company and prefer to promote employee dependence on supervisors rather than independent action or entrepreneurship. Internal development of new products and technologies and interunit coordination are very important to these firms.[154] This is the case at Rubbermaid, a company known for producing such mundane products as trash cans and dustpans. Yet, Rubbermaid's record for innovation is anything but mundane. The company brings out new products at the rate of one a day.[155] The HR strategies most appropriate to steady-state firms emphasize efficiency, detailed work planning, internal grooming of employees for promotion and long-term career development, centralization, and a paternalistic attitude (reflected, for example, in preferential recall of laid-off employees when the economic environment improves).

Porter's Business Unit Strategies

Two well-known business unit strategies were formulated by Porter[156] and Miles and Snow.[157] Both of these may be used to analyze which HR strategies represent the best fit with a firm's business strategy.

Porter has identified three types of business unit strategies that help a firm cope with competitive forces and outperform other firms in the industry. For each of these strategies, outlined in Figure 1.4, a certain set of HR strategies would fit best.[158]

The *overall cost leadership strategy* is aimed at gaining a competitive advantage through lower costs. Financial considerations and budgetary constraints play a critical role here in shaping HR strategies. Cost leadership requires aggressive construction of efficient plant facilities (which requires sustained capital investment), intense supervision of labor, vigorous pursuit of cost reductions, and tight control of distribution costs and overhead. Firms that have successfully pursued a low-cost leadership strategy include Briggs & Stratton, Emerson Electric, Texas Instruments, Black & Decker, and DuPont.[159]

Low-cost firms tend to emphasize structured tasks and responsibilities, products designed for easy manufacture, and the need to predict costs with minimal margin of error. The HR strategies that fit a low-cost orientation emphasize efficient, low-cost production; reinforce adherence to rational, highly structured procedures to minimize uncertainty; and discourage creativity and innovation (which may lead to costly experimentation and mistakes). Thus, effective HR strategies include carefully spelling out the work that each employee needs to do, job-specific training, hiring workers with the necessary technical qualifications and skills, paying employees on the basis of job held, and relying on performance appraisals as a control tool to weed out low performers.

A firm with a *differentiation business strategy* attempts to achieve a competitive advantage by creating a product or service that is perceived as unique. Some common characteristics of such firms are strong marketing abilities, an emphasis on product engineering and basic research, a corporate reputation for quality products, and amenities that are attractive to highly skilled labor. Approaches to differentiating can take many forms; among them are design or brand image (Fieldcrest in top-of-the-line towels and linens; Mercedes-Benz in automobiles); technology (Hyster in lift trucks; Fisher in stereo components; Coleman in camping equipment); fea-

Figure 1.4

Business Strategy	Common Organizational Characteristics	HR Strategies
Overall cost leadership	■ Sustained capital investment and access to capital ■ Intense supervision of labor ■ Tight cost control requiring frequent, detailed control reports ■ Low-cost distribution system ■ Structured organization and responsibilities ■ Products designed for ease in manufacture	■ Efficient production ■ Explicit job descriptions ■ Detailed work planning ■ Emphasis on technical qualifications and skills ■ Emphasis on job-specific training ■ Emphasis on job-based pay ■ Use of performance appraisal as a control device
Differentiation	■ Strong marketing abilities ■ Product engineering ■ Strong capability in basic research ■ Corporate reputation for quality or technological leadership ■ Amenities to attract highly skilled labor, scientists, or creative people	■ Emphasis on innovation and flexibility ■ Broad job classes ■ Loose work planning ■ External recruitment ■ Team-based training ■ Emphasis on individual-based pay ■ Use of performance appraisal as developmental tool
Focus	Combination of cost-leadership and differentiation strategy directed at a particular strategic target	Combination of HR strategies above

Source: Common organizational characteristics: Porter, M. E. (1980). *Competitive Strategy*, 40–41. New York: Free Press.

Selected HR Strategies That Fit Porter's Three Major Types of Business Strategies

tures (Jenn-Air in electric ranges); customer service (IBM in computers); and dealer networks (Caterpillar Tractor in construction equipment).

Differentiation provides a competitive advantage because of the brand loyalty it fosters. Consumers who are brand loyal are less sensitive to changes in price. This enables the differentiator to enjoy higher profit margins, which in turn allow it to invest in activities that are costly and risky but that enhance the perceived superiority of its products or services. These activities include extensive research, experimentation with new ideas and product designs, catering to the needs of different customers, and supporting creative initiatives by managers and employees.

HR strategies that fit a differentiation strategy emphasize innovation, flexibility, renewal of the workforce by attracting new talent from other firms, opportunities for mavericks, and reinforcement (rather than discouragement) of creative flair. The specific HR strategies that are likely to benefit differentiators include the use of broad job classes, loose work planning, external recruitment at all levels, team-based learning, emphasis on what the individual can do (rather than on the job title held) as a basis for pay, and reliance on performance appraisal as a developmental (rather than a control) device.

The *focus strategy* relies on both a low-cost position and differentiation, with the objective of serving a narrow target market better than other firms. The firm seeks to achieve differentiation either from better meeting the needs of the particular target, or from lowering costs in serving this target, or both.[160] Firms that have used this strategy successfully include Illinois Tool Works (in the specialty market for fasteners), Gymboree (a national franchise providing creative activities and accessories for children under the age of 5), Fort Howard Paper (manufacturer of specialized industrial grade papers), and Porter Paint (producer of paints for professional housepainters).

The HR strategies likely to fit the focus strategy best would be somewhere in the middle of those described for low-cost producers and differentiators. At Illinois Tool Works (ITW), for instance, the chairman stresses working hand-in-hand with customers both to find out what they want and to learn how ITW can help them lower their operating costs. HR strategies reflect this focus by boosting efficiency to hold costs down. ITW's business is decentralized into 200 fairly small operating units, headed by managers whose pay is largely tied to sales and profits at their individual operations. The company's workers are nonunion, which helps to hold costs down. To keep ITW's products geared to customer needs, management puts heavy emphasis on R&D. ITW's R&D spending of almost $40 million a year keeps creativity high; ITW holds over 4,000 active patents.[161]

Miles and Snow's Business Strategies

Miles and Snow created another well-known classification of business unit strategies.[162] They characterize successful businesses as primarily adopting either a defender or a prospector strategy.

Defenders are conservative business units that prefer to maintain a secure position in relatively stable product or service areas instead of looking to expand into uncharted territory. Defenders attempt to protect their market share from competitors rather than engage in new-product development. Defenders tend to be highly formalized and to emphasize cost control, and to operate in a stable environment. Many defenders develop an elaborate internal system for promoting, transferring, and rewarding workers that is relatively isolated from the uncertainties of the external labor market. In exchange for a long-term commitment to the firm, employees are rewarded with job security and the expectation of upward mobility through the ranks. Defenders discourage risk-taking behaviors because they prefer reliability to innovation.

The HR strategies that best fit defenders' needs, categorized according to six major strategic HR choices we saw in Figure 1.2 earlier, are summarized in Figure 1.5 on page 32. These strategies include work flows emphasizing managerial control and reliability, staffing and employee separation policies designed to foster long-term employee attachment to the firm, performance appraisals focused on managerial control and hierarchy, structured training programs, and compensation policies that emphasize job security.

Unlike defenders, whose success comes primarily from efficiently serving a stable market, the prospector's key objective is to find and exploit new product and market opportunities.[163] *Prospectors* emphasize growth and innovation, development of new products, and an eagerness to be the first in new-product or market areas, even if some of these efforts fail. The prospector's

Figure 1.5

Strategic HR Area	Defender Strategy	Prospector Strategy
Work flows	■ Efficient production ■ Control emphasis ■ Explicit job descriptions ■ Detailed work planning	■ Innovation ■ Flexibility ■ Broad job classes ■ Loose work planning
Staffing	■ Internal recruitment ■ HR department makes selection decision ■ Emphasis on technical qualifications and skills ■ Formal hiring and socialization process	■ External recruitment ■ Supervisor makes selection decision ■ Emphasis on fit of applicant with culture ■ Informal hiring and socialization process of new employees
Employee separations	■ Voluntary inducements to leave ■ Hiring freeze ■ Continuing concern for terminated employee ■ Preferential rehiring policy	■ Layoffs ■ Recruit as needed ■ Individual on his or her own ■ No preferential treatment for laid-off workers
Performance appraisal	■ Uniform appraisal procedures ■ Used as control device ■ Narrow focus ■ High dependence on superior	■ Customized appraisals ■ Used as developmental tool ■ Multipurpose appraisals ■ Multiple inputs for appraisals
Training	■ Individual training ■ On-the-job training ■ Job-specific training ■ "Make" skills	■ Team-based or cross-functional training ■ External training ■ Generic training emphasizing flexibility ■ "Buy" skills
Compensation	■ Fixed pay ■ Job-based pay ■ Seniority-based pay ■ Centralized pay decisions	■ Variable pay ■ Individual-based pay ■ Performance-based pay ■ Decentralized pay decisions

Source: Gómez-Mejía, L. R. (2003). Compensation strategies and Miles and Snow's business strategy taxonomy. Unpublished report. Management Department, Arizona State University.

Selected HR Strategies That Fit Miles and Snow's Two Major Types of Business Strategies

strategy is associated with flexible and decentralized organizational structures, complex products (such as computers and pharmaceuticals), and unstable environments that change rapidly.

The HR strategies that match the strategic orientation of prospectors, also summarized in Figure 1.5, involve work flows that foster creativity and adaptability; staffing and employee separation policies that focus on the external labor market; customized, participative employee appraisals used for multiple purposes (including employee development); training strategies targeting broad skills; and a decentralized compensation system that rewards risk taking and performance. The Issues and Applications feature titled "Lincoln Electric and Hewlett-Packard: Defender and Prospector" discusses how these two firms have successfully used HR strategies to support their opposite business strategies.

Issues and Applications

Lincoln Electric and Hewlett-Packard: Defender and Prospector

To get a better idea of what it means for a company to be a defender or a prospector, let us look at the activities of two companies: Ohio-based Lincoln Electric, a manufacturer of electrical products; and Hewlett-Packard, the Palo Alto, California, electronics manufacturer that put Silicon Valley on the high-tech map.

Lincoln Electric

Lincoln Electric is a classic defender. It has carved out a niche in the electrical products industry (the manufacture of electric arc-welding generators, welding equipment, and supplies) and has "defended" it for over 70 years through continuous efforts to improve production processes and product quality, cut costs, lower prices, and provide outstanding customer service. Lincoln is best known for its incentive system, which rewards high-quantity, high-quality output with wages and bonuses that average over *twice* the national average for comparable work classifications. Lincoln's HR strategies fit with the company's strategy because Lincoln has created a secure market share with moderate, steady growth. It relies heavily on internally developed human resources. Employees are carefully selected, placed, and trained, and they are expected to be with the company for much, if not all, of their careers.

The appropriate role for the HR department at Lincoln is clear. Selection, placement, appraisal, and long-term training assistance are key services. In addition, the HR department must constantly maintain the fit between job design and the incentive system. Lincoln is a tightly integrated company that requires predictable, planned HR inputs and regular maintenance.

Hewlett-Packard

Hewlett-Packard (HP) began with the notion that high returns were possible from moving products as rapidly as possible from basic design to the market. It is a company well suited to the rapid expansion of a growing industry—a true prospector—with small, changing product divisions as its basic organizational building blocks. (The company has over 60,000 employees in more than 60 divisions or units.) A new-product idea or offshoot is evolved, a self-contained division is created, and a market is pursued as long as HP has a distinctive design or technological advantage. When products reach the stage where successful competition turns primarily on cost, HP may move out of the arena and turn its attention to a new design or an entirely new product.

HR units at both the division and the corporate level have the constant task of starting new groups, and finding and deploying managerial and technical resources. In this setting, HR departments perform an essentially entrepreneurial role, helping to identify and quickly develop (through rapid movement and alternative assignments) crucial human resources. Key human resources are brought in from the outside and invested in myriad units and divisions, as well as developed internally. Thus, the overall HR strategy at Hewlett-Packard can be characterized as acquiring human resources.

Source: Based on Miles, R. E., and Snow, C. C. (1984). Designing strategic human resources systems. *Organizational Dynamics 13*(1), 43–46.

Fit with the Environment

In addition to reinforcing overall organizational strategies, HR strategies should help the organization better exploit environmental opportunities or cope with the unique environmental forces that affect it. The relevant environment can be examined in terms of four major dimensions: (1) *degree of uncertainty* (how much accurate information is available to make appropriate business decisions); (2) *volatility* (how often the environment changes); (3) *magnitude of change* (how drastic the changes are); and (4) *complexity* (how many different elements in the environment affect the firm, either individually or together). For example, much of the computer and high-tech industry is very high on all four of these dimensions:

- **Degree of uncertainty.** Compaq thought consumers would continue to pay a premium price for its high-performance computers. The company was proved wrong in the 1990s as low-cost competitors such as Dell, Packard Bell, and AST quickly cut into Compaq's market.
- **Volatility.** IBM paid dearly when demand for its mainframe computers declined drastically in the late 1980s and it was caught unprepared.

- **Magnitude of change.** The advent of each successive new generation of computer microprocessor chips (for example, Intel's 386, 486, Pentium) has almost immediately rendered all previously sold machines obsolete. In 2002 Polaroid was forced to declare bankruptcy as quick adoption of digital cameras turned its main product (instant photography) obsolete almost overnight.
- **Complexity.** The number and variety of competitors in the computer industry, both domestically and overseas, have grown dramatically in recent years. The life of a product seldom extends more than three years now, as new innovations drive previous equipment and software out of the market.

Before formulating and implementing HR strategies, a firm needs to examine how low or high it is on each of these environmental dimensions. As Figure 1.6 shows, firms that are high on these four dimensions are more likely to benefit from HR strategies that promote flexibility, adaptiveness, quick response, transferability of skills, the ability to secure external talent as needed, and risk sharing with employees through variable pay.

Conversely, firms facing environments that are low on uncertainty, volatility, magnitude of change, and complexity benefit from HR strategies that allow for an orderly, rational, and routine approach to dealing with a relatively predictable and stable environment. The "old" AT&T (before divestment), much of the airline and trucking industry before deregulation, utilities, and government bureaucracies fall at the low end of the scale on these four dimensions. Figure 1.6 shows that the HR strategies that fit firms operating under these conditions tend to be rather mechanistic: detailed work planning, job-specific training, fixed pay, explicit job descriptions, centralized pay decisions, and the like.

Figure 1.6

Environmental Dimension	Low	High
Degree of Uncertainty	■ Detailed work planning ■ Job-specific training ■ Fixed pay ■ High dependence on superior	■ Loose work planning ■ Generic training ■ Variable pay ■ Multiple inputs for appraisals
Volatility	■ Control emphasis ■ Efficient production ■ Job-specific training ■ Fixed pay	■ Flexibility ■ Innovation ■ Generic training ■ Variable pay
Magnitude of Change	■ Explicit job descriptions ■ Formal hiring and socialization of new employees ■ "Make" skills ■ Uniform appraisal procedures	■ Broad job classes ■ Informal hiring and socialization of new employees ■ "Buy" skills ■ Customized appraisals
Complexity	■ Control emphasis ■ Internal recruitment ■ Centralized pay decisions ■ High dependence on superior	■ Flexibility ■ External recruitment ■ Decentralized pay decisions ■ Multiple inputs for appraisals

Sources: Based on Gómez-Mejía, L. R., and Balkin, D. B. (2002). *Management.* New York: Irwin/McGraw-Hill; Gómez-Mejía, L. R., and Balkin, D. B. (1992). *Compensation, organizational strategy, and firm performance.* Cincinnati, OH: South-Western; Gómez-Mejía, L. R., Balkin, D. B., and Milkovich, G. T. (1990). Rethinking your rewards for technical employees. *Organizational Dynamics, 18*(4), 62–75; Gómez-Mejía, L. R. (1992). Structure and process of diversification, compensation strategy, and firm performance. *Strategic Management Journal, 13,* 381–397.

Selected HR Strategies for Firms Low and High on Different Environmental Characteristics

Fit with Organizational Characteristics

Every firm has a unique history and its own way of doing business. To be effective, HR strategies must be tailored to the organization's personality. The features of an organization's personality can be broken down into five major categories.

The Production Process for Converting Inputs into Output

Firms with a relatively routine production process (such as large-volume steel mills, lumber mills, and automobile plants) tend to benefit from HR strategies that emphasize control, such as explicit job descriptions and job-specific training. The opposite is true for firms with nonroutine production processes (such as advertising firms, custom printers, and biotechnology companies). These firms benefit from flexible HR strategies that support organizational adaptability, quick response to change, and creative decision making. These flexible strategies may include broad job classes, loose work planning, and generic training.

The Firm's Market Posture

Firms that experience a high rate of sales growth and engage in product innovation destined for a wide market segment tend to benefit from HR strategies that support growth and entrepreneurial activities. These HR strategies include external recruitment ("buying" skills), decentralized pay decisions, and customized appraisals. The opposite is true for firms with low rates of growth and limited product innovation destined for a narrow market segment. These firms tend to benefit more from HR strategies that emphasize efficiency, control, and firm-specific knowledge. Such strategies include internal recruitment ("making" skills), on-the-job training, and high dependence on superiors.

The Firm's Overall Managerial Philosophy

Companies whose top executives are averse to risk, operate with an autocratic leadership style, establish a strong internal pecking order, and are inwardly rather than outwardly focused may find that certain HR practices match this outlook best. The HR strategies most often used in these kinds of firms include seniority-based pay, formal hiring and socializing of new employees, selection decisions made by the HR department, and use of top-down communication channels. The HR strategies that fit a managerial philosophy high on risk taking, participation, egalitarianism, and an external, proactive environmental orientation include variable pay, giving supervisors a major role in hiring decisions, up-and-down communication channels, and multiple inputs for performance appraisals.

The Firm's Organizational Structure

Some HR strategies fit very well with highly formalized organizations that are divided into functional areas (for example, marketing, finance, production, and so on) and that concentrate decision making at the top. The HR strategies appropriate for this type of firm include a control emphasis, centralized pay decisions, explicit job descriptions, and job-based pay. Firms whose organizational structures are less regimented will benefit from a different set of HR strategies, including informal hiring and socializing of new employees, decentralized pay decisions, broad job classes, and individual-based pay.

The Firm's Organizational Culture

Two important dimensions of a firm's culture should be considered when formulating and implementing HR strategies: entrepreneurial climate and moral commitment. Companies that foster an *entrepreneurial climate* benefit from supporting HR strategies such as loose work planning, informal hiring and socializing of new employees, and variable pay. Firms that discourage entrepreneurship generally prefer a control emphasis, detailed work planning, formal hiring and socializing of new employees, and fixed pay.

A strong emphasis on *moral commitment*—the extent to which a firm tries to foster a long-term emotional attachment between the firm and its employees—is also associated with certain supporting HR strategies. These include an emphasis on preventive versus remedial disciplinary action to handle employee mistakes, employee protection, and explicit ethical codes to monitor and guide behavior. Firms that are low on moral commitment usually rely on an authoritarian relationship between employee and company. HR strategies consistent with this orientation include an emphasis on discipline or punishment to reduce employee mistakes, employment at will (discussed in Chapters 3 and 14), and informal ethical standards.

Fit with Organizational Capabilities

Distinctive competencies The characteristics that give a firm a competitive edge.

A firm's organizational capabilities include its **distinctive competencies,** those characteristics (such as technical ability, management systems, and reputation) that give the firm a competitive edge. For instance, Mercedes-Benz automobiles are widely regarded as superior because of the quality of their design and engineering. Wal-Mart's phenomenal success has been due, at least in part, to its ability to track products from supplier to customer better than its competitors can.

HR strategies make a greater contribution to firm performance the greater the extent to which (1) they help the company exploit its specific advantages or strengths while avoiding weaknesses, and (2) they assist the firm in better utilizing its own unique blend of human resource skills and assets.

The following examples illustrate how one type of HR strategy—compensation strategy—may be aligned with organizational capabilities.[164]

- Firms known for excellence in customer service tend to pay their sales force only partially on commission, thereby reducing their sales employees' potential for abrasive behaviors and overselling.
- Smaller firms can use compensation to their advantage by paying low wages but being generous in stock offerings to employees. This strategy allows them to use more of their scarce cash to fuel future growth.
- Organizations may take advantage of their unused capacity in their compensation strategies. For example, most private universities offer free tuition to faculty and their immediate family. With average tuition at private colleges exceeding $13,000 a year, this benefit represents a huge cash savings to faculty members, thereby allowing private universities to attract and retain good faculty with minimal adverse impact on their cost structure.

Choosing Consistent and Appropriate HR Tactics to Implement HR Strategies

As noted earlier, even the best-laid strategic HR plans may fail when specific HR programs are poorly chosen or implemented.[165] In addition to fitting with each of the four factors just described (organizational strategy, environment, organizational characteristics, and organizational capabilities), a firm's HR strategies must be mutually consistent. That is, HR strategies are more likely to be effective if they reinforce one another rather than work at cross-purposes. For instance, many organizations are currently trying to improve their performance by structuring work in teams. However, these same organizations often continue to use a traditional performance appraisal system in which each employee is evaluated individually. The appraisal system needs to be overhauled to make it consistent with the emphasis on team performance.

Because it is not always possible to know beforehand if an HR program will meet its objectives, a periodic evaluation of HR programs is necessary. The Manager's Notebook titled "But Will It Work?" lists a series of important questions that should be raised to examine the appropriateness of HR programs. These questions should be answered as new programs are being chosen and while they are in effect. (A Manager's Notebook feature appears in every chapter in this book.)

MANAGER'S NOTEBOOK

Customer-Driven HR

But Will It Work? Questions for Testing the Appropriateness of HR Programs Before Implementation

HR programs that look good on paper may turn out to be disasters when implemented because they conflict too much with company realities. To avoid this kind of unpleasant surprise, it is important to ask the following questions *before* implementing a new HR program.

1. Are the HR Programs Effective Tools for Implementing HR Strategies?
   - ✔ Are the proposed HR programs the most appropriate ones for implementing the firm's HR strategies?
   - ✔ Has an analysis been done of how each of the past, current, or planned HR programs contributes to or hinders the successful implementation of the firm's HR strategies?
   - ✔ Can the proposed HR programs be easily changed or modified to meet new strategic considerations without violating either a "psychological" or a legal contract with employees?
2. Do the HR Programs Meet Resource Constraints?
   - ✔ Does the organization have the capacity to implement the proposed HR programs? In other words, are the HR programs realistic?
   - ✔ Are the proposed programs going to be introduced at a rate that can be easily absorbed, or will the timing and extent of changes lead to widespread confusion and strong employee resistance?
3. How Will the HR Programs Be Communicated?
   - ✔ Are the proposed HR programs well understood by those who will implement them (for example, line supervisors and employees)?
   - ✔ Does top management understand how the proposed programs are intended to affect the firm's strategic objectives?
4. Who Will Put the HR Programs in Motion?
   - ✔ Is the HR department playing the role of an internal consultant to assist employees and managers responsible for carrying out the proposed HR programs?
   - ✔ Is top management visibly and emphatically committed to the proposed programs?

The HR Department and Managers: An Important Partnership

This book takes a managerial approach to human resources and HR strategy. All managers—regardless of their functional area, their position in the hierarchy, and the size of the firm for which they work—must deal effectively with HR issues because these issues are at the heart of being a good manager.

The role of a company's human resources department is to support, not to supplant, managers' HR responsibilities. For instance, the HR department may develop a form to help managers measure the performance of subordinates, but it is the managers who conduct the actual evaluation. Stated another way, the HR department is primarily responsible for helping the firm meet its business objectives by designing HR programs, but managers must carry out these programs. This means that every manager is a human resource manager.

There is widespread consensus that HR professionals need to know their organization's business thoroughly—not only in terms of people, but also in terms of the economic, financial, environmental, and technological forces affecting it.[166] Rather than playing a staff role, they should become internal consultants known for their expertise and ability to help solve the HR problems faced by line managers. They should also be able to merge HR activities effectively with the firm's business needs.[167]

For the sake of the firm, managers and the HR department need to work together closely. Unfortunately, lack of cooperation has traditionally been a problem, and even today it is not uncommon for managers and HR professionals to view each other negatively. These negative perceptions often create a communication gap and hinder the establishment of an effective partnership between the two groups. Figure 1.7 (page 38) lists the five sets of competencies HR professionals need to be considered full strategic partners in running the business.

Companies can take certain steps to foster an effective partnership between managers and the HR department.[168] Specifically, companies should:

- Analyze the people side of productivity rather than depend solely on technical solutions to problems. This requires that managers be trained in certain HR skills. It also requires encour-

Figure 1.7

Leadership
- Understand the nature and styles of leadership, and display appropriate leadership characteristics in performance of professional responsibilities.
- Demonstrate leadership at multiple performance levels:
  - Individual
  - Team
  - Unit or organization

Knowledge of the Business
- Understand corporate business (structure, vision and values, goals, strategies, financial and performance characteristics).
- Understand the unit's business, including special knowledge of competitors, products, technology, and sources of competitive advantage.
- Understand internal and external customers.
- Understand the environment (external and internal) of corporation and individual businesses.
- Understand:
  - Key business disciplines
  - Nature, scope, and HR implications of business globalization
  - Information technology as it affects competitiveness and business processes

HR Strategic Thinking
- Understand the strategic business planning process.
- Understand and be able to apply a systematic HR planning process.
- Be able to select, design, and integrate HR systems or practices to build organizational mind-set, capability, and competitive advantage for the business.
- Be able to develop and integrate business unit HR strategies within framework of corporate HR strategies.

Process Skills
- All HR professionals should be competent in key corporate processes and understand management processes critical to particular business units.
- Understand key process skills such as consulting, problem solving, evaluation/diagnosis, workshop design, and facilitation.
- Understand the basic principles, methodologies, and processes of organizational change and development. Facilitate and manage organizational change.
- Balance, integrate, and manage under conditions of uncertainty and paradox.

HR Technologies
- All HR professionals should have a generalist perspective on HR systems and practices as they relate to achievement of business competitive advantage.
- Generalists are capable of designing, integrating, and implementing HR systems to build organizational capability and create business competitive advantage.
- Specialists are capable of designing/delivering leading-edge practices to meet competitive business needs.
- All HR professionals are capable of measuring effectiveness of HR systems and practices.

Source: Adapted with permission from Boroski, J. W. (1990). Putting it together: HR planning in "3D" at Eastman Kodak, *Human Resource Planning, 13*(1), 54. Copyright 1990 by The Human Resource Planning Society.

Competencies Required of HR Department to Become a Full Strategic Partner

aging managers to value human resources as a key element in organizational effectiveness and performance.

- View HR professionals as internal consultants who can provide valuable advice and support that improve the management of operations. In other words, rather than thinking of the HR department as a group responsible for enforcing bureaucratic procedures, view it as a source of expertise capable of assisting managers in solving personnel-related problems, planning for the future, and improving utilization of productive capacity.
- Instill a shared sense of common fate in the firm rather than a win/lose perspective among individual departments and units. This means developing incentives for managers and HR professionals to work together to achieve common goals.
- Require some managerial experience as part of the training of HR professionals. This requirement should make HR staff more sensitive to and cognizant of the problems managers face.
- Actively involve top corporate and divisional managers in formulating, implementing, and reviewing all HR plans and strategies in close collaboration with the HR department. This should increase top management's commitment to the effective implementation of these plans.
- Require senior HR executives to participate on an equal basis with other key managers from the various functional areas (marketing, finance) involved in charting the enterprise's strategic direction.

Companies should also periodically conduct an **HR audit** to evaluate how effectively they are using their human resources. The audit, which is typically conducted by the HR department, deals with a broad set of questions, including:

HR audit
A periodic review of the effectiveness with which a company uses its human resources. Frequently includes an evaluation of the HR department itself.

- Is the turnover rate exceptionally low or high?
- Are the people quitting good employees who are frustrated in their present job, or are they marginal performers?
- Is the firm receiving a high return on the money it spends on recruitment, training, and pay-for-performance plans?
- Is the firm complying with government regulations?
- How well is the company managing employee diversity?
- Is the HR department providing the services that line managers need?
- Are HRM policies and procedures helping the firm accomplish its long-term goals?

The HR audit addresses these and other important issues systematically so that effective programs can be maintained and ineffective programs corrected or eliminated.

Specialization in Human Resource Management

Over the past three decades, the size of the typical HR department has increased considerably. This increase reflects both the growth and complexity of government regulations and a greater awareness that HR issues are important to the achievement of business objectives.

Many colleges and universities now offer specialized degrees in human resources at the associate, bachelor's, master's, and doctoral levels. The Society for Human Resource Management (SHRM), which has almost 60,000 members, has set up a certification institute to offer HR professionals the opportunity to be certified officially at the PHR (Professional Human Resources) or SPHR (Senior Professional Human Resources) level. SHRM certification requires a certain amount of experience and mastery of a body of knowledge as indicated by successful completion of a comprehensive examination. (For additional information and application materials, write to the Society at 1800 Duke Street, Alexandria, VA 22314 or visit the Web site at www.shrm.org.) Other organizations whose members specialize in a particular area of HRM are WorldatWork (previously the American Compensation Association), the Human Resource Planning Society, and the American Society for Training and Development.[169]

In recent years, the compensation of HR specialists has increased faster than other jobs, and for some HR jobs pay is sharply on the rise, reflecting greater professionalization and increasing awareness by business that a well-managed HR function may help the firm achieve a sustainable competitive advantage. Whereas HR directors have a median annual income of $78,968, the top jobs in this field pay more than $500,000. Among the specialized subfields, executive trainers (median pay = $117,600), corporate compensation directors (median pay = $109,975), benefit directors (median pay = $105,865), and corporate security managers (median pay = $102,500, a new position added by many firms following the September 11, 2001, attacks) are paid the most.[170]

Summary and Conclusions

Human Resource Management: The Challenges

The major HR challenges facing managers today can be divided into three categories: environmental challenges, organizational challenges, and individual challenges.

The environmental challenges are rapid change, rise of the Internet, workforce diversity, economic globalization, legislation, evolving work and family roles, skill shortages, and the rise of the service sector.

The organizational challenges are choosing a competitive position, decentralization, downsizing, organizational restructuring, the rise of self-managed work teams, the increased number of small businesses, organizational culture, advances in technology, and the rise of outsourcing.

The individual challenges involve matching people with the organization, treating employees ethically and engaging in socially responsible behavior, increasing individual productivity, deciding whether to empower employees, taking steps to avoid brain drain, and dealing with issues of job insecurity.

Planning and Implementing Strategic HR Policies

Correctly done, strategic HR planning provides many direct and indirect benefits for a company. These include the encouragement of proactive (rather than reactive) behavior; explicit communication of company goals; stimulation of critical thinking and ongoing examination of assumptions; identification of gaps between the company's current situation and its future vision; the encouragement of line managers' participation in the strategic planning process; the identification of HR constraints and opportunities; and the creation of common bonds within the organization.

In developing an effective HR strategy, an organization faces several challenges. These include putting in place a strategy that creates and maintains a competitive advantage for the company and reinforces the overall business strategy; avoiding excessive concentration on day-to-day problems; developing strategies suited to unique organizational features; coping with the environment in which the business operates; securing management commitment; translating the strategic plan into action; combining intended and emergent strategies; and accommodating change.

A firm's strategic HR choices are the options available to it in designing its human resources systems. Firms must make strategic choices in many HR areas, including work flows, staffing, employee separations, performance appraisal, training and career development, compensation, employee rights, employee and labor relations, and international management.

Selecting HR Strategies to Increase Firm Performance

To be effective, HR strategies must fit with overall organizational strategies, the environment in which the firm is operating, unique organizational characteristics, and organizational capabilities. HR strategies should also be mutually consistent and reinforce one another.

The HR Department and Managers: An Important Partnership

Responsibility for the effective use of human resources lies primarily with managers. Hence, all managers are personnel managers. HR professionals' role is to act as internal consultants or experts, assisting managers to do their jobs better.

Over the past three decades, the size of the typical HR department has increased considerably. This increase reflects both the growth and complexity of government regulations and a greater awareness that HR issues are important to the achievement of business objectives.

Key Terms

ability, 19
brain drain, 20
business unit strategy, 28
corporate strategy, 28
decentralization, 11
distinctive competencies, 36
downsizing, 11
empowerment, 19
environmental challenges, 3
HR audit, 39
human resources (HR), 2
human resource strategy, 2
human resource tactic, 2
individual challenges, 17
line employee, 3
manager, 3
motivation, 19
organizational challenges, 10
organizational culture, 13
outsourcing, 16
productivity, 18
quality of work life, 19
staff employee, 3
strategic HR choices, 24
strategic human resources (HR) planning, 20
total quality management (TQM), 10

Discussion Questions

1. According to an analysis of the most recent 2000–2003 recession conducted by a team of academics, U.S. businesses are adopting a dual approach to deal with economic fluctuations: boost output by lifting productivity (through better technology, careful selection of employees, more training opportunities, etc.) and hire temporary workers to adjust to swings in demand. Thus, "companies can quickly lay off temps when demand slows. But these same businesses can give real raises to the remaining workers commensurate with faster productivity."[171] Do you think these policies may lead to perceived inequities? From a human resource perspective, do you support these policies? Explain.
2. Which of the environmental, organizational, and individual challenges identified in this chapter will be most important for human resource management in the twenty-first century, in your opinion? Which will be least important? Use your own experiences in your answer.
3. In a recent national survey of HR executives in more than 400 companies, most respondents reported that the priorities of top management at their firms are to counter competition, cut costs, and improve performance. Yet only 12 percent of these HR executives said that their department had a major responsibility for improving productivity, quality, and customer service in their com-

panies. What do you think are some of the reasons for this gap between top management's priorities and the responsibility of the HR department? What are some of the consequences of this gap? Outline several ways in which HR departments can align themselves with their company's strategic goals. How do you think an HR department can gain top management's support for *its* programs and goals?

4. According to a 2002 survey by *USA Today*/CNN/Gallup poll, only 10 percent of respondents think American corporations can be trusted to look out for the interests of their employees. In a recent cover story, *USA Today* notes that "dozens of the largest companies—from Polaroid to IBM to Cisco Systems—have canceled severance, halted health benefits, withdrawn job offers, changed pension plans or issued misleading audit reports. The result? A troubling erosion in the trust that workers place in our nation's business institution."[172] What impact is lack of employee trust likely to have on a company? What HR policies can a company put in place to increase the level of trust?
5. In recent years much of the outsourcing of HR services has gone to consulting firms, which also do auditing work. According to a 2002 study by three well-known college professors who examined 3,000 proxy statements, the more consulting a company bought from its auditor the more likely its earnings met or beat Wall Street expectations. Thus, "if you want impressive earnings, hire your auditor as a consultant too."[173] Do you think this is mere coincidence? What may account for this observed empirical relationship?
6. A study by Professors Judiesch and Lyness of the City University of New York's Baruch College found that adjusting for factors such as age, gender, education, and job factors, employees who take leave under the Family and Medical Leave Act (FMLA) of 1993 were heavily penalized. (The FMLA permits employees to take unpaid leave of up to 12 weeks for family or medical reasons.) Employees who took leave were less likely to be promoted than non-leave takers, received lower job performance ratings for the year in which they took time-off, and received smaller salary increases than their peers with similar low rating.[174] What may account for these findings? Based on your opinion, what does this say in terms of attempts to induce changes in HR practices via government intervention? Explain.
7. 3M's competitive business strategy is based on innovation. 3M requires that at least 25 percent of its annual sales come from products introduced over the previous five years, a goal it often exceeds. Specific HR programs adopted to implement this strategy include the creation of a special fund that allows employees to start new projects or follow up on ideas. 3M's "release time" program, in which workers are given time off during the day to pursue their own interests, is given credit for the creation of new products that management would not have thought of by itself. In addition, 3M's appraisal process encourages risk taking. A senior manager at 3M says, "If you are threatened with dismissal after working on a project that fails, you will never try again." What other types of HR policies might 3M institute to spur product innovation?
8. Many believe that top managers care little about human resources compared to such areas as marketing, finance, production, and engineering. What might account for this perception, and what would you do to change it?

There is a variety of additional material available on the Web site that accompanies this text. You can access this information by visiting the Web site at **www.prenhall.com/gomez.**

Emerging Trends Case 1.1

YOU MANAGE IT!

At Risk from Smoking: Your Job

Concern with protecting employee health has been increasing in many quarters. The clear manifestation of this may be found in tough new measures used by employers to prevent workers from smoking. Smokers have been banned from lighting up on airplanes, at work, and in restaurants. Now a nicotine habit could cost a smoker a job. For example, St. Cloud, Florida (population 19,000), requires applicants for city jobs to swear they've been tobacco free for a year. New hires can't smoke or dip and can be tested to make sure they're not cheating. (Current employees are exempt.)

Other Florida cities have similar laws, but none go as far: North Miami bans smokers from applying for city jobs, too, but relents after they're hired; Coral Gables won't let smokers be cops.

Boosters say the restrictions mean fewer lost workdays, higher productivity, and lower health insurance costs. Eric Nieves, St. Cloud's human resources director, says 6 percent to 12 percent of the $1.2 million the city spends on health insurance is related to health problems caused by smoking.

But civil rights advocates say saving money is not worth the loss of privacy. Smoking is a health risk, "but so is high blood pressure and cholesterol," says Angie Brooks of the American Civil Liberties Union, which is considering whether to file suit. "It's a very slippery slope."

And some say the law will make hiring harder. Says public works director Bob MacKichan, "I could have the most qualified person there is, but now I don't even get to see the application."

Critical Thinking Questions

1. Many people believe that policies such as the ones described in the case represent an unacceptable degree of employer intrusion into the personal lives of employees. Do you agree? Explain.
2. Although many companies claim that zero-tolerance, no-smoking policies are enforced for the well-being of employees, some critics argue that the real reason behind these policies is to save on insurance costs. This "false pretense" makes both smokers and nonsmokers more cynical of the firm's real intentions when it comes to explanations concerning incentive programs, introduction of new technology, layoffs, restructuring, and the like. If you were asked to justify adoption of a zero-tolerance, no-smoking policy, how would you do it?
3. An alternative to the policy described here is to require smokers to pay a higher insurance premium, in a sense asking them to pay for the cost of their habit. Do you think this is a better policy? Explain.

Team Exercises

A firm considering adoption of a zero-tolerance, no-smoking policy has set up an internal task force consisting of two executives, the HR manager, and two employees to discuss the pros and cons of implementing such a policy. Students divide into groups of five to role-play this situation and provide recommendations to the firm's CEO (played by instructor).

Class is divided up into groups of five with some groups representing smokers who wish to defend their right to smoke and some groups representing nonsmokers who wish to argue for their right to a smoke-free, working environment. Groups meet separately and then present their position in class, with the instructor acting as a mediator.

Source: Adapted with permission from Tse, K., and Foust, D. (2002, April 15). At risk from smoking: Your job. *BusinessWeek*, 12.

YOU MANAGE IT!

Emerging Trends Case 1.2

Greater Security or Looking for Dirty Laundry?

When you are interviewing someone for employment, do you wonder whether the candidate has a criminal background? A drug problem? Has the candidate lied about his or her credentials?

That's more likely than you might think. American Background Information Services Inc. (ABI), based in Winchester, Virginia, found undisclosed criminal backgrounds on 12.6 percent of the people it screened.

That number is typical, other experts say. "Ten to 20 percent of applicants flat out lie," says Randy Baker, HR manager at Birch Telecomm in Emporia, Kansas.

About 8.3 percent of applicants screened have a criminal history, and 23 percent have misrepresented their employment or education credentials, says Blair Cohen, CEO of InfoMart Inc., an employment screening company based in Atlanta. Other security firms show figures that are almost twice as high.[175]

In some industries, the numbers are staggering. Telemarketing applicants have a criminal rate of 30 percent to 40 percent, according to Kit Fremin, owner of Background Check International LLC in Temecula, California. Before September 11, 2001, most companies were checking criminal history or credit reports, says Jason B. Morris, president and CEO of Background Information Services Inc. in Cleveland. But the terrorist attacks on the World Trade Center and the Pentagon have since provoked a booming business among employment screening companies.

For instance,

- ASI Business Solutions, a computer software company in King of Prussia, Pennsylvania, outsources searches of criminal histories, motor vehicle reports, education credentials, and three previous employers for all new hires, says HR manager Donna Polier. The company adds a full credit report search for individuals applying for management positions, she says.
- ViaSat, a satellite communications company and government contractor in Carlsbad, California, does extensive background checks on both permanent and temporary employees. "We've always outsourced, but it's expensive [because] they charge per state. So if a candidate has moved around, it can cost up to $300," says Cathy Akin, vice president of HR. ViaSat would prefer to handle the employment

and education verifications in-house, if it had the staff to do so, she says. "These are relatively easy things to do."

- Birch Telecomm's Baker thinks he could do a more thorough job of calling previous employers himself, although he says he is comfortable with the company's employment screening vendor. The vendor usually calls only the HR department and never speaks with the candidate's previous manager, he says.
- Ryan's Family Steak Houses Inc., based in Greer, South Carolina, has done background checks on its managers for many years but only began running background checks on hourly team members three years ago, says Eddie Tallon, director of internal audit and security. "There was not an incident. We are a very proactive company in the security arena and felt as though this would be another way to provide a safe and secure environment for our customers and team members," he says. Ryan's hires a vendor to do Social Security number traces and criminal background checks on all employees, as well as credit checks on cashiers and managers, Tallon says.

Under the nation's heightened security concerns, companies that already were outsourcing background checks are looking to do more extensive searches on new hires or to screen current employees. One large company wants to do a second check on every employee hired in the past two years for federal criminal history, nationwide wants and warrants, identity verification, and international searches, Cohen says.

Requests for international searches are on the rise, says Kevin McCrann, operations manager at Accurate Information Systems Inc., in Massapequa, New York. "The cost of doing international searches is much higher," he says. Whereas his firm charges $15 per U.S. county for a criminal search, international searches start at $35 and can go as high as $135, he says. International searches are definitely on the rise, but the problem is that few nations keep as complete records as the United States does, says Gary W. Schneider, ABI executive vice president. Even in those nations that have the capacity for good record keeping, such as Great Britain, tight privacy laws can make finding anything out nearly impossible, says Pre-employ.com's Mather.

One company has received venture capital funds from the CIA to screen out potential criminals and security risks. This company, Systems Research and Development (SRD), scans massive amounts of data for hidden connections—such as a casino employee who has the same phone number as a known cheat. SRD calls its approach Nora, for "non-obvious relationship awareness." The idea is to draw on disparate sources of information—employment applications, transaction records, customer listings, "wanted lists" and more—to unearth hidden links; when suspicious connections turn up, SRD's clients can investigate further.

Critical Thinking Questions

1. Some people believe that security measures, such as those outlined in this feature, violate the privacy rights of prospective and current employees and that they create a climate where Big Brother is watching over you. Do you agree? Explain.
2. One potential problem with security screening systems is that people with minor pecadilloes (for instance, being late on two credit payments) may be penalized unfairly, perhaps even without their knowledge. What kinds of policies should a firm put in place to decide what is a serious or a trivial security concern? Explain.
3. One troubling aspect of security screening systems is the potential for false alarm, particularly when private security firms are paid to identify and investigate current or prospective employees and customers who may be security risks. And there is always a possibility that consciously or unconsciously racial or ethnic profiling may occur. What can a company do to avoid the problem of mistakes being made and potential discrimination as a result of security screening? Explain.

Team Exercise

A manufacturing company making automobile parts is about to hire an outside vendor to screen all current and prospective employees for security risks. A committee has been set up within the company to decide what criteria should be used to select such a firm, and the instructions that should be given to the chosen vendor as to the type of information that should be gathered. Students divide up into groups of five to role-play this situation, and provide a report to the entire class.

Students are divided into teams and asked to do a "security screening" on any public figure of their choice using publicly available information, most of it obtainable through the Internet. Each team will then provide a report to the entire class, explaining how the information was obtained, the inferences drawn from that information, and the difficulties or challenges faced in gathering this information.

Source: Adapted from Mayer, M. (2002, January). Background checks in focus. *HR Magazine*, 10–15. See also Weber, T. (2002, January 11). To find security risks, company sifts data seeking obscure links. *Wall Street Journal*, A-1; and Armour, S. (2002b, June 19). Security checks worry workers. *USA Today*, A-1.

YOU MANAGE IT!

Discussion Case 1.3

Managers and HR Professionals at Sands Corporation: Friends or Foes?

Sands Corporation is a medium-sized company located in the Midwest. It manufactures specialized computer equipment used in cars, serving as a subcontractor to several automobile manufacturers as well as to the military. Federal contracts are an important part of Sands' total sales. In 1965 the firm had 130 employees. At that time, the personnel department had a full-time director (who was a high school graduate) and a part-time clerk. The department was responsible for maintaining files, placing recruitment ads in the newspaper at management's request, processing employment applications and payroll, answering phones, and handling other routine administrative tasks. Managers and supervisors were responsible for most personnel matters, including whom to hire, whom to promote, whom to fire, and whom to train.

Today Sands employs 700 people. Personnel, now called the human resources department, has a full-time director with a master's degree in industrial relations, three specialists (with appropriate college degrees and certifications: one in compensation, one in staffing, and one in training and development), and four personnel assistants. Sands' top management believes that a strong HR department with a highly qualified staff can do a better job of handling most personnel matters than line supervisors can. It is also convinced that a good HR department can keep line managers from inadvertently creating costly legal problems. One of Sands' competitors recently lost a $5 million sex discrimination suit, which has only strengthened Sands' resolve to maintain a strong HR department.

Some of the key responsibilities the company assigns to its HR department are:

- **Hiring** The HR department approves all ads, screens all applicants, tests and interviews candidates, and so forth. Line supervisors are given a limited list of candidates (usually no more than three) per position from which to choose.
- **Workforce diversity** The HR department ensures that the composition of Sands' workforce meets the government's diversity guidelines for federal contractors.
- **Compensation** The HR department sets the pay range for each job based on its own compensation studies and survey data of salaries at similar companies. The department must approve all pay decisions.
- **Employee appraisal** The HR department requires all supervisors to complete annual appraisal forms on their subordinates. The department scrutinizes these appraisals of employees' performance closely; it is not uncommon for supervisors to be called on the carpet to justify performance ratings that are unusually high or low.
- **Training** The HR department conducts several training programs for employees, including programs in improving human relations, quality management, and the use of computer packages.
- **Attitude surveys** The HR department conducts an in-depth attitude survey of all employees each year, asking them how they feel about various facets of their job, such as satisfaction with supervisor and working conditions.

Over the past few weeks several supervisors have complained to top executives that the HR department has taken away many of their management rights. Some of their gripes are:

- The HR department ranks applicants based on test scores or other formal criteria (for example, years of experience). Often the people they pick do not fit well in the department and/or do not get along with the supervisor and co-workers.
- Excellent performers are leaving because the HR department will not approve pay raises exceeding a fixed limit for the job title held, even when a person is able to perform duties beyond those specified in the job description.
- It takes so long to process the paperwork to hire new employees that the unit loses good candidates to competitors.
- Much of the training required of employees is not focused on the job itself. These "canned" programs waste valuable employee time and provide few benefits to the company.
- Supervisors are afraid to be truthful in their performance ratings for fear of being investigated by the HR department.
- Attitude survey data are broken down by department. The HR department then scrutinizes departments with low scores. Some supervisors feel that the attitude survey has become a popularity contest that penalizes managers who are willing to make necessary (but unpopular) decisions.

The HR department director rejects all of these accusations, arguing that supervisors "just want to do things their way, not taking into account what is best for the company."

Critical Thinking Questions

1. What seems to be the main source of conflict between supervisors and the HR department at Sands Corporation? Explain.
2. Do you believe that managers should be given more autonomy to make personnel decisions such as hiring, appraising, and compensating subordinates? If so, what are some potential drawbacks to granting them this authority? Explain.
3. How should Sands' top executives deal with the complaints expressed by supervisors? How should the director of the HR department deal with the situation? Explain.

Team Exercise

The CEO of Sands Corporation has called a meeting of four managers, all of whom have lodged some of the complaints noted in the case, and four members of the HR department (the director and three specialists). The instructor or a student acts as the CEO in that meeting. The exercise is carried out as follows: (a) Each side presents its case, with the CEO acting as moderator. (b) The two groups then try to agree on how Sands' HR department and managers can develop a closer working relationship in the future. The two groups and the CEO may conduct this exercise in separate groups or in front of the classroom.

Video Shorts Case 1.4

YOU MANAGE IT!

The Strategic Role of Human Resource Management

The six videos in this series contain live footage of Manhattan area HR professionals at work in the dotcom sector, the music and hotel industries, and the market research business. These scenes cut to the heart of people's real-life concerns in today's workplace. As you listen to the shows' guests offer their expert commentary, you will gain insight into HR's emerging role as strategic partner and change agent. It might be useful to note that the entire series was filmed shortly after the September 11, 2001 terrorist attack on the World Trade Center, at a time of particularly high unemployment for New York City.

Welcome to the first installment of television's weekly newsmagazine show, *SPOTLIGHT Inside HR*. You will meet anchorperson Meg Allen, your host for this series, along with guests Martin Buckingham, associate director of human resources at HotJobs.com, and Jenny Herman, director of education and development at Loews Hotels. *SPOTLIGHT*'s undercover cameras will take you for an inside look at Hot Jobs HR; where a merger/acquisition deal with Yahoo! is on the table and the company is facing the challenge of employee retention. Later on in the show you'll be joining Meg's guests as they discuss the surveillance tape you have just seen.

As you watch, it might be useful to note the following: Hot jobs was founded in 1996 as both a Web site and a recruitment software package that would allow clients to create a private job board. Since then, over 9,000 businesses and nearly 3 million job seekers have used Hot Jobs. Shortly before taping, Hot Jobs was planning to merge with TMP Worldwide, Inc., parent of rival Monster.com. Now, six months later, the company finds itself on the verge of accepting a hostile bid by Yahoo!. Aside from the legal ramifications of this merger/acquisition deal, Hot Jobs HR specialists will have to address the human needs of its 700 employees during this upheaval. Additionally, Hot Jobs, like almost every other New York City enterprise, is still reeling from the impact of the World Trade Center tragedy.

This week the surveillance crew finds Jackson Doone, one of Hot Jobs' "star" senior programmers looking to HR for some concrete answers about his own future and the future of his team. During his six year tenure at Hot Jobs, Jackson has earned great compensation and has become accustomed to all the industry perks that go with his position. Not only is he worried about what the merger with Yahoo! means for him, but he is anxious about losing his top staff to the competition. Actually, he has recently received an offer himself.

Daryl Hulme, a member of the Hot Jobs HR team, has agreed to see Jackson on short notice. She is well aware that since the deal with Yahoo! has been on the table, rumors about what will happen have been spreading fast. Jackson is obviously on edge. When he asks her what to tell his staff, Daryl cannot give him clear-cut answers. She knows that employee retention is crucial right now. Jackson lets her know that Hot Jobs will lose people if they are kept in the dark much longer. What kinds of pressure do you think he is under right now? What kinds of pressure do you think Daryl Hulme is feeling right now? You might observe that, rather than responding defensively, she suggests several steps Jackson can take to feel more in control. She is trying to help him stay focused. Why do you suppose she recommends that he "test the waters" and see what the job market holds? Daryl advises him to be honest with his team members and enlists his cooperation as a high-level employee. Notice that even though she must sense his impatience, she is boosting his ego, even now. Consider why she might be doing this. Remember that, as an HR professional, one of her strategic goals is to help Hot Jobs management retain talented people. The one thing that arouses Jackson's interest is the possibility of offering a retention bonus. But when Daryl goes on to explain the existing legal restrictions, he seems frustrated. As the scene ends, decide whether this has been a helpful conversation from Jackson's perspective.

During the discussion segment of the show, Martin Buckingham speaks candidly about the counseling role HR personnel at Hot Jobs have had to take on as the Yahoo! deal goes through its final stages. He concedes that it is hard to keep morale up when layoffs and restructuring may be ahead. Perhaps because Hot Jobs is a relatively young company with a young staff, most people there are facing a corporate transition for the first time.

Jenny Herman likens this situation to the downturn that the hotel industry faced recently in the wake of September 11. As you listen, consider whether this is an appropriate comparison. With cuts in staff and reduced hours at many Loews hotels, quick decisions had to be made. Unlike Hot Jobs, Loews Hotels has been in existence since 1946 and employs over 2,500 people at 17 locations. Management decisions are usually decentralized at Loews, giving individual hotels maximum flexibility, but during this crisis all decisions were centralized, allowing the executive board to control emergency measures. This served to boost spirits and give people a sense that their leadership was strong. HR was integral to strategic solutions during this time. Employees came through for one another, even starting a hardship fund for those who had lost their jobs or could not pay the rent due to salary cuts. HR was able to spread the word via an internal newsletter.

In times of change, HR must remain a strategic partner, taking action that will result in corporate success, while at the same time filling the needs of employees who feel threatened. It is truly a balancing act.

Critical Thinking Questions

1. Do you agree with *SPOTLIGHT* panelists Jenny Herman of Loews and Martin Buckingham of Hot Jobs that Daryl Hulme did a good job? How is she protecting the interests of the company? How is she protecting the interests of the employee as well as fostering commitment?
2. Hot Jobs Associate Director of HR Martin Buckingham is apprehensive that this period of transition will affect the focus of the Hot Jobs staff, resulting in lower productivity and the loss of some of the company's best people. Why is this especially significant at an Internet company like Hot Jobs?
3. If you were in Jackson's place, what would you do? Why?
4. Host Meg Allen feels that communication during a time of corporate flux is especially important. Using Jackson and Daryl as examples, would you say that Hot Jobs enjoys good communication between its line mangers and HR managers? Explain.
5. According to Martin Buckingham, all HR strategies affecting Hot Jobs employees "trickle down" from the specific vision of the CEO. How does this affect HR's role in executing and formulating strategy? How does this differ from Loews Hotels?

Part II: The Contexts of Human Resource Management

Managing Work Flows and Conducting Job Analysis

Challenges

After reading this chapter, you should be able to deal more effectively with the following challenges:

1. **Describe** bureaucratic, flat, and boundaryless organizational structures and the business environments in which each is most appropriate.
2. **List** the factors influencing worker motivation that are under managers' control.
3. **Conduct** job analysis and prepare job descriptions and specifications.
4. **Apply** flexible work designs to situations in which employees have conflicts between work and family, or employers face fluctuating demand for their products.
5. **Develop** policies and procedures to protect human resource information system data so that employees' privacy rights are maintained.

The powerful forces of technology and global competition are forcing managers to rethink all aspects of business. Work is in a state of flux as companies change basic work processes, job requirements and expectations, and organizational structures to focus more on customers' needs.

One important change is the practice of using work teams instead of individual workers as the basic work unit. Today many workers spend much of their time on a team established to satisfy customers' needs. For example:

- Southwest Airlines is able to prepare an aircraft from landing to takeoff in 20 minutes by using work teams to unload, service, and load the aircraft. This is one-third the time it takes Southwest's competitors to load and unload their planes and helps explain why Southwest is one of the most profitable airlines.[1]

- General Motors slashed the development time it takes to produce a full mock-up of a car from 12 weeks to two by using collaborative engineering teams that share design information between auto parts suppliers and engineering units within the company. The time saved frees up workers to think more creatively and come up with three or four more alternative designs per car.[2]
- Contract manufacturer SCI Systems is using collaborative software tools to form virtual teams to connect its employees with its customers and suppliers. When a customer such as Dell Computer places an order, SCI can deal with its suppliers and Dell in real time to manage how the computer is built to suit the customer's needs. These teams allow SCI to build products faster according to the specific requirements of each customer.[3]

THE MANAGERIAL PERSPECTIVE

This chapter is about managing work, which is a highly dynamic process. Managers design structures to organize work into departments, teams, and jobs so that work is performed efficiently and provides a valuable product or service for a customer. Human resource specialists assist managers by keeping track of and documenting the changes for the content of each job through a process called *job analysis.* In this chapter we explore why job analysis is important to managers and why it is the bedrock of most human resource programs.

Like work teams, organizations are fundamentally groups of people. The relationships among these people can be structured in different ways. In this chapter we describe how top managers decide on the most appropriate structure for the organization as a whole and for the flow of work within the organization. Although you may never be asked to redesign your organization, it is likely that your company will eventually undergo structural change because such change is necessary for survival. It is important that you understand structural issues so that you can see the big picture and take an active role in implementing changes.

Work can be viewed from three different perspectives: the entire organization, work groups, and individual employees. We examine each of these perspectives and their implications for human resource management. We also discuss job analysis (a critical HR activity) and the use of contingent workers and alternative work schedules to create a flexible workforce. An understanding of job analysis gives managers a tool to measure how much and what types of work are necessary to achieve organizational objectives. We conclude the chapter with a discussion of human resource information systems.

Work: The Organizational Perspective

Organizational structure
The formal or informal relationships between people in an organization.

Work flow
The way work is organized to meet the organization's production or service goals.

Organizational structure refers to the formal or informal relationships between people in an organization. **Work flow** refers to the way work is organized to meet the organization's production or service goals. In this section we discuss the relationship between strategy and organizational structure, the three basic organizational structures, and the uses of work flow analysis.

Strategy and Organizational Structure

An organization develops a business strategy by establishing a set of long-term goals based on (1) an analysis of environmental opportunities and threats and (2) a realistic appraisal of how the business can deploy its assets to compete most effectively. The business strategy selected by management determines the structure most appropriate to the organization.[4] Whenever management changes its business strategy, it should also reassess its organizational structure.

Recall from Chapter 1 that a company would select a *defender strategy* when it is competing in a stable market and has a well-established product. For example, a regulated electric utility company might adopt such a strategy. Under a defender strategy, work can be efficiently organized into a structure based on an extensive division of labor, with hierarchies of jobs assigned to functional units such as customer service, power generation, and accounting. Management is centralized and top management has the responsibility for making key decisions. Decisions are implemented from the top down via the chain of command. Workers are told what to do by supervisors, who in turn are handed directions from middle managers, who take orders from the company's top executives.

A company would select a *prospector strategy* when operating in uncertain business environments that require flexibility. Companies that are experiencing rapid growth and launching many new products into a dynamic market are likely to select such a strategy. In companies with a prospector strategy, control is decentralized so that each division has some autonomy to make decisions that affect its customers. Workers who are close to the customer are allowed to respond quickly to customers' needs without having to seek approval from supervisors.

Management selects HR strategies to fit and support its business strategies and organizational structure. Here are some examples of strategic HR choices regarding structure and work flows that companies have made to achieve cost efficiency and product quality.

- General Electric (GE) signed a 10-year maintenance deal with British Airways in 1998 to do engine maintenance and overhaul work. The maintenance agreement will help British Airways save costs by outsourcing this work to GE, which builds, designs, and maintains commercial aircraft engines as a core business.[5]
- Kodak in the early 1990s eliminated several layers of middle management through early retirements, then delegated these laid-off managers' responsibilities to teams of engineers and technicians. Kodak management wanted to differentiate its product from the competition based on quality and believed that a reorganized product development process could help it reach that goal.[6]

A Question of Ethics

Implicit in this chapter is the view that organizational change is necessary for survival. However, organizational change often places individual employees under considerable stress, particularly the stress resulting from having to learn new skills and job requirements constantly. Is the organization ethically responsible for protecting employees from these stressful changes?

Designing the Organization

Designing an organization involves choosing an organizational structure that will help the company achieve its goals most effectively. There are three basic types of organizational structure: bureaucratic, flat, and boundaryless (Figure 2.1 on page 50).

Bureaucratic Organization

Companies that adopt a defender business strategy are likely to choose the **bureaucratic organizational structure.** This pyramid-shaped structure consists of hierarchies with many levels of management. It uses a top-down or "command and control" approach to management in which managers provide considerable direction to and have considerable control over their subordinates. The classic example of a bureaucratic organization is the military, which has a long pecking order of intermediate officers between the generals (who initiate combat orders) and the troops (who do the fighting on the battlefield).

Bureaucratic organizational structure
A pyramid-shaped organizational structure that consists of hierarchies with many levels of management.

A bureaucratic organization is based on a *functional division of labor*. Employees are divided into divisions based on their function. Thus, production employees are grouped in one division, marketing employees in another, engineering employees in a third, and so on. Rigid boundaries separate the functional units from one another. At a bureaucratic auto parts company, for instance, automotive engineers would develop plans for a new part and then deliver its specifications to the production workers.

Rigid boundaries also separate workers from one another and from their managers because the bureaucratic structure relies on *work specialization*. Narrowly specified job descriptions clearly mark the boundaries of each employee's work. Employees are encouraged to do only the work specified in their job description—no more and no less. They spend most of their time working individually at specialized tasks and usually advance only within one function. For example, employees who begin their career in sales can advance to higher and higher positions in sales or marketing but cannot switch into production or finance.

Figure 2.1

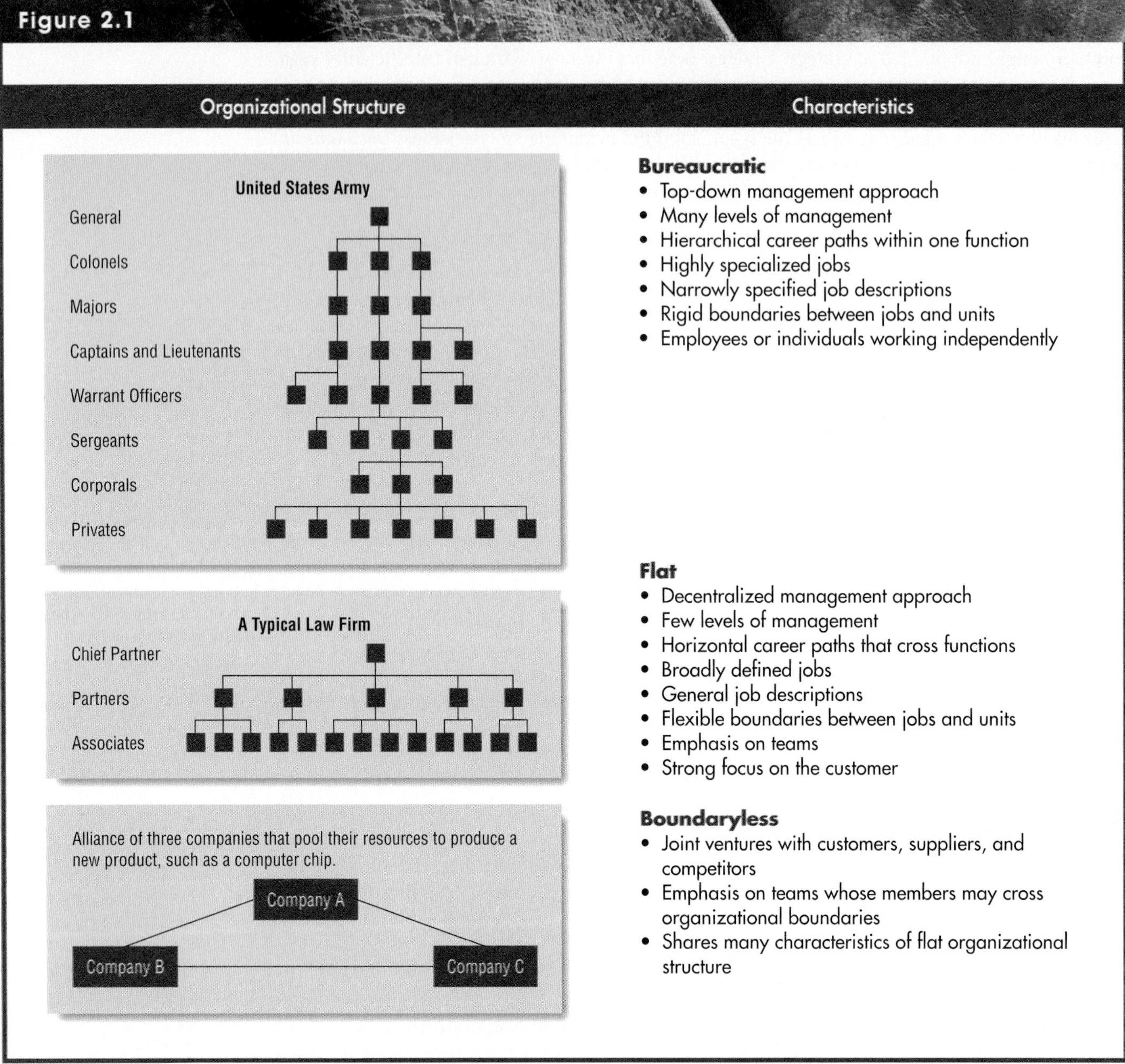

Organizational Structures

The bureaucratic structure works best in a predictable and stable environment. It is highly centralized and depends on front-line workers performing repetitive tasks according to managers' orders. In a dynamic environment, this structure is less efficient and sometimes disastrous.

Flat Organization

Flat organizational structure An organizational structure that has only a few levels of management and emphasizes decentralization.

A company that selects the prospector business strategy is likely to choose the **flat organizational structure.** A flat organization has only a few levels of managers and emphasizes a decentralized approach to management. Flat organizations encourage high employee involvement in business decisions. Nucor (a Charlotte, North Carolina, steel company) has a flat organizational structure. Though Nucor has over 5,000 employees, only three levels separate the front-line steel workers from the president of the company. Headquarters staff consists of a mere 30 people in a modest cluster of offices.[7]

Flat organizations are likely to be divided into units or teams that represent different products, services, or customers. The purpose of this structure is to create independent small businesses that can respond rapidly to customers' needs or changes in the business environment. For example, Hewlett-Packard (HP), a large manufacturer of computers, is organized into about 60 different product-based business units. Each HP unit behaves like a minibusiness that is responsible for generating a profit for the overall company, and employees within each unit feel as if they are working for a small company. The flat organizational structure has fostered an entrepreneurial culture that has enabled HP to innovate and sustain itself at the cutting edge of technology.

The flat organizational structure reduces some of the boundaries that isolate employees from one another in bureaucratic organizations. Boundaries between workers at the same level are reduced because employees are likely to be working in teams. In contrast to workers at bureaucratic organizations, employees of a flat organization can cross functional boundaries as they pursue their careers (for instance, starting in sales, moving to finance, and then into production). In addition, job descriptions in flat organizations are more general and encourage employees to develop a broad range of skills (including management skills). Boundaries that separate employees from managers and supervisors also break down in flat organizations, where employees are empowered to make more decisions.

Flat organizational structures can be useful for organizations that are implementing a total quality management (TQM) strategy that emphasizes customer satisfaction. Implementing a TQM strategy may require changing work processes so that customers can receive higher-quality products and better service. For example, an auto insurance company may change its claims adjustment process to speed up reimbursement to customers. Rather than using 25 employees who take 14 days to process a claim, the company may create a claims adjustment team that works closely with the customer to take care of all the paperwork within three days.

The flat structure works best in rapidly changing environments because it enables management to create an entrepreneurial culture that fosters employee participation.

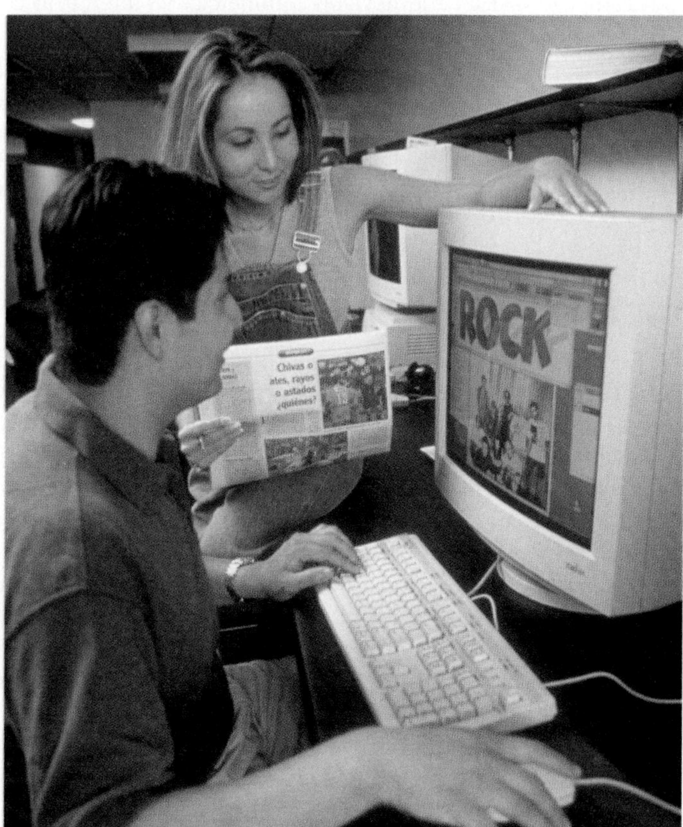

La Opinion, *a newspaper based in Los Angeles, California, has a flat organizational structure that supports workers who must keep up with the fast pace of the news business. Here graphic designers work together to devise an eye-catching page design.*

Boundaryless Organization

Boundaryless organizational structure
An organizational structure that enables an organization to form relationships with customers, suppliers, and/or competitors, either to pool organizational resources for mutual benefit or to encourage cooperation in an uncertain environment.

A **boundaryless organizational structure** enables an organization to form relationships with customers, suppliers, and/or competitors, either to pool organizational resources for mutual benefit or to encourage cooperation in an uncertain environment. Such relationships often take the form of joint ventures, which let the companies share talented employees, intellectual property (such as a manufacturing process), marketing distribution channels (such as a direct sales force), or financial resources. Boundaryless organizational structures are most often used by companies that select the prospector business strategy and operate in a volatile environment.

Boundaryless organizations share many of the characteristics of flat organizations. They break down boundaries between the organization and its suppliers, customers, or competitors. They also strongly emphasize teams, which are likely to include employees representing different companies in the joint venture. For example, a quality expert from an automobile manufacturing company may work closely with employees at one of the company's auto parts suppliers to train them in specific quality management processes.

Companies often use a boundaryless organizational structure when they (1) collaborate with customers or suppliers to provide better-quality products or services; (2) are entering foreign markets that have entry barriers to foreign competitors, or (3) need to manage the risk of developing an expensive new technology. The boundaryless organization is appropriate in these situations because it is open to change, facilitates the formation of joint ventures with foreign companies, and reduces the financial risk to any one organization. Here are some examples of boundaryless organizational structures:

- Paramount and Twentieth Century Fox film studios collaborated to produce, market, and distribute the expensive and ultimately successful epic movie *Titanic*, which broke box office records around the world in the late 1990s. The collaboration was necessary: The production costs of the movie (over $200 million) were too steep for one film company to risk without putting the studio in financial jeopardy.
- Airbus Industries is a boundaryless organizational design that consists of a partnership of European firms from four countries (France, Germany, England, and Spain) that worked together to market and develop commercial jet aircraft to compete with Boeing, the world's leading producer of passenger jets.
- Sun Microsystems, a producer of computer workstations and servers, has formed a partnership with America Online, the largest provider of online services for computers. The partners' goal is to create a combination of services and products that lets companies obtain all their software and online services over the Internet, instead of buying software in boxes. The strength of this partnership could pose a major threat to Microsoft's strong market position.[8]

Work Flow Analysis

Work flow analysis
The process of examining how work creates or adds value to the ongoing processes in a business.

We said earlier that work flow is the way work is organized to meet the organization's production or service goals. Managers need to do **work flow analysis** to examine how work creates or adds value to the ongoing business processes. (*Processes* are value-adding, value-creating activities such as product development, customer service, and order fulfillment.[9]) Work flow analysis looks at how work moves from the customer (who initiates the need for work) through the organization (where employees add value to the work in a series of value-creating steps) to the point at which the work leaves the organization as a product or service for the customer.

Each job in the organization should receive work as an input, add value to that work by doing something useful to it, and then move the work on to another worker. Work flow analysis usually reveals that some steps or jobs can be combined, simplified, or even eliminated. In some cases, it has resulted in the reorganization of work so that teams rather than individual workers are the source of value creation.

Work flow analysis can be used to tighten the alignment between employees' work and customers' needs. It can also help a company make major performance improvements through another program called *business process reengineering*.

Business Process Reengineering

The term *reengineering* was coined by Michael Hammer and James Champy in their pioneering book *Reengineering the Corporation*. Hammer and Champy emphasize that reengineering should not be confused with restructuring or simply laying off employees in an effort to eliminate layers of management.[10] **Business process reengineering (BPR)** is not a quick fix but rather a fundamental rethinking and radical redesign of business processes to achieve dramatic improvements in cost, quality, service, and speed.[11] Reengineering examines the way a company does its business by closely analyzing the core processes involved in producing its product or delivering its service to the customer. By taking advantage of computer technology and different ways of organizing human resources, the company may be able to reinvent itself.[12]

Business process reengineering (BPR)
A fundamental rethinking and radical redesign of business processes to achieve dramatic improvements in cost, quality, service, and speed.

BPR uses work flow analysis to identify jobs that can be eliminated or recombined to improve company performance. Figure 2.2 shows the steps involved in processing a loan application at IBM Credit Corporation before and after BPR. Before the BPR effort, work flow analysis showed that loan applications were processed in a series of five steps by five loan specialists, each of whom did something different to the loan application. The entire process took an average of six days to complete, which gave customers the opportunity to look elsewhere for financing.[13] For much of that time, the application was either in transit between the loan specialists or sitting on someone's desk waiting to be processed.

Using BPR, the jobs of the five loan specialists were reorganized into the job of just one generalist called the deal structurer. The deal structurer uses a new software program to print out a standardized loan contract, access different credit checking databases, price the loan, and add boilerplate language to the contract. With the new process, loan applications can be completed in four hours instead of six days.[14]

Critics of reengineering claim that over half of reengineering projects fail to meet their objectives while causing pain to companies and employees in the form of layoffs and disruptions to established work patterns.[15] However, a survey by CSC Index, a leading reengineering consulting firm, reported that reengineering is very popular in both the United States and Europe. The survey of 621 large European and U.S. companies found that 69 percent of U.S. firms and 75 percent of European firms are already engaged in reengineering and over half of the remaining companies are thinking about embarking on a reengineering project.[16]

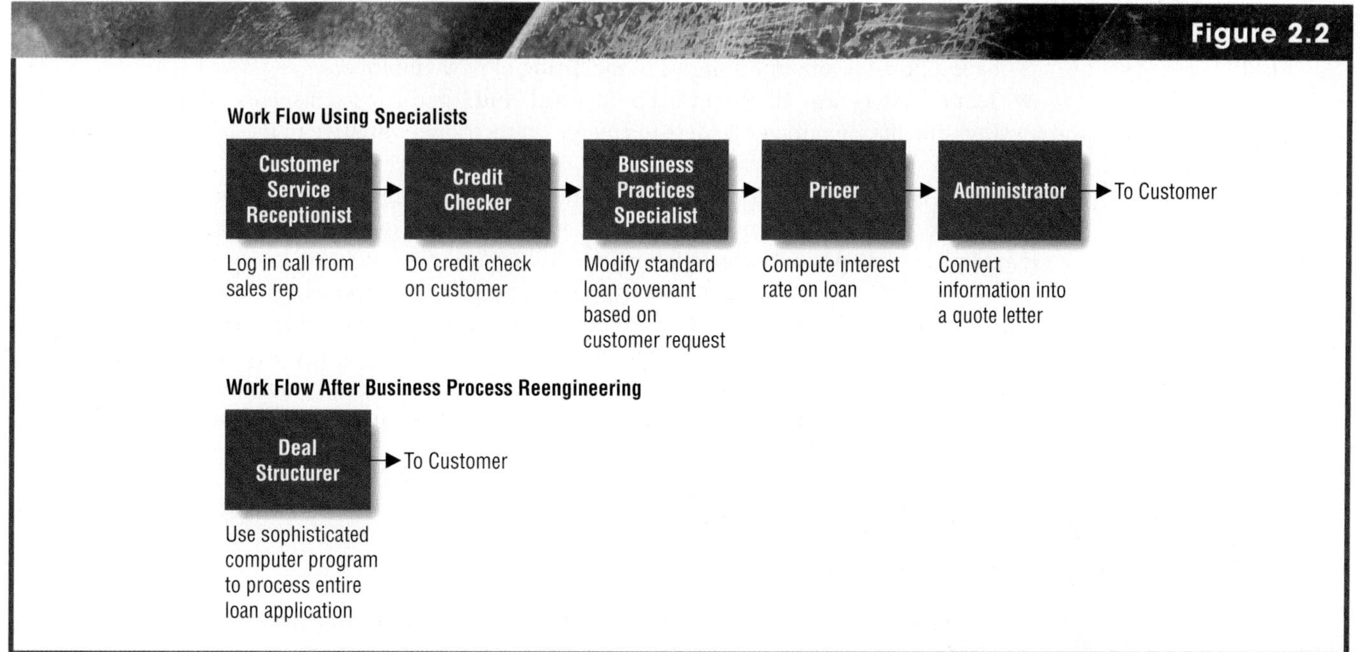

Processing a Loan Application at IBM Credit Corporation Before and After BPR

Work: The Group Perspective

We turn now to an examination of work from the perspective of employee groups. In the flat and boundaryless organizational structures, teamwork is an imperative. Indeed, as we have seen, teams are the basic building blocks of both structures.

Team
A small number of people with complementary skills who work toward common goals for which they hold themselves mutually accountable.

What exactly is a team and how does it operate? A **team** is a small number of people with complementary skills who work toward common goals for which they hold themselves mutually accountable.[17] The size of most teams ranges from 6 to 18 employees.[18] Unlike *work groups*, which depend on a supervisor for direction, a team depends on its own members to provide leadership and direction.[19] Teams can also be organized as departments. For example, a company may have a product development team, a manufacturing team, and a sales team.

Several types of teams are used in organizations today. The type that is having the most impact on U.S. companies is the self-managed team.

Self-Managed Teams

Self-managed team (SMT)
A team responsible for producing an entire product, a component, or an ongoing service.

Organizations are implementing self-managed work teams primarily to improve quality and productivity and to reduce operating costs. **Self-managed teams (SMTs)** are responsible for producing an entire product, a component, or an ongoing service. In most cases, SMT members are cross-trained on the different tasks assigned to the team.[20] Some SMTs have members with a set of complex skills—for example, scientists and engineers with training in different disciplines. Members of the SMT have many managerial duties, including work scheduling, selecting work methods, ordering materials, evaluating performance, and disciplining team members.[21]

One company that has switched over to SMTs is the San Diego Zoo. The zoo's employees traditionally had very narrow and well-defined job responsibilities: Keepers did the keeping and gardeners did the gardening. Then the zoo decided to develop bioclimatic zones, in which plants and animals are grouped together in cageless enclosures that resemble their native habitats. Because the zones themselves are interdependent, the employees who manage them must work together. For instance, the humid 3.5-acre Tiger River exhibit is run by a seven-member team of mammal and bird specialists, horticulturists, and maintenance and construction workers.[22]

HRM practices are likely to change in the following ways when SMTs are established:[23]

- Peers, rather than a supervisor, are likely to evaluate individual employee performance.
- Pay practices are likely to shift from pay based on seniority or individual performance to pay focused on team performance (for example, team bonuses).[24]
- Rather than being based solely on input from managers and HR staff, team members may have a decisive amount of input in the hiring of new employees.
- Team leaders are likely to step forward and identify themselves. For example, SEI Investments encourages leaders to emerge on their own initiative in its self-managed teams.[25]

Self-managed teams have made some impressive contributions to the bottom lines of companies that have used them. For instance, after implementing SMTs, Shenandoah Life found it could process 50 percent more applications and customer service requests with 10 percent fewer employees.[26] Xerox plants using SMTs are 30 percent more productive than Xerox plants organized without them.[27] Boeing used SMTs to reduce the number of engineering problems in the development of the new 777 passenger jet by more than half.[28] For a look at how self-managed teams work at Lucent Technologies, a manufacturer of telecommunications products, see the Issues and Applications feature titled "Lynn Mercer's Teams at Lucent" below.

Issues and Applications

Lynn Mercer's Teams at Lucent

Lynn Mercer is the cellular-phone factory manager at Lucent Technologies. She is dedicated to the concept of self-managed teams and has worked hard to make them succeed. The teams in her operation decide how the work should be done, what improvements are needed, and who should

perform them. She notes that she just sets the mission of the factory, and the rest is up to the teams. Lucent's teams elect their own leaders and are exceptionally flexible so they can adapt to the ever-changing needs of the cellular-phone industry. Mercer wants this flexibility because team members truly understand their customers' needs.

Mercer explains that, although all instructions are still written down in her team-managed factory, every individual can make online changes to a procedure if the individual's team agrees. Not only do teams have the power to change procedures, others can also learn from them and do not have to reinvent the wheel. Team members learn many different tasks and skills and how to perform them well. The results have been remarkable. Mercer's factory has not missed a deadline in over two years, and labor costs remain a very low percentage of total costs.

Sources: Nahavandi, A. (2000). *The art and science of leadership* (2nd ed.). Upper Saddle River, NJ: Prentice Hall, 163. Adapted from T. Pezinger Jr. (March 7, 1997). How Lynn Mercer manages a factory that manages itself, *Wall Street Journal*, B1.

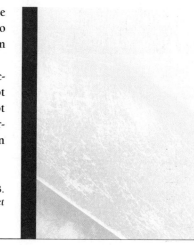

Because team members often initially lack the skills necessary for the team to function successfully, it may take several years for an SMT to become fully operational.[29] A company can hasten this evolution by using its HR department to train employees in the skills required of team members. Three areas are important:[30]

1. **Technical skills** Team members must be cross-trained in new technical skills so that they can rotate among jobs as necessary. Team members who are cross-trained give the team greater flexibility and allow it to operate efficiently with fewer workers.
2. **Administrative skills** Teams do much of the work done by supervisors in organizations that don't have teams. Therefore, team members need training in such management/administrative skills as budgeting, scheduling, monitoring and evaluating peers, and interviewing job applicants.
3. **Interpersonal skills** Team members need good communication skills to form an effective team. They must be able to express themselves effectively in order to share information, deal with conflict, and give feedback to one another.[31]

Other Types of Teams

In addition to the SMT, businesses use other types of teams: the problem-solving team, the special-purpose team, and the virtual team.[32] The **problem-solving team** consists of volunteers from a unit or department who meet one or two hours per week to discuss quality improvement, cost reduction, or improvement in the work environment. The formation of problem-solving teams does not affect an organization's structure because these teams exist for only a limited period; they are usually disbanded after they have achieved their objectives. Problem-solving teams are often used when organizations decide to pursue a TQM effort; the teams focus on making improvements in the quality of a product or service.

Problem-solving team
A team consisting of volunteers from a unit or department who meet one or two hours per week to discuss quality improvement, cost reduction, or improvement in the work environment.

The **special-purpose team** or **task force** consists of members who span functional or organizational boundaries and whose purpose is to examine complex issues—for example, introducing a new technology, improving the quality of a work process that spans several functional units, or encouraging cooperation between labor and management in a unionized setting. An example of a special-purpose team is the quality of work life (QWL) program, which consists of team members (including union representatives and managers) who collaborate on making improvements in all aspects of work life, including product quality. The QWL program at Ford and General Motors has focused on improving product quality, whereas the QWL program between the United Steel Workers of America and the major steel companies has concentrated on developing new ways to improve employee morale and working conditions.[33]

Special-purpose team
A team or task force consisting of workers who span functional or organizational boundaries and whose purpose is to examine complex issues.

For more on problem-solving teams, refer to the Manager's Notebook titled "Tips on Managing Problem-Solving Teams."

MANAGER'S NOTEBOOK

Customer-Driven HR

Tips on Managing Problem-Solving Teams

Managers should be able to use problem-solving teams consisting of employees with cross-functional skills to solve challenging organizational issues. In designing and managing such teams, the following are some important points to consider:

- If the team is expected to implement new ideas, include members from different levels of the organization. Creating a team with members from different levels (front-line employees and supervisors, for example) can also foster cooperation and reduce barriers between employees and managers.
- Monitor the team to ensure that the free exchange of ideas and creativity is not stifled if managers and employees are on the same team.
- Select members for their expertise and diverse perspectives but also for their ability to compromise and solve problems collaboratively.
- Allow the team enough time to complete its task. The more complex the problem, and the more creative the solution needs to be, the more large blocks of time the members will need.
- Coordinate with other managers to free up time for the members.
- Provide clear goals and guidelines on what you expect the team to do. Tell them what they can and cannot address.

Source: Nahavandi, A., and Malekzadeh, A. R. (1999). *Organizational behavior*. Upper Saddle River, NJ: Prentice Hall, 276.

Virtual team
A team that relies on interactive technology to work together when separated by physical distance.

The **virtual team** uses interactive computer technologies such as the Internet, groupware (software that permits people at different computer workstations to collaborate on a project simultaneously), and computer-based videoconferencing to work together despite being separated by physical distance.[34] Virtual teams are similar to problem-solving teams because they do not require full-time commitment from team members. The difference is that virtual team members interact with each other electronically, rather than face-to-face.[35]

Virtual teams allow organizations to position individuals who might not be otherwise available on teams because of their part-time nature and flexibility in accommodating distance. For example, a management consulting firm working on a project out of its San Francisco office for a local bank could involve financial specialists from its New York and Chicago offices on the project team. This type of team also makes it possible for companies to cross organizational boundaries by linking customers, suppliers, and business partners in a collaborative effort that can increase the quality and speed with which the new product or service is brought to market. In writing this textbook, the authors (university professors) formed a virtual team with the publishing company's editors and also with the design specialists who created the graphics and visual images for the text.

Work: The Individual Perspective

The third and final perspective from which we will examine work flows and structure is that of the individual employee and job. We look first at the various theories of what motivates employees to achieve higher levels of performance and then at different ways jobs can be designed to maximize employee productivity. In the next section we look at job analysis, the gathering and organization of information concerning the tasks and duties of specific jobs. The section concludes with a discussion of job descriptions, which are one of the primary results of job analysis.

Motivating Employees

Motivation can be defined as that which energizes, directs, and sustains human behavior.[36] In HRM, the term refers to a person's desire to do the best possible job or to exert the maximum effort to perform assigned tasks. An important feature of motivation is that it is behavior directed toward a goal.

Motivation
That which energizes, directs, and sustains human behavior. In HRM, a person's desire to do the best possible job or to exert the maximum effort to perform assigned tasks.

Motivation theory seeks to explain why employees are more motivated by and satisfied with one type of work than another. It is essential that managers have a basic understanding of work motivation because highly motivated employees are more likely to produce a superior-quality product or service than employees who lack motivation.

Two-Factor Theory

The *two-factor theory of motivation*, developed by Frederick Herzberg, attempts to identify and explain the factors that employees find satisfying and dissatisfying about their jobs.[37] The first set of factors, called motivators, are internal job factors that lead to job satisfaction and higher motivation. In the absence of motivators, employees will probably not be satisfied with their work or motivated to perform up to their potential. Some examples of motivators are:

- The work itself
- Achievement
- Recognition
- Responsibility
- Opportunities for advancement

Notice that salary is not included in the motivator list. Herzberg contends that pay belongs among the second set of factors, which he calls *hygiene* or *maintenance factors*. Hygiene factors are external to the job; they are located in the work environment. The absence of a hygiene factor can lead to active dissatisfaction and demotivation and, in extreme situations, to avoidance of the work altogether. Hygiene factors include the following:

- Company policies
- Working conditions
- Job security
- Salary
- Employee benefits
- Relationships with supervisors and managers
- Relationships with co-workers
- Relationships with subordinates

According to Herzberg, if management provides the appropriate hygiene factors, employees will not be dissatisfied with their jobs, but neither will they be motivated to perform at their full potential. To motivate workers, management must provide some motivators.

Two-factor theory has two implications for job design:

- Jobs should be designed to provide as many motivators as possible.
- Making (external) changes in hygiene factors such as pay or working conditions is not likely to sustain improvements in employee motivation over the long run unless (internal) changes are also made in the work itself.

Work Adjustment Theory

Every worker has unique needs and abilities. *Work adjustment theory* suggests that employees' motivation levels and job satisfaction depend on the fit between their needs and abilities and the characteristics of the job and the organization.[38] A poor fit between individual characteristics and the work environment may lead to reduced levels of motivation. Work adjustment theory proposes that:

- A job design that one employee finds challenging and motivating may not motivate another employee. For example, a mentally disabled employee may find a repetitive job at a fast-food restaurant highly motivating and challenging, but a college graduate may find the same job boring.

- Not all employees want to be involved in decision making. Employees with low needs for involvement may fit poorly on a self-managed team because they may resist managing other team members and taking responsibility for team decisions.

Goal-Setting Theory

Goal-setting theory, developed by Edwin Locke, suggests that employees' goals help to explain motivation and job performance.[39] The reasoning is as follows: Because motivation is goal-directed behavior, goals that are clear and challenging will result in higher levels of employee motivation than goals that are ambiguous and easy.

Because it suggests that managers can increase employee motivation by managing the goal-setting process, goal-setting theory has some important implications for managers:[40]

- Employees will be more motivated to perform when they have clear and specific goals. A store manager whose specific goal is to "increase store profitability by 20 percent in the next six months" will exert more effort than one who is told to "do the best you can" to increase profits.
- Employees will be more motivated to accomplish difficult goals than easy goals. Of course, the goals must be attainable; otherwise the employee is likely to become frustrated. For example, an inexperienced computer programmer may promise to deliver a program in an unrealistic amount of time. The programmer's manager may work with her to establish a more realistic, yet still challenging, deadline for delivering the program.
- In many (but not all) cases, goals that employees participate in creating for themselves are more motivating than goals that are simply assigned by managers. Managers may establish mutually agreed-upon goals with employees through a management by objectives (MBO) approach (discussed in Chapter 7) or by creating self-managed teams that take responsibility for establishing their own goals.
- Employees who receive frequent feedback on their progress toward reaching their goals sustain higher levels of motivation and performance than employees who receive sporadic or no feedback. For example, a restaurant manager can motivate servers to provide better service by soliciting customer feedback on service quality and then communicating this information to employees.

Job Characteristics Theory

Developed by Richard Hackman and Greg Oldham, *job characteristics theory* states that employees will be more motivated to work and more satisfied with their jobs to the extent that jobs contain certain core characteristics.[41] These core job characteristics create the conditions that allow employees to experience critical psychological states that are related to beneficial work outcomes, including high work motivation. The strength of the linkage among job characteristics, psychological states, and work outcomes is determined by the intensity of the individual employee's need for growth (that is, how important the employee considers growth and development on the job).

There are five core job characteristics that activate three critical psychological states. The core job characteristics are:[42]

1. **Skill variety** The degree to which the job requires the person to do different things and involves the use of a number of different skills, abilities, and talents.
2. **Task identity** The degree to which a person can do the job from beginning to end with a visible outcome.
3. **Task significance** The degree to which the job has a significant impact on others—both inside and outside the organization.
4. **Autonomy** The amount of freedom, independence, and discretion the employee has in areas such as scheduling the work, making decisions, and determining how to do the job.
5. **Feedback** The degree to which the job provides the employee with clear and direct information about job outcomes and performance.

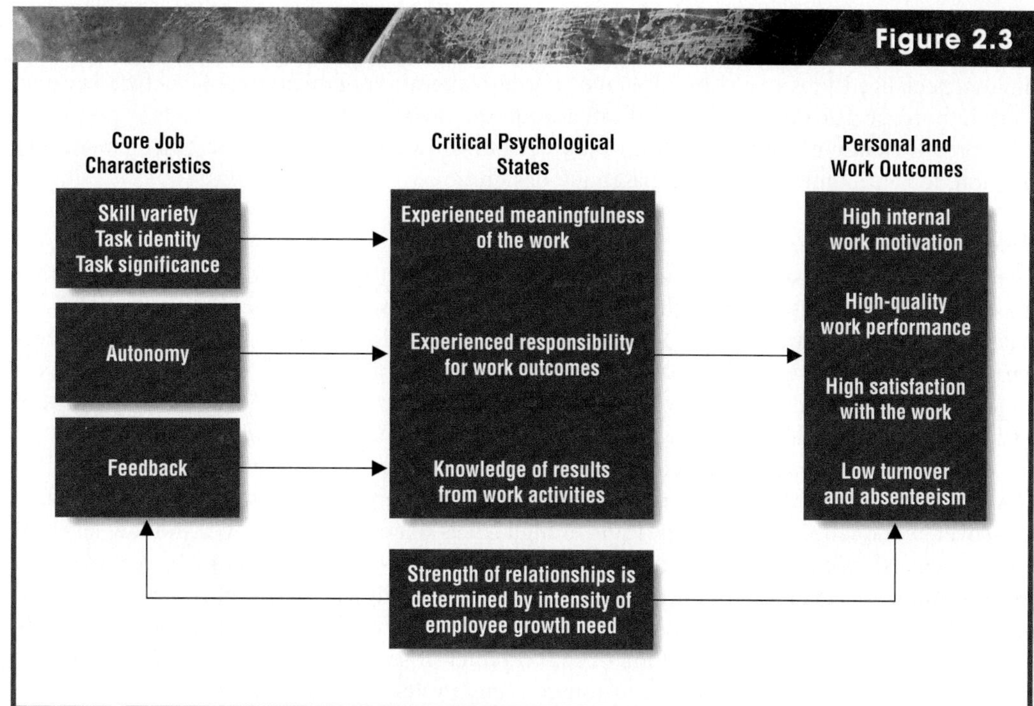

The Job Characteristics Theory of Work Motivation

The three critical psychological states affected by the core job characteristics are:[43]

1. **Experienced meaningfulness** The extent to which the employee experiences the work as important, valuable, and worthwhile.
2. **Experienced responsibility** The degree to which the employee feels personally responsible or accountable for the results of the work.
3. **Knowledge of results** The degree to which the employee understands on a regular basis how effectively he or she is performing the job.

Skill variety, task identity, and task significance are all linked to experienced meaningfulness of work, as Figure 2.3 shows. Autonomy is related to experienced responsibility and feedback to knowledge of results.

A job with characteristics that allow an employee to experience all three critical psychological states provides internal rewards that sustain motivation.[44] These rewards come from having a job where the person can learn (knowledge of results) that he or she has performed well on a task (experienced responsibility) that he or she cares about (experienced meaningfulness).[45] In addition, this situation results in certain outcomes that are beneficial to the employer: high-quality performance, higher employee satisfaction, and lower turnover and absenteeism. Job characteristics theory maintains that jobs can be designed to contain the characteristics that employees find rewarding and motivating.

Designing Jobs and Conducting Job Analysis

All the theories of employee motivation suggest that jobs can be designed to increase motivation and performance. **Job design** is the process of organizing work into the tasks required to perform a specific job.

Job design
The process of organizing work into the tasks required to perform a specific job.

Job Design

There are three important influences on job design. One is work flow analysis, which (you will recall) seeks to ensure that each job in the organization receives work as an input, adds value to that work, and then passes it on to another worker. The other two influences are business strategy and the organizational structure that best fits that strategy. For example, an emphasis on highly specialized jobs could be expected in a bureaucratic organizational structure because work in bureaucratic organizations is built around the division of labor.

We will examine five approaches to job design: work simplification, job enlargement, job rotation, job enrichment, and team-based job design.

Work Simplification

Work simplification assumes that work can be broken down into simple, repetitive tasks that maximize efficiency. This approach to job design assigns most of the thinking aspects of work (such as planning and organizing) to managers and supervisors, while giving the employee a narrowly defined task to perform. Work simplification can utilize labor effectively to produce a large amount of a standardized product. The automobile assembly line, where workers engage in highly mechanical and repetitive tasks, exemplifies the work simplification approach.

Although work simplification can be efficient in a stable environment, it is less effective in a changing environment where customers demand custom-built products of high quality. Moreover, work simplification often leads to high levels of employee turnover and low levels of employee satisfaction. (In fact, where work simplification is used, employees may feel the need to form unions to gain some control over their work.) Finally, higher-level professionals subjected to work simplification may become so specialized in what they do that they cannot see how their job affects the organization's overall product or service. The result can be employees doing work that has no value to the customer. Many professional employees in highly specialized jobs became casualties of corporate restructurings over the last decade because organizations discovered such work did not provide value to consumers.

Work simplification is not to be confused with *work elimination*. Companies trying to eliminate work challenge every task and every step within a task to see if there is a better way to get the work done. Even if parts of the work cannot be eliminated, some aspect of the job may be simplified or combined with another job. Oryx—a Dallas, Texas–based oil and gas producer—saved $70 million in operating costs in one year after it set up teams to take a fresh look at its operations. The teams discovered many procedures, reviews, reports, and approvals that had little to do with Oryx's business and could easily be eliminated. Work elimination is similar to BPR, though it differs in that work elimination typically focuses on particular jobs and processes rather than on overhauling the entire company.[46]

Job Enlargement and Job Rotation

Job enlargement and job rotation are used to redesign jobs to reduce fatigue and boredom among workers performing simplified and highly specialized work. **Job enlargement** expands a job's duties. For example, auto workers whose specialized job is to install carpets on the car floor may have their job enlarged to include the extra duties of installing the car's seats and instrument panel.[47]

Job enlargement
The process of expanding a job's duties.

Job rotation rotates workers among different narrowly defined tasks without disrupting the flow of work. On an auto assembly line, for example, a worker whose job is installing carpets would be rotated periodically to a second workstation where she would install only seats in the car. At a later time period she might be rotated to a third workstation, where her job would be to install only the car's instrument panels. During the course of a day on the assembly line, the worker might be shifted at two-hour intervals among all three workstations.

Job rotation
The process of rotating workers among different narrowly defined tasks without disrupting the flow of work.

Both job enlargement and job rotation have limitations because these approaches focus mainly on eliminating the demotivating aspects of work and, thus, improve only one of the five core job characteristics that motivate workers (skill variety).

Job Enrichment

Job enrichment is an approach to job design that directly applies job characteristics theory (see Figure 2.3) to make jobs more interesting and to improve employee motivation. **Job enrichment** puts specialized tasks back together so that one person is responsible for producing a whole product or an entire service.[48]

Job enrichment
The process of putting specialized tasks back together so that one person is responsible for producing a whole product or an entire service.

Job enrichment expands both the horizontal and the vertical dimensions of a job. Instead of people working on an assembly line at one or more stations, the entire assembly line process is abandoned to allow workers to assemble an entire product, such as a kitchen appliance or radio.[49] For example, at Motorola's Communications Division, individual employees are now responsible for assembling, testing, and packaging the company's pocket radio-paging devices. Previously, these products were made on an assembly line that broke the work down into 100 different steps and used as many workers.[50]

Job enrichment gives employees more opportunities for autonomy and feedback. It also gives them more responsibilities that require decision making, such as scheduling work, determining work methods, and judging quality.[51] However, the successful implementation of job enrichment is limited by the production technology available and the capabilities of the employees who produce the product or service. Some products are highly complex and require too many steps for one individual to produce them efficiently. Other products require the application of so many different skills that it is not feasible to train employees in all of them. For example, it could take an employee a lifetime to master all the skills necessary to assemble a Boeing 777 aircraft.

Team-Based Job Designs

Team-based job designs focus on giving a team, rather than an individual, a whole and meaningful piece of work to do.[52] Team members are empowered to decide among themselves how to accomplish the work.[53] Team members are cross-trained in different skills, then rotated to do different tasks within the team. Team-based job designs match best with flat and boundaryless organizational structures.

One company that emphasizes team-based job design is GM's Saturn division, located in Spring Hill, Tennessee. The process of assembling the Saturn car is accomplished by self-managed teams of 8 to 15 workers. Each team takes responsibility for managing itself. It interviews and hires new team members, manages its own budget, and receives reports on the amount of waste it generates so that it can develop plans to utilize its materials more effectively.[54]

Job Analysis

After a work flow analysis has been done and jobs have been designed, the employer needs to define and communicate job expectations for individual employees. This is best done through **job analysis,** which is the systematic gathering and organization of information concerning jobs. Job analysis puts a job under the microscope to reveal important details about it. Specifically, it identifies the tasks, duties, and responsibilities of a particular job.

Job analysis
The systematic process of collecting information used to make decisions about jobs. Job analysis identifies the tasks, duties, and responsibilities of a particular job.

- A *task* is a basic element of work that is a logical and necessary step in performing a job duty.
- A *duty* consists of one or more tasks that constitute a significant activity performed in a job.
- A *responsibility* is one or several duties that identify and describe the major purpose or reason for the job's existence.

Thus, for the job of administrative assistant, a task might be completing a travel authorization form, which is part of the duty to keep track of the department's travel expenses, which is part of the responsibility to manage the departmental budget.

Job analysis provides information to answer the following questions: Where does the work come from? What machines and special equipment must be used? What knowledge, skills, and abilities (KSAs) does the job holder need to perform the job? How much supervision is necessary? Under what working conditions should this job be performed? What are the performance expectations for this job? On whom must the job holders depend to perform this job? With whom must they interact? Job analysis can answer these questions, thereby giving managers valuable information that can help them develop more effective HRM policies and programs, as described in the remaining chapters of this text.

Who Performs Job Analysis?

Depending on the technique selected, job analysis is performed either by a member of the HR department or by the *job incumbent* (the person who is currently assigned to the job in question). In some businesses a manager may perform the job analysis.

Teams at GM's Saturn division, such as this team of interior designers for Saturn's S-series, manage their own activities. Each team interviews and hires team members, manages its own budget, keeps track of the waste it generates, and finds ways to increase its efficiency.

Methods of Gathering Job Information

Companies use several methods to gather job information: interviews, observation, diaries, and questionnaires. Factors such as cost and job complexity will influence the choice of method.

- **Interviews** The interviewer (usually a member of the HR department) interviews a representative sample of job incumbents using a structured interview. The structured interview includes a series of job-related questions that is presented to each interviewee in the same order.
- **Observation** An individual observes the job incumbent actually performing the job and records the core job characteristics from observation. This method is used in cases where the job is fairly routine and the observer can identify the job essentials in a reasonable amount of time. The job analyst may videotape the job incumbent in order to study the job in greater detail.
- **Diaries** Several job incumbents may be asked to keep diaries or logs of their daily job activities and record the amount of time spent on each activity. By analyzing these diaries over a representative period of time (perhaps several weeks), a job analyst is able to capture the job's essential characteristics.
- **Questionnaires** The job incumbent fills out a questionnaire that asks a series of questions about the job's knowledge, skill, and ability requirements, duties, and responsibilities. Each question is associated with a quantitative scale that measures the importance of the job factor or the frequency with which it occurs. A computer can then tally the scores on the questionnaires and create a printout summarizing the job's characteristics. The computerized method of gathering job information with questionnaires is the most expensive method.

The Uses of Job Analysis

Job analysis measures job content and the relative importance of different job duties and responsibilities. Having this information helps companies comply with government regulations and defend their actions from legal challenges that allege unfairness or discrimination. As we will see in Chapter 3, the generic defense against a charge of discrimination is that the contested decision (to hire, to give a raise, to terminate) was made for job-related reasons. Job analysis provides the documentation for such a defense. For instance:

- A company may be able to defend its policy of requiring sales representatives to have a valid driver's license if it can show via job analysis that driving is an essential activity in the sales rep's job. Otherwise, under the Americans with Disabilities Act (see Chapter 3), the employer may be asked to make a reasonable accommodation for a blind job applicant who asserts his rights to be considered for the job.

- The owner of a fast-food restaurant who pays an assistant manager a weekly salary (without any overtime pay) may be able to defend herself from charges of an overtime pay violation with a job analysis proving that the assistant manager job is exempt from the overtime provisions of the Fair Labor Standards Act (see Chapter 10). The owner can prove this by showing that most of the job duties and responsibilities involve supervising and directing others rather than preparing food and providing service to customers.

In addition to establishing job relatedness for legal purposes, job analysis is also useful for the following HR activities:

- **Recruitment** Job analysis can help the HR department generate a higher-quality pool of job applicants by making it easy to describe a job in newspaper ads that can be targeted to qualified job applicants. Job analysis also helps college recruiters screen job applicants because it tells them what tasks, duties, and responsibilities the job entails.
- **Selection** Job analysis can be used to determine whether an applicant for a specific job should be required to take a personality test or some other kind of test. For example, a personality test that measures extroversion (the degree to which someone is talkative, sociable, active, aggressive, or excitable) may be justified for selecting a life insurance sales representative. (Such a job is likely to emphasize customer contact, which includes making "cold calls" on potential new accounts.) Job analysis may also reveal that the personality test measuring extroversion has a weak relationship to the job content of other jobs (for example, lab technician) and should not be used as part of the selection process for those jobs.
- **Performance appraisal** The performance standards used to judge employee performance for purposes of promotion, rewards, discipline, or layoff should be job related. Under federal law, a company is required to defend its appraisal system against lawsuits and prove the job relatedness of the performance criteria used in the appraisal.
- **Compensation** Job analysis information can be used to compare the relative worth of each job's contributions to the company's overall performance. The value of each job's contribution is an important determinant of the job's pay level. In a typical pay structure, jobs that require mastery of more complex skills or that have greater levels of responsibility pay more than jobs that require only basic skills or have low amounts of responsibility.
- **Training and career development** Job analysis is an important input for determining training needs. By comparing the knowledge, skills, and abilities that employees bring to the job with those that are identified by job analysis, managers can identify their employees' skill gaps. Training programs can then be put in place to improve job performance.

The Techniques of Job Analysis

Figure 2.4 on page 64 lists eight major techniques of job analysis. Detailed descriptions of these techniques are beyond the scope of this book. However, we briefly describe four of them—task inventory analysis, the critical incident technique, the position analysis questionnaire, and functional job analysis—to give you a sense of what job analysis entails. For a set of general guidelines on conducting a job analysis effectively, see the Manager's Notebook on page 64 titled "Guidelines for Conducting a Job Analysis."

Task Inventory Analysis *Task inventory analysis* is actually a collection of methods that are offshoots of the U.S. Air Force task inventory method.[55] The technique is used to determine the **knowledge, skills, and abilities (KSAs)** needed to perform a job successfully. The analysis involves three steps: (1) interview, (2) survey, and (3) generation of a task by KSA matrix.

Knowledge, skills, and abilities (KSAs)
The knowledge, skills, and abilities needed to perform a job successfully.

The interview step focuses on developing lists of tasks that are part of the job. Interviews are conducted both with workers who currently hold the job and with their managers. The goal of the interviews is to generate specific descriptions of individual tasks that can be used in the task inventory survey.

The survey step involves generating and administering a survey consisting of task statements and rating scales. The survey might ask respondents—the current job holders—to rate each task on importance, frequency, and training time needed. Whether the survey is sent to a

Figure 2.4

Technique	Employee Group Focused On	Data-Collection Method	Analysis Results	Description
1. Task Inventory Analysis	Any—large number of workers needed	Questionnaire	Rating of tasks	Tasks are rated by job incumbent,* supervisor, or job analyst. Ratings may be on characteristics such as importance of task and time spent doing it.
2. Critical Incident Technique	Any	Interview	Behavioral description	Behavioral incidents representing poor through excellent performance are generated for each dimension of the job.
3. Position Analysis Questionnaire (PAQ)	Any	Questionnaire	Rating of 194 job elements	Elements are rated on six scales (for example, extent of use, importance to job). Ratings are analyzed by computer.
4. Functional Job Analysis (FJA)	Any	Group interview/ questionnaire	Rating of how job incumbent relates to people, data, and things	Originally designed to improve counseling and placement of people registered at local state employment offices. Task statements are generated and then presented to job incumbents to rate on such dimensions as frequency and importance.
5. Methods Analysis (Motion Study)	Manufacturing	Observation	Time per unit of work	Systematic means for determining the standard time for various work tasks. Based on observation and timing of work tasks.
6. Guidelines-Oriented Job Analysis	Any	Interview	Skills and knowledge required	Job incumbents identify duties as well as knowledge, skills, physical abilities, and other characteristics needed to perform the job.
7. Management Position Description Questionnaire (MPDQ)	Managerial	Questionnaire	Checklist of 197 items	Managers check items descriptive of their responsibilities.
8. Hay Plan	Managerial	Interview	Impact of job on organization	Managers are interviewed regarding such issues as their responsibilities and accountabilities. Responses are analyzed according to four dimensions: objectives, dimensions, nature and scope, accountability.

* The term *job incumbent* refers to the person currently filling a particular job.

The Techniques of Job Analysis

sample of the workers or to all of them will depend on the number of workers and the economic constraints on the job analysis.

The final step is the creation of a task by KSA matrix, which is used to rate the extent to which a variety of KSAs are important for the successful completion of each task. An abbreviated example of a KSA rating matrix is presented in Figure 2.5. Ratings in the matrix are usually determined by subject matter experts, who might include supervisors, managers, consultants, and job incumbents.

Task inventory analysis has two major advantages. First, it is a systematic means for analyzing the tasks in a particular situation. Second, it uses a tailor-made questionnaire rather than an already prepared stock questionnaire. The technique can be used to develop job descriptions and performance appraisal forms, as well as to develop or identify appropriate selection tests.

Figure 2.5

Sample Task by KSA Matrix

Rating Scale
Importance of characteristics for successful performance of task

1	2	3	4	5
Very Low	Low	Medium	High	Very High

	Worker Characteristics									
Job Task	Mathematical Reasoning	Analytical Ability	Ability to Follow Directions	Memory	Comprehension—Oral	Comprehension—Written	Expression—Oral	Expression—Written	Problem-Solving Ability	Clerical Accuracy
1. Reviews production schedules to determine correct job sequencing										
2. Identifies problem jobs and takes corrective action										
3. Determines need for and provides special work orders										
4. Maintains log book and makes required assignments										
5. Negotiates with foremen to determine critical dates for emergency situations										
6. Analyzes material availability and performs order maintenance										
7. Prepares job packets										
8. Maintains customer order file										
9. Negotiates with Purchasing to ensure material availability										
10. Determines product availability for future customer orders										
11. Determines promise dates and provides to customer										
12. Determines adequacy of materials given document forecast										

Critical Incident Technique. The *critical incident technique (CIT)* is used to develop behavioral descriptions of a job.[56] In CIT, supervisors and workers generate behavioral incidents of job performance. The technique involves the following four steps: (1) generate dimensions, (2) generate incidents, (3) retranslate, and (4) assign effectiveness values. In the generating dimensions step, supervisors and workers identify the major dimensions of a job. "Dimensions" are simply aspects of performance. For example, interacting with customers, ordering stock, and balancing the cash drawer are the major dimensions of a retail job. Once they have agreed on the job's major dimensions, supervisors and workers generate "critical incidents" of behavior that represent high, moderate, and low levels of performance on each dimension. An example of a critical incident of high performance on the dimension "interacting with customers" might be:

When a customer complained to the clerk that she could not find a particular item, seeing no one else was in line, this clerk walked with the customer back to the shelves to find the item.

An example of low performance on the same dimension might be:

When a customer handed the clerk a large number of coupons, the clerk complained out loud to the bagger that he hated dealing with coupons.

The last two steps, retranslation and assigning effectiveness values, involve making sure that the critical incidents generated in the first two steps are commonly viewed the same way by other employees.

The CIT provides a detailed behavioral description of jobs. It is often used as a basis for performance appraisal systems and training programs, as well as to develop behaviorally based selection interview questions. The appendix to Chapter 7 gives you the opportunity to develop critical incidents.

Position Analysis Questionnaire (PAQ). The PAQ is a job analysis questionnaire that contains 194 different items. Using a five-point scale, the PAQ seeks to determine the degree to which the different items, or job elements, are involved in performing a particular job.[57] The 194 items are organized into six sections:

1. **Information input** Where and how a worker gets information needed to perform the job.
2. **Mental processes** The reasoning, decision-making, planning, and information-processing activities involved in performing the job.
3. **Work output** The physical activities, tools, and devices used by the worker to perform the job.

MANAGER'S NOTEBOOK

Customer-Driven HR

Guidelines for Conducting a Job Analysis

Conducting a job analysis requires managers to take five steps:

1. **Determine the desired applications of the job analysis.** For example, if used as a basis for performance appraisal, job analysis should collect data that are representative of differing levels of job performance. If used as a basis for determining training needs, then job analysis should collect information on the necessary knowledge, skills, and abilities that lead to effective job performance.
2. **Select the jobs to be analyzed.** Factors that make specific jobs appropriate for job analysis include the stability or obsolescence of job content (rapidly changing jobs require more frequent job analysis). Entry-level jobs (which require selection tools that determine who gets hired and who gets rejected) are also analyzed regularly.
3. **Gather the job information.** Within budget constraints, collect the desired information using the most appropriate job-analysis technique.
4. **Verify the accuracy of the job information.** Both the job incumbents and their immediate supervisors should review the job information to ensure that it is representative of the actual job.
5. **Document the job analysis by writing a job description.** Document the job-analysis information in a job description that summarizes the job's essential duties and responsibilities, as well as the knowledge, skills, and abilities necessary for the job. This document allows managers to compare different jobs on various dimensions and is an important part of many HR programs.

Source: Adapted from Gatewood, R. D., and Feild, H. S. (2001). *Human resource selection* (5th ed.) Fort Worth, TX: Harcourt College Publishers.

4. **Relationships with other persons** The relationships with other people required in performing the job.
5. **Job context** The physical and social contexts in which the work is performed.
6. **Other characteristics** The other activities, conditions, and characteristics relevant to the job.

A computer analyzes the completed PAQ and generates a score for the job and a profile of its characteristics.

Functional Job Analysis. Functional job analysis, a technique used in the public sector, can be done by either interview or questionnaire.[58] This technique collects information on the following aspects of the job:[59]

1. What the job incumbent does to people, data, and things.
2. The methods and techniques the job incumbent uses to perform the job.
3. The machines, tools, and equipment used by the job incumbent.
4. The materials, projects, or services produced by the job incumbent.

The results of functional job analyses are published by the U.S. federal government in the *Dictionary of Occupational Titles (DOT)*.[60] The DOT contains standard and comprehensive descriptions of about 20,000 jobs and has helped to bring about more uniformity in the job titles used in different sections of the country. The DOT listings also facilitate the exchange of statistical information about jobs.

Job Analysis and the Legal Environment

Because job analysis can be the basis on which a firm wins or loses a lawsuit over how it selects or appraises employees, it is important that organizations carefully document their job-analysis efforts.

There are two important questions regarding job analysis. First: Which job analysis method is best? Although there are many job-analysis techniques, there is no clear choice as to which is best. Some, like task inventory analysis and Guidelines-Oriented Job Analysis, were developed to satisfy legal requirements, but there is no legal basis to prefer one to another. The *Uniform Guidelines* published by the Equal Employment Opportunity Commission state that a job analysis should be done but do not specify a preferred technique.

As a general rule, the more concrete and observable the information, the better. Thus, job-analysis approaches that provide specific task or behavioral statements, such as task inventory analysis or CIT, may be preferable. CIT can be very expensive because of the time commitment required of supervisors and workers.

Given the lack of a single best technique, the choice of job-analysis technique should, within economic constraints, be guided by the purpose of the analysis. For example, if the major purpose for the analysis is the redesign of jobs, then an analysis focusing on tasks would probably be best. But if the major purpose is the development of a training program, a behaviorally focused technique would probably be best.

Job Analysis and Organizational Flexibility

The second question regarding job analysis is: How does detailed job-analysis information fit into today's organizations, which need to be flexible and innovative to remain competitive?

Whatever technique is used, job analysis is a static view of the job as it currently exists, and a static view of jobs is at odds with current organizational trends emphasizing flexibility and innovativeness. For instance, America West Airlines attempts to keep labor costs down by having employees do a variety of tasks. The same person may be a flight attendant, ticket agent, and baggage handler all in the same week. And almost all jobs today are affected by the constant advances in information and communication technologies. Such factors can render even the most thorough job analysis virtually useless after a very short time.

In an organizational environment of change and innovation, it is better to focus job analyses on *worker* characteristics than on *job* characteristics. The tasks involved in jobs may change, but such employee characteristics as innovativeness, team orientation, interpersonal skills, and communication skills will likely remain critical to organizational success. Unfortunately, most job-analysis techniques are not focused on discovering worker characteristics unless the characteristics are directly related to the immediate tasks. But, because the importance of fit with the organization is being increasingly recognized as a factor that should be considered in selection,[61] job analysis may become more focused on underlying employee factors.[62] Sun Microsystems, Toyota (USA), and AFG Industries are some of the organizations that have expanded job analysis to emphasize fit between prospective employees and the organization.

Job Descriptions

Job description
A written document that identifies, describes, and defines a job in terms of its duties, responsibilities, working conditions, and specifications.

A **job description** is a summary statement of the information collected in the job-analysis process. It is a written document that identifies, defines, and describes a job in terms of its duties, responsibilities, working conditions, and specifications. There are two types of job descriptions: specific job descriptions and general job descriptions.

A *specific job description* is a detailed summary of a job's tasks, duties, and responsibilities. This type of job description is associated with work flow strategies that emphasize efficiency, control, and detailed work planning. It fits best with a bureaucratic organizational structure with well-defined boundaries that separate functions and the different levels of management. Figure 2.6 shows an example of a specific job description for the job of service and safety supervisor. Note that this job description closely specifies the work that is unique to a person who will supervise *safety* employees. The specific job knowledge of safety regulations and Red Cross first-aid procedures included in this job description make it inappropriate for any other type of supervisor (for example, a supervisor at a local supermarket).

The *general job description*, which is fairly new on the scene, is associated with work flow strategies that emphasize innovation, flexibility, and loose work planning. This type of job description fits best with a flat or boundaryless organizational structure in which there are few boundaries between functions and levels of management.[63]

Only the most generic duties, responsibilities, and skills for a position are documented in the general job description.[64] Figure 2.7 on page 70 shows a general job description for the job of "supervisor." Note that all the job duties and responsibilities in Figure 2.7 apply to the job of *any* supervisor—one who supervises accountants, engineers, or even the safety employees managed by the service and safety supervisor in Figure 2.6.

The driving force behind a move toward general job descriptions may be a TQM program or business process reengineering.[65] For example, the Arizona Public Service (APS), a public utility, moved toward general job descriptions after discovering that it had 1,000 specific job descriptions for its 3,600 workers.[66] This massive number of specific job descriptions erected false barriers among work functions, choked off change, and prevented APS from providing high levels of customer service. By using general job descriptions, APS was able to reduce the number of its job descriptions to 450.

An even more impressive application of general job descriptions is seen at Nissan, the Japanese auto manufacturer. Nissan has only one general job description for all its hourly wage production employees.[67] By comparison, some of the divisions of General Motors have hundreds of specific job descriptions for their hourly production workforce. This fact is partially explained by the vigilance of the United Auto Workers' Union (UAW) in defending the rights of its members to work in specific jobs.

Elements of a Job Description

Job descriptions have four key elements: identification information, job summary, job duties and responsibilities, and job specifications and minimum qualifications.[68] Figures 2.6 and 2.7 show how this information is organized on the job description.

To comply with federal law, it is important that job descriptions document only the essential aspects of a job. Otherwise, qualified women, minorities, and persons with disabilities may be unintentionally discriminated against for not meeting specified job requirements. For example, a valid driver's license should not be put in the job description if the job can be modified so that it can be performed by a person with physical disabilities without a driver's license.

Identification Information. The first part of the job description identifies the job title, location, and source of job-analysis information; who wrote the job description; the dates of the job analysis and the verification of the job description; and whether the job is exempt from the

Figure 2.6

Job Title: Service and Safety Supervisor

DIVISION: Plastics
DEPARTMENT: Manufacturing
SOURCE(S): John Doe WAGE CATEGORY: Exempt
JOB ANALYST: John Smith VERIFIED BY: Bill Johnson
DATE ANALYZED: 12/26/03 DATE VERIFIED: 1/5/04

Job Summary

The SERVICE AND SAFETY SUPERVISOR works under the direction of the IMPREGNATING & LAMINATING MANAGER: **schedules** labor pool employees; **supervises** the work of gardeners, cleaners, waste disposal, and plant security personnel; **coordinates** plant safety programs; **maintains** daily records on personnel, equipment, and scrap.

Job Duties and Responsibilities

1. **Schedules** labor employees to provide relief personnel for all manufacturing departments; **prepares** assignment schedules and **assigns** individuals to departments based on routine as well as special needs in order to maintain adequate labor levels through the plant; **notifies** Industrial Relations Department weekly about vacation and layoff status of labor pool employees, contractual disputes, and other employment-related developments.
2. **Supervises** the work of gardeners, cleaners, waste disposal, and plant security personnel; **plans** yard, cleanup, and security activities based on weekly determination of needs; **assigns** tasks and responsibilities to employees on a daily basis; **monitors** progress or status of assigned tasks; **disciplines** employees.
3. **Coordinates** plant safety programs; **teaches** basic first-aid procedures to security, supervisory, and lease personnel in order to maintain adequate coverage of medical emergencies; **trains** employees in fire fighting and hazardous materials handling procedures; **verifies** plant compliance with new or changing OSHA regulations; **represents** division during company-wide safety programs and meetings.
4. **Maintains** daily records on personnel, equipment, and scrap; **reports** amount of waste and scrap to cost accounting department; **updates** personnel records as necessary; **reviews** maintenance checklists for towmotors.
5. **Performs** other miscellaneous duties as assigned.

Job Requirements

1. Ability to apply basic principles and techniques of supervision.
   a. Knowledge of principles and techniques of supervision.
   b. Ability to plan and organize the activities of others.
   c. Ability to get ideas accepted and to guide a group or individual to accomplish the task.
   d. Ability to modify leadership style and management approach to reach goal.
2. Ability to express ideas clearly both in written and oral communications.
3. Knowledge of current Red Cross first-aid operations.
4. Knowledge of OSHA regulations as they affect plant operations.
5. Knowledge of labor pool jobs, company policies, and labor contracts.

Minimum Qualifications

Twelve years of general education or equivalent; one year supervisory experience; and first-aid instructor's certification.

OR

Substitute 45 hours classroom supervisory training for supervisory experience.

Source: Jones, M. A. (1984, May). Job descriptions made easy. *Personnel Journal*. Copyright May 1984. Reprinted with the permission of *Personnel Journal*. ACC Communications, Inc., Costa Mesa, California; all rights reserved.

Example of a Specific Job Description

overtime provision of the Fair Labor Standards Act or subject to overtime pay rates. To be certain that the identification information ensures equal employment opportunities, HR staff should:

- Make sure the job titles do not refer to a specific gender. For example, use the job title "sales representative" rather than "salesman."
- Make sure job descriptions are updated regularly so that the date on the job description is current. Job descriptions more than two years old have low credibility and may provide flawed information.

Figure 2.7

Job Title: Supervisor

DIVISION: Plastics
DEPARTMENT: Manufacturing
SOURCE(S): John Doe, S. Lee
JOB ANALYST: John Smith
DATE ANALYZED: 12/26/03

WAGE CATEGORY: Exempt
VERIFIED BY: Bill Johnson
DATE VERIFIED: 1/5/04

Job Summary

The SUPERVISOR works under the direction of the MANAGER: **plans** goals; **supervises** the work of employees; **develops** employees with feedback and coaching; **maintains** accurate records; **coordinates** with others to achieve optimal use of organizational resources.

Job Duties and Responsibilities

1. **Plans** goals and allocates resources to achieve them; **monitors** progress toward objectives and adjusts plans as necessary to reach them; **allocates** and **schedules** resources to assure their availability according to priority.
2. **Supervises** the work of employees; **provides** clear instructions and explanations to employees when giving assignments; **schedules** and assigns work among employees for maximum efficiency; **monitors** employees' performance in order to achieve assigned objectives.
3. **Develops** employees through direct performance feedback and job coaching; **conducts** performance appraisals with each employee on a regular basis; **provides** employees with praise and recognition when performance is excellent; **corrects** employees promptly when their performance fails to meet expected performance levels.
4. **Maintains** accurate records and documents actions; **processes** paper work on a timely basis, and with close attention to details; **documents** important aspects of decisions and actions.
5. **Coordinates** with others to achieve the optimal use of organizational resources; **maintains** good working relationships with colleagues in other organizational units; **represents** others in unit during division or corporatewide meetings.

Job Requirements

1. Ability to apply basic principles and techniques of supervision.
   a. Knowledge of principles and techniques of supervision.
   b. Ability to plan and organize the activities of others.
   c. Ability to get ideas accepted and to guide a group or individual to accomplish the task.
   d. Ability to modify leadership style and management approach to reach goal.
2. Ability to express ideas clearly in both written and oral communications.

Minimum Qualifications

Twelve years of general education or equivalent; and one year supervisory experience.

OR

Substitute 45 hours classroom supervisory training for supervisory experience.

Source: Jones, M. A. (1984, May). Job descriptions made easy. *Personnel Journal*. Copyright May 1984. Reprinted with the permission of *Personnel Journal*, ACC Communications, Inc., Costa Mesa, California; all rights reserved.

Example of a General Job Description

- Ensure that the supervisor of the job incumbent(s) verifies the job description. This is a good way to ensure that the job description does not misrepresent the actual job duties and responsibilities. (A manager who is familiar with the job may also be used to verify the description.)

Job Summary. The job summary is a short statement that summarizes the job's duties, responsibilities, and place in the organizational structure.

Job Duties and Responsibilities. Job duties and responsibilities explain what is done on the job, how it is done, and why it is done.[69]

Each job description typically lists the job's three to five most important responsibilities. Each responsibility statement begins with an action verb. For example, the job of supervisor in Figure 2.7 has five responsibilities that start with the following action verbs: plans, supervises, develops, maintains, and coordinates. Each responsibility is associated with one or more job duties, which also start with action verbs. For example, the supervisor job in Figure 2.7 has two job duties associated with the responsibility of "plans goals": (1) monitors progress toward objectives, and (2) allocates and schedules resources. The job duties and responsibilities statement is probably the most important section of the job description because it influences all the other parts of the job description. Therefore, it must be comprehensive and accurate.

Job Specifications and Minimum Qualifications. The **job specifications** section lists the worker characteristics (KSAs) needed to perform a job successfully. The KSAs represent the things that an employee who has mastered the job can do.

Job specifications
The worker characteristics needed to perform a job successfully.

When documenting KSAs it is important to list only those that are related to successful job performance. It is inappropriate to list what a specific job incumbent knows that is not related to the job. For example, a current computer programmer may have mastered some programming languages that are not necessary for job performance. These should not be included in the job description.

The *minimum qualifications* are the basic standards a job applicant must have achieved to be considered for the job. These can be used to screen job applicants during the recruiting and selection process. Minimum requirements must be carefully specified to avoid discriminating against job applicants. Here are some things to watch for when documenting minimum qualifications:

- A college degree should be used as a minimum qualification only if it is related to the successful performance of the job. For example, a bachelor's degree may be a minimum qualification for an accountant in a major accounting firm, but it is not likely to be necessary for the job of shift supervisor in a fast-food restaurant. The same logic applies to requirements for all other education standards, including a high school diploma or an advanced college degree.
- Work experience qualifications should be carefully specified so that they do not discriminate against minorities or persons with disabilities. For example, the job description in Figure 2.7 provides for a substitute of 45 classroom hours of supervisory training for the one year of work experience minimum qualification. This provision allows people who have been excluded from employment opportunities in the past to be considered for the position. This flexibility allows the company to consider diverse job applicants, who are less likely to meet the work experience qualification.

The Flexible Workforce

One of the imperatives for many modern organizations is flexibility. We have seen how organizations can be structured and jobs designed to maximize this flexibility. In this section we examine two additional strategies for ensuring flexibility. First, we look at the practice of using contingent workers. Second, we examine flexible work schedules. Flexible work schedules let employers use talented employees who might otherwise be unavailable for employment.

Contingent Workers

There are two types of workers: core workers and contingent workers. A company's **core workers** have full-time jobs and enjoy privileges not available to contingent workers. Many core workers expect a long-term relationship with the employer that includes a career in the organization, a full array of benefits, and job security. In contrast, the jobs of **contingent workers** are based on the employer's convenience and efficiency needs. Firms hire contingent workers to help them deal with temporary increases in their workload or to do work that is not part of their core set of capabilities. Contingent workers are easily dismissed when an organization no longer needs their services. When the business cycle moves into a downturn, the contingent workers are the first employees to be discharged. They thus provide a buffer zone of protection for the core workers. For example, in some large Japanese corporations core workers' jobs are protected by a large contingent workforce that can be rapidly downsized when business conditions change.

Core workers
An organization's full-time employees.

Contingent workers
Workers hired to deal with temporary increases in an organization's workload or to do work that is not part of its core set of capabilities.

Contingent workers include temporary employees, part-time employees, outsourced subcontractors, contract workers, and college interns. According to the U.S. Bureau of Labor Statistics in the United States, contingent workers made up 24 percent of the total labor force in 2001. This number includes approximately 22 million part-time employees, 9 million contract workers, and 1.2 million temporary employees. The jobs held by contingent workers are diverse, ranging from secretaries, security guards, sales clerks, and assembly-line workers to doctors, college professors, engineers, managers, and even chief executives.

Temporary Employees

Temporary employment agencies provide companies with *temporary employees* (or "temps") for short-term work assignments. Temps work for the temporary employment agency and are simply reassigned to another employer when their current job ends. Temporary employees are used to fill in for employees who are sick or on family leave. They can also be used to increase output when demand is high and to do work that is peripheral to the core employees' work. Manpower, the largest of the 7,000 U.S. temporary employment agencies, is also the nation's largest private employer, with almost 750,000 people on its payroll.[70]

Temporary employees provide employers with two major benefits:

- Temps on average receive less compensation than core workers. Temporary employees are not likely to receive health insurance, retirement, or vacation benefits from the company that uses their services. They generally do not receive these benefits from the temporary agency either. For example, as layoffs mounted in the 1990s, the total payroll for professionals and managers employed by temporary firms more than tripled.[71] However, many managers working at temp jobs earn 50 percent less than they earned as core workers.[72]
- Temporary employees may be highly motivated workers since many employers choose full-time employees from the ranks of the top-performing temps. Because temps can be screened for long-term career potential in an actual work setting and be easily dismissed if the company determines that they have low potential, hiring temps helps employers reduce the risk of selecting employees who prove to be a poor fit.

Employers should understand the legal limits of using a temporary worker on a long-term basis. Microsoft learned that temporary employees are not meant to be long-term members of the company. Several thousand Microsoft temps who held long-term positions but were employed through a temporary agency ("Permatemps") filed a class action lawsuit, claiming that Microsoft treated them as full-time workers in every way except in terms of compensation and benefits. Specifically, they claimed that they were denied access to valuable stock-purchase benefits that were available to core employees. A federal court of appeals ruled that workers who were on Microsoft's payroll for more than a few months—even if placed by temporary agencies—should be considered common-law employees who are entitled to the same benefits that permanent employees receive.[73]

Temporary employees are being used with increasing regularity throughout the world. In France, one in five workers is on a temporary or part-time contract, and in Britain more than 25 percent of the workforce is part-time. Almost 33 percent of new jobs created in Spain in 2000 were for temporary workers.[74]

Part-Time Employees

Part-time employees work fewer hours than full-time core employees. Employers have the flexibility to schedule these people for work when they are needed. Part-time jobs offer far fewer employee benefits than full-time jobs, thus providing substantial savings to employers. Traditionally, part-timers have been employed by service businesses that have a high variance in demand between peak and off-peak times. For example, restaurants and markets hire many part-time employees to provide service to customers during peak hours (usually evenings and weekends).

Companies are finding many new applications for part-time workers. For example, UPS has created 25-hour-per-week part-time jobs for shipping clerks and supervisors who sort packages at its distribution centers. Companies that downsize their workforces to reduce payroll costs have been known to restructure full-time core jobs into part-time positions.

In a special type of part-time employment called **job sharing**, a full-time job is divided between two or more people to create two part-time jobs. The people in the job-sharing arrangement divide the job's responsibilities, hours, and benefits among themselves. During a downscaling of its workforce, Du Pont used job sharing between employees in its management, research, and secretarial areas to avoid layoffs.[75]

Job sharing
A work arrangement in which two or more employees divide a job's responsibilities, hours, and benefits among themselves.

Outsourcing/Subcontracting

As we saw in Chapter 1, outsourcing (sometimes called *subcontracting*) is the process by which employers transfer routine or peripheral work to another organization that specializes in that work and can perform it more efficiently. Employers that outsource some of their nonessential work gain improved quality and cost savings. Outsourcing agreements may result in a long-term relationship between an employer and the subcontractor, though it is the employer who has the flexibility to renew or end the relationship at its convenience.[76]

Outsourcing is the wave of the future as more and more companies look to the "virtual corporation" as an organizational model.[77] A *virtual company* consists of a small core of permanent employees and a constantly shifting workforce of contingent employees.

Consistent with the outsourcing trend, human resource activities are being outsourced by organizations. For example, payroll, benefits, training, and recruiting are often outsourced to external service providers.[78] Previously these outsourced activities were performed in-house. In fact, human resource outsourcing is a fast-growing $80 billion industry in 2002, and total annual industry revenues increased 33 percent over that of the previous year.[79] While outsourcing routine human resource activities such as payroll produces efficiencies, the outsourcing of critical HR systems such as training or performance evaluation may lead to a loss of control over important systems or a loss of opportunity to learn from one's best human resource practices that could achieve fundamental improvements in other human resource activities. Clearly, human resource outsourcing is no panacea and the implications of outsourcing an HR activity should be carefully weighed in terms of benefits and costs before the decision to outsource or retain an HR activity is made.

A Question of Ethics

Many employees and union representatives complain bitterly about the practice of outsourcing work, particularly to foreign countries. Part of the complaint is that companies do this to avoid paying fair wages and providing employee benefits that U.S. workers expect. Is this an ethical issue? If so, on what basis should companies make outsourcing decisions?

Establishing the right relationship with service vendors is very important for companies that decide to outsource. While some companies view their outsourced vendors as strategic partners, others caution that, ultimately, company and vendor do not have identical interests. For example, UOP, an Illinois-based engineering firm that develops technology used to build oil refineries, sued Andersen Consulting, the information-technology firm UOP had hired to streamline and improve some of its work processes. UOP sued for $100 million in damages, alleging breach of contract. UOP's president and CEO claimed that "the difference between what Andersen promised us . . . and what it actually delivered is staggering."[80] The lesson is that it pays to communicate clearly and specifically with vendors from the beginning.[81]

One company that relies on outsourcing as a source of competitive advantage is Benetton, the Italian multinational corporation that makes clothing sold in 110 countries. Benetton views itself as a "clothing services" company rather than as a retailer or manufacturer.[82] The company outsources a large amount of clothes manufacturing to local suppliers but makes sure to provide its subcontractors with the clothes-making skills that Benetton views as crucial to maintaining quality and cost efficiency.[83]

The Manager's Notebook "Advantages and Disadvantages of Outsourcing an HR Activity" provides some useful information on factors to consider before outsourcing or retaining an HR activity such as training, benefits administration, and recruiting.

Emerging Trends — MANAGER'S NOTEBOOK

Advantages and Disadvantages of Outsourcing an HR Activity

There are both advantages and disadvantages to outsourcing an HR activity to a firm that specializes in providing an HR service to customers. A manager should consider the costs and benefits before deciding to outsource or retain a specific HR activity. Here are some important factors to consider:

Outsourcing Advantages

- An outsourcing firm can provide better-quality people and the most current practices and information pertaining to an activity or task. Because the HR activity is the core mission of the outsourcing firm, it can specialize in doing it very well. For example, a firm that specializes in training employees on the use of word processing software is likely to be able to train employees to use the most recent upgrades on the software that contains the newest features and applications.
- Outsourcing certain tasks can result in a reduction in administrative costs because the outsourcer can do the task more efficiently and gain economies of scale by virtue of having a large network of customers.
- Outsourcing specific activities and employees that do not fit with company culture may be useful to preserve a strong culture or employee morale. An example of this would be outsourcing the benefits administration activity at a law firm, where the law firm culture is shared by people who are trained as attorneys.

Outsourcing Disadvantages

- Deploying an HR activity to an outsourcing firm may lead to losing control of an important activity, which can be a costly problem. For example, by outsourcing employee recruiting to an external recruiting firm, the client company may experience missed deadlines on time-sensitive projects if the recruiting firm has other more important clients to serve.
- Outsourcing an HR activity may result in losing the opportunity to gain knowledge and information that could benefit other company processes and activities. For example, outsourcing executive training and development to a company that provides a standardized training package can result in a lost opportunity to learn about the unique aspects of a firm's way of shaping leadership with respect to its own culture.

Source: Kaplan, J. (2002, January 14). The realities of outsourcing. *Network World*, 33; and Baron, J., and Kreps, D. (1999). *Strategic human resources: Frameworks for general managers*. New York: John Wiley & Sons.

Contract Workers

Contract workers are employees who develop work relationships directly with an employer (instead of with a subcontractor through an outsourcing arrangement) for a specific piece of work or time period.[84] Contract workers are likely to be self-employed, supply their own tools, and determine their hours of employment. Sometimes contract workers are called *consultants* or *freelancers*. Because contract workers are not part of the company headcount, managers can rely on their services to get around company restrictions on staffing policies intended to avoid payroll costs.

Many professionals with specialized skills become contract workers.[85] Hospitals use contract workers as emergency room physicians. Universities use them as adjunct professors to teach basic courses. U.S. West, one of the Baby Bell telecommunications companies, uses contract workers for many of its HR jobs.

Contract workers can often be more productive and efficient than in-house employees because freelancers' time is usually not taken up with the inevitable company bureaucracy and meetings. They can also give companies a fresh outsider's perspective. However, for all the benefits of using contract workers, they do pose some administrative challenges. It is not always easy to motivate a freelancer for whom you are one of several clients, each with urgent projects and pressing deadlines.

College Interns

One of the newest developments in the contingency work area is the use of *college interns*, college students who work on full-time or part-time assignments of short duration (usually for one academic semester or summer) to obtain work experience. Some interns are paid, some are not. Employers use interns to provide support to professional staff. Sometimes interns work a trial run for consideration as a potential core employee after graduation from college. Large companies that use college interns include IBM and General Electric (which have internships for electrical engineers), the Big Six accounting firms (which use interns on auditing engagements with clients), and Procter & Gamble (which uses interns in its sales and marketing areas).

College interns are also used extensively by small companies that want to attract employees who will grow with the company. For instance, at Seal Press, a small publishing company in Seattle, Washington, a woman who started as a marketing intern went on to become marketing assistant and is now marketing director. Editorial interns log in and read unsolicited manuscripts, write detailed reader's reports, and sometimes attend staff meetings. Because the work is challenging, there is a long waiting list of applicants.

Flexible Work Schedules

Flexible work schedules alter the scheduling of work while leaving intact the job design and the employment relationship. Employers can use flexible work schedules to modify the traditional nine-to-five Monday-through-Friday work schedule to provide advantages for both themselves and employees. Employers may get higher levels of productivity and job satisfaction.[86] Employees may feel that they are trusted by management, which can improve the quality of employee relations (see Chapter 13).[87] Employees with flexible work schedules may also experience less stress by avoiding rush hour traffic.

The three most common types of flexible work schedules are flexible work hours, compressed workweeks, and telecommuting.

Flexible Work Hours

Flexible work hours give employees control over the starting and ending times of their daily work schedules. Employees are required to put in a full 40-hour workweek at their onsite workstation, but have some control over the hours when they perform the work. **Flexible work hours** divide work schedules into **core time,** when all employees are expected to be at work, and *flexible time* **(flextime),** when employees can choose to organize work routines around personal activities.

Flexible work hours
A work arrangement that gives employees control over the starting and ending times of their daily work schedules.

Core time
Time when all employees are expected to be at work. Part of a flexible work hours arrangement.

Flextime
Time during which employees can choose not to be at work. Part of a flexible work hours arrangement.

Companies that use flexible work hours vary in the degree of flexibility they offer to employees. Hewlett-Packard's policy gives workers the flexibility to arrive at work between 6:30 A.M. and 8:30 A.M. and leave after they put in eight hours of work. Hewlett-Packard's core hours are between 8:30 A.M. and 2:30 P.M.[88] Meetings and team activities take place in this core time.

Compressed Workweeks

Compressed workweeks alter the number of workdays per week by increasing the length of the workday to 10 or more hours. One type of compressed workweek schedule consists of four 10-hour workdays. Another consists of four 12-hour workdays in a four days on/four days off schedule. This schedule gives workers two four-day blocks of time off every 16 days.[89]

Compressed workweeks provide employers with two main advantages. First, they create less potential for disruptions to businesses that provide 24-hour-per-day services, such as hospitals and police forces. Second, they lower absenteeism and tardiness rates at companies with work sites in remote locations that require long commutes to work (for example, off-shore oil drilling platforms).

Compressed workweeks offer both advantages and disadvantages to employees. The major advantage is that they give employees three- or four-day weekends to spend with their families or engage in personal interests. However, employees who work a compressed workweek may experience increased levels of stress and fatigue.[90] Employers should select employees for whom a longer workday will not interfere with job performance.

Telecommuting

Telecommuting provides flexibility in both the hours and the location of work. Personal computers, modems, fax machines, e-mail, and the Internet (which connects computers in an international network) have created the opportunity for millions of people in the United States to work out of a home office.[91] Telecommuting allows employees to cultivate tailored lifestyles while working a full-time job.[92]

Telecommuting
A work arrangement that allows employees to work in their homes full-time, maintaining their connection to the office through phone, fax, and computer.

Jill Smith telecommutes from her home as a reservation agent for JetBlue Airways.

Telecommuting gives employers the flexibility to hire talented employees who might not otherwise be able to offer their services. For instance, it lets workers with child-rearing responsibilities work out of their homes. Employers also save on office space costs with telecommuting. However, telecommuting does present several challenges to managers. We discuss these in detail in Chapter 13.

Human Resource Information Systems

As we have seen, many organizations are choosing nontraditional structures, designing work to break down barriers among employees, and using a variety of techniques to ensure workforce flexibility. While these strategies are very potent for increasing organizational effectiveness, they can make it difficult to keep track of all the people who work for the organization. Fortunately, computer hardware and software have made keeping track of human resources much easier.

Human resource information system (HRIS)
A system used to collect, record, store, analyze, and retrieve data concerning an organization's human resources.

Human resource information systems (HRIS) are systems used to collect, record, store, analyze, and retrieve data concerning an organization's human resources.[93] Most of today's HRIS are computerized, so we will focus on these. Although it is beyond the scope of this book's managerial approach to discuss the technical details of the HRIS, it is worth briefly exploring two relevant issues: the applications of HRIS and the management of security and privacy issues related to HRIS.

HRIS Applications

A computerized HRIS contains computer hardware and software applications that work together to help managers make HR decisions.[94] The hardware may be a mainframe computer or a fairly inexpensive personal computer. The software may be a custom-designed program or an off-the-shelf (prepackaged) applications program. (The latter is more likely to be used on personal computers.) Figure 2.8 shows some HRIS software applications currently available to business. These include:

Figure 2.8

Selected Human Resource Information Systems Applications

Applicant tracking
Basic employee information
Benefits administration
Bonus and incentive management
Career development/planning
Compensation budgeting
EEO/AA compliance
Employment history
Goal-setting system
Health and safety
Health insurance utilization
Hiring procedures
HR planning and forecasting
Job descriptions/analysis
Job evaluation
Job posting
Labor relations planning
Payroll
Pension and retirement
Performance management
Short- and long-term disabilities
Skills inventory
Succession planning
Time and attendance
Travel costs
Turnover analysis

Source: Dzamba, A. (2001, January). What are your peers doing to boost HRIS performance? *HR Focus*, 5–6; Kavanagh, M., Gueutal, H., and Tannenbaum, S. (1990). *Human resource information systems: Development and application*, 50. Boston: PWS-Kent. Reproduced with the permission of South-Western College Publishing.

- **Employee information** An employee information program sets up a database that provides basic employee information: name, sex, address, phone number, date of birth, race, marital status, job title, and salary. Other applications programs can access the data in the employee information database for more specialized HR uses.
- **Applicant tracking** An applicant tracking program can automate some of the labor-intensive activities associated with recruiting job applicants. These activities include storing job applicant information so that multiple users can access it and evaluate the applicant, scheduling interviews with different managers, updating the status of the job applicant (such as whether the applicant has received other job offers or has special personal circumstances such as a dual-career marriage), generating correspondence (for example, a job offer or a rejection letter), and producing the necessary equal employment opportunity (EEO) records required by the government.
- **Skills inventory** A skills inventory keeps track of the supply of job skills in the employer's workforce and searches for matches between skill supply and the organization's demand for job skills. The skills inventory can be used to support a company's policy of promotion from within.
- **Payroll** A payroll applications program computes gross pay, federal taxes, state taxes, Social Security, other taxes, and net pay. It can also be programmed to make other deductions from the paycheck for such items as employee contributions to health insurance, employee contributions to a tax-deferred retirement plan, and union dues.
- **Benefits administration** A benefits application program can automate benefits recordkeeping, which can consume a great deal of time if done manually. It can also be used to administer various benefit programs or to provide advice about benefit choices (for example, determining when an employee will have enough deferred compensation in his or her retirement fund to be able to consider early retirement). Benefits software can also provide an annual benefits statement for each employee.

HRIS Security and Privacy

The HR department must develop policies and guidelines to protect the integrity and security of the HRIS. Unauthorized users of HRIS can create havoc. In one case, an executive who worked for a brokerage house tapped into her company's HRIS to get employee names and addresses for her husband, a life insurance agent who used the information to mail solicitations to his wife's colleagues. The solicited employees brought a million-dollar class-action suit against the company for invasion of privacy.[95] In another case, a computer programmer tapped into a computer company's HRIS, detected the salaries of a number of employees (including top managers and executives), and disclosed this information to other employees. The situation became very disruptive as angry employees demanded to know why large pay discrepancies existed.[96]

To maintain the security and privacy of HRIS records, companies should:

- Limit access to the HRIS by controlling access to the computer and its data files. Rooms that house computers and sensitive databases should be locked. Sometimes the data can be encoded so that they are not understandable to an unauthorized user.
- Permit access to different portions of the database with the use of passwords and special codes. For example, a manager may receive authorization and a special code to tap into the skills inventory database but may not be granted permission to access sensitive medical information in the benefits database.
- Grant permission to access employee information only on a need-to-know basis.
- Develop policies and guidelines that govern the utilization of employee information and notify employees how this policy works.
- Allow employees to examine their personal records to verify their accuracy and make corrections if necessary.

Summary and Conclusions

Work: The Organizational Perspective

A firm's business strategy determines how it structures its work. Under a defender strategy, work can be efficiently organized into a functional structure based on division of labor, with hierarchies of jobs assigned to functional units. Under a prospector strategy, decentralization and a low division of labor are more appropriate. The bureaucratic organizational structure is likely to be most effective when an organization is operating in a stable environment. The flat and the boundaryless organizational structures are more likely to be effective when organizations operate in uncertain environments that require flexibility.

Work flow analysis examines how work creates or adds value to ongoing business processes. It helps managers determine if work is being accomplished as efficiently as possible. Work flow analysis can be very useful in TQM programs and business process reengineering.

Work: The Group Perspective

Flat and boundaryless organizational structures are likely to emphasize the use of self-managed teams (SMTs), small work units (between 6 and 18 employees) that are responsible for producing an entire product, a component, or an ongoing service. Businesses also use two other types of team designs. Problem-solving teams consist of volunteers from a unit or department who meet one or two hours per week to discuss quality improvement, cost reduction, or improvement in the work environment. Special-purpose teams consist of members who span functional or organizational boundaries and whose purpose is to examine complex issues. Virtual teams allow geographically separated employees to collaborate together on projects or special problems by interacting on the computer or via other technology.

Work: The Individual Perspective

Motivation theory seeks to explain how different job designs can affect employee motivation. Four important work motivation theories are the two-factor, work adjustment, goal-setting, and job characteristics theories.

Designing Jobs and Conducting Job Analysis

Job design is the process of organizing work into the tasks required to perform a specific job. Different approaches to job design are work simplification, job enlargement, job rotation, job enrichment, and team-based job designs.

Job analysis is the systematic process of gathering and organizing information concerning the tasks, duties, and responsibilities of jobs. It is the basic building block of many important HR activities. Job analysis can be used for purposes of legal compliance, recruitment, selection, performance appraisal, compensation, and training and career development. Given the lack of a single best job-analysis technique, the choice of technique should be guided by the purposes of the analysis.

Job descriptions are statements of a job's essential duties, responsibilities, working conditions, and specifications. They are derived from job analysis. Job descriptions, which can be specific or general, have four elements: identification information, job summary, job duties and responsibilities, and job specifications and minimum qualifications.

The Flexible Workforce

Flexible work designs help managers deal with unexpected jolts in the environment and accommodate the needs of a diverse workforce. To maintain flexibility in the workforce, employers can use contingent workers (temporary employees, part-time employees, outsourced subcontractors, contract workers, and college interns). They can also alter work with flexible work schedules (flexible work hours, compressed workweeks, and telecommuting).

Human Resource Information Systems

Human resource information systems (HRIS) are systems used to collect, record, store, analyze, and retrieve relevant HR data. HRIS data matched with the appropriate computer software have many applications that support HR activities. These include applicant tracking, skills inventories, payroll management, and benefits administration. It is important that the HR department develop policies to protect the security of the HRIS data and the privacy rights of its employees.

Key Terms

boundaryless organizational structure, 52
bureaucratic organizational structure, 49
business process reengineering (BPR), 53
contingent workers, 71
core time, 75
core workers, 71
flat organizational structure, 50
flexible work hours, 75
flextime, 75
human resource information system (HRIS), 76
job analysis, 61
job description, 68
job design, 59
job enlargement, 60
job enrichment, 60
job rotation, 60
job sharing, 73
job specifications, 71
knowledge, skills, and abilities (KSAs), 63
motivation, 57
organizational structure, 48
problem-solving team, 55
self-managed team (SMT) force, 54
special-purpose team, 55
team, 54
telecommuting, 75
virtual team, 56
work flow, 48
work flow analysis, 52

Discussion Questions

1. When American Greetings Corporation, the Cleveland greeting card and licensing company, redesigned about 400 jobs in its creative division, it asked workers and managers to reapply for the new jobs. Everyone was guaranteed a position and no one took a pay cut. Employees now develop products in teams instead of in assembly-line fashion and are free to transfer back and forth among teams that make different products instead of working on just one product line, as they did in the past. Give some reasons why you think American Greetings restructured its work to be performed in teams. Would the teams at American Greetings be considered self-managed work teams? Why or why not?
2. Why is it so difficult to predict whether a new employee will be a highly motivated employee? What factors can influence employee motivation?
3. Are job descriptions really necessary? What would happen if a company decided not to use any job descriptions at all?
4. Are managers likely to question the work commitment of their contingent workers? What might be the consequences for management when the majority of a company's workforce consists of temporary employees and contract workers?
5. What are the drawbacks to using flexible work hours from the organization's perspective? Compressed workweeks? Telecommuting? How should the HR department deal with these challenges?
6. Some management experts do not agree that a virtual team is really a team at all. Based on the definition of a team, what properties of a virtual team satisfy the definition of a team? Do any aspects of a virtual team give rise to doubts over whether it satisfies the definition of a true team? Suppose you needed to organize a virtual team of consultants working in different cities to do an important project for a client. What human resource management practices could you apply that would influence the virtual team members to behave as if they were on a true team, such as a self-managed or problem-solving team?
7. A recent trend more and more companies are embracing is to outsource all or most of their human resource management activities. Do you agree or disagree with this trend? What risks is a company taking when it decides to outsource its entire set of human resource management activities? Try to describe a situation in which it is more beneficial to retain most of the human resource management activities within a company so that HR is provided by the human resource management department.

8. In recent years there has been an increase in the number of companies that have wrongly classified an "employee" as a "contract worker" and, consequently, were taken to court by workers who believed they were entitled to certain rights and privileges enjoyed by individuals who were given "employee" status. What are some of the rights and privileges that are given to employees but not to contract workers? What advantages do employers gain with contract workers over regular employees? How could a contract worker prove to the courts that he or she is really an employee and was wrongly classified as a contract worker?

There is a variety of additional material available on the Web site that accompanies this text. You can access this information by visiting the Web site at **www.prenhall.com/gomez.**

YOU MANAGE IT!

Emerging Trends Case 2.1

Virtual Teamwork at IBM

Virtual teamwork is all in a day's work for John Patrick, who has organized a number of these initiatives at IBM since 1993. Back then, the Internet made barely a blip on corporate radar screens. As one of IBM's senior strategists, Patrick had been experimenting with programs for browsing files on computer systems connected around the world. IBM was then a large, lumbering company in trouble, and Lou Gerstner had been brought in as CEO from the outside to invigorate the venerable computer firm.

Skipping from file to file on the Internet, Patrick became convinced that IBM needed to get involved with this emerging phenomenon. So he drafted a "Get Connected" memo about new ways to communicate in the digital world—including now-commonplace techniques such as assigning each employee an e-mail address and creating a corporate Web site. Patrick's ideas resonated with employees all over IBM. "People didn't know where I reported in the company, and they didn't care," remembers Patrick. "We shared a common vision that the Internet was going to change everything and that IBM should be a leader."[a]

A grass-roots group of IBMers from a wide variety of functions, units, and locations flocked to Patrick's e-mail discussion list to join the Get Connected team. They had "no budget, no head count, no authority," he says. "Everything we did was informal."[b] In just six months, this virtual team designed IBM's corporate Web site, which went live in May 1994. Later that year, a team of volunteers from 12 different IBM businesses worked with Patrick to create the company's first exhibit at Internet World, a major industry trade show.

Not long afterward, IBM developed an official Internet strategy and created a task force for implementation. When the company established an Internet division, Patrick was named vice president of Internet technology. Since then, his Get Connected virtual team has branched out to help more than 10,000 IBM business customers harness the power of the Internet to communicate with their customers. Patrick's newest project, Web Ahead, is a virtual team effort to develop innovative cutting-edge Internet applications.[c]

Critical Thinking Questions

1. Why was the use of virtual teams successful in this particular situation at IBM?
2. What do you think are the key advantages of virtual teams over other types of teams discussed in this chapter?
3. One drawback of virtual teams is the limited opportunity for face-to-face communication among team members. Why could this be a serious problem?

Team Exercise

Assume that in one of your human resource management courses your professor expects you to form a virtual team with four of your fellow students to make a 30-minute presentation to your class on the topic of "mutual fund investment strategies for retirement funds." Your professor requires that all the work on this challenging project be done as a virtual team and without any face-to-face meetings. Within your discussion group come up with ways to deal with these issues involving a virtual team: How would you organize the virtual team? Is a virtual team leader necessary? On what basis would you select students to be members of your virtual team? How would you make sure that everyone did their assigned task so that a high-quality presentation results from your mutual efforts?

Sources: A. Nahavandi, and Malekzadeh, A. R. (1999). *Organizational behavior*. Upper Saddle River, NJ: Prentice Hall, 297.

[a]Ransdell, E. (1997, October–November). IBM grassroots revival. *Fast Company*, 188.

[b]Oringel, A. (1998, March 2). John Patrick Reinventing Big Blue. www.developer.com/news/profiles/022598-patricks.

[c]Ibid.

Customer-Driven HR Case 2.2

YOU MANAGE IT!

Employees Write Their Own Job Titles for Customers

Traditionally, job titles have been used to show an employee's relative rank within the company pecking order. Employees who have customer contact are issued business cards that show their job title on the business card. Thus, a job title with "vice president" in it indicates that the job incumbent is an executive in the firm. Or a job title such as "associate engineer" indicates that the employee is at the bottom of the engineering job hierarchy, below other employees who have titles such as "senior engineer" or "principal engineer." The breaking down of hierarchies and barriers within companies due to the Internet and the need to become more customer focused has influenced the practice of using job titles. The latest idea is to give two job titles to an employee: One job title reflects the employee's internal role within the company and the second job title is a customer-focused one. The customer-focused job title is descriptive and individualistic and lets employees have fun and creativity with designing their job title. Here are some creative examples of customer-focused job titles:

- **Chief Talent Scout**: Xcelerate, a Fort Lauderdale, Florida–based company uses this title for the person in charge of recruiting.
- **Director of Privacy**: This title is used at DoubleClick, an Internet services company, for the person responsible to protect customers' privacy as well as the company's own intellectual property such as copyrighted software code.
- **Director of Consumer Delight & Loyalty**: San Francisco–based Relect.com uses this title for the employee who is responsible for marketing new products and services.
- **Senior Vice President of Great People**: This title has been used in several firms for the top executive responsible for human resources.
- **Sultan of Sound Bites**: This title has been used in a large public company to communicate information to members of the investment community regarding company performance and future business prospects.

Critical Thinking Questions

1. How important are job titles? What would happen if there were no job titles? What would happen if everyone in a company had the same job title, such as "associate"? Some companies actually have such a policy.
2. What problems do you foresee when a company adopts a policy of customer-focused job titles and lets employees develop their own unique titles? How should the process of developing customer-focused job titles be managed?

Team Exercise

Some companies use generic job titles in order to minimize the differences between employees that arise due to differences in rank, status, experience, and salary levels. The justification for these generic job titles is that they help to remove barriers to communication caused by differences in rank and status, so that more information sharing and collaboration between employees are likely to occur. For example, one of the major telecommunications companies gives the generic job title of "member of technical staff" (MTS for short) to all engineering employees from the most recently hired college graduate with a B.S. in engineering and with no work experience to the most established engineer with a Ph.D. degree, 20 patented inventions, and 20 years of work experience at the firm. Assume you are the manager of engineering at this telecommunications company and a group of engineers is requesting that you allow them to use customer-focused job titles. Some examples of the titles that they have proposed include "thought leader," "czar of debugging," and "inventor extraordinaire." Discuss this proposal with your team members and develop an approach to deal with this employee request. Determine first whether you will encourage or discourage employees to use customer-focused job titles and explain the basis for your decision. Next, decide what guidelines you will use to manage the adoption of job titles if you have decided that it makes sense to use customer-focused job titles.

Source: Conlin, M. (2000, August 28). Write your own job title. *BusinessWeek*, 148.

YOU MANAGE IT!

Discussion Case 2.3

Roche Group Pharmaceuticals Switches to Research Teams That Collaborate

How does a giant pharmaceutical company deal with genomics technology, which involves a host of innovations that will revolutionize how medicines get developed? By making a fresh start in how it manages scientists who work on research projects. One of the key breakthroughs at Roche Group, a large Swiss pharmaceutical company with research facilities in New Jersey, is to emphasize collaboration between research teams instead of encouraging competition between the teams, as previously occurred.

For years the Roche Group pitted veteran scientific teams against one another. Team competition was a component of its proud, tough-minded culture that had helped the firm develop blockbuster drugs such as Valium and Librium. But it wasn't working anymore. For Roche to move forward, the company needed to wipe away its gladiator mentality (to the "victor" go all the spoils) and replace it with a warmer style of teamwork—especially in the chaotic, booming new field of genomics.

In the mid-1990s, research scientists at Roche were divided into competing teams—with a mandate to fight one another for resources. Teams took on names that were medically interesting or outright heroic. Glucogen jostled against Camelot, Tsunami, and other rivals.

Competition between teams at first energized the teams. Teams made banners and worked late into the night on scientific projects. But as Roche's internal wars stretched on, the ultracompetitive approach became less appealing. Faltering projects became almost impossible to abandon because scientists' careers were so wrapped up in them. Researchers were tempted to hoard technical expertise they picked up along the way, since sharing the knowledge might allow others to catch up.

Finally, Roche disbanded its intramural competition in 1998 in favor of a more collaborative approach. "If you have just a few drug-discovery targets," says Nader Fotouhi, a vice president for discovery chemistry, "the competing-team approach can work. But if you have a large number of targets, it can't work."

An example of how the new collaborative approach is working is provided in Roche's New Jersey GeneChip lab. Researcher Hongjin Bian has won worldwide acclaim during the past three years for developing savvy ways of handling the GeneChips and reading the results. She has been encouraged to share her techniques with Roche colleagues as far away as Europe and Japan. With the old system, her insights might well have been kept secret.

Critical Thinking Questions

1. What do you consider to be the advantages of team competition within a large company? Why do you think team competition was viewed positively at Roche when scientists were working with older technologies that predated GeneChip technology for developing new pharmaceutical products?
2. Do you think it is likely that teams are able to compete and cooperate at the same time? What are the barriers that make it difficult for competition and cooperation to occur simultaneously between different teams?
3. What human resource management practices would you expect to facilitate a behavioral change in attitudes of team members so that they are motivated to abandon competitive behaviors (i.e., withholding information, aggressive behavior, squandering resources that another team could better put to good use) and adopt more collaborative behaviors (i.e., sharing information, friendly behavior, economizing on resources so that more are available for other teams) in dealing with other teams within a company?

Team Exercise

In a group with several other students assume you have been retained as consultants to the director of research at a laboratory at Roche that uses the latest genomics technology to develop new pharmaceutical products. The research teams at the laboratory are still not collaborating as well as expected because the old employee behaviors and attitudes embedded in the former culture of competition are difficult to extinguish and replace with collaborative attitudes and behaviors that are now desired by management. Develop a plan of change using human resource management practices that you expect will deepen and intensify the collaborative attitudes and culture as well as reduce the incidence of competitive behaviors that are no longer welcome at Roche's genomics laboratory. Which human resource practices (i.e., training, staffing, reward systems, discipline, work flow, or other practices) are the most important ones that your group has decided to recommend with respect to the plan of change? Try to be specific when describing the practices and the necessary steps you would take to implement them.

Source: Anders, G. (2002, January). Roche's new scientific method. *Fast Company*, 60–67.

Customer-Driven HR Case 2.4

YOU MANAGE IT!

Writing a Job Description

Job descriptions are useful tools that document job content and can aid decisions for recruitment, staffing, training, compensation, and human resource planning. The purpose of this skill-building activity is to give you some experience writing a job description. In preparation carefully read the section in this chapter titled "Job Descriptions" and refer to the figures in that section that provide examples of a specific job description and a general job description.

Next, select a job and write a job description. Ideally, your job description should be based on a job you are familiar with—one at which you are currently employed or recently experienced is the best candidate for this exercise. It could be a part-time or full-time job. If you have no work experience to draw from for this exercise, then ask a friend or relative to provide detailed information about his or her job.

Once you have chosen the job for this exercise you are ready to begin.

Critical Thinking Questions

1. What do you see as the main differences between a specific job description and a general job description?
2. Suppose several people are employed in the same job as the one for which you are writing a job description. Would it be necessary to write a different job description for each person who works in the same job?
3. Carefully follow the format for the "Specific Job Description" provided in Figure 2.6 when writing the job description for the job you selected. Make sure that you include in your job description the following elements: (1) job title and identification information, (2) job summary, (3) job duties and responsibilities, (4) job requirements, and (5) minimum qualifications. Check your work to make sure the style of your job description matches the example in the text as closely as possible.

Team Exercise

Work with a partner or a small group of three to four people and exchange job descriptions with a partner or group member. Read each other's job descriptions and make suggestions for improvements based on the example provided in the text. Take turns discussing the suggested revisions with your partner or group so that each person receives some feedback on his or her job description. Make revisions to your job description as needed to improve it. It is normal for a job description to go through several revisions before the document is finished. Now examine the job description you just wrote and revised. Discuss with your partner or group how this job description could be applied to making decisions in the organization that offers the job. Next, discuss what additional steps would be needed to finalize the job description before it could actually be used as a basis for employment decisions in a company.

Understanding Equal Opportunity and the Legal Environment

Challenges

After reading this chapter, you should be able to deal more effectively with the following challenges:

1. **Explain** why compliance with HR law is an important part of doing business.
2. **Follow** changes in HR law, regulation, and court decisions.
3. **Manage** within equal employment opportunity laws and understand the rationale and requirements of affirmative action.
4. **Make** managerial decisions that will avoid legal liability.
5. **Know** when to seek the advice of legal counsel on HRM matters.

Which Company Would You Rather Work For?

Company A

A class-action sexual harassment suit at a large Texas-based furniture rental company is being pursued by the EEOC on behalf of women who alleged that male managers created a hostile work environment for women. A senior executive was quoted as saying, "Women should be home taking care of their husbands and children." This same senior executive was observed smacking female employees' butts. Other company managers were accused of forcing female employees to quit and tearing up job applications from women. A 2000 company newsletter pictured 66 managers—all male.[1]

Company B

A female employee of a convention services firm was subjected to a company vice president's crude sexual comments and gestures. When she asked the vice president to stop the offensive behavior, he retaliated and profanely criticized her work. After the female employee reported this harassment to the director of human resources, an investigation followed and the director found the complaint valid. The firm gave the vice president a written reprimand and suspended him without pay for seven days. The employer promised the female employee she would never have to work with the vice president again and offered to pay for counseling she might need related to the incident.[2]

If You Were a Judge, Which Employer Would You Find Guilty of Discrimination?

Company X

Wayne, an African American employee, was transferred to a warehouse in Marietta, Georgia, a facility that stores aircraft parts for a large, military defense company. At his new job site he noticed antiblack graffiti scrawled on the restroom walls. His white colleagues harassed him, as did his manager who called him "boy." Wayne complained to his supervisor who was no help. The supervisor, instead, assigned Wayne to collecting parts to be boxed; collecting the parts required Wayne to walk about 10 miles a day. Meanwhile, his white colleagues who had less job seniority remained at their computer terminals where Wayne previously worked. One day, Wayne and two other black co-workers found "back to Africa tickets" on their desks; company management did nothing about this incident.[3]

Company Y

A manufacturer requires newly hired machine repairpersons to have a minimum of four years' work experience. An African American applicant who did not have this experience was denied employment. At the time, only one of the 31 machine repairpersons was African American. On investigation, you learn that the company had previously hired machine repairpersons without this experience on an emergency basis and that these employees had worked out just fine.[4]

THE MANAGERIAL PERSPECTIVE

Managers must understand the legal issues that affect the practice of HRM because many of their decisions are constrained to some extent by law. They should consider legal issues when making the following decisions:

- Which employees to hire
- How to compensate employees
- What benefits to offer
- How to accommodate employees with dependents
- How and when to fire employees

Legal constraints on HR practices have become increasingly more complex, in large part because of new employment laws and recent court decisions that interpret existing laws. The new employment laws mainly affect people with disabilities and those who seek a medical leave of absence from work. The court decisions relate to numerous issues such as worker safety and sexual harassment. Changes in the law have made HR decisions more difficult and risky—thereby increasing the cost of poor decisions.

HR managers consult and advise managers about the legal aspects of a personnel decision. Legal concerns are not the only priority in employment decisions but are heavily considered along

with other factors such as timeliness, product quality, and economic efficiency. The dynamism of the legal environment means that managers must seek the advice of HR specialists who, in turn, add value to management decisions with their expertise in employment laws and regulations.

In this chapter we examine the various aspects of HR law and regulation. First, we look at why managers must understand the HR legal environment. Next we explore several challenges that managers face when they try to comply with the law. Then we discuss *equal employment opportunity (EEO)* law, the enforcement mechanisms in place to ensure compliance, and several other laws that affect HRM. Finally, we describe ways for the effective manager to avoid potential legal pitfalls.

We need to start with a caveat. As with any legal issue you face, you should seek the advice of a qualified attorney to grapple with specific legal questions or problems relating to HRM. There are many lawyers who specialize in labor and employment law. However, you should not feel that you cannot make *any* decisions without specific legal counsel, and it is a mistake to let legal considerations become so important that you end up making poor business decisions. One goal of this chapter is to give you enough information to know when you need to seek legal counsel.

Why Understanding the Legal Environment Is Important

Understanding and complying with HR law is important for three reasons. It helps you do the right thing, realize the limitations of your firm's HR and legal departments, and minimize your firm's potential liability.

Doing the Right Thing

First and foremost, compliance with the law is important because it is the right thing to do. While you may disagree with the specific applications of some of the laws we discuss, the primary requirement of all these laws is to mandate good management practice. The earliest of the EEO laws requires that male and female employees who do the same job for the same organization receive the same pay. This is the right thing to do. The most recent EEO law requires that applicants or employees who are able to perform a job should not be discriminated against because of a disability. This, too, is the right thing to do.

Operating within these laws has benefits beyond simple legal compliance. Compensation practices that discriminate against women not only create potential legal liability but also lead to poor employee morale and low job satisfaction, which can in turn lead to poor job performance. Discriminating against qualified employees with disabilities makes no sense; in discriminating, the organization hurts itself by not hiring and retaining the best employees. McDonald's has taken the lead in hiring youth with learning disabilities. This is socially responsible and has created a positive impression among many customers.[5]

Realizing the Limitations of the HR and Legal Departments

A firm's HR department has considerable responsibilities with respect to HR law. These include keeping records, writing and implementing good HR policies, and monitoring the firm's HR decisions. However, if managers make poor decisions, the HR department will not always be able to resolve the situation. For instance, if a manager gives a poor employee an excellent performance rating, the HR department cannot undo the damage and provide the documentation necessary to support a decision to terminate the employee.

Nor can a firm's legal department magically solve problems created by managers. One of the key functions of legal counsel, whether internal or external, is to try to limit damage after it has occurred. Managers should work to prevent the damage from happening in the first place.

Members of the HR department support managers who have to make HR decisions with legal implications. HR staff may monitor managers' decisions or act as consultants. For example:

- A supervisor wants to discharge an employee for unexcused absences and consults the HR department to determine if there is enough evidence to discharge this person for "just cause." The HR department can help the manager and the company avoid a lawsuit for "wrongful discharge."
- A manager receives a phone call from a company that is inquiring about the qualification of a former employee. The manager is not sure how much information in the former employee's work history to reveal, so she seeks the HR department's advice. HR can help the manager and the company avoid a lawsuit for defamation (damage to an employee's reputation as a result of giving out false information to a third party).

Limiting Potential Liability

Considerable financial liabilities can occur when HR laws are broken or perceived to be broken. Typical court awards to victims of age, sex, race, or disability discrimination range from $50,000 to $300,000 depending on the size of the employer. Nonetheless, individual awards can actually be much larger. In 2001 the U.S. federal appeals court upheld a jury verdict awarding Troy Swinton $1.03 million for punitive damages, back wages, and emotional stress for racial discrimination suffered at U.S. Mat in Woodinville, Washington. The only African American employee out of 140 employees, Swinton was subjected to a regular stream of racial "jokes" and slurs during his six months of employment.[6] Also, in 2001, a California court awarded Lachi Richards, a civil engineer diagnosed with multiple sclerosis, $925,00 in emotional distress damages and $476,00 in economic damages in a disability discrimination suit against her former employer CH2M Hill, an international engineering firm. Richards tried to devise with her employer a "reasonable accommodation" to her work schedule to cope with her debilitating illness. But, instead, she was met with a hostile work environment. She was accused of trying to "milk" the company when she asked for accommodations, such as making doors easier to open, removing furniture from the hall so she could get her wheelchair through the office, and allowing better access to the elevator, library, supply room, and hallways.[7]

Organizations may also face a public relations nightmare when discrimination charges are publicized. In highly publicized cases in the early 1990s, several individual store managers and employees of Denny's restaurant chain were alleged to have discriminated against African American customers. Not only did the company subsequently have to pay $46 million to

After some scathing publicity about its treatment of minorities, Denny's has made huge strides. Akin Olajuwon (brother of the basketball star) is the company's second-largest franchise owner. Minorities own over one-third of the franchise restaurants, and Fortune *named it one of the best companies for Asians, blacks, and Hispanics to work for in 1998.*

African American patrons and $8.7 million in legal fees to settle these complaints, but the company's image with customers was damaged as well.[8] In recent years, though, Denny's has made major strides: As of 1998 minorities owned 35 percent of the company's 737 franchises, and an African American, Akin Olajuwon, owns 63 franchised restaurants, which makes him Denny's second-largest franchisee. In 1993 only one franchised restaurant was owned by an African American.[9]

In another highly publicized case, Texaco paid approximately $150 million to settle a racial discrimination lawsuit filed by some of the company's African American employees. The company's image also suffered when tape recordings revealed that some employees had engaged in blatant acts of racism. Since the settlement, Texaco has made significant progress in its minority hiring practices and diversity efforts.[10]

Challenges to Legal Compliance

Several challenges confront managers attempting to comply with HR law. These include a dynamic legal landscape, the complexity of regulations, conflicting strategies for fair employment, and unintended consequences.

A Dynamic Legal Landscape

The Appendix to this chapter contains a table listing all the laws discussed throughout this text. A quick scan of that table clearly demonstrates that many laws affect the practice of HRM. Several of these laws have been passed in the last decade.

The opinions handed down in court cases add to this dynamic environment. For example, in 1971 the Supreme Court handed down a landmark civil rights decision in a case titled *Griggs v. Duke Power*.[11] Among other things, this decision placed a heavy burden of proof on the employer in an employment discrimination case. Normally, a Supreme Court decision sets a precedent that the Court is then very reluctant to overturn. However, in a 1989 case, the Court revised the standard it had set in *Griggs*, making it more difficult for an employee to win a discrimination case.[12] Then, in 1991, Congress passed a lengthy amendment to the Civil Rights Act of 1964 (discussed later in this chapter) that returned to the burden-of-proof standard established in the *Griggs* decision.

These fast-paced changes are not limited to issues of courtroom procedure. Sexual harassment has been a topic of major concern since it was propelled into the national spotlight by the 1991 Clarence Thomas–Anita Hill confrontation. Sexual harassment regulations were adopted by the Equal Employment Opportunity Commission (EEOC) in the early 1980s and accepted by the Supreme Court in 1986. Since then, companies, lawyers, and judges have been attempting to figure out just what they mean and require. Opinions on these issues vary widely, which means that different courts have made differing decisions about what constitutes sexual harassment. Until the Supreme Court makes several more rulings, or Congress clarifies the underlying law, managers will need to pay close attention to the unfolding developments.

The Complexity of Laws

HR law, like most other types of law, is very complex. Each individual law is accompanied by a set of regulations that can be lengthy. For instance, the Americans with Disabilities Act (1990) is spelled out in a technical manual that is several hundred pages long. To make matters even more complex, one analysis has concluded that there may be as many as 1,000 different disabilities affecting over 43 million Americans.[13] It is very difficult for an expert in HR law, much less a manager, to understand all the possible implications of a particular law.

Nonetheless, the gist of most HR law is fairly straightforward. Managers should be able to understand the basic intention of all such laws without too much difficulty and can easily obtain the working knowledge they need to comply with those laws in the vast majority of situations.

Conflicting Strategies for Fair Employment

Society at large, political representatives, government employees, and judges all have different views regarding the best ways to achieve equitable HR laws. One of the major debates in this area centers on the competing strategies used to further the goal of **fair employment**—the situation in which employment decisions are not affected by illegal discrimination. The plain language of most civil rights law prohibits employers from making decisions about employees (hiring, performance appraisal, compensation, and so on) on the basis of race, sex, or age. Thus, one strategy to reach the goal of fair employment is for employment decisions to be made without regard to these characteristics. A second strategy, **affirmative action,** aims to accomplish the goal of fair employment by urging employers to hire certain groups of people who were discriminated against in the past. Thus, affirmative action programs require that employment decisions be made, at least in part, on the basis of characteristics such as race, sex, or age. Obviously, there is a conflict between these two strategies—one proposing that only "blind" hiring practices are fair, the other proposing that fairness requires organizations to make an effort to employ certain categories of people (Figure 3.1).

Fair employment
The goal of EEO legislation and regulation: a situation in which employment decisions are not affected by illegal discrimination.

Affirmative action
A strategy intended to achieve fair employment by urging employers to hire certain groups of people who were discriminated against in the past.

While the battle resulting from these competing strategies is being played out throughout society, the main legal struggle has occurred in the Supreme Court. Based on a series of Supreme Court decisions, the following conclusions seem warranted:

- The affirmative action strategy has been upheld. Specifically, employers are permitted to base employment decisions, in part, on a person's race, sex, age, and certain other characteristics.
- To be permissible, the employment decision cannot be made solely on the basis of these characteristics. Further, the people considered for the position should be "essentially equally qualified" on job-relevant characteristics before these other characteristics are permitted to play a role in the employment decision.
- The one situation in which affirmative action is not permitted is during layoffs. For instance, a white teacher should not be laid off to save the job of a Latino teacher, even if this means that minorities will be underrepresented in the postlayoff workforce.
- Courts may order an affirmative action program with specific quotas when an organization has a history of blatant discrimination.

A Question of Ethics

Is it ethical to refuse to give preferential treatment to minorities and women, who have been widely discriminated against in the past?

Unintended Consequences

It is very common for a law, a government program, or an organizational policy to have numerous unanticipated consequences, some of which turn out to be negative. HR law is certainly not immune to this phenomenon. For example, the Americans with Disabilities Act (ADA) was pri-

Figure 3.1 Competing Strategies for Fair Employment

Ideal Behavior Strategy

Best way to achieve fair employment is to make decisions without regard to:
- Race
- Sex
- Religion
- National origin
- Color
- Age
- Disability

→ Goal: Fair employment ←

Affirmative Action Strategy

Best way to achieve fair employment is to make decisions, at least in part, on the basis of:
- Race
- Sex
- Religion
- National origin
- Color
- Age
- Disability

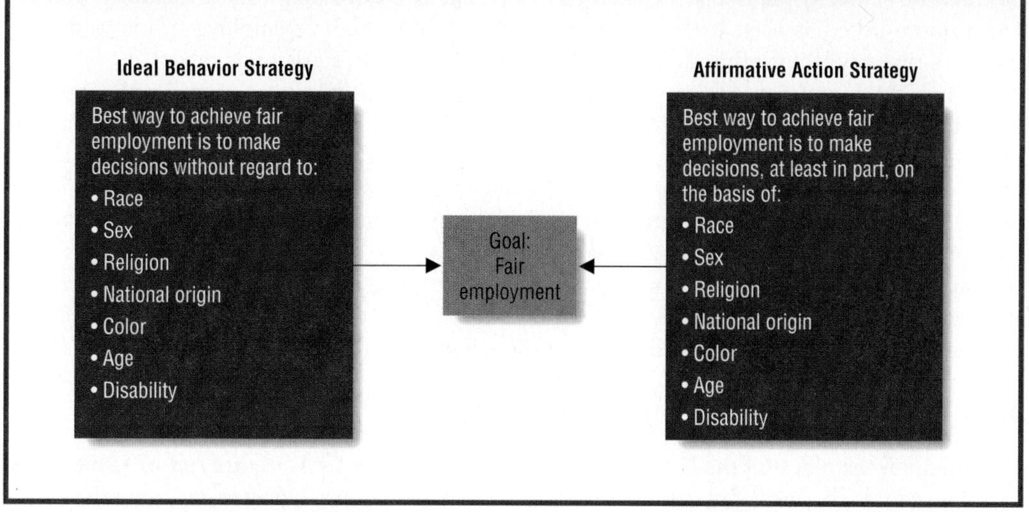

marily intended to increase the possibility of employment for people with physical and/or mental disabilities. However, since the law has gone into effect, job applicants have filed relatively few ADA complaints. Rather, current employees injured on the job have filed the majority of complaints. Traditionally, state workers' compensation laws (see Chapter 12) regulate the benefits given to employees injured on the job, including income continuation. Nobody intended the ADA to become a national workers' compensation law, but that appears to be just what is happening. The challenge to managers is to anticipate and deal with both the intended and unintended consequences of law.

Equal Employment Opportunity Laws

The laws that affect HR issues can be divided into two broad categories: (1) equal employment opportunity laws and (2) everything else. We will spend the bulk of this chapter on the EEO laws because these are the ones that most affect a manager's day-to-day behavior. In addition, the EEO laws cut across almost every other issue that we discuss in this text. The other laws tend to be more specifically focused, and we discuss them in the context in which they apply. For instance, we discuss the laws governing union activities in Chapter 15 and the Occupational Safety and Health Act (OSHA) in Chapter 16.

The major EEO laws are the Equal Pay Act of 1963, Title VII of the Civil Rights Act of 1964, the Age Discrimination in Employment Act of 1967, and the Americans with Disabilities Act of 1990. The Civil Rights Act of 1964 has been amended through the years, most recently in 1991. The theme that ties these laws together is simple: Employment decisions should not be based on characteristics such as race, sex, age, or disability.

The Equal Pay Act of 1963

Equal Pay Act (1963)
The law that requires the same pay for men and women who do the same job in the same organization.

The first of the civil rights laws was the **Equal Pay Act,** which became law in 1963. It requires that men and women who do the same job in the same organization should receive the same pay. "Same pay" means that no difference is acceptable.

Determining whether two employees are doing the same job can be difficult. The law specifies that jobs are the same if they are equal in terms of skill, effort, responsibility, and working conditions. Thus, it is permissible to pay one employee more than another if the first employee has significant extra job duties, such as supervisory responsibility. Pay can also be different for different work shifts. The law also specifies that equal pay is required only for jobs held in the same geographical region. This allows an organization to make allowances for the local cost of living and the fact that it might be harder to find qualified employees in some areas.

The law contains several explicit exceptions. First, it does not prohibit the use of a merit pay plan. That is, an employer can pay a man more if he is doing a better job than his female coworker. In addition, companies are permitted to pay for differences in quantity and quality of production. Seniority plans also are exempted; a company that ties pay rates to seniority can pay a man more if he has been with the company longer than a female employee. Finally, the law indicates that any factor other than sex may be used to justify different pay rates.[14]

When the Equal Pay Act was passed, the average female employee earned only about 59 cents for each dollar earned by the average male worker. While this gap has narrowed in the intervening years, to about 77 cents in 1999,[15] this average differential remains troubling, and in some jobs it is much higher. For instance, 30-year-old male sales representatives earned $60,000 in 2001 whereas their female counterparts in sales, doing the same amount and same kind of work, earned only $36,000 at the same age.[16] Some states, such as Washington and Illinois, have responded to this issue by requiring that civil service employers pay equally for work of comparable worth.[17] Understanding equal pay and comparable worth requires more knowledge of compensation decisions, so we will return to these issues in Chapter 10.

Title VII
Section of the Civil Rights Act of 1964 that applies to employment decisions; mandates that employment decisions not be based on race, color, religion, sex, or national origin.

Title VII of the Civil Rights Act of 1964

Although not the oldest of the civil rights laws, **Title VII of the Civil Rights Act of 1964** is universally seen as the most important passed to date. This law was enacted in the midst of the seething civil rights conflicts of the 1960s, one year after the civil rights march on Washington at which Dr. Martin Luther King, Jr., delivered his "I Have a Dream" speech.

Before passage of the Civil Rights Act of 1964, open and explicit discrimination based on race, particularly against African Americans, was widespread. *Jim Crow laws* legalized racial segregation in many southern states. The act itself had several sections, or titles, all of which aim to prohibit discrimination in various parts of society. For instance, Title IX applies to educational institutions. Title VII applies to employers who have 15 or more employees, as well as to employment agencies and labor unions.

General Provisions

Title VII prohibits employers from basing employment decisions on a person's race, color, religion, sex, or national origin. The heart of the law, Section 703(a), is reprinted in Figure 3.2. Note that employment decisions include "compensation, terms, conditions, or privileges of employment."

Title VII clearly covers persons of any race, any color, any religion, both sexes, and any national origin. However, as court cases and regulations have grown up around this law, so has the legal theory of a **protected class.** This theory states that groups of people who suffered discrimination in the past require, and should be given, special protection by the judicial system. Under Title VII, the protected classes are African Americans, Asian Americans, Latinos, Native Americans, and women. While it is not impossible for a nonprotected-class plaintiff to win a Title VII case, it is highly unusual.

Protected class
A group of people who suffered discrimination in the past and who are given special protection by the judicial system.

Discrimination Defined

Despite the negative connotation the word has acquired, **discrimination** simply means making distinctions—in the HR context, distinctions among people. Therefore, even the most progressive companies are constantly discriminating when they decide who should be promoted, who should receive a merit raise, and who should be laid off. What Title VII prohibits is making discriminations among people based on their race, color, religion, sex, or national origin. Specifically, it makes two types of discrimination illegal.

Discrimination
The making of distinctions. In HR context, the making of distinctions among people.

The first type of discrimination, **disparate treatment,** occurs when an employer treats an employee differently because of his or her protected-class status. Disparate treatment is the kind of treatment that you probably first think of when considering discrimination. For instance, Robert Frazier, who is a bricklayer's assistant and an African American, was fired after quarreling with a white bricklayer. However, Frazier's employer did not discipline the white bricklayer at all, even though he had injured Frazier by throwing a broken brick at him. A federal court judge ruled that Frazier had been treated more harshly because of his race and, thus, suffered from disparate treatment discrimination.[18]

Disparate treatment
Discrimination that occurs when individuals are treated differently because of their membership in a protected class.

The second type of discrimination, **adverse impact** (also called *disparate impact*), occurs when the same standard is applied to all applicants or employees, but that standard affects a protected class more negatively (adversely). For example, most police departments around the United States have dropped their former requirement that officers be of a minimum height because the equal application of that standard has an adverse impact on women, Latinos, and

Adverse impact
Discrimination that occurs when the equal application of an employment standard has an unequal effect on one or more protected classes. Also called *disparate impact*.

Figure 3.2

Title VII of the Civil Rights Act of 1964

Section 703. (a) It shall be an unlawful employment practice for an employer—

(1) to fail or refuse to hire or to discharge any individual, or otherwise to discriminate against any individual with respect to his compensation, terms, conditions, or privileges of employment, because of such individual's race, color, religion, sex, or national origin; or

(2) to limit, segregate, or classify his employees or applicants for employment in any way which would deprive or tend to deprive any individual of employment opportunities or otherwise adversely affect his status as an employee, because of such individual's race, color, religion, sex, or national origin.

Asian Americans (that is, any given height standard will rule out more women than men, and more Latinos and Asian Americans than African Americans and nonminority individuals). Figure 3.3 summarizes the distinctions between disparate treatment and adverse impact.

The adverse impact definition of discrimination was confirmed in a very important 1971 Supreme Court case that we have already discussed, *Griggs v. Duke Power*.[19] Griggs was an African American employee of the Duke Power Company in North Carolina. He and other African American employees were refused promotions because Duke Power, on the day that Title VII took effect, had implemented promotion standards that included a high school diploma and passing scores on two tests, one of general intellectual ability and one of mechanical ability. The Supreme Court ruled that such standards, even though applied equally to all employees, were discriminatory because (1) they had an adverse impact on a protected class (in this case, African Americans) and (2) Duke Power was unable to show that the standards were related to subsequent job performance.

Griggs v. Duke Power has some important implications. Under the *Griggs* ruling, courts may find that a company is acting in a discriminatory manner even though it works hard to ensure that its HR decision processes are applied equally to all employees. If the outcome is such that a protected class suffers from adverse impact, then the organization may be required to demonstrate that the standards used in the decision process were related to the job. In October 1993, Domino's Pizza lost a case in which it attempted to defend a "no-beard policy." The appellate court ruled that the policy had an adverse effect on African Americans because almost half of male African Americans suffer from a genetic condition that makes shaving very painful or impossible. Almost no white men suffer from this malady. Therefore, African Americans are more adversely affected by this requirement than whites are.[20] Domino's could have won this case if it had shown that not having a beard was necessary for good job performance. It could not, so the court ruled the no-beard policy a violation of Title VII.

In an earlier (1975) case, *Albemarle Paper Company v. Moody*, the Supreme Court established procedures to help employers determine when it is appropriate to use employment tests as a basis for hiring or promoting employees. The Court ruled that employers can use an employment test only when they can demonstrate that the test is a valid predictor of job performance. Thus, *Albemarle* places the burden of proof on the employer to prove that a contested test (for example, a test that has an adverse impact on a protected class) or other selection tool is a valid predictor of job success.[21]

Defense of Discrimination Charges

When a discrimination case makes it to court, it is the responsibility of the plaintiff (the person bringing the complaint) to show reasonable evidence that discrimination has occurred. The legal term for this type of evidence is *prima facie,* which means "on its face." In a disparate treat-

Two Kinds of Discrimination

Figure 3.3

Disparate Treatment	Adverse Impact
Direct discrimination	Indirect discrimination
Unequal treatment	Unequal consequences or results
Decision rules with a racial/sexual premise or cause	Decision rules with racial/sexual consequences or results
Intentional discrimination	Unintentional discrimination
Prejudiced actions	Neutral actions
Different standards for different groups	Same standards, but different consequences for different groups

Source: Adapted from Ledvinka, J., and Scarpello, V. G. (1991). *Federal regulation of personnel and human resource management* (2nd ed.). Boston: PWS-Kent. Reproduced with the permission of South-Western College Publishing. Copyright 1991 by PWS-Kent. All rights reserved.

ment lawsuit, to establish a prima facie case the plaintiff only needs to show that the organization did not hire her (or him), that she appeared to be qualified for the job, and that the company continued to try to hire someone else for the position after rejecting her. This set of requirements, which originated from a court case brought against the McDonnell-Douglas Corporation, is often called the *McDonnell-Douglas test.*[22] In an adverse impact lawsuit, the plaintiff only needs to show that a restricted policy is in effect—that is, that a disproportionate number of protected-class individuals were affected by the employment decisions.

One important EEOC provision for establishing a prima facie case that an HR practice is discriminatory and has an adverse impact is the **four-fifths rule.** The four-fifths rule comes from the EEOC's *Uniform Guidelines on Employee Selection Procedures*, an important document that informs employers how to establish selection procedures that are valid and, therefore, legal.[23]

Four-fifths rule
An EEOC provision for establishing a prima facie case that an HR practice is discriminatory and has an adverse impact. A practice has an adverse impact if the hiring rate of a protected class is less than four-fifths the hiring rate of a majority group.

The four-fifths rule compares the hiring rates of protected classes to those of majority groups (such as white men) in the organization. It assumes that an HR practice has an adverse impact if the hiring rate of a protected class is less than four-fifths of the hiring rate of a majority group. For example, assume that an accounting firm hires 50 percent of all its white male job applicants for entry-level accounting positions. Also assume that only 25 percent of all African American male job applicants are hired for the same job. Applying the four-fifths rule, there is prima facie evidence that the accounting firm has discriminatory hiring practices because 50 percent × 4/5 = 40 percent, and 40 percent exceeds the 25 percent hiring rate for African American men.

Once the plaintiff has established a prima facie case, the burden of proof switches to the organization. In other words, the employer is then placed in a position of proving that illegal discrimination did not occur. This can be very tough to prove. Suppose that a sales manager interviews two applicants for a sales position, a man and a woman. Their qualifications look very much the same on paper. However, in the interview the man seems to be more motivated. He is hired, and the rejected female applicant files a disparate treatment discrimination suit. She can, almost automatically, establish a prima facie case (she was qualified, she was not hired, the company did hire someone else). Now the sales manager has to prove that the decision was based on a judgment about the applicant's motivation, not on the applicant's sex.

While these cases can be difficult, employers do win their share of them. There are four basic defenses that an employer can use:

- **Job relatedness** The employer has to show that the decision was made for job-related reasons. This is much easier to do if the employer has written documentation to support and explain the decision. In our example, the manager will be asked to give specific job-related reasons for the decision to hire the man for the sales job. As we noted in Chapter 2, job descriptions are particularly useful for documenting the job-related reasons for any particular HR decision.
- **Bona fide occupational qualification** A **bona fide occupational qualification (BFOQ)** is a characteristic that must be present in all employees for a particular job. For instance, a film director is permitted to consider only females for parts that call for an actress.
- **Seniority** Employment decisions that are made in the context of a formal seniority system are permitted, even if they discriminate against certain protected-class individuals. However this defense requires the seniority system to be well established and applied universally, not just in some circumstances.
- **Business necessity** The employer can use the business necessity defense when the employment practice is necessary for the safe and efficient operation of the organization and there is an overriding business purpose for the discriminatory practice. For example, an employee drug test may adversely impact a disadvantaged minority group, but the need for safety (to protect other employees and customers) may justify the drug-testing procedure.

Bona fide occupational qualification (BFOQ)
A characteristic that must be present in all employees for a particular job.

Of these four defenses, the job-relatedness defense is the most common because of the strict limitations courts have placed on the BFOQ, seniority, and business necessity defenses.

Title VII and Pregnancy

In 1978 Congress amended Title VII to state explicitly that women are protected from discrimination based either on their ability to become pregnant or on their actual pregnancy. The

Pregnancy Discrimination Act of 1978 requires employers to treat an employee who is pregnant in the same way as any other employee who has a medical condition.[24] For instance, an employer cannot deny sick leave for pregnancy-related illnesses such as morning sickness if the employer allows sick leave for other medical conditions such as nausea-related illnesses. The law also states that a company cannot design an employee health benefit plan that provides no coverage for pregnancy. These are strict requirements, as evidenced by the following cases.

In one case that applied the Pregnancy Discrimination Act, a woman who worked at the U.S. Postal Service (USPS) claimed she was subjected to pregnancy discrimination when she was not reappointed after she had served a one-year appointment. The USPS cited her absences from work and that she was considered a high-risk pregnancy and should be doing only light-duty work. However, the EEOC found the complainant was treated less favorably than comparative employees based on her pregnancy. The basis of the EEOC's ruling was that the law requires the employer to treat pregnant employees just as it treats other employees with temporary impairments.[25]

In another pregnancy discrimination case, plaintiff Deitra Golson worked as a delinquent loan collector for Green Tree Financial Servicing Corp., and her monthly production goals were generally outstanding until the start of her pregnancy. Later, when Golson was forced to miss work for pregnancy-related problems, her performance fell short of her goals, and she was placed on a 90-day probation. During this probationary period Golson improved her performance numbers but was fired anyway for failing to meet specific performance goals. The court awarded Golson a total of $261,500 in compensatory damages, punitive damages, and back pay. It reasoned that Golson was treated differently than nonpregnant employees with respect to performance goals following a medical leave, and she was fired without being allowed to complete her 90-day probationary period.[26]

A female police officer in Pinellas Park, Florida, claimed she experienced pregnancy discrimination when she was demoted to dispatcher after becoming pregnant and requesting light duty. She showed evidence that her male supervisor informed her that he was forced to hire women, and he specifically gave women the least desirable shifts and days off to punish them if they became pregnant. The city settled in favor of the complainant and reinstated her as police officer.[27]

Sexual Harassment

The Title VII prohibition of sex-based discrimination has also been interpreted to prohibit sexual harassment. In contrast to the protection for pregnancy, the sexual harassment protection was not an amendment to the law but rather a 1980 EEOC interpretation of the law.[28] The EEOC's defini-

U.S. law requires employers to treat pregnant employees in the same way as any other employees with a medical condition. In addition, the Family and Medical Leave Act of 1993 requires certain employers to provide up to 12 weeks' unpaid leave to eligible employees who adopt a child or need to care for a sick parent, child, or spouse.

tion of sexual harassment is given in Figure 3.4. Also shown in the figure is the definition of general harassment that the EEOC issued in 1993. The majority of harassment cases filed to date have dealt with sexual harassment, but this may change in the future.[29] Courts appear to be extending sexual harassment definitions to other protected classes, such as race, age, and disability.

There are two broad categories of sexual harassment. The first, **quid pro quo sexual harassment,** covers the first two parts of the EEOC's definitions. It occurs when sexual activity is demanded in return for getting or keeping a job or job-related benefit.[30] For instance, a buyer for the University of Massachusetts Medical Center was awarded $1 million in 1994 after she testified that her supervisor had forced her to engage in sex once or twice a week over a 20-month period as a condition of keeping her job.[31]

Quid pro quo sexual harassment
Harassment that occurs when sexual activity is required in return for getting or keeping a job or job-related benefit.

The second category, **hostile work environment sexual harassment,** occurs when the behavior of co-workers, supervisors, customers, or anyone else in the work setting is sexual in nature and the employee perceives the behavior as offensive and undesirable.[32] Consider this example from a Supreme Court case decided in 1993.[33]

Hostile work environment sexual harassment
Harassment that occurs when the behavior of anyone in the work setting is sexual in nature and is perceived by an employee as offensive and undesirable.

Teresa Harris was a manager at Forklift Systems, Inc., an equipment rental firm in Nashville, Tennessee. Her boss was Charles Hardy, the company president. Throughout the two and one-half years that Harris worked at Forklift, Hardy made such comments to her as "You're a woman, what do you know?" and "We need a man as the rental manager." He suggested in front of other employees that the two of them "go to the Holiday Inn to negotiate her raise." When Harris asked Hardy to stop, he expressed surprise at her annoyance but did not apologize. Less than one month later, after Harris had negotiated a deal with a customer, Hardy asked her in front of other employees, "What did you do, promise the guy . . . some [sex] Saturday night?" Harris quit her job at the end of that month.

The issue the Court had to decide was whether Hardy violated the sexual harassment regulations based on Title VII. Lower courts had held that Hardy's behavior was certainly objectionable, but that Harris had not suffered serious psychological harm and that Hardy had not created a hostile work environment. The Supreme Court disagreed, holding that the behavior only needed to be such that a "reasonable person" would find it to create a hostile or abusive work environment. Figure 3.5 on page 96 lists the tests that the Supreme Court said should be considered by judges and juries in deciding whether certain conduct creates a "hostile work environment" and is thus prohibited by Title VII.

Some cases of sexual harassment have involved groups of employees who have lodged hostile work environment claims. In 1998 Mitsubishi Motor Manufacturing of America paid out

A Question of Ethics

Some businesses thrive on a sexual theme. For example, "Hooters" attracts customers by marketing a sexual environment. Many ad campaigns have explicit sexual themes. Are such marketing efforts ethical? What effect might these public images have on the working environment at the company that uses them?

Figure 3.4

EEOC Definitions of Harassment

1980 Definition of Sexual Harassment

Unwelcome sexual advances, requests for sexual favors, and other verbal or physical conduct of a sexual nature constitute sexual harassment when:

1. submission to such conduct is made either explicitly or implicitly a term or condition of an individual's employment;
2. submission to or rejection of such conduct by an individual is sued as a basis for employment decisions affecting such individual; or
3. such conduct has the purpose or effect of unreasonably interfering with an individual's work performance or creating an intimidating, hostile, or offensive working environment.

1993 Definition of Harassment

Unlawful harassment is verbal or physical conduct that denigrates or shows hostility or aversion toward an individual because of his or her race, color, religion, gender, national origin, age or disability, or that of his/her relatives, friends, or associates, and that:

1. has the purpose or effect of creating an intimidating, hostile, or offensive working environment;
2. has the purpose or effect of unreasonably interfering with an individual's work performance; or
3. otherwise adversely affects an individual's employment opportunities.

Do You Have a Hostile Work Environment?

Figure 3.5

The Supreme Court listed these questions to help judges and juries decide whether verbal and other nonphysical behavior of a sexual nature create a hostile work environment.

- How frequent is the discriminatory conduct?
- How severe is the discriminatory conduct?
- Is the conduct physically threatening or humiliating?
- Does the conduct interfere with the employee's work performance?

$34 million to settle a sexual harassment case brought by the EEOC on behalf of more than 300 female employees. Among their complaints were being groped, gestured to, urged to reveal their sexual preferences, and exposed to sexually explicit pictures.[34] The following year in 1999 Ford Motor Company achieved a settlement with women in two Chicago area factories in regard to their sexual harassment complaints. The female employees claimed there existed a long-term pattern of groping, name-calling, and partying with strippers and prostitutes. The carmaker agreed to set aside $7.5 million to compensate victims of harassment and $10 million more to provide diversity training to managers and male workers.[35] Mitsubishi had changed its image as a leader in corporate forgiveness of sexual harassment in 1998 to a model corporate citizen four years later in 2002. Mitsubishi made improvements that included a zero tolerance policy for sexual harassment and provided training for all employees about the illegality of harassment and how to investigate complaints when they arise.[36]

Sexual harassment cases are not only expensive, but they also can be highly disruptive to business and political organizations. Consider the disruption to the executive branch of the U.S. government when Paula Jones sued President Clinton for sexual harassment. She alleged that the president made an unwanted sexual advance toward her in 1991 while he was the governor of Arkansas and she was a state employee. In 1999 President Clinton paid $850,000 to settle the suit.[37]

Although most sexual harassment cases involve women as victims, the number of cases in which men are the victims is increasing.[38] In 1995 a federal judge awarded a man $237,257 for being sexually harassed by a female supervisor at a Domino's Pizza restaurant. The female supervisor made unwelcome sexual advances to the male subordinate, creating a hostile work environment. When the man threatened to report the supervisor's inappropriate conduct to top management, he was fired.[39]

Courts also consider same-sex harassment improper work-related behavior. Joseph Oncale, an oil-rig worker who alleged that fellow male workers physically and verbally abused him with sexual taunts and threats, was allowed to bring a sexual harassment lawsuit against his employer. Despite arguments to the contrary, a court reviewing the *Oncale* case ruled in 1998 that same-sex harassment, not just that between the sexes, can be the basis for a sexual harassment lawsuit.[40]

As Figure 3.6 (page 398) indicates, sexual harassment is a major EEO issue for employers. A recent Harris survey found that 31 percent of women reported that they had been sexually harassed in the workplace.[41] According to the EEOC, plaintiffs filed 15,475 cases of sexual harassment with federal and state agencies in 2001 (Figure 3.6). Men filed approximately 13 percent of those cases.

The Manager's Notebook titled "Reducing Potential Liability for Sexual Harassment" spells out some ways to prevent or correct instances of sexual harassment.

MANAGER'S NOTEBOOK

Reducing Potential Liability for Sexual Harassment

To reduce the potential liability of a sexual harassment suit, managers should:

- **Establish a written policy prohibiting harassment.**
- **Communicate the policy and train employees in what constitutes harassment.**

- Establish an effective complaint procedure.
- Quickly investigate all claims.
- Take remedial action to correct past harassment.
- Make sure that the complainant does not end up in a less desirable position if he or she needs to be transferred.
- Follow up to prevent continuation of harassment.

Source: Commerce Clearing House. (1991). *Sexual harassment manual for managers and supervisors*. Chicago: Commerce Clearing House.

Managers should be aware of recent U.S. Supreme Court sexual harassment rulings that directly affect employer liability in sexual harassment cases. First, an employer may be held liable for the actions of supervisors toward their subordinate employees even if the offense is not reported to top management.

Second, the Supreme Court has established an employer defense against sexual harassment claims. The employer must prove two items:

- It exercised reasonable care to prevent and correct sexual harassment problems in a timely manner.[42]
- The plaintiff failed to use the internal procedures for reporting sexual harassment.[43]

If the employee reasonably believes that reporting the offensive conduct is not a viable option, then the employer cannot take advantage of the defense. The internal procedures, then, must consist of fair investigations.[44] The Manager's Notebook entitled "How to Handle a Sexual Harassment Investigation" provides some guidelines to managers for investigating an employee's complaint of an alleged instance of sexual harassment.

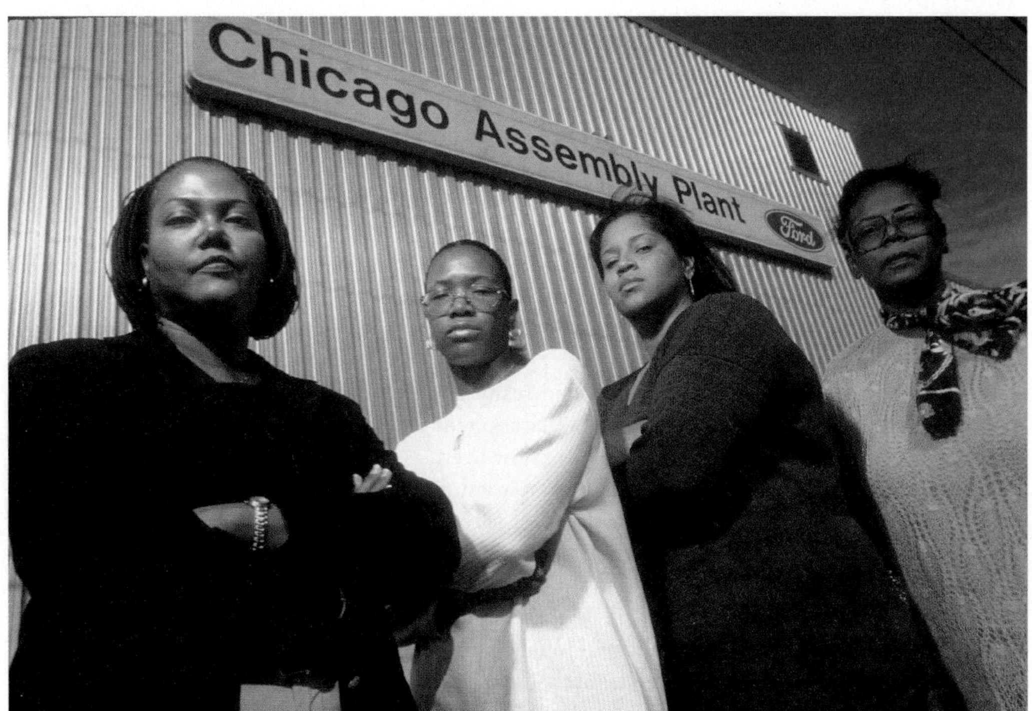

Female employees at two Ford plants claimed groping and name-calling created a hostile environment. The suit resulted in a large settlement to compensate the victims of sexual harassment.

Number of Sexual Harassment Charges in the United States from 1992 to 2001.

Source: The U.S. Equal Employment Opportunity Commission (2002). http://www.eeoc.gov/stats/harass.html.

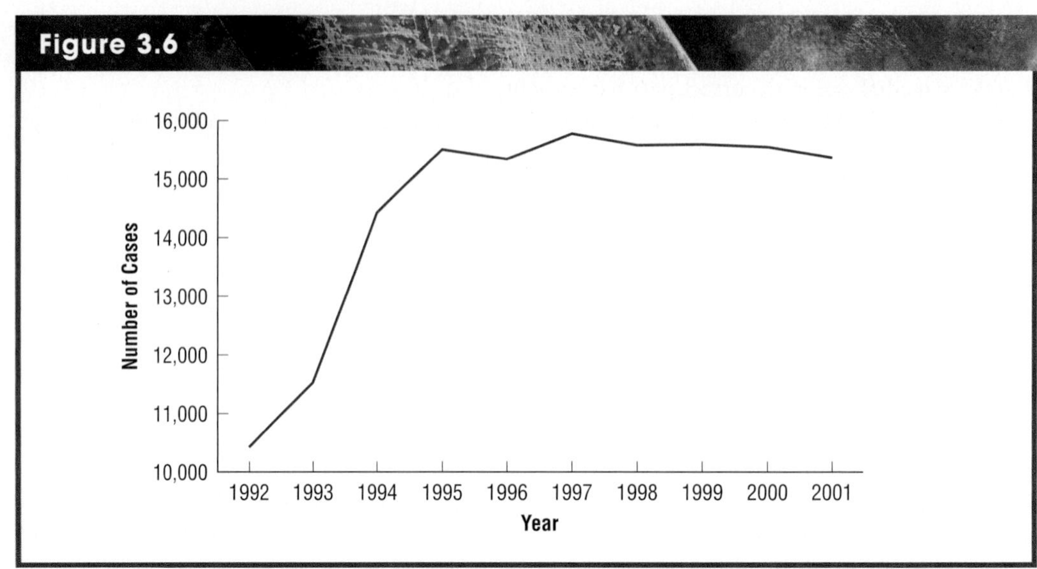

MANAGER'S NOTEBOOK

How to Handle a Sexual Harassment Investigation

When an employee brings a complaint of sexual harassment to a manager, the manager has the responsibility to investigate the complaint. Failure to investigate a sexual harassment complaint can result in an employer liability if the case goes to court. Here are some guidelines for conducting an investigation into sexual harassment:

- **Timeliness.** Managers should respond quickly, within 24 to 48 hours of a complaint of sexual harassment. Reacting later than that risks the company being considered negligent because it left the employee exposed to harassment.
- **Documentation.** Managers should ask open-ended questions to get as much detail as possible about the harassment. Notes taken during the interview should be rewritten or typed after the meeting is concluded. The manager should write the report based on notes from the interview with the complainant.
- **Employee agreement.** After the manager documents the facts in the report, the manager should go over the events with the complainant to see if there is anything that should be added. There should be documentation of the employee's agreement with the manager's version of the events.
- **Resolution.** Managers should ask what end result the employee is seeking. Those with a genuine complaint usually say they want the harassment to stop. Those with a personal vendetta are often looking to have the alleged perpetrator fired.
- **Findings of fact.** The manager should interview witnesses who can corroborate or discredit the allegations of sexual harassment. The manager should then interview the alleged harasser. The accused should have the opportunity to defend himself or herself. A "findings of fact" document should be recorded to represent all the facts in the complaint; when this document is completed, the investigation is considered completed.
- **Remedy.** The employer is only obligated to take steps reasonably likely to stop the harassment. The employer has the right to determine an appropriate course of action. An effective sexual harassment policy gives managers the flexibility to choose from a range of various sanctions that depends on the seriousness of the harassment. These sanctions can range from a written

warning to the harasser to stop, to a transfer elsewhere in the firm or demotion, to termination of the harasser.

Source: Covey, A. (2001, July). How to handle harassment complaints. *HR Focus*, 5–6; Segal, J. (2001, October). HR as judge, jury, prosecutor and defender. *HRMagazine*, 141–154.

To safeguard against sexual harassment claims, experts recommend that employers develop a zero-tolerance sexual harassment policy, successfully communicate the policy to employees, and ensure that victims can report abuses without fear of retaliation.[45]

The Civil Rights Act of 1991

In 1991, believing that the Supreme Court was beginning to water down Title VII, Congress passed a comprehensive set of amendments to Title VII. Together, these amendments are known as the *Civil Rights Act of 1991*. Although the legal aspects of these amendments are fairly technical, their impact is very real for many organizations. Among the most important effects of the 1991 amendment are:

- **Burden of proof** As we noted earlier, the employer bears the burden of proof in a discrimination case. Once the applicant or employee files a discrimination case and shows some justification for it, the organization has to defend itself by proving that it had a good job-related reason for the decision it made. This standard was originally established in the *Griggs v. Duke Power* decision in 1971. Then a 1989 Supreme Court case, *Wards Cove Packing Co. v. Antonio,* had the effect of placing more of the burden of proof on the plaintiff.[46] The 1991 law reinstates the *Griggs* standard.
- **Quotas** To avoid adverse impact, many organizations (including the Department of Labor) had developed a policy of adjusting scores on employment tests so that a certain percentage of protected-class applicants would be hired. The 1991 law amending Title VII prohibits **quotas,** which are employer adjustments of hiring decisions to ensure that a certain number of people from a certain protected class are hired. Thus, quotas, which had received mixed reviews in Supreme Court decisions before 1991, are now explicitly forbidden. Employers who have an affirmative action program that gives preference to protected-class candidates have to walk a very fine line between "giving preference" (which is permissible) and "meeting a quota" (which is forbidden).
- **Damages and jury trials** The original Title VII law allowed successful plaintiffs to collect only back pay awards. However, racial minorities were also able to use an 1866 law to collect punitive and/or compensatory damages. **Punitive damages** are fines awarded to a plaintiff to punish the defendant. **Compensatory damages** are fines awarded to a plaintiff to compensate for the financial or psychological harm the plaintiff has suffered as a result of the discrimination. The 1991 law extended the possibility of collecting punitive and compensatory damages to persons claiming sex, religious, or disability-based discrimination. Such damages are capped at $50,000 to $300,000, depending on the size of the employer.[47] In addition, the law allows plaintiffs to request a trial by jury.

Quotas
Employer adjustments of hiring decisions to ensure that a certain number of people from a certain protected class are hired.

Punitive damages
Fines awarded to a plaintiff in order to punish the defendant.

Compensatory damages
Fines awarded to a plaintiff to compensate for the financial or psychological harm the plaintiff has suffered.

Some believe that by expressly forbidding quotas, the Civil Rights Act of 1991 has prohibited a very useful mechanism for reducing discrimination in employment decisions. Many organizations had found that the best way to prevent adverse impact was to use a combination of quotas and cognitive ability testing. That is, the employer would select a certain percentage of applicants from various groups, and then choose the highest performers on cognitive ability tests from each group. This employment strategy resulted in both the maintenance of a quality work force and the greater participation of minorities in that workforce. Yet, by outlawing quotas, the Civil Rights Act of 1991 has prohibited this option.[48]

Executive Order 11246

Executive orders are policies that the president establishes for the federal government and organizations that contract with the federal government. Executive Order 11246 (as amended by Executive Order 11375), issued by President Johnson in 1965, is *not* part of Title VII. It does,

Executive order
A presidential directive that has the force of law. In HR context, a policy with which all federal agencies and organizations doing business with the federal government must comply.

however, prohibit discrimination against the same categories of people that Title VII protects. In addition, it goes beyond the Title VII requirement of no discrimination by requiring covered organizations (firms with government contracts over $50,000 and 50 or more employees) to develop affirmative action programs to promote the employment of protected-class members. For instance, government contractors such as Northrop Grumman and Lockheed Martin are required to have active affirmative action programs.

The Age Discrimination in Employment Act of 1967

Age Discrimination in Employment Act (1967) The law prohibiting discrimination against people who are 40 or older.

The **Age Discrimination in Employment Act (ADEA)** prohibits discrimination against people who are 40 or older. When first enacted in 1967, it protected people aged 40 to 65. Subsequently, it was amended to raise the age to 70, and in 1986 the upper age limit was removed entirely.

The majority of ADEA complaints are filed by employees who have been terminated. For instance, a 57-year-old computerized control salesman for GE Fanuc Automation was the only employee terminated during a "reduction in force"; he was replaced by six younger sales representatives. He brought a lawsuit, claiming that he was fired because of his age, and a Detroit jury awarded him $1.1 million in damages and lost wages and benefits.[49] Employers can also lose lawsuits as a result of ill-informed workplace humor. Employers have lost several age discrimination cases because terminated employees had evidence that supervisors had told jokes about old age.[50]

An important amendment to the ADEA is the *Older Workers Benefit Protection Act (OWBPA)* of 1990, which makes it illegal for employers to discriminate in providing benefits to employees based on age. For example, it would be illegal for employers to provide disability benefits only to employees who are age 60 or less or to require older disabled employees to take early retirement. Another OWPA provision makes it more difficult for firms to ask older workers in downsizing and layoff situations to sign waivers in which they give up their right to any future age-discrimination claims in exchange for a payment.[51]

The Americans with Disabilities Act of 1990

Americans with Disabilities Act (1990) The law forbidding employment discrimination against people with disabilities who are able to perform the essential functions of the job with or without reasonable accommodation.

The most recent of the major EEO laws is the **Americans with Disabilities Act (ADA).** Signed into law in 1990 and gradually implemented since then, ADA has three major sections. Title I contains the employment provisions; Titles II and III concern the operation of state and local governments and places of public accommodation such as hotels, restaurants, and grocery stores. The employment provisions began to be enforced for the approximately 264,000 U.S. employers with 25 or more employees on July 26, 1992, and for the approximately 666,000 U.S. employers with 15 or more employees on July 26, 1994.[52]

The central requirement of Title I of the ADA is as follows:

> Employment discrimination is prohibited against *individuals with disabilities* who are able to perform the *essential functions* of the job with or without *reasonable accommodation.*

Three parts of this requirement need definition.

Individuals with Disabilities

Individuals with disabilities Persons who have a physical or mental impairment that substantially affects one or more major life activities.

For the purposes of ADA, **individuals with disabilities** are people who have a physical or mental impairment that substantially affects one or more major life activities. Some examples of major life activities are:[53]

- Walking
- Speaking
- Breathing
- Performing manual tasks
- Sitting
- Lifting
- Seeing
- Hearing
- Learning
- Caring for oneself
- Working
- Reading

Obviously, persons who are blind, hearing impaired, or wheelchair bound are individuals with disabilities. But the category also includes people who have a controlled impairment. For instance, a person with epilepsy is disabled even if the epilepsy is controlled through medication. The impairment must be physical or mental and not due to environmental, cultural, or economic disadvantages. For example, a person who has difficulty reading due to dyslexia is considered disabled, but a person who cannot read because he or she dropped out of school is not. Persons with communicable diseases, including those who are HIV-positive (infected with the virus that causes AIDS), are included in the definition of individuals with disabilities.

ADA coverage is only extended to people with disabilities that impair a major life activity. It does not provide remedies to people with disabilities that impair only a work activity. This limitation of ADA coverage was decided in a 2002 Supreme Court decision when an employee at a Toyota plant in Kentucky, whose carpal tunnel syndrome restricted her ability to use pneumatic tools at work, sought a remedy under the ADA. It was denied by the court.[54]

In addition, the ADA protects persons who are *perceived* to be disabled. For instance, an employee might suffer a heart attack. When he tries to return to work, his boss may be scared that the workload will be "too much" and refuse to let him come back. The employer would be in violation of the ADA because he perceives the employee as disabled and is discriminating against him on the basis of that perception.

Two particular classes of people are explicitly *not* considered disabled: individuals whose current use of alcohol is affecting their job performance and those who use illegal drugs (whether they are addicted or not). However, those who are recovering from their former use of either alcohol or drugs are covered by ADA.

A 1999 Supreme Court decision clarified who is entitled to ADA protection. The court ruled that a person is not considered disabled under the ADA if his or her impairment is corrected and does not substantially limit a major life activity. For example, it held that two female job applicants for a pilot position with United Airlines could not claim ADA protection for the disability of poor eyesight. The women's uncorrected eyesight was below United's 20/100 uncorrected vision requirement for pilots; their corrected vision with glasses was 20/20. The court found that because the women's vision could be corrected with glasses they were not disabled under the terms of the act and denied them a remedy.[55] This decision is likely to affect ADA coverage of other impairments that can be corrected, such as hearing loss, high blood pressure, or asthma.

Essential Functions

The EEOC separates job duties and tasks into two categories: essential and marginal. **Essential functions** are job duties that every employee must do or must be able to do to be an effective employee. *Marginal functions* are job duties that are required of only some employees or are not critical to job performance. The following examples illustrate the difference between essential and marginal functions:

Essential functions
Job duties that each person in a certain position must do or must be able to do to be an effective employee.

- A company advertises a position for a "floating" supervisor to substitute when regular supervisors on the day, night, and graveyard shifts are absent. The ability to work any time of the day or night is an essential job function.
- A company wishes to expand its business with Japan. In addition to sales experience, it requires all new hires to speak fluent Japanese. This language skill is an essential job function.
- In any job requiring computer use, it is essential that the employee have the ability to access, input, or retrieve information from the computer terminal. However, it may not be essential that the employee be capable of manually entering or visually retrieving information because technology exists for voice recognition input and auditory output.
- A group of chemists working together in a lab may occasionally need to answer the telephone. This is considered a marginal job duty if not every one of the chemists can answer the phone because the other chemists can do so.

ADA requires that employers make decisions about applicants with disabilities solely on the basis of their ability to perform essential job functions.

Reasonable Accommodation

Organizations are required to take some reasonable action to allow disabled employees to work for them. The major aspects of this requirement are:

Reasonable accommodation
An action taken to accommodate the known disabilities of applicants or employees so that disabled persons enjoy equal employment opportunity.

- Employers must make **reasonable accommodation** for the known disabilities of applicants or employees so that disabled people enjoy equal employment opportunity.[56] For example, an applicant who uses a wheelchair may need accommodation if the interviewing site is not wheelchair accessible.

- Employers cannot deny a disabled person employment to avoid providing the reasonable accommodation, unless providing the accommodation would cause an "undue hardship." Undue hardship is a highly subjective determination, based on the cost of the accommodation and the employer's resources. For instance, an accommodation routinely provided by large employers (such as specialized computer equipment) may not be required of small employers because the small employers do not have the large employer's financial resources.
- No accommodation is required if the individual is not otherwise qualified for the position.
- It is usually the obligation of the disabled individual to request the accommodation.
- If the cost of the accommodation would create an undue hardship for the employer, the disabled individual should be given the option of providing the accommodation. For instance, if a visually impaired person applies for a computer operator position in a small company that cannot afford to accommodate the applicant, then the applicant should be given the option to provide the accommodating technology. (It should be noted, though, that the President's Committee on Employment of People with Disabilities reports that 20 percent of accommodations do not cost anything at all, and less than 4 percent cost more than $5,000.[57]) The Manager's Notebook titled "Designing Flexible Work Areas to Accommodate Employees with Disabilities" describes some of the ways that employers can design flexible work areas to accommodate employees with disabilities.

MANAGER'S NOTEBOOK

Designing Flexible Work Areas to Accommodate Employees with Disabilities

By planning ahead when designing work areas, employers can easily accommodate employees with disabilities. Here are some tips for designing flexible work areas:

- **Use panel systems so that work spaces can be easily modified and work surface heights can be raised or lowered as needed.**
- **Install electronically controlled work surfaces and tables.**
- **Lower storage areas or install storage areas that are mobile.**
- **Install adjustable keyboard pads that adjust easily with little hand pressure.**
- **Install adjustable lighting with variable intensity that can add more or less light to the work space as needed.**

Source: Reprinted, by permission of publisher, from *HR Focus*, (1992, July). Some quick tips to make workspaces more flexible, *69*, 12–14.

A wide variety of accommodations is possible, and they can come from some surprising sources. For example, Kreonite, Inc., a small family-owned business (about 250 employees) that manufactures specialized photographic film, has been committed to employing persons with disabilities. Several of Kreonite's employees are deaf. Kreonite turned to a local not-for-profit training center for someone to teach sign language to its hearing employees. The training was free, and 30 Kreonite employees volunteered to attend.[58]

Some additional examples of potential reasonable accommodations that the EEOC has suggested are:[59]

- Reassigning marginal job duties.
- Modifying work schedules.
- Modifying examinations or training materials.

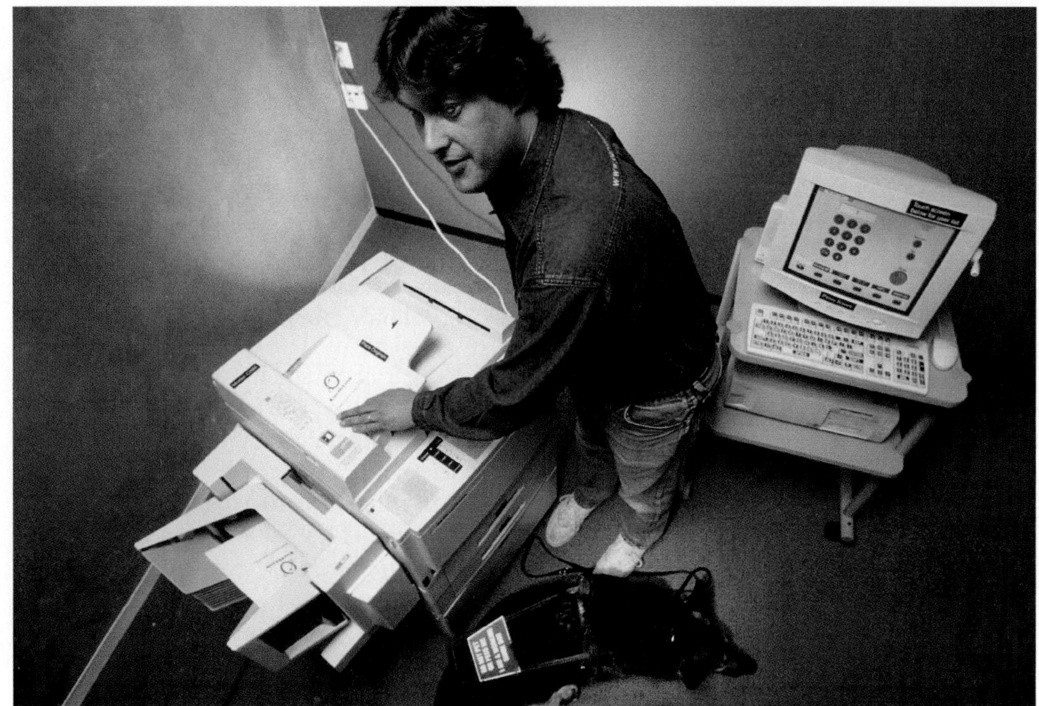

David Redman, a blind office worker, uses a braille-labeled copy machine that his employer purchased in order to provide a reasonable accommodation for him under the ADA.

- Providing qualified readers and interpreters.
- Permitting use of paid or unpaid leave for treatment.

As we noted earlier in the chapter, the main focus of the ADA and its accompanying regulations is the hiring process. However, the majority of complaints filed so far involves situations in which current employees have become disabled on the job. According to the EEOC, the total number of disability cases filed under the ADA in 2001 was 16,470. The two largest categories of cases were emotional and psychiatric impairments and back injuries, both of which are difficult to diagnose and treat.[60] Managers need to be prepared to deal with a set of issues not anticipated by the lawmakers and regulators who created and passed the ADA.

The Vocational Rehabilitation Act of 1973

The *Vocational Rehabilitation Act* is the precursor to the ADA. However, this act applied only to the federal government and its contractors. Like Executive Order 11246, the Vocational Rehabilitation Act not only prohibits discrimination (in this case, on the basis of disability) but also requires that the covered organizations have an affirmative action plan to promote the employment of disabled individuals. Familiarity with this law is useful to organizations attempting to comply with the ADA because it has led to over 20 years' worth of court and regulatory decisions based on the same central prohibition against disability-based discrimination.

The Vietnam Era Veterans Readjustment Act of 1974

One additional EEO law deserves brief mention. The *Vietnam Era Veterans Readjustment Act of 1974* prohibits discrimination against Vietnam-era veterans (those who served in the military between August 5, 1964, and May 7, 1975) by federal contractors. It also requires federal contractors to take affirmative action to hire Vietnam-era veterans.

EEO Enforcement and Compliance

The enforcement of EEO laws is the responsibility of the executive branch of government, which is headed by the president. In this section we describe the regulatory agencies that enforce the various EEO laws, as well as some of the plans that have been used to comply with affirmative action requirements.

Regulatory Agencies

Two agencies are primarily responsible for the enforcement of EEO law: the Equal Employment Opportunity Commission (EEOC) and the Office of Federal Contract Compliance Programs (OFCCP).

Equal Employment Opportunity Commission (EEOC)

Equal Employment Opportunity Commission (EEOC)
The federal agency responsible for enforcing EEO laws.

The **Equal Employment Opportunity Commission (EEOC),** which was created by Title VII, has three major functions. The first is processing discrimination complaints. The second is issuing written regulations. The third is information gathering and dissemination.[61]

In processing discrimination complaints, the EEOC follows a three-step process:

- **Investigation** An applicant or employee who thinks that he or she has been discriminated against begins the process by filing a complaint with the EEOC. The EEOC then notifies the company that a complaint has been filed, and the company becomes responsible for ensuring that any records relating to the complaint are kept safe. The EEOC usually finds itself with a backlog, so it may take up to two years to begin investigating the complaint. And the number of cases is rapidly accelerating, increasing 4.6 percent from 1989 to 1990 and 21.6 percent from 1992 to 1993.[62] In 2001, 80,840 cases were filed with the EEOC, compared to 62,100 in 1990.

  Of the 80,840 total charges filed with the EEOC in 2001, the common types of discrimination of all filings were:[63]
  - Race: 28,912 or 35.8%
  - Sex/Gender: 25,140 or 31.1%
  - Age: 17,405 or 21.5%
  - Disability: 16,470 or 20.4%
  - National Origin: 8,025 or 9.9%
  - Religion: 2,127 or 2.6%
  - Equal Pay: 1,251 or 1.5%

  The average processing time for private sector charge filings at the EEOC was 182 days in 2001, which is an improvement of 34 days over the previous year.

  After conducting the investigation, the EEOC determines if it is likely that the company did in fact violate one or more EEO laws. Complainants are always free to file a lawsuit, but the courts are unlikely to rule in their favor without the EEOC's backing.
- **Conciliation** If the EEOC finds that an EEO law was probably violated, it attempts to resolve the case through conciliation. **Conciliation** consists of negotiation among the three parties involved: the complainant, the employer, and the EEOC. The goal of conciliation is to reach a fair settlement while avoiding a trial.
- **Litigation** If conciliation is not possible, the EEOC can choose between two courses of action. The EEOC does not have the power to compel an employer to pay compensation or any other kind of damages; this can be done only as the result of a court's decision. Because pursuing a lawsuit is very expensive, the EEOC takes this course of action only in a relatively small percentage of cases. If the EEOC chooses not to pursue the case, it issues a right-to-sue letter to the complainant, who is then free to pursue court action with the blessing (if not the financial or legal support) of the EEOC.

Conciliation
An attempt to reach a negotiated settlement between the employer and an employee or applicant in an EEO case.

In addition to resolving complaints, the EEOC is responsible for issuing regulations and guidelines. These documents put "meat on the bones" of the individual laws. For instance, when the EEOC decided that sexual harassment was prohibited by Title VII, it issued regulations defining what sexual harassment is (see Figure 3.4) and what it expects employers to do in response to employee complaints of harassment. Similarly, when the ADA was signed into law in 1990, the EEOC was given the responsibility of issuing regulations that would inform employers exactly what they would (and would not) be expected to do to comply with the law. The EEOC Web site (www.EEOC.gov) also provides a list of its regulations. Figure 3.7 lists some of the most prominent EEOC regulations.

The EEOC also gathers information to monitor the hiring practices of organizations. It does this by requiring organizations with 100 or more employees to file an annual report (EEO-1) indicating the number of women and minorities who hold jobs in nine different job categories.

Figure 3.7

Principal EEOC Regulations

Sex discrimination guidelines
Questions and answers on pregnancy disability and reproductive hazards
Religious discrimination guidelines
National origin discrimination guidelines
Interpretations of the Age Discrimination in Employment Act
Employee selection guidelines
Questions and answers on employee selection guidelines
Sexual harassment guidelines
Record keeping and reports
Affirmative action guidelines
EEO in the federal government
Equal Pay Act interpretations
Policy statement on maternity benefits
Policy statement on relationship of Title VII to 1986 Immigration Reform and Control Act
Policy statement on reproductive and fetal hazards
Policy statement on religious accommodation under Title VII
Disability discrimination guidelines

Source: Adapted from Ledvinka, J., and Scarpello, V. G. (1991). *Federal regulation of personnel and human resource management* (2nd ed.). Boston: PWS-Kent. Reproduced with the permission of South-Western College Publishing.

The EEOC examines this information to identify patterns of discrimination that may exist in organizations.

Finally, the EEOC disseminates posters to employers. These posters explain to workers how to protect themselves from employment discrimination and how to file a complaint. The EEOC requires employers to display the posters in a prominent place (such as the company cafeteria).

Office of Federal Contract Compliance Programs (OFCCP)

The **Office of Federal Contract Compliance Programs (OFCCP)** is responsible for enforcing the laws and executive orders that apply to the federal government and its contractors. Specifically, it enforces Executive Order 11246 and the Vocational Rehabilitation Act, which both go beyond prohibiting discrimination to requiring affirmative action programs by covered employers.

Office of Federal Contract Compliance Programs (OFCCP)
The federal agency responsible for monitoring and enforcing the laws and executive orders that apply to the federal government and its contractors.

Many of the regulations written by the OFCCP are very similar to those issued by the EEOC. However, there are two major differences between the enforcement activities of the two agencies. First, in contrast to the EEOC, the OFCCP actively monitors compliance with its regulations. That is, it does not wait for an employee or applicant to file a complaint. Rather, it requires covered employers to submit annual reports on the state of their affirmative action program. Second, unlike the EEOC, the OFCCP has considerable enforcement power. Being a government contractor is considered a privilege, not a right. The OFCCP can take away that privilege if it determines that an employer is not complying with the law. It can also levy fines and other forms of punishment.

Affirmative Action Plans

An affirmative action plan is required of all government agencies and businesses that do a significant amount of work for the government. There are three steps to developing an affirmative action plan: conducting a utilization analysis, establishing goals and timetables, and determining action options.

Utilization Analysis

The first step in developing an affirmative action plan is conducting a *utilization analysis* to describe the organization's current work force relative to the pool of qualified workers in the labor force. There are two parts to conducting this analysis. The first involves determining the demographic composition of the current work force by dividing all the jobs in the organization into classifications. For instance, all management jobs are placed in one classification, all clerical and secretarial jobs in a second, all sales positions in a third, and so on. The percentage of persons from each protected class working in each of these classifications is then determined.

The second part is determining the percentage of those same protected classes in the available labor market. In gathering this information, organizations need to consider the eight different pieces of information listed in Figure 3.8. For instance, what percentage of qualified and available managers are women? What percentage are African Americans? What percentage are Asian Americans? The OFCCP offers guidelines for determining these figures. If the available figures are significantly higher than the currently employed in any category, the protected groups are said to be underutilized in that job category.

Goals and Timetables

The second step is setting goals and timetables for correcting underutilization. The OFCCP explicitly requires that rigid numerical quotas *not* be set. Rather, the employer should take into consideration the size of the underutilization, how fast the workforce turns over, and whether the work force is growing or contracting. Another consideration in setting goals and timetables is the types of actions the employer intends to take.

Action Plans

The final step in developing an affirmative action plan is deciding exactly what affirmative actions to take. The OFCCP suggests the following guidelines:

- Recruiting protected-class members.
- Redesigning jobs so that the underrepresented workers are more likely to be qualified.
- Providing specialized training sessions for underprepared applicants.
- Removing any unnecessary barriers to employment. For instance, a company located in an area not served by public transportation might consider providing van service from certain areas so that potential applicants who do not have reliable transportation can become employees.

The central concern for organizations is determining how much (if any) preference they should give to applicants who belong to an underutilized protected class. For instance, a few years ago there was a job opening in the transportation department of Santa Clara County, California. After going through the normal selection process, the candidates for promotion were ranked according to their performance on tests and in interviews. County rules allowed any of the top seven candidates to be chosen. The supervisors were poised to choose the employee ranked second—Paul Johnson, a white man. Diane Joyce, a white woman who was ranked fourth, called the county's affirmative action officer and ended up with the job.

Johnson filed suit. His argument was straightforward: Title VII prohibits discrimination based on sex, and he did not get the job because he is a man. This is a classic case of alleged **reverse discrimination,** discrimination that occurs as the result of an attempt to recruit and hire more people from the protected classes. In this case, the job classification to which the person was to be promoted had 238 positions, none of which were held by women. Johnson pursued his case all the way to the U.S. Supreme Court. In 1987 the Court ruled that Santa Clara County's decision was permissible.[64]

Reverse discrimination Discrimination against a nonprotected-class member resulting from attempts to recruit and hire members of protected classes.

The Supreme Court has decided over a dozen reverse discrimination cases since the first one in 1977.[65] Although the Court has favored the affirmative action strategy side of the tension outlined in Figure 3.1, almost all of these cases were decided by 6–3 or 5–4 margins. Because new justices are added to the Supreme Court fairly regularly, how these kind of cases will be decided in the future is very much an open question.

The United States is not the only country with affirmative action. Other countries have created similar policies to provide employment or educational opportunities for disadvantaged groups. For example, India has tried to improve the status of the untouchables, the lowest caste in its society, by providing them with preferential treatment in employment and education. This policy has had mixed results because it has enraged some members of the higher castes.

Figure 3.8

Components of an Eight-Factor Availability Analysis

Determine the percentage of protected-class members for each of the following groups of people:

- Local population
- Local unemployed workers
- Local labor force
- Qualified workers in the local labor market
- Qualified workers in the labor market from which you recruit
- Current employees who might be promoted into the job classification
- Graduates of local education and training programs that prepare people for this job classification
- Participants in training programs sponsored by the employer

Malaysia has favored the Islamic Malays over the Chinese (who on average are wealthier and more highly educated than the Malays) for jobs and higher education opportunities. Significant numbers of Chinese Malaysians have responded to this policy by emigrating to Asia and North America.[66] Other countries have disadvantaged groups in their population but have decided not to create employment policies favorable to these groups. For example, France has a large population of Algerians who have been historically disadvantaged, but it has avoided remedying the high Algerian unemployment rate with a policy similar to affirmative action in the United States. In Great Britain, the government's Commission for Racial Equality concluded that most British firms do little to ensure equal employment opportunity beyond verbal support for the idea.[67]

Other Important Laws

We have concentrated on equal employment opportunity laws in this chapter because they have a broad effect on almost all HR issues and, as such, are highly likely to influence managers' behavior. The other HR laws, listed in the Appendix to this chapter and discussed elsewhere in the book, are much more narrowly focused. These include laws that affect compensation and benefit plans (state workers' compensation laws, the Social Security Act, the Fair Labor Standards Act, the Employee Retirement and Income Security Act, the Consolidated Omnibus Budget Reconciliation Act, and the Family and Medical Leave Act), union–management relations (the Wagner Act, the Taft-Hartley Act, and the Landrum-Griffin Act), safety and health issues (the Occupational Safety and Health Act), and layoffs (the Worker Adjustment and Retraining Act).

Four laws not addressed elsewhere deserve brief mention. The *Immigration Reform and Control Act of 1986* was intended to reduce the inflow of illegal immigrants to the United States. The law has one provision that affects employers. To discourage the hiring of illegal immigrants, the law mandates that employers hire only people who can document that they are legally permitted to work in the United States. The Employment Eligibility Verification (I-9) form specifies which documents employers need to see from new employees. It appears that the major impact of the Immigration Reform and Control Act has been the creation of a market for fake documents.

A Question of Ethics

Is it ethical for a U.S. employer to require all employees to speak only English at the workplace?

The *Immigration Act of 1990* was legislated to make it easier for skilled immigrants to enter the United States. This law represents a modification of previous U.S. immigration policy, which favored immigrants who either (1) had family members who are U.S. citizens or (2) were leaving a country that was assigned a large quota of immigrants to the United States based on historical trends.[68]

The *Drug-Free Workplace Act of 1988* requires that government contractors try to ensure that their workplaces are free from drug use. Employers are required to prevent the use of illegal drugs at their work sites and to educate their employees about the hazards of drug use. While the law does not mandate drug testing, it—along with other more narrowly focused laws and regulations—has led to a general acceptance of drug testing, both of current employees and applicants, across the United States.[69] About 98 percent of *Fortune* 200 companies now conduct some form of drug testing.[70]

The *Uniformed Services Employment and Reemployment Rights Act of 1994* protects the rights of people who take short leaves from a private-sector employer to perform military service (such as reserve duty). The law protects these employees' seniority rights and benefits. It also protects them from employer discrimination in hiring, promotion, or layoff decisions.

Avoiding Pitfalls in EEO

The great majority of employees and job applicants in the United States fall into one or more protected classes. This means that almost any decision made by a manager that affects a worker's employment status can be challenged in a court of law. In most cases, sound management practices will not only help managers avoid EEO lawsuits but will also contribute to the organization's bottom line. Five specific management practices are recommended: providing training, establishing a complaint resolution process, documenting your decisions, being honest, and asking applicants only for information that you need to know.

Provide Training

One of the best ways to avoid EEO problems is to provide training. Two types of training are appropriate. First, the HR department should provide supervisors, managers, and executives with regular updates on EEO and other labor issues, since this area of law is in a constant state of flux.[71] The Supreme Court regularly decides cases that affect HR practice. Although managers can try to read periodicals or search the Web to obtain current information, most find their everyday demands too taxing to allow time for this. Regular, focused training sessions conducted by the HR department are the most efficient method of communicating this information to managers.

Second, employers should focus on communicating to employees their commitment to a discrimination-free work environment. For instance, all employees need to be instructed in what sexual harassment is, how to stop it before it becomes a problem, and what to do if it does become a problem. Honeywell has a council of employees with disabilities, one function of which is to promote awareness of disability issues throughout the company.[72]

Establish a Complaint Resolution Process

Every organization should establish a process for the internal resolution of EEO and other types of employee complaints. It is much less expensive to resolve these concerns if the EEOC, OFCCP, and legal counsel are not involved. More important, employee morale and satisfaction can be improved when employees are able to pass along their concerns to upper-level management. (We describe complaint resolution systems in detail in Chapters 13 and 15.)

Once in place, the complaint resolution process should be followed correctly. AT&T avoided liability in a sexual harrassment case because it was able to show that it had acted promptly to remedy the problem once management had been informed of it.[73] The Issues and Applications feature titled "Alternative Dispute Resolution Methods at Marriott and the EEOC" describes how Marriott and the EEOC have taken the lead in experimenting with new ways to resolve employee EEO complaints.

Issues and Applications

Alternative Dispute Resolution Methods at Marriott and the EEOC

Ron Wilensky, vice president for employee relations for Marriott International, was not satisfied with the company's "Guarantee of Fair Treatment" program, which instructed employees with complaints to go first to their immediate supervisor, then to the supervisor's manager, and so on up the ladder if necessary. Based on his experience with three *Fortune* 500 companies that had similar policies, he estimated that 75 percent of employees bypass such a policy and consult an attorney. To verify his hunch, he established a committee to examine employee satisfaction with the Guarantee of Fair Treatment. The results indicated that employees did not trust the policy. Instead, they wanted a system that would give those with grievances a chance to air their concerns before impartial listeners and have those concerns addressed promptly—without fear of retribution.

To give employees what they want, Wilensky and his committee have been experimenting with three dispute resolution systems.

1. **Mutual agreement through mediation** A neutral person, typically an expert in dispute resolution, meets with both parties to the conflict and tries to arrange a negotiated settlement. Since 80 to 90 percent of litigation is settled out of court anyway, the goal is to reduce attorney fees and other associated costs.
2. **A helping hot line** Wilensky found that it was difficult to track employee grievances across so many different geographical locations, so Marriott uses a toll-free 800-number hot line at 300 of its food service locations. Available 24 hours a day, 7 days per week, the hotline is intended to be used only to report cases of perceived wrongful discharge, discrimination, and harassment. Marriott promises to initiate an investigation within three days of receiving the complaint.
3. **A panel of peers** In 50 Marriott locations, employees have an opportunity to air their grievance before a panel of their peers. The panel is chosen at random from a group of specially trained volunteers. The panel has the authority to make final, binding decisions on all grievances brought before it.[A]

The EEOC also uses alternative dispute resolution systems. It relies on mediation to achieve faster resolution of its large backlog of cases. The EEOC chairwoman, Ida L. Castro, recently made a strong commitment to use mediation by increasing the mediation budget by $13 million in 1999 to expand the use of mediation in each EEOC district office.[B]

Source: [A]Wilensky, R., and Jones, K. M. (1994, March). Quick response key to resolving complaints. *HRMagazine*, 42–47. Reprinted with the permission of *HRMagazine*, published by the Society for Human Resource Management, Alexandria, VA; [B]Leonard, B. (1999, February). A new era at the EEOC. *HRMagazine*, 54–62.

Document Decisions

It is widely understood and accepted that all financial transactions and decisions need to be well documented. Documentation is necessary so that these decisions can be audited and summarized, problem areas identified, and solutions implemented.[74] The same rationale can be applied to decisions made about employees. The nature of any HR decision, and the rationale for it, should be clearly documented. Both the EEOC and OFCCP have certain reporting requirements. Employers that have a sound human resource information system in place do not find it difficult to comply with these requirements. One important type of documentation is performance appraisal. As we will see in Chapter 7, there are many good reasons for conducting appraisals, only one of which is to provide documentation in case of a lawsuit.

Nonetheless, the legal reason is an important one. In a discrimination case the generic charge is that the employer has based a decision in whole or in part on a non-job-related characteristic (age, sex, race, religion, and so on). The employer's generic defense is that it had a job-related reason for its decision. This defense is much easier to establish if the employer can provide written documentation to support its claim.

Be Honest

Typically, applicants and employees will not file an EEO complaint unless they think they have been mistreated. Perceptions of mistreatment often result from situations in which employees' or applicants' expectations have not been met. Imagine the following scenario: A 50-year-old employee has consistently received excellent performance evaluations over a 20-year period. He is then abruptly terminated by his manager for poor work performance. This employee is likely to file a lawsuit because over time he has developed the expectation that he is a valued

Figure 3.9

Subject of Question	Examples of Acceptable Questions	Examples of Unacceptable Questions	Comments
Name	"What is your name?" "Have you worked for this company under another name?"	"What was your maiden name?"	Questions about an applicant's name that may indicate marital status or national origin should be avoided.
Age	"Are you at least 18 years old?" "Upon employment, all employees must submit legal proof of age. Can you furnish proof of age?"	"What is your date of birth?" "What is your age?"	A request for age-related data may discourage older workers from applying.
Race, Ethnicity, and Physical Characteristics	"After employment, the company must have a photograph of all employees. If employed, can you furnish a photograph?" "Do you read, speak, or write a foreign language?"	"What is your race?" "What are your height and weight?" "Would you please submit a photograph with your application for identification purposes?" "What is the color of your hair? Your eyes?" "What language do you commonly use?" "How did you acquire your ability to read, write, or speak a foreign language?"	Information relative to physical characteristics may be associated with sexual or racial group membership.
Religion	A statement may be made by the employer of the days, hours, and shifts worked.	"What is your religious faith?" "Does your religion keep you from working on weekends?"	Questions that determine applicants' availability have an exclusionary effect because of some people's religious practices.
Gender, Marital Status, and Family	"If you are a minor, please list the name and address of a parent or guardian." "Please provide the name, address, and telephone number of someone who should be contacted in case of an emergency."	"What is your sex?" "Describe your current marital status." "List the number and ages of your children." "If you have children, please describe the provisions you have made for child care." "With whom do you reside?" "Do you have any dependents or relatives who should be contacted in case of an emergency?" "Do you prefer being referred to as Miss, Mrs., or Ms.?"	Direct or indirect questions about marital status, children, pregnancy, and childbearing plans frequently discriminate against women and may be a violation of Title VII.
Physical Conditions	"Are you willing to take a physical exam if the nature of the job for which you are applying requires one?"	"Do you have any physical disabilities, defects, or handicaps?" "How would you describe your general physical health?" "When was your last physical exam?"	A blanket policy excluding the disabled is discriminatory. Where physical condition is a requirement for employment, employers should be able to document the business necessity for questions on the application form relating to physical condition.

Examples of Acceptable and Unacceptable Questions Asked on Application Forms or During Interviews

Figure 3.9

Subject of Question	Examples of Acceptable Questions	Examples of Unacceptable Questions	Comments
Military Service	"Please list any specific educational or job experiences you may have acquired during military service that you believe would be useful in the job for which you are applying."	"Please list the dates and type of discharge you may have received from military service."	Minority service members have a higher percentage of undesirable military discharges. A policy of rejecting those with less than an honorable discharge may be discriminatory.
Hobbies, Clubs, and Organizations	"Do you have any hobbies that are related to the job for which you are making application?" "Please list any clubs or organizations in which you are a member that relate to the job for which you are applying."	"Please list any hobbies you may have." "Please list all clubs and other organizations in which you are a member."	If questions on club/organization memberships are asked, a statement should be added that applicants may omit those organizations associated with age, race, sex, or religion.
Credit Rating	None.	"Do you own your own car?" "Do you own or rent your residence?"	Use of credit rating questions tends to have an adverse impact on minority group applicants and has been found unlawful. Unless shown to be job-related, questions on car ownership, home ownership, length of residence, garnishments of wages, etc., may violate Title VII.
Arrest Record	"Have you ever been convicted of a crime related to the job you will be expected to perform?" Example: A conviction of embezzlement is related to the job of bank loan officer.	"Have you ever been arrested for a crime?"	Asking if an applicant has ever been arrested violates the applicant's Title VII rights because such questions adversely affect minority applicants.

Source: Adapted from Gatewood, R. D., and Feild, H. S. (2001). *Human resource selection*, 5th ed. Fort Worth, TX: Harcourt College Publishers. Copyright © 2001 by the Harcourt College Publishers, reproduced by permission of the publisher and Bland, T., and Stalcup, S. (1999, March). Build a legal employment application. *HRMagazine*, 129–133.

employee, and he now believes that the only possible reason for his termination is his age. While it may be painful in the short term, providing honest feedback to employees is a good management practice that may reduce legal problems in the long run.

Ask Only for Information You Need to Know

Major sources of potential lawsuits are the application and interview phases of the hiring process. The general rule is that companies should ask only for information that is related to job performance. For instance, you should not ask about an applicant's religious affiliation, although you may ask if a person can work on specific days of the week. Similarly, you can ask if the applicant is capable of performing the essential physical aspects of the job (preferably specifically listed), but asking general questions about health would probably be interpreted as a violation of the ADA. Figure 3.9 gives several more examples of appropriate and inappropriate questions to ask on an application form or during an interview.

Summary and Conclusions

Why Understanding the Legal Environment Is Important

Understanding and complying with human resource law is important because (1) it is the right thing to do, (2) it helps you realize the limitations of your firm's HR and legal departments, and (3) it helps you minimize your firm's potential liability.

Challenges to Legal Compliance

HR law is challenging for four reasons. Laws, regulations, and court decisions are all part of a dynamic legal landscape. The laws and regulations are complex. The strategies for fair employment required by the laws and regulations sometime compete with, rather than reinforce, one another. And laws often have unanticipated or unintended consequences.

Equal Employment Opportunity Laws

The following are the most important EEO laws: (1) Equal Pay Act of 1963—prohibits discrimination in pay between men and women performing the same job in the same organization. (2) Title VII of the Civil Rights Act of 1964—prohibits employers from basing employment decisions on a person's race, color, religion, sex, or national origin. It has been amended or interpreted to prohibit discrimination based on pregnancy (the Pregnancy Discrimination Act of 1978) and sexual harassment. Most recently, it has been amended by the Civil Rights Act of 1991, which places the burden of proof in a discrimination case squarely on the defendant (employer), prohibits the use of quotas, and allows for punitive and compensatory damages as well as jury trials. Executive Order 11246 prohibits discrimination against the same categories of people that Title VII protects but also requires that government agencies and contractors take affirmative action to promote the employment of persons in protected classes. (3) Age Discrimination in Employment Act of 1967—prohibits discrimination against employees who are 40 years old or older. (4) Americans with Disabilities Act of 1990—prohibits discrimination against individuals with disabilities who can perform the essential functions of a job with or without reasonable accommodation. The Vocational Rehabilitation Act of 1973, the precursor to ADA, applied only to government agencies and contractors. (5) Vietnam Era Veterans Readjustment Act of 1974—prohibits discrimination against Vietnam-era veterans by federal contractors and requires federal contractors to take affirmative action to hire Vietnam-era veterans.

EEO Enforcement and Compliance

Two main agencies are responsible for enforcing EEO laws. The Equal Employment Opportunity Commission (EEOC) enforces EEO laws. It processes discrimination complaints, issues written regulations, and gathers and disseminates information. The Office of Federal Contract Compliance Programs (OFCCP) enforces the laws and executive orders that apply to the federal government and its contractors. The OFCCP also monitors the quality and effectiveness of affirmative action plans.

Other Important Laws

The Immigration Reform and Control Act of 1986 requires employers to document the legal work status of their employees. The Immigration Act of 1990 makes it easier for skilled immigrants to enter the United States. The Drug-Free Workplace Act of 1988 requires that government contractors try to ensure that their workplaces are free of drug use. The Uniformed Services Employment and Reemployment Act of 1994 protects the rights of private sector employees who take short leaves to perform military service.

Avoiding Pitfalls in EEO

Employers can avoid many pitfalls associated with HR law by engaging in sound management practices. Among the most important of these practices are training, establishing an employee complaint resolution system, documenting decisions, communicating honestly with employees, and asking job applicants only for information the employer needs to know.

Key Terms

adverse impact, 91
affirmative action, 89
Age Discrimination in Employment Act (1967), 100
Americans with Disabilities Act (1990), 100
bona fide occupational qualification (BFOQ), 93
compensatory damages, 99
conciliation, 104
discrimination, 91
disparate treatment, 91
Equal Employment Opportunity Commission (EEOC), 104
Equal Pay Act (1963), 90
essential functions, 101
executive order, 99
fair employment, 89
four-fifths rule, 93
hostile work environment sexual harassment, 95
individuals with disabilities, 100
Office of Federal Contract Compliance Programs (OFCCP), 105
protected class, 91
punitive damages, 99
quid pro quo sexual harassment, 95
quotas, 99
reasonable accommodation, 101
reverse discrimination, 106
Title VII (Civil Rights Act of 1964), 90

Discussion Questions

1. Why should managers be concerned with understanding HR law instead of leaving it to the experts?
2. Explain why HR decisions are heavily regulated. Based on your analysis of current social forces, what new laws or regulations do you think will be passed or issued in the next few years?
3. You own a small construction business. One of your workers is 55 years old and had heart bypass surgery about six months ago. He wants to come back to work, but you are concerned that he will not be able to handle the job's physical tasks. What should you do? What are you prohibited from doing? What laws apply in this case?
4. What three steps are involved in developing an affirmative action program? How much flexibility does an employer have in developing the specific points in such a program?
5. What is adverse impact? How does it differ from adverse treatment?
6. Should employers have a policy that prevents employees from dating each other? Would such a policy be legal? Would it be ethical?
7. How can an individual show prima facie evidence for adverse impact discrimination? How would an employer defend itself from this evidence?
8. Suppose you are a plant manager and one of your employees has trouble controlling his anger and experiences wide swings in emotions due to bipolar disorder (a medical condition). You are aware that he has been under the treatment of a psychiatrist. This employee recently threatened other employees with violence and you placed him on leave until his psychiatrist indicates to you that his emotional condition has stabilized. Can the angry employee use the ADA to seek a reasonable accommodation and get reinstated to his job or a modified one? If you need further information to assess this issue, what information would that be?
9. What are bona fide occupational qualifications (BFOQ)? What is a business necessity? Can race be a BFOQ? Can it be a business necessity? Why or why not?
10. "Sexual harassment is a problem that occurs between two employees. The company should not be held liable for the actions of misbehaving employees." Do you agree or disagree? Explain your answer.
11. Many companies in the United States have recently put an end to the practice of giving an annual employee Christmas party due to complaints by employees with non-Christian religious backgrounds or spiritual values who claimed the Christmas party was a discriminatory employment practice. These dissident employees argued that the employer who celebrated by paying for an employee Christmas party favored Christianity over other religions and belief systems. Do you think non-Christian employees are treated illegally or unethically when the employer decides to give a Christmas party for all the employees? What is the basis of your decision? What would be a reasonable accommodation that an employer could make to satisfy both the Christian and non-Christian employees?

There is a variety of additional material available on the Web site that accompanies this text. You can access this information by visiting the Web site at **www.prenhall.com/gomez.**

Emerging Trends Case 3.1

YOU MANAGE IT!

The Importance of Tolerance in the Workplace After the Events of September 11

The September 11, 2001, attacks on the World Trade Center in New York and the Pentagon in Washington, DC, motivated the need to protect the workplace from discrimination based on religious and ethnic origins of employees. The EEOC has reported a significant increase in the number of charges of alleged discrimination based on religion and/or national origin. Many of the charges have been filed by individuals who are perceived to be Muslim, Arab, South Asian, or Sikh. These charges commonly allege harassment and discharge.

Title VII of the Civil Rights Act of 1964 prohibits workplace discrimination based on religion, ethnicity, country of origin, race, and color. Such discrimination is prohibited in any aspect of employment, including recruitment, hiring, promotion, benefits, training, job duties, and termination.

Workplace harassment is also prohibited by Title VII. In addition, an employer must provide a reasonable accommodation for religious practices unless doing so would result in undue hardship.

Read the following situations regarding hiring and employment decisions and answer the questions that follow:

Incident 1: Wearing a Head Scarf on a Temporary Assignment

Susan is an experienced clerical worker who wears a hijab (head scarf) in conformance with her Muslim beliefs. ABC Temps places Susan in a long-term assignment with one of its clients. The client contacts ABC and requests that it instruct Susan to remove her hijab while working at the front desk, or ABC must provide a person who does not need to wear the hijab at work, effectively displacing Susan from her job. According to the client, Susan's religious attire violates the firm's dress code and presents the "wrong image" because it is a very conservative firm. Should ABC comply with its client's request?

Incident 2: Religious Accommodation for Prayer

Three of the 10 Muslim employees in X-Cell Instruments' 30-person template design division approach their manager and ask that they be allowed to use a conference room in an adjacent building for prayer. Until making the request, those employees prayed at their work stations. What should the manager at X-Cell Instruments do?

Incident 3: Is It Harassment or Joking?

Muhammad, who is Arab American, works for Friendly Motors, a large used car business. Muhammad meets with his manager and complains that Bill, one of his co-workers, regularly calls him names like "the ayatollah," "the local terrorist," and "camel jockey," and has intentionally embarrassed him in front of customers by claiming he is incompetent. When confronted with these allegations, Bill claimed he was just joking with Muhammad, that he dubs co-workers with names such as "shorty," "dude," and "stinky," and has never had any complaints from them. Instead they are amused by Bill's colorful names. How should the manager deal with this situation?

Critical Thinking Questions

1. In incident 1, does it make a difference whether ABC Temps or the client asks Susan to remove her head scarf? What should ABC Temps do if the client refuses to withdraw its request that Susan not wear the head scarf at its office?
2. In incident 2, if the conference room is needed for business purposes, can the manager at X-Cell deny the use of the room for religious purposes? What would be an appropriate accommodation to the Muslim employees so they are able to conduct their prayers if the conference room is almost always used for business meetings?
3. In incident 3, should the manager accept Bill's defense, that he was only joking and that Muhammad needs to lighten up and learn to appreciate the American sense of humor, where nicknames are part of having fun at the workplace? When does a joke stop being funny and turn into a case of harassment?

Team Exercise

Assume you are a manager in a company and you noticed a significant increase in complaints by Arab and Muslim employees that they are being harassed and shunned by the other employees. With three or four of your fellow classmates develop an approach to deal with this pattern of hostile employee behavior toward Arab and Muslim employees. Should harassment be treated as a "special case" as a consequence of the U.S. president's war on terrorism, or should it be treated as any other instance of harassment? Make sure you are able to defend your approach.

Source: The U.S. Equal Employment Opportunity Commission (2002, May 14).

Questions and answers about employer responsibilities concerning the employment of Muslims, Arabs, South Asians, and Sikhs. www.eeoc.gov/facts/backlash-employer.html; *HR Focus*. (2001, November). The growing importance of tolerance in the workplace, 3–5.

YOU MANAGE IT! Discussion Case 3.2

Does the ADA Protect the Rights of Able-Bodied Applicants, Too?

Can an able-bodied job applicant seek protection under the Americans with Disabilities Act (ADA)? An appeals court recently ruled that a job applicant does not need to be disabled to apply for the protection of the ADA.

When an applicant interviewed for a position as a grinder with an Oklahoma steel firm, an initial interviewer allegedly told him that he was the best-qualified candidate for the job. The applicant was then asked to fill out an application form that questioned whether he had ever received worker's compensation or if he had physical defects that precluded him from performing certain jobs. He answered the first question with a number of details regarding past injuries but left the second question blank. The applicant was not given the job and he sued the company for violating the ADA. Initially, the lower court determined that he had no standing under the law because he was not disabled.

However, the court of appeals disagreed. The court pointed out that the ADA's purpose is to prevent all preemployment questions that would identify and exclude persons with disabilities. However, the ADA does not limit the prohibition on preemployment inquiries to people with disabilities. Even if the applicant was not disabled, the questions on the application were improper, and the applicant was harmed as a result. Therefore, the court held that the applicant could sue for discrimination under the ADA.

Critical Thinking Questions

1. After reading this case, when do you think is the appropriate time for a manager to ask a job applicant health and medical questions?
2. Review the text discussion and this case. Do you think employers have a right to screen out job applicants who have disabilities that could limit their job performance? For example, should a building contractor have the right to screen out job applicants with back problems so he or she can select employees who are able to perform physically demanding labor, such as lifting heavy building materials? Do you think a building contractor can require a job applicant to pass a physical exam to work on a construction job? If so, when should the medical exam be given?

Team Exercise

With a group of five of your fellow students identify a specific job in which the work takes place under strenuous working conditions, such as offshore oil drilling laborer, fisherman on an Alaskan fishing boat, wildfire crew member for the U.S. Forest Service, driver of an 18-wheel tractor trailer truck that transports perishable foods over long distances, or lifeguard at a California public beach on the Pacific Ocean. Your task is to develop some useful questions that can be used in an interview to screen out candidates who do not have the physical strength or energy level to effectively perform physically demanding work. With your team members carefully examine each question to make sure it does not violate the ADA or other employment laws that protect the employee rights described in this chapter. Refer to some of the examples of acceptable and unacceptable questions asked in interviews or application forms in Figure 3.9. When you are finished, be prepared to share your interview screening questions that relate to the job with your instructor and other classmates.

Source: Adapted from Long, S. E. (1999, March). Able applicant can protest medical questions. *HR Focus*, 3.

Emerging Trends Case 3.3 — YOU MANAGE IT!

Are Women Breaking Through the Glass Ceiling?

"Glass ceiling" refers to invisible or artificial barriers that prevent women and people of color from advancing above a certain level in an organization. It describes the situation in which women are greatly underrepresented in the top-management ranks in American corporations as well as organizations in other countries. In the United States, women represent 30 percent of all managers but less than 5 percent of executives.

The glass ceiling does not represent a typical form of discrimination that consists of entry barriers to women and minorities within organizations. Rather, it represents a subtle form of discrimination that includes gender stereotypes, lack of opportunities for women to gain job experiences necessary for advancement, and lack of top-management commitment to providing resources to promote initiatives that support an environment for women to advance to the top executive ranks.

As an invisible barrier, the glass ceiling is difficult to crash through legislation. Informal networking and mentoring are often mentioned as ways of increasing opportunities for women to become executives. However, cross-gender relationships between a male mentor and a female employee may be discouraged by the sexual tensions that arise in such relationships, because they can become close, blurring the distinction between their professional and personal lives. In some instances, a mentoring relationship with a younger female may threaten the established male with the potential for a career-wrecking allegation of sexual harassment in which the woman is viewed as the victim because she ranks lower in the hierarchy. While same-gender female mentoring relationships are less likely to be as problematic as the cross-gender ones, they depend on the availability of senior female executives willing and able to nurture high-potential women. Because some senior women who have made it to the top can be resentful of junior women who appear to be having an easier time in their career advancement, pioneering women who made it to the top are not always willing to become mentors.

Despite the glass ceiling, by 2002 the number of women who achieved the position of chief executive officer (CEO) or chairman of a major *Fortune* 500 corporation in the United States was much greater than the number of women as top executives in large corporations in 1997. During 2002, here are some women executives who have clearly broken through the glass ceiling:

- Carly Fiorina, CEO of Hewlett-Packard
- Andrea Jung, CEO of Avon, a large cosmetics firm
- Charlotte Beers, chairman of J. Walter Thompson, one of the world's largest advertising firms
- Patricia Russo, CEO of Lucent Technologies
- Anne Mulcahy, CEO and chairman of Xerox
- Oprah Winfrey, chairman of Harpo Entertainment Group
- Marjorie Scardino, CEO of Pearson

Critical Thinking Questions

1. Go to the Web sites of Avon (www.Avon.com), Lucent Technologies (www.lucent.com), Hewlett-Packard (www.hp.com), and Xerox (www.xerox.com) and explore those sites to learn more about the women who are either the CEO or chairperson at these companies. Several of the Web sites have a "biography of executives" feature to click on to learn more about the CEO and other top executives. Another possibility is to use a search engine such as Yahoo! and search on the company name and name of the CEO or chairperson to gather some background on the careers of executive women. Based on the information you gather, develop a rationale to explain how these women overcame the "glass ceiling" and attained the top executive role in a major U.S. corporation.
2. Some male senior executives avoid becoming mentors to younger women because of their fear of possible sexual harassment claims against them (as retribution for a romantic relationship that ends badly) or office gossip suggesting the mentoring pair are having a romance. Do you think it is reasonable for male executives to have fears about what could evolve or be suggested about professional relationships with female managers? How could a woman seeking a mentor go about cultivating a mentoring relationship with a male senior executive, being aware that some men have reservations about establishing close professional relationships with women due to office gossip or the possibility of a romantic relationship that results in the male having to defend himself against charges of sexual harassment?

Team Exercise

With a team of four or five students, develop an HR plan to break down some of the glass ceiling barriers in an organization that is male dominated at the upper ranks. Some examples of male-dominated industries include high technology (Intel, Texas Instruments, and Cisco Systems, for example), defense (Boeing, Lockheed Martin, and General Dynamics, for example), and energy (Exxon, BP-Amoco, and Chevron, for example). Think of specific HR activities that could "add value" to the firm by breaking down barriers to women who are seeking to become executives in the organization. Some HR functions that could provide fruitful sources include training, recruitment and selection, compensation, benefits, work systems, HR planning, performance appraisal, employee relations, and discipline. Be prepared to present and defend your plan to other members of your class.

Sources: Bell, M., McLaughlin, M., and Sequeira, J. (2002, April). Discrimination, harassment, and the glass ceiling: Women executives as change agents. *Journal of Business Ethics*, 65–76; and Haben, M. (2001, April/May). Shattering the glass ceiling. *Executive Speeches*, 4–10.

YOU MANAGE IT! Discussion Case 3.4

Applying EEO Laws to Management Decisions

This exercise is designed to help you increase your skills in applying EEO laws and regulations to some situations similar to those you may face as a manager who is expected to be responsive to employees' concerns. Read the following two situations and be prepared to answer the questions that follow.

Incident 1: The Obese Employee

The service department of Computer Universe maintained the computers for many small and large businesses in the area. The large clients who provided lucrative contracts were given special attention and service. One such client demanded a change in the specialist who serviced its computers.

Fran Stone, the computer service manager, was dumbfounded when a large client demanded that John Zurn be removed from the account. When Fran asked why, the client claimed that John was incompetent. When she asked the client to elaborate on the claim, the true reason emerged. Forced to answer, the client said, "That fat slob couldn't service my chair." To avoid the loss of this account, Fran assigned another service specialist to replace John.

John Zurn took great pride in his work and was pleased with the list of prestigious clients he worked for. He enjoyed his work and got along fine with everyone but was constantly uneasy about his weight. At 5 feet, 8 inches, he weighed 350 pounds. To help cope with his concerns, John joined the National Association to Advance Fat Acceptance. He is now convinced more than ever that fat people can be excellent at whatever they do. Fran's decision to remove John from this prestigious account is a serious setback for John's newfound confidence.

Incident 2: Was the Pregnant Teacher Unfairly Treated?

An assistant professor of management, Jane Mangalo, in her third year of an initial three-year appointment was reappointed for another three years. However, the university's personnel committee, consisting of elected faculty from different disciplines, wrote in her letter of reappointment that she needed to work on improving her teaching performance. The same committee will decide whether to grant her tenure during the last year of her second three-year appointment.

Jane Mangalo was extremely angered by the negative reference to her teaching performance in the letter of reappointment. She had received excellent ratings from students in all but one semester. During that semester, she was pregnant and suffered from such severe nausea and weakness that she had to use an intravenous line continuously and to sit in one place in the classroom, which prevented her from writing on the blackboard or using the projector as she led case discussions.

The problem went away after she had the baby. However, apparently, some students complained about how she taught the class that semester. Jane believed that she did the university a favor by teaching rather than going on disability leave and that the negative reference to her teaching performance in the letter of reappointment constituted discrimination against the disabled.

When the committee found evidence of weak teaching performance in one semester, it decided to include in Jane's reappointment letter the standard phrase used in such cases, encouraging her to work on improving her teaching performance. When the committee wrote the letter, it was unaware of Jane's condition during the sole semester in which the evidence of weak teaching performance appeared. Although Jane's temporary medical problem was mentioned in the portfolio of materials that the committee reviewed, the reference to it was overlooked.

Critical Thinking Questions

1. In incident 1, is an obese employee protected by any of the EEO laws? Do you think that John's work reassignment was job-related or due to discriminatory treatment? Support your conclusion.
2. In incident 2, is a pregnant employee protected by any of the EEO laws or other laws of the workplace? Which one(s)? Do you think that Jane's performance evaluation was fair or that she was a victim of discrimination? Support your conclusions.
3. Suppose you are a manager in incident 1. How would you have handled the situation when the client complained about John's obesity?
4. Assume you are the department chairperson in incident 2. How would you explain to Jane the committee's assessment that her teaching needs improvement?

Team Exercise

Work in a small group of three to four students to discuss the following questions:

- Should physical appearance matter in making employment decisions such as work assignments, pay raises, or performance reviews?
- Should a company have a policy that explicitly protects the rights of people who are obese, are physically unattractive, or have nontraditional appearances (having characteristics of both sexes such as a transsexual or a cross-dresser, for example)?
- What are the pros and cons of such a policy?

Source: Adapted from Powell, G. N. (1984), *Gender and diversity in the workplace*. Thousand Oaks, CA: Sage Publications, pp. 118–119, 130–131.

Appendix to Chapter 3

Human Resource Legislation Discussed in This Text

The laws are listed in chronological order.

Law	Year	Description	Chapter(s)
Workers' Compensation Laws	Various	State-by-state laws that establish insurance plans to compensate employees injured on the job	12, 15, 16
Social Security Act	1935	Payroll tax to fund retirement benefits, disability and unemployment insurance	12
Wagner Act	1935	Legitimized labor unions and established the National Labor Relations Board	14, 15
Fair Labor Standards Act	1938	Established minimum wage and overtime pay	10, 15
Taft-Hartley Act	1947	Provided some protections for employers and limited union power; permitted states to enact right-to-work laws	15
Landrum-Griffin Act	1959	Protects union members' right to participate in union affairs	15
Equal Pay Act	1963	Prohibits unequal pay for same job	3, 10
Title VII of Civil Rights Act	1964	Prohibits employment decisions based on race, color, religion, sex, and national origin	3, 4, 5, 7, 14, 16, 17
Executive Order 11246	1965	Same as Title VII; also requires affirmative action	3
Age Discrimination in Employment Act	1967	Prohibits employment decisions based on age when person is 40 or older	3, 5
Occupational Safety and Health Act	1970	Establishes safety and health standards for organizations to protect employees	14, 16
Employee Retirement Income Security Act (ERISA)	1974	Regulates the financial stability of employee benefit and pension plans	12, 16
Job Training Partnership Act	1982	Provides block money grants to states, which pass them on to local governments and private entities that provide on-the-job training	8
Vietnam-Era Veterans Readjustment Act	1974	Prohibits federal contractors from discriminating against Vietnam-era veterans and encourages affirmative action plans to hire Vietnam veterans	3
Pregnancy Discrimination Act	1978	Prohibits employers from discriminating against pregnant women	3, 16
Consolidated Omnibus Budget Reconciliation Act (COBRA)	1985	Requires continued health insurance coverage (paid by employee) following termination	12
Immigration Reform and Control Act	1986	Prohibits discrimination based on citizenship status; employers required to document employees' legal work status	3, 17
Worker Adjustment and Retraining Act (WARN)	1988	Employers required to notify workers of impending layoffs	6
Drug-Free Workplace Act	1988	Covered employers must implement certain policies to restrict employee drug use	3, 16
Americans with Disabilities Act (ADA)	1990	Prohibits discrimination based on disability	3, 4, 5, 14, 16
Civil Rights Act	1991	Amends Title VII; prohibits quotas, allows for monetary punitive damages	3, 5
Family and Medical Leave Act	1993	Employers must provide unpaid leave for childbirth, adoption, illness	12, 15
Uniformed Services Employment and Reemployment Rights Act	1994	Employers must not discriminate against individuals who take leave from work to fulfill military service obligations	3

Law	Year	Description	Chapter(s)
Health Insurance Portability and Accountability Act	1996	Employees are allowed to transfer their coverage of existing illnesses to new employer's insurance plan	12

Laws discussed briefly:

Byrnes Antistrikebreaking Act—Chapter 15
Coal Mine Health and Safety Act—Chapters 4, 16
Employee Polygraph Protection Act—Chapter 5
Immigration Act of 1990—Chapter 3
Norris-LaGuardia Act—Chapter 15
Older Workers Benefit Protection Act of 1990—Chapter 3
Railway Labor Act—Chapter 15

Managing Diversity

Challenges

After reading this chapter, you should be able to deal more effectively with the following challenges:

1. **Link** affirmative action programs to employee diversity programs to ensure that the two support each other.
2. **Identify** the forces that contribute to the successful management of diversity within the firm.
3. **Reduce** potential conflict among employees resulting from cultural clashes and misunderstandings.
4. **Draw** a profile of employee groups that are less likely to be part of the corporate mainstream and develop policies specifically targeted to these groups' needs.
5. **Implement** HR systems that assist the firm in successfully managing diversity.

The second-grade schoolteacher posed a simple problem to the class: "There are four blackbirds sitting in a tree. You take a slingshot and shoot one of them. How many are left?"

"Three," answered the seven-year-old European with certainty. "One subtracted from four leaves three."

"Zero," answered the seven-year-old African with equal certainty. "If you shoot one bird, the others will fly away."

Which child answered correctly? Clearly, the answer depends on your cultural point of view. For the first child, the birds in the problem represented a hypothetical situation that required a literal answer. For the second child, the birds in the problem had a relationship to known behavior that could be expected to occur.[1]

THE MANAGERIAL PERSPECTIVE

To succeed as a manager in the twenty-first century, you must work effectively with people who are different from you. The labor force is becoming more diverse in terms of ethnicity, race, sex, sexual orientation, disability, and other cultural factors. The managerial challenge is learning how to take advantage of this diversity while fostering cooperation and cohesiveness among dissimilar employees. The HR department may help you meet this challenge by developing training programs, offering assistance and advice, establishing fair selection procedures, and the like. But in the end, the line manager is the person who interacts face-to-face with diverse employees on a daily basis. In this chapter we explore diversity issues that affect managers and the skills needed to make employee diversity a source of competitive advantage.

The blackbird story clearly illustrates one of the most important truths of HRM: People with different life experiences may interpret reality very differently. By the time people enter an organization, their *cognitive structure*—the way they perceive and respond to the world around them—has been largely determined. This cognitive structure is shaped both by unique personal experiences (with family, peers, school system) and by the socializing influences of the person's culture, and it operates both at home and in the workplace.

Managing workforce diversity in a way that both respects the employee and promotes a shared sense of corporate identity and vision is one of the greatest challenges facing organizations today. In this chapter we examine what diversity is, what its challenges are, and how to manage it. By the end of the chapter, you will understand diversity issues better and have some ideas of how to handle them successfully.

What Is Diversity?

Although definitions vary, **diversity** simply refers to human characteristics that make people different from one another. The English language has well over 23,000 words to describe personality[2] (such as "outgoing," "intelligent," "friendly," "loyal," "paranoid," and "nerdy"). The sources of individual variation are complex, but they can generally be grouped into two categories: those over which people have little or no control and those over which they have some control.[3]

Diversity
Human characteristics that make people different from one another.

Individual characteristics over which a person has little or no control include biologically determined characteristics such as race, sex, age, and certain physical attributes, as well as the family and society into which he or she is born. These factors exert a powerful influence on individual identity and directly affect how a person relates to other people.

In the second category are characteristics that people can adopt, drop, or modify during their lives through conscious choice and deliberate efforts. These include work background, income, marital status, military experience, political beliefs, geographic location, and education.

It is important to keep in mind the distinction between the sources of diversity and the diversity itself. Without this distinction, stereotyping tends to occur. Essentially, stereotyping is assuming that group averages or tendencies are true for each and every member of that group. For instance, employees who have had significant military experience are generally more accepting of an authoritarian management style than those who have not had such experience. However, if you conclude that *all* veterans favor authoritarian leadership, you will be wrong. While veterans *on average* are more accepting of authority, there may be, as Figure 4.1 (page 122) shows, very wide differences among veterans on this score. True, veterans *on the whole* show this characteristic to a greater degree than nonveterans, but the differences *within* each group are far greater than the average difference between groups. In fact, many veterans develop a distaste for authoritarian management *because* of their military experience, and many nonveterans prefer an authoritarian leadership style.

If you take this example and substitute any two groups (male-female, young-old, and so on) and any individual characteristic (aggressiveness, flexibility, amount of education), you will find in the vast majority of cases that the principle illustrated by Figure 4.1 holds true. In fact, it is

Group Versus Individual Differences on Acceptance of Authoritarian Leadership

Figure 4.1

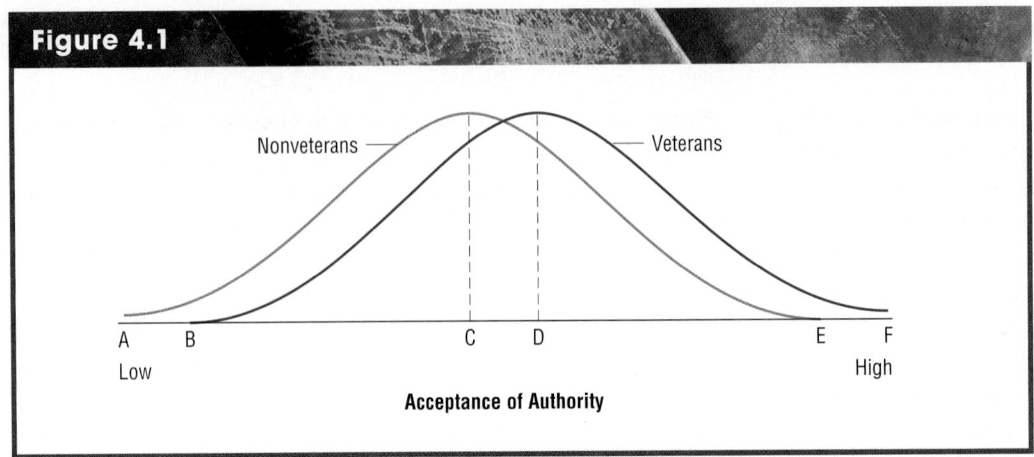

very difficult to identify individual characteristics that do *not* have a substantial overlap between two groups. The main point of this discussion is to emphasize that while employees are diverse, a relatively small amount of this diversity is explained by their group membership.

As we proceed through this chapter, we will point out some characteristics that are typical of specific groups. Such depictions are both valuable and dangerous. They are valuable because they alert managers to diversity in their employees. But they are dangerous because it is very easy to fall into the trap of assuming that a group tendency is true of all individual employees. The effective manager sees his or her employees as individuals, not as members of a particular group. As we saw in Chapter 3, it is illegal to base employment decisions on certain group characteristics. These laws merely codify an important principle of effective management: Treat people as individuals, not as representatives of a group.

Why Manage Employee Diversity?

Unless effectively managed, the presence of diversity among employees may create misunderstandings that have a negative impact on productivity and teamwork. It may also result in overt or subtle discrimination by those who control organizational resources against those who do not fit into the dominant group.

In addition to being illegal, excluding certain people from participation in an organization because of their group membership is counterproductive because it prevents effective people from contributing to or remaining with the organization. Consider Chris Powell, a young African American man. After graduating from college, he landed a sales job at Ford Motor Company. Eager to advance, he often asked his supervisors for feedback. "I'd go and seek their counsel, but they would just say I was doing a fine job and should keep on doing it," Powell says. "No one offered any advice on how to get to the next step."

Then Powell's division was asked to push a slow-selling car. One of Powell's white co-workers learned that Ford was offering some promotion money to help salespeople with the sales pitch. The co-worker tapped into the fund and won the contest. "That information came from someone who was watching out for him—and it gave him the edge," says a disappointed Mr. Powell. After three years at Ford, with no promotion in sight, Powell quit.[4]

To survive and prosper in an increasingly heterogeneous society, organizations must capitalize on employee diversity as a source of competitive advantage. For example, Computer Associates International hires software developers from many nationalities, filling jobs where there is an extreme shortage of personnel.[5] Because many of these employees are non-English speakers, Computer Associates offers free courses in English as a second language.[6] Avon Products provides another example of how firms capitalize on diversity. Avon uses its diversity to create a competitive advantage, using feedback from its workforce to adapt to women's changing needs quickly and effectively. The input of Avon's minority employees—almost one-third of its workforce—helped the firm find a successful niche in an industry that tends to ignore the beauty needs of women of color.[7] ATT provides formal recognition and support to employee networks formed around a characteristic of diversity (such as the Asian Pacific Islanders' Business Resource Group) if the networks present a business plan to management showing their value to the company.[8]

Affirmative Action Versus Managing Employee Diversity

Many people perceive *management of diversity* as a new label for affirmative action. In reality, these are two very distinct concepts.[9] *Affirmative action* first emerged from government pressures on business to provide greater opportunities for women and minorities. **Management of diversity,** in contrast, recognizes that traditional firms, where white men are the majority, are becoming a thing of the past. There is a growing awareness that a key factor in corporate performance is how well *nontraditional employees* such as women and minorities can be fully integrated and work effectively with one another and with their white male counterparts. For this reason, many organizations specify diversity as the ability to effectively use the talents of people from various backgrounds, experiences, and perspectives.[10] (See Figure 4.2 for examples of how several organizations have chosen to define diversity.)

Management of diversity
The set of activities involved in integrating nontraditional employees (women and minorities) into the workforce and using their diversity to the firm's competitive advantage.

The push behind managing employee diversity originated and found its strongest advocates among private corporations in the 1990s. It has continued today as the government's commitment to affirmative action has waned. Most corporations now see diversity management as a business

Figure 4.2

Society for Human Resource Management (SHRM): "To celebrate diversity is to appreciate and value individual differences. SHRM strives to be the leader in promoting workplace diversity. Although the term is often used to refer to differences based on ethnicity, gender, age, religion, disability, national origin and sexual orientation, diversity encompasses an infinite range of individuals' unique characteristics and experiences, including communication styles, physical characteristics such as height and weight, and speed of learning and comprehension."

Microsoft Corporation: "At Microsoft, we believe that diversity enriches our performance and products, the communities in which we live and work, and the lives of our employees. As our workforce evolves to reflect the growing diversity of our communities and global marketplace, our efforts to understand value and incorporate differences become increasingly important. At Microsoft, we have established a number of initiatives to promote diversity within our organization, and to demonstrate this commitment in communities nationwide."

Texas Instruments (TI): Texas Instruments defines diversity as "effectiveness at using the talents of people of different backgrounds, experiences, and perspectives is key to our competitive edge . . . Diversity is a core TI value; valuing diversity in our workforce is at the core of the TI Values statement . . . Every tier must work to create an environment that promotes diversity . . . Each TI business will develop diversity strategies and measurements. . . ."

BankBoston: "Diversity at BankBoston is defined broadly to include group differences (based on age, race, gender, sexual orientation, disabilities, parental status or job group, for instance) and individual differences, including communications style, career experience, and other variables. Our goal is to create an environment that is inclusive, drawing upon the strength of the diversity of our workforce to exceed the expectations of BankBoston's customers."

Harvard Pilgrim Healthcare: "Harvard Pilgrim Healthcare is committed to increasing the diversity of staff at all levels while paying special attention to improving the representation of women and minorities in key positions; to creating an inclusive respectful and equitable environment; to serving our diverse members with culturally sensitive services; and to changing the organizational culture through leadership, policies, and practices."

Computer Sciences Corporation (CSC): "We value the diversity of our employees and the unique perspectives they bring to CSC. Diversity at CSC includes functional roles within the company, the markets and industries we serve, our length of service, geographic location, educational background, age, race, gender, ethnicity and whether we joined CSC independently or through an acquisition. By valuing differences, we demonstrate our commitment to treating everyone with fairness and respect."

Source: Society for Human Resource Management (2003, Feb. 13). Where HR meets the world. How should my organization define diversity? www.shrm.org/diversity.

Examples of How Several Organizations Have Chosen to Define Diversity

Avon's global workforce and leadership consist mainly of women. It has more female managers than any other Fortune *500 company, including the president of its U.S. Product Marketing Group, Andrea Jung.*

necessity rather than a means to achieve social goals or meet government requirements (as many saw affirmative action)[11] Several factors provide a rationale for diversity management. These include demographic trends, the need to view diversity as an asset, and marketing concerns.

Demographic Trends

The changing composition of the labor force is altering the employee landscape at a very rapid pace. Figure 4.3 presents data on the growth rates of various demographic groups and on their relative participation in the workforce. Historical data are given for 1990 through 2000; projections are used for 2000 through 2010. We will refer to the data in this figure when we discuss specific groups later in this chapter. In the next decade or so, we will see a dramatic growth rate in people aged 55 or older (46.6 percent). Asian Americans, Hispanic Americans, and other ethnic minorities have shown very rapid growth rates since 1990, and these are projected to continue at a fast pace into the end of the decade. Both groups have registered increases in workforce participation in recent years, and these are also expected to continue. White Americans will still make up a substantial majority of the workforce in the year 2010 (69.2 percent) but less of a majority than in 1990 (79.1 percent). Women's participation rates are expected to keep rising and men's to go on declining.

Note that the data contained in the figure are national. If we focus on the larger metropolitan areas, where most business takes place, the changes have been even more dramatic. Of the top 25 markets, "minorities" now make up a majority of the population in 18.[12] Most corporations are located within or near these metropolitan areas and are highly dependent on the local nonwhite labor supply to meet their needs.[13] In some states—most notably California, where nonwhites account for more than half of the population—the future is already here.

Many Americans think of employee diversity in terms of poor minorities and women occupying relatively unskilled and low-paying positions, with professional and managerial jobs held by white men. This stereotype, while true in the past, is rapidly eroding. At Bell Laboratories, for instance, American-born physicists are in the minority. At Schering-Plough's research labs, the first language of biochemists is less likely to be English than Korean, Hindi, Chinese, Japanese, German, Russian, Vietnamese, or Spanish. Most U.S. doctorates in engineering are granted to people whose native language is not English and who came to the United States from non-European countries. A recent study shows that the earnings of the more than 25 million immigrants who have come to the United States since the mid-1970s reach the average earnings of the native-born U.S. population within 15 years of arrival. The poverty rate of those who remain in the country for 15 to 20 years is less than the rate for people born in the United States.[14] The average income difference between natives and foreign born in 2002 was approximately 12 percent, which is far lower than most people believe.[15]

Figure 4.3

	Level		Percentage Change		Percent Distribution	
	2000	2010	1990–2000	2000–2010	2000	2010
AGE						
16–24	22,715	26,081	1.0	14.8	17.9	16.1
25–54	99,974	104,994	13.2	5.0	70.2	71.0
55 and older	18,175	26,646	21.0	46.6	12.9	16.9
SEX						
Man	75,247	82,221	9.0	9.3	53.4	52.1
Woman	65,616	75,500	15.5	15.1	46.6	47.9
RACE						
African Americans	16,603	20,041	20.8	20.7	11.8	12.7
Asian Americans and Others	6,687	9,636	43.7	44.1	4.7	6.1
Hispanic Americans	15,368	20,947	43.4	36.3	10.9	13.3
Non-Hispanic White Americans	102,963	109,118	5.3	6.0	73.1	69.2

Source: Bureau of Labor Statistics, Employment Projections Home Page (2003). stats.bls.gov.

Civilian Labor Force by Sex, Race, and Hispanic Origin (numbers in thousands)

Of the more than 20 million jobs projected to be created over the next decade, 75 percent will be filled by women and minorities. This means that firms must actively compete to attract and retain educated and talented workers from those groups: Most large corporations across different industries are eagerly trying to create receptive environments for nontraditional employees. For instance, Lucent Technologies, Chase Manhattan, Marriott International, FedEx, Xerox, Sun Microsystems, Colgate, Palmolive, Merck, and DuPont, among others, have at least one minority member on their board of directors and close to one-fifth of officials and managers who are minority group members.[16] Together, these demographic changes make it imperative that employers plan for the central role that diversity management will play in the twenty-first century. At IBM diversity permeates every facet of management and technical operations: 57 percent of IBM's board of directors are women, multicultural, and/or non-U.S. born; and 40 percent of IBM's top 54-member Worldwide Executive Council are women, multicultural, or non-U.S. born. Members of IBM's Worldwide Executive Council guide specific corporatewide diversity initiatives. The council is held accountable for recruiting, retaining, and advancing all talent and, most important, linking IBM's diversity initiatives to the global marketplace.[17]

Diversity as an Asset

Once, diversity in the workforce was thought to lead to garbled communications and conflict and, thus, a less efficient workplace. Today, many firms realize that diversity can actually enhance organizational effectiveness. Employee diversity can improve organizational functioning by stimulating greater creativity, better problem solving, and greater system flexibility.[18] Rosabeth Kanter, a well-known business consultant based at Harvard University, notes that most innovative firms purposely establish heterogeneous work groups "to create a marketplace of ideas, recognizing that a multiplicity of points of views need to be brought to bear on a problem."[19]

- **Greater creativity** Employee diversity can stimulate consideration of less obvious alternatives. Consider the following true story:

  A Hispanic man and a white woman were members of a task force advising the CEO on a planned organizational downsizing. These two people suggested that the recommendation of the task force majority to lay off 10 percent of the workforce would devastate morale. The majority, who were white men, initially felt that these two members were allowing their "soft hearts" to interfere with the need to make a hard-nosed business decision. Upon further consideration, the CEO decided not to lay off employees and opted instead for a plan proposed by these two dissenters. The plan proposed to reduce labor costs by offering early retirement, unpaid vacations, and stock in the firm to employees in exchange for a 5 percent salary cut. Most employees reacted very positively to the plan, with many reporting that it increased their loyalty and commitment to the firm.[20]

- **Better problem solving** Homogeneous groups are prone to a phenomenon called *groupthink*, in which all members quickly converge on a mistaken solution because they share the same mind-set and view the problem through the lens of conformity.[21] In a heterogeneous group with a broader and richer reservoir of experiences and cultural perspectives, the potential for groupthink shrinks.
- **Greater system flexibility** In today's rapidly changing business environments, flexibility is an important characteristic of successful firms. If properly managed, employee diversity can infuse more flexibility into the firm. The existence of diversity at different levels generates more openness to new ideas in general and greater tolerance for different ways of doing things.

Marketing Concerns

Most successful firms realize that effective management of a diverse workforce can lead to better marketing strategies for a multicultural, multiethnic population. For example:

- Much of Wal-Mart's substantial growth has come in urban areas, prompting the retailer to diversify its 960,000 workforce so that it mirrors its market. Forty-two percent of Wal-Mart officials and managers are minorities. "Customers want to come to a store where they feel comfortable," says Rose Reze (in yellow, left center of picture on page 127), a regional vice president in Southern Florida.[22]
- Greyhound greatly improved its profits by targeting Mexican Americans and setting up joint ventures with Mexican companies to serve the $200 million a year cross-border market.[23]
- American Express Company and Merrill Lynch & Co. use African American employees to hold workshops and networking receptions in venues such as black museums to attract black investors. The new tactics seem to be working. Within two years of launching the program 68 percent of AmEx new business has come from black clients.[24]
- Verizon has been successful in tapping the Hispanic market. In 2001, Verizon established the Multilingual Call Center, which has been addressing over 310,000 calls per month in Spanish. "Our customer satisfaction ratings are over 95 percent satisfactory, and we are still improving," says Ana Garcia-Piedra, director of Multilingual Sales and Solutions at Verizon. Through the Multilingual Call Center, "We've not only assembled employees who speak 'the language,' but we've been able to leverage their cultural connections to the respective communities where they reside," adds Oscar Gomez, vice president of the Office of Diversity at Verizon.[25]

Challenges in Managing Employee Diversity

Although employee diversity offers opportunities that can enhance organizational performance, it also presents managers with a new set of challenges. These challenges include appropriately valuing employee diversity, balancing individual needs with group fairness, dealing with resistance to change, ensuring group cohesiveness and open communication, avoiding employee resentment and backlash, retaining valued performers, and maximizing opportunity for all.

Valuing Employee Diversity

In some ways, the idea that diversity is good runs counter to the "melting pot" tradition—the notion that individuals should assimilate into the U.S. mainstream. The melting pot tradition

Wal-Mart's workforce is an outgrowth of its customer orientation. Its workforce, a reflection of its diverse customer base, helps Wal-Mart to address minority customers' needs more effectively than its competitors can.

makes some people uncomfortable with differences.[26] According to consultant Jo VanderKloot, a major obstacle to managing diversity is embedded in "one of the hidden rules in American culture . . . that you don't comment on differences, because the differences mean a deficiency."[27]

The *"difference as deficiency" perspective* (which assumes that everyone, regardless of culture or race, should strive to be alike) has given way to *"difference as better" advocacy* in many quarters. Indeed, much of the rationale behind affirmative action in the 1970s and 1980s was based on the melting pot principle: Opening the corporate doors to women and minorities would give them the chance to assimilate into the existing corporate culture and learn the behaviors, skills, and strategies of the white men who had created and still maintained that culture.[28]

The difference debate has become highly charged and politicized. Those who oppose diversity argue that the United States is losing the common ground necessary to a viable society, while those who advocate diversity argue that assimilation wrongly assumes a hierarchy of skills and behaviors with white men at the top and women and minorities below them. Organizations often find themselves attacked from both sides and frustrated in their attempts to manage employee diversity effectively. As one divisional manager of a major corporation says:

> I feel like as a company we are walking on eggshells all the time. No matter what we do someone will find it offensive. If we use the term "diversity" some people accuse us of trying to enforce political correctness. If we don't openly celebrate diversity, others will accuse us of being sexists and racists. This is a no-win proposition.[29]

Nonetheless, prejudice is still alive and well, so businesses and the people in them need to make progress to truly value the contributions of women and minorities. For instance, a recent analysis of Equal Employment Opportunity Commission data by Rutgers University Law School shows that although discrimination has fallen overall, employees in some regions are still highly biased. The researchers report that in Washington State, for example, 25 percent of employers with more than 50 workers still intentionally discriminate against women. And, in Georgia, almost 40 percent of larger employers discriminate racially, while 30 percent display a bias against women.[30]

A Question of Ethics

Many organizations have policies requiring that members of certain demographic groups (such as women and African Americans) sit on certain (or all) committees. Are there any dangers to such a policy? Could the potential benefits outweigh the potential costs?

Individual Versus Group Fairness

An issue closely related to the "difference is divisive versus better" debate is how far management should go in adapting HR programs to diverse employee groups. Should the company make the ability to speak Spanish a condition of employment for first-line supervisors who manage a large number of Latino employees? Should management require that appraisals of all

African American employees be reviewed by an African American manager? Should the firm be more lenient about punctuality and deadlines for employees whose cultures are not time sensitive? Should management make dress code exceptions for employees who view coats and ties as European customs that do not fit their lifestyles? These questions are not hypothetical; in some organizations, they are being seriously debated.

Universal concept of management
The management concept holding that all management practices should be standardized.

Cultural relativity concept of management
The management concept holding that management practices should be molded to the different sets of values, beliefs, attitudes, and behaviors exhibited by a diverse workforce.

The extent to which a **universal concept of management,** which leads to standardized management practices, should be replaced by a **cultural relativity concept of management,** which calls for molding management practices to the workforce's different sets of values, beliefs, attitudes, and patterns of behaviors, is an extraordinarily complex question. The proponents of universalism believe that fitting management practices to a diverse workforce sows the seeds for a permanent culture clash in which perceived inequities lead to intense workplace conflict. For instance, when the Lotus software company extended benefits coverage to homosexual couples, unmarried heterosexual employees living with a partner felt that they had been unfairly left out. Conversely, the proponents of relativity argue that failure to adapt HR practices to the needs of a diverse population may alienate much of the workforce and reduce their potential contributions.

Resistance to Change

Although employee diversity is a fact of life, the dominant groups in organizations are still composed of white men. Some argue that a long-established corporate culture is very resistant to change and that this resistance is a major roadblock for women and minorities seeking to survive and prosper in a corporate setting.

Group Cohesiveness and Interpersonal Conflict

Although employee diversity can lead to greater creativity and better problem solving, it can also lead to open conflict and chaos if there is mistrust and lack of respect among groups. This means that as organizations become more diverse, they face greater risks that employees will not work together effectively. Interpersonal friction rather than cooperation may become the norm.

Segmented Communication Networks

A Question of Ethics

Many managers and executives use golfing as an opportunity to combine business and pleasure. How could this practice damage an organization's diversity efforts? Are there any recreational activities that could enhance diversity efforts?

Shared experiences are often strongly reinforced by *segmented communication channels* in the workplace. One study found that most communication within organizations occurs between members of the same sex and race. This was found to be true across all professional categories, even at the top, where the number of women and minorities is very small.[31]

The presence of segmented communication poses three major problems to businesses. First, the organization cannot fully capitalize on the perspectives of diverse employees if they remain confined to their own groups. Second, segmented communication makes it more difficult to establish common ground across various groups.[32] Third, women and minorities often miss opportunities or are unintentionally penalized for not being part of the mainstream communication networks.

Resentment

Although affirmative action is now decades old, it remains clouded in controversy. At the heart of this debate is the fact that equal employment opportunity (EEO) was imposed by government rather than self-initiated. In the vast majority of U.S. organizations, it was a forced change rather than a voluntary one. The response to this forced change was, in many cases, grudging compliance.[33]

One side effect of forced compliance has been the reinforcement of a belief among some managers and mainstream employees that organizations have to compromise their standards to comply with EEO laws. Some have seen EEO laws as legislating a "forced diversity" that favors political solutions over performance and/or competence.

Given this background, it is perhaps not surprising that twice as many white men as women and minorities feel that promotions received by the latter groups can be attributed to affirmative action.[34] This belief presents two problems. First, women and minorities in positions of authority and responsibility may not be taken as seriously as white men are. Second, the belief that white men are getting the short end of the stick may provoke some of them to vent their frustration against those employees (women and minorities) whom they believe are getting an unfair advantage.

It is important that managers deal with these issues because affirmative action is here to stay. A poll conducted by *Fortune* magazine in the mid-1990s found that 96 percent of CEOs would not change their affirmative action efforts, even if all federal enforcement was abolished.[35] By 2003, other polls confirmed that big business's commitment to affirmative action continues to be strong, even though most firms now prefer to use "diversity" rather than "affirmative action."[36]

Backlash

Some white men feel that they have been made the scapegoats for society's ills and that they have to defend themselves against encroachments by those using their gender or ethnicity to lay claim to organizational resources (such as promotions, salaries, and job security). Thus, while women and minorities may view a firm's "cultural diversity policy" as a commitment to improving their chances for advancement, white men may see it as a threat. Derogatory phrases such as "white male bashing" are often used by those who feel threatened by the diversity concept. Clearly, firms face a major challenge in trying to grapple with this backlash—which may be unwarranted, because white men still enjoy considerable advantages.[37] It is doubtful that a firm can effectively manage employee diversity if its white male employees (some of whom may be in positions of power) are hostile toward the concept.

Retention

The job satisfaction levels of women and minorities are often lower than those of white men. The main complaint among female and minority employees is that they lack career growth opportunities. The perception that their upward mobility is thwarted grows stronger at higher levels as women and minorities bump up against the **glass ceiling,** an invisible barrier in the organization that prevents them from rising to any higher position. Lower job satisfaction translates into higher resignation rates, with a resulting loss of valuable talent and greater training costs because of high turnover.

Glass ceiling
The intangible barrier in an organization that prevents female and minority employees from rising to positions above a certain level.

Competition for Opportunities

As minorities grow both proportionately and absolutely in the U.S. population, competition for jobs and opportunities is likely to become much stronger. Already there are rising tensions among minorities jockeying for advancement. Employers are being put into the uncomfortable position of having to decide which minority is most deserving.[38] Consider the following examples:

- "Blacks have been too successful at the expense of everyone else," grumbles Peter Rogbal, a Mexican American captain in the San Francisco Fire Department. "Other groups have been ignored to placate the black community."
- In Los Angeles, black and white members of the Laborers Local 300 sued to overturn a plan giving Latinos preference in winning unskilled construction work.
- One diversity expert notes that "African-Americans, who suffered tremendously for their political gains worry that Hispanics will stomp on them during their climb to greater power. Latinos wonder whether blacks will make room."[39]

A Question of Ethics

What ethical problems might arise from giving preferential treatment to certain employees based on their group membership?

There are no fail-proof techniques for effectively handling these challenges. There is, however, one principle that managers should always keep in mind: Treat employees as individuals, not as members of a group. With this principle as a guide, many of these challenges become much more manageable.

We now turn to a discussion of the concerns of specific employee groups. As you read this material, remember that discussions such as these necessarily make broad generalizations that can easily be misused. Our purpose is to give you some idea of the complexity of employee diversity, not to stereotype individuals.

Diversity in Organizations

The elements of diversity—such as race, ethnicity, and sex—tend to have a profound impact on how people relate to one another. In this section we discuss (in alphabetical order) the groups that are most likely to be "left out" of the corporate mainstream. Of course, one individual may belong to several of these groups. For instance, a person could be an Amerasian (of American and Vietnamese parentage) woman who is legally blind (disabled) and who came to the United States five years ago (foreign born). This example highlights the limitations of group-based descriptions. And over time many of the social and legal barriers that kept ethnic groups apart have come down so that there are millions of people with mixed heritages. For this reason, the Census Bureau in 2000 allowed Americans to classify themselves into multiple racial categories. Nevertheless, the distinction between white versus black, Asian, or Hispanic still lingers in the United States, whether or not a person has mixed ancestry. Halle Berry, the first African American with an Oscar for best actress (awarded in 2002), the child of a white mother and a black father, put it bluntly: "I got called 'zebra' and 'oreo cookie' in school. My mother taught me wisely: 'When you leave this house, people will assume you are black and you will be discriminated against. So accept being black, embrace it.' "[40]

African Americans

African Americans constitute approximately 12 percent of the U.S. workforce (see Figure 4.2 on page 123). After enduring centuries of forced slavery, they continued to experience outright discrimination until the 1960s. Although there are still significant barriers to black advancement—including both blatant and subtle discrimination—many improvements have taken place in the last three decades. Since the passage of the Civil Rights Act of 1964, the number of African American officials, managers, technicians, and skilled craftspeople has tripled while the number in clerical positions has quadrupled and the number in professional jobs has doubled.[41] However, a significant percentage of African Americans (perhaps as high as 15 percent) are among the "hardcore" unemployed.

African Americans face two major problems in organizations. First, explicit, intentional racism still exists some 40 years after the first civil rights victories.[42] African Americans are not the only group to suffer from blatant racism, but it is safe to say that they are the group that suffers the most. The persistence of the Ku Klux Klan and other white supremacy organizations serves as a constant reminder, to both African Americans and U.S. society as a whole, that the struggle for civil rights is not over. Managers need to be careful to reassure their African American employees, and the entire organization, that racist views will not be tolerated in the workplace.

The second problem African Americans face as a group is less educational preparation than whites.[43] This is not an issue unique to blacks. People of Hispanic origin also have less educational preparation for the workplace than whites do. In 2002, both blacks and Hispanics showed approximately half of the college graduation rate of whites. Because of the increasing importance of technology and information in the U.S. economy, the discrepancy between the wage rates of college-educated and non-college-educated workers is growing. Therefore, the differential in educational preparation between African Americans (and Hispanic Americans) and whites puts the former at a major disadvantage in the labor market.

Although discrimination continues to be a problem and blacks are at a significant economic disadvantage in comparison to whites, there is reason for optimism. An analysis of 291 metropolitan areas in 2002 indicated that all but 19 of these areas were more integrated than in 1990. Most recent census figures indicate a record-low black poverty rate (22 percent versus 36 percent 20 years earlier) and a record-high black median household income ($30,000, about 20 percent higher than 20 years earlier). During the past three decades black household incomes have increased almost twice as fast as whites' incomes. Controlling for inflation, among married-couple households, some 51 percent of African Americans had incomes of $50,000 or more. In 1980, barely one of two blacks over age 25 held a high school diploma. In 2003, nearly four of five, or just under 80 percent had a high school diploma; and for blacks in the 25–29 age group, it was 86 percent, which was the same as for whites. And in less than 20 years, the number of black college graduates has doubled.[44] African Americans' share of management jobs has increased at least five-fold since 1966.[45]

Asian Americans

Americans of Asian descent constitute approximately 4.7 percent of the U.S. workforce. Their representation in the labor force increased by approximately 44 percent from 1990 to 2000 and is projected to increase by another 44 percent by 2010 (see Figure 4.2 on page 123). Just as the term "Hispanics" applies to a range of people, "Asian Americans" include a wide variety of races, ethnic groups, and nationalities (for instance, Japanese, Chinese, Koreans, Indians, and Pakistanis).[46] Although Asian Americans have done well in technical fields and are very well represented in institutions of higher education, they are underrepresented in top corporate positions. Employer discrimination probably accounts for this to some extent, for Asian Americans are often stereotyped as being too cautious and reserved to lead.[47] They also suffer from the belief held in some quarters that, because of their educational attainments, they are an advantaged group and, therefore, do not deserve special consideration in hiring and promotion decisions. As a result, they are less likely to benefit from programs intended to improve the employment conditions of women and other minorities. Finally, one survey found that 40 percent of African Americans and Hispanic Americans and 27 percent of whites saw Asian Americans as "unscrupulous, crafty, and devious in business."[48] For all these reasons, some Asian Americans are relegated to technical and support positions that require minimal interpersonal interactions and offer limited opportunities for advancement.

John Yang, a vice president at Hewlett-Packard, notes that although Asians are well represented in the high-technology industry, they seldom make it to the upper echelons. Those Asians who are at the top rung of high-tech companies often started their own companies, like Charles Wand of New York's Computer Associates.[49]

Most Asian immigrants to the United States today are from the Philippines, Indonesia, Sri Lanka, and Thailand. At least half of these immigrants are women, many of whom end up working for very low wages in high-pressure industries like the garment business.[50] Since the terrorist attacks of September 11, 2001, South Asian Americans, including Indian Americans and Pakistani Americans and especially Sikh Americans (a religious group often mistakenly believed to be Arab because many Sikh men wear turbans and long beards), have reported several hundred cases of harassment and discrimination at work.[51]

People with Disabilities

There are approximately 43 million people with disabilities in the United States, 15 million of whom are actively employed and 6 million of whom subsist on Social Security payments and disability insurance.[52] At least 3.7 million people with severe disabilities are at work.[53] The remainder are either unemployed (presumably supported by their families) or under working age. People who are physically disabled face four main problems at work.

First, social acceptance of disabilities has not advanced much since the dark ages.[54] Many people still view people with disabilities with suspicion, even scorn, feeling that those who are physically impaired should stay away from the work world and let "normal" people assume their duties. At a more subtle level, co-workers may not befriend employees with disabilities because they simply do not know how to relate to them. Even extroverts can suddenly become shy in front of a person with a disability.

Second, people with disabilities are often seen as being less capable than others. This misconception persists even though people who are legally blind and deaf can perform many tasks just as well as those with normal sight and hearing, and modern technology allows many paralyzed people to run computers.

Third, many employers are afraid to hire people with disabilities or put them in responsible positions for fear that they may quit when work pressures mount. This myth persists despite the fact that absenteeism and turnover among such employees are only a fraction of those of other employees. For instance, Marriott International reports that turnover among employees with disabilities is only 8 percent annually, compared to 105 percent for workers in general.[55] Pizza

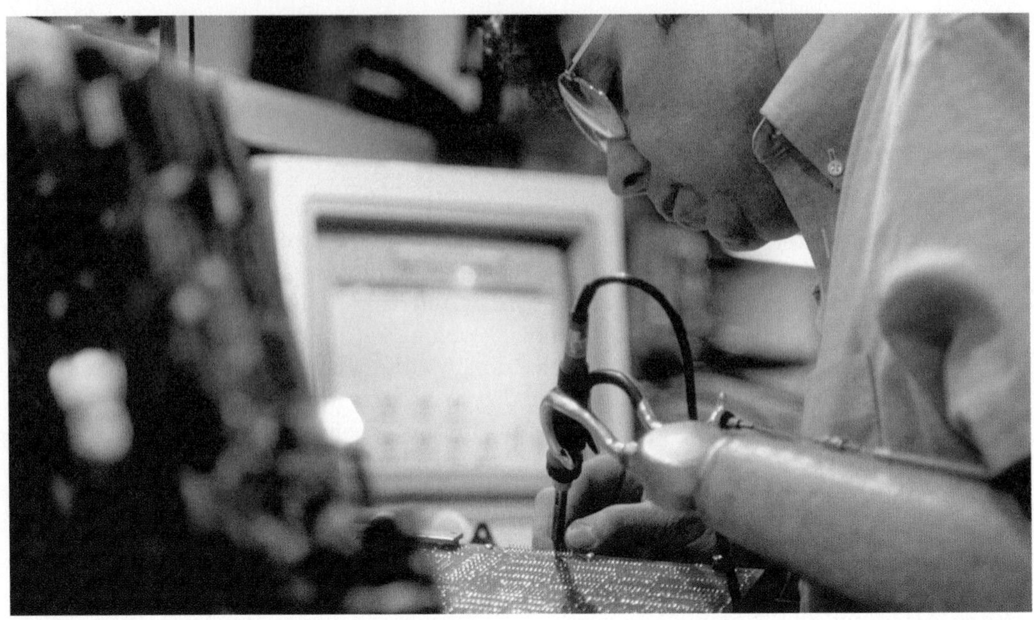

Many companies over-estimate the costs of accommodating employees with disabilities. Studies indicate that accommodation costs an average of $200 to $500—costs that are often outweighed by the lower absenteeism and turnover rates of workers with disabilities.

Hut has also found a huge difference in turnover rates: 20 percent for employees with disabilities versus more than 200 percent for employees without disabilities.[56]

Fourth, many employers have overestimated the costs of accommodating employees with disabilities ever since the passage of the Americans with Disabilities Act in 1990. In fact, employers have found that accommodations are usually simple and cheap, costing on average between $200 and $500 across different firms.[57] For instance, Griener Engineering, Inc., in Irving, Texas, installed a lighter-weight door on the women's restroom and raised a drafting table by putting bricks under its legs. Hewlett-Packard provides, among other things, Braille books, interpreters, and text telephone (TTY) service in which an operator transcribes a hearing person's response that is transmitted and read by a deaf person on a text telephone screen.[58] In 2002, the U.S. Supreme Court established a clear distinction between a physical impairment and a disability under the Americans with Disabilites Act (ADA). For example, Ella Williams, an assembly-line worker at a Toyota plant, was unable to work with power tools after she developed crippling pain in her wrists, neck, and shoulders from repetitive motions. The Sixth Circuit Court of Appeals in Cincinnati said her injury was akin to having "damaged or deformed limbs," and it ruled Toyota should have accommodated her by giving her work as an inspector. Toyota appealed the decision to the U.S. Supreme Court. Citing the so-called "toothbrush test," the Supreme Court ruled that to be disabled a worker must have difficulties in doing everyday tasks. According to Justice O'Connor, "Even after [Williams's] condition worsened, she could still brush her teeth, wash her face, bathe, tend her flower garden, fix breakfast, do laundry and pick up around the house." This suggests that Williams did not have a true disability but rather a physical impairment. Thus, she was not entitled to the antidiscrimination protection of ADA.[59]

The Foreign Born

Approximately 11 percent of the U.S. population is foreign born, although in some areas such as California, southern Texas, southern Florida, and in New York City the proportion reaches close to one-fourth of the population.[60] Reliable statistics are hard to find because of illegal immigration and census undercounts (fearing legal reprisal, many undocumented workers wish to remain incognito), but at least 30 million immigrants have come to the United States over the past 30 years.[61] In addition, half a million foreign students on temporary visas are attending U.S. universities at any one time, spending about $11 billion a year on tuition and living expenses.[62] Many of these people remain in the United States after obtaining their degrees. Regardless of their parents' legal status, all children born in the United States are automatically U.S. citizens under the U.S. Constitution.

The United States is a nation of immigrants, and those coming to the country increase the U.S. supply of labor. Many people continue to view the United States as a land of opportunity because political barriers are low and opportunities for advancement are great. Nonetheless, many immigrants face significant barriers because of their language difficulties, race or ethnicity (most are non-Europeans), and cultural differences. Many illegal immigrants work very hard in jobs with low wages and often do not collect benefits. In addition, they often meet with resentment from whites and other minorities who feel that the newcomers are taking jobs away from them. In the end, despite political debates about illegal immigration and louder and more frequent calls after September 11, 2001, to curb immigration violations as a top government priority, the fact is that American industry depends on workers who have crossed the border to take jobs that nonimmigrant Americans refuse to accept at the going wages.[63] For instance, nearly 40 percent of the workers who rebuilt the Pentagon after its damages from terrorist attack on September 11, 2001, were Hispanic immigrants. As remarked in 2002 by Tom Donohue, president of the U.S. Chamber of Commerce (representing thousands of U.S. firms of all sizes across the 50 states), "If tomorrow we send them [illegal aliens] all home, this economy would stop. They are hard workers, they are important workers. . . ."[64]

Certain myths about foreign-born workers need to be debunked. First, it is not true that all immigrants are uneducated. An Urban Institute study, which screened newcomers from countries such as Mexico and El Salvador, found that 79 percent of adult immigrants had high school diplomas and 33 percent had college degrees.[65] Second, there is not a higher proportion of immigrants on public assistance today than at the beginning of the century. In 1909, more than 50 percent of welfare recipients were immigrants; today only 9 percent of immigrant families receive public assistance. This figure compares to 7.4 percent of households headed by the native born.[66] Third, most foreign born are not at a great economic disadvantage versus native born. In fact, the income difference between a household led by a foreign-born resident and a household led by a native-born resident in the United States is only about 12 percent ($36,000 versus $41,000 annually), which is amazingly low considering the additional hurdles an immigrant faces in learning a new language, adapting to a new culture, and coping with employment discrimination, among other difficulties.[67] Fourth, large-scale immigration does not occur only in the United States. World migration has increased dramatically during the past 25 years.[68] Stroll through the streets of Paris, Vancouver, Amsterdam, Johannesburg, London, Madrid, Kuwait City, or San Jose to see the mix of people of different nationalities who live and work there, often with dubious legal status (see the Manager's Notebook on "Diversity on a Global Scale").

Emerging Trends

MANAGER'S NOTEBOOK

Diversity on a Global Scale

Growing employee diversity is a trend not only in the United States but globally as well. Currently there are hundreds of millions of people who live outside the country of their birth. Immigration is now the major component of demographic change in many developed countries. In the United States, according to the latest U.S. Census Bureau projection, the population will grow by 129 million, but if immigration stops it would increase by 54 million. The United States is not alone. From 1996 to 2002, the United States received 27 percent of the world's international migrants, yet Western Europe received almost as many (21 percent). If it were not for immigration, Europe would lose about 28 million people over the next 50 years. Although less publicized, large-scale migration is also occurring within Africa (for instance, between South Africa and its neighbors), some Arab countries (for example, more than half of the workforce in Kuwait comes from neighboring countries), between Hong Kong and mainland China, in the Caribbean (at least a million illegal Haitians live in the Dominican Republic), in Central America (there are at least a million Nicaraguans in Costa Rica, or about 20 percent of the population), and in South America (there has been heavy migration from Colombia to Venezuela and from Paraguay to Argentina during the past 20 years). Governments around the world have not been able to stem this tide because labor moves toward areas with better wages and employment conditions, and employers are willing to hire immigrants to reduce costs. In fact, it has not been uncommon for governments during the last few years to pass restrictive immigration legislation. (Hong Kong has passed very strict laws on border controls with mainland China and has made it extremely difficult for mainland Chinese to obtain permanent residency.) At the same time, these same governments tend to look the other way when it comes to implementation (in most countries immigrants do the kinds of jobs natives would rather not do). Eventually this will reshape many of the notions that we currently have about race as people from different backgrounds commingle. In the meantime, firms need to find ways to manage this growing diversity more effectively.

Source: Doyle, R. (2002, Feb.). Assembling the future: How international migrants are shaping the 21st Century. *Scientific American*, 30; Baker, S., Cappel, K., and Carlisle, K. (2002, March 18). Crime and politics: Suddenly it is the hottest of issues—and linked closely to immigration. *Business Week*, 50–51. Associated Press (2002, Jan. 11). Hong Kong to oust immigrants. *Arizona Republic*, A-15.

Finally, there is no evidence that crime rates are higher among illegal aliens. For instance, although in some European countries crime has been falling (such as in Italy and Germany) while immigration has skyrocketed, recent polls show that natives believe crime to be on the rise. As noted by a commentator, "The presumption that immigrants are guilty is becoming almost automatic."[69] Much prejudice is directed not only toward Arabs and people of color but also toward Europeans from countries that are not members of the European Union (EU), including Romania and pieces of the former Yugoslavia.[70] Yet, as population continues to decline in EU countries, they are becoming increasingly dependent on this influx of foreign labor. This means that in the EU effective management of diversity is becoming necessary to achieve greater overall organizational success. This shows that effective management of diversity is becoming necessary to achieve greater overall organization success in many parts of the world.

Homosexuals

Although early research dating from the 1940s suggested that about 10 percent of the population is gay, there is considerable debate about the true percentage, with estimates ranging from 1 to 2 percent to 10 percent.[71] In recent years gay advocacy groups have become very outspoken about their rights, arguing that sexual preference should not be a criterion for personnel-related decisions. But homosexuality is still taboo in many workplaces.

Gays have little legal protection at present. There is no federal law to prevent overt discrimination against homosexuals, and only six states (Connecticut, Massachusetts, Minnesota, New Jersey, Wisconsin, and Hawaii) have such antidiscrimination laws on their books. Currently, the U.S. military has a controversial "don't ask, don't tell" policy that prevents gay soldiers from openly discussing their sexual orientation but also prohibits inquiries about the sexual orientation of new or current enlistees. Many other organizations have explicit or implicit policies against the hiring or retention of homosexuals, even if they do not discuss their homosexuality.

Homosexuals face three key problems in the workplace. The first is outright refusal to hire or retain homosexual employees (which is not illegal in most states). The second is intolerance from workers or managers in companies that do not have explicit policies forbidding discrimination against gays. Third, AIDS has added fear to prejudice. These problems have a chilling effect that causes many gay people to stay in the closet for fear of being fired or ostracized at work.

In most jobs sexual preference per se is not likely to affect work performance, so companies that practice discrimination in hiring or promotion may be robbing themselves of valuable employees. Still, in firms that do not practice discrimination or have explicit policies against it (such as Apple Computer), managers may face difficulties in integrating openly gay employees into heterosexual teams that are intolerant of homosexuals.

Latinos (Hispanic Americans)

The label *Hispanic* is of recent vintage, encompassing those individuals whose declared ancestors or who themselves came from Latin American countries. The label *Latino* is the term that these groups (both in the United States and abroad) have traditionally used for cultural self-definition and to distinguish their cultural identity from that of non-Latino North Americans. The label *Hispanic*, the official label used by the U.S. government, is "essentially a term of convenience for administrative agencies and researchers."[72]

A mistake people sometimes make is to equate the term *Hispanic* with race, something that many Latinos find offensive. Latinos include people of European descent (there are at least 70 million of them in Latin America) and African descent (there are at least 25 million living in the Spanish-speaking Antilles and the Caribbean basin), as well as Latin Indians (who make up a very large proportion of the Mexican and Andean population), Asians (there are probably 10 million Asians of Hispanic descent), and a very large number of people of mixed origin. In fact, most Latinos do not divide people into exclusive racial categories (for example, white or black), but see them as a blend of various racial traits. In some Spanish-speaking Caribbean countries like Cuba, Puerto Rico, and the Dominican Republic, there may be as many as 10 different terms to designate people of mixed African and European descent based on physical features. In short it is very difficult to draw a portrait of a "typical" Latino.[73]

There are at least 35 million Latinos in the United States, with more estimates as high as 45 million.[74] Reliable numbers are difficult to find because many are not included in census figures. Their percentage distribution in workforce participation is expected to reach 12.7 percent by 2010 (see Figure 4.2 on page 123). The U.S. Latino population is very diverse. Under this umbrella one finds individuals whose families were in the United States before the country's independence and others who arrived a month ago. Many Latinos are professionals and entrepreneurs; others are unskilled laborers and farmers. One also finds large differences in income. At the high end of the scale are upper- and middle-class Cubans who came to the United States in the aftermath of the 1959 Cuban Revolution; on the low end are migrant workers.[75]

Latinos face a number of problems in the U.S. workplace. One is language.[76] More than any other immigrant group (perhaps because of their segregated urban enclaves, large numbers, and geographical proximity to Latin America), Latinos tend to retain their native language as the primary language at home. As a result, many have a limited proficiency in English, which hinders employment opportunities and can be a source of discrimination at work. Second, cultural clashes may occur because of value differences. Some Latinos see non-Latino North Americans as unemotional, insensitive, self-centered, rigid, and ambitious to the point where they live to work rather than the other way around. Meanwhile, non-Latinos often complain that with Latinos "punctuality, absenteeism, planning, and scheduling can be a lot more loose than one would expect."[77]

Third, Latinos of African or Latin American Indian descent (many of whom migrate to the United States because of their extreme poverty at home) often face an additional hurdle: racial discrimination because of their skin color. This may occur both within the Latino community and in the larger society.

All of these challenges do not negate the noteworthy progress that Latinos have made in recent years. The largest 500 Latino-owned firms in the United States export more than $1 billion worth of goods each year, generating many U.S. jobs in the process.[78] Almost a quarter of the *Fortune* 1000 firms have some Latino senior executives, with 70 serving as executive officer. Latinos occupy 181 board seats in these companies, double the 1993 number. Hispanic middle-class households (those earning $40,000 to $140,000 annually) have grown 71 percent during the past 20 years, with 13 percent of Latino families reporting incomes of more than $75,000. Total Hispanic purchasing power has reached nearly $500 billion. The proportion of college graduates is now 20 percent, an increase of 43 percent over two decades.[79]

Older Workers

The U.S. workforce is getting older. The average U.S. worker is 38, expected to reach close to 42 by the year 2010, and 45 percent of employees are currently over the age of 40. Older workers face several important challenges in the workplace. First, the United States is a youth-oriented culture that has not yet come to terms with its changing demographics.[80] Starting around the age of 40, but particularly after the age of 50, employees encounter a number of stereotypes that may block their career advancement. Partly because of this reason, the number of age bias claims against private sector employers filed with the Equal Employment Opportunity Commission has recently reached 22 percent of all discrimination claims in a given year.[81] Among the most common negative assumptions about older workers are that they are:

- Less motivated to work hard.
- "Dead wood."
- Resistant to change and cannot learn new methods.
- "Fire proof."[82]

These negative characterizations are not supported by research. In fact, one of the most stunning economic achievements in U.S. business in the last decade—the turnaround of manufacturing productivity and growth—has been accomplished at plants staffed predominantly by older assembly-line workers.[83] Furthermore, some recent surveys show that the absenteeism rate for those 55 and over (4.2 days per year) was almost identical to the absenteeism rate of other age groups (3.9).[84] Recent studies also show that older workers are just as committed to their jobs as younger workers.[85] Many successful companies have implemented programs to use the knowledge and wisdom of older workers to mentor employees. In the words of an HR consultant, "These companies are striking gold in a silver mine by leveraging senior workers as knowledge champions."[86]

Second, *generational conflict* may arise. Older workers sometimes feel that their position and status are threatened by "young bucks" eager to push "over-the-hill" employees out of the way. This tension can negatively affect the cohesiveness of teams and work units. It can also sour the relationship between boss and subordinate.

Third, even if in good health, this group is more susceptible to physical problems. Often older workers are forced to step down from their jobs because the firm cannot and/or will not find appropriate opportunities for them to use their seasoned judgment, knowledge, and ability to serve as mentors for new workers. Although an illegal practice that is difficult to prove in court, older workers are often targeted for layoffs because they earn more money.[87]

Many companies find that accommodating the physical problems and limitations of aging workers pays off.[88] At Alcoa's plant in Davenport, Iowa, where the average age of workers is 47, strains and sprains were becoming a chronic problem. Since the company asked all 2,500 workers to attend a "back class," injuries have declined.[89] It is important to point out, however, that most older workers, particularly those in nonphysical jobs, function as well as they did 20 or 30 years ago. This fact underscores our general theme that it is necessary for managers to treat employees as individuals, not as members of a group or class.

Women

One of the most important U.S. demographic changes over the past 30 years has been the influx of women into the workforce. Since 1970, the percentage of women in the labor force has more than doubled. The projected rate for women in the workforce is expected to reach 48 percent by 2010 (see Figure 4.2 on page 123).[90] Unfortunately, women's earnings have not mirrored this participation trend. After falling to a low of 59 percent of male earnings in 1975, the female-to-male earnings ratio rose slowly and is now approximately 73 percent, just 10 points above its level in 1920 (63 percent), when only 20 percent of women were in the labor force.[91]

There may be reason for optimism, however. Women's share of top-management jobs has increased at least threefold during the last three decades.[92] The hiring of Carly Fiorina to the top spot at Hewlett-Packard, in an industry that has traditionally been notorious for male domination, is a good example of how times may be changing.[93] Other recent examples of women moving to the top include the appointment of Patricia Russo as CEO of Kodak, Carole Black as CEO of Lifetime Entertainment Services, Ann Mulcahy as CEO of Xerox, Margaret Whitman as CEO of eBay, and Abigail Johnson as CEO of Fidelity.[94] And 55 percent of employed women bring in half or more of their total household income.[95]

Still, there is no doubt that most women still earn considerably less than their male counterparts. Other than overt sex discrimination (which is, of course, illegal), several factors may account for the earnings differential between women and men and women's lack of upward mobility. These include biological constraints and social roles, a male-dominated corporate culture, exclusionary networks, and sexual harassment.

Biological Constraints and Social Roles

Obviously, only women can become pregnant and give birth. But even after three decades of feminism, women continue to encounter a fairly rigid set of expectations regarding their roles and behavior that extend far beyond these biological constraints. Women are still primarily responsible for taking care of the children and performing most household duties, while men are still expected to "bring home the bacon" and handle yard work. In survey after survey, men say a woman's place is in the home.[96] A conducted study in the late 1990s estimates that full-time working women still spend three times the amount of time spent by men on household duties.[97]

Perhaps reflecting these societal norms, organizations have traditionally failed to be flexible enough to meet the needs of working women. Only a tiny proportion of companies provide day care and other support options (such as job sharing and reduced work hours for employees with young children). For this reason, many talented and highly educated women are forced to curtail their career aspirations and/or quit the organization in their late 20s or early to mid-30s—crucial years in one's career—if they wish to have a family. Practically all male top managers are married and have children, whereas the majority of women who make it to the top are single and childless.

A Male-Dominated Corporate Culture

Most women perceive a male-dominated corporate culture as an obstacle to their success.[98] However, most sex differences are not related to performance, particularly in white-collar occupations, where sheer physical strength is seldom required.

A number of studies have shown that men tend to emerge in leadership positions in U.S. culture because they are more likely than women to exhibit traits that are believed to "go hand-in-hand" with positions of authority. These traits include (1) more aggressive behaviors and tendencies; (2) initiation of more verbal interactions; (3) focusing of remarks on "output" (as opposed to "process") issues; (4) less willingness to reveal information and expose vulnerability; (5) a greater task (as opposed to social) orientation; and (6) less sensitivity, which presumably enables them to make tough choices quickly.[99] Thus, cultural expectations may create a self-fulfilling prophecy, with individuals exhibiting the "female traits" of focusing on process, social orientation, and so on more likely to be relegated to operational and subordinate roles.

Exclusionary Networks

Many women are hindered by lack of access to the **old boys' network,** the informal relationships formed between male managers and executives. As we noted earlier in this chapter, most communication at work takes place within groups of members of the same sex. This happens even at the highest organizational levels. Because most high-level positions are filled by men, women are often left out of the conversations that help men get ahead.[100] During a gender-awareness workshop at Corning, for example, women executives complained that their male colleagues never invited them to lunch. These women felt that they were missing out on the opportunity to get vital insider gossip, such as news of an employee's imminent transfer or of the boss's interest in a new product category.[101]

Old boys' network
An informal social and business network of high-level male executives that typically excludes women and minorities. Access to the old boys' network is often an important factor in career advancement.

Sexual Harassment

Women have to confront sexual harassment to a much greater extent than men do. Women have had to forfeit promising careers because they would not accept the sexual advances of men in positions of power and did not feel they had any recourse but to quit their jobs.[102] Anita Hill's testimony at the Clarence Thomas Supreme Court confirmation hearings in October 1991 was a national turning point on this issue. Since the hearing, many more women have come forward with complaints about sexual harassment in the workplace.

For instance, a group of 23 women at Salomon Smith Barney's branch office in Garden City, New York, alleged that the branch office had a "boom-boom-boom" room in the basement where male brokers and managers gathered to engage in fraternity-house antics that their female co-workers found offensive and harassing.[103] In a recent case involving Wal-Mart, which is still pending, a 10-year employee, 36-year-old Kim Miller, claims her male supervisors referred to her as "bitch" and talked about which female customers they would like to get into bed. The sexual talk allegedly turned toward her and included offers to get her pregnant. Once, when Miller was working in the tire-and-mounting unit, she claims she walked in on her male co-

Male and Female Views of Sexual Harassment

Source: Deutschman, A. (1991, November). Dealing with sexual harassment. *Fortune*, 145.

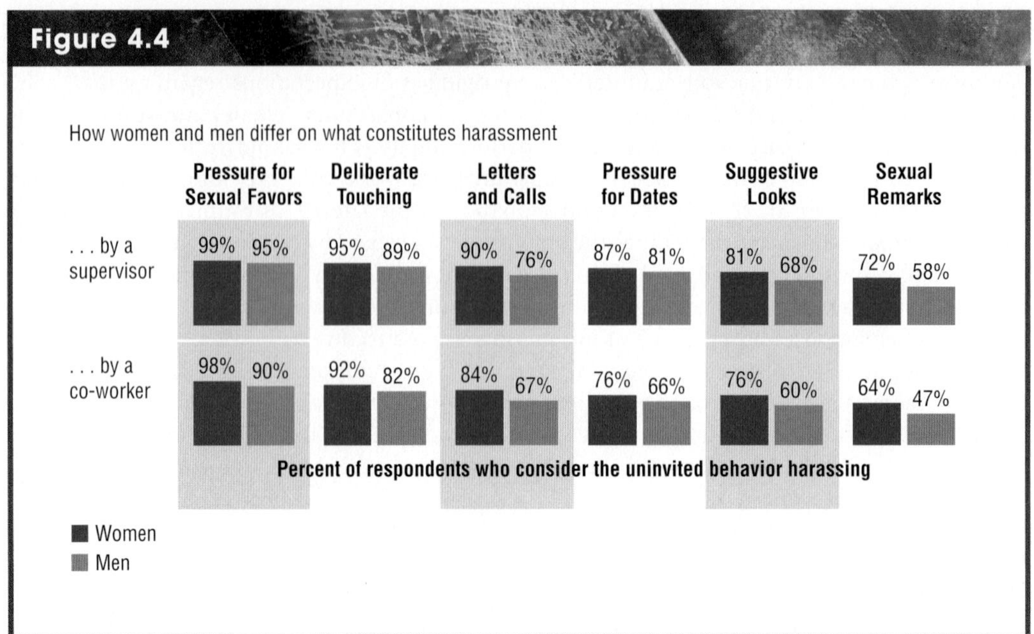

workers huddled over a porn video in the customer lounge.[104] In 2002, one in five civil suits concerned harassment or discrimination, compared with one in 20 at the time of Anita Hill's testimony 11 years earlier. Sexual harassment litigation is also occurring in Europe.[105] Currently more than 100 insurance firms in the United States offer employment practice liability insurance, which covers employers' legal costs, damages, and settlements in lawsuits for discrimination and harassment.[106]

Businesses have been getting tougher on this issue by crafting stronger sexual harassment policies and setting up intensive seminars for employees. These educational efforts are particularly important because men and women often have different notions of what kind of behavior constitutes sexual harassment (Figure 4.4). DuPont's anti–sexual harassment program, titled "A Matter of Respect," uses video scenes of sexual harassment to get male and female employees to discuss specific actions. For instance, in one scene a woman sales representative is ready to close an important deal with a client in a hotel dining room when the client asks, "Why don't we go upstairs and talk about this some more?" At this point the trainer stops the video and encourages the group to discuss what the woman should do.[107]

Improving the Management of Diversity

Organizations that have made the greatest strides in successfully managing diversity tend to share a number of characteristics. These factors are a commitment from top management to valuing diversity, diversity training programs, employee support groups, accommodation of family needs, senior mentoring and apprenticeship programs, communication standards, organized special activities, diversity audits, and a policy of holding management responsible for the effectiveness of diversity efforts.

In recent years, *Fortune* has published a list of the "50 Best Companies for Asians, Blacks, and Hispanics." The judges consider many of the factors just mentioned. A sample of these firms selected in 2002 appears in Figure 4.5.

Top-Management Commitment to Valuing Diversity

It is unlikely that division managers, middle managers, supervisors, and others in positions of authority will become champions of diversity unless they believe that the chief executive officer and those reporting to the CEO are totally committed to valuing diversity. Xerox, DuPont,

Figure 4.5

Sample of 2002 Top Companies	Board of Directors	Top 50 Paid	Officials and Managers	Workforce	Asian Black Hispanic Native Americans	Minorities as a % of New Hires	Summary
Adventica	4 of 11	7 of 50	31.1%	48%	4.3% 11.2% 32.2% 0.3%	48%	The owner of Denny's proves its commitment to minorities after it was plagued by discrimination suits in the mid-1990s. The restaurant chain tops *Fortune*'s list five years in a row. It was ranked among the top five companies for African Americans; ranked 4 in percent of total purchasing from minority businesses; and ranked 1 in percent of charitable giving primarily benefiting minorities.
Xerox	2 of 15	9 of 50	23.6%	29.8%	5.1% 16.1% 7.9% 0.7%	40%	The black employees have filed a class-action lawsuit against Xerox, yet top guns have reiterated their commitment to diversity, with minorities 40% of new hires.
SBL Communications	3 of 21	3 of 50	29.1%	37.2%	4.2% 19.7% 12.6% 0.7%	47%	SBC spends $2.4 billion with minority-owned companies annually. It also provides scholarships for its suppliers to attend classes.
Lucent Technologies	1 of 7	7 of 50	21.7%	27.7%	10.5% 11.3% 5.4% 0.7%	32%	Minorities account for half of all management-track employees.
Hilton Hotels	1 of 14	4 of 50	28.8%	57.0%	7.8% 20.6% 28.1% 0.5%	59%	Almost 60% of new hires are minorities and close to a third assume managerial/professional positions.
PepsiCo	3 of 13	11 of 51	14.5%	25.4%	2.1% 13.2% 9.8% 0.9%	31%	One of our 50 Most Powerful Women in Business, Indian-born Indra Nooyi became even more powerful when she was named president of this soft drink giant in May.
Applied Materials	2 of 10	12 of 50	27.3%	40.1%	22.9% 6.5% 10.4% 0.3%	45%	The Silicon Valley maker of chip-manufacturing equipment earns its place with strong numbers in almost all categories. It's one of the top five companies for Asian Americans and counts 12 minorities among its 50 best-paid employees.
Levi Strauss	2 of 14	11 of 50	34.6%	56.4%	7.8% 9.9% 38.3% 0.4%		The jeans maker has struggled in the marketplace but is one of the top five companies for minority managers.
S.C. Johnson & Sons	2 of 10	8 of 50	11.7%	12.2%	1.5% 5.9% 4.4% 0.4%	21%	The 115-year-old family-owned company, maker of products like Sara Lee and Windex, is making a concerted effort to improve diversity in its upper minorities and offering them full-tuition M.B.A. fellowships.
Verizon Communications	3 of 16	3 of 50	19.9%	28.5%	3.4% 18.6% 6.1% 0.4%		The telecom company targets and prepares promising low-ranking minority employees for advancement. Verizon also provides training programs specifically for minorities.

Source: www.fortune.com (2002). Entire list of 50 firms with detailed information in each may also be found in that Web site.

Sample of 10 Best Companies for Asian, Black, and Hispanic Employees

Corning, Procter & Gamble, Avon, the *Miami Herald*, Digital Equipment Corporation, U.S. West, and other pacesetters in the successful management of diversity all have CEOs who are fully dedicated to putting this ideal into practice. For example, Avon has established a multicultural participation council (which includes the CEO) that meets regularly. Similarly, in a startling 10-page color brochure, the CEO of Corning announced that management of diversity is one of Corning's three top priorities, alongside total quality management and a higher return to shareholders. At IBM, departing CEO Lou Gerstner was very active and visible in directing diversity initiatives. He often met with IBM's board of directors and the senior management team to discuss diversity issues and held senior management accountable for recruitment, retention, and advancement of minorities and women.[108]

Diversity Training Programs

Diversity training programs Programs that provide diversity awareness training and educate employees on specific cultural and sex differences and how to respond to these in the workplace.

Supervisors need to learn new skills that will enable them to manage and motivate a diverse workforce. Ortho-McNeil Pharmaceutical, Hewlett-Packard, Wells Fargo, Kaiser Permanente, Microsoft, and other companies have developed extensive in-house **diversity training programs** that provide awareness training and workshops to educate managers and employees on specific cultural and sex differences and how to respond to these in the workplace.[109] A recent survey of CEOs found that the most common reason for implementing diversity training programs was "tapping diverse customers and markets" (44 percent). Only 2.9 percent of respondents indicated the avoidance of litigation as a reason.[110]

Much experimentation in this type of training is occurring around the United States.[111] DuPont has sponsored an all-expense-paid conference for African American managers to discuss the problems they encounter and how they can contribute more to the firm. AT&T has offered homophobia seminars designed to help straight employees feel comfortable working alongside openly gay employees and to eliminate offensive jokes and insults from the workplace.[112] Corning has introduced a mandatory four-day awareness training program for some 7,000 salaried employees—a day and a half for gender awareness, two and a half days for ethnic awareness.[113] In one of the most creative programs of this kind, Ethicon, Inc., a subsidiary of Johnson & Johnson that makes sutures, requires each supervisor to assume the identity of an employee of different ethnicity or sex and role-play accordingly.

At least a dozen big corporations, including Hewlett-Packard, DuPont, and Eastman Kodak, have introduced "diversity kits" aimed at employees' young children.[114] The companies give the kits to their employees and suggest that they share the information with their children. As Julie Baskin Brooks, a former manager of diversity at Xerox, notes, if society starts sensitizing people to diversity issues at a young age, "then maybe we won't have this mess when they are in their 20s."[115]

In 2002, the Society for Human Resource Management (SHRM) issued a report that examines diversity training programs. According to that report, diversity training "is a fundamental component of a diversity initiative and represents an opportunity for the organization to inform and educate senior management and staff about diversity."[116] However, this report also notes that frequently these programs fall short of expectations. Several factors undermine the effectiveness of these programs.[117]

First, the training may have come at a time when employees were preoccupied with more urgent priorities (such as downsizing, increased work level, or launching a new product under tight deadlines). Second, if employees perceive that external forces such as a court order or a politician's decree have prompted the training, they may resist. Third, if the training poses some as perpetrators and others as victims, those who feel blamed may be defensive. And fourth, if diversity is seen as the domain of a few groups (people of color and women, for example), everyone else may feel left out and view the initiative as being for others, not for them.

To avoid these four problems, SHRM provides recommendations including holding focus groups with people who may find fault with the training; creating a diversity council that represents a cross section of employees with a wide range of views and attitudes; and exploring ways to deliver the training that do not use a typical classroom format (such as one-on-one coaching to help managers deal with diversity challenges or interventions at team meetings on request).[118]

Support Groups

Some employees perceive corporate life as insensitive to their culture and background, perhaps downright hostile. The perception of an attitude that says "You don't belong here" or "You are here because we need to comply with government regulations" is largely responsible for the high turnover of minorities in many corporations.

To counteract these feelings of alienation, top management at many firms (such as FedEx, Bank of America, Allstate Insurance, DuPont, Marriott and Ryder) has been setting up **support groups.** These groups are designed to provide a nurturing climate for diverse employees who would otherwise feel shut out. These groups also provide a way for employees with the same ethnic or racial background or sexual orientation to find one another in the vast corporate bureaucracy. Figure 4.6 (Employee Resource Groups at Microsoft) lists such groups at Microsoft. As you

Support group
A group established by an employer to provide a nurturing climate for employees who would otherwise feel isolated or alienated.

Figure 4.6

The **African American** employee resource group began in 1989 and is dedicated to supporting the continued growth of African American employees at Microsoft. The group is also committed to reaching out to the African American community.

The **Attention Deficit Disorder** (ADD) group works to improve and enhance the lives of Microsoft employees and families affected by Attention Deficit/Hyperactivity Disorder through education, advocacy, and support.

The **Chinese** employee resource group was established in 1992 and now has members from China, Taiwan, Hong Kong, and North America.

The **Dads** group is an employee-driven initiative whose purpose is to equip and empower Microsoft fathers to more effectively balance their work with their family life.

The **Deaf and Hard of Hearing** group works to ensure that professional opportunities, corporate events, and corporate resources are accessible to individuals with hearing loss.

The **Filipino** group's mission is to share Microsoft's technology with the Filipino community and to encourage more Filipinos to become involved in the software industry.

The **Gay, Lesbian, Bisexual, and Transgender** group. Microsoft's oldest employee resource group dating back to 1988, pursues Microsoft's vision of equal opportunity for all employees without regard to sexual orientation.

The **Hispanic** employee resource group seeks to promote the Latino presence within Microsoft by active involvement with the recruitment and development of Latino employees, educational involvement at the college and high school levels, social interactions, and special events.

The **Indian** employee resource group is for employees from or interested in India. This group focuses on fostering activities through which members can share diverse cultural traditions and values.

The **Korean** employee resource group is dedicated to supporting the continued growth of Korean employees at Microsoft and providing support to the Korean community outside of Microsoft.

The **Native American** group's members work to impact Native American communities outside Microsoft and to increase the number of Native Americans within the organization itself. Members coordinate an annual volunteer mentor program for local area Native American youth that reaches about 10 students each year. Completion of the mentor program is celebrated with a traditional Pow Wow sponsored in part by Microsoft.

Working **Single Parents** have a lot of company at Microsoft, and this employee resource group helps bring them together for support, advice, and encouragement.

The **Taiwanese** employee resource group was established in 2000. The group supports Taiwanese employees at Microsoft and welcomes members interested in Taiwan.

Another active employee resource group works to attract, develop, and keep great **Women** at Microsoft. Founded in 1990, this employee group works to promote solutions for the issues that affect women in business.

Working Parents are a growing constituency at Microsoft and this group seeks to increase awareness for the issues that impact working parents and to present workable solutions to employees of Microsoft.

Source: Reprinted with permission from www.microsoft.com/diversity (2002).

Employee Resource Groups at Microsoft

see, these groups are truly diverse: for example, Attention Deficit Disorder people, Deaf and Hard of Hearing, Single-Parents, and Working Parents, in addition to various ethnic groups. Examples in other companies include Black Employee Network at American Express, the Women's Advisory Group at 3M, and the Asian Pacific Islanders' Business Resource Group at AT&T.[119]

A Question of Ethics

To what extent should employers be responsible for the appropriate care of their employees' children?

Accommodation of Family Needs

Firms can dramatically cut the turnover rate of their female employees if they are willing to help women handle a family and career simultaneously. Employers can use the following options to assist women in this endeavor. Unfortunately, most organizations do not yet offer these services.[120]

Day Care

Perhaps the best way to make it easier for women to keep their jobs after starting a family is to provide day care. Although the number of U.S. firms providing day-care support is increasing (see Manager's Notebook, "Round-the-Clock Day Care"), it is still true that most firms do not see day care as the company's responsibility.[121] The U.S. government has a "hands off" policy on day care. This is in sharp contrast with most other industrialized countries, where the government takes an active role in the provision of day care. (For more details, see the Issues and Applications feature titled "What European Countries Do for Mum, Maman, Mütter, and More . . .".)

MANAGER'S NOTEBOOK

Emerging Trends

Round-the-Clock Child Care

When Natalie Biggs works the night shift at Palace Station Casino in Las Vegas, her 5-year-old son enjoys a slumber party—even if it's a school night. Biggs, a change-booth operator, drops Donovan off at one of Station Casino's four 24-hour child-care centers. Developed and run by Dallas-based Children's Choice Learning Centers, they boast all the resources of a well-equipped child-care facility—playrooms, classrooms, game areas, and playgrounds—as well as full-fledged dormitories for boys and girls who need to stay the night. "I bring him in a little early, so he can play with his friends before going to bed," says Biggs. When she picks him up at 7:00 A.M., Donovan has already had breakfast and is dressed for school. Children's Choice has been a godsend for Biggs who moved to Las Vegas from Philadelphia in June 2000. "I don't have any family here," says Biggs, "and Donovan loves the center."

Launched just three years ago, Children's Choice Learning Centers has already developed six all-day centers serving 15 clients, with another 12 opening this year. The facilities benefit casino employees in Nevada, Louisiana, and Iowa, and hospital workers in Nevada, Missouri, and Texas. The company will open two new $4 million, 21,000-square-foot centers: one at MGM Grand/New York-New York in Las Vegas, the other at Medical City Dallas Hospital. President and CEO Leslie Wulf predicts Children's Choice will open as many as 150 centers in the next five to seven years.

Another company, Massachusetts-based Bright Horizons Family Solutions, runs round-the-clock child-care facilities for Toyota in Kentucky, for S.C. Johnson in Wisconsin, and two Ford Motor Co./United Auto Workers Family Service Learning Centers and is currently developing the child-care component at 11 more.

Children's Choice operates on a zero-cost model for employers. Companies contract for a certain number of slots, but Children's Choice makes the capital investment ($3.5 million on average) to build the center.

Source: Adapted with permission from Ashton, A. (2002, February). Round-the-clock child care. *Working Mother*, 64.

Issues and Applications

What European Countries Do for Mum, Maman, Mütter, and More . . .

- When it comes to creating a family-friendly workplace, more than an ocean separates U.S. and European companies. Unlike the United States, many European countries have provisions for maternity leave, child care, and flexible schedules—and they've had them in place for years. For example:
- Germany adopted its maternity leave law back in 1878. German women receive six weeks' prenatal leave at full pay and eight weeks postnatal leave, also at full pay. After mothers return to work, they get time off to breastfeed. In addition, there is a three-year parental leave for all working parents, both male and female.
- Sweden was the first nation to broaden extended postnatal maternity leave to "parental leave," for either the mother or the father, or for both alternately. Today Swedish parents are guaranteed a one-year leave of absence after childbirth. The first half is reserved for the mother, who receives 90 percent of her salary from social security.
- Denmark, with the highest level of publicly funded services in Europe, offers women 18 weeks' maternity leave, four weeks before the birth and 14 weeks afterward. Men can take 10 days' leave after their baby is born, and parental leave policy allows either the mother or the father to take an additional 10 weeks off after the birth.
- France leads the pack in day-care support. In addition to getting at least 16 weeks' maternity leave at 84 percent of their salaries, working mothers can bring their children to state-run day-care centers called *crèches*, which are open 11 hours a day and cost between $3.00 and $17.50 daily.
- Some European companies, such as National Westminster Bank (NWB) in London, have career break policies that allow employees to take a multiyear leave after the birth of a child. During that period the employee remains in contact with the company, fills in for vacationing employees, and participates in training. At NWB, career breaks of six months to seven years are available to staff at all grades.

"What we tend to find in Europe," says a coordinator of Daycare Trust in London, "is that the more government involvement there is in these issues, the more likely there is to be involvement by employers." In the United States it is up to individual companies to provide family-friendly programs. This creates some pockets of work-family innovation, but there is no national trend toward providing these kinds of services.

Alternative Work Patterns

Employers like Quaker Oats, IBM, Ciba-Geigy, and Pacific Telesis Group have been willing to experiment with new ways to help women balance career goals and mothering, and thereby have retained the services of many of their top performers.[122] As we saw in Chapter 2, these programs come in a variety of forms, including flexible work hours, flextime, and telecommuting. One type of program that is becoming more evident is job sharing where two people divvy up what normally is one person's full-time job. A survey in 2002 of more than 1,000 companies by consulting firm Hewitt Associates found that 28 percent of the organizations offer job sharing, up from 12 percent in 1990.[123] (See Manager's Notebook "Fair Shares.") Another option is extended leave. A rare benefit, **extended leave** allows employees to take a sabbatical from the office, sometimes up to three years, with benefits and the guarantee of a comparable job on return. Some companies require leave-takers to be on call for part-time work during their sabbatical.[124]

Extended leave
A benefit that allows an employee to take a long-term leave from the office, while retaining benefits and the guarantee of a comparable job on return.

Customer-Driven HR

MANAGER'S NOTEBOOK

Fair Shares

Two moms, alternating at one job. It's the ideal setup for women who want to cut their job work hours without stalling their careers while having more home work hours. How is it done?

For better or worse, Hilary Hausman and Sarah Moore are joined together on the job. Almost always, they'll tell you, it's for the better—better than working full-time and sacrificing time with their families, and better than working part-time and stalling their careers. Job sharing—two people in one position on alternate days—makes a lot of sense for mothers who want to cut hours without being "mommy tracked." Over the past decade, job sharing has caught on: In a survey of more than 1,000 companies by consulting firm Hewitt Associates, 28 percent of the organizations offer job sharing, up from just 12 percent in 1990. And almost all the companies on our 100 Best list have a job-sharing option.

Many working mothers must multitask. Distractions creep into the workday: phone calls to school between meetings, trips to the bank at lunchtime. But job sharers can usually take care of these tasks on their days off. "When I'm at work, my mind is completely on the job," says Moore. This plan doesn't benefit just job sharers—it's a huge plus for employers. Says veteran job-share supervisor Paul Anovick, "I would be satisfied if they delivered 100 percent, but really, they deliver 200 percent."

Job-share teams stress that they're one person, but the fact is that two people together can handle with minimal anxiety situations that would be incredibly stressful for single employees. "It's up to us to make the job-share work, even when obstacles present themselves," says Moore. "We tend to overdeliver."

So do most successful job sharers, and it's a bargain for employers. Typically, job sharers split salary, and health, vacation, and retirement benefits 50-50—a better deal than many part-timers get. But two people working 25 to 30 hours a week with one day of overlap, as Hausman, Moore, and the vast majority of job sharers do, bring more to the workplace than a single employee could. "Any one person who works sixty hours a week would tend to burn out," says Moore.

"Hilary and Sarah are a classic case of two and two making five," says the boss. "I get 20 percent more out of them than I would out of a single human." What's more, if the job sharers take staggered vacations, the position is always at least partially covered.

Source: Adapted with permission from Newman, A. M. (2002, February). *Working Mother*, 64–76.

These alternative work patterns are often collectively labeled the *mommy track*. This term can be negative or positive, depending upon how the company views its female employees who need assistance in combining a career with motherhood.[125] The less common term *daddy track* has arisen to describe the career paths of men who opt to spend some time raising their children. A survey conducted for the benefits consulting firm Robert Half International indicated that 74 percent of the men surveyed would accept slower career development in exchange for more time to spend with their families.[126] In addition, 21 percent of men report that they would prefer to stay home caring for family members if they did not need a paycheck.[127]

Senior Mentoring Programs

Senior mentoring program
A support program in which senior managers identify promising women and minority employees and play an important role in nurturing their career progress.

Some companies encourage **senior mentoring programs,** in which senior managers identify promising women and minority employees and play an important role in nurturing their career progress.[128] At Marriott, for instance, newly hired employees with disabilities are paired with Marriott managers who serve as their coaches. Honeywell and 3M team up experienced executives with young women and minorities to give them advice on career strategies and corporate politics, as do Xerox and DQE Corporation, a Pittsburgh utilities firm.[129]

Apprenticeships

Apprenticeship
A program in which promising prospective employees are groomed before they are actually hired on a permanent basis.

Apprenticeships are similar to senior mentoring programs, except that promising prospective employees are groomed before they are actually hired on a permanent basis. As with senior mentoring, company managers are encouraged to become actively involved in apprenticeship programs. For example, Sears has established an apprenticeship program that gives students hands-on training in skills like basic electronics and appliance repair. The best students are hired for ten hours a week to work at a Sears Service Center. This on-the-job training is integrated into the school curriculum, and the most talented students are hired upon completion of the program.

Technology and Diversity

E-mail and the Internet can diminish stereotypes for potential recruits, employees, and business owners because the interaction focuses on the content, not the color, sex, or cultural background of the communicators. Betty A. Ford discovered how the anonymity of the Web helps her sell hand-tailored boxer shorts through her online site City Boxers. Ford, a black entrepreneur, knew that in a physical retail store her sex and color should not matter, but they would hinder her ability to sell her product. In contrast, Ford notes that on the Web "people make their decision on what the boxer shorts look like, not on who's selling them."[130]

Communication Standards

Certain styles of communication may be offensive to women and minority employees. Examples are the use of "he" when referring to managers and "she" when referring to secretaries, inadequately representing or ignoring minorities in annual reports, failure to alphabetize ethnic groups' titles (Asian, Latino, etc.), and using terms, such as *protected classes* and *alien*, that may have a precise legal meaning but are offensive to those being described. To avoid these problems, organizations should set *communication standards* that take into account the sensitivities of a diverse employee population.

Businesses should also set policies to prevent any use of technology that promotes stereotyping. For instance, a firm should have a clear policy that prohibits e-mail containing racial, sexist, or homophobic comments and jokes. If handled well, such policies reinforce top management's commitment to diversity.

Organized Activities

All the programs we have discussed here may be supplemented by social events that celebrate diversity.[131] For instance, Pillsbury regularly offers ethnic cuisine and specialty events in the Pillsbury cafeteria. The Microsoft Windows Platform Division hosts Equal Access Benefit Concerts at major industry conferences exclusively for the IT community. Past celebrity entertainers include Sinbad, Ziggy Marley and the Melody Makers, Kool and the Gang (featuring JT Taylor), the Brian Setzer Orchestra, the B-52's, and Santana. Equal Access tickets have become "must haves" at expos such as Comdex, Windows World, and Networld+Interop. More than 13,500 IT professionals have attended a Windows Platform Division Equal Access Benefit performance in past years.[132]

Diversity Audits

Often the roots of an employee diversity problem (such as high turnover of minority employees) are not immediately evident. In these instances, research in the form of a **diversity audit** may be necessary to uncover possible sources of bias. When Xerox discovered that women and minorities early in their careers with the company were less likely to hold positions that successful managers had held when they were at lower levels, the company concentrated on assigning promising women and minorities to jobs with greater fast-track potential. Microsoft has developed an index that measures the success or failure of specific diversity activities and strategies over time and their impact on the organization.[133] Detailed information on the index appears at www.microsoft.com/diversity.

Diversity audit
A review of the effectiveness of an organization's diversity management program.

Management Responsibility and Accountability

Management of diversity will not be a high priority and a formal business objective unless managers and supervisors are held accountable for implementing diversity management and rewarded for doing so successfully. At the very minimum, successful diversity management

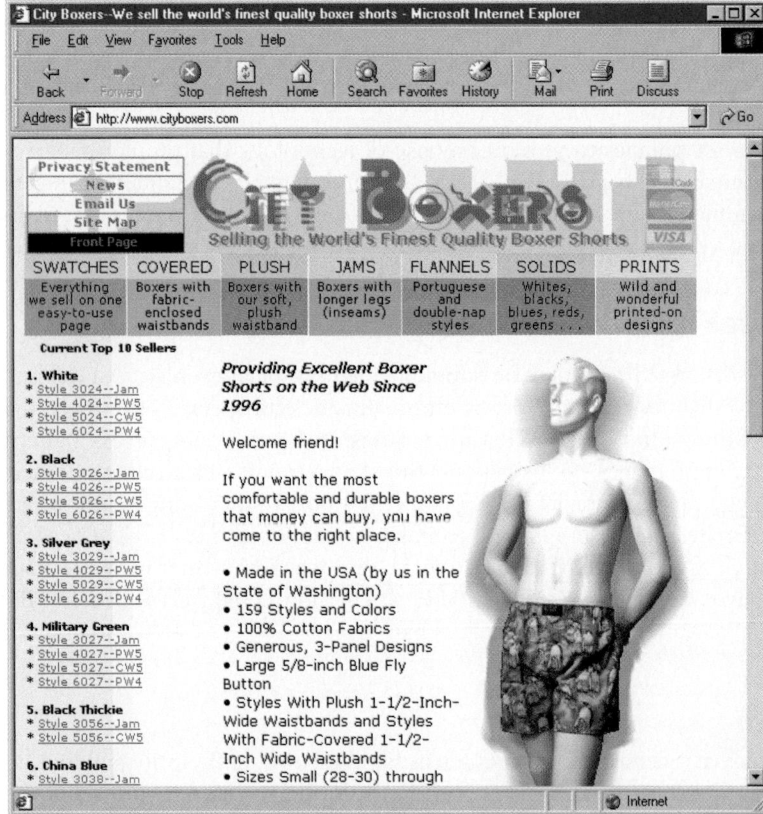

City Boxers' owner Betty Ford launched her boxer shorts business on the Web to bypass traditional sex and racial stereotypes that could hinder product sales.

Source: Crockett, R. (1998, October 5). Invisible—and loving it. *BusinessWeek*, 124–125.

should be one of the factors in the performance appraisal system for those in positions of authority. For instance, at Garrett Company, a manufacturer of jet engines, bonus pay is tied to a supervisor's record on managing diversity.

Some Warnings

Two potential pitfalls must be avoided if diversity management programs are to be successful. These are (1) avoiding the appearance of "white male bashing" and (2) avoiding the promotion of stereotypes.

Avoiding the Appearance of "White Male Bashing"

Disproving the accusation that managing diversity is just another catchphrase for providing opportunities for women and minorities *at the expense of white men* is crucial to the successful management of diversity programs. Otherwise, these programs are likely to engender resentment, heighten anxieties, and inflame the prejudices of those who feel threatened. A delicate balancing act is required because, given limited resources, some competition is inevitable. At the very least, management should continually emphasize the positive aspects of capitalizing on employee diversity by framing it as something that (1) must be done to gain a competitive advantage and (2) is in the best interests of all employees. Training programs, if properly designed, may be used as efficient vehicles to convey these messages. Another approach is to use rewards. For instance, Whirlpool distributed an extra $2,700 to each employee in its Benton Harbor, Michigan, plant in a single year in response to productivity and quality improvements. The plant has a significant minority population, and the group incentive induced all employees to work closely together in what they saw as a win-win effort.[134]

For some guidelines on what HR professionals and company managers can do to avoid the appearance of "white male bashing" and increase the positive response to the firms diversity program, see the Manager's Notebook titled "Preventing Diversity Backlash."

MANAGER'S NOTEBOOK

Preventing Diversity Backlash

Many organizations that have instituted diversity programs have experienced adverse reactions from employee groups, particularly white men. Here are some guidelines for HR professionals and company managers who are attempting to manage diversity without adversity.

1. Adopt an inclusive definition of diversity that addresses all kinds of differences among employees including (but not limited to) race and gender. A broader definition of diversity will invite participation and lower resistance.
2. Make sure that top management is not only committed to establishing a diversity program but also communicates that commitment directly to all employees. Top executives should also let managers know why diversity is important to the company's bottom line and global competitiveness.
3. Involve everyone, including white men, in designing the diversity program. White men will be less resistant to these programs if they are included on the task forces, panels, and other groups the company sets up to look at diversity issues and decide how the company should handle them.
4. Avoid stereotyping groups of employees, such as white men, when explaining cultural or ethnic differences. Although the airing of stereotypes is a common facet of diversity training workshops, trainers should direct trainees away from focusing on any group as "the culprit" and affirm the value of each person's individual experience and viewpoint.
5. Recognize and reward white men who are part of the solution rather than blaming men who are part of the problem. Many white men who have long been advocates for diversity feel they are not being recognized for it.
6. Avoid one-shot training efforts that stir up emotions without channeling them in productive directions. Use ongoing training that encompasses diversity as only one facet of needed change in the corporate culture.
7. Ensure that employees perceive minorities and women as competing successfully on their own rather than receiving favorable treatment.

Source: Adapted from Merritt (2002), SHRM (2002a, b, d) *Fortune* (1999, April 26). Special section on minority business enterprises, 130–153; Merritt, J. (2002, March 11). Guess who's pushing a bold plan for diversity? Big business. *BusinessWeek*, 56–58; Society for Human Resource Management (SHRM). (2002a, February 13). Diversity training. www.shrm.org/diversity; Society for Human Resource Management (SHRM). (2002b, February 13). What if your diversity training is successful? www.shrm.org/diversity; Society for Human Resource Management (SHRM). (2002d, February 13). Where AR meets the world: How should my organization define diversity? www.shrm.org/diversity.

Avoiding the Promotion of Stereotypes

As we discussed earlier, an inherent danger in diversity programs is inadvertent reinforcement of the notion that one can draw conclusions about a particular person based simply on his or her group characteristics. Remember, differences between individuals *within* any given group are almost always greater than the "average" or typical differences *between* any two groups. **Cultural determinism**—promoting the idea that one can infer an individual's motivations, interests, values, and behavioral traits based on that individual's group memberships—robs employees of their individuality and creates a divisive mind-set of "them versus us."

Unfortunately, cultural awareness programs and other diversity training activities tend (unintentionally) to overdramatize diversity. This may lead participants to hold assumptions regarding groups that are totally incorrect (and most likely offensive) when applied to specific employees.[135]

Cultural determinism
The idea that one can successfully infer an individual's motivations, interests, values, and behavioral traits based on that individual's group memberships.

Every employee deserves to be treated as an individual who has a unique set of needs experiences, motivations, interests, and capabilities. The result of diversity efforts should always be to promote the value of individuals. It may be necessary to discuss group differences and characteristics as a means to that end, but those discussions should never be the stopping point. Managers who remember and apply this basic tenet will be able to take full advantage of the abilities of all their employees.

Summary and Conclusions

What Is Diversity?

Diversity refers to human characteristics that make people different from one another. Today's labor force is highly diverse. If effectively managed, this diversity can provide the organization with a powerful competitive edge because it stimulates creativity, enhances problem solving by offering broader perspectives, and infuses flexibility into the firm.

Challenges in Managing Employee Diversity

An organization confronts significant challenges in making employee diversity work to its advantage. These include (1) genuinely valuing employee diversity, (2) balancing individual needs with group fairness, (3) coping with resistance to change, (4) promoting group cohesiveness, (5) ensuring open communication, (8) retaining valued performers, and (9) managing competition for opportunities.

Diversity in Organizations

Some groups are likely to be left out of the corporate mainstream. African Americans still face a certain amount of explicit racism and tend to be less educationally prepared for the workplace. Asian Americans confront two stereotypes—one saying they are too cautious and reserved to lead, and another saying they are unscrupulous in business—as well as the feeling that they are too educated to merit special consideration as a minority. Full social acceptance is still denied to people with disabilities, who are often incorrectly perceived as being less capable than others, more prone to quit their jobs under pressure, and costly to accommodate in the workplace.

Foreign-born workers face language and cultural barriers and sometimes ethnic/racial prejudice. They are often resented by Americans of all races, who believe they are taking their jobs.

Homosexuals sometimes face outright discrimination (the refusal to hire or retain them as employees) and ostracism from coworkers or managers. Latinos face language and cultural difficulties and, in some cases, racial discrimination.

Older workers encounter negative stereotypes about their abilities, energy, and adaptability, as well as some physical problems and resentment from younger workers. Women often fare badly in male-dominated corporate cultures that display masculine leadership biases and have old boys' networks that exclude women. They are also subject to sexual harassment to a much greater degree than men.

Improving the Management of Diversity

Organizations that have capitalized the most on their diverse human resources to gain a competitive advantage tend to have top management committed to valuing diversity; solid, ongoing diversity training programs; support groups that nurture nontraditional employees; and policies that accommodate employees' family needs. They also have senior mentoring and apprenticeship programs to encourage employees' career progress, set communication standards that discourage discrimination, celebrate diversity through organized activities, use diversity audits to uncover bias, and hold their managers responsible for effectively implementing diversity policies.

Some Warnings

There are two pitfalls in diversity management programs that managers must be careful to avoid: (1) giving the appearance of "white male bashing" and (2) unintentionally promoting stereotypes.

Key Terms

Discussion Questions

1. In 2002, Rent-A-Center, based in Plano, Texas, was slapped with a sex discrimination and harassment case "that is allegedly so big and so extreme that the federal government is trying to block the proposed settlement—something it has not done in at least 30 years."[136] Rent-A-Center is the nation's largest rent-to-own furniture and home appliance company, employing 4,600 women. While the company is offering a $12.25 million payment to women plaintiffs, the EEOC believes the offer is inadequate and could undercut cases elsewhere. The allegations? Men pushing women out of jobs and literally destroying women's job applications. Sworn statements quote a senior executive as saying, "Women should be home taking care of their husbands and children." Some women accused executives of "smacking their butts." As circumstantial evidence of a negative climate against women, those employees who feel aggrieved pull out the company newsletter, picturing 66 managers—all males. According to one of the women's attorneys, Jerome Schlicter, "It's the most remarkable example of a mentality that was supposed to have gone out of American business 50 years ago."[137] Why do many firms wait until being faced with a legal suit to respond to diversity issues rather than handling them proactively?
2. The United States is often viewed by outsiders as a litigious society, where everyone has a lawyer and is willing to sue someone else on the slightest basis. Until recently, Europeans believed that sexual harassment suits are just part of this American penchant for litigation. Europeans saw flirting between a male supervisor and a female subordinate as natural chivalry at work. Yet according to *The Economist*, "Europe may be following America's often flamboyant practices in such matters."[138] The tripling of such cases in Britain during the past 10 years is an indication that sexual harassment is no longer an American phenomena. Why do you think this is happening overseas? Explain.
3. Women and ethnic minorities are often lumped together as a single class. What do these two groups have in common? What are the major differences between them? Explain.
4. Conflicts among minority groups may arise as they compete for a limited number of jobs and promotion opportunities. What can firms do to avoid these kinds of conflict?
5. Some people still believe that the best way—and perhaps the only fair way—to manage is to treat all employees equally regardless of their sex, race, ethnicity, physical impairment, and other personal characteristics. Do you agree? Explain.
6. When a long-time contract employee for Pacific Gas & Electric in Tracy, California, was the first in his unit to be laid off, he claimed that the others—an African American woman and a man of Indian descent—had been kept on (even though they were less qualified than he was) because PG&E was intent on creating a more diverse workplace. "I feel like I'm losing out," this white male employee said. PG&E claimed his race and sex had nothing to do with his being laid off. What can companies do to keep white males from feeling victimized by diversity efforts and training programs instead of valued as "diverse" employees in their own right?
7. James L. Schneider, owner of a small computer design and software consulting company in San Francisco, complains that he has a difficult time competing with firms that bring foreign software engineers into the United States to do similar work for one-third the price Schneider charges. "American citizens are out on the street," Schneider says. "In the competitive world, it is difficult to bid against people who work at substantially lower rates."

   On the other side of the coin, many U.S. computer companies fear that if they do not hire foreign talent, then competitors in other countries will. What is your position on these opposite views? Explain.
8. Doug Dokolosky, a former IBM executive who specializes in coaching women, argues that "to reach the top requires sacrifice and long hours. If that is your ambition, forget things like balancing work and family. . . ." Do you agree with Dokolosky that most U.S. firms just pay lip service to family accommodation policies? Can you think of any noteworthy exceptions?

There is a variety of additional material available on the Web site that accompanies this text. You can access this information by visiting the Web site at **www.prenhall.com/gomez.**

YOU MANAGE IT!

Discussion Case 4.1

Making Time for a Baby

At age 27 a woman's chances of getting pregnant begin to decline. At age 20, the risk of miscarriage is about 9 percent; it doubles by age 35, then doubles again by the time a woman reaches her early forties. At age 42, 90 percent of a woman's eggs are abnormal. As many women have become dedicated to their careers—putting off having children to focus on their work—there has been a 100 percent rise in the past 20 years of childless women ages 40 to 44. Economist Sylvia Ann Hewlett states in her new book, *Creating a Life: Professional Women and the Quest for Children* (Talk Miramax Books), that many ambitious young women who hope to have kids are heading down a bad piece of road if they think they can spend a decade establishing their careers and wait until 35 or beyond to establish their families.

Women have been debating for a generation how best to balance work and home life, but somehow each new chapter starts a new fight, and Hewlett's book is no exception. In 1989, when Felice Schwartz discussed in *Harvard Business Review* how to create more flexibility for career women with children (she never uses the phrase *mommy track* herself), her proposals were called "dangerous" and "retrofeminist" because they could give corporations an excuse to derail women's careers. Slow down to start a family, the skeptics warned, and you run the risk that you will never catch up.

And so, argues Hewlett, many women embraced a "male model" of single-minded career focus, and the result is "an epidemic of childlessness" among professional women. She conducted a national survey of 1,647 "high-achieving women," made up of 1,168 who earn in the top 10 percent of income of their age group or hold degrees in law or medicine and another 479 who are highly educated but are no longer in the workforce. What she learned shocked her. She found that 42 percent of high-achieving women in corporate America—companies with 5,000 or more employees—were still childless after age 40. That ratio was 49 percent of women who earn $100,000 or more. Many other women were able to have only one child because they started their families too late. "They've been making a lot of money," says Dr. David Adamson, a leading fertility specialist at Stanford University, "but it won't buy back the time."

Recent census data support Hewlett's research: Childlessness has doubled in the past 20 years, so that 20 percent of women between ages 40 to 44 are childless. For women that age and younger with graduate and professional degrees, the figure is 47 percent. This group certainly includes women for whom having children was never a priority. For them, the opening of the workforce offered many new opportunities, including the opportunity to define success in realms other than motherhood. But Hewlett argues that many other women did not actually choose to be childless. When she asked women to recall their intentions at the time they were finishing college, Hewlett found that only 14 percent said that they definitely did not want to have children.

For most women whom Hewlett interviewed, childlessness was what one called "a creeping non-choice." Time passes, work is relentless. The travel, the hours—relationships are hard to sustain. By the time a woman marries and feels settled enough in her career to think of starting a family, it may often be too late. "They go to a doctor, take a blood test and are told the game is over before it even begins," says L.A.'s Madsen. "They are shocked, devastated and angry." Women generally know their fertility declines with age; they just don't realize how much and how fast.

According to Hewlett, "In just 30 years we've gone from fearing our fertility to squandering it—and very unwittingly."

Critical Thinking Questions

1. The book by Hewlett suggests a problem for women in their twenties: The best years for having children coincide with the best years for establishing a career. How do you think women should handle this situation? What role should men play when their partners face this predicament? Explain.
2. Some people believe that organizations should share some of the responsibility for childbearing, which is absolutely necessary for a society's self-preservation. Concepts such as the "mommy track," "baby paid sabbatical," and "child care at work" have been proposed as ways that firms can fulfill this responsibility. Do you agree? Do you think firms would offer such programs voluntarily without government mandate? Explain.
3. Many managers look negatively at a "résumé gap"—the duration of time a person is not in the workforce. Women who take time off to raise a family are often at a disadvantage in a competitive hiring situation. Although few managers would admit it, they might not hire a woman of

childbearing age or promote her to a more responsible position for fear that she might become pregnant. How can a firm deal with these potential biases? Explain.

Team Exercise

Assume that top executives of a high-technology firm would like to offer women more opportunities to balance career and family. These executives believe that attracting and retaining talented women will give the firm a competitive advantage. Students divide into groups of six, preferably three males and three females, to role-play this situation and develop some recommendations for top management. Instructor may play the role of CEO.

Source: Adapted with permission from Horowitz, J. M., Rawe, J., and Song, S. (2002, April 15). Making time for a baby. *Time*, 49–58.

Discussion Case 4.2

YOU MANAGE IT!

Living in America After September 11

Racial profiling is not new in the United States. Many German Americans faced it during World War I, Japanese Americans were put into concentration camps during World War II, African Americans are often targeted by police for routine traffic violations, and Hispanic Americans often have to deal with immigration raids. Within five months of the terrorist attacks of September 11, 2001, there was a 150 percent increase in the number of "biased incidents" against people who appear to be Muslim. What's it like being an Arab American businessman today? Just ask the number-one retailer of U.S. flags.

Fawaz Ismail heard the whooping sound of a police siren as he cruised his topaz Mercedes out of the parking lot of his favorite Afghan restaurant on a mid-September afternoon. It was just a routine stop, the officer told him. He needed to see some I.D. What the policeman didn't explain—but what Ismail fully understood—was that being an Arab American in suburban Virginia, just a stone's throw from the Pentagon and a few miles from Washington, DC—was about to get complicated.

Ismail obliged, handing over his driver's license along with two American-flag lapel pins, the same ones his company provides to the White House, among other customers. He supplies most government agencies and all but a few foreign embassies in Washington. He even designed a special 50th anniversary flag for the CIA.

"When you see President Bush on TV, these are the exact pins he's wearing," Ismail told the cop. "But I can't take these," the officer parried. "Then give them to your friends," said Ismail before he smiled and drove off.

To some people Fawaz Hassan "Tony" Ismail looks Greek. To others he could pass for Italian or Latino. But to a jittery cop in the aftermath of September 11, the 40-year-old Palestinian American CEO of Alamo Flags, the country's largest retail-flag enterprise, fits the racial profile of the potential terrorist.

It's an experience shared by many Arabs and Muslims these days. In the weeks that followed the September attacks, the nation's 3 million Arab American citizens endured a barrage of bigotry, anger, and suspicion. Passengers have refused to board planes with Arab travelers—or anyone that remotely resembles an Arab. Formerly cordial neighbors have vandalized Arab homes. Self-proclaimed patriotic zealots have attacked Arab men, women, and children in the streets. The American-Arab Anti-Discrimination Committee logged more than 440 hate crimes and cases of discrimination and harassment against Arabs and Muslims within two months of September 11. Unfortunately, other "foreign-looking" people have also suffered from hate crimes after September 11, 2001. For instance, an Asian Indian gas-station attendant was killed in Arizona by an assassin who later bragged to police about killing terrorists.

Critical Thinking Questions

1. Stereotypes often play an important role in how people react to others. Whether or not it is a conscious policy, "racial profiling" based on stereotypes may lead to discrimination. What can a firm do to deal with this potential problem? Explain.
2. Security concerns have grown enormously important since September 11, 2001, and the federal government keeps these concerns alive through frequent warnings. It is impossible to keep an eye on everybody, so there is the possibility that only "high-risk" groups such as Arab Americans or those who look foreign are explicitly targeted for close monitoring. These people, of course, would feel ostracized for acts they had nothing to do with. What should a firm do to deal with this type of prejudice?
3. If you were a person who fit a certain stereotype, what would you do at work to prevent being a target of racial profiling? And if you think you have been such a target, what did you do to defend yourself? Explain.

Team Exercise

An airline has reported several cases in which pilots and flight attendants have refused to fly when Arab Americans are on the plane, even after they have undergone exhaustive security screening. A recent case was well publicized when one of President Bush's top security advisers, who happens to be Arab American, was forced to leave the plane. There have also been situations in which employees have refused to work with Arab American colleagues. Students divide up into groups of five and role-play a situation in which the company CEO asks a team of senior pilots to recommend how to handle such incidents.

Source: Adapted with permission from Simmons, J. (2002, January 7). Living in America. *Fortune*, 92–94.

YOU MANAGE IT!

Discussion Case 4.3

Conflict at Northern Sigma

Northern Sigma, a hypothetical high-technology firm headquartered in New York, develops and manufactures advanced electronic equipment. The company has 20 plants around the United States and 22,000 employees, 3,000 of whom work at a single site in Chicago that is responsible for research and development. About half of the employees at that facility are scientists and engineers. The other half are support personnel, managers, and market research personnel. Corporate executives are strongly committed to hiring women and minorities throughout the entire organization, but particularly at the Chicago site. The company has adopted this policy for two reasons: Women and minorities are severely underrepresented in the Chicago plant (making up only about 13 percent of the workforce), and it is becoming increasingly difficult to find top-notch talent in the dwindling applicant pool of white men.

Phillip Wagner is the general manager of the Chicago plant. In his most recent performance evaluation he was severely criticized for not doing enough to retain women and minorities. For the past two years, the turnover rate for these groups has been three times higher than that for other employees. Corporate executives estimate that this high turnover rate is costing at least $1 million a year in training costs, lost production time, recruitment expenses, and so forth. In addition, more than 70 charges of discrimination have been filed with the EEOC during the past three years alone—a much higher number of complaints than would be expected given the plant's size and demographic composition.

Under pressure from headquarters, Wagner has targeted the turnover and discrimination problems as among his highest priorities for this year. As a first step, he has hired a consulting team to interview a representative sample of employees to find out (1) why the turnover rate among women and minorities is so high and (2) what is prompting so many complaints from people in these groups. The interviews were conducted in separate groups of 15 people each. Each group consisted either of white men or a mix of women and minorities. A summary of the report prepared by the consultants follows.

Women and Minority Groups

A large proportion of women and minority employees expressed strong dissatisfaction with the company. Many felt they had been misled when they accepted employment at Northern Sigma. Among their most common complaints:

- Being left out of important task forces.
- Personal input not requested very often—and when requested, suggestions and ideas generally ignored.
- Contributions not taken very seriously by peers in team or group projects.
- Need to be 10 times better than white male counterparts to be promoted.
- Lack of respect and lack of acknowledgment for work experience.
- A threatening, negative environment that discourages open discussion of alternatives.
- Supervisors often arrogant, insensitive, domineering, and patronizing.
- Frequent use of demeaning ethnic- or gender-related jokes.
- Minimal career support once hired.

White Male Groups

Most white men, particularly supervisors, strongly insisted that they were interested solely in performance and that neither race nor sex had anything to do with how they treated their staff members or fellow employees. They often used such terms as equality, fairness, competence, and color-blindness to describe their criteria for promotions, assignments, selection for team projects, and task force membership. Many of these men felt that, rather than being penalized, women and minorities were given "every conceivable break."

The consulting team asked this group of white men specific questions concerning particular problems they may have encountered at work with women and the three largest minority groups in the plant (African Americans, Asian Americans, and Latinos). The most common comments regarding the white men's encounters with each of these groups follow.

African Americans

- Frequently overreact.
- Expect special treatment because of their race.
- Unwilling to blend in with the work group, even when white colleagues try to make them feel comfortable.

- Like to do things on their own terms and schedules.
- Do not respond well to supervision.

Asian Americans

- Difficult to figure out what they really think; very secretive.
- Passive-aggressive: One can never tell when they are upset, but they have their way of getting back at you when you least expect it.
- Very smart with numbers, but have problems verbalizing ideas.
- Stoic and cautious; will not challenge another person even when that person is blatantly wrong.
- Like to be left alone; do not want to become supervisors even if this means an increase in pay.
- Prone to express agreement or commitment to an idea or course of action, yet are uncommitted to it in their hearts.

Latinos

- Many can barely speak English.
- Often volatile and emotional.
- More concerned with their extended family than with work; work is often incidental to them and they exhibit little attachment to the firm.
- Often have a difficult time handling structured tasks as employees, yet become dogmatic and authoritarian in supervisory positions.
- Have a difficult time at work dealing with women whom they expect to be submissive and passive.
- Very lax about punctuality and schedules.
- Difficult to tell when they really mean "yes" because they have many ways of saying "yes"; quite often "yes" really means "maybe" or "no," but they just do not want to offend you. Yet you are still expected to figure out their true response.
- Tend to be verbal rather than analytical.

Women

- Most are not very committed to work and are inclined to quit when things don't go their way.
- Often more focused on interpersonal relationships than on work performance.
- Respond too emotionally when frustrated by minor problems, thus unsuited for more responsibility.
- Sensitive and unpredictable.
- Moody.
- Tend to misinterpret chivalry as sexual overtures.
- Indecisive.
- Cannot keep things confidential and enjoy gossip.

Phillip Wagner was shocked at many of these comments. He had always thought of his plant as a friendly, easygoing, open-minded, liberal, intellectual place because it has a highly educated workforce (most employees have college degrees, and a significant proportion have advanced graduate degrees). He is now trying to figure out what to do next.

Critical Thinking Questions

1. What consequences are likely to result from the problems at the Northern Sigma plant? Explain your answer.
2. Should Wagner be held responsible for these problems? Explain.
3. What specific recommendations would you offer Wagner to improve the management of diversity at the Chicago plant?

Team Exercise

The class divides into groups of three to five students. Each group should discuss what recommendations it would make to Wagner. After 10 to 15 minutes, each group should present its recommendations to the class. How different are the recommendations from group to group? What principles from the chapter were you able to apply to this problem?

Part III: Staffing

Recruiting and Selecting Employees

Challenges

After reading this chapter, you should be able to deal more effectively with the following challenges:

1. **Understand** the supply and demand of HR.
2. **Weigh** the advantages and disadvantages of internal and external recruiting.
3. **Distinguish** among the major selection methods and use the most legally defensible of them.
4. **Make** staffing decisions that maximize the hiring and promotion of the best people.
5. **Understand** the legal constraints on the hiring process.

Specialty Cabinets Company had rapidly expanded from a two-person operation to a small business with 28 employees. This thriving business catered to those who needed high-end cabinet work in custom-built homes or office buildings. Specialty had been able to attract highly trained carpenters because of the pay and the collegial work environment. However, the company's president realized that Specialty needed to hire an additional manager to cope with the expanded number of employees and projects. She gave George Zoran, a senior supervisor with strong interpersonal skills, the responsibility for hiring the new manager.

George posted the notice of an opening on the company bulletin board and put an ad in the "Help Wanted" section of the classified ads of the local newspaper. Soon he received numerous applications from candidates inside and outside the company. George made some telephone calls to screen for candidates who should be interviewed personally. He then scheduled and conducted several interviews.

George was particularly impressed with one candidate, Tim Wells. Tim had never worked in carpentry, but George thought Tim seemed personable and had sufficient managerial experience and ambition to handle the job. Interestingly, George also learned that Tim was the son of an old school friend. He thoroughly enjoyed telling Tim about hunting trips he had taken with Tim's father.

On the next round of interviews, George took Tim on a tour of the business operation and offered him the position. George was confident that Tim would be a great addition to the company. Unfortunately, his expectations proved overly optimistic.

Other workers complained about Tim's lack of woodworking experience. They also complained that Tim did not ask for their opinion when he should have. For instance, Tim did not have the knowledge to plan schedules that ensured project deadlines would be met and he did not ask for advice. As a result, his employees recently had to work long hours over a holiday weekend to meet a critical deadline. The workers wondered why George had hired Tim, and Tim wondered why George had led him to believe he could succeed in the job.

THE MANAGERIAL PERSPECTIVE

Although HR managers may be responsible for designing employee recruitment and selection systems in many firms, all managers need to understand and use these systems. After all, attracting and hiring the right kind and level of talent are critical elements of business effectiveness. Stocking a company with top talent has been described as the single most important job of management.[1] The abilities of attracting and hiring effective employees are also key elements of a successful management career. As the Specialty Cabinets example demonstrates, managers may be in charge of recruiting or have a key role in the process. If they do not attract and hire the right people, managers can hurt the organization.

The focus of this chapter is on understanding and conducting effective recruitment and selection. As you think back to the situation at Specialty Cabinets, consider these important questions:

- Who should make the hiring decision?
- What characteristics should a firm look at when deciding whom to hire, and how should those characteristics be measured?
- Should managers consider how a potential employee "fits" with the firm's culture in addition to that employee's skill level?

In this chapter we explore how managers plan recruitment efforts effectively by assessing the supply of and demand for human resources. Then we examine the hiring process in detail, the challenges managers face in hiring and promoting, and recommendations for dealing with those challenges. Finally, we evaluate specific methods for making hiring decisions and the legal issues that affect hiring decisions.

Human Resource Supply and Demand

Labor supply is the availability of workers who possess the required skills that an employer might need. **Labor demand** is the number of workers an organization needs. Estimating future labor supply and demand and taking steps to balance the two require planning.

Labor supply
The availability of workers with the required skills to meet the firm's labor demand.

Human resource planning (HRP) is the process an organization uses to ensure that it has the right amount and the right kinds of people to deliver a particular level of output or services in the future. Firms that do not conduct HRP may not be able to meet their future labor needs (a labor shortage) or may have to resort to layoffs (in the case of a labor surplus).

Labor demand
How many workers the organization will need in the future.

Human resource planning (HRP)
The process an organization uses to ensure that it has the right amount and the right kind of people to deliver a particular level of output or services in the future.

A failure to plan can lead to significant financial costs. For instance, firms that lay off large numbers of employees are required to pay higher taxes to the unemployment insurance system, whereas firms that ask their employees to work overtime are required to pay them a wage premium. (We discuss both of these issues in detail in Chapter 2.) In addition, firms sometimes need to do HRP to satisfy legally mandated affirmative action programs (see Chapter 3). In large organizations HRP is usually done centrally by specially trained HR staff.

Figure 5.1 summarizes the HRP process. The first HRP activity entails forecasting labor demand. Labor demand is likely to increase as demand for the firm's product or services increases and to decrease as labor productivity increases (because more output can be produced with fewer workers, usually because of the introduction of new technology).

The second part of the HRP process entails estimating labor supply. The labor supply may come from existing employees (the *internal* labor market) or from outside the organization (the *external* labor market).

After estimating labor demand and supply for a future period, a firm faces one of three conditions, each of which requires a different set of responses. In the first scenario, the firm will need more workers than will be available. A variety of approaches can then be used to increase the labor supply available to a specific firm. These include training or retraining existing workers, grooming current employees to take over vacant positions (*succession planning*), promoting from within, recruiting new employees from outside the firm, subcontracting part of the work to other firms, hiring part-timers or temporary workers, and paying overtime to existing employees.

Which approach or approaches are appropriate will depend on their relative costs and how long the labor shortage is expected to last. For instance, if demand exceeds supply by only a small amount and this situation is deemed temporary, paying overtime may be less expensive than hiring new workers, which entails extra costs for training and legally mandated benefits (such as Social Security payments and workers' compensation insurance).

Human Resource Planning

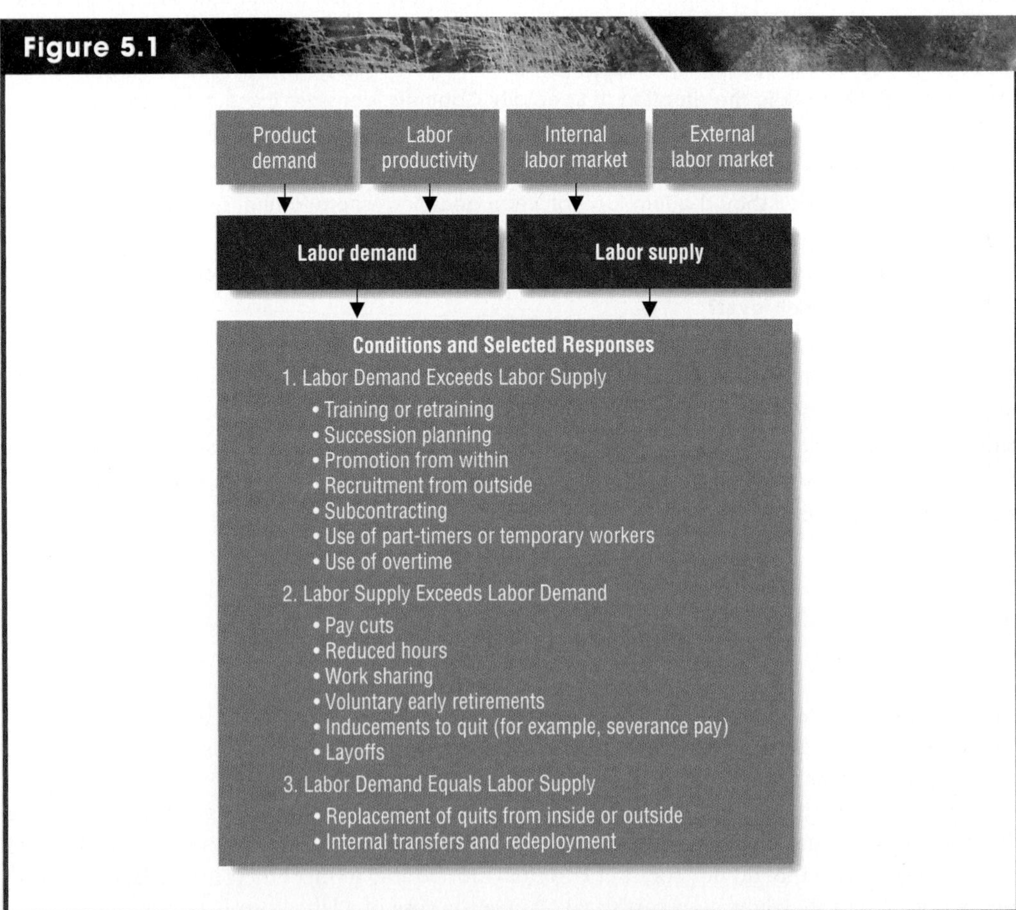

In the second scenario, labor supply is expected to exceed labor demand. This excess means that the firm will have more employees than it needs. Firms may use a variety of measures to deal with this situation. These include pay cuts, reducing the number of hours worked, and work sharing (all of which may save jobs). In addition, the firm may eliminate positions through a combination of tactics, including early retirement incentives, severance pay, and outright layoffs. (We discuss these issues in detail in Chapter 6 and 13.) If the labor surplus is expected to be modest, the firm may be better off reducing the number of hours worked instead of terminating employees. Under federal law, the latter option would force the firm to pay more into the unemployment compensation insurance program. Furthermore, reducing hours worked rather than laying off workers can avoid additional recruiting and training costs when the demand for labor increases.[2] (The Controllers Report 2002).

In the third scenario, labor demand is expected to match labor supply. The organization can deal with this situation by replacing employees who quit with people promoted from the inside the business or hired from the outside. The firm may also transfer or re-deploy employees internally, with training and career development programs designed to support these moves.

A Simplified Example of Forecasting Labor Demand and Supply

Figure 5.2 shows an example of how a large national hotel chain with 25 units forecasts its labor demand for 16 key jobs two years ahead. Column A indicates the number of employees who currently hold each of these jobs. Column B calculates the present ratio of employees to hotels—that is, the number of current employees divided by the current number of hotels (25). The hotel chain expects to add seven additional hotels by the year 2006 (for a total of 32). In column C, the expected number of employees for each job in 2006 is calculated by multiplying the current ratio of employees to hotels (column B) by 32. For instance, in 2003 there were nine resident managers for 25 hotels, or a ratio of 0.36 (9 ÷ 25). When the number of hotels expands to

Figure 5.2

Example of Predicting Labor Demand for a Hotel Chain with 25 Hotels

	A Number of Employees (2003)	B Ratio of Employees/Hotels (Calculated as Column A ÷ 25)	C Projected 2006 Labor Demand for 32 Hotels (Calculated as Column B x 32)*
Key Positions			
General Manager	25	1.00	32
Resident Manager	9	.36	12
Food/Beverage Director	23	.92	29
Controller	25	1.00	32
Assistant Controller	14	.56	18
Chief Engineer	24	.96	31
Director of Sales	25	1.00	32
Sales Manager	45	1.80	58
Convention Manager	14	.56	18
Catering Director	19	.76	24
Banquet Manager	19	.76	24
Personnel Director	15	.60	19
Restaurant Manager	49	1.96	63
Executive Chef	24	.96	31
Sous Chef	24	.96	31
Executive Housekeeper	25	1.00	32
Total	379		486

*These figures are rounded.

32 in 2006, it is forecasted that 12 resident managers will be needed (0.36 × 32 = 11.52, or 12.0 after rounding).

The same hotel chain's labor supply prediction is found in columns A to D of Figure 5.3. Column A shows the percentage of employees in each of the 16 key jobs who left the firm during the past two years (2001 to 2003). Multiplying this percentage by the number of present employees in each of these key jobs produces an estimate of how many current employees will have quit by 2006. For example, 38 percent of general managers quit between 2001 and 2003. Because there are now 25 employees holding this job, it is forecasted that by 2006, ten of them will have left the firm (0.38 × 25 = 9.5, rounded to 10).

The projected turnover for each job is shown in column C. This means that by 2006, 15 of the current general managers (25 minus 10; see column D) will still be working for the company. Because the projected labor demand for general managers in 2006 is 32 (see Figure 5.2), 17 new general managers (32 minus 15) will have to be hired by 2006.

In the past, many firms avoided HRP, simply because their staffs were too swamped with everyday paperwork to manage the planning process effectively. For example, FedEx used to rely on a 20-page employment application. Completing the form and then checking it for accuracy was a difficult and time-consuming process. Many applicants had to be called back when errors were later found in their application materials. Imagine the labor and paper involved in this process at FedEx when you consider that the organization hires 25,000 new hourly workers each year. These excesses ended when FedEx moved to a paperless Web-based system for

Figure 5.3

	Supply Analysis				Supply-Demand Comparison	
	A	B	C	D	E	F
	% Quit* (1998–2000)	Number of Present Employees (See Figure 5.2, Column A)	Projected Turnover by 2006 (Column A x Column B)	Employees Left by 2006 (Column B - Column C)	Projected Labor Demand in 2006 (See Figure 5.2, Column C)	Projected New Hires in 2006 (Column E - Column D)
Key Positions						
General Manager	38	25	10	15	32	17
Resident Manager	77	9	7	2	12	10
Food/Beverage Director	47	23	11	12	29	17
Controller	85	25	21	4	32	28
Assistant Controller	66	14	9	5	18	13
Chief Engineer	81	24	16	8	31	23
Director of Sales	34	25	9	16	32	16
Sales Manager	68	45	30	15	58	43
Convention Manager	90	14	13	1	18	17
Catering Director	74	19	14	5	24	19
Banquet Manager	60	19	12	7	24	17
Personnel Director	43	15	6	9	19	10
Restaurant Manager	89	49	44	5	63	58
Executive Chef	70	24	17	7	31	24
Sous Chef	92	24	22	2	31	29
Executive Housekeeper	63	25	16	9	32	23
Total Employees		379	257	122	486	364

*These figures are rounded.

Example of Predicting Labor Supply and Required New Hires for a Hotel Chain

prospective hires to complete and human resource managers to evaluate.[3] This Web-based system eliminated paper, immediately caught errors as a job candidate was completing the employment application form, and reduced by more than 50 percent the time a candidate needed to complete the application form and recruiters to examine it, all this without increasing the number of HR recruiting staff. Because the Web-based system saved recruiters the time of examining application forms, they had time to check an applicant's references—something not often done under the former system. Furthermore, the Web-based job application system was integrated with the human resource information system (HRIS) so that human resource supply and demand data could be automatically updated. Many software companies, such as PeopleSoft, Lawson, SAP, and Oracle, now offer powerful computer-based HRP programs.[4]

Forecasting Techniques

Two basic categories of forecasting techniques are quantitative and qualitative. The example described in Figure 5.2 is a highly simplified version of a *quantitative technique*. A variety of mathematically sophisticated quantitative techniques has been developed to estimate labor demand and supply.[5]

Although used more often, quantitative forecasting models have two main limitations. First, most rely heavily on past data or previous relationships between staffing levels and other variables, such as output or revenues. Relationships that held in the past may not hold in the future, and it may be better to change previous staffing practices than to perpetuate them.

Second, most of these forecasting techniques were created during the 1950s, 1960s, and early 1970s and were appropriate for the large firms of that era, which had stable environments and workforces. They are less appropriate today, when firms are struggling with destabilizing forces such as rapid technological change and intense global competition. These forces are creating major organizational changes that are difficult to predict from past data. For instance, a clothing manufacturer that typically sells its goods to retail stores may decide to expand its audience by selling its clothes to consumers via the Web. The business may need to recruit people with technological and other skills that were previously unnecessary.

Unlike quantitative techniques, qualitative techniques rely on experts' qualitative judgments or subjective estimates of labor demand or supply. The experts may include top managers, whose involvement in and support of the HRP process is a worthwhile objective in itself. One advantage of qualitative techniques is that they are flexible enough to incorporate whatever factors or conditions the expert feels should be considered. In other words, unlike quantitative methods, qualitative techniques are not constrained by past relationships. However, a potential drawback of these techniques is that subjective judgments may be less accurate or lead to rougher estimates than those obtained through quantitative methods.

HR personnel are typically the people most likely to make formal use of techniques for forecasting labor supply and demand. However, all managers should understand the basics of forecasting techniques, some of which can be used for purposes other than predicting labor supply and demand. For those interested in learning more about quantitative and qualitative forecasting, Figure 5.4 (page 160) outlines some important techniques and their main advantages and disadvantages.

The Hiring Process

Once the firm has determined its staffing needs, it needs to hire the best employees to fill the available positions. As Figure 5.5 (page 161) shows, the hiring process has three components: recruitment, selection, and socialization.

Recruitment is the process of generating a pool of qualified candidates for a particular job. The firm must announce the job's availability to the market and attract qualified candidates to apply. The firm may seek applicants from inside the organization, outside the organization, or both.

Recruitment
The process of generating a pool of qualified candidates for a particular job; the first step in the hiring process.

Selection is the process of making a "hire" or "no hire" decision regarding each applicant for a job. The process typically involves determining the characteristics required for effective job

Figure 5.4

Methods of Forecasting Demand

Quantitative Techniques

- **Regression analysis** Statistically identifies historical predictors of workplace size. Future demand for human resources is predicted using an equation.
- **Ratio analysis** Examines historical ratios involving workforce size (such as number of customers relative to number of employees) and uses ratios to predict future demand for human resources.

Judgmental Techniques

Information is collected and subjectively weighed to forecast the demand for human resources.

- **Top-down approach** Prediction made by top management.
- **Bottom-up approach** Lower-level managers each make their own initial estimates, which are then consolidated, and the process continues up through higher levels of management. Top management makes final estimates.

Methods of Forecasting Supply

Quantitative Techniques

- **Markov analysis** Estimates the internal supply of labor by turning movement of labor into transition probabilities.

Judgmental Techniques

- **Executive reviews** Top management makes judgments about who should be promoted, reassigned, or let go. The process can clarify where there may be surpluses or shortages of managers.
- **Succession planning** Identifies workers who are ready or will soon be qualified to replace current managers. Can highlight development needs and areas where there may be a shortage of management-level labor.
- **Vacancy analysis** Judgments are made about likely employee movements. Shortages or surpluses of labor can be anticipated by comparing these judgments to estimates of demand.

Source: Adapted from Heneman, H. G., and Heneman, R. L. (1994). *Staffing organizations.* Middleton, WI: Mendata House.

Selection
The process of making a "hire" or "no hire" decision regarding each applicant for a job; the second step in the hiring process.

performance and then measuring applicants on those characteristics. The characteristics required for effective job performance are typically based on a job analysis (see Chapter 2). Depending on applicants' scores on various tests and/or the impressions they have made in interviews, managers determine who will be offered a job. This selection process often involves the establishment of *cut scores*; applicants who score below these levels are considered unacceptable.

Socialization
The process of orienting new employees to the organization or the unit in which they will be working; the third step in the hiring process.

The staffing process is not, and should not be, complete once applicants are hired or promoted. To retain and maximize the human resources who were so carefully selected, organizations must pay careful attention to socializing them. **Socialization** involves orienting new employees to the organization and to the units in which they will be working. It is important that new employees become familiar with the company's policies, procedures, and performance expectations. Socialization can make the difference between a new worker's feeling like an outsider and feeling like a member of the team. Although socialization is a crucial part of the hiring process, it is an ongoing activity that continues after hiring. We discuss the socialization process in more detail in Chapter 8.

Challenges in the Hiring Process

Most people would agree that the best-qualified candidates should be hired and promoted. In the long run, hiring the best candidates makes a tremendous contribution to the firm's performance. It has been estimated that above-average employees are worth about 40 percent of their salary more to the organization than average employees.[6] Thus, an above-average new hire in a sales job with a $40,000 salary would be worth $16,000 more to the organization than an average employee hired for the same position. Over 10 years, the above-average employee's added value to the company would total $160,000!

The potential negative consequences of poor hiring decisions are equally graphic. Poor hiring decisions are likely to cause problems from day one. Unqualified or unmotivated workers will probably require closer supervision and direction. They may require additional training yet never reach the required level of performance. They may also give customers inaccurate information or give customers a reason to do business with competitors.

All of this underscores a simple point: If a company makes the right hiring decision to begin with, it will be far better off. For this reason, it is essential that line managers and possibly other line workers be involved in the hiring process. Although the HR department has an active role to play in recruiting, selecting, and socializing new employees, line personnel also need to play a central role in this process. In the end, it is the line managers who will actively be supervising the new hires, and these managers often have job-related insights that members of the HR department may lack. Further, line workers will interact with and be the peers of the new hire, and these workers have intimate knowledge of what is required to do the job well.

Despite the obvious importance of selecting the best available talent, the hiring process is fraught with challenges. The most important of these are:

- Determining which characteristics that differentiate people are most important to performance.
- Measuring those characteristics.
- Evaluating applicants' motivation levels.
- Deciding who should make the selection decision.

Figure 5.5

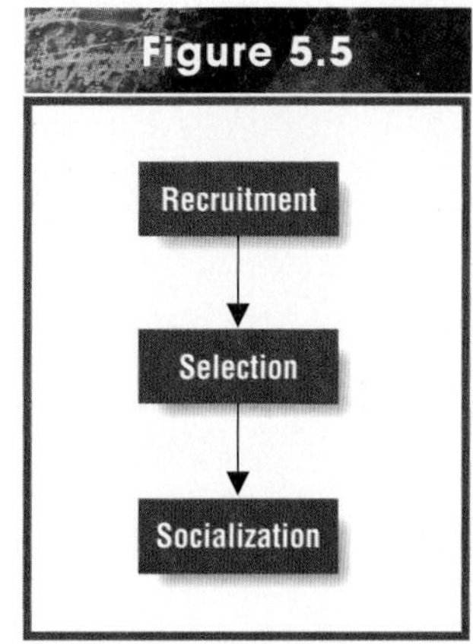

The Hiring Process

Determining the Characteristics Most Important to Performance

For several reasons, the characteristics a person needs to perform a job effectively are not necessarily obvious. First, the job itself is very often a moving target. For instance, the knowledge, skills, and abilities (KSAs—see Chapter 2) necessary for a good computer programmer right now are certainly going to change as hardware and software continue evolving. Second, the organization's culture may need to be taken into account. Arrowhead Central Credit Union in San Bernardino, California, focuses on candidates' attitudes and personality in its hiring process to see how employees fit with the organization. The senior vice president at Arrowhead Central states, "We've learned from experience that you can teach skills, but you cannot teach attitude."[7]

Similarly, the Reprovich-Reynolds Group, a consulting firm in Pasadena, California, evaluates job candidates to determine their fit with an organization's culture. The consulting firm contends that if a candidate fits well with the culture, he or she will do well, even with a modicum of technical skill. However, if fit with the organizational culture is off the slightest, employees "will never be able to build and forge a solid enough relationship with their colleagues to leverage their technical skill set."[8]

Third, different people in the organization often want different characteristics in a new hire. For example, upper-level managers may want the new manager of an engineering group to be financially astute, whereas the engineers in the group may want a manager with technical expertise.

Measuring the Characteristics That Determine Performance

Once it is determined that a set of characteristics is important for job performance, how are those characteristics to be measured? Suppose that mathematical ability is considered critical. You cannot infer from looking at someone what level of mathematical ability he or she possesses.

Rather, you must administer some test of mathematical ability. Some tests are better than others at predicting job performance, and they can vary widely in cost.

The Motivation Factor

Most of the measures used in hiring decisions focus on *ability* rather than *motivation*. There are countless tests of mathematical ability, verbal ability, and mechanical ability. But, as the following equation makes clear, motivation is also critical to performance:

$$\text{Performance} = \text{Ability} \times \text{Motivation}$$

This equation shows that a high ability level can yield poor job performance if it is combined with low motivation. Likewise, a high level of motivation cannot offset a lack of ability. (We will discuss another influence on performance, system factors, in Chapter 7.) The performance equation makes conceptual sense, and recent empirical work supports the importance of both ability and motivation in determining performance. For instance, the early career success of M.B.A. graduates has been found to be a function of both ability and motivation levels.[9]

Unfortunately, motivation is very difficult to measure. Many employers try to assess motivation during the employment interview, but (as we will see later in this chapter) there are numerous problems with this method. In addition, motivation seems to be much more dependent on context than ability is. If you are a typical student, your motivation to work hard in a class depends to a large extent on whether you like the course content, how much you like and respect your instructor, and how grades are determined. Your academic ability is fairly stable from course to course, but your motivation level is much more variable. Work situations are just as variable: How much you like your job responsibilities, how well you get along with your boss, and how you are compensated all affect your level of effort.

Who Should Make the Decision?

In many organizations, the HR department routinely makes staffing decisions, particularly for entry-level jobs. There are two good reasons for letting the HR department run the staffing process. The first (and more important) is that the organization must ensure that its employment practices comply with the legal requirements described in Chapter 3, and making HR staff responsible for all hiring decisions can help avoid problems in this area. The second reason is convenience. Since the HR staff is usually responsible for processing initial contacts with applicants and is often the repository of information about applicants, many organizations find it easier to let the HR department follow through and make hiring decisions.

However, having the HR department play the central role in hiring has one obvious drawback: This system leaves the line personnel out of a process that is critical to the operation's effectiveness. It is the line personnel, after all, who are intimately familiar with the line jobs and who must work with the candidates selected in the hiring process.

If an organization decides to involve line employees in hiring decisions, which ones should it consult? There are at least three separate groups. The first, and most obvious, are the managers who will be supervising the new hire. The second group consists of the new hire's co-workers. The third group, where applicable, is the new hire's subordinates. As we saw in the Specialty Cabinets Company example that opened this chapter, these groups do not necessarily share the same view of what characteristics are important in the new employee.

An interesting example of a company that heavily involves subordinates in hiring decisions is Semco, a Brazilian manufacturing firm. Semco is well known for its egalitarian culture and policies. The company has no receptionists, secretaries, standard hierarchies, or executive privileges. It lets workers set their own hours and salary and asks subordinates to help hire their own managers. In his book *Maverick*, Semco's owner, Ricardo Semler, describes a group "grilling" of a Semco manager being considered for promotion to general manager of another unit:

> Anatoly Timoshenko was going into the arena, and the lions were hungry. Gathered in a meeting room at Santo Amaro was as antagonistic a group of people as he was likely to face in peacetime. If he was lucky, they would be his future subordinates.[10]

Meeting the Challenges of Effective Staffing

As we noted earlier, choosing the right person for a job can make a tremendous positive difference in productivity and customer satisfaction. Choosing the wrong person can result in sluggish operations and lost customers. For these reasons it is important that each step of the staffing process—recruitment, selection, and socialization—be managed carefully. We discuss the first two of these three steps next.

Recruitment

The aim of recruitment is to attract *qualified* job candidates. We stress the word *qualified* because attracting applicants who are unqualified for the job is a costly waste of time. Unqualified applicants need to be processed and perhaps even tested or interviewed before it can be determined that they are not qualified. To avoid these costs, the recruiting effort should be targeted solely at applicants who have the basic qualifications for the job.

The recruitment process is really a sales activity. A job candidate is your customer when you are trying to sell the job to him or her. Some keys to successfully approaching recruitment as a sales activity are presented in the Manager's Notebook: Customer-Driven HR, "Making the Sale with a Customer-Driven Approach to Recruitment."

Customer-Driven HR

MANAGER'S NOTEBOOK

Making the Sale with a Customer-Driven Approach to Recruitment

Why do people buy? Fundamentally, people buy something because they are sold on how that "something" will be a benefit to them. A buy decision is typically a choice among alternatives that is based on a comparison of desirable and undesirable characteristics. Some characteristics may be explicit, such as price; other characteristics are more subjective, such as brand and reputation.

As with the purchase of a product or service, recruitment involves candidates making a buy decision about your job opening. Recruitment is a sales activity in which you are trying to get new and promising talent to buy into your organization. Recruitment is your opportunity to sell the organization and the job, maybe even the community, to the job candidates. Treating the applicants as customers will help to maximize the chances that they will buy into and choose your job and organization.

Following are key questions that can help you to take a more customer-oriented approach to recruitment. The questions are divided into the categories of *preparation* for the recruitment activity, the *process* of the recruitment activity, and the actual recruitment *encounter.* These questions need to be answered by everyone involved in the recruiting process.

Preparation

- Why do you work for your organization?
- What are the advantages of working here?
- What are the best things about working for this organization?
- What are the career opportunities here?
- What gets recognized and rewarded?
- What are the positives about living in the community?

Process

- Do you treat applicants as your customers?
- Are interviews scheduled around the applicant's preferences?
- Would applicants describe their visit as positive and pleasant or as a series of hoops to jump through?

- Do you welcome each applicant?
- Are applicants treated as guests or as widgets to be processed?
- Are assessments, such as testing or interviews, explained so that applicants understand the purpose and the reason the assessments are needed?
- Are there interview expenses that aren't paid for because you want to reduce costs?

Encounter

- What are the most important things the applicant is looking for in a job?
- What are the most important things the applicant is looking for in an organization?
- What are the most important things the applicant is looking for in a community?
- If the applicant could change something about his or her current job, what would it be?

Once you understand the applicant's needs and preferences based on answers to encounter questions such as those just listed, think about how those needs and preferences can be met. To effectively respond to each applicant's needs and preferences requires in-depth understanding of what the job, organization, and community have to offer. Adequately addressing the *preparation* stage is critical.

If the selection process determines that the applicant's qualifications fit the needs of the job and an offer is made, hopefully the applicant will "buy" your offer. However, even for applicants who are not offered a position or who say "no" to your offer, there may be benefits to treating them as customers. In perceiving themselves as customers throughout the recruitment process, even applicants who are not hired will nevertheless have a positive impression of the organization. They may become customers of the organization's products or services as well as recommend the organization to others as a potential employer. Positive impressions can be the direct result of a customer approach to recruitment.

Source: Partially adapted with permission from Bozell, J. (2002). Cut to the chase. *Nursing Management*, 33, 39–40.

Sources of Recruiting

A great number of recruitment sources are available to organizations.[11] The most prominent of these sources are:

- **Current employees** Many companies have a policy of informing current employees about job openings before trying to recruit from other sources. Internal job postings give current employees the opportunity to move into the firm's more desirable jobs. However, an internal promotion automatically creates another job opening that has to be filled.
- **Referrals from current employees** Studies have shown that employees who were hired through referrals from current employees tended to stay with the organization longer and displayed greater loyalty and job satisfaction than employees who were recruited by other means.[12] Dr Pepper/Seven Up, Inc., counts on employee referrals to help identify top job candidates.[13] Approximately 40 percent of new hires at Dr Pepper/Seven Up come from employee referrals, and the company pays a $500 bonus to a worker if a referral is hired and achieves the performance goals for the position. However, current employees tend to refer people who are demographically similar to themselves, which can create equal employment opportunity (EEO) problems.
- **Former employees** A firm may decide to recruit employees who previously worked for the organization. Typically, these are people who were laid off, although they may also be people who have worked seasonally (during summer vacations or tax season, for example). Because the employer already has experience with these people, they tend to be safe hires. Forming an online alumni network could be a simple and cost-effective way to maintain a hiring pool of competitive candidates.[14] When returning to work for a former employer, rehires tend to stay longer than new hires and they cost less to bring back on board because rehires have already been through the selection process. In addition, new hires are less productive than rehires in the first quarter of work. Need someone who can quickly get out of the gate and be up to

speed? Consider rehiring a former employee. Furthermore, a network of former employees can be a source of employee referrals because they are familiar with the company, its culture, and its values.

- **Print and radio advertisements** Advertisements can be used both for local recruitment efforts (newspapers) and for targeted regional, national, or international searches (trade or professional publications). For instance, clinical psychologists often find jobs through listings in the American Psychological Association's monthly newspaper.
- **Internet advertising and career sites** Employers are increasingly turning to the Web as a recruitment tool because online ads are relatively cheap, are more dynamic, and can often produce faster results than newspaper help-wanted ads. In addition, the reach of the Internet has expanded dramatically, so companies can connect with people all over the world who are looking for jobs.[15]

The Web is not only an economical, efficient means to recruit, it is also a convenient tool for job seekers. Thousands of career Web sites exist and almost all are free to people searching for jobs. One of the best known sites, Monster.com, lists approximately 1 million jobs.[16] Job seekers can search for jobs by industry, geographic location, and in some cases, by job description. The common practice of going through the Sunday help-wanted ads with a highlighter in hand is rapidly becoming a thing of the past. Figure 5.6 lists some sites that might be helpful to you when looking for a job.

- **Employment agencies** Many organizations use external contractors to recruit and screen applicants for a position. Typically, the employment agency is paid a fee based on the salary offered to the new employee. Agencies can be particularly effective when the firm is looking for an employee with a specialized skill. Another advantage of employment agencies is that they often seek out candidates who are presently employed and not looking for a new job, which indicates that their current employer is satisfied with their performance.
- **Temporary workers** Temporary workers seem to be everywhere in the workforce. They allow an organization to get through the ups and downs of the business cycle without making permanent hiring decisions. There was an average of 2.9 million temporary employees on the job in 1998, an increase of 9 percent from the previous year.[17] However, according to the Bureau of Labor Statistics (BLS), as a percentage of the labor force, less than 10 percent of workers are classified as temporary or contract workers.[18] This percentage has remained steady since 1995, the year the BLS began tracking temporary or contract workers.

In addition to providing some flexibility given fluctuating business cycles, the increase in the number of temporary workers may also be due to employers using temporary workers as a way to avoid paying benefits. That is, temporary workers can be used as a means to cut labor costs and make more money. However, the use of temporary workers as a means of cost cutting can lead to abuse, unfair treatment, and, as we saw in Chapter 3, potential legal liability. There is no job security for temporary workers. Surveys find that over half of temporary workers would prefer the security and benefits that come with a permanent job.[19] However, after proving their value to the organization as temporary workers, many of them are hired as permanent employ-

Figure 5.6 A Sampling of Job Search Sites

www.careerbuilder.com	Access to more than 2 million job postings on various Web sites
www.ajb.dni.us	The job bank of the Department of Labor
www.careermosaic.com	Job postings and industry information such as professional association listings
www.careerpath.com	Weekly listings from approximately 90 newspapers and from employer Web sites
www.monster.com	Popular Web site for job postings and résumés

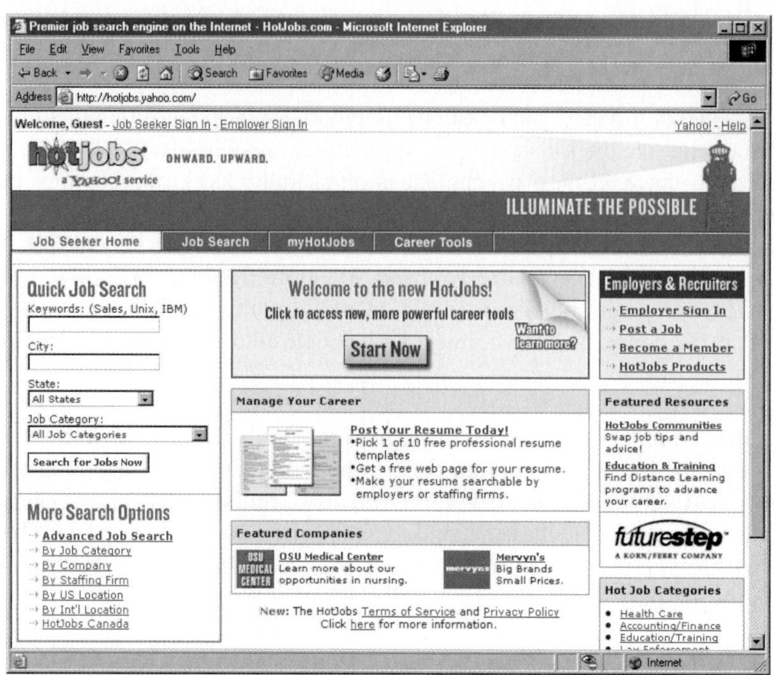

Web sites such as hotjobs.com are exploding in popularity as job seekers hop onto the Web in search of their perfect job.

ees. While in the minority, some people prefer the freedom and variety that go along with being a temporary worker.

- **College recruiting** Your school probably has a job placement office that helps students make contacts with employers. Many larger employers have college recruiting programs that target certain colleges and universities and certain majors. Students whose majors are accounting, engineering, computer programming, and information systems at the undergraduate level and those with graduate degrees in business and law are often considered the most desirable candidates because of the applied training they have received.

A couple of years ago a tight labor market meant that companies were offering signing bonuses of thousands of dollars and recruiting college graduates more aggressively than ever before. However, the country slipped into an economic recession that was compounded by the terrorist attack of September 11, 2001. Nonetheless, college recruiting remains a vital means for organizations to bring in new people with fresh and innovative ideas. Furthermore, a labor surplus due to economic recession appears to be a nonissue for many organizations because the skills they are looking for do not seem to be readily available on the market. Although the battle to attract top talent may have cooled a bit, it will heat up again soon.[20] In addition to economic recovery, the demand for labor will increase due to demographics. Specifically, by 2010 there is predicted to be a severe labor shortage as older workers retire and fewer younger workers will be in the labor force due to slow population growth between 1966 and 1985.[21] Thus, college recruiting is likely to remain an important recruiting source for the forseeable future. You might think that college recruiting may change in its nature and shift from face-to-face meetings to Web-based interactions. This is certainly taking place with many organizations relying on the Internet to recruit college students. For example, Hewlett-Packard has a Web site specifically focused on college recruiting at www.jobs.hp.com. However, savvy organizations recognize that the Internet cannot do the entire recruiting job.[22] There is value in interacting with college students, developing relationships, and generating interest in the college pool of candidates. Company visits to college campuses, job fairs, and various relationships such as internships are likely to continue for the long term.

In Japan, where some large companies offer lifetime employment, college recruitment is practically the only way employers can bring in new blood. Competition among college students to gain access to the largest companies is fierce. For instance, college students routinely send "information request postcards" to prospective employers beginning in December of their junior year. A student may mail well over 1,000 cards to prospective employers, with 40 to 50 cards sent to employers the student really wants to impress. The companies send the students information, including an invitation to come to the company's "information sessions."[23]

- **Customers** An innovative recruitment source is the organization's customers, who are already familiar with the organization and what it offers.[24] Customers can be more valuable than simply as buyers and consumers of a product or service.[25] Interested customers can help to improve processes and the relationship can evolve into an employment relationship. These people, who must be happy with the organization's product or service because they have remained customers, may bring more enthusiasm to the workplace than other applicants who are less familiar with the organization. Also, customers have been the recipients of the firm's product or service and, therefore, may have valuable insights into how the organization could be improved. There may be reason to view the children of customers as potential job candidates. As the owner of a coffee shop in Indianapolis, Indiana, Kassie Ritman recruits customers' children for employment.[26] Not only does knowing the parents give Kassie some insight into the values and background of the children, but also she believes she is accorded additional respect and is viewed as an authority figure because she knows the parents.

The appropriateness of these and other sources depends on the type of job to be filled and the state of the economy. When the unemployment rate is high, companies find it easy to attract qualified applicants. When it is low, organizations need to be more resourceful in locating qualified applicants.

Small U.S. firms often find it difficult to recruit qualified applicants even when the unemployment rate is high. In a survey of 519 small businesses, more than a quarter of the respondents said finding qualified and motivated employees was among their top three business worries.[27] Bad hires can be catastrophic for small businesses, which do not have the luxury of being able to reassign workers who are not well suited for their positions.[28]

How do employers evaluate the effectiveness of different recruitment sources? One way is to look at how long employees recruited from different sources stay with the company. Studies show that employees who know more about the organization and have realistic expectations about the job tend to stay longer than other applicants.[29] For instance, potential flight attendants who are familiar with the job realize that the position's glamorous, jet-setting image is offset by its many not-so-attractive aspects: dealing with difficult passengers, flying the same route over and over, living out of a suitcase, and working odd schedules. The first three recruitment sources we discussed—current employees, employee referrals, and former employees—are likely to turn up applicants with realistic expectations of the job.

Another way of evaluating recruitment sources is by their cost. The organization should carefully consider the most cost-effective recruiting method for a particular situation. There are substantial cost differences between advertising and using cash awards to encourage employee referrals and between hiring locally and hiring beyond the local area (which entails relocating the new employee). When it is necessary to go outside the local area to get employees it may make sense for company managers to travel to other cities and conduct employment interviews there rather than to pay transportation expenses for applicants to visit the company site.

Managers can increase the HR department's effectiveness by giving HR personnel continuous feedback on the quality of the various recruitment sources. For example, managers can set up a simple spreadsheet (as shown in the accompanying table on page 168) with recruiting sources in the rows and effectiveness measures (say, on a scale of 1 to 10) in the columns. Alternatively, the columns might track various outcomes from each of the recruitment sources, such as number of employment offers, number of acceptances, turnover at one year, and employee performance ratings at one year. Managers themselves might update the grid periodically or delegate this task to individuals or team members, who will then interpret the grid and provide recommendations to the HR department. (Some data, such as performance ratings, may be confidential and appropriate only for management consideration.)

Nontraditional Recruiting

Recruiting new workers, a task often taken for granted or ignored when unemployment rates are high, is a central concern for managers in U.S. organizations when unemployment rates are low. Even though at the time of this writing, the U.S. economy is still in recovery from a recession and

Source	Number of Employment Offers	Number of Acceptances	Total Cost	Turnover After 1 Year	Average Performance Rating at 1 Year
Referrals					
Print ads					
Internet ads and career sites					
Agencies					
College recruitment					
Customers					

from the terrorist attack of September 11, 2001, the economic downturn is not expected to last. In the longer term, a labor shortage is expected because the baby boomer generation is nearing retirement and relatively fewer young people are entering the workforce.[30] Furthermore, even in times of high employment and a general labor surplus, there can be shortages of labor with particular skills or in particular areas. Many organizations are currently facing difficulty obtaining qualified labor, and many more organizations will face a labor shortage in years to come.

When faced with a labor shortage, companies spend more to advertise job openings via radio, the Web, billboards, television, and print media and at job fairs. Many firms also use employment agencies and employee leasing firms to recruit and select new hires. In addition, many companies recruit from nontraditional labor pools and use innovative methods to attract new employees.

Nontraditional labor pools can include prisoners, welfare recipients, senior citizens, and workers from foreign countries. For example, the health care industry has been facing a labor shortage due to a rapid increase in the number of health care jobs combined with a decline in interest in the health care area by job candidates.[31] Due to this shortage, some hospitals have been importing workers from Canada, Europe, and Asia. In Rapid City, South Dakota, a regional hospital has been employing unskilled laborers from the Philippines to work in its environmen-

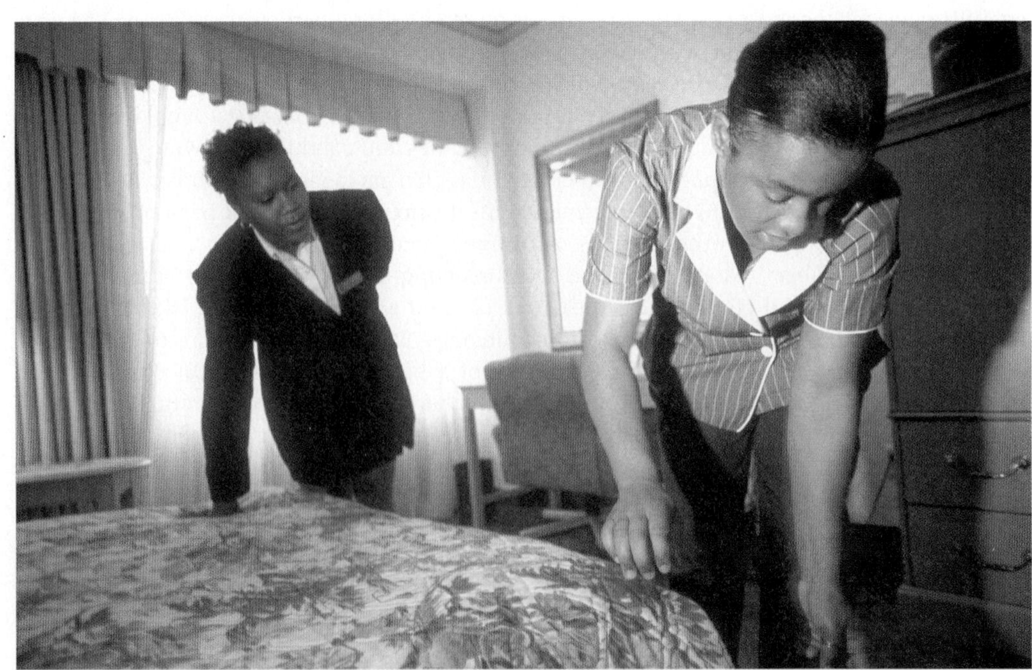

Mariott's recruiting efforts include offering training programs to new employees. Lisa Jackson, a mother of two who had never held a job, received six weeks of training before she began working for a local Marriott hotel.

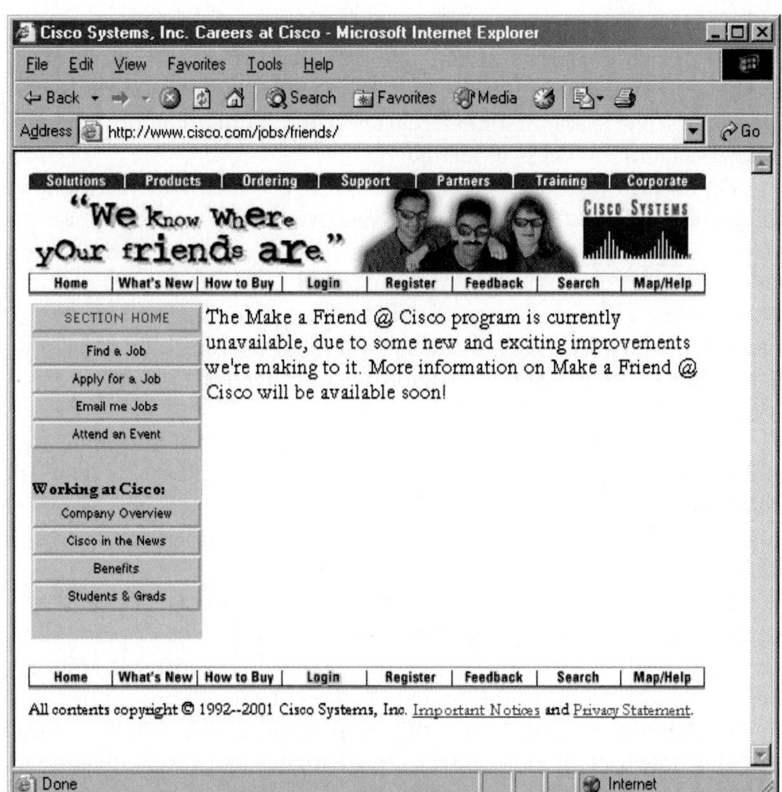

Cisco's "friends" program is an innovative way to recruit—the company's employees help potential recruits understand what it is like to work at Cisco.

tal services area. The Filipinos have H2B (unprofessional) visas and aren't allowed to work for a single employer for more than 11 consecutive months. The hospital has an employee-sharing arrangement with a local hotel in order to satisfy the rules. This additional effort is considered to be worth it by the hospital in order to bring employees on board who are considered to be excellent and courteous workers. St. Mary's Hospital in Richmond, Virginia, has been addressing the labor shortage problem using a more local source of nontraditional labor. The hospital turned to the indigent population as a possible source of labor. The largest recruitment source has been the Salvation Army's rehabilitation program for alcoholics and drug addicts between the ages of 30 and 60. The staff of 80 in the environmental services area includes 10 workers from this program. Marriott International recruits welfare recipients by offering a six-week unpaid training program to those who are interested in a career.[32]

Although nontraditional labor pools are a useful source of labor, potential employees from these groups often lack experience and education and may lack the necessary social skills to interact with customers and co-workers effectively. Many companies cannot or do not want to tackle such a training burden, so a number of nonprofit organizations provide training support. Companies that partner with nonprofit organizations benefit by finding additional labor. Society also benefits when people who lack opportunities are given training and a job.

An example is the 10-year partnership between Binding Together, a program run by a nonprofit group, and the Darvin Group, a New York printing company.[33] Binding Together provides vocational training for homeless adults and people with a history of substance abuse. Darvin actively recruits people who have graduated from the Binding Together program. In fact, 50 percent of its production staff—from machine operators to managers—are program graduates.

A labor shortage is not characteristic across time or across countries. For example, unemployment rates of 15 percent were common in the early 1980s. Because of an economic recession in Japan, the unemployment rate for 15- to 19-year-olds in Japan was running at approximately 10 percent.[34] This rate is comparable to or lower than the rate in the United States for the same age group, but it is a high rate for Japan where near zero unemployment has been the norm. Education officials are concerned about the unemployment and claim that a 51 percent increase in juvenile crime in 1998 and another 10 percent increase in the first half of 1999 were an effect of the joblessness.[35]

External Versus Internal Candidates

Hiring both external and internal candidates has benefits and drawbacks. Hiring externally gives the firm the advantage of fresh perspectives and different approaches. Sometimes it also makes economic sense to search for external specialists rather than bear the expense of training current workers in a new process or technology.

On the downside, current employees may see externally recruited workers as "rookies" and, therefore, discount their ideas and perspectives. When this is the case, people brought in to rejuvenate a department or firm will have only a limited impact. Another disadvantage is that external workers need time to become familiar with the firm's policies and procedures. It may take weeks before a new recruit has learned the job. Bringing in someone from the outside can also cause difficulties if current workers resent the recruit for filling a job they feel should have gone to a qualified internal worker. In addition, the outsider's style may clash with the work unit's culture.

Internal recruiting, usually in the form of promotions and transfers, also has its advantages and disadvantages. On the positive side, it is usually less costly than external recruiting. It provides a clear signal to the current workforce that the organization offers opportunities for advancement. And internal recruits are already familiar with the organization's policies, procedures, and customs.

MetLife, for example, uses its intranet for its internal recruitment program. The program, entitled Careers in Motion, enables managers to post job openings and allows employees to search for MetLife openings across the country. This intranet approach makes it possible for employees to access privately and at any time the job opportunities posted as opposed to traditional internal recruitment through job openings posted on bulletin boards in public areas.[36]

One drawback of internal recruiting is that it reduces the likelihood of introducing innovation and new perspectives. Another is that workers being promoted into higher-level jobs may be undercut in their authority because they are so familiar with their subordinates. For example, former co-workers may expect special treatment from a supervisor or manager who used to be a colleague.

Recruiting Protected Classes

An integral part of many organizations' recruitment efforts, both externally and internally, involves attracting women, minorities, people with disabilities, and other employees in the protected classes. While the Equal Employment Opportunity Commission guidelines stipulate only that government employers and government contractors must have written affirmative action policies, many private sector employers believe that such policies make good business sense for them. It stands to reason, for instance, that newspapers with diverse readerships would want to increase the diversity of their editorial and reporting staffs.

A good rule of thumb for companies wanting to increase the diversity of their workforce is to target their audience through media or recruitment methods that focus on minorities, rather than relying on the message that it wants to recruit minorities. When a company puts too much emphasis on hiring of minorities in ads, candidates may feel resentful or believe they are being hired simply to fill a quota. Recruitment experts say that minority candidates should be addressed the same way all candidates are.[37] The restaurant chain, Old Country Buffet, for example, found that radio ads can be an effective minority recruitment tool.[38] When opening a restaurant in San Francisco, the company had difficulty recruiting employees. The restaurant asked their current Hispanic employees which radio stations they listened to. These employees were also given the advertising copy and they translated it into Spanish. The result? Within two days of running the ads, the restaurant was fully staffed.

Planning the Recruitment Effort

To be effective, recruitment should be tied to HRP.[39] As we saw earlier in this chapter, HRP involves a comparison of present workforce capabilities with future demands. The analysis might indicate, for example, a need for 10 more staff personnel given the firm's expansion plans and anticipated market conditions. This information should play a key role in determining the level of the recruitment effort.

Once HRP has been performed, an important question remains: How many candidates should the recruitment effort attempt to attract for each job opening? The answer depends on *yield ratios*, which relate recruiting input to recruiting output. For example, if the firm finds that

Figure 5.7

Sample Library Job Search Sources

Source	Description
The Career Guide: Dun's Employment Opportunities Directory	Lists companies by geographic area, industry, and disciplines hired; lists educational and experience requirements
Standard & Poor's Register of Corporations, Directors and Executives	Lists more than 50,000 corporations, most privately owned
Moody's Investment Services Manuals	Presents information from company reports and other sources
The Dictionary of Occupational Titles	Provides information on job responsibilities and required education and experience levels

Source: Walberg, M. (1995, March 20). Job hunters find library offers company data, search assistance. *Arizona Republic*, E5.

it has to make two job offers to get one acceptance, this offer-to-acceptance ratio indicates that approximately 200 offers will have to be extended to have 100 offers accepted. Perhaps the interview-to-offer ratio has been 3:1. This ratio indicates that the firm will have to conduct at least 600 interviews to make 200 offers. Other ratios to consider are the number of invitations-to-interview ratio and the number of advertisements or contacts-to-applicant ratio. Each firm sets its own number of candidates to number of job openings ratio. The desired level of recruitment effort may be higher if the firm wishes to be particularly selective in making employment offers.

Planning Your Job Search

Our major concern in this section is recruitment. However, the flip side of recruitment is the job search process in which people search for the right employer. Are you looking for your first job or a change in your career? A place to start your job search is the local library. Figure 5.7 lists and briefly describes some of the major sources of information to help formulate your search. In addition, online and CD-ROM searches are available at many libraries.

Selection

Given the pool of candidates that results from the recruitment effort, selection is the mechanism that determines the overall quality of an organization's human resources. To understand the impact of selection practices, consider what happens when the wrong person is hired or promoted. How do you, as a customer, like being served by someone who is slow and inept? How would you, as a line supervisor, like to deal with the problems caused by a worker who cannot perform necessary tasks on a production line? These direct effects of poor selection practice are only the beginning. Hiring the wrong person can also cause friction among staff as other workers become resentful of having to pick up the slack for inept employees. Inappropriate hires may even lead better employees to seek employment elsewhere. All of these effects have economic ramifications.[40]

In fact, the economic value of good selection procedures is higher than most people realize. For example, the federal government's use of ability testing for entry-level jobs has been estimated to save the government over $15 billion per year.[41] This amazing figure is derived from the cumulative effects of modest job performance increases by people hired because they scored better than average on the selection test. Continually hiring people who perform, say, 20 percent above average can make a tremendous difference to an organization that hires many workers.

To further understand the benefits of good selection, managers need to consider the risks of poor selection, particularly for smaller businesses. For example, a payroll manager was terminated two months after being hired and accused of embezzling more than $30,000 from the organization.[42] The candidate had submitted a fraudulent résumé and a background check was not done. As this example shows, the cost of a poor selection could severely hamper a small or fledgling company or even put it out of business.

A variety of tools can be used in the selection process. Before we consider these techniques, though, you should be aware of two concepts important for selection tools: reliability and validity.

Reliability and Validity

Reliability
Consistency of measurement, usually across time but also across judges.

Reliability refers to consistency of measurement, usually across time, but also across judges. If a measure produces perfectly consistent results, that measure is perfectly reliable. For example, if you take a math test every week for five weeks and always obtain the same score, then that measure of your mathematical skill level would be considered to be perfectly reliable. Likewise, if five different interviewers all judged you to have the same level of social skill, the interjudge reliability would be perfect.

However, perfect reliability is rarely if ever achieved. Measurement almost always involves some error and that error is "noise," or unreliability. The greater the amount of noise in a measure, the harder it is to determine the true signal that the measure is trying to detect. For instance, the less similar your test scores on the math test you took repeatedly, the more difficult it is to determine your true mathematical skill level. Also, the less agreement across interview judges, the more difficult it is to determine your true level of social skill. Conceptually, reliability is the amount of noise in a measure, but operationally, reliability is assessed by the level of similarity of agreement in scores over time or among judges.

The error with which something is measured can be broken down into two types: deficiency error and contamination error.[43] *Deficiency error* occurs when a component of the domain being measured is not included in the measure. Not including subtraction questions in a test of basic math skills would yield a deficient measure: one that does not capture the true level of basic math skill.

Contamination error occurs when a measure includes unwanted influences. For example, an interviewer may be under undue time pressure from other job duties and not take the time to accurately assess a job candidate. Alternatively, a job candidate may be exceptional at creating a favorable first impression that sways an interviewer's assessment of her job skills. Or, an interviewer might rate an average job candidate lower than average because of the contrast with an outstanding candidate who preceded him.

Selection measures, whether tests, interviews, or some other techniques, are meant to measure job-related qualifications. Reliability is an index of how much error has influenced the measures.

Validity
The extent to which the technique measures the intended knowledge, skill, or ability. In the selection context, it is the extent to which scores on a test or interview correspond to actual job performance.

Validity is the extent to which the technique measures the intended knowledge, skill, or ability. In the selection context, this means that validity is the extent to which scores on a test or interview correspond to actual job performance. Validity is at the heart of effective selection. It represents how well the technique used to assess candidates for a certain job is related to performance in that job. A technique that is not valid is useless and may even present legal problems. In fact, documentation of the validity of a selection technique is central to that technique's legal defensibility. When discrimination in hiring practices is charged, the critical evidence will be the job relatedness (validity) of the selection technique.[44]

There are typically two basic strategies for demonstrating the validity of selection methods: content and empirical. A *content validity* strategy assesses the degree to which the content of the selection method (say, an interview or a test) is the representative of job content. Job knowledge tests are often validated using a content validation strategy. For instance, applicants for the job of commercial airline pilot are required to take a series of exams administered by the Federal Aviation Administration. These exams assess whether the candidates have the necessary knowledge to pilot safely and effectively. However, passing these tests does not guarantee that the applicant has the other abilities necessary to perform well in the cockpit.

An *empirical validity* strategy demonstrates the relationship between the selection method and job performance. Scores on the selection method (say, interview judgments or test scores) are compared to ratings of job performance. If applicants who receive higher scores on the selection method also turn out to be better job performers, then empirical validity has been established.

There are two types of empirical (also known as criterion-related) validity: concurrent and predictive.[45] *Concurrent validity* indicates the extent to which scores on a selection measure are related to job performance levels, when both are measured at roughly the same time. To illustrate, say that a company develops a test to use for hiring additional workers. To see how well the test might indicate job performance levels, the company gives the test to its current workforce. The company then correlates the test scores with the performance appraisal scores that supervisors just completed. The correlation between the test scores and job performance scores indicates the concurrent validity of the test because both the test and job performance scores were measured concurrently in time.

Predictive validity indicates the extent to which scores on a selection measure correlate with future job performance. For example, the company gives the test to all applicants and then checks their job performance level 12 months later. The correlation between the test scores and job performance in this case indicates the predictive validity of the test because the selection measure preceded the assessment of job performance.

Even if empirical validity is the goal when developing or choosing a selection measure, all measures should have content validity.[46] That is, what is being measured to assist in making the hiring decision should be job related. The starting point for establishing job-related content is a job analysis (see Chapter 2). However, content validity does not necessarily guarantee empirical validity. For instance, a measure that is content valid but so difficult that no one can earn a passing score will probably not be found to have empirical validity. Further, if empirical validity is assessed, the two forms, concurrent and predictive, each have their advantages and disadvantages.

Concurrent validation can be done relatively quickly and easily. However, the validity found with the concurrent approach may not be a good estimate of how valid a measure may be when used for assessing job applicants. To illustrate, current workers may not be representative of job applicants. To illustrate, current workers may not be representative of job applicants in that they may be older and tend to be white and male. Further, current workers may not be as motivated when taking an employment test as job applicants would be. We see, then, that concurrent validity may not be a good estimate of how valid a selection measure might be in practice.

In contrast, predictive validation most closely matches the hiring problem of trying to predict who will develop into the best performers for the organization. However, determining the predictive validity of a measure requires a fairly large number of people, at least 30, for whom both selection and job performance scores are available. Further predictive validity cannot be determined until job performance is measured, perhaps 6 to 12 months later.

Before we proceed to examine specific selection methods, we need to emphasize an important point concerning reliability and validity. Selection methods can be reliable but not valid; however, selection methods that are not reliable cannot be valid. This fact has a great deal of practical significance. Whether someone has an M.B.A. or not can be measured with perfect reliability. But if having an M.B.A. is not associated with improved job performance, attainment of an M.B.A. is not a valid selection criterion for that job. It seems clear that more highly motivated applicants make better employees, but if the selection method used to measure motivation is full of errors (not reliable), then it cannot be a valid indicator of job performance.

Selection Tools As Predictors of Job Performance

In this section we look at the most commonly used methods of selection, in no particular order. Each approach has its limitations as well as its advantages.

Letters of Recommendation

In general, letters of recommendation are not highly related to job performance because most are highly positive.[47] This does not mean that *all* letters of recommendation are poor indicators of performance, however. A poor letter of recommendation may be very predictive and should not be ignored.

A content approach to considering letters of recommendation can increase the validity of this selection tool. This approach focuses on the content of the letters rather than on the extent

A Question of Ethics

Suppose you are asked to write a recommendation letter for a friend whom you like but consider unreliable. Would it be ethical for you to write a positive reference even though you anticipate that your friend will not be a good employee? If not, would it be ethical for you to agree to write the letter knowing that you will not be very positive in your assessment of your friend's abilities?

of their positivity.[48] Assessment is done in terms of the traits the letter writer attribute to the job candidate.[49] For example, two candidates may produce equally positive letters, but the first candidate's letter may describe a detail-oriented person, while the second candidate's letter describes someone who is outgoing and helpful. The job to be filled may require one type of person rather than the other. For example, a job in customer relations requires an outgoing and helpful person, whereas clerical work requires someone who is good at details.

A more proactive approach to increasing the validity and usefulness of letters as well as verbal references (see "Reference Checks", p. 182) is to focus the reference on key job competencies. Rather than asking a reference broad questions, such as "Tell me what you think of this job candidate?," ask the reference about the applicant's skill in areas relevant to the job opening. Ask the reference for specific examples of what he or she has observed the candidate do when confronted with situations similar to conditions the applicant will confront if hired. By focusing references on job-relevant characteristics, you will be more likely to obtain written and verbal references that are valid and useful to your task of hiring a great worker.[50]

Application Forms

Organizations often use application forms as screening devices to determine if a candidate satisfies minimum job specifications, particularly for entry-level jobs. The forms typically ask for information regarding past jobs and present employment status.

A recent variation on the traditional application form is the *biodata form*.[51] This is essentially a more detailed version of the application form in which applicants respond to a series of questions about their background, experiences, and preferences. Responses to these questions are then scored. For instance, candidates might be asked how willing they are to travel on the job, what leisure activities they prefer, and how much experience they have had with computers. As with any selection tool, the biodata most relevant to the job should be identified through job analysis before the application form is created. Biodata have moderate validity in predicting job performance.

Ability Tests

Various tests measure a wide range of abilities, from verbal and qualitative skills to perceptual speed. *Cognitive ability tests* measure a candidate's potential in a certain area, such as math, and are valid predictors of job performance when the abilities tested are based on a job analysis.

A number of studies have examined the validity of *general cognitive ability* (*g*) as a predictor of job performance. General cognitive ability is typically measured by summing the scores on tests of verbal and quantitative ability. Essentially, g measures general intelligence. A higher level of g indicates a person who can learn more and faster and who can adapt quickly to changing conditions. People with higher levels of g have been found to be better job performers, at least in part because few jobs are static today.[52]

Some more specific tests measure physical or mechanical abilities. For example, the *physical ability tests* used by police and fire departments measure strength and endurance. The results of these tests are considered indicators of how productively and safely a person could perform a job's physical tasks. However, companies can often get a more direct measure of applicants' performance ability by observing how well they perform on actual job tasks. These types of direct performance tests, called *work sample tests*, ask applicants to perform the exact same tasks that they will be performing on the job. For example, one of Levi Strauss's work sample tests asks applicants for maintenance and repair positions to disassemble and reassemble a sewing machine component.[53]

Work sample tests are widely viewed as fair and valid measures of job performance, as long as the work samples adequately capture the variety and complexity of tasks in the actual job. Work sample tests scores have even been used as criteria for assessing the validity of general mental ability selection measures.[54] However, physical ability measures have been found to screen out more women and minorities than white men. Physical preparation before the testing has been found to reduce this adverse impact significantly.[55]

Personality Tests

Personality tests assess *traits*, individual workers' characteristics that tend to be consistent and enduring. Personality tests were widely used to make employee selection decisions in the 1940s and 1950s,[56] but today they are rarely used to predict job-related behaviors.[57] The arguments against using personality tests revolve around questions of reliability and validity. It has been argued that traits are subjective and unreliable,[58] unrelated to job performance,[59] and not legally acceptable.[60]

Perhaps the main reason personality tests fell out of favor is that there is no commonly agreed-upon set of trait measures. Many traits can be measured in a variety of ways, and this lack of consistency produces problems with reliability and validity. However, recent research on personality measurement has demonstrated that personality can be reliably measured[61] and summarized as being composed of five dimensions.[62] The "big five" factors, now widely accepted in the field of personality psychology, follow:[63]

- **Extroversion** The degree to which someone is talkative, sociable, active, aggressive, and excitable.
- **Agreeableness** The degree to which someone is trusting, amiable, generous, tolerant, honest, cooperative, and flexible.
- **Conscientiousness** The degree to which someone is dependable and organized and conforms and perseveres on tasks.
- **Emotional stability** The degree to which someone is secure, calm, independent, and autonomous.
- **Openness to experience** The degree to which someone is intellectual, philosophical, insightful, creative, artistic, and curious.

Of the five factors, conscientiousness appears to be most related to job performance.[64] It is hard to imagine a measure of job performance that would not require dependability or an organization that would not benefit from employing conscientious workers. Conscientiousness is thus the most generally valid personality predictor of job performance.

The validity of the other personality factors seems to be more job specific, which bring us to two warnings about personality tests. First, whether or not personality characteristics are valid predictors of job performance depends on both the job and the criteria used to measure job performance. As with all selection techniques, a job analysis should be done first to identify the personality factors that enhance job performance. Second, personality may play little or no role in predicting performance on certain measures, such as the number of pieces produced on a factory line (which may depend largely on such factors as speed of the production line). However, personality factors may play a critical role in jobs that are less regimented and demand teamwork and flexibility. Clearly, then, selection procedures should take both personality and the work situation into account.[65] Some types of people may be better suited for some work situations than for others. The Issues and Applications feature titled "Staffing International Positions—A Learning Opportunity" highlights an individual characteristic that may make an important difference in an international setting. Recent studies have found that personality can be an accurate predictor of the performance of not only job candidates[66] but also college students.[67]

Staffing International Positions—A Learning Opportunity

Issues and Applications

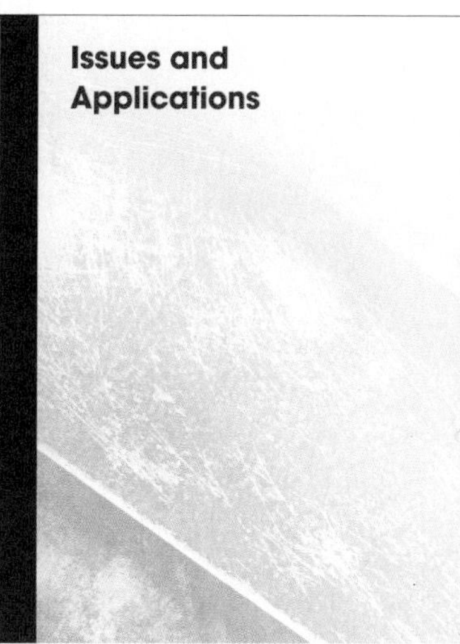

The global economy has forced managers to deal with other countries' cultures and business practices. For individuals, the most extreme cultural adaptation is an assignment to live and work in another country. But what determines how successful these people will be in their adopted setting and culture? Even organizations experienced with international assignments do not have stellar records in terms of effectively selecting or preparing expatriates (those who live and work in a foreign country). However, there seems to be some consensus among managers concerning what it takes to achieve business objectives in an international context: adaptability. Fortunately, learning orientation is an indicator of someone's adaptability and can be both measured and developed.

Learning orientation is based on a belief that personal characteristics can be developed and improved. For a person with a high learning orientation level, performance of a task is an opportunity to learn and improve, not an indicator of the level of his or her ability. A learning orientation would be indicated by someone who strongly agrees with a statement such as "I am willing to select a challenging work assignment that I can learn a lot from" and strongly disagrees with a

statement such as "It is more satisfying to work at things I do well than to struggle with those that might be beyond my abilities."

Learning orientation is critical for an expatriate manager. Working in another culture will result in a host of experiences that may not go well on the first try. However, accomplishing organizational goals within the social, legal, and market conditions of another country requires the manager to gradually increase understanding and appreciation of the new environment. Initial difficulties must be embraced as learning opportunities. If the manager withdraws from situations after initial problems, neither learning nor success is likely to occur.

A number of studies demonstrate the importance of a learning orientation in a domestic organizational environment, but there is good reason to believe that it is at least as important in an international context. The degree of learning orientation can be fairly easy and inexpensively measured with questionnaires and situational exercises. Use of learning orientation could give an expatriate manager program a competitive edge.

Source: Porter, G., and Tansky, J. W. (1999). Expatriate success may depend on a "learning orientation": Considerations for selection and training. *Human Resource Management, 8*, 47–60.

Psychological Tests

Retail chains, banks, and other service sector companies have long used pencil-and-paper psychological tests to weed out applicants who might steal on the job. Today, there are broader psychological tests designed to gauge, for example, whether a job applicant has a strong work ethic or will be motivated or defeated by the challenges of the job. These broad tests attempt to uncover likely behavior with questions such as: "Would you agree that to be successful, luck is more important than hard work?" Wet Seal, Inc. (a women's wear retailer in Irvine, California) has since 1990 spent $100,000 a year on psychological testing developed to select more motivated employees. Within the first six months of using these tests, store managers were reporting that newer hires seemed "more willing to go the extra mile" for customers.[68] Although Wet Seal and other employers, including Burger King and JP Food Services,[69] have had success using psychological tests as selection instruments, employers need to be careful in the use of these types of exams. The questions and scoring methods must be the same for all applicants, and they must be job related rather than general inquisitions into employees' personal lives.

Honesty Tests

Two recent surveys, the National Retail Security Survey and the Annual Retail Theft Survey, indicate that retailers' losses due to employee theft have surpassed losses due to shoplifting. Total inventory shrinkage for U.S. retailers in 2000 was $32.2 billion, translating into 68 percent of total annual sales lost to shrinkage.[70] In the past, companies often used polygraph tests as part of the preemployment screening process. The polygraph measures the interviewee's pulse, breathing rate, and galvanic skin response (perspiration) while he or she is asked a series of questions. The theory is that these physiological measures will change when the interviewee is not telling the truth. However, the passage of the federal Employee Polygraph Protection Act in 1988 has eliminated the use of polygraph tests by most employers.

Honesty or integrity tests are designed to identify job applicants who are likely to engage in theft and other undesirable behavior. Integrity tests can now be administered in a variety of forms, including paper and pencil, via telephone, and via the Internet, among others. Depending on the depth and length of the honesty test, the cost of a test can range from approximately $8 to $14.[71] The typical test measures attitudes toward honesty, particularly whether the applicant believes that dishonest behavior is normal and not criminal.[72] For example, the test might measure the applicant's tolerance for theft by other people and the extent to which the applicant believes most people steal regularly.

A study by independent researchers appears to confirm the validity of honesty testing.[73] They found that scores on the honesty test taken by applicants for positions at a retail convenience store chain were moderately tied to actual incidences of theft. Specifically, those who scored more poorly on the honesty test were more likely to steal from their employer. Additionally, a recent study reported by one of the major honesty test publishers supports the validity of the measure. Specifically, a retailer began using an integrity test in 600 of its 1,900 locations. Within one year there was a 35 percent drop in the rate of inventory shrinkage in the stores using the test while there was a 10 percent rise in the shrinkage rates in the stores not using the tests.[74]

Nevertheless, honesty tests are controversial. Most of the arguments against integrity testing center on the issue of false-positive results: people who are honest but score poorly on the tests. Typically, at least 40 percent of the test takers receive failing marks.[75] The following items are representative of questions that might be found on the many integrity tests available on the market.

Typical Items from Integrity Tests

Issues and Applications

The following are typical questions used in integrity tests and were supplied by the Chicago-based Pearson Reid London House.

- Do you believe a person who writes a check for which he knows there is no money in the bank should be refused a job in which honesty is important?
- Do you think a person should be fired by a company if it is found that he helped the employees cheat the company out of overtime once in a while?
- If you found a $10 bill while standing in a line of 20 people at a restaurant, how many people would you ask whether they had lost the money?
- If you found a $100 bill while standing in a line of 20 people at a restaurant, how many people would you ask whether they had lost the money?
- Do you believe that most people are honest?
- Do you think that the way a company is run is more responsible for employee theft than the attitudes and tendencies of employees themselves?
- What percentage of people do you think cheat on their income tax returns?
- Would you ever consider buying something from somebody if you knew the item had been stolen?

Interviews

Although the job interview is probably the most common selection tool, it has often been criticized for its poor reliability and low validity.[76] Countless studies have found that interviewers do not agree with one another on candidate assessments. Other criticisms include human judgment limitations and interviewer biases. For example, one early study found that most interviewers make decisions about candidates in the first two or three minutes of the interview.[77] Snap decisions can adversely affect an interview's validity because they are made based on limited information. More recent research, however, indicates that interviewers may not make such hasty decisions.[78]

Another criticism is that traditional interviews are conducted in such a way that the interview experience is very different from interviewee to interviewee. For instance, it is very common for the interviewer to open with the following question: "Tell me about yourself." The interview then proceeds in a haphazard fashion depending on the applicant's answer to that first question. Essentially, each applicant experiences a different selection method. Thus, it is not surprising that traditional interviews have very low reliability. However, it is possible to increase the effectiveness of traditional, unstructured job interviews by following the guidelines presented in the "Manager's Notebook titled "Unstructured Does Not Mean Unprepared: Making the Most of the Hiring Interview."

MANAGER'S NOTEBOOK

Unstructured Does Not Mean Unprepared: Making the Most of the Hiring Interview

Managers can increase the effectiveness of unstructured interviews by focusing on six simple tasks.

- **Be prepared.** The Boy Scouts' motto could just as well be the interviewer's. Lack of preparation is the most common and costly mistake interviewers make. At least a day in advance, use the interviewee's résumé and discussions with key personnel to create an interview agenda and take at least 15 minutes to review this agenda before the appointment.
- **Put applicants at ease in the first few minutes.** Few things are more unsettling to an interviewee than being ushered into an office and watching his or her interviewer make business phone calls or have an impromptu meeting with a colleague. Take care of business before greeting interviewees and put them at ease with some pleasant small talk before rushing into the interview questions.
- **Don't be ruled by snap judgments or stereotypes.** Stereotyping is bad for the manager and bad for the company. Curb your tendency to rush to judgment and always keep in mind that you are dealing with an individual, not a type.
- **Ask results-oriented questions.** Ask questions that are designed to uncover not only what the job candidate has done but also what the results of the person's actions have been.
- **Don't underestimate the power of silence.** Many interviewers make the mistake of jumping in during any pause in the dialogue to discuss their own views on management and the company. Silences can be a time when the interviewee is absorbing information and forming a question or comment, and these are usually worth waiting for.
- **Close the interview with care.** Some interviewers let the session drift on until both parties begin to flounder about or lose interest. Others close an interview abruptly when interrupted by a phone call or a colleague. It's best to plan a time limit for the interview and to bring it to a natural close rather than let an outside event terminate the conversation prematurely.

Source: Excerpted, with permission of the publisher, from Uns, A. (1988). *88 mistakes interviewers make and how to avoid them*. New York: Amacom Books.

Structured interview
Job interview based on a thorough job analysis, applying job-related questions with predetermined answers consistently across all interviews for a job.

Dissatisfaction with the traditional unstructured interview has led to an alternative approach called the structured interview.[79] The **structured interview** is based directly on a thorough job analysis. It applies a series of job-related questions with predetermined answers consistently across all interviews for a particular job.[80] Figure 5.8 gives examples of the three types of questions commonly used in structured interviews:[81]

- **Situational questions** try to elicit from candidates how they would respond to particular work situations. These questions can be developed from the critical incident technique of job analysis: Supervisors and workers rewrite critical incidents of behavior as situational interview questions, then generate and score possible answers. During the interview, candidates' answers to the situational questions are scored on the basis of the possible answers already generated.[82]
- **Job knowledge questions** assess whether candidates have the basic knowledge needed to perform the job.

Figure 5.8

Examples of Structured Interview Questions

Type	Example
Situational	You are packing things into your car and getting ready for your family vacation when you realize that you promised to meet a client this morning. You did not pencil the meeting into your calendar and it slipped your mind until just now. What do you do?
Job knowledge	What is the correct procedure for determining the appropriate oven temperature when running a new batch of steel?
Worker requirements	Some periods are extremely busy in our business. What are your feelings about working overtime?

- **Worker requirements questions** assess candidates' willingness to perform under prevailing job conditions.

Structured interviews are valid predictors of job performance.[83] A number of factors are probably responsible for this high level of validity. First, the content of a structured interview is, by design, limited to job-related factors. Second, the questions asked are consistent across all interviewees. Third, all responses are scored the same way. Finally, because a panel of interviewers is typically involved in conducting the structured interview, the impact of individual interviewers' idiosyncrasies and biases is limited.

Structured interviews have been used very successfully at several large companies, including Philip Morris U.S.A. and Virginia Natural Gas Company. At these companies interviewing panels range from two to six members and typically include an HR professional, the hiring manager, and the person who will be the candidate's manager. The panels often also include key people from other departments who have to work very closely with the new hire.

The usual practice is to interview all candidates over a one- or two-day period. This makes it easier to recall interviewee responses and compare them equitably. Immediately after an interview, panel members rate the interviewee using a one- to two-page sheet that lists important job dimensions along with a five-point rating scale. After each interviewer has rated the candidate, one member of the panel—usually either the HR professional or the hiring manager—facilitates a discussion in which the panel arrives at a group rating for the candidate. After all applicants have been interviewed, the panel creates a rank order of acceptable job candidates.[84]

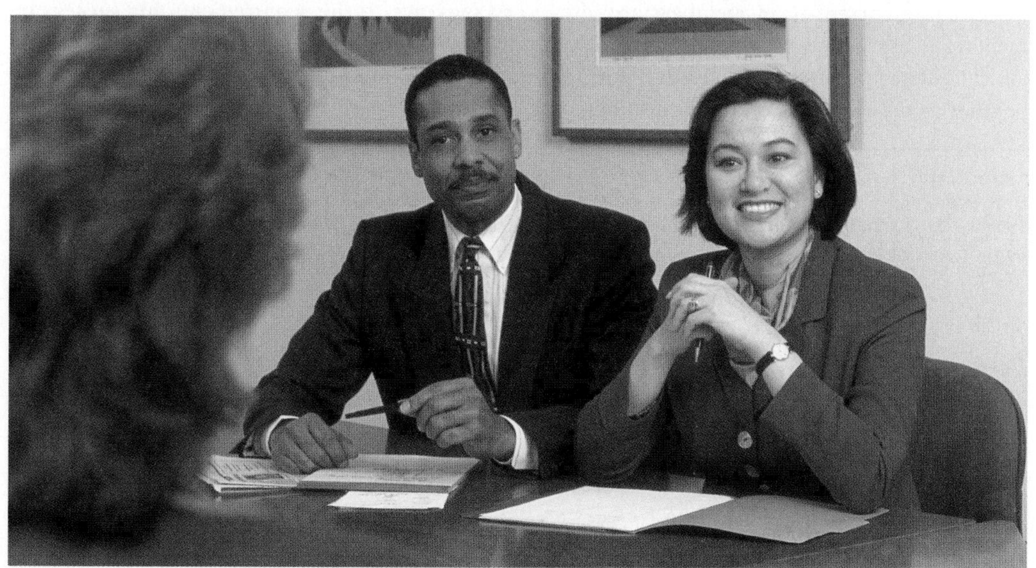

In a structured interview process, a panel of interviewers asks each potential candidate the same job-related questions. The results of this type of interview are valid predictors of job performance.

If the structured interview is so effective, why is the traditional interview much more popular? One reason is that many equate the panel format of structured interviews with a stress test. Another is that organizations find the traditional interview quite useful, probably because it serves more functions than just selection.[85] For example, it can be an effective public relations tool in which the interviewer gives a positive impression of the organization. Even a candidate who is not hired may retain this positive impression.

In addition, the unstructured interview may be a valid predictor of the degree to which a candidate will fit with the organization. Although the concept of "fit" is somewhat ambiguous,[86] what we are referring to here is the match between the candidate's values and traits and the chemistry of the organization or work unit. A good fit helps make things run smoothly and efficiently and is related to job satisfaction and intention to stay with the organization.[87] Fit with the organization can be particularly important in team situations, which is why some companies have started to conduct "team interviews." For more details, see the Issues and Applications feature titled "Hiring for Teamwork: What to Look For."

Issues and Applications

Hiring for Teamwork: What to Look For

Teamwork situations require team members to communicate and work toward common goals. Specific technical skills, which are often the central concern when selecting people to work in individual jobs, may be much less important in team situations. What characteristics, then, should employers look for when hiring people who will work on a team? Although much research remains to be done, preliminary findings indicate that effective team members should be able to:

- **Recognize and resolve conflict** Conflict can destroy a team's effectiveness. Team members must have the ability to deal with and resolve the disagreements and clashes that are bound to occur.
- **Participate and collaborate in problem solving** Teams are often expected to solve their own problems rather than look to supervisors for answers.
- **Communicate openly and supportively** Teams need open communication, and team members need to support one another. The inability to communicate, or a tendency to communicate negatively, could be detrimental to team effectiveness.
- **Coordinate and synchronize activities** Team operations require the cooperation of all team members and the coordination of various tasks.

In addition, effective team members usually have the following personality characteristics:

- **Conscientiousness** Team members must be able to depend on one another. Someone who does not follow through can cause problems for the entire group effort.
- **Agreeableness** Team members need to be flexible and tolerant if they are to meld into an effective unit.

Because current team members are often very sensitive to the requirements for success on their team, a number of companies are now conducting "team interviews" to determine whether job candidates possess the necessary skills and traits. Such interviews are likely to become more popular as the emphasis on teamwork increases.

Source: Cardy, R. L., and Stewart, G. L. (1997). Quality and teams; Implications for HRM theory and research. In D. B. Fedor and S. Ghosh (Eds.), *Advances in the management of organization quality*, 2. Greenwich, CT: JAI Press; Stevens, M. J., and Campion, M. A. (1994). The knowledge, skill, and ability requirements for teamwork: Implications for human resource management. *Journal of Management, 20*, 503–530.

Finally, unstructured interviews may be better than structured interviews for screening out unsuitable applicants.[88] Many times a candidate who seemed "fine" on paper reveals some disturbing qualities during an unstructured interview (Figure 5.9). Human judgment may be subject to error and bias, but people can be quite good at assessing a candidate's fit with their organization.

Whether employers choose to use structured or unstructured interviews, they need to make sure their interview questions are not illegal. Companies that ask job applicants certain ques-

Figure 5.9

Unusual Job Interview Behaviors

The impression you make through your behavior at a job interview is critical to your being favorably considered for the job. No matter how stellar your résumé, inappropriate behavior during the interview can ruin your chances for a job offer. The following are some real situations that indicate how unusual (even bizarre) the behavior of some job seekers can be.

- The applicant wore a Walkman and said she could listen to me and the music at the same time.
- A balding candidate abruptly excused himself and returned to the office a few minutes later wearing a hairpiece.
- The applicant asked to see the interviewer's résumé to determine if the interviewer was qualified to judge his capabilities for the job.
- The interviewee announced she hadn't had lunch and proceeded to eat a hamburger and french fries in the interviewer's office—wiping the ketchup on her sleeve.
- When I asked the candidate about his hobbies, he stood up and started tap dancing around my office.
- After arriving for a morning interview, the candidate asked to use the employer's phone. She called her current employer, faked a coughing fit, and called in sick to her boss.
- In response to the interviewer's offer to answer questions, a job seeker replied, "What happens if I wake up in the morning and don't feel like going to work?"
- A candidate interrupted a discussion of work hours and the office environment to say that he would take the job only if he could move his desk to the courtyard outside.
- Asked what he would like to do in his next position, a candidate replied, "I'll tell you what I don't want to be doing—sitting in boring meetings, doing grunt work, and having to be nice to people all day long."
- Question: "Why do you want this job?" Answer: "I've got a big house, a big car, and a big credit card balance. Pay me and I'll be happy."

tions (for example, their race, creed, sex, national origin, marital status, or number of children) either on application forms or in the interview process run the risk of being sued.

To operate within the limits of the law, interviewers should remember the nine don'ts of interviewing:[89]

1. Don't ask applicants if they have children, plan to have children, or what child-care arrangements they have made.
2. Don't ask an applicant's age.
3. Don't ask whether the candidate has a physical or mental disability that would interfere with doing the job. The law allows employers to explore the subject of disabilities only *after* making a job offer that is conditioned on satisfactory completion of a required physical, medical, or job skills test.
4. Don't ask for such identifying characteristics as height or weight on an application.
5. Don't ask a female candidate for her maiden name. Some employers have asked this to ascertain marital status, another topic that is off limits in interviewing both men and women.
6. Don't ask applicants about their citizenship.
7. Don't ask applicants about their arrest records. You are, however, allowed to ask whether the candidate has ever been convicted of a crime.
8. Don't ask if a candidate smokes. Because there are numerous state and local ordinances that restrict smoking in certain buildings, a more appropriate question is whether the applicant is aware of these regulations and is willing to comply with them.
9. Don't ask a job candidate if he or she has AIDS or is HIV-positive.

The key point to remember is not to ask questions that are peripheral to the work itself. Rather, interviewers should stay focused on the objective of hiring someone who is qualified to perform the tasks required by the job.

Assessment center
A set of simulated tasks or exercises that candidates (usually for managerial positions) are asked to perform.

Assessment Centers

An **assessment center** is a set of simulated tasks or exercises that candidates (usually for managerial positions) are asked to perform. Observers rate performance on these simulations and make inferences regarding each candidate's managerial skills and abilities. Many organizations, including Deloitte & Touche, PricewaterhouseCoopers, and the BBC, use assessment centers for external recruitment and for internal promotion.[90] Responses to a European survey indicate that over half of larger organizations (more than 1,000 employees) use assessment centers.[91]

Although expensive, the assessment center appears to be a valid predictor of managerial job performance.[92] Assessment centers may be well worth the price when the costs of poor hiring or promotion decisions are high, as in the hiring of police officers or fire fighters.[93] However, given a tight budget, the cost of an assessment center can be prohibitive. For example, the State of Maryland used to require the use of assessment centers in hiring public school principals, but that requirement was recently dropped because the expense of $1,200 to $1,500 per candidate became too onerous.[94]

Assessment centers are usually conducted off premises, last from one to three days, and may include up to six candidates at a time. Most assessment centers evaluate each candidate's abilities in four areas: organizing, planning, decision making, and leadership. However, there is considerable variability in what exercises an assessment center includes, how these are conducted, and how they are scored.[95]

The *in-basket exercise* is probably the exercise most widely associated with assessment centers. An in-basket exercise includes the kinds of problems, messages, reports, and so on that might be found in a manager's in-basket. The candidates are asked to deal with these issues as they see fit, and then are assessed on how well they prioritized the issues, how creative and responsive they were in dealing with each one, the quality of their decisions, and other factors. Performance on an in-basket exercise can be highly revealing. Often it points up the skills of a candidate who might otherwise have appeared average.[96]

Assessment centers have been used to help select frontline workers as well as managers. For instance, the British telecommunications firm, Mercury Communications, used assessment centers to recruit 1,000 customer service assistants for its new site near Manchester. The assessment center activities involved simulated call-handling and decision-making exercises. Mercury's managers believe these assessment centers are very effective in screening for the skills important to customer-service representatives. These include listening skills, sensitivity to customers, and the ability to cope in a high-pressure environment.[97]

A Question of Ethics

Some experts contend that urinalysis is an invasion of privacy and, therefore, should be prohibited unless there is reasonable cause to suspect an employee of drug use. Is it ethical for companies to insist that applicants undergo urinalysis? Suppose a company that wants to save on health insurance costs decides to test the cholesterol levels of all job applicants to eliminate those susceptible to heart attacks. Would this practice be ethical? Would it be legal?

Drug Tests

Preemployment drug testing typically involves asking job applicants to undergo urinalysis as part of routine selection procedures. Applicants whose test results are positive are usually eliminated from further consideration. Alternatively, they may be given the option of taking another test at their own expense if they challenge the test's outcome.[98]

The purpose of preemployment drug testing is to avoid hiring people who may become problem workers. However, applicants may avoid detection of drug use if they remain drug-free for a sufficient period of time before taking the test. The extent to which this type of cheating occurs is not known, but a significant percentage of applicants (about 12 percent) do have positive drug test results.

An important issue in preemploying drug testing is its effectiveness. Do drug test results correlate to an applicant's later job performance? The answer is yes. In one study done by the U.S. Postal Service, urine samples were taken from more than 5,000 job applicants, but the results were not used in hiring. Six months to one year later, it was found that the applicants who had positive tests were absent 41 percent more often and fired 38 percent more often than those who did not. It appears that drug testing is a valid predictor of job performance.[99]

Reference Checks

One of the best methods of predicting the future success of prospective employees is to look at their past employment record. Fear of defamation suits has often caused companies to not provide job-related information on former employees. However, checking employees' references is an employer's best tactic for avoiding negligent hiring suits, in which the employer is held liable for injuries inflicted by an employee while on the job. What should companies do?

Courts in almost every state have held that employers—both former and prospective—have a "qualified privilege" to discuss an employee's past performance. But to enjoy that privilege, a company must follow three rules. First, it must determine that the inquirer has a job-related need to know. Second, the former employer must release only truthful information. Third, EEO-related information (such as an employee's race or age) should not be released.[100]

Background Checks

Background checks can be distinguished from reference checks and can include, depending on the job opening, criminal-background checks, verifications of academic achievements, driving histories, immigration status checks, and Social Security checks. A primary motivation for organizations to conduct background checks was to avoid a lawsuit charging negligent hiring. However, after the terrorist attack of September 11, 2001, organizations are broadening their screening efforts out of a concern for security. The Patriot Act, passed in November 2001, requires background checks on people who work with certain toxins and bans felons and illegal aliens, among others, from working with these materials.[101] The need for background checks is also underscored by the frequency with which misinformation is submitted on job application forms. HireRight, a company that conducts background checks, has estimated that 34 percent of application forms contain outright lies concerning work experience, education, and required skills. HireRight also finds that about 9 percent of applicants falsify college degrees and list jobs and employers that don't exist.[102] These data certainly support conducting background checks. Description of the major types of background checks that might be conducted is presented in the Manager's Notebook: Emerging Trend, "Looking for Trouble."

MANAGER'S NOTEBOOK

Looking for Trouble

A variety of checks can be done to verify the accuracy of information provided by an applicant or worker, or to confirm that the person has the skills or experience needed to perform the job. Following are the major types of background checks.

- **Criminal record.** Almost all employers who screen their employees search for convictions in countries where the person has lived.
- **Social Security check.** This check, which looks at the names and addresses associated by credit bureaus with an applicant's Social Security number, helps confirm the applicant's identity.
- **Employment history.** Employers verify the dates of employment, title, and salary history.
- **Education.** Employers verify degrees, professional licenses, and certifications.
- **Driving record.** This is checked if the job involves driving.
- **Credit reports.** Companies generally don't look at applicants' personal credit reports unless their credit management is relevant to the job.
- **Workers' compensation claims.** Employers tend to be cautious about looking at these records because of strict state laws about how they can be used.
- **Civil court records.** These searches are rare and usually focus on job-related lawsuits.

Source: Adapted and used with permission from Steen, M. (2002, March 25). Under security. *San Jose Mercury News*, E, 1.

Handwriting Analysis

Graphology, the study of handwriting for the purpose of measuring personality or other individual traits, is routinely used to screen job applicants in Europe, the birthplace of the technique. Analysis can involve assessment of over 300 aspects of handwriting, including the slope of the letters, the height at which the letter *t* is crossed, and the pressure of the writing. Although graphology is not as widely used in the United States as it is in Europe, it is estimated that over 3,000 U.S. organizations use the procedure as part of their screening process. Furthermore, the covert and occasional use of graphology may be even more widespread and may be growing.[103] The important question, of course, is whether handwriting is a valid predictor of job performance. Research on this issue indicates that the answer is no.

One study collected handwriting samples from 115 real estate associates and gave them to 20 graphologists, who scored each sample on a variety of traits, such as confidence, sales drive, and decision making.[104] Later, these results were compared with the subject's actual performance ratings as well as with objective performance measures such as total sales volume. There was a fair amount of consistency across graphologists' judgments of the handwriting samples (reliability). However, none of the judgments made by the graphologists correlated with any of the performance measures, so graphology cannot be considered a valid measure. This conclusion is echoed by other research on graphology.[105] Thus, it should not be used as an employment screening device, and you should be wary when you see graphology touted as a valuable selection tool in magazines and other popular press outlets.[106]

Combining Predictors

Organizations often use multiple methods to collect information about applicants. For instance, managers may be selected on the basis of past performance ratings, an assessment center evaluation, and an interview with the manager to whom they will be reporting.

How should these pieces of information be combined to make an effective selection decision? There are three basic strategies. The first requires making a preliminary selection decision after completion of each method. This approach is called *multiple hurdle strategy* because an applicant has to clear each hurdle before moving on to the next one. Those who do not clear the hurdle are eliminated from further consideration.

Both of the remaining approaches require collecting all the information before making any decision; the difference is in how that information is combined. In a *clinical strategy* the decision maker subjectively evaluates all of the information and comes to an overall judgment. In a *statistical strategy* the various pieces of information are combined according to a mathematical formula, and the job goes to the candidate with the highest score.

The multiple hurdle strategy is often the choice when a large number of applicants must be considered. Usually, the procedure is to use the less-expensive methods first to screen out clearly unqualified applicants. Research studies indicate that a statistical strategy is generally more reliable and valid than a clinical strategy,[107] but many people—and probably most organizations—prefer a clinical strategy.

Selection and the Person/Organization Fit

Many companies have successfully used the various selection tools to hire above-average employees who have made a significant contribution to the firm's bottom line.[108] However, the traditional approach to selection may not be sufficient for a growing number of organizations. In many companies activities and decisions are decentralized, and workers find themselves working in cross-functional teams.[109] In these situations, candidates' job skills (as measured by selection tests) may not be as important as their ability to perform effectively in an empowered and high-involvement environment.

For this reason, some companies have been searching for a way to measure the degree of "fit" between job candidates and the organization.[110] However, there are at least two concerns regarding measures of fit in the selection process. First, it is not clear that an organization could defend a discrimination lawsuit by pointing to "lack of fit" instead of "lack of job-specific skills." Second, most research has validated selection methods by using supervisor evaluations of job performance on specific job-relevant characteristics. Thus, although we know which selection tools predict job-specific performance, we do not know how well they predict organizational fit.

Reactions to Selection Devices

In the last several pages we have discussed how well the various selection tools predict job performance. Next, we consider reactions to selection tools. How do applicants and managers respond to the selection methods we have discussed? The answer is clearly important, because these responses may be the determining factor in a decision to file a lawsuit.

1. **Applicant Reactions to Selection Devices** Applicants are a major customer of selection systems; they want and may demand fair selection devices. Moreover, applicants' reactions to selection methods can influence their attraction to and opinions of an organization and their decision to accept or reject an offer of employment.[111] Applicants' reactions to selection tools also influence their willingness to purchase the company's products.[112]

   To which selection tests do applicants respond most favorably and least favorably? Some interesting findings have emerged. For example, despite the increasing use of personality assessment devices as predictors, many job applicants believe that personality traits are "fakeable" and not job relevant. In addition, applicants perceive biodata, which have substantial validity, as irrelevant and invasive; they generally respond negatively to cognitive ability measures also. They respond most favorably to job simulations (for example, assessment center exercises) and interviews.
2. **Manager Reactions to Selection Systems** Managers need selection systems that are quick and easy to administer and that deliver results that are easy to understand. However, very little research has considered manager reactions to selection systems. One study surveyed 635 managers from 38 agencies in state government.[113] The study assessed the managers' perceptions of various factors related to the selection process, including selection methods. These findings were used to revise selection systems and other HR practices in those agencies.

A central issue is the extent to which an organization should balance the traditional measures of reliability and validity with the measures of applicants' and managers' reactions in determining which selection methods to use. Clearly, reliability and validity cannot be jettisoned completely. A reasonable balance between the traditional criteria of reliability and validity and the quality criteria of applicants'/managers' reactions needs to be maintained.

Legal Issues in Staffing

Legal concerns can play an exceptionally important role in staffing, particularly in selection. A number of legal constraints, most notably federal legislation and its definition of illegal discrimination, affect selection.

Discrimination Laws

The Civil Rights Act of 1964 and its extension, the Civil Rights Act of 1991, provide broad prohibition against discrimination based on race, color, sex, religion, and national origin. These laws, which state that such discrimination in *all terms and conditions* of employment is illegal, affect selection as well as many other organizational programs, including performance appraisal and training.

To lower the chances of lawsuits claiming discrimination, firms should ensure that selection techniques are job related. In other words, the best defense is evidence of the validity of the selection process. For example, if a minority group member turned down for a job claims discrimination, the organization should have ample evidence to document the job relatedness of its selection process. This evidence should include job analysis information and evidence that test scores are valid predictors of performance.

The Age Discrimination in Employment Act of 1967 and the 1978 amendments to the act prohibit discrimination against people aged 40 and older. Again, the organization needs evidence of the validity of the selection process if older applicants are turned away—particularly if comparable but younger applicants are hired.

The Americans with Disabilities Act (ADA) of 1991 extends the Vocational Rehabilitation Act of 1973 and provides legal protection for people with physical or mental disabilities. ADA requires employers to provide reasonable accommodations for people whose disabilities may prevent them from adequately performing essential job functions, unless doing so will create an undue hardship for the organization. Thus, employers need to determine what constitutes a job's essential functions. Although the law does not clearly define "reasonable accommodation," the courts may deem reasonable such actions as modifications in schedules, equipment, and facilities. In terms of selection, ADA prevents employers from asking applicants if they have a disability and prohibits the requirement of medical examinations before making job offers. However, an employer can ask applicants if they can perform a job's essential functions. Also, job offers can be made contingent on the results of a medical examination.

Affirmative Action

Affirmative action must also be considered. Federal Executive Order 11246 requires organizations that are government contractors or subcontractors to have affirmative action programs in place. These programs are designed to eliminate any underutilization that might occur in an organization's employment practices (see Chapter 3). Affirmative action is not the same as the equal employment opportunity required by the Title VII of Civil Rights Act and related legislation. Making job-related selection decisions while not discriminating against subgroups is not the same as setting utilization goals. However, organizations that are not government contractors or subcontractors can lose the privilege of selecting employees solely on the basis of expected job performance if they are found guilty of discrimination. In that case, they can be ordered to put an affirmative action program in place.

Negligent Hiring

The final legal issue in staffing concerns claims of *negligent hiring*. Negligent hiring refers to a situation in which an employer fails to use reasonable care in hiring an employee, who then commits a crime while in his or her position in the organization. Because claims of negligent hiring have increased over the years,[114] managers need to be particularly sensitive to this issue. For example, Avis Rent A Car hired a man without thoroughly checking his background; the man later raped a female co-worker. Avis was found guilty of negligent hiring and had to pay damages of $800,000. Had the company carefully checked the information provided in the man's job application, it would have discovered that he was in prison when he claimed he was attending high school and college. Employers are responsible for conducting a sound investigation into applicants' backgrounds. Factors such as gaps in employment or admission of prior criminal convictions should prompt closer investigation. To avoid liability for negligent hiring, employers should:[115]

- Develop clear policies on hiring as well as on disciplining and dismissing employees. The hiring policy should include a thorough background check of applicants, including verification of educational, employment, and residential information.
- Check state laws regarding hiring applicants with criminal records. What is legal in this area varies widely among states.
- Learn as much as possible about applicants' past work-related behavior, including violence, threats, lying, drug or alcohol abuse, carrying of weapons, and other problems. Keep in mind that privacy and discrimination laws prohibit inquiries into an applicant's personal, non-work-related activities. Behavioral problems may be investigated only in the context of their possible effect on job performance.

Summary and Conclusions

Human Resource Supply and Demand

HRP is the process an organization uses to ensure that it has the right amount and right kinds of people to deliver a particular level of output or services at some point in the future. HRP entails using a variety of qualitative or quantitative methods to forecast labor demand and labor supply and then taking actions based on those estimates.

The Hiring Process

The hiring process consists of three activities: recruitment, selection, and orientation.

Challenges in the Hiring Process

The hiring process is filled with challenges. These include (1) determining which characteristics are most important to performance, (2) measuring these characteristics, (3) evaluating applicants' motivation, and (4) deciding who should make hiring decisions.

Meeting the Challenge of Effective Staffing

Because choosing the right person for a job can have a tremendous positive effect on productivity and customer satisfaction, it is important that each step of the hiring process be managed carefully.

The Recruitment Process

Recruiting should focus on attracting qualified candidates, internally and/or externally. Recruiting efforts should be tied to the firm's HRP efforts. To ensure proper fit between hires and their jobs and to avoid legal problems, firms should conduct job analyses.

The Selection Process

Many selection tools are available. These include letters of recommendation, application forms, ability tests, personality tests, psychological tests, interviews, assessment centers, drug tests, honesty tests, reference checks, and handwriting analysis. The best (and most legally defensible) selection tools are both reliable and valid.

Legal Issues in Staffing

Several federal legal issues govern staffing practices. The Civil Rights Act, the Age Discrimination Act, and the Americans with Disabilities Act all prohibit various forms of discrimination. Executive Order 11246 spells out affirmative action policies. Employers must also take steps to protect themselves from negligent hiring litigation.

Key Terms

Discussion Questions

1. Smith & Nephew DonJoy, Inc., is a small but fast-growing manufacturer of medical devices in the north end of San Diego County. Because of the recent downsizing of Southern California's aerospace and defense industries, each job opening at DonJoy draws five times more applications than it did just a few years ago. An engineering position is likely to generate as many as 300 applicants. You would think that under these conditions finding employees would be easy, but the selective layoffs made during the downsizings and the need for people to seek new career paths have created a glut of less-than-qualified applicants. What selection tool(s) can DonJoy use to get the most qualified employees from its huge pool of applicants? In general, which selection tool(s) do you think are the best predictors of job performance?
2. Should applicants be selected primarily on the basis of ability or on personality/fit? How can fit be assessed?
3. After returning to Los Angeles from Montana, a former LA police officer thought it would be relatively simple to gain reinstatement in the police force. After all, he had served in the LAPD for 10 years and had won commendations and the respect of his peers and supervisors. Yet two years after his return, this former officer still had not regained his job. Why? Because he is a white man and he scored 98 on the oral portion of his entrance exam.

   As of August 1993, the only way for a white man to land a job with the LAPD was to score a perfect 100. The lowest eligible score for a Latino man was 96, for an African American man it was 95, and for all female candidates it was 94. This scoring was established when the city agreed to establish goals for recruiting minority and female officers.

   Do you think there are other ways the LAPD can recruit qualified minority and female employees that will not negatively affect white male recruits? Explain. In general, how would you design a selection process to achieve a diverse workforce and hire the most qualified workers?
4. Julie Watkins has worked in her new position writing software documentation for three months. At first, she was excited about joining the fast-paced, growing software industry, but now she is having doubts. She keeps hearing about how important her job is to the company, but she does not understand how her work contributes to the whole. Her exposure to the company is limited to her department colleagues (other technical writers), the employee cafeteria, and the payroll office. What could Watkins's company have done to make her see the whole picture and gain an understanding of and commitment to how the company works?
5. Interviewing unqualified applicants can be a frustrating experience and a waste of time for managers, peers, or

whoever is responsible for interviewing. How can the HR department minimize or eliminate this problem?

6. You work for a medium-sized, high-tech firm that faces intense competition on a daily basis. Change seems to be the only constant in your workplace, and each worker's responsibilities shift from project to project. Suppose you have the major responsibility for filling the job openings at your company. How would you go about recruiting and selecting the best people? How would you identify the best people to work in this environment?

There is a variety of additional material available on the Web site that accompanies this text. You can access this information by visiting the Web site at **www.prenhall.com/gomez.**

YOU MANAGE IT!

Emerging Trends Case 5.1

Security: A Question of Balance?

Concern for security has increased in workplaces across the country following the terrorist attack of September 11, 2001. Specifically, the attack highlighted the need to do background checks on all employees. According to HireRight, an Internet-based screening firm, approximately 85 percent of major firms check backgrounds of job applicants. Security is a central concern in certain situations and the U.S. government has taken steps to assure that adequate background checks take place in these situations. For example, the Patriot Act places limits on people who can work with toxic materials. In addition, the U.S. Food and Drug Administration recently issued voluntary guidelines on workplace safety and security. The guidelines were issued in recognition of the importance of security of the food and drug production and distribution systems. The guidelines recommend that employers obtain and verify work references, addresses, and phone numbers. Also, the guidelines ask companies to consider performing criminal background checks and checking applicant names against the FBI's terrorist watch list. Furthermore, the guidelines recommend checking on the immigration status of prospective employees, if appropriate, among other things. These guidelines were developed with input from the Grocery Manufacturers of America and security and military experts. The result is a comprehensive but workable approach.

In addition to the recent concern about terrorism, background checks and other preemployment screens, such as integrity tests, are routinely done to limit employee criminal acts such as theft and violence. However, these checks are not free and place additional hurdles in the way of recruiting needed labor. On the other hand, how can a price be put on security?

Critical Thinking Questions

1. Background checks are commonly done for job applicants, not usually for current employees. However, some companies are taking a more comprehensive approach to security and checking backgrounds of current employees, particularly if an employee is being promoted or is suspected of misconduct.[a] Should background checks be used on current employees? When and under what circumstances? What about using other screens, such as honesty tests, usually associated with preemployment inquiries, on current workers?
2. The state of California passed a law in January 2002 that requires employers to give a copy of the results of a background check to any applicant or employee subjected to the check. If you live in California or any state that requires the same, would it change the responses you gave to each of the questions in item 1? Why would it change your responses?
3. Background checks may be perceived by some people as an invasion of privacy. Why would this perception be a concern? What could be done to eliminate or reduce this perception?
4. Discrimination is a concern that arises regarding security efforts, such as background checks. Should certain nationalities be targeted for checks or for more thorough checks than other nationalities? Why or why not? What about developing a profile of characteristics associated with, say, theft, violence, or terrorism? Would you recommend the use of such profiles? Why or why not?

Team Exercise

1. Consider the various types of background checks presented in the Manager's Notebook: "Looking for Trouble."
   a. Allocate members of your team to research the costs of each of the various types of background checks.
   b. When would you recommend using each type of check and why? Specifically, identify examples of jobs for

which each type of background check would be of value. What would be gained in each situation? Would the benefits offset the costs? Are there some types of checks that your team wouldn't recommend for one or more types of jobs or situations? Explain. Provide a summary to the rest of the class.

2. Security concerns include employee theft and violence.
   a. In regard to employee theft, research has found that employees often follow the model of their supervisor.[b] If the supervisor tends to take things from the employer, a culture in which such dishonesty is acceptable can be established. With such a culture, would focusing screening on lower-level employees solve the theft problem? If not, what would you recommend?
   b. As a security concern, violence is often approached with controls such as two-way mirrors and video cameras. However, these vigilance approaches don't really address underlying causes. Violence can sometimes occur from people not employed by the organization. Background checks of prospective employees can lower the chances of problems of having someone who will cause violence within the workforce. However, studies have found that threat to employees from outsiders is related to frustrations with level of service and with the perception of the organization that lowers social controls (for example, a dirty, unpleasant, and cluttered environment). Given these conditions, what steps would your team recommend to lowers the chances of violence being instigated by outsiders?
   c. Share your recommendations in (a) and (b) with the rest of the class.

Source: Adapted from Hernan, P. (2002). Looking for trouble: Employees' backgrounds face closer scrutiny in the wake of Sept. 11. *Industry Week*, 25, 15(3).

[a] Steen, M. (2002, March 25). Under security. *San Jose Mercury News*, E1.

[b] *Security Director's Report* (2002, April). New crime data suggest effective countermeasures, 1.

Discussion Case 5.2

YOU MANAGE IT!

Automated Hiring

"It was wonderful!" says Linda Prince, an HR administrator with Procter & Gamble. She was referring to the use of an interactive voice response (IVR) system for hiring. An IVR system incorporates a toll-free phone number that candidates may call anytime from anywhere. Usually, a toll-free listing is published in local newspapers and a Touch-Tone phone is required. The IVR system presents automated questions and can screen candidates based on experience, availability, and match with characteristics needed for the job and with the organization's culture. If the candidate answers the automated screening questions satisfactorily, the IVR program can schedule an in-person interview.

Note, however, that IVR is not cheap. Given an average of 25 questions and employer phone costs of 40 to 50 cents per minute, a typical call might take about eight minutes and cost approximately $4.00.

P&G used an IVR system to search for production technicians for a manufacturing plant. The company set criteria so callers could disqualify themselves. Candidates who were disqualified had been convicted of a felony, did not have a high school diploma or its equivalent, declined to rotate shifts, or rejected the starting salary. Those who passed the initial screening took an automated skill test. Candidates who passed that test were scheduled for a face-to-face interview. Ms. Prince's assessment is that the IVR system provided more opportunity to job candidates because the phone lines were rarely busy and were accessible 24 hours a day, seven days a week. Also the system may have been more effective than human beings at quickly screening out inappropriate applicants and saving the cost of further processing for those candidates.

Critical Thinking Questions

1. Do you agree with the assertions that an IVR system provides job candidates with more opportunity and may be more efficient than human beings at screening out inappropriate candidates? Is P&G's IVR system something you would want to use in the hiring process of an organization for which you work or will work? Explain.
2. In what circumstances do you think IVR should or should not be used? For example, is it appropriate if you manage a small business and need to hire two people?
3. An increasing number of companies believe the selection process has a public relations element to it. They view applicants as potential customers so they try to give all applicants a positive view of the organization regardless of how the hiring decision turns out. The applicant's satisfaction with the selection process is an important measure if the business holds this viewpoint. Do you think the IVR system is a useful tool for firms that have the applicant-as-customer perspective? Explain.

Source: Adapted from Thaler-Carter, R. E. (1999). Reach out and hire someone. *HRMagazine*, May, 8–12.

YOU MANAGE IT!

Emerging Trends Case 5.3

Online Recruitment

The Internet is increasingly becoming a tool used to recruit job applicants. However, the features of this approach are still emerging and some sectors are just beginning to use the Internet in recruitment and selection. Although the Internet offers convenience, it's not without problems.

A recent survey found that 89 percent of *Fortune* 500 companies have a career section on their corporate Web site.[a] About 75 percent of these career sections provide job postings and accept electronic applications. Although many companies allow off-line job applications, there is a trend away from this and a trend toward completely digital applications, certainly among large corporations. Another trend is the use of online prescreening tools to separate qualified from unqualified candidates.

The Riverside County Human Resources Department in California provides an example of a public sector agency that has recently implemented online job applications.[b] The HR Web page contains job listing, benefits information, and application information. Current county employees and external job seekers can submit résumés online and see video clips of employees talking about what it is like to live and work in the county.

Perhaps Riverside County HR's most innovative feature is its inclusion of online testing to prescreen applicants. Depending on the position an applicant is seeking, an online test may include over 100 items but provide immediate feedback to the applicant as well as quick and easy generation of a list of qualified finalists for the HR department to further consider. In contrast, the typical approach to preemployment testing had involved taking a test that was only offered at particular times during the year. Furthermore, HR department staff had to manually update approximately 125,000 applicant records per year. This updating will now be done automatically.

Critical Thinking Questions

1. Although it may seem that employers have free and easy access to electronic résumés, this isn't accurate. Many employers now face the cost of wading through a glut of electronic résumés, many of which are part of an indiscriminate submission of résumés from people who aren't really interested in the organization or who don't fit well with the organization. In other words, there's a lot of junk! This problem can become particularly costly for smaller organizations. For example, Eric Starkman, president of Starkman Inc., a New York public relations firm, has decided that his organization will no longer accept electronic résumés.[c] The result? The quantity of résumés has been dramatically reduced but the quality has increased.

   Mr. Starkman's approach is contrary to the trend away from paper résumés, but it does point out a real issue.
   a. Do you agree with Starkman's approach? Why or why not?
   b. How could you manage or reduce the amount of "junk" résumés and job applications?
2. The online approach is convenient, unless you don't have access to the Web, and not everyone does. Should people who do not have Web access be provided an alternative to online application? Or do you assume that those people without Internet access wouldn't be good job candidates? For what type of jobs might this assumption be true?

Team Exercise

1. Online prescreening offers a convenient and efficient way of determining whether an applicant has the needed qualifications, but it is an assessment that can be easily falsified. An applicant could seek answers elsewhere or even have someone else take the online test. For those who passed its online testing, the Riverside County Human Resources Department followed up with a paper-and-pencil form of the test. They found 3 percent of the applicants appeared to have falsified their online performance.
   a. Considering that 3 percent isn't a large percentage, do you think falsification in the online application process is an issue? Why or why not?
   b. Are there situations or jobs in which falsification would be a more serious concern? Describe.
   c. Report your conclusions to the rest of the class.
2. Online tests can be developed in-house or developed by an outside company that specializes in designing tests for preemployment screening. Essentially, this is a make-or-buy decision, but it can get complex. Some of the relevant factors to consider include the number of job openings, the extent of in-house expertise, and the establishment of validity. The pricing structure for companies that develop tests differs, with some charging for test development while others don't charge for development but have a higher per-test fee.
   a. As a team develop a decision-making strategy to help determine whether, depending on the situation, it would be better to "make" or "buy" preemployment screening tests.
   b. Assume that a discrimination in hiring lawsuit has been filed and the validity of your test is in question. Would it be better to have a test that was internally or externally developed? Why?
   c. Share your strategy and opinions with the rest of the class.

3. Online tests provide immediate feedback to applicants. However, what if the preemployment screen includes a personality test? A score and its interpretation in regard to personality or psychological makeup can be sensitive and possibly volatile information. Should personality or psychological measures be included in preemployment screening? Divide your team in half with each half taking a different position on the issue. Also consider in the debate that if personality or psychological assessments are included, how should feedback on test performance be handled?

Sources: [a]Human Resource Department Management Report (2002). Latest trends in recruiting via the corporate Web site. March newsletter of the Institute of Management & Administration. [b]Bingham, B., Ilg, S., and Davidson, N. (2002). Great candidates fast: On-line job application and electronic processing—Washington State's new Internet application. *Public Personnel Management, 31*, 53; and Mooney, J. (2002). Preemployment testing on the Internet: Put candidates a click away and hire at modem speed. *Public Personnel Management, 31*, 4. [c]Maher, K. (2002, January 29). Career journal—The jungle: How to apply online. *Wall Street Journal, 13*, 8.

Emerging Trends Case 5.4

YOU MANAGE IT!

Clone or Complement? What to Look for in a Team

In many organizations that have moved to a team structure, the team is the principal unit where work gets done. However, most organizations recruit and hire as though there was one job description and the team didn't exist. The reality is that people have natural strengths or tendencies and, therefore, end up playing different roles on a team. For example, some people are naturally empathetic and focused on interpersonal issues. Others are focused on and most comfortable with technical aspects. Others like the excitement of identifying new concepts and solutions but aren't cut out for dealing with the operational details needed to carry them through. Recent research has found that allowing people to play to their strengths can yield maximum performance and employee satisfaction.[a]

Critical Thinking Questions

1. If there are distinct roles to be played on a team, how would you go about recruiting and hiring for them?
2. The characteristics needed by individual team members depend on the team and the strengths and weaknesses of others who are on the team. In other words, the situation is much more dynamic than assuming that there is one static job with a single set of qualifications. How could you model or include this dynamic and interactive nature in the recruitment and hiring process?

Team Exercise

As a team, identify the roles that you think are important for teams in the workplace.

1. Identify the skills needed to perform each role.
2. In addition to skills, a natural tendency or motivation to perform in a particular type of role can be critical. How could you measure the motivation needed for each role?
3. How could you measure the skills needed for each role?
4. How could you effectively recruit for the various positions or roles?
5. Present your recruitment and selection plan to the rest of the class.

Source: [a]Black, B. (2002). The road to recovery. *Gallup Management Journal, 1*, 10–12.

Video Shorts Case 5.5

YOU MANAGE IT!

Recruitment and Placement

Welcome once again to *SPOTLIGHT Inside HR*. In this week's broadcast you'll be going behind the scenes with Paul Fiolek, vice president of human resources at Bertelsman BMG, where he faces the possibility that the wrong person has been hired for a job. Later on in the show Cheryl Brie, director of recruitment at Focus Pointe, joins Paul and host Meg Allen to discuss the scene captured on tape by *SPOTLIGHT*'s surveillance cameras.

As you listen, you might want to keep in mind the following: Bertelsman, one of the world's top music distributors, counts Santana, The Dave Matthews Band, and TLC among its long list of recording artists. With 200 branches and over

11,000 employees worldwide, BMG also holds a 20 percent stake in Jive Records, home to The Backstreet Boys, Britney Spears, and N Sync. Currently it owns the rights to some 700,000 songs.

Paul Fiolek has been at BMG for over 10 years and has weathered many of the fickle music industry's incarnations. Watch as Paul takes on Sylvie Aronson, senior director, Music Placement, at BMG. Sylvie, with the help of three supervisors, manages a 50-person department dedicated to placing new artist singles in film and TV spots. Despite the music industry's ongoing difficulties, this division has been growing steadily and has started branching off into creative placement beyond the boundaries of television and movies. Sylvie was granted approval to hire an additional staff member whose connections and experience would contribute to this effort. The new employee is proving to be counterproductive. He lacks experience and does not have the necessary contacts. Sylvie is convinced that BMG's hiring process is at fault, and she is fuming.

Enter Sylvie. She lets Paul know right away that she is not happy. She accuses HR of having "dropped the ball," sending her candidates who did not meet the criteria specified by her department. Sylvie feels that had HR approved a higher salary for the position they might have succeeded in attracting more qualified people. She questions HR's decision to limit its advertising to *Rolling Stone Magazine*. Paul counters by telling her that the recruitment process is a partnership between line management and HR and that the final decision is always the department's to make. He points out that 60 responses to the ad were received and that, although Sylvie was sent only three candidates, she clearly had the option of telling HR that none of them were qualified. Sylvie feels she was pressured into making a decision by time constraints. Is it possible that she simply does not know how to rectify this mistake and is attempting to get HR to take care of it for her?

Sylvie does not back down and the conversation begins to go around in circles. Paul lets his temper get the better of him and lectures her, saying that she does not listen. Do you think his words and his tone are justified? Note that during the entire course of his exchange with Sylvie, the interests of BMG never leave Paul's mind. As an HR vice president, he must always balance the needs of shareholders, management, and employees. He must be able to see the larger picture in order to assess the value not only of this department but also of this particular job and this particular position. Sylvie only sees her needs and what she believes are the needs of the Music Placement Department at BMG. Ideally, there should be no split between the two. Paul comments later on in the show that he felt he had to "educate" Sylvie. What do you think he meant?

As *SPOTLIGHT* comes to a close, Meg Allen introduces the technological aspect of recruitment into the discussion. Both Paul Fiolek and Cheryl Brie of Focus Pointe, a market research service with a staff of 200, agree that online recruiting has had a dramatic effect on the hiring process. The trend in today's marketplace is to use the Internet more and more as a source for talent. While Bertelsman may use a company specializing in video interviews to search for top executives around the country, Focus Pointe is more likely to rely on networking and newspaper ads. Finally, however, Cheryl and Paul concur that nothing will ever replace the experience of meeting a job candidate "face-to-face."

Critical Thinking Questions

1. Do you agree with Cheryl Brie that Sylvie Aronson is "looking to place blame" on the HR department? If you do agree, how would you have reacted to Sylvie's accusations? If you do not agree with Cheryl Brie, explain why you feel Sylvie is correct in her assessment of the HR department's role in this instance.
2. Describe the steps that Bertelsman BMG would need to take in order to rewrite the job specifications for this opening. Why might this be useful to you as an HR manager? If you feel it would not be useful, explain why.
3. Do you think running an ad in *Rolling Stone Magazine* was a wise choice for drawing outside candidates to fill the position that Sylvie had open in her department? What are some other sources that could have used to attract qualified people? When considering alternatives, remember that you have a limited budget.
4. What type of an interview do you feel would be best suited to this dynamic Music Placement Department? Why?
5. Paul Fiolek's conversation revealed a great deal about the formal structure of Bertelsman BMG's HR department. Bertelsman is a giant in the music and entertainment industry. Analyze how this might have both a positive and a negative influence on hiring practices.
6. (Optional) Taking into account the comments you have just heard on *SPOTLIGHT* and the information in your text, how do you think online recruiting might impact on your own job search after graduation?

Managing Employee Separations, Downsizing, and Outplacement

Challenges

After reading this chapter, you should be able to deal more effectively with the following challenges:

1. **Identify** the costs and benefits associated with employee separations.
2. **Understand** the differences between voluntary and involuntary separations.
3. **Avoid** problems in the design of early retirement policies.
4. **Design** HRM policies for downsizing the organization that are alternatives to a layoff; and, when all else fails, develop a layoff program that is effective and fair to the firm's stakeholders.
5. **Understand** the significance and value of outplacement programs.

Place yourself in the following situation:

You're a member of the key management staff at Storage Way, an Internet data storage and restoration service company. A layoff announcement, the fourth in the past 12 months, has just been made by CEO Kim Fennell. The company has been rocked by the sluggish economy and most of its competitors are no longer in business or are going out of business. This fourth layoff will reduce the number of employees at Storage Way another 40% and the headcount will dwindle to 38. The Vice President of sales and marketing just left the company and some senior staff members also left during the past couple of months. Yet, the CEO is firmly positive about the future of the company. He says there is no cash problem in the company and that despite the layoffs, the company would still be able to service present and future customers.

The layoff looks like its going to hit sales and marketing the hardest, but engineering will also be affected. It is up to you to develop and implement a layoff policy immediately. As you draft the policy, consider the following questions.

- **What criteria should you use to determine who will be laid off?** Should you base the layoff decision on seniority? If so, would the company lose more top-performing employees? But if the layoff is based on merit, do you have an accurate system to measure performance? Will this system be defensible if angry employees challenge it in court?
- **How much notice should be given to employees who will be laid off?** Should they be given as much advance notice as possible? Or would giving advance notification create performance problems as current employees search for new jobs?
- **How will security be provided to our remaining employees and protect the business from sabotage or theft by employees who are losing their jobs?** Will you have to deal with disgruntled former employees? Should armed guards be hired to escort laid-off employees out of the building? What message would that send to remaining employees and the media?
- **How should news of the layoff be communicated to the employees who will be let go?** Should they be told about the layoff in a memo or let them read about it in the newspaper? Should a general meeting be held to inform the affected employees? Who should be responsible for telling employees that they have been selected for discharge?
- **When should the media be told about the layoffs?** How can rumors be controlled that may appear in the media? How can investors, distributors, and customers be informed that the company is committed to doing business with them and that the layoff will not hurt the company's relationship with them?
- **How will the remaining workforce, the "survivors," feel about working for the company after the layoff?** Will they still be motivated to perform? Will they remain committed to the company? How can the anger and grief they will be feeling be dealt with?
- **What kind of services can be provided to laid-off employees to help them find other jobs?** Should a company be retained that can supply these services? Can the laid-off employees' be offered benefits for a certain period of time to help ease the pain?

THE MANAGERIAL PERSPECTIVE

As the opening vignette suggests, relationships between employers and employees are constantly subjected to change in today's business environment. Global competition and new technologies such as the Internet have changed the rules of competition, forcing many firms to become increasingly productive with smaller workforces. In addition, in the late 1990s and early 2000s the number of U.S. employees who quit jobs voluntarily increased as employees searched for and found better opportunities in a tight labor market.

Managers must not only develop skills to help an employee who leaves the company voluntarily, but they must also aid employees who have been fired for cause or are being let go for economic reasons. A manager skilled at ending the employment relationship with an employee may leave the door open in the future to reestablish the relationship when conditions change. A badly managed ending to the employment relationship can have severe consequences. It can damage a firm's reputation in its industry or community and limit its ability to attract the scarce, talented employees that it may need in the future.

The previous chapter discussed the management aspects of employee *inflow* into an organization (HR planning, recruitment, selection, and placement decisions). This chapter deals with the sometimes more unpleasant task of managing an organization's outflow of human resources. We explore the process leading up to an employee's exit from the firm and how to manage that process effectively.

What Are Employee Separations?

Employee separation
The termination of an employee's membership in an organization.

Turnover rate
The rate of employee separations in an organization.

An **employee separation** occurs when an employee ceases to be a member of an organization.[1] The **turnover rate** is a measure of the rate at which employees leave the firm. Companies try to monitor and control their turnover rate so that they can, in turn, monitor and control the costs of replacing employees. For example, replacing a U.S. Navy fighter pilot may cost more than $1,000,000.[2] In 1999 the overall turnover rate of information technology (IT) professionals was 20 percent and replacement costs averaged $33,000.[3] In 2002, it has been estimated that there are over 800,000 unfilled information technology position[4] In the health care industry, the turnover rate has been estimated to be 20.4 percent—the highest in a decade.[5] An excessively high turnover rate compared to the industry standard is often a symptom of problems within the organization.

Employee separations can and should be managed. Before we discuss the management of separations, however, it is beneficial to examine both the costs and the benefits of separations.

The Costs of Employee Separations

The costs of employee separations depend on whether managers intend to eliminate the position or to replace the departing employee. By eliminating positions, the company can reduce costs in the long run. This is why many companies in the last decade have downsized their labor forces. However, if not done correctly, layoffs can appear to provide an economic fix in the short term but cause problems for the organization in the long term. Furthermore, even when positions are eliminated, the separation costs can be considerable. For example, as Figure 6.1 shows, from 1993 to 1998 AT&T announced five job cuts to streamline its operations. The separations cost the company billions of dollars. In addition to the monetary cost, AT&T lost talented people, and company morale was crippled. To shore up morale, AT&T executives took a generous approach in its last round of job cuts, offering rich buyout incentives to attract volunteers. As AT&T spokeswoman Adele Ambrose explained, "We wanted to send the right message to our employees, that we need to get cost-competitive but we wanted to be generous to them and express that we care about them."[6]

The cost of turnover can differ across organizations, and some costs associated with turnover can be difficult to estimate. For example, an organization's geographic location may necessitate a particularly high cost of recruiting new employees, which causes the cost of turnover in that organization to be unusually high. Losing customers due to an employee quitting or the loss of talent on productivity or on a research and development all may result in costs that are tremendous but difficult to estimate. Although turnover costs can differ across organizations and can include aspects that are difficult to quantify, it is common to estimate the cost of a turnover from a conservative 25 percent[7] to 150 percent of the lost employee's annual com-

Figure 6.1

Date Announced	Job-Cut Goal	Number of Employees, Jan. 1 of Each Year	Charge Taken (in billions)
Aug. 1993	4,000	313,000	No charge
Feb. 1994	15,000	309,000*	No charge
Sept. 1995	8,500	302,000	$1.6†
Jan. 1996	40,000	301,000	$6.0†
Jan. 1998	18,000	128,000**	$1.0 (estimated)

*Acquired McCaw Cellular Communications in 1993.
**After spinning off Lucent Technologies and NCR in 1997.
†Total charge includes restructuring and consolidation.

Source: Schiesel, S. (1998, February 8). AT&T: A leaner company without a crash diet. *New York Times*, www.nytimes.com/library/financial/Sunday/archive/.

AT&T's Job Cuts: 1993 Through 1998

pensation.[8] Looking at the most conservative end of that range, at an average salary of $30,000, the cost of a turnover would be $6,000. For a company with 1,000 employees and a 20 percent turnover rate, the annual cost of turnover would be at least $1,200,000—not a trivial cost, and it could be much higher depending on the situation. Figure 6.2 presents some of the costs associated with replacing an employee. The costs can be categorized as *recruitment costs, selection costs, training costs*, and *separation costs*. Recognize that even these costs do not capture all of the costs that can be associated with turnover (such as lowered productivity, loss of knowledge and talent, loss of customers, negative impact on remaining workers, and so on).

Recruitment Costs

The costs associated with recruiting a replacement may include advertising the job vacancy and using a professional recruiter to travel to various locations (including college campuses). To fill executive positions or technologically complex openings, it may be necessary to employ a search firm to locate qualified individuals, who most likely are already employed. A search firm typically charges the company a fee of about 30 percent of the employee's annual salary.

Selection Costs

Selection costs are associated with selecting, hiring, and placing a new employee in a job. Selection can involve interviewing the job applicant, which includes the costs associated with travel to the interview site and the productivity lost in organizing the interviews and arranging meetings to make selection decisions. For example, a law firm's decision to hire a new associate may involve the participation of many junior associates as well as senior partners. Each of these lawyers may charge clients hundreds of dollars per hour for his or her time. If several meetings are called after the interviews are completed, these lawyers lose valuable time that they could have spent working for their clients.

Other selection costs involve testing the employee and conducting reference checks to make sure the applicant's qualifications are legitimate. Finally, the company may have to pay relocation costs, which include the costs of moving the employee's personal property, travel costs, and sometimes even housing costs. Housing costs may include the costs of selling one's previous house and the transaction costs of buying a house in a more expensive market.

Training Costs

Organizations incur costs in providing new employees with the knowledge necessary to perform on the job. Most new employees need some specific training to do their job. For example, sales representatives need training on the company's line of products. Training costs also include the costs associated with an orientation to the company's values and culture. Also important are direct training costs—specifically, the cost of instruction, books, and materials for training courses. The cost of training someone in technical software skills, for instance, can be as high as $30,000 or more.[9] Finally, while new employees are being trained, they are not performing at the level of fully trained employees, so some productivity is lost. For example, new computer programmers may write fewer lines of code in a given amount of time than experienced programmers do.

Separation Costs

A company incurs separation costs for all employees who leave, whether or not they will be replaced. The largest separation cost involves compensation in terms of pay and benefits. Most

Figure 6.2

Recruitment Costs	Selection Costs	Training Costs	Separation Costs
■ Advertising	■ Interviewing	■ Orientation	■ Separation pay
■ Campus visits	■ Testing	■ Direct training costs	■ Benefits
■ Recruiter time	■ Reference checks	■ Trainer's time	■ Unemployment insurance cost
■ Search firm fees	■ Relocation	■ Lost productivity during training	■ Exit interview
			■ Outplacement
			■ Vacant position

Human Resource Replacement Costs

companies provide *severance pay* (also called *separation pay*) for laid-off employees. Severance pay may add up to several months' salary for an experienced employee. For example, IBM laid off 170 employees in its San Jose, California, disk drive plant. The affected workers were given 8 to 26 weeks of separation pay, depending on their length of service. However, recent surveys of employers indicate that technical and professional employees receive a median of three weeks' pay and nonexempt employees typically receive two weeks' pay as severance.[10] Nearly 80 percent of 1,000 companies included in one survey reported that they have a severance plan. Although length of service is the main factor in determining the amount of severance pay, many companies also use formulas that take into account factors such as salary, grade level, and title.

Less frequently, employees may continue to receive health benefits until they find a new job. In addition, employers who lay off employees may also see their unemployment insurance rates go up. Companies are penalized with a higher tax if more of their former employees draw benefits from the unemployment insurance fund in the states in which they do business.

Other separation costs are associated with the administration of the separation itself. Administration often includes an **exit interview** to find out the reasons why the employee is leaving (if he or she is leaving voluntarily) or to provide counseling and/or assistance in finding a new job. It is now common practice in larger firms to provide departing employees with **outplacement assistance,** which helps them find a job more rapidly by providing them with training in job-search skills. Finally, employers incur a cost if a position remains vacant and the work does not get done. The result may be a reduction in output or quality of service to the firm's clients or customers. For example, because of labor shortages in many U.S. cities in the early 2000s, it is not unusual for restaurants to experience a shortage of cooks and servers. Regular customers may be dissatisfied with the slow service at the understaffed restaurants and go to different ones with better service.

Exit interview
An employee's final interview following separation. The purpose of the interview is to find out the reasons why the employee is leaving (if the separation is voluntary) or to provide counseling and/or assistance in finding a new job.

Outplacement assistance
A program in which companies help their departing employees find jobs more rapidly by providing them with training in job-search skills.

Conducting exit interviews is a challenge because it is often difficult to get departing employees to speak honestly about the company, usually because they do not want to "burn their bridges behind them." The Manager's Notebook titled "Excelling at Exit Interviews" gives some tips for eliciting truthful responses.

MANAGER'S NOTEBOOK

Excelling at Exit Interviews

1. Start with the assumption that open and honest responses will not be easily obtained.
2. Use skilled interviewers, preferably from the HR department. In very small or family-run companies where this is impossible, paper-and-pencil questionnaires can be mailed to an ex-employee's home. This may not be a disadvantage because these kinds of surveys tend to produce more candid answers.
3. Assure departing employees that any comments they make will be held confidential (except those that concern potential legal issues) and that their responses won't endanger their chances of getting a good job reference.
4. Start with routine departure basics, such as when benefits will end, before moving to the heart of the interview: why the employee is leaving.
5. Ask open-ended questions and avoid appearing to be the company's interrogator or defender.
6. Before taking any action, make sure the feedback from exit interviews correlates with other available information, such as employee surveys or peer and supervisor reviews.
7. Take action. People are more likely to feel their comments make a difference at companies that have a history of responding to ex-employees' perspectives.

Source: Saia, R. (1999, January 25). Parting shots. *Computerworld*, 58; Rasmusson, E. (1998, November). How a quitter can help your company, *Sales & Marketing Management*, 96; and Brotherton, P. (1996, August). Exit interviews can provide a reality check. *HRMagazine*, 45–50.

The Benefits of Employee Separations

Although many people see separations negatively, they have several benefits. When turnover rates are too low, few new employees will be hired and opportunities for promotion are sharply curtailed. A persistently low turnover rate may have a negative effect on performance if the workforce becomes complacent and fails to generate innovative ideas. A certain level of employee separations is a good and necessary part of doing business, and the benefits of employee separations to the organization include the following: Labor costs are reduced; poor performers are replaced; innovation is increased; and opportunities for greater diversity are enhanced.

Employees may receive some potential benefits from a separation, too. An individual may escape from an unpleasant work situation and eventually find one that is less stressful or more personally and professionally satisfying.

Reduced Labor Costs

An organization can reduce its total labor costs by reducing the size of its workforce. Although separation costs in a layoff can be considerable, the salary savings resulting from the elimination of some jobs can easily outweigh the separation pay and other expenditures associated with the layoff.

Replacement of Poor Performers

An integral part of management is identifying poor performers and helping them improve their performance. If an employee does not respond to coaching or feedback, it may be best to terminate him or her so that a new (and presumably more skilled) employee can be brought in. The separation of poor performers creates the opportunity to hire good performers in their place.

Increased Innovation

Separations create advancement opportunities for high-performing individuals. They also open up entry-level positions as employees are promoted from within. An important source of innovation in companies is new people hired from the outside who can offer a fresh perspective. Such individuals may be entry-level college graduates armed with the latest research methods, or they may be experienced managers or engineers hired from leading research laboratories.

The Opportunity for Greater Diversity

Separations create opportunities to hire employees from diverse backgrounds and to redistribute the cultural and gender composition of the workforce. Increasing its workforce diversity allows an organization to take advantage of a diverse workforce (see Chapter 4) while maintaining control over its hiring practices and complying with the government's Equal Employment Opportunity Commission policies.

Types of Employee Separations

Employee separations can be divided into two categories. Voluntary separations are initiated by the employee. Involuntary separations are initiated by the employer. When employees leave voluntarily, they are less likely to take their former employers to court for wrongful discharge. To protect themselves against legal challenges by former employees, employers must manage involuntary separations very carefully with a well-documented paper trail.

Voluntary Separations

Voluntary separation
A separation that occurs when an employee decides, for personal or professional reasons, to end the relationship with the employer.

Voluntary separations occur when an employee decides, for personal or professional reasons, to end the relationship with the employer. The decision could be based on the employee's obtaining a better job, changing careers, or wanting more time for family or leisure activities. Alternatively, the decision could be based on the employee's finding the present job unattractive because of poor working conditions, low pay or benefits, a bad relationship with a supervisor, and so on. In most cases, the decision to leave is a combination of having attractive alternatives and being unhappy with aspects of the current job.

Voluntary separations can be either *avoidable* or *unavoidable*. Unavoidable voluntary separations result from an employee's life decisions that extend beyond an employer's control, such as a spouse's decision to move to a new area that requires a relocation for the employee. However, recent studies show that approximately 80 percent of voluntary separations are avoidable, and many of those are due to staffing mistakes. By investing in quality HRM recruiting, selection, training, and development programs (see Chapters 5 and 8), companies can avoid many mistakes involving a poor match between the employee and the job.[11]

There are two types of voluntary separations: quits and retirements.

Quits

The decision to *quit* depends on (1) the employee's level of dissatisfaction with the job and (2) the number of attractive alternatives the employee has outside the organization.[12] The employee can be dissatisfied with the job itself, the job environment, or both. For example, if the hours and location of a job are unattractive, an employee may look for a job with better hours and a location closer to home.

In recent years some employers have been using pay incentives to encourage employees to quit voluntarily. Employers use these *voluntary severance plans*, or *buyouts*, to reduce the size of their workforce while avoiding the negative factors associated with a layoff. The pay incentive may amount to a lump-sum cash payment of six months to two years of salary, depending on the employee's tenure with the company and the plan's design. For example, Connecticut Mutual Life Insurance Company used an employee buyout to reduce the size of its workforce after it merged with Massachusetts Mutual Life Insurance. Workers with three years or more were given three weeks of pay for each year of service, with a minimum of 26 weeks of pay and a maximum of 76 weeks.[13]

Retirements

Like a quit, a *retirement* is initiated by the employee. However, a retirement differs from a quit in a number of respects. First, a retirement usually occurs at the end of an employee's career. A quit can occur at any time. (In fact, it is in the early stages of one's career that a person is more likely to change jobs.) Second, retirements usually result in the individual's receiving retirement benefits from the organization. These may include a retirement income that is supplemented with personal savings and Social Security benefits. People who quit do not receive these benefits. Finally, the organization normally plans retirements in advance. HR staff can help employees plan their retirement, and managers can plan in advance to replace retirees by grooming current employees or recruiting new ones. Quits are much more difficult to plan for.

Most employees postpone retirement until they are close to 65 because that is the age at which they are entitled to full Social Security and Medicare benefits from the government (see Chapter 12).[14] Without these benefits, many workers would find it difficult to retire. It is illegal for an employer to force an employee to retire on the basis of age.

Many *Fortune* 500 companies have found *early retirement incentives* an effective way to reduce their workforce. These incentives make it financially attractive for senior employees to retire early. Along with buyouts, they are used as alternatives to layoffs because they are seen as a gentler way of downsizing. We discuss the management of early retirements in detail later in this chapter.

Involuntary Separations

An **involuntary separation** occurs when management decides to terminate its relationship with an employee due to (1) economic necessity or (2) a poor fit between the employee and the organization. Involuntary separations are the result of very serious and painful decisions that can have a profound effect on the entire organization and especially on the employee who loses his or her job.

Involuntary separation
A separation that occurs when an employer decides to terminate its relationship with an employee due to (1) economic necessity or (2) a poor fit between the employee and the organization.

Although managers implement the decision to dismiss an employee, the HR staff makes sure that the dismissed employee receives "due process" and that the dismissal is performed within the letter and the spirit of the company's employment policy. Cooperation and teamwork

As the baby boomer generation continues to age, a record-breaking number of employees will retire. The American Association of Retired Persons (AARP) helps lobby to protect the rights of retirees and offers counseling services such as financial advice.

between managers and HR staff are essential to effective management of the dismissal process. HR staff can act as valuable advisers to managers in this arena by helping them avoid mistakes that can lead to claims of wrongful discharge. They can also help protect employees whose rights are violated by managers. There are two types of involuntary separations: discharges and layoffs.

Discharges

A *discharge* takes place when management decides that there is a poor fit between an employee and the organization. The discharge is a result of either poor performance or the employee's failure to change some unacceptable behavior that management has tried repeatedly to correct. Sometimes employees engage in serious misconduct, such as theft or dishonesty, which may result in immediate termination.

Managers who decide to discharge an employee must make sure they follow the company's established discipline procedures. Most nonunion companies and all unionized firms have a *progressive discipline procedure* that allows employees the opportunity to correct their behavior before receiving a more serious punishment. For example, an employee who violates a safety rule may be given a verbal warning, followed by a written warning within a specified period of time. If the employee does not stop breaking the safety rule, the employer may choose to discharge the employee. Managers must document the occurrences of the violation and provide evidence that the employee knew about the rule and was warned that its violation could lead to discharge. In this way, managers can prove that the employee was discharged for just cause. Chapter 14 details the criteria that managers can use to determine if a discharge meets the standard of just cause.*

An example from the business pages illustrates how costly discharging an employee can be if handled poorly or without due process. Sandra McHugh won $1.1 million in damages in an age discrimination lawsuit against her employer.[15] McHugh was forced out of her job because of her age—which was 42 at the time of her discharge from the company.

The Manager's Notebook: Emerging Trend "To Terminate or Not to Terminate: That's an Important Question" offers further consideration of how the termination decision should be approached.

*In some jurisdictions, it is possible for management to discharge an employee based on evidence that does not meet the standard of just cause. However, the authors recommend meeting this standard as a good business practice.

Emerging Trends

MANAGER'S NOTEBOOK

To Terminate or Not to Terminate: That's an Important Question

Discharging an employee can be an emotional and critical event for all parties involved. The decision to terminate needs to be approached carefully and rationally. No manager wants a termination to lead to a wrongful discharge lawsuit (see Chapter 14 for a consideration of management's legal right to terminate). The following points can help you decide whether to terminate and, if so, how to carry it out.

1. **Sometimes it's a no-brainer**. Has the employee been stealing from the company? Does the worker unnecessarily cause trouble? Does the person feel that he or she is so much better than everyone else that being part of the team is beneath him or her? If these types of problems exist, the worker may simply deserve to be fired. If there were no errors in hiring, these unpleasant terminations may not have to be made. However, hiring decisions cannot all be perfect.
2. **Sometimes it's not so blatant**. Even if all hiring decisions were perfect, changes in workers, in the job, the marketplace, and the general economy may dictate that termination is necessary. It may be that the worker just doesn't fit with the job or organization any longer. Or performance may no longer be adequate due to changes in job requirements or budgetary constraints. The following points can help assure that you carry out the termination as defensibly as possible.
   a. **Contractual rights?** Confirm that the worker does not have a contract that would limit the organization's right to fire the worker. Contractual rights might, for example, be extended in an letter offering employment, in an employee handbook, or in personnel policies.
   b. **Legal liability?** Are there circumstances that $$$pose a potential legal liability to the organization? For example, did the employee recently file a workers' compensation claim? If so, a termination might appear to be retaliation against the worker. Is the worker covered by employment discrimination laws, for example, due to age, race, gender, national origin, or religion? These laws do not preclude termination for poor performance or for business reasons. They just preclude personnel decisions being made on the basis of age, race, gender, and so on. If the worker is covered by these laws, be sure that the termination is based on legitimate and nondiscriminatory factors and that the reasons for termination can be documented.
   c. **Is it fair?** How have other similarly situated employees been treated? Is there written documentation of a performance problem (if that is the basis for the termination)? Has the employee been notified of the problem and been given an opportunity to improve? Should you offer assistance to the employee in transitioning to a new job? The answers to these and related questions can help you gauge the fairness of a termination action. Fairness may not be a legal requirement (although it can be in some jurisdictions), but people who have been treated fairly are less likely to pursue lawsuits. But if they do, such lawsuits are less likely to stand up to legal scrutiny if you have made sure that you have treated people fairly.

Sources: Adapted from Schmitt, J. (2002). Some people just need firing. *Contractor, 49*, 14; and Bee, L., and Mastman, G. L. (2002). Fair treatment in firings avoids suits. *National Underwriter Property & Casualty, 106*, 20(3).

Layoffs

A *layoff* differs from a discharge in several ways. In a layoff, employees lose their jobs because a change in the company's environment or strategy forces it to reduce its workforce. Global competition, reductions in product demand, changing technologies that reduce the need for workers, and mergers and acquisitions are the primary factors behind most layoffs.[16] In contrast, the actions of most discharged employees have usually been a direct cause of their separation.

Layoffs have a powerful impact on the organization. They can affect the morale of the organization's remaining employees, who may fear losing their jobs in the future. In addition, layoffs can affect a region's economic vitality, including the merchants who depend on the workers' patronage

A Question of Ethics

What can a company do to help a community when it decides to close a plant that is important to the community's economic prosperity?

to support their businesses. When layoffs happen, the entire community may suffer. This was the case when National Cash Register (NCR) closed many plants in the Dayton, Ohio, area in the 1990s. Dayton's economic prosperity collapsed when it lost 20,000 high-paying jobs due to a failed merger between NCR and AT&T.[17] More recently, a layoff at Dell Computer had a severe impact on a community. On February 15, 2001, Dell Computer Corporation fired 1,700 workers in the first major layoff in the company's history.[18] Three months later, another 4,000 jobs were eliminated. Nearly all of the cuts were made at Dell's central Texas facility in Round Rock, a city north of Austin. Laid-off workers, crying and carrying their belongings, were led out of the building by security. More than the emotional impact, the financial impact on many workers was dramatic. Hank Watson is an example. A sales manager at Dell, his annual salary was greater than $100,000. After being laid off, he received less than $1,200 per month in unemployment benefits and it was four months before he found a job as a waiter. The thousands of laid-off Round Rock workers found it hard to replace the income they had made with Dell. The local market was saturated with thousands of other people who had similar résumés. The local real estate market is an indicator of the collective impact of the Dell layoffs. The Round Rock real estate market is made up of approximately 30 to 35 percent Dell employees, but the higher end of the market is made up almost entirely of Dell employees. In 2002, the number of homes valued over $250,000 that are for sale has increased tenfold in one year, and nothing at this end of the market is selling.[19] Even a local deli's sandwich sales decreased by 25 percent. The greater the dependence of a local economy on one employer, the more devastating a layoff can be to that community.

Investors may be affected by layoffs as well. The investment community may interpret a layoff as a signal that the company is having serious problems. This, in turn, may lower the price of the company's stock on the stock market. Finally, layoffs can change a company's image. They can hurt a company's standing as a good place to work and make it difficult to recruit highly skilled employees who can choose among numerous employers. For example, the layoffs of thousands of aerospace engineers from defense contractors such as General Dynamics, Lockheed Martin, and Northrop Grumman may make it difficult for these companies to attract the best new engineering graduates.

Nissan, the Japanese car manufacturer, may also have difficulty attracting talented engineers and professionals after announcing the closing of five factories and the layoff of thousands of employees in Japan. Plant closings and large-scale layoffs are rare in Japan and almost unheard of in its automobile industry.[20]

Downsizing
A company strategy to reduce the scale (size) and scope of its business in order to improve the company's financial performance.

Layoffs, Downsizing, and Rightsizing

It is appropriate at this point to clarify the difference between a layoff and two concepts that are frequently (but sometimes mistakenly) associated with it: downsizing and rightsizing. A company that adopts a **downsizing** strategy reduces the scale (size) and scope of its business to

Managers who discharge an employee for a bad cause can cost their company thousands—or even millions—of dollars. Sandra McHugh, who was fired because of her age, won over $1 million in damages.

improve its financial performance.[21] When a company decides to downsize, it may choose layoffs as one of several ways of reducing costs or improving profitability.[22] In recent years many firms have done exactly this, but we want to emphasize that companies can take many other measures to increase profitability without resorting to layoffs.[23] We discuss these measures later in this chapter.

Rightsizing involves reorganizing a company's employees to improve their efficiency.[24] An organization needs to rightsize when it becomes bloated with too many management layers or too many bureaucratic work processes that add no value to its product or service. For example, companies that reconfigure their front-line employees into self-managed work teams may find that they are overstaffed and need to reduce their headcount to take advantage of the efficiencies provided by the team structure. The result may be layoffs, but layoffs are not always necessary. As with downsizing strategy, management may have several alternatives to layoffs available when it rightsizes its workforce. However, whatever the label, the result is that people are losing their jobs. The important thing is to be sure not to be a victim of a layoff, a rightsizing, or a downsizing. The Manager's Notebook: Emerging Trend titled "Don't Be a Layoff Victim: Tips for Keeping Your Job" offers some pointers that may help you establish your value to an organization so that a termination axe will fall elsewhere.

Rightsizing
The process of reorganizing a company's employees to improve their efficiency.

Managing a layoff is an extremely complex process. Before we examine the specifics, however, it is useful to examine an important alternative to layoffs: early retirements.

Emerging Trends — MANAGER'S NOTEBOOK

Don't Be a Layoff Victim: Tips for Keeping Your Job

In most organizations, jobs are not guaranteed. Even the most seemingly stable organizational environment can be rocked by market and economic forces. Rather than being passive and fatalistic, there are steps you can take to help assure that, if things get rough, you will be retained. These are no guarantees, but the following may prove helpful.

- **Looks count!** A T-shirt and jeans topped with a backward facing baseball cap may have been your attire for college but is likely not acceptable for business. You don't need to dress like a fashion model, but unprofessional dress will be noticed.
- **Be a member of the team**. You might get by doing the minimum amount of work to hold your job, but not when layoff decisions loom. Accept being on that project committee or volunteer to do it. You will likely learn something, meet others in the organization, and create opportunities to positively portray yourself in the organization. If you can't do another task or aren't sure if you can handle the workload, be honest about it. Point out what other projects or teams you are on and that you may not be able to give adequate attention to everything. This allows for discussion of duties and priorities and shows that you take your responsibilities seriously. It will probably come off much better than generating an excuse that may appear lame and evasive.
- **Performance matters**. Whatever performance measures are used in your work setting, be sure your performance is competitive. You may take on more difficult tasks or you may be detail oriented. If the result is that your performance is not competitive, you need to change so that it is. The performance management system and those who don't know you may not take complexity or accuracy into account.
- **Choose your battles**. You won't always agree with others and you may experience unfairness. However, you need to choose your battles carefully. Being right will do you little good if the person you just battled with is the golfing partner of the manager assigned the task of making layoff decisions.
- **Be courteous**. Be complimentary—it costs nothing! Thank staff people for their efforts. You might thrive in a demanding and callous environment, but your workers likely won't. Offer praise when it is merited and thank people for their assistance. Treat people in a friendly and courteous manner and you will find that worker reactions can change from explanations for why something can't be done to finding a way to make it happen.

- **Own up to your mistakes**. If you made an error, left out important data, or forgot an appointment, don't blame others. It may seem easy to locate blame for a mistake on one of your workers. However, you may pay for it eventually in terms of loss in worker loyalty and your reputation. Owning up to your mistakes will be looked upon positively by others.
- **People gossip, so make sure it's positive** Most work settings are like small towns: Informally, they run on gossip. If you are always late or disappear on Friday afternoons, it's sure to be noticed, eventually, by everyone. People gossip. Try to conduct yourself so that what is said about you is positive and doesn't cause you problems. Recognizing the prevalence and the effects of informal communication can be helpful to you in other ways. For example, have lunch with your workers and listen to what they have to say. If they open up with you, you could learn more from one luncheon meeting than from any formal meetings. Be careful not to add to the gossip and say anything negative about anyone.

Source: Adapted with permission from Solomon, G. (2002). How to keep your job in a tight market: Maybe you can't make yourself indispensable, but there's plenty you can do to ensure that colleagues and staff like having you around. *Medical Economics, 79*, 104(2).

Managing Early Retirements

When a company decides to downsize its operation, its first task is to examine alternatives to layoffs. As we mentioned earlier, one of the most popular of these methods is early retirement. In recent years companies such as IBM, Exxon Mobil, DuPont, AT&T, Hewlett-Packard,[25] Bell Atlantic,[26] and GTE[27] have used early retirement to reduce the size of their workforce.

The Features of Early Retirement Policies

Early retirement policies consist of two features: (1) a package of financial incentives that makes it attractive for senior employees to retire earlier than they had planned and (2) an *open window* that restricts eligibility to a fairly short period of time. After the window is closed, the incentives are no longer available.[28]

The financial incentives are usually based on a formula that accelerates senior employees' retirement eligibility and increases their retirement income. It is not unusual for companies to provide a lump-sum payment as an incentive to leave. Many companies also offer the continuation of health benefits so that early retirees enjoy coverage until they are eligible for Medicare at age 65. However, as companies have opened the early retirement window to more and more employees in recent years, they have had to scale back once generous severance packages. For instance, when IBM announced its early retirement policy in 1991, it allowed any employee with 30 years of service to retire with full retirement benefits regardless of age. Employees who accepted the offer received a lump sum of one year's salary. By 1993 departing employees got a maximum of 26 weeks' pay plus only six months' paid medical coverage.[29]

Early retirement policies can reduce the size of a company's workforce substantially. DuPont experienced a 10 percent reduction and Exxon Mobil experienced a 15 percent reduction in their workforces with early retirement policies.[30]

Avoiding Problems with Early Retirements

Managing early retirement policies requires careful design, implementation, and administration. When not properly managed, early retirement policies can cause a host of problems. Too many employees may take early retirement, the wrong employees may leave, and employees may perceive that they are being forced to leave, which may result in age discrimination complaints.

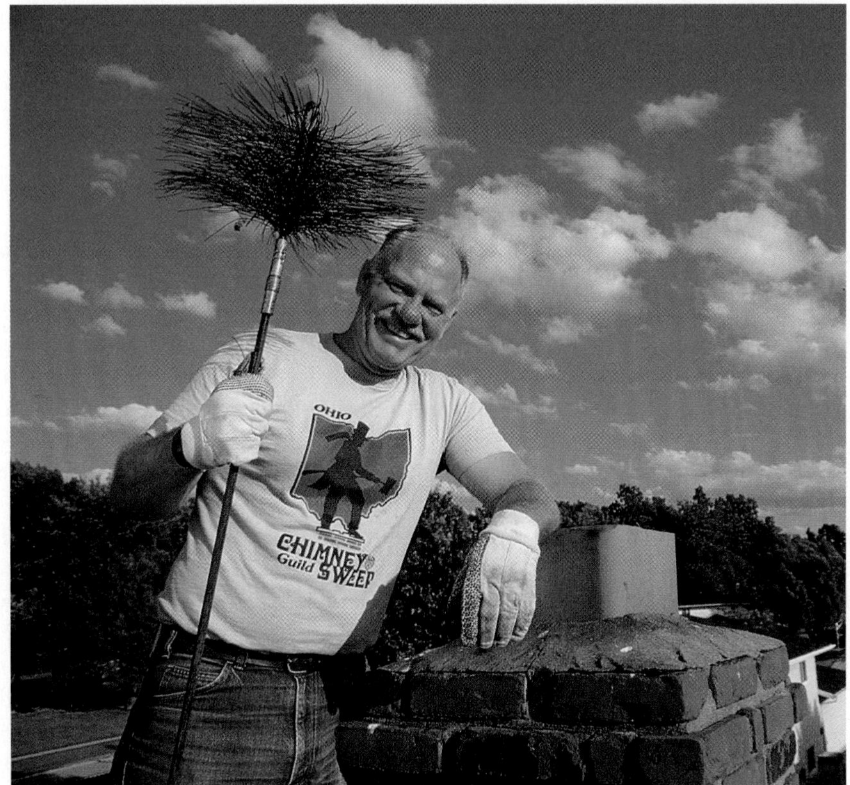

After 13 years as a fuels buyer with BP America, Inc., Ron Colvin started his own business as a chimney sweep. Colvin is happy to be out of corporate life and is making decent money. The only problem: "It gets lonely, working by yourself," he says.

DuPont was surprised in 1985 when 12,000 of its employees, about twice as many as expected, elected to take advantage of the company's early retirement incentives.[31] One way to avoid excess resignations is to restrict eligibility to divisions that have redundant employees with high levels of seniority (instead of making the policy available to all employees throughout the corporation). Another way is to ask senior employees how they would respond to a specific early retirement plan. This survey could then be used to predict the number of senior employees who would retire if the incentives were made available. If the survey shows that too many would leave, the incentives could be fine-tuned so that a controlled number of employees take early retirement.

Sometimes the most marketable employees with the best skills can easily find another job and decide to "take the money and run." To avoid this situation and keep its most valuable people, the company can develop provisions to hire back retired employees as temporary consultants until suitable replacements can be promoted, hired, or trained.

Early retirement programs must be managed so that eligible employees do not perceive that they are being forced to retire and consequently file age discrimination charges. Situations that could be interpreted as coercive include the following:

- A longtime employee who has performed satisfactorily over many years suddenly receives an unsatisfactory performance evaluation.
- A manager indicates that senior employees who do not take early retirement may lose their jobs anyway because a layoff is likely in the near future.
- Senior employees notice that their most recent pay raises are quite a bit lower than those of other, younger workers who are not eligible for early retirement.

An example demonstrates how a lack of sensitivity on the part of management can result in litigation. A former employee who sued IBM for age discrimination was awarded $315,000 in compensatory damages because he convinced the jury that he was forced to take early retirement.[32] The employee introduced evidence showing that his job had been reclassified after he voiced some reservations about taking early retirement. Shortly after that, he claimed, he received a warning that his next performance evaluation would be considered unsatisfactory.

Managers can avoid lawsuits by following one simple guideline: All managers with senior employees should make certain that they do not treat senior employees any differently than other employees. HR staff members play an important role here by keeping managers aware of the letter and the spirit of the early retirement policy so that they do not (consciously or unconsciously) coerce senior employees during the open window period.

Managing Layoffs

Typically, an organization will institute a layoff when it cannot reduce its labor costs by any other means. Figure 6.3, which presents a model of the layoff decision and its alternatives, shows that managers should first try to reduce their labor costs by using alternatives to layoffs, such as early retirements and other voluntary workforce reductions. After managers make the decision to implement a layoff, they must concern themselves with the outplacement of the former employees.

An important influence on the likelihood of a layoff is the business's HR strategy (see Chapter 1). Companies with a lifelong employment HR strategy are less likely to lay off employees because they have developed alternative policies to protect their permanent employees' job security. The best-known examples of firms with lifelong employment policies are the large Japanese corporations, which employ about one-third of Japanese workers. In the United States a few companies (such as FedEx Corporation) have firm no-layoff policies. FedEx has never had a layoff in its U.S. operation, which includes 124,000 employees.[33] Its no-layoff policy means that the organization is committed to preserving jobs and benefits as much as possible. FedEx has dealt with the recent economic recession by relying on attrition, deferring purchases, instituting a hiring freeze, limiting employee travel, and deferring bonuses. Most workers, at FedEx or anywhere, would probably agree that these cutbacks are better than losing their jobs. Most firms, however, have market-driven HR strategies that permit layoffs when alternatives are not available.

Alternatives to Layoffs

Most organizations search for alternative cost-reduction methods before turning to layoffs. A recent survey found attrition, which reduces the size of the workforce by not replacing workers

The Layoff Decision and Its Alternatives

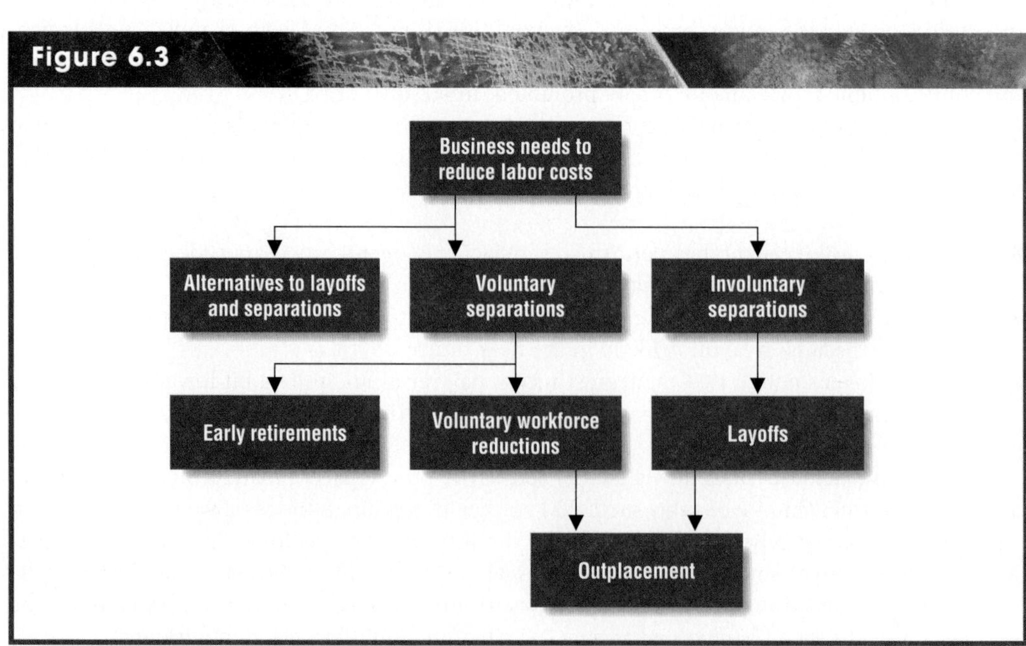

who leave the organization, to be the common strategy.[34] Other approaches include employment freezes, not renewing contract workers, and encouraging employees to take time off voluntarily. Figure 6.4 shows the major alternatives to layoffs. These include employment policies, changes in job design, pay and benefits policies, and training. Managers can use these alternatives both to reduce labor costs and to protect the jobs of full-time employees.

Employment Policies

The first alternatives to layoffs that managers are likely to consider are those that intrude the least on the day-to-day management of the business. These alternatives usually focus on adjustments to employment policies.

The least disruptive way to cut labor costs is through **attrition.** By not filling job vacancies that are created by turnover, improvements can be made on the bottom line. After contract negotiations with the United Auto Workers Union, DaimlerChrysler made clear its plan to trim its workforce through attrition and workers who take early retirement packages.[35]

Attrition
An employment policy designed to reduce the company's workforce by not refilling job vacancies that are created by turnover.

When greater cost reductions are needed, a **hiring freeze** may be implemented. Many universities have used hiring freezes to balance their budgets in years of fiscal restraint. Temporary employees, part-time employees, student interns, co-ops, and subcontracted employees may also be eliminated to protect the jobs of permanent full-time employees.

Hiring freeze
An employment policy designed to reduce the company's workforce by not hiring any new employees into the company.

Other employment policies aim to decrease the number of hours worked and, therefore, the number of hours for which the company must pay its employees. Workers may be encouraged to take voluntary (unpaid) time off or leaves of absence, or they may be asked to put in a shorter workweek (for example, 35 hours rather than 40).

The strategic application of employment policies to provide job security for a firm's full-time, core employees is called a *rings of defense* approach to job security. Under this approach, headcounts of full-time employees are purposely kept low. An increase in the demand for labor will be satisfied by hiring part-time and temporary employees or subcontracting work to freelancers. For example, Axcelis is a manufacturer of tools used in the semiconductor industry. It has a core of 2,000 full-time permanent workers but uses temporary workers and contract workers as a buffer against changes in market conditions.[36] Given a downturn in the market, the company has reduced the number of noncore workers from 500 last year to approximately 50 now. The advantage of this approach is that it provides some stability and security, at least for the core employees. This security can pay off in the form of workers who feel more comfortable and can, therefore, be more innovative—an important competitive characteristic in many industries. However, the increasing use of temporary, or contingent, workers as a strategy to smooth out variations in demand for labor means that more workers are vulnerable and treated as expendable by employers. Furthermore, the use of contingent workers can mean that customer service and productivity can suffer because of contingent workers' possible inexperience and lack of sufficient loyalty and commitment to the company.

Figure 6.4

Employment Policies	Changes in Job Design	Pay and Benefits Policies	Training
■ Reduction through attrition ■ Hiring freeze ■ Cut part-time employees ■ Cut internships or co-ops ■ Give subcontracted work to in-house employees ■ Voluntary time off ■ Leaves of absence ■ Reduced work hours	■ Transfers ■ Relocation ■ Job sharing ■ Demotions	■ Pay freeze ■ Cut overtime pay ■ Use vacation and leave days ■ Pay cuts ■ Profit sharing or variable pay	■ Retraining

Alternatives to Layoffs

The use of contingent workers as a buffer labor force is a strategy that has extended beyond the United States primarily through U.S. foreign operations. Although other countries do not yet use contingent workers to the extent that companies in the United States do, they are catching up with this practice, particularly in poor countries where there are few labor protection laws. As noted by John Challenger, CEO of the Challenger Gray & Christmas personnel firm, for some countries the transition to a contingent workforce can be difficult. For example, Japan has been facing very difficult times, but the use of workers as a contingent buffer has put it at odds with its own value system. $$$ stated, "If you're over 40 and lose your job, it's almost impossible to find your way back into the workforce. You would be lucky to get 30% of your former pay. This is a society that values age more than the United States, but older people are treated worse than they are here."[37]

Changes in Job Design

Managers can use their human resources more cost-effectively by changing job design and transferring people to different units of the company. Alternatively, they may relocate people to jobs in different parts of the country where the cost of living and salaries are lower. The cost of relocating an employee plus the fact that some employees do not want to move sometimes make this alternative problematic. Another practice, common in unionized companies, allows a senior employee whose job is eliminated to take a job in a different unit of the company from an employee with less seniority. This practice is called *bumping*.

Companies can also use *job sharing* (which we discussed in Chapter 2) when it is possible to reconfigure one job into two part-time jobs. The challenge here is to find two people willing to share the job's hours and pay. Finally, as a last resort, highly paid workers may be demoted to lower-paying jobs.

A Question of Ethics

Is it ethical for top managers to receive cash bonuses while at the same time asking lower-level employees to accept a pay freeze?

Pay and Benefits Policies

As one way of reducing costs, managers can enforce a *pay freeze* during which no wages or salaries are increased. Pay freezes should be done on an across-the-board basis to avoid accusations of discrimination. These policies can be augmented by reductions in overtime pay and policies that ask employees to use up their vacation and leave days. Many state governments have enforced annual pay freezes on their employees. Unfortunately, pay freezes often cause some top-performing, highly marketable employees to leave the company.

A more radical and intrusive pay policy geared toward reducing labor costs is a *pay cut*. This action can be even more demoralizing to the workforce than a pay freeze and should be used only if employees are willing to accept it voluntarily as an alternative to layoffs. Unions in several U.S. industries have accepted wage reductions in return for job security. For example, in 1994 the unions that represent the pilots and machinists at United Airlines accepted a 15 percent pay cut in exchange for 55 percent of the company stock and three of 12 seats on the board of directors.[38] The impetus for this innovative agreement was the employees' desire for job security, because United Airlines management had been considering a major downsizing that would include layoffs of union members. By 1996 United Airlines reported healthy profits that were well received by the investment community and resulted in a doubling of the value of its stock.

A long-term pay policy that may protect workers from layoffs entails structuring compensation so that profit sharing (the sharing of company profits with employees) or variable pay (pay contingent on meeting performance goals) makes up a significant portion of employees' total compensation (around 15 to 20 percent). When the business cycle hits a low point, the company can save up to about 20 percent of the payroll by not paying out profit sharing or variable pay, but still retain its employees by paying them the salary portion of their total compensation. Few companies in the United States use this approach, but it is very common in Japan.

Training

By retraining employees whose skills have become obsolete, a company may be able to match newly skilled workers with available job vacancies. Without this retraining, the workers might have been laid off. For example, IBM has retrained some of its production workers in computer programming and placed them in jobs requiring this skill.

Nontraditional Alternatives to Layoffs

In their attempt to avoid layoffs, some companies have come up with innovative alternatives.

- Hugh Aaron's small East Coast plastics company had been plagued by cyclical layoffs for years. Finally Aaron took a daring step. He promised employees he would eliminate all future layoffs if they agreed to work overtime or take on new job tasks whenever necessary. To avoid burnout and understaffing when business was strong, Aaron called in retirees who were happy to mix with the old gang, and he relied on college students to fill in during the busy summer months. As a result of the program, employee morale reached new heights.
- Sidney Harman, chairman of Harman International Industries, Inc., employs 1,500 production workers in California's San Fernando Valley. Harman has succeeded in creating an internal labor buffer for periods of slack demand. He has dubbed his idea *OLE,* an acronym for offline employment. Production workers who would otherwise be idle during downturns are employed making clock faces from scrap wood or working in one of Harman's new outlet stores. More work has been brought back inside the plants (rather than jobbed out to outside companies). In addition, Harman regularly pulls workers off the line and puts them into training programs.

Implementing a Layoff

Once the layoff decision is made, managers must implement it carefully. A layoff can be a traumatic event that affects the lives of thousands of people. The key issues that managers must settle are notifying employees, developing layoff criteria, communicating to laid-off employees, coordinating media relations, maintaining security, and reassuring survivors of the layoff.

Notifying Employees

The **Worker Adjustment and Retraining Notification Act (WARN)** requires U.S. employers with 100 or more employees to give 60 days' advance notice to employees who will be laid off as a result of a plant closing or a mass separation of 50 or more workers.[39] This law, passed in 1988, was designed to give workers more time to look for a new job. Employers who do not notify their employees must give them the equivalent of 60 working days of income. Employers who lay off fewer than 50 employees have greater flexibility as to when they can notify the affected employees.

Worker Adjustment and Retraining Notification Act (WARN) of 1988
A federal law requiring U.S. employers with 100 or more employees to give 60 days' advance notice to employees who will be laid off as a result of a plant closing or a mass separation of 50 or more workers.

There are several arguments in favor of giving at least several weeks' notice before a layoff. It is socially and professionally correct to extend employees this courtesy. Also, this treatment is reassuring to the employees who will remain with the company. But there are also arguments in favor of giving no notification. If the labor relations climate is poor, there is the potential for theft or sabotage to company equipment. In addition, the productivity of employees who are losing their jobs may decline.[40]

The requirements for layoff notification tend to be more restrictive in European countries than in the United States. For example, in Sweden management must give at least 60 days' advance notice in layoffs of five or more workers, while in France as few as two workers must get at least 45 days' notification.[41] Figure 6.5 (page 210) lists advance notice requirements in several other European nations.

Developing Layoff Criteria

A Question of Ethics

How much notice of a layoff should a company be obligated to give?

In planning and implementing a layoff, it is essential that the criteria for dismissal be clear. When the criteria are clearly laid out, the managers responsible for determining who will be laid off can make consistent, fair decisions. The two most important criteria used as the basis for layoff decisions are seniority and employee performance.

Seniority, the amount of time an employee has been with the firm, is by far the most commonly used layoff criterion. It has two main advantages. First, seniority criteria are easily applied; managers simply examine all employees' dates of hire to determine the seniority of each (in years and days). Second, many employees see the seniority system as fair because (1) managers cannot play "favorites" under a seniority-based decision and (2) the most senior employees have the greatest investment in the company in terms of job rights and privileges

Requirements of Advance Notice for Collective Dismissals in Selected European Countries

Figure 6.5

Country	Notice Requirements
Belgium	30 days
Denmark	30 days
Germany	30 days
Greece	30 days
Ireland	30 days
Italy	22 to 32 days
Luxembourg	60 to 75 days
Netherlands	2 to 6 months
United Kingdom	30 to 90 days (if at least 10 workers are involved)

Source: Ehrenberg, R. G., and Jakubson, G. H. (1988). *Advance notice provisions in plant closing legislation.* Kalamazoo, MI: W. E. Upjohn Institute for Employment Research.

(they have accrued more vacation and leave days, and have more attractive work schedules, for example).

There are disadvantages to using the "last in, first out" method, however. The firm may lose some top performers, as well as a disproportionate amount of women and minorities—who are more likely to be recent hires in certain jobs. Nonetheless, the courts have upheld seniority as the basis for layoff as long as all employees have equal opportunities to obtain seniority.

Despite efforts to retain senior employees during a layoff, many choose to leave. In the late 1990s, droves of talented senior managers and executives quit their firms because the bull market made them wealthy enough to retire early. To combat this senior "brain drain" trend, Deloitte Consulting launched a Senior Leader's program that allows senior partners in the firm to downshift from full-time to part-time consulting or mentoring. That way, the firm can retain the talent and knowledge of these highly skilled partners and the employees have the flexibility to pursue other endeavors.[42]

When the workforce is unionized, layoff decisions are usually based on seniority. This provision is written into the labor contract. However, when the workforce is nonunion and especially when cuts must be made in professional and managerial employees, it is not unusual for companies to base layoff decisions on performance criteria or on a combination of performance and seniority. Using performance as the basis for layoffs allows the company to retain its top performers in every work unit and eliminate its weakest performers. Unfortunately, performance levels are not always clearly documented, and the company may be exposed to wrongful discharge litigation if the employee can prove that management discriminated or acted arbitrarily in judging performance. Because of these legal risks, many companies avoid using performance as a basis for layoff.

If a company has taken the time to develop a valid performance appraisal system that accurately measures performance and meets government guidelines, then there is no reason why appraisal data cannot be used as the basis for layoff. For example, IBM used performance as the basis for layoffs of its professional workforce in a 1990s downsizing effort.[43] When using this criterion, managers should take the employee's total performance over a long period of time into account. Managers who focus on one low performance appraisal period and ignore other satisfactory or exceptional performance appraisals could be viewed as acting arbitrarily and unfairly. We discuss this topic in detail in the next chapter.

Communicating to Laid-Off Employees

It is crucial to communicate with the employees who will be laid off as humanely and sensitively as possible. No employee likes being told he or she will be discharged, and the way a manager handles this unpleasant task can affect how the employee and others in the organization accept the decision. A yes/no test for assessing how well a layoff has been conducted is presented in the Manager's Notebook: Customer-Driven HR titled "Test Your Layoff Savvy: How Well Did You Do?"

Customer-Driven HR

MANAGER'S NOTEBOOK

Test Your Layoff Savvy: How Well Did You Do?

The following yes/no items were designed to assess how well a layoff was conducted. These same items can be used to guide how a layoff should be conducted. The greater the number of "no" responses, the poorer the layoff was conducted.

Yes/No

_____ 1. Management frequently communicated with employees during the layoff period.
_____ 2. Management clearly explained the reasons for the layoffs.
_____ 3. Management kept a visible profile during the layoff period.
_____ 4. Our company provided outplacement services to the laid-off employees.
_____ 5. Our company told each employee of his or her termination in private.
_____ 6. Management has spelled out a clear "where we go from here" message to remaining employees.
_____ 7. Managers and supervisors report that employee productivity is at least as good as prelayoff levels.
_____ 8. We have retained nearly all valued employees in the aftermath of layoffs (i.e., they haven't quit).
_____ 9. Management concluded the layoffs without dragging them on for months.
_____ 10. There is not a significant amount of talk among employees about possible future layoffs.
_____ 11. Our company has not significantly reduced career development programs and training opportunities during or after the layoff period.
_____ 12. Our company has undertaken a review following the layoffs to identify potentially overstressed departments.

Source: Adapted with permission from *Security Director's Report*, (2002). Is your corporate climate breeding future thieves? January Newsletter, 6–7, 10–11.

Laid-off employees should first learn of their fate from their supervisor in a face-to-face private discussion. Employees who learn about their dismissal through a less personal form of communication (for example, a peer or a memo) are likely to be hurt and angry. The information session between supervisor and employee should be brief and to the point. The manager should express appreciation for what the employee has contributed, if appropriate, and explain how much severance pay and what benefits will be provided and for how long. This information can be repeated in greater detail at a group meeting of laid-off employees and should be documented in a written pamphlet handed out at the meeting.

The best time to hold the termination session is in the middle of the workweek. It is best to avoid telling workers they are being laid off during their vacation or right before a weekend, when they have large blocks of time on their hands.[44]

One example of how *not* to communicate a layoff is provided by the following example: A petroleum company brought employees together for a rather unsettling meeting. Each employee was given an envelope with the Letter A or B on it. The A's were told to stay put while the B's were ushered into an adjacent room. Then, en masse, the B's were told that they were being laid off.

Coordinating Media Relations

Rumors of an impending layoff can be very dangerous to the workforce's morale as well as to the organization's relations with customers, suppliers, and the surrounding community. Top managers, working with HR staff members, should develop a plan to provide accurate information about the layoff to external clients (via the media) as well as the workforce (via internal communications).[45] In this way, managers can control and put to rest rumors that may exaggerate the extent of the firm's downsizing efforts. It is also important that direct communication take place with the employees directly affected by the layoff *and* the surviving employees and that all communication be coordinated with press releases to the media. In addition, HR staff must prepare to answer any questions that employees or the media may have regarding outplacement, severance pay, or the continuation of benefits.

Maintaining Security

In some situations a layoff may threaten company property. Laid-off employees may find themselves rushed out of the building, escorted by armed guards, and their personal belongings delivered to them later in boxes. Although such treatment may seem harsh, it may be necessary in certain industries (such as banking and computer software) where sabotage could result in substantial damage.

For instance, Timothy Lloyd worked for Omega Engineering, Inc., a company that designs and manufactures instruments and process control devices. After he was dismissed but before his last day at the company, Lloyd allegedly set a "program bomb" in the company's computer system. About two weeks after his last day, the bomb deleted key files from Omega's database, resulting in $10 million in damage. Al DiFrancesco, Omega's director of human relations, noted that the company could have avoided the problem with better security, but "hindsight is 20/20. . . ." As a result of the damage, Omega tightened its security policies and procedures to safeguard against disgruntled employees.[46]

In most cases security precautions are probably not necessary when implementing a layoff, and using armed guards and other heavy-handed tactics will only lead to hard feelings and resentment. Treating laid-off employees with dignity and respect generally reduces the potential for sabotage.

Reassuring Survivors of the Layoff

A sometimes neglected aspect of layoff implementation is developing plans to deal with the layoff's survivors. An organization may lose the cost savings of a layoff if survivor productivity drops as a result of the layoff.[47] Survivors of a layoff may initially have low morale and experience stress. This problem could be made worse if the layoff was not handled well. A recent survey found that nearly 50 percent of employees report that they learned of a layoff by word of mouth or a rumor.[48] Furthermore, 50 percent of employees rated management below average on how well it recognizes the value of the remaining employees. Many will have lost important friendships in the layoff. Some may feel the same emotions experienced by survivors of tragedies: guilt ("Why not me?"), anger ("This is not fair"), and anxiety ("Am I next?").[49] The following reactions of layoff survivors express some of the feelings of anger and depression that are very common:

- "Stop telling us to work smarter. Show us how. . . . Stop blaming us! We've been loyal to the company. We've worked hard and did everything we were told. We've moved for the company, we've traveled for the company, and we've taken on extra work for the company. And now you say we did wrong. You told us to do it. Management told us to do it! And the company did pretty well while we did it. Stop blaming us!"[50]
- "You see a lot of good people being let go and that's very demoralizing, to know that an excellent person is being let go."
- "They're padding their pockets. In the good times the bonuses and everything go to the top executives, and during the bad times the workers get cut out. The company hasn't shown me that they care as much about me."[51]
- "Of course, it's upsetting to see co-workers go. You're sitting at your desk and you look to the side and there's an empty chair. And you can't help but wonder, 'Why wasn't it me?'"

To cope with these feelings, the survivors may try to "escape." It is not unusual to see a sharp increase in absenteeism as well as turnover of key people who leave to work for competitors.

Companies can minimize problems in this area by developing special programs for survivors. One simple but critical step is to educate the retained employees about the organization's financial situation.[52] (Pay for Performance Report, 2002). If retained workers understand the economic reasons for the layoff, they may be more likely to blame the bad times on external factors rather than finding some way to blame management. Furthermore, understanding the causes for the layoff may motivate workers to help the organization make it through the rough time. Besides this kind of education, retained workers may need an infusion of energy and a reminder that they are still part of a team.

Windy City Fieldhouse is a company that organizes team-building events, some of which are specifically designed to boost morale following a layoff.[53] (Enright, 2002). For example, to build comradery and trust among layoff survivors who may be experiencing guilt, the company might use a competitive game called Puzzling Planks. The exercise is a team competition involving a pile of boards that fit together to make three-dimensional figures. The point of the exercise is to get people to again feel their contributions are important and that they are a part of a team and an organization. Other team-building exercises organized by Windy City Fieldhouse might involve more physical exercises, such as obstacle courses.

In addition to such organized events, there are simple suggestions that can help you create a more fun, upbeat, and energetic climate among layoff survivors.[54] (Enright, 2002). For example, host a simple end-of-the-week breakfast—bagels, cream cheese, juice, and coffee should do it. Arrange for a pot-luck luncheon or picnic. Hold a monthly raffle in which a drawing is held for a product, gift certificate, or an afternoon off! Add some games, such as guessing the number of pennies in a jar. The point of all of these activities is to infuse some energy and fun to a workplace that may be suffering from a layoff and to send a message to survivors that management cares about and recognizes them.

Outplacement

As we mentioned at the beginning of this chapter, outplacement is an HR program created to help separated employees deal with the emotional stress of job loss and provide assistance in finding a new job.[55] Outplacement activities are often handled by consulting firms retained by the organization, which pays a fee based on the number of outplaced employees. Companies are often willing to pay for outplacement because it can reduce some of the risks associated with layoffs, such as negative publicity or an increased likelihood that unions will attempt to organize the workforce.[56] Employers who provide outplacement services tend to give the goal of social responsibility a high priority as part of their HR strategy.

The Goals of Outplacement

The goals of an outplacement program reflect the organization's need to control the disruption caused by layoffs and other employee separations. The most important of these goals are (1) reducing the morale problems of employees who are about to be laid off so that they remain productive until they leave the firm, (2) minimizing the amount of litigation initiated by separated employees, and (3) assisting separated employees in finding comparable jobs as quickly as possible.[57]

Outplacement Services

The most common outplacement services are emotional support and job-search assistance. These services are closely tied to the goals of outplacement.

Emotional Support

Outplacement programs usually provide counseling to help employees deal with the emotions associated with job loss—shock, anger, denial, and lowered self-esteem. Because the family may suffer if the breadwinner becomes unemployed, sometimes family members are included in the counseling as well.[58] Counseling also benefits the employer because it helps to defuse some of the hostility that laid-off employees feel toward the company.

Job-Search Assistance

Employees who are outplaced often do not know how to begin the search for a new job. In many cases, these people have not had to look for a job in many years.

An important aspect of this assistance is teaching separated employees the skills they need to find a new job. These skills include résumé writing, interviewing and job-search techniques, career planning, and negotiation skills.[59] Outplaced employees receive instruction in these skills from either a member of the outplacement firm or the HR department. In addition, the former employer sometimes provides administrative support in the form of clerical help, phone answering, access to e-mail, and fax services.[60] These services allow laid-off employees to use computers to prepare résumés, post résumés on the Web or send them via fax and e-mail, and to use copiers to copy résumés.

The use of outplacement has become a global HR management practice. Several large corporations in Great Britain have recently restructured their operations, eliminating thousands of jobs. British Telecom has cut its workforce by 40,000, and Midland Bank has eliminated 10,000 jobs over the past decade.[61] An important part of these downsizing strategies is the use of outplacement services to smooth the affected employees' transition to a new job. Similarly, Japanese corporations use outplacement firms to find jobs for surplus workers.[62]

Summary and Conclusions

What Are Employee Separations?

Employee separations occur when employees cease to be members of an organization. Separations and outplacement can be managed effectively. Managers should plan for the outflow of their human resources with thoughtful policies. Employee separations have both costs and benefits. The costs include (1) recruitment costs, (2) selection costs, (3) training costs, and (4) separation costs. The benefits are (1) reduced labor costs, (2) replacement of poor performers, (3) increased innovation, and (4) the opportunity for greater diversity.

Types of Employee Separations

Employees may leave either voluntarily or involuntarily. Voluntary separations include quits and retirements. Involuntary separations include discharges and layoffs. When an employee is forced to leave involuntarily, a much greater level of documentation is necessary to show that a manager's decision to terminate the employee was fair and consistent.

Managing Early Retirements

When downsizing an organization, managers may elect to use voluntary early retirements as an alternative to layoffs. Early retirement programs must be managed so that eligible employees do not perceive that they are being forced to retire.

Managing Layoffs

Layoffs should be used as a last resort after all other cost-cutting alternatives have been exhausted. Important considerations in developing a layoff policy include (1) notifying employees, (2) developing layoff criteria, (3) communicating to laid-off employees, (4) coordinating media relations, (5) maintaining security, and (6) reassuring survivors of the layoff.

Outplacement

No matter what policy is used to reduce the workforce, it is a good idea for the organization to use outplacement services to help separated employees cope with their emotions and minimize the amount of time they are unemployed.

Key Terms

attrition, 207
downsizing, 202
employee separation, 195
exit interview, 197
hiring freeze, 207
involuntary separation, 199
outplacement assistance, 197
rightsizing, 203
turnover rate, 195
voluntary separation, 198
Worker Adjustment and Retraining Notification Act (WARN), 209

Discussion Questions

1. After eight years as a marketing assistant for the New York office of a large French bank, Sarah Schiffler was told that her job, in a non-revenue-producing department, was being eliminated. Her choices: She could either be laid off (with eight months' severance pay) or stay on and train for the position of credit analyst, a career route she had turned down in the past. Nervous about making mortgage payments on her new condo, Sarah agreed to stay, but after six months of feeling miserable in her new position, she quit. Was her separation from the bank voluntary or involuntary? Can you think of situations in which a voluntary separation is really an involuntary separation? What are the managerial implications of such situations?
2. What are the advantages and disadvantages of using seniority as the basis for layoff? What alternatives to seniority are available as layoff criteria?
3. Would an employer ever want to increase the rate of employee turnover in a company? Why or why not?
4. What advantages might an organization have if it takes a customer-oriented approach to conducting layoffs?
5. In an age when more and more companies are downsizing, an increasingly important concept is "the virtual corporation." The idea is that a company should have a core of owners and managers, but that, to the greatest degree possible, workers should be contingent—temporary, part-time, or on short-term contracts. This gives the corporation maximum flexibility to shift vendors, cut costs, and avoid long-term labor commitments. What are the advantages and disadvantages of the virtual corporation from the point of view of both employers and workers?
6. Under what circumstances might a company's managers prefer to use layoffs instead of early retirements or voluntary severance plans as a way to downsize the workforce?
7. Under what set of conditions should a company lay off employees without giving them advance notice?
8. "The people who actually have the face-to-face contact with the person who is being laid off are not the ones who made the decision. They often did not have any input into which of their people would go," says a technician at a firm that experienced large-scale layoffs. What role should managers—who have the "face-to-face" contact with employees—play in implementing a layoff? Do you think managers and HR staff members always agree on how employee separations should be handled? Why or why not?
9. Managing survivors in a layoff is important. As a manager, what concerns would you have about the surviving workforce after a layoff? How can the HR management staff be of assistance in providing support for the survivors to a layoff?
10. Why should management be concerned with helping employees retire from their organization successfully?
11. Organizations have worked hard to develop teams as a cohesive and effective framework in the workplace. What can a layoff do to this framework and to the sense of cohesiveness? What could you do to manage these problems?

There is a variety of additional material available on the Web site that accompanies this text. You can access this information by visiting the Web site at **www.prenhall.com/gomez.**

Customer-Driven HR Case 6.1

YOU MANAGE IT!

Severance Payback: Employees as Customers or as Expendable Commodities?

Filtronic Comtek Inc., based in Maryland, makes microwave equipment for the telecommunications industry. The company abruptly closed its machining and manufacturing operation in Merrimack, New Hampshire. Approximately 250 workers were laid off without the 60-day notice legally mandated by the Worker Adjustment and Retraining Notification Act. Instead of complying with the law, the company paid the penalty of a 60-day severance package for each worker. However, when it paid the severance packages, it made a miscalculation and overpaid workers between \$700 and over \$1,000 per person.

About a month later, the company realized its mistake. The company sent letters to each of the laid-off workers telling them they were legally obligated to return the overpaid money. In March 2002, a letter from a lawyer recently employed by Filtronic was sent to the laid-off workers. Each letter looked like a lawsuit with the term "Settlement Offer" boldly stamped across the top and Filtronic Comtek Inc. versus the employee's name on a subject line. The lawyer said that no litigation has yet been filed, but the company might pursue this option.

Critical Thinking Questions

1. Do you think that the company should pursue repayment of the excessive severance package? Why or why not?
2. The company's lawyer has stated that the organization is sympathetic with the hardship that repayment may pose on the former employees. So the company is willing to accept a payment plan of four equal monthly payments.
   a. Do you think the payment plan offer is a good idea? Why or why not?

   The company is presenting the payment plan option as evidence of its sympathetic and customer-oriented approach to the laid-off workers. Do you agree that Filtronic Comtek is taking a customer-oriented approach to its former workers? Why or why not?
3. Some of the former workers are experiencing financial difficulties and don't know how they can pay the money back. For example, Debbie Burnard is a single parent with three children. After being laid off, she came down with pneumonia and other health difficulties. She now has $900 in medical bills to pay and receives $300 every two weeks in unemployment benefits. She panicked when she received the letter from Filtronic's lawyer and doesn't know how she can repay the money, even on the payment plan. The money was spent months ago.

   Should Filtronic Comtek somehow take ability to repay into account? How might it go about this?

Team Exercise

Most of the former employees of Filtronic Comtek aren't about to repay the money and some of them cannot financially do so. One former worker, Mark Boulanger, views the request for repayment as harassment and is angry over it. He is considering hiring a lawyer.

On the other hand, the company's lawyer has pointed out that if the error had been that workers were underpaid, there would have been outrage and insistence that they be paid what was due. He also states that the company owes it to its shareholders to recover the money.

Some broader contextual information may also be helpful in this case. A New Hampshire Labor Department representative has recommended to the company that it no longer pursue repayment. The representative has questioned whether the company has lost sight that it is dealing with human beings. The company has 17 facilities throughout the world, including one in Maryland that it bought last year for $20 million.

Divide the class into two halves: one side taking the former employee perspective and the other side taking the company perspective. Each side should identify key arguments in support of its position. Pick representatives of each position and have them debate (1) whether Filtronic should be pursuing repayment and (2) what should be done if the company embraces a customer orientation in how it deals with employees.

Source: Adapted from Leighton, B. (March, 2002). Laid-off Filtronic Comtek workers told to refund severance overpayments. *The Telegraph*, Nashua, NH.

YOU MANAGE IT! Customer-Driven HR Case 6.2

Recognizing the Importance of Workers: Layoffs as a Last Resort

Workers' salaries are a big expense in most organizations. Cutting jobs would seem to be a fiscally rational way to quickly and significantly reduce expenses. Layoffs may appear to make sense in the short term and on paper but not really in the long term. Consider the negative fallout associated with a major layoff of 8,500 workers at Cisco Systems Inc. Following this cost-cutting measure, worker productivity dropped and resulted in sales per employee of $470,000 in October 2001, down from $710,000 a year previously. Some organizations are beginning to realize that layoffs can begin a negative spiral and can bring tremendous costs to the organization, such as lowering morale, productivity, and loyalty, and the possibility of sabotage and loss of customers. These companies are searching for creative but effective alternatives to downsizing. As FedEx spokesperson, Gree Rossiter, has stated, people are what differentiate a company and are simply too important to put at risk.

As an alternative to layoffs, some companies are seeking other ways to cut costs while retaining their most important asset—their employees. For example, job sharing, shortened workweeks, and pay cuts are among the strategies being used to stave off or, hopefully, to eliminate the need for layoffs. For example, Acxiom Corp., a database and information management company with over 5,000 employees, utilized pay cuts to avoid the need for layoffs. As an initial cost-cutting move, Acxiom imposed a mandatory 5 percent cut in pay for all employees earning less than $25,000. In exchange, employees were given stock options in the amount of salary that had been forfeited. A voluntary pay cut was offered shortly thereafter in which workers could forfeit up to an additional 15 percent of salary in exchange for double that amount in stock options. More than one-third of employees volunteered for the additional pay cut. Acxiom estimates that the mandatory and voluntary pay cuts allowed the company to lay off half the number of employees it otherwise would have had to lay off. Axciom did end up laying off 400 workers—7 percent of its workforce. The executive in charge of organizational effectiveness for Axciom, Jeff Standridge, stated, "The intangible benefit is that 85 percent of our employee population became stockholders in the company. They have skin in the game, and now the company's future can be determined by people with a greater stake in the company." When Acxiom expands employment again, it will give preference to the laid-off workers, avoiding some of the costs associated with recruiting and training new employees.

Accenture Ltd., a global information technology consulting company, took a different approach to delay the need for layoffs. The company offered a one-year sabbatical program in which employees would receive 20 percent of their salaries and all of their benefits. Employees can do anything while on a sabbatical—except work for a competitor. The sabbatical program was popular in the United States with 2,200 signing up, filling up all places in the U.S. program so it is now closed. Accenture has extended the program to employees in the United Kingdom, Sweden, Germany, and Japan. The primary goal of the program is trimming short-term costs while keeping access to talented employees. Unfortunately, Accenture did still have to resort to layoffs, affecting 2,500 employees.

Other companies, such as FedEx and Lincoln Electric, have firm philosophies of no layoffs. Someday layoffs may be needed at these companies, but it would occur only as a last resort. The intent of these companies is to create a deeply loyal and productive workforce.

Critical Thinking Questions

1. In addition to the examples just mentioned, what else could organizations do to avoid or limit layoffs? Generate possibilities by brainstorming, referring to this chapter, as well as by finding additional company examples.
2. Prioritize your alternatives to layoffs. What would you do first, second, and so on?
3. Given that you are in a management position in an organization, describe how you would provide the sequential strategy to employees you gave in your answer to question 2. Would you use meetings, newsletters, and so on? Draft the description or announcement that would frame this sequential strategy and place it in a context. For example, what's the purpose(s) of the strategy?
4. Do you think a sequential strategy could be an effective management tool? Explain.

Team Exercise

As described in this case, some companies are convinced that layoffs should be avoided. However, layoffs can certainly reduce short-term costs and can be positively responded to by the stock market for publicly traded firms. On the other hand, pursuing alternatives to layoffs is not without its risks. For example, some bitterness was experienced by Acxiom after it laid off workers. How would you, for example, like to take a pay cut and then lose your job?

Divide your team into halves, one side taking a prolayoff position, the other an antilayoff position. Debate whether steps should be taken to avoid layoffs.

Source: Adapted from King, J. (2002). Working alternatives to job cuts. *Computerworld*, 36, 24–25.

Emerging Trends Case 6.3 — YOU MANAGE IT!

Turnover Redux

Turnover can have a crippling effect on organizations. For example, the grocery retailer, Kroger, calculates that its employee turnover rate is such that its cost was $80 million last year. As with other companies, Kroger is recognizing the cost that turnover can exact and is taking steps to try to control it. To help reduce its turnover rate, Kroger has begun a pilot study aimed at hiring workers who will have a lower propensity to quit. Specifically, Kroger has set up kiosks in selected stores where job seekers can electronically fill out an application form. Application can also be made online via the Internet. The pattern of responses to questions on the application are analyzed with a computer model designed to predict the likely retention rate of each applicant. For example, applicants might be asked to provide the last name of their supervisor from two jobs ago. The assumption is that if someone can accurately provide this information, he or she is more likely to have stronger ties in the workplace and stay in the job longer. The application system also does other screening tasks, including background checks. Kroger may be moving from doing this in a pilot project to a fully working employment program in the future. Kroger said that it is planning other actions in an attempt to wrestle down its turnover rate.

Critical Thinking Questions

1. Kroger's emphasis on the application process focuses on characteristics of workers as an important causal factor in

turnover. Do you think that its approach will be effective? Why or why not?

2. Are there system characteristics that might be important determinants of retention and turnover? In other words, what factors about jobs or organizations might be important in determining whether someone decides to quit or stay with an employer?
3. For the system factors you identified in question 2, what would you recommend Kroger do about each? Are there some factors that may be difficult or impossible to change?

Team Exercise

Lowering turnover requires understanding the causes of turnover and then doing something about them. The following simple model can guide your efforts in identifying and managing factors underlying turnover decisions.

As depicted in the model, there are worker characteristics that may be directly related to turnover. Consider the Kroger example. There may be some types of people who just tend to stay longer in a job than others. Likewise, there may be characteristics of the job and organization that are directly linked to turnover decisions. However, in addition to these direct effects, employee characteristics and system characteristics can jointly influence turnover decisions through their degree of fit with each other.

a. As a team, identify worker characteristics and system characteristics that may influence turnover through their degree of fit (or misfit). In addition, identify worker characteristics and system characteristics that may have a direct influence on turnover decisions.
b. Design survey questions or interview questions that could be used to measure each of the characteristics you listed in the preceding question. Determine how you could measure the turnover probability part of the model. (Hint: Consider asking people to judge the extent to which they would like to quit their current job or ask them to consider a time when they did quit a job.)
c. If you have access to an organization, try out your survey or interview items. Consider asking family members, friends, and fellow students to complete the survey or interview. How does your model hold up? For example, did turnover happen or does it seem more likely to occur when worker characteristics and system characteristics are present that you thought should be related to turnover? Does turnover appear more likely when there is poor fit among the worker characteristics and system characteristics? Share your findings with the rest of the class.
d. How could Kroger use the model and the survey or interview items you generated? Specifically, generate a systematic process for the company to follow to identify causal factors of turnover at Kroger. (Hint: Consider using exit interview and surveys.) Share your proposed process with the rest of the class.
e. Kroger seems to be taking the position that worker characteristics may be the most important factor affecting turnover. Divide your team into worker proponents and system proponents and debate which factor is more important and has a greater impact on turnover decisions. Which would appear to be more easily managed? Is there an advantage to including both factors, as in the model depicted? Is there an advantage to including the factor of fit?

Source: Adapted from Perotta, P. (2002). Kroger is piloting an electronic application. *Supermarket News, 50*, 17+.

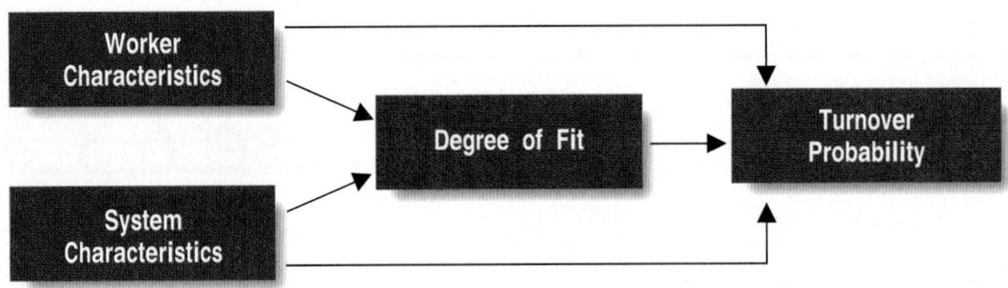

YOU MANAGE IT!

Emerging Trends Case 6.4

Layoff and Security

A surprising number of Americans have lost their jobs. In October 2001, 415,000 people were laid off, the largest monthly total in four years. How were those people treated? Recent surveys indicate that the majority of people are dissatisfied with how their layoff was conducted.[a] This dissatisfaction goes beyond losing a job. It concerns how the layoff was handled. People who have been laid off usually describe it as being made to feel like a criminal.[b] It is little wonder that such feelings occur when standard business practice seems to be to treat laid-off employees as threats. The common layoff procedure involves the following:[c]

1. A brief meeting is held with the employee to tell her of the elimination of her job and to inform her about the existence of benefits and severance, if any. In some companies this meeting is conducted by an HR representative who is not familiar to the worker. In effect, the worker is terminated by a stranger. Simultaneously, the employee's access to the company computer system and e-mail is denied.
2. Immediately upon concluding this brief meeting, the employee is escorted through cleaning out her work space and walked to the door.

The purpose is security. Do some people steal data and sabotage equipment after being terminated? Of course, some do! But the probability isn't high. For example, the director of global staffing at National Semiconductor Corporation estimates that employees informed of being laid off who might pose a security threat are one out of 300 to 400 employees.[d]

Critical Thinking Questions

1. What message is being sent to workers being laid off by following the standard procedure just described?
2. What effect would this standard approach to laying off workers have on the retained workers? A recent survey of such layoff survivors found over 25 percent saying their layoff was handled poorly and nearly 50 percent said they found out about the layoff through informal rumors rather than through official communication.[e] These conditions can make the organization vulnerable to retaliatory theft and sabotage from layoff survivors. Explain how the process by which a layoff is conducted could have these negative effects.
3. It has been recommended that employers should take a more enlightened and customer-oriented approach to laying off workers. For example, it has been suggested that employers establish electronic alumni networks. These networks would allow former workers to keep in touch with the company and with each other.[f] Furthermore, the network could provide a source for new hires that would have limited recruiting and training costs.

   Identify characteristics of a more customer-oriented approach to conducting layoffs. What steps would be involved? Identify major guidelines and characteristics of your proposed process.

Team Exercise

Telling someone his position is being eliminated can be a difficult and emotionally draining task. Role-play laying off a worker with one member of your team taking the role of manager and another member taking the role of worker. Other team members should observe the interaction and provide feedback to the person playing the manager as to how the interaction went and how it might be improved. Conduct the role-play using the standard approach and again using the customer-oriented approach you developed in item 3 of the critical thinking questions. Which approach seemed to work more effectively?

Balancing security concerns with customer-oriented treatment can be difficult. Divide your team in half and debate the advantages and disadvantages of the security-driven standard approach to conducting layoffs with your customer-oriented approach. Share the key advantages and disadvantages with the rest of the class.

Sources: [a]*HR Focus.* (2002, January). If you must lay off workers: Consider the long-term consequences, 79, 8. [b]Jorgenson, B. (2002). Being shown the door: Management must weigh the pros and cons of this touchy layoff procedure. *Electronic Business, 28,* 38. [c]Doler, K. (2002). Layoffs have become a nasty business. *Electronic Business, 28,* 6. [d]Jorgenson (2002). [e]*Security Director's Report.* (2002). Is your corporate climate breeding future thieves? January Newsletter, 6–7, 10–11; [f]*Human Resource Management Report.* (2002). What's your department's policy on rehiring laid-off employees? February Newsletter, *1,* 13–14.

Discussion Case 6.5

YOU MANAGE IT!

Managing Outplacement at Rocky Mountain Oil

Rocky Mountain Oil has announced that it will reduce the scale of its U.S. operations and eliminate several hundred administrative positions at its Denver headquarters. The organization wants to provide outplacement assistance to the employees who will lose their jobs. However, it does not want to spend much money on outplacement.

The company has formed an outplacement committee consisting of top managers most of whom come from the operations and financial units of the business. The committee has provided a recommendation for an outplacement program that has been accepted by Rocky Mountain's CEO, Barbara Robinson. This program consists of two parts. First, each laid-off employee's immediate supervisor will provide counseling and emotional support to his or her laid-off employees. All supervisors will receive an outplacement counseling packet that includes the recent article "Ten Easy Steps to Help Employees Deal with Losing Their Jobs." Trailers will be placed at the far end of the company parking lot to serve as temporary offices for former employees, who can use them while searching for jobs and receiving counseling from their former supervisors.

Second, the outplacement program will help former employees develop job-search skills. Each employee will be given a copy of the book *What Color Is Your Parachute?*, which provides tips on how to conduct a job search. In addition, each employee will be offered the opportunity to take a course at nearby Black Rock Junior College called "Introduction to Personnel Management," in which students learn to write a résumé, gain information about the labor market, and gather tips on how to interview. Rocky Mountain Oil will pick up the cost of tuition (about $100 per employee) for the course.

Shortly after the CEO approved the outplacement program, Rocky Mountain Oil's director of human resources, Karen Sinclair, read a copy of the memo announcing the program. Sinclair had not been invited to be a member of the outplacement committee. After she finished reading the memo, Ms. Sinclair thought to herself, "That's what happens when you let accountants design a human resource program."

Critical Thinking Questions

1. Do you see any problems with the outplacement program at Rocky Mountain Oil?
2. What did Karen Sinclair mean by her statement?
3. What improvements to the design of the outplacement program do you think need to be made?

Team Exercise

Students form pairs, one role-playing Barbara Robinson and the other playing Karen Sinclair. Each tries to convince the other of the advantages of the outplacement program she prefers.

Part IV: Employee Development

Appraising and Managing Performance

Challenges

After reading this chapter, you should be able to deal more effectively with the following challenges:

1. **Explain** why performance appraisal is important and describe its components.
2. **Discuss** the advantages and disadvantages of different performance rating systems.
3. **Manage** the impact of rating errors and bias on performance appraisals.
4. **Discuss** the potential role of emotion in performance appraisal and how to manage its impact.
5. **Identify** the major legal requirements for appraisal.
6. **Use** performance appraisals to manage and develop employee performance.

The time for the annual performance appraisal was fast approaching at Milo Engineering, and the head of one of the departments was not looking forward to it. The appraisal system seemed to be sound, yet many employees seemed to dislike and distrust the process. Under the appraisal system each department employee reviewed the performance of his or her peers. All employees submitted an annual report listing their individual activities and accomplishments. The reports were then distributed to all 22 employees in the department. In this way, each employee rated all department employees (except for themselves) on multiple dimensions of job performance. Once completed, the employees submitted the appraisal forms to the department head who did the formal evaluation.

The department head used the peer ratings as advisory input into his evaluation, but he usually didn't vary that much from the average of the peer judgments. This year, Milo's CEO informed managers that tight budgetary conditions meant there was no money available for merit raises. So, high performance ratings would not result in a high pay increase and low ratings would not lead to a lower pay increase. The department head had actually been relieved to get this bad news. Why? The lack of merit pay meant that the performance ratings wouldn't be that important, and people should not be concerned about them. He didn't realize how wrong he was!

Because the peer ratings took a great deal of time, employees complained. They were particularly bitter because the ratings would not result in salary changes. Further, the department head discovered that at least one person violated the rules and rated herself quite favorably. In addition, that person and another one gave everyone in the department poor ratings, presumably to make themselves look better by comparison. The department head eliminated the ratings of these two employees. Further, he decided that because merit money was not at stake, he would, instead of having the usual face-to-face meetings, simply provide employees a written summary of how peers judged their performance.

After the evaluations were distributed, people in the department were upset. Many felt that they had spent more time on rating performance than the department head had. Some people even filed formal grievances over their appraisals, arguing that their peers had evaluated them unfairly and the department head had done nothing to rectify the bias.

The department head was surprised at the negative reaction to the appraisal process. He concluded that performance appraisal is a losing proposition: Even when it does not matter, people get angry and waste your time with complaints and grievances.

THE MANAGERIAL PERSPECTIVE

The situation at Milo Engineering (a real organization given a fictitious name) illustrates common problems with performance appraisal—the process of assessing employee performance and diagnosing and improving performance problems. Maintaining and improving your performance and the performance of other people in the organization will be an important part of your role as a manager. To conduct this process, you may rely on appraisal forms and systems that are often designed by HR personnel. Although these forms and systems are key elements of the appraisal process, they are only a starting point.

To appraise effectively, you must also spot performance problems, provide constructive feedback, and take action to improve performance. Mastering these critical skills is not easy. Measuring and managing performance are two of the most difficult issues a manager faces. As a result, many managers become disillusioned and avoid appraisal issues as much as possible. However, managers must measure performance and provide meaningful feedback to employees if employees are to improve—even if salary dollars are not at stake. We all need, want, and deserve feedback regarding how we are doing in the workplace.

As the chapter opener suggests, accurate measurement of employee performance is necessary for effective management. Our first goal in this chapter is to acquaint you with the foundation, design, and implementation of performance measurement systems. Our second is to describe the principles of effective performance management.

What Is Performance Appraisal?

Performance appraisal
The identification, measurement, and management of human performance in organizations.

Performance appraisal, as shown in Figure 7.1, involves the *identification, measurement,* and *management* of human performance in organizations.[1]

- **Identification** means determining what areas of work the manager should be examining when measuring performance. Rational and legally defensible identification requires a measurement system based on job analysis, which we explored in Chapter 2. The appraisal system, then, should focus on performance that affects organizational success rather than performance-irrelevant characteristics such as race, age, or sex.

- **Measurement**, the centerpiece of the appraisal system, entails making managerial judgments of how "good" or "bad" employee performance was. Good performance measurement must be consistent throughout the organization. That is, all managers in the organization must maintain comparable rating standards.[2]
- **Management** is the overriding goal of any appraisal system. Appraisal should be more than a past-oriented activity that criticizes or praises workers for their performance in the preceding year. Rather, appraisal must take a future-oriented view of what workers can do to achieve their potential in the organization. This means that managers must provide workers with feedback and coach them to higher levels of performance.

Figure 7.1

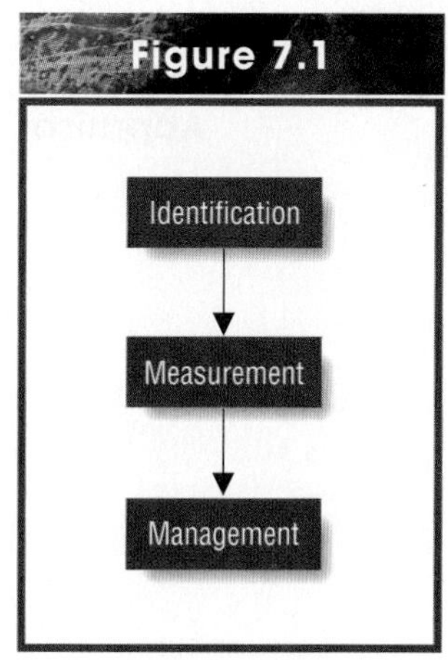

A Model of Performance Appraisal

The Uses of Performance Appraisal

Organizations usually conduct appraisals for *administrative* and/or *developmental* purposes.[3] Performance appraisals are used administratively whenever they are the basis for a decision about the employee's work conditions, including promotions, termination, and rewards. Developmental uses of appraisal, which are geared toward improving employees' performance and strengthening their job skills, include counseling employees on effective work behaviors and sending them for training.

Appraisals are conducted only once per year in most organizations. According to a recent survey, fewer than 20 percent hold performance reviews twice per year and 10 percent conduct reviews on a quarterly basis.[4] Furthermore, appraisals are typically based on supervisors' subjective judgments[5] rather than on objective indicators of performance, such as number of units produced. This has led many to conclude that appraisals are full of errors. For example, annual appraisals can place an excessive burden on the memory of a person who has to rate multiple workers. Also, supervisors' judgments may be influenced by stereotypes and other personal beliefs or perceptions.[6]

For these and other reasons, dissatisfaction with appraisal is rampant. Most surveys of raters, ratees, and even HR professionals find that people generally believe the performance appraisal process is unsuccessful.[7] Given dissatisfaction with the traditional process of rating people on various dimensions, some companies are moving away from using rating forms and are focusing instead on listening to workers and coaching them on how to improve.[8] For example, a management consultant has recently recommended that managers would be better off not focusing on numbers on a rating form but would benefit in providing meaningful feedback to workers about their performance and how to improve.[9] Further, some people staunchly oppose the practice of performance appraisal as a hopelessly flawed and demeaning method of trying to improve performance.[10] For example, it has recently been argued that performance appraisal should be eliminated as a practice in organizations because of the problems and errors in evaluating performance.[11]

However, people need some sort of assessment to improve. Whether the performance is in the workplace, in the classroom, or on a playing field, you have to gauge how you are performing to learn how to improve and, later, to assess whether you have improved. Figure 7.2 on page 224 lists several reasons, from both the employer's and employee's perspectives, why appraisal is valuable despite the criticisms that have been leveled against it.

Because of its value, written appraisal remains an important activity in most organizations. The challenge is to manage the appraisal system so that it furthers the goals of performance improvement and worker development. In the next two sections, we explain the issues and challenges involved in the first two steps of performance appraisal, identification and measurement. We conclude the chapter by discussing how managers can use the results of appraisal to improve employee performance.

Identifying Performance Dimensions

The first step in the performance appraisal process (see Figure 7.1) is identifying what is to be measured. This process seems fairly simple at first glance. In practice, however, it can be quite complicated. Consider the following example:

The Benefits of Performance Appraisal

Figure 7.2

Employer Perspective
1. Despite imperfect measurement techniques, individual differences in performance can make a difference to company performance.
2. Documentation of performance appraisal and feedback may be needed for legal defense.
3. Appraisal provides a rational basis for constructing a bonus or merit system.
4. Appraisal dimensions and standards can help to implement strategic goals and clarify performance expectations.
5. Providing individual feedback is part of the performance management process.
6. Despite the traditional focus on the individual, appraisal criteria can include teamwork and the teams can be the focus of the appraisal.

Employee Perspective
1. Performance feedback is needed and desired.
2. Improvement in performance requires assessment.
3. Fairness requires that differences in performance levels across workers be measured and have an effect on outcomes.
4. Assessment and recognition of performance levels can motivate workers to improve their performance.

Source: Cardy, R. L., and Carson K. P. (1996). Total quality and the abandonment of performance appraisal: Taking a good thing too far? *Journal of Quality Management*, 193–206.

Dimension
An aspect of performance that determines effective job performance.

Nancy manages a newly formed group of information technology workers who assist with technology-related issues across the organization. As part of her job as manager, Nancy has to allocate raises based on performance. How she assesses performance is up to her. Nancy decides to take a participative approach rather than unilaterally deciding which aspects, or **dimensions,** determine effective job performance. In a meeting with her team of technology experts, they start generating dimensions of performance. One of the first suggested is the *quality of work* done. For example, whether a problem with a computer is really diagnosed and solved is, they all agree, an important dimension of performance. However, Nancy realized that some of the workers she supervises took three times longer than others to complete assignments, so she offered *quantity of work performed* as another dimension. The team agreed that quantity was another dimension of performance. One of the technology workers volunteered that how well someone interacted with their peers and "customers" inside the organization was pretty important. The team added *interpersonal effectiveness* as another performance dimension.

Raising and considering additional work dimensions might continue until Nancy and her team have identified all the dimensions—maybe a total of six or eight—they think adequately capture performance. They may work on drafts of the list of dimensions until a final version is agreed upon. The dimensions in this example are quite general, and the team might also decide to make the dimensions more specific by adding definitions of each dimension and behavioral descriptions of performance at various levels on each dimension.

As you have probably realized, the process of identifying performance dimensions is very much like the job-analysis process described in Chapter 2. In fact, job analysis is the mechanism by which performance dimensions should be identified.

Identification of performance dimensions is the important first step in the appraisal process. If a significant dimension is missed, employee morale is likely to suffer because employees who do well on that dimension will not be recognized or rewarded. If an irrelevant or trivial dimension is included, employees may perceive the whole appraisal process as meaningless.

Management experts point out that what is measured should be directly tied to what the business is trying to achieve.[12] What is being measured should be meaningful and controllable because measurement should be viewed as a management tool, not a measurement exercise. Performance dimensions usually have been identified by conducting a job analysis. However, in an attempt to tightly connect performance appraisal to strategy, many organizations are now identifying performance dimensions based on the strategic objectives of the organization. For example, Southwest Washington Medical Center now links corporate strategic goals to employee performance goals. This approach to identifying performance dimensions makes sure that everyone is working together toward common goals rather than at cross-purposes with each other.[13]

In sum, either job analysis or strategy can be used as a basis for identifying performance dimensions. The job-analysis approach identifies performance dimensions based on what workers currently do in the organization. The strategy-based approach identifies dimensions based on goals and where the organization intends to go.

Measuring Performance

Measuring employee performance involves assigning a number to reflect an employee's performance on the identified characteristics or dimensions.[14] Technically, numbers are not mandatory. Labels such as "excellent," "good," "average," and "poor" might be used instead. But these grades could just as well be numbered 1 through 4, and you would still need to decide what grade is appropriate for a given employee.

It is often difficult to quantify performance dimensions. For example, "creativity" may be an important part of the advertising copywriter's job. But how exactly does one measure creativity—by the number of ads written per year, by the number of ads that win industry awards, or by some other criterion? These are the issues that managers face when trying to evaluate an employee's performance.

Measurement Tools

Numerous techniques for measuring performance have been developed over the years. Today managers have a wide array of appraisal formats from which to choose. Here we discuss the formats that are most common and legally defensible. These formats can be classified in two ways: (1) the type of judgment that is required (relative or absolute), and (2) the focus of the measure (trait, behavior, or outcome). Figure 7.3 summarizes these format classifications.

Relative and Absolute Judgments

Measures of employee performance can be classified on the basis of whether the type of judgment called for is relative or absolute.

Appraisal systems based on **relative judgment** ask supervisors to compare an employee's performance to the performance of other employees doing the same job. Providing a *rank order* of workers from best to worst is an example of a relative approach. Another type of relative judgment format classifies employees into groups, such as top third, middle third, or lowest third.

Relative judgment
An appraisal format that asks supervisors to compare an employee's performance to the performance of other employees doing the same job.

Relative rating systems have the advantage of forcing supervisors to differentiate among their workers. Without such a system, many supervisors are inclined to rate everyone the same, which destroys the appraisal system's value. For example, one study that examined the distribution of performance ratings for more than 7,000 managerial and professional employees in two large manufacturing firms found that 95 percent of employees were crowded into just two rating categories.

Most HR specialists believe that the disadvantages of relative rating systems outweigh their advantages, however.[15] First, relative judgments (such as ranks) do not make clear how great or small the differences between employees are. Second, such systems do not provide any absolute information, so managers cannot determine how good or poor employees at the extreme rank-

Figure 7.3 Appraisal Formats

Classified by . . .	Example
The type of judgment required	Relative or absolute
The focus of the measure	Trait, behavior, or outcome

ings are. For example, relative ratings do not reveal whether the top-rated worker in one work team is better or worse than an average worker in another work team. The worst-rated worker in one team may be a better performer than the average-rated workers in another team that has a poorer overall level of performance. This problem is illustrated in Figure 7.4. Marcos, Jill, and Frank are the highest-ranked performers in their respective work teams. However, Jill, Frank, and Julien are actually the best overall performers.

Third, relative ranking systems force managers to identify differences among workers where none may truly exist.[16] This can cause conflict among workers if and when ratings are disclosed. Finally, relative systems typically require assessment of overall performance. The "big picture" nature of relative ratings makes performance feedback ambiguous and of questionable value to workers who would benefit from specific information on the various dimensions of their performance. For all these reasons, there is a growing trend to use relative rating systems only when there is an administrative need (for example, to make decisions regarding promotions, pay raises, or termination).[17]

Absolute judgment
An appraisal format that asks supervisors to make judgments about an employee's performance based solely on performance standards.

Unlike relative judgment appraisal formats, **absolute judgment** formats ask supervisors to make judgments about an employee's performance based solely on performance standards. Comparisons to the performance of co-workers are not made. Typically, the dimensions of performance deemed relevant for the job are listed on the rating form, and the manager is asked to rate the employee on each dimension. An example of an absolute judgment rating scale is shown in Figure 7.5.

Theoretically, absolute formats allow employees from different work groups, rated by different managers, to be compared to one another. If all employees are excellent workers, they all can receive excellent ratings. Also, because ratings are made on separate dimensions of performance, the feedback to the employee can be more specific and helpful.

Although often preferable to relative systems, absolute rating systems have their drawbacks. One is that all workers in a group can receive the same evaluation if the supervisor is reluctant to differentiate among workers. Another is that different supervisors can have markedly different evaluation standards. For example, a rating of 6 from an "easy" supervisor may actually be lower in value than a rating of 4 from a "tough" supervisor. But when the organization is handing out promotions or pay increases, the worker who received the 6 rating would be rewarded.

Nonetheless, absolute systems do have one distinct advantage: They avoid creating conflict among workers. This, plus the fact that relative systems are generally harder to defend when legal issues arise, may account for the prevalence of absolute systems in U.S. organizations.

It is interesting to note, though, that most people *do* make comparative judgments among both people and things. That is, they tend to make evaluative judgments in relative rather than absolute terms. A political candidate is better or worse than opponents, not good or bad in an absolute sense. Your favorite brand is better than others, not a 5.6 on some scale of brand quality. If comparative judgments are the common and natural way of making judgments, it may be that supervisors can be more accurate when making relative ratings than when making absolute ratings.[18]

Rankings and Performance Levels Across Work Teams

Figure 7.4

Actual	Ranked Work	Ranked Work	Ranked Work
10 (High)		Jill (1)	Frank (1)
9			Julien (2)
8		Tom (2)	Lisa (3)
7	Marcos (1)	Sue (3)	
6	Uma (2)		
5			
4	Joyce (3)	Greg (4)	
3	Bill (4)	Ken (5)	Jolie (4)
2	Richard (5)		Steve (5)
1 (Low)			

Figure 7.5

PERFORMANCE REVIEW

Three-month (H&S) ☐ Annual (H-Only) ☐
Six-month (H&S) ☐ Special (H&S) ☐
H = Hourly S = Salaried

_______________ Employee Name

☐☐☐☐☐☐☐☐☐ Social Security # Hourly ☐ Salaried ☐

For probationary employee review: Do you recommend that this employee be retained? Yes ☐ No ☐

_______________ Classification/Classification Hire Date

Review period: From ____________ To ____________

_______________ Department/Division

For each applicable performance area, mark the box that most closely reflects the employee's performance.

1 = unacceptable 2 = needs improvement 3 = satisfactory 4 = above average 5 = outstanding

PERFORMANCE AREA	1	2	3	4	5
Ability to make job-related decisions					
Accepts change					
Accepts direction					
Accepts responsibility					
Attendance					
Attitude					
Compliance with rules					
Cooperation					
Cost consciousness					
Dependability					

PERFORMANCE AREA	1	2	3	4	5
Effective under stress					
Initiative					
Knowledge of work					
Leadership					
Operation and care of equipment					
Planning and organizing					
Quality of work					
Quantity of acceptable work					
Safety practices					
SUPERVISOR'S OVERALL APPRAISAL					

For overall appraisals at the 1 or 2 level: Is the employee to remain or be placed on probationary status? Yes ☐ No ☐

If yes, what is the approximate date of next performance review? ____________

JOB STRENGTHS AND SUPERIOR PERFORMANCE INCIDENTS: ____________

AREAS FOR IMPROVEMENT: ____________

PROGRESS ACHIEVED IN ATTAINING PREVIOUSLY SET GOALS: ____________

SPECIFIC OBJECTIVES TO BE UNDERTAKEN PRIOR TO NEXT REVIEW FOR IMPROVED WORK PERFORMANCE: ____________

SUPERVISOR COMMENTS: ____________

EMPLOYEE COMMENTS: ____________

Use separate sheet, if necessary, for additional comments by supervisor or employee. Please note on form if separate sheet is used.

Signing a review does not indicate agreement, only acknowledgment of being reviewed.

Employee's Signature ____ Date ____ Rating Supervisor's Signature ____ ☐☐☐☐☐☐☐☐☐ Social Security # ____ Date ____

Second Level Supervisor's Signature ____ Date ____ Department Head's Signature ____ Date ____

Sample of Absolute Judgment Rating Scale

Trait, Behavioral, and Outcome Data

In addition to relative and absolute judgments, performance measurement systems can be classified by the type of performance data on which they focus: trait data, behavioral data, or outcome data.

Trait appraisal instrument
An appraisal tool that asks a supervisor to make judgments about worker characteristics that tend to be consistent and enduring.

Trait appraisal instruments ask the supervisor to make judgments about *traits*, worker characteristics that tend to be consistent and enduring. Figure 7.6 presents four traits that are typically found on trait-based rating scales: decisiveness, reliability, energy, and loyalty. Although a number of organizations use trait ratings, current opinion is unfavorable. Trait ratings have been criticized for being much too ambiguous[19] and for leaving the door open for conscious or unconscious bias. In addition, trait ratings (because of their ambiguous nature) are less defensible in court than other types of ratings.[20] Definitions of reliability for example, can differ dramatically across supervisors, and the courts seem to be sensitive to the "slippery" nature of traits as criteria. Another difficulty with trait formats is choosing from among the hundreds of possible traits those that should be included in the rating instrument.

Assessment of traits also focuses on the *person* rather than on the *performance,* which can make employees defensive. Trait ratings imply that poor performance resides within the person and, therefore, are equivalent to ratings of the person's worth. From the limited research done in this area, it seems that this type of person-focused approach is not conducive to performance development. Measurement approaches that focus more directly on performance, either by evaluating behaviors or results, are generally more acceptable to workers and more effective as development tools.

Despite these problems, trait ratings may be more effective than many believe. After all, traits are simply a shorthand way of describing a person's behavioral tendencies. Thus, trait judgments can be based on behavior, which would make them less error laden than critics suggest. We routinely make trait judgments about others, and it is rare for someone to be described other than through his or her traits. If you doubt this, perform the following experiment:

Let's say a classmate has asked you to describe one of your professors. Also imagine that this professor does magic tricks to maintain class interest and to accentuate lecture points, sparks lively discussion, and is known for wearing outrageous costumes. Would your initial response to your classmate consist of a list of behaviors that you've seen the professor engage in? Not likely! You'd more likely use the words "lively," "wild," "entertaining," "engaging," "crazy"—all trait terms. You might follow up this assessment with some behavioral description, but probably more for the purpose of enjoyable storytelling than anything else. The point is that we routinely make trait judgments about others; they are a powerful way of describing people. Because we do

Sample Trait Scales

Figure 7.6

Rate each worker using the scales below.

Decisiveness

1 2 3 4 5 6 7
Very low — Moderate — Very high

Reliability

1 2 3 4 5 6 7
Very low — Moderate — Very high

Energy

1 2 3 4 5 6 7
Very low — Moderate — Very high

Loyalty

1 2 3 4 5 6 7
Very low — Moderate — Very high

it all the time, we also may be quite good at it. Nonetheless, because traits focus on the person rather than performance many experts do not recommend using trait judgments for feedback purposes. Also, as mentioned earlier, trait judgments can be ambiguous, so they can pose legal defensibility concerns.

Behavioral appraisal instruments focus on assessing a worker's behaviors. That is, instead of ranking leadership ability (a trait), the rater is asked to assess whether an employee exhibits certain behaviors (for example, works well with coworkers, comes to meetings on time). In one type of behavioral instrument, Behavioral Observation Scales, supervisors record how frequently the various behaviors listed on the form occurred.[21] However, ratings assessing the value rather than the *frequency* of specific behaviors are more commonly used in organizations. Probably the best-known behavioral scale is the Behaviorally Anchored Rating Scale (BARS). Figure 7.7 is an example of a BARS scale used to rate the effectiveness with which a department manager supervises his or her sales personnel. Behaviorally based rating scales are developed with the *critical incident technique*. We describe the critical incident technique in the Appendix to this chapter.

Behavioral appraisal instrument
An appraisal tool that asks managers to assess a worker's behaviors.

The main advantage of a behavioral approach is that the performance standards are concrete. Unlike traits, which can have many facets, behaviors across the range of a dimension are

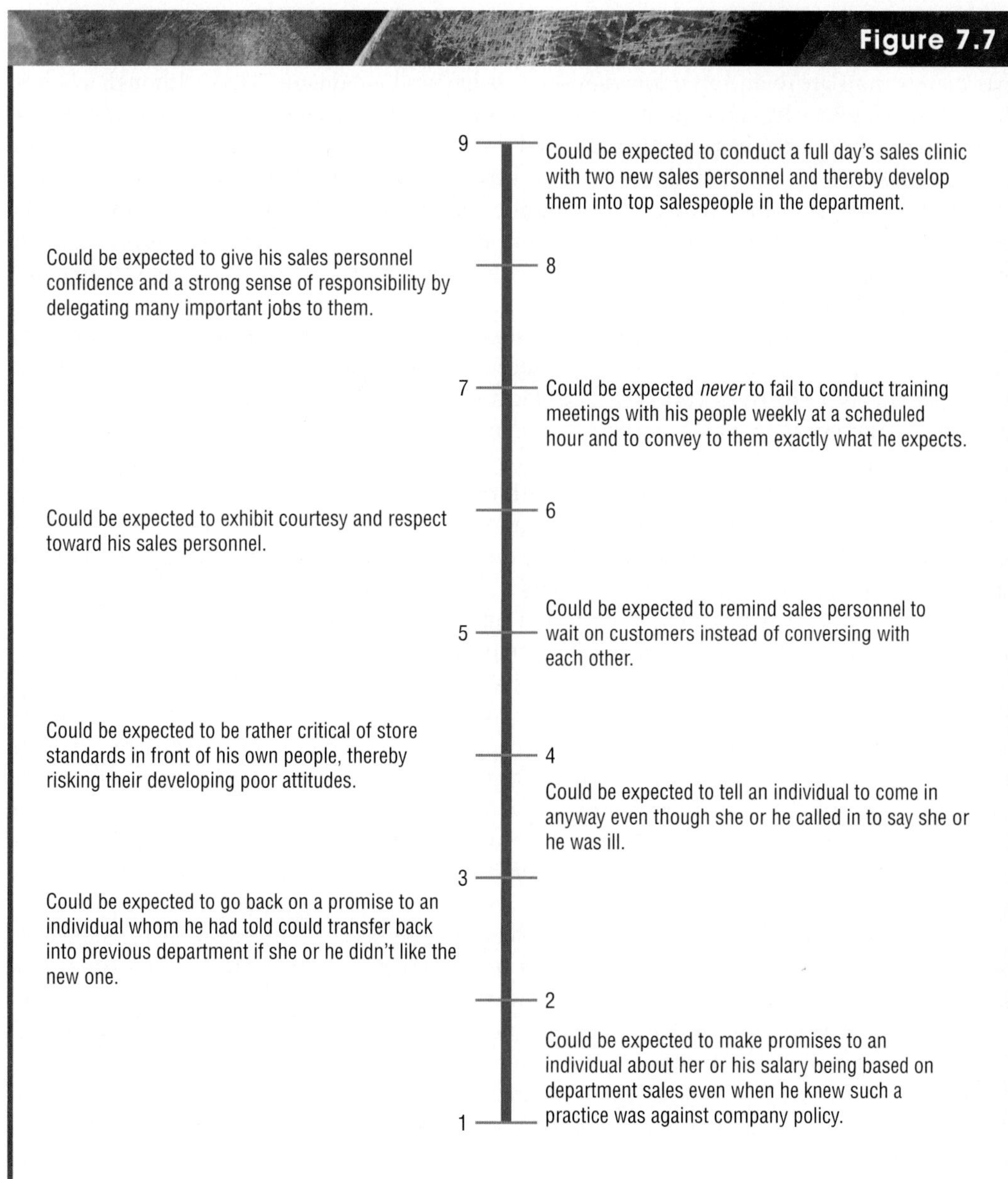

Sample BABS Used to Rate a Sales Manager

Source: Campbell, J. P., Dunnette, M. D., Arvey, R. D., and Hellervik, L. V. (1973). The development and evaluation of behaviorally based rating scales. *Journal of Applied Psychology*, 15–22. © 1973 by the American Psychological Association. Reprinted with permission.

included directly on the behavioral scale. This concreteness makes BARS and other behavioral instruments more legally defensible than trait scales, which often use such hard-to-define adjectives as "poor" and "excellent." Behavioral scales also provide employees with specific examples of the types of behaviors to engage in (and to avoid) if they want to do well in the organization. In addition, behavioral scales encourage supervisors to be specific in their performance feedback. Finally, both workers and supervisors can be involved in the process of generating behavioral scales.[22] This is likely to increase understanding and acceptance of the appraisal system.

Behavioral systems are not without disadvantages, however. Most notably, the development of behavioral scales can be very time consuming, easily taking several months. Another disadvantage of behavioral systems is their specificity. The points, or *anchors,* on behavioral scales are clear and concrete, but they are only examples of behavior a worker *may* exhibit. Employees may never exhibit some of these anchor behaviors, which can cause difficulty for supervisors at appraisal time. Also, significant organizational changes can invalidate behavioral scales. For example, computerization of operations can dramatically alter the behaviors that workers must exhibit to be successful. Thus, the behaviors painstakingly developed for the appraisal system could become useless or, worse, operate as a drag on organizational change and adaptation. Workers will be unwilling to make changes in their work behaviors when the criteria by which their performance is judged are not changed as well.

Another potential difficulty is many supervisors' belief that a behavioral focus is an unnatural way of thinking about and evaluating workers. As we discussed earlier, traits are a more natural way to think about others. Supervisors required to make behaviorally based evaluations may merely translate their trait impressions into behavioral judgments. Thus, although a behavioral approach seems less ambiguous, it may require mental gymnastics that can introduce error into ratings. No research has directly examined this issue, but one study has found a preference among both supervisors and workers for a trait-based system over a behaviorally based system.[23] The "unnaturalness" of a behavioral orientation may underlie this preference. However, the behavioral scales can help clarify what is being measured and what behavior succeeds in an organization. Even if taking a behavioral perspective seems unnatural at first, it is a valuable skill that can easily be learned.

Outcome appraisal instruments
An appraisal tool that asks managers to assess the results achieved by workers.

Management by objectives (MBO)
A goal-directed approach to performance appraisal in which workers and their supervisors set goals together for the upcoming evaluation period.

Outcome appraisal instruments ask managers to assess the results achieved by workers, such as total sales or number of products produced. The most prevalent outcome approaches are **management by objectives (MBO)**[24] and naturally occurring outcome measures. MBO is a goal-directed approach in which workers and their supervisors set goals together for the upcoming evaluation period. The rating then consists of deciding to what extent the goals have been met. With *naturally occurring outcomes,* the performance measure is not so much discussed and agreed to as it is handed to supervisors and workers. For example, a computerized production system used to manufacture cardboard boxes may automatically generate data regarding the number of pieces produced, the amount of waste, and the defect rate.

The outcome approach provides clear and unambiguous criteria by which worker performance can be judged. It also eliminates subjectivity and the potential for error and bias that goes along with it. In addition, outcome approaches provide increased flexibility. For example, a change in the production system may lead to a new set of outcome measures and, perhaps, a new set of performance standards. With an MBO approach, a worker's objectives can easily be adjusted at the beginning of a new evaluation period if organizational changes call for new emphases. Perhaps the most important thing is that outcomes can easily be tied to strategic objectives.[25] (Behaviors can also be linked to strategic objectives, but developing behavioral measures linked to strategic objectives may be more involved and less immediate than outcome measures.)

Are outcome-based systems, then, the answer to the numerous problems with the subjective rating systems discussed earlier? Unfortunately, no. Although objective, outcome measures may give a seriously deficient and distorted view of worker performance levels. Consider an outcome measure defined as follows: "the number of units produced that are within acceptable quality limits." This performance measure may seem fair and acceptable. But consider further that production involves the use of some complex equipment that not everyone is good at troubleshooting. As long as the equipment is running fine, even an inexperienced worker can attend the machine and accrue impressive production numbers. However, when the machine is not running properly, it can take several hours—sometimes an entire shift—to locate the problem and resolve it. If you were a manager faced with this situation, would you not put your best workers on the problem? Of course, you would. But consider what would happen to those workers' performance records. Your best workers could actually end up looking like the worst workers in terms of the amount of product produced.

This situation actually occurred at a manufacturer of automobile components.[26] To resolve the issue, management concluded that supervisors' subjective performance judgments were superior to objective outcome measures. The subjective ratings differed radically from the outcome measures. But in this case, the subjective ratings were found to be related to workers' scores on job-related tests whereas no such relationship was found for the outcome measures. Clearly, in some situations human judgment is superior to objective measures.

Another potential difficulty with outcome-based performance measures is the development of a "results at any cost" mentality.[27] Using objective measures has the advantage of focusing workers' attention on certain outcomes, but this focus can have negative effects on other facets of performance. For example, an organization may use the number of units produced as a performance measure because it is fairly easy to quantify. Workers concentrating on quantity may neglect quality and follow-up service to the long-term detriment of the organization. Although objective goals and other outcome measures are effective for increasing performance levels, these measures may not reflect the entire spectrum of performance.[28]

Measurement Tools: Summary and Conclusions

Our discussion so far makes it clear that there is no single best appraisal format. Each approach has positive and negative aspects. Figure 7.8 summarizes the strengths and weaknesses of each approach in the areas of administration, development, and legal defensibility. The choice of appraisal system should rest largely on the appraisal's primary purpose.

Managers must understand each appraisal format to choose the best tool for the purpose. For example, say that your main management concern is obtaining desired results. An outcome approach would be best for this purpose. However, when outcomes are not adequately achieved, further evaluation may be needed to diagnose the problem.

For example, a manager could use a behavioral evaluation to determine if a salesperson is using the right behaviors to achieve the desired results. The manager could assess the sales representative's behavior by considering dimensions such as greeting the customer and identifying customer needs and preferences. In sum, an outcome format can be a good way of measuring performance for the purpose of rewarding top performers. A behavioral format may be needed, however, if the purpose is performance improvement.

Most appraisal systems were developed on the premise that companies could reduce or eliminate rater errors by using the right appraisal format. However, rating formats make little difference in the actual ratings that are obtained. In fact, empirical evidence suggests that the type of tool does not make that much difference in the accuracy of ratings.[29]

If formats do not have much impact on ratings, what does? Not surprisingly, it's the person doing the rating. Characteristics such as the rater's intelligence, familiarity with the job,[30] and

A Question of Ethics

Is it appropriate for organizations to evaluate and compensate employees according to objective measures of performance, even though performance is at least partially determined by factors beyond their control? Should a salesperson, for instance, be paid completely on commission even in the midst of a recession that makes it practically impossible to sell enough to make a decent living?

Figure 7.8

Evaluation of Major Appraisal Formats

	CRITERIA		
Appraisal Format	**Administrative Use**	**Developmental Use**	**Legal Defensibility**
Absolute	0	+	0
Relative	++	-	-
Trait	+	-	- -
Behavior	0	+	++
Outcome	0	0	+

- - Very poor - Poor 0 Unclear or mixed + Good ++ Very good

ability to separate important from unimportant information[31] influence rating quality. A number of studies indicate that raters' ability and motivation levels are the critical factors in rating employees effectively.

Challenges to Effective Performance Measurement

How can managers ensure accurate measurement of worker performance? The primary means is to understand the barriers that stand in the way. Managers confront at least five challenges in this area:

- Rater errors and bias
- The influence of liking
- Organizational politics
- Whether to focus on the individual or the group
- Legal issues

Rater Errors and Bias

Rater error
An error in performance appraisals that reflects consistent biases on the part of the rater.

A **rater error** is an error in performance appraisal that reflects consistent biases on the part of the rater. One of the most prominent rater errors is *halo error,* the tendency to rate similarly across dimensions.[32] Suppose you are buying a refrigerator. If you are most interested in one particular feature—say, the versatility of shelving arrangement—you would commit a halo error if you allowed a particular model's shelving versatility to influence your ratings of its other features (appearance, energy efficiency, and so on). Similarly, raters commit halo errors in performance measurement when they allow the rating they give on one performance dimension to influence the ratings they give on other dimensions. Despite the word's angelic connotations, "halo" can cause uniformly negative ratings as well as uniformly positive ones.

There are at least two causes of halo error:[33] (1) A supervisor may make an overall judgment about a worker and then conform all dimensional ratings to that judgment, and/or (2) a supervisor may make all ratings consistent with the worker's performance level on a dimension that is important to the supervisor. To return to the computer programmer example we used earlier: If Nancy rates Luis low on all three performance dimensions (quality of programs written, quantity of programs written, and interpersonal effectiveness) even though his performance on quality and quantity is high, then she has committed a halo error.

Another type of rater error is *restriction of range error,* which occurs when a manager restricts all of his or her ratings to a small portion of the rating scale. A supervisor who restricts ranges tends to rate all workers similarly. Three different forms of range restriction are common: *leniency errors*, or restricting ratings to the high portion of the scale; *central tendency errors,* or using only the middle points of the scale; and *severity errors,* or using only the low portion of the rating scale.

Suppose that you are an HR manager reviewing the performance ratings given by the company's supervisors to their subordinates. The question is: How can you tell how accurate these ratings are? In other words, how can you tell what types of rating error, if any, have colored the ratings? The answer is that it is very difficult to tell. Let us say that a supervisor has given one of her subordinates the highest possible rating on each of five performance dimensions. There are at least three possible explanations. The employee may actually be very good on one of the dimensions and has been rated very high on all because of this (halo error). Or the rater may only use the top part of the scale (leniency error). Or the employee may be a very good all-around worker (accurate). Although sophisticated statistical techniques have been developed to investigate these possibilities, none is practical for most organizations or managers. Further, current research indicates that "errors" in ratings can sufficiently represent "true" ratee performance levels (the "accurate" possibility presented previously) such that rater errors are *not* good indicators of inaccuracy in rating.[34] Taking steps to remove rater errors from ratings or to train raters to avoid rater errors may not improve the accuracy of ratings and are not recommended practices.

Personal bias may also cause errors in evaluation. Consciously or unconsciously, a supervisor may systematically rate certain workers lower or higher than others on the basis of race, national origin, sex, age, or other factors. Conscious bias is extremely difficult, if not impossible, to eliminate. Unconscious bias can be overcome once it is brought to the rater's attention. For example, a supervisor might be unconsciously giving higher evaluations to employees who went to his alma mater. When made aware of this leaning, however, he may correct it.

Blatant, systematic negative biases should be recognized and corrected within the organization. Negative bias became an issue at the U.S. Drug Enforcement Agency (DEA) in the early 1980s when a lawsuit, *Segar v. Civiletti,* established that African American agents were systematically rated lower than white agents and, thus, were less likely to receive promotions and choice job assignments. The DEA failed to provide supervisors with any written instructions on how to evaluate agents' performance, and virtually all the supervisors conducting the evaluations were white.[35]

The problem of error and bias in ratings is obviously of more than academic interest. A major difficulty in performance measurement is ensuring comparability in ratings across raters.[36] **Comparability** refers to the degree to which the performance ratings given by various supervisors in an organization are similar. In essence, the comparability issue is concerned with whether or not supervisors use the same measurement yardsticks. What one supervisor considers excellent performance, another may view as only average.

Comparability
In performance ratings, the degree to which the performance ratings given by various supervisors in an organization are similar.

One of the most effective ways to deal with errors and bias is to develop and communicate evaluation standards via **frame-of-reference (FOR) training,**[37] which uses fictitious behavioral examples of performance that a worker might exhibit. These performance examples are presented to raters, either in writing or on videotape. Videotape presentations of performance examples are more expensive but probably more realistic than paper descriptions of performance. Lucent Technologies uses videotapes of performance episodes as part of its rater training program.[38] After watching a videotaped performance episode, Lucent trainees describe the performance situation and its consequences and evaluate the central performer.

Frame-of-reference (FOR) training
A type of training that presents supervisors with fictitious examples of worker performance (either in writing or on videotape), asks the supervisors to evaluate the workers in the examples, and then tells them what their ratings should have been.

After rating the performance presented on videotape or paper, the trainees in a typical FOR session would then be told what their ratings should have been. Discussion of which worker behaviors represent each dimension (and why) follows. This process of rating, feedback, and discussion is succeeded by the presentation of another example. Again, rating, feedback, and discussion follow. The process continues until the supervisors develop a common frame of reference for performance evaluation.

FOR training has consistently been found to increase the accuracy of performance ratings.[39] Perhaps even more important, it develops common evaluation standards among supervisors. This makes comparability among various supervisors' ratings possible and is critical to lowering bias in ratings.

The FOR training procedure does have a number of drawbacks, though. One glaring problem is the expense, which can be prohibitive owing to the amount of time and number of people involved. Another drawback of the FOR approach is that it can be used only with behaviorally based appraisal systems.

The Influence of Liking

Liking can cause errors in performance appraisals when raters allow their like or dislike of an individual to influence their assessment of that person's performance. Liking plays a potent role in performance measurement because both liking and ratings are person-focused. The two may be at odds, however. Liking is emotional and often unconscious, whereas formal ratings are—or should be—nonemotional and conscious. Because liking is unconscious, it seems to be established very quickly,[40] which may allow it to influence (bias) more conscious evaluations that occur later.

Although there is much to be learned in this area, field studies have found rater liking and performance ratings to be substantially correlated.[41] Recent work has found the correlation between liking and performance ratings to be an issue no matter who the rater is, but liking appears to have a stronger influence on ratings made by peers and subordinates than it does on those made by supervisors.[42] Findings of a correlation might indicate that performance ratings are biased by rater liking. However, good raters may tend to like good performers and dislike poor performers.

The fundamental question, of course, is whether the relationship between liking and performance ratings is appropriate or biased.[43] It is appropriate if supervisors like good performers better than poor performers. It is biased if supervisors like or dislike employees for reasons other than their performance and allow these feelings to contaminate their ratings. It is often very difficult to separate these two possibilities.[44] Nonetheless, most workers appear to believe that their supervisor's liking for them influences the performance ratings they receive.[45] The perception of bias can cause communication problems between workers and supervisors and lower supervisors' effectiveness in managing performance.

Precautions

Given the potentially biasing impact of liking, it is critical that supervisors manage their emotional reactions to workers. The first step in managing any emotional reaction is recognizing the presence of the emotion. Managers should be aware of their emotional reactions to workers so that they can guard against their influence.

To ensure that they evaluate workers on performance rather than liking, managers should keep a performance diary for each worker.[46] This diary, which should record behavioral incidents observed by the supervisor, can serve as the basis for evaluation and other managerial actions. An external record of worker behaviors can dramatically reduce error and bias in ratings.

Recordkeeping should be done routinely—for example, daily or weekly. Keeping records of employee performance is a professional habit worth developing, particularly to safeguard against litigation that challenges the fairness of appraisals.[47] To prevent error and bias, the record should reflect what each worker has been doing, not opinions or inferences about the behavior. Further, the record should present a balanced and complete picture by including all performance incidents—positive, negative, or average. A good question to ask yourself is whether someone else reading the record would reach the same conclusion about the level of performance as you have.

Keeping employee performance records may seem like a time-consuming task, but the time spent keeping such records may be less than anticipated and the benefits greater. In one field study of such recordkeeping, supervisors reported that the task took five minutes or less per week.[48] More important, the majority of supervisors reported that they would prefer to continue, rather than discontinue, the recording of behavioral incidents. This preference for additional paperwork may seem unusual until one considers the benefits derived from the process. By compiling a weekly record, they did not have to rely much on general impressions and possibly biased memories when conducting appraisals. In addition, the practice signaled workers that appraisal was not a personality contest. Finally, the diaries provided a legal justification for the appraisal process: The supervisor could cite concrete behavioral examples that justified the rating.

Two warnings are in order here. First, performance diaries are not guarantees against bias due to liking, because supervisors can be biased in the type of incidents they choose to record. However, short of intentional misrepresentation, the keeping of such records should help reduce both actual bias and the perception of bias.

Second, some managers use performance diaries in place of intervention and discussion because it is less uncomfortable, initially, to record a performance problem than to discuss it with the employee. Documenting problems is fine and even useful for creating a legally defensible case if the employee must be terminated. However, it is unfair to keep a secret running list of "offenses" and then suddenly unveil it to the employee when he or she commits an infraction that can't be overlooked. The message for managers is simple: If an employee's behavior warrants discussion, the discussion should take place immediately.[49]

Here's how one company used performance diaries both to aid performance appraisal and to enhance employee coaching:

> In its drive to revamp its performance appraisal system, Azteca Foods, Inc., a 125-employee company, asked its 25 managers to begin keeping a daily log of each employee's performance. Every time an employee did something negative (like arriving late to work or missing an assignment deadline) or something positive (like making a notable contribution) the manager was expected to write it down and give immediate feedback. While this procedure may sound time-consuming, the company found the payback worth the extra effort. At appraisal time managers were able to bring up concrete examples of what an employee did instead of saying "You've done a good (or inadequate) job." The procedure also fosters communication between managers and subordinates and motivates workers to continuously improve performance.[50]

Although liking can be a source of bias in performance appraisals, it can also be the direct result of good performance. Managers tend to like employees who have a positive attitude, who get along well with their co-workers, and who perform consistently well.

Organizational Politics

Thus far we have taken a *rational perspective* on appraisal.[51] In other words, we have assumed that the value of each worker's performance can be estimated. Unlike the rational approach, the *political perspective* assumes that the value of a worker's performance depends on the agenda, or goals, of the supervisor.[52] In other words, the political approach to appraisal holds that performance measurement is a goal-oriented activity and that the goal is seldom accuracy. Consider the following quote from an executive with extensive experience in evaluating his subordinates:

> As a manager, I will use the review process to do what is best for my people and the division. . . . I've got a lot of leeway—call it discretion—to use this process in that manner. . . . I've used it to get my people better raises in lean years, to kick a guy in the pants if he really needed it, to pick up a guy when he was down or even to tell him that he was no longer welcome here. . . . I believe that most of us here at _____ operate this way regarding appraisals.[53]

The distinction between the rational and political approaches to appraisal can best be understood by examining how they differ on various facets of the performance appraisal process.

- The *goal* of appraisal from a rational perspective is accuracy. The goal of appraisal from a political perspective is *utility*, the maximization of benefits over costs given the context and agenda. The value of performance is relative to the political context and the supervisor's goals. For example, a supervisor may give a very poor rating to a worker who seems uncommitted in the hopes of shocking that worker into an acceptable level of performance. Or the supervisor may give positive ratings to workers in an attempt to reduce complaints and conflict. In these circumstances, it is clear that the goal of appraisal is not accuracy.
- The *roles* played by supervisors and workers also differ in the rational and political approaches. The rational approach sees supervisors and workers largely as passive agents in the rating process: Supervisors simply notice and evaluate workers' performance. Thus, the accuracy of supervisors is critical to the attainment of accurate evaluations. In contrast, the political approach views both supervisors and workers as motivated participants in the measurement process. Workers actively try to influence their evaluations, either directly or indirectly.

The various persuasion techniques that workers use to alter the supervisor's evaluation are direct forms of influence. For example, just as a student tells a professor that he needs a higher grade to keep his scholarship, a worker might tell her boss that she needs an above-average rating to get a promotion. Indirect influences on ratings include a variety of behaviors in which workers engage to influence how supervisors notice, interpret, and recall events.[54] Behaviors ranging from flattery to excuses to apologies all are examples of how workers attempt to influence supervisors' impressions. The following quote from a consulting group manager demonstrates how employees in the organization used impression-management tactics:[55]

> Phone calls from customers praising a consultant's performance were rarely received except during the month before appraisals. These phone calls were often instigated by the consultants to highlight their importance.

- From a rational perspective, the *focus* of appraisal is measurement. Supervisors are flesh-and-blood instruments[56] who must be carefully trained to measure performance meaningfully. The evaluations are used in decisions about pay raises, promotions, training, and termination. The political perspective sees the focus of appraisal as management, not accurate measurement. Appraisal is not so much a test that should be fair and accurate as a management tool with which to reward or discipline workers.
- *Assessment criteria*, the standards used to judge worker performance, also differ between the rational and political approaches. The rational approach holds that a worker's performance should be defined as clearly as possible. Without a clear definition of what is being assessed and clear standards for its assessment, accurate assessment is impossible. In the political approach, the definition of what is being assessed is left ambiguous so that it can be bent to the current agenda. Thus, ambiguity ensures the necessary flexibility in the appraisal system.
- Finally, the *decision process* involved in performance assessment differs between the rational and political approaches. In the rational approach, supervisors make dimensional and overall assessments based on specific behaviors they have observed. For instance, in the computer programmer example we have been using, Nancy would rate each programmer on each dimension and then combine all the dimensional ratings into an overall evaluation. In the political approach, it is the other way around: Appropriate assessment of specifics follows the overall assessment. Thus, Nancy would first decide who in her group should get the highest rating (for whatever reason) and then justify that overall assessment by making appropriate dimensional ratings.

A Question of Ethics

Performance appraisal is a management tool. As such, managers often use the tool to benefit themselves or the company. For example, a manager may use overly positive performance ratings as a reward for someone who spear-headed a project for the manager. Likewise, a manager may use overly harsh ratings as punishment for someone who objected to a project the manager promoted. Do you think such use of the appraisal system is acceptable? Why?

Appraisal in most organizations seems to be a political rather than a rational exercise.[57] It appears to be used as a tool for serving various and changing agendas; accurate assessment is seldom the real goal. But should the rational approach be abandoned because appraisal is typically political? No! Politically driven assessment may be common, but that does not make it the best approach to assessment.

Accuracy may not be the main goal in organizations, but it is the theoretical ideal behind appraisal.[58] Accurate assessment is necessary if feedback, development, and HR decisions are to be based on employees' actual performance levels. Basing feedback and development on managerial agendas is an unjust treatment of human resources. Careers have been ruined, self-esteem lost, and productivity degraded because of the political use of appraisal. Such costs are difficult to assess and to ascribe clearly to politics. Nonetheless, they are very real and important for workers.

Individual or Group Focus

Just as we have assumed throughout this chapter that the performance measurement process is rational, we have also assumed that the appropriate focus is the individual employee. This is largely a reflection of our Western culture. We value the rugged individual, the superstar, the person who stands out from the crowd. Our entire economic system is based on competition and survival of the fittest. However, in organizations, teamwork and cooperation are necessary for the achievement of common goals. Indeed, as we have seen in earlier chapters, teams are becoming increasingly common in the U.S. workplace.

If the organization has a team structure, managers need to consider team performance appraisal at two levels: (1) individual contribution to team performance and (2) the performance of the team as a unit.[59] To properly assess individual contributions to team performance, managers and employees must have clear performance criteria relating to traits, behaviors, or outcomes. Behavioral measures are typically most appropriate for assessing individual contributions to team performance because they are more easily observed and understood by team members and others who interact with the team.

The individual contribution measures could be developed with the input of team members. However, a good starting point is the set of competencies for individual contribution to team performance identified in recent research.[60] The following example describes the use of these competencies at Pfizer, a large pharmaceutical company. Peers assess team members online in the finance area of Pfizer.[61]

> The assessment is based on a four-dimensional model of collaboration, communication, self-management, and decision making. Feedback reports are used as a discussion point to improve the functioning of teams. Over time, there has been significant improvement in the average level of ratings given to team members.

The Manager's Notebook entitled "Measuring the Performance of Teams" presents a seven-step process recommended by management consultant Jack Zigon. Whatever measures are already in existence or are developed for measuring team performance, here are some points to keep in mind:

First, the measurement system needs to be balanced. For example, although financial objectives may be apparent and easy to develop as criteria, these kinds of objectives are measured in such a way that they do not reflect the concerns of customers.

Another point to keep in mind is that outcome measures may need to be complemented with measures of process. For example, achieving a result may be important but so, too, is interpersonal relations. With a balance of measures, it should be clear to team members that achieving outcomes by running roughshod over peers and customers is not acceptable performance.

One more point to keep in mind concerning the development of team performance measures is that the measures must reflect criteria that the teams can influence. It will do no good to develop measures of performance over which teams have no control.[62]

Emerging Trends — MANAGER'S NOTEBOOK

Measuring the Performance of Teams

1. **Review existing measures to make sure the team is aware of the measures and has commitment and responsibility to achieving them.**
2. **Identify interim checkpoints at which team progress or achievements can be assessed.**
3. **Identify what the team and team members must do to achieve the desired team-level results.**
4. **Prioritize team goals according to relative importance.**
5. **Develop any needed measures of interim and final team and individual performance.**
6. **Develop team and individual performance standards so that everyone has a clear understanding of performance expectations.**
7. **Determine how the performance management system will work. Who will be the raters? How will feedback be provided?**

Source: Adapted from Denton, K. D. (2001). Better decisions with less information. *Industrial Management, 43*, 21.

Assessing the performance of a team as a unit means that managers must measure performance at the team, not individual, level. Unfortunately, performance in teams doesn't always go along as rationally or as smoothly as hoped. The Manager's Notebook entitled "Team Performance Management: Tactics for the Disgruntled Employee" explores ways in which a team can help to manage the behavior of a team member who is disgruntled and a disruptive influence. Team members may be the best sources for identifying and developing team level criteria. Going to team members to help develop criteria encourages their participation in selecting measures that they feel they can directly influence.

MANAGER'S NOTEBOOK

Emerging Trends

Team Performance Management: Tactics for the Disgruntled Employee

Work can't always be smooth and rational. Sometimes the workplace can be disrupted and negatively impacted by someone who is acting out emotionally. For example, a worker may exhibit aggressive behavior toward others and may even exhibit physical aggression by hitting doors or kicking boxes. Such a worker might not freely exchange information and may, therefore, make it difficult for other workers to get their jobs done. Disgruntled behavior could be caused by any number of things including frustrations with the workplace, drug dependencies, and personality disorders. Whatever the reasons, the behaviors of such a worker can intimidate others and can cause concern over whether the aggressiveness might escalate or become focused on someone. Unfortunately, such negative situations can sometimes fester and not be dealt with by management. Why? Dealing with such a problem requires confrontation and many people prefer to avoid confrontation. In addition, in an empowered and team-based environment, a disgruntled worker may be viewed as a problem for peers to resolve. And, if the worker exhibiting the interpersonal difficulties happens to be able to achieve results, management might look the other way.

In sum, there is a variety of possible causes for disgruntled behavior and many reasons why it may be allowed to continue. However, something must be done about the aggressive behavior. Not only may productivity be negatively affected, but morale can also spiral downward and trust in management can plummet if the problem isn't effectively dealt with. The following are possible tactics that a team may use to deal with a member exhibiting hostile behavior. First, however, is safety. If it is felt that the hostility level is such that there may be a threat to personal safety, then internal security should be present during any meeting.

1. **Peer Confrontation with Supervisor.** If the problem team member is unpredictable and hostile, it may be best for the work team to confront the supervisor, not the difficult team member. The supervisor must be made to understand how the difficult worker's behavior is negatively impacting the team. Even in an empowered and team-based setting, management cannot ignore performance difficulties that a team is having trouble wrestling with. If the supervisor does not take meaningful action in a timely fashion, the team should be prepared to go to a higher level of management.
2. **Team Guerilla Tactic.** If management is nonresponsive, an alternative approach is for people on the work team to schedule appointments with an employee assistance program representative or with the human resources department. The point of scheduling these appointments is not to directly solve the problem. Rather, the point is to bring about a situation in which the counselor or human resource representative is an advocate for the work team and its problem. Furthermore, the purpose of scheduling multiple meetings is to gain the attention and action of management by virtue of the amount of time team members are spending away from their work.
3. **Policy Development.** A policy should be put in place that clearly makes a hostile work environment unacceptable. The policy should include sections on prevention and intervention. In a traditional work environment, the development of such a policy would likely rest with management and/or human resource management. However, in an empowered team structure, although management may still take responsibility for final wording and implementation of such a policy, team members may need to bring forth the idea and do some benchmarking. Whatever the specifics of the policy, hitting doors and kicking boxes would likely be considered unsafe and hostile behavior.
4. **Team Performance Appraisal.** A dimension such as "interpersonal relations" or "team player" is often included in most team-structured work situations. In some organizations,

teams are responsible for conducting their own appraisals on team members. Whoever is responsible for conducting the appraisal and providing feedback, it is certainly legitimate to hold a hostile co-worker accountable. Hostile behavior and not sharing information would certainly be relevant to performance on this dimension.

5. **Discipline and Action Plan.** Whether it is the responsibility of the team or the supervisor to determine discipline, the thrust of these tactics is to get to the point where appropriate disciplinary action is taken. Depending on the situation, a written warning or loss of a day's pay may be enough of a contingency that the problem worker's behavior changes. In addition to discipline, an action plan that includes goals and additional meeting times would be in order.

Source: Adapted with permission from Raphael, T. (2002). Dealing with disgruntled employees. *Workforce*, *80*, 12–14.

Two final points: First, experts recommend that individual performance still be assessed, even within a team environment, because U.S. society is so strongly focused on individual performance.[63] Second, there is no consensus as to what type of appraisal instrument should be used for team evaluations. The best approach may include internal and external customers making judgments across both behavioral and outcome criteria.[64]

Legal Issues

The major legal requirements for performance appraisal systems are set forth in Title VII of the Civil Rights Act of 1964, which prohibits discrimination in all terms and conditions of employment (see Chapter 3). This means that performance appraisal must be free of discrimination at both the individual and group levels. Some courts have also held that performance appraisal systems should meet the same *validity* standards as selection tests (see Chapter 5). As with selection tests, *adverse impact* may occur in performance evaluation when members of one group are promoted at a higher rate than members of another group based on their appraisals.

Probably the most significant court test of discrimination in performance appraisal is *Brito v. Zia Company*, a 1973 U.S. Supreme Court case. In essence, the Court determined that appraisal is legally a test and must, therefore, meet all the legal requirements regarding tests in organizations. In practice, however, court decisions since *Brito v. Zia* have employed less stringent criteria when assessing charges of discrimination in appraisal.

Appraisal-related court cases since *Brito v. Zia* suggest that the courts do not wish to rule on whether appraisal systems conform to all accepted professional standards (such as whether employees were allowed to participate in developing the system).[65] Rather, they simply want to determine if discrimination occurred. The essential question is whether individuals who have similar employment situations are treated differently.

The courts look favorably on a system in which a supervisor's manager reviews appraisals to safeguard against the occurrence of individual bias. In addition, the courts take a positive view of feedback and employee counseling to help improve performance problems. A recent analysis of 295 court cases involving performance appraisal found judges' decisions to be favorably influenced by the following additional factors:[66]

- Use of job analysis
- Providing written instructions
- Allowing employees to review appraisal results
- Agreement among multiple raters (if more than one rater was used)
- The presence of rater training

In the extreme, a negative performance appraisal may lead to the dismissal of an employee. Management's right to fire an employee is rooted in a legal doctrine called *employment at will*. Employment at will is a very complex legal issue that depends on laws and rulings varying from state to state. We discuss employment at will fully in Chapter 14. Here, it is enough to say that managers can protect themselves from lawsuits by following good professional practice. If they provide subordinates with honest, accurate, and fair feedback about their performance, and then make decisions consistent with that feedback, they will have nothing to fear from ongoing questions about employment at will.

Managing Performance

The effective management of human performance in organizations requires more than formal reporting and annual ratings. A complete appraisal process includes informal day-to-day interactions between managers and workers as well as formal face-to-face interviews. Although the ratings themselves are important, even more critical is what managers do with them. In this section we discuss the third and final component of performance appraisal, performance management.

The Appraisal Interview

Upon completing the performance rating, the supervisor usually conducts an interview with the worker to provide feedback—one of the most important parts of the appraisal process. Many managers dread the performance appraisal, particularly if they do not have good news to impart. The HR department or an external group, such as a management association or consulting group, can help managers by offering training in conducting interviews, providing role-play practice, and offering advice on thorny issues. Figure 7.9 summarizes several communication "microskills" that managers need to effectively conduct an appraisal interview.

Performance reviews are sometimes separated into two sessions: one to discuss performance, the other to discuss salary.[67] (This practice is common in Great Britain, where 85 percent of large companies split the appraisal meeting.) The logic behind this system was based on two assumptions. First, managers cannot simultaneously be both a coach and a judge. Thus, the manager was expected to play the coach role during the performance development meeting and the judge role during the salary meeting. Second, if performance and salary discussions were combined, employees probably would not listen to their performance feedback because their interest would be focused on salary decisions.

However, research has found that discussion of salary in an appraisal session has a *positive* impact on how employees perceive the appraisal's usefulness.[68] There are at least two reasons for this. First, when money is at stake, the manager is much more likely to take the tasks of appraisal and feedback seriously. Managers who have to justify a low salary increase will probably take time to carefully support their performance assessments, and this more detailed feedback should make the appraisal session more valuable to the employee. Second, including the salary discussion can energize the performance discussion. Feedback, goal setting, and making action plans can become a hollow and meaningless exercise when salary implications are divorced from the session.

In sum, it appears that the best management practice is to combine development and salary discussion into one performance review. Informal performance management throughout the appraisal period requires a combination of judgment and coaching. To be most effective, judgment and coaching should also be used together in the formal review session.

Performance Improvement

Because formal appraisal interviews typically are conducted only once a year,[69] they may not always have substantial and lasting impact on worker performance.[70] Much more important than the annual interview is informal day-to-day performance management. Supervisors who manage performance effectively generally share four characteristics. They:

- Explore the causes of performance problems.
- Direct attention to the causes of problems.
- Develop an action plan and empower workers to reach a solution.
- Direct communication at performance and provide effective feedback.[71]

Each of these characteristics is critical to achieving improved and sustained performance levels.

Figure 7.9

Face-to-face communication during the performance appraisal interview can be more effective if managers use "microskills"—communication factors that must be present for effective interpersonal communication. Several examples follow:

Skills	Benefit	Description	Example
Nonverbal Attending	Suggests interest and active listening.	Rater sits with a slight forward, comfortable lean of the upper body, maintains eye contact, and speaks in a steady and soothing voice.	While the ratee is speaking, the rater looks at the person and gently nods head to signal interest.
Open and Closed Questions	Appropriate use of open and closed questions can ensure an effective flow of communication during an interview.	Open questions encourage information sharing and are most appropriate early in an interview or in complex, ambiguous situations. Closed questions evoke short responses and are useful for focusing and clarifying.	Open questions start with words like "Could," "Would," "How," "What," or "Why." Closed questions start with words like "Did," "Is," or "Are."
Paraphrasing	Paraphrasing can clarify and convey to the ratee that you are listening actively.	A paraphrase is a concise statement in your own words of what someone has just said. It should be factual and nonjudgmental.	You might begin by saying "If I have this right . . ." or "What you're saying is . . ." and end with "Is that correct?" or "That's what you are saying?"
Reflection of Feeling	Shows that you are trying to understand the emotional aspect of the workplace. The empathy and sensitivity of such reflection can open up communication and allow the interview to move more meaningfully to task-related issues.	Similar to paraphrase, a reflection of feeling is a factual statement of the emotions you sense the other person is feeling. Be cautious about using this technique insincerely or with those who need professional help.	Start by saying something like "It sounds like you're feeling . . ." End as you would a paraphrase ("Is that right?").
Cultural Sensitivity	Communication is more effective when you are sensitive to the possible influence of cultural differences.	Pay attention to cultural differences that may influence how another person communicates and how you might communicate with others.	When dealing with employees from a culture that is highly formal, avoid addressing them in the workplace by their first names. Doing so may signal disrespect.

Sources: Adapted from Kikoski, J. F. (1998). Effective communication in the performance appraisal interview: Face-to-face communication for public managers in the culturally diverse workplace. *Public Personnel Management, 27,* 491–513; and Ivey, A. B., Ivey, M. B., and Simek-Downing, L. (1987). *Counseling and psychotherapy: Integrating skills, theory, and practice* (2nd ed). Upper Saddle River, NJ: Prentice Hall.

Communication Skills for the Appraisal Interview

Exploring the Causes of Performance Problems

Exploring the causes of performance problems may sound like an easy task, but it is often quite challenging. Certainly, the worker may be directly responsible for his or her performance. However, performance can be the result of many factors, some of which are beyond the worker's control. In most work situations, though, observers tend to attribute the causes to the worker.[72] That is, supervisors tend to blame the worker when they observe poor performance, while workers tend to blame external factors. This tendency is called *actor/observer bias*.[73] The experience of baseball teams provides an analogy. When a team is losing, the players (workers/actors) point to external causes such as injuries, a tough road schedule, or bad weather. The manager (supervisor/observer) blames the players for sloppy execution in the field. And the team's owner and the sportswriters (top management/higher observers) hold the manager responsible for the team's poor performance.

It is important that managers determine the causes of performance deficiencies accurately for three reasons. First, determination of causes can influence how performance is evaluated. For example, a manager is likely to evaluate an episode of poor performance very differently if he thinks it was due to low effort than if he thinks it was due to poor materials. Second, causal determination can be an unspoken and underlying source of conflict between supervisors and their workers. Supervisors often act on what they believe are the causes of performance problems. This is only rational. But when the supervisor's perception significantly differs from the worker's, the difference can cause tension. Third, causal determinations affect the type of remedy selected; what is thought to be the cause of a performance problem determines what is done about it. For instance, very different actions would be taken if poor performance was thought to be the result of inadequate ability rather than inadequacies in the raw materials.

How can the process of determining the causes of performance problems be improved? A starting point is to consider the possible causes consciously and systematically. Traditionally, researchers believed that two primary factors, ability and motivation, determined performance.[74] A major problem with this view is that situational factors external to the worker, such as degree of management support, also affect worker performance.[75]

A more inclusive version of the causes of performance embraces three factors: ability, motivation, and situational factors. The *ability* factor reflects the worker's talents and skills, including characteristics such as intelligence, interpersonal skills, and job knowledge. *Motivation* can be affected by a number of external factors (such as rewards and punishments) but is ultimately an internal decision: It is up to the worker to determine how much effort to exert on any given task. **Situational factors** (or **system factors**) include a wide array of organizational characteristics that can positively or negatively influence performance. System factors include quality of materials, quality of supervisor, and the other factors listed in Figure 7.10.[76]

Situational factors or system factors
A wide array of organizational characteristics that can positively or negatively influence performance.

Performance depends on all three factors. The presence of just one cause is not sufficient for high performance to occur; however, the absence or low value of one factor can result in poor performance. For example, making a strong effort will not result in high performance if the worker has neither the necessary job skills nor adequate support in the workplace. But if the worker doesn't put forth any effort, low performance is inevitable, no matter how good that worker's skills and how much support is provided.

In determining the causes of performance problems, managers should carefully consider situational factors. The factors in Figure 7.10 are only a starting point; they are too generic for use in some situations. For best results, supervisors should use this list as a basis for generating their own job-specific lists of factors. Involving workers in creating the lists will both produce examples that supervisors may not have been aware of and send a signal that managers are serious about considering workers' input. The supervisor and worker (or work team) can go over the list together to isolate the causes of any performance difficulties.

Examples of situational constraints/facilitators that managers face can include factors such as clerical support, excessive reporting requirements, and the performance of subordinates and co-workers.[77] Only some of these situational factors are under the control of a manager. For

Situational (System) Factors to Consider in Determining the Causes of Performance Problems

Figure 7.10

- Poor coordination of work activities among workers.
- Inadequate information or instructions needed to perform a job.
- Low-quality materials.
- Lack of necessary equipment.
- Inability to obtain raw materials, parts, or supplies.
- Inadequate financial resources.
- Poor supervision.
- Uncooperative co-workers and/or poor relations among people.
- Inadequate training.
- Insufficient time to produce the quantity or quality of work required.
- A poor work environment (for example, cold, hot, noisy, frequent interruptions).
- Equipment breakdown.

example, subordinate performance may have more to do with the manager than with anything else. To determine whether a factor is truly in the person or system category, managers must consider the organizational context.

Finally, supervisors should also consider using self-review, peer reviews, and subordinate reviews on an annual or semiannual basis. **Self-review,** in which workers rate themselves, allows employees input into the appraisal process and can help them gain insight into the causes of performance problems. For example, there may be a substantial difference in opinion between a supervisor and an employee regarding one area of the employee's evaluation. Communication and possibly investigation are warranted in such a case. In some situations, people can find themselves having to rely on self-appraisal as a guide to managing performance. The Manager's Notebook entitled "Performance Self-Management" considers the essentials of setting up a performance self-management system.

Self-review
A performance appraisal system in which workers rate themselves.

Emerging Trends

MANAGER'S NOTEBOOK

Performance Self-Management

The employment relationship has shifted from a long-term relationship between a loyal worker and an employer offering a secure position to a more independent and temporary arrangement. Some people, for example, have shifted from the role of traditional employee to an internal consultant or to a freelance service provider. Greater independence and a shorter-term relationship may mean little, if any, meaningful performance feedback, at least from a traditional performance management system. In the long term, being called in or not to work on various projects may provide the ultimate performance feedback. However, if you are in the role of consultant or freelancer, you need more immediate performance feedback and you may need to set up the performance measurement and feedback system yourself.

Here are some of the basics that should be addressed in setting up a system to measure your own performance as a manager.

- **Define Performance.** What exactly am I trying to achieve?
- **Identify Measures.** What are the key indicators of my performance? How should my success be measured and who should do the measuring? Keep the measures simple and quantifiable, but you might also want to include some narrative or verbal feedback. Narrative and verbal feedback can help you understand the ratings and assist in your development.
- **What Standard?** Not every project or client is the same. Some may want perfection and some may want to cut costs and sacrifice. Find out whether this project or client merits clearing all hurdles by a mile or simply getting over them. Although you might want to maximize your performance at all times on all dimensions, it is not always possible to do so. This standard may simply not fit or be appropriate in some situations.
- **Feedback.** How do you obtain your own performance feedback? How often? From whom or where?

Source: Adapted from Simon, N. J. (2002). Whose fault is it anyway? *Competitive Intelligence Magazine, 5*, 55–57.

When a supervisor and a worker cannot resolve their disagreement, performance assessments from additional sources, such as peers and subordinates, may be useful. In a **peer review,** workers at the same level of the organization rate one another. For instance, peer review played a central role in the appraisal process at Milo Engineering, the business featured in our opening vignette. In a **subordinate review,** workers review their supervisors. If peers' and subordinates' judgments converge with the supervisor's, then it is likely that the supervisor's judgment is correct. If peers' and subordinates' judgments do not match the supervisor's, it may be that the supervisor is not aware of or sensitive to the impact of certain factors on the worker's performance.

Peer review
A performance appraisal system in which workers at the same level in the organization rate one another.

Subordinate review
A performance appraisal system in which workers review their supervisors.

More and more companies are using peer review as a performance appraisal system. W. L. Gore & Associates, the company known by outdoors enthusiasts for its Gore-Tex fabric, has used peer review since its founding over 30 years ago. At Gore, every employee is ranked by peers on the basis of his or her contributions to the company's goals. The peers in this case are committees of 6 to 10 co-workers. Because W. L. Gore limits the size of its 40-odd plants to fewer than 200 people, co-workers tend to be familiar with one another's work. The rankings, called "contribution lists," may be compiled several times a year. They begin at the team level, asking about each group, "Who is the most valuable contributor to this function? Who is the next most valuable?" and so on.

In addition to feedback from within the organization, companies are increasingly looking to customers as a valuable source of appraisal. Traditional top-down appraisal systems may encourage employees to perform only those behaviors that supervisors see or pay attention to. Thus, behaviors that are critical to customer satisfaction may be ignored.[78]

Indeed, customers are often in a better position to evaluate the quality of a company's products or services than supervisors are. Supervisors may have limited information or a limited perspective, while internal and external customers often have a wider focus or greater experience with more parts of the business. Figure 7.11 presents an example of a customer appraisal form.

360° feedback The combination of peer, subordinate, and self-review.

The combination of peer, subordinate, and self-review and sometimes customer appraisal, termed **360° feedback,** is rapidly becoming a common approach to performance appraisal. One reason for the increase in 360° feedback is the trend for fewer management layers. With so many more employees reporting to one supervisor, it is just not possible for the supervisor to gauge everyone's work accurately. Another reason is that the old system where the supervisor alone reviews performance is out of sync with today's emphasis on teamwork and participative management.[79]

Further, feedback from one source is easy to discount, but a message from many sources is hard to ignore.[80] Companies around the world are embracing the 360° appraisal process, but not without problems. For example, by the middle of 1998, 2.6 percent of 70 multinational companies with offices in Asia had introduced 360° appraisals in the Asian part of their operation.[81] This figure was a substantial increase from only a handful of companies two years earlier.

However, local Asian companies have been slower to jump on the 360° appraisal bandwagon. For example, Hong Kong managers are reluctant because there is a feeling that negative evaluation of subordinates could reflect badly on the manager but higher ratings could indicate

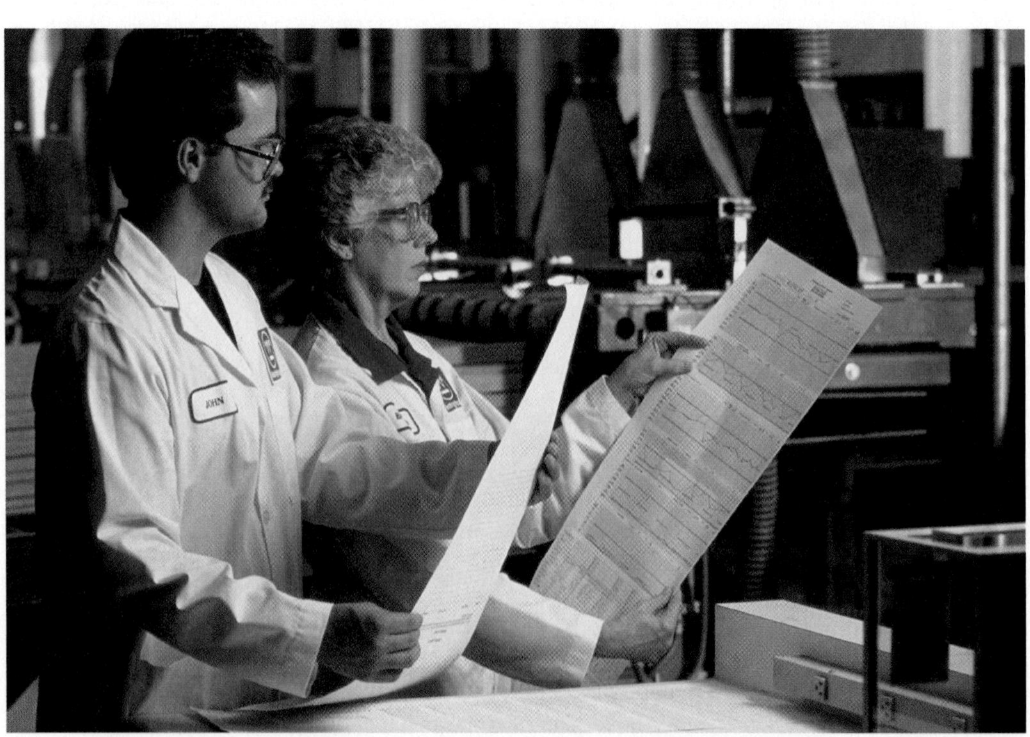

Employees use peer ratings to appraise co-workers. Review by employees familiar with each other's work can result in an accurate assessment of performance.

Figure 7.11

Name: ______________________________

This survey asks your opinion about specific aspects of the products and services you received. Your individual responses will remain confidential and will be compiled with those of other customers to improve customer service. Please use the following scale to indicate the extent to which you agree with the statement. Circle one response for each item.

1 = Strongly Disagree
2 = Disagree
3 = Neutral
4 = Agree
5 = Strongly Agree
? = Unsure

If you feel unable to adequately rate a specific item, please leave it blank.

QUALITY

I had to wait an unreasonable amount of time for my requests to be met .... 1 2 3 4 5 ?

The products I have received have met my expectations.......... 1 2 3 4 5 ?

My requests were met on or before the agreed upon deadline.......... 1 2 3 4 5 ?

The products I have received have generally been error free.......... 1 2 3 4 5 ?

SERVICE/ATTITUDE

When serving me, this person:

Was helpful.......... 1 2 3 4 5 ?

Was cooperative in meeting my requests.......... 1 2 3 4 5 ?

Communicated with me to understand my expectations for products.......... 1 2 3 4 5 ?

Was uncooperative when I asked for revisions/additional information.......... 1 2 3 4 5 ?

Told me when my requests would be filled.......... 1 2 3 4 5 ?

When necessary, sufficiently explained to me why my expectations could not be met.......... 1 2 3 4 5 ?

Kept me informed about the status of my request.......... 1 2 3 4 5 ?

CUSTOMER SATISFACTION

How would you rate your overall level of satisfaction with the *service* you have received?

1 = Very Dissatisfied
2 = Dissatisfied
3 = Neutral
4 = Satisfied
5 = Very Satisfied

What specifically could be done to make you more satisfied with the *service*?

____
____
____

How would you rate your overall level of satisfaction with the *products* you have received?

1 = Very Dissatisfied
2 = Dissatisfied
3 = Neutral
4 = Satisfied
5 = Very Satisfied

What specifically could be done to make you more satisfied with the *products*?

____
____
____

Customer Appraisal Form

Source: Cardy, R. L., and Dobbins, G. H. (1994). *Performance appraisal: Alternative perspectives.* Cincinnati, OH: South-Western.

that the rater is too soft. There is also hesitation to implement 360° systems in China because the Chinese culture includes great respect for authority and peer and subordinate evaluation suggests a relinquishment of authority. The feedback potential of a 360° appraisal system is great, but managers need to be aware of the cultural minefields that may make implementation of such a system difficult.

The shift to a 360° system can be a major change that requires careful planning to be successful. Many organizations have implemented 360° appraisal systems because it seems to be the popular thing to do rather than out of a desire to provide feedback and promote the development of employees. If the goal is simply putting in place a feedback instrument, it is doubtful that the system will be implemented and maintained in a way that will lead to maximal effectiveness. Recent surveys found that 360° review systems can be associated with a decrease in market value of an organization.[82] Such findings regarding the possible negative effects of the 360° approach doesn't mean it is a bad approach. The importance of the system's purpose and how it is implemented is, however, underscored as a critical factor. Just jumping on the 360° bandwagon isn't a strategy that can be expected to pay off. The Manager's Notebook titled "Key Steps in Implementing 360° Appraisal" provides steps to follow that should result in an effective and acceptable system.

MANAGER'S NOTEBOOK

Key Steps in Implementing 360° Appraisal

To create a successful 360° appraisal program, companies should proceed as follows:

1. Top management communicates the goals of and need for 360° appraisal.
2. Employees and managers are involved in the development of the appraisal criteria and appraisal process.
3. Employees are trained in how to give and receive feedback.
4. Employees are informed of the nature of the 360° appraisal instrument and process.
5. The 360° system undergoes pilot testing in one part of the organization.
6. Management continuously reinforces the goals of the 360° appraisal and is ready to change the process when necessary.

Source: Adapted from Milliman, J. F., Zawacki, R. A., Norman, C., Powell, L., and Kirksey, J. (1994, November). Companies evaluate employees from all perspectives. *Personnel Journal*, 99–103.

Collecting performance appraisals from many sources can be time consuming and expensive. Consider the costs that a 360° system can involve:

Situation: 400 employees each receive feedback from 12 raters using a questionnaire that takes, on average, 30 minutes to fill out.

Total Time Calculation: 30 minutes × 12 raters per ratee = 6 rater hours
6 rater hours × 400 ratees = 2,400 hours
2,400 hours ÷ 8 hours per workday = 300 workdays

If the average daily salary is $200, then the rater-time cost for administering the 360° system would be $60,000.

Companies can significantly reduce the time need for 360° appraisal by putting the appraisal system on-line. Computerizing the system can streamline the process and reduce the amount of time raters need to devote to the evaluation task. For example, with an automated system a 90-item questionnaire may take only 30 minutes to complete, compared to 45 minutes for a paper questionnaire. The evaluations may also be better because the rating task demands less time from the raters.

Computerizing the 360° system can reduce many other costs as well. These include:

- **Paper costs.** In a computerized system, the costs of paper and paper handling are trivial. In a traditional system, they are quite high. For example, at one airline that conducts 360° appraisal each rater receives 47 pieces of paper (including instructions, rating forms, and envelopes). Each of the 16,000 employees also receives 9 to 21 pages of feed-back on their own performance. The paper costs certainly add up. By computerizing its appraisal system, this airline could save nearly 1 million pages of paper per year.
- **Administrative overhead.** Going online can greatly reduce administrative overhead. One expert has estimated that computerizing the 360° system decreases the number of people dedicated to managing the system from three full-time employees per 1,000 participants to one employee per 2,000 participants.[83]

Directing Attention to the Causes of Problems

After supervisor and worker have discussed and agreed on the causes of performance problems, the next step is to take action to control them. If certain factors affect performance positively, managers should try to ensure that those factors are present as much as possible. In the more common case of constraining factors, managers should try to reduce or eliminate them.

Figure 7.12

How to Determine and Remedy Performance Shortfalls

Cause	Questions to Ask	Possible Remedies
Ability	Has the worker ever been able to perform adequately? Can others perform the job adequately, but not this worker?	Train Transfer Redesign job Terminate
Effort	Is the worker's performance level declining? Is performance lower on all tasks?	Clarity linkage between performance and rewards Recognize good performance
Situation	Is performance erratic? Are performance problems showing up in all workers, even those who have adequate supplies and equipment?	Streamline work process Clarify needs to suppliers Change suppliers Eliminate conflicting signals or demands Provide adequate tools

Source: Adapted from Schermerhorn, J. R., Gardner, W. I., and Martin, T. N. (1990). Management dialogues: Turning on the marginal performer. *Organizational Dynamics, 18*, 47–59; and Rummler, G. A. (1972). Human performance problems and their solutions. *Human Resource Management, 19*, 2–10.

Depending on whether the cause of performance problems is related to ability, effort, or situational characteristics, very different tactics are called for. As Figure 7.12 makes clear, different remedies are required for different categories of performance shortfalls. Leaping to a remedy like training (a common reaction) will not fix a problem that is caused by ability and will be a waste of the organization's resources.[84]

Developing an Action Plan and Empowering Workers to Reach a Solution

Effective performance management requires empowering workers to improve their performance. The traditional management approach of supervisors giving orders and workers following them usually does not lead to maximum performance levels. The newer empowerment approach requires supervisors to take on the role of coach rather than director and controller.[85] As in a sports team, the supervisor-as-coach assists workers in interpreting and reacting to the work situation. The role is not necessarily one of mentor, friend, or counselor. Rather, it is that of enabler. The supervisor-as-coach works to ensure that the necessary resources are available to workers and helps employees identify an action plan to solve performance problems. For example, the supervisor may suggest ways for the worker to eliminate, avoid, or get around situational obstacles to performance. In addition to creating a supportive, empowered work environment, coach/supervisors clarify performance expectations; provide immediate feedback; and strive to eliminate unnecessary rules, procedures, and other constraints.[86] The most effective performance may result from being specific about desired outcomes but not giving too many details about how the worker should strive to reach these goals.[87] Too much detail is contrary to an empowered approach and may stifle and demoralize an employee. The Manager's Notebook entitled "Coaching Effectiveness" provides an example assessment of the coaching function.

Customer-Driven HR

MANAGER'S NOTEBOOK

Coaching Effectiveness

When managers are reluctant to be good coaches to their workers, adding to the managers performance appraisal a measure of how well they are coaching their workers can change all that.

Including coaching as a dimension in the appraisal of managers signals the importance that the organization places on coaching and helps assure that it is done as well as possible. Here is an example of the items used by a company to assess how well the coaching function is being carried out. Workers' assessments on these items are used by the company to reward the coaching strengths of managers and to identify areas needing development.

Use the scale below to respond to each of the following items.

1	2	3	4	5
Never	Seldom	Sometimes	Frequently	Always

- My coaching sessions are held every month.
- My coaching sessions are long enough.
- My coach sets challenging but achievable performance goals for me to accomplish.
- My coach sets too many performance goals for me to accomplish.
- My coach shares with me his/her thoughts and feelings, not only facts.
- My coach asks for and appreciates my ideas and suggestions.
- My coaching sessions are stimulating and help me do my job better.
- Because of my coach's position, I would be afraid to question his/her decisions.
- Because of my coach's personality, I would be afraid to question his/her decisions.
- My coach plays favorites when resolving conflicts.
- When my coach delegates work to me, he/she checks and rechecks the smallest details to my frustration and annoyance.
- My coach provides me with the skills and knowledge to be successful.
- My coach is eager to explore my career path in the organization and what I need to do to get there.
- My coach continuously keeps me informed about where the organization is going and keeps me updated on what the other departments and branches are doing.

General Comments:

Source: Adapted with permission from O'Connor, T. J. (2002). Performance management via coaching: Good coaching can help guarantee profitable results and happy employees in an uncertain economy. *Electrical Wholesaling*, *83*, 39(3).

Directing Communication at Performance

Communication between supervisor and worker is critical to effective performance management. Exactly what is communicated and how it is communicated can determine whether performance improves or declines.

It is important that communication regarding performance be directed at the performance and not at the person. For example, a worker should not be asked why he is such a jerk! It is usually much more effective to ask the worker why his performance has been ineffective lately. Open-minded communication is more likely to uncover the real reason for a performance problem and thus pave the way for an effective solution.

The Manager's Notebook titled "Give-and-Take! Tips for Better Performance Reviews" gives tips on providing for and receiving performance feedback. As a future manager, you will be on both the giving and the receiving end of the performance feedback process, so it is important to learn to do both well.

MANAGER'S NOTEBOOK

Customer-Driven HR

Give-and-Take! Tips for Better Performance Reviews

Performance appraisal is usually put off, avoided, and not done well by many managers. However, effective appraisal is something that every employee should receive. Here are tips that might help managers do a more effective job of reviewing performance.

- **Start with the raw data.** Review quantifiable data and critical incidents of performance. You should have a system for recording and retrieving performance information and use it to make your performance ratings. If you don't have such a system or don't use it, it can appear to workers that your performance evaluations are subjective, based on personality or other factors, or biased.
- **Make sure you are evaluating performance on appropriate dimensions.** Perhaps the job has substantially changed and the job analysis and performance appraisal systems haven't kept pace. Are the dimensions on which you are evaluating the person still relevant?
- **Beware of rating biases.** Avoid the "recency effect." That is, do not emphasize minor things because they were recent while there may be other more important things that occurred months ago. Also avoid the tendency to attribute the cause of poor performance to be the worker. Make sure you have your facts straight and have an accurate understanding of the situation surrounding the worker's performance.
- **Support ratings with written comments.** Employees will want and deserve to know the basis for the levels they were rated. You need to provide explanation and justification for your performance judgments.
- **Evaluate several or all of your people at one time, if possible.** Doing performance assessments on multiple people at the same time can help assure that you are using the standards consistently for everyone.
- **Stick with performance and stay away from inferences about cause.** Evaluate observed performance but stay focused solely on performance. For example, a worker may have a problem with absences and lateness. You must give this worker appropriate feedback and, perhaps, explain why absences and lateness are problems in the workplace. (You shouldn't wait for a formal performance review session to provide this kind of feedback to the workers.) However, you need to confine yourself to dealing only with performance. To offer your conjecture or inferences concerning the cause(s) of performance problems may get you into legal difficulty. For example, offering your conclusion that the absences and late arrivals may be due to a drug or alcohol dependency may form the basis of a legal situation in which the employee claims she or he is perceived by you to be disabled. Even if drug or alcohol dependency was not part of the picture, the employee could conceivably argue that he or she should be protected by the Americans with Disabilities Act, since your perception was that he or she had a drug or alcohol problem. Stay with performance and you'll avoid such legally sticky messes.
- **Be consistent across workers.** If two workers have been late to work but it is mentioned in the performance review of only one of them, you are asking for trouble. People talk and compare and even an inadvertent difference could be interpreted to be evidence of unfairness and bias.

Source: Adapted with permission from *Pay for Performance Report* (2002). Two tools to boost a sub-par performance management process. January Newsletter of the Institute of Management and Administration, 2–4.

Summary and Conclusions

What Is Performance Appraisal?

Performance appraisal is the identification, measurement, and management of human performance in organizations. Appraisal should be a future-oriented activity that provides workers with useful feedback and coaches them to higher levels of performance. Appraisal can be used administratively or developmentally.

Identifying Performance Dimensions

Performance appraisal begins by identifying the dimensions of performance that determine effective job performance. Job analysis is the mechanism by which performance dimensions should be identified.

Measuring Performance

The methods used to measure employee performance can be classified in two ways: (1) whether the type of judgment called for is relative or absolute, and (2) whether the measure focuses on traits, behavior, or outcomes. Each measure has its advantages and disadvantages. But it is clear that the overall quality of ratings is much more a function of the rater's motivation and ability than of the type of instrument chosen.

Managers face five challenges in managing performance: rater errors and bias; the influence of liking, organizational politics; whether to focus on the individual or the group; and legal issues (including discrimination and employment at will).

Managing Performance

The primary goal of any appraisal system is performance management. To manage and improve their employees' performance, managers must explore the causes of performance problems, direct manager and employee attention to those causes, develop action plans and empower workers to find solutions, and use performance-focused communication.

Key Terms

absolute judgment, 226
behavioral appraisal instrument, 229
comparability, 233
dimension, 224
frame-of-reference (FOR) training, 233
management by objectives (MBO), 230
outcome appraisal instruments, 230
peer review, 243
performance appraisal, 222
rater error, 232
relative judgment, 225
self-review, 243
situational factor or system factors, 242
subordinate review, 243
360° feedback, 244
trait appraisal instrument, 228

Discussion Questions

1. AT ARCO Transportation, a $1 billion division of Atlantic Richfield, employees are hired, promoted, and appraised according to how they fulfill the performance dimensions most valued by the company. One of these performance dimensions is "communication"—specifically, "listens and observes attentively, allowing an exchange of information" and "speaks and writes clearly and concisely, with an appropriate awareness of the intended audience." Would you say that ARCO appraises performance based on personality traits, job behavior, or outcome achieved? On which of these three aspects of performance do you think workers should be appraised?
2. Superficially, it seems preferable to use objective performance data (such as productivity figures), when available, rather than subjective supervisory ratings to assess employees. Why might objective data be less effective performance measures than subjective ratings?
3. How important are rating formats to the quality of performance ratings? What is the most important influence on rating quality?
4. What is comparability? How can it be maximized in performance appraisal?
5. "Occasionally an employee comes along who needs to be reminded who the boss is, and the appraisal is an appropriate place for such a reminder." Would the manager quoted here be likely to use a rational or a political approach to appraisal? Contrast the rational and political approaches. To what extent is it possible to separate the two?
6. Do you think performance appraisal should be done? Is it worth the cost?
7. What criteria do you think should be used to measure team performance? What sources should be used for the appraisal? Should individual performance still be measured? Why or why not?
8. You're the owner of a 25-employee company that has just had a fantastic year. Everyone pulled together and worked hard to achieve the boost in company profits. Unfortunately, you need to sink most of those profits into paying your suppliers. All you can afford to give your workers is a 3 percent pay raise across the board. At appraisal time, how would you communicate praise for a job well done coupled with your very limited ability to reward such outstanding performance? Now assume you can afford to hand out some handsome bonuses or raises. What would be the best way to evaluate employees when *everyone* has done exceptional work?
9. Would you design a performance appraisal system based on behaviors, outcomes, or both? Why would you design it in this way?

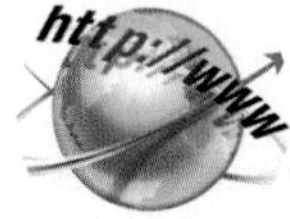

There is a variety of additional material available on the Web site that accompanies this text. You can access this information by visiting the Web site at **www.prenhall.com/gomez.**

Discussion Case 7.1

YOU MANAGE IT!

How Well Do You Play Your Roles?

The growing reality in many workplaces today is that people really do not have a static "job." In many cases, employees' jobs are highly dynamic and often vary depending on the project. This variability is especially true if employees work in teams. For example, on one project an employee may play the role of technical expert and another member may take on the role of a team leader. On another project that same worker may work to keep team communication open and the project on schedule, whereas someone else may act as the technical expert. In a dynamic work environment, traditional appraisal based on job descriptions may be sorely inadequate. People with the same job title could be performing substantially different roles. Further, the roles they play may differ across projects and over time. As a result, important performance issues may not be captured by traditional performance appraisal.

One approach to solving this deficiency is to appraise people on the roles they perform at work. Role-based performance appraisal is used in a handful of companies and initial results indicate that the system captures important aspects of performance that are not measured with a traditional appraisal system. HR personnel and managers developed measures for roles such as "Team Player," "Innovator;" and "Job." Brief descriptions of these roles and the types of measures used for each are shown next.

Role	Measure
Team player	Responsive to needs of others in team
	Making sure his or her work group succeeds
Innovator	Creating better processes
	Coming up with new ideas
Job	Quantity of work output
	Quality of work output

Critical Thinking Questions

1. What other roles and additional measures do you think would be useful for role-based appraisal?
2. Rafael wants to put more emphasis on being a team player while Sarah wants to delve into making creative contributions for the coming appraisal period. However, both need to continue to perform their job functions.
   a. Design a system that would allow people choice in what they do and, thus, have flexibility in what they are held accountable for.
   b. Do you think people should be given the chance to place greater or lesser weight on various roles they might play? Why or why not?
3. What advantage might a role-based appraisal system offer to the organization? To the worker?
4. One company that pilot tested role-based appraisal found that although the organization's mission was to promote teamwork, the team player ratings were poor. Assume you are a manager in the company. You realize that the stated values of the business do not match the business activities, so the current emphasis on teamwork is unfair. What would you do to rectify this problem?

Source: Welbourne, T. M., Johnson, D. E., and Erez. A. (1998). The role-based performance scale: Validity analysis of a theory-based measure. *Academy of Management Journal, 41*, 540–555.

Customer-Driven HR Case 7.2

YOU MANAGE IT!

Performance Review Software: Making a Difficult Job Easier or Making Things Worse?

Most all workers want and deserve to know how they are doing. But many managers dread appraising the performance of workers and either put it off or not do it very well. However, everyone wants and deserves to know how they are doing. A growing number of companies are offering technology that promises to solve this problem. Software can now not only make the rating task paperless and as easy as point and click, but also generating feedback and performance improvement suggestions can be entirely automated. For example, PerformaWorks is a company that offers a software package, called eWorkbench, that allows 360° appraisal by bosses, peers, subordinates, and even customers.[a] The software is designed to evaluate employees on goals tied to the organization's objectives. The software can calculate the extent to which each employee has contributed to those objectives and, therefore, to the organization's bottom line. The program provides an electronic means for aligning everyone with the same mission and making sure everyone is working toward the same organizational goals. KnowledgePoint is another company that offers an electronic appraisal tool. The KnowledgePoint software is Web based and focuses on goals and competencies that can be generic or customized (see www.performancereview.com). In addition, depending on rating levels, the software generates a narrative performance summary to hand to the worker that describes performance levels on competencies or goals and suggests actions the worker should take to improve performance.

Critical Thinking Questions

1. What advantages might there be to using the types of software just described for evaluating the performance of workers? Are there rational advantages, such as speed? What about political advantages, such as a manager being able to blame a poor performance review on the software?
2. What disadvantages might there be to using the electronic approach to performance reviews? Examine this issue from the perspectives of both managers and employees.
3. The major vendors of hosted online performance appraisal systems include KnowledgePoint, Softscape, PerformaWorks, and SuccessFactors.com. These applications can vary in price depending on the number of employees and degree of functionality desired. However, a price of around $100,000 is typical for a midsized firm.[b] The electronic approach offers savings in time and labor. A traditional (paper-based) approach to performance appraisal has been estimated to cost $1,500 per employee,[c] with some of the sources of this cost being time spent (1) setting goals and objectives, (2) conducting reviews, (3) designing, printing, copying, filing, and distributing appraisal forms, (4) training supervisors to conduct appraisals, and (5) dealing with postappraisal appeals and grievances. An electronic approach might eliminate the costs of designing, printing, and so on, but the approach may not influence the other sources of cost. Do you think the costs of the online performance appraisal systems are worth it? Why? Consider expected costs and benefits to provide a rationale for your answer.
4. Examine the steps involved in reviewing performance. Considering these steps as separable parts of a bundle of performance review actions, are there parts that make sense to do electronically and automatically? Are there other parts that shouldn't be done that way? Go back to the lists of advantages and disadvantages you identified in your response to questions 1 and 2. Examine these advantages and disadvantages to see if some are particularly associated with making certain steps in the review process electronic and automatic. Given the pattern that you find in regard to advantages and disadvantages associated with certain steps, build an electronic performance review system that you think would be maximally effective (for example, work efficiently, be accepted, provide useful information, and so on). What parts would be electronic? What steps would be automated? Which would not? Describe your proposed system and your rationale for it to the rest of the class.

Team Exercise

Divide your team into proponents and antagonists in regard to taking an electronic and automated approach to reviewing performance. Debate the merits and drawbacks of the electronic approach. Structure your debate around the perspectives of key constituents (for example, managers, workers, and customers). Also consider a rational versus a political approach in considering the pluses and minuses. Also consider key criteria (such as acceptance of the feedback, ease of use, impact on performance, and so on).

Is there a clear outcome to your debate? Should performance reviews be electronic and automated or not? Describe the outcome of your debate to the rest of the class and explain some of the conclusions that led to this outcome.

[a]Parker, V. L. (2000, December 31). Software for hard task: Job reviews/Raleigh company sells it. *The News & Observer*, E1.
[b]*Managing HR Information Systems*. (2001). Latest software puts performance appraisal online and cuts costs. February Newsletter of the Institute of Management and Administration, 12–14.
[c]Dutton, G. (2002). Making reviews more efficient and fair. *Workforce*, *80*, 76. www.performancereview.com.

YOU MANAGE IT! Customer-Driven HR Case 7.3

From Formal Appraisal to Informal Feedback and Development: The Power of Coaching

Performance management is often viewed as an annual evaluative snapshot that is linked to an expected sum of money. As such, it has been likened to the task of doing taxes[a]: Nobody looks forward to doing it, filling out the forms is a pain, but we all hope that the result leads to a nice check. Performance management can and should be much more than an exercise linked to compensation. Performance management should focus on improving performance and helping people to develop their maximum potential to perform. One way to achieve this is through coaching workers. For performance potential to be realized, managers need to be more than evaluators and bureaucrats who complete forms. They need to embrace the role of coach.

ABC Electrical Supply (fictitious name, real company) provides an example of an organization that has made coaching a priority and a key part of how performance is managed.[b] ABC used its performance appraisal system as a means to assure that coaching would be taken seriously and done well. Effective coaching is a collaboration between manager and worker in which short- and long-term goals are discussed and set. Then feedback, reviews, and potential solutions are exchanged. In short, coaching involves a partnership focused on performance. Done well, coaching can improve performance, lead to greater learning and understanding, and improve trust and loyalty. ABC considers coaching as a continuing and informal process; the formal coaching program includes a monthly meeting between manager and subordinate. The monthly meetings are focused on sharing business-related information and evaluation of progress on individual performance goals. These performance goals are identified by first considering the overall organizational strategy and related department goals. Individual performance goals are then generated that fit with and contribute to this context. To help make sure that coaching is on track and being done effectively, ABC has workers annually appraise the performance of coaches. The appraisal survey used by ABC is presented in the You Manage It! below. The assessments provided on this survey are then used with each manager/coach to identify coaching development needs and to reinforce coaching strengths.

Critical Thinking Questions

1. A major difficulty in implementing effective performance coaching programs is the resistance of managers to perform the role of coach. Why do you think managers might be reluctant to take on this role? How would you go about implementing a coaching program that would eliminate or reduce the resistance of managers?
2. An old saying relevant to performance appraisal is "What gets measured gets done." Do you think that the performance coaching program at ABC, or any organization, could work without being made part of the manager's evaluation? Do you think it should be part of the appraisal of managers? Why or why not?
3. How would you handle a manager who doesn't coach very well (for example, the manager has poor interpersonal skills and has difficulty giving effective feedback)?
4. How do you think a manager who believes that performance coaching takes away from more important tasks and is a waste of time should be handled?

Team Exercise

As a team, brainstorm the aspects of coaching that you think are important. You can start by looking at the survey used by ABC Electrical Supply but focus more on the actual coaching sessions. What would you want a coach to do? What should a coach do? Once you have identified these aspects, develop rating scales to use for assessing these aspects. What type of rating scales should be used? Why?

Have someone in your team role-play the part of a worker and someone else play the role of manager/coach. Use the rating scales you developed to rate the coaching performance and to help direct feedback to the person playing this role. Do you think that this process of evaluation and feedback could lead to improved coaching? How would you recommend that your rating scales be used? For example, should observers use the rating scales, or should they be completed by the worker or manager?

Performance is often a team-level issue, even though it is composed of individual performers. How would you recommend that coaching take place at a team level? Would your rating scales need to be modified for use with a team of workers?

Share your rating scales and recommendations for their use with the rest of the class.

---

[a] *Pay for Performance Report*. (2002). Performance management: Make it work, make it fun. March Newsletter of the Institute of Management and Administration.

[b] O'Connor, T. J. (2002). Performance management via coaching: Good coaching can help guarantee profitable results and happy employees in an uncertain economy. *Electrical Wholesaling*, *83*, 39(3).

Emerging Trends Case 7.4

YOU MANAGE IT!

Tightening the Appraisal Noose

Performance standards have been tightening at many companies over the past year.[a] The recent economic downturn has led to companies being concerned with reducing costs and obtaining top performance from workers. Furthermore, the prevalence of layoffs has resulted in a pool of unemployed workers that includes some who are very talented and well trained. This puts organizations in the position to demand better performance from their current workers, to dismiss workers who aren't performing satisfactorily, and to bring in new workers if current workers' performance is not satisfactory.

Capital One Financial Corporation, a credit card company, provides an example of an organization in which performance standards have been tightened and performance-based dismissals have been occurring at a fast pace.[b] A Capital One spokesperson has stated that the company has tightened performance standards over the past year and that more workers are now being dismissed for poor performance. The company points out that the more stringent performance standards and dismissals mean that top-performing employees can be better rewarded for their efforts and that the company is better positioned to meet its financial goals. However, many workers would disagree that the strategy is a positive change and have accused the company of conducting a disguised layoff.

According to a former Capital One employee: "People just disappear. . . . One day someone is here, the next day the desk is empty and the phone is dead." Some former employees claim that they were fired even though they received good performance reviews. One former employee said that a very generous severance package was offered but believes the termination couldn't be justified. A job placement firm in Virginia, the home state of Capital One, has been working with a lot of former Capital One employees and concludes that the company is engaged in an across-the-board reduction in force. The company denies this and points to approximately 100 job openings posted on the company's Web site. The facts are that the company did hire 4,000 workers in the past year. However, accounting for the number of people voluntarily or involuntarily leaving the organization, the net gain in employment was 900. Once hired, Capital One employees receive performance appraisals twice a year, from both supervisors and peers. The company has stated that a more disciplined approach is now taken in managing performance. The company is trying to differentiate among the performance levels of people who previously may have been lumped together in the performance management process.

Critical Thinking Questions

1. Do you think the performance appraisal system at Capital One was too lenient in the past?
2. Could the performance management system at Capital One now be too harsh? How can you tell?
3. The Labor Department reported on Tuesday, May 7, 2002, that productivity in the first quarter of 2002 was at its highest level in 19 years. In part, the productivity increase has been due to cutting labor costs, such as through layoffs, but also to increasing the output per worker.[c]
   a. Do you think there may be a relationship between companies, such as Capital One, taking a more stringent approach in performance appraisal and the upturn in productivity? Explain.
   b. If there is a link between the more disciplined approach to measuring and managing performance and productivity gains, why do you think that is? For example, has productivity increased because organizations have managed to clear out deadwood? Or has productivity increased because workers are frantically and stressfully working in a state of fear that they might be next to be terminated?

Team Exercise

Trying to wring out cost reductions and output improvements by more stringently measuring and managing performance can have advantages and disadvantages. For example, productivity might be improved but at a cost of lowered employee satisfaction and loyalty.

Divide your team into two sides, one promoting the advantages of a more stringent approach to performance appraisal and the other promoting the disadvantages. Debate the extent to which the approach leads to positive or negative outcomes. You can look at this issue from short- and long-range perspectives, and from the perspectives of a company, employees, and society at large. Can your team reach a consensus on whether it recommends the approach?

Share with the rest of the class the advantages and disadvantages identified by your team. Indicate your conclusion about the stringent approach and your rationale for the recommendation.

---

[a]*Financial Executive*. (2002). Doing smarter performance reviews, *18*, 12.
[b]Hayard, C. (2002, April 13). Firings on rise at Capital One: Firm cites tougher performance rules. *Richmond Times-Dispatch*, A, 1.
[c]*Arizona Republic*. (2002, May 8). Productivity up most in 19 years as companies cut payrolls, D1.

YOU MANAGE IT!

Emerging Trends Case 7.5

Implementing the Balanced Scorecard Concept

The balanced scorecard concept was introduced 10 years ago by David Norton and Harvard Business School Professor Robert Kaplan. The thrust of the balanced scorecard is that financial measures do not adequately capture how effectively an organization is performing, so other dimensions need to be included. Specifically, customer service, process characteristics, and innovation are the additional dimensions typically included in a balanced scorecard approach. The purpose of the balanced scorecard is to give a broader perspective on performance than the perspective provided by simple financial outcomes. Although financial outcomes are a critical measure of effectiveness, the other dimensions can provide an early indication of how well things are operating. For example, problems in customer service and process difficulties may show up long before an impact on financial outcomes is seen. In addition to a broader view of effectiveness and an early warning system of sorts, the balanced scorecard is meant to tie performance measures to the strategic direction of the organization. What aspects of each of the dimensions should be measured is an issue that should be addressed with the strategy of the organization firmly in mind. Everything can't be measured, and even if it could, there would be too much information and a lack of focus. The key performance measures, those measures that link to the organization's mission, must be identified.[a]

The balanced scorecard has been applied to the performance of functions or to units. For example, the balanced scorecard concept can be used to generate performance measures that align with the strategy of the organization. The balanced scorecard has been used at a broader level than the individual worker. However, the concept can be used to align individual performance with strategic goals and to develop a broad perspective of the performance effectiveness of individual workers.

Critical Thinking Questions

1. Apply the balanced scorecard approach to measuring individual performance. A scorecard typically has four quadrants, with each quadrant focusing on a particular dimension. Try using the following labels for the four quadrants:
   a. outcomes/results (in place of financial measures)
   b. behaviors/actions (in place of process characteristics)
   c. customer service
   d. learning/development/growth (in place of innovation)

   For each of the four quadrants, identify example performance measures.
2. Using this quadrant framework, generate measures that fit a particular strategy. For example, you might select customer service, sales, low cost, or high quality as strategic goals for an organization. Select or generate a strategy and identify performance measures for each quadrant that fit with the strategic goal.
3. Given the four-quadrant scorecard you just developed, assign relative weights to the quadrants. Not all aspects may be equally important and the weight placed on a dimension depends on the context and the purpose for measures on that dimension. For your strategic context, determine the relative weight, or importance, of the dimensions in the four quadrants. You might allocate 100 points across the four dimensions as a way to represent the weighting system. Once you have identified the weights, how could they be used in the performance measurement system?
4. For the scorecard you developed, indicate which performance measures are laggards and which would be leading indicators. What actions should you take as a manager if a worker isn't exhibiting adequate performance on a leading indicator? On a lagging indicator?

Team Exercise

Applying the balanced scorecard approach to the measurement of individual performance offers the promise of a broader perspective on performance and alignment of individual performance with strategic goals. However, making the balanced scorecard approach operational and effective at the individual level is a large task.

As a team, develop an implementation plan for a balanced scorecard approach to measuring individual performance. Include whatever aspects you think are important, but be sure to address the following issues.

- **Who should evaluate?** Is the balanced scorecard best used as a self-appraisal tool? If others should be included as sources of appraisal, who should be included? Should some measures or quadrants be evaluated by some sources and not others? Identify the best sources for each quadrant.
- **Technology.** What type of system will your balanced scorecard be? The typical more macro-approach to the balanced scorecard can be accomplished electronically (see www.balancedscorecard.com). Should the individual level approach be, for example, Web based?
- **Training?** Do you think training will be needed to effectively implement the system? If so, describe.
- **Feedback.** Feedback is critical to performance improvement. How often will feedback be provided in your system and who will provide it?
- **Rollout.** Will you implement it across the board or do a pilot test?

---

[a]Cameron, P. (2002). The balancing act: Even in today's volatile economic climate, many organizations are turning to the balanced scorecard to help steer their organization in the right direction. *CMA Management, 75*, 28(4).

Appendix to Chapter 7

The Critical Incident Technique: A Method for Developing a Behaviorally Based Appraisal Instrument

The critical incident technique (CIT) is one of many types of job-analysis procedures. The CIT is often used because it produces behavioral statements that make explicit to an employee what is required and to a rater what the basis for an evaluation should be.

CIT Steps

The following steps are involved in a complete CIT procedure:

1. **Identify the major dimensions of job performance.**
   This can be done by asking a group of raters and ratees to brainstorm and generate dimensions relevant to job performance. Each person lists, say, three dimensions. The group members then combine their lists and eliminate redundancies.
2. **Generate "critical incidents" of performance.**
   For each dimension, the group members should list as many incidents as they can think of that represent effective, average, and ineffective performance levels. Each person should think back over the past 6 to 12 months for examples of performance-related behaviors that they have witnessed. Each incident should include the surrounding circumstances or situation.

   If you are having trouble generating incidents, you might want to think of the following situation:

   Suppose someone said that person A, whom you feel is the most effective person in the job, is a poor performer. What incidents of person A's behavior would you cite to change the critic's opinion?

   Try to make sure that the incidents you list are observable *behaviors* and not *personality characteristics* (traits).
3. **Double-check that the incidents represent one dimension.**
   This step is called *retranslation*. Here you are trying to make sure there is clear agreement on which incidents represent which performance dimension. If there is substantial disagreement among group members, this incident may need to be clarified. Alternatively, another dimension may need to be added or some dimensions may need to be merged.

   In the retranslation process, each person in the group is asked to indicate what dimension each incident represents. If everyone agrees, the group moves on to the next incident. Any incidents on which there is disagreement are put to the side for further examination at the end of the process. At that time they may be discarded or rewritten.
4. **Assign effectiveness to each incident.**
   Effectiveness values are assigned to all the incidents that survived retranslation. How much is incident "A" worth in our organization, on, say, an effectiveness scale of 1 (unacceptable) to 7 (excellent)? All group members should rate each incident. If there is substantial disagreement regarding the value of a certain behavior, that behavior should be discarded.

NOTE: Disagreement on incident values indicates differences in valuative standards or lack of clarity in organizational policy. 0 in valuative standards can be a fundamental problem in appraisal. The CIT procedure can help to reduce these differences.

The following are some CIT worksheets for you to try your hand at. The dimensions included are a subset of those generated in a research project conducted for a hospital that wanted a common evaluation tool for all nonnursing employees.*

Critical Incidents Worksheet
Job Title:
Job Dimension: Knowledge of Job—Understanding of the position held and the job's policies, techniques, rules, materials, and manual skills.
Instructions: Provide at least one behavioral statement for each performance level.
1. Needs improvement:
2. Satisfactory:
3. Excellent:
4. Outstanding:

Critical Incidents Worksheet
Job Title:
Job Dimension: Initiative—The enthusiasm to get things done, energy exerted, willingness to accept and perform responsibilities and assignments; seeks better ways to achieve results.
Instructions: Provide at least one behavioral statement for each performance level.
1. Needs improvement:
2. Satisfactory:
3. Excellent:
4. Outstanding:

Critical Incidents Worksheet
Job Title:
Job Dimension: Personal Relations—Attitude and response to supervision, relationships with coworkers, flexibility in working as part of the organization.
Instructions: Provide at least one behavioral statement for each performance level.
1. Needs improvement:
2. Satisfactory:
3. Excellent:
4. Outstanding:

Critical Incidents Worksheet
Job Title:
Job Dimension:
Dependability—Attention to responsibility without supervision, meeting of deadlines.
Instructions: Provide at least one behavioral statement for each performance level.
1. Needs improvement:
2. Satisfactory:
3. Excellent:
4. Outstanding:

The jobs covered ranged from floor sweeper and clerical worker to laboratory technician and social worker. Of course, the behavioral standards for each dimension differed across jobs—an excellent floor sweeper behavior would not be the same as an excellent lab technician behavior. The dimensions included in the worksheets appear fairly generic, though, and are probably applicable to jobs in most organizations. You may want to develop more specific dimensions or other dimensions altogether.

Remember, after generating incidents, your group should determine agreement levels for the dimension and value for each incident. An easy way to do this is for one person to recite an incident and have everyone respond with dimension and value. This process could be informal and verbal or formal and written.

*Goodale, J. G., and Burke, R. J. (1975). Behaviorally based rating scales need not be job specific. *Journal of Applied Psychology, 60*, 389–391.

Training the Workforce

Challenges

After reading this chapter, you should be able to deal more effectively with the following challenges:

1. **Determine** when employees need training and the best type of training given a company's circumstances.
2. **Recognize** the characteristics that make training programs successful.
3. **Weigh** the costs and benefits of a computer-based training program.
4. **Design** job aids as complements or alternatives to training.
5. **Understand** how to socialize new employees effectively.

Training is usually conducted when employees have a skill deficit or when an organization changes a system and employees need to learn new skills. But what about learning better ways to do business—even when employees are highly skilled and systems are established? And rather than focus on individuals' learning skills, maybe teams of employees can learn from each other. Johnson Controls has developed one approach to training that might serve as a model for empowered work environments.

Johnson Controls is a global market leader in automotive systems and facility management and control. The company's automotive business is based in Plymouth, Michigan, and the organization employs more than 57,000 people at 275 facilities around the world. The company's training and development group, the Leadership Institute, sponsors an event that enables workers to learn from each other. The program, called Team Rally, began in 1996 with the participation of 31 North American teams. The event in 1999 involved 125 teams from around the world.

In the Team Rally competition, teams use entertaining skits to demonstrate how they improved operations or service at Johnson Controls. Some teams use parodies of television (*Gilligan's Island*) or movies (*Star Wars*) to entertain and present the teams' project results in improving productivity or quality and decreasing waste. One 1998 team entertained the participants with a skit that showed how their improvements generated annual savings of more than $6 million. Teams are judged on their results, how efficiently they share improvements with other employee facilities, and other factors.

Although entertaining, the team competition trains employees to use current systems more effectively. The Team Rally program won't work in all situations (for example, when a system is being changed and people need to learn the new skills that will be needed), but it is a powerful tool for training employees on how to improve the use of current systems.

Source: Adapted from Roznowski, D. (1999, August 19). Johnson Controls employees help to reduce cost, waste, and increase safety, quality through team rally event. *PR Newswire Association, Inc.*

THE MANAGERIAL PERSPECTIVE

As the opening vignette suggests, successful organizations and managers realize that people are a key resource in maintaining competitive advantage. These organizations and managers view employee training as an investment in their people, not an expense. As a manager, you will want your staff to have the best skills and the broadest understanding of the organization and its customers. This chapter examines key training issues and the training process, identifies the major types of training available, and explores how to evaluate the effectiveness of training. Your understanding of these training basics can pay off for you, your workers, and your organization.

Key Training Issues

Johnson Controls' program illustrates some of the important training issues facing today's organizations. Specifically:

- **How can training keep pace with a changing organizational environment?** Johnson Controls confronts this challenge by taking an empowered approach to training in which teams of employees learn from each other. However, as equipment and techniques change, employees may have to receive training directed by managers (known as a top-down approach to training). Many organizations are turning to computerized options as an efficient means for delivering training. The computerized approach may not be the answer in all situations. For example, in a service-oriented organization, customer service skills training might be most effective if it is conducted face-to-face with people to give the trainee an experience that is much closer to reality.
- **Should training take place in a classroom setting or on the job?** Classroom training may lack realism and not be as effective as training that occurs while on the job. However, on-the-job training can cause slowdowns that decrease production or irritate customers. Johnson Controls trains employees off the job at its Team Rally events, although the training is relevant to the job. Some organizations use *virtual reality (VR)* technology to maximize the relevance of classroom training. However, this approach may not be applicable or cost-effective in other organizations. For example, it would be difficult to use VR to improve teamwork or people skills because VR training is typically an individual experience.

- **How can training be effectively delivered worldwide?** Many of today's organizations conduct operations around the world. Consistent quality of products or service is critical to organizational survival in today's competitive markets. Johnson Controls' Team Rally event involves employees from around the world. Unfortunately, achieving uniformity worldwide can be difficult. VR training provides organizations with a realistic and effective training tool that can easily be used worldwide. Solutions for companies that cannot afford VR training might include computer-, teleconference-, or video-based training.
- **How can training be delivered so that trainees are motivated to learn?** Lectures and workbooks may have outstanding content but be totally ineffective if they do not engage the trainees or motivate them to learn. The entertaining and competitive format of Johnson Controls' Team Rally event motivates employees to learn performance improvement techniques. Other engaging delivery media might include VR, videos, and multimedia displays.

In this chapter we discuss how organizations confront the challenges of training. First, we distinguish between training and development. Then we discuss the major challenges managers face in trying to improve workers' performance through training. Next we offer some suggestions on managing the three phases of the training process, explore selected types of training, and consider ways to maximize and evaluate training effectiveness. We close the chapter with a section on what is arguably the most important training opportunity: the orientation of new employees.

Training Versus Development

Training
The process of providing employees with specific skills or helping them correct deficiencies in their performance.

Development
An effort to provide employees with the abilities the organization will need in the future.

Although training is often used in conjunction with development, the terms are not synonymous. **Training** typically focuses on providing employees with specific skills or helping them correct deficiencies in their performance.[1] For example, new equipment may require workers to learn new ways of doing the job or a worker may have a deficient understanding of a work process. In both cases, training can be used to correct the skill deficit. In contrast, **development** is an effort to provide employees with the abilities the organization will need in the future.

Figure 8.1 summarizes the differences between training and development. In training, the focus is solely on the current job; in development, the focus is on both the current job and jobs that employees will hold in the future. The scope of training is on individual employees, whereas the scope of development is on the entire work group or organization. That is, training is job specific and addresses particular performance deficits or problems. In contrast, development is concerned with the workforce's skills and versatility.[2] Training tends to focus on immediate organizational needs and development tends to focus on long-term requirements. The goal of training is a fairly quick improvement in workers' performance, whereas the goal of development is the overall enrichment of the organization's human resources. Training strongly influences present performance levels, whereas development pays off in terms of more capable and flexible human resources in the long run.

Keep in mind one other distinction between training and development: Training can have a negative connotation. The result is that people might appreciate an opportunity for development but resent being scheduled for training.[3] Why? Training often implies that a person has a skill

Training Versus Development

Figure 8.1

	Training	Development
Focus	Current job	Current and future jobs
Scope	Individual employees	Work group or organization
Time Frame	Immediate	Long term
Goal	Fix current skill deficit	Prepare for future work demands

deficit, so employees may view their selection for training as a negative and embarrassing message rather than an improvement opportunity.

Changing this perception can be difficult. To help make the change, a company can focus on the improvement potential offered through training rather than correction of skill deficit. In other words, the "training" is portrayed as development. Although this tactic muddies the distinction between training and development, the two terms are often used interchangeably in practice. Given the rapid rate of change in many workplaces, training is becoming a necessity. The culture of organizations, then, needs to change so that training is viewed positively.

It is essential to remember these differences when generating and evaluating training programs. For example, using a training approach to affect a long-range issue is likely to be futile. Similarly, taking a development approach to improve current job performance problems will probably prove ineffective. In this chapter we focus on training. Development is the subject of Chapter 9.

Challenges in Training

The training process brings with it a number of questions that managers must answer. These are:

- Is training the solution to the problem?
- Are the goals of training clear and realistic?
- Is training a good investment?
- Will the training work?

Is Training the Solution?

A fundamental objective of training is the elimination or improvement of performance problems. However, not all performance problems call for training. Performance deficits can have several causes, many of which are beyond the worker's control and would, therefore, not be affected by training.[4] For example, unclear or conflicting requests, morale problems, and poor-quality materials cannot be improved through training.

Before choosing training as the solution, managers should carefully analyze the situation to determine if training is the appropriate response.

Are the Goals Clear and Realistic?

To be successful, a training program must have clearly stated and realistic goals. These goals will guide the program's content and determine the criteria by which its effectiveness will be judged. For example, management cannot realistically expect that one training session will make everyone a computer expert. Such an expectation guarantees failure because the goal is unattainable.

Unless the goals are clearly articulated before training programs are set up, the organization is likely to find itself training employees for the wrong reasons and toward the wrong ends. For example, if the goal is to improve specific skills, the training needs to be targeted to those skill areas. Magazine publisher Condé Nast is now working to identify and address specific goals for training. However, the director of employee programs at Condé Nast notes: "Prior to last year, we were offering generic training and employees were signing up on a self-selection basis."[5] The director of employee programs believes that goal-driven training teaches skills that are more relevant to workers' jobs. As a result, the company and the employee benefit.

In contrast, the company's training goal may be to provide employees with a broader understanding of the organization. For example, IDG, a highly decentralized publisher with offices around the world, provides three training seminars per year on the interdependent nature of the functions in the organization.[6] Employees selected for the training, mainly those in managerial positions, learn how to interact with other departments more effectively. As these examples show, the training goals should determine the type of training offered—a simple idea worth remembering.

A Question of Ethics

Some companies reimburse the educational expenses of employees who take classes on their own. In an era when people can count less and less on a single employer to provide them with work over the course of their careers, do you think employers have a responsibility to encourage their employees to pursue educational opportunities?

Is Training a Good Investment?

Training can be expensive. Consider the impressive figure of $57 billion. That's the amount that was spent on formal training in the United States in 2001, a 5 percent increase over the $54 billion spent in 2000.[7] Despite these impressive figures, current economic conditions are causing a reduction in training budgets in a number of organizations. The Manager's Notebook entitled "Cutting Training Costs but Maintaining Training Effectiveness" offers ways to reduce training costs that don't sacrifice the quality of the training. In addition to some belt tightening in training budgets, how this money is being spent is changing. Expenditures on seminars and conferences have increased 59 percent over the past three years. Investment in e-learning, or training conducted via the Internet, is projected to grow rapidly and be used by 60 percent of companies within two years.[8] The average amount spent on training per employee was $704 in 2000, up 4 percent from 1999.[9]

MANAGER'S NOTEBOOK

Emerging Trends

Cutting Training Costs but Maintaining Training Effectiveness

A tighter economy has translated into smaller budgets for training in many organizations. Doing away with training altogether may mean losing a competitive edge, or worse, losing the business. It isn't easy to maintain effectiveness when budgets are shrunk, but it is possible. Here are some tactics from training professionals to reduce costs.

- **Look inside.** Employees in the organization may be a rich source of training expertise. Rather than paying top dollar for outside talent, it is possible that some of the best subject matter experts are already in the organization. Furthermore, the relevance of the training when it comes from someone inside the organization can be built in and not present a problem. A director of training and education at a Florida automotive company had to eliminate training or find a low-cost alternative.[a] The 400-employee company now relies entirely on internal expertise for its training resource. Another internal approach to increasing skill levels is to use coaching and mentoring. Coaches and mentors could be people in supervisory and management roles or people with particular areas of expertise. Thus, training could be done within the top-down hierarchical structure in the organization or could be a peer-based process.
- **Do you need it?** Limit training to what is really needed. Given tighter budgets, a number of companies have shifted from a strategy of a wide variety of types of training to focusing on a couple of key areas.
- **Give training a strategic alignment.** Make sure training efforts are tied to strategic goals. The investment in training will pay off in moving the organization forward to the extent that it is linked with strategy. If proposed training doesn't seem related to goals of the organization, the training and its cost should likely be eliminated.
- **Consider e-learning.** Electronic approaches to training aren't always the answer, but they do offer an alternative that can lower costs. Organizations might be able to save 50 percent to 70 percent of the cost of training by replacing the traditional instructor-led approach with an e-learning approach.[b] Most of the savings are due to reducing lost work hours and eliminating housing and travel costs.

Source: [a]Adapted from *Managing Training & Development*. (2002). The five most effective strategies for improving training programs, March Newsletter of the Institute of Management and Administration. [b]Adapted from *Payroll Manager's* Report. (2002). How to train your staff on a smaller training budget. May Newsletter of the Institute of Management and Administration.

It isn't really the cost, per se, that should be the important issue as much as the effectiveness of the investment.

In some cases, training may be appropriate but not cost-effective. Before beginning a training program, managers must weigh the cost of the current problem against the cost of training to eliminate it. It could be that the training cure is more costly than the performance ailment—in which case alternatives to training must be considered.

Not conducting training can be a costly choice. A federal appeals court recently upheld a judgment against an employer because it failed to train its managers about the basic requirements of discrimination law. Phillips Chevrolet, Inc. was found guilty of age discrimination. A general manager who had ultimate hiring authority admitted that he often considered the age of applicants when making hiring decisions and wasn't aware that it was an illegal practice. The courts stated that the failure of the organization to train its managers in the basics of discrimination law was an "extraordinary mistake" and justified the conclusion that the company was recklessly indifferent to antidiscrimination law.[10] The court awarded $50,000 in punitive damages. The company probably realizes now that the cost required to train its managers in discrimination law was little relative to the cost levied against it for not providing that training.

Determining whether training is a good investment requires measuring the training's potential benefits in dollars. Training that focuses on "hard" areas (such as the running and adjustment of machines) that have a fairly direct impact on outcomes (such as productivity) can often be easily translated into a dollar value. Estimating the economic benefits of training in "softer" areas—such as teamwork and diversity training—is much more challenging. However, demonstrating the value of a training investment is important, particularly when budgets are tight. Only approximately 7 percent of organizations collect data and estimate their return on their investments in training.[11] Although not a dollar estimate, whether trainees learn what is covered in the training and then apply the new skills and knowledge back on the job can be indicators of the effectiveness of training. Even learning and application measures of effectiveness are estimated to be conducted by 38 percent and 14 percent of organizations, respectively.[12] Although evaluation may be lacking, the best companies try to maximize return on their training investment by aligning their training with their mission, strategy, and goals.[13] However, only an analysis of costs and benefits will indicate if a training investment, no matter how well planned and positioned, was worth it or is worth continuing.

Will Training Work?

There are many types of training programs in widespread use. Some are computerized, others use simulations, and still others use the traditional lecture format. Some types of training are more effective than others for some purposes and in some situations. Designing effective training remains as much an art as a science, however, because no single type of training has proved most effective overall.

Beyond the type of training and its content, a number of contextual issues can determine a training program's effectiveness. For example, an organizational culture that supports change, learning, and improvement can be a more important determinant of a training program's effectiveness than any aspect of the program itself. Participants who view training solely as a day away from work are unlikely to benefit much from the experience. The Manager's Notebook entitled "Transfer of Training: Moving from Learning to Doing" offers steps you can take to ensure that what you learn in training is applied in your work. In addition to the importance of the active involvement of participants, if participants' managers do not endorse the content and purpose of the training, it is unlikely that the training program will have any influence on work processes. Consider the following training success story.

Customer-Driven HR — MANAGER'S NOTEBOOK

Transfer of Training: Moving from Learning to Doing

Training is meant to make positive changes in the workplace. For those changes to occur, not only must learning happen, but also the lessons learned need to be transferred to the workplace. If the

lessons are learned but don't translate into improved on-the-job behavior, then the transfer of training hasn't occurred.

There are many reasons why training may not transfer back to the workplace. For example, upper management may not visibly support the change being promoted by the training. Without management "walking the talk," it's not likely that the trainees will embrace the lessons and apply them to the workplace. Furthermore, the lessons may be compelling, but the culture of the workplace may work against any changes. There may simply not be enough time to apply the lessons. The work environment may be too chaotic and unstructured for any lessons from training to take hold and make positive changes.

The following suggestions are steps that can be taken to maximize the chances that lessons from training transfer back to the workplace.

- *Be a teacher.* Be a link between the training and people in your area of the workplace. If you teach others what was learned in the training, you will help to spread the training and will practice and reinforce what you learned.
- *Assign yourself homework.* Set specific goals that apply the lessons learned in the training.
- *Develop your own job aids.* Placing a key model, terms, or steps learned in training on a convenient and easily seen spot, such as a tent card on your desk, can help remind you of the core message of the training.
- *Get a training partner.* A partner can help provide support for applying the lessons from training. Overcoming obstacles to transfer of training can be more easily accomplished with a partner than by yourself.
- *Ask for help.* If you need help in transferring the training lessons, you might ask your manager or the HR department for help. Additional materials, follow-up sessions, or other forms of organizational support may be available.

Source: Adapted with permission from Janove, J. W. (2002). Use it or lose it: Training is a waste of time and money if managers don't transfer lessons learned to their daily work lives. *HRMagazine, 47*, 99(4).

The Men's Wearhouse is an off-price retailer of men's business clothing. Despite the increasing size of the service sector (see Chapter 1), management of retail personnel is often poor and turnover is high. Further, training is often nonexistent, and the industry is increasingly competitive. In this context, the Men's Wearhouse has established itself as a quality clothier with a high growth and earnings rate and substantial growth in its stock value. Its approach to training differentiates the Men's Wearhouse from its major competitors. The company has constructed a 35,000-square-foot training center and offers

The Men's Wearhouse invests time and money to train its employees and the results are positive. The company retains its employees longer, has fewer inventory losses, and has lower security costs than its competitors.

programs such as "Suits University" and "Selling Accessories U." Three or four days of training are typically provided each year to both new and seasoned employees.

The company's training investment is substantially greater than that made by others in the industry. However, it seems to pay off well. First, although specific figures aren't available, the employee turnover rate is significantly lower than that of its competitors. Second, the "shrink" (lost inventory due to error or theft) is about one-third of the industry average. Also, the company's decision makers believe that if they create a corporate culture that supports employees, they don't need to spend money on security devices. In fact, the Men's Wearhouse spends nothing on security—no monitors or electronic tagging. Experts claim that the Men's Wearhouse's commitment to training has played a key role in its success.[14]

Finally, training will not work unless it is related to organizational goals. A well-designed training program flows from the company's strategic goals; a poorly designed one has no relationship to—or even worse, is at cross-purposes with—those goals. It is the manager's responsibility to ensure that training is linked with organizational goals.

Managing the Training Process

Effective training can raise performance, improve morale, and increase an organization's potential. Poor, inappropriate, or inadequate training can be a source of frustration for everyone involved. To maximize the benefits of training, managers must closely monitor the training process.

As Figure 8.2 shows, the training process consists of three phases: (1) needs assessment, (2) development and conduct of training, and (3) evaluation. In the *needs assessment phase,* managers determine the problems or needs that the training must address. In the *development and conduct phase,* training personnel design the most appropriate type of training and offer it to the workforce. In the *evaluation phase,* managers assess the training program's effectiveness. In the pages that follow, we provide recommendations for maximizing the effectiveness of each of these phases.

In large organizations, input of managers is very important for determining what training is needed (phase 1), but the actual training (phase 2) is usually provided by either the organization's own training department or an external resource (such as a consulting firm or a local university). After the training program is completed, managers are often called on to determine whether the training has been useful (phase 3). In small businesses, the manager may be responsible for the entire process, although external sources of training may still be used.

The Training Process

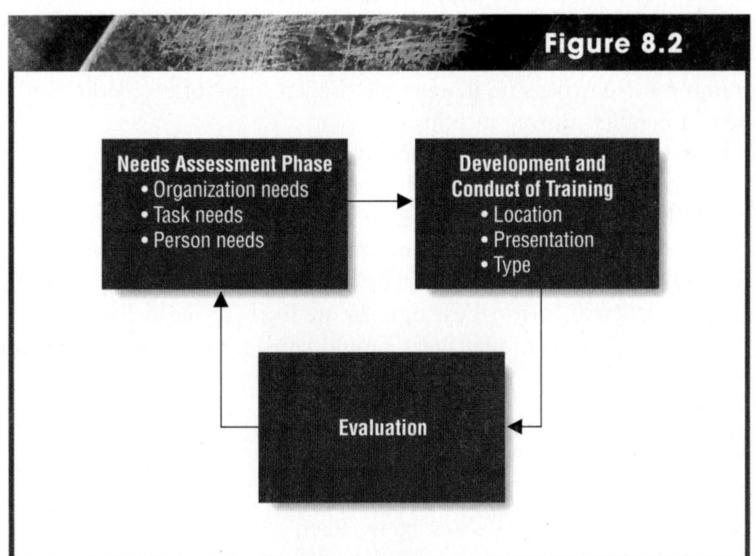

The Assessment Phase

The overall purpose of the assessment phase is to determine if training is needed, and if so, to provide the information required to design the training program. Assessment consists of three levels of analysis: organizational, task, and person.

The Levels of Assessment

Organizational analysis examines broad factors such as the organization's culture, mission, business climate, long- and short-term goals, and structure. Its purpose is to identify both overall organizational needs and the level of support for training. Perhaps the organization lacks the resources needed to support a formal training program, or perhaps the organization's strategy emphasizes innovation. In both cases, the organizational analysis that reveals such information plays a major role in determining whether training will be offered and the type of training (or alternative to training) that would be most appropriate. If a lack of resources prevents formal training, a mentoring program might be used as an alternative. An innovative environment may call for a training program focused on encouraging workers' creativity.

Task analysis is an examination of the job to be performed. It focuses on the duties and tasks of jobs throughout the organization to determine which jobs require training. A recent and carefully conducted job analysis should provide all the information needed to understand job requirements. These duties and tasks are then used to identify the knowledge, skills, and abilities (KSAs) required to perform the job adequately (see Chapter 2). Then the KSAs are used to determine the kinds of training needed for the job.

Person analysis determines which employees need training by examining how well employees are carrying out the tasks that make up their jobs.[15] Training is often necessary when there is a discrepancy between a worker's performance and the organization's expectations or standards. Often a person analysis entails examining worker performance ratings and then identifying individual workers or groups of workers who are weak in certain skills. The source of most performance ratings is the supervisor, but (as we saw in Chapter 7) a more complete picture of workers' strengths and weaknesses may be obtained by expanding the sources to include self-assessment by the individual worker and performance assessments by the worker's peers.[16]

As we noted in Chapter 4, performance problems can come from numerous sources, many of which would not be affected by training. The only source of a performance problem that training can address is a deficiency that is under the trainee's control.[17] Because training focuses on changing the worker, it can improve performance only when the worker is the source of a performance deficiency. For example, sales training will improve sales only if poor sales techniques are the source of the problem. If declining sales are due to a poor product, high prices, or a faltering economy, sales training is not going to help.

It is important to note that when we talk about the worker as the source of performance problems, we are not referring only to deficiencies in hard areas such as KSAs directly connected to the job. Sometimes the deficiencies occur in such soft areas as diversity, ethics, and AIDS awareness, and they, too, require training to correct. For example, the Eddie Bauer company in Seattle trains all new employees on its standards for conduct at meetings. The purposes of the training are to make sure that people show respect for each other and to reduce the possibility of gender conflicts during meetings.[18]

Training is not the only option available for responding to a worker deficiency. For example, if decision makers determine that the training needed to bring workers up to desired levels would be too costly, transferring or terminating the deficient workers may be the more cost-effective course. Strict KSA requirements can then be used to select new employees and eliminate the performance gap. The obvious drawbacks of terminating or replacing employees deemed deficient is that these options are likely to harm commitment and morale in the workforce. For this reason, managers should consider training as preferable to transfer or termination.

Clarifying the Objectives of Training

The assessment phase should provide a set of objectives for any training program that might be developed following the assessment. Each objective should relate to one or more of the KSAs identified in the task analysis and should be challenging, precise, achievable, and understood by all.[19] Pfizer, Inc., for example, gears its training to the competencies it has identified for jobs from entry level to the most senior positions.[20] Similarly, Booz, Allen, & Hamilton maps the competencies needed from entry level to senior management positions to a suite of training courses.

Whenever possible, objectives should be stated in behavioral terms and the criteria for judging the training program's effectiveness should flow directly from the behavioral objectives. Suppose the cause of a performance deficiency is poor interpersonal sensitivity. The overall objective of the training program designed to solve this problem, then, would be to increase interpersonal sensitivity. Increasing "interpersonal sensitivity" is a noble training goal, but the term is ambiguous and does not lead to specific content for a training program or to specific criteria by which the training's effectiveness can be judged. Stating this objective in behavioral terms requires determining what an employee will know, do, and not do after training. For example, the employee will greet customers and clients by name, refrain from sexual humor that could be perceived as harassing, and show up for all meetings on time.[21]

Figure 8.3 shows how the overall objective of sensitivity training provides a starting point that can be broken down into dimensions (specific aspects of job performance) for which specific behavioral goals can then be developed. The overall objective in the figure is to increase the interpersonal sensitivity of supervisors in their relations with production employees. First, this overall objective is divided into two dimensions: listening and feedback skills. Then specific behaviors that are part of these dimensions are identified, both to guide the training effort and to help evaluate whether the training has been successful.

The Training and Conduct Phase

The training program that results from assessment should be a direct response to an organizational problem or need. Training approaches vary by location, presentation, and type.

Location Options

Training can be carried out either on the job or off the job. In the very common *on-the-job training (OJT)* approach, the trainee works in the actual work setting, usually under the guidance of an experienced worker, supervisor, or trainer. At the Los Alamos National Laboratory of the U.S. Department of Energy, for instance, training often relies on one-on-one coaching, hands-on demonstrations, and practice. Before setting the training in motion, however, management at this New Mexico–based facility carefully considers the task employees are being trained for, the level of training needed, the number of trainees, and the availability of instructional settings and resources.

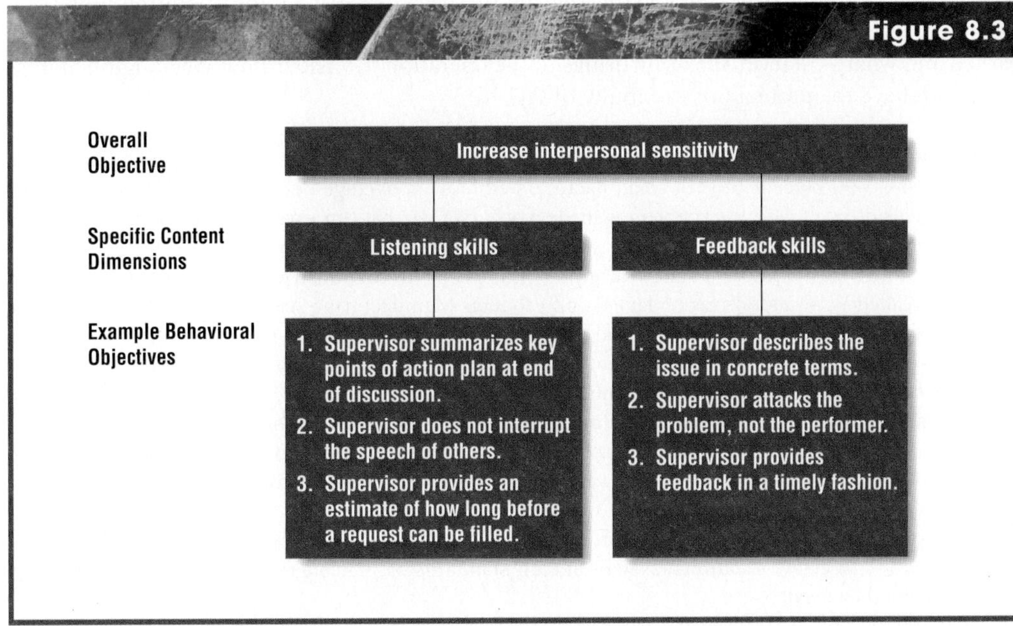
Figure 8.3
Overall Objective
Increase interpersonal sensitivity
Specific Content Dimensions
Listening skills
Feedback skills
Example Behavioral Objectives
1. Supervisor summarizes key points of action plan at end of discussion.
2. Supervisor does not interrupt the speech of others.
3. Supervisor provides an estimate of how long before a request can be filled.
1. Supervisor describes the issue in concrete terms.
2. Supervisor attacks the problem, not the performer.
3. Supervisor provides feedback in a timely fashion.

Example of Development of Behavioral Training Objectives

Job rotation, apprenticeships, and internships are all forms of OJT.

- *Job rotation*, as we saw in Chapter 2, allows employees to gain experience in different kinds of narrowly defined jobs in the organization. It is often used to give future managers a broad background.
- *Apprenticeships,* OJT programs typically associated with the skilled trades, derive from the medieval practice of having the young learn a trade from an experienced worker. In Europe, apprenticeships are still one of the major ways for young men and women to gain entry to skilled jobs. In the United States, apprenticeships are largely confined to adults wanting to work in certain occupations, such as carpentry and plumbing. These apprenticeships generally last four years, and the apprentice's pay starts at about half that of the more experienced "journey workers." While there are some shining examples of youth apprenticeship programs, such as the Cornell University–funded youth Apprenticeship Demonstration Project, only 27 states have apprenticeship agencies and only 2 percent of U.S. high school graduates enter apprenticeships for skilled jobs. One of the consequences of this lack of youth apprenticeship programs is the rapidly shrinking pool of skilled labor in the United States.[22]
- Just as apprenticeships are a route to certain skilled blue-collar jobs, *internships* are a route to white-collar or managerial jobs in a variety of fields. Internships are opportunities for students to gain real-world job experience, often during summer vacations from school. Although most internships offer very low or no pay, student interns can often gain college credits and, possibly, the offer of a full-time job after graduation.

OJT has both benefits and drawbacks. This type of training is obviously relevant to the job because the tasks confronted and learned are generated by the job itself. Very little that is learned in the context of OJT would not transfer directly to the job. OJT also spares the organization the expense of taking employees out of the work environment for training and usually the cost of hiring outside trainers because company employees generally are capable of doing the training. On the negative side, OJT can prove quite costly to the organization in lost business when on-the-job trainees cause customer frustration. (Have you ever been caught in a checkout line that moves like molasses because a trainee is operating the cash register?) Even if only a handful of customers switch to a competitor because of dissatisfaction with trainee service, the cost to the organization can be substantial. Errors and damage to equipment that occur when a trainee is on the job may also prove costly. Another potential drawback is that trainers might be top-notch in terms of their skills but inadequate at transferring their knowledge to others. In other words, those who can, cannot always teach.

Finally, the quality and content of OJT can vary substantially across organizations. This variability makes it difficult for employers to judge the skill level of a potential worker from another organization. A new worker may claim that he or she received OJT for operating a piece of machinery or conducting a task, but the employer can be left wondering what the worker really learned and what skill level she or he brings to the operation. Consider how Washington State is trying to relieve the problem of variability of OJT.

> Washington is home to 1,300 wood products manufacturers, the vast majority of which are small operations—90 percent of these manufacturers employ an average of 16 people. Finding qualified workers is difficult, and the problem is made worse by OJT that can vary substantially in quality and content across employers.
>
> To address this problem, a statewide group of 87 people from industry, schools, and unions formed a team called Washington's Secondary Wood Products Manufacturing Advisory Team (SWPMT). The team wrote skill standards for the wood products industry, identified needed skills (that is, the team did a *task analysis*—see *"The Assessment Phase"* in this chapter), and then wrote descriptions of the required knowledge and skills. The team's next step is to develop a curriculum and training based on these standards. Thus, a standard training experience will replace the spotty OJT that currently characterizes the industry. Certification based on the skill standards will provide workers with a way to communicate the skills they have achieved and provide employers a way of knowing the skill levels of their workforce.[23]
>
> The work of SWPMT in Washington is linked to the National Skills Standards Board. The goal of the board is to create a national system of skill standards so that businesses can obtain the skilled workforce they need.[24]

Off-the-job training is an effective alternative to OJT. Common examples of off-the-job training are formal courses, simulations, and role-playing exercises in a classroom setting. One advantage of off-the-job training is that it gives employees extended uninterrupted periods of study. Another is that a classroom setting may be more conducive to learning and retention because it avoids the distractions and interruptions that commonly occur in an OJT environment. The big disadvantage of off-the-job training is that what is learned may not transfer back to the job. After all, a classroom is not the workplace, and the situations simulated in the training may not closely match those encountered on the job. Also, if employees view off-the-job training as an opportunity to enjoy some time away from work, not much learning is likely to take place.

Presentation Options

Trainers use a variety of presentation techniques in training sessions. The most common presentation techniques are slides and videotapes, teletraining, computers, simulations, virtual reality, and classroom instruction and role-plays.

Slides and Videotapes. Slides and videotapes can be used either off-the-job or in special media rooms in an organization's facility. Slides and videotapes provide consistent information and, if done well, can be interesting and thought provoking. However, these presentation media do not allow trainees to ask questions or receive further explanation (although new advances in videotape technology are permitting some interaction between the observer and the medium). Many companies prefer to use slides, film, or tapes to supplement a program led by a trainer, who can answer individuals' questions and flesh out explanations when necessary.

Teletraining. A training option that is particularly useful when trainees are dispersed across various physical locations is teletraining.[25] Satellites are used to beam live training broadcasts to employees at different locations. In addition to the video reception, the satellite link can allow trainees to ask questions of the instructor during the broadcast.

Two disadvantages of teletraining are the need for an expensive satellite connection and the difficulty of scheduling the broadcast so that everyone will be able to attend. AT&T Productivity

The wood products industry needs a trained workforce. Washington State's Secondary Wood Products Manufacturing Advisory Team has developed skill standards to help meet this need.

Training overcomes these drawbacks in an innovative way.[26] The satellite broadcast of a training program is put on videotape, and the video is edited to eliminate the live questions and discussion. The video is then made available at sites where people still need to receive the training. At a specified delivery time the training instructor is available via conference call to introduce the sections of the videotape and to respond to questions. This method makes the trainer's expertise available to trainees without requiring him or her to redeliver the entire training program.

Computers. With the widespread availability of personal computers, both small and large businesses are finding computer-training to be a cost-effective medium. There are numerous potential advantages to computer-based training. In particular, if a job requires extensive use of computers, then computer-based training is highly job related and provides for a high degree of transfer of training back to the job. Computers also have the advantage of allowing trainees to learn at a comfortable pace. As a trainer, the computer never becomes tired, bored, or short-tempered. Further, advancing technology is making the computer a truly multimedia training option in which text can be combined with film, graphics, and audio components.

Many organizations are using computer-based training because of its advantages. For instance, it is much easier and cheaper to transfer information via computer to employees in various places than it is to transfer employees to a central location to receive training or to send trainers to multiple locations.

Computer-based training can range from the use of a CD-ROM to training over the Internet. A number of companies are still exploring what type of computer-based training works best for them. Figure 8.4 spotlights three of Red Lobster's computer-based training techniques and their benefits and drawbacks. Jim Plyant, the director of operations for Red Lobster, sees computers as

Computer-Based Training at Red Lobster

Red Lobster uses a range of computer-based training programs to meet its training goal of helping people build and use their skills, not just memorize and, later, forget. Although the systems have drawbacks, the pros greatly outweigh the cons.

Figure 8.4

Examples of Training Techniques

- **Point-of-sale training** To acquaint managers and servers with the restaurant chain's point-of-sale system, a computer serves as the "cash register." Trainees work through a computerized training session on point-of-sale techniques at their own pace and can review points or steps if they miss them the first time. Red Lobster supplements the program with a videotape and workbook.
- **Simulation** Red Lobster also uses a computer-based program that approximates a walkthrough of a real job. Jim Plyant, Red Lobster's director of operations, contends that the program feels and appears like the real job function.
- **Computer-based tutorials** Red Lobster also uses tutorials to provide employees with the information and skills they need when they need them.

Computer-Based Training Benefits and Drawbacks

Benefits	Drawbacks
More cost-effective than classroom training	Many programs do not assess employees' progress so managers cannot measure the employee's skill level.
Time efficient	Many programs lack a feedback mechanism to help employees determine how much they have learned.
Targeted at crucial skills	
Allows employees to progress at their own pace	
Does not hamper productivity	

Source: Adapted from Prewitt, M. (1998). FS/TEC'98: Darden execs share ins, outs of computer training. *Nation's Restaurant News, 32*, 57, 72.

an efficient way of training workers that does not slow productivity or push people too hard. He recognizes that many people might prefer learning in a situation where they are face-to-face with a teacher. However, there is no time for classrooms in the fast-paced seafood restaurant.

Although there are numerous types of computer-based training, Web-based training is fast becoming the training method of choice. The decline in business travel after the terrorist attack of September 11, 2001, made the prospect of online training more appealing. It is estimated that the e-learning market in the United States will increase from $2.3 billion in 2000 to $14.7 billion by 2004 and the global market will hit $23 billion by 2004.[27]

Using the Internet or company intranet for training, e-learning has been increasing in popularity for obvious reasons. This approach offers not only the content but also administers the training. E-learning also offers a way to standardize training across far-flung employees and centers of operation.[28] Perhaps the most apparent reason is the elimination of travel and lodging costs. Add to that the benefit to individuals who can access training at any time and from any place where an Internet connection is available, it is not surprising that organizations are adopting an e-learning approach. E-learning is a success story at many organizations.

American General Inc., a Houston-based company, provides a successful example of e-learning. Within two years of starting e-learning, American General now has more than half of its corporate training completed online and offers more than 500 courses on the Web. As a result of the online training, the company has thus far reduced its training costs by 20 percent. An online training course at American General costs $10 per person whereas the average cost per person for a classroom course is $65.[29]

Not all e-learning applications have worked out so successfully. Some organizations have found the e-learning promise to be a dream that couldn't be fully realized, at least in the short term.[30] There can be technology problems, such as integration among elements of an e-learning system. In addition, product limitations, inadequate support services, and financial problems of vendors can all cause difficulty for an e-learning initiative.[31] Costs can be greater than expected. For example, an e-learning management system—the software that acts as a course catalog and registrar's office—can cost from $250,000 to $350,000.[32] Probably the biggest potential hurdle to an e-learning initiative is failure to realize that it is a change that needs to be carefully implemented if it is to be successfully adopted by an organization. The Manager's Notebook entitled "Implementing E-Learning: To Be Effective, Be Sensitive to Your Employee/Customer Needs" presents suggestions for successfully implementing an e-learning initiative.

Customer-Driven HR

MANAGER'S NOTEBOOK

Implementing E-Learning: To Be Effective, Be Sensitive to Your Employee/Customer Needs

E-learning offers the promise of training anytime and anywhere and at a reduced price due to no travel or lodging costs. However, e-learning has not been an instant success, nor has it delivered the promised just-in-time and tailored training. Part of the difficulty is recognizing that the e-learning approach is a change from the norm and, as with anything new, there needs to be careful attention to implementation. If a new approach can be used on a small scale and shown to be effective, the small successes can lead to broad-scale adoption. Here are some suggestions for implementing e-learning that can maximize the effectiveness of this training approach.

- *Identify groups most likely to benefit from an e-learning initiative.*
  The Geographically Disadvantaged. If training usually occurs in certain locations, is there a group of employees for whom attending training is a major disruption due to travel time and cost? If so, this group of employees could be a target for an e-learning initiative.
  The Well Trained. Some employees may be familiar with substantial portions of the course material. The e-learning approach allows employees to search for and focus on only the blocks of information they need, making the approach more efficient than traditional training.
  Those Under Time Pressure. Leaving work to attend a program at a different location, perhaps for several days, just doesn't fit into everyone's schedule. For people with demanding job

requirements, e-learning is a viable option that doesn't require leaving work. Furthermore, e-learning has the potential to be more a continuous process integrated with work and less of a separate event than traditional training.

- *Show them the money*. E-learning can cut training costs by eliminating travel and lodging expenses. Demonstrating these cost savings can gain buy-in for the approach.
- *Target pilot group*. For an e-learning pilot run, you could target managers who have a large number of employees in disparate locations, have high training bills, or are supporters of training.

Source: Adapted with permission from Schlag, P. V. (2002). The trainer's ally: E-learning doesn't mean harm. It just wants to help. *T + D*, *56*, 18(3).

In regard to e-learning, it is necessary to recognize that the sophistication of the technology does not make any guarantees about the content of the training.

If the content preparation is poor, the training experience will be poor as well. Further, training employees in complex skills or concepts may be best accomplished through interaction with experienced people. Also, in instances when a job's duties do not require the use of a computer, computer-based training may hinder the learning process.[33]

Finally, remember that computer-based training is not an all-or-nothing proposition. For example, a trainer might supplement e-learning with a live workshop to maximize the advantages of each approach.[34] The computerized portion can promote learning by allowing trainees to make mistakes and search for correct choices privately. The workshop can help trainees practice and reinforce their skills through vehicles such as interactive role playing. A number of organizations are successfully taking a blended or "b-learning" approach in which e-learning is supplemented with classroom instruction.[35] Developing effective interpersonal skills, for example, may be best learned in a classroom setting and could later be reinforced via online training. AT&T provides an example of blending e-learning and traditional classroom instruction.[36] The business-to-business sales portion of the organization now uses a blended approach to learn and apply new skills. Workshop concepts are reinforced with online material, and online support provides information on best practices and strategies. Promotion to higher levels of sales responsibility require not just completing the workshop but also demonstrating successful use of skills in the field as determined from submission of action plans and success stories. The b-learning approach by AT&T takes the emphasis off course completion and places it on supplying the skill on a day-to-day basis.

Simulation
A device or situation that replicates job demands at an off-the-job site.

Simulations. Particularly effective in training are **simulations,** devices or situations that replicate job demands at an off-the-job site. Organizations often use simulations when the information to be mastered is complex, the equipment used on the job is expensive, and/or the cost of a wrong decision is quite high. A dramatic example of a training simulation program is FATS, developed by FireArms Training Systems of Duluth, Georgia, and now used by more than 300 law enforcement agencies in the United States.[37] The FATS program uses a microcomputer (a PC) and a 10-foot video screen to confront police officers-in-training with the sights and sounds of a number of situations commonly encountered in police work. For example, a dangerous suspect is fleeing on a crowded street. Should the officer shoot at the suspect and risk injuring or killing innocent bystanders? FATS gives police trainees the opportunity to practice making such snap decisions in a safe but realistic setting.

The airline industry has long used simulators to train pilots. Unlike FATS, flight simulations often include motion in addition to visual and auditory realism. This aspect substantially increases the cost of the simulation but makes the training even more realistic. The airline industry is fine-tuning a major simulator for air traffic control personnel. The NASA Ames Research Center has developed a virtual control tower simulator with a price tag of approximately $10 million. Viewers can see any airport in the world outside the control tower's 12 glass windows in a 360-degree view. The tower can simulate any time of day or night, any weather pattern, and the movement of up to 200 aircraft and ground vehicles.

The simulator can train air traffic controllers safely and rigorously. In addition, air traffic planners can experiment with different flight patterns and their impact on efficiency and safety.

Air traffic control simulators, though costly, can improve a company's bottom line. Delta's use of an air traffic control simulator to train its personnel has helped the airline save approximately $20 million.

One of the first tasks for the simulator will be to test possible locations for a new runway at the San Francisco airport.[38]

Another type of simulation confronts trainee doctors with an accident victim arriving at the emergency room. The trainees choose from a menu of options, with the patient dying if the decision is delayed too long or is incorrect.

Traditionally, simulators have been considered separate from computer-based training. With advances in multimedia technology, however, the distinctions between these two methods have blurred considerably.

A new product is a recent example of the melding of computerized and simulator types of training. Greg Merril founded HT Medical, a company that specializes in the simulation technology for health-care professionals, based on the simple but profound idea that flight simulator technology could apply to the medical field.[39] In mid-1998 HT Medical brought its first computer-based simulation product to the market. The device is called a CathSim Intravenous Training System and gives medical personnel the chance to practice giving shots before giving them to a real patient. As a result, nurses and doctors get a realistic experience without practicing on animals or humans. In addition, the CathSim provides trainees with report cards on their effectiveness and allows supervisors to track trainees' progress.

The CathSim works with a PC and includes a small robotic box, called AccuTouch, which is about the size of a paperback book. A computer program allows users to select from a variety of options, such as whether the patient is an elderly woman or a drug user. The program then presents on screen a number of materials and needle sizes to choose from. After that, the trainee inserts a real needle into the AccuTouch box. The box has a rubber-like substance and mimics resistance and other factors of a real patient's arm. If the needle is inserted improperly the computer program may yell "ow" in response.

The CathSim unit currently sells for $6,000. Within two months after its release, 7,500 of the approximately 10,000 U.S. medical organizations had contacted Merril's company about acquiring a CathSim.[40]

Few studies have been done on the effectiveness of simulations, but the limited data available indicate that this training method does have a positive impact on job performance. For example, one study found that pilots who trained on simulators become proficient at flight maneuvers nearly twice as fast as pilots who trained only in the air.[41] The importance of this difference is underscored by the fact that the cost of simulator training is only about 10 percent of the cost of using the real equipment to train pilots.

Virtual reality (VR)
The use of a number of technologies to replicate the entire real-life working environment in real time.

Virtual Reality. Virtual reality (VR) uses a number of technologies to replicate the entire real-life working environment rather than just several aspects of it, as in simulations. Within these three-dimensional environments, a user can interact with and manipulate objects in real time.

The CathSim allows medical personnel to practice in a simulation environment rather than on humans or animals.

The military uses VR training and continues to invest in the technology. For example, the U.S. Army awarded a $45 million contract to the University of Southern California in August 1999 to improve VR training.[42] The work at USC is focused on making the virtual environments more realistic and team based. The goal is to have whole task squads, rather than an individual at a time, experience the VR battle scenarios and interact.

Advances in VR technology are also occurring in the private sector. For instance, Motorola's Semiconductor Product Sector tested a VR training system developed by Modis Training technologies.[43] Modis is an Arizona company that specializes in recreating plant floors in VR, complete with production lines and equipment. The test results were positive: Motorola trainees made fewer mistakes and learned faster with the virtual training. The average learning time dropped from 6 weeks to 1.5 weeks. Because a mistake on a semiconductor production line can cost half a million dollars, Motorola is willing to invest in virtual training, which is expensive to develop. In the long run the company's investment seems modest compared to the cost savings of fewer production mistakes.

Tasks that are good candidates for VR training are those that require rehearsal and practice, working from a remote location, or visualizing objects and processes that are not usually accessible. VR training is also excellent for tasks in which there is a high potential for damage to equipment or danger to individuals.

For example, forestry students in Alvdalen, Sweden, practice in a virtual tree harvester before operating the real machine.[44] Researchers found that students who received VR training were more confident and productive when they started operating the real machine. In contrast, students who trained in the real machine (a behemoth that has a 33-foot arm and can carry 90-foot pine trees) were much more nervous and dangerous. A harvesting machine costs approximately $400,000 and damage to it or the environment could be expensive. Wouldn't you rather put in a few hours on the virtual equipment before being responsible for the real thing?

The initial use of VR technology in employee training appears quite successful. The immersion of trainees in a virtual world may be the key to this success.[45] The VR experience provides a sense of self-location in a simulated environment in which objects appear solid and can be navigated around, touched, lifted, and so on. This sense of immersion is probably connected to the excitement and motivation that VR trainees often report.

One drawback of VR training has been that the technology is meant for one individual user at a time rather than multiple participants. Thus, VR training has not been applicable to team training situations. This limitation may soon be overcome, however. As indicated earlier, the military is investing in VR technology that can incorporate interaction among team members. Technological advances in the military sector tend to spill over into the private sector. With the prevalence of teams in the workplace, the demand for this type of VR capability will be high.

Classroom Instruction and Role-Plays. Classroom lectures are used in many organizations to impart information to trainees. Although widely viewed as "boring," classroom instruction can be exciting if other presentation techniques are integrated with the lecture. For example, a videotape could complement the discussion by providing realistic examples of the lecture material. In-class case exercises and role-plays (both of which are found throughout this book) provide an opportunity for trainees to apply what is being taught in the class and transfer that knowledge back to the job. Solving and discussing case problems helps trainees learn technical material and content, and role-plays are an excellent way of applying the interpersonal skills being emphasized in the training. If done well, role-plays give trainees the opportunity to practice the skills they've been studying via books, video, computer, or some other medium.[46]

Types of Training

As we noted earlier, there are many approaches to training. We focus here on the types of training that are commonly used in today's organizations: skills, retraining, cross-functional, team, creativity, literacy, diversity, crisis, and customer service.

Skills Training. When we think of training, most of us probably envision a program that focuses on particular skill needs or deficits. Indeed, this type of training is probably the most common in organizations. The process is fairly simple: The need or deficit is identified via a thorough assessment. Specific training objectives are generated, and training content is developed to achieve those objectives. The criteria for assessing the training's effectiveness are also based on the objectives identified in the assessment phase.

To understand how skills training programs are developed, let us examine a classic example of skills training. In 1992, 10 percent of all complaints to IBM's CEO centered on the handling of telephone calls. Because customer service is one of IBM's top priorities, the CEO knew he had to take action. He appointed a project team composed of both line managers and trainers to investigate the situation. This arrangement was designed to ensure that line personnel would take the project team's recommendations and actions seriously. (Programs that come out of the "black box" of the HR department are sometimes discounted by line managers.)

The project team did a careful assessment. A survey of IBM customers revealed that 70 percent of customer contact was via telephone.[47] Additionally, a formal survey of over 10,000 IBM customers revealed that shoddy phone handling was the biggest complaint. As Figure 8.5 shows, analysis of the survey responses indicated that customers' most frequent complaints were that they could not reach a knowledgeable person and that their calls were not being returned. The

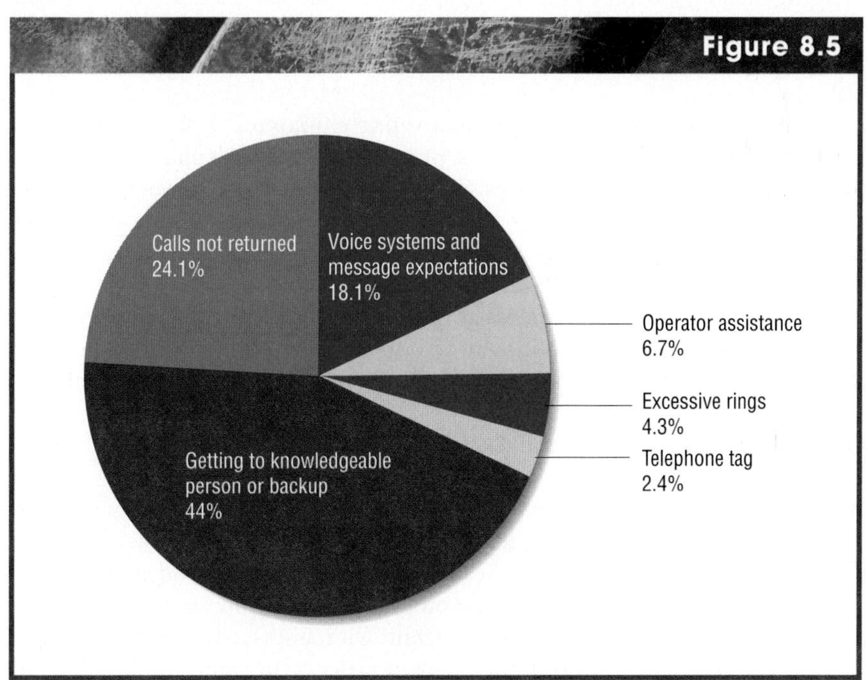

Sources of Customer Dissatisfaction with IBM Telephone Service

Source: Estabrooke, R. M., and Fay, N. F. (1992). Answering the call of "tailored training." *Training, 29*, 85–88. Reprinted with permission from the October 1992 issue of *Training*. Copyright 1992. Lakewood Publications, Minneapolis, MN. All rights reserved. Not for resale.

Figure 8.6

Interoffice Memo

Over all, the rating of our telephone service by customers and internal users is poor. Together, we are going to fix this problem, and fix it fast.

IBM Senior Vice President's Memo to All Managers

Source: Estabrooke, R. M., and Fay, N. F. (1992). Answering the call of "tailored training." *Training, 29,* 85–88. Reprinted with permission from the October 1992 issue of *Training*. Copyright 1992. Lakewood Publications. Minneapolis, MN. All rights reserved. Not for resale.

project team then conducted a survey of IBM employees and found that while more than 75 percent knew how to put a customer on hold, fewer than 5 percent knew how to forward a call. The team also found that most professional employees felt that they did not need telephone skills because calls from customers should be handled by the secretarial staff. Based on these survey results, the team categorized the telephone interaction problem into two broad categories: (1) not using phone features and (2) not treating customers with professional courtesy.

The team presented its findings and recommended a training strategy to senior management. The senior vice president in charge of the team, who agreed that telephone interactions were a problem to be taken seriously, issued the stern memo reprinted in Figure 8.6. Any employee receiving this memo clearly got the message that telephone skills were now a main issue at IBM. The strong support of top management forced line employees to take the issue seriously and helped the project team obtain funds for the training program.

The project team divided employees into two groups on the basis of how often they used the phone system and then tailored the training to each group. The "intensive" group was composed of employees such as secretaries and operators, the "casual" group of engineers, managers, and other professionals. The intensive group was relatively small in number but accounted for most of the phone interaction with customers. It was important that this group be both courteous and well acquainted with the phone system. The casual group needed not only to understand the basics of the phone system but also had to be trained in telephone etiquette.

Training for the intensive user group involved broad-based coverage of expected behaviors and instruction in the phone system's specific operational features. Among the training program's features: a videotape of good and poor role models of phone interaction shown to secretaries and switchboard operators, a computer-based training program that covered details of the phone system as well as courtesy skills, and pamphlets and other reference materials. Depending on their current levels of skill and knowledge, trainees took from three to nine hours to complete the program.

The casual users required a substantially different approach for three reasons. First, they did not need the same level of knowledge as the intensive group because they had much less phone interaction with customers. Second, the cost of intensive training for the approximately 150,000 professional employees who fell into the casual group would be prohibitive. Third, the casual users were not motivated to improve their telephone skills because they did not see a problem in their phone performance. These employees' training package, then, was designed to be brief and entertaining. A videotape shown at departmental meetings provided an overview of the topic. In addition, a brief and humorous audiotape that could be played in the car or on the job emphasized the desired behaviors. An abbreviated version of the computer-based training program focusing on only the key elements of phone operation was included in the casual users' package. Pamphlets and other reference sources were also provided. The project team assumed that most casual users would select the product they preferred and spend perhaps an hour with the material.

Other HR activities focused on motivating employees to solve the phone communication problem. For example, the senior vice president selected telephone effectiveness as one of five key annual performance measures. Additionally, the project team's staff made random calls monthly to assess each business unit's phone effectiveness. Figure 8.7, which can serve as a model for any kind of skill improvement training program, summarizes the process followed by the training project team at IBM.

The program was quite successful. After one year, customer satisfaction with IBM's telephone responsiveness increased by nearly 10 percent. While the long-term goal is 100 percent satisfaction, a 10 percent increase in the first year of a program is certainly a healthy improvement.

IBM's program offers several lessons:

- In some organizational settings, the most important step in building commitment to training may be the inclusion of people who have a great deal of informal or political power in the organization. If someone is politically strong enough to torpedo an instructional effort, it may be best to include him or her in the program's training design from the outset.
- The idea of beginning a training program with assessments at the organizational, task, and person levels may be more academic than realistic. In reality, problems often suddenly come

Figure 8.7

Steps to Skill Improvement at IBM

1. Build in commitment.
   - Gain support of management.
2. Thoroughly analyze the problem.
   - Is it important?
   - What is the real problem?
3. Gain line support.
4. Develop training strategies.
   - Is there more than one group of employees that needs training?
   - Design materials appropriate to each group's needs and motivation levels.
5. Develop motivational strategies.
   - Take steps to heighten awareness of issue.
   - Signal importance of issue through measurement and recognition programs.

to light in organizations, and something must be done about them quickly if the organization is to remain competitive.

- Multiple forms of a training package may be needed for different groups of trainees. Some employee groups may need detailed knowledge and a high level of skills in a particular area, while others may need only broad familiarity and basic skills. Tailoring the training to each group's skill requirements maximizes the training's effectiveness.
- Providing trainees with materials such as pamphlets and reference guides can help to ensure that the training results in improved performance. These sorts of materials, **job aids,** are external sources of information that workers can access quickly when they need help in making a decision or performing a specific task.[48] Their use is growing rapidly for a few reasons. First, job aids reduce the need to memorize many details and therefore decrease errors and bolster efficiency. Second, although job aids cannot replace formal training programs, they can supplement training and help ensure that the training transfers back to the job. Third, they are relatively inexpensive and can be developed and delivered quickly.

Job aids
External sources of information, such as pamphlets and reference guides, that workers can access quickly when they need help in making a decision or performing a specific task.

Retraining. A subset of skills training, *retraining* focuses on giving employees the skills they need to keep pace with their job's changing requirements. For instance, however proficient garment workers may be at a traditional skill such as sewing, they will need retraining when the company invests in computerized sewing equipment. Unfortunately, even though retraining is much cited in the media as an item at the top of the corporate agenda, many companies rush to upgrade their equipment without taking comparable steps to upgrade their employees' skills. They erroneously believe that automation means a lower-skilled workforce when, in fact, it often requires a more highly skilled one.

One company that takes retraining seriously is Nabisco Group Holdings. It gives workers faced with new technology the option of accepting early retirement or receiving retraining. Other significant developments on the retraining front have been spearheaded by creative partnerships between labor unions and employers. For instance, the Garment Industry Development Corporation consolidates union and industry efforts. Its Super Sewer program teaches a worker all the operations necessary to make a garment using computerized pattern making.[49]

Retraining not only involves getting the presently employed up to speed but also providing training assistance to displaced (laid-off) and unemployed workers. Several government initiatives have provided funding for retraining for displaced workers. *The Job Training Partnership Act (JTPA) of 1982,* the largest single training program financed by the federal government, gives block grants to states, which pass them on to local governments and private entities that provide on-the-job training.

Unfortunately, retraining efforts do not appear to be as effective as some would hope. Government statistics show that only 7 to 12 percent of dislocated workers take advantage of JTPA retraining programs. Furthermore, not all the people who go through retraining complete the program or benefit from it.[50] Critics also point out that the JTPA's placement rate is a disappointing 50 percent.

Cross-Functional Training. Traditionally, organizations have developed specialized work functions and detailed job descriptions. However, today's organizations are emphasizing versatility rather than specialization. The Issues and Applications feature titled "Street Legal: From the Racetrack to Passenger Cars" spotlights a cross-functional training program at Ford Motor Company. Training workers in multiple functions or disciplines is, thus, becoming increasingly popular.

Issues and Applications

Street Legal: From the Racetrack to Passenger Cars

Ford Motor Company's 2000 Lincoln LS sedan has been praised for its nimbleness and sure-footed handling. The five Ford engineers who worked on the car's chassis and aerodynamic styling were part of Ford's Racing Team, a cross-training program that supports the efforts of racing teams around the world. More importantly, the program requires Ford's production engineers to work with race engineers.

According to Neil Ressler, Ford vice president for research and vehicle technology, this type of cross-training teaches some of their youngest and most talented production engineers "to be bold, to be imaginative, and to be nimble-thinking." He further points out that "these invaluable skills are passed on to the most important people of all, our customers."

One of the engineers on the 2000 Lincoln worked with the Newman-Haas racing team, co-owned by actor Paul Newman. The engineer also got to work with the legendary Mario Andretti. The racing experiences had a substantial impact on the design of the Lincoln. The engineers paid close attention to the balance of the weight between the front and rear of the car. The car's aerodynamics were borrowed from the racing domain.

In addition, working on a race team teaches production engineers to be more adaptive, to work under pressure, and to make quick changes. The cross-training program participants typically return to Ford with a more flexible attitude that enables them to get more done.

Source: Adapted from Brennan, M. (1999 July 8). Ford sends its engineers to school at the racetrack. *Detroit Free Press*, C3.

Cross-functional training
Training employees to perform operations in areas other than their assigned job.

Cross-functional training involves training employees to perform operations in areas other than their assigned job. There are many approaches to cross-functional training. For example:

- Job rotation can be used to provide a manager in one functional area with a broader perspective than he or she would otherwise have.
- Departments can trade personnel for periods of time so that each worker or set of workers develops an understanding of the other department's operation.
- **Peer trainers,** high-performing workers who double as internal on-the-job trainers, can be extraordinarily effective in helping employees develop skills in another area of operation.[51]

Peer trainers
High-performing workers who double as internal on-the-job trainers.

Peer trainers must be selected carefully. Aside from having top-notch skills, they must be patient and motivated to teach others. An effective way to choose motivated people is simply to ask workers if they would like to be a peer trainer and then select the best volunteers. Some organizations promote the peer-trainer role as an honor and offer a tangible reward to sweeten the added responsibility. At Walt Disney's parks, peer trainers are paid extra while they are instructing and bear a trainer designation on their name badges as they move around the park. Volunteers at some companies such as national retailer T.J. Maxx undergo a formal training program to become successful peer trainers.

Because some workers, and even some managers, balk at the idea of cross-functional training, they should be instructed in the importance of such training and the benefits it can provide. Among these benefits:

- The more adaptable workers are, the more valuable they become to the organization. Adaptability increases both workers' job security and the organization's "depth on the bench."

The analogy to baseball is apt. Suppose a baseball team does not have a trained replacement for a particular player. When that player is injured, the coach has a problem because there is no one on the bench who can effectively play that position. Similarly, an organization is in trouble if a worker who leaves, is promoted, or becomes ill cannot quickly be replaced with someone else who can do the job. Cross-functional training can provide the talent base that ensures operations will continue to run smoothly.

- Versatile employees can better engineer their own career paths.
- When promotions aren't available, broader exposure and responsibility can motivate workers.
- Training coworkers can clarify a worker's own job responsibilities.
- A broader perspective increases workers' understanding of the business and reduces the need for supervision.[52] This broader understanding allows workers to anticipate the effects of possible actions on the entire operation and to use cross-departmental ties to solve problems collectively.
- When workers can fill in for other workers who are absent, it is easier to use flexible scheduling, which is increasingly in demand as more employees want to spend more time with their families. Often the absence of one skilled worker can disrupt production and increase costs for the company.

Employees 50 years or older may be particularly valuable when it comes to cross-functional versatility.[53] Older workers have often performed a variety of jobs, which will have naturally provided them with a good amount of cross-functional experience. They also tend to have a broader perspective on the organization's operations. For these reasons, older workers are often quick studies in a cross-functional training program and make effective peer trainers.

Team Training. Many organizations are grouping more and more of their work around teams. Companies are realizing increased productivity, effectiveness, and efficiency through work teams.[54] Team training can be divided into two areas based on the two basic team operations: content tasks and group processes.[55] *Content tasks* directly relate to a team's goals—for example, cost control and problem solving. *Group processes* pertain to the way members function as a team—for example, how team members behave toward one another, how they resolve conflicts, and how extensively they participate. Unlike traditional individual training, team training goes beyond the content skills and includes group processes.[56]

Surprisingly, little is known about how to train teams most effectively. The following initial findings can be used to guide team training efforts:

- Team members should be trained in communication skills (both speaking and listening) that encourage respect for all team members.
- Training should emphasize the interdependence of team members.
- Instruction should instill the recognition that team goals and individual goals are not always the same and provide strategies for dealing with conflicts that will inevitably arise between the two.
- Flexibility should be emphasized because teamwork almost always causes unexpected situations.[57]

One type of training that has become increasingly popular for developing teamwork, particularly among managerial and supervisory employees, is outdoor experiential training. Companies such as IBM, General Electric, and DuPont periodically take hundreds of employees out of the office and into the woods in hopes of building teamwork, increasing communication skills, and boosting self-esteem. Many of these experiential training programs resemble Outward Bound, the rigorous outdoor adventure course, although they are less physically demanding.

Creativity Training. As a means of tapping their workers' innovative potential, many organizations have been turning to creativity training. According to *Training* magazine, the number of organizations with 100 or more employees that offer creativity training doubled from 16 percent in 1986 to 32 percent in 1990.[58] In 1995 this figure was 35 percent.[59]

Creativity training is based on the assumption that creativity can be learned. There are several approaches to teaching creativity, all of which attempt to help people solve problems in new

Brainstorming
A creativity training technique in which participants are given the opportunity to generate ideas openly, without fear of judgment.

ways.[60] One common approach is the use of **brainstorming,** in which participants are given the opportunity to generate ideas as wild as they can come up with, without fear of judgment. Only after a good number of ideas have been generated are they individually submitted to rational judgment in terms of their cost and feasibility. Creativity is generally viewed as having two phases: imaginative and practical.[61] Brainstorming followed by rational consideration of the options it produces satisfies both of these phases. Figure 8.8 presents some other approaches to increasing creativity.

Because people often find it difficult to break out of their habitual ways of thinking, creativity trainers provide exercises designed to help them see things in a new way. In one innovative program provided by a Dallas-based creativity consultant, half a dozen gifted, outgoing youngsters from a Dallas school are cloistered with up to 30 top managers in day-long sessions. The adults vent their business problems—and the kids give them advice. The adult participants have found talking to kids about these problems helpful because, as an executive from Texas Utilities Mining put it, "They didn't have any preconceived ideas."[62]

Some companies, such as Pfizer, Inc. (now merged with Warner-Lambert) and Progressive Corporation, use art as inspiration for problem solving and to spark creativity among employees.[63] Both companies expose employees to art through museum workshops or displaying art in its facilities. The Boyer Corporation has a company art program designed to promote "out-of-the-box" thinking. The purpose of the art programs is to get employees thinking about different alternatives and perspectives so they can be more creative in their work.

Skeptics criticize creativity training, saying there is no way to measure its effectiveness. They also say that training in a soft skill like creativity might make people feel good but does not produce any lasting change in their work performance. It is true that documenting the bottom-line results of creativity training is nearly impossible. Yet some companies have found impressive results. For example, Frito-Lay says a cost-management program done in conjunction with creative problem-solving training saved more than $500 million in a five-year period. And when a team of DuPont's top engineers was stumped at why new technology worked in the lab but faltered in a manufacturing plant, creativity trainers came to the rescue. After employees at the plant were trained in creative thinking techniques, the technology worked as planned.

Of course, creativity training is not a magic solution to all problems. No training program is. And while a training program can help stimulate creativity, the more important factor in generating creative solutions is an organizational environment that supports creativity.[64]

Literacy Training. The abilities to write, speak, and work well with others are critical in today's business environment. Unfortunately, many workers do not meet employer requirements in these areas. For example, although most workplace materials require a tenth- or eleventh-grade reading level, about 20 percent of Americans between the ages of 21 and 25 cannot read at even an eighth-grade level.[65] The American Management Association reported that one in three job

Techniques to Increase Creativity

Figure 8.8

Creativity can be learned and developed. The following techniques can be used to improve a trainee's skill in generating innovative ideas and solutions to problems.

1. **Analogies and Metaphors** Drawing comparisons or finding similarities can improve insight into a situation or problem.
2. **Free Association** Freely associating words to describe a problem can lead to unexpected solutions.
3. **Personal Analogy** Trying to see oneself as the problem can lead to fresh perspectives and, possibly, effective solutions.
4. **Mind Mapping** Generating topics and drawing lines to represent the relationships among them can help to identify all the issues and their linkages.

Source: Adapted from Higgins, J. M. (1994). *101 creative problem solving techniques: The handbook of new ideas for business.* Winter Park, FL: New Management Publishing Company.

applicants tested for jobs in 1995 lacked sufficient reading or math skills to perform the job he or she was seeking. In the face of these problems, it is surprising that less than 20 percent of U.S. companies offer literacy training of any kind.[66]

Before proceeding further, it is important to clarify some definitions. The term **literacy** is generally used to mean the mastery of *basic skills*—that is, the subjects normally taught in public schools (reading, writing, arithmetic, and their uses in problem solving). It is important to distinguish between general literacy and functional literacy. *General literacy* is a person's general skill level, while *functional literacy* is a person's skill level in a particular content area. An employee is functionally literate if he or she can read and write well enough to perform important job duties (reading instruction manuals, understanding safety messages, filling out order slips). The most pressing issue for employers is not the general deficiencies in the workforce but rather their workers' ability to function effectively in their jobs. For example, a generally low level of reading ability may be cause for societal concern, but it is workers' inability to understand safety messages or fill out order slips that is the immediate concern for business. Functional illiteracy can be a serious impediment to an organization's productivity and competitiveness. For instance, the Occupational Safety and Health Administration (see Chapter 16) believes that there is a direct correlation between illiteracy and some workplace accidents.

Literacy
The mastery of basic skills (reading, writing, arithmetic, and their uses in problem solving).

Functional literacy training programs focus on the basic skills required to perform a job adequately and capitalize on most workers' motivation to get help or advance in a particular job. These programs use materials drawn directly from the job. For example, unlike a reading comprehension course (which teaches general reading skills), functional training teaches employees to comprehend manuals and other reading materials they must use on the job.

Working in concert with unions, government agencies, and schools, companies have devised a number of programs to remedy deficiencies in basic skills. These programs fall into three basic categories:

- **Company in-house programs** These programs are conducted solely or primarily for company employees. One of the earliest in-house programs was begun in the 1960s at Polaroid Corporation. Polaroid's program focuses on a range of basic literacy and arithmetic skills. Employees are assessed by their supervisors and the HR department, and those with reading skills below the fourth-grade level enter a tutorial program that takes four hours per week. Instruction is tailored to the individual's job.

  Companies that offer literacy training must vigorously advertise and promote their programs to reach the employees who need them. Many firms do this through company newsletters or bulletin-board announcements.

- **Company/local schools programs** Many companies join with a local high school or community college in a partnership aimed at improving workers' literacy. In these partnerships, companies and/or unions pay the tuition for workers to attend classes at local schools. Some companies allow workers up to six hours off per week to attend classes. Sometimes several companies are involved in the partnership, as in the Newark Literacy Campaign, the Alliance for Education in Worcester, Massachusetts, and the Memphis Literacy Coalition.

  In Phoenix, the Public Works and Personnel Departments worked with local community colleges and a county literacy volunteer group to develop a curriculum for city employees.[67] The well-received program has been successful despite its relatively low cost, which averages about $2.25 per employee contact hour. More than 950 employees from 13 departments have participated in the program.[68] Gains in literacy help the organization and improve employees' personal and professional quality of life. Figure 8.9 on page 282 presents some suggestions, based on the experience of the City of Phoenix, for implementing a successful literacy program.

- **Company/local or state government programs** In some areas, local or state government has supplied the major initiative for literacy programs. The South Carolina Institute for Work Force Excellence is one of the most extensive partnership programs between state government and the state's leading employers. In the first year after the South Carolina legislature passed a broad education reform measure, 338 initiative programs enrolling more than 3,000 people were held across the state. A third of the people enrolled work for Springs Industries, Inc., the state's largest employer. Other major participating companies are Campbell Soup, Digital Equipment, and Sun Oil.[69]

A Question of Ethics

Are companies ethically responsible for providing literacy training for workers who lack basic skills? Why or why not?

Suggestions for the Successful Implementation of a Literacy Program

Figure 8.9

1. Be sensitive in your approach to skills assessment. Assessments can be a source of stress for employees.
2. Tie the curriculum as closely as possible to what workers do. For example, tie reading back to understanding a workplace memo.
3. Include both managers and employees in the development stage of the program.
4. Align the program with company objectives and job requirements.
5. Be flexible about when and where training is held and provide incentives for participation.
6. Provide for self-paced learning. Workers will have very different skill levels and learning abilities.
7. Use a variety of training tools.
8. Provide ongoing feedback.
9. Ensure employee confidentiality.
10. Get the support of top management for the program.

Source: Adapted from Hays, S. (1999). Basic skills training 101. *Workforce, 78*, 76–78.

Diversity Training. Ensuring that the diverse groups of people working in a company get along and cooperate is vital to organizational success. As we saw in Chapter 4, *diversity training programs* are designed to teach employees about specific cultural and sex differences and how to respond to these in the workplace. Diversity training is particularly important when team structures are used. Diversity training efforts can be difficult for white males because they may perceive that the training is directed at or against them.[70] To be successful, diversity training efforts need to include and be sensitive to all groups. Diversity training that focuses on individual strengths and weaknesses rather than on differences between groups can be a positive experience for all employees. A recent survey of *Fortune* 1000 companies found that the majority of firms offer diversity training with an average of 5 hours of diversity training per employee.[71] The majority of people surveyed also reported that the diversity efforts yielded improvements in corporate culture, recruitment, and client relations. (See Chapter 4 for additional information about this type of training.)

Crisis Training. Unfortunately, accidents, disasters, and violence are part of life. Events such as plane crashes, chemical spills, and workplace violence can wreak havoc on organizations. Yet many companies are ill prepared to deal with the tragedies and their aftermath. Consider the case of Pan Am, which made one mistake after another when trying to cope with a terrorist attack that resulted in the death of everyone aboard one of its flights. The following are just some of the mistakes Pan Am made:[72]

- The airline informed one family of their daughter's death by leaving a message on their answering machine.
- A family awaiting the arrival of their only child's body was told that their "shipment" had arrived. At the local airport the family was met by a forklift driver at a building marked "livestock."
- A flight attendant who was supposed to work on the doomed flight was so upset that she asked to be excused from her next flight. She was told that if she didn't fly she would be fired.

Ironically, Pan Am had practiced responding to a mock crash only two months earlier. As is too often the case, however, the crisis management training didn't address the human elements of a crisis.

In addition to after-the-fact crisis management, *crisis training* can focus on prevention. For example, organizations are becoming increasingly aware of the possibility of workplace violence, such as attacks by disgruntled former employees or violence against spouses. Prevention training often includes seminars on stress management, conflict resolution, and team building.[73]

Customer Service Training. Organizations are increasingly recognizing the importance of meeting customers' expectations, particularly those companies that have a quality focus. In addition to establishing philosophies, standards, and systems that support customer service, these companies often provide customer service training to give employees the skills they need to meet and exceed customer expectations. Sometimes the market forces a company to realize the importance of customer service. Denny's, the nation's largest family restaurant chain, has been learning the importance of customer service. Denny's was hit with racial bias lawsuits that resulted in a $46 million settlement in 1994. The restaurant chain was found guilty of discrimination by offering poorer and slower service to minority than to majority group members. However, the media attention to the case may have highlighted for some unscrupulous people the legal jackpot that poor service might provide. Thus, Denny's and other family-style restaurants include listening, communicating, and responding to customers as part of their training.[74] Training for customer service may be a way to not only increase profits but also to decrease the chances of a discrimination lawsuit.

The Evaluation Phase

In the evaluation phase of the training process, the effectiveness of the training program is assessed. Companies can measure effectiveness in monetary or nonmonetary terms. Whatever the terms, the training should be judged on how well it addressed the needs it was designed to address. For example, a business may evaluate a training program designed to increase workers' efficiency by assessing its effects on productivity or costs, but not in terms of employee satisfaction.

All too often the evaluation phase of the training process is neglected. This is tantamount to making an investment without ever determining if you're receiving an adequate (or any) return on it. Granted, collecting the necessary data and finding the time to analyze training results may be difficult. But at the very least companies should estimate the costs and benefits of a training program, even if these cannot be directly measured. Without such information, training's value cannot be demonstrated, and upper management may feel there is no compelling reason to continue the training effort. The Manager's Notebook entitled "Is It Worth It? The ROI of Training" presents the basic steps needed to estimate the return on an investment in training.

Emerging Trends

MANAGER'S NOTEBOOK

Is It Worth It? The ROI of Training

Does it make a difference? How effective is it? What's the bottom line? These questions are important when it comes to training and have taken on increased importance given the current context of economic uncertainty and tight budgets. Investments in training may not be made without estimates that substantiate positive returns on those investments.

Return on investment (ROI) is calculated using this formula:

$$\text{ROI} = \frac{(\text{Training Benefits} - \text{Training Costs})}{\text{Training Costs}} \times 100$$

$$= \frac{\text{Net Training Benefits}}{\text{Training Costs}} \times 100$$

Some suggestions regarding ROI of training:

- ***Plan ahead.*** **If you want to show that a training program has a positive impact on the bottom line, make sure that the training is needed and will be tied to business results. If analysis of a proposed training effort indicates it is not needed or has no link to business results, then do not follow through with the program.**
- ***Determine what you will measure.*** **The measures by which the effectiveness of a training program will be assessed need to be carefully chosen. The measures need to fit with the thrust or purpose of the training but also need to be relevant to the business.**

- *Design how the effectiveness of training will be assessed.* A group of employees that did not receive training can serve as a control group. Another possibility is to contrast measured results of the linked business activity after training with measured results of the same business activity before training.
- *Convert nonmonetary measures to dollar terms.* To estimate ROI, all measures must be placed into the same dollar metric. Some measures may not easily translate into a dollar value, but estimates can be made. For example, the cost/benefit of a unit of performance or a change in attitude or in loyalty may need to be estimated.

Source: Adapted from *Managing Training & Development*. (2001). True training ROI: Going beyond smile sheets. August Newsletter of the Institute of Management and Administration, *1*, 6–7, 10; and *Human Resource Department Management Report*. (2002). Four quick steps to proving the ROI of your HR self-service applications. May Newsletter of the Institute of Management and Administration, *1*.

The evaluation process followed by Allied Signal's Garrett Engine Division provides an excellent illustration of how to measure training's effectiveness. Personnel responsible for training at Garrett Engine assessed its effectiveness at the four levels presented in Figure 8.10. At level 1, trainees rated the course and instructor at the time of training. At level 2, participants were given an after-training test. The results of these tests were compared against scores on a pretest and against the scores achieved by a group of workers who did not go through the training (the *control group*). At level 3, trainees' use of their new skills and knowledge back on the job were compared against the job performance of the control group. At level 4, the evaluation team examined the critical issue of whether the training made a real difference to the company's bottom line.

In general, the outcomes of the first three levels of measurement were positive. At level 1, trainees gave high ratings to the course and instructor. The test at level 2 indicated that the performance of employees who had received training was higher than that of the employees who had not. The same result was achieved at level 3. Nonetheless, the big question remained: Did the training have a positive dollar impact on the company?

To answer this question, the Garrett training team measured performance before and after training for both trained and untrained groups of maintenance workers in terms of response time to job requests and job-completion time. It was assumed that if the maintenance teams were responding and completing jobs more quickly, the equipment would be down less time and Garrett Engine Division would save money. The maintenance department had already calculated the cost of equipment downtime, and this figure was used to translate downtime into dollar amounts. As Figure 8.11 shows, the after-training downtime for the training group, at $1,156, was $55 less than that for the control group, at $1,211. This $55 value appears to be the monetary benefit of the training experience. Although this may seem like a small amount, it represents the savings *per job*, and the team completed on average 55 jobs per week. The total cost of the team-building training was estimated to be $5,355. A monthly return on investment (ROI)

Four Measurement Levels Employed by Garrett Engine Division

Figure 8.10

Level	Type of Measurement
1	Participants' reaction to the training at the time of the training.
2	Participants' learning of the content of the training.
3	Participants' use of their new skills and knowledge back on the job.
4	Company's return on the training investment.

Source: Pine, J., and Tingley, J. C. (1993). ROI of soft skills training. *Training, 30*, 55–60. Reprinted with permission from the February 1993 issue of *Training*.

Figure 8.11

Performance Levels of Training and Control Groups at Garrett Engine Division

	Response Time	Completion Time	Total Down Time	Estimated Cost
Training Group				
Before training	4.8 hours	13.6 hours	18.4 hours	$1,341
After training	4.1 hours	11.7 hours	15.8 hours	$1,156
Control Group[a]				
Before training	4.4 hours	11.6 hours	16.0 hours	$1,165
After training	4.4 hours	11.7 hours	16.1 hours	$1,211

[a]The control group was not trained. The numbers cited here for the control group were compiled before and after the training group underwent training.

Source: Pine, J., and Tingley, J. C. (1993). ROI of soft skills training. *Training, 30*, 55–60. Reprinted with permission from the February 1993 issue of *Training*. Copyright 1993. Lakewood Publications, Minneapolis, MN. All rights reserved. Not for resale.

calculation using these figures is presented in Figure 8.12. In the short run, the training certainly appeared to pay off.

Although the financial return on training expenditures is important, it is not always the most appropriate measure of effectiveness. A better measurement might be whether the training resulted in attaining the business goal.[75] In a competitive fight for survival, achieving business goals may be more important than a cost/benefit analysis.

Also, the purpose of evaluation may be more than assessment.[76] For example, measures of training effectiveness might serve as a source of learning and motivation if they are provided as feedback to trainees. A business could use data on behavioral change, for instance, to give workers feedback about their work-related improvements.

Legal Issues and Training

Like all other HRM functions, training is affected by legal regulations. The major requirement here is that employees must have access to training and development programs in a nondiscriminatory fashion. Equal opportunity regulations and antidiscrimination laws apply to the training process, just as they do to all other HR functions.

As we discussed in Chapter 3, determining whether a training program has adverse impact is a primary means of deciding if a process is discriminatory. If relatively few women and minori-

Figure 8.12

ROI After Four Average Workweeks at Garrett Engine Division

	$55 (average savings per job)
x	55 (jobs per week)
x	4 (number of weeks)
=	$12,100 (benefits)
-	$5,355 (cost of training)
=	$6,745 (net benefits)

$\frac{6{,}745}{5{,}355} = 1.26 = 126\%\ \text{ROI}$

Source: Pine, J., and Tingley, J. C. (1993). ROI of soft skills training. *Training, 30*, 55–60. Reprinted with permission from the February 1993 issue of *Training*. Copyright 1993. Lakewood Publications, Minneapolis, MN. All rights reserved. Not for resale.

ties are given training opportunities, it would appear that there is discrimination in terms of development offered to different groups of employees. This situation could trigger an investigation and the company may have to demonstrate that development opportunities are offered on a job-relevant and nondiscriminatory basis.

A Special Case: Orientation and Socialization

Orientation
The process of informing new employees about what is expected of them in the job and helping them cope with the stresses of transition.

It is possible, though difficult to prove, that the most important training opportunity occurs when employees start with the firm. At this time managers have the chance to set the tone for new employees through **orientation,** the process of informing new employees about what is expected of them in the job and helping them cope with the stresses of transition. Orientation is an important aspect of the socialization stage of the staffing process as briefly discussed in Chapter 5.

Although many people use the terms *orientation* and *socialization* synonymously, we define socialization as a long-term process with several phases that helps employees acclimate themselves to the new organization, understand its culture and the company's expectations, and settle into the job. We view orientation as a short-term program that informs them about their new position and the company.

The socialization process is often informal and, unfortunately, informal can mean poorly planned and haphazard. A thorough and systematic approach to socializing new employees is necessary if they are to become effective workers. The first step should be an orientation program that helps new employees understand the company's mission and reporting relationships and how things work and why.

Socialization can be divided into three phases: (1) anticipatory, (2) encounter, and (3) settling in.[77] At the *anticipatory stage,* applicants generally have a variety of expectations about the organization and job based on accounts provided by newspapers and other media, word of mouth, public relations, and so on. A number of these expectations may be unrealistic and, if unmet, can lead to dissatisfaction, poor performance, and high turnover.

Realistic job preview (RJP)
Realistic information about the demands of the job, the organization's expectations of the job holder, and the work environment.

A **realistic job preview (RJP)** is probably the best method of creating appropriate expectations about the job.[78] As its name indicates, an RJP presents realistic information about the demands of the job, the organization's expectations of the job holder, and the work environment. This presentation may be made either to applicants or to newly selected employees before they start work. For example, a person applying for a job selling life insurance should be told up front about the potentially negative parts of the job, such as the uncertain commission-based income and the need to try to sell insurance to personal acquaintances. Of course, the positive parts of the job, such as personal autonomy and high income potential, should also be mentioned.

RJPs can be presented orally, in written form, on videotape, or, occasionally in a full-blown work sample. For instance, at Toyota USA's Georgetown (Kentucky) plant, job simulations and work samples are used to demonstrate to applicants the repetitive nature of manufacturing work and the need for teamwork. Studies have found RJPs to have beneficial effects on important organizational outcomes such as performance and turnover.[79]

In the *encounter phase,* the new hire has started work and is facing the reality of the job. Even if an RJP was provided, new hires need information about policies and procedures, reporting relationships, rules, and so on. This type of information is helpful even for new employees who have had substantial experience elsewhere because the organization or work unit often does things somewhat differently than these employees are used to. In addition, providing systematic information about the organization and job can be a very positive signal to new workers that they are valued members of the organization.

During the *settling-in phase,* new workers begin to feel like part of the organization. If the settling in is successful, the worker will feel comfortable with the job and his or her role in the work unit. If it is unsuccessful, the worker may feel distant from the work unit and fail to develop a sense of membership in the organization. An *employee mentoring program,* in which an established worker serves as an adviser to the new employee, may help ensure that settling in is a success.[80] (We talk about mentoring programs at length in Chapter 9.) For example, Bojangles', a quick-service restaurant business, has developed a "buddy system" to help orient

Figure 8.13

Socialization—Do It Yourself!

WHAT'S THE PATH TO SUCCESS?
Get to know people in the organization, especially those who can tell you what it takes to succeed. Make it a goal to get to know four new people in the first two weeks on the job.

GET FEEDBACK.
Have a meeting with your boss within the first month to get an informal sense of how you are performing so far.

DO IT.
Pick a reasonable project and complete it within your first two months on the job. Completing the project will not only show initiative, it will probably introduce you to other parts of the organization and further immerse you in the culture.

WHAT DO YOU DO?
Write your own job description within the first two months on the job. Indicate what it is you really do in this job. This description can be used as a way to check with others, including your boss, as to whether that is what you should be doing. At the very least, people may be impressed with your motivation and diligence.

RENEW AND GO FOR IT AGAIN.
Treat months three and four like the first two months on the job. Commit to reenergizing yourself and renewing your enthusiasm for your new job. Get to know even more people, pick another project, and get more feedback!

Source: Adapted from *Detroit News*. (1998, June). Guide gives advice to new hires, L1.

new employees and reduce employee turnover. The system ensures that each new hire is assigned a mentor who acts as a sounding board and advisor on career issues.[81]

Unfortunately, not all organizations take an active role in orienting new workers. As a new hire, you may find that you have to take the lion's share of the responsibility for socialization yourself. Take a look at Figure 8.13 for ideas on how to do this.

Even the most extensive socialization program won't make new hires feel at ease if their immediate supervisors are not supportive during their adjustment period. See the Manager's Notebook titled "Building New Workers' Confidence" for a list of actions managers can take to make new employees feel at home in the organization.

MANAGER'S NOTEBOOK

Building New Workers' Confidence

A positive experience in the first few days on the job can be critical to the new hire's motivation and success in the organization. Employee orientation, whether it is a large-scale endeavor or a one-on-one process, can help create a positive perception of the organization. Studies have found well-planned orientation to pay off in terms of fewer employee mistakes, lower turnover, better work attitude, and improved communication. Here are steps you can take to create a positive orientation experience.

Give a call. Ask the new employee's supervisor or a coworker to call a few days before his or her start date as a welcome and to answer any questions. This simple preliminary call can reduce first-day anxiety.

Let them know the rules. You or another designated person should inform the new worker about any written or unwritten rules. For example:

✓ Is there a dress code?
✓ Is there a mission statement?

✓ What are the department goals? How is success measured?
✓ Where do you get office supplies?
✓ Where should the worker park?
✓ Is there an e-mail policy?
✓ Is there a sexual harassment or discrimination policy?

Explain who's who. Provide a list of important people and places and their phone numbers. You might include items on this list such as the mailroom, receptionist, maintenance, technical support, security, and key colleagues.

Do it with class. Given a number of new hires, organize an orientation class and provide an opportunity for them to meet each other and realize they're not alone. Cover the employee manual and any necessary administrative work. If available, show a company video introducing them to the organization and its top managers.

Do the tour. Take new hires on a tour of the operation and help them to learn their way around.

Help them hit the ground running. Make sure they have all necessary keys and identification.

Make it fun. Welcome them to their new work area with a basket of gift-wrapped office supplies. This inexpensive gesture can make the first day more like a celebration.

Source: Adapted from Belaiche, M. (1999, Spring). A well-planned orientation makes a difference. *Canadian Manager*, 23–24.

The key point for managers is this: The socialization process may take months, not a day or so. Intracorp, a managed-care and work/life services company, has developed a socialization process called New Directions that recognizes the time it takes to orient employees.[82] The program was implemented to help reduce turnover in the first year of employment.

The New Directions program is divided into four phases.

- **Phase one** acclimates workers by providing expectations and product training.
- **Phase two** is a one-day training session that gives new hires information on the company's history, strategy, policies, and benefits.
- **Phase three** spans the first three months on the job and focuses on training workers about the market, its customers, and business plans.
- **Phase four** carries on through at least six months and consists of interim reviews and feedback.

The program has helped reduce the company's high turnover rate for first-year employees. A number of other companies, such as Texas Instruments, have similar programs.[83]

Summary and Conclusions

Training Versus Development

Although training and development often go hand in hand and the terms are often used interchangeably, the terms are not synonymous. Training typically focuses on providing employees with specific skills and helping them correct deficiencies in their performance. Development is an effort to provide employees with the abilities that the organization will need in the future.

Challenges in Training

Before embarking on a training program, managers must answer several important questions: (1) Is training the solution to the problem? (2) Are the goals of training clear and realistic? (3) Is training a good investment? (4) Will the training work?

Managing the Training Process

The training process consists of three phases: assessment, development and conduct of training, and evaluation. In the assessment phase, organizational, task, and person needs are identified and the goals of training are clarified. Several options are available during the training phase. Training can take place either on the job or off the job and can be delivered through a variety of techniques (slides and videotapes, teletraining, computers, simulations, virtual reality, classroom instruction, and role-plays). The most appropriate type of training (for example, skills, retraining, cross-functional, team, creativity, literacy, diversity, crisis, or customer service) should be chosen to achieve the stated objectives. In the evaluation phase, the costs and benefits of the training program should be assessed to determine its effectiveness.

A Special Case: Employee Socialization and Orientation Organizations should pay particular attention to socializing employees. The first step in socializing them is orientation, or informing new employees about what is expected of them in the job and helping them cope with the inevitable stresses of transition. Companies and managers who recognize that socialization is a long-term process and should be carefully planned will benefit from lower turnover.

Key Terms

brainstorming, 280
cross-functional training, 278
development, 260
job aids, 277
literacy, 281
orientation, 286
peer trainers, 278
realistic job preview (RJP), 286
simulation, 272
training, 260
virtual reality (VR), 273

Discussion Questions

1. Performance problems seem all too common in your workplace. People do not seem to be putting forth the needed effort, and interpersonal conflict on the work teams seems to be a constant. Is training the answer? If so, what kind of training should be done? What other actions may be appropriate?
2. How effective do you think training can be in raising employee motivation?
3. An HR manager recalls a longtime employee who came to her in tears because she heard a rumor that workers would soon be required to use new equipment with a video screen that provided information in text form. The worker knew her inability to read would be discovered and feared she would lose her job.

   Many workers who are illiterate would not be so forthright—partly out of embarrassment, partly out of fear. Another HR manager notes, "They will ask for directions many times, even though the instruction manual is alongside their machine. . . . Some workers always seem to be having problems with their eyesight or their glasses. . . . The truth is that they simply cannot read." How would you go about identifying workers who should receive literacy training? Discuss the differences between general illiteracy and functional illiteracy and how you would decide which of these issues a training program should address.
4. How important is it that the effectiveness of a training program be measured in dollar terms? Why is it important to measure training effectiveness in the first place?
5. Training provides workers with skills needed in the workplace. However, many organizations have dynamic environments in which change is the norm. How can training requirements be identified when job duties are a moving target?
6. Simuflite, a Texas aviation training company, expected to whip the competition with FasTrak, its computer-based training (CBT) curriculum for corporate pilots. Instead, the new venture sent Simuflite into a nose dive. In traditional ground-school training, pilots ask questions and learn from "war stories" told by classmates and instructors. With FasTrak, they sat in front of a computer for hours absorbing information. Their only interaction was in tapping the computer screen to provide answers to questions, and that novelty wore off very quickly. Pilots grew bored with the CBT ground school.

   What does Simuflite's experience suggest about the limitations of interactive media and CBT? In what situations is CBT most likely to be beneficial to trainees?
7. According to one survey, trainees list the following as some of the traits of a successful trainer: knowledge of the subject, adaptability, sincerity, and sense of humor. What other traits do you think trainers need to be successful in the training situation?
8. Jim Sullivan, an operator of successful restaurants for nearly 30 years, has recently stated that the most critical step of adult education is not to learn but to unlearn. He contends that new behaviors will never be used until the old ones are unlearned. Many academic scholars agree with him.

As a simple example, let us say you are a restaurant manager and you want your waitstaff to provide customers with a stand-up list of appetizers. You bring in the staff, tell them what you want them to do, and present a video covering the correct way to use stand-up menus.

No doubt, you have provided training. Why, then, are the staff not using the stand-up appetizer menus a week later? The answer is simple. The training did not cover what needed to be unlearned—the habit of initially interacting with customers by asking whether they are ready to order. The workers need to replace the ingrained behavior with the new behavior of providing the stand-up menu.

Changing a typical way of doing something is difficult. Unlearning and replacing with a new behavior works best if there is a motivating context. For example, the shift to providing stand-up menus might occur most quickly if the waitstaff is made aware of the slim profits in selling entrees versus appetizers. Now the staff is more likely to get on board with this simple change.

a. Do you think unlearning is an important step in learning? Why or why not?

b. How can unlearning be accomplished? If you were responsible for training people in a new way of doing things, how would you go about the "unlearning" phase?

c. Unlearning implies that trainees are not blank slates. However, most training programs do not take this into account. Describe a training program in which you could add the step of unlearning.

9. How to evaluate the return on investment in training is a question that is commonly asked of personnel at the American Society for Training and Development. The results-oriented business mentality places pressure to show that training offers a positive return on investment. The assumption, of course, is that the impact of training can and should be captured financially.

In stark contrast to this trend, Taco, Inc., a privately owned manufacturer of pumps and valves, takes a much more qualitative, if not philosophical, approach to measuring training effectiveness. The company offers impressive educational opportunities. More than six dozen courses are offered in an on-site learning center. The facility cost the company $250,000 to build and the education delivery amounts to $300,000 in annual direct expenses and lost productivity. Asked to place a dollar value on the return from the training, the chief executive simply points to the return in the form of employee attitude.

a. What do you think is the best or most appropriate measure of the return on investment for training? Why?

b. In what situations, if any, would a financial measure of return be inappropriate?

c. Evaluate the Taco, Inc. approach to evaluating training effectiveness. Do you agree with its approach?

d. With your partner or team, develop an approach for evaluating the effectiveness of training from a customer perspective. You might want to start with the four levels of measurement presented in this chapter and apply them to a customer perspective.

Sources: Adapted from Sullivan, J. (1998). Why training doesn't work . . . and what operators better do about it. *Nation's Restaurant News, 32*, 54, 138; and Lei, D., Slocum, J. W., and Pitts, R. A. (1999). Designing organizations for competitive advantage: The power of unlearning and learning. *Organizational Dynamics, 27*, 24–38.

Source: Adapted from Calvacca, L. (1999). The value of employee training. *Folio: The Magazine for Magazine Measurement, 27*, 186–187; and Pffier, J. (1999). Seven practices of successful organizations: Part 2. *Health Forum Journal, 42*, 55.

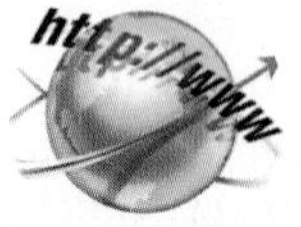

There is a variety of additional material available on the Web site that accompanies this text. You can access this information by visiting the Web site at **www.prenhall.com/gomez.**

YOU MANAGE IT! Customer-Driven HR Case 8.1

Adventure Team Building: Real Substance or Candy?

Trust, risk taking, problem solving, and interpersonal relations are important for the effective performance of teams but can sometimes be problem areas. Some organizations have approached these types of team development areas with outdoor adventure, ropes courses, and sports activities. However, a critical issue is whether these types of experiences really improve the performance of teams in the workplace. Sometimes the experiences don't go as planned. Furthermore, whether these types of experiences really improve the performance of teams in the workplace seems more an issue of belief than of hard evidence. Consider the fire walking adventure hosted by Burger King.

Burger King was looking for a team-building experience and decided on a fire walking exercise as a means to engender risk taking and comradery among Burger King staff members. Fire walking involves walking barefoot across coals that are approximately 1,200 degrees Fahrenheit. Unfortunately, the team-building exercise left participants with first and second-degree burns on their feet. Still, the managers responsible for orchestrating the exercise were positive about the program and emphasized the dedication and courage the staff exhibited.

In addition to fire walking, other intense team-building experiences, such as rope climbing and military maneuvers, hold out the promise of developing trust among team members. However, these programs can be expensive because they usually involve travel to off-site resorts. But do these programs work? Critics of these approaches claim they are quick fixes that can't solve long-term or deep-seated problems. Stephen Covey, a well-known management consultant, refers to these approaches as "cotton candy" and only "cosmetic."

Critical Thinking Questions

1. Do you think intense team-building exercises are worthwhile? Why or why not?
2. Do you agree with Burger King's management that the fire walking program was overall positive?
3. It is typically assumed that the more closely the training experiences match the workplace situation, the greater the chance that the training will transfer to the workplace. For example, the more closely training equipment matches workplace equipment, the fewer the problems should be in transferring the training to the workplace. However, with outdoor adventures and other forms of intense team-building exercises, the training situation does not at all match the workplace situation for most workers, unless they walk on fire or climb ropes as part of their jobs.

   Do you think this lack of correspondence between the training and work situations may be a problem for transfer of training for intense team-building exercises? Explain.

Team Exercise

A number of people have experienced some form of intense team-building experience, such as rope or rock climbing. Have members of your team contact friends, family, and neighbors to locate people who have been through this type of training. Interview these people to get a sense of the exercise they went through, what the point of it was, and how well they think it worked. Collect these experiential descriptions and share them with the rest of the class. Can any conclusions be drawn from these experiences? What other information, in addition to these subjective assessments, would help you decide if intense team-building exercises are worth it?

Source: Adapted from McMaster, M. (2002). Roping in the followers: High-dollar, high-excitement team-building courses may be the last thing your sales force needs. *Sales & Marketing Management, 154*, 36(4).

Customer-Driven HR Case 8.2

YOU MANAGE IT!

The Service Profit Chain: Take Care of Your People and They'll Take Care of the Customers

Monical Pizza, a company located in Illinois, was experiencing sluggish sales, high debt, and rising turnover in the mid-1990s. The president of Monical Pizza, Harry Bond, was searching for a way to improve the performance of the organization when he ran across a 1994 *Harvard Business Review* article entitled "Putting the Service-Profit Chain to Work." The article views profitability as a function of customer loyalty that, in turn, is a function of employee satisfaction and loyalty. The message to Bond and Monical Pizza was to improve employee satisfaction, which would cause employee loyalty and performance to also improve. Customer satisfaction would then follow and lead to improved profitability. Bond took the message to heart and decided that performance improvement at Monical required an internal focus rather than an external focus. Monical made the move to an employee-centric organization and funded the effort by transferring dollars from its media budget into training and development. The company literally shifted its focus to its employees by reallocating budgets.

Monical's focus on employee satisfaction took shape on a number of fronts. Employee satisfaction was included as a measure that determines the amount of management bonus pay. The company completely revised its training program in 1999 and now includes an 8- to 12-week program. The training includes "soft skills" such as communication, recognition, and conflict resolution. The point of the training is to provide managers the skills they need to create a positive work environment for employees.

Implementation of the Service Profit Chain model is ongoing at Monical Pizza, but there are indicators of success.

Turnover improved by 80 percentage points in 2001. Revenue is up and the company is expanding by two to four stores per year. According to President Bond, there is "... a strong, definitive correlation between employee satisfaction, reduced turnover, greater guest satisfaction and our improved financial performance."

Critical Thinking Questions

1. Employee satisfaction is the critical issue in the Service Profit Chain model. Identify positive effects that might be associated with higher employee satisfaction. For example, turnover, as demonstrated by Monical Pizza, might be lowered as a result of improved employee satisfaction. What other positive outcomes might result from improved employee satisfaction?
2. Can you identify additional steps that Monical Pizza could take to further improve employee satisfaction? If you were a consultant hired by Monical Pizza, what would be your recommendations for additional cost-effective actions that would improve employee satisfaction?
3. Is there a downside to a focus on employee satisfaction? That is, can a focus on employee satisfaction lead to negative business outcomes? Explain.

Team Exercise

Divide your team in two groups, one focusing on costs, the other focusing on benefits. Using responses to question 2, the cost group should estimate the costs associated with the various actions that might be taken to improve employee satisfaction. The benefits group should estimate the increased profits or cost savings associated with the various positive outcomes identified in question 1. For example, can you find information on the typical cost of turnover? If you assume, say, a 40 percent reduction turnover for a 500-employee operation, what then might be the dollar benefit to the organization?

Put together the actions and identify which outcomes would seem to be most likely linked to each action. Add your estimates of dollar costs and benefits. Which actions would you recommend based on a potential return or breadth of impact? Share your analysis and recommendations with the rest of the class.

Source: Adapted from Crecca, D. H. (2002). By the book: Monical Pizza Corp. applies Harvard's service profit chain model, driving retention and profiting. *Chain Leader*, 6, 50(3).

YOU MANAGE IT! Emerging Trends Case 8.3

Training Before Employment: How Honda Keeps Firing on All Cylinders

Honda wanted to build a new factory to manufacture its popular and highly rated Odyssey minivan and engine. What it ended up doing is starting from scratch with workers who did not have any experience in building cars! Yet, within two years vehicles were rolling off the line, and within three years it is scheduled to go into full production. How did Honda do it? In a word—training.

Honda was approached by many states that wanted to be home to the new factory. Alabama was chosen because of the availability of labor and the state's offer to partner with Honda in recruitment and training. The state of Alabama allocated $30 million for training and the funds paid for a 62,000-square-foot Honda training center in Lincoln, Alabama. The facility has modern classrooms and replicas of Honda equipment. The Alabama operation provided Honda with an opportunity to make a fresh start and build new processes and a new workforce from scratch. However, between December 1999 and April 2002, 1,500 employees had to be found and trained.

A strategy to Honda's successful launch of this new plant was preemployment training. In conjunction with state labor and training agencies, Honda advertised a free training program that was a precondition for applying for a job with the auto manufacturer. Participants were required to have a high school degree or equivalent and two years of work experience. The training involves attending two one-hour sessions per week for six weeks. The first half of the training is classroom instruction on topics such as math and precision measuring. This initial portion of the training also includes a videotape presentation that conveys the speed and repetitive nature of the manufacturing work. Some people decide the work isn't for them and Honda has experienced about a 15 percent dropout rate. The final three weeks involves intense hands-on training. Participants are carefully observed by 40 assessors who rate each applicant's speed, accuracy, and ability to follow instructions. Completing the training is not a guarantee of employment—it's only an opportunity to apply for a job. However, the majority of graduates of the training get full-time jobs. Honda views putting in the time and effort by an applicant to complete the program as an indication of his or her commitment level.

The free training offer resulted in 18,000 people responding. In conjunction with state agencies, some applicants were eliminated due to lack of education or experience. The program has been training 340 people every six weeks and has graduated over 2,600. There is a backlog of over 1,000 candidates.

Honda considers the plan a success. Honda managers claim they are achieving the same level of performance with a totally inexperienced workforce as Honda operations in which 50 percent of the workforce had auto manufacturing experience. The preemployment training is largely given the credit for the positive results. The training provides skills but also gives people an opportunity to see if they really want to pursue this type of work.

Critical Thinking Questions

1. Do you think it is fair for Honda to offer the training with no guarantee of employment? Why do you think so many people are willing to put in the time and effort needed to complete the preemployment training?
2. Honda focused on classroom and hands-on experiences for its preemployment training approaches at a time when electronic approaches, such as e-learning, were receiving a great deal of attention as the new, effective, and less costly approach to training. Why do you think Honda chose the training approaches it did?
3. Given you had input over how preemployment training was to be delivered, what would you recommend? Specifically, would you recommend an e-learning approach, a more traditional classroom and hands-on approach such as used by Honda, or an approach that blends the two? Identify the characteristics that would drive your recommendation. For example, what characteristics of the work, of the training participants, and of the organization would be important in determining how preemployment training should be delivered? List contingency factors and explain how each factor would suggest a particular approach to delivering preemployment training.

Team Exercise

Honda's assessment of the effectiveness of its preemployment training program seems subjective. As discussed in this chapter, the effectiveness of training can be assessed at a number of levels. Certainly, impact on business results and ROI estimates are important outcomes, but other levels of impact can be important, too.

1. For each possible level of analysis, identify how you could go about assessing the effectiveness of Honda's preemployment training. What measures or data would you need? Would you use a control group? A before–after comparison? Comparisons with other plants? Share your assessment approaches for each level with the rest of the class.
2. Divide your team in half with one group responsible for costs and the other group for benefits. Identify the various cost items and benefits that might be involved in a preemployment effort such as Honda's. Estimate the costs and benefits and calculate an ROI for the program. (Note: The assessors involved in Honda's preemployment training are actually part-time state employees, not Honda employees.) Would your ROI calculation be affected by including the assessors on Honda's payroll? What if the facility costs had to be borne by Honda? Would your ROI calculations indicate that Honda would have still pursued this program?

Source: Adapted from Grossman, R. I. (2002). Made from scratch: When Honda built a plant in Alabama it also built a workforce using local workers who had no experience in making cars. *HRMagazine*, *47*, 44(7).

Emerging Trends Case 8.4

YOU MANAGE IT!

Eureka! Lessons from the Ranch

Creativity. It is a term that evokes an image of warm and fuzzy artistic expression. However, many organizations are realizing that creativity, in the form of cold, hard, innovativeness that is related to business results, is a necessity for competing in crowded and turbulent markets. Linking creativity to business performance is the special niche of a unique place called the Eureka Ranch.

The Eureka Ranch is an operation started by Doug Hall, a former marketing executive for Procter & Gamble. What sets Eureka Ranch apart from other creativity training programs is that it is based on careful statistical analysis of companies that generated business ideas and inventions. Through research on the experience of clients such as Pepsi, Nike, and Walt Disney, the ranch has identified some key factors related to creativity that lead to a business payoff. These factors fall under the general categories of marketing and creativity and are summarized here.

Marketing

Benefit. The product or service has to have an obvious benefit. It has to be something that cuts through the information overload of customers.

Credibility. The benefit has to be believable due to, for example, the company's reputation, guarantee, or testimonials.

Uniqueness. The product or service needs to be different from what is already available.

Creativity

Related and unrelated stimuli. Ideas can be generated by things that are related and converge as well as by things that are unrelated and diverge.

Diversity in thinking. Mixing together people who are diverse in their ways of thinking and problem solving, not necessarily diverse in demographics, can lead to more and varied ideas.

Fear elimination. People hold back because they are afraid of ridicule and other possible negative outcomes. Fear must be eliminated if creativity and effective implementation of new ideas are to be successful.

Critical Thinking Questions

1. A creativity program at Eureka Ranch can cost anywhere from nothing for a free trial sampling of its service to $150,000 for a full training program that includes an artificial intelligence program capable of evaluating the probability of marketplace success of your idea. Do you think this training is worth it? Explain.
2. Creativity is something that sounds like a positive and desirable characteristic. Are there situations in which you would *not* want employees to be creative? Describe these situations.
3. Consider each of the key factors promoted by Eureka Ranch. How could you apply them in efforts in your own organization to generate ideas for products or services that will add to the bottom line?

Team Exercise

Eureka Ranch approaches creativity as something that can be learned. However, creativity can also be an individual difference characteristic in which some people are just naturally more creative and others less so.

Divide your team in half with each half taking a training or individual difference approach to creativity. How would you manage and promote creativity from each perspective? Identify key structures and processes in your system. The two groups should share the systems that were generated. Next, as an entire team, address how you would manage and promote creativity if it is both an individual difference as well as something that can be learned.

Source: Adapted from Kaplan-Leiserson, E. (2001). Eureka! *T + D, 55*, 50–61.

YOU MANAGE IT!

Video Shorts Case 8.5

Training and Development

In today's show, *SPOTLIGHT* host Meg Allen takes us straight to the heart of the hotel industry—customer service. Jenny Herman, director of training and development at Loews Hotels, and Martin Buckingham, associate director of human resources at Hot Jobs.com, are today's guests. Watch along with them, as *SPOTLIGHT*'s undercover tape reveals how Jenny turns a confrontational meeting with marketing director, Danielle Jacobs, into an opportunity for both corporate and personal growth.

As you listen, it might be useful to note the following: Known throughout the United States and Canada for its friendly service, Loews employs over 2,500 people and is currently planning its largest expansion ever. Loews has recently opened five new properties, with more in various stages of development.

Danielle has come into Jenny's office to let her know, in no uncertain terms, that the new hotel employees are not up to par. She has been with Loews for over 15 years and is used to running a close-knit, efficient department. Since the opening of five new hotels, the marketing team has been busier than ever, coming up with special guest packages like Loews Loves Pets and Generation G. The recent hiring of new personnel at the hotel sites was supposed to make rolling out her department's new programs easier, but she feels that it is making everything worse. The customer complaints that have been received reflect badly on her and on her marketing staff. Moreover, she feels that since the expansion she no longer has the inside track on the training process for all the new guest programs her department is rolling out.

When Danielle enters, you will notice the exchange of greetings is very brief and both women seem prepared to defend their turf. Danielle clearly wants to deflect any blame for guest complaints from herself. Why do you think Jenny is careful to offer alternative explanations for the downfall in service before revealing that she is aware of the complaints and has evidence that it is very likely newly hired personnel who were at fault?

As training and development is clearly a function of HR, Danielle wants to know why the new employees have not been trained properly or "recoached." In response, Jenny shares with Danielle that, although the New Hire Certification Process is "cutting edge in the hotel industry," it is not working as well as management had hoped it would. It seems that the program will have to be revised. She also tells Danielle that "mystery shoppers" used in researching the complaints supported her belief that it was new employees who were making mistakes. But Danielle is not satisfied and presses Jenny, asking whether there isn't some way that an employee who is falling short can be observed. She doesn't stop there, suggesting that maybe the worker could be talked to and be helped. Consider why, at this juncture, Jenny invites Danielle to be a member of the Training Task Force. If you watch Jenny's face you might almost see a smile. Danielle wants to have input and gladly accepts. Analyze what has happened in the communication between these two dedicated Loews professionals.

We have already seen that each of the Loews branded programs is documented in Loews Core Standards and gotten a glimpse of just how important ongoing training is in the hotel industry. In the discussion segment of the show it is made clear that training is key at Hot Jobs as well. According to Martin Buckingham, Hot Jobs does needs analysis to decide exactly what kind of training program would be best and follows up with constant monitoring. Employees at Hot Jobs are encouraged to give and receive constructive feedback on an ongoing basis in place of a more formal system that might entail an annual review. Think about why this seems particularly well suited to a dot-com company. Right now, there is a diversity training program in place at Hot Jobs in order to educate everyone to value the way others think. Of course, because Hot Jobs is in the throws of a merger with Yahoo!, HR has had to turn much of its training effort to giving managers the tools they need to get through this period of turmoil.

HR has many training methods available today, including mentoring and management development programs that enable people to develop themselves and achieve both personal and professional goals. As *SPOTLIGHT*'s Meg Allen says, "Your employees are your customers."

Critical Thinking Questions

1. How was HR management at Loews able to determine that the customer complaints were most likely due to a training problem? Why was this strategically important to HR?
2. Now that you have been inside HR at both Loews Hotels and Hot Jobs, recommend one "off-the-job training and development technique" for each company. Why do you think this technique would be most effective?
3. What basic steps would you advise Jenny Herman to take in managing strategic organizational renewal at Loews? She has shared some of the programs already in place as the company expands, but there may be some basic ground rules for leading change that would help her to improve results.
4. As a new employee at Loews, do you think you would enjoy being part of a mentoring program? Why? As an employee who has worked at Loews for 20 years, do you think you would enjoy being part of a mentoring program? Why?
5. HR at Hot Jobs favors ongoing constructive feedback as a means of performance appraisal. In your opinion is there an alternate method of performance appraisal that might work well at Hot Jobs? Why? If you feel that your method may be even better than feedback, feel free to say so!

Developing Careers

Challenges

After reading this chapter, you should be able to deal more effectively with the following challenges:

1. **Establish** a sound process for helping employees develop their careers.
2. **Understand** how to develop your own career.
3. **Identify** the negative aspects of an overemphasis on career development.
4. **Understand** the importance of dual-career issues in career development.
5. **Develop** a skills inventory and a career path.
6. **Establish** an organizational culture that supports career development.

Steve, a technician at GCX for the past six years, was once an excellent performer. Over the past few years, however, he has grown increasingly frustrated and disillusioned. He expected to move up in the company, but it isn't happening.

When his department supervisor retired last year, Steve thought that he would be promoted into the position. He told Natalie, the unit manager, of his interest, and she assured him that he would be given every consideration. The next thing Steve knew, someone from outside the company had been offered the job.

Steve was disappointed and angry, and the lack of an explanation didn't help. He didn't understand why he had been passed over. He had consistently been a top performer. He knew the technical end of the business as well as anyone, and he always achieved his performance objectives. What did he have to do to get into management?

After a couple of weeks of quietly seething, Steve decided to ask Natalie point blank why he had not been offered the supervisor's job. Natalie seemed quite surprised at Steve's eagerness to be promoted. She told him that she hadn't thought his interest in the supervisory position was very strong and that an outsider got the job simply because he had better credentials. She advised Steve to keep trying; sooner or later, something would open up.

Steve was no closer to understanding what he needed to do to get promoted. When he got home that night, he made some phone calls about job openings he had seen advertised. Maybe he could advance faster somewhere else. Even if he didn't leave GCX, he thought, he sure wasn't going to go out of his way for the company anymore. He had some sick days coming and he planned on using them soon.

Allessandra relaxed at home after two long, interesting days. Her company, a large telecommunications firm, had sent her to an assessment center for an evaluation of her strengths and weaknesses as a potential middle-level manager. Currently, she was the head of a sales office located in Des Moines, Iowa, and was responsible for the surrounding metropolitan area.

Her experience at the assessment center could not have been better. After a day and a half of various activities, she had met with the consultants who operate the center. They told her that she definitely had the characteristics her company was looking for in a future manager. She had a few weak areas—most notably, confidence in pushing her ideas in the face of opposition—but she already knew this and was working on overcoming her timidity. They told her that the report she received would also be given to her boss, as well as to the HR manager responsible for management development activities. She knew that although it might take a year or two for a position to become available, she was on her way up.

THE MANAGERIAL PERSPECTIVE

Steve's experience, unfortunately, is much more common than Allessandra's: Workers often have goals and aspirations that their organizations do not know about. Whether these goals are reasonable or unrealistic, lack of progress toward them can have a strongly negative effect on performance.

Giving employees opportunities to grow and develop can ensure that your workforce keeps pace with the demands of the changing business environment. In addition, if you make this kind of investment in your employees, you are more likely to keep workers instead of seeing them lured away by competitors.

The employer and employee often share the responsibility for career development. In your job as a manager, then, you are likely to be partially responsible for your career development and for your workers' career development. As part of that responsibility, you may become involved in a formal or informal mentor relationship. In this chapter we investigate how you can help manage others' career development and your own. First, we define career development. Second, we explore some of the major challenges connected with career development and offer some approaches to help managers avoid problems in this area. We conclude by discussing self-development.

What Is Career Development?

As we noted in Chapter 8, career development is different from training. Career development has a wider focus, longer time frame, and broader scope. The goal of training is improvement in performance; the goal of development is enriched and more capable workers. **Career development** is not a one-shot training program or career-planning workshop. Rather, it is an ongoing organized and formalized effort that recognizes people as a vital organizational resource.[1]

Career development
An ongoing and formalized effort that focuses on developing enriched and more capable workers.

The career development field, though relatively young, has seen tremendous change, largely because career opportunities and paths are less structured and predictable than they were two decades ago.[2] Instead of job security and career-long tenure with one organization, downsizing and technological change now characterize the business world.

Survey results indicate that business realities such as downsizing and rapid change have affected employees' career attitudes.[3] A national survey of more than 1,000 adults found that only 56 percent think long-term career advancement depends on staying with an employer for a long time. An increasing number of workers, especially those with college degrees or annual salaries greater than $50,000, believe job hopping is an acceptable way to advance their careers. John Challenger, CEO of the outplacement firm Challenger Gray & Christmas, said that over half of his firm's clients found jobs in new industries in the fourth quarter of last year, a 10-year peak. He points out that most skills are transferable to other industries and that those skills are frequently more critical in other industries than in employees' current jobs. The Manager's Notebook: Emerging Trend, "Making the Switch: Changing Industries, Not Careers," examines why people may want to change the industry they work in, yet keep their career focus. The feature also includes suggestions to help make the transition from one industry to another as successful as possible.

MANAGER'S NOTEBOOK

Emerging Trends

Making the Switch: Changing Industries, Not Careers

People contemplate a work-related change for a variety of reasons. Individuals who lose their jobs due to downsizing may be looking at how they can make a new start in another field. Even those who have survive downsizings in their organizations may be looking for a more secure work environment. Or people may simply want a change in their work environment. However, a radical career change isn't a practical option in many cases. A career change may mean developing new skills and functional expertise. It could entail obtaining a degree or certificate in an unfamiliar area. However, a change in industries may not require a whole new set of skills.

Why change industries? Because the grass may be greener in some other industry. The following industries are projected to be growth areas.

- *Health care*. Health-related businesses, such as hospitals, clinics, and biotech firms, are projected to be great opportunities for employees.
- *Government*. The demand for labor is expected to increase because 45 percent of senior U.S. government executives are expected to retire by 2005.
- *Education*. More than 2 million teachers are expected to retire by 2008.
- *Security and insurance*. After the terrorist attacks of September 11, 2001, the fields of both security and insurance are experiencing an upsurge in demand but insufficient labor to meet it.

Although there may be some industries that you find very appealing, you may not know how to break into them. Recruiters and headhunters often screen out people who don't have industry experience. The following points can help you to successfully make the switch to a new industry.

- *Networking*. Organizations are often deluged with résumés when a job opening is posted, particularly when a posting is done electronically. However, being a friend of a friend who happens to be a manager in the industry you are targeting may lead to worthwhile job leads. A recent survey found the majority of new hires came from employee referrals. In addition to job leads, use your network of friends, family, and business acquaintances to help you effectively portray your skills and experiences in a way that is relevant to your target industry.
- *Learn the lingo*. Some industries, such as biotech, have a great number of buzzwords. Learn the language used in the industry if you want to fit in and not signal that you are an outsider.
- *Do your homework*. Information on almost any company in any industry can be found on the Internet.
- *Know yourself*. What are your interests and values? What are you willing to give up and what isn't negotiable to you? Answering these questions can help you determine if the industry and

companies you are targeting will be a good fit for you. Knowing if you are willing to take a pay cut for a job in a more rural setting or if you thrive on a fast-paced environment will help you to quickly determine if opportunities are right for you.

- *Burn no bridges.* Soon after you land a job and start working in the targeted industry, it's possible you may discover the grass isn't greener there and you may view your industry switch as a mistake. Given this possibility, keep in touch with former colleagues and be familiar with developments in the industry you left. Keeping your contacts and knowledge base current can be your insurance against total loss of employment.

Source: Adapted with permission from Harrington, A. (2002). Make that switch. *Fortune*, *145*, 159+.

The uncertain business environment and changing employee attitudes hamper career development efforts. Even so, career development remains an important activity. It can play a key role in helping managers recruit and retain the skilled, committed workforce an organization needs to succeed.[4] But it can only do so if it meets the dynamic needs of employers and employees.

In the 1970s, most organizations instituted career development programs to help meet organizational needs (such as preparing employees for anticipated management openings) rather than to meet employees' needs.[5] Today, career development usually involves meeting employee and employer needs. Figure 9.1 shows how organizational and individual career needs can be linked to create a successful career development program. Many organizations view career development as a way of preventing job burnout (see Chapter 16), improving the quality of employees' work lives, and meeting affirmative action goals.[6]

This changed emphasis has largely resulted from a combination of competitive pressures (such as downsizing and technological changes) and workers' demands for more opportunities for growth and skill development.[7] This combination has made career development a more difficult endeavor than it used to be. There is no longer a strict hierarchy of jobs from which a career path can easily be constructed. Career development today involves workers' active participation in thinking through the possible directions their careers can take.

An organization must make career development a key business strategy if it intends to survive in an increasingly competitive and global business environment.[8] In the information age, companies will compete more on their workers' knowledge, skill, and innovation levels than on the basis of labor costs or manufacturing capacity.[9] Because career development plays a central

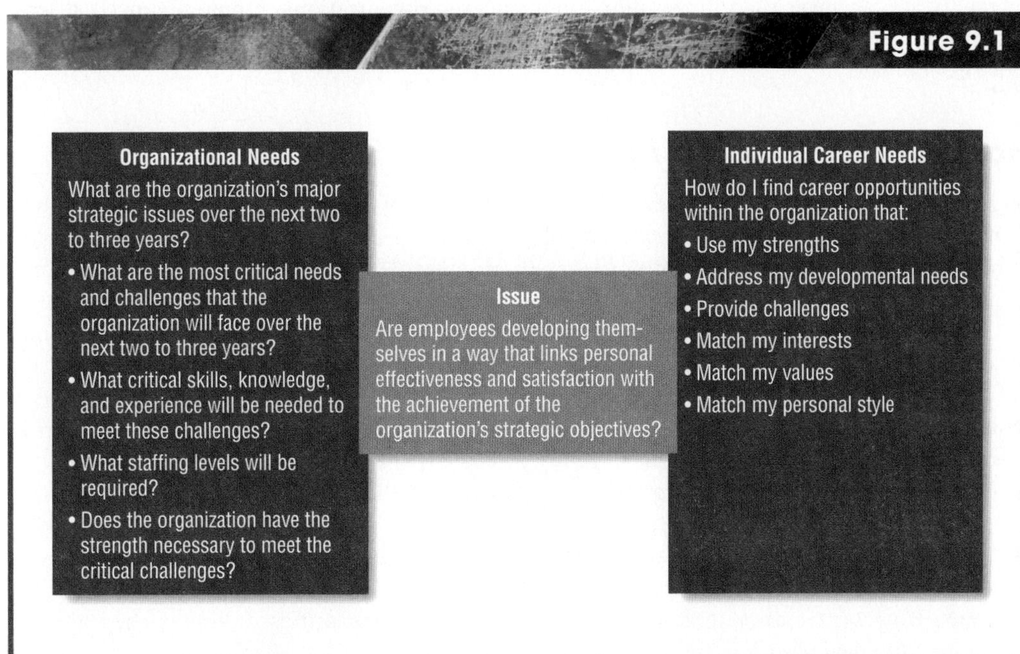

Figure 9.1
Organizational Needs
What are the organization's major strategic issues over the next two to three years?
• What are the most critical needs and challenges that the organization will face over the next two to three years?
• What critical skills, knowledge, and experience will be needed to meet these challenges?
• What staffing levels will be required?
• Does the organization have the strength necessary to meet the critical challenges?
Issue
Are employees developing themselves in a way that links personal effectiveness and satisfaction with the achievement of the organization's strategic objectives?
Individual Career Needs
How do I find career opportunities within the organization that:
• Use my strengths
• Address my developmental needs
• Provide challenges
• Match my interests
• Match my values
• Match my personal style

Career Development System: Linking Organizational Needs with Individual Career Needs

Source: Gutteridge, T. G., Leibowitz, Z. B., and Shore, J. E. (1993). *Organizational career development: Benchmarks for building a world-class workforce.* Reprinted with permission from *Conceptual Systems*, Silver Springs, MD.

role in ensuring a competitive work force, it cannot be a low-priority program offered only during good economic times.

Challenges in Career Development

Although most businesspeople today agree that their organizations should invest in career development, it is not always clear exactly what form this investment should take. Before putting a career development program in place, management needs to consider three major challenges.

Who Will Be Responsible?

A Question of Ethics

How much responsibility does a company have for managing its employees' careers? Can a company take too much responsibility for employee career development? In what ways might this be harmful to employees?

The first challenge is deciding who will be ultimately responsible for career development activities. In traditional, bureaucratic organizations development was something done "for" individual employees. For instance, the organization might have an assessment center to identify employees who have the characteristics necessary to hold middle- and upper-management positions. Once identified, these individuals would be groomed through a variety of programs: special project assignments, positions in international divisions, executive training programs, and so on. The individual employee, while certainly not kept in the dark about the company's plans, would not actively participate in the development decisions.

In contrast, many modern organizations have concluded that employees must take an active role in planning and implementing their own personal development plans. The mergers, acquisitions, and downsizings of the 1980s and 1990s led to layoffs in managerial ranks and managers' realization that they cannot depend on their employers to plan their careers for them. Added to this economic turmoil is the empowerment movement, which shifts decision-making responsibility down through the organizational hierarchy. Both of these trends have led companies to encourage their employees to take responsibility for their own development. We will look at strategies for personal development at the end of this chapter.

Career development can occur in many ways in today's organizations. In an increasing number of organizations, career development responsibility is being shifted to the employee. Although an employee empowerment approach to development can be positive, it can be negative if taken too far. Giving employees total responsibility for managing their own careers can create problems in today's flatter organizations, where opportunities to move up through the hierarchy are far fewer than in traditional bureaucratic organizations. Employees need at least general guidance regarding the steps they can take to develop their careers, both within and outside the company.

How Much Emphasis Is Appropriate?

So far, we have presented career development as a positive way for companies to invest in their human resources. However, too great an emphasis on career enhancement can be detrimental to organizational effectiveness.[10] Employees with an extreme careerist orientation can become more concerned about their image than their performance.

It is difficult to pinpoint where an employee's healthy concern for his or her career becomes excessive. However, there are certain warning signs managers should watch for:

- Is the employee more interested in capitalizing on opportunities for advancement than in maintaining adequate performance?
- Does the employee devote more attention to managing the impressions he or she makes on others than to reality?
- Does the employee emphasize networking, flattery, and being seen at social functions over job performance? In the short run, people who engage in these tactics often enjoy advancement. However, sooner or later they run into workplace duties or issues they are not equipped to deal with.

For better or for worse, studies have found that such strategies are effective in helping employees advance through the organization.[11]

Managers should also be aware that a career development program can have serious side effects—including employee dissatisfaction, poor performance, and turnover—if it fosters unrealistic expectations for advancement.

How Will the Needs of a Diverse Workforce Be Met?

To meet the career development needs of today's diverse workforce, companies need to break down the barriers some employees face in achieving advancement. In 1991 the first major government study of the glass ceiling revealed that women and minorities are held back not only from top executive positions but also from lower-level management positions and directorships. The study revealed that women and minorities are frequently excluded from informal career development activities such as networking, mentoring, and participation in policy-making committees. In addition to outright discrimination, some of the practices that contribute to their exclusion are informal word-of-mouth recruitment, companies' failure to sensitize and instruct managers about equal employment opportunity requirements, lack of mentoring, and the too-swift identification of high-potential employees.[12]

Barriers to the advancement of minorities and women continue to exist nearly 10 years after the initial government study of the glass ceiling. The Office of Federal Contract Compliance Programs (OFCCP) enforces antidiscrimination laws covering federal contractors. The OFCCP began monitoring the pay and promotion practices of companies doing business with the government in 1991. It has found problems in about half of the companies it has audited.[13]

However, some of these difficulties have to do with gender- or race-based pay differences rather than with mobility and promotion opportunities.[14] A recent survey found evidence of a glass ceiling at universities.[15] Although the number of women in faculty positions increased from 22.5 percent in 1974 to 1975 to 33.8 percent in 1997 to 1998, most women were in the lower ranks. In 1997 to 1998, only 18.7 percent of those at the top faculty rank of full professor were women.

A confidential internal report at Coca-Cola identified barriers to diversity, particularly for African Americans.[16] The report identified not only a glass ceiling wherein few black employees made it to senior levels in the company but also *glass walls*. The notion of glass walls refers to the channeling of minorities and women into non-revenue-generating areas of the organizations. The areas, such as community relations and HR, are less likely than areas such as finance or marketing to lead to senior management positions. Of course, the phenomenon of glass ceilings and walls is not unique to Coca-Cola. For example, as observed by a female president of an insurance company, "It's kind of a male club of senior executives—lots of women in management roles, lots of women running service departments and the like, but not a lot of them in that upper echelon."[17] To improve promotion opportunities, the Coca-Cola report recommends actions such as a mentoring program, a statement of philosophy regarding diversity, and executive accountability for improving diversity.

Interestingly, the glass ceiling phenomenon may account, in part, for the explosive growth in small businesses in the United States. Approximately one-third of U.S. businesses, or 8 million, are female owned. However, that number is likely to change: Female-owned businesses are being created at twice the rate of all businesses.[18] A study of female business owners found that a significant number were motivated to start their own companies because of frustration with the corporate world and barriers to advancement.

There are signs of improvement in advancement opportunities for women and minorities. For example, a 1999 U.S. Office of Personnel Management report found that 52 percent of promotions over the past year went to women.[19] Currently, approximately 43 percent of the federal workforce are female. Of these 716,000 women, 22 percent are employed at a senior grade level (earning up to $125,000 annually) up from 13 percent in 1993. Although the glass ceiling isn't broken in the public sector, it seems that it is at least being raised.

Evidence suggests that in the private sector the glass ceiling may be cracking in some industries. For instance, in 1999 Carleton "Carly" Fiorina became the CEO of Hewlett-Packard.[20] Fiorina contends that the glass ceiling no longer exists in the information technology industry. She points out that the demand for computer scientists, engineers, and programmers is so great

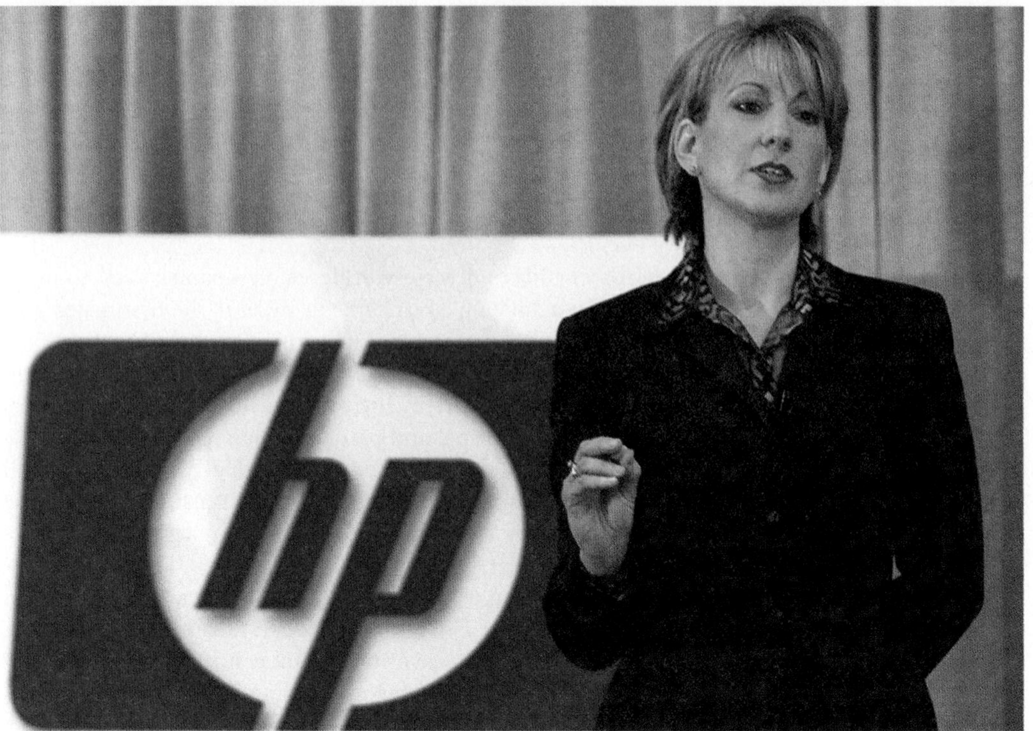

Carly Fiorina, Hewlett-Packard's president and CEO, is one of the few females to hold a high-ranking executive position in a Fortune *1,000 company. She believes that the glass ceiling is cracking in high-technology businesses.*

that companies cannot afford to be biased against women and minorities. This sentiment is echoed by women in other industries. Jill Campbell, vice president of operations for Cox Communications, says that she never hit a glass ceiling. She largely attributes her successful career at Cox to a mentor who helped guide and support her efforts in the organization.[21] Likewise, a hospital president, Susan Stout Tamme, says that she never experienced a glass ceiling in her health care career.[22]

Although advancement of women in fields such as information technology, health care, and engineering is notable, the glass ceiling still exists over all. Consider this sobering fact: In the *Fortune* 1,000 companies, women hold only 2.7 percent of the highest-ranking executive positions.[23] Even in the health care arena, where there are many opportunities for advancement, there nevertheless seems to be a glass ceiling. For example, Counsuelo Diaz, CEO of a health care organization, observes that the health care industry is still largely controlled by men who, perhaps subconsciously, gravitate toward and are most comfortable with candidates who are also white males.[24] In her opinion, women and minorities may have to deal with the glass ceiling for a long time to come.

Other countries may have even stronger barriers to the advancement of women than the United States. "Career Advancement and Asian Women: The Glass Ceiling Overseas" examines the glass ceiling in Asia.

Issues and Applications

Career Advancement and Asian Women: The Glass Ceiling Overseas

Trying to get ahead in the business world can be difficult, particularly if you are a woman in Asia. Women in China, Vietnam, Korea, Japan, Hong Kong, and other Asian countries may face even stronger barriers to advancement than do their American counterparts.

Take, for instance, Japan. In that culture, women are expected to marry young and devote themselves to child rearing. It is difficult for Japanese women to keep full-time positions after they have children because company support is usually nonexistent and Japanese management is male centered.[a] Almost half of Japan's workforce is female, but only a few are on a career track. Most Japanese women work at part-time jobs that offer little security or advancement potential. Of the 54,000 board members who run the companies listed on the Japanese stock exchange, only 196 are women.[b] Even Hong Kong, considered one of the more progressive Asian countries with respect to workplace practices, has few female managers. About 22 percent of all managers are women, up from 16 percent in 1993.[c]

The attitudes toward female advancement may be so culturally ingrained that many Asian women may consider them natural and acceptable. Some Asian women deny that barriers to their workforce advancement exist. Some go even further, seemingly condoning these barriers. For example, a female vice president at an Asian bank recently told a reporter that male executives probably had the physical stamina to work longer hours than females. A Thai finance company director agreed with her husband's decision to hire a male instead of a female engineer for his construction firm because women lack the requisite physical strength and should not be subjected to leering workmen and other job site hazards.[d]

Perhaps not so coincidentally, applications by Asian women to American business schools have been on a substantial upswing.[e] For example, the number of Asian women applying for admission to Yale's business school has increased 132 percent in the past six years, whereas applications over all have risen 67 percent. Applications from Asian women to the MBA program at the University of Chicago have increased 72 percent over the past two years.[f] Many of these women hope that their improved skills and educational status will help them to shatter the glass ceiling when they return to their home countries.[g] If that does not work, many U.S. companies with a presence in Asia are hiring Asian women to work for them there.

Sources: [a]Yamaguchi, M. (1999, February 9). Japan shuns career women. *Arizona Republic*, E10. [b]Ibid. [c]Marshall, S. (1999, May 21). Executive action: Women stereotyping women—Compounding glass ceiling, some women may construct their own workplace barriers. *Asian Wall Street Journal*, P3. [d]Ibid. [e]Schellhardt, T. D. (1999, June 1). Managers and managing: Asian women seeking MBAs at U.S. schools. *Wall Street Journal*, 4. [f]Ibid. [g]Ibid.

Another employee group that may need special consideration is **dual-career couples.** Nearly 80 percent of all couples are working couples. The two-income family is replacing the single-income family as the norm.[25] When both members of a couple have career issues at stake, personal lives can complicate and become intertwined with occupational lives. A career opportunity for one member that demands a geographic move can produce a crisis for both the couple and their companies. Rather than waiting until they reach such a crisis point to resolve competing career issues, it is better for the couple to plan their careers and discuss how they will proceed if certain options become available. This approach also reduces the possibility of abrupt personnel losses for organizations.

Dual-career couple
A couple whose members both have occupational responsibilities and career issues at stake.

Some of the organizational approaches used to deal with the needs of dual-career couples include flexible work schedules, telecommuting (both discussed in Chapter 4), and child-care services (see Chapter 12). These kinds of practices have become more common over the past decade. A recent report by the Hay Group, a worldwide management consulting firm, concluded that the trends of more flexible and family-oriented benefits are expected to continue.[26] However, the possible career impact of choosing to have more flexibility in how you accomplish work assignments needs to be carefully considered. For example, telecommuting may maximize your immediate convenience, but what might be the longer-term impact on your career opportunities? Perhaps the less you are seen around the workplace, the less your name might be thought of when opportunities arise. The Manager's Notebook: Customer-Driven HR entitled, "Working Away from Work: Getting the Job Done, but What About Your Career?" examines the choice of working remotely.

Customer-Driven HR — MANAGER'S NOTEBOOK

Working Away from Work: Getting the Job Done, but What About Your Career?

Technology now offers the option of getting work done without going to the workplace. A 2001 survey of technology professionals found 96 percent would like to work from home, at least part of the time. Furthermore, 39 percent stated they would be willing to take a pay cut to be able to work from home. On the downside, most of the respondents also recognized that they may have to accept a slower rate of career development in exchange for the benefit of working from home.

You need to recognize that options such as telecommuting and virtual work can have a negative impact on your career development. However, the following steps can help you to reduce or eliminate any negative effects to your career or the careers of your employees.

- *Determine what's best for you.*
  Are you an independent worker? Do you like flexibility? If so, working virtually may be for you. But working from home may not be for you if you prefer a great deal of structure and direction. Do you like face-to-face interaction and working on a team? If so, working from home may not be for you.
  Are you new to the job, function, or industry? If so, a lot can be learned by observing, which you won't be able to do working from home. Lack of opportunity to observe can slow your rate of learning and advancement.
- *Manage your home workspace.*
  Do you tend to be a workaholic? If you do, you will need to manage your work at home so that your focus on job and career is kept in balance. For example, place a door on your home workspace and use it! At the end of your workday, close that door and don't open it again until the next day. The same approach to electronic devices, such as phones and computers, can help you to keep your home and work life in proper balance.
- *Stay connected.*
  Even though you may be effective at working virtually, you need to continue to network and communicate. Being out of sight may mean that you are also out of mind when it comes to opportunities for development and advancement. Make sure you stay in touch with people and schedule occasional face-to-face meetings at the workplace.

Source: Adapted from Schettler, J. (2002). Techie Telecommute. *Training, 39*, 20(1); and Fulton, M. L. (2002). Working virtually. *Searcher, 10*, 50(5).

Some companies have also begun counseling couples in career management. These proactive programs, which involve both the employee and his or her spouse or significant other, have typically been reserved for executives and others who are considered key personnel in the organization.[27] First, each partner individually comes up with his or her goals and action plans. Then the partners are brought together to share their agendas and work through any conflicts. Professional counselors offer possible solutions and alternatives.[28] The result of the process—a joint career plan—is then provided to the organization. Employees and their partners benefit from this approach by formulating a mutually agreeable plan, and the organization benefits by increasing the probability of retaining key employees. Indeed, recent findings underscore the importance of and potential benefits of dual-career counseling and spousal support services.[29] The levels of work stress and job satisfaction experienced by dual-career workers are significantly influenced by the spouse's level of support; over the long term, lack of spousal support can have a negative influence on job performance and even cause a worker to leave his or her job.

Experts strongly recommend counseling and mentoring for dual-career couples facing an overseas assignment, a more common experience than ever before.[30] Without an active career support program, the employee may refuse the overseas assignment because of dual-career issues or the expatriate may perform the assignment inadequately. These possibilities cost an organization dearly because high performers are often selected for such duties and the assignment typically involves hefty training, housing, and moving expenses.

Providing career development and support that involves the expatriate spouse or significant other can reduce an organization's risk.[31] For example, an organization may make the transition to a new place and culture easier for the couple by offering the spouse help such as membership in professional organizations, tuition reimbursement, job-search assistance, and transportation to conferences.

Whether at home or on an overseas assignment, a dual-career couple's concerns relating to family issues has been linked to stress, depression, and anxiety for both men and women.[32] At least one member of a dual-career couple may have to spend work time on personal issues and problems. A growing number of companies are going beyond typical family-friendly benefits and offering *work-life programs* as a way to ease the stress of dual-career couples.[33] Worklife programs are outsourced counseling and referral services that may offer assistance ranging from finding child care (offered by companies such as Procter & Gamble and Aetna) to finding a kennel for your pet (Starbucks) or providing a lawyer's advice (U.S. Bancorp).

Marriott International, for example, wants employees to be cheerful so they can offer effective customer service. Marriott has given its employees a work-life program since 1996 at a cost of about $12.00 per employee per year. Considering the cost savings from factors such as lower absenteeism, Marriott estimates that it receives a 400 percent return on its investment. Work-life programs can assist all workers, not just workers who are part of a dual-career couple, but dual-career partners may benefit the most from the program.

Meeting the Challenges of Effective Career Development

Creating a development program almost always consists of three phases: the assessment phase, the direction phase, and the development phase (Figure 9.2). Although presented separately in Figure 9.2, the phases of development often blend together in an actual program.

The Assessment Phase

The *assessment phase* of career development involves activities ranging from self-assessment to organizationally provided assessment. The goal of assessment, whether performed by employees themselves or by the organization, is to identify employees' strengths and weaknesses. This kind of clarification helps employees (1) to choose a career that is realistically obtainable and a good fit and (2) to determine the weaknesses they need to overcome to achieve their career goals. Figure 9.3 lists some tools that are commonly used for self-assessment and for organizational assessment.

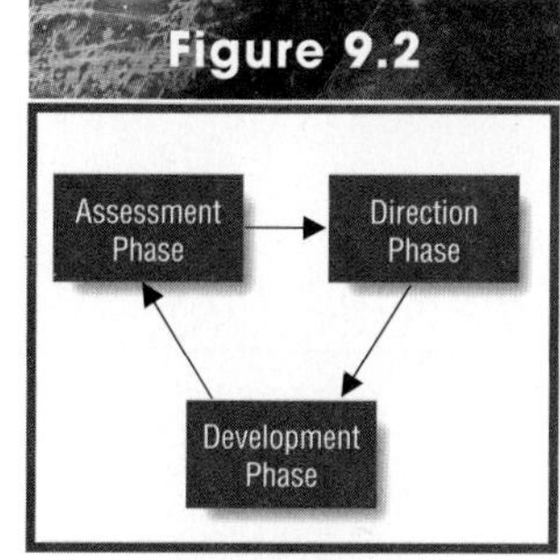

The Career Development Process

Self-Assessment

Self-assessment is increasingly important for companies that want to empower their employees to take control of their careers. The major tools used for self-assessment are workbooks and workshops.

Career workbooks have been very popular for decades. Generic workbooks were commonly used in the 1970s, but tailored workbooks gained in popularity in the 1980s.[34] In addition to the exercises included in a generic career workbook, tailored workbooks might contain a statement of the organization's policies and procedures regarding career issues as well as descriptions of the career paths and options available in the organization.

Career-planning workshops, which may be led either by the company's HR department or by an external provider such as a consulting firm or local university, give employees information about career options in the organization. They may also be used to give participants feedback on

Figure 9.3

Common Assessment Tools

Self-Assessment	Organizational Assessment
Career workbooks	Assessment centers
Career-planning workshops	Psychological testing
	Performance appraisal
	Promotability forecasts
	Succession planning

their career aspirations and strategy. Participation in most workshops is voluntary, and some organizations hold these workshops on company time to demonstrate their commitment to their workforce.

Whether done through workbooks or workshops, self-assessment usually involves doing skills assessment exercises, completing an interests inventory, and clarifying values.[35]

- As their name implies, *skills assessment exercises* are designed to identify an employee's skills. For example, a workbook exercise might ask the employee to compile a brief list of his or her accomplishments. Once the employee has generated a set of, say, five accomplishments, he or she then identifies the skills involved in making each accomplishment a reality. In a workshop situation, people might share their accomplishments in a group discussion, and then the entire group might help identify the skills underlying the accomplishments.

  Another skills assessment exercise presents employees with a list of skills they must rate on two dimensions: their level of proficiency at that skill and the degree to which they enjoy using it. A total score is then generated for each skill area—for example, by multiplying the proficiency by the preference rating. Figure 9.4 shows an example of this approach to skills assessment. Scores below 6 indicate areas of weakness or dislike, whereas scores of 6 or above indicate areas of strength. The pattern of scores can guide employees regarding the type of career for which they are best suited.

Sample Skills Assessment Exercise

Figure 9.4

Use the scales below to rate yourself on each of the following skills. Rate each skill area both for your level of proficiency and for your preference.

Proficiency:

1	2	3
Still learning	OK — competent	Proficient

Preference:

1	2	3
Don't like to use this skill	OK — Don't particularly like or dislike using this skill	Really enjoy using this skill

Skill Area	Proficiency	×	Preference	=	Score
1. Problem solving	____		____		____
2. Team presentation	____		____		____
3. Leadership	____		____		____
4. Inventory	____		____		____
5. Negotiation	____		____		____
6. Conflict management	____		____		____
7. Scheduling	____		____		____
8. Delegation	____		____		____
9. Participative management	____		____		____
10. Feedback	____		____		____
11. Planning	____		____		____
12. Computer	____		____		____

- An *interest inventory* is a measure of a person's occupational interests. Numerous off-the-shelf inventories can give employees insight into what type of career will best fit their interests. One of the best-known inventories is the Strong Vocational Interest Inventory.[36] The interest inventory asks people to indicate how strong or weak an interest they have in activities such as dealing with very old people, making a speech, and raising money for charity. Responses to items on the inventory are then scored to identify the occupations in which the individual has the same interests as the professionals employed in those fields.
- *Values clarification* involves prioritizing personal values. The typical values-clarification exercise presents employees with a list of values and asks them to rate how important each value is to them. For example, employees may be asked to prioritize security, power, money, and family in their lives. Knowing their priority values can help employees make satisfying career choices.

Organizational Assessment

Some of the tools traditionally used by organizations in selection (see Chapter 5) are also valuable for career development. Among these are assessment centers, psychological testing, performance appraisal, promotability forecasts, and succession planning.

- *Assessment centers* are situational exercises—such as interviews, in-basket exercises, and business games—that are often used to select managerial talent. Although assessment centers have traditionally been used for selection, companies are increasingly using them as part of their career development programs. A developmentally oriented assessment center stresses giving feedback and direction to the worker.[37] The assessment center measures competencies needed for a particular job and provides participants with feedback about their strengths and weaknesses in the competency areas as uncovered in the exercises. This feedback increases employees' understanding of their skills and helps them develop realistic career goals and plans.

  Somewhat surprisingly, there have been few empirical studies of the effectiveness of assessment centers for developmental purposes.[38] However, the limited number of studies do indicate that assessment centers have significant and positive effects on participants, even months after the assessment center exercise.
- Some organizations also use *psychological testing* to help employees better understand their skills and interests. Tests that measure personality and attitudes, as well as interest inventories, fall into this category.[39]
- *Performance appraisal* is another source of valuable career development information. Unfortunately, appraisals are frequently limited to assessment of past performance rather than oriented toward future performance improvements and directions. Future-oriented performance appraisal can give employees important insights into their strengths, their weaknesses, and the career paths available to them.
- **Promotability forecasts** are decisions made by managers regarding the advancement potential of their subordinates. These forecasts allow the organization to identify people who appear to have high advancement potential.[40] The high-potential employees are then given developmental experiences (such as attending an executive training seminar) to help them achieve their advancement potential.

  For example, in 1988 AT&T launched a companywide computerized program to track high-potential managers and equip them with the right experiences to face business challenges in the years ahead. The emphasis in this Leadership Continuity Program (LCP) is on development, not promotion in the near term. Participants accept assignments that will prepare them for increased responsibilities. Candidates are selected for LCP on the basis of three criteria: sustained strong performance, overall high standing in relation to peers, and a demonstrated potential to perform at least four salary levels above their current level.[41]
- **Succession planning** focuses on preparing people to fill executive positions. Formally, succession planning means examining development needs given a firm's strategic plans. That is, the formal approach identifies the organization's future direction and challenges and then derives the competencies new leaders need.[42] Then the organization identifies internal and external target candidates. Once a short list of executives is created, the candidates are

Promotability forecast
A career development activity in which managers make decisions regarding the advancement potential of subordinates.

Succession planning
A career development activity that focuses on preparing people to fill executive positions.

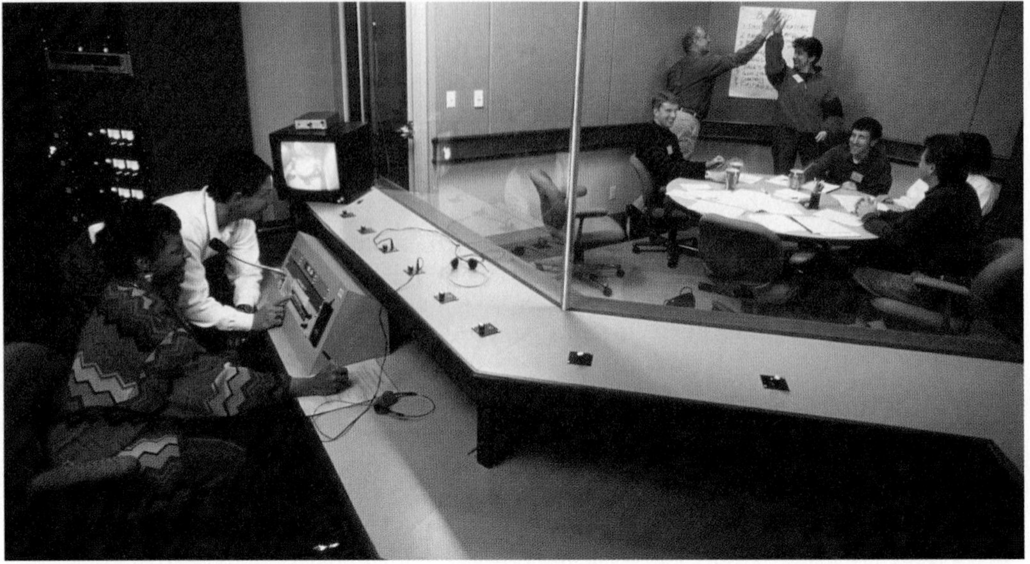

Some companies ask outside consultants to evaluate their internal candidates for promotion. Here psychologists at the Center for Creative Leadership assess candidates' leadership skills through one-way glass.

researched and tracked using the required competencies as evaluation areas. This tracking and monitoring process continues indefinitely so that an up-to-date list is available when inevitable turnover in leadership occurs. Succession planning is necessary when the organization needs key positions filled without interruption. Without it, the business may sacrifice profitability and stability as the price for not being prepared.

Although the formal approach is advisable, most succession planning is done informally. Informal succession planning means high-level managers identify and develop their own replacements. The employees identified as having upper-management potential may then be given developmental experiences that help prepare them for the executive ranks, such as workshops on the organization's values and mission.

Succession planning is one of the trickiest challenges in the area of career development. Organizations have often been accused of discriminating against women and minorities when filling high-level positions. Rather than outright discrimination, it is usually the informality of much succession planning that makes companies unwittingly exclude these groups as candidates. Formal succession planning programs, such as those in place at 3M and Westpac Banking Corporation (Australia's largest bank), can make the identification of high-potential employees and replacement candidates a more egalitarian procedure.

What employee characteristics and experiences predict success at the managerial and executive levels? The earliest work in this area was done by researchers at AT&T.[43] For example, one study examined the influence of various educational characteristics on management performance two decades later. The study found that college major and extent of extracurricular activities were significantly related to later management performance. Grades were found to predict managers' overall motivation levels, with the grades themselves reflecting more the manager's work ethic than the degree of skill or knowledge obtained in various courses.

A more recent study examined the extent to which demographic, human capital, motivational, and organizational variables predict executive career success.[44] The researchers divided career success into objective (for example, pay level) and subjective (for example, job satisfaction) components. The researchers concluded that educational level, quality and prestige of the university, and major were all related to the pay levels of a sample of 1,388 executives. Interestingly, ambition was negatively related to job satisfaction, with the more ambitious executives indicating less satisfaction in their current positions.

Personality characteristics are also a determinant of success in higher-level management jobs. For example, one study examined the effects of both personality and cognitive abilities on the current earnings of managers, and concluded that such characteristics as creativity, sociability, self-reliance, and self-control are strongly related to managers' success as determined by pay level.[45] Recent research suggests that some of the "big five" personality characteristics are related to measures of career success, such as salary, promotions, and career satisfaction.[46] For example, extraversion was positively related to all measures of career success, whereas neuroticism was a negative factor for career satisfaction. Thus, managers should consider these characteristics, as well as level of technical knowledge and motivation, when preparing their promotability forecasts and conducting succession planning.

In small companies succession planning is crucial because the sudden departure or illness of a key player can cause the business to flounder. Yet just as some people shy away from drafting a will for fear of recognizing their own mortality, some small-business owners shy away from succession planning for fear of recognizing that they will not always be in control of their business. Other small-business owners are too caught up in the daily pressures of running a business to plan for the future. A poll of 800 business owners revealed that only about one fourth of small-business owners have a succession plan, and just half of those owners have formalized the plan by committing it to paper.[47]

In doing succession planning, small-business owners—whether aged 20 or 50—should consider whether they want to keep the business in the family, recruit an outside manager to run it, sell it to a key executive, or put it on the market. At Lavelle Company (a building materials company in Fargo, North Dakota), founder George Lavelle used these considerations as a starting point for fleshing out a detailed succession plan. He wanted to involve all six of his sons who worked in the business in succession planning, so he took them to a succession program at The Center for Family Business in Cleveland in 1980, 13 years before he retired in 1993. Shortly after, he also decided to hire and groom an outsider to serve as president when he retired. He made this move because he thought that none of his sons should be pressured to assume the top leadership role before he was ready. Lavelle also avoided the emotional task of choosing which son to appoint as successor. Instead he left the decision to an executive committee, which includes the new president and several of Lavelle's sons. In praise of his father's deliberate planning, the eldest son acknowledges, "We are probably the envy of other companies in our position."[48]

The Direction Phase

The *direction phase* of career development involves determining the type of career that employees want and the steps they must take to realize their career goals. Appropriate direction requires an accurate understanding of one's current position. Unless the direction phase is based on a thorough assessment of the current situation, the goals and steps identified may be inappropriate. For example, a task force assembled by the Healthcare Financial Management Association reviewed credentials, experience, and other data for more than 5,000 senior finance executives. They also reviewed certification standards and graduate school curricula and worked with two panels of experts. Through this review, the task force developed the competency model shown in Figure 9.5.

The association is currently working on ways to use the competency model in career development by focusing on the type of role the person desires. For example, someone who aspires to be the leader of an enterprise may need to develop the highest competency levels in the area of leading others. Someone aspiring to the role of business advisor might be best served by developing a balanced portfolio of competencies. The association is defining the levels of competencies within each area and the pattern of levels appropriate for various roles.

The direction phase, represented by the competencies, should be based on a careful assessment of what is needed in the profession. Further, career development direction should not be a stand-alone effort. To be effective, career development must be integrated with other HRM efforts, such as staffing, performance appraisal, and training.

As one manager who participated in a recent study by PricewaterhouseCoopers quoted Mark Twain: "Never try to teach a pig to sing. It wastes your time and annoys the pig."[49] In other words, for your organization's development efforts to be successful, you need to first make sure that you are hiring people who generally match your skill requirements and culture. The two major approaches to career direction are individual counseling and various information services.

Individual Career Counseling

Individual career counseling refers to one-on-one sessions with the goal of helping employees examine their career aspirations.[50] Topics of discussion might include the employee's current

A Competency Growth Model for Healthcare Financial Managers: Basis for Career Development Direction

Figure 9.5

A Healthcare Financial Management Association task force identified behavioral characteristics having to do with the skill, knowledge, social, trait, or motive qualities needed to excel in the profession. These competencies were grouped into the following three components:

COMPONENT 1: UNDERSTANDING THE BUSINESS ENVIRONMENT

Competencies:

1. Strategic thinking—the ability to integrate knowledge of the industry with an understanding of the long range vision of an organization.
2. Systems thinking—an awareness of how one's role fits within an organization and knowing when and how to take actions that support its effectiveness.

COMPONENT 2: MAKING IT HAPPEN

Competencies:

1. Results orientation—the drive to achieve and the ability to diagnose inefficiencies and judge when to take entrepreneurial risks.
2. Collaborative decision making—actions that involve key stakeholders in the decision-making processes.
3. Action orientation—going beyond the minimum role requirements to boldly drive projects and lead the way to improved services, processes, and products.

COMPONENT 3: LEADING OTHERS

Competencies:

1. Championing business thinking—the ability to energize others to understand and achieve business-focused outcomes. Fostering an understanding of issues and challenges through clear articulation and agenda setting.
2. Coaching and mentoring—the ability to release the potential of others by actively promoting responsibility, trust, and recognition.
3. Influence—the ability to communicate a position in a persuasive manner, thus generating support, agreement, or commitment.

Source: Adapted from *Healthcare Financial Management*. (1999). Dynamic healthcare environment demands new career planning tools, *52*, 70–74.

job responsibilities, interests, and career objectives. Although career counseling is frequently conducted by managers or HR staff members, some organizations, such as Coca-Cola and Disneyland, use professional counselors.[51]

The days in which career counseling means face-to-face interaction with a professional counselor or manager may be numbered. Career counseling is now available online at sites such as www.careerexperience.com and www.careerJournal.com. The Dow Jones' Careerjournal.com site, for example, focuses on executive-level job hunters and offers career counseling and résumé evaluation. The service is not entirely virtual, however. Although material is submitted online, interaction with a career counselor is via phone. Currently, a conversation costs $79.00 and one hour of phone counseling is offered for $119.00.[52] Personality and other career assessment testing and phone consultation are offered for $219.00.

When line managers conduct career counseling sessions, the HR department generally monitors the sessions' effectiveness and provides assistance to the managers in the form of training, suggested counseling formats, and the like. There are several advantages to having managers conduct career counseling sessions with their employees. First, managers are probably more aware of their employees' strengths and weaknesses than anyone else. Second, knowing that managers understand their employees' career development concerns can foster an environment of trust and commitment.

Unfortunately, assigning career counseling responsibility to managers does not guarantee that the task will be carried out carefully. As with performance appraisal and many other important HR activities, managers may treat employee career development simply as a paper-shuffling exercise unless top management signals its strong support for development activities. If managers only go through the motions, there is likely to be a negative impact on employee attitudes, productivity, and profits.

Information Services

As their name suggests, information services provide career development information to employees. Determining what to do with this information is largely the employee's responsibility. This approach makes sense, given the diversity of the interests and aspiration of employees in today's organizations.

The most commonly provided information services are job-posting systems, skills inventories, career paths, and career resource centers.

- **Job-posting systems** are a fairly easy and direct way of providing employees with information on job openings. The jobs available in an organization are announced ("posted") on a bulletin board, in a company newsletter, through a phone recording or computer system, or over a company's intranet. This is the practice at 3M and at NCR, the AT&T company that develops information systems and products.[53] Whatever the media used for the posting, it is important that all employees have access to the list. All postings should include clear descriptions of both the job's specifications and the criteria that will be used to select among the applicants. Such information helps employees determine whether they are qualified for the position. In addition, information on how the criteria will be applied to fill the position should be supplied. Doing so alleviates employees' fears that selection may be a political process.

  Job-posting systems have the advantage of reinforcing the notion that the organization promotes from within.[54] This belief not only motivates employees to maintain and improve their performance but also tends to reduce turnover.

Job-posting system
A system in which an organization announces job openings to all employees on a bulletin board, in a company newsletter, or through a phone recording or computer system.

- **Skills inventories** are company-maintained records with information such as employees' abilities, skills, knowledge, and education.[55] The company can use this comprehensive, centralized HR information system to get an overall picture of its workforce's training and development needs, as well as to identify existing talent in one department that may be more productively employed in another.

  Skills inventories can prove valuable for employees as well. Feedback regarding how they stack up against other employees can encourage them to improve their skills or seek out other positions that better match their current skill levels.

Skills inventory
A company-maintained record of employees' abilities, skills, knowledge, and education.

- **Career paths** provide valuable information regarding the possible directions and career opportunities available in an organization. A career path presents the steps in a possible career and a plausible timetable for accomplishing them. Just as a variety of paths may lead to the same job, so may starting from the same job lead to very different outcomes. Figure 9.6 provides an example of alternative career paths that a bus person in the hotel business might follow.

  To be realistic, career paths must specify the qualifications necessary to proceed to the next step and the minimum length of time employees must spend at each step to obtain the necessary experience. This information could be generated by computer.

Career path
A chart showing the possible directions and career opportunities available in an organization; it presents the steps in a possible career and a plausible timetable for accomplishing them.

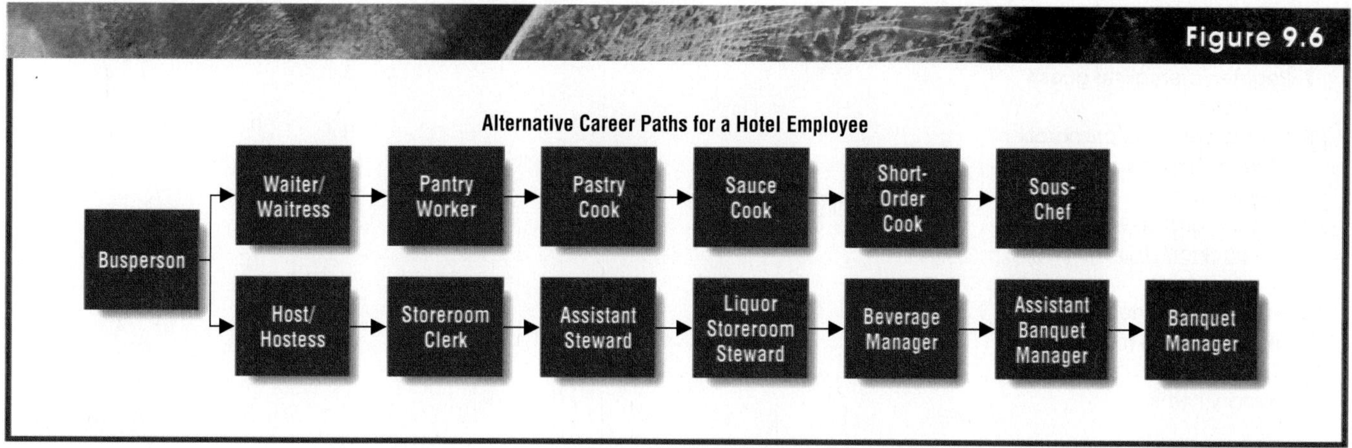

Alternative Career Paths for a Hotel Employee

This is a generic example of alternative career paths. Actual career paths should specify a time frame for each job.

Figure 9.7 presents examples of two survey forms that might be used to collect career path information. Form A asks employees to indicate how important certain skills are for the performance of their job. The skills included on the form can be determined by examining job-analysis information and by interviewing individual employees. Employee responses can then be used to develop lists of critical and desirable skills for each job. The abbreviated list of skills in Form A is based on jobs in the hotel industry.

Form B asks employees to judge the extent to which experience in other jobs in the organization is needed to perform their current job adequately. The lowest-level jobs, which still involve the skill requirements uncovered with the use of Form A, would not require previous job experience within the organization. Higher-level or more complex jobs would likely require more job experience.

Career resource center A collection of career development materials such as workbooks, tapes, and texts.

- A **career resource center** is a collection of career development materials such as workbooks, tapes, and texts. These resources might be maintained by the HR department either in its offices or in an area that is readily accessible to employees. Companies with many locations might publicize the availability of these materials and lend them to employees who express interest. Some colleges and universities maintain career resource centers, and many consulting firms (particularly those specializing in employee outplacement) provide career develop-

Figure 9.7

FORM A: SKILL REQUIREMENTS

Instructions: A list of various skills that apply to various jobs is presented below. Use the scale provided to indicate the extent to which each skill is applicable to your current position.

	Circle the Most Appropriate Number			
	Not applicable	**Somewhat desirable useful at times**	**Very desirable but not essential**	**Critical—could not perform job without it**
Skills				
1. Determine daily/forecasted production and service equipment requirements.	1	2	3	4
2. Clean guest rooms.	1	2	3	4
3. Set up, break down, and change over function rooms.	1	2	3	4
4. Handle security problems.	1	2	3	4
5. Clean public areas/ restrooms.	1	2	3	4
6. Assist in menu development.	1	2	3	4
7. Register/preregister guests into hotel.	1	2	3	4
8. Participate in the preparation of sauces, soups, stews, and special dishes.	1	2	3	4
9. Prepare and serve salads, fruit cocktails, fruits, juices, and so on.	1	2	3	4
10. Participate in the rating of meats and other dishes.	1	2	3	4
11. Care for, clean, and distribute laundry items.	1	2	3	4

(continued)

Two Career Path Information Forms

Figure 9.7

FORM B: EXPERIENCE REQUIREMENTS

Instructions: A list of work experience by job titles is presented below. Use the scale provided to indicate for each item: (a) how important previous experience in this work is for the successful performance of your current job duties; and (b) the amount of experience that constitutes adequate training or exposure so that you are able to function efficiently in your current position.

Circle the Most Appropriate Number

	Importance of Requirement			**Minimum Experience**				
	Not very important	**Very desirable but not essential**	**Critical—could not perform job without it**	**0–6 mos**	**7–11 mos**	**1–2 yrs**	**3–5 yrs**	**6 yrs**
Work Experience								
1. *Storeroom Clerk:* Accurately compute daily food costs by assembling food invoices, totaling food requisitions, taking monthly inventory of food storeroom, and so on.	1	2	3	1	2	3	4	5
2. *Liquor Storeroom Steward:* Maintain adequate levels of alcoholic beverages and related supplies; properly receive, store, and issue them to user departments.	1	2	3	1	2	3	4	5
3. *Pantry Worker:* Prepare and serve to waiters salads, fruit cocktails, fruit juices, and so on.	1	2	3	1	2	3	4	5
4. *Pastry Cook:* Prepare mixes for baking cakes, pies, soufflés, and so on.	1	2	3	1	2	3	4	5
5. *Short-Order Cook:* Prepare short-order foods in assigned restaurant areas.	1	2	3	1	2	3	4	5
6. *Sous Chef:* Assist executive chef in all areas of kitchen production; directly supervise the operations of the kitchen in his or her absence.	1	2	3	1	2	3	4	5
7. *Waiter or Waitress:* Take food and beverage orders from customers and serve them in a restaurant or lounge.	1	2	3	1	2	3	4	5
8. *Beverage Manager:* Supervise and schedule personnel as required and maintain budgeted liquor cost and supplies for the lounge and/or banquet functions.	1	2	3	1	2	3	4	5
9. *Assistant Banquet Manager:* Assist in the coordination and successful completion of all banquet functions, such as coordinating staffing requirements, ensuring that function room is properly set and tidied, and keeping banquet manager fully informed of all problems or unusual matters.	1	2	3	1	2	3	4	5

Figure 9.7 continued

ment materials as well. Career resource centers can help people identify for themselves their strengths and weaknesses, career options, and educational and training opportunities.

The Development Phase

Meeting the requirements necessary to move up in an organization can require a great deal of growth and self-improvement. The *development phase,* which involves taking actions to create and increase skills to prepare for future job opportunities, is meant to foster this growth and self-improvement. The most common development programs offered by organizations are mentoring, coaching, job rotation, and tuition assistance.

Mentoring

Mentoring
A developmentally oriented relationship between senior and junior colleagues or peers that involves advising, role modeling, sharing contacts, and giving general support.

Mentoring is a developmentally oriented relationship between senior and junior colleagues or peers. Mentoring relationships, which can occur at all levels and in all areas of an organization, generally involve advising, role modeling, sharing contacts, and giving general support. Mentoring can be either voluntary and informal or involuntary and formal. Informal mentoring is generally more effective than mentoring done solely as a formal responsibility,[56] though there are situations in which a formal mentoring program may be the better choice.

Mentoring has been found to make a real difference in careers, with executives who were mentored early in their careers tending to make more money at a younger age and more likely to follow a career plan than those who were not mentored. Research findings support the conclusion that effective mentoring can improve outcomes such as performance levels, promotion rates, upward mobility, income, and job satisfaction.[57] For mentors, particularly those nearing retirement, the mentoring role can offer new challenges and reignite enthusiasm and motivation. A recent survey of mentors found that the supervisors are often considered the most effective mentors.[58] However, survey respondents also view the roles of supervisor and mentor quite differently, with the supervisor focused on results and the mentor on the person. Mentees report that mentors build confidence, stimulate learning, and serve as a role model and sounding board.

There are, it should be noted, some problems with informal mentoring as a development program. Women employees are often reluctant to initiate a relationship with a potential male mentor because such an appeal may be misconstrued as a sexual advance. And with the increasing attention being paid to sexual harassment in the workplace, male managers may be even more hesitant to take on a female protégé. Formal mentoring programs can help counter this reluctance.

Formal programs may also offer advantages to minority employees. When the American Society of Association Executives (ASAE) found it faced an uphill battle attracting racial and ethnic minority members, it launched a mentoring program to augment the association's diversity program. The ASAE invited chief executives in the Washington, DC, area to nominate minority colleagues in the developmental stages of their careers as candidates for a pilot mentoring program. Fourteen finalists were selected from among 54 applicants and then were paired off with ASAE fellows and former members of the ASAE board of directors. One of the finalists, Reuben Blackwell IV, noted, "The best encouragement for young African Americans and people of color is to see men and women like themselves succeeding in their careers." Successful formal mentoring programs, such as the ASAE's, involve much more than simply bringing mentor and protégé together.[59]

Some organizations are combining job shadowing with mentoring.[60] Job shadowing involves a junior person observing a more senior employee for a set duration. For example, Edward Jones blends shadowing with mentoring in its GoodKnight Plan. The program pairs a noninvestment representative with a successful veteran for about one year. The new representative is gradually provided the opportunity to take on a percentage of the veteran's accounts before opening his or her office. The company has found the production level of representatives who went through the GoodKnight Plan to be at a level in their first year that isn't reached by representatives who didn't go through the program until their second or third year. Target is another organization blending shadowing with mentoring. Target provides a 15-week Business Analyst Program in which new analysts shadow a mentor. The mentor acclimates the new hires to the Target culture and provides tasks and feedback. By the end of the program, the new analysts can manage their own category of merchandise.

While formal mentoring programs are more likely to be found at large companies, some small companies have developed more informal, but equally intensive, mentoring programs. Ed Fu, the owner of a growing computer consulting firm, Fu Associates, takes a personal interest in training a select group of talented employees. He calls it "Fu-izing." Each new hire starts out working directly with a mid-level employee. After new hires have been on the job for several months, Fu chooses from among them designers to serve on projects for which he is the senior systems analyst.

Like women and minorities in large firms, people who work for a small business or are self-employed may find it difficult to find a mentor. These people can benefit from membership in professional and trade associations. This form of "group mentoring" may complement individual mentoring or serve as a substitute for it.

Membership in professional organizations is an effective career development tool. While research is limited, it is clear that association membership provides important networking opportunities, and many a career has been advanced as a result of networking. Interestingly, skill development does not appear to be an important benefit of trade group membership, probably because most people look to their workplaces for skill development. Even though most professional organizations emphasize the educational content of their functions, the social process and networking opportunities seem to be much more important to members.[61]

Coaching

Employee *coaching* consists of ongoing, sometimes spontaneous, meetings between managers and their employees to discuss the employee's career goals and development. Working with employees to chart and implement their career goals enhances productivity and can spur a manager's own advancement. Then why do so many managers give short shrift to employee coaching? For one thing, in today's flatter organizations managers have more people under their supervision and less time to spend on developing each employee. For another, as we noted earlier, managers tend to view "employee development" as a buzz phrase unless top management clearly and strongly supports it. Finally, most managers are ill-prepared to coach employees and feel uncomfortable in the role.[62] Many managers view their role as one of providing answers, pointing out weaknesses, diagnosing problems, and solving them. This role is effective if the purpose is judgment or assessment, but it is not conducive to effective coaching.

Coaching need not be the ordeal many managers think it is. The secret is to take advantage of what some HR consultants have called "coachable moments"—opportunities that occur in the midst of ongoing work for valuable, if brief, career counseling. Here are five common cues from employees that can open the door to coachable moments:

1. An employee demonstrates a new skill or interest.
2. An employee seeks feedback.
3. An employee expresses an interest in a change in the organization.
4. An employee is experiencing a poor job fit.
5. An employee mentions a desire for development opportunities.[63]

Given the occurrence of such coachable moments, what should you do? That is, how do you go about being an effective coach for someone? The Manager's Notebook titled "Effective Coaching Techniques" gives a set of simple but powerful tips for being a great coach.

MANAGER'S NOTEBOOK

Effective Coaching Techniques

1. **Create a coaching context**
   ✓ Identify your purpose in the coaching role as supporting the employee's overall development and effectiveness.

- ✓ Set parameters. State whether you want to focus only on increasing his or her effectiveness in the department or would entertain a broader view.

2. **Actively listen to the person**
   - ✓ Limit interruptions from others and from yourself.
   - ✓ Reflect back to the person what you heard, not how you would solve the problem.
3. **Ask questions**
   - ✓ View the goal of the interaction as helping the employee to find a path or answer that works best for him or her.
   - ✓ Don't give advice but take the tougher role of asking questions that open up new possibilities or explore assumptions.
4. **Give useful feedback**
   - ✓ Let the employee identify his or her weaknesses or difficulties to overcome. Your input should help clarify and prioritize what needs to be done.

Source: Adapted from Mobley, S. A. (1999). Judge not: How coaches create healthy organizations. *Journal for Quality and Participation*, 22, 57–60.

Sometimes employees coach one another. This was what 10 African American sales reps in Xerox's Washington, DC, office began doing in 1971. One of the company's few African American sales reps had left the company abruptly, and his colleagues, fearing that his departure had to do with race, banded together to form a survival network they called the Corporate Few. Meeting in each other's apartments, they coached one another on presentation skills, sales techniques, and pricing strategies. The three most senior sales reps tutored the others on the nuances of Xerox's culture. When the network widened and spawned similar groups at other Xerox offices, Xerox's top brass took notice. Then-president David T. Kearns learned about the network and openly supported it. Today Xerox is widely acclaimed for its acceptance and advancement of minorities. Ten percent of the company's vice presidents are African American and the internal African American network is thriving.[64]

Job Rotation

Job rotation involves assigning employees to various jobs so that they acquire a wider base of skills. Broadened job experience can give workers more flexibility to choose a career path. And, as we discussed in Chapter 8, employees can gain an even wider and more flexible experience base through cross-functional training.

In addition to offering more career options for the employee, job rotation results in a more broadly trained and skilled workforce for the employer. However, job rotation programs have some disadvantages. They do not suit employees who want to maintain a narrow and specialized focus. From the organization's perspective, they can slow down operations as workers learn new skills. While the development benefits of job rotation may be high in the long run, firms should be aware of the short run and intermediate costs. From an employee's perspective, the opportunity of job rotation may be a survival mechanism. Specifically, downsizing in an organization may focus on eliminating an obsolete area. When employees broaden their skills through job rotation, they help ensure their longevity and usefulness to the organization.

Tuition Assistance Programs

Organizations offer *tuition assistance programs* to support their employees' education and development. Tuition and other costs of educational programs (ranging from seminars, workshops, and continuing education programs to degree programs) may be entirely covered, partially covered, or covered contingent upon adequate performance in the program.

A survey of educational reimbursement programs revealed that 43 percent of these plans reimbursed less than 100 percent of tuition. Typically, there is a fixed limit—such as 75 percent of tuition—for all courses. Some companies vary the percentage of tuition funds reimbursed according to the relevance of the course to organizational goals. For instance, a business-book publishing company might encourage its editors to take professional courses related to the business, such as economics and marketing, by reimbursing these courses at 100 percent. However, if editors want to take courses on sign language interpretation, art history, or English literature, the company might reimburse only 50 percent of the tuition.

Self-Development

We conclude this chapter by examining how to manage your personal career.

When an employer does not routinely offer development programs, it is essential that employees work out their own development plan. Employees who neglect to do this risk stagnation and obsolescence. One of the first issues to wrestle with is whether your current job fits with your career plans. The Manager's Notebook: Customer-Driven HR entitled "Career Self-Management" presents questions you can use to assess whether your job places you on a career track that is good for you.

Customer-Driven HR

MANAGER'S NOTEBOOK

Career Self-Assessment

Career self-assessment has rapidly become the norm in many organizations. But how do you evaluate where you're at in your career? And how can you know if your current job puts you on track for reaching your career goals? The following questions can help you make your own career assessments.

- *Does what you're doing for work resonate with your values?* Make a list of your values and judge how well what you are doing at work fits with these values. Are there serious mismatches on values that are most central to you?
- *Do you find your work to be meaningful?* Whatever you do, is it something that you feel makes a positive contribution? For example, does your work allow you to make a positive difference for your customers, organization, or community, and is this effect important to you?
- *How does your organization treat you?* Do you feel you are treated with dignity and respect at work?
- *How do you use your talents at work?* Are you doing what you are good at? Is it what you like to do? Are your contributions appreciated?
- *What is your manager like?* Does your manager support your career growth? Does he or she help your own efforts to develop yourself?
- *What is your life like?* Do you feel in balance? Are you satisfied with the quality of your life? Are there things missing?

Thoughtfully answering the foregoing questions can help you determine if you are on a positive career track or if you need to make some changes. Not every answer can be positive or positive to the maximum degree, but too many negative responses may be a signal that where you are at now isn't contributing to your career.

Source: Adapted with permission from Kaplan-Leiserson, E. (2002). A love match: Do you love your job? Does it love you? *T+D, 56,* 14(2).

Even if your current job fits well with your career plans, a downsizing or merger may put you at risk of being terminated. It has happened to many people. Planning for your career should include a consideration of how you can demonstrate that you make a difference to the organization. The suggestions in the Manager's Notebook titled "An Ounce of Prevention: Ensuring Your Survival" on pages 318 and 319 can help you make this case if you find that your job and career are vulnerable to the fallout from business decisions such as mergers and downsizings.

MANAGER'S NOTEBOOK

An Ounce of Prevention: Ensuring Your Survival

When the dust of the merger, downsizing, or budget cut settles, will you be a survivor? The decision of who stays or goes may be made by an outside consultant who never met you but bases decisions on estimated contributions versus compensation. The following suggestions should help ensure that your career with your present organization isn't brought to an abrupt and early end.

I. **Assess yourself.**
   A. *How are your job skills?*
   Are your information technology skills sufficient for you to be independent, or do you require the cost of a support person to assist you with document preparation and distribution, voice and electronic communication, and so on? Benchmark how your skills compare with your peers in your organization and in other organizations. If you have skill deficiencies, take appropriate steps to correct them: Mentoring or further education may be appropriate.[a]
   B. *How important is your role?*
   Would profits or customer satisfaction be negatively affected if your job or department were eliminated? If your skills are cutting edge but your job or department makes you vulnerable, you need to reposition yourself. Short of leaving the organization, perhaps you can transfer to a more significant part of the organization or develop projects and ties with other departments. These relationships may lead to a transfer or be a safety net if the axe falls.[a]
   C. *What do you contribute?*
   It can be difficult to demonstrate that you and your experience make a difference to customers and to the bottom line, but one or more of the following options may prove useful.
      1. Have you become quicker or more productive? Determine what one hour of your time is worth and construct a chart showing how much the organization is now saving because the task or project is completed more quickly.
      2. Can you show an increase in customer satisfaction associated with your efforts? You may not be able to associate customer satisfaction ratings directly with your performance, but you should have a file of any customer testimonials. You may also want to consider asking customers to put in writing that your performance was a positive factor in their interaction with the organization. Depending on your position, these customers may be internal (for instance, peers from other departments) or external.
      3. If you're in a management position, do employees like you and tend to stick with you? If so, you might be able to show how much you save the organization by a lower than average turnover rate.[b]

II. **Cultivate a positive relationship with your boss and your boss's boss.**
   A boss sometimes has a great deal of discretion over who stays and who goes. Whom do they decide to sacrifice? It only makes sense—those who lack the "soft skills" (such as interpersonal abilities) and who are difficult to manage and oppose the manager and his or her direction would be prime candidates. Being someone your boss can count on can make the difference between survival and sacrifice. It may also be worthwhile to make sure your boss is aware of your contributions. Maybe an occasional update through an e-mail or informal chat is in order. However, avoid looking like a braggart.[b] A matter-of-fact presentation that identifies the problem and what you did about it may work best.

III. **Get plugged into the networks.**
   Be sure to work on your reputation with others both inside and outside of the organization. If others in the organization aren't aware of your skills and contributions, the grapevine may consider you expendable. If you have a positive reputation with external organizations you

will probably be the one who gets calls from headhunters and will have an easier time of finding another position if the axe does fall.[a]

Sources: [a]Kennedy, M. M. (1999). How do you prove you make a difference? *Across the Board*, *36*, 44–48; [b]Master, M. (1999). And did I mention . . .? *Across the Board*, *36*, 62.

Developing your career involves more than just assuring your survival in your organization. Successfully managing your career development means recognizing and developing for yourself the skills needed to advance in today's workplace. The Manager's Notebook: Emerging Trend, "Guidelines for Today's Leaders," identifies some of the characteristics needed for effective management in today's competitive and dynamic environment. Developing these characteristics in yourself can help you to achieve a positive and rewarding career.

Emerging Trends — MANAGER'S NOTEBOOK

Guidelines for Today's Leaders

Today's business environment is more dynamic, competitive, and global than ever before. Success in this environment requires a change in the traditional command-and-control approach to managing. The following points can help guide you to being an effective leader in today's business environment.

- *Take an entrepreneurial perspective.* What are the needs in the marketplace and how can they be better served? Who are your organization's customers and how can you better anticipate their needs? These types of questions direct managers to customer-driven solutions. Being externally driven and looking for solutions rather than complaining about problems will lead to positive things for the organization and for your career.
- *Embrace chaos.* Things can change quickly in today's business world. Rather than being a threat, change is now a routine part of the workplace. Effective performance as a leader requires that you be willing to adapt and try new approaches. Decisions need to be viewed as tactical adjustments rather than permanent answers. Given today's fast-paced environment, you have to make the best decisions with the information immediately available and then you need to move forward. It will not do any good for your organization or your career to dwell on past decisions and how things might have been different if other information had been available.
- *Some risk is needed.* Today's effective leaders are not risk averse. However, they also do not act blindly and rashly. The possibility of failure has to be accepted as part of the path to learning and success. However, getting accurate information and attending to details will increase your chances of making the best choices.
- *Breadth is the key.* Adaptability and a customer focus are characteristics highly valued in today's organizations. The ability to partner with others and to come up with ways to get things done may be more important than specialist skills. You can make positive contributions to your organization and career by viewing everything as your job. Stop and think carefully before taking the position whether something is part of your job.
- *Soft skills can make or break you.* Based on their knowledge and experience, many senior-level managers believe that soft skills are a necessity when it comes to management-level positions. Strong interpersonal skills are essential for managers to effectively hire, lead, mentor, and retain employees in today's dynamic and team-based workplaces.

Source: Adapted from Kacena, J. F. (2002). New leadership directions. *Journal of Business Strategy*, *23*, 21–23; and Executive update. (2002), *T+D*, *56*, 19.

In addition to effective personal characteristics and behaviors, career development can be significantly influenced by situational opportunities. For example, teams, particularly cross-functional or organization-wide teams, can provide a great career development opportunity.[65] Broad teams allow you to gain a wider understanding and perspective of the organization. Furthermore, such teams provide excellent opportunities for adding valuable contacts to your network.

Figure 9.8 lists a set of suggestions to help employees enhance their own development and increase their opportunities for advancement. The *development suggestions* focus on personal growth and direction, while the *advancement suggestions* focus on the steps employees can take to improve their promotability in the organization.

Development Suggestions

The development suggestions in Figure 9.8 are based on the assumption that the organization does not offer development programs. However, these suggestions are relevant even when the company provides development activities.

1. **Create your own personal mission statement.** Like an organizational mission statement, a *personal mission statement* should indicate the business you would like to be in and the role you would like to play.[66] You should see the statement as changeable over time, not a commandment to which you must blindly adhere regardless of situational or personal factors.

   The process of developing the statement can reveal personal values and preferences you may not have realized you have. Once completed, the mission statement should help you set your strategic direction, clarify your priorities, and avoid investing time and energy in pursuits that are not instrumental to achieving your mission.
2. **Take responsibility for your own direction and growth.** You should not place all of your hopes in a company-provided development program. Things change, and steps in a career path can be eliminated as a result of downsizing or reorganizing. Organizations may also eliminate or replace development programs. Such changes could be devastating for people who place their future entirely in the hands of their organization.
3. **Make enhancement, rather than advancement, your priority.** Organizational flattening and downsizing mean that there will be fewer opportunities for advancement in the coming years. Even today direct upward paths to desired higher-level positions are rare. It is best to accept this reality and search for opportunities to broaden your skills in the short term. Enhancing your skills in the short run should lead to advancement in the longer run.
4. **Talk to people in positions to which you aspire and get their suggestions on how to proceed.** People who are currently in the kind of job you desire can give you valuable insight into the job and what you must do to make it to that level. Talking to people is also a good way of networking and keeping your name on people's lips.
5. **Set reasonable goals.** As with any major undertaking, it is best to set reasonable goals along the way to your ultimate goal. Breaking your career aspirations into smaller, more manage-

Figure 9.8

Development	Advancement
1. Create your own personal mission statement.	1. Remember that performance in your function is important, but interpersonal performance is critical.
2. Take responsibility for your own direction and growth.	2. Set the right values and priorities.
3. Make enhancement your priority rather than advancement.	3. Provide solutions, not problems.
4. Talk to people in positions to which you aspire and get suggestions on how to proceed.	4. Be a team player.
5. Set reasonable goals.	5. Be customer oriented.
6. Make investment in yourself a priority.	6. Act as if what you're doing makes a difference.

Source: Advancement suggestions adapted from Matejka, K., and Dunsing, R. (1993). Enhancing your advancement in the 1990s. *Management Decision, 31*, 52–54.

Suggestions for Self-Development

able goals can help you take the necessary steps toward accomplishing your ultimate goal. It is important to make these minigoals reasonable and achievable. Expecting too much too soon can lead to disillusionment and frustration.

6. **Make investment in yourself a priority.** When multiple demands are made on your time and attention, it is easy to neglect self-development activities. It is important to remind yourself that these activities are actually investments in yourself and your future, and that no one else is likely to make those investments for you.

Advancement Suggestions

The advancement suggestions in Figure 9.8 focus on the steps you can take to improve your chances of being considered for advancement. The development suggestions are fundamental and provide the necessary base, but the advancement suggestions provide the necessary attitudes and organizational presence.

1. **Remember that performance in your function is important, but interpersonal performance is critical.** Advancing in an organization requires excellent interpersonal skills. The abilities to communicate (both one-on-one and to groups), to collaborate, to listen, to summarize, and to write concise reports and memos are essential to being considered a viable candidate for advancement.
2. **Set the right values and priorities.** Your worth to an organization increases after you have discovered the organization's values and priorities and aligned yourself with them. For example, some organizations place a high value on collaboration and teamwork, while others emphasize independence and individual contribution. Aligning your behavior with the organization's values improves your chances for advancement.[67]
3. **Provide solutions, not problems.** Nobody likes to hear complaints. So, rather than voicing complaints and pointing out problems, take some time to think issues through and offer potential solutions. You'll be perceived as a much more valuable member of the organization.
4. **Be a team player.** You should not try to steal the limelight for your work group's accomplishments. Rather, you should try to shine the spotlight on the group's efforts. When you do, you'll be viewed as a facilitator rather than a grandstander. However, you should be sure that those responsible for evaluating your performance know of your personal accomplishments. One way to balance these concerns is to refuse to seek public praise for your performance but not be afraid to call attention to your successes when appropriate.
5. **Be customer oriented.** Always keep in mind that anyone with whom you have an exchange is your "customer." Whether these interactions are internal or external, understanding and satisfying customer needs should be a top priority. When you take a customer-orientation approach to your job, the organization will recognize you as a high-quality representative who can be expected to accomplish things.
6. **Act as if what you are doing makes a difference.** A sure way to be overlooked for advancement is to display an apathetic or negative attitude. Not all tasks or projects to which you are assigned will spur your interest, but if you approach these activities with a positive attitude, others will see you as a contributor and a valuable team player.

Summary and Conclusions

What Is Career Development?

Career development is an ongoing organized and formalized effort that focuses on developing enriched and more capable workers. It has a wider focus, longer time frame, and broader scope than training. Development must be a key business strategy if an organization is to survive in today's increasingly competitive and global business environment.

Challenges in Career Development

Before putting a career development program in place, management needs to determine (1) who will be responsible for development, (2) how much emphasis on development is appropriate, and (3) how the development needs of a diverse workforce (including dual-career couples) will be met.

Meeting the Challenges of Effective Development

Career development is a continuing cycle of three phases: an assessment phase, a direction phase, and a development phase. Each phase is an important part of developing the workforce.

In the assessment phase, employees' skills, interests, and values are identified. These assessments may be carried out by the workers themselves, by the organization, or by both. Self-assessment is often done through career workbooks and career-planning workshops. Organizational assessment is done through assessment centers, psychological testing, performance appraisal, promotability forecasts, and succession planning.

The direction phase involves determining the type of career that employees want and the steps they must take to make their career goals a reality. In this phase workers may receive individual career counseling or information from a variety of sources, including a job-posting system, skills inventories, career paths, and career resource centers.

The development phase involves taking actions to create and increase employees' skills and promotability. The most common development programs are mentoring, coaching, job rotation, and tuition assistance programs.

Self-Development

In situations in which the employer does not routinely offer development programs, employees must take an active role in their own development. To do otherwise is to risk stagnation and obsolescence.

Key Terms

career development, 297
career path, 311
career resource center, 312
dual-career couple, 303
job-posting system, 311
mentoring, 314
promotability forecast, 307
skills inventory, 311
succession planning, 307

Discussion Questions

1. It has been argued that training can lead to turnover, but career development can reduce it. Differentiate between training and career development. Why might training lead to turnover whereas career development might improve retention? Explain.
2. How would you go about retaining and developing older employees who are part of a dual-career couple?
3. Today's organizations are flatter and offer fewer opportunities for advancement. How do you think careers should be developed in this type of organizational environment?
4. In a recent survey of 925 men and women with MBAs, it was found that "traditional" married men—those who have children and whose wives do not work—earn on average 20 percent more per year than family men without children and with employed wives. Yet only 21 percent of the managers surveyed said they were in this type of traditional family structure. By contrast, 39 percent are in "posttraditional" family units, and these workers express greater satisfaction with their careers. What challenges do these posttraditional family units pose to company career development plans? How can companies meet these challenges?
5. People who adopt a careerist strategy focus on career advancement through political machinations rather than excellent performance. Experts have pointed out four ways in which workers try to influence their superiors' opinions of them: favor doing (doing a favor for a superior in hopes that the favor will someday be returned), opinion conformity (agreeing with superiors in order to build trust and a relationship), other enhancement (flattery), and self-presentation (portraying oneself as having very desirable traits and motives).

   In what other ways might employees try to influence their superiors' opinions of them? How can managers tell when an employee is sincere? What criteria should be used when deciding which employees to promote?
6. Companies use various tactics to encourage managers to make employee development a top priority. At Honeywell, for instance, a prestigious award worth $3,000 is given to those managers who contribute strongly to their unit's profitability, who assist the career development of at least three people, and who have excellent records as mentors of diverse employee groups. Winners gain companywide recognition as well as the financial reward. What do you think of this policy of tying financial rewards to people development? What are some other ways companies can hold managers accountable for developing those they supervise?

There is a variety of additional material available on the Web site that accompanies this text. You can access this information by visiting the Web site at **www.prenhall.com/gomez.**

Customer-Driven HR Case 9.1

YOU MANAGE IT!

Mentoring: Great Investment or Sunk Cost?

Mentoring looks like a highly effective career development tool. Survey results indicate that 77 percent of companies report that mentoring programs are effective in increasing retention and more than 60 percent of college students list mentoring as a criterion for selecting an employer after graduation. Furthermore, 75 percent of executives indicate that mentoring played a key role in their careers. It would appear that mentoring can lead to improved recruitment, career success, and retention. However, approximately 90 percent of formal mentoring programs dissolve. To be successful, there may be more to mentoring than it may at first appear.

Although surveys indicate that the majority of mentoring programs run into problems, there are a number of organizations that have very successful mentoring programs. For example, Deloitte & Touche, a company with over 90,000 employees and a presence in over 130 countries, includes mentoring as one of its guiding principles. One of the keys to the success of its mentoring program seems to be how it has embedded mentoring into its culture. The firm begin emphasizing mentoring during new employee orientation. The majority of mentoring that occurs at Deloitte & Touche is informal and self-directed. The organization fosters an environment in which mentoring is nurtured as a natural occurrence rather than bureaucratically imposed.

To be a success, a mentoring program requires active and responsible management. Perhaps most important is that everyone needs to understand the purpose for a mentoring program and that time and resources are necessary and must be provided for the program. People also need to be comfortable with the role of mentor and have the skills needed to effectively perform in this role. Thus, training is likely to be needed if a mentoring program is to be successful. And, if mentoring is to be taken as an important and serious activity, then it needs to be managed in a way that clearly conveys this message. Specifically, there should be positive feedback and other contingencies tied to doing mentoring well. However, there should be negative feedback and contingencies if a manager is doing a poor job of mentoring and losing people to the labor marketplace. If mentoring effectiveness isn't measured and meaningful feedback and contingencies linked to the measure, then people can rightly develop the perception that mentoring is not really important in the organization.

Critical Thinking Questions

1. Do you think a mentoring program is worth it? Why or why not?
2. Mentoring may be more effective for some employees than for others. For example, women can sometimes encounter obstacles in organizations that can slow down their advancement. Given this situation, a mentoring program for women may be more useful and offer a greater return on investment than a mentoring program for men. Should mentoring programs be developed for all employees or just for select groups? What problems might be encountered if mentoring programs were put in place for some groups of employees but not for others?
3. There are various online systems to facilitate mentoring programs. Using the Internet, explore what is available, how much the programs cost, and what they do. Would you recommend an online mentoring program? Would you use an online system for all aspects of a mentoring program? Explain.

Team Exercise

As a team, develop a management system designed to maximize the success of a mentoring program. In your system, be sure to address the following.

- Mentor characteristics and selection
- How mentors and mentees are paired
- Any training that will be provided
- Performance measurement
- Performance management—feedback and contingencies

How could you evaluate the effectiveness of the mentoring program? What measures would you recommend? Could you estimate return on investment for a mentoring program?

Source: Adapted from Barbian, J. (2002). The road best traveled. *Training*, *39*, 38(4).

YOU MANAGE IT! Customer-Driven HR Case 9.2

Capitalizing on Techno Savvy: Putting Mentoring in Reverse

Mentoring has been used for years by forward-looking companies as a way to pass on experience and knowledge in an organization. Traditionally, the direction of mentoring has been from older, more experienced workers providing input to younger, less experienced workers. However, many young and entry-level workers in today's organizations have better understanding and skills in the technology domain than do their managers. That's why a number of organizations are putting their traditional approach to mentoring in reverse with their younger employees mentoring their experienced managers. The purpose for the reverse mentoring is to spread technical expertise and to help more experienced managers better understand a more youthful perspective.

Jack Welch, former CEO of General Electric, is the person generally credited with introducing formal reverse mentoring. In 1999 Welch ordered 500 of his top managers to find workers who were Internet savvy and to pair with them as mentors. Welch included himself in this effort and committed blocks of time to learn about things such as Internet bookmarks and competitor Web sites. From this beginning, organizations are now expanding the reverse mentoring concept to a variety of topics. An outcome of reverse mentoring may be the growing realization that mentoring is about sharing knowledge and expertise, no matter who has it, so that this knowledge within an organization can be leveraged to full advantage.

Critical Thinking Questions

1. What topics, other than technology, would be appropriate for the reverse mentoring approach?
2. College students pursue internships at companies. The reverse mentoring concept leads to the possibility that some companies may learn as much or more from some college students as the students learn from the experience with the company. Do you think it is possible to shift the internship model into a two-way street of information sharing? How would each side benefit from such an approach? Would students in this approach need particular kinds of skills? How would you propose that students be selected for such opportunities?
3. Mentoring and reverse mentoring can be seen as particular directions of knowledge sharing. Would peer-to-peer mentoring be possible? What about customer to employee? Could the traditional concept of mentoring be expanded to something similar to 360-degree appraisal (see Chapter 7)? If so, how would it change the nature and purpose of mentoring?

Team Exercise

Although reverse mentoring can be a great concept, it can pose problems when trying to put it into operation. For example, the ego of the more experienced manager may get in the way of effectively learning what the less experienced worker has to offer. Likewise, the less experienced worker may need to develop patience and an understanding of what is more or less important in the organizational context.

As a team, confront the reality that reverse mentoring isn't just going to happen. What steps would you recommend that would help assure that reverse mentoring works effectively? For example, would you recommend training? What kind? For whom? Have team members search for examples of reverse mentoring in organizations. How well is the program working and what was done to implement it? Share your recommendations and findings with the rest of the class.

Source: Greengard, S. (2002). Moving forward with reverse mentoring. *Workforce, 81*, 15.

YOU MANAGE IT! Emerging Trends Case 9.3

Get Rid of Those Bad Habits

Why do some people seem to move upward in their careers while others seem to work hard to simply maintain their current level? One reason may be the behavioral tendencies or habits that people develop. Some behavioral tendencies may keep people from moving ahead in their careers or even worse sabotaging their own chances for career advancement. For example, some people are uncomfortable with success and with increasing responsibility for managing others. This fear may unknowingly cause people to make errors and, therefore, save them from the discomfort of further advancement.

There are many other examples of behavioral tendencies that might be considered bad habits when it comes to career opportunities. Ironically, some of these habits were good habits that helped people to get ahead during the early stages of their career, but they became "bad" habits and worked against them later. Here's how a good habit becomes a bad habit. People who have developed the habit of analyzing decisions and allocating time and effort based on a strict belief in a rational system, particularly early in their careers, often do not see the value in networking and office politics. If performance is evaluated and rewarded on anything other than objective outcomes, the result for people with this perspective is the perception of unfairness or discrimination. A simple and objective view of performance can be a positive characteristic very early in your career. However, organizational reality quickly dictates that performance is broader than can be measured by objective outputs and subjective factors. Getting things done with and through other people becomes an important part of what constitutes performance.

Another tendency that can end up as a bad habit for your career is the avoidance of conflict. Some people who avoid confrontation early in their careers find this can be a successful strategy. However, dealing with conflict can be part of organizational life and confrontation may be needed to reach a solution or to drive the creative process. The habitual unwillingness or inability to deal with tension and conflict can hold people back from advancement in their careers.

Critical Thinking Questions

1. Identify other tendencies that could be bad habits for career advancement. Describe how each tendency could be a bad habit when it comes to moving forward in a career.
2. For each tendency identified in your answer to question 1, try to determine what might be the cause of each tendency. For example, the avoidance of conflict might result from a lack of self-confidence or a lack of experience and skills for dealing with situations when confrontation is necessary. Make a table of behavioral tendencies and possible causes.
3. Given the table resulting from your response to question 2, identify how the bad habit might be overcome. For example, would training be a solution? If so, what type of training?

Team Exercise

Contact people you know in management positions and ask them to describe behavioral tendencies of people that got in the way of their career advancement. Before contacting these managers, your team needs to generate the questions that will be used so that everyone will be asking the same questions. You might also ask managers what became of the person and what, if anything, they think could have been done to alter the person's bad habit. In addition, make note of the type of industry or workplace in which each behavioral tendency occurred and was viewed as a problem.

As a team, compile the information gathered from your sample of managers. Describe the bad habits to the rest of the class, explaining why they were a problem in that work context. Share any examples of solutions to the bad habits.

Whether a characteristic is positive or negative can be largely determined by the situation in which the characteristic occurs. In the case of behavioral tendencies (those that were identified in the preceding Critical Thinking Exercise 1 or those identified by your management sample), are there some work contexts or types of industries in which these habits might not be considered as "bad?" Are bad habits really just an issue of inappropriate fit between work situations and people, or are there habits that are universally bad? Discuss as a team and share your conclusions with the rest of the class.

Source: Adapted from *HRMagazine*. (2002) The 12 bad habits that hold good people back. *47*, 93(2).

Emerging Trends Case 9.4 — YOU MANAGE IT!

Head Start for Careers

Employees are an important resource and, just like any valuable resource, organizations and industries compete for them. Usually we think of competition for employees occurring during recruitment and hiring. However, some industries are vying for employees at a much earlier point than recruitment. For example, the hotel industry has been active in developing future employees by offering programs beginning as early as elementary school. These programs are meant to influence career decisions of students and can continue through high school. The School-to-Work Opportunities Act was passed by Congress in 1994 and provides states with funds to support School-to-Work programs.

The School-to-Work programs offer industry speakers and field trips. Job shadowing is another technique that can be used as part of a program to influence career decisions. Job shadowing assigns a student to a worker and the student "shadows" and observes what the employee does. You can find more information on job shadowing at www.jobshadow.org.

A proactive approach has been used to supplement these techniques by the hotel industry in Florida. The Florida hoteliers host a summer program for high school teachers that pays them a stipend and offers them continuing education credits. This program educates teachers about the hotel industry and its career opportunities. The teachers leave the summer program with brochures and other materials that have been prepared for sharing with students when the teachers return to their classrooms in the fall.

Critical Thinking Questions

1. We usually don't think about anyone's career starting until after high school or college. Does the approach described here push concerns about career down to an age that is too early? Do you think this "head start" approach to influencing career choices is a good thing? Why or why not?
2. The description identified some techniques that can be used to make early influences on career decisions. Identify other techniques that might be useful.
3. Find additional information on job shadowing. What is Groundhog Shadow Day?

Team Exercise

As a team, examine the costs and benefits of a program designed to provide early influence on career decisions. Specifically, identify the techniques you would suggest your organization use. Estimate the costs associated with each technique. Identify measures that could be used to assess how well the techniques and overall program worked. In other words, how could you tell if your efforts were effective? Develop criteria that would allow you to assess effectiveness at various levels (e.g., participant reactions, self-report of intended career choice, actual career choice, etc.). Which criteria would you recommend? How long must the organization wait before effectiveness of the program can be estimated with each measure? Do you think that a monetary estimate of ROI could be made? Describe.

Share your criteria and how you would measure effectiveness with the rest of the class.

Source: Maladecki, R. (2002). Hotel-education programs help industry find future employees. *Hotel and Motel Management, 217*, 10.

Part V:

Compensation

Managing Compensation

Challenges

After reading this chapter, you should be able to deal more effectively with the following challenges:

1. **Identify** the compensation policies and practices that are most appropriate for a particular firm.
2. **Weigh** the strategic advantages and disadvantages of the different compensation options.
3. **Establish** a job-based compensation scheme that is internally consistent and linked to the labor market.
4. **Understand** the difference between a compensation system in which employees are paid for the skills they use and one in which they are paid for the job they hold.
5. **Make** compensation decisions that comply with the legal framework.

Sigma, Inc. is a medium-sized biotechnology firm specializing in genetic engineering. The firm was founded in 1996 by a college professor, Dr. Roger Smith, who left academia to start a new company in a promising young field. The venture has been a resounding success. In spite of the bear market at the start of this new century, Sigma's stock price increased a hundredfold over its original value from 1996 to 2003, and the number of its employees increased to 350 in 2003. Smith is still Sigma's chief executive officer and continues to be actively involved in all hiring and pay decisions. He repeatedly tells his line managers that Sigma "will pay whatever it takes to hire the best talent in the market."

During the past year Smith has noticed an erosion in Sigma's "family atmosphere" and an increase in the number of dissatisfied employees. Despite Sigma's generous compensation package, pay appears to be a major concern. There have been three pay-related complaints during the past week alone, and Smith suspects this is only the tip of the iceberg. The first complaint came from a software developer who has been with Sigma for five years. He is upset that another developer was recently hired at a salary 15 percent higher than his. Smith explained that such starting salaries are necessary to attract top experienced programmers from other firms in a very tight labor market. The second complaint came from a software engineer who feels that Sigma's best technical people—the lifeblood of a biotechnology firm—are discriminated against in pay because supervisors (who, in his words, are often "failed engineers") receive 30 percent more pay. The third complaint was filed by a head secretary who has been with Sigma from the start. She is angry that janitors are getting more money than she is, and she is not satisfied with Smith's explanation that it is difficult to hire and retain reliable people who are willing to clean up and dispose of dangerous chemicals.

In addition, a 49-year-old engineer who was purportedly terminated for poor performance has just filed an age discrimination suit against the company, arguing that the firm is replacing older, higher-earning employees with Indian employees on temporary visas who are willing to work at much lower wages.

THE MANAGERIAL PERSPECTIVE

Sigma's experience raises several important questions that managers and HR personnel must face in designing and administering compensation programs, such as the following:

- Who should be responsible for making salary decisions?
- Should pay be dictated by what other employers are paying?
- What types of activities should be rewarded with higher salaries?
- What criteria should be used to determine salaries?
- Which employee groups should receive special treatment when scarce pay resources are allocated?

The pay system is one of the most important mechanisms that firms and managers can use to attract, retain, and motivate competent employees to perform in ways that support organizational objectives. It also has a direct bearing on the extent to which labor costs detract from or contribute to business objectives and profitability.

The HR department plays an important role in designing administrative rules and procedures to ensure fair allocation of pay, control labor costs, and maintain parity with competitor's pay levels for similar jobs. However, organizations face many choices in terms of which pay policies and practices to use. The challenge for top managers, in consultation with HR personnel, is to pick those that are most appropriate to the firm. Most managers at all levels of the organization enjoy some discretion in making pay decisions for subordinates. Such decisions should be equitable and relate to criteria such as unique skills, performance level, and the flexibility to perform multiple tasks.

In the first part of this chapter, we define the components of compensation and examine the nine criteria used to develop a compensation plan. Then we explore the process of designing a compensation plan and the legal and regulatory influences on compensation.

What Is Compensation?

As Figure 10.1 shows, an employee's **total compensation** has three components. The relative proportion of each (known as the *pay mix*) varies extensively by firm.[1] The first and (in most firms) largest element of total compensation is **base compensation,** the fixed pay an employee receives on a regular basis, either in the form of a salary (for example, a weekly or monthly pay-

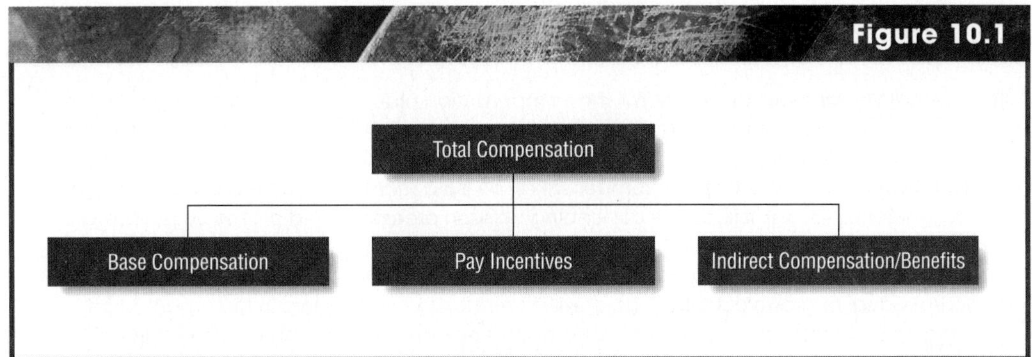

The Elements of Total Compensation

check) or as an hourly wage. The second component of total compensation is **pay incentives,** programs designed to reward employees for good performance. These incentives come in many forms (including bonuses and profit sharing) and are the focus of Chapter 11. The last component of total compensation is *benefits,* sometimes called *indirect compensation.* Benefits encompass a wide variety of programs (for example, health insurance vacations, and unemployment compensation), the costs of which approach 41 percent of workers' compensation packages.[2] A special category of benefits called *perquisites,* or perks, are available only to employees with some special status in the organization, usually upper-level managers. Common perks are a company car, a special parking place on company grounds, and company-paid country club memberships. Chapter 12 discusses benefit programs in detail.

Compensation is the single most important cost in most firms. Personnel costs are as high as 60 percent of total costs in certain types of manufacturing environments and even higher in some service organizations (for example, labor costs amount to approximately 80 percent of the U.S. Postal Service's budget). This means that the effectiveness with which compensation is allocated can make a significant difference in gaining or losing a competitive edge. For instance, a high-tech firm that provides generous compensation to managerial and marketing personnel but underpays its research and development staff may lose its ability to innovate because competitors constantly pirate away its best talent. Thus, *how much* is paid and *who* gets paid what are crucial strategic issues for the firm; they affect the cost side of all financial statements and determine the extent to which the firm realizes a low or high return on its payroll dollars.[3]

Total compensation
The package of quantifiable rewards an employee receives for his or her labors. Includes three components: base compensation, pay incentives, and indirect compensation/benefits.

Base compensation
The fixed pay an employee receives on a regular basis, either in the form of a salary or as an hourly wage.

Pay incentive
A program designed to reward employees for good performance.

Designing a Compensation System

An employee's paycheck is certainly important for its purchasing power. In most societies, however, a person's earnings also serve as an indicator of power and prestige and are tied to feelings of self-worth. In other words, compensation affects a person economically, sociologically, and psychologically.[4] For this reason, mishandling compensation issues is likely to have a strong negative impact on employees and, ultimately, on the firm's performance.[5]

The wide variety of pay policies and procedures presents managers with a two-pronged challenge: to design a compensation system that (1) enables the firm to achieve its strategic objectives and (2) is molded to the firm's unique characteristics and environment.[6] We discuss the criteria for developing a compensation plan in the sections that follow and summarize these options in Figure 10.2 on page 330. Although we present each of these as an either/or choice for the sake of simplicity, most firms institute policies that fall somewhere between the two poles.

Internal Versus External Equity

Fair pay is pay that employees generally view as equitable. There are two forms of pay equity. **Internal equity** refers to the perceived fairness of the pay structure within a firm. **External equity** refers to the perceived fairness of pay relative to what other employers are paying for the same type of labor.

Internal equity
The perceived fairness of the pay structure within a firm.

External equity
The perceived fairness in pay relative to what other employers are paying for the same type of labor.

The Nine Criteria for Developing a Compensation Plan

Figure 10.2

1. **Internal Versus External Equity** Will the compensation plan be perceived as fair within the company, or will it be perceived as fair relative to what other employers are paying for the same type of labor?
2. **Fixed Versus Variable Pay** Will compensation be paid monthly on a fixed basis—through base salaries—or will it fluctuate depending on such preestablished criteria as performance and company profits?
3. **Performance Versus Membership** Will compensation emphasize performance and tie pay to individual or group contributions, or will it emphasize membership in the organization—logging in a prescribed number of hours each week and progressing up the organizational ladder?
4. **Job Versus Individual Pay** Will compensation be based on how the company values a particular job, or will it be based on how much skill and knowledge an employee brings to that job?
5. **Egalitarianism Versus Elitism** Will the compensation plan place most employees under the same compensation system (egalitarianism), or will it establish different plans by organizational level and/or employee group (elitism)?
6. **Below-Market Versus Above-Market Compensation** Will employees be compensated at below-market levels, at market levels, or at above-market levels?
7. **Monetary Versus Nonmonetary Awards** Will the compensation plan emphasize motivating employees through monetary rewards like pay and stock options, or will it stress nonmonetary rewards such as interesting work and job security?
8. **Open Versus Secret Pay** Will employees have access to information about other workers' compensation levels and how compensation decisions are made (open pay), or will this knowledge be withheld from employees (secret pay)?
9. **Centralization Versus Decentralization of Pay Decisions** Will compensation decisions be made in a tightly controlled central location, or will they be delegated to managers of the firm's units?

In considering internal versus external equity, managers can use two basic models: the distributive justice model and the labor market model.

The Distributive Justice Model

The *distributive justice model* of pay equity holds that employees exchange their contributions or input to the firm (skills, effort, time, and so forth) for a set of outcomes. Pay is one of the most important of these outcomes, but nonmonetary rewards like a company car may also be significant. This social-psychological perspective suggests that employees are constantly (1) comparing what they bring to the firm to what they receive in return and (2) comparing this input/outcome ratio with that of other employees within the firm. Employees will think they are fairly paid when the ratio of their inputs and outputs is equivalent to that of other employees whose job demands are similar to their own.

Some employees compare their input/outcome ratio to that of employees in other firms, but most compare themselves to their peers in the same organization. From this perspective, then, the compensation system's key task is to ensure that salaries and wages are set so that employees perceive a fair input/outcome balance within the firm and, to a lesser extent, outside it.

The Labor Market Model

According to the *labor market* model of pay equity, the wage rate for any given occupation is set at the point where the supply of labor equals the demand for labor in the marketplace (W_1 in Figure 10.3). In general, the less employers are willing to pay (low demand for labor) and the lower the pay workers are willing to accept for a given job (high supply of labor), the lower the wage rate for that job.[7]

The actual situation is a great deal more complicated than this basic model suggests however. People base their decisions about what jobs they are willing to hold on many more factors

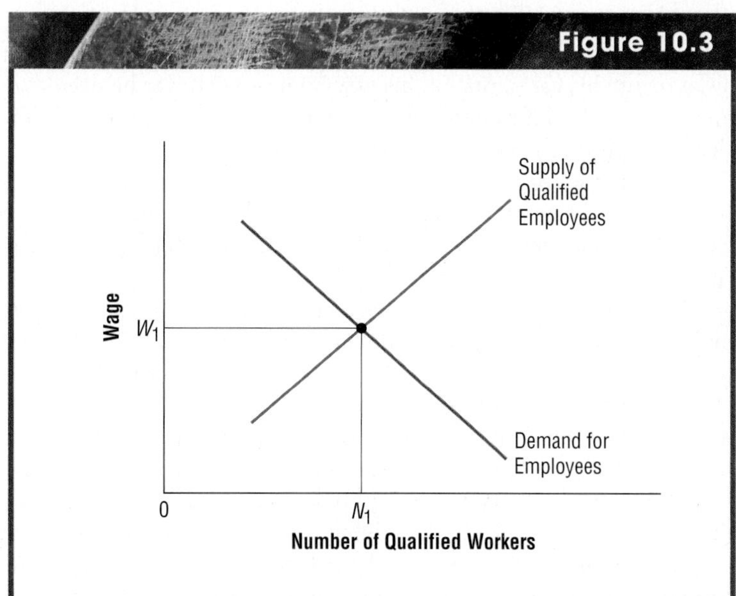

The Labor Market Model

than just pay. The organization's location and the job's content and demands are just two of these factors. Moreover, the pay that an employer offers is based on many factors besides the number of available people with the skills and abilities to do the job. These factors include historical wage patterns, the presence or absence of unions, and internal organizational politics. A complete exploration of this topic is beyond the scope of this book. However, the basic point of the labor market model is that external equity is achieved when the firm pays its employees the "going rate" for the type of work they do.[8] A firm cannot stray too far in either direction from the market wage. If it offers pay much below the going rate, it may be unable to attract and retain qualified workers. If it pays much more than the going rate, it may be unable to charge competitive prices for its product because its labor costs are too high.

Balancing Equity

Ideally, a firm should try to establish both internal and external pay equity, but these objectives are often at odds. For instance, universities sometimes pay new assistant professors more than senior faculty who have been with the institution for a decade or more,[9] and firms sometimes pay recent engineering graduates more than engineers who have been on board for many years.[10]

You may wonder why the senior employees accept lower pay instead of leaving and competing for higher-paying positions elsewhere. Senior faculty are usually tenured, which means they would give up job security if they went to another university. Furthermore, both college professors and engineers work in fields where the knowledge base is constantly changing, making recent graduates (who are more likely to be aware of new developments in their field) somewhat more valuable employees.

In addition to balancing internal and external equity, many firms have to determine which employee groups' pay will be adjusted upward to meet (or perhaps exceed) market rates and which groups' pay will remain at or under market. This decision is generally based on each group's relative importance to the firm. For example, marketing employees tend to be paid more in firms that are trying to expand their market share and less in older firms that have a well-established product with high brand recognition.

In general, emphasizing external equity is more appropriate for newer, smaller firms in a rapidly changing market. These firms often have a high need for innovation to remain competitive and are dependent on key individuals to achieve their business objectives.[11] Much of the relatively new high-tech industry fits this description.

For instance, with a sales growth rate of at least 40 percent annually during the last few years, Dell Computer's CEO Michael Dell claims the number-one priority for the company is hiring and retaining scarce talent. The CEO is not afraid to get in on the act, according to Dell's HR

Director Andy Esparza. "I'll call Michael or e-mail him to say, 'We've got a recruit who has a couple of competing offers. Would you call him?' " says Esparza. "And he'll pick up the phone right away, or use his car phone on his way home—whatever he needs to do to make that call. He is a great closer." Dell negotiates with each prospective employee to devise a compensation package that depends on the person's value to the company.[12]

A greater emphasis on internal equity is more appropriate for older, larger, well-established firms. These firms often have a mature product, employees who plan to spend most of their career with the firm, and jobs that do not change often. Much of the regulated utilities industry fits this description.

When faced with this dilemma, an increasing number of firms have opted to offer large "sign-on bonuses" to new employees to entice good candidates without disrupting the existing salary schedules. A recent survey of 348 large and small firms that use sign-on bonuses indicated 80 percent of them use bonuses to sign on professional staff and executives; 70 percent to sign midlevel managers and information technology personnel; 60 percent for sales, lower-level managers, and technical staff; and 20 percent for clerical workers. In a sense the new employee receives a big pay raise "up front"—in many cases 25 percent or more of annual salary—and the company avoids the need to reduce posted salary differentials between junior and senior employees.[13]

Another interesting twist to the balancing equity dilemma in recent years is the practice of companies facing uncertain financial futures showering large amounts of "retention bonuses" on key employees. The objective is to retain needed expertise without having to raise the entire salary schedule—which might hasten the firm's demise. For instance, in 2002 Kmart spent upward of $92 million in retention bonuses for 9,700 key employees as it filed for bankruptcy protection. Other recent well-publicized cases of companies that did the same include Enron, Polaroid, Bradlees Inc., and Aerovox, Inc.[14]

The company has to be careful that employees do not see the sign-on bonus and the retention bonus as attempts to deal with the balancing equity dilemma in an underhanded fashion, which would just add fuel to the fire.

Fixed Versus Variable Pay

Firms can choose to pay a high proportion of total compensation in the form of base pay (for example, a predictable monthly paycheck) or in the form of variable pay that fluctuates according to some preestablished criterion. For example, Citibank pays its employees (except for those at the highest executive ranks) almost exclusively in the form of fixed compensation or base pay. In contrast, Anderson Windows pays its employees up to 50 percent of their total compensation in the form of a bonus based on company profits for the year. On average, approximately 75 percent of firms in 2002 were offering some form of variable pay.[15]

There is a great deal of variation in the way firms answer the fixed versus variable pay question. On average, 10 percent of an employee's pay in the United States is variable. This compares to 20 percent in Japan. However, the range is huge in both countries—from 0 percent up to 70 percent. For select employee groups (such as sales), variable pay can be as high as 100 percent.[16] In general, the proportion of variable pay increases as an employee's base pay increases, indicating that those in higher-level positions earn more but their overall compensation is more subject to risk. For employees earning more than $750,000 a year in base pay, variable compensation is close to 90 percent of base pay. For those earning less than $25,000 a year in base pay, this percentage drops to less than 5 percent.[17]

As we discuss in Chapter 11, variable compensation takes many forms, including individual bonuses, team bonuses, profit sharing, and stock ownership programs. The higher the proportion of variable pay, the more *risk sharing* there is between the employee and the firm. This means a trade-off between income security and the potential for higher earnings.[18]

Fixed pay is the rule in the majority of U.S. organizations largely because it reduces the risk to both employer and employee. However, variable pay can be used advantageously in smaller companies, firms with a product that is not well established, companies with a young professional workforce that is willing to delay immediate gratification in hopes of greater future returns, firms supported by venture capital, organizations going through a prolonged period of cash shortages, and companies that would otherwise have to institute layoffs because their revenues are volatile.

Apple Computer provides an excellent example of a firm that used variable pay to its own and its employees' advantage. Employees were willing to work for low salaries for several years in exchange for company stock; many of those who persevered became millionaires after the value of Apple's stock went sky high in the mid-1980s. Similarly, many Wal-Mart store managers who worked for years at a low salary plus Wal-Mart stock became wealthy when the company's stock value soared. Some economists attribute the small rise in unemployment in the recession during 2001–2002, particularly after September 11, 2001, to a two-thirds drop in the amount of bonuses received by workers. "Nobody likes losing a bonus but it may be the price for saving jobs," according to one observer.[19] Among the largest companies that say flexibility helped minimize layoffs during the most recent recession are Rockwell International Corp. and Agilent Technologies. But it also seems to work among smaller firms. Consider the following case of WR Hambrecht:

> WR Hambrecht, a San Francisco–based boutique investment bank, announced a base salary cap of $60,000 for its investment bankers and certain other employees in 2002. The balance of their compensation comes from profit sharing and bonuses, both to be determined by each department's manager based on performance. This limits Hambrecht's payroll expenses in a long downturn—no profits, no sharing—while simultaneously rewarding the best employees and encouraging others to leave. "Without spending more money, they're reallocating their funds to the people who are bringing money into the firm," says Bill Coleman, senior vice president for compensation at research firm Salary.com. Hambrecht says it has been able to avert new layoffs and hasn't seen significant defections.[20]

Not all variable-pay plans work out well for employees, however. Employees at two airlines, People Express and America West, found that the stock they received in lieu of a higher salary was almost worthless when they tried to cash it in. More recently, employees at Enron and Global Crossing saw their stockholdings drop from $90 to about 50 cents per share within months, partly due to company mismanagement and partly due to corruption at the top.[21]

Performance Versus Membership

A special case of fixed versus variable compensation involves a choice between performance and membership.[22] A company emphasizes performance when a substantial portion of its employees' pay is tied to individual or group contributions and the amount received can vary significantly from one person or group to another. The most extreme forms of *performance-contingent compensation* are traditional piece-rate plans (pay based on units produced) and sales commissions. Other performance-contingent plans use awards for cost-saving suggestions, bonuses for perfect attendance, or merit pay based on supervisory appraisals. All these options are provided on top of an individual's base pay (see Chapter 11).

Firms that emphasize *membership-contingent compensation* provide the same or a similar wage to every employee in a given job, as long as the employee achieves at least satisfactory performance. Employees receive a paycheck for logging in a prescribed number of hours of work per week (normally 40). Typically, salary progression occurs by moving up in the organization, not by doing the present job better.

The relative emphasis placed on performance versus membership depends largely on the organization's culture and the beliefs of top managers or the company's founder. For instance, 3M's CEO has noted that the most important managerial value at 3M is that human beings are endowed with the urge to create, to bring into being something that has never existed before . . . [therefore] rewards have to be tied directly to successful innovation . . . the worst thing we could do with [innovators] is to base their rewards on how well they fit into some preconceived management mold."[23] 3M's encouragement of innovation has paid off. In what has become a legend in the field of product development, one of its chemists developed the immensely popular adhesive Post-It™ Notes after getting tired of having bookmarks fall out of his hymnal at church. It took a year of tinkering to develop the final product, but 3M provided the chemist with the time to tinker and a handsome bonus for the final result.[24]

Most companies that emphasize performance tend to be smaller than 3M. They are usually characterized by fewer management levels, rapid growth, internal competition among people and groups, readily available performance indicators (see Chapter 7), and strong competitive pressures.[25]

Job Versus Individual Pay

Most traditional compensation systems assume that in setting base compensation a firm should evaluate the value or contributions of each job, not how well the employee performs it.[26] Under this system, the job becomes the unit of analysis for determining base compensation, not the individual(s) performing that job. This means that the minimum and maximum values of each job are set independently of individual workers, who must be paid somewhere in the range established for that job. For instance, an unemployed Ph.D. in chemistry may accept a job as a janitor and do an outstanding job of keeping the building clean and well organized. Yet he may be paid $6.50 an hour—not because he does not deserve more, given his credentials and janitorial performance, but because this is the maximum hourly pay set for this job. He can get paid more only by being promoted, and this could take years.

Rather than basing pay on a narrowly defined job, companies may choose to emphasize an individual's abilities, potential, and flexibility to perform multiple tasks in setting his or her pay. For example, the chemistry Ph.D. may be offered a job at $20 per hour because he can do many things that are as necessary to the organization as cleaning, such as helping in the lab and drafting reports. In this type of **knowledge-based pay or skill-based pay** system, employees are paid on the basis of the jobs they *can* do or the talents they have that can be successfully applied to a variety of tasks and situations.[27] Thus, the more hats an individual can wear, the more pay he or she will receive. Employees' base compensation increases as they become able to perform more duties successfully.

Knowledge-based pay or skill-based pay
A pay system in which employees are paid on the basis of the jobs they can do or talents they have that can be successfully applied to a variety of tasks and situations.

While the traditional job-centered pay system is still predominant, more and more firms are opting for a knowledge-based approach. Proponents argue that knowledge-based pay provides greater motivation for employees, makes it easier to reassign workers to where they are most needed, reduces the costs of turnover and absenteeism because other employees can assume missing employees' duties, and provides managers with much more staffing flexibility. However, critics maintain that a skill-based system may lead to higher labor costs, loss of labor specialization, greater difficulty in selecting applicants because the qualifications are less specific, and a chaotic workplace where "the left hand doesn't know what the right hand is doing."[28]

How, then, should managers approach the job versus individual pay option? Research suggests that neither approach is always preferable; the better choice depends on the prevailing conditions at the firm. A job-based pay policy tends to work best in situations where:

- Technology is stable.
- Jobs do not change often.
- Employees do not need to cover for one another frequently.
- Much training is required to learn a given job.
- Turnover is relatively low.
- Employees are expected to move up through the ranks over time.
- Jobs are fairly standardized within the industry.

The automobile industry fits most of these criteria. Individual-based compensation programs are more suitable when:

- The firm has a relatively educated workforce with both the ability and the willingness to learn different jobs.
- The company's technology and organizational structure change frequently.
- Employee participation and teamwork are encouraged throughout the organization.
- Opportunities for upward mobility are limited.
- Opportunities to learn new skills are present.
- The costs of employee turnover and absenteeism in terms of lost production are high.[29]

Individual-based pay plans are common in manufacturing environments that rely on continuous-process technologies.[30]

Elitism Versus Egalitarianism

Firms must decide whether to place most of their employees under the same compensation plan (an **egalitarian pay system**) or to establish different compensation plans by organizational level and/or employee group (an **elitist pay system**). For example, in some firms only the CEO is eligible for stock options.[31] In other companies even the lowest-paid worker is offered stock options. Some companies offer a wide menu of pay incentives only to specific employee groups[32] (such as salespeople), while others make these available to most employees. At Ben & Jerry's Homemade Holdings, Inc., the Vermont-based ice cream company, the compensation system is linked to company prosperity. When the company does well, everyone does well. The profit-sharing plan awards the same percentage to all employees, from the top to the bottom.[33]

Egalitarian pay system
A pay plan in which most employees are part of the same compensation system.

Elitist pay system
A pay plan in which different compensation systems are established for employees or groups at different organizational levels.

The egalitarianism versus elitism choice is important because it creates an impression of what it takes to succeed in the firm and the type of work managers value. A traditional organizational hierarchy is reinforced if compensation plans and perks vary with one's place in the hierarchy.[34] For instance, in one large computer firm based in the Midwest, average compensation was perfectly correlated with the floor on which one worked in corporate headquarters: the higher the floor, the higher the pay. In addition, there were four dining rooms in the building and employees could use only the one assigned to them; an observer could immediately tell a person's rank (and prestige level) by where he or she had lunch.

The trend in recent years has been toward more egalitarian compensation systems[35] both in the United States and overseas. For example, in 2003 approximately 29 percent of U.S. companies provided stock options to most employees, which is a steep increase over a few years earlier. As discussed in the following chapter, foreign companies have begun moving to this strategy in the past few years to maintain parity with the United States.[36] Why? A company that has fewer differences between employee levels and fewer compensation plans, allows employees to increase their earnings without moving into management, and keeps status-related perks to a minimum enjoys distinct benefits. The most significant of these are a focus on joint task accomplishment, more consultation between subordinates and supervisors, and better cooperation among employees.

Nonetheless, both systems have their advantages and disadvantages. Egalitarianism gives firms more flexibility to deploy employees in different areas without having to change their pay levels. It can also reduce barriers between people who need to work closely together. Elitist pay structures tend to result in a more stable workforce because employees make more money only by moving up through the company.

Elitist compensation systems are more prevalent among older, well-established firms with mature products, a relatively unchanging market share, and limited competition. Egalitarian compensation systems are more common in highly competitive environments, where firms frequently take business risks and try to expand their market share by continually investing in new technologies, ventures, and products.

Emerging Trends

MANAGER'S NOTEBOOK

Global Convergence in Approaches to Compensation

Not long ago, employees were paid one way in the United States, another way in the United Kingdom, and a different way in Japan. For example, in the United States employees may receive a significant portion of their pay in the form of stocks, whereas in the United Kingdom almost all employees would be paid a fixed salary, and in Japan up to one-fifth of compensation would be in the form of profit sharing. And in other places around the world, there were plenty of other approaches in corporate compensation practices as well as in retirement, health care, and other benefits programs. But things are changing.

Increasingly, these differences are narrowing or disappearing altogether as leading companies take a similar global approach in designing their pay and benefit plans for employees at all levels, whether they work in Singapore or Sao Paulo. This is one of the chief findings of the 2002 Worldwide Total Remuneration (WWTR) study conducted by Towers & Perrin, which highlights compensation practices in 25 countries, plus Hong Kong SAR. Companies are discovering that global compensation strategies can achieve cost savings through standardization of programs, tap new financing opportunities available in capital markets, and meet the needs of internationally mobile employees. The WWTR study says that compensation and benefit practices once familiar only to executives are becoming increasingly available to other employees within the organization regardless of country. This trend is evident with two types of variable pay: variable bonus linked to individual performance and long-term incentives (LTI) programs, especially stock-based plans, both of which have grown dramatically in recent years across all 25 countries surveyed (for more on this, see related discussion in Chapter 11). The study cites several factors that are likely to encourage further similarities in global remuneration practices. These factors include greater access to information (particularly through the Web), lower cost of living differences in the European Union, a common currency in the euro zone, more liberal legislation in many countries giving firms greater freedom to set compensation policies, and local and regional companies that are beginning to imitate the practices of global companies.

However, convergence does not mean conformity. Convergence refers to similarity in compensation practices across countries. As the changes just listed evolve globally, they are not expected to eliminate the significant tax, accounting, and legal issues in individual countries. Moreover, each country has its own cultural, historic, and social policies that can influence the relationship between employers and employees.

Source: Towers Perrin Monitor. (2002, January). Available at www.towers.com/towerspublications/publication/Monitor/mon0201.htm.

A Question of Ethics

Some people argue that it is wrong for CEOs to earn multimillion-dollar salaries while some of their employees are earning the minimum wage or being laid off. Some suggest that a firm's top earner should earn no more than 20 times what the lowest-ranked employee earns. What do you think?

Below-Market Versus Above-Market Compensation

The below-market versus above-market compensation decision is crucial for two reasons.[37] First, employees' pay relative to alternative employment opportunities directly impacts the firm's ability to attract workers from other companies. Pay satisfaction is very highly correlated with pay level, and dissatisfaction with pay is one of the most common causes of employee turnover. Second, the choice has an important cost component. The decision to pay above market for all employee groups allows the firm to hire the "cream of the crop," minimize voluntary turnover, and create a climate that makes all employees feel they are part of an elite organization. This has traditionally been the choice for "blue-chip" firms like IBM, Microsoft, and Procter & Gamble. However, few companies can afford such a policy. Instead, most firms recognize the importance of certain groups explicitly by paying them above market and cover these costs by paying other groups below market. For example, many high-tech firms compensate their R&D workers quite well while paying their manufacturing employees below-market wages.

In general, above-market pay policies are more prevalent among larger companies in less competitive industries (like utilities) and among companies that have been performing well and, therefore, have the ability to pay more. In addition, companies that are trying to grow rapidly in a tight labor market must consider paying above-market wages. For instance, Goldman Sachs increased its workforce by 42 percent within a two-year period in the late 1990s. Its pay is at the top of the scale, with executive secretaries, for example, earning $50,000 a year.[38] We emphasize again that the trend is not for more firms to offer above-market pay in terms of salary but rather to offer above-market premium in any form of variable pay, which is not guaranteed and in some cases may be subject to a sudden drop. That means an employee's total compensation may be well above the market in one year and well below the market in the next year, depending on stock prices, profitability, difficulty of achieving the performance target needed to receive incentive, and the like. However, most firms try to protect star performers from such ups and downs to ensure they do not leave during bad years.[39] Unions, which we discuss in detail in Chapter 15, also contribute to above-market pay. Unionized workers receive approximately 9 to 14 percent higher wages than similar nonunionized workers do.[40]

At-market wages are typical in industries that are both well established and highly competitive (for example, grocery store and hotel chains). Firms paying below market tend to be small, young, and nonunionized. They often operate in economically depressed areas and have a higher proportion of women and minorities in the workforce. Growing firms making risky business decisions that leave them short of cash may also offer a lower base salary relative to the market.

Monetary Versus Nonmonetary Rewards

One of the oldest debates about compensation concerns monetary versus nonmonetary rewards. Unlike cash or payments that can be converted into cash in the future (such as stocks or a retirement plan), nonmonetary rewards are intangible. Such rewards include interesting work, challenging assignments, and public recognition.[41]

Many surveys have shown that employees rank pay low in importance. For example, a large-scale survey found that only 2 percent of Americans declared that pay is a very important aspect of a job.[42] This finding should be viewed with skepticism, however. Most people may find it culturally desirable to downplay the importance of money. In the words of a compensation researcher, "whether sorrowing or raging, reformers throughout Western history have attacked the love of money as the root of all evil—the source of many of the disorders we encounter in life."[43] Two well-known commentators add, "pay may rank higher than people care to admit to others—or to themselves. In practice, it appears that good old-fashioned cash is as effective as any reward that has yet been invented."[44]

Most HRM researchers and practitioners agree that pay symbolizes what the organization values and signals the activities it wants to encourage. For instance, most research-oriented universities base faculty pay primarily on the number of papers a faculty member has published in leading academic journals. The result: Teachers at these universities spend a great deal of time writing papers for publication. Furthermore, employees at all levels do those things that they believe will be rewarded with pay raises.

The relative importance of monetary versus nonmonetary rewards is illustrated by a recent study of more than 1,000 large to midsized firms (conducted by *Fortune* magazine in 2002) to identify the 100 best places to work and how they got that way. Figure 10.4 on page 338 lists a sample of 12 such firms and how they reward employees. Milton Moskowitz, an analyst at *Fortune* magazine, notes that "compensation is still certainly key. But the list also reflects the level of trust, pride, and camaraderie that employees share with management and their peers, as well as what practices the company has in place to support those things."[45]

Nonetheless, organizations do face a choice concerning how much emphasis to place on money and how much to place on other rewards such as high job security.[46] For instance, Amway, a distributor of cleaning products through home-based franchises, is well known for emphasizing monetary rewards, while companies such as SAS Institute and Southwest Airlines are pacesetters in providing nonmonetary rewards. However, these firms also provide strong monetary incentives.

In general, companies that emphasize monetary rewards want to reinforce individual achievement and responsibility. Those that emphasize nonmonetary rewards prefer to reinforce commitment to the organization. Thus, a greater emphasis on monetary rewards is generally found among firms facing a volatile market with low job security, firms emphasizing sales rather than customer service, and firms trying to foster a competitive internal climate rather than long-term employee commitment. A greater reliance on nonmonetary rewards is usually found in companies with a relatively stable workforce, those that emphasize customer service and loyalty rather than fast sales growth, and those that want to create a more cooperative atmosphere within the firm.[47]

Open Versus Secret Pay

Firms vary widely in the extent to which they communicate openly about worker's compensation levels and company compensation practices. At one extreme some firms require employees to sign an oath that they will not divulge their pay to co-workers; the penalty for breaking the oath is termination. At the other extreme, every employee's pay is a matter of public record; in

Figure 10.4

Company	Number of Employees	% Minorities	% Women	Training hrs/yr	
TD Industries www.tdindustries.com	1,368	33%	8%	32	Employees, called partners, own this construction company that installs air conditioning in tall buildings. An above-par sick-pay plan: two weeks after one year; 12 weeks at full pay after three years.
Alston & Bird www.alston.com	1,338	21%	57%	40	A model progressive law firm. In addition to a regular bonus, employees receive a bonus by meeting objectives for teamwork, community service, customer service, and learning technical skills.
Microsoft www.microsoft.com	49,675	24%	26%	NA	The huge tech company keeps team spirit high. Every department has a budget used for such things as Seattle Mariners games and whale watching in San Juan Islands.
Deloitte & Touche www.us.deloitte.com	29,154	23%	45%	76	Associates of this professional-services firm have a mentor for career growth. The consulting arm sets aside one day a month to hand out accolades to employees.
Intuit www.intuit.com	6,587	21%	49%	60	The maker of Quicken provides workers with on-site dental services, yoga classes, and home-loan assistance. When a new product failed, the company threw a celebration to help the team learn from mistakes.
Alcon Laboratories www.alconlabs.com	11,695	25%	49%	45	This medical technology firm keeps employees happy with a casual, egalitarian culture, tons of paid time off, 50% discounts on laser eye surgery, and a generous profit-sharing plan that has made 76 millionaries to date.
Whole Foods Market www.wholefoodmarket.com	21,514	33%	43%	35	The natural and organic foods retailer opened its first market in Manhattan in 2002 and had a two-for-one stock split—good for employees, since all are eligible for stock options. Work teams that cut costs share in the savings.
Sun MicroSystems www.sun.com	39,020	35%	34%	45	The computer system company held the line on layoffs until after September 11, 2001, when it cut 9% of its workforce. But it has held on to amenities like on-site dry cleaning and auto and bike maintenance.
Pfizer, Inc. www.pfizer.com	89,936	22%	47%	NA	Acquisition of Warner-Lambert led to an 8% cut in this U.S. pharmaceuticals company's workforce; great severance terms helped ease the pain for some, as did a $5,000 retraining allowance.

Sample of Best Places to Work and How They Reward Employees

Figure 10.4

Company	Number of Employees	% Minorities	% Women	Training hrs/yr	
Starbucks www.starbucks.com	59,541	26%	60%	40	The coffee chain provides medical, dental, and vision coverage to all workers, including part-timers. Stores in New York, Washington, DC, and Pennsylvania brewed free coffee for relief workers after September 11, 2001.
Genentech www.genentech.com	4,859	31%	52%	32	The 25-year-old biotech firm showers employees with unique perks: company bicycles, a rental library of audio books, an on-site hair salon, free espresso, and weekly social gatherings.
Four Seasons Hotel www.fourseasons.com	25,326	63%	42%	35	Upscale hotel chain's housekeeping staff makes nearly 50% more than the market average. Workers also get complimentary hotel stays, with 50% discounts on food and beverages.
Carlson Companies www.carlson.com	46,596	31%	51%	28	Hospitality chain (Radisson hotels, T.G.I. Friday's) offers on-site child care, free car detailing, and walking trails at its 300-acre headquarters. Its Regent Wall Street motel gave meals to 20,000 emergency workers at the World Trade Center.
Merck & Co. www.merck.com	73,399	26%	55%	40	Women rank high in management at this drug manufacturer where perks include tuition reimbursement, terrific health services, on-site video rentals, oil changes, and child care serving nearly 1,000 kids in four centers.

Source: Fortune's Best Companies to Work For (2002). See www.fortune.com/lists/bestcompanies/snap_502.html.

Figure 10.4 continued

public universities this information may even be published in the student newspaper. Many organizations are somewhere in between: They do not publish individual data but they do provide information on pay and salary ranges.

Open pay has two advantages over secret pay.[48] First, limiting employees' access to compensation information often leads to greater pay dissatisfaction because employees tend to overestimate the pay of coworkers and superiors. In other words, when compensation is secret, people tend to feel more underpaid than they really are. Second, open pay forces managers to be more fair and effective in administering compensation because bad decisions cannot be hidden and good decisions can serve as motivators to the best workers.

But open pay has a downside. First, it forces managers and supervisors to defend their compensation decisions publicly. As we will see later in this chapter, personal judgments play a major role in deciding who gets paid what in any pay system. Regardless of good-faith attempts to explain these judgments, it may be impossible to satisfy everyone (even those who are doing very well may feel that they should be doing better). Second, the cost of making a mistake in a

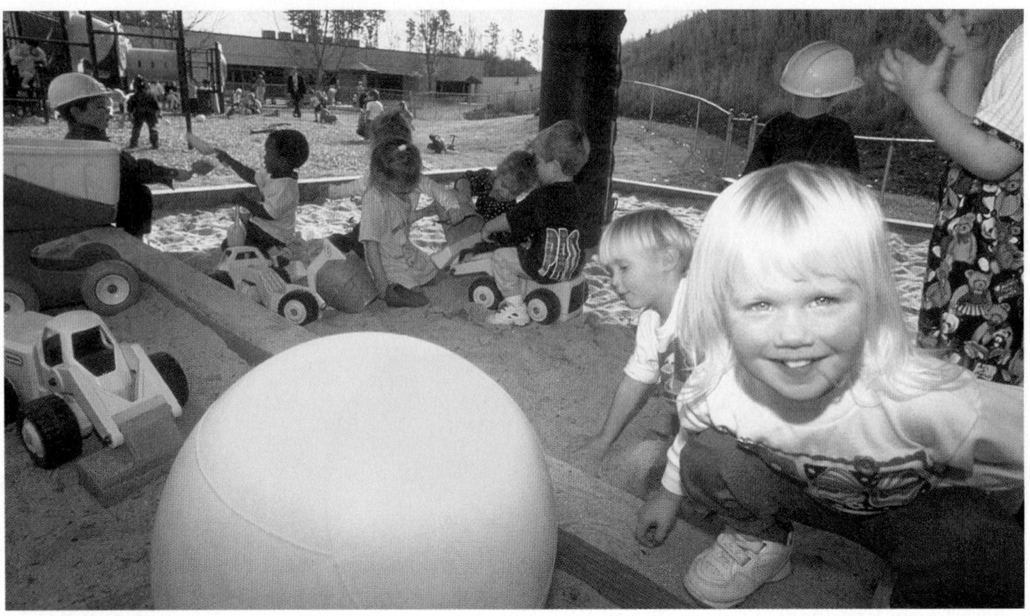

SAS Institute, a statistical software firm, pays its employees competitive salaries but also emphasizes its nonmonetary rewards, which include day care, a fitness center, an on-site health-care facility, and M&Ms every Wednesday. Its productive workforce is loyal and service oriented.

pay decision increases when pay is open. Third, to avoid time-consuming and nerve-wracking arguments with employees, managers may eliminate pay differences among subordinates despite differences in performance levels. The result may be turnover of the better performers, who feel underpaid.

So, despite its potential benefits, open pay is not appropriate for every organization. Recent research suggests that greater pay openness is more likely to be successful in organizations with extensive employee involvement and an egalitarian culture that engenders trust and commitment.[49] This is because open pay can foster perceptions of fairness and greater motivation only in a climate that nurtures employee relations. In more competitive climates, it may unleash a destructive cycle of conflict and hostility that is difficult to stop.

Centralization Versus Decentralization of Pay Decisions

Organizations must decide where pay decisions will be made. In a centralized system, pay decisions are tightly controlled in a central location, normally the HR department at corporate headquarters. In a decentralized system, pay decisions are delegated deep down into the firm, normally to managers of each unit. What are the advantages of centralization versus decentralization of pay decisions?

Centralized pay is more appropriate when it is cost-effective and efficient to hire compensation specialists who can be located in a single place, and made responsible for salary surveys, benefits administration, and recordkeeping.[50] If the organization faces frequent legal challenges, it may also be prudent to centralize major compensation decisions in the hands of professionals. In addition, companies tend to centralize the compensation function during periods of decline to control expenses.

There are some potential negative consequences of too much centralized control. A centralized system maximizes internal equity, but does not handle external equity (market) concerns very well. Thus, large and diverse organizations are better served by a decentralized pay system. For example, Mars, Inc., a worldwide leader in the candy market with estimated annual revenues of $11 billion and 30,000 employees, has only two HR people at corporate headquarters. Each Mars unit is responsible for its own pay decisions. This system is part of Mars's HR resource strategy to minimize corporatewide rules, regulations, and red tape.[51]

Summary

Compensation is a complex topic that has a significant impact on organizational success. You may be feeling a bit overwhelmed by the number of decisions that companies need to make in designing and implementing a compensation system. In practice, however, the nine issues we have discussed are not independent of one another. For instance, if circumstances dictate that paramount attention be given to external equity, then decisions on the other issues will follow from that. Pay for the job (as opposed to the individual) will be necessary because the job is the basis of the external comparison and market wages are by definition associated with external equity. Monetary rather than nonmonetary rewards will probably be used because money is the usual measure of external equity. And, as we have just seen, external equity is easier to manage in a decentralized system.

In short, the good news is that there are not as many separate compensation systems as the nine options might suggest. The bad news is that none of these options is a simple either/or decision. Rather, each pair of criteria defines two end points on a continuum, with many possibilities between them.

One final point: We discuss the role of unions in detail in Chapter 15. However, it is important to note here that compensation policies that apply to a unionized workforce are subject to negotiation and bargaining. Thus, managers in union shops are often severely restricted in what they can and cannot do with regard to compensation issues.

Compensation Tools

For the past 100 years, companies have used numerous techniques to decide who should get paid what. The goal of all these tools is to produce pay systems that are equitable and that allow the firm to attract, retain, and motivate workers while keeping labor costs under control. Despite their diversity, compensation tools can be grouped into two broad categories depending on the unit of analysis used to make pay decisions: job-based approaches and skill-based approaches.

The first category, *job-based approaches*, includes the most traditional and widely used types of compensation programs.[52] These plans assume that work gets done by people who are paid to perform well-defined jobs (for example, secretary, bookkeeper). Each job is designed to accomplish specific tasks (for example, typing, recordkeeping) and is normally performed by several people. Because all jobs are not equally important to the firm and the labor market puts a greater value on some jobs than on others, the compensation system's primary objective is to allocate pay so that the most important jobs pay the most.

A simplified example of a typical job-based pay structure appears in Figure 10.5 on page 342. It shows the pay structure of a hypothetical large restaurant with 87 employees performing 18 different jobs. These 18 jobs are grouped into six **pay grades,** with pay levels ranging from $6.50 an hour for jobs in the lowest grades to a maximum of $32.00 an hour for the job in the highest grade (chef). Employees are paid within the range established for the grade at which their job is classified. Thus, a dishwasher or a busser would be paid between $6.50 and $7.25 an hour (Grade 1).

Pay grades
Groups of jobs that are paid within the same pay range.

The second type of pay plan, the *skill-based approach,* is far less common. It assumes that workers should be paid not according to the job they hold, but rather by how flexible or capable they are at performing multiple tasks. Under this type of plan, the greater the variety of job-related skills workers possess, the more they are paid. Figure 10.6 (page 342) shows a simple example of a skill-based approach that could be used as an alternative to the job-based approach depicted in Figure 10.5. Workers who master the first set of skills (Block 1) receive $7 an hour; those who learn the skills in Block 2 (in addition to those in Block 1) receive $8.50 an hour; those who acquire the skills in Block 3 (in addition to those in Blocks 1 and 2) are paid $11.50 an hour; and so on.

In the sections that follow, we discuss these two major types of compensation programs in greater depth. Because compensation tools and pay plans can be very complex, we avoid many of the operational details, focusing instead on these programs' intended uses and their relative strengths and weaknesses. Excellent sources that provide step-by-step procedures of how to implement such programs are available elsewhere.[53]

Job-Based Compensation Plans

There are three key components of developing job-based compensation plans: achieving internal equity, achieving external equity, and achieving individual equity. Figure 10.7 on page 343 sum-

Pay Structure of a Large Restaurant Developed Using a Job-Based Approach

Figure 10.5

	Jobs	Number of Positions	Pay
GRADE 6	Chef	2	$21.50–$32.00/hr.
GRADE 5	Manager	1	$12.50–$22.00/hr.
	Sous-Chef	1	
GRADE 4	Assistant Manager	2	$8.50–$13.00/hr.
	Lead Cook	2	
	Office Manager	1	
GRADE 3	General Cook	5	$7.50–$9.00/hr.
	Short-Order Cook	2	
	Assistant to Lead Cook	2	
	Clerk	1	
GRADE 2	Server	45	$7.00–$8.00/hr.
	Hostess	4	
	Cashier	4	
GRADE 1	Kitchen Helper	2	$6.50–$7.25/hr.
	Dishwasher	3	
	Janitor	2	
	Busser	6	
	Security Guard	2	

marizes how these are interrelated and the steps involved in each component. The large majority of U.S. firms rely on this or a similar scheme to compensate their workforce.[54]

Job evaluation
The process of evaluating the relative value or contribution of different jobs to an organization.

Achieving Internal Equity: Job Evaluation

Job-based compensation assesses the relative value or contribution of different jobs (*not* individual employees) to an organization. The first part of this process, referred to as **job evaluation,** is

Pay Schedule of a Large Restaurant Designed Using a Skill-Based Approach

Figure 10.6

Skill Block	Skills	Pay
5	■ Create new items for menu ■ Find different uses for leftovers (e.g., hot dishes, buffets) ■ Coordinate and control work of all employees upon manager's absence	$24.00/hr.
4	■ Cook existing menu items following recipe ■ Supervise kitchen help ■ Prepare payroll ■ Ensure quality of food and adherence to standards	$18.00/hr.
3	■ Schedule servers and assign workstations ■ Conduct inventory ■ Organize work flow on restaurant floor	$11.50/hr.
2	■ Greet customers and organize tables ■ Take orders from customers ■ Bring food to tables ■ Assist in kitchen with food preparations ■ Perform security checks ■ Help with delivery	$8.50/hr.
1	■ Use dishwashing equipment ■ Use chemicals/disinfectants to clean premises ■ Use vacuum cleaner, mop, waxer, and other cleaning equipment ■ Clean and set up tables ■ Perform routine kitchen chores (e.g., making coffee)	$7.00/hr.

Figure 10.7

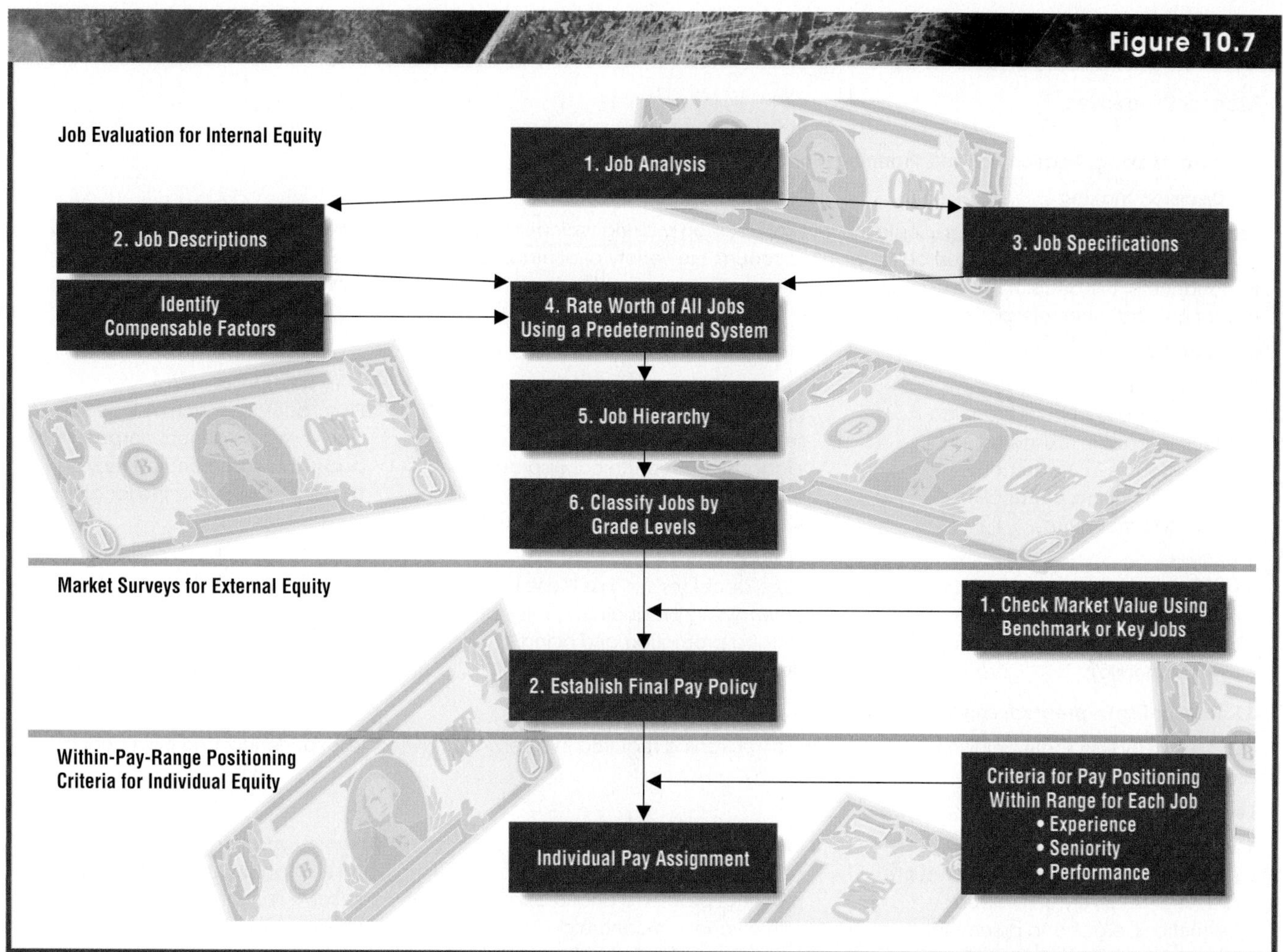

The Key Steps in Creating Job-Based Compensation Plans

composed of six steps intended to provide a rational, orderly, and systematic judgment of how important each job is to the firm. The ultimate goal of job evaluation is to achieve internal equity in the pay structure.

Step 1: Conduct Job Analysis. As we discussed in Chapter 2, job analysis is the gathering and organization of information concerning the tasks, duties, and responsibilities of specific jobs. In this first step in the job-evaluation process, information is gathered about the duties, tasks, and responsibilities of all jobs being evaluated. Job analysts may use personal interviews with workers, questionnaires completed by employees and/or supervisors, and business records (for example, cost of equipment operated and annual budgets) to study the what, how, and why of various tasks that make up the job. Sample items from a commonly used job analysis questionnaire, the Position Analysis Questionnaire, appear in Figure 10.8 on page 344. For each question, the job analyst considers what is known about the job and decides which of the five descriptions is most appropriate.

Step 2: Write Job Descriptions. In the second step in the job-evaluation process, the job-analysis data are boiled down into a written document that identifies, defines, and describes each job in terms of its duties, responsibilities, working conditions, and specifications. This document is called a *job description*. (You will recall this term from Chapter 2.)

Step 3: Determine Job Specifications. *Job specifications* consist of the worker characteristics that an employee must have to perform the job successfully. These prerequisites are drawn from the job analysis, although in some cases they are legally mandated (for example, plumbers must have a plumbing license). Job specifications are typically very concrete in terms of necessary

Figure 10.8

Mental Processes

Decision Making, Reasoning, and Planning/Scheduling

36. Decision making

Using the response scale below, indicate the level of decision making typically involved in the job; considering the number and complexity of the factors that must be taken into account, the variety of alternatives available, the consequences and importance of the decisions, the background experience, education, and training required, the precedents available for guidance, and other relevant considerations.

Level of Decision

1 *Very limited*
(e.g., decisions such as those in selecting parts in routine assembly, shelving items in a warehouse, cleaning furniture, or handling automatic machines)

2 *Limited*
(e.g., decisions such as those in operating a wood planer, dispatching a taxi, or lubricating an automobile)

3 *Intermediate*
(e.g., decisions such as those in setting up machines for operation, diagnosing mechanical disorders of aircraft, reporting news, or supervising auto service workers)

4 *Substantial*
(e.g., decisions such as those in determining production quotas or making promoting and hiring decisions)

5 *Very substantial*
(e.g., decisions such as those in approving an annual corporate budget, recommending major surgery, or selecting the location for a new plant)

37. Reasoning in problem solving

Using the response scale below, indicate the level of reasoning required in applying knowledge, experience, and judgment to problems.

Level of Reasoning in Problem Solving

1 *Very limited*
(use of common sense to carry out simple or relatively uninvolved instructions, e.g., hand assembler or mixing machine operator)

2 *Limited*
(use of some training and/or experience to select from a limited number of solutions the most appropriate action or procedure in performing the job, e.g., sales clerk, electrician apprentice, or library assistant)

3 *Intermediate*
(use of relevant principles to solve practical problems and to deal with a variety of concrete variables in situations where only limited standardization exists, such as that used by supervisors or technicians)

4 *Substantial*
(use of logic or scientific thinking to define problems, collect information, establish facts, and draw valid conclusions, such as that used by petroleum engineers, personnel directors, or chain store managers)

5 *Very substantial*
(use of logical or scientific thinking to solve a wide range of intellectual and practical problems, such as that used by research chemists, nuclear physicists, corporate presidents, or managers of a large branch or plant)

Source: Purdue Research Foundation, West Lafayette, IN 47907-1650. Used with permission.

Sample Items from Position Analysis Questionnaire

years and type of prior work experience, level and type of education, certificates, vocational training, and so forth. They are usually included on job descriptions.

Step 4: Rate Worth of All Jobs Using a Predetermined System. After job descriptions and job specifications are finalized, they are used to determine the relative value or contributions of different jobs to the organization. This job evaluation is normally done by a three- to seven-person committee that may include supervisors, managers, HR department staff, and outside consultants. Several well-known evaluation procedures have evolved over the years, but the *point factor system* is used by the vast majority of firms.[55]

The point factor system uses **compensable factors** to evaluate jobs. Compensable factors are work-related criteria that the organization considers most important in assessing the relative value of different jobs. One commonly used compensable factor is knowledge. Jobs that require more knowledge (acquired either through formal education or through informal experience) receive a higher rating and, thus, more compensation. Although each firm can determine its own compensable factors, or even create compensable factors suitable to various occupational groups or job families (clerical, technical, managerial, and so on), most firms adopt compensable factors from well-established job-evaluation systems. Two point factor systems that are almost universally accepted are the *Hay Guide Chart Profile Method* and the Management Association of America (MAA) *National Position Evaluation Plan* (formerly known as the NMTA point factor system). The Hay Method, which is summarized in Figure 10.9 uses three compensable factors to evaluate jobs: know-how, problem solving, and accountability. The MAA (NMTA) plan has three separate units: Unit I for hourly blue-collar jobs; Unit II for nonexempt clerical, technical, and service positions; and Unit III for exempt supervisory, professional, and management-level positions. The MAA (NMTA) plan includes 11 factors divided into four broad categories (skill, effort, responsibility, and working conditions). The Unit I plan is summarized in Figure 10.10 on page 346.[56]

Compensable factors
Work-related criteria that an organization considers most important in assessing the relative value of different jobs.

In both systems each compensable factor is assigned a scale of numbers and degrees. The more important factors are given higher point values and the less important factors lower values. For instance, as Figure 10.11 on page 347 shows, the highest possible points under the MAA (NMTA) system are for experience, with each degree of experience worth 22 points. The value of

Figure 10.9

Hay Compensable Factors

Know-How

Know-how is the sum total of every kind of skill, however acquired, necessary for acceptable job performance. This sum total, which comprises the necessary overall "fund of knowledge" an employee needs, has three dimensions:

1 Knowledge of practical procedures, specialized techniques, and learned disciplines.
2 The ability to integrate and harmonize the diversified functions involved in managerial situations (operating, supporting, and administrative). This know-how may be exercised consultatively as well as executively and involves in some combination the areas of organizing, planning, executing, controlling, and evaluating.
3 Active, practicing skills in the area of human relationships.

Problem Solving

Problem solving is the original "self-starting" thinking required by the job for analyzing, evaluating, creating, reasoning, and arriving at conclusions. To the extent that thinking is circumscribed by standards, covered by precedents, or referred to others, problem solving is diminished and the emphasis correspondingly is on know-how.

Problem solving has two dimensions:

1 The environment in which the thinking takes place.
2 The challenge presented by the thinking to be done.

Accountability

Accountability is the answerability for an action and for the consequences thereof. It is the measured effect of the job on end results. It has three dimensions:

1 Freedom to act—the degree of personal or procedural control and guidance.
2 Job impact on end results.
3 Magnitude—indicated by the general dollar size of the areas(s) most clearly or primarily affected by the job (on an annual basis).

Source: Courtesy of The Hay Group, Boston, MA.

Figure 10.10

Skill

1. **Knowledge** Measures the level of learning or equivalent formal training applied in a given type of work.
2. **Experience** Measures the amount of time usually needed before being able to perform a job's duties with no more than normal supervision.
3. **Initiative and ingenuity** Indicates the extent to which independent judgment and decision making are exercised on the job.

Effort

4. **Physical demand** Measures how much and how often duties include lifting heavy materials, moving them, and working in difficult positions.
5. **Mental attention or visual demand** Measures how much fatigue occurs from work that is visually or mentally intense, concentrated, and exacting.

Responsibility

6. **Equipment or process** Measures the damage to equipment or process that would probably result from error or carelessness.
7. **Material, product, or service quality** Refers to losses that would likely occur through spoilage, waste, and negligence in processing, inspection, testing, or delivery of service.
8. **Safety of others** Measures the extent to which a job involves protecting others from injury or health hazards.
9. **Work of others or as a member of quality/process team** Refers to the extent of responsibility for assisting, instructing, or directing others or involvement in quality or process teams that impact other operations within the company.

Job Conditions

10. **Working conditions** Measures the degree of exposure to such elements as dust, heat, noise, or fumes.
11. **Hazards** Concerns the risk of injury from materials, tools, equipment, and locations that remains even after protective and safety measures have been taken.

Source: MAA (formerly NMTA) National Position Evaluation Plan.

MAA National Position Evaluation Plan's 11 Compensable Factors (Unit 1—The Manufacturing, Maintenance, Warehousing, Distribution, and Service Positions)

the other two MAA (NMTA) skill factors is 14 points per degree. All other factors are worth either 5 or 10 points per degree.

This scale allows the evaluation and compensation committee to assign a number of points to each job on the basis of each factor degree. For example, using the MAA (NMTA) table in Figure 10.11, let us assume that job X is rated at the fifth degree for physical demand (50 points), equipment or process (25 points), material or product (25 points), safety of others (25 points), and work of others (25 points); at the fourth degree for mental or visual demand (20 points), working conditions (40 points), and hazards (20 points); at the second degree for experience (44 points); and at the first degree for knowledge (14 points) and initiative and ingenuity (14 points). The total points for this job across all 11 MAA (NMTA) compensable factors is, thus, 302.

Job hierarchy
A listing of jobs in order of their importance to the organization, from highest to lowest.

Step 5: Create a Job Hierarchy. The four steps described thus far produce a **job hierarchy,** a listing of jobs in terms of their relative assessed value (from highest to lowest). Figure 10.12 on page 348 illustrates a job hierarchy for office jobs in a typical large organization. Column 1 of the figure shows the total points assigned to each job in descending order. These range from a high of 300 for customer service representative to a low of 60 for receptionist.

Step 6: Classify Jobs by Grade Levels. For the sake of simplicity, most large organizations classify jobs into grades as the last step in the job-evaluation process. For instance, at Control Data Corporation, a manufacturer of computer equipment, thousands of jobs have been grouped

Figure 10.11

Factor	POINTS ASSIGNED TO FACTOR DEGREES				
	1st Degree	2nd Degree	3rd Degree	4th Degree	5th Degree
Skill					
1. Knowledge	14	28	42	56	70
2. Experience	22	44	66	88	110
3. Initiative and Ingenuity	14	28	42	56	70
Effort					
4. Physical Demand	10	20	30	40	50
5. Mental or Visual Demand	5	10	15	20	25
Responsibility					
6. Equipment or Process	5	10	15	20	25
7. Material or Product	5	10	15	20	25
8. Safety of Others	5	10	15	20	25
9. Work of Others	5	10	15	20	25
Job Conditions					
10. Working Conditions	10	20	30	40	50
11. Hazards	5	10	15	20	25

Source: MAA (formerly NMTA) National Position Evaluation Plan.

MAA National Position Evaluation Plan: Points Assigned to Factor Degrees

into fewer than 20 grades.[57] Typically, the job hierarchy is reduced to a manageable number of grade levels, with the assigned points used to determine where to set up dividing lines between grades. For example, column 2 in Figure 10.12 shows how the hierarchy of 18 clerical jobs is divided into five grade levels. All jobs in a given grade are judged to be essentially the same in terms of importance because the points assigned to each are very close in number.

Other job-evaluation systems are the *ranking system* (in which the evaluation committee puts together a hierarchy of job descriptions from highest to lowest based on an overall judgment of value); the *classification system* (in which the committee sorts job descriptions into grades without using a point system, as in the federal civil service job classification system); *factor comparison* (a complex and seldom-used variation of the point and ranking systems); and *policy capturing* (in which mathematical analysis is used to estimate the relative value of each job based on the firm's existing practices).

You should keep two key aspects of our discussion so far in mind. First, job evaluation is performed internally and does not take into account the wage rates in the marketplace or what other firms are doing. Second, job evaluation focuses only on the value of the tasks that make up each job, not the people performing them. The MAA (NMTA) booklet distributed to all employees whose jobs are evaluated under that system makes this very explicit: "The plan does not judge anyone as an individual; it does not rate anyone's ability to perform a job. It [evaluates] each job according to a simple set of [compensable] factors . . . that are applied in exactly the same way to all jobs."[58]

Achieving External Equity: Market Surveys

To achieve external equity, firms often conduct *market surveys*. The purpose of these surveys is to determine the pay ranges for each grade level. An organization may conduct its own salary surveys, but most purchase commercially available surveys. Consulting firms conduct literally hundreds of such surveys each year for almost every type of job and geographical area.

Similarly, the federal government regularly conducts salary surveys on a regional and national basis for 777 occupations. The results are currently available for free on the Internet (Bureau of Labor Statistics, 2003, National Employment and Wage Estimates by Occupation and Industry, www.lib.gsu.edu/collections/govdocs/stats.htm).

Figure 10.12

Hierarchy of Clerical Jobs, Pay Grades, and Weekly Pay Range for a Hypothetical Office

	1 Points	2 Grade	3 Weekly Pay Range
Customer Service Representative	300	5	$500–$650
Executive Secretary/ Administrative Assistant	298		
Senior Secretary	290		
Secretary	230	4	$450–$550
Senior General Clerk	225		
Credit and Collection Clerk	220		
Accounting Clerk	175	3	$425–$475
General Clerk	170		
Legal Secretary/Assistant	165		
Senior Word Processing Operator	160		
Word Processing Operator	125	2	$390–$430
Purchasing Clerk	120		
Payroll Clerk	120		
Clerk-Typist	115		
File Clerk	95	1	$350–$400
Mail Clerk	80		
Personnel Clerk	80		
Receptionist	60		

Why spend time and money on internal job evaluations when market data can be used to determine the value of jobs? There are two reasons. First, most companies have jobs that are unique to the firm and therefore cannot be easily matched to market data.[59] For instance, the job of "administrative assistant" in Company Y may involve supporting top management in important tasks (for example, making public appearances for an executive when he or she is not available), whereas in Company Z it may involve only routine clerical duties. Second, the importance of a job can vary from firm to firm. For example, the job of "scientist" in a high-tech firm (where new-product creation is a key to competitive advantage) is usually far more important than in a mature manufacturing company (where scientists are often expected to perform only routine tests).

Using market surveys to link job-evaluation results to external wage/salary data generally involves two steps: benchmarking and establishing a pay policy.

Benchmark or key jobs
A job that is similar or comparable in content across firms.

Step 1: Identify Benchmark or Key Jobs. To link the internal job-evaluation hierarchy or grade-level classification to market salaries, most firms identify **benchmark or key jobs**—that is, jobs that are similar or comparable in content across firms—and check salary surveys to determine how much these key jobs are worth to other employers. The company then sets pay rates for nonkey jobs (for which market data are *not* available) by assigning them the same pay range as key jobs that fall into the same grade level.

An example will help here. Let's say five of the jobs in our office example in Figure 10.12 are identified as key. (These are briefly described in Figure 10.13.) The company purchases a salary survey for office workers in the area showing both average weekly pay and the 25th, 50th, and 75th percentiles in weekly pay for these key jobs. For example, Figure 10.14 (page 350) shows that 25 percent of the customer service representatives in organizations included in the survey earn $400 per week or less, 50 percent earn $500 or less, and 75 percent earn $650 or less. The average weekly salary in the area for this job is $495. The company uses these market data to assign a pay range for all jobs that were evaluated as at the same grade level as the key job of customer service representative—in this case, executive secretary and senior secretary. But first it needs to establish a pay policy.

Figure 10.13

Sample Benchmark Jobs for Office Personnel

Customer Service Representative Establishes and maintains good customer relations and provides advice and assistance on customer problems.

Credit and Collection Clerk Performs clerical tasks related to credit and collection activities; performs routine credit checks, obtains supplementary information, investigates overdue accounts, follows up by mail and/or telephone to customers on delinquent payments.

Accounting Clerk Performs a variety of routine accounting clerical work such as maintaining journals, subsidiary ledgers, and related reports according to well-defined procedures or detailed instructions.

Word Processing Operator Operates word processing equipment to enter or search, select, and merge text from a storage device or internal memory for continuous or repetitive production of copy.

Clerk-Typist Performs routine clerical and typing work; follows established procedures and detailed written or oral instructions; may operate simple types of office machines and equipment.

Source: 1994 AMS Foundation *Office, Secretarial, Professional, Data Processing and Management Salary Report*, AMS Foundation, 550 W. Jackson Blvd., Suite 360, Chicago, IL 60661. See also Salary Wizard (2003). Salary report for administrative support, and clerical job categories. Hrcom.salary.com/salarywizard.

Step 2: Establish a Pay Policy. Because market wages and salaries vary widely (look again at Figure 10.14), the organization needs to decide whether to lead, lag, or pay the going rate (which is normally defined as the midpoint of the wage/salary distribution in the survey). A firm's **pay policy** is determined by how it chooses to position itself in the pay market. The hypothetical firm shown in Figure 10.12, for example, decided to set a pay policy pegging the minimum pay for each grade to the 50th percentile and the maximum pay to the 75th percentile in the market (see column 3 of Figure 10.12). Some firms use more complex methods to achieve the same objective.

Pay policy
A firm's decision to pay above, below, or at the market rate for its jobs.

Customer-Driven HR

MANAGER'S NOTEBOOK

How Much Is a Position Worth in the Marketplace?

Salary survey data were commonly obtained by the HR department. These data were then used as part of the job evaluation process to set salary schedules for various positions. But technology is making this process almost obsolete. Line managers can now instantly access salary data analyzed by location, by industry, and by work experience for hundreds of positions. This is possible through online compensation surveys; two of them are Salary Source and Survey Finder.

Salary Source (www.salarysource.com)

Using Salary Source, a manager can assess the current market value for any of nearly 350 positions. Salary Source uses multiple survey sources. With Salary Source, the user is guaranteed to receive data for every position from at least three different surveys. Salary Source allows the user to specify data required for a city among more than several thousand cities in the United States and U.S. territories. Using current market pay movement factors, the data can be adjusted to reflect the current date or any date specified up to 12 months in the future.

Survey Finder (hrcom.salary.com)

The Survey Finder enables HR professionals and line managers to search from a database of hundreds of up-to-date compensation surveys offered from more than 100 independent vendors. Users may purchase certain surveys, apply to participate, or express interest in purchasing all available compensation surveys directly online from the Survey Finder. The Survey Finder's database includes surveys from major human resource consulting firms, compensation consulting firms, survey companies, and industry associations. To make searches easier, the Survey Finder catalogs every survey according to industrial, geographic, and employee population.

Sources: Salary Source (www.salarysource.com) and Survey Finder (hrcom.salary.com/surveyfinder).

Achieving Individual Equity: Within-Pay-Range Positioning Criteria

After the firm has finalized its pay structure by determining pay ranges for each job, it must perform one last task: Assign each employee a pay rate within the range established for his of her job. Companies frequently use previous experience, seniority, and performance appraisal ratings to determine how much an employee is to be paid within the stipulated range for his or her job. The objective of this last step is to achieve individual equity. **Individual equity** refers to fairness in pay decisions for employees holding the same job.

Individual equity
The perceived fairness of individual pay decisions.

Evaluating Job-Based Compensation Plans

As we noted earlier, job-based compensation programs are widely used. These systems are rational, objective, and systematic, all features that minimize employee complaints. They are also relatively easy to set up and administer. However, they have several significant drawbacks, specifically:

- Job-based compensation plans do not take into account the nature of the business and its unique problems. For example, jobs are harder to define and change more rapidly in small, growing companies than in larger, more stable companies (such as those in the insurance industry). Heavy reliance on job-evaluation procedures and surveys assumes a universal perspective that may not be relevant to the firm.
- The process of establishing job-based compensation plans is much more subjective and arbitrary than its proponents suggest. These plans may provide a façade of objectivity to cover what is essentially a series of judgment calls.
- Job-based systems are less appropriate at higher levels of an organization, where it is more difficult to separate individual contributions from the job itself. At managerial and professional levels, the employee helps define the job. To force people to conform to a narrowly defined job description robs the organization of much-needed creativity.
- As the economy has become more service oriented and the manufacturing sector has continued to shrink, jobs have become more broadly defined. As a result, job descriptions are often awash in generalities. This makes it more difficult to evaluate the relative importance of jobs.
- Job-based compensation plans tend to be bureaucratic, mechanistic, and inflexible. Once an internal pay structure is put in place, it is difficult to change. Thus, firms cannot easily adapt their pay structure to a rapidly changing economic environment. In addition, because they rely on fixed salary and benefits associated with each level in the hierarchy, these plans tend

Figure 10.14

Market Salary Data for Selected Benchmark Office Jobs

	WEEKLY PAY PERCENTILE			
Benchmark Jobs	**25th**	**50th**	**75th**	**Weekly Pay Average**
1. Customer Service Representative	$400	$500	$650	$495
2. Credit and Collection Clerk	$400	$450	$550	$455
3. Accounting Clerk	$370	$425	$475	$423
4. Word Processing Operator	$380	$390	$430	$394
5. Clerk-Typist	$330	$350	$400	$343

to result in layoffs to save on costs during economic downturns. Japanese firms, which rely less on job-based compensation plans and often provide 20 percent to 30 percent of their employees' pay in variable form, have greater flexibility to absorb the economy's ups and downs.

- The job-evaluation process is biased against those occupations traditionally filled by women (clerical, elementary school teaching, nursing, and the like). Although empirical studies are inconclusive on this issue, critics often use vivid examples to make their point, such as sanitation jobs (garbage collectors) in New York City being evaluated higher than teaching jobs.
- Wage and salary data obtained from market surveys are not definitive. After adjusting for job content, company size, firm performance, and geographic location, differences ranging from that 35 percent to 300 percent in the pay of identical jobs within the same industry are not uncommon.[60] One researcher has concluded: "Clearly, the pay practices of firms in the same industry are often widely divergent. . . . No doubt, this means that employers, on the basis of a carefully selected survey sample, can justify widely divergent pay practices (a point frequently ignored when competitive pay is analyzed and discussed)."[61] To make the point with an example, consider an information technology (IT) director position requiring a minimum of five years' experience, a bachelor's degree, and supervision of 10 or more programmers and systems analysts. For firms of similar size and in cities with similar cost of living, in 2002 the median salary for an IT director was $90,000 per year. However, some earned well over $500,000 annually whereas others earned less then $50,000.[62]
- In determining internal and external equity, it is the employees' perceptions of equity that count, not the assessments of job-evaluation committees and paid consultants. Job-based compensation plans assume that the employer can decide what is equitable for the employee. Because equity is in the eye of the beholder, this approach may simply rationalize an employer's pay practices rather than compensate employees according to their contributions.

Despite all these criticisms, job-based compensation plans continue to be widely used, probably because there are no alternative systems that are both cost efficient and generally applicable. Skill-based pay, which we describe later in this chapter, offers an alternative approach, but it is costly and its uses are limited.

Suggestions for Practice

Rather than dismissing job-based compensation plans completely, it is more realistic to take steps to reduce the potential problems associated with them. In developing a job-based pay plan, the firm should take the following recommendations into account:

- **Think strategically in making policy decisions concerning pay.** Tools are a means to an end, not an end in themselves. For example, it may be in the firm's best interests to design a certain number of jobs very broadly and flexibly. The firm may also find it advantageous to pay at the top of the market for critical jobs that are central to its mission and at the low end of the market for jobs it considers less important. In short the firm's business and HR strategy should drive the use of compensation tools rather than the other way around.
- **Secure employee input.** Employee dissatisfaction will be reduced to the extent that employees have a voice in the design and management of the compensation plan. A simple, straightforward way to solicit employee input is to use computers. Computer-assisted job-evaluation systems allow employees to describe their jobs in a way that can be synthesized, displayed, rearranged, and easily compared. This approach offers two benefits. First, it gives employees a chance to describe what they do. This tends to improve the acceptability of job-evaluation results (although it does not eliminate the need for evaluative judgments to develop a job hierarchy). Second, it offers an inexpensive way to update job descriptions and to incorporate these changes into the system regularly (for example, yearly).
- **Increase each job's range of pay while expanding its scope of responsibility.** This approach, commonly called **job banding**, entails replacing narrowly defined job descriptions with broader categories (bands) of related jobs.[63] For instance, Fine Products, Inc., a consumer products company, collapsed 13 separate plant, regional, and production manager job titles down to four jobs with increased responsibility. The range within each band was set at approximately 90 percent (from $28,500 to $54,500 for "Band C," for instance).[64]

Job banding
The practice of replacing narrowly defined job descriptions with broader categories (bands) of related jobs.

This permits employees to receive a substantial pay raise without having to change jobs or get promoted. Banding has three potential benefits. First, it gives the firm more flexibility because jobs are not narrowly defined. Second, during periods of slow growth, the firm can reward top performers without having to promote them. Third, the firm may save on administrative costs because with banding there are fewer layers of staff and management.

- **Examine statistical evidence periodically to ensure that the job-evaluation system is doing what it is supposed to.** For instance, high turnover or difficulty in hiring employees in certain job classifications may be a good indicator that job evaluation is not working properly.
- **Expand the proportion of employees' pay that is variable (bonuses, stock plans, and so forth).** Variable-pay programs provide the firm with the flexibility to reduce costs without resorting to layoffs. A large firm may prevent thousands of layoffs by devoting as little as 10 percent of an employee's pay to a variable-pay pool that rewards workers during good times and serves as a "shock absorber" during bad times.
- **Establish dual-career ladders for different types of employees so that moving into management ranks or up the organizational hierarchy is not the only way to receive a substantial increase in pay.** In some situations, such as in a large organization with multiple business units and several layers of management, a tall job hierarchy is appropriate; in others, a relatively flat hierarchy with much room for salary growth (based, for instance, on performance and seniority) makes more sense. Figure 10.15 is an example of a dual-career ladder.

Skill-Based Compensation Plans

Unlike job-based compensation plans, skill-based compensation plans use skills as the basis of pay.[65] All employees start at the same pay rate and advance one pay level for each new skill they master.[66]

Three types of skills may be rewarded. Employees acquire *depth skills* when they learn more about a specialized area or become expert in a given field. They acquire *horizontal* or *breadth skills* when they learn more and more jobs or tasks within the firm and *vertical skills* when they acquire "self-management" abilities, such as scheduling, coordinating, training, and leadership. Skill-based pay has been adopted by a wide range of industries, such as telecommunications (AT&T and Northern Telecom), insurance (Shenandoah Life Insurance), hotels (Embassy Suites), and retailing (Dayton Hudson).[67]

Example of a Dual-Career Ladder

Figure 10.15

Band	Managerial	Individual Contributor
13	President	
12	Executive Vice President	Vice President for Research
11	Vice President	Executive Consultant
10	Assistant Vice President	Senior Consultant
9	Director	Consultant
8	Senior Manager	Senior Adviser
7	Manager	Adviser
6		Senior Specialist
5		Specialist
4		Senior Technician
3		Senior Administrative Support, Technician
2		Administrative Support Senior Manufacturing Associate
1		Clerical Support, Manufacturing Associate

Source: LeBlanc, P. (1992). Banding the new pay structure for the transformed organization. *Perspectives in Total Compensation, 3*(8). American Compensation Association, Scottsdale, AZ. Used with permission of the author, Peter V. LeBlanc, of Sibson & Company.

Skill-based pay offers several potential advantages to the firm.[68] First, it creates a more flexible workforce that is not straitjacketed by job descriptions specifying work assignments for a given job title. Second, it promotes cross-training, thus preventing absenteeism and turnover from disrupting the work unit's ability to meet deadlines. Third, it calls for fewer supervisors, so management layers can be cut to produce a leaner organization. Fourth, it increases employees' control over their compensation because they know in advance what it takes to receive a pay raise (learning new skills).

Skill-based pay does pose some risks to the organization and this may help explain why only a relatively small proportion (5 to 7 percent) of all firms use it.[69] First, it may lead to higher compensation and training costs that are not offset by greater productivity or cost savings. This can happen when many employees master many or all of the skills and thus receive a higher wage than they would under a job-based pay rate. Second, unless employees have the opportunity to use all the skills they have acquired, they may become "rusty." Third, when employees hit the top of the pay structure, they may become frustrated and leave the firm because they have no further opportunity to receive a pay raise. Fourth, attaching monetary values to skills can become a guessing game unless external comparable pay data are available. Finally, skill-based pay may become part of the problem it is intended to solve (extensive bureaucracy and inflexibility) if an elaborate and time-consuming process is required to monitor and certify employee skills.

In short, skill-based pay is no panacea. To avoid cost overruns, perceptions of unfairness, and a highly regimented system, managers must carefully fit a skill-based pay system into their entire HR strategy. For example, to justify the additional training expenditures associated with skill-based pay, HR development should receive high priority in the firm's strategic plan. Such programs are more likely to work in organizations staffed with employees who are interested in learning multiple jobs rather than in beating the game to receive higher pay.

One final observation about skill-based pay: This is the pay system that many new and small businesses use by default. An entrepreneur who needs additional help hires people because of what they can do. Those who can do more things are more valuable to a growing business. Because flexibility is crucial for continued growth, flexible employees are more highly valued and paid accordingly. When a business is fairly new, of course, there is no formalized system relating specific skills to specific compensation values. However, at some point the company must systematize its compensation structure. It is then that the design issues described earlier become critical.

The Legal Environment and Pay System Governance

The legal framework exerts substantial influence on the design and administration of compensation systems. The key federal laws that govern compensation criteria and procedures are the Fair Labor Standards Act, the Equal Pay Act, and the Internal Revenue Code. In addition to these, each state has its own sets of regulations that complement federal law. Labor laws may also limit managerial discretion in setting pay levels.

The Fair Labor Standards Act

The **Fair Labor Standards Act (FLSA)** of 1938 is the compensation law that affects most pay structures in the United States. To comply with the FLSA, employers must keep accurate records of earnings and hours worked by all covered employees and must report this information to the Wage and Hour Division of the U.S. Department of Labor. Most businesses are covered by the FLSA, except those with only one employee or annual gross sales under $500,000.

Fair Labor Standards Act (FLSA)
The fundamental compensation law in the United States. Requires employers to record earnings and hours worked by all covered employees and to report this information to the U.S. Department of Labor. Defines two categories of employees: exempt and nonexempt.

The FLSA defines two categories of employees: exempt and nonexempt. **Exempt employees** are not covered by the provisions of the act; **nonexempt employees** are. Exempt categories include professional, administrative, executive, and outside sales jobs. The Department of Labor provides guidelines to determine if a job is exempt or nonexempt. Managers are often tempted to classify as many jobs as possible as exempt to avoid some of the costs associated with nonexempt status, principally the minimum wage and overtime payments. However, there are heavy penalties for employers who unfairly classify nonexempt jobs as exempt.

Exempt employee
An employee who is not covered by the provisions of the Fair Labor Standards Act. Most professional, administrative, executive, and outside sales jobs fall into this category.

Nonexempt employee
An employee who is covered by the provisions of the Fair Labor Standards Act.

Minimum Wages

The minimum wage set by the FLSA is currently $5.15 per hour, although at the time of this writing Congress was considering a substantial increase in the minimum wage spread out over a number of years (2003 U.S. Master™ Wage-Hour Guide). Minimum wage legislation is controversial. Those in favor believe that it raises the standard of living for the poorest members of society. Those who oppose it argue that it results in higher levels of unemployment and poverty among low-skilled workers because it discourages firms from hiring and/or retaining workers. Opponents also claim that minimum wages encourage U.S. firms to open overseas plants in low-wage countries (such as Mexico and the Philippines), thereby creating more unemployment at home. This debate has not yet been resolved, probably because the minimum wage is set at a much lower level than most U.S. firms are willing to pay. However, the debate is being rekindled by a growing number of local governments passing "living wage" (wage needed to secure a decent standard of living) legislation that sets the minimum wage at a much higher level than the federal minimum of $5.15 per hour. For instance, in 2003 the city of Santa Cruz, California, requires a minimum hourly wage of $12.55 per hour. See You Manage It! Emerging Trends, "How Much Is a Living Wage" on page 359.

Overtime

The FLSA requires that nonexempt employees be paid one and a half times the standard wage for each hour they work over 40 hours a week. This provision was intended to stimulate hiring by making it more costly to expand production using existing employees. In fact, however, many firms would rather pay overtime than incur the costs associated with hiring additional employees (recruitment, training, benefits, and so on).

The Equal Pay Act

The Equal Pay Act (EPA) was passed in 1963 as an amendment to the FLSA. As we discussed in Chapter 3, it requires that men and women be paid the same amount of money if they hold similar jobs that are "substantially equal" in terms of skill, effort, responsibility, and working conditions. The EPA includes four exceptions that allow employers to pay one sex more than the other: (1) more seniority; (2) better job performance; (3) greater quantity or quality of production; and (4) certain other factors, such as paying extra compensation to employees for working the night shift. If there is a discrepancy in the average pay of men and women holding similar jobs, managers should ensure that at least one of the four exceptions to the EPA applies. If none of the four applies, the company may face stiff penalties in the form of legal costs and back pay to affected employees.

As more women move into jobs traditionally filled by men, the issue of comparable worth has entered the spotlight.

Comparable Worth

Equal pay should not be confused with comparable worth, a much more stringent form of legislation enacted in some countries and used in a few public jurisdictions in the United States. **Comparable worth** calls for comparable pay for jobs that require comparable skills, effort, and responsibility and have comparable working conditions, even if the job content is different. For instance, if a company using the point factor job-evaluation system we described earlier finds that the administrative assistant position (held mostly by women) receives the same number of points as the shift supervisor position (held mostly by men), comparable worth legislation would require paying employees in these jobs equally, even though they might be exercising very different skills and responsibilities.

Comparable worth
A pay concept or doctrine that calls for comparable pay for jobs that require comparable skills, effort, and responsibility and have comparable working conditions, even if the job content is different.

The considerable controversy surrounding comparable worth legislation centers mainly on how it should be implemented rather than on its main goal of pay equity between the sexes. Supporters of comparable worth legislation favor using job-evaluation tools to advance pay equity, pointing out that many private firms already use this method to set wages. Opponents argue that job evaluations are inherently arbitrary and that they do not take sufficient account of jobs' market value. For example, comparable worth proponents have often said that markets treat nurses unfairly because society links the profession to women's unpaid nurturing role in the family. Despite all the problems with implementation, comparable worth is already being used in many countries, including Britain, Canada, and Australia.[70]

Role of the Office of Federal Contract Compliance (OFCCP)

Although not its primary charge, the OFCCP may evaluate compensation in an effort to monitor compliance with EEO. This agency has extensive powers because it may revoke federal government contracts from employers—a costly loss in revenue for many firms.

During the past 35 years, OFCCP has focused most of its efforts on the implementation of affirmative action plans (see Chapter 3). Recently, however, that emphasis seems to have shifted to more focused investigations of pay disparities by gender and race. Since the last edition of this book was published, the OFCCP has sent out approximately 60,000 forms to employers asking for compensation data by EEO category (i.e., officials and managers, professionals, clerical, rates, etc.).[71] As seen in the Manager's Notebook entitled "Pay Disparities Move to the Forefront," this trend is likely to reduce part of the pay gap. Nevertheless, a gap remains that is substantial no matter what the occupation.

Emerging Trends — MANAGER'S NOTEBOOK

Pay Disparities Move to the Forefront in Federal Compliance Reviews of EEO Regulations

It is becoming common for the Office of Federal Contract Compliance (OFCCP), as part of its routine compliance reviews, to request compensation data from employers and to hold those contractors accountable for disparities that may exist. Costly settlements are becoming commonplace. Some recent settlements, resulting from routine reviews, have included the following:

- Computer Science Corporation at Edwards Air Force Base in California, under a settlement reached with OFCCP, agreed to pay $734,000 to 55 women and 17 minority employees. The settlement was a result of a routine compliance review by the OFCCP.
- Roche Diagnostics Corporation agreed to pay $155,000 to 23 minority and women managers to settle pay disparities found during an OFCCP compliance review of the Indianapolis medical equipment manufacturer. At the time of the OFCCP review, Roche had just merged with Boehringer Mannheim Corporation, and it was determined that some of the newly merged minority and women employees were underpaid as compared to white men who had been doing the same work at Roche.
- Boeing Company, the second largest federal contractor, reached a settlement agreeing to corporate-wide elimination of pay disparities affecting women and minorities, including $4.5 million

in back pay and salary adjustments. Although the settlement was a result of pay disparity claims brought by the OFCCP against Boeing's facilities in Philadelphia, Huntsville, Alabama, and Long Beach, California, the settlement also sought to remedy pay disparities at Boeing's Wichita, Kansas, Tulsa, Oklahoma, and Seattle facilities and for low-level and midlevel executives throughout the company.

Source: Reprinted with permission from Stillson, C. A., and Mohler, K. M. (2001). History still in the making—the continuing struggle for equal pay. *Worldatwork Journal*, 10(1), 1–8.

The Internal Revenue Code

Internal Revenue Code (IRC) The code of tax laws that affects how much of their earnings employees can keep and how benefits are treated for tax purposes.

The **Internal Revenue Code (IRC)** affects how much of their earnings employees can keep. It also affects how benefits are treated for tax purposes, as we discuss in Chapter 12. The IRC requires the company to withhold a portion of each employee's income to meet federal tax obligations (and, indirectly, state tax obligations, which in most states are set as a percentage of the federal tax deduction).

Tax laws change from time to time, and these changes affect an employee's take-home pay as well as what forms of compensation can be sheltered from taxes. An employer's failure to take advantage of IRC legislation may result in wasted payroll dollars. For instance, the tax laws currently treat capital gains (profits) on the sale of stock as ordinary income. This reduces the motivational value of stock as a long-term pay incentive because employees bear more risk with stock than with a cash-based form of pay. However, setting the capital gains tax below the tax on ordinary income could make stock more attractive to employees as a pay incentive.

Summary and Conclusions

What Is Compensation?

Total compensation has three components: (1) base compensation, the fixed pay received on a regular basis; (2) pay incentives, programs designed to reward good performance; and (3) benefits or indirect compensation, including health insurance, vacations, and perquisites.

Designing a Compensation System

An effective compensation plan enables the firm to achieve its strategic objectives and is suited to the firm's unique characteristics as well as to its environment. The pay options managers need to consider in designing a compensation system are (1) internal versus external equity, (2) fixed versus variable pay, (3) performance versus membership, (4) job versus individual pay, (5) egalitarianism versus elitism, (6) below-market versus above-market compensation, (7) monetary versus nonmonetary rewards, (8) open versus secret pay, and (9) centralization versus decentralization of pay decisions. In all situations, the best choices depend on how well they "fit" with business objectives and the individual organization.

Compensation Tools

There are two broad categories of compensation tools: job-based approaches and skill-based approaches. The typical job-based compensation plan has three components: (1) To achieve internal equity, firms use job evaluation to assess the relative value of jobs throughout the firm. (2) To achieve external equity, they use salary data on benchmark or key jobs obtained from market surveys to set a pay policy. (3) To achieve individual equity, they use a combination of experience, seniority, and performance to establish an individual's position within the pay range for his or her job.

Skill-based compensation systems are more costly and more limited in use. Skill-based pay rewards employees for acquiring depth skills (learning more about a specialized area), horizontal or breadth skills (learning about more areas), and vertical skills (self-management).

The Legal Environment and Pay System Governance

The major federal laws governing compensation practices are the Fair Labor Standards Act (which governs minimum wage and overtime payments and provides guidelines for classifying employees as exempt or nonexempt); the Equal Pay Act (which prohibits pay discrimination based on gender); and the Internal Revenue Code (which specifies how various forms of employee pay are subject to taxation). Some countries and municipalities have comparable worth legislation, which calls for comparable pay for jobs that require comparable skills, effort, and responsibility and have comparable working conditions, even if the job content is different.

Key Terms

base compensation, 328
benchmark or key jobs, 348
comparable worth, 355
compensable factors, 345
egalitarian pay system, 335
elitist pay system, 335
exempt employee, 354
external equity, 329
Fair Labor Standards Act (FLSA), 353
individual equity, 350
internal equity, 329
Internal Revenue Code (IRC), 356
job banding, 351
job evaluation, 342
job hierarchy, 346
knowledge-based pay or skill-based pay, 334
nonexempt employee, 354
pay grades, 341
pay incentive, 329
pay policy, 349
total compensation, 328

Discussion Questions

1. Some companies have a policy of selectively matching external offers to prevent employees from leaving the company. What are the pros and cons of such a policy? Explain.
2. As we approach the mid-2000s, the wealthiest 5 percent of Americans earned more than 20 percent of total household income, up from about 15 percent in 1970. Salaries for the top 5 percent of the workforce have increased dramatically in recent years while those for the lowest 33 percent have decreased after adjusting for inflation. For example: the average physician in private practice in the United States nets $231,080 per year; the average orthopedic surgeon earns $386,000 per year. Nine medical professors at Cornell, Columbia, and Stanford Universities earn more than $1 million each per year. The typical partner in a law firm receives annual pay of $178,080. At last count, 5,043 professors in the United States were receiving more than $110,000 for a nine-month academic year salary.

   Some people believe that these large salaries and growing inequalities in the labor market are unfair and show that the labor market does not work. Do you agree? Explain your answer.
3. Seventeen years ago a brash young engineer in a large chemical company handed her boss a four-page list of the promotions she expected to gain every two years as she rose through the ranks. She hoped for a vice presidency eventually, which would put her only half a dozen rungs below chairman at this title-stingy company. The engineer has held nine jobs so far, but the last three have kept her at the director's level. The company is restructuring and this talented 48-year-old woman is getting discouraged. What kind of nonmonetary rewards can the company offer to keep her from leaving? She is also one of the few female engineers in the company, and she just found out through the grapevine that a male engineer at her rank is getting paid 25 percent more than she is. How would you determine if this pay difference meets at least one of the four exceptions to the Equal Pay Act?
4. One observer argues that external equity should always be the primary concern in compensation, noting that it attracts the best employees and prevents the top performers from leaving. Do you agree?
5. During 2002–2003, many firms laid off thousands of workers, froze employees' pay, and eliminated all bonuses. Yet, many of these firms targeted "key employees" they retained by paying them huge compensation increases, creating large "inequities" within the workforce, even among employees not targeted as key but performing the same job. What are the pros and cons of such a policy? Explain.
6. The United States faces a severe teacher shortage in the hard sciences (biology, chemistry, physics) and mathematics. To help alleviate the shortage, the New York City Board of Education hired 730 new teachers from Canada, Austria, Italy, Spain, and the Caribbean during 2001–2003. Many believe the teacher shortage is due to a single salary schedule for all teachers regardless of field, as well as due to using a seniority scale for paying more to teachers based on how long they have been teaching. Teachers' unions are opposed to any form of "salary discrimination" by field (e.g., paying English and history teachers less than biology and chemistry teachers) on the grounds that all teachers perform the same job. Mr. Iftimie Simon, a mathematics teacher in New York who immigrated from Romania, says, "It reminds me of a communist system—they want everybody to be the same." Then again, he adds, "Even in Communist Romania teachers advanced on merit, not seniority."[72] Do you agree that all teachers perform the same job regardless of field and, thus, should be subject to the same salary schedule? Explain.
7. According to a consultant, the quality of many surveys is low, in part because firms are deluged with requests from consulting companies to complete surveys in exchange for access to the results. This results in firms filling out surveys carelessly or not responding to many of the surveys at all. Also, instead of using their more experienced compensation people to complete surveys, firms often

assign the task to entry-level HR employees or even clerical personnel. As a result, the responses provided may not be as thorough or complete as when surveys are completed by more experienced professional staff.[73] As a manager, how would you know if the salary survey data is accurate?

8. A compensation analyst from a mid-sized oil and gas company rarely has the time to call different survey vendors to discuss discrepancies between pay averages for the same jobs. Instead, he chooses the number with which he is most comfortable based on gut feeling. Because of time pressures, he has to rely on judgment and experience to make a reasonable recommendation as to what is a "competitive offer." Do you think this is a good practice.[74]

There is a variety of additional material available on the Web site that accompanies this text. You can access this information by visiting the Web site at **www.prenhall.com/gomez.**

YOU MANAGE IT!

Emerging Trends Case 10.1

A Little Less in the Envelope This Week

A decade ago, no other firm treated its employees better than IBM. Big Blue's generous compensation packages offered medical coverage that was virtually free, cushy pensions, and salaries that rose dependably each year. Today those guarantees are gone.

IBM replaced these guaranteed compensation packages with more pay-for-performance plans and leaner benefits. This change began in the early 1990s and became an urgently needed change during the late 1990s' war for talent. A workaholic up-and-comer at IBM in the 1990s could exceed every goal and still wind up with the same raise as the incompetent in the next office. Even worse, fewer than 1,000 employees (in a company with 413,000 employees at the time) had stock options. In a climate that was all about risk and reward, IBM was more about security and one-size-fits-all pay.

So IBM instituted rigorous performance reviews, widened its stock options to 70,000 workers, and made an average of 10 percent of employee pay variable—meaning it could swell or shrink depending on the worker's performance and the company's performance. Benefits were also overhauled. Recently, IBM announced a new pension plan, which saved the company millions but caused anger among employees, many of whom complained of losing as much as half of their benefits. Health coverage cost employees as much as $157 a month. Says 37-year-old IBM engineer Jeff Zitz, who estimates his pension under the new plan could take as much as an 80 percent hit: "Halfway through my career, they changed the deal."

Now, blue-collar and white-collar employees across Corporate America are realizing just how much their deals have changed, too. Nowhere is the shift in risk more painfully obvious, to those affected as well as those who fear being affected in the same way, than at Enron Corp., where employees saw their retirement savings wiped out while executives at the top cashed in.

But you don't have to work at a company that's bankrupt and under siege by federal investigators to feel at least some of the pain. In 2003, for example, many workers at companies as diverse as Ford Motor Company and Texas Instruments Inc. won't see a penny in bonuses—something that during the boom was a slam-dunk, swelling pay by 10 percent to 70 percent. At Gap Inc., salaries are frozen, while at Bethlehem Steel and Wyndham Hotels, company matches to 401(k) plans have been cut. At Lockheed Martin Corp., employees have been squeezed to pay more of the soaring health-care costs: For some, the employee portion of premiums has tripled in the past seven years. Co-pays on doctor visits and prescription drugs have doubled. Robert M. Handshuh, a 45-year-old Lockheed Martin project manager, says his 2 percent raises won't begin to offset the spike in his portion of increased health-care costs. "I'm barely holding my own in the last two years," he says.

Critical Thinking Questions

1. Not long ago, an ideal job was working in a large corporation that "prided itself on offering employees some insulation from the vagaries of the business cycle with a panoply of benefits and a steady, if slow, climb in pay."[a] As noted previously, opportunities for these kinds of jobs are rapidly fading. Why do you think this is happening? Explain the basis for your answer.
2. "Now, a company's attitude is that you have to take a percent of the risk with them," says Hewitt Associates LLC compensation expert Ken Abosch. "There's no question that most corporations have turned away from fixed forms of compensation in favor of variable forms. There

has been an abandonment of entitlement programs."[b] Do you think this is a good trend or a bad trend? Explain.

3. For the past 80 years, job evaluation as a compensation tool was designed to assess the value of each job rather than to evaluate the person doing the job, prompting a flat pay schedule for all incumbents in a particular job. Some HR experts believe that the emerging trend just discussed has created a new ballgame, where pay inequality has become "normal." Employers are using variable pay to lavish financial resources on their most prized employees, creating a kind of corporate star system. "How do you communicate to a workforce that isn't created equally? How do you treat a workforce in which everyone has a different deal?" asks Jay Schuster of Los Angeles–based compensation consultants Schuster-Zingheim & Associates Inc. If you were asked these questions, how would you answer them? Explain.

Team Exercise

The HR director of a large manufacturing plant has called a meeting of several divisional managers to come up with a plan on how to explain to employees that their annual cash bonus last year (which averaged $10,000) will go down to zero this year. Part of the concern the HR director has is that about 10 percent of employees received huge bonuses this year amounting to 25 percent of base pay, even though the rest received zero bonus. In addition, many employees believe that while they have been penalized by the ups and downs of variable pay, most executives are insulated from risk and some have even received special stipends. Students divide into groups of five to role-play this situation and develop a plan for explaining to employees why this is happening.

Source: Reprinted with permission from Conlin, M., and Berner, R. (2002, February 18). A little less in the envelope this week. *BusinessWeek*, 64–66. [a]Ibid., p. 65. [b]Ibid., p. 66.

Emerging Trends Case 10.2

YOU MANAGE IT!

How Much Is a Living Wage?

Jerome Gibbons works about 60 hours a week, just as he did five years ago, but with one difference. Back then Gibbons held two demanding jobs—as a wheelchair attendant at Los Angeles International Airport and as a security guard in an office tower. He still works 40 hours a week at the airport, but thanks to the city's five-year-old "living wage" ordinance, which raised the minimum wage for firms that contract with the city, his hourly pay has jumped from $5.75 to $9.54. He has been able to drop his second job and now studies at a local college for what he hopes will be a better job as a counselor to substance abusers. Gibbons, 31, who is unmarried, says of the city-mandated pay raise: "It makes paying bills easier and going to school easier."

More and more low-wage workers like Gibbons are finding hope for a better life as the living-wage movement gains momentum. Devoted to the principle that people who work full time should not live in poverty, the living-wage campaigning won its first success in Baltimore, Maryland, in 1994, and has since spread to 81 other cities and counties—including Boston and Santa Fe, New Mexico—as well as such institutions as universities and school boards. Living-wage proposals are pending in dozens of other localities, from Santa Monica, California, to New York City.

These laws generally require that contractors who work for local governments—and in some places, businesses that receive subsidies and tax breaks—must pay employees enough to raise their income above the federal poverty level of $18,100 for a family of four. That works out to more than $8 an hour—though some cities with high living costs like Santa Cruz, California, require hourly wages as high as $12.55. (The federal minimum wage is $5.15 per hour.)

Some cites are attempting more sweeping reforms. In 2002, New Orleans voters approved by 2–1 a referendum that would require every private employer in the city to pay at least $6.15 an hour. Activists went to court to ask a judge to strike down a 1997 state law banning local minimum wages. The judge ruled that banning minimum wages was unconstitutional (five other states have similar law), so New Orleans is free to force higher wages pending a review by the Louisiana Supreme Court.

A more ambitious ordinance by the Santa Monica city council would impose a living wage not only on its contractors but also on hotels and other major businesses located in a 1.5-square-mile "coastal zone," adjacent to its famous beach.

Critical Thinking Questions

1. The living-wage movement is generating organized resistance, notably among hotel and restaurant owners and other employers of low-wage workers. Do you agree that these employers should be actively opposed to this type of legislation? Explain.
2. Do you think it is a good idea to ease poverty through the passage of "living wage" legislation? What do you see as the pros and cons? Explain.
3. Some people believe that local businesses owe something to the community for the favors they get on the grounds that private hotels, restaurants, and shops often receive indirect support from local governments through tax

abatements and other subsidies and, thus, they should give something back in the form of a living wage. What is your position on this? Explain.

Team Exercise

A group of five human resource executives from various hotels in a large tourist area expected to introduce "living wage" legislation meet to discuss how the law may be challenged. At the same time, a group of five community activists is meeting to garner support for the proposed legislation. Students divide into groups of five, some into the HR executive group and some into the community activist group. Each group must develop a plan to convince others that the proposed law is a good idea or a bad idea. Make sure you clearly articulate your arguments in favor or against the proposed legislation.

Source: Reprinted with permission from Roston, E. (2002, April 8). How much is a living wage? *Time*, 52–54. See also Koretz, G. (2002, April 22). The case for living wage laws. *BusinessWeek*, 26.

YOU MANAGE IT!

Discussion Case 10.3

An Academic Question

Mountain States University is a medium-sized public university with 21,000 students and 1,200 faculty members. The College of Business Administration is the largest one on campus, with 8,000 students and 180 faculty members. For the past few years, the dean has had to deal with a large number of dissatisfied faculty who complain that they are underpaid relative to newly hired faculty. Many of the complainants are senior tenured professors who refuse to engage in committee activities beyond the minimum service requirements and who are seldom in their offices because they feel aggrieved. They teach six hours a week, spend two hours in the office, and then disappear from campus. Recently, the head of the college's faculty council compiled some statistics and sent these to the dean, demanding "prompt action to create more equity in the faculty pay structure." The average salary statistics are shown in the table below.

	1986		1992	
Rank	**New Hires**	**Current**	**New Hires**	**Current**
Full professors	$47,000	$42,000	$68,000	$56,000
Associate professors	$39,000	$36,000	$62,000	$51,000
Assistant professors	$34,000	$30,000	$52,000	$48,000
	1998		**NOW**	
Rank	**New Hires**	**Current**	**New Hires**	**Current**
Full professors	$79,000	$62,000	$86,900	$66,340
Associate professors	$73,000	$61,000	$80,300	$65,270
Assistant professors	$61,000	$59,000	$70,150	$63,130

The dean replied that he has little choice but to make offers to new faculty that are competitive with the market and that the university will not give him enough funds to maintain equitable pay differences between new and current faculty or between higher and lower ranks.

Critical Thinking Questions

1. Based on the data collected by the faculty council, name three compensation problems that exist at Mountain States University.
2. Is the dean's explanation for decreased pay differences by rank and/or seniority justifiable?

3. How would you suggest the dean deal with senior faculty who feel underpaid?

Team Exercise

A group of six faculty members has come to see the dean to express dissatisfaction with pay compression at the college. All six represent current faculty; two are assistant professors, two are associate professors, and two are full professors. Students divide into groups of seven and role-play this situation as the dean attempts to deal with the pay complaints raised by the faculty. The dean doesn't have the money to correct the pay-compression problem, yet he can't afford to alienate the faculty.

Discussion Case 10.4

YOU MANAGE IT!

Reckoning the Cost of Stock Options

Although the stock of Yahoo! went down 8 percent since CEO Terry Semel took the reins in 2001, the Internet portal handed Semel 1 million stock options in 2002 on top of the 10 million he already owned. And why not? Although Semel's $254,853 salary took a bite out of 2001's bottom line, the estimated $194 million value of his stock options—assuming the stock earns a 10 percent annual return—will never appear as an expense on the official income statement. Similarly, Cisco's annual options grants increased from 245 million to 320 million over three years without any negative impact on the company's net earnings. In fact, because options "don't hit the income statement, corporations view them as free," says Elizabeth Fender, a director of corporate governance at TIAA-CREF, a large pension fund that manages $270 billion.

Because options require no cash outlays, companies argue that not reporting the value of stock options on the accounting statements is appropriate. Moreover, they say that by granting employees an ownership stake, options align the interests of shareholders and employees as no other form of compensation can.

While the employees make out well when they exercise the options, making them shareholders, the previous shareholders suffer when those options are exercised. Here's why. Exercise options turn into stock, which increases the number of shares outstanding. With earnings now spread over more shares, earnings per share decline, reducing every shareholder's slice of the earnings pie. That's okay with the employees who exercised the options because before they were not getting any slice, but the original shareholders get a smaller slice than before the employees exercised the options. Companies with rapidly rising earnings might avoid this dilution. More often, though, corporate treasurers buy back stock on the open market to avoid issuing extra shares. If the company spends $25 for a share it sells to an employee for $10, there's a cash drain. The impact doesn't show up in the earnings statement, but it does hurt the cash balance. What would be the effect on earnings if options were treated as an expense? According to *BusinessWeek*, the effect could be large. For instance, Cisco's losses in 2001 would have almost tripled (from $1.01 billion to $2.7 billion) had the cost of the options been added to the bottom line.

Critical Thinking Questions

1. As earnings decline, companies tend to be generous with new options to compensate employees, while conserving cash. Do you think this is a good practice? Explain.
2. Some people believe that compensating employees with stock options instead of "hard" money (such as a monthly salary) may result in employees being penalized for bad management. For example, the average price of options granted by Cisco to employees in 2001 was $39.93. But because those options were only worth $17.00 in 2003, in effect they were worthless because employees could only make a gain if the price had exceeded the so-called "strike price"—the price at which they were originally granted, or $39.93 on average. Do you agree or disagree? Explain.
3. Many employees do not understand the risk they incur with their pay and are often led to believe that their "net worth" is higher than it really is, as there are no guarantees with variable pay plans. What is the company's responsibility in communicating and training employees about properly understanding "at-risk" compensation programs? Do you think it is in the company's interest to be clear and explicit about the risk inherent in such plans? Explain.

Team Exercise

Business is lobbying against moves by the U.S. Congress and the International Accounting Standards (IAS) to count the value of options against the bottom line. They claim that stocks are very effective in tying the interest of employees to the interests of the firm and that counting options as an expense will greatly limit firms' flexibility to attract, retain, and motivate employees who have the potential to increase the firm's earnings. A group of five business executives has come together to present their views as to why such a move by the U.S. Congress and IAS is not a good one. Students divide into groups of five and role-play this situation. The group then presents its recommendations to the instructor, who will play the role of a congressional representative.

Source: Reprinted with permission from Tergesen, A. (2002, April 15). Reckoning the cost of stock options. *BusinessWeek*, 114–116.

Rewarding Performance

Challenges

After reading this chapter, you should be able to deal more effectively with the following challenges:

1. **Recognize** individual and group contributions to the firm by rewarding high performers.
2. **Develop** pay-for-performance plans that are appropriate for different levels in an organization.
3. **Identify** the potential benefits and drawbacks of different pay-for-performance systems and choose the plan that is most appropriate for a particular firm.
4. **Design** an executive compensation package that motivates executives to make decisions that are in the firm's best interests.
5. **Weigh** the pros and cons of different compensation methods for sales personnel and create an incentive plan that is consistent with the firm's marketing strategy.
6. **Design** an incentive system to reward excellence in customer service.

Century Telephone Company bases its employees' annual pay raises on how well they perform their job duties. For the past 10 years, these "merit raises" have averaged 4.5 percent of base pay. About two years ago the HR department conducted an employee attitude survey. One of its most striking findings: More than 75 percent of employees felt that pay raises and performance were unrelated. In response, top managers asked the HR staff to determine if pay raises were indeed based on performance (as required by policy) or on some other unrelated factors. Surprisingly, the data showed that employees were right: Supervisors rated more than 80 percent of their workers as "excellent," and there was only minimal differentiation in the percentage raises received by individual employees.

Top management concluded that supervisors were equalizing performance ratings and raises, sidestepping their responsibility to reward employees on the basis of performance.

To remedy the situation, Century instituted a new procedure a year ago. Under this new system, supervisors must distribute employee performance ratings as follows: excellent (top 15 percent), very good (next 20 percent), good (next 20 percent), satisfactory (next 35 percent), marginal or unsatisfactory (lowest 10 percent). Pay raises are pegged to these performance classifications, with employees at the top receiving a 10 percent raise and those at the bottom receiving nothing.

Shortly after the system was put in place, it became obvious that something had gone wrong. A large number of employees could not understand how or why their performance had "dropped" compared to the previous year. Many believed that favoritism played a big role in who received pay increases. Irate employees hounded their supervisors, who in turn complained that increased tension was poisoning interpersonal relationships and interfering with performance.

THE MANAGERIAL PERSPECTIVE

Most employees believe that they should be rewarded to recognize their relative performance. The HR department in many firms is responsible for designing mechanisms that support managers in linking employee's pay to performance. Managers generally decide who should receive more rewards than others based on merit. Those rewards may be given based on individual, team, business unit, or corporate performance criteria. At the top of the organizational pyramid, the board of directors is responsible for choosing executive compensation packages that are competitive and induce executives to make decisions that are in the best interest of the organization.

Attempting to motivate employees with pay incentives can backfire, as the experience at Century Telephone (a real company given a fictitious name) shows. Nonetheless, the use of pay incentives is increasing. In 1988 the number of U.S. companies offering pay for performance (chiefly in the form of bonus) to all salaried employees was 47 percent. At the turn of the millennium, experts estimate that close to 95 percent of U.S. companies do so.[1]

What these numbers do not tell us is the mushrooming of creative incentive plans that are being implemented. For instance, almost half of the publicly traded "Best Companies" in *Fortune*'s list offer stock options to every category of employee. Other firms are experimenting with all kinds of "perks" for nonexecutives. For example, JM Family Enterprises in Florida offers top performers free haircuts, manicures, and day trips to the Bahamas on the company yacht. Kingston Technology Co., Inc., besides buying free monthly lunches, offers quarterly performance-based bonuses that sometimes exceed the typical employee's full year's salary.[2]

During the recession from 2000 to 2003, when most firms were faced with tight budgets and declining stock prices, almost 90 percent of firms introduced some sort of employee recognition program. Typically these programs involve presentation of awards at banquets or luncheons and written articles about recipients in the company newsletter and in Web page displays, among other public announcements.[3] Many troubled companies have introduced retention bonuses (Enron being an awesome example) to prevent key employees from leaving.[4] Retention bonuses are somewhat controversial because they may be perceived as rewards for poor performance (on the assumption that key employees may be partly responsible for the firm's decline). An example that has fueled this controversy is Kmart. Before Kmart filed for bankruptcy protection in 2002, the firm gave more than $30 million in retention and relocation "loans" (including $18 million to nine top executives) to selected senior officers. The "loans" may be forgiven by Kmart. For example, Charles C. Conaway, chief executive officer, walked away with a $5 million "forgiven" loan shortly after Kmart filed for Chapter 11 protection.[5]

In this chapter we discuss the design and implementation of pay-for-performance (incentive) systems. First, we address the major challenges facing managers in their attempts to link pay and performance. Second, we offer a set of general recommendations to deal with these challenges. Third, we describe specific types of pay-for-performance programs and the advantages and dis-

Kingston Technology Co., Inc. owners John Tu and David Sun believe in creating a work environment that motivates employees. To reward top performers, Kingston offers creative incentives, such as free lunches and hefty bonuses.

advantages of each. We conclude with a discussion of unique pay-for-performance plans for two important employee groups, executives and sales personnel.

Pay for Performance: The Challenges

Most workers believe that those who work harder and produce more should be rewarded accordingly. If employees see that pay is not distributed on the basis of merit, they are more likely to lack commitment to the organization, decrease their level of effort, and look for employment opportunities elsewhere.[6]

In Chapter 10, we examined the process of classifying jobs into hierarchies. Jobs at the top of the hierarchy contribute more to the organization and, therefore, receive higher compensation than jobs at the bottom of the hierarchy. In this chapter, we are concerned with how effectively employees within the same job classification perform their tasks. **Pay-for-performance systems,** also called **incentive systems,** reward employee performance on the basis of three assumptions:[7]

Pay-for-performance system or incentive system
A system that rewards employees on the assumptions that (1) individual employees and work teams differ in how much they contribute to the firm; (2) the firm's overall performance depends to a large degree on the performance of individuals and groups within the firm; and (3) to attract, retain, and motivate high performers and to be fair to all employees, the firm needs to reward employees on the basis of their relative performance.

1. Individual employees and work teams differ in how much they contribute to the firm—not only in what they do but also in how well they do it.
2. The firm's overall performance depends to a large degree on the performance of individuals and groups within the firm.
3. To attract, retain, and motivate high performers and to be fair to all employees, a company needs to reward employees on the basis of their relative performance.

These assumptions seem straightforward and acceptable. However, it is widely recognized that incentive systems can create negative consequences for firms. Thus, before talking about specific types of pay-for-performance plans, we will discuss eight challenges facing organizations that want to adopt an incentive system.

The "Do Only What You Get Paid For" Syndrome

To avoid the charge that pay is distributed on the basis of subjective judgments or favoritism, pay-for-performance systems tend to rely on objective indicators of performance.[8] This may lead some managers to use whatever "objective" data are available to justify pay decisions. Unfortunately, the closer pay is tied to particular performance indicators, the more employees tend to focus on those indicators and neglect other important job components that are more difficult to measure. Consider the following examples:

- In some school systems where teachers' pay has been linked to students' scores on standardized tests, teachers spend more time helping students do well on the tests than helping them understand the subject matter. As one expert has noted, "When you interview the teachers, they tell you they would like to teach other things, but they feel they have to teach to the test [because] they are afraid that a poor showing by their pupils will result in negative evaluations for themselves or their schools."[9]
- Administrators in many colleges and universities rely on student ratings to evaluate faculty performance, even though many people believe that this measure reflects popularity more than quality of instruction.
- Many brokerage houses pay more than 50 percent of a broker/analyst's compensation in the form of commissions generated on the stocks they pick. The commission system sometimes leads analysts to push stocks that pay the highest commissions, even if these are a poor investment for clients. This potential conflict of interest has exposed brokerage houses to significant legal risks and, in some cases, costly court settlements in favor of customers.[10]
- Part of the reason for the scandals associated with Arthur Andersen (one of the five largest accounting firms with 85,000 employees) and subsequent legal problems may have been due to the way its managers were rewarded for volume of revenues generated through consulting and accounting fees. This may have led managers to poorly monitor their clients (and in some cases approve of outright fraud) for fear of losing lucrative contracts.[11] Other companies are also being investigated for "playing" with accounting numbers used to reward executives with bonuses. Although Enron is perhaps the prime example, other firms include Xerox, Qwest, and IBM.[12]

Negative Effects on the Spirit of Cooperation

The experiences of Century Telephone Company clearly show that pay-for-performance systems may provoke conflict and competition while discouraging cooperation.[13] For instance, employees may withhold information from a colleague if they believe that it will help the other person get ahead. Those who are receiving less than they feel they deserve may try to "get back" at those who are receiving more, perhaps by sabotaging a project or spreading rumors. Internal competition may set off rivalries that lead to quality problems or even cheating.

Lack of Control

As we noted in Chapter 7, employees often cannot control all of the factors affecting their performance. Some examples of factors beyond an employee's control are the supervisor, performance of other work group members, the quality of the materials the employee is working with, working conditions, the amount of support from management, and environmental factors.[14]

For instance, many medical doctors in group practice now receive a substantial portion of their pay in the form of a bonus. Yet, because doctors are often reimbursed through insurance companies that run managed care programs, the doctors have little control over the revenues they can distribute as a bonus in a group practice setting. Doctors commonly complain that managed care bureaucrats try to slash revenues as doctors' overhead costs rise. As a result, the managed care system pressures physicians to see more patients in less time. In addition, "[n]urses and pharmacists are allowed to poach on [doctors'] territory."[15] Union membership is soaring among doctors as many see such a situation as demoralizing and inequitable.[16]

Difficulties in Measuring Performance

As we saw in Chapter 7, assessing employee performance is one of the thorniest tasks a manager faces, particularly when the assessments are used to dispense rewards.[17] At the employee level, the appraiser must try to untangle individual contributions from those of the work group while avoiding judgments based on a personality bias (being a strict or a lenient rater), likes and dislikes, and political agendas. At the group or team level, the rater must try to isolate the specific contributions of any given team when all teams are interdependent.[18] Appraisers experience the same difficulties in attempting to determine the performance of plants or units that are interrelated among themselves and with corporate headquarters. In short, accurate measures of performance are not easy to achieve, and tying pay to inaccurate measures is likely to create problems.

Psychological Contracts

Once implemented, a pay-for-performance system creates a psychological contract between the employee and the firm.[19] A *psychological contract* is a set of expectations based on prior experience, and it is very resistant to change.

Breaking a psychological contract can have damaging results. For instance, when a computer products manufacturer changed the terms of its pay-for-performance program three times in a two-year period, the result was massive employee protests, the resignation of several key managers, and a general lowering of employee morale.

Two other problems may arise with respect to the psychological contract. First, because employees feel entitled to the reward spelled out in the pay-for-performance plan, it is difficult to change the plan even when conditions call for a change. Second, it is sometimes hard to come up with a formula that is fair to diverse employee groups.

The Credibility Gap

Employees often do not believe that pay-for-performance programs are fair or that they truly reward performance, a phenomenon called the *credibility gap*.[20] Some recent studies indicate that as many as 75 percent of a typical firm's employees question the integrity of pay-for-performance plans.[21] If employees do not consider the system legitimate and acceptable, it may have negative rather than positive effects on their behavior. For instance, merit pay for teachers has been a favorite topic of political candidates over the past 20 years, but the merit pay systems that have been implemented have generally received low marks from teachers and unions.[22] In one North Carolina pilot project, outsiders sat in on classes three times a year to review teachers' performance. Teachers complained that the reviews were subjective and that bad teachers just cleaned up their act for the evaluation.[23]

Similar problems have been reported in Europe. In a well-intended attempt by the British government to reward good teaching, "superhead" teachers can earn up to $140,000 a year, a big change from a system where teachers were stuck at the $46,000-a-year level. The bumper pay raises are linked to exam results, lower truancy rates, and improved mathematical and literacy rates. Even though no teacher would receive a pay cut (that is, there is only upside potential to earn more money), teachers' unions have vigorously opposed the program. They argue that teachers cannot always be blamed if pupils do badly and that the bonus received may depend more on luck than performance.[24]

When HR departments create performance management programs or purchase them "off the shelf" from consulting firms, managers and employees often do not feel a sense of ownership. Because they feel no ownership, managers and employees lack credibility in the programs. According to a well-known human resource consultant, "In most companies performance management programs are imposed on supervisors who, in turn, impose them on their employees. Often, the HR organization owns the plan and is assigned accountability for this imposition. In effect, performance management is pushed on employees, and supervisors try to manage their performance. Unfortunately, the result is a battlefield on which supervisors and employees prepare strategies and tactics to get the highest possible performance rating by arguing contentiously about ratings."[25]

Job Dissatisfaction and Stress

Pay-for-performance systems may lead to greater productivity but lower job satisfaction.[26] Some research suggests that the more pay is tied to performance, the more the work unit begins to unravel and the more unhappy employees become.[27] The Issues and Applications feature titled "Incentives That Backfired: The Case of Lantech" illustrates how incentives can raise stress along with productivity.

Issues and Applications

Incentives That Backfired: The Case of Lantech

Lantech, a small manufacturer of machinery in Kentucky, learned through firsthand experience how incentive plans can backfire:

> Incentive pay encourages workers to improve quality, cut costs, and otherwise enhance the corporate good. Right? Well, that's the way it's supposed to work. In the real world, pay for performance can also release passions that turn workers into rival gangs, so greedy for extra dollars they will make another gang's numbers look bad to make their own look good. Such was the experience of Pat Lancaster, the chairman of Lantech. . . . To his dismay, Lancaster discovered that the lust for bonus bucks grew so overheated and so petty that one of his workers tried to stiff a competing division for the toilet paper bill.
>
> "Incentive pay is toxic," says Lancaster, "because it is so open to favoritism and manipulation."
>
> At one point, each of the company's five manufacturing divisions was given a bonus determined by how much profit it made. An individual worker's share of the bonus could amount to as much as 10 percent of his or her regular pay. But the divisions are so interdependent, it was very difficult to sort out which division was entitled to what profits. "That led to so much secrecy, politicking, and sucking noise that you wouldn't believe it," says CEO Jim Lancaster, Pat's son. For example, the division that built standard machines and the one that added custom design features to those machines depended on each other for parts, engineering expertise, and such. So inevitably the groups clashed, each one trying to assign costs to the other and claim credit for revenues.
>
> "I was spending 95 percent of my time in conflict resolution instead of on how to serve our customers," recalls Pat. The divisions wrangled so long over who would get charged for overhead cranes to haul heavy equipment around the factory floor that Lantech couldn't install those useful machines until 1992, several years later than planned. At the end of each month, the divisions would rush to fill orders from other parts of the company. Such behavior created profits for the division filling the order but, unfortunately, generated piles of unnecessary and costly inventory in the receiving division. Some employees even argued over who would have to pay for the toilet paper in the common restrooms.
>
> So Lantech has finally abandoned individual and division performance pay, and relies instead on a profit-sharing system in which all employees get bonuses based on salary. Furious passions have subsided, and the company is doing just fine now, says the senior Lancaster.

Source: Reprinted from Nulty, P. (1995, November 13). Incentive pay can be crippling, *Fortune*, 235.

Potential Reduction of Intrinsic Drives

Pay-for-performance programs may push employees to the point of doing whatever it takes to get the promised monetary reward and in the process stifle their talents and creativity. Thus, an organization that puts too much emphasis on pay in attempting to influence behaviors may reduce employees' *intrinsic drives*. One expert argues that the more a firm stresses pay as an incentive for high performance, the less likely it is that employees will engage in activities that benefit the organization (such as overtime and extra special service) unless they are promised an explicit reward.[28]

A Question of Ethics

How much consideration should the organization give to the psychological health of its employees when designing a pay-for-performance system?

Meeting the Challenges of Pay-for-Performance Systems

Properly designed pay-for-performance systems present managers with an excellent opportunity to align employees' interests with those of the organization. The following recommendations can help to enhance the success of performance programs and avoid the pitfalls we just discussed.

Link Pay and Performance Appropriately

Piece-rate system
A compensation system in which employees are paid per unit produced.

There are few cases in which managers can justify paying workers according to a preestablished formula or measure. Traditional **piece-rate systems,** in which workers are paid per unit produced, represent the tightest link between pay and performance. Many piece-rate systems have been abandoned because they tend to create the kinds of problems discussed earlier, but there are situations in which piece-rate plans are appropriate. The primary requirement is that the employee has complete control over the speed and quality of the work. For example, it is appropriate to pay typists for the number of pages they type *if* they can work at their own pace. However, most typists should not be paid on a piece-rate basis because they often have other responsibilities (for example, handling telephone calls) and are subject to constant interruptions. Interestingly enough, the Internet is creating a new type of piece-rate system in which employees have control over the speed and quality of work. It has allowed many firms, particularly high-tech companies, to have employees work elsewhere (including at home), thereby saving office space, overhead, and supervisory time. Many of the employees work on a contract basis so the company saves on benefits. Employees enjoy the flexibility of working on their own time, and the firm has access to a larger labor pool (such as people with young children, workers with disabilities, students, those who live away from the larger metropolitan areas, and even workers overseas).

Use Pay for Performance as Part of a Broader HRM System

Pay-for-performance programs are not likely to achieve the desired results unless they are accompanied by complementary HRM programs. For instance, performance appraisals and supervisory training usually play a major role in the eventual success or failure of a pay-for-performance plan. As we saw in Chapter 7, performance ratings are often influenced by factors other than performance. Because a defective appraisal process can undermine even the most carefully conceived pay plan, supervisors should be rigorously trained in correct rating practice.

Poor staffing practices can also damage the credibility of a pay-for-performance program. For instance, if employees are hired because of their political connections rather than for their skills and abilities, other employees will get the message that good performance is not that important to the organization.

Employees should also receive training to make them more productive so they are able to earn more. For instance, Edward Jones of St. Louis, operator of more than 4,000 stock brokerage offices, is one of the most profitable and highest-paying firms in the business. It also spends a minimum of $50,000 per employee on training.[29]

Build Employee Trust

Even the best-conceived pay-for-performance program can fail if managers have a poor history of labor relations or if the organization has a cutthroat culture. Under these conditions, employees are not likely to attribute rewards to good performance, but rather to chance or good impression management. If a pay-for-performance program is to have a chance of succeeding, managers need to build employee trust, which may require making major changes in the organization's climate.[30]

Building trust can be a tall order, particularly in companies where cynicism rules. Managers should start by answering these questions from their employees' perspective:

- Does it pay for me to work longer, harder, or smarter?
- Does anyone notice my extra efforts?

If the answers are no, managers need to go all out to show that they care about employees and are aware of the work they do. Even more important, they need to keep employees informed and involved when making any changes in management or the compensation plan.[31]

Employees must be educated to understand the risk inherent in variable pay plans as they become more widespread. This education may not only help sustain morale if results of variable pay are disappointing to employees, but it could also prevent expensive legal challenges from disappointed employees. For instance, there's a pending legal case by a dozen current and former employees of WorldCom against broker Salomon Smith Barney, which was responsible for overseeing WorldCom's employee stock option program. The employees accused Salomon Smith Barney of pressing them into risky investment strategies that resulted in considerable losses and high tax bills when company shares fell. Most of the employees affected by these losing investments say the brokers discouraged diversification and did not fully explain the risks should WorldCom's stock decline.[32]

Promote the Belief That Performance Makes a Difference

Because of the problems noted earlier, managers may shy away from using pay to reward performance.[33] However, unless an organization creates an atmosphere in which performance makes a difference, it may end up with a low-achievement organizational culture. In a sense, then, pay-for-performance systems are the lesser of two evils because without them, performance may drop even lower.[34]

Use Multiple Layers of Rewards

All pay-for-performance systems have advantages and disadvantages. For instance, bonuses or pay raises given to individual employees are more motivating than some other incentives because they allow employees to see how their personal contributions led to a direct reward. At the same time, though, they tend to create more internal competition, which leads to less cooperation. Bonuses given to teams or work units promote cooperation because they foster a sense of common interest, but they also prevent individual employees from linking the reward to their own efforts and thus reduce the reward's motivational impact.

Because all pay-for-performance systems have positive and negative features, providing different types of pay incentives for different work situations is likely to produce better results than relying on a single type of pay incentive. With a multiple-layers-of-reward system, the organization can realize the benefits of each incentive plan while minimizing its negative side effects. For instance, at AT&T Credit, variable pay (in the form of bonuses) is based on 12 measures reflecting the performance of both regional teams and the entire business unit. Team members must meet their individual performance goals to qualify for variable pay.[35]

Increase Employee Involvement

An old saying among compensation practitioners is: "Acceptability is the ultimate determinant of success in any compensation plan." When employees do not view a compensation program as legitimate, they will usually do whatever they can to subvert the system—from setting maximum production quotas for themselves to shunning coworkers who receive the highest rewards. The best way to increase acceptance is to have employees participate in the design of the pay plan.[36] Employee involvement will result in a greater understanding of the rationale behind the plan, greater commitment to the pay plan, and a better match between individual needs and pay-plan design.[37]

At B.F. Goodrich's plant in Terre Haute, Indiana, employee involvement is an integral part of a plantwide pay-for-performance plan called PLUS (Performance Lets Us Share). When the plant (which used to manufacture the compound for phonograph records) switched to producing a variety of plastic compounds, it had to put in place new processes, new goals, and new pay plans for its workforce. From the beginning, a task force of employees was involved in crafting a plan that would reward workers for achieving the new performance goals. Management was so pleased with the task force's work that it adopted a formal employee-involvement structure that encourages employees to make and carry out their own suggestions. In the first year PLUS was implemented, the plant averaged five ideas per employee and workers earned bonuses in 9 out of 12 months.[38]

Employee participation in designing the plan is not the same as employee dispensation of the rewards. Managers should still control and allocate rewards because employees may not be able to separate self-interest from effective pay administration. Managers can, however, solicit employee input by instituting an appeal mechanism that allows workers to voice their complaints about how rewards have been distributed. Such a mechanism is likely to enhance the perceived fairness of the system, particularly if a disinterested third party acts as an arbitrator and is empowered to take corrective actions.[39] A good appeals system may also help the organization avoid the costly legal fees and penalties in back pay that may result when disputes are resolved through litigation. Employers can also use the Web to communicate how the incentive plan works and to "personalize" it. (See the Manager's Notebook entitled "Incentive on Management on the Web.")

Use Motivation and Nonfinancial Incentives

This chapter focuses on financial awards, which are managers' biggest concern in administering incentive plans. However, nonfinancial rewards can be used effectively to motivate employee performance.[40] One of the most basic facts of motivation is that people are driven to obtain the things they need or want. Although pay is certainly a strong motivator, it is not an equally strong motivator for everyone. Some people are more interested in the nonfinancial aspects of their work.

Nonfinancial rewards include public and nonpublic praise, honorary titles, expanded job responsibilities, paid and unpaid sabbatical leaves, mentoring programs, and 100 percent tution reimbursements.[41] Even if it is impossible to provide a financial reward for a job well done, many employees appreciate overt recognition of excellent performance.

Types of Pay-for-Performance Plans

A firm may use a variety of approaches to reward performance. As Figure 11.1 shows, pay-for-performance plans can be designed to reward the performance of the individual, team, business unit or plant, entire organization, or any combination of these. All of these plans have advantages and disadvantages, and each is more effective in some situations than in others. Most organizations are best served by using a variety of plans to counterbalance the potential drawbacks of any single plan.

Individual-Based Plans

At the most micro level, firms attempt to identify and reward the contributors of individual employees. *Individual-based pay plans* are the most widely used pay-for-performance plans in industry.[42]

Merit pay
An increase in base pay, normally given once a year.

Of the individual-based plans commonly used, merit pay is by far the most popular; its use is almost universal.[43] **Merit pay** consists of an increase in base pay, normally given once a year.

Pay-for-Performance Programs

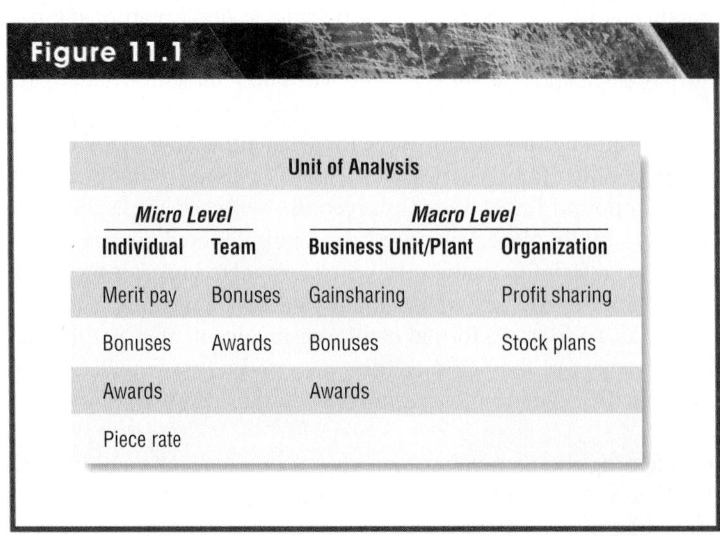

Unit of Analysis			
Micro Level		*Macro Level*	
Individual	**Team**	**Business Unit/Plant**	**Organization**
Merit pay	Bonuses	Gainsharing	Profit sharing
Bonuses	Awards	Bonuses	Stock plans
Awards		Awards	
Piece rate			

Supervisors' ratings of employees' performance are typically used to determine the amount of merit pay granted. For instance, subordinates whose performance is rated "below expectations," "achieved expectations," "exceeded expectations," and "far exceeded expectations" may receive 0 percent, 3 percent, 6 percent, and 9 percent pay raises, respectively. Once a merit pay increase is given to an employee, it remains a part of that employee's base salary for the rest of his or her tenure with the firm (except under extreme conditions, such as a general wage cut or a demotion).

Customer-Driven HR — MANAGER'S NOTEBOOK

Incentive Management on the Web

The Web is being used to communicate incentive programs to managers and employees. With 125 software developers, Synygy Inc. (www.synygy.com) is perhaps the largest provider of "incentive management" software. According to A. Stiffler, president and CEO of Synygy, "With the 100-percent Web-based version of Synygy Compensation, any global company now has the power and flexibility to centrally manage its thousands of incentive compensation plans for salaried employees, executives, suppliers, channel partners, and customers throughout the world. Now, the strategic goals of a company are easily incorporated into variable pay plans to drive the behaviors of employees, partners, and customers!"

This software is currently being introduced by many large corporations, including General Electric, Johnson & Johnson, and Hewlett-Packard, among others. Hewlett-Packard (HP) introduced this software in 2002 to manage incentive plan participants in 30 countries, with calculation and reporting of results in 40 different currencies. HP also uses Web capabilities to deliver reports and information globally to executives via the Internet.

"Incentive compensation can motivate and reward desired performance in employees, but only if people understand the plan and get quick and consistent feedback on their performance," says the global HR director of Hewlett-Packard. He adds, "[this software] helps us deliver accurate timely incentive information on a worldwide basis, providing our executives with valuable analysis on their progress in managing their business objectives."

This type of software is intended for use not only by the HR department but also by all managers and employees who are part of the incentive program. It can instantly provide the following information:

- Personalized documents that offer a complete overview of the plan's nuances and an individual employee's historical earnings
- Summary sheets of incentive features for quick reference
- Report mock-ups that show how to read the report to understand the payout, how it was calculated, and what data were used to calculate it
- Case studies that illustrate how hypothetically representative plan participants are affected by changes in the incentive plan
- Exercises so that participants can "learn by doing"
- "What-if" personalized simulations so that incentive plan participants can see which strategies result in the highest payout for them (and, therefore, for the company)

Sources: www.synygy.com/news (April, 2002); and Stiffler, M. A. (2001, January–February). Incentive compensation and the Web. *Compensation and Benefits Review*, 15–18.

Individual **bonus programs** (sometimes called **lump-sum payments**) are similar to merit pay programs but differ in one important respect. Bonuses are given on a one-time basis and do not raise the employee's base pay permanently. Bonuses tend to be larger than merit pay increases because they involve lower risk to the employer (the employer is not making a permanent financial commitment). Bonuses can also be given outside the annual review cycle when

Bonus program or lump-sum payment
A financial incentive that is given on a one-time basis and does not raise the employee's base pay permanently.

employees achieve certain milestones (for example, every month that Continental ranks among the top five airlines in on-time arrivals, employees receive a check for at least $65) or offer a valuable cost-saving suggestion. A recent survey shows that 92 percent of firms offer special one-time spot awards, and 28 percent provide lump-sum payments to their employees. These types of bonuses often exceed 5 percent of annual salary.[44]

Award
A one-time reward usually given in the form of a tangible prize.

Awards, like bonuses, are one-time rewards but tend to be given in the form of a tangible prize, such as a paid vacation, a television set, or a dinner for two at a fancy restaurant.

Advantages of Individual-Based Pay-for-Performance Plans

There are four major advantages to individual-based plans:

Expectancy theory
A theory of behavior holding that people tend to do those things that are rewarded.

- **Performance that is rewarded is likely to be repeated.** A widely accepted theory of motivation, known as **expectancy theory,** is often used to explain why higher pay leads to higher performance. People tend to do those things that are rewarded. Money is an important reward to most people, so individuals tend to improve their work performance when a strong performance-pay linkage exists.[45] In other words, because employees value money as a reward, they will work harder to achieve or exceed a performance level if they believe that they will receive money for doing so.
- **Individuals are goal oriented and financial incentives can shape an individual's goals over time.** Every organization is interested not only in the level at which employees perform but also in the focus of their efforts. A pay incentive plan can help make employees' behavior consistent with the organization's goals.[46] For instance, if an automobile dealer has a sales employee who sells a lot of cars, but whose customers rarely return to the dealership, the dealer might implement a pay incentive plan that gives a higher sales commission for cars sold to repeat buyers. This plan would encourage the sales staff to please the customer rather than just sell the car.
- **Assessing the performance of each employee individually helps the firm achieve individual equity.** An organization must provide rewards in proportion to individual efforts. Individual-based plans do exactly this. If individuals are not rewarded, high performers may leave the firm or reduce their performance level to make it consistent with the payment they are receiving.
- **Individual-based plans fit in with an individualistic culture.** National cultures vary in the emphasis they place on individual achievement versus group achievement (see Chapter 17). The United States is at the top of the list in valuing individualism, and U.S. workers expect to be rewarded for their personal accomplishments and contributions. This cultural orientation is likely to enhance the motivational value of a pay-for-performance system designed for U.S. employees.

In contrast, the Japanese do not tend to reward individual performance. "It's against their ethic," says a consultant with Tasa, Inc., which has conducted executive searches for the U.S. offices of many Japanese concerns. That ethic has its costs outside Japan. Japanese banks in New York, for instance, often have trouble recruiting and keeping first-rate U.S. managers, who are used to reaping rewards for their accomplishments.[47] Economic pressures seem to be moving the Japanese toward a more "American" model. In a land that once guaranteed employment for life, no job is secure and fixed salaries are being slowly replaced by individual-based pay-for-performance plans. In a 2002 survey, 70 percent of Japanese leaders said they plan to cut wages and that only top performers may be able to keep (or exceed) their prior earnings.[48]

Disadvantages of Individual-Based Pay-for-Performance Plans

Many of the pitfalls of pay-for-performance programs are most evident at the individual level. Two particular dangers are that individual plans may (1) create competition and destroy cooperation among peers and (2) sour working relationships between subordinates and supervisors. And because many managers believe that below-average raises are demoralizing to employees and discourage better performance, they tend to equalize the percentage increases among employees, regardless of individual performance. This, of course, defeats the very purpose of an incentive plan.

Other disadvantages of individual-based plans include the following:

- **Tying pay to goals may promote single-mindedness.** Linking financial incentives to the achievement of goals may lead to a narrow focus and the avoidance of important tasks, either because goals are difficult to set for these tasks or because their accomplishment is difficult to measure at the individual level. For instance, if a grocery store sets a goal of happy and satisfied customers, it would be extremely difficult to link achievement of this goal to individual employees. Individual-based plans have a tendency to focus on goals that are easy to measure even if these goals are not very important to the organization. They also tend to encourage people to "play it safe" by choosing to accomplish more modest goals instead of riskier goals that are harder to achieve.
- **Many employees do not believe that pay and performance are linked.** Although practically all organizations claim to reward individual performance, it is difficult for employees to determine to what extent their companies really do so. As we saw in Chapter 7, many managers use the performance appraisal process for reasons other than accurately measuring performance.[49] So it should come as no surprise that many surveys over the past three decades have found that up to 80 percent of employees do not see a connection between personal contributions and pay raises.[50] The beliefs underlying this perception, many of which have proved to be very resistant to change, are summarized in Figure 11.2.
- **Individual pay plans may work against achieving quality goals.** Individuals rewarded for meeting production goals often sacrifice attention to product quality. Individual-based plans

Figure 11.2

Factors Commonly Blamed for the Failure of Individual-Based Pay-for-Performance Systems

- Performance appraisal is inherently subjective, with supervisors evaluating subordinates according to their own preconceived biases.
- Regardless of the appraisal form used, supervisors tend to manipulate the ratings.
- Merit systems emphasize individual rather than group goals, and this may lead to dysfunctional conflict in the organization.
- To maintain an effective working relationship with all subordinates and prevent interpersonal conflict within the team, the supervisor may be reluctant to single out individuals for special recognition with pay.
- The use of a specified time period (normally one year) for the performance evaluation encourages a short-term orientation at the expense of long-term goals.
- Supervisors and employees seldom agree on the evaluation, leading to interpersonal confrontations.
- Supervisors often do not know how to justify a particular pay raise recommendation to an employee.
- Increments in financial rewards are spaced in such a way that their reinforcement value for work behaviors is questionable. For example, becoming twice as productive now has little perceived effect on pay when the employee must wait a whole year for a performance review.
- Individual merit pay systems are less appropriate for the service sector, where many people in the United States work. In knowledge-based jobs (such as "administrative assistant"), it is even difficult to specify what the desired product is.
- Supervisors typically control a rather limited amount of compensation, so merit pay differentials are normally quite small and, therefore, of questionable value.
- A number of bureaucratic factors that influence the size and frequency of merit pay (for example, position in salary range, pay relationships within the unit and between units, and budgetary limitations) have little to do with employee performance.
- Performance appraisals are designed for multiple purposes (training and development, selection, work planning, compensation, and so forth). When a system is used to accomplish so many objectives, it is questionable whether it can accomplish any of them well. It is difficult for the supervisor to play the role of counselor or adviser and evaluator at the same time.

Source: Updated (2003) from Balkin, D. B., and Gómez-Mejía, L. R. (Eds.). (1987). *New perspectives on compensation*, 159. Upper Saddle River, NJ: Prentice Hall.

also work against quality programs that emphasize teamwork because individual programs generally do not reward employees for helping other workers or coordinating work activities with other departments.

At the extreme, incentives may tempt individuals to act in an unscrupulous, unacceptable manner. In some jurisdictions, for example, police reportedly began to issue speeding tickets to motorists going 1 mph over the posted speed limit after cash incentives for citing speeding motorists went into effect. Although these drivers were technically in violation of the law, most car speedometers are not that accurate, often deviating by a 5-mph range.[51]

- **Individual-based programs promote inflexibility in some organizations.** Because supervisors generally control the rewards, individual-based pay-for-performance plans promote dependence on supervisors. Thus, these plans tend to prop up traditional organizational structures, which make them particularly ineffective for firms trying to take a team approach to work.

Conditions Under Which Individual-Based Plans Are Most Likely to Succeed

Despite the challenges they present to managers, rewards based on individual performance can be highly motivating. Individual-based pay-for-performance plans are most likely to be successful under the following conditions:

- **When the contributions of individual employees can be accurately isolated.** Identifying any one person's contributions is generally difficult, but it is more easily done for some jobs than for others. For instance, a strong individual incentive system can work well with salespeople because it is relatively easy to measure their accomplishments in a timely manner. In contrast, research scientists in industry are generally not offered individual-based performance incentives because they typically work so closely together that individual contributions are hard to identify.
- **When the job demands autonomy.** The more independently employees work, the more it makes sense to assess and reward the performance of each individual. For example, the performance of managers of individual stores in a large retail chain like Gap can be rated fairly easily, whereas the performance of the HR director in a large company is much more difficult to assess.
- **When cooperation is less critical to successful performance or when competition is to be encouraged.** Practically all jobs require some cooperation, but the less cooperation needed, the more successful an individual-based pay program will be. For example, less employee cooperation is expected of a stockbroker than of a pilot in an Air Force squadron.

Team-Based Plans

In an attempt to increase the flexibility of their workforces, a growing number of firms are redesigning work to allow employees with unique skills and backgrounds to tackle projects or problems together. For instance, at Compaq Computer Corp., as many as 25 percent of the company's 16,000 employees are on teams that develop new products and bring them to market.[52] Employees in this new system are expected to cross job boundaries within their team and to contribute in areas in which they have not previously worked. Other companies that have implemented a team approach to job and work design are Clairol/Bristol-Myers Squibb, Hershey Chocolate (North America), Newsday/Times Mirror, Pratt & Whitney/United Technologies, General Motors, TRW, Digital Equipment, Shell Oil, and Honeywell.[53] A team-based compensation system can provide integral support for effective team arrangements. Based on his experience at Kraft General Foods, one observer has noted that "in terms of support for team activity, nothing is symbolically more important than compensation."[54]

Team-based pay plans normally reward all team members equally based on group outcomes. These outcomes may be measured objectively (for example, completing a given number of team projects on time or meeting all deadlines for a group report) or subjectively (for example, using the collective assessment of a panel of managers). The criteria for defining a desirable outcome

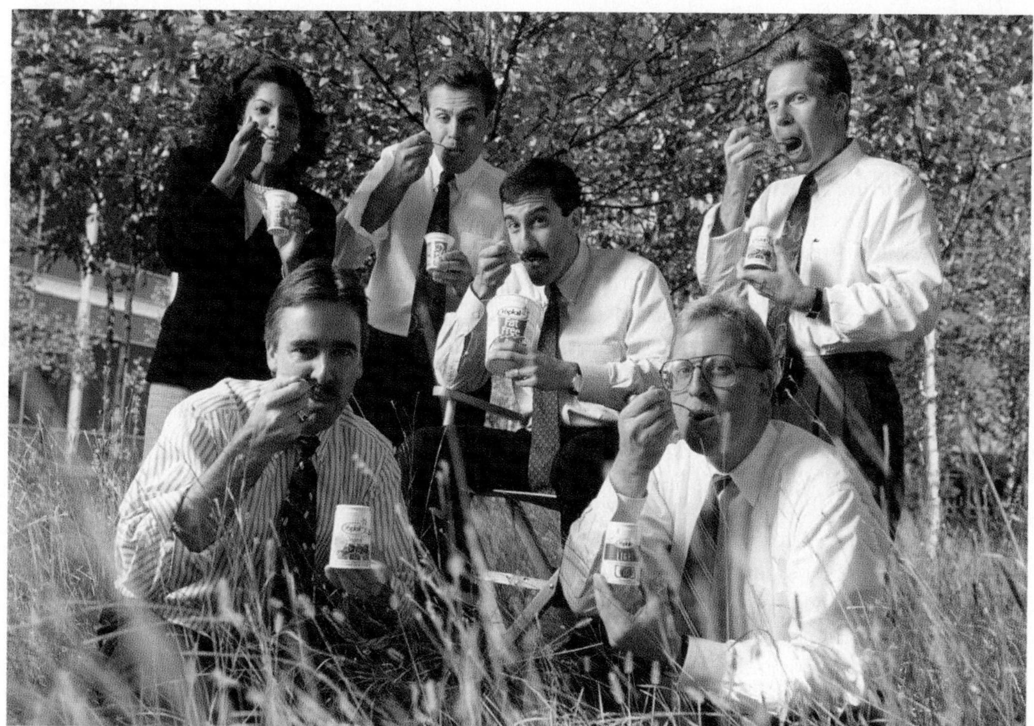

A team of young managers at Yoplait Yogurt has built the company into a thriving business by setting tougher goals for themselves than the parent company, General Mills, set for them. When the team exceeded these goals, its managers collected bonuses of $30,000 to $50,000, about half their annual salaries.

may be broad (for example, being able to work effectively with other teams) or narrow (for example, developing a patent with commercial applications). As in individual-based programs, payments to team members may be made in the form of a cash bonus or in the form of noncash awards such as trips, time off, or luxury items.

Some firms allow the team to decide how its bonus will be distributed within the group. One such firm is Johnsonville Foods (JF), which produces specialty sausage products. JF's monthly bonus program, Great Performance Shares, provides bonuses to teams whose contributions have helped the company achieve "great performance." Work crews (rather than the supervisor) decide the amount team members should receive based on their contributions. At Texas Instruments, teams get a lump-sum amount to divide among members.[55]

Advantages of Team-Based Pay-for-Performance Plans

When properly designed, team-based incentives have two major advantages.

- **They foster group cohesiveness.** To the extent that team members have the same goals and objectives, work closely with one another, and depend on one another for the group's overall performance, team-based incentives can motivate group members to behave and think as a unit rather than as competing individuals. In this situation, each worker is more likely to act in a way that benefits the entire group.[56]
- **They aid performance measurement.** A number of studies have shown that performance can be measured more accurately and reliably for an entire team than for individuals.[57] This is true because less precise measurement is required when an individual's performance does not need to be identified and evaluated in relation to others in a group.

Disadvantages of Team-Based Pay-for-Performance Plans

Managers need to be aware of potential pitfalls with team-based plans. This may account for the limited adoption of these types of incentives, which are used by firms about a third as often as individual-based incentives.[58] These are:

- **Possible lack of fit with individualistic cultural values.** Because most U.S. workers expect to be recognized for their personal contributions, they may not react well to an incentive system in which individual efforts take a back seat to the group effort, with all team members rewarded equally. On the other side of the coin, individual incentives are likely to fail in societies with a collective orientation. The Japanese, for example, are far less comfortable with individual risk than Americans are. Nonetheless, in a striking display of cultural insensitivity, many U.S. companies have introduced high-risk individual incentives to their Japanese subsidiaries. These plans have generally failed.[59]

- **The free-riding effect.** In any group, some individuals put in more effort than others. In addition, ability levels differ from one person to the next. Those who contribute little to the team—either because of low effort or limited ability—are *free riders*.[60]

  When all team members (including free riders) are rewarded equally for a group outcome, there are likely to be complaints of unfairness. (Think what would happen in a classroom study group if the same grade were given to all group members.) The result may be conflict rather than the cooperation the plan was intended to foster, with supervisors having to step in to judge who is contributing what.[61] Supervisory intercession, of course, negates the worth of team-based incentives and may produce a very negative climate of accusation and infighting.

  To minimize the free-riding effect, some companies have been adjusting pay incentives to encourage individual performance within teams. Unisys sets annual base pay raises on performance reviews by a team coach and three peers chosen by the employee. All team members can also receive up to 20 percent of base pay as a team bonus. AT&T Universal Card created wider differences in base salaries after employees in a 200-member team demanded greater recognition of their individual performances.[62]
- **Social pressures to limit performance.** Although group cohesiveness may motivate all team members to increase their effort and work to their full potential—both positively through encouraging a supportive team spirit and negatively through reproaching those who do not carry their share of the weight—it can also dampen team productivity. When the labor relations climate is hostile or the firm has a history of broken promises, group dynamics may result in the setting of artificial performance limits. When commercial airline pilots want to express a grievance, for instance, they sometimes agree among themselves to fly "by the book." This means that they follow every rule without exception, leading to an overall work slowdown. This is a very effective strategy because the airline can hardly complain publicly that its pilots are following the rules. Group dynamics may also encourage team members to try to beat the game—cheating to get the reward, for instance—as a way to get back at management.[63]
- **Difficulties in identifying meaningful groups.** Before they decide how to distribute rewards based on team performance, managers must define a *team*. Coming up with a definition can be tricky because various groups may be highly interdependent, making it difficult to identify which ones did what. Also, a person may be a member of more than one team, and teams may change members frequently. For instance, while the editor of the book you are reading now is a member of the editorial team, she works closely with the production team (to produce the book), the art team (to develop the art program and design), the photo team (to research and get permission to reprint the photos in the book), the marketing team (to make the book meet its audience's expectations and demands) and, finally, the sales force (to sell the book to your instructor and help with customer service).
- **Intergroup competition leading to a decline in overall performance.** A team may become so focused on maximizing its own performance that it ends up competing with other teams. The results can be quite undesirable. For instance, the manufacturing group may produce more units than the marketing group can possibly sell, or the marketing group may make sales commitments that manufacturing is hard pressed to meet on schedule.[64]

Conditions Under Which Team-Based Plans Are Most Likely to Succeed

Although managers need to be aware of the potential disadvantages of team-based plans, they should also be on the lookout for situations conducive to their successful use. Such plans are likely to be successful under the following circumstances:

- **When work tasks are so intertwined that it is difficult to single out who did what.** This is often the case in research and development labs, where scientists and engineers work in teams. It is also the case with firefighter crews and police units, which often think of themselves as one indivisible entity.

- **When the firm's organization facilitates the implementation of team-based incentives.** Team-based incentives are appropriate when:
  1. **There are few levels in the hierarchy, and teams of individuals at the same level are expected to complete most of their work with little dependence on supervisors or upper management.** Both public-sector and private-sector organizations that have had to lay off workers to maintain efficiency and profitability have found that teamwork becomes a necessity. For instance, when the city of Hampton, Virginia, underwent a massive downsizing and restructuring that resulted in the loss of several layers of supervision, it had to redesign its work. The city created self-managed teams and incorporated team-based pay into a multilayered pay-for-performance plan.[65]
  2. **Technology allows for the separation of work into relatively self-contained or independent groups.** This can be done more easily in a service unit (such as a telephone repair crew) than in a large manufacturing operation (such as a traditional automobile assembly line).
  3. **Employees are committed to their work and are intrinsically motivated.** Such workers are less likely to shirk responsibility at the expense of the group, so free riding is not a serious concern. Intrinsic motivation is often found in not-for-profit organizations, whose employees are emotionally committed to the organization's cause.
  4. **The organization needs to insist on group goals.** In some organizations this is a paramount need. For example, high-tech firms often find that their research scientists have their own research agendas and professional objectives—which are frequently incompatible with those of the firm or even their peers. Team-based incentives can focus such independent-minded employees' efforts on a common goal.[66]
- **When the objective is to foster entrepreneurship in self-managed work groups.** Sometimes, to encourage innovation and risk taking within employee groups, a firm will give certain groups extensive autonomy to perform their task or achieve certain objectives. This practice is often referred to as *intrapreneuring* (a term coined by Gifford Pinchot, who published a book with that title in 1985). Intrapreneuring means creating and maintaining the innovation and flexibility of a small-business environment within the confines of a large bureaucratic structure.[67] In an intrapreneuring environment, management often uses team-based incentives as a hands-off control mechanism that allows each group to assume the risk of success or failure, as entrepreneurs do.

The formation of self-managed teams and the use of team-based pay plans are not limited to large companies. When The Published Image, a custom newsletter publisher with 26 employees, experienced extremely rapid growth at the expense of low quality, low employee morale, and high turnover, the firm's founder, Eric Gershman, decided on a radical reorganization. To combat employees' belief that their job was to please the boss instead of the customer, he divided employees into four largely autonomous teams, each with its own clients and staff of sales, editorial, and production workers. Published Image managers-turned-coaches field questions and rate the teams for timeliness and accuracy. A monthly score of 90 or higher entitles team members to biannual bonuses, which can add up to 15 percent of their base pay.[68] Figure 11.3 on page 378 summarizes the advantages and disadvantages of individual- and team-based pay-for-performance plans.

Plantwide Plans

Plantwide pay-for-performance plans reward all workers in a plant or business unit based on the performance of the entire plant or unit. Profits and stock prices are generally not meaningful performance measures for a plant or unit because they are the result of the entire corporation's performance. Most corporations have multiple plants or units, which make it difficult to attribute financial gains or losses to any single segment of the business. Therefore, the key performance indicator used to distribute rewards at the plant level is plant or business unit efficiency, which is normally measured in terms of labor or material cost savings compared to an earlier period.

Figure 11.3

Advantages and Disadvantages of Individual- and Team-Based Pay-for-Performance Plans

	Individual-Based Plans	Team-Based Plans
Advantages	■ Rewarded performance is likely to be repeated ■ Financial incentives can shape a person's goals ■ Can help the firm attain individual equity ■ Fit an individualistic culture	■ Fosters group cohesiveness ■ Aids performance measurement
Disadvantages	■ Can promote single-mindedness individualistic culture ■ Disbelief that pay and performance are linked ■ May work against achieving quality goals ■ May promote inflexibility	■ Possible lack of fit with ■ May lead to free-riding effect ■ Group may pressure members to limit performance ■ Hard to define a team ■ Intergroup competition

Gainsharing
A plantwide pay-for-performance plan in which a portion of the company's cost savings is returned to workers, usually in the form of a lump-sum bonus.

Plantwide pay-for-performance programs are generally referred to as **gainsharing** programs because they return a portion of the company's cost savings to the workers, usually in the form of a lump-sum bonus. Three major types of gainsharing programs are used. The oldest is the *Scanlon Plan*, which dates back to the 1930s. It relies on committees of employees, union leaders, and top managers to generate and evaluate cost-saving ideas. If actual labor costs are lower than expected labor costs over an agreed-on period (normally one year), the difference is shared between the workers (who, as a group, usually receive 75 percent of the savings) and the firm (which usually receives 25 percent of the savings). A portion of the savings may also be set aside in a rainy day fund.

The second gainsharing program, the *Rucker Plan*, uses worker–management committees to solicit and screen ideas. These committees are less involved and simpler in structure than those used by the Scanlon Plan. But the cost-saving calculation in the Rucker Plan tends to be more complex because the formula encompasses not only labor costs but also other expenses involved in the production process.

The last type of gainsharing program, *Improshare* ("*Im*proved *pro*ductivity through *shar*ing"), is a relatively new plan that has proved easy to administer and communicate. First, a standard is developed—based on either studies by an industrial engineering group or some set of base-period experience data—that identifies the expected number of hours required to produce an acceptable level of output. Any savings arising from production of this agreed-on output in fewer than the expected hours are shared between the firm and the workers.

Advantages of Plantwide Pay-for-Performance Plans

The primary rationale for gainsharing programs can be traced to the early work of Douglas McGregor,[69] a colleague and collaborator of Joseph Scanlon, founder of the Scanlon Plan. According to McGregor, a firm can be more productive if it follows a participative approach to management—that is, if it assumes that workers are intrinsically motivated, can show the company better ways of doing things if given the chance, and enjoy being team players.

In contrast to individual-based incentive plans, gainsharing does not embrace the idea that pay incentives motivate people to produce more. Rather, gainsharing suggests that cost savings result from treating employees better and involving them intimately in the firm's management. The underlying philosophy is that competition between individuals and teams should be avoided, that all workers should be encouraged to use their talents for the plant's common good, that employees are willing and able to contribute good ideas, and that the financial gains generated when those ideas are implemented should be shared with employees.

Gainsharing plans can provide a vehicle to elicit active employee input and improve the production process. They can also increase the level of cooperation across workers and teams by giving everyone a common goal. In addition, gainsharing plans are subject to fewer measurement difficulties than individual- or team-based incentives. Because gainsharing plans do not require managers to sort out the specific contributions of individuals or interdependent teams, it is easier both to formulate bonus calculations and to achieve worker acceptance of these plans.[70]

Gainsharing plans have been lauded not only for increasing organizational productivity but also for improving quality in manufacturing firms that previously relied on individual-incentive or piece-rate plans. When Tech Form Industries (TFI), a Shelby, Ohio–based producer of tubular exhaust systems, realized that its individual-based incentive plans were driving quality—and its business—down the tubes, it discontinued its piece-rate system and, with employee involvement, developed a companywide gainsharing plan. Within three years, returns of defective products went down by 83 percent, direct labor hours spent on repairs decreased by 50 percent, and grievances declined by 41 percent. The transition from an individual-based incentive system to gainsharing required many steps, the first of which was to negotiate with the United Steel Workers union to fashion salary packages that were at least comparable to the piecework plan.[71]

Disadvantages of Plantwide Pay-for-Performance Plans

Like all other pay-for-performance plans, plantwide gainsharing programs may suffer from a number of difficulties, among them:

- **Protection of low performers.** The free-rider problem can be very serious in plants where rewards are spread across a large number of employees. Because so many people work together in a plant, it is less likely that peer pressure will be used to bring low performers into the fold.
- **Problems with the criteria used to trigger rewards.** Although the formulas used to calculate bonuses in gainsharing plans are generally straightforward, four problems may arise. First, once the formula is determined, employees may expect it to remain the same forever. A too-rigid formula can become a management straitjacket, but managers may not want to risk employee unrest by changing it. Second, improving cost savings will not necessarily improve profitability because the latter depends on many uncontrollable factors (such as consumer demand). For example, an automobile production facility can operate at high efficiency, but if it is producing a car that is in low demand, that plant's financial performance will not look good. Third, when gainsharing is first instituted, it is easier for inefficient than for efficient plants or business units to post a gain. This is because opportunities for dramatic labor-cost savings are much higher in the less efficient units.[72] Thus, gainsharing programs may seem to penalize already efficient units, which can be demoralizing to those who work in them. Fourth, there may be only a few labor-saving opportunities in a plant. If these are quickly exhausted, further gains will be difficult to achieve.
- **Management–labor conflict.** Many managers feel threatened by the concept of employee participation. When the gainsharing program is installed, they may be reluctant to give up their authority to committees, thus creating conflict and jeopardizing the program's credibility. In addition, only hourly workers are included in many gainsharing plans. The exclusion of salaried employees may foster hard feelings among them.

Conditions Favoring Plantwide Plans

A number of factors affect the successful implementation of gainsharing programs.[73] These are:

- **Firm size.** Gainsharing is more likely to work well in small to midsize plants, where employees can see a connection between their efforts and the unit's performance.
- **Technology.** When technology limits improvements in efficiency, gainsharing is less likely to be successful.
- **Historical performance.** If the firm has multiple plants with varying levels of efficiency, the plan must take this variance into account so that efficient plants are not penalized and inefficient plants rewarded. It is difficult to do this where there are scanty historical records. In these cases, past data are insufficient for establishing reliable future performance standards making it difficult to implement a gainsharing program.
- **Corporate culture.** Gainsharing is less likely to be successful in firms with a traditional hierarchy of authority, heavy dependence on supervisors, and a value system that is antagonistic

to employee participation. Gainsharing can be used effectively in a firm that is making the transition from a more autocratic to a more participative management style, but it probably cannot lead the charge as a stand-alone program.

- **Stability of the product market.** Gainsharing is most appropriate in situations where the demand for the firm's product or service is relatively stable. Under these circumstances, historical data may be used to forecast future sales reliably. When demand is unstable, the formulas used to calculate bonuses may prove unreliable and force management to change the formula, which is likely to lead to employee dissatisfaction. For example, increases in total output that occur as efficiency improves may create an inventory surplus that the market cannot absorb. When this happens, management may have little money to distribute or, even worse, may have to lay off employees as a cost-cutting measure.

Corporatewide Plans

The most macro type of incentive programs, *corporatewide pay-for-performance plans,* reward employees based on the entire corporation's performance. The most widely used program of this kind is **profit sharing,** which differs from gainsharing in several important ways:[74]

Profit sharing
A corporatewide pay-for-performance plan that uses a formula to allocate a portion of declared profits to employees. Typically, profit distributions under a profit-sharing plan are used to fund employees' retirement plans.

- In a profit-sharing program, no attempt is made to reward workers for productivity improvements. Many factors that affect profits (such as luck, regulatory changes, and economic conditions) have little to do with productivity, and the amount of money employees receive depends on all of these factors.
- Profit-sharing plans are very mechanistic. They make use of a formula that allocates a portion of declared profits to employees, normally on a quarterly or annual basis, and do not attempt to elicit worker participation.
- In the typical profit-sharing plan, profit distributions are used to fund employees' retirement plans. As a result, employees seldom receive profit distributions in cash. (This deferral of profit-sharing payments is commonly done for tax reasons.) Profit sharing that is distributed via a retirement plan is generally viewed as a benefit rather than an incentive. Some companies do have profit-sharing programs that are true incentives, however. A notable case is Andersen Corporation, the Minnesota-based manufacturer of windows and patio doors. Employees have received up to 84 percent of their annual salary in a lump-sum check at the end of the year from Andersen's profit-sharing pool.[75]

Employee stock ownership plan (ESOP)
A corporatewide pay-for-performance plan that rewards employees with company stocks, either as an outright grant or at a favorable price that may be below market value.

Like profit sharing, **employee stock ownership plans (ESOPs)** are based on the entire corporation's performance—in this case, as measured by the firm's stock price. ESOPs reward employees with company stock, either as an outright grant or at a favorable price that may be below market value.[76] Employers often use ESOPs as a low-cost retirement benefit for employees because stock contributions made by the company are nontaxable until the employee redeems the stock.[77] Employees whose retirement plans are based on ESOPs are exposed to risk, however, because the price of the company's stock may fluctuate as a result of general stock market activity or mismanagement of the firm.

Risk was not in the mind of most stock-owning employees as the stock market sky-rocketed during the 1990s. Examples of firms that offer ESOPs to all employees who saw at least a tripling of their original value during the 1990s include Amgen, Arrow Electronics, Autodesk, Hewlett-Packard, Intel, Lucent Technologies, Marriot International, Merck, Sun Microsystems, and Whole Foods Market.[78] However, many employees were shocked to find that during the recession from 2000 to 2003 the value of their stockholdings declined by a third or more within a year and, in some cases, in a matter of months. For instance, employees holding Xerox stock saw its value drop from $64 to $7 per share between late 2000 and mid-summer 2001. Suffering even more, employees who worked for Enron saw their company-invested wealth disappear almost overnight as Enron's stock dropped from $90 early in 2001 to $10 dollars by November 2001, and then to pennies as the company went through bankruptcy proceedings and faced charges of massive accounting fraud in 2002.[79]

Firms in the United States have led the world in employee stock ownership plans (ESOPs), particularly in industries such as high technology. Now, multinational firms and foreign firms are extending stock ownership opportunities to their employees at home and abroad. DuPont is giving its employees around the world 200 stock options each as part of the company's 200th anniversary celebration, starting in July 2003.[80] Other companies offering stock options to employees include Siemens and SAP in Germany, Marconi and British Telecom in the United Kingdom, and Suez Lyonnaise des Eaux and Alcatel in France.[81] And many foreign governments are establishing the legal framework to permit such plans, which until recently were unknown outside the United States. (See the Manager's Notebook entitled "The Worldwide Growth of Employee Ownership Phenomenon.") This also means that "ultimately, and unfortunately, there is no real shortcut to a country by country analysis of these issues prior to implementation," according to Baker & McKenzie (a major compensation consulting firm).[82] For example, depending on the specific country, many U.S. companies are surprised to find that, contrary to U.S. practice:[83]

- Option gains may be included in mandatory severance payments.
- Suspending vesting during a maternity leave may not be legal.
- Excluding part-time employees from participating in the plan based solely on the criterion that they are part time may be impermissible.
- An employee's consent and/or notification to a government agency may be required before information necessary to determine an option grant is collected and transferred to a U.S. database.
- The company may have to provide stock options to all employees, regardless of their rank as employees or managers, and seniority may be a mandatory criterion to decide who gets how much.

Emerging Trends — MANAGER'S NOTEBOOK

The Worldwide Growth of Employee Ownership Phenomenon

Employers throughout the world are embracing various employee equity-based compensation plans and many foreign governments are changing their tax laws, securities laws, and other laws to facilitate—or at least reduce—impediments to these types of incentive programs. There are examples of companies in places as varied as Estonia, Brazil, Japan, and Finland extending equity in various forms as incentive compensation to employees.

Most countries are removing barriers and, in many cases, actively supporting development of employee ownership opportunities for local employees of foreign corporations and employees of domestic enterprises. Examples:

- A high-level commission of the Chinese government has been charged with crafting a regulatory infrastructure for employee stock options.
- The U.K. government, as part of its stated policy goal of doubling the level of employee ownership, passed a law creating a new type of pretax employee share scheme dubbed the All Employee Share Ownership Plan (AESOP). The United Kingdom also enacted a new program to encourage the use of stock options in entrepreneurial enterprises.
- India recently liberalized rules allowing information technology, pharmaceutical, and biotechnology companies to offer stock options to employees.
- Last year, South Korea passed a law actively encouraging stock-based incentives, which the government described as "an optimal tool to raise worker productivity because it aligns employee and employer goals."
- Taiwan's Securities and Futures Commission recently approved the use of employee stock options. The Far Eastern Economic Review commented on these and similar developments in the region as follows: "As Asian companies compete head on with multinationals in global markets, they are discovering they need to offer multinational-style compensation packages." They went on to note that mainstream companies throughout corporate Asia are "supplementing

employees' salaries with the right to buy cheap shares in the company. The benefits to shareholders—not to mention companies and staff—could prove impressive."

- **Denmark, Switzerland, Australia, Ireland, Singapore, the Netherlands, Brazil, and Chile, among others, have all recently enacted similar changes in tax laws to facilitate, or affirmatively encourage, the use of stock-based incentive plans.**

Sources: Adapted with permission from Butler, M. J. (2001, 2nd Quarter). Worldwide growth of employee ownership phenomena. *Worldatwork Journal*, *10*(2), 1–5.

Advantages of Corporatewide Pay-for-Performance Plans

Corporatewide pay-for-performance plans have distinct advantages, several of which are economic rather than motivational. These are:

- **Financial flexibility for the firm.** Both profit sharing and ESOPs are variable compensation plans: Their cost to the firm is automatically adjusted downward during economic downturns. This feature allows the firm to retain a larger workforce during a recession. In addition, these plans allow employers to offer lower base compensation in exchange for company stock or a profit-sharing arrangement. This feature gives the firm "float," or flexibility to direct scarce cash where it is most needed. ESOPs may also be used to save a foundering company—one whose cash is running out or is facing a hostile takeover bid. Weirton Steel, Hyatt Clark, Polaroid, and Chevron have effectively used ESOPs for this purpose.[84]
- **Increased employee commitment.** Employees who are entitled to profit sharing and ESOPs are more likely to identify themselves with the business and increase their commitment to it. Many consider the sharing of profits between the firm's owners and workers as a just distribution of income in a capitalistic society.
- **Tax advantages.** As noted earlier, both profit sharing and ESOPs enjoy special tax privileges. In essence, they allow the firm to provide benefits (discussed in detail in Chapter 12) that are subsidized in part by the federal government. Although these types of plans are sometimes blamed for the loss of enormous amounts in tax revenues, it can be argued that they let firms that cannot afford to pay employees high salaries grow and prosper, thereby creating more jobs and tax revenues in the long run. Apple Computer, Sun Microsystems, Oracle Corporation, Quantum Corporation, and Microsoft might not be around today were it not for tax-subsidized ESOPs and profit-sharing plans.

Disadvantages of Corporatewide Pay-for-Performance Plans

Like all other pay-for-performance programs, corporatewide plans have their drawbacks:

- **Employees may be at considerable risk.** Under profit-sharing or ESOP plans, workers' financial well-being may be threatened by factors beyond their control. Often workers are not fully aware of how much risk they face because the factors affecting profits or stock prices can be very complex. The more reliant long-term employees are on these programs for savings (for their children's college tuition, their own retirement, or some other purpose), the more vulnerable they are to the firm's fate.

  Many employees of *Fortune* 500 firms saw their life savings take a huge fall after the bull market turned into a bear market late in 2000. As the Enron case travels through the legal and legislative process, it has become evident that employers can subject employees to great financial risk when they impose restrictions that prohibit them from selling or diversifying their company stock until a certain age or when they are allowed to bet 100 percent of their long-term savings on their company stock. Unfortunately, such stipulations attached to stock ownership plans are widespread and not unique to Enron.[85] Among entrepreneurial firms, the risk can be huge: Many of these firms do not survive past five years so the stock employees own may not be worth the paper it is printed on.[86]
- **Limited effect on productivity.** Because the connection between individual goal achievement and firm performance is small and difficult to measure, corporatewide programs are not likely

to improve productivity. However, they should reduce turnover if seniority strongly affects how much an employee is entitled to under the plan.

- **Long-run financial difficulties.** Both profit sharing and ESOPs often appear painless to the company in the short run, either because funds are not paid out to employees until retirement or because employees are paid in "paper" (company stock). This illusion may induce managers to be more generous with these types of compensation than they should be, leaving future management generations with less cash available, lower profits to distribute to investors, and a firm that has decreased in value.

Conditions Favoring Corporatewide Plans

A number of factors influence the successful implementation of corporatewide pay-for-performance plans:

- **Firm size.** Although they may be used at firms of any size, profit sharing and ESOPs are the plans of choice for larger organizations, in which gainsharing is less appropriate.[87]
- **Interdependence of different parts of the business.** Corporations with multiple interdependent plants or business units often find corporatewide plans most suitable because it is difficult to isolate the financial performance of any given segment of the corporation.
- **Market conditions.** Unlike gainsharing, which requires relatively stable sales levels, profit-sharing and ESOP programs are attractive to firms facing highly cyclical ups and downs in the demand for their product. The structuring of these incentives helps the firm cut costs during downturns. (This is why these programs are often called "shock absorbers.") Employees (except those who are closer to retirement) are not immediately affected by these fluctuations in short-term earnings because most profit-sharing benefits are deferred until retirement.
- **The presence of other incentives.** Because corporatewide pay-for-performance plans are unlikely to have much motivational impact on individuals and teams within the firm, they should not be used on their own. When used in conjunction with other incentives (for example, individual and team bonuses), corporatewide programs can promote greater commitment to the organization by creating common goals and a sense of partnership among managers and workers.

As future managers, you should be aware of the types of pay-for-performance plans, their advantages and disadvantages, and favorable conditions for each kind of plan. Figure 11.4 on page 384 summarizes the conditions that favor individual, team, plantwide, and corporatewide pay-for-performance plans.

Designing Pay-for-Performance Plans for Executives and Salespeople

Executives and salespeople are normally treated very differently than most other types of workers in pay-for-performance plans. Because pay incentives are an important component of these employees' total compensation, it is useful to examine their special compensation programs in some detail. It is also useful to examine how companies are rewarding excellence in customer service—a key source of competitive advantage today.

Executives

Leaders of major U.S. corporations pocketed smaller pay packages in 2002 than at any time since 1989, mostly because of the sudden drop in stock prices during 2001 (which accounted for almost one-half of their total pay). Yet, the 15 highest-paid chiefs were each earning on average $108.8 million in annualized pay in 2002.[88] And while long-term income of CEOs of *Fortune* 500 firms had dropped on average by about 18 percent during the bear market of 2001 to 2003, CEOs did not fare worse than most Americans whose wealth invested in their companies for retirement was also closely tied to the stock market.[89] Employees at Procter & Gamble

Conditions That Favor Various Pay-for-Performance Plans

Figure 11.4

Type of Plan	Favorable Conditions
Individual-Based Plans	■ The contributions of individual employees can be accurately isolated ■ The job demands autonomy ■ Successful performance does not depend on cooperation, or competition should be encouraged
Team-Based Plans	■ Work tasks are so intertwined that it is difficult to single out who did what ■ The firm's organization supports the implementation of team-based incentives ■ The firm's objective is to foster entrepreneurship in self-managed work groups
Plantwide Plans	■ Firm size is small to midsize ■ Technology does not limit efficiency improvements ■ Clear records of historical performance are available ■ Corporate culture supports participative management ■ A stable product market is present
Corporatewide Plans	■ Firm size is large ■ Different parts of the business are interdependent ■ A relatively unstable (cyclical) product market is present ■ Other incentives are present

and Coca-Cola had 80 percent or more of their retirement wealth in the stocks of their respective companies before they tanked in 2001.[90]

According to some estimates, each of the *Fortune* 500 CEOs could live to age 95 among the top 2 percent of Americans if he or she saved just one year's pay. At the higher end, some could have $1.2 million a year for life by saving one year's pay.[91] CEOs earn approximately 240 times what the average employee makes, up from 42 times in 1980, and far more than in any other industrialized nation both on absolute and relative grounds. That is, U.S. CEOs make more money than CEOs in other countries and they earn more compared to what the average worker does than CEOs from other nations earn. For instance, in Japan the CEO is paid 33 times what the average Japanese worker is paid.[92]

Until the most recent bear market, the trend has been for CEO pay to be less in the form of salary and more in the form of long-term income. Between 1995 and 1999, CEO salary as a proportion of total pay dropped by almost 20 percent while long-term income grew by almost 20 percent. This trend was the result of several forces, including favorable tax treatment for long-term income (for the CEO, stock gains are tax deferred and when stocks are cashed they are taxed at the capital gains rate, which is lower than the rate on salary and bonuses); stock grants not counted as an expense in the balance sheet; a rapidly rising stock market; and investor calls for greater CEO accountability (unlike salary, long-term income is not assured and reflects growth in shareholder value).

Ironically the trend toward greater emphasis on long-term income to reward executives has had several unintended consequences.

First, a bull market (as in the 1990s) can make CEO pay soar, fueling the belief that CEO pay is out of control. During the 1991–2001 decade, the nation's corporate elite saw their average pay increase by more than 550 percent, almost 20 times faster than raises to the typical worker.[93]

Second, because executives may decide at any time to cash the stock options they received years earlier, it is difficult to see the link between CEO pay and firm performance. For example, Lawrence J. Ellison, CEO of Oracle Corporation, received a "windfall" of $706 million in 2001, even though for Oracle that year had been a disaster (the total return to Oracle's shareholders declined 57 percent during 2001). The huge amount received by Ellison (which exceeds the gross domestic product of many countries) came from exercising long-held stock options, and his decision to cash them in in 2001 probably had nothing to do with Oracle's poor showing in 2001. In other words, it is difficult to see the chronological tie between stock-based pay and firm performance because of the time between receiving and cashing a stock option. Many complex methods have been devised by academics to estimate the true linkage of long-term income to firm performance, yet these are arcane, often controversial, and the results tend to be inconsistent.[94]

And, third, when the stock market changes from bull to bear, firms face the problem of what to do with executives whose stocks "are under water" (i.e., the current market price is below the price when they were provided to the executive, so the options have become worthless). Many firms believe that "underwater" options are demotivating to executives and could make those executives an attractive recruitment target by competitors. To deal with this possibility, firms might make new additional grants to compensate the executive for the loss of value of previously granted stocks, cancel and reissue stock options to ensure they are not under water, or buy underwater stock with cash.[95] This strategy may reinforce the notion that top executives incur little risk with their pay while employees are often asked to bear the brunt of employment and compensation risk because they are more likely to be laid off and see their bonus cut during a downturn.[96]

A large number of plans are used to link executives' pay to firm performance, but there is little agreement on which is best. The disagreement is only heightened by the huge sums of money involved (close to a median or 3 million annually in total among *Fortune* 500 firms)[97] and the weak or inconsistent correlation between executive earnings and firm performance.[98]

Salary and Short-Term Incentives

The amount of executives' base pay increases as firms get larger[99]—practically all CEOs of *Fortune* 500 firms earn a base of at least half a million dollars a year with an average of $1.6 million in cash compensation annually based on 2002 estimates.[100] Executives' bonuses are usually short-term incentives linked to the firm's specific annual goals. More than 90 percent of U.S. firms reward executives with year-end bonuses, but the criteria used to determine these bonuses vary widely.

A Question of Ethics

Do you think it is ethical for a company to give its CEO and its other top executives multimillion-dollar pay packages that are not closely tied to the company's performance?

Two major concerns are often expressed regarding executives' annual bonuses. First because executives are likely to maximize whatever criteria are used to determine their bonuses, they may make decisions that have short-term payoffs at the expense of long-term performance. For instance, long-term investments in research and development may be crucial to the firm's success in introducing new products over time. Yet if bonus calculations treat such investments as costs that reduce net income, executives may be tempted to scale back R&D. Second, many bonus programs represent salary supplements that the CEO can expect to receive regardless of the firm's performance. For instance, an examination of the *Wall Street Journal's* executive pay survey in 2002 shows that during the previous year (characterized by a major economic downturn) approximately three-fourths of the CEOs in the survey received a substantial bonus. And if we focus on companies with a drop of total shareholder return of 40 percent or more, we find that a surprising number of those CEOs received a bonus in excess of half a million dollars during the same period (including, for instance, Aplera, Crown Cork & Seal, Continental Airlines, and Boeing).[101]

The almost automatic payment of lavish bonuses to top executives has led to much resentment among middle managers. One vice president at a major bank expressed a common middle-management frustration: "It disturbs me when someone on high dictates that no matter how hard you work or what you do, you're only going to get a 6 percent increase, and if you don't like it, you can take a hike. Yet whatever they've negotiated for themselves—10 percent, 20 percent, or 30 percent—is a different issue from the rest of the staff."

Long-Term Incentives

Most executives also receive long-term incentives, either in the form of equity in the firm (stock-based programs) or a combination of cash awards and stock. A brief description of the most commonly used executive long-term incentive plans appears in Figure 11.5 on page 386.

The primary criticism of long-term incentive plans is that they are not very closely linked with executive performance. There are three reasons for this. First, even executives themselves

Figure 11.5

Stock-Based Programs

Stock Options Allow the executive to acquire a predetermined amount of company stock within a stipulated time period (which may be as long as 10 years) at a favorable price.

Stock Purchase Plans Provide a very narrow time window (usually a month or two) during which the executive can elect to purchase the stocks at a cost that is either less than or equal to fair market value. (Stock purchase plans are commonly available to all employees of the firm.)

Restricted Stock Plans Provide the executive with a stock grant requiring little, if any, personal investment in return for remaining with the firm for a certain length of time (for example, four years). If the executive leaves before completing the specified minimum length of service, all rights to the stock are forfeited.

Stock Awards Provide the executive with "free" company stock, normally with no strings attached. Often used as a one-time-only "sign-on" bonus for recruitment purposes.

Formula-Based Stock Stock provided to the executive either as a grant or at a stipulated price. Unlike other stock-based programs, the value of the stock to the executive when he or she wishes to redeem it is not its market price but one calculated according to a predetermined formula (normally book value, which is assets minus liabilities divided by the number of outstanding shares). Used when the board believes that the market price of an organization's stock is affected by many variables outside the control of the top-management team.

Junior Stock Stock whose value is set at a lower price than common stock, so that the executive is required to spend less cash up front to acquire it. Unlike the owners of common stock, the owners of junior stock have limited voting and dividend rights. However, junior stock can be converted to common stock upon achievement of specific performance goals.

Discounted Stock Options Stock with a strike price lower than the market value of the stock at the date of the grant. Introduced during recent bear market (2001–2003) where there was a reasonable probability that the market value of the stock will rise slowly or may drop.

Tracking Stock Options A class of shares linked to the performance of a specific business or unit of the parent company rather than linked to the performance of the corporation as a whole.

Programs That Combine Cash Awards and Stocks

Stock Appreciation Rights (SARs) Provide the executive with the right to cash or stocks equal to the difference between the value of the stock at the time of the grant and the value of that same stock when the right is exercised. Thus, the executive is rewarded for any increase in the value of the stock, although no stock was actually granted by the firm. No investment on the executive's part is required. May be offered alone or mixed with stock options.

Performance Plan Units Under this plan, the value of each share is tied to a measure of financial performance such as earnings per share (EPS). For example, for every 5 percent increase in EPS, the firm may provide the executive with $1,000 for every share he or she owns. Therefore, if EPS increases by 15 percent the executive will receive $3,000 for each share owned. The payment may be made in cash or common stocks.

Performance Share Plans Offer the executive a number of stocks based on profitability figures using a predetermined formula. The actual compensation per share depends on the market price per share at the end of the performance or award period.

Phantom Stock Pays executives a bonus proportional to the change in prices of company stocks, rather than changes in profitability measures. A phantom stock is only a bookkeeping entry because the executive does not receive any stock per se. The executive is awarded a number of shares of phantom stock to track the cash reward that will be received upon attaining the performance objectives. The award may be equal to the appreciation or the value of the share of phantom stock.

Source: Updated version (2003) of chart appearing in Gómez-Mejía, L. R., and Balkin, D. B. (1992). *Compensation, organizational strategy, and firm performance*, 219, Cincinnati, OH: South-Western. Copyright 1992 by South-Western Publishing. All rights reserved. See also Fox, R. D., and Hauder, E. A. (2001). Sending out an SOS—Methods for companies to resuscitate underwater stock options. *Worldatwork Journal, 10*(2), 7–12; Pitt, H. (2002, April 5). Pitt calls for stricter control of options. *Wall Street Journal*, A-4; Ledford, G. E., Harper, D., and Schuler, J. (2001). Beyond plain vanilla—New flavors in stock option use. *Worldatwork Journal, 10*(2), 10–16; and Byrne, J. A. (2002, April 15). Pay related wealth: Winners and losers. *BusinessWeek*, 83.

Commonly Used Long-Term Executive Incentive Plans

rarely know how much their equity in the firm is worth because its value depends on stock prices at redemption. Second, the executive is likely to have very little control over the value of a company's stock (and thus the worth of his or her own long-term income) because stock prices tend to be highly volatile. (As noted earlier, depending on the time period, this can benefit the executive as during the decade of the 1990s or hurt the executive as during the first half of the 2000s.) Third, designing long-term incentive plans involves many judgment calls, and these are not always addressed in a manner consistent with achieving the firm's long-term strategic objectives. The major questions that firms should address in designing executive long-term programs are listed in Figure 11.6.

Perks

Perquisites ("perks") Noncash incentives given to a firm's executives.

In addition to cash incentives, many executives receive a large number of **perquisites or "perks."** These may include a wide array of "special deals" such as physical exams, financial counseling, club memberships, company plane, airline VIP clubs, chauffer service, and concierge service, among other similar perquisites. These may keep the executive happy, but they are seldom linked to business objectives.[102] They are also an easy target of criticism for those who feel that executive compensation is already excessive and who believe that perks are a form of "stealth wealth," representing "a hidden way [for executives] to increase their compensation."[103] "CEOs are getting far more skilled at hiding this [pay] stuff," says William Patterson, director of the AFL-CIO's Office of Investment. "There is far more anger because of the surreptitious disclosure [of perks]."[104] Two recent cases have provoked much media attention. One case is Fleet Boston Financial Corp.'s CEO, Terrence Murray, who will collect an annual pension of $5.8 million on his retirement in 2003. This is more than double what the normal company formula would have paid, despite the fact that Fleet Boston shares underperformed the average for similar banks during the prior decade. Once he steps down, Murray also will enjoy lifetime use of a corporate aircraft for as much as 150 hours a year, a car and driver when requested, an office and assistant, a company-paid home security system, and financial planning. His wife and guests can take free flights even if he stays behind. The other case of excessive perks often cited in the media is that of Jack Welch who stepped down as CEO of GE in 2001. The company has guaranteed him a high interest rate of 12 percent on his deferred compensation account (much higher than the going market rate) and other perks (such as a special life insurance policy and use of GE's plane). These perks are estimated at nearly $9 million a year for as long as he lives.[105]

There are no easy answers to these criticisms. Executive compensation will probably always be more an art than a science because of all the factors that must be considered and each firm's unique conditions. Nonetheless, it is safe to say that an executive compensation plan is more likely to be effective if (1) it adequately balances rewarding short-term accomplishments with motivating the executive to consider the firm's long-term performance, (2) the incentives provided are linked to the firm's overall strategy (for example, fast growth and risky investments

Figure 11.6

Key Strategic Pay Policy Questions in the Design of Executive Long-Term Income Programs

1. How long should the time horizon be for dispensing rewards?
2. Should length of service be considered in determining the amount of the award?
3. Should the executive be asked to share part of the costs and, therefore, increase his or her personal risk?
4. What criteria should be used to trigger the award?
5. Should there be a limit on how much executives can earn or a formula to prevent large unexpected gains?
6. How often should the awards be provided?
7. How easy should it be for the executive to convert the award into cash?

Sources: Makri, M., and Gómez-Mejía, L. R. (2002). Rewarding executives. In Silzer, R. (Ed.), *The 21st Century Executive* (pp. 200–228). San Francisco: Jossey-Bass; Grabke-Rundell, A., and Gómez-Mejía, L. R. (2002). Power as a determinant of executive compensation. *Human Resource Management Review, 12*, 3–23; and Deya-Tortella, B., Gómez-Mejía, L. R., De Castro, J., and Wiseman, R. (2002). Rethinking executive stock option plans. Paper presented at the Academy of Management Annual Conference, Denver, CO.

versus moderate growth and low business risks), (3) the board of directors can make informed judgments about how well the executive is fulfilling his or her role, and (4) the executive has some control over the factors used to calculate the incentive amount.[106]

Directors and Shareholders as Equity Partners

The board of directors is responsible for setting executive pay. Traditionally, the board members have been paid in cash. In recent years, however, the relative elements of director compensation have changed fundamentally, as we see a shift toward payment in stock and stock options to tie the financial interests of directors to those of the firm and thus increase their incentive to monitor the executives more closely. Close to 85 percent of firms include at least some stock as part of the annual compensation of directors, with $45,000 in stock on average per director.[107]

Although in theory this change in director compensation is a good idea, two well-known researchers warn us that it could be tantamount to the fox watching the chicken. In other words, boards may be tempted to act in a self-serving manner because in most cases the board sets its own compensation.[108] For instance, directors may set lower performance targets for the granting of stock options. And even if the board acts in good faith with the best interest of shareholders in mind, the appearance of a conflict of interest would always loom in the background.[109]

Salespeople

Sales professionals, working with the marketing staff, are responsible for bringing revenues into the company. There are several reasons why setting up a compensation program for salespeople is so much different from setting up compensation programs for other types of employees.[110]

- The spread in earnings between the lowest- and highest-paid salespeople is usually several times greater than the earnings spread in any other employee group within the company.
- The reward system for salespeople plays a supervisory role because these employees generally operate away from the office and may not report to the boss for weeks at a time.
- Perceptions of pay inequity are a lesser concern with this group than with others because few employees outside the company's marketing organization have knowledge of either sales achievement or rewards.
- Sales compensation is intimately tied to business objectives and strategies.
- The performance variation among salespeople tends to be quite large. Most organizations rely on relatively few stars to generate most of the sales.
- The salesperson generally works alone and is personally accountable for results.
- Accurate market data on pay practices and levels are extremely difficult to find for salespeople, and commercial salary surveys are usually unreliable.

Sales professionals may be paid in the form of *straight salary* (with no incentives), *straight commission* (in which all earnings are in the form of incentives), or a *combination plan* that mixes the two. Straight salary is most appropriate when maintaining good customer relations and servicing existing accounts are the key objectives, with increased sales a secondary goal. Straight commission is most appropriate when the key objective is to generate greater sales volume through new accounts. Only one-fourth of all firms use either a straight-salary or straight-commission method. Three-quarters use a combination of the two, though the relative proportion of salary versus incentives varies widely across firms. The trend has been to put more emphasis on commissions in a mixed plan.[111]

As the Manager's Notebook titled "Salary? Commission? Or Both? A Guide to Compensating Salespeople" shows, all three sales compensation methods have their pros and cons. The main criterion that should determine the type of plan chosen is overall marketing philosophy, which is derived from the firm's business strategies.[112] If increased sales is the major goal and these sales involve a one-time transaction with the customer and little expectation of a continuing relationship, then a greater proportion of incentives in the pay mix is appropriate. If customer service is crucial and the sales representative is expected to respond to clients' needs on a long-term basis, then greater reliance on straight salary is appropriate. For example, used car salespeople are often paid in the form of straight commission, while sales representatives for highly technical product lines (which often require extensive customer service) tend to be paid on straight salary.

MANAGER'S NOTEBOOK

Salary? Commission? Or Both? A Guide to Compensating Salespeople

Straight-Commission Sales Compensation Plan

Advantages

- Effective for generating new accounts
- Sales force is highly motivated to sell the product
- High performers' contributions are recognized with pay
- Sales representatives become entrepreneurial and require minimal supervision
- Selling costs are efficiently controlled
- Plan administration is simple
- Fixed costs are kept to a minimum

Disadvantages

- Sales volume is emphasized over profits
- Customer service may be neglected
- Sales representative may overstock the customer
- Offers less economic security to sales force
- Provides less direct control over sales force
- Top-performing sales representatives may outearn other employees, including executives
- Possible resistance to changes in sales territories
- Possible focus on products that require the least effort to sell

Straight-Salary Sales Compensation Plan

Advantages

- Secure income
- Sales force is willing to perform nonselling activities
- Plan administration is simple
- Sales force is less likely to overstock customers
- Low resistance to change in sales territories
- Low employee turnover rates
- Sales force treated as salaried professional
- More cooperation and less competition in sales force

Disadvantages

- Low motivational impact
- Difficult to attract or retain top sales performers
- More sales managers are needed to provide supervision
- Sales representatives may focus on products that require least effort to sell

Combination Sales Compensation Plan

Advantages

- Incorporates advantages of both straight-salary and straight-commission plans
- Recognizes both selling and nonselling activities with pay
- Can offer both economic security and monetary incentives to sales representatives
- Greater variety of marketing goals can be supported with plan

Disadvantages

- Plan is more complicated to design
- Sales force may become confused and try to accomplish too many objectives

- Plan is more difficult and costly to administer
- Sales representatives may receive unanticipated windfall earnings

Source: Updated version (2003) of chart appearing in Gómez-Mejía, L. R., and Balkin, D. S. (1992). *Compensation, organizational strategy, and firm performance*. Cincinnati, OH: South-Western. Reproduced with the permission of South-Western College Publishing.

Rewarding Excellence in Customer Service

More and more companies are using incentive systems to reward and encourage better customer service. A survey of 1,400 employers revealed that 35 percent of the respondents factor customer satisfaction into their formula for determining incentive payments. Another third are considering doing so. Common measures of customer satisfaction used to determine incentive payments are customer surveys, records of on-time delivery of products and services, and number of complaints received.[113]

Customer service rewards may be individual-, team-, or plant-based. For example, Storage Technology in Louisville, Colorado, uses customer service as part of its formula to distribute gainsharing monies to all employees covered by the plan. To ensure that sales representatives and managers do not shortchange the customer for the sake of increasing sales and short-term profits, IBM introduced a plan where 40 percent of incentive earnings are tied to customer satisfaction. IBM uses a survey to determine if buyers are happy with the local sales team.[114] AT&T Universal Card provides a $200 on-the-spot bonus for employees who deal effectively with customers' complaints on the phone; phone calls are randomly monitored for this purpose.[115]

Summary and Conclusions

Pay-for-Performance: The Challenges

Pay-for-performance (incentive) programs can improve productivity, but managers need to consider several challenges in their design and implementation. Employees may be tempted to do only what they get paid for, ignoring those intangible aspects of the job that are not explicitly rewarded. Cooperation and teamwork may be damaged if individual merit pay is too strongly emphasized. Individual merit systems assume that the employee is in control of the primary factors affecting his or her work output, an assumption that may not be true. Individual performance is difficult to measure, and tying pay to inaccurate performance measures is likely to create problems. Pay incentive systems can be perceived as an employee right and can be difficult to adapt to the organization's changing needs. Many employees do not believe that good performance is rewarded (the credibility gap). Emphasizing merit pay can place employees under a great deal of stress and lead to job dissatisfaction. Finally, merit pay may decrease employees' intrinsic motivation.

Meeting the Challenges of Pay-for-Performance Systems

To avoid the problems sometimes associated with pay-for-performance systems, managers should (1) link pay and performance appropriately, (2) use pay for performance as part of a broader HRM system, (3) build employee trust, (4) promote the belief that performance makes a difference, (5) use multiple layers of rewards, (6) increase employee involvement, and (7) consider using nonfinancial incentives. Employee participation in the design of the plan can enhance its credibility and long-term success.

Types of Pay-for-Performance Plans

There are four types of incentive programs. At the level of individual employees, merit pay (which becomes part of base salary) and bonuses and awards (given on a one-time basis) determined via supervisory appraisals are most common. At the next level, team-based plans reward the performance of groups of employees who work together on joint projects or tasks, usually with bonuses and noncash awards. At the level of the plant or business unit, gainsharing is the program of choice. Gainsharing rewards workers based on cost savings, usually in the form of a lump-sum bonus. At the fourth and highest level of the organization—the entire corporation—profit sharing and employee stock option plans (ESOPs) are used to link the firm's performance with employees' financial rewards. Both plans are commonly used to fund retirement programs.

Designing Pay-for-Performance Plans for Executives and Salespeople

Two employee groups, top executives and sales personnel, are normally treated very differently than most other workers in pay-for-performance plans. Short-term annual bonuses, long-term incentives, and perks may be used to motivate executives to make decisions that help the firm meet its long-term strategic goals. Sales employees are revenue generators, and their compensation system is normally used to reinforce productive behavior. A reliance on straight salary for salespeople is most appropriate where maintaining customer relations and servicing existing accounts are the key objectives. A heavy reliance on straight commission is most appropriate if the firm is trying to increase sales. Most firms use a combination of the two plans. In today's globally competitive marketplace, many firms are also using incentive programs to reward customer service.

Key Terms

Discussion Questions

1. This chapter identifies three assumptions underlying pay-for-performance plans. Do you believe these assumptions are valid?
2. How can a pay-for-performance system increase the motivation of individual employees and improve cooperation at the same time?
3. One observer notes that "the problem with using pay as an incentive is that it is such a powerful motivational weapon that management can easily lose control of the situation." Do you agree? Why or why not?
4. Some companies have introduced "business literacy" programs on the assumption that pay-for-performance programs will work only if employees are aware of what brings money into the firm. Most employees are totally unaware of their company's financial situation. Companies like PepsiCo, Sears, and State Farm have used pictorial representations called "learning maps" or "business games." Learning maps chart the flow of revenues and costs and explain how the company makes money. Other similar maps describe their customers' businesses. Business games teach employees how the business works, asking them to respond to a variety of challenges facing the company and, hence, providing a better understanding of what makes the firm perform better or worse. Economic "value trees" sometimes are used. These trees begin with return on capital and flow through each financial and nonfinancial measure that affects returns.[116] Skeptics believe these programs are a way for the company to sell employees on the notion of more work for the same or less pay and to justify layoffs as a business strategy to save on costs. Do you think these programs can help employees see the connection between individual/team performance and organizational profitability? Do you think the credibility of pay-for-performance plans improves or declines as a result of these programs? Explain.
5. An insurance company compensates its work teams by awarding an annual bonus based on three factors: productivity, customer satisfaction, and quality of work in one of its teams; four members came up with a way to speed up claims payments that boosted customer satisfaction and productivity and also satisfied quality goals. In this situation, is a bonus for the entire 10-member team justified? How can the insurance company make sure that free riders (low performers) do not benefit from the productivity of others in the group and that those who do the most work will be rewarded appropriately?
6. In 2002, Ford announced some of the details concerning the firing of former CEO Jacques A. Nasser, which followed a $5.4 billion loss during his last year in the job.[117] In addition to an annual pension for life of nearly $1 million (he is only 53 years old) and performance bonuses through 2003, he received full payment on stock granted to him in 2001. It isn't known how many shares he received, but his 2000 award is now worth $5.8 million.[118] This type of "golden parachute" or "sweet severance" package is not unusual when a corporation terminates a CEO for lackluster performance. Why do you think boards of directors approve of such deals for disgraced CEOs on the way out, when most employees who are laid off receive at most a few weeks' severance pay? Is this practice in the company's best interest? Explain.
7. A committee of top-level CEOs of the largest French firms made a recommendation that top executive pay should remain secret in France (unlike the United States where by law it must be disclosed for all publicly traded firms). Their rationale? French CEOs earn up to 50 percent less pay than their American and British counterparts for firms of similar size, in the same industry, and for similar performance levels. In a press conference,

Marc Viénot, Honorary Chairman of Société Générale, remarked that "Revealing it would just help rivals lure French CEOs away with better pay packages . . . [Besides] Americans like bragging about their pay, and the French don't."[119] Do you agree with the committee's decision and its rationale? Explain.

8. A customer survey for Landmark Company reports that people do not trust what sales representatives say about their firm's products. How might you use the compensation system to help change this negative image?

There is a variety of additional material available on the Web site that accompanies this text. You can access this information by visiting the Web site at **www.prenhall.com/gomez.**

YOU MANAGE IT!

Emerging Trends Case 11.1

Forced Ranking: Tough Love or Overkill?

According to Worldatwork (which represents approximately 10,000 compensation professionals), about 20 percent of employers already use a formal performance ranking system to distribute rewards, and this proportion seems to be growing rapidly.

Forced rankings—also known as forced grading and performance ranking programs—are either loved or hated by HR professionals and corporate executives, and for most employees they create a lot of stress and anxiety. These systems rank employees by categories, often into a top 5 percent, middle 90 percent, and bottom 5 percent, although the percentage distributions among the three ranks can vary. The stars at the top receive plenty of rewards; the bottom dwellers may be warned or terminated; and the middle may receive cost-of-living increases.

Some employers see these programs as ways to identify and clear out underperformers so they can focus on those who make the best contribution to the bottom line. Other employers, especially during these recessionary times, believe forced rankings wreak havoc on corporate culture and are heartless "house cleaning" exercises that fail to take all aspects of employees' contributions into account.

Those in Favor of Forced Ranking

Jack Welch, former CEO of General Electric, is probably the best-known proponent of forced rankings. Welch, in a letter to GE shareholders, wrote:

"Not removing the bottom 10 percent early in their careers is not only a management failure, but false kindness as well—a form of cruelty—because inevitably a new leader will come into a business and take out that bottom 10 percent right away, leaving them—sometimes midway through a career—stranded and having to start over somewhere else."

Another supporter of forced ranking is Carly Fiorina, Hewlett-Packard's CEO, who introduced a new evaluation process at HP based on performance rankings. In her words, "We're going back to performance management the way it was originally intended to be."

And Geoffrey Colvin, CEO of Motorola, remarked, "We can't all be above average. . . . Every company needs to get rid of underperformers, and most managers won't until they have to."

Those Opposed to Forced Ranking

Those who dislike the forced ranking system believe it undermines productivity. "I think it promotes employee dissatisfaction and discontent," contends Patricia Gurne, a managing partner with the law firm Coastes Davenport & Gurne (Washington, DC). She believes forced rankings are self-defeating because they set artificial categories for employees. According to her, this is similar to the practice of college professors who decide to give only two A grades in a class, regardless of how students actually perform. With forced ranking, "There have to be employees who are graded as unsatisfactory even if the entire workforce is actually performing up to standards."

"Today, forced ranking can actually encourage average or mediocre performance," according to Brent Longnecker, from the staffing services company Resources Connection (Costa Mesa, California). In Longnecker's opinion, forced ranking can inspire competition that results in "intense internal conflict [that] can destroy any semblance of employee teamwork and cooperation." He also believes forced ranking "forces evaluators to make determinations on a person-versus-person basis rather than a person-to-established-standards basis." He feels this takes management away from a focus on "preestablished objectives, job standards, and toward evaluations based on personal attributes." This, in turn, can lead to problems including in-fighting, management subjectivity, and lawsuits.

Brian Anderson, senior consultant at Watson Wyatt (Bethesda, Maryland), warns that forced rankings "can be toxic to a culture" pitting employees one against another, effectively destroying any hopes for teamwork and collaboration.

Critical Thinking Questions

1. Forced rankings are not new. Their use is documented as far back as World War I. It fell in disfavor in the 1930s and, until the start of this new century, it was almost unheard of in most companies, particularly "blue-chip" firms. Why do you think so many companies have "rediscovered" forced ranking and are pushing it as an antidote to low productivity and inefficiency? Explain.
2. Considering the stark views of those who favor and those who oppose forced ranking systems, which side would you take? Explain.
3. Do you believe that forced rankings that provide lavish rewards to top performers are perceived as unfair by most employees? What can a company do to ensure that ranking systems are viewed as equitable? Explain.

Team Exercise

You are part of a group of five divisional executives of a large conglomerate; your group has been asked by the company CEO to explore implementation of forced ranking systems in the years ahead. Students divide into groups of five to role-play this situation and present the CEO with your recommendations as to whether or not forced rankings should be adopted. Justify your rationale carefully.

Sources: Adapted with permission from *HR Focus* (2002, February). Forced rankings: Tough love or overkill? 79(2), 11.

Discussion Case 11.2

YOU MANAGE IT!

Loafers at Lakeside Utility Company

Lakeside Utility Company provides electrical power to a county with 50,000 households. Pamela Johnson is the manager in charge of all repair and installation crews. Each crew consists of approximately seven employees who work closely together to respond to calls concerning power outages, fires caused by electrical malfunctions, and installation of new equipment or electric lines. Fourteen months ago Johnson decided to implement a team-based incentive system that will award an annual bonus to each crew that meets certain performance criteria. Performance measures include indicators such as average length of time needed to restore power, results of a customer satisfaction survey, and number of hours required to complete routine installation assignments successfully. At the end of the first year, five crews received an average cash bonus of $12,000 each, with the amount divided equally among all crew members.

Soon after Johnson announced the recipients of the cash bonus, she began to receive a large number of complaints. Some teams not chosen for the award voiced their unhappiness through their crew leader. The two most common complaints were that the teams working on the most difficult assignments were penalized (because it was harder to score higher on the evaluation) and that crews unwilling to help out other crews were being rewarded.

Ironically, members of the crews that received the awards also expressed dissatisfaction. A surprisingly large number of confidential employee letters from the winning teams reported that the system was unfair because the bonus money was split evenly among all crew members. Several letters named loafers who received "more than their share" because they were frequently late for work, took long lunches and frequent smoking breaks, and lacked initiative. Johnson is at a loss about what to do next.

Critical Thinking Questions

1. What major issues and problems concerning the design and implementation of pay-for-performance systems does this case illustrate? Explain.
2. Are team-based incentives appropriate for the type of work done by Johnson's crews?
3. Might it be desirable to use a combination of team-based and individual incentives at Lakeside Utility Company? How might such a plan be structured?

Team Exercises

Students form pairs. One student takes the role of Pamela Johnson, the other the role of an HRM consultant Johnson has hired to help her decide what to do next. Role-play the meeting between the two. Johnson explains what has happened and the consultant reacts.

The class divides into groups of five students each. One of the students takes the role of a consultant hired by Pamela Johnson to help her decide what to do. The remaining four students take the roles of line workers, each from a different crew. The consultant is gathering information from the crews about how they feel about the bonus system and what changes they would like to see.

YOU MANAGE IT!

Discussion Case 11.3

Playing the Compensation Game

The following situations emerged in very different organizational settings after incentives were introduced to reward good employees:

- After the discovery of insect parts in its pea packages, Green Giant designed a bonus plan to reward employees for removing insect parts from the vegetables. Green Giant abandoned the incentive plan when it learned that employees were bringing insect parts from home, putting them into the vegetables, and then removing them to get their bonuses.
- A software developer had problems with a different kind of bug: software program glitches. Like Green Giant, the company installed an incentive plan to reward programmers for finding and removing the bugs. Initially, the plan seemed successful. But, as in Green Giant's case, the developer's performance numbers hid the problem—employees were, in fact, creating the very bugs the incentive plan was paying them to remove.
- Sunbeam had hired Al Dunlap as CEO to restructure the company and turn around its performance, as he had done at Scott Paper in the mid-1990s. To support that objective, the company compensated Dunlap with a pay package rich in stock options. By late 1996, the new CEO had clearly met his goals: the stock value had returned more than 130 percent to the shareholders. Then in 1998 the Securities and Exchange Commission launched an investigation of Sunbeam's accounting practices coincident with a dramatic decline in stock value. By June 1998, the stock was selling at $3.75, down from a 1996 high of $53. Dunlap had met his goal of improving the short-run value of the company but was unable to find a buyer as he had done at Scott Paper. Sunbeam's board eventually fired him as CEO.
- In 1805, an army private deserted from the Lewis and Clark expedition on its trek across North America. Because desertion is serious business, one captain decided to offer a reward to ensure that the private was punished: $10 to anyone who brought the private back alive, or $20 for the private's scalp. The captain got exactly what he was willing to pay for: lots and lots of scalps.

Critical Thinking Questions

1. What is the common thread across the widely different examples of "pay for performance" given above?
2. What are some of the pros and cons of linking pay to objective criteria that are important to the organization such as quality control measures, profitability, and low turnover?
3. Alfie Kohn, a well-known management consultant and writer, argues that "the failure of any incentive program is due less to a glitch in that program than to the inadequacy of the psychological assumptions that ground all such plans."[120] Kohn believes that stock options, piece rates, commission, bonuses, and even rewards such as employee-of-the-month programs, vacations, and praise are bribes that can cause more harm than good. Do you agree? Explain.
4. How would you prevent the problems that arose at Green Giant, the software developer, and Sunbeam and still reward good performance? Explain.
5. Assuming you are a top executive at Green Giant and the software developer, would you punish the employees who engaged in those unethical acts, the managers that devised the incentive system, or both?
6. Some people believe that most employees will act ethically even though they have a chance to take advantage of an incentive system through inappropriate behaviors. Do you agree?

Team Exercise

Divide the class into groups of three to five students. One set of teams will defend the proposition that incentives can be beneficial to a firm by reinforcing desired behaviors. Another set of teams will defend the position that in most cases incentives promote a "let's beat the game" attitude among employees that leads to poor performance.

Source: Adapted with permission from Bloom, M. (1999). The art and context of the deal: A balanced view of executive incentives. *Compensation and Benefits Review, 31*(1), 25–31.

Video Shorts Case 11.4

YOU MANAGE IT!

Compensation

In today's show Cheryl Brie, director of recruitment at Focus Pointe and a frequent guest on *SPOTLIGHT*, joins host Meg Allen. *SPOTLIGHT*'s undercover crew captures Cheryl as she tackles the sometimes thorny issue of compensation. Later on they will discuss the film footage shot at Focus Pointe with guest Paul Fiolek, of human resources at Bertelsman BMG.

As you watch Cheryl interact with recruiter Angelo Hernandez, the following background may help you better assess the scene: Focus Pointe, a provider of qualitative research services and facilities, employs a staff of 200. A leader in the market research industry, Focus Pointe offers its clients deluxe, state-of-the-art facilities and expert in-house recruiting of consumer, medical, and business-to-business respondents. In order to distinguish itself from its competitors, Focus Pointe uses a unique triple-screening process to ensure that respondents meet the specifications of their clients.

Cheryl Brie is joined by another HR staff member at Focus Pointe, Chona Castillo. They have both come to this meeting with Angelo prepared to try to work things out. Angelo has been at the company for six years and has kept a steady number of "high-end" recruits, including physicians and business professionals, coming in. But lately his numbers have fallen off. Since his compensation is based in part on the number of recruits the client accepts as focus group participants, this means he is making less money than he used to. He wants an explanation from the company as to why more of his recruits are being rejected than in the past. Think about your reaction when you hear him ask for a raise, while at the same time acknowledging that he is not "making the numbers." You will observe that he just can't understand why his candidates aren't being let into "the room," even though he admits that the policy at Focus Pointe has not changed. He is angry and feels he has to look out for himself and his own financial needs. Consider Cheryl's responses, from an HR perspective, throughout this meeting.

Cheryl and Chona are both consistent with their position that he has delivered the "high-quality recruits and the numbers" in the past and that they are ready to compensate him for the talent he brings to the recruiting task. Why is this important? Cheryl suggests that perhaps Angelo's backward slide is a matter of reeducation, retraining, or better communication with his supervisor to make sure he is getting all the information he needs. Do you think Angelo is really listening to Cheryl or do you think his focus is more on what he wants to say?

As the meeting comes to an end, Cheryl has agreed to pay Angelo $5.00 more per recruit and give him a 4 percent salary increase, but he has to earn it by getting his numbers back up within three months. If at the end of the three months he has not made the numbers, they will have to renegotiate. Angelo got his raise, for now, but did he learn anything?

After viewing the clip, Meg Allen directs the audience to the discussion segment of the show. Cheryl reiterates that Angelo needed retraining to justify his raise and to get his performance up to par. Paul Fiolek would not have given Angelo the increase in compensation. Consider the difference in staffing strategies and requirements at a conglomerate like BMG versus a small business like Focus Pointe. You might ask yourself whether you think Angelo is a good candidate for retraining.

Managing employee compensation is one of HR's most important and most difficult roles. As Paul Fiolek points out, it often happens in the case of commission-based pay that the compensation levels off due to industry changes or strategic changes within the corporation. People cannot be expected to remain satisfied when this happens. However, there are many things HR can do to keep people motivated and happy, including the offering of bonuses and less traditional perks such as gym packages, babysitting, or, as Meg Allen suggests, better cafeteria food!

Critical Thinking Questions

1. Would you have given Angelo a pay raise up front? What are your reasons?
2. As an HR professional, how would you go about setting pay rates at Focus Pointe? If you have time, you might search one of the pay data Web sites in your text and find out what recruiters earn.
3. How are incentive plans best used? Why are they well suited to a company like Focus Pointe? Why do you think the sales incentive plan at Focus Pointe is a combination plan?
4. Can you think of a strategic sales incentive to keep recruiters motivated at Focus Pointe?
5. How can line management be helpful to HR in establishing strategic pay plans?

Designing and Administering Benefits

Challenges

After reading this chapter, you should be able to deal more effectively with the following challenges:

1. **Explain** the significance of employee benefits to both employers and employees.
2. **Design** a benefits package that supports the firm's overall compensation strategy and other HRM policies.
3. **Distinguish** between a defined benefit retirement plan and a defined contribution retirement plan and recognize the situations in which each is most appropriate.
4. **Discuss** how traditional health insurance plans and managed-care health insurance plans work and the advantages and disadvantages of each.
5. **Develop** cost-containment strategies for the different types of employee benefits.
6. **Understand** the administrative complexities of providing a full array of benefits to the work force and suggest ways to deliver benefits effectively.
7. **Recognize** the HR department's key role in keeping accurate records of employee benefits and informing employees about their benefits.

Today's HR managers face a number of challenges that did not exist a decade ago. One of these challenges is managing the rapidly increasing costs of employee benefits. Although health-care costs have received the most attention, the costs of many other employee benefits are also increasing. At the same time, benefits have become crucial to attracting, retaining, and motivating employees. A report by the National Study of the Changing Work Force found that 43 percent of employees who changed jobs rated employee benefits as "very important" in their decision, while only 35 percent said the same for salary or wages.

The following examples give some idea of the many ways companies are managing employee benefits in difficult times. Some companies are:

- **Cutting benefits costs wherever they can** IBM recently changed the basis of its pension from a traditional plan that uses a fixed formula for retirement income based on an employee's seniority and last five years of salary to a new type of pension called a "cash balance" plan. The cash balance plan sets aside the same amount of savings for an employee each year instead of accelerating the contributions toward the end of an employee's career as the traditional plans do. The new plan reduces the amount of resources needed to fund a pension and makes it more predictable for the company. It also makes it easier for employees to change jobs and take the full value of the retirement account with them, which was not the case with the traditional pension plan.

Although younger employees who are more likely to change jobs favored the cash balance plan, older IBM employees with 20 or more years of experience felt betrayed by the new plan design. Why? Their expected retirement income would be significantly less than their expected income under the traditional plan.[1] As a result, IBM faced its first serious union organization threat in many years. Disappointed employees with seniority considered organizing a union that could help them bargain with management to shift back to the original plan.[2]

- **Providing cutting-edge benefits** By providing innovative, cutting-edge benefits that satisfy specific employee needs, a company is in a better position to attract and retain talented employees who are in scarce supply. Delta Air Lines recently offered to provide computers and Internet access at the homes of all of its 72,000 employees for $12 a month. Delta wanted to make it easier for its pilots and flight attendants to schedule their flights while away from their office.[3] Sun Microsystems provides concierge services that give personal assistance to busy employees. For a small fee the concierge service will pick up groceries, take the car for scheduled maintenance, provide dry cleaning and laundry pickup and delivery, order and deliver flowers, and provide other personal services for employees. Interlock Resources, a Clayton, Missouri, software company, provides complete meals so employees do not need to leave the company at meal times. President and CEO Wayne Haar noted: "Having food on site makes it easy for our staff to stay in for lunch or dinner. Our kitchen is stocked with our employees' favorite foods, snacks and beverages, which they select and order through a local grocery store's Internet site."[4]

Offering benefits that give employees a sense of security while containing costs might seem to be mutually exclusive goals. The challenge is for managers and HR professionals to work together to (1) give employees meaningful benefit choices that match their needs, (2) keep the costs of these benefits under control, and (3) ensure that employees are fully informed of their benefit options.

THE MANAGERIAL PERSPECTIVE

In the United States, unlike most other developed countries, the employer provides most of an employee's benefits. The benefits, which are part of a group benefit plan, are designed to safeguard employees and their families against problems due to sickness, accidents, or retirement. More than almost any other issue addressed in this text, an organization's HR staff controls benefits programs. Still, managers must be familiar with benefits for several reasons:

- **Benefits issues are important to employees** Managers must help employees understand and make the best use of their benefits. For instance, if an employee has a child who needs urgent medical attention, the employee's manager should be able to explain the company's medical benefits to ensure that the employee obtains all available coverage.
- **Benefits are a powerful recruiting tool** Managers at firms that offer enticing benefits can use this advantage to recruit high-quality applicants.
- **Benefits help retain talented employees** Firms that offer an attractive benefits package to employees give managers an advantage because the package often helps reduce turnover.
- **Certain benefits play a part in managerial decisions** Some benefits—such as vacations, family and medical leave, and sick days—give employees scheduling flexibility. Managers need to be aware of these benefits to effectively manage work schedules.

- **Benefits are important to managers** Managers need to be aware of their own benefit options. Some decisions, particularly those concerning retirement plans, have long-term consequences. Good decisions in this area made early in a career can affect quality of life at the end of and after a career.

However, understanding benefit plan designs is not an easy task. As we see in the chapter, cost-control measures, the need to offer benefits that attract and retain employees, and new laws and regulations have led to many changes in the design of benefit programs.

In this chapter we explain benefits in detail. We begin with an overview of employee benefits and the relationship of benefits to the rest of the compensation package. Second, we examine strategies for designing benefits programs. Next, we describe the scope and significance of two categories of employee benefits programs: legally required benefits and voluntary benefits. Finally, we discuss some important issues in benefits administration.

An Overview of Benefits

Employee benefits are group membership rewards that provide security for employees and their family members. They are sometimes called **indirect compensation** because they are given to employees in the form of a plan (such as health insurance) rather than cash. A benefits package complements the base-compensation and pay-incentives components of total compensation. According to the U.S. Bureau of Labor Statistics, benefits cost U.S. companies about $12,160 per year for the average employee.[5] Figure 12.1 shows how the benefit dollar is divided in the average firm.

Employee benefits or indirect compensation
Group membership rewards that provide security for employees and their family members.

Employee benefits protect employees from risks that could jeopardize their health and financial security. They provide coverage for sickness, injury, unemployment, and old age and death. They may also provide services or facilities that many employees find valuable, such as child-care services or an exercise center.

In the United States the employer is the primary source of benefits coverage. The situation is quite different in other countries, where many benefits are sponsored by the government and

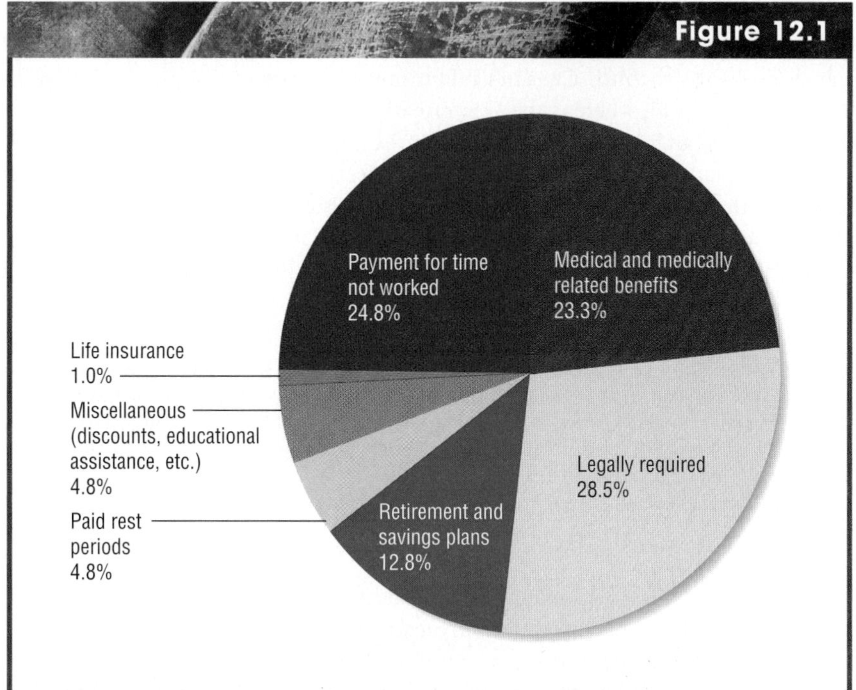

How the Benefit Dollar Is Spent

Source: U.S. Bureau of Labor Statistics (2001). Employer costs for employee compensation.

funded with taxes. For example, in the United States employers voluntarily provide their employees with health insurance, while in Canada health insurance is a right bestowed on all citizens by the country's national health system. For a brief summary of Canada's health-care policy, see the Issues and Applications feature titled "Benefits Across the Border: A Look at Canada's Health-Care System."

The benefits package offered by a firm can support management's efforts to attract employees. When a potential employee is choosing among multiple job offers with similar salaries, a firm offering an attractive benefits package will be ahead of the pack. For example, Swedish Medical Center, a hospital in Denver, Colorado, uses its on-site child-care center as a recruiting tool to attract high-quality staff.[6] It is one of only two hospitals in its region that offer this benefit.

Issues and Applications

Benefits Across the Border: A Look at Canada's Health Care System

When Tommy Bettis from Arkansas broke his arm and cut his head while helping to repair the garage of his Ontario friend, Kristopher Goering, Bettis received emergency care at a Canadian hospital by presenting Goering's health card. Although this case involved an emergency occurring in Canada, thousands of Americans are routinely borrowing Canadian health cards to get medical care.

Why are ailing Americans going to another country and using illegal means to get health care there? Because in Canada health care is free. In the debate on U.S. health-care reform, the U.S. media have alternately portrayed Canada's national health-care system as a medical miracle or as a bureaucratic nightmare. The truth seems to be somewhere in between. Yet, from the vantage point of 44 million uninsured residents of the United States—many of whom are employed full- or part-time—Canada's system is more in the miracle category.

Canada's national system covers all residents' medical and hospital bills and is funded through income taxes (top bracket: 48 percent on income over $50,000) and through a payroll tax on employers. Doctors and hospitals are reimbursed directly by provincial governments according to a negotiated schedule of fees, while patients pay nothing—except higher taxes than U.S. citizens. (In fact, Americans take home the largest percentage of their gross pay among all industrialized nations.) Health-care expenditures are 40 percent lower per capita than in the United States, however, and the burden is lighter for employers, too. Consider Ford Motor Company of Canada. In 1990 it spent $41 million on coverage for its 22,000 workers, or about $65 per vehicle produced—many times less than what its U.S. parent pays for health coverage for U.S. employees. But does Canada get more out of its health system for less? Statistics seem to say so: Canada boasts the eighth-highest life expectancy in the world, 77.03 years as opposed to 75.22 for the United States, which ranks thirty-third. Canada's infant mortality rate of 7.9 per 1,000 live births is the tenth lowest in the world, whereas the U.S. rate of 10 per 1,000 is twenty-first.

Is there a catch in the Canadian system? Canadians sometimes have to wait for nonemergency procedures, but rarely for run-of-the-mill services. Also, in Canada, recession has cut into tax revenues, so the system is facing a financial crunch. But there is one rising cost Canada can do something about: the cost of Americans using the system illegally. Canadian officials are cracking down on health-care fraud, seizing the cards of ineligible users and making a bigger effort to collect for medical services provided to nonresidents.

Sources: Weber, J. (1998, August 31). Canada's health-care system isn't a model anymore. *BusinessWeek*, 36. Multinational Division, Sedwick Noble Lowndes (1996). *The 1995 guide to pensions and labor law in Europe, Japan, and the U.S.A.* Chicago, IL; and Farnsworth, C. H. (1993, December 20). Americans filching free health care in Canada. *New York Times*, A1; Crossette, B. (2001, October 11). Canada's health care shows strains. *New York Times*, A12.

Benefits can also help management retain employees. Benefits that are designed to increase in value over time encourage employees to remain with their employer. For instance, many companies make contributions to employees' retirement funds, but these funds are available only to employees who stay with the company for a certain number of years. For this reason,

Stride Rite offers its employees a flexible benefits program that includes child-care benefits, such as a company-sponsored day care center that focuses on bringing the elderly and the very young together.

benefits are sometimes called "golden handcuffs." An excellent example of the power of benefits to retain employees is the U.S. military, which provides early retirement benefits to personnel who put in 20 years of service. This "20 years and out" retirement provision allows retired military people to start a second career at a fairly young age with the security of a lifelong retirement income to supplement their earnings. These generous benefits help the armed forces retain valuable officers and professionals who would otherwise be attracted to higher-paying civilian jobs.[7]

Basic Terminology

Before we proceed, let us define some basic terms that we will use throughout this chapter:

- **Contributions** All benefits are funded by contributions from the employer, the employee, or both. For example, vacations are an employer-provided benefit: The salary or wages paid to the employee during the vacation period come entirely from the employer. Premiums for health-care insurance are often paid partly by the employer and partly by the employee.
- **Coinsurance** Payments made to cover health-care expenses that are split between the employer's insurance company and the employee. For instance, under an 80/20 insurance plan, the employer's insurance company would pay 80 percent of the employee's health-care costs and the employee would pay the remaining 20 percent.
- **Copayment** A small payment that the employee pays, usually $5 to $15 dollars, for each office visit to a physician under the health plan. The health plan pays for additional medical expenses that exceed the copayment at no cost to the employee.
- **Deductible** An annual out-of-pocket expenditure that an insurance policyholder must make before the insurance plan makes any reimbursements. For instance, the 80/20 plan described previously may also have a $500 deductible, in which case the employee would be responsible for the first $500 of medical expenses before the insurance company makes its 80 percent coinsurance payment.
- **Flexible benefit programs** A **flexible benefits program,** also called a **cafeteria benefits program,** allows employees to select the benefits they need most from a menu of choices. Unlike employers that try to design a one-size-fits-all benefits package, employers with a flexible benefits program recognize that their employees have diverse needs that require different benefits packages. A 30-year-old married female employee with a working spouse and small children is likely to need child-care benefits and may be willing to forgo extra paid vacation days in exchange for this benefit. A 50-year-old married male employee with grown children may prefer a larger employer contribution to his retirement plan.

Contributions
Payments made for benefits coverage. Contributions for a specific benefit may come from the employer, employee, or both.

Coinsurance
Payments made to cover health-care expenses that are split between the employer's insurance company and the insured employee.

Copayment
A small payment made by the employee for each office visit to a physician under a health plan. The health plan pays for additional medical expenses that exceed the copayment at no cost to the employee.

Deductible
An annual out-of-pocket expenditure that an insurance policyholder must make before the insurance plan makes any reimbursements.

Flexible or cafeteria benefits program
A benefits program that allows employees to select the benefits they need most from a menu of choices.

The Cost of Benefits in the United States

The cost of employee benefits in the United States has increased dramatically over the decades as businesses have offered more and more benefits. As Figure 12.2 shows, the cost of employee benefits as a percentage of an employer's payroll increased from 3 percent in 1929 to about 37.5 percent in 2000.[8] This growth can be explained by a combination of factors, including federal tax policy, federal legislation, the influence of unions, and the cost savings of group plans.

Federal Tax Policy

Since the 1920s, the federal government has provided favorable tax treatment for group benefit plans that meet certain standards (discussed later in this chapter).[9] Employers who meet the tax policy guidelines receive tax deductions for their benefits expenditures.

Employees also receive favorable treatment under the tax policy because they receive many of their benefits on a *tax-free* basis. For example, employees receive their employer's contribution to a health insurance plan tax-free. In contrast, self-employed individuals have to pay for health insurance out of their taxable income. Other benefits are received on a *tax-deferred* basis. For example, employee contributions to a qualified retirement plan (up to a maximum amount) may be tax-deferred until the employee retires, at which time the person may be taxed at a lower rate. Federal tax policy on benefits has encouraged employees to demand additional benefits because each additional dollar a company allocates for benefits has more value than a dollar allocated as cash compensation, which is taxed as ordinary income.

Federal Legislation

In 1935, federal legislation decreed that all employers must provide Social Security and unemployment insurance benefits to their employees. We take a closer look at these benefits later in this chapter. At this point, we only wish to make the point that federal law requires some benefits and that federal legislation will probably continue to cause significant growth in the cost of benefits.

Union Influence

Unions have been in the forefront of the movement to expand employee benefits for the last half century. In the 1940s, powerful unions such as the United Auto Workers and the United Mine Workers obtained pensions and health insurance plans from employers. In recent years, unions have been asking for dental-care coverage, extended vacation periods, and unemployment benefits beyond those required by federal law.

Cost of Employee Benefits in the United States, 1929-2000.

Source: U.S. Chamber of Commerce, 1996. *Employee benefits 1996*. Washington, DC: U.S. Chamber of Commerce; Jusko, J. (2002, April), Benefits costs below average. *Industry Week*, 18.

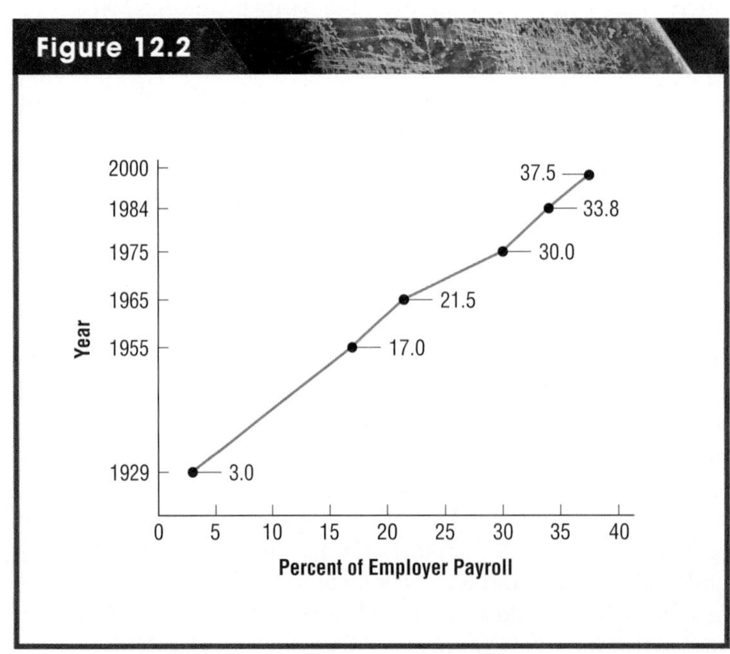

Once benefit patterns are established in unionized firms, these same benefits tend to spread to nonunionized companies, which often wish to avoid union organization drives.

Cost Savings of Group Plans

Employers can provide benefits for much less money than employees would pay to obtain them on their own. When insurance companies can spread risk over a large group of individuals, they can reduce the cost of benefits per person. This fact causes employees to put considerable pressure on their employers to provide certain benefits.

Types of Benefits

Benefits can be organized into six categories. These categories, which we examine in detail later in this chapter, are:

1. **Legally required benefits** U.S. law requires employers to give four benefits to all employees, with only a few exceptions: (1) Social Security, (2) workers' compensation, (3) unemployment insurance, and (4) family and medical leave. All other benefits are provided by employers voluntarily.
2. **Health insurance** Health insurance covers hospital costs, physician charges, and the costs of other medical services. Because of its importance, health insurance is usually considered separately from other types of insurance.
3. **Retirement** Retirement benefits provide income to employees after they retire.
4. **Insurance** Insurance plans protect employees or their dependents from financial difficulties that can arise as a result of disability or death.
5. **Paid time off** Time-off plans give employees time off with or without pay, depending on the plan.
6. **Employee services** Employee services are tax-free or tax-preferred services that enhance the quality of employees' work or personal life.

Figure 12.3 shows the percentage of full-time U.S. employers providing selected benefits plans. As the figure makes clear, large- and medium-sized private firms (those that employ more

Figure 12.3

	Medium and Large Private Firms* 1997	Small Private Firms** 1996	State and Local Governments 1998
Health Insurance	76	64	86
Retirement Plans			
Defined Benefit Plans	50	15	90
Defined Contribution Plans	57	38	14
Insurance Plans			
Life Insurance	87	62	89
Long-Term Disability Insurance	43	22	34
Time-Off Plans			
Paid Vacations	95	86	67
Paid Holidays	89	80	73
Paid Sick Leave	56	50	96
Flexible Benefits Plans	13	4	5

*Firms employing 100 workers or more.

**Firms employing fewer than 100 workers.

Source: U.S. Department of Labor, Bureau of Labor Statistics (1999). *Employee benefit survey*; U.S. Department of Labor, Bureau of Labor Statistics (2000). *Employee benefits in state and local governments, 1998.*

Percentage of Employers Providing Selected Benefit Plans

than 100 individuals) and state and local governments offer a wider variety of benefits than small businesses do.

The growth of benefits over the years, coupled with increased benefits costs, has encouraged employers to hire more part-time or temporary employees when their business grows. Companies often do not provide benefits to part-time employees and temporary employees.

The Benefits Strategy

To design an effective benefits package, a company needs to align its benefits strategy with its overall compensation strategy. The benefits strategy requires making choices in three areas: (1) benefits mix, (2) benefits amount, and (3) flexibility of benefits. These choices provide a blueprint for the design of the benefits package.

The Benefits Mix

Benefits mix
The complete package of benefits that a company offers its employees.

The **benefits mix** is the complete package of benefits that a company offers its employees. There are at least three issues that should be considered when making decisions about the benefits mix: the total compensation strategy, organizational objectives, and the characteristics of the workforce.[10]

The total compensation strategy issue corresponds to the "below-market versus above-market compensation" decision we discussed in Chapter 10. The company must choose the market in which it wants to compete for employees and then provide a benefits package attractive to the people in that market. In other words, management tries to answer the question: Who are my competitors for employees and what kinds of benefits do they provide?

A Question of Ethics

Most larger employers provide some sort of retirement fund for their employees. Do you think that companies are ethically bound to offer this benefit? Does the financial condition (good or poor) or size of the firm make any difference to your analysis?

For example, a high-tech firm may want to attract people who are risk takers and innovators. The firm's management may decide not to offer retirement benefits because high-tech companies are usually considered desirable places to work by people in their 20s, and people this young are generally not concerned about retirement. As an upstart challenger to IBM, Apple Computer chose not to offer retirement benefits because management did not think this benefit would attract the entrepreneurial employees it wanted.[11]

The organization's objectives also influence the benefits mix. For instance, if the company philosophy is to minimize differences between low-level employees and top management, the benefits mix should be the same for all employees. If the organization is growing and needs to retain all its current personnel, it needs to ensure that it offers the benefits its workforce desires.

Finally, the characteristics of the workforce must be considered when choosing the benefits mix. If the firm's workforce consists largely of parents with young children, it is likely that child-care and other family-friendly benefits will be important. A professional workforce will probably want more say in decisions about its retirement funds. A unionized workforce is likely to demand a guaranteed retirement plan.

Benefits Amount

The benefits amount choice governs the percentage of the total compensation package that will be allocated to benefits compared to the other components of the package (base salary and pay incentives). This choice corresponds to the "fixed versus variable pay" decision covered in Chapter 10. Once management determines the amount of money available for all benefits, it can establish a benefits budget and decide on the level of funding for each part of the benefits program. Management will then know how much it can contribute for each benefit and how much it will need to ask employees to pay toward that benefit. In larger companies these calculations are usually performed by the benefits administrator, while smaller companies often hire a benefits consultant to do the math.

A company that focuses on providing job security and long-term employment opportunities is likely to devote a large portion of its compensation dollars to benefits. One company that prides itself on its excellent employee benefits is Procter & Gamble (P&G). Its profit-sharing plan—the oldest such plan in continuous operation in the United States—was started in 1887.

P&G was also one of the first companies to offer all its employees comprehensive sickness, disability, and life insurance programs.[12] Figure 12.4 lists the 10 U.S. companies that provide the most generous benefits, including extensive medical coverage, lengthy vacations, and lavish pension and profit-sharing plans.

Figure 12.4

1. Xerox*
2. Quaker Oats*
3. John Hancock
4. DaimlerChrysler
5. Merck*
6. Bell Atlantic
7. AT&T*
8. Citibank
9. Johnson & Johnson
10. Hewlett-Packard

Companies with the Best Benefits

* Company offers a flexible benefits plan.

Source: Alderman, L., and Kim, J. (1996, January). Get the most from your company benefits. *Money*, 102–106.

Flexibility of Benefits

The *flexibility of benefits choice* concerns the degree of freedom employees have to tailor the benefits package to their personal needs. This choice corresponds to the "centralization versus decentralization of pay" decision described in Chapter 10. Some organizations have a relatively standardized benefits package that gives employees few options. This system makes sense in organizations that have a fairly homogeneous workforce. In these firms a standardized benefits package can be designed for a "typical" employee. However, because of the changing demographics of the U.S. workforce—more women working full-time, dual-career marriages, and single-parent families—there is now a greater variety of employee needs. In organizations that cannot develop a "typical" employee profile, a decentralized benefits package that emphasizes choice will probably be more effective. We discuss flexible benefits packages in detail at the end of this chapter.

Legally Required Benefits

With only a few exceptions, all U.S. employers are legally required to provide Social Security, workers' compensation, and unemployment insurance coverage for their employees—benefits that are designed to give the workforce a basic level of security. The employer pays a tax on an employee's earnings for each of these three required benefits. In the case of Social Security, the employee also pays a tax to fund the benefit. A fourth legally required benefit has been added in recent years: Employers must offer unpaid leave to employees in certain family and medical circumstances.

Social Security

Social Security provides (1) income for retirees, the disabled, and survivors of deceased workers and (2) health care for the aged through the Medicare program. Established by the Social Security Act in 1935, Social Security is funded through a payroll tax paid in equal amounts by the employer and the employee. The Social Security tax in 2002 was 7.65 percent of an employee's annual earnings on the first $84,900 of income. This means that both the employer and employee pay a tax of 7.65 percent on the employee's earnings. The Social Security tax actually has two components: a tax of 6.2 percent to fund the retirement, disability, and survivor benefits, and a tax of 1.45 percent to fund Medicare. Employees who earn more than $84,900 are taxed at 1.45 percent of all their additional earnings. This 1.45 percent tax is also matched by the employer.

Social Security
A government program that provides income for retirees, the disabled, and survivors of deceased workers, and health care for the aged through the Medicare program.

To be eligible for full Social Security benefits, a person must have worked 40 quarter-year periods (which equals 10 years of total employment) and have earned a minimum of $870 per quarter. Figure 12.5 on page 406 spells out the provisions of the four Social Security benefits—retirement income, disability income, Medicare, and survivor benefits—and who is eligible to receive them.

Retirement Income

Social Security provides retirement income to people who retire at age 65. Workers who retire between ages 62 and 64 receive benefits reduced by as much as 20 percent.

The retirement income provided by Social Security averages about 25 percent of one's earnings in the final year before retirement at age 65. This means that people need to develop other sources of postretirement income if they want to maintain a lifestyle similar to the one they enjoyed before retirement. These sources might include a company-provided pension plan, personal savings, or another job. According to the Social Security Administration, people who retired at age 65 in 2002 could expect a monthly Social Security check ranging from $568 to

Figure 12.5

Benefit	Eligibility	Provisions
Retirement income	■ Age 65–67 (full benefits) *or* ■ Age 62–64 (benefits reduced up to 20 percent)	Monthly payments for life beginning at retirement. Average benefit provides about 25 percent of earnings prior to retirement.
Disability income	■ Totally and continuously disabled for 5 months. ■ Disability should be expected to last at least 12 months or result in death.	Monthly payments comparable to retirement benefits as long as totally disabled. Provisions for payments to dependents.
Medicare	■ Age 65 *or* ■ Receiving Social Security disability payments for 24 months.	Covers hospital expenses, nursing home and home health agency expenses, subject to a deductible payment. Medical expenses are covered, subject to monthly premium.
Survivor benefits	■ Family members of the deceased person, including widow or widower age 60 or over, child or grandchild under age 18, or dependent parent age 62 or over.	Monthly payments related to the deceased worker's primary Social Security retirement benefit.

Source: Adapted from the 2002 Social Security online Web site www.ssa.gov.

Social Security Benefits

$1,660, depending on their preretirement earnings. In the future the minimum age for receiving Social Security benefits will increase. For people born after 1950, the minimum retirement age for full benefits will be 66, and for individuals born in 1960 or later, it will be age 67. The average monthly retirement income provided by Social Security in 2002 was $874 for an individual and $1,454 for a retired married couple.

Disability Income

For people who become disabled and cannot work for at least 12 months, Social Security provides a monthly income comparable to retirement benefits. Because the level of disability income averages only about 30 percent of one's earnings from the job, workers need to derive disability income from other sources. These sources include short- and long-term disability insurance and personal savings and investments.

Medicare

Medicare
A part of the Social Security program that provides health insurance coverage for people aged 65 and over.

Medicare provides health insurance coverage for people 65 and older. Medicare has two parts. Part A covers hospital costs. People who pay an annual deductible ($812 in 2000) receive up to 60 days of hospital expenses covered under Medicare. Part B, for which individuals pay a monthly fee ($54.00 in 2000), covers medical expenses such as doctors' fees and the cost of medical supplies. The deductibles and monthly fees for Medicare are adjusted periodically as the cost of medical care increases.

Survivor Benefits

A deceased employee's surviving family members may receive a monthly income if they qualify. Survivor benefits are related to the deceased worker's primary retirement benefit. Those eligible to receive survivor benefits are (1) widows and widowers age 60 and over, and (2) widows and widowers of any age who care for a child age 16 or younger, an unmarried child or grandchild younger than age 18, or a dependent parent age 62 or over.

Workers' Compensation

Workers' compensation
A legally required benefit that provides medical care, income continuation, and rehabilitation expenses for people who sustain job-related injuries or sickness. Also provides income to the survivors of an employee whose death is job related.

Workers' compensation provides medical care, income continuation, and rehabilitation expenses for people who sustain job-related injuries or sickness. "Workers' comp" also provides income to the survivors of an employee whose death is job related.

Workers' compensation is designed to provide a *no-fault remedy* to workers who are injured on the job. This means that even workers who were wholly at fault for their accidents can still receive a benefit. Employers who provide workers' compensation coverage cannot be sued by injured employees.

Workers' compensation is administered by state governments and is required by 47 of 50 states for all employees, including part-time workers. In South Carolina, Texas, and New Jersey, workers' comp is elective. It is funded by a payroll tax, the proceeds of which go to a state workers' compensation fund or to a private insurance company. Only the employer pays for workers' compensation. Although the average workers' compensation cost is only about 1 percent of total payroll expense, companies in accident-prone industries may pay more than 25 percent of their payroll in workers' compensation taxes.[13]

The rates that employers pay for workers' compensation are based on three factors: (1) the risk of injury for an occupation, (2) the frequency and severity of the injuries sustained by a company's workforce (called the company's injury *experience rating*), and (3) the level of benefits provided for specific injuries within the state where the company is located. Because the company's experience rating is based on its own safety record, managers have an incentive to design and promote a safe work environment: A better safety record leads directly to a lower payroll tax rate. Some states offer greater benefits to injured workers, which leads to higher workers' comp taxes assessed on employers in those states. States with the highest workers' compensation costs are Oklahoma, Louisiana, Rhode Island, Texas, and Florida.[14]

Small businesses in industries such as construction and food service have had great difficulty dealing with cost increases in workers' compensation taxes resulting from increasing claims. Consider the following examples:

- Workers' compensation costs for William Solburg, the owner of a small construction company near Tallahassee, Florida, have skyrocketed. More than 25 percent of his total payroll costs go to cover workers' compensation insurance, and he foresees a significant increase in the near future. Solburg is uncertain whether his business can survive much longer with workers' compensation costs rising so quickly.[15]
- At Olsten Corporation, a Westbury, New York, temporary employee service firm, workers' compensation costs tripled in a recent four-year period. Some of these cost increases came about because certain Olsten employees filed fraudulent claims for alleged long-term disabilities. When Olsten hired a detective agency to monitor a worker out on disability for a back injury, the camera caught him changing a tire on his car, a job that required bending over and heavy lifting.[16]

Some small companies are fighting back by banding together to form *self-insurance* pools. L.E. Mason Company, a Boston maker of lighting fixtures and other construction materials, joined a self-insurance group because its rates were 40 percent below Mason's alternatives. Here's how a self-insurance fund works: A fund's member companies, often in the same industry, band together and hire an administrator. The administrator contracts with actuaries, investment managers, health-care providers, and anyone else necessary to perform the functions of an insurance company. Fund members share one another's risk, paying losses out of premiums and investment returns. A typical fund member has between 60 and 100 employees and pays between $50,000 and $100,000 a year for coverage. As of 2000, 35 states allowed self-insurance funds, up from 20 in 1986.

Self-insurance funds are not the answer for all companies. In firms that go it alone, HR staff can help managers control workers' compensation costs in several important ways:

- The HR department should stress safe work procedures by impressing upon employees the importance of safety (see Chapter 16). Many accidents are caused by carelessness, ignorance of safe work practices, personal problems, or the use of alcohol or drugs. HR staff should train managers and supervisors to communicate and enforce the company's safety program. Employees who disregard safe work practices should be disciplined.[17]
- The HR department should audit workers' compensation claims. Managers should challenge any claim they suspect is fraudulent or not job related. For example, a manager can ask an injured worker to submit to a drug test. A positive result from the drug test can be a reason

A Question of Ethics

One way for companies to lower their workers' compensation costs is to move from a state with a high workers' compensation tax rate to one with a lower rate. Is this a legitimate reason for moving a business? What other ethical issues should employers think about when trying to decrease workers' comp costs?

for denying a claim. Or after a serious accident a safety specialist could conduct an investigation at the scene of the accident. Information gathered from the investigation may reveal inconsistencies in the story that may indicate the employee's claim is fraudulent.[18]

- HR should manage how workers' comp benefits work with employers' health insurance benefits when workers sustain job-related injuries. HR should establish controls so that duplicate medical benefits are not paid out to employees.
- HR staff should design jobs and work assignments so that there are fewer risks of injuries such as back strain and repetitive motion injuries. For example, employees can have their video display terminals adjusted daily to avoid strain on the arms and wrists.[19]
- HR can encourage workers who are partially disabled to return to work under a *modified duty plan*. Under such a plan, a manager or HR staff member works with injured employees to develop modified tasks that they can perform until they are ready to handle their regular job. For instance, a maintenance worker with a back injury might be assigned to help schedule the work orders. Modified duty plans can save the company money on benefits that provide income continuation for employees who may be needlessly postponing the return to employment.

Unemployment Insurance

Unemployment insurance
A program established by the Social Security Act of 1935 to provide temporary income for people during periods of involuntary unemployment.

The Social Security Act of 1935 established **unemployment insurance** to provide temporary income for people during periods of involuntary unemployment. The program is part of a national wage stabilization policy designed to stabilize the economy during recessionary periods. The logic underlying this policy is fairly simple: If unemployed workers have enough income to maintain their consumption of basic goods and services, the demand for these products will be sustained, which ultimately will preserve the jobs of many people who might otherwise be added to the ranks of the unemployed.

Unemployment insurance is funded by a tax paid by employers on all employees' earnings. The tax averages 6.2 percent on the first $7,000 earned by each employee.[20] The proceeds of the tax are split between the state government and the federal government, which provide different services for the unemployed. The federal government levies a tax of 0.8 percent, a rate that does not change from employer to employer. In contrast, the state's assessment ranges from at or near zero to more than 10 percent (the average is about 5.4 percent). All the states give employers an experience rating comparing the employer's contributions to the unemployment insurance fund against the benefits drawn by the employer's workers from the fund over a period of time. This system allows the state to lower the unemployment tax rate for employers that discharge only a small number of employees, and raise it for those that discharge large numbers of employees for any reason (including layoffs).

To be eligible for unemployment insurance, employees must meet several qualifications. First, they must be available for and actively seeking employment. Second, they must have worked a minimum of four quarter-year periods out of the last five quarter-year periods and have earned at least $1,000 during those four quarter-year periods combined. Finally, they must have left their job involuntarily.

Employees may be disqualified for unemployment insurance benefits for several reasons. The following people are not eligible for unemployment insurance:

- An employee who quits voluntarily.
- An employee who is discharged for gross misconduct (for example, for failing a drug test).
- An employee who refuses an offer of suitable work (that is, a job and pay level comparable to the employee's previous position).
- An employee who participates in a strike (48 of 50 states deny benefits to strike participants).
- A person who is self-employed.[21]

Unemployment benefits were designed to cover an employee's basic living expenses but not to be a disincentive against actively seeking employment. For this reason, unemployment benefits seldom cover more than 50 percent of lost earnings, and people discharged from high-paying jobs generally receive only a small fraction of their lost earnings. States have developed their own schedules for unemployment benefits and cap them at a maximum level that ranges from about $100 to $400 per week. Unemployment benefits last for 26 weeks, although in states with persistently high unemployment rates, extensions of benefits in 13-week periods may be given. In addition, some companies provide **supplemental unemployment benefits (SUB)** to their laid-off employees. These benefits are most often written into the union contract.

Supplemental unemployment benefits (SUB)
Benefits given by a company to laid-off employees over and above state unemployment benefits.

It is interesting to compare the level of replacement income and duration of benefits provided by unemployment insurance in the United States to the benefits provided to unemployed workers in other countries.[22]

- United States: 50% of salary for 6 months
- Italy: 80% of salary for 6 months
- Japan: 80% of salary for 10 months
- France: 75% of salary for 60 months
- Germany: 60% of salary for 12 months
- Sweden: 80% of salary for 15 months

As can be seen by this international comparison, the amount and duration of unemployment benefits are modest in the United States compared to other countries. In the United States, government policy is designed to encourage unemployed workers to actively seek employment, and it views generous benefits as suppressing an employee's motivation to search for a new job.

Containing the costs of unemployment insurance is an important priority for management. The HR department can make significant contributions here by establishing practices that lower the firm's experience rating. Here are some useful HR practices in this area:

- HR planning can tell management whether an increase in the company's workload is due to short-term or long-term causes. Short-term increases in the workload should be handled by hiring temporary employees or consultants rather than by creating full-time positions. Because neither temporary employees nor consultants can claim unemployment benefits, it costs the company nothing to let them go when the workload decreases. If the increased workload appears to be long-term, however, the company may decide to hire more full-time employees.
- The employee benefits administrator should audit all unemployment claims filed by former employees. Employers have the right to appeal these claims, and in about half the cases they win.
- Managers or members of the HR department should conduct exit interviews with all discharged employees to (1) come to a mutual understanding on the reason for termination and (2) advise them that the company will fight unemployment claims not made for good reason. For example, if an employee discharged for theft makes a claim for unemployment benefits, the company will contest the claim.

Unpaid Leave

Employees occasionally need long periods of time off to take care of their families or their own health problems. Until recently, most employers refused to give workers unpaid leaves for any reason other than the birth of a child. The **Family and Medical Leave Act of 1993 (FMLA)**, enacted under the Clinton administration, now requires most employers to provide up to 12 weeks' unpaid leave to eligible employees for the following reasons.[23]

Family and Medical Leave Act of 1993 (FMLA)
A federal law that requires employers to provide up to 12 weeks' unpaid leave to eligible employees for the birth or adoption of a child; to care for a sick parent, child, or spouse; or to take care of health problems that interfere with job performance.

- The birth of a child.
- The adoption of a child.
- To care for a sick spouse, child, or parent.
- To take care of the employee's own serious health problems that interfere with effective job performance.

The FMLA applies only to businesses with 50 or more employees and to employers with multiple facilities that have 50 workers within a 75-mile radius. The law requires employers to give employees returning from FMLA leave the same job they held before taking the leave or an equivalent job. Employers must maintain coverage of health insurance and other employee ben-

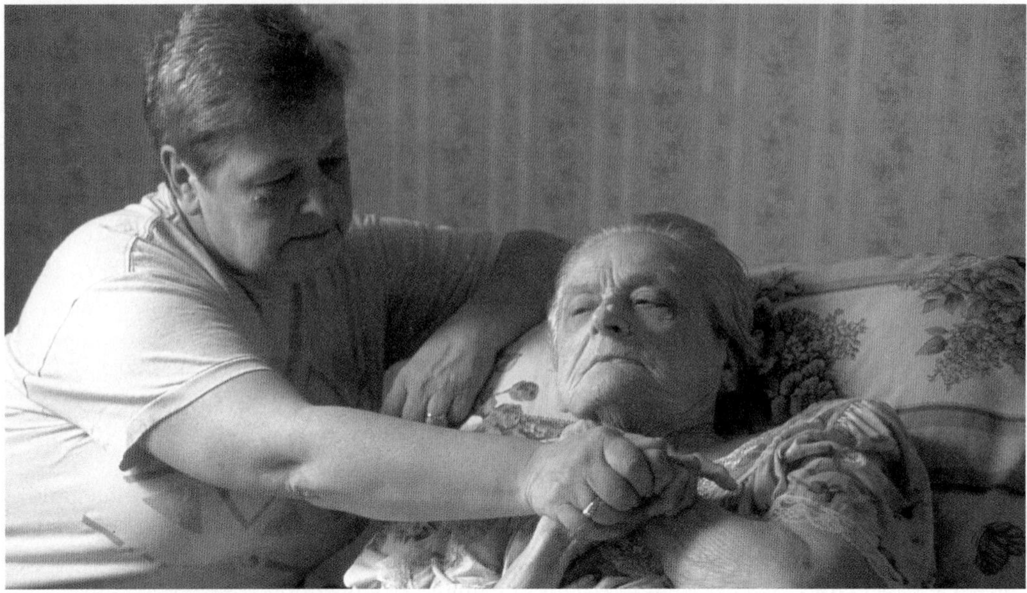

The Family and Medical Leave Act of 1993 requires most employers to provide up to 12 weeks' unpaid leave to eligible employees who adopt a child; who need to care for a sick spouse, parent, or child; or who must take care of their own serious health problems that interfere with job performance.

efits while the employee is on FMLA leave.[24] Employees are eligible to take FMLA leave after accumulating one year of service with their employer. "Highly compensated" employees—those at the top 10 percent of the pay scale and who tend to be the company's top managers—are not eligible for FMLA leave because it may be a hardship for the employer to replace them for a 12-week period.

The FMLA forces companies to develop contingency plans to keep their operations running with a minimum of disruption and added cost when employees are on leave. Managers may want to consider (1) cross-training some workers to cover for employees on leave or (2) hiring temporary workers.[25]

Mandatory unpaid leave also forces companies to confront some troublesome issues, such as:

- Can employees substitute accrued sick days for unpaid leave?
- What sort of illnesses are serious enough to justify a leave?[26]
- How can FMLA leave be coordinated with other laws such as the Americans with Disabilities Act?
- Just what constitutes an "equivalent" job when a leavetaker returns and finds his or her job filled?

The last question was the subject of a Wisconsin lawsuit filed well before the FMLA was passed. Elizabeth Marquardt returned from maternity leave to find that her Milwaukee-based employer, Kelley Company, had eliminated her job as credit manager during a restructuring. Kelley gave Marquardt a new job with the same pay and benefits. However, the new job involved supervising one employee instead of four, and unlike the old position, it included about 25 percent clerical work. Marquardt resigned the next day. Kelley claimed that the reassignment was intended to sidestep Marquardt's longstanding problems with customers. But a Wisconsin appeals court ruled that the jobs were not equivalent because Marquardt's "authority and responsibility were greatly reduced in the new position." HR professionals and line managers will have to work together to avoid such court challenges.[27] The Manager's Notebook titled "What to Do When an Employee Returns from FMLA Leave" specifies an employer's duties and obligations.

What effects has the FMLA had on business operations? A major Department of Labor survey on the FMLA completed in 2000 examined the impact of the law on business during an 18-month period in 1999 and 2000. The key findings were (1) 6 percent of eligible employees took FMLA leave during this 18-month period; (2) about 88 percent of employers stated that FMLA had no effect on company profitability or growth; (3) the most common reasons for taking leave were for personal health problems (52 percent), care for a new child (18 percent), and care for an ill parent (13 percent), and (4) the most frequently used method to cover the work for an employee taking leave was to assign the work temporarily to other employees (98 percent). The second most frequently cited method was to hire an outside temporary replacement to do the work (41 percent).[28]

Emerging Trends

MANAGER'S NOTEBOOK

What to Do When an Employee Returns from FMLA Leave

Employers have both duties and rights when an employee returns from FMLA leave. Here are some key points to consider:

1. Although an employer is not required to hold an employee's specific position open for an indefinite period of time, the employee is entitled to an "equivalent" job when he or she returns. Under FMLA an equivalent position is one that is virtually identical to the former position in terms of pay, benefits, and working conditions. The job must also have the same or substantially similar duties and responsibilities.
2. On returning from FMLA the employee must receive any unconditional pay raises, such as cost-of-living increases, given to other employees during the leave period. The employee must also be given all benefits accrued at the time his or her leave began, such as paid vacation, sick leave, or personal leave, unless this has been substituted for FMLA leave.
3. An employer is not required to apply the time taken for FMLA to seniority or length of service schedules that are used to determine pay increases, promotions, or other rewards unless the employer's policy is to recognize all unpaid leave taken by employees as an input to seniority.
4. Employers are not required to provide an equivalent position to a returning employee who took FMLA leave if the employee is laid off during the leave period, or his or her work shift is eliminated. Similarly, if an employee would have been terminated because of misconduct or incompetence that occurred before the leave, the employer isn't required to reinstate the employee after the leave.

Source: Adapted from Flynn, G. (1999, April). What to do after an FMLA leave. *Workforce*, 104–107.

Voluntary Benefits

The benefits provided voluntarily by employers include health insurance, retirement benefits, other types of insurance plans, time off, and employee services. Future legislation may move some of these benefits from the voluntary category to the legally required category.

Health Insurance

Health insurance provides health-care coverage for both employees and their dependents, protecting them from financial disaster in the wake of a serious illness. Because the cost of individually obtained health insurance is much higher than that of an employer-sponsored group health plan, many people could not afford health insurance if it were not provided by their employer. As Figure 12.3 shows, 76 percent of large- and medium-sized private businesses in the United States offer health insurance to their employees. However, only 64 percent of small firms (those with fewer than 100 employees) do so. It has been estimated that about 44 million people in the United States do not have any health insurance coverage.[29]

During the early 1990s, U.S. health-care costs increased at an astonishing 10 percent to 20 percent per year. By 1997 spending on health care accounted for about 14 percent of the U.S.

gross domestic product (GDP). This is the highest percentage found in any country in the world. For example, per capita health spending in the United States exceeds that of Canada by 44 percent, of Germany by 30 percent, and of the United Kingdom by 104 percent. And unlike the United States, these countries provide health-care coverage for all their citizens. Figure 12.6 compares health-care expenditures across the 24 countries that were members of the Organization for Economic Cooperation and Development (OECD) in 1997.

Obviously, cost containment of health spending will be an important issue for companies and the nation for many years. The benefits specialist in the HR department can make an important contribution to the bottom line by keeping spending on health insurance under control. For example, many companies are now requiring employees to make larger contributions toward the cost of their health insurance.

Consolidated Omnibus Budget Reconciliation Act of 1985 (COBRA)
Legislation that gives employees the right to continue their health insurance coverage for 18 to 36 months after their employment has terminated.

The health insurance benefits that a company offers are significantly affected by the **Consolidated Omnibus Budget Reconciliation Act (COBRA) of 1985,** which gives employees the right to continue their health insurance coverage after their employment has terminated. Employees and their dependents are entitled to 18 to 36 months' additional coverage from the group health insurance plan after separation from the organization. The former employee (or relative of the employee) must pay the full cost of coverage at the group rate, which is still considerably less than the individual rate that could be purchased from a health insurance company on the open market. All employees who are covered by an organization's health-care plan are also covered by COBRA provisions.

Health Insurance Portability and Accountability Act (HIPAA)
A federal law that protects an employee's ability to transfer between health insurance plans without a gap in coverage due to a preexisting condition.

Preexisting condition
A medical condition treated while an employee was covered under a former employer's health plan and requires treatment under a new employer's different health plan.

The ability of an employee to transfer between health insurance plans without a gap in coverage due to a preexisting condition is protected by a federal law enacted in 1996 called the **Health Insurance Portability and Accountability Act (HIPAA).** A **preexisting condition** is a medical condition that was treated while the employee was covered under a former employer's health plan and requires further treatment under a new employer's different health plan. Under HIPAA an employee earns a credit of coverage for every month he or she is covered by the former employer's health insurance plan. When an employee earns 12 months of credit with the former employer, he or she is immediately covered by the new employer's health plan and cannot be denied coverage due to a preexisting condition.[30]

Health Spending in Various Countries 1997
Source: OECD health data (1999), www.oecd.org.

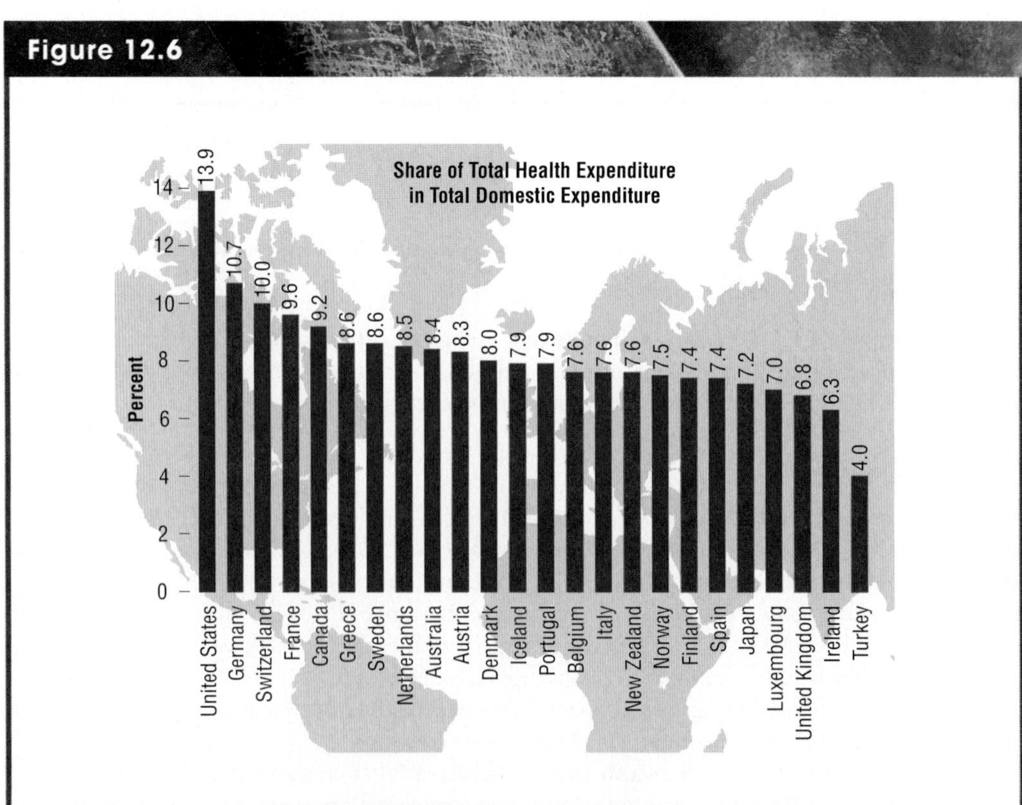

There are three common types of employer-provided health insurance plans: (1) traditional health insurance, (2) health maintenance organizations (HMOs), and (3) preferred provider organizations (PPOs). Figure 12.7 summarizes the differences among these plans.

Traditional Health Insurance

Provided by an insurance company that acts as an intermediary between the patient and health-care provider, *traditional health insurance plans* (also called *fee-for-service plans*) develop a fee schedule based on the cost of medical services in a specific community. They then incorporate these fees into the costs of insurance coverage. The best-known examples of traditional health insurance plans are the Blue Cross and Blue Shield organizations. Traditional health insurance covers hospital and surgical expenses, physicians' care, and a substantial portion of expenses for serious illnesses. In 2002 traditional health plans were selected by 7 percent of employees who had health insurance coverage.[31]

Traditional health insurance plans have several important features. First, they include a deductible that a policyholder must meet before the plan makes any reimbursements. Second they require a monthly group rate (also called a **premium**) paid to the insurance company. The premium is usually paid partially by the employer and partially by the employee. Third, they provide for coinsurance. The typical coinsurance allocation is 80/20 (80 percent of the cost is covered by the insurance plan and 20 percent is picked up by the employee). The deductible, premium, and coinsurance can be adjusted, so the employer's and employee's costs of health-care insurance vary depending on how the parties agree to allocate the costs.

Premium
The money paid to an insurance company for coverage.

Traditional plans give employees the greatest amount of choice in selecting a physician and a hospital. However, these plans have several disadvantages. First, they often do not cover regular checkups and other preventive services. Second, calculating the deductible and coinsurance allocation requires a significant amount of paperwork. Each time they visit a physician, employees must fill out claims forms and obtain bills with long, itemized lists of services. This can be frustrating for patients and costly to physicians, who often need to hire clerical workers solely to process forms.

Figure 12.7

Issue	Traditional Coverage	Health Maintenance Organization (HMO)	Preferred Provider Organization (PPO)
Where must the covered parties live?	May live anywhere.	May be required to live in an HMO-designated service area.	May live anywhere.
Who provides health care?	Doctor and health-care facility of patient's choice.	Must use doctors and facilities designated by HMO.	May use doctors and facilities associated with PPO. If not, may pay additional copayment/deductible.
How much coverage of routine/ preventive medicine?	Does not cover regular checkups and other preventive services. Diagnostic tests may be covered in part or full.	Covers regular checkups, diagnostic tests, and other preventive services with low or no fee per visit.	Same as HMO if doctor and facility are on approved list. Copayment and deductibles are much higher for doctors and facilities not on list.
What hospital care costs are covered?	Covers doctors' and hospitals' bills.	Covers doctors' bills; covers bills of HMO-approved hospitals.	Covers bills of PPO-approved doctors and hospitals.

Source: Milkovich, G., and Newman, J. (2002). *Compensation* (7th ed.), 473. Homewood, IL: Irwin McGraw-Hill.

Employer-Provided Health Insurance Plans

Health Maintenance Organizations (HMOs)

Health maintenance organization (HMO)
A health-care plan that provides comprehensive medical services for employees and their families at a flat annual fee.

A **health maintenance organization (HMO)** is a health-care plan that provides comprehensive medical services for employees and their families at a flat annual fee. People covered by an HMO have unlimited access to medical services because the HMO is designed to encourage preventive health care to reduce ultimate costs. (The "stitch in time saves nine" analogy applies here.) HMO members pay a monthly premium, plus a small copayment or deductible. Some HMOs have no copayment or deductible. The HMOs' annual flat fee per member acts as a monetary disincentive to the HMOs' participatory doctors, who might otherwise be tempted to give patients unnecessary medical tests or casually refer them to expensive medical specialists. In 2002, HMOs were selected by 23 percent of employees who have health insurance coverage.[32]

HMOs have two major advantages. First, for a fixed fee, people covered by the HMO receive most of their medical services (including preventive care) without incurring coinsurance or deductibles or having to fill out claims forms. Second, HMOs encourage preventive health care and healthier lifestyles.

The major disadvantage of HMOs is that they restrict people's ability to select their physicians and the hospitals at which they receive medical services. The HMO may service a limited geographic area, which may restrict who can join the plan. People may be forced to leave their existing doctor and choose one from a list of those who belong to the HMO. In the case of serious illnesses, the specialists consulted must also belong to the HMO, even if there are doctors in the area with better reputations and stronger qualifications. In addition, some consumer groups have criticized HMOs for skimping on patient care to save money on medical costs.

To deal with the problem of patients being denied health-care services by administrators under an HMO, federal lawmakers have proposed a "Patient's Bill of Rights," which is intended to protect patients from abuses of cost-control policies. Although federal lawmakers continue to debate this issue, 38 states now have laws allowing patients to appeal medical decisions to external review boards that have independent experts. In addition, seven states led by Texas have passed laws giving patients the right to sue HMOs, and 26 more are considering such legislation.[33]

Preferred Provider Organizations (PPOs)

Preferred provider organization (PPO)
A health-care plan in which an employer or insurance company establishes a network of doctors and hospitals to provide a broad set of medical services for a flat fee per participant. In return for the lower fee, the doctors and hospitals who join the PPO network expect to receive a larger volume of patients.

A **preferred provider organization (PPO)** is a health-care plan in which an employer or insurance company establishes a network of doctors and hospitals to provide a broad set of medical services for an annual flat fee per participant. The fee is lower than that which doctors and hospitals normally charge their customers for the bundle of services, and the monthly premium is lower than that charged by a traditional plan for the same services. In return for charging a lower fee, the doctors and hospitals who join the PPO network expect to receive a larger volume of patients. Members of the PPO can use it for preventive health care (such as checkups) without paying a doctor's usual fee for the service. PPOs collect information on the utilization of their health services so that employers can periodically improve the plan's design and reduce costs. In 2002, PPOs were selected by 70 percent of employees who have health insurance coverage.[34]

PPOs combine some of the best features of HMOs (managed health care and a wide array of medical services for a fixed fee) with the flexibility of the traditional health insurance plan. They include provisions that allow their members to go outside the PPO network and use non-PPO doctors and medical facilities. People who select non-PPO doctors and hospitals pay additional fees in the form of deductibles and copayments determined by the PPO. Because PPOs have few of the disadvantages of traditional health insurance plans or HMOs, they are expected to continue growing rapidly.

Millions of employees have no health insurance coverage because they are self-employed or work for small businesses whose owners offer no health benefits to reduce costs. These persons who are uncovered by employer-sponsored health insurance plans will need to find their own health insurance coverage. The Manager's Notebook entitled "Tips for Obtaining Your Own Health Insurance" should provide some useful insights for those who are seeking health insurance coverage.

Customer-Driven HR

MANAGER'S NOTEBOOK

Tips for Obtaining Your Own Health Insurance

The cost of buying your own health insurance can be more expensive than the cost for employee coverage with an employer-sponsored plan. That's because an employer can spread the risks of an illness or injury over a large group of employees so that the costs are more predictable than for an individual. Here are some ways an individual can find health insurance coverage at a reasonable cost when no employer-sponsored plan is provided.

- **Form your own small group.** Even for small groups, the health insurance policies are less costly than the cost of an individual policy. Group policies cost 20 percent to 50 percent less than individual policies. For example, in New Jersey two employees can form a group as long as each employee works a minimum of 25 hours per week. In the state of Washington self-employed people can form a group of one and have a wider selection of policies with more competitive prices.
- **Join an association that has group coverage.** In some areas, such as Rochester, New York, the local chamber of commerce offers some of the best health insurance options for individuals without employer coverage.
- **Check out prices on the Web.** In most states, eHealthInsurance.com can give you immediate quotes from several companies, including many Blue Cross/Blue Shield plans, and will spell out what benefits you will get for the price.
- **Take advantage of COBRA provisions.** If you have left a company that provided health insurance benefits coverage, and your employer had more than 20 employees, the company is required by law to let you continue your health insurance coverage for up to 18 months. In order to receive this health insurance coverage under the COBRA law you need to pay the full cost of the health insurance plus an additional 2 percent in administrative expenses. COBRA coverage may be useful if you need to stay under the care of your current doctors. However, because company plans often have more features than an individual may need, you may find a better deal by shopping around for a health plan with only the basic features that you need.

Source: Adapted from Lankford, K. (2001, February). The best of health: Finding a policy you can afford when you're on your own. *Kiplinger's*, 82–86.

Health Insurance Coverage of Employees' Partners

Traditionally, health insurance benefits have been offered only to employees and their spouses or dependents. Today, however, employers are being asked to offer the same health insurance benefits to employees' domestic partners—that is, unmarried heterosexual or homosexual partners.

So far, only a handful of companies and municipalities allow employees to include domestic partners in their health insurance coverage, and most of these limit coverage to gay and lesbian employees. But among the firms that offer such benefits are some of the most prestigious names in U.S. business: Silicon Graphics, Microsoft, Viacom, Apple Computer, and Warner Bros. Companies that also cover unmarried heterosexual couples include Ben & Jerry's Homemade, Levi Strauss, and the Federal National Mortgage Association.

Most of corporate America, however, is resisting the pressure to extend health insurance benefits to domestic partners for a number of reasons. First, some companies fear that they will end up footing the bill for more AIDS-related expenses if they offer health benefits to gay partners. Second, companies fear that employees will abuse the domestic partner benefits by signing up a friend or a string of partners. Finally, companies worry about pitting gay and straight employees against each other, since most current plans offer benefits only to same-sex couples.

Most of these fears seem unfounded. Research shows that, in fact, health-care costs for gay partners and unmarried heterosexual couples are often lower than those for married couples.

Moreover, many homosexual employees do not sign up for the benefits because they want to keep their sexual orientation private. Employers can protect themselves against abuse by asking eligible employees to file affidavits of "spousal equivalency" showing a history of living together and sharing assets. The question of pitting heterosexual employees against gay and lesbian employees may become moot because the growing threat of discrimination lawsuits may force employers to offer coverage to all domestic partners in the near future.[35]

Health-Care Cost Containment

A company's HR benefits manager can control health-care costs by designing (and modifying) health insurance plans carefully and developing programs that encourage employees to adopt healthier lifestyles. Specifically, HR staff can:

- **Develop a self-funding arrangement for health insurance** A company is self-funding when it puts the money it would otherwise pay in insurance premiums into a fund to pay employee health-care expenses. Under this type of plan, the employer has an incentive to assume some responsibility for employees' health. Self-funding plans can be designed to capture administrative efficiencies that translate into lower costs for the same services provided by a traditional health insurance plan.[36]
- **Coordinate health insurance plans for families with two working spouses** HR staff can encourage spouses who have duplicate coverage under two different insurance plans to establish a cost-sharing arrangement. Many companies, such as General Electric, require employees whose working spouses decline their own employers' health insurance to pay a significantly higher premium than nonworking spouses or those who cannot get insurance elsewhere.[37]
- **Develop a wellness program for employees** A *wellness program* assesses employees' risk of serious illness (for example, heart disease or cancer) and then teaches them how to reduce that risk by changing some of their habits (such as diet, exercise, and avoidance of harmful substances such as alcohol, tobacco, and caffeine).[38] Adolph Coors Company, the Colorado-based beer producer, has a wellness program composed of six areas: health hazard appraisal, exercise, smoking cessation, nutrition and weight loss, physical and cardiovascular rehabilitation, and stress and anger management. It has been estimated that Coors' wellness program returns $3.37 to the company for each dollar spent on it.[39]

Retirement Benefits

After retiring, people have three main sources of income: Social Security, personal savings, and retirement benefits. Because Social Security can be expected to provide only about one fourth of preretirement earnings, retirees must rely on retirement benefits and personal savings to maintain their standard of living. Retirement benefits support an employee's long-term financial goal of achieving a planned level of retirement income.

An important service that the HR department can provide to employees nearing retirement is preretirement counseling. *Preretirement counseling* sessions give employees information about their retirement benefits so that they can plan their retirement years accordingly.[40] A benefits specialist can answer questions like:

- What will my total retirement income be when Social Security is added to it?
- Would I be better off taking my retirement benefits in the form of a lump sum or as an annuity (a fixed amount of income each year)?
- What would be the tax effects on my retirement benefits if I earn additional income from a part-time job?

Retirement benefit plans that are "qualified" by the Internal Revenue Service receive favorable tax treatment under the Internal Revenue Code. To qualify, the retirement plan must be available to broad classes of employees and must not favor highly compensated workers over lower-paid workers. Under a qualified retirement plan, employees pay no taxes on the contributions made to the plan until these funds are distributed at retirement. Also, the earnings on the fund's investments accumulate without being taxed each year. Employers may also take a tax deduction for the annual contributions they make to a qualified retirement plan.

ERISA

The major law governing the administration of retirement benefits in the United States is the **Employee Retirement Income Security Act (ERISA).** Passed in 1974, ERISA protects employees' retirement benefits from mismanagement.[41] The key provisions of ERISA cover who is eligible for retirement benefits, vesting, and funding requirements.

Employee Retirement Income Security Act (ERISA)
A federal law established in 1974 to protect employees' retirement benefits from mismanagement.

- **Eligibility for retirement benefits** ERISA requires that the minimum age for participation in a retirement plan cannot be greater than 21. However, employers may restrict participation in the retirement plan to employees who have completed one year of service with the company.
- **Vesting** A guarantee that accrued retirement benefits will be given to retirement plan participants when they retire or leave the employer is called *vesting*. Under current ERISA rules, employee vesting rules must conform to one of two schedules: (1) full vesting after five years of service; or (2) 20 percent vesting after three years of service and a further 20 percent vesting each year thereafter, until the employee is fully vested at seven years of service. Employers are allowed to vest employees faster than this if they wish. Vesting pertains only to employer contributions to the retirement plan. Any contributions the employee has made to the plan are always the employee's property, along with any earnings that have accumulated on those contributions. These employee-provided funds, and any employer contributions that are vested, are said to be **portable**—that is, they stay with the employee as he or she moves from one company to another.
- **Funding requirements and obligations** In addition to establishing guidelines for a retirement plan's minimum funding requirements, ERISA requires that retirement plan administrators act prudently in making investments with participants' funds. Plans that do not meet ERISA funding standards are subject to financial penalties from the Internal Revenue Service.

Vesting
A guarantee that accrued retirement benefits will be given to retirement plan participants when they retire or leave the employer.

Portable benefits
Employee benefits, usually retirement funds, that stay with the employee as he or she moves from one company to another.

To protect employees from an employer's possible failure to meet its retirement obligations, ERISA requires employers to pay for plan termination insurance, which guarantees the payment of retirement benefits to employees even if the plan terminates (either because of poor investment decisions or because the company has gone out of business) before they retire. Termination insurance for defined benefit plans (discussed next) is provided by the **Pension Benefit Guaranty Corporation (PBGC),** a government agency.

Pension Benefit Guaranty Corporation (PBGC)
The government agency that provides plan termination insurance to employers with defined benefit retirement programs.

Defined Benefit Plans

A **defined benefit plan,** also called a **pension,** is a retirement plan that promises to pay a fixed dollar amount of retirement income based on a formula that takes into account the average of the employee's last three to five years' earnings before retirement. The amount of annual income provided by defined benefit plans increases with the years of service to the employer. For example, based on a final five-year preretirement average salary of $50,000, Eastman Kodak's pension plan pays a retired employee with 30 years of service $20,523 per year at age 65. Merck, the pharmaceutical giant, pays an employee with the same salary and 30 years of service $24,000 per year at age 65.[42] Medium and large companies are more likely to provide a pension plan for their workers: 50 percent of these firms offer a defined contribution plan, compared to only 15 percent of small businesses (see Figure 12.3 on page 403).

Defined benefit plan or pension
A retirement plan that promises to pay a fixed dollar amount of retirement income based on a formula that takes into account the average of the employee's last three to five years' earnings prior to retirement.

Under a defined benefit plan, the employer assumes all the risk of providing the promised income to the retiree and is likely to make all of the financial contributions to the plan. Defined benefit plans are most appropriate for firms that want to provide a secure and predictable retirement income for employees. Michigan-based Dow Chemical is one such company.[43] They are less appropriate for firms that stress risk taking and want employees to share in the risk and responsibility of managing their retirement assets.

Most companies that use defined benefit plans for retirement provide the maximum retirement income only after an employee has spent an entire career of 30 to 35 years with the company. Those who change jobs by moving to different companies are penalized with much lower retirement incomes. Employees currently entering the labor market expect to change jobs and employers several times. Defined benefit plans are less attractive to these employees because few will spend an entire career at one company. Consequently, there has been a decline in the number of companies offering defined benefit plans for their employees' retirement.[44]

Defined Contribution Plans

Defined contribution plan
A retirement plan in which the employer promises to contribute a specific amount of funds into the plan for each participant. The final value of each participant's retirement income depends on the success of the plan's investments.

A **defined contribution plan** is a retirement plan in which the employer promises to contribute a specific amount of funds into the plan for each participant. For example, a defined contribution plan may require the employer to contribute 6 percent of the employee's salary into the plan each pay period. Some defined contribution plans also allow or require employees to make additional contributions to the plan. The retirement income that the participants receive depends on the success of the plan's investments and therefore cannot be known in advance.[45] Companies that value employee risk taking and participation are likely to offer defined contribution plans. Under these plans, employees and employers share both risk and responsibility for retirement benefits. Employees may need to decide how to allocate their retirement funds from different investment choices that represent various levels of risk. Because they require fewer obligations from employers than defined benefit plans, most of the new retirement plans established in recent years have been defined contribution plans.

There is a dark side to this trend toward defined contribution plans. Whereas highly educated and highly paid employees may benefit from such risk-taking arrangements, defined contribution plans are likely to be devastating for low-wage workers, according to a report by the Senate Labor and Human Resources Committee. By the year 2020, more than 50 million U.S. men and women will be of retirement age, but many will not be able to retire because as low-wage earners, they could not afford to invest in the defined contribution plans established by their employers. Many of these low-wage workers are women.[46]

Figure 12.8 summarizes the most common defined contribution retirement plans: the 401(k) plan, the individual retirement account (IRA), the simplified employee pension (SEP), and the profit-sharing Keogh. These plans all have tax benefits that can prove very valuable in the long run.

401(k) Plan. To understand the features and benefits of a *401(k) plan* (as well as other tax-deferred retirement plans), consider the following situation. Suppose you want to save $100 per

Figure 12.8

Plan	Available to	Appropriate for	Maximum Contribution	Tax Break on Contributions Earnings
401(k)	Employees of for-profit businesses	Everyone who qualifies	15 percent of salary up to $11,000 in 2002	Yes/Yes
IRA	Anyone with earned income	Those without company pension plans or who have put the maximum into their company plan	100 percent of salary up to $3,000; $6,000 if joint with spouse	Sometimes/Yes
SEP	The self-employed and employees of small businesses	Self-employed person who is a sole proprietor	100 percent of gross self-employment income or $40,000, whichever is less	Yes/Yes
Profit-Sharing Keogh	The self-employed and employees of unincorporated small businesses	Small-business owner who is funding a plan for self and employees	Same as SEP	Yes/Yes

Source: Adapted from Wang, P. (1999, March). Get the max from your 401(k). *Money*, 78–84; Internal Revenue Service employee retirement plans corner. www.irs.gov/bus-info/ep/retirement.html.

A Comparison of Defined Contribution Retirement Plans

month for your retirement, you are in the 28 percent federal income tax bracket, and the money you invest will earn 8 percent per year. If you save the money out of your salary and put it into a personal savings account, the $1,200 that you set aside each year would, in effect, be reduced to $864 because of taxes (Figure 12.9). With one year's interest, that $864 would grow to $891. Each year the investment earnings would also be taxed at the 28 percent rate. If you continue to set aside $1,200 each year in a personal account, your retirement fund would grow to $67,514 in 30 years.

With tax-deferred retirement plans like the 401(k), the money you save each month is not taxed. Therefore, each year you are saving the full $1,200 you put into your retirement account. In addition, the earnings on your investment are not taxed. After the first year, the value of your account would be $1,251 (compared to $864 under the personal account scenario). After 30 years, the value would grow to $141,761, more than twice the size of the personal account. When you retire and draw the funds, your withdrawals will be taxed at your retirement tax rate.

Anyone who works for a for-profit business is eligible to participate in a 401(k) plan.[47] Most companies that establish 401(k) plans will match 25 percent to 100 percent of employee contributions up to 6 percent of the employee's salary.[48] In 2002 the maximum employee annual contribution that could be made to a 401(k) plan was 15% of salary up to a limit of $11,000. The contribution limit to 401(k) plans will increase by $1,000 increments per year between 2003 ($12,000 contribution limit) and 2006 ($15,000 limit).[49] Employees in not-for-profit companies can also save for retirement with a 403(b) retirement plan, which has the same features as the 401(k) plan. The 403(b) plan lets employees in not-for-profit organizations take advantage of the same retirement savings opportunities as those offered to employees in the for-profit sector who are eligible to participate with a 401(k) plan.[50]

The 401(k) plan's matching feature makes it attractive to both employers and employees. Employees benefit by accumulating tax-deferred retirement funds; employers benefit by reducing their risk, since there is no payment required when the employee leaves or retires. Usually,

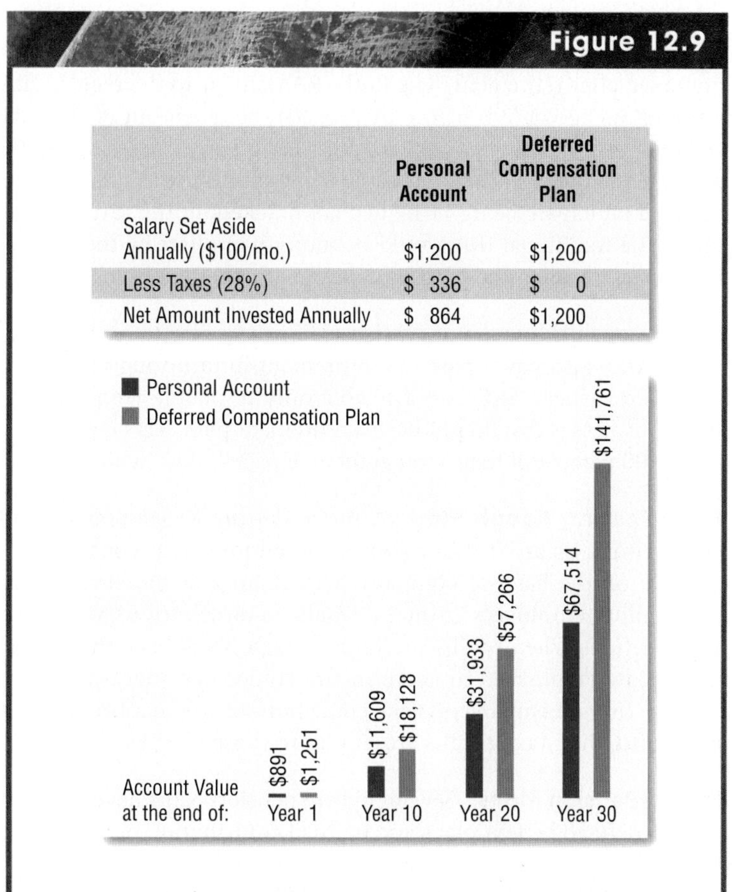

	Personal Account	Deferred Compensation Plan
Salary Set Aside Annually ($100/mo.)	$1,200	$1,200
Less Taxes (28%)	$ 336	$ 0
Net Amount Invested Annually	$ 864	$1,200

Personal Account versus Deferred Compensation Plan

Source: State of Tennessee. *Introduction to the deferred compensation programs.*

employees are free to decide individually how they wish to invest their funds. The basic choice is between an investment strategy with a high potential return, but the risk of a low or even a negative return, and a strategy with low risk and a low to moderate return. Investing in the stock market is an example of the first investment strategy; investing in a savings account is an example of the second.

One controversial aspect of 401(k) plans is a practice that permits many large companies to provide their matching contribution to an employee's 401(k) contribution in the form of company stock. For example, Procter & Gamble, Pfizer, General Electric, and McDonald's use company stock for matching an employee's 401(k) contribution.[51] An employee who has a large portion of her retirement savings in the stock of one company puts her retirement investment at considerable risk. This risk became apparent in 2001 with the bankruptcy of Enron, a large energy company, and the subsequent collapse of its stock price that wiped out the retirement savings of thousands of Enron employees.[52] Even worse, Enron restricted employees from selling their stock until they were close to retirement age. If possible, employees should try to reallocate their 401(k) savings in company stock to other less risky investment choices when it is permitted to do so.

IRA. An *individual retirement account (IRA)* allows people in 2002 to contribute up to $3,000 per year tax free (or $6,000 per year into a joint account with a spouse). Unlike the other defined contribution plans, IRAs are personal savings plans—that is, employers do not contribute to them. As with the 401(k) plan, the interest on an IRA account is tax deferred until the employee cashes it in at retirement. This tax-free benefit is eliminated for employees who participate in a qualified retirement plan with their employer and/or employees who have an adjusted gross income of at least $44,000 (single people) or $64,000 (married people filing a joint return). However, there are no such restrictions on the IRA's tax-deferred earnings. IRAs are available to both those without company pension plans and those who have contributed the maximum to their company plan. The IRA contribution maximum for individuals is scheduled to increase to $4,000 in 2005 and $5,000 in 2008.

In 1998 a new version of the IRA called the *Roth IRA* became available. The Roth IRA allows people to contribute up to $3,000 per year of after-tax income into a savings plan in which the accumulation of interest on the contributions is not taxed and the distributions of income are not taxed after retirement. The Roth IRA (similar to the regular IRA) requires a person to attain a minimum age of 59½ before income can be taken out of the savings without a penalty. Roth IRAs are restricted to people with adjusted gross incomes of less than $110,000 as a single person or $160,000 for married people filing joint returns. The Roth IRA is advantageous for people who anticipate being in higher tax brackets in the future, because the tax savings possible under the traditional IRA would be more than offset by the tax-free distributions of retirement income taken when the person moves to a higher tax bracket.[53]

SEP. A *simplified employee pension (SEP)* is similar to an IRA, but while IRAs are available to people who also participate in a retirement fund through their employer (subject to the limits described earlier), SEPs are available only to people who are self-employed or who work for small businesses that do not have a retirement plan. Those who are eligible for an SEP can invest up to 100 percent of their annual income or $40,000 (whichever is less) on a tax-deferred basis.

Profit-Sharing Keogh Plan. A *profit-sharing Keogh plan* provides for the same maximum contribution as an SEP but allows the employer to contribute to an employee's retirement account on the basis of company performance as measured by profits. Profit-sharing Keogh plans allow employers to make smaller contributions when profits are modest and larger contributions when profits are high. Keogh plans have three main advantages. First, because they allow employees to share in the company's success, they foster a sense of teamwork. Second, they let employers make contributions to the retirement plan that reflect their ability to pay. Third, their tax benefits are similar to those of SEPs.

Hybrid Pension Plans. Several hybrid pension plans have sprung up to address the limitations of both defined benefit plans and defined contribution plans. Defined benefit plans reward long-term service in a world in which employees are more and more mobile. And while defined contribution plans offer greater portability than defined benefit plans, defined contribution plans are tied more to investment returns than to job performance. Thus, fast-trackers who move from job to job may end up with less retirement income than those who work in a company with a traditional pension plan. One of the most popular hybrid plans developed to bridge these two types of pensions is the *cash balance plan,* which works like this: Employees are credited with a certain amount of money for their tax-deferred retirement account each year, based on their annual pay. These contributions are compounded using an agreed-upon interest rate (such as the interest rate on five-year Treasury bills). The employees take the cash balances with them when they change jobs. One drawback of cash balance plans is the time-consuming and expensive recordkeeping required for individual accounts. Another problematic issue is the effect on employees when a company decides to convert from a traditional pension plan to a cash balance pension plan. In some cases the cash balance plan provides lower retirement income than traditional pensions for more senior employees. As described in the vignette at the start of this chapter, IBM made this switch without giving employees who were close to retirement age the chance to remain with the traditional plan. The affected employees protested strongly, threatening to organize a union to protect their interests.[54]

Despite these potential drawbacks, cash balance plans are becoming popular because they are effective for retaining younger employees. Duracell International and Bank of America are two companies that have cash balance plans.[55]

Insurance Plans

A wide variety of insurance plans can provide financial security for employees and their families. Two of the most valued company-provided insurance benefits are life insurance and long-term disability insurance.

Life Insurance

Basic *term life insurance* pays a benefit to the survivors of a deceased employee. The typical benefit is one or two times the employee's annual income. For example, both Citicorp and AT&T offer their employees life insurance that will pay one year's salary to their survivors. In most cases, company-provided term life insurance policies cover workers only while they are employed by the organization. Companies with a flexible benefits policy may allow employees to purchase insurance beyond the basic level. An employee with a nonworking spouse, for example, may need a benefit of three to five years' salary to provide for his or her survivors. Approximately 87 percent of medium and large businesses provide a life insurance benefit to full-time employees.

Long-Term Disability Insurance. Employees who experience a serious injury away from the job (for example, in an auto accident) may not be able to perform their job duties for a long period of time. These employees need replacement income to cover the earnings lost while they are recovering from the accident or, if they are permanently disabled, for the rest of their lives. Workers' compensation does not provide disability income for people who have had off-duty accidents, and Social Security provides only a modest level of disability income to cover the most basic needs.

Long-term disability insurance provides replacement income to disabled employees who cannot perform their essential job duties. An employee is eligible to receive disability benefits after being disabled for six months or more. These benefits range from 50 percent to 67 percent of the employee's salary.[56] For example, Xerox provides 60 percent replacement income under its long-term disability insurance plan, while IBM provides 67 percent.[57] Employees who are disabled for less than six months are likely to receive replacement income under a sick leave policy (discussed later in this chapter). Employees can also purchase short-term disability insurance, which provides coverage until the long-term coverage takes over.

With Social Security benefits added to long-term disability insurance benefits, an employee's total replacement income is likely to be 70 percent to 80 percent of his or her salary. Long-term disability insurance plans usually take Social Security into account and are designed so that disabled employees do not receive more than 80 percent of their salary from these combined sources—the theory being that a higher percentage might be a disincentive to return to work. Approximately 43 percent of medium and large companies offer long-term disability insurance benefits to their workers (see Figure 12.3 on page 403).

Paid Time Off

Paid time off provides breaks from regularly scheduled work hours so that employees can pursue leisure activities or take care of personal or civic duties. Paid time off includes sick leave, vacations, severance pay, and holidays. Paid time off is one of the most expensive benefits for the employer. A survey by the U.S. Chamber of Commerce found that paid time off costs U.S. employers 13.1 percent of total payroll.[58]

Sick Leave

Sick leave provides full pay for each day that an employee experiences a short-term illness or disability that interferes with his or her ability to perform the job. Employees are often rewarded with greater amounts of sick leave in return for long-term service to the company. According to the U.S. Bureau of Labor Statistics, employers with sick leave benefits provide an average of 15 days of sick leave for employees with one year of full-time service to the company. Many employers allow employees to accumulate sick leave over time. For example, an employee with ten years on the job may accumulate 150 sick days if he or she has not used any sick time (10 years × 15 days per year of sick leave = 150 days). This accumulated sick leave coverage would be more than enough to give the employee full replacement income for the first six months of a serious illness, after which long-term disability coverage takes over.

Some companies allow retiring employees to collect pay for accumulated sick leave and vacation time. For example, when John Young retired as the CEO of Hewlett-Packard, he collected $937,225 in lieu of unused sick pay and vacation leave accumulated during his 34 years with the company.[59]

An HR benefits specialist must monitor and control sick leave benefits to prevent employees from using sick leave to take care of personal business or to reward themselves with a "mental health day" off from work. The HR department should consider instituting the following guidelines:

- Set up a "wellness pay" incentive program that monetarily rewards employees who do not use any sick days. Wellness programs may also encourage employees to adopt healthier lifestyles and file for fewer health benefits. For example, Quaker Oats provides bonuses of as much as $500 for employees who exercise, shun smoking, and wear seat belts.[60]
- Establish flexible work hours so that employees can take care of some personal business during the week, thereby decreasing their need to use sick days for this reason.
- Reward employees with a lump sum that represents their unused sick days when they leave or retire from the organization. Alternatively, give employees the chance to accrue vacation days as a percentage of unused sick leave.
- Allow employees to take one or two personal days each year. This helps to discourage employees from regarding sick days as time off to which they are entitled even if they do not get sick.
- Establish a paid time off (PTO) bank, which is a policy that pools time off in a bank of days that employees use for vacation, sick leave, personal days, and floating holidays. PTO programs allow employees to choose how they will use their time off without feeling the pressure to justify their absence to the boss. With PTOs, employees can take time off for any reason as long as it is scheduled with supervisors. Time off can also be used for unplanned reasons such as sickness and emergencies.[61]

Vacations

Employers provide paid vacations to give their employees time away from the stresses and strains of the daily work routine. Vacation time allows employees to recharge themselves psychologically and emotionally and can lead to improved job performance.[62] Many companies reward long-term service to the company with more vacation time. For example, Hewlett-Packard employees with one year of service are eligible for 15 days' vacation; after 30 years of service, they are entitled to 30 days.

Figure 12.10 is an international comparison of the annual number of paid vacation days that employees receive from their companies after one year of service. U.S. employees average about 10 days (two weeks) of paid vacation. This is the same as in Japan, but far less than in most

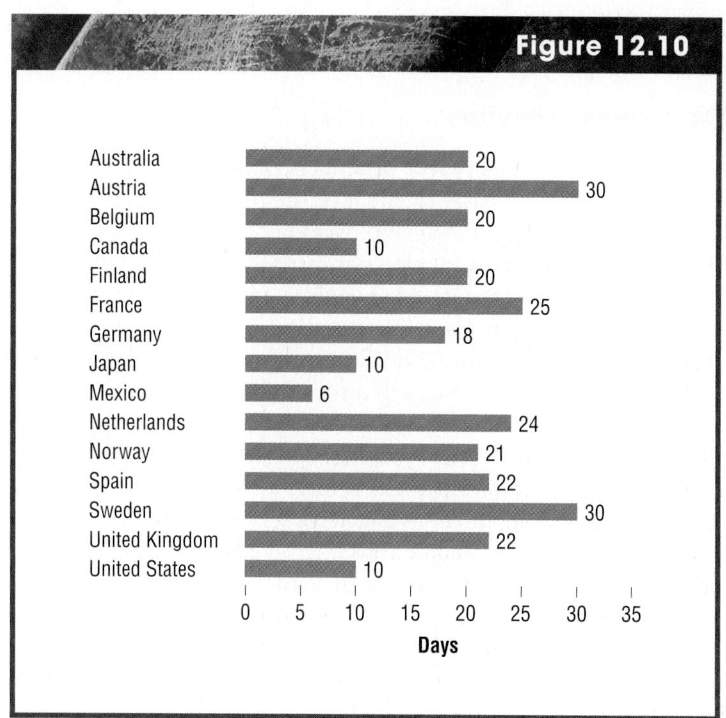

Annual Number of Vacation Days in Various Countries for Employees with One Year of Service

Source: Reprinted, by permission of the publisher, from *HR Focus*. May 1992.

European Union nations. For example, French workers receive 25 days (five weeks) and Swedish workers receive 30 days (six weeks) of paid vacation. Many European countries have laws stipulating the number of paid vacation days that workers must receive, but the United States has no such laws.

Some U.S. businesses are starting to offer employees *sabbatical leave,* which is an extended vacation with pay. Sabbaticals, which can be considered a vacation with a purpose, help employees improve their skills or provide a service to the community. Sabbaticals are very common for college and university faculty, for whom they are a tradition. In the business world, where they are much newer, they are most likely to be found in the high-tech industries, where employee skills become obsolete rapidly and need to be renewed. At Intel, for example, engineers and technical employees who have worked for the company for seven years are entitled to an eight-week paid sabbatical in addition to their annual paid vacation. Employees have used these sabbaticals to continue their education, teach in public schools or colleges, or do volunteer work for nonprofit organizations.[63]

Severance Pay

While not typically thought of as a benefit, the severance pay given to laid-off employees is also a form of paid time off. The type of severance pay offered varies widely. Some organizations offer one month's pay for each year the employee has worked for them, often capped at one year's salary. Severance pay is provided to cushion the shock of termination and to finance the employee's search for a new position.

Severance policies are not limited to large companies. In a recent survey, 66 percent of all companies with fewer than 100 employees said they had a severance policy.[64]

Holidays and Other Paid Time Off

Many employers give their employees paid holidays or pay extra to employees who are required or volunteer to work on holidays. In the United States, employers provide an average of 10 paid holidays per year to employees. Other countries provide similar or more paid holidays with an average of 9 paid holidays in the United Kingdom, 11 in Brazil, 17 in Japan, and 19 in Mexico.[65] While they are not required to, many employers also provide paid leave for jury duty. In manufacturing environments where employees work on tight time schedules, many employers provide (either voluntarily or through a union contract) time for employees to eat, clean up, and get dressed. Some union contracts (particularly those in railroad and other transportation firms) also stipulate that employees will be paid if they are scheduled for work even though no work is available.

Employee Services

The last category of employee benefits is *employee services*, which employers provide on a tax-free or tax-preferred basis to enhance the quality of employees' work or personal life. Figure 12.11 lists some well-known employee services. These include child care, health club memberships, subsidized company cafeterias, parking privileges, and discounts on company products.

Companies are taking a fresh look at employee services and their value to employees. For years, employers offered services tentatively and experimentally, often as kind of a side dish to the main course of medical and health insurance and pension plans. But today companies are using a wide array of services to attract and retain employees, particularly if they cannot offer competitive salaries or raises. John Hancock Mutual Life Insurance of Boston recruits prospective employees with a heavy emphasis on its variety of benefits, including flexible scheduling, dependent-care services, fitness center, and take-home food from the company cafeteria.[66] Andersen Consulting provides concierge services as a benefit for its busy consultants who spend a lot of time away from home traveling on consulting projects. Concierge services take care of personal errands for employees such as car care, taking clothes to the cleaners, event planning, gift buying, and ticket purchasing. This support helps decrease employee stress by reducing the time busy employees spend on personal tasks.[67]

Some companies offer unconventional services. For example, one increasingly popular employee service is free self-defense classes. Model Muggings of Boston, a firm that specializes in teaching self-defense techniques, has seen considerable growth in the demand for its on-site classes. When book publisher Houghton Mifflin began offering Model Muggings classes at its Boston site, 210 of 800 workers signed on immediately.[68]

One of the most valued employee services today is child care.[69] Currently, about 5 percent of U.S. employers provide some child-care benefits, and this percentage is likely to increase because of the growing number of single parents and dual-career households with children.[70]

Companies that decide to offer child-care services have several options. The most expensive is an on-site child-care center. The Issues and Applications feature titled "Children: On-Site at Stride Rite" explores how this system works at the Massachusetts shoe manufacturer. Other child-care options include subsidizing employee child-care costs at off-site child-care centers and establishing a child-care referral service for working parents.[71] Because child care is expen-

Selected Tax-Free or Tax-Preferred Employee Benefits or Services

Figure 12.11

1. Charitable contributions
2. Counseling
   - Financial
   - Legal
   - Psychiatric/psychological
3. Tax preparation
4. Education subsidies
5. Child adoption
6. Child care
7. Elder care
8. Subsidized food service
9. Discounts on merchandise
10. Physical awareness and fitness programs
11. Social and recreational opportunities
12. Parking
13. Transportation to and from work
14. Travel expenses
    - Car reimbursement
    - Tolls and parking
    - Food and entertainment reimbursement
15. Clothing reimbursement/allowance
16. Tool reimbursement/allowance
17. Relocation expenses
18. Emergency loans
19. Credit union
20. Housing
21. Employee assistance programs
22. On-site health services
23. Credit unions
24. Concierge services

Source: *HR Focus*. (2000, June). What benefits are companies offering now? 5–7.

sive, employers usually subsidize 50 percent to 75 percent of the costs and require employees to pay the rest.[72]

Issues and Applications

Children: On-Site at Stride Rite

The following excerpt describes the origins of Stride Rite's on-site day-care center a quarter of a century ago.

> In the early 1970s the neighborhood surrounding Stride Rite's corporate headquarters and factory on Harrison Avenue in Boston's Roxbury neighborhood was showing signs of decay. Crime was common, housing was in disrepair, and business was leaving the area for more stable surroundings. Each time the then-chairman, Arnold Hiott, looked out his office window, he noticed small children wandering in the streets unattended, with little to occupy their time.
>
> Hiott decided that it would make sense to convert some of the company's empty manufacturing space into a child-care center so the neighborhood children would have somewhere to go and something constructive to do. Under his direction and vision, corporate America's first on-site day-care center was born in 1971—years before most companies even considered the idea—as Hiott offered employees the opportunity to bring their own children to the center. Hiott's vision set the tone for the company's corporate culture, which is based on respect for workers and maintaining working conditions that demonstrate that respect.
>
> When the company's headquarters moved to Cambridge, Massachusetts, in 1981, the child-care center moved with it. The facility has expanded into an intergenerational center, in which youngsters and seniors can spend their time together while family members work.
>
> Fees are set at 14 percent of income with a maximum of $140 a week for child care and $100 a week for elder care. These care facilities have a positive effect on the retention and morale of current employees and on the community at large.
>
> Good child care is so tied to the company's commitment to employees' quality of life that when it entered into a joint manufacturing venture with Thailand-based Bangkok Rubber Co. three years ago, Stride Rite insisted that its new Thai partner open a day-care center for employees there, too.[a]

In 1998, the company spent close to $500,000 funding its child-care programs. The company's continued commitment to child care and elder care, coupled with other family-friendly benefits, such as school holiday camps and an on-line grocery delivery service, have landed it a spot on *Working Woman's* list of "100 Best Places to Work for Working Women" seven times.[b]

Sources: [a]Excerpted from *Personnel Journal* (1993, January). Benefits built on base of on-site care, 60. Copyright January 1993. Reprinted with the permission of *Personnel Journal*, ACC Communications, Inc., Costa Mesa, CA: all rights reserved. [b]*Working Woman* (1999, September). 100 best companies for working mothers. www.workingmother.com/100best/companies/stride.html.

Administering Benefits

We conclude this chapter by examining two critical issues in the administration of employee benefits: (1) the use of flexible benefits and (2) the importance of communicating benefits to employees. The HR department usually takes the lead in administering benefits, but managers need to help communicate options to employees, provide advice occasionally, keep records (vacation time, sick days), and be prepared to call on the HR department if disputes arise.

Flexible Benefits

As we have seen, employees have different benefits needs, depending on a number of factors: age, marital status, whether the employee's spouse works and has duplicate benefits coverage, and the presence and ages of children in the household. A flexible benefits program allows employees to choose from a selection of employer-provided benefits such as vision care, dental care, health insurance coverage for dependents, additional life insurance coverage, long-term disability insurance, child care, elder care, more paid vacation days, legal services, and contributions to a 401(k) retirement plan.[73]

As Figure 12.3 shows, 13 percent of large- and medium-sized U.S. employers have a flexible benefits plan in place, among them TRW Systems, Educational Testing Services, DaimlerChrysler, and Bell Atlantic.[74] In the future, as the workforce becomes even more diverse, it is likely that more companies will implement flexible benefits plans.

Types of Flexible Benefits Plans

The three most popular flexible benefits plans are modular plans, core-plus options plans, and flexible spending accounts.[75]

Modular plans consist of a series of different bundles of benefits or different levels of benefits coverage designed for different employee groups. For example, Module A might be the basic package paid for entirely by employer contributions. It would include only the most essential benefits and would be designed for single employees. Module B might include everything in Module A plus additional benefits such as family coverage under the health insurance plan, dental care, and child care. This module might be designed for married employees with young children and could require both employer and employee contributions.

Core-plus options plans consist of a core of essential benefits and a wide array of other benefits options that employees can add to the core. The core is designed to provide minimum economic security for employees, and usually includes basic health insurance, life insurance, long-term disability insurance, retirement benefits, and vacation days. Core-plus options plans give employees "benefits credits" that entitle them to "purchase" the additional benefits that they want. In most cases, all employees receive the same number of credits and may use them either to purchase higher levels of coverage in the core benefits package or to purchase additional benefits such as dental care or child care.

Flexible spending accounts are individual employee accounts funded by the employer, the employee (with pretax dollars), or both. Employees "pay" for the combination of benefits from their accounts. The result can be added take-home pay because employees do not pay taxes on the dollars that they have spent on benefits from their flexible spending accounts. Employee benefits administrators must design flexible spending accounts that conform to the rules specified in Section 125 of the Internal Revenue Code, which governs which benefits are exempt from taxes and which are not. For example, educational benefits and van pooling cannot be included in a flexible spending account because they are taxable benefits.

Challenges with Flexible Benefits

Flexible benefits offer employees the opportunity to tailor a benefits package that is meaningful to them at a reasonable cost to the company. However, they do pose some challenges to benefits administrators. These are:

1. **Adverse selection** The *adverse selection* problem occurs when enough employees use a specific benefit more than the average employee does. Intensive use of a benefit can drive up the benefit's cost and force the employer either to increase spending on benefits or reduce the amount of coverage it provides. For example, employees who know they will need expensive dental work may select a dental-care option instead of some other benefit. Or employees who know they have a high probability of an early death (due to a health condition such as high blood pressure or even a terminal condition such as cancer) may choose extra life insurance coverage. In both cases, the cost of the insurance coverage will eventually be driven up.

   Benefits administrators can deal with the adverse selection problem by placing restrictions on benefits that are likely to result in adverse selection problems. For instance, the company might require those applying for higher life insurance coverage to successfully pass a physical examination. They can also bundle a broad package of benefits together into modules to ensure a more balanced use of each benefit.[76]
2. **Employees who make poor choices** Sometimes employees make a poor choice of benefits and later regret it. For example, an employee who selects additional vacation days instead of long-term disability insurance is likely to regret his choice if he experiences a long-term ill-

ness that exceeds his accumulated amount of sick leave. Benefits administrators can manage this problem by (1) establishing core benefits that minimize an employee's risks and (2) communicating benefits choices effectively so that employees make appropriate choices.

3. **Administrative complexity** A flexible benefits program is difficult to administer and control. Employees must be kept informed of changes in the cost of benefits, the coverage of benefits, and their utilization of benefits. They must also be given the opportunity to change their benefits selection periodically. In addition, the potential for errors in recordkeeping is high. Fortunately, computer software packages can help the HR department manage the recordkeeping aspect of benefits administration. Benefits consultants can assist HR staff in selecting and installing these software programs.

Benefits Communication

Benefits communication is a critical part of administering an employee benefits program. Many employees in companies with excellent benefits packages have never been informed of the value of these benefits and are therefore likely to underestimate their worth.[77] The two major obstacles to effective benefits communication are (1) the increasing complexity of benefits packages and (2) employers' reluctance to devote enough resources to explain these complex packages to employees.

Traditionally, benefits have been communicated via a group meeting during new-employee orientation or a benefits handbook that describes each benefit and its level of coverage. In today's dynamic world of employee benefits, however, more sophisticated communication media (such as videotape presentations and computer software that generates personalized benefits status reports for each employee) are needed. Here are a few of the approaches employers are taking to inform employees about additions to or changes in their benefits:

- General Electric (GE) uses its benefits Web site to give its employees access to benefits information 24 hours a day. GE's benefits Web site has reduced the number of calls to its benefits department by 25,000 calls per month, resulting in substantial cost savings of $175,000 per month. GE reported that a telephone inquiry to the benefits department cost $8.00, whereas a Web site inquiry cost only $1.00.[78]

Figure 12.12

Benefits Web Sites
Lets employees access information about their benefits from home, a hotel, or anywhere with an Internet connection. Employees can also enroll in a different HMO health insurance plan, for example, on the Web site without having to go to the company benefits office and wait for an appointment with a benefits specialist.

Colorful Fliers or Newsletters
Can be mailed to employees' homes so they can read them at leisure.

Audio-Visual Presentations
Slides and videos that present concepts in an upbeat fashion can ensure that employees at different locations receive the same information.

Toll-Free Number
Lets employees call to enroll in a benefits program or hear automated information about these programs 24 hours a day.

Computer Software Package
Allows employees to play "what-if" scenarios with their benefits. For example, they can determine the amount that will be deducted from their paychecks if they enroll in medical plan A as opposed to plan B, or how much money they would save by age 60 if they contribute 6 percent a year to the 401(k) plan.

Sources: Families and Work Institute, 1992. Reprinted by permission; and Cohen, A., and Cohen, S. (1998, November/December). Benefits Websites: Controlling costs while enhancing communication. *Journal of Compensation and Benefits*, 11–18.

Selected Methods of Employee Benefits Communication

- In its innovative 15½-minute video, the Los Angeles County Employees Retirement Association (LACERA) uses a Sam Spade–type detective character to "crack the case" of confusing retirement plans. During the course of the video the animated detective discovers what confusing terms like *noncontributory* and *defined benefits* mean—and so do LACERA's 500 new hires each month.[79]

Figure 12.12 lists some of the ways a company can keep its employees informed about their benefits or answer questions about coverage.

Summary and Conclusions

An Overview of Benefits

Benefits are group membership rewards that provide security for employees and their families. Benefits cost companies about $12,160 per year for the average employee. The cost of employee benefits has increased dramatically in recent years. Although benefits programs are usually centrally controlled in organizations, managers need to be familiar with them so they can counsel employees, recruit job applicants, and make effective managerial decisions.

The Benefits Strategy

The design of a benefits package should be aligned with the business's overall compensation strategy. The benefits strategy requires making choices in three areas: (1) benefits mix, (2) benefits amount, and (3) flexibility of benefits.

Legally Required Benefits

The four benefits that almost all employers must provide are Social Security, workers' compensation, unemployment insurance, and unpaid family and medical leave. These benefits form the core of an employee's benefits package. All other employer-provided benefits are designed to either complement or augment the legally required benefits.

Voluntary Benefits

Businesses often provide five types of voluntary benefits to their employees: (1) Health insurance provides health care for workers and their families. The major types of health insurance plans are traditional health insurance, health maintenance organizations (HMOs), and preferred provider organizations (PPOs). (2) Retirement benefits consist of deferred compensation set aside for an employee's retirement. Funds for retirement benefits can come from employer contributions, employee contributions, or a combination of the two. The Employee Retirement Income Security Act (ERISA) is the major law governing the management of retirement benefits. There are two main types of retirement benefit plans: defined benefit plans and defined contribution plans. In a defined benefit plan, the employer promises to provide a specified amount of retirement income to an employee. A defined contribution plan requires employees to share with their employer some of the risk of and responsibility for managing their retirement assets. The most popular defined contribution plans are 401(k) plans, individual retirement accounts (IRAs), simplified employee pension plans (SEPs), and profit-sharing Keogh plans. (3) Insurance plans protect employees or their survivors from financial disaster in the case of untimely death, accidents that result in disabilities, and serious illnesses. Two kinds of insurance likely to be included in a benefits package are life insurance and long-term disability insurance. (4) Paid time off, which gives employees a break to pursue leisure activities or take care of personal and civic duties, includes sick leave, vacations, severance pay, holidays, and other paid time off. (5) Employee services consist of a cluster of tax-free or tax-preferred services that employers provide to improve the quality of their employees' work or personal life. One of the most valued employee services is child-care benefits.

Administering Benefits

Two important issues involving benefits administration are the use of flexible benefits and communicating benefits to employees. Although the benefits administration is likely to be performed by an HR benefits specialist, managers need to understand their companies' benefits package well enough to help communicate benefits to their employees and keep records.

Key Terms

benefits mix, 404
coinsurance, 401
Consolidated Omnibus Budget Reconciliation Act of 1985 (COBRA), 412
contributions, 401
copayment, 401
deductible, 401

defined benefit plan or pension, 417
defined contribution plan, 418
employee benefits or indirect compensation, 399
Employee Retirement Income Security Act (ERISA), 417
Family and Medical Leave Act of 1993 (FMLA), 409
flexible or cafeteria benefits program, 401
Health Insurance Portability and Accountability Act (HIPAA), 412
health maintenance organization (HMO), 414
Medicare, 406
Pension Benefit Guaranty Corporation (PBGC), 417
portable benefits, 417
preexisting condition, 412
preferred provider organization (PPO), 414
premium, 413
Social Security, 405
supplemental unemployment benefits (SUB), 409
unemployment insurance, 408
vesting, 417
workers' compensation, 406

Discussion Questions

1. How might the increasing diversity of the workforce affect the design of employee benefits packages in large companies?
2. The United States mandates only four benefits, yet U.S. employers provide many other benefits—such as health insurance, retirement benefits, and paid vacations—voluntarily. Why do so many employers provide these benefits even though they are not legally required to do so?
3. What are the advantages and disadvantages of enacting a federal law that requires all employers to provide health insurance for their workers?
4. How do managed-care health insurance plans (HMOs and PPOs) differ from traditional fee-for-service health insurance plans? What are the costs and benefits of each to the employer? To the employee?
5. Why should younger employees (those in their 20s and 30s) care about retirement benefits?
6. Why is cost containment such an important issue in employee benefits programs?
7. As pointed out in the chapter, some countries legislate the provision of more generous employment benefits than the United States does. What are the pros and cons of such an approach?
8. A growing trend in the United States is outsourcing the administration of employee benefits to a company that specializes in this area. What are the advantages and disadvantages of outsourcing benefits administration?
9. Should HR staff recommend particular investments (such as mutual funds) to employees for their 401(k) plans? Why or why not?
10. Only a small percentage of part-time and temporary employees in the United States receive health insurance and retirement benefits compared to employees with full-time jobs. How serious a problem is this? Which people do you think are most likely to be affected by this lack of benefits coverage? What, if anything, can be done about this situation?
11. Some benefits experts claim that unemployment insurance and workers' compensation benefits create a disincentive to work. Why do you think they say this? Do you agree or disagree with this position?
12. According to the international comparison of vacation days given to employees presented in Figure 12.10 on page 423, the United States provides some of the fewest vacation days to employees compared to the amount of vacation days available in most other countries. What factors could account for this discrepancy of vacation days given to American employees compared to their counterparts in other countries?

There is a variety of additional material available on the Web site that accompanies this text. You can access this information by visiting the Web site at **www.prenhall.com/gomez.**

YOU MANAGE IT!

Emerging Trends Case 12.1

Communicating Benefits at the Kraft Intranet Café

Kraft Foods has designed a Web site that communicates a variety of employment policies, including employee benefits information, to its employees. Kraft calls its Web site the Intranet Café because it is fun, friendly, and easy to use and reinforces Kraft's identity as a food company. The intranet is a network that uses Internet technology to link all the computers within the company, but has security barriers that prevent nonemployees from viewing the site.

Kraft Intranet Café's "HR Online" page gives employees the ability to update their personal employee benefits information and learn about benefits programs such as 401(k) retirement benefits, vacation eligibility, or even how to find a doctor in the network of approved physicians in the managed health insurance plan.

One of the most innovative features of the Kraft Intranet Café's "HR Online" page is the information on employee benefits in the area of work/life support that provides resources for women and men trying to balance child-rearing or elder-care responsibilities with professional goals. Kraft employees find information, forms, and contact names for its benefits programs online. Here are some of the programs and their features that are available to employees online:

- ***Maternity leave*** Exempt employees are given maternity leave after disability leave. These new mothers are also given gradual return to the workplace when needed and additional financial assistance for child care.
- ***Sick days for care of dependents*** Most salaried employees can use up to 50 percent of their paid sick days for the care of a sick child, spouse, or parent.
- ***Relocation services*** To help assess the readiness of a family to relocate, the company provides training to bring forward the issues the family needs to consider.
- ***Education reimbursement*** Full-time employees may qualify for 100 percent education reimbursement if course work relates directly to job function. Scholarships for employees' children are also available.
- ***Flexible work arrangements*** With agreement from individual supervisors, an employee can determine a work schedule that balances the needs of the department with a personal situation. Options include working at home, flextime, part-time, and job sharing.

Critical Thinking Questions

1. What are the advantages of using a Web site over using more traditional methods of providing information and enrollment forms for employee benefits programs? What are the disadvantages of using Web sites for this purpose?
2. If Web sites become the dominant source of learning about benefits plans for employees nationwide, what impact would this have on the profession of HRM? Do you think there will be fewer or more opportunities in the area of employee benefits and what would those opportunities be?

Team Exercise

With a group of four or five students discuss how a Web site similar to the one used at Kraft Foods could be used to post information about pay to employees. What type of pay information could be posted on the Web site? What type of pay information should be kept off the Web site and only given out on a "need to know" basis? Why do you think it is more problematic and controversial to use a Web site for pay information than for employee benefits information?

Source: Adapted from Isaacson, K. (1998, Winter). Finding work/life solutions at the Kraft Intranet Café. *ACA Journal*, 19–20.

YOU MANAGE IT!

Emerging Trends Case 12.2

Employee Retirement Savings in 401(k) Plans Collapse at Enron

Marie Thibaut spent 15 years as an administrative assistant at Enron in Houston, Texas. During that time, she dutifully put 15% of her salary into a 401(k) retirement plan, investing the entire amount in the company's rapidly climbing stock. Enron then matched that investment with yet more company shares. By the winter of 2000, she had amassed close to $500,000 in stock, enough for the 61-year-old divorcée to begin contemplating retirement. "My children told me I should diversify," Thibaut said. "But all the mutual funds were going down, and I just kept going up." She's not going up any longer. In 2001

Enron declared bankruptcy and Thibaut was out of work, a victim of one of the worst corporate collapses in history. Her 401(k) is worth just $22,000.

That depressing story has been repeated thousands of times at Enron, Lucent, Nortel, and other technology companies whose stocks have retreated after the Internet bubble burst in 2000. But, despite the punishing market and calls for diversification, workers continue to pour a huge portion of their retirement money into their employer's shares of stock. Benefits consulting firm Hewitt Associates estimates that at the end of 2001 almost 30% of the $71 billion in assets in some 1.5 million 401(k) plans were invested in the stock of the sponsoring company. At some places the proportion is even higher. Microsoft employees keep 46% of their 401(k) funds in company stock. At Enron, the figure was 62%. At Coca-Cola 81% of employees' 401(k) funds are in company stock. To make matters worse, many of these retirement plans, like Enron's, restrict the sale of stock. For example, Enron employees were not able to sell their company stock until they reached 50 years of age.

As every undergraduate business student who has taken a basic course in finance knows, it is very risky to put a large percentage of a person's retirement funds into the stock of one company—doing that violates the basic financial principle of asset diversification. So why have millions of Americans made this mistake with their retirement funds?

First, many Americans have not taken a basic course in finance and are unaware of the risk of owning so much of a single stock, especially when it is the stock in a company that they believe they know—the company where they work.

Moreover, companies should be matching employees' 401(k) contributions in cash, not in stock. But stock matches are cheaper and many executives think it is fine for their employees to hold big stakes in the stock of their company. Many of these executives also hold large amounts of company stock, but they are far wealthier than ordinary employees and are better able than those employees to withstand the investment risk when the company stock plunges.

Unbalanced, one-stock 401(k) plans violate every safety-and-soundness principle of investing, according to New Jersey Senator Jon Corzine, who was formerly cochair of the investment firm Goldman Sachs. For example, defined benefit pension plans are not permitted to put more than 10% of their money into a single stock according to the regulations governing pension plans. Institutional investors, such as mutual funds and insurance firms, generally set a cap at 5% of their money in any one company stock.

These standards of prudence are backed by both academic studies and common sense, Corzine says. Employees counting on company stock may get lucky for a few years. But, over time, they run a higher and higher risk of major loss.

Critical Thinking Questions

1. Why do many employers of large companies such as Enron and Coca-Cola decide to give the matching contributions to their employees' 401(k) plans in the form of company stock instead of cash? Do you think this human resource practice is ethical? Explain your position.
2. Suppose your employer fully matched your contribution to your 401(k) plan in company stock. What can you do to reduce your investment risk? Would it be a good idea not to contribute any money to your company's 401(k) plan? Do you think it would be a good idea to diversify your savings between your company 401(k) plan and a personal IRA plan that you start? What other investment strategies might you want to explore?

Team Exercise

With a group of four or five students discuss the merits of making a government policy to regulate company 401(k) retirement plans to protect employees' retirement savings from disasters such as what happened to employees at Enron. Here are some possible regulations for you to discuss in your group: (1) regulation to require that companies have a ceiling of no more than 20% of company stock to be applied to any single employee's 401(k) retirement plan; and (2) a regulation permitting employees to be able to sell the company stock from their employer matching contribution after a one-year waiting period, so that an employee could use the sale of the stock to buy mutual funds or bonds that are less risky. Regulations of an employee benefit such as 401(k) plans unfortunately may lead to unexpected consequences. What unexpected consequences could occur as a result of legislation that regulates 401(k) plans? Finally, be prepared to let the class know if your group recommends in favor of 401(k) plan regulations to protect employee retirement plans or recommends in favor of rejecting any regulations. Give your reason for your group decision.

Sources: Adapted from Kahn, J. (2002, January 7). When 401(k)s are KO'd. *Fortune*, 104; Quinn, J. (2002, January 21). 401(k)s and the Enron mess. *Newsweek*, 25; and *The Economist*. (2001, December 15). When labor and capital don't mix: Enron's demise unmasks conflicts in company pension plans, 60.

YOU MANAGE IT!

Issues and Exercises Case 12.3

Keeping Workers' Compensation Costs Under Control

Oregon Retirement Apartments is an apartment complex in Portland, Oregon, that provides housing, meals, and some assisted living services for its residents. Approximately 300 residents live in the facility. Fifty people work for the complex: a professional staff of administrators and social workers and an operations staff consisting of food service employees, housekeepers, building and maintenance workers, and night managers. Oregon Retirement Apartments tries to provide a rich social and cultural life for its residents (most of whom are in their 70s and 80s) so that they can live independently in a pleasant environment.

Barbara Spector, the facility's executive director, is very concerned about employees who abuse workers' compensation. This concern results from an incident involving Pat O'Toole, a housekeeping employee who filed a claim for workers' compensation benefits for a work-related back injury. Barbara suspected that Pat's injury did not occur on the job and therefore contested the claim. The investigation that followed showed that the claim was indeed false; Pat had sustained her back injury in a skiing accident, not during work hours. The investigation also revealed Pat's long history of filing workers' compensation claims with previous employers. According to files maintained by the state government, Pat has filed a total of 12 workers' compensation claims over her employment life.

After the incident with Pat, Barbara decided to establish a new hiring policy: People with a high likelihood of filing workers' compensation claims will not be hired. She justifies this policy change by citing her responsibility for containing the cost of workers' compensation insurance (which is adjusted according to the safety record of a company's workforce). The new policy requires Oregon Retirement's HR staff to examine the workers' compensation records of all job applicants at the same time that their references are checked. The services of a local HR consulting firm are used to scan the workers' compensation database for evidence of an applicant's previous claims. Job applicants who have filed three or more workers' compensation claims are considered a "high risk" and dropped from the applicant pool.

Critical Thinking Questions

1. Is Barbara Spector's policy of rejecting job applicants who have filed three or more workers' compensation claims fair? Is it ethical?
2. What impact does the Americans with Disabilities Act (see Chapter 3) have on an employment practice that rejects applicants who have previously filed workers' compensation claims? Could this practice discriminate against people with disabilities?

Team Exercises

With a partner or a small group, develop some alternative employment practices to help Barbara Spector avoid hiring people who are likely to misuse workers' compensation benefits.

Discuss the following situation with your partner or group: During a job interview, an applicant reports that he has never applied for workers' compensation benefits. After hiring the applicant, the employer checks on this information and finds out that the employee lied. What should the company do?

YOU MANAGE IT!

Issues and Exercises Case 12.4

Managing Employee Benefits with Fair Procedures

One of the most important aspects of managing employee benefits is ensuring that the company uses fair procedures to apply the benefit to employees. The purpose of this exercise is to give you some practice in developing skills to handle some ethical or administrative challenges involving employee benefits that a manager or HR specialist could encounter. When determining if your proposed benefit procedure is fair, make sure you consider all the parties involved in the decision before you choose the best alternative. Read each of the following scenarios before answering the questions that follow:

Scenario 1

Sue is a 55-year-old employee at Company A. Her children are out of college and her parents are deceased. Company A offers a child-care program to all employees along with an elder-care program. However, Sue, like many other employees at Company A, currently has no need for these services and will not need them in the future. Should the firm retain these benefits programs or get rid of them? Should the company offer alternate benefits for employees who have no use for such services?

Scenario 2

Dan is the manager of employee benefits at Company B. He noticed that some employees use sick leave as a way to take care of personal business such as caring for a sick child, having a dental appointment, or catching up on work at home. Currently each employee is entitled to one sick leave day per month. To improve efficiency, Dan eliminated the sick leave benefit and replaced it with six personal leave days that employees can take on a discretionary basis by notifying their supervisor in advance. Dan reasoned that under the former sick leave policy employees who play by the rules and only use leave when they are sick are penalized, whereas under the new personal leave benefit policy everybody has access to personal leave days to use for illnesses or other reasons for taking leave. Employees are not rewarded with days off for withholding the truth under this new benefit policy. Do you agree or disagree with Dan's decision?

Scenario 3

Frank works 25 hours per week at Company C, a mail-order firm, in the packaging department. He receives no benefits other than those required by the law. Frank does the same work as three other full-time employees who work in his department. These full-time employees qualify for pensions, health insurance, long-term disability, child-care, and vacations—none of which are provided to Frank. Is it ethical or fair to not provide benefits to part-time employees, even if they are doing the same work as full-time employees? Assume that Frank would like to work full-time, wants to receive the benefits, and feels frustrated because he is not eligible to receive them. Remember, too, that the firm is not legally required to pay Frank's or other part-time employees' benefits. The company justifies its position because it saves money on benefits costs by hiring part-time employees, including Frank.

Critical Thinking Questions

1. In each of the three scenarios determine what the benefits issues are. For example, in scenario 1 does it make sense to get rid of a benefit that some employees use and others do not use? How important is this benefit? In scenario 2, is it better to eliminate a benefit that a few abuse and replace it with a different one, or should a different tactic be employed? In scenario 3, do part-time employees deserve the same benefits as full-time employees or different ones?
2. Assume you are a manager in each of the three scenarios. How would you manage the benefits procedures in each situation? Assume you want to be as fair as possible to the employees in your unit. What would you do? How would you determine if the employees view your solution as a fair one?

Team Exercise

Work with a small group of three or four students to develop a fair benefits procedure or policy for each of the three scenarios. For scenario 1 develop a benefits procedure or policy for the situation when employees are not able to use a benefit that is provided by the employer. For scenario 2 develop a procedure or policy that addresses employee abuse of sick-leave benefits. For scenario 3 develop a procedure or policy for the situation when part-time employees receive reduced benefits compared to full-time employees. Note the areas of agreement and disagreement within your group discussion. How important do you think the manager's decision-making *process* for achieving the benefits procedure or policy is?

Source: Adapted from Nkomo, S. M., Fottler, M. D., and McAfee, R. B. (2000). *Applications in human resource management* (4th ed.), 216–219. Cincinnati, OH. South-Western.

Part VI: Governance

Developing Employee Relations

Challenges

After reading this chapter, you should be able to deal more effectively with the following challenges:

1. **Outline** how good employee relations and communications can contribute to business goals.
2. **Describe** the three types of programs used to facilitate employee communications.
3. **Explain** the various appeals procedures through which employees can challenge management actions.
4. **Understand** how employee assistance programs can help employees deal with personal problems that may interfere with job performance.
5. **Summarize** the technological innovations that allow managers to disseminate information quickly and explain how information dissemination influences an organization's employee relations.

Nancy is a customer service manager for a copier company. She started about four years ago as a customer service representative. In her job she occasionally came into contact with customers who would "hit" on her or make suggestive comments, but she was always able to handle those situations. Usually, a diplomatic brush-off was enough. Now, however, she faces a situation that she does not know how to handle.

It all began six months ago when she was promoted to her current position of customer service manager. She really likes the job and the company, and hopes to be promoted further. The problem is her boss. Steve was largely responsible for her promotion, and Nancy feels indebted to him. But after about two months, she realized that his attention to her went beyond work. He began to tell her about his marriage problems and commented that he found her very attractive. After all the help he had given her, Nancy hesitated to tell him directly that she was not interested in him romantically. But after he started sending flowers and asking her out, she finally asked him to stop.

That did not work. In fact, things got much worse. Steve's requests became more direct, and now they had threats attached. Specifically, he told her that if she did not begin a relationship with him, he would not only not recommend her for any further promotions, but he also would try to get her terminated. Nancy feels trapped. She knows that Steve is well liked by his colleagues, and she is afraid that if she complains about him, she will only lose her job sooner.

Then she read in the monthly newsletter about the company's employee relations program. One of the program's goals is to give employees confidential access to an employee relations specialist who can help them resolve interpersonal problems on the job. Nancy called the confidential hot line and set up an appointment with a counselor. She is looking forward to explaining her dilemma to someone who is impartial and in a position to help her.

THE MANAGERIAL PERSPECTIVE

Dealing successfully with a problem like Nancy's requires effective employee relations—the subject of this chapter. Companies with strong employee relations benefit because their employees are highly motivated to expend their best efforts. In exchange, the employees expect to be treated fairly and recognized for their achievements. To develop and sustain relations, employers must keep employees informed of company policies and strategies. That way, employees can learn new behaviors or skills as needed and understand the workings of the firm more fully. In addition, employers must have policies that allow employees to discuss problems with or communicate important information to company representatives that can respond effectively.

As a future manager, you will play a key role in employee relations. You must listen to your employees' concerns and feelings, observe their experiences, and help keep employees informed about changes in the business and the effects of such changes.

HR specialists also play a crucial role in employee relations. If they develop communication policies and procedures that apply appropriate communication tools in a timely manner, employees can access more abundant, higher quality information and can communicate more effectively with management. Managers and HR specialists must work in partnership to ensure that the communication policies and procedures bolster employee relations.

In this chapter we explore how managers and employee relations specialists can work together to coordinate an employee relations program. Next, we present a model of communication and explore specific policies that give employees access to important information. Finally, we examine some programs for recognizing employees' individual and team contributions to company goals.

The Roles of the Manager and the Employee Relations Specialist

Good *employee relations* involve providing fair and consistent treatment to all employees so that they will be committed to the organization. Companies with good employee relations are likely to have an HR strategy that places a high value on employees as stakeholders in the business. Employees who are treated as *stakeholders* have certain rights within the organization and can expect to be treated with dignity and respect. For example, Johnson & Johnson, a company known for its excellent employee relations, is committed to a philosophy of respect for the individual. To foster good employee relations, managers must listen to and understand what employees are saying and experiencing, keep them informed about what management plans to do with the business, and tell them how those plans may affect their jobs. They should also give employees the freedom to air grievances about management decisions. There may be good reasons for not changing the decision, but management should at least listen to the grievances.

Employee relations representative
A member of the HR department who ensures that company policies are followed and consults with both supervisors and employees on specific employee relations problems.

Employee relations policy
A policy designed to communicate management's thinking and practices concerning employee-related matters and prevent problems in the workplace from becoming serious.

Effective employee relations require cooperation between managers and **employee relations representatives.** These specialists are members of the HR department who act as internal consultants to the business. They try to ensure that company policies and procedures are followed and advise both supervisors and employees on specific employee relations problems. **Employee relations policies** provide channels to resolve such problems before they become serious.

For example, an employee whose supervisor has denied her request for two weeks' vacation (to which she is entitled according to the employee handbook) may ask the employee relations representative to speak to her supervisor and clarify why she is being denied her preferred vacation time. Or a supervisor may request assistance because he suspects that one of his subordinates has an alcohol abuse problem that is affecting job performance. In both these cases, the employee relations representative will try to resolve the problem within the letter and spirit of the appropriate employment policy, while carefully balancing the interests of the supervisor, the employee, and the company.

Employee relations representatives may also develop new policies that help maintain fairness and efficiency in the workplace. The client in this situation may be a top manager who needs assistance in drafting a new policy on smoking in the workplace or the hiring of employees' spouses and other relatives.

Developing Employee Communications

Many companies have found that the key to a good employee relations program is a *communication channel* that gives employees access to important information and an opportunity to express their ideas and feelings. When supervisors are familiar with employment policies and employees are aware of their rights, there is less opportunity for misunderstandings to arise and productivity to drop.

Because corporations are very complex, they must develop numerous communication channels to move information up, down, and across the organizational structure. For instance, Intel provides many communication channels that allow employees and managers to speak with one another and share information. Managers communicate with their employees by walking around and talking to them informally, sponsoring newsletters, and providing a Web site with key employment policies. Employees give feedback to managers through e-mail, memos, meetings, and other forms of face-to-face communication. As today's organizations have delegated more responsibilities and decision-making authority to employees, the importance of making more information available to employees has increased substantially.[1]

Types of Information

Two forms of information are sent and received in communications: facts and feelings. *Facts* are pieces of information that can be objectively measured or described. Examples are the cost of a computer, the daily defect rate in a manufacturing plant, and the size of the deductible payment in the company-sponsored health insurance policy. Recent technological advances have made factual information more accessible to more employees than ever before. Facts can be stored in databases and widely distributed to employees by networks of personal computers.

Feelings are employees' emotional responses to the decisions made or actions taken by managers or other employees. Managers who implement decisions must be able to anticipate or respond to the feelings of the employees who are affected by those decisions. If they cannot or do not, the plan may fail. For example, a public university changed its health insurance coverage without consulting the employees affected by the change. When these employees learned of their diminished coverage, they responded so negatively that the manager of employee benefits resigned. (The health insurance policy was subsequently changed to be more favorable to the employees.)

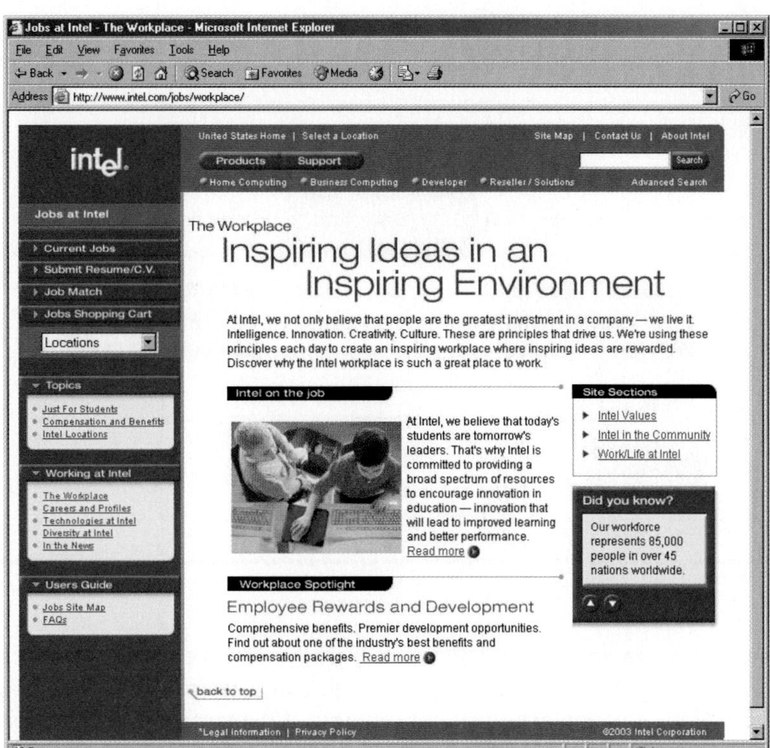

Intel has strong relations with its employees because it places a strong emphasis on two-way honest communication.

A company must be especially careful of employees' feelings when it is restructuring or downsizing and laying off a considerable portion of its workforce. A production employee at a large East Coast manufacturing firm remembers how top management kept issuing memos that said, in effect, "we're doing fine, we're doing fine," and then suddenly announced layoffs. Survivors of the layoff were shocked and hurt and became highly distrustful of management.[2]

Organizations need to design communication channels that allow employees to communicate facts and feelings. In many cases, these channels must provide for face-to-face communication because many feelings are conveyed nonverbally. Employees cannot write on a piece of paper or record on a computer database their complex emotional reactions to a decision that they fear will cost them their jobs.

How Communication Works

Figure 13.1 is a simple representation of the communications process within an organization. Communication starts with a *sender*, who has a message to send to the *receiver*. The sender must *encode* the message and select a *communication channel* that will deliver it to the receiver. In communicating facts, the message may be encoded with words, numbers, or digital symbols; in communicating feelings, it may be encoded as body language or tone of voice.

Some communication channels are more appropriate than others for sending certain messages. For example, memos are usually not very effective for sending information that has a lot of feeling in it. A more effective channel for conveying strong emotions is a meeting or other form of face-to-face communication.

Communication is not effective unless the receiver is able to *decode* the message and understand its true meaning. The receiver may misinterpret a message for many reasons. For example, the message may be filled with technical jargon that makes it difficult to decode, the receiver may misinterpret the sender's motives for sending the message, or the sender may send a message that lends itself to multiple interpretations.

Because of the strong possibility of miscommunication, important communications should include opportunities for *feedback* from the receiver. This way the sender can clarify the message if its true meaning is not received. In addition, noise in the sender's or receiver's environment may block or distort the message. *Noise* is anything that disrupts the message: inaccurate com-

The Communications Process Within an Organization

Figure 13.1

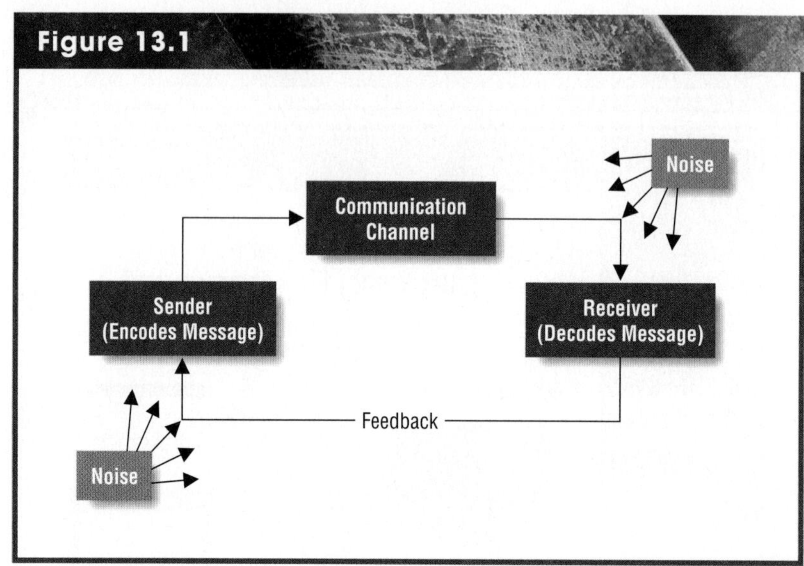

munication by the sender, fatigue or distraction on the part of the receiver, or actual noise that distorts the message (other people talking, traffic, telephone ringing). Very often noise takes the form of information overload. For example, if the receiver gets 100 e-mail messages in one day, she may not read the most important one very carefully because she is overwhelmed by the barrage of information.

Communications that provide for feedback are called *two-way communications* because they allow the sender and receiver to interact with each other. Communications that provide no opportunity for feedback are one-way. Although ideally all communications should be interactive, this is not always possible in large organizations, where large amounts of information must be distributed to many employees. For example, top executives at large companies do not usually have the time to speak to all the employees they need to inform about a new product about to be released. Instead, they may communicate with the employees via a memo, report, or e-mail. In contrast, top executives at small businesses have much less difficulty communicating with their employees. The Manager's Notebook titled "How to Communicate Useful Feedback to Employees" offers tips for managers who want to improve the communication process of giving and receiving feedback. (Note that we offered additional information on giving feedback during performance appraisals in Chapter 7.)

MANAGER'S NOTEBOOK

How to Communicate Useful Feedback to Employees

Here are some ways to communicate useful feedback to subordinates and other employees.

- **Focus on specific behaviors.** Provide feedback that lets employees know what specific behaviors are effective or need improvement. That way, they are able to sustain and intensify the desired behaviors and are motivated to change those that may be inappropriate. Avoid vague statements such as "you have a bad attitude." It is better to give more specific feedback such as "you ignored the customer when she tried to get your attention."
- **Keep the feedback impersonal.** Try to keep the feedback descriptive rather than judgmental or evaluative. To do this, focus on job-related behaviors rather than make value judgments about the employee's motivations. Rather than telling an employee "you are incompetent," it would be preferable to say, "I noticed some gaps in your product knowledge when you gave a presentation to the marketing group."

- **Give the feedback at the appropriate time and place.** The best time to give feedback is right after the person who should receive the feedback engages in the behavior at issue. A manager who waits months until the formal performance appraisal to give the feedback has lost an opportunity to coach and motivate an employee to improve at the time the behavior was observed. Similarly, the appropriate place to provide critical feedback is in private. Giving negative feedback publicly can humiliate the person being critiqued and is likely to provoke anger rather than the intended result of the message. Conversely, giving positive feedback in front of others can be motivational not only to the person who is being praised, but also to others who may learn from the good example set by the employee whose behaviors are positively recognized.
- **Focus negative feedback on behaviors that can be controlled by the employee.** When giving negative feedback to another employee, focus on behaviors that the employee can control. For example, it may be appropriate for a manager to criticize an employee who is late arriving at a team meeting. However, if the manager asked the employee to handle a customer service problem that took longer to solve than originally anticipated, the criticism about tardiness may be unfair.

Sources: Adapted from Nahavandi, A., and Malekzadeh, A. B. (1999). *Organizational Behavior,* 437–438. Upper Saddle River, NJ, Prentice Hall, and Robbins, S. P. and Hunsaker P. L. (1996). *Training in Interpersonal Skills* (2nd ed.), 73–75. Upper Saddle River, NJ, Prentice Hall.

Downward and Upward Communication

Employee relations specialists help to maintain both downward communication and upward communication in an organization. **Downward communication** allows managers to implement their decisions and to influence employees lower in the organizational hierarchy. It can also be used to disperse information controlled by top managers. **Upward communication** allows employees at lower levels to communicate their ideas or feelings to higher-level decision makers. Unfortunately, many organizations erect serious barriers in their upward communication channels. For example, in many companies it is considered disloyal for an employee to go "over the head" of an immediate supervisor and communicate with a higher-level executive about a problem.

Downward communication
Communication that allows managers to implement their decisions and to influence employees lower in the organizational hierarchy.

Upward communication
Communication that allows employees at lower levels to communicate their ideas and feelings to higher-level decision makers.

One final but very important note concerning communication in general: The U.S. economy is shifting from an industrial base to an information base. This revolution is as significant as the move from an agrarian to an industrial economy over a century ago. In an industrial economy, production processes are the focus of concern. In an information economy, communication (the production and transmission of information) is the focus. How information is communicated, both internally and externally, is becoming more and more important to organizational success. A strong symbol of this transition is the rise of Microsoft, the software giant. Software is almost pure information; it has no tangible aspect. Yet the person who supplies most of the world's operating system software (the kind that controls a computer's operation and directs the processing of programs) and application software (the specific programs run on the computer)—Bill Gates, the founder and CEO of Microsoft—is reportedly one of the wealthiest people in the United States.

Encouraging Effective Communications

Working with supervisors and managers, employee relations representatives can aid effective communications by developing and maintaining three types of programs: information dissemination, employee feedback, and employee assistance.

Information Dissemination Programs

Information is a source of power in organizations. In traditional top-down hierarchies, top managers zealously guard information as their special preserve. But the information age has forced many businesses to forge a new set of rules. Today organizations depend more and more on knowledge workers to produce their product or service. **Knowledge workers** (for example, programmers, writers, educators) transform information into a product or service and need large amounts of information to do their jobs effectively. For these workers, the dissemination of information throughout the organization is critical to providing high-quality service and products to the organization's customers.

Knowledge worker
A worker who transforms information into a product or service.

Information dissemination involves making information available to decision makers, wherever they are located. Employees who have access to abundant information are more likely to feel empowered and are better able to participate in decision making. Information dissemination also helps managers adopt more participative leadership styles and work configurations, leading to greater employee involvement and, ultimately, to better employee relations.

Information dissemination
The process of making information available to decision makers, wherever they are located.

The most important methods of disseminating information to employees are employee handbooks, written communications, audiovisual communications, electronic communications, meetings, retreats, and informal communications.

The Employee Handbook

The *employee handbook* is probably the most important source of information that the HR department can provide. It sets the tone for the company's overall employee relations philosophy,[3] informing both employees and supervisors about company employment policies and procedures and communicating employees' rights and responsibilities. The handbook lets employees know that they can expect consistent and uniform treatment on issues that affect their job or status in the company. It also tells supervisors how to evaluate, reward, and discipline their employees. It can protect supervisors and the company from making uninformed and arbitrary decisions that may hurt the workforce's morale or lead to litigation from angry employees.

Employee handbooks contain information issues such as employee benefits, performance evaluation, dress codes, employment of family members, smoking, probationary employment periods, drug-testing procedures, family leave policies, sexual harassment, discipline procedures, and safety rules.[4] Handbooks need to be updated annually to reflect the current legal environment and to remain consistent with the company's overall employee relations philosophy.

A Question of Ethics

Some companies attempt to restrict the behavior of employees while they are off the job. The most common restriction is a prohibition against smoking. Less common is a prohibition against public drinking. Is it ethical for a company to try to control its employees' behavior while they are not on the job?

Although sometimes considered a tool for only large corporations, small businesses can also benefit from the use of employee handbooks. For example, a restaurant owner recently discharged an employee who did not pay for a meal, even though there was no written policy on meals and the owner had previously allowed some other employees to eat meals at the restaurant. The ex-employee took the owner to court over this misunderstanding. The owner spent over $7,000 in legal fees defending the decision to discharge the ex-employee. This dispute could have been avoided if an "employee meals" policy had been distributed in an employee handbook. Unfortunately, the owner did not think an employee handbook was necessary.[5]

Court decisions in some states have suggested that employee handbooks may constitute an implied contract between employer and employee that restricts the employer's freedom to discharge employees without just cause. To avoid such restrictive interpretations by the courts, employers should include at the end of their handbook a disclaimer stating that employees can be discharged for any reason or no reason and that the handbook does not constitute an employment contract, but rather it is a set of guidelines.[6] Some firms go even further to protect themselves: They ask all new employees to sign an employee handbook acknowledgment form stating they have received the handbook; will refer to it for company rules, regulations, and policies; and understand that it is in no way a contract. Figure 13.2 shows a sample employee handbook acknowledgment form.[7] Not surprisingly, such forms have been controversial because the legal protection they provide the employer also tends to undermine the goodwill the handbook was designed to foster.

Still, employee handbooks can help prevent or solve problems in the workforce. Figure 13.3 (page 442) shows how a firm might communicate an enlightened nepotism policy through its employee handbook. (**Nepotism** is the practice of favoring relatives over others in the workplace.) The policy communicated in Figure 13.3 protects the rights of family members but balances those rights with the company's need to avoid conflicts of interest that could affect the efficiency of its business.

Nepotism
The practice of favoring relatives over others in the workplace.

Figure 13.2

TJP INC. EMPLOYEE HANDBOOK ACKNOWLEDGMENT FORM

This employee handbook has been given to ______________________
on (date) ______________________
by ______________________ (title) ______________________
Employee's effective starting date ______________________
Employee's pay period ______________________
Employee's hours and workweek are ______________________
Welcome to TJP, Inc. Below is a list of your benefits with their effective date:

Benefit	**Effective Date**
Hospitalization ______________________	__________
Life insurance ______________________	__________
Retirement ______________________	__________
Vacation ______________________	__________
Sick leave ______________________	__________
Holidays ______________________	__________
Personal days ______________________	__________
Bereavement ______________________	__________
Workers' compensation ______________________	__________
Social Security ______________________	__________
Your first performance appraisal will be on ______________________	__________

I understand that my employee handbook is for informational purposes only and that I am to read and refer to the employee handbook for information on employment work rules and company policies. TJP, Inc. may modify, revoke, suspend or terminate any and all policies, rules, procedures, and benefits at any time without prior notice to company employees. This handbook and its statements do not create a contract between TJP, Inc. and its employees. This handbook and its statements do not affect in any way the employment-at-will relationship between TJP, Inc. and its employees.

(Employee's signature) ______________________
(Date) ______________________

Sample Employee Handbook Acknowledgment Form

Source: Reprinted, by permission of the publisher, from *Management Review*, June 1993.

In family-owned businesses in which owners often groom sons, daughters, or other family members to take over the company, nepotism is taken for granted. In these situations, the question becomes: How much nepotism is okay? It is not uncommon for company owners to put their children in positions of power and grant them pay, titles, and privileges denied to more experienced or qualified company employees. Naturally, this antagonizes nonfamily employees. Family business consultants Craig E. Aronoff and John L. Ward recommend that family members meet the following three qualifications before making the family business a permanent career:

- Get an education appropriate for the job sought.
- Work three to five years outside the family business.
- Start in an existing, necessary job within the family business and honor precedents for pay and performance.[8]

Written Communications: Memos, Financial Statements, Newsletters, and Bulletin Boards

There are many other forms of written communication besides the employee handbook. *Memos* are useful for conveying changes in policies or procedures. For example, when there is a change in coverage of a specific type of medical procedure, the affected group of employees can be notified by written memo. In addition, the company should disseminate *financial reports* to make

Figure 13.3

Nepotism Policy

Section 1. **Family Member Employment.** The company considers it an unlawful employment practice regarding a member of an individual's family working or who has worked for the Company to:

a. Refuse to hire or employ that individual;
b. Bar or terminate from employment that individual; or
c. Discriminate against that individual in compensation or in terms, conditions, or privileges of employment.

Section 2. **Conflict of Interest.** The Company is not required to hire or continue in employment an individual if it:

a. Would place the individual in a position of exercising supervisory, appointment, or grievance adjustment authority over a member of the individual's family, or in a position of being subject to the authority that a member of the individual's family exercises; or
b. Would cause the Company to disregard a bona fide occupational requirement reasonably necessary to the normal operation of the Company's business.

Section 3. **Member of an Individual's Family.** Member of an individual's family includes wife, husband, son, daughter, mother, father, brother, brother-in-law, sister, sister-in-law, son-in-law, daughter-in-law, father-in-law, mother-in-law, aunt, uncle, niece, nephew, stepparent, or stepchild of the individual.

Source: Adapted from Decker, K. H. (1989). *A manager's guide to employee privacy: Policies and procedures,* 231–232. New York, Wiley.

Sample Nepotism Policy Statement from an Employee Handbook

employees knowledgeable about the company's performance. Shareholders are routinely given this information, but employees should receive it, too, because it is an important source of feedback on their aggregate performance.[9]

One activity for which the HR department is likely to have direct responsibility is the production and distribution of an employee newsletter. The *newsletter* is usually a short monthly or quarterly publication designed to keep employees informed of important events, meetings, and transitions and to provide inspirational stories about employee and team contributions to the business (Figure 13.4).[10] Newsletters help foster community spirit in a company or unit. The advent of desktop publishing packages for personal computers has made newsletter production and distribution feasible for even the smallest of companies. For example, Valleylab, a medical instruments manufacturer in Colorado, started a newsletter to inform its employees about quality improvements made by various employee teams under its total quality management (TQM) program. Some managers use a simple *bulletin board* to post current team performance data and comparisons with outside competitors or other teams with the company. Moreover, a common feature of a company Web site is to have an *electronic bulletin board* that contains announcements of interest to employees that can be posted quickly and can be viewed by all the employees regardless of their location. For example, an employee who anticipates the start of a one-year international assignment may want to post an announcement on the electronic bulletin board that he is willing to sublease his home to a person for a year with an enhanced likelihood of having the message reach more employees this way. Also, reprints of stories about the company and its employees published in the news media can be posted or linked on the electronic bulletin board for all to read.

Audiovisual Communications

New technologies have made it possible to disseminate information that goes beyond the printed word. Visual images and audio information are powerful communication tools. The widespread use of videocassette recorders (VCRs) in the home allows companies to distribute videotapes to employees when they need to convey important information. Managers at the Rocky Flats Nuclear Weapons Arsenal in Denver used prerecorded videotapes quite successfully to announce a downsizing (due to defense cuts) that would result in the layoff of several thousand employees. Each employee received a videotape containing a message from top executives explaining the reasons for the workforce reduction and the company's new mission. The tape also included a personal message from then-President George Bush explaining why the end of

Figure 13.4
Sample Employee Newsletter
Source: Pearson Education.

the Cold War meant a change in the U.S. government's spending priorities. In this case, audiovisual communication helped to maintain employee morale despite all the changes and uncertainty at the company.

Teleconferencing allows people with busy schedules to participate in meetings even when they are a great distance away from the conference location (or one another). Through video cameras and other sophisticated equipment, teleconferencing makes it possible for employees at remote locations to interact with one another as if they were all seated in the same conference room. One four-hour video conference that keeps five people off an airplane and out of hotels and restaurants could save a company at least $5,000.

Teleconferencing
The use of audio and video equipment to allow people to participate in meetings even when they are a great distance away from the conference location or one another.

With teleconferencing systems ranging in price from $10,000 to $40,000, however, the costs are still prohibitive for many companies. Fortunately, advances in computers and phone networks may soon make it possible to equip desktop computers with a camera and videoconfer-

Videoconferencing works well to connect workers in several locations. With telecommunications and video technology workers hear and see each other when they meet.

encing circuit board for as little as $1,000 to $1,500. Besides making videoconferencing more affordable, desktop systems promise to make the technology less intimidating to managers and employees.[11] Another way companies can teleconference affordably is to rent the equipment as needed. For instance, Kinko's rents rooms equipped with teleconferencing equipment in many of its locations.

Electronic Communications

Voice mail
A form of electronic communication that allows the sender to leave a detailed voice message for a receiver.

Advances in electronic communications have made interactive communications possible even when the sender and receiver are separated by physical distance and busy schedules. With **voice mail,** an employee can avoid playing "telephone tag" with busy managers and instead leave a detailed voice message for them. The sender can also transmit a prerecorded voice mail message to some or all the people within the company's telephone network. For example, an executive can send a personalized greeting to a large group of employees. In addition, the receiver can leave different voice mail messages for different types of callers by creating a menu of messages.

Like any technology, voice mail has some drawbacks. Many people still dislike speaking to a machine. And this machine has plenty of potential for misuse. People often use it to screen calls, avoiding callers they do not want to talk to by pretending they are not there. This is fine in private life, but screening too many calls at the office can create problems. The following guidelines can help managers cut down on potential abuses of the voice mail system:[12]

- **Limit message capacity** To discourage long-winded voice mail messages, set the individual message capacity for 60 seconds.
- **Do not leave people in limbo** Sometimes it is necessary to screen calls. However, screening does not mean not returning calls for five or six days. To prevent the screening habit, some companies have a policy stipulating that answering machines cannot be turned on when employees are in their offices.
- **Do not allow voice mail to be used as a crutch** Senders who are supposed to phone someone with unpleasant news should not wait until the person is out to lunch so they can leave the message on voice mail.
- **Make sure everyone understands the system** This includes temporary employees, people from other departments, and new hires.
- **Respect the caller** Employees who will be away from the office on business, or on vacation and not checking their messages, should leave a message for the callers telling them how to reach a colleague who is taking their calls.[13]

Electronic mail, or **e-mail,** allows employees to communicate with each other via written electronic messages sent through personal computer terminals linked by a network. In addition, e-mail allows employees to offer feedback to anyone in the organization, no matter what that person's rank. E-mail is a very fast way to convey important business results or critical events to a large number of employees.[14] It also permits the sharing of large information databases among employees and even members of different organizations. E-mail has made it possible for professors at different universities worldwide to collaborate on research studies, write manuscripts, and share data as quickly as if they were working next door to each other at the same university. Interorganizational electronic communication is likely to increase significantly in the coming years, thanks to the rise of the Internet.

Electronic mail (e-mail)
A form of electronic communication that allows employees to communicate with each other via electronic messages sent through personal computer terminals linked by a network.

Despite its many advantages, e-mail has created some problems for managers. One problem is that, through ease of use, e-mail contributes to information overload. "Fifty percent of e-mail is a complete waste of time," says the assistant director of fire and aviation at the U.S. Forestry Service. "People create mailing lists and send one document to 50 people when only five people need to see it." To combat this problem, the U.S. Forestry Service's system typically allows space for only 30 to 50 messages; senders often have their memos sent back to them if the receiver's mailbox is full. Another problem is people's tendency to print out every message they get, causing exactly the kind of paper blitz that e-mail is supposed to prevent.[15]

Firms that set up e-mail systems with the idea of boosting productivity are sometimes dismayed to find that they are actually *lowering* productivity. Ira Chaleff, president of International Business Technology U.S., a Washington, DC–based management consulting firm, recommends the following guidelines for using e-mail productively:

- Establish an e-mail improvement team to develop protocols and procedures for getting the most out of the system.
- Create electronic files for messages that need to be saved and organize them in subject folders for quick retrieval.
- Set up a common folder or electronic bulletin board to which senders can route reports and memos intended for general distribution. An electronic bulletin board can save considerable system space and time.[16]
- Shut off the computer beep that alerts the receiver to incoming messages to prevent constant interruptions of work.
- Assume that your e-mail from a company computer will be read by management. Use other communication channels for private or controversial messages.
- Protect sensitive documents with encryption software so that private information is not accessible to hackers or other unintended receivers.

The thorniest problem managers confront with e-mail requires consultation with HR professionals. This is the tendency of employees to view their e-mail messages as private property, sacrosanct from employer inspection. This assumption can lead them to use e-mail to communicate about off-hours activities or to spread rumors, misinformation, and complaints speedily throughout the organization. Some managers have been shocked to find that disgruntled employees have developed grievance Web sites that encourage workers to use e-mail to sabotage managers' plans.[17] For these reasons, employers sometimes decide to monitor their employees' e-mail. Employees usually resent this, regarding it as an invasion of their privacy.[18] A survey taken in 2001 of 435 employers sponsored by the American Management Association found that about 62 percent of the employers exercise their legal right to monitor employees' e-mail.[19] For more information about grievance sites on the Web see the Issues and Applications feature titled "How Managers Can Use Grievance Sites to Quell Dissent."

A Question of Ethics

Should companies have the right to read and monitor their employees' e-mail?

Issues and Applications

How Managers Can Use Grievance Sites to Quell Dissent

Managers may be horrified by complaints posted on online grievance sites, yet if they can get past the angry tone of these messages there is valuable information embedded within them. Kyle Shannon, co-founder of e-commerce consultancy Agency.com, logged onto one of the grievance sites at Vault.com and read a slew of messages left by some of his employees who did not reveal their identities. One message said, "I saw people cry at work regularly," written by a woman who claims she quit after eight months with Agency. Another message stated, "I managed a team of five developers that, except for one person, were not capable of doing the work required of them. Upper management was clueless."

These grievance sites are a new phenomenon that allows tech-savvy employees to vent their anger and frustration with their company anonymously on the Internet and share this information with other employees. These forums range from message boards at Vault.com and Yahoo.com to company-specific sites like United.com (a site for peeved United Airlines employees and customers) and Walmartyrs.com (for employees who feel alienated by Wal-Mart employment policies). Management understandably is not enamored with all this airing of dirty company laundry in a display for all the world to see. Some firms such as Morgan Stanley, an investment bank, have gone as far as barring employees from accessing Vault.com at the workplace.

However, instead of banning the "gripe sites" managers would be better off logging on to them. If nothing else, "it's a free focus group," suggests Bob Rosner, founder of a grievance site called Working Wounded and author of a book by the same name. Rosner suggests to not invest too much importance in individual postings but rather to look for themes that point to problems in the organization. He encourages managers to identify themselves and to "try to start a discussion and see what flows from these complaints."

Making even a small improvement from the grievance site can have a significant effect on the company's morale. Witness the impact of Kyle Shannon's visit to Vault.com. After perusing the angry messages, Shannon tapped out his response: "I can assure you that we take the messages on these boards very seriously." He apologized to workers who were having a "poor experience," acknowledged Agency's growing pains, and promised he would "listen to the issues and address them as quickly as possible." A few months later Shannon started his own discussion forum on Vault.com and encouraged Agency workers to use it. They did. Then Shannon hired a new "vice president of people management" to smooth relations with employees. Almost immediately the angry tone of the messages in Agency's grievance site at Vault.com began to taper off.

Source: Adapted from Simons, J. (2001, April 2). Stop moaning about gripe sites and log on. *Fortune*, 181–182.

For example, when setting up Epson America's e-mail system, e-mail administrator Alana Shoars reassured 700 nervous Epson employees that their e-mail would be private. When Shoars found out that her supervisor was copying and reading employees' e-mail messages, she complained—and lost her job. She filed suit, but the judge agreed with the company. Because state privacy statutes did not make specific reference to e-mail or the workplace, the judge said, the law did not protect electronic messages in the office. Epson has since notified employees that it cannot guarantee e-mail privacy, citing in part its need to protect itself from computer crime. Unless HR staff members develop e-mail policies that are explicit and reasonable, employee relations may suffer.[20] A company may violate employee privacy if it captures its employees' electronic profiles when they visit the company Web or intranet site and then sells those profiles to marketers. The marketers may in turn send unwanted marketing messages by e-mail, telephone, and junk mail to employees who match the target market profile.[21]

Multimedia technology
A form of electronic communication that integrates voice, video, and text, all of which can be encoded digitally and transported on fiber optic networks.

Multimedia technology—integrating voice, video, and text, all of which are encoded digitally and can be transported on fiber optic networks—make it possible to interact with video images of employees located across the country or around the world as if they were in the same room.

Multimedia technology has potential applications in many areas. One is in employee training programs (see Chapter 8). For example, pilots can develop aviation skills on a multimedia flight simulator without risking an accident to the plane. Many textbooks now offer multimedia disks that help students learn skills and apply the information they've learned from the text.[22] These multimedia programs include voice and video clips and ask the student to make a decision from a menu of possible choices. After making a decision, the student can see the outcome on video.

Another application of multimedia technology is in telecommuting, a trend that is already changing the face of companies across the nation.[23] More and more employees are working with company-equipped computer systems and faxes in their homes.[24] The accompanying Manager's

Notebook, "Five Keys to Managing Telecommuters," addresses the managerial implications of this new workplace development.

MANAGER'S NOTEBOOK

Five Keys to Managing Telecommuters

Telecommuting must be carefully planned. The following suggestions can make managing telecommuters a little easier:

- Select telecommuters with care, considering the work habits of the employee and the type of work involved. People who are not very self-motivated may not be able to manage their time well at home.
- Maintain schedules and make sure telecommuters stick to deadlines. Although it is okay for telecommuters to work off-hours, they should be available for consultation when the company needs them.
- Make sure the technology works. Without the right compatibility between employer's and telecommuters computer systems, there will be delays in communication and traffic tie-ups on the electronic highway.
- Have home-based workers come in to the office on a regular basis so they can attend meetings and interact with managers. Doing so not only keeps these employees in the flow but also helps combat their feelings of isolation.
- Develop a well-planned telecommuting contract that includes performance expectations with measurable results. Managers of telecommuters must develop new skills and learn to transition from managing with a focus on employee's behaviors and time to one with an emphasis on managing by results.

Sources: Based on Grensing Pophal, L. (1999, January). Training supervisors to manage teleworkers. *HRMagazine*, 67–72; McCude, J. (1998, February). Telecommuting revisited. *Management Review*, 10–16; and *HR Focus*. (2002, May). Time to take another look at telecommuting, 6–7.

Meetings

Formal meetings are opportunities for face-to-face communication between two or more employees and are guided by a specific agenda. Formal meetings facilitate dialogue and promote the nurturing of personal relationships, particularly among employees who may not interact frequently because they are separated by organizational or geographic barriers.

Meetings take place at different organizational levels. For example, staff meetings allow managers to coordinate activities with subordinates in their units.[25] Division or corporate meetings involve issues that have a larger impact, and may include managers or employees from all divisions across the corporation. For instance, when a company like Microsoft decides to unveil a new product, organization-wide meetings are sometimes used to make sure that everyone in the organization is communicating the same message. Task force meetings may be called to discuss specific goals such as a change in marketing strategy or compensation policies.

It has been estimated that managers and executives spend as much as 70 percent of their time in meetings.[26] Poorly managed meetings can be a colossal waste of time that lower a company's productivity. Think about what it might cost for several highly paid executives to spend three hours at a meeting without accomplishing their objectives—and then multiply that amount by 260 workdays a year. However, meetings do not have to be a necessary evil. Here are some guidelines for making meetings more productive:

1. Decide whether it is even necessary to hold a meeting. If a matter can be handled by a phone call or memo, do not schedule a meeting.

IBM's Joanna Dapkevich, a part-time manager who telecommutes, relies on multimedia technology to meet with her staff. The company made her telecommuting arrangements clear and workable. The results have been positive: Her team's morale is the highest in the division and its customer service ratings have improved significantly.

2. Make meeting participation match the meeting's purpose. For instance, if a meeting is being held for the purpose of sharing information, a large group might be appropriate. For a problem-solving session, a smaller group is usually more productive.
3. Distribute a carefully planned agenda before the meeting. This will provide participants with purpose and direction and give them a chance to plan their own contributions.
4. Choose an appropriate meeting space and time. It is difficult for people to accomplish much when they are crowded into a small room with notepads balanced on their laps. Holding a meeting in a room that is too large may encourage participants to spread out and not develop the necessary cohesion. Timing is crucial, too. At meetings scheduled in the hour before lunch, attendees may be listening to their stomachs growl rather than to their colleagues. Some managers like to schedule meetings in the morning, when people are more alert. To encourage promptness, they set a time that is not exactly on the hour—such as 10:10 instead of 10:00 A.M.
5. In the case of a problem-solving or policy-setting meeting, close with an action plan and follow up with a memo outlining what happened at the meeting and what steps need to be taken.[27]

Skillful management of the dynamics among meeting participants is even more important than logistics. It is inevitable that some participants will attempt to dominate the proceedings with either helpful or negative contributions. Meeting leaders must strive to establish an atmosphere in which everyone feels at ease—one in which differences of opinion are encouraged and treated with respect.

Further clouding the air in the conference room are gender differences. Women often complain that they find it difficult to get, and hold, the floor in meetings with male colleagues. Sociolinguist Deborah Tannen has found that women and men have different communication styles that lead to misunderstandings both at work and at home.[28] Cultural differences also crop up in the meeting room. In a U.S. business meeting, the focus tends to be on action. In contrast, the objective of Japanese business meetings is to gather information or to analyze data before planning action. In Italy, meetings are often a way for managers to demonstrate their authority and power.[29]

In addition to scheduled formal meetings with specific work-related goals, managers can use informal meetings to build personal relationships among employees. Friday social hours have become a regular part of business at high-technology companies, including Cisco Systems and Sun Microsystems. At these social hours, technical employees talk among themselves and with managers and marketing staff about projects and share information that may not be communicated through formal channels. This practice has spread to many other types of businesses.

Retreats

A *retreat* is an extended meeting in which the company takes employees to a relaxing location such as a mountain lodge or an oceanside resort, where they mix business with recreational activities like golf, tennis, or sailing. Some retreats are designed to develop creative ideas for long-term planning or for implementing changes in business practices. Others, such as the outdoor adventures organized by Outward Bound, encourage employees to develop interpersonal skills by involving them in such activities as mountain climbing or whitewater rafting, where they are forced to be interdependent. These intense shared experiences can foster mutual appreciation among co-workers. A retreat can also be an excellent way of improving employee relations. For example, one medium-sized law firm in the Denver area used a retreat to improve relations between partners and associates. All the firm's members spent two days at a mountain lodge talking in small groups about ways to improve their relationships with one another. These discussions brought into the open many touchy issues that had been simmering. In the retreat setting, the firm's members could deal with them constructively.

Many family businesses are discovering the value of retreats. Two brothers, Steve and Elliott Dean, bought all the stock in their father's company, Dean Lumber Company in Gilmer, Texas. Three years later Steve realized that he had been so busy with day-to-day affairs that he had not spoken with family members about his plans for the company's future. The solution: a family retreat at which all 15 members of the Dean clan gathered for two days to discuss Steve's vision for Dean Lumber, helped by a facilitator from the Family Business Institute at Baylor University in Waco, Texas. The retreat, which included a preretreat screening, facilities with meals, the facilitator, and guest speakers, cost the Deans $5,000.

Most family business consultants recommend using a nonfamily facilitator at the first retreat, to get the process going and keep emotions from running too high. Later on the role of facilitator can be rotated among family members. To help the Dean family get a grip on the issue of succession, for example, the facilitator asked the group to pretend that Steve and Elliott had been killed in a plane crash and asked what they would do. This proved a shocking exercise for the brothers because it made them realize how very little short- or long-term planning they had done.[30]

In addition to using retreats to air important issues, many family businesses use them to set up a *family council*, an organizational and strategic planning group whose members regularly meet to decide values, policy, and direction.

Informal Communications

Sometimes called the "grapevine," **informal communications** consist of information exchanges without a planned agenda that occur informally among employees. Many informal communications take place among employees who form friendships or networks of mutual assistance at the water fountain or in the hallway, company cafeteria, offices, or parking lot. Informal communications pass along information that is usually not available through more formal communication channels—for example, the size of upcoming merit pay increases, who is in line for a big promotion, who has received an outside job offer, and who has gotten a low performance evaluation and is upset about it.

Informal communications
Also called "the grapevine." Information exchanges without a planned agenda that occur informally among employees.

Informal communications can be the source of creative ideas. Qwest, a regional telecommunications company, has designed a new research facility to take advantage of the benefits of informal communication. The architect designed "breakout rooms" and hallways to optimize spontaneous interactions between technicians and scientists so that informal groups can brainstorm together to solve technical problems and generate ideas.

When organizations allow too much information to be communicated informally, there is a good chance that it will be distorted by rumor, gossip, and innuendo. The result may be poor employee morale and poor employee relations. To guard against this, the HR department and managers need to monitor informal communications and, when necessary, clarify them through more formal channels. One effective way to monitor informal communications is through **management by walking around (MBWA).** MBWA, championed by Tom Peters and Robert Waterman in their wildly successful book *In Search of Excellence*, is a management technique in which the manager walks around the company so that employees at all levels have an opportunity to offer suggestions or voice grievances. This management style is used to build rapport with employees and monitor morale at IBM and many other companies.[31]

Management by walking around (MBWA)
A technique in which managers walk around and talk to employees informally to monitor informal communications, listen to employee grievances and suggestions, and build rapport and morale.

Employee Feedback Programs

To provide upward communications channels between employees and management, many organizations offer **employee feedback programs.** These programs are designed to improve management-employee relations by (1) giving employees a voice in decision making and policy formulation and (2) making sure that employees receive due process on any complaints they lodge

Employee feedback program
A program designed to improve employee communications by giving employees a voice in policy formulation and making sure that they receive due process on any complaints they lodge against managers.

against managers. The HR department not only designs and maintains employee feedback programs but is also expected to protect employee confidentiality in dealing with sensitive personal issues. HR personnel are also charged with ensuring that subordinates are not subject to retaliation from angry managers.

The most common employee feedback programs are employee attitude surveys, appeals procedures, and employee assistance programs. Here we discuss the first two kinds of programs, which are intended to resolve work-related problems. We discuss employee assistance programs (EAPs), which are designed to help employees resolve personal problems that are interfering with their job performance, later in this chapter.

Employee Attitude Surveys

Employee attitude survey
A formal anonymous survey designed to measure employee likes and dislikes of various aspects of their jobs.

Designed to measure workers' likes and dislikes of various aspects of their jobs, **employee attitude surveys** are typically formal and anonymous. They ask employees how they feel about the work they do, their supervisor, their work environment, their opportunities for advancement, the quality of the training they received, the company's treatment of women and minorities, and the fairness of the company's pay policies. An excerpt from an employee attitude survey is reproduced in Figure 13.5. The survey responses of various subgroups can be compared to those of the total employee population to help managers identify units or departments that are experiencing poor employee relations.

Making specific improvements in employee relations can avert acts of sabotage or labor unrest (such as strikes, absenteeism, and turnover) that are directly attributable to strains between subordinates and managers. For example, in analyzing attitude survey data, a chain of retail stores in the Midwest found that employees at one store had much lower levels of satisfaction than the employees at any other store in the chain. The chain's top managers immediately realized this was the same store that had experienced several serious acts of sabotage. Instead of retaliating against employees, corporate management set out to solve the store's supervision problems with training and mediation.

To manage an employee attitude survey effectively, managers should follow three rules. First, they should tell employees what they plan to do with the information they collect and then

Excerpt from an Employee Attitude Survey

Figure 13.5

To What Extent Am I Satisfied With . . .

	Highly Satisfied		Satisfied		Highly Dissatisfied
1. my pay and bonus	1	2	3	4	5
2. my benefits—over all	1	2	3	4	5
3. my chance to get a promotion or a better job	1	2	3	4	5
4. having a sense of well-being on the job	1	2	3	4	5
5. the respect and recognition I receive from management	1	2	3	4	5
6. my job security	1	2	3	4	5
7. the morale of my division	1	2	3	4	5
8. the degree of responsibility and autonomy I have in doing my work	1	2	3	4	5
9. the opportunity to have my ideas adopted	1	2	3	4	5
10. working with highly talented and capable people	1	2	3	4	5
11. interdivisional cooperation and communication	1	2	3	4	5

Source: Goodrich & Sherwood Company, 521 Fifth Avenue, New York, NY 10175. Used with permission.

inform them about the results of the survey. There is no point in surveying opinions unless the firm intends to act on them. Second, managers should use survey data ethically to monitor the state of employee relations, both throughout the company and within employee subgroups (such as women, accountants, or newly hired workers), and to make positive changes in the workplace. They should not use the information they collect to fire someone (for example, a supervisor whose workers are unhappy) or to take away privileges. Finally, to protect employee confidentiality and maintain the integrity of the data, the survey should be done by a third party, such as a consulting firm.

The application of the Internet with custom-designed software provides employee attitude survey feedback on a just-in-time basis. For example, eePulse, an Ann Arbor, Michigan, company, produces weekly reports of employee job satisfaction and other work attitude measures for its clients based on taking the pulse of various employee subgroups with an e-mail survey. The Web-based attitude survey lets managers identify the factors that cause declines in employee satisfaction more rapidly than is possible with traditional paper-and-pencil surveys.[32]

In which countries are workers the most satisfied with their jobs and their employers? According to a recent survey (Figure 13.6), Swiss workers are the happiest, whereas Japanese workers are the least happy. The United States falls in the middle range—at about the same level as Germany and Sweden, two countries known for their enlightened approaches to management.[33]

Appeals Procedures

Providing a mechanism for employees to voice their reactions to management practices and challenge management decisions will enhance employees' perception that the organization has fair employment policies. Organizations without an effective set of appeals procedures increase their risk of litigation, costly legal fees, and back-pay penalties to employees who use the courts to obtain justice.[34] Effective appeals procedures give individual employees some control over the decisions that affect them and help to identify managers who are ineffective or unfair.

Appeals procedure
A procedure that allows employees to voice their reactions to management practices and to challenge management decisions.

Some of the most common management actions appealed by employees are:

- The allocation of overtime work
- Warnings for safety rule violations
- The size of merit pay increases
- The specification of job duties

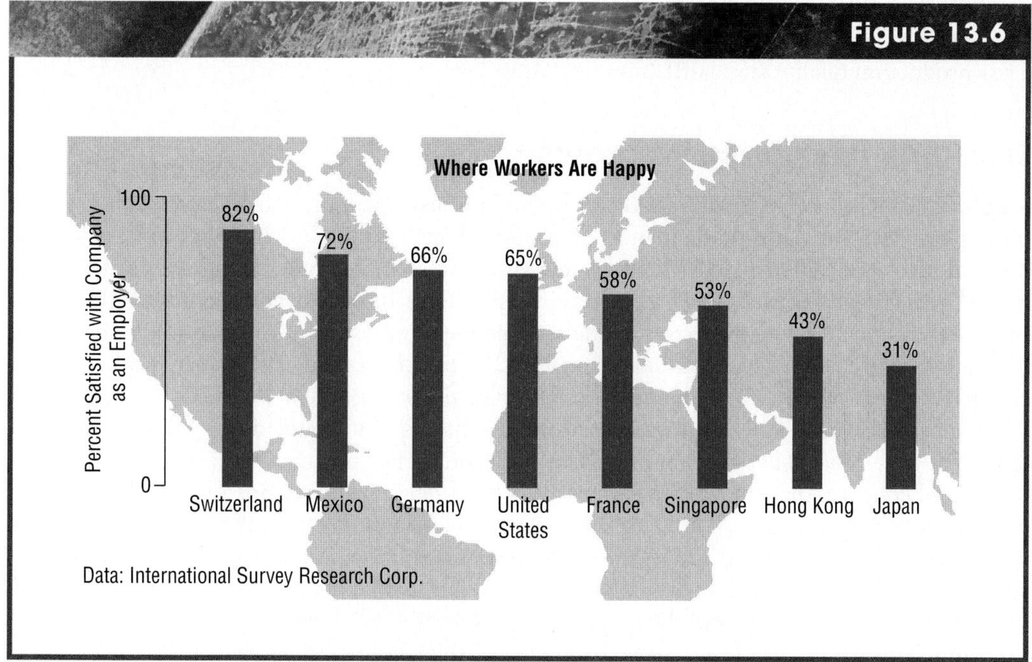

International Comparisons of Employee Satisfaction

Source: Reprinted from June 24, 1996 issue of *BusinessWeek* by special permission, copyright © by The McGraw-Hill Companies, Inc.

- The employer's reimbursement for medical expense claims filed by employees
- Performance evaluations

Managers may choose from several different types of appeals procedures that vary in formality.[35] The most informal is an *open-door program*. Although the specifics of open-door programs vary from company to company, the common theme is that all employees have direct access to any manager or executive in the organization. Lucent Technologies' open-door policy has been much admired. A Lucent employee can walk into the office of any manager, up to and including the CEO, and ask for an opinion on a complaint or any other problem worrying the employee. The manager consulted must conduct a fair investigation into both sides of the issue and provide an answer within a specified period of time. For example, an employee who is dissatisfied with his or her performance evaluation may seek a second opinion from another manager. The open-door policy has two major benefits: It makes employees feel more secure and committed to Lucent, and it makes managers less likely to act arbitrarily.

Like the open-door policy, a *speak-up program* is informal and flexible. It differs in that it prescribes specific steps for the employee to take in bringing a work problem to management's attention. CIGNA, a financial services and insurance company, has a speak-up program called Speak Easy that guarantees employees access to higher levels of management, but only after they bring their problems to the attention of their immediate supervisor (Figure 13.7).

The grievance panel and the union grievance procedure are the most formal mechanisms used by organizations to handle employee complaints. *Grievance panels* are used in nonunion firms. They are composed of the complaining employee's peers and managers other than the employee's direct manager. The grievance panel conducts an investigation into the grievance brought before it. Grievance panels are typically the last step in the appeal process. For example, Honeywell's grievance panel, called the Management Appeals Committee, is asked to resolve a grievance only if solutions have not been found at earlier steps involving, first, the employee's supervisor and, second, an employee relations representative.

The *union grievance procedure* is the appeals procedure used by all employees working under a union contract. Like the grievance panel procedure, it entails multiple steps leading to a final and binding decision made by a neutral decision maker called an arbitrator. The union grievance procedure is an important feature of labor contracts, and we explain it in greater detail in Chapter 15.

Organizations should use a mix of appeals procedures. For instance, a company might implement an open-door policy to deal with fairly simple problems that can be resolved quickly (such as determining whether an employee violated a safety rule). Next, it might institute an employee assistance program to deal with sensitive problems that involve an employee's privacy (such as a terminal illness). Finally, it might set up a grievance panel to examine complex problems affecting employee relations within a group or organizational unit (such as the definition of a fair production quality standard).

Employee Assistance Programs

Employee assistance program (EAP)
A company-sponsored program that helps employees cope with personal problems that are interfering with their job performance.

Employee assistance programs (EAPs) help employees cope with personal problems that are interfering with their job performance. These problems may include alcohol or drug abuse, domestic violence, elder care, AIDS and other diseases, eating disorders, and compulsive gambling.[36] Organizations with EAPs publicize the programs to employees and assure them that their problems will be handled confidentially. When an employee's personal problem interferes with job performance, the individual is considered a *troubled employee*.[37] In a typical company about 10 percent of the total employee population at any given time is troubled.

Figure 13.8 (page 454) shows some of the symptoms of a troubled employee. A troubled employee generally behaves inconsistently in terms of attendance, quality of work, attention to detail, and concern for personal appearance.[38] A great deal of the person's energy is devoted to coping with a personal crisis that he or she may want to keep secret from the company. Until this personal problem is resolved, the employee will be in emotional and/or physical pain and the company will be deprived of the full benefit of his or her skills. It is, therefore, in the interests of both the troubled employee and the employer to resolve the problem.

Four steps are involved in the operation of an EAP (Figure 13.9 on page 454):

Figure 13.7

Speak Easy

Speak Easy is a special program which gives you the opportunity to talk to management about work-related concerns. Speak Easy, with the support of CIGNA Corporation management, ensures an open line of communication and guarantees a timely response.

Through the Speak Easy Program, you may want to:

- Comment on your treatment as an employee.
- Describe a specific situation that is affecting your performance or the way you feel about your job.

Management wants to hear what you have to say . . . so Speak Easy.

Here's how the program works:

Phase I This is the first and most direct way to raise issues about your job or work situation. Go to your supervisor or manager and ask to talk over problems or questions. He or she is committed to listen and give you a fair and honest answer.

But if your supervisor or manager disagrees, cannot correct the situation, or is unwilling to change an earlier decision, Phase I offers you another step.

At your request, your supervisor will arrange interview(s) with additional levels of your management, including the top company official of your department or location. You will be invited to present your concerns, and every effort will be made to resolve your issue.

Phase II Phase II has been designed for privately raising the matters not resolved in Phase I. You may be unhappy with the course of action taken or feel the matter is too touchy to go through your supervisor. Phase II will give you another audience—someone not directly involved in the situation. But it's important to note that this phase is normally **not a replacement for Phase I employee-management discussions**.

In Phase II of the program, your issues will be kept strictly confidential and reviewed impartially by the Speak Easy Coordinator. Only the coordinator will know your identity if you choose.

All you do is pick up a Speak Easy envelope located in holders throughout your office and fill in the pertinent information. . . . Then drop the completed form and envelope in the mail. You can expect a prompt response from the coordinator, so long as your signature, home address, and phone number are on the form. Otherwise, you cannot be contacted and advised of the results of the coordinator's review.

If, for some reason, the review cannot be continued without revealing your name, the coordinator will tell you. It will be your decision whether or not to continue.

Please remember the sole responsibility of the Speak Easy Coordinator is to make sure that your situation is dealt with fairly and equitably.

Phase III This is the final step if you still aren't completely satisfied with the decision. This phase gives you direct access to the Head of your Operating Group or Staff Organization.

If after using Phases I and II, you are not satisfied with the decision about your situation, you may send a Speak Easy form or a letter fully stating the issue to the Head of your Operating Group or Staff Organization with a copy to your Speak Easy Coordinator.

The situation will be immediately reviewed and you will be informed promptly of the final resolution of your appeal. If the review supports the previous opinions or decisions, these will be upheld; if not, the prior decision will be modified.

Source: Excerpt from CIGNA's "Speak Easy" Brochure. Reprinted with permission of the CIGNA Corporation.

Excerpt from CIGNA's Speak Easy Brochure

1. The first step is identifying troubled employees and referring them for counseling. About half of all referrals are self-referrals by employees who realize they are in a crisis and need help, but want to keep their problem confidential. The other half are made by supervisors who observe some of the symptoms of a troubled employee. When job performance is deficient, the EAP referral is usually linked to the company's discipline procedure—it may be the last step taken before the employee is dismissed. Employees have the right to refuse to participate in the EAP, but refusal may mean termination if the problem has a significant negative impact on their work. In fact, though, many employees appreciate the company's willingness to help them through EAP counseling.
2. The second step after referral is a visit with an EAP counselor, who interviews the employee to help identify the problem. In the case of a complex personal problem like alcohol abuse, employees may strongly deny having a problem. The counselor, however, is trained to iden-

Symptoms of a Troubled Employee

Figure 13.8

1. Excessive absenteeism patterns: Mondays, Fridays, days before and after holidays
2. Unexcused absences
3. Frequent absences
4. Tardiness and early departures
5. Altercations with co-workers
6. Causing injuries to other employees through negligence
7. Poor judgment and bad decisions
8. Unusual on-the-job accidents
9. Increased spoilage and breaking of equipment through negligence
10. Involvements with the law—for example, a DWI (driving while intoxicated) conviction
11. Deteriorating personal appearance
12. Obsessive behavior such as inappropriate discussion of personal problems with customers

Source: Adapted from Filipowicz, C. A. (1979). The troubled employee: Whose responsibility? *Personnel Administrator, 24*(6), 8. Reprinted with the permission of *HRMagazine* (formerly *Personnel Administrator*) published by the Society for Human Resource Management. Alexandria, VA, and Wojcik, J. (1998, November 23). Signs may foreshadow workplace violence. *Business Insurance*, 41.

tify the problem and arrange for treatment. The location of an EAP can be at an on-site facility, with counselors available on the company premises, or an off-site facility. Off-site EAP facilities can provide counseling services to employees by the use of an 800 telephone line with counselors on call on a 24-hour per day basis. However, because EAPs are driven by relationships between counselors and employees, a recent survey by consulting firm EAP Support Systems found that overall use of off-site EAP programs was one-third less than that of on-site EAP programs.[39]

3. The third step is to solve the problem. Sometimes the EAP counselor is able to help the employee do this in a short time (three sessions or fewer). For example, an employee in financial difficulty may need only short-term counseling in how to manage personal finances. Some problems, however, take longer to resolve. For these, the EAP counselor will send the troubled employee to an outside agency equipped to provide the necessary treat-

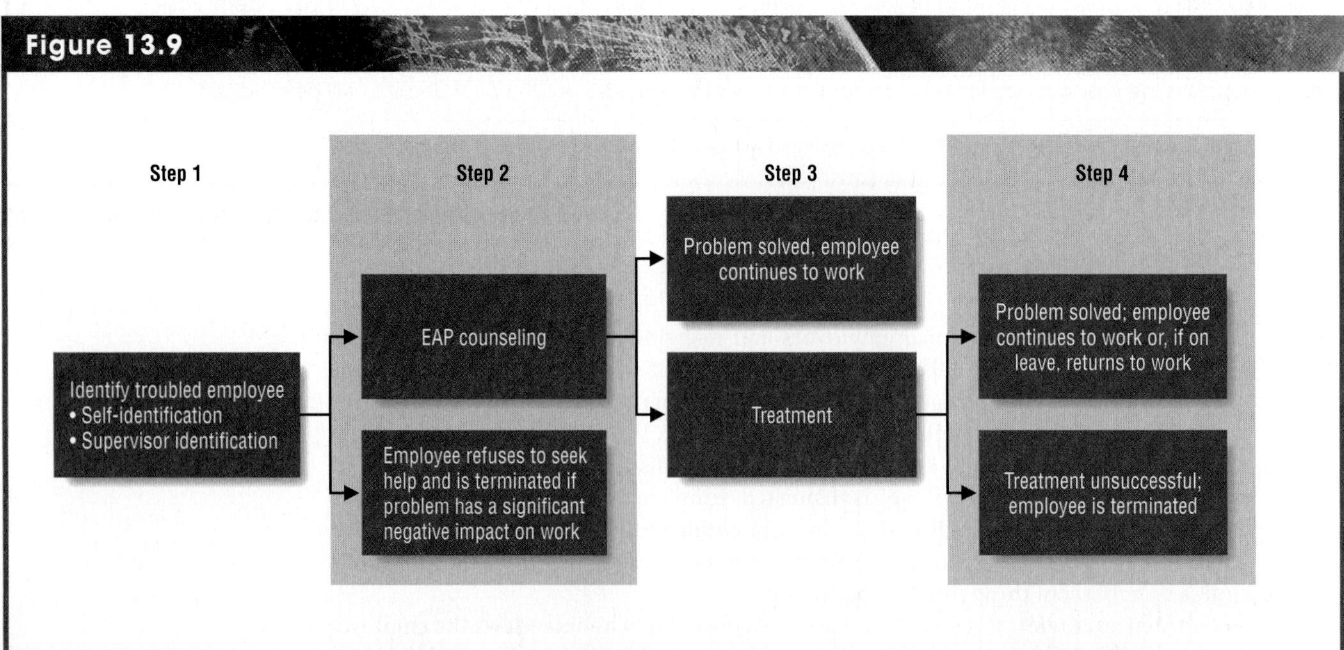

An Employee Assistance Program

ment. The counselor will try to find a service that best fits the employee's needs and is also cost-effective. For example, an EAP counselor who determines that an employee needs treatment for alcoholism must decide if the employee should receive inpatient residential treatment, receive outpatient treatment, or attend Alcoholics Anonymous (AA) meetings.[40] Inpatient residential treatment may require a 30-day hospitalization period that costs about $15,000. The other two alternatives cost much less.

4. The fourth and final step depends on the outcome of the treatment. If the employee has been placed on leave and the treatment is successful, the employee is allowed to return to work. In some cases, treatment does not require the employee to take a leave of absence; the employee remains on the job while being treated and continues after treatment has been successfully concluded. If the treatment is unsuccessful and the difficulty continues to disrupt the employee's work performance, the employer usually terminates the employee.

EAPs can help employees suffering from anxiety and stress due to restructurings or downsizings. The EAP at Rohm & Haas, a specialty chemical company headquartered in Philadelphia, played an important role in easing the effects of downsizing the company's production facility. When employment was cut from 800 to about 550, the company negotiated with its EAP vendor for an on-site psychologist who, in addition to maintaining office hours at the plant, sat in on management meetings and walked around the plant talking to employees. At GTE, EAPs are used to identify and provide support for managers who are dealing with people who are being let go or transferred.[41]

In the United States there are more than 12,000 EAPs; 75 percent of *Fortune* 500 companies use them[42] to deal with a wide variety of problems. Gambling casinos in the Atlantic City, New Jersey, area have used EAPs to deal with the high incidence of alcohol- and drug-related performance problems that employees in the gambling industry experience. The EAP for the Association of Flight Attendants, which represents flight attendants from 19 airlines, has an unusually large number of individuals seeking help for weight loss.[43]

EAPs contribute to effective employee relations because they represent a good-faith attempt by management to support and retain employees who might otherwise be dismissed because of poor performance. The annual cost per employee of an EAP runs about $30 to $40.[44] However, employers gain financial benefits that outweigh their out-of-pocket EAP expenses in terms of savings on employee turnover, absenteeism, medical costs, unemployment insurance rates, workers' compensation rates, accident costs, and disability insurance costs. One study showed that the rate of problem resolution for EAPs is about 78 percent.[45] PricewaterhouseCoopers consultants estimate that each dollar invested in an EAP could return four to seven times that amount in cost reductions.[46]

Employee Recognition Programs

Companies operating in global markets need employees who continuously improve the way they do their jobs to keep the company competitive. Employees are more likely to share their ideas for work improvements when managers give them credit for their contributions. **Employee recognition programs** can enhance employee relations by communicating that the organization cares about its employees' ideas and is willing to reward them for their efforts.[47] The HR department can help here by developing and maintaining formal employee recognition programs such as suggestion systems and recognition awards.

Employee recognition program
A program that rewards employees for their ideas and contributions.

Suggestion Systems

A *suggestion system* is designed to solicit, evaluate, and implement suggestions from employees and then reward the employees for worthwhile ideas.[48] Although the reward is often monetary, it does not have to be. It might instead be public recognition, extra vacation time, a special parking spot, or some other benefit. Suggestion systems have been successfully implemented in such diverse organizations as hospitals, universities, the U.S. Postal Service and other branches of government, and private-sector companies such as BP Amoco, Eastman Kodak, Black & Decker,

Simon & Schuster, and Lincoln Electric Company.[49] Firms that use suggestion systems in the United States average approximately 10 suggestions per 100 employees. Although this yield of suggestions appears modest, management experts indicate that many incremental workplace improvements are normally made outside of a formal suggestion system.[50]

Managers should adhere to three guidelines when designing a suggestion system. They should:

- Use a suggestion evaluation committee to evaluate each suggestion fairly and provide an explanation to employees why their suggestions have not been used.
- Implement accepted suggestions immediately and give credit to the suggestion's originator. The company newsletter can be used to publicly recognize employees whose suggestions have resulted in improvements.
- Make the value of the reward proportional to the suggestion's benefit to the company. For example, a loan manager at Bank of America who made a suggestion that saved the bank $363,520 a year received a cash award of $36,520 for her idea.[51]

Suggestion systems, long a part of U.S. business, have become more popular globally in recent years. For example, Japanese companies such as Toyota, Honda, and Mitsubishi have successfully gathered numerous suggestions from their employees resulting in significant improvements in their products (including automobiles). At Honda employees who provide suggestions that result in quality improvements earn points that can be applied to prizes such as a new Honda Accord or two international airline tickets.[52]

Recognition Awards

Recognition awards give public credit to people or teams who make outstanding contributions to the organization. These people or teams may become role models for others by communicating what behaviors and accomplishments the company values. McDonald's Employee of the Month award consists of a notice posted in each restaurant for all employees and customers to see. IBM employees who make major contributions are recognized in a host of different ways, ranging from a simple thank-you letter from a division manager to a cash award of $150,000 (given to two company scientists who won the Nobel Prize in science).

The recognition of teams and people who make important quality contributions can be either monetary or nonmonetary. For example, FedEx allows supervisors to confer instant cash awards to employees for quality efforts.[53] FedEx has earned the Malcolm Baldrige National Quality Award, the highest recognition of quality that a U.S. company can receive.

A recognition award can be initiated by a manager or by an internal customer of an individual or a team, with nominees evaluated by a recognition and awards committee. To emphasize that quality improvement should be continuous, there should be no limit on the number of times that a person or team can receive a recognition award.

A recognition award should be a celebration of the team or individual's success that encourages all organization members to work toward the organization's goals.[54] Recognition awards that focus attention on team or individual accomplishments include:

- A company-paid picnic to which all team members and their families are invited.
- T-shirts, coffee mugs, or baseball caps with a team insignia encouraging team commitment.
- A company-paid night on the town (such as dinner at a nice restaurant or tickets to a concert or sports event) for an employee and his or her spouse.[55]
- A plaque engraved with the names of individuals or teams that have made outstanding contributions.
- A donation in the name of an employee to the charity of his or her choice.

Recognition programs can serve purposes other than providing positive feedback to employees.[56] A Phoenix area hotel rewarded employees who made outstanding contributions with a free night's stay at the hotel. Not only was this a valued prize, but it also gave employees the chance to view their organization from the customer's perspective. Management hoped that this experience would prompt new suggestions for improving customer service.

Recognition in front of one's peers is a powerful way to motivate employees.

Although public recognition can be a powerful tool to sustain employee and team motivation, the Manager's Notebook "Guidelines for Public Recognition Rewards" shows managers how to avoid pitfalls with public recognition awards. For example, when a reward appears to be motivated by favoritism or becomes a popularity contest rather than clear recognition of excellent performance, it can depress rather than improve company morale.[57]

Customer-Driven HR — MANAGER'S NOTEBOOK

Guidelines for Public Recognition Rewards

Public recognition rewards can have a high upside impact on employee and team levels of motivation if they are administered well. Most employees find it very rewarding to be recognized and honored in front of their peers. However, a public reward that is poorly administered due to favoritism or being perceived as a popularity contest can demotivate employees and embarrass the recipient of the reward. Here are some key points to keep in mind when administering public recognition rewards to employees.

- **Have clear reward criteria.** Reward criteria that are clear, unambiguous, and well communicated to employees beforehand are likely to result in an employee perception of fairness and deservedness of the reward on the part of its recipient.
- **Ensure that judges of the recognition reward are not personally related to the recipient.** The individuals on the committee who determine the winner of the public recognition reward should have an arm's-length relationship to the reward recipient. For example, if an employee's supervisor or co-worker is on the rewards committee, this person may need to excuse himself or herself from the voting to avoid a perception of favoritism.
- **The presentation of the reward should be given on a sincere basis.** The speaker who presents the reward to the recipient in front of peers should focus on giving a sincere message of appre-

ciation to the employee being honored. The presenter should avoid engaging in theatrics and exaggerated gestures that make the recipient feel undeserving and embarrassed.

- **Try to personalize the reward if possible.** Rewards that are personalized to the needs of the recipient have the greatest impact on motivation. An employee who loves sports will probably appreciate tickets to a baseball game more than tickets to hear an orchestra play classical music. A personalized plaque given in a public ceremony will have longer-lasting memory value than cash because the cash is soon spent whereas the plaque remains in an employee's office or in his or her home.

Sources: Adapted from Wiscombe, J. (2002, April). Rewards get results. *Workforce*, 42–48; and Ginther, C. (2000, August). Incentive programs that really work. *HRMagazine*, 117–120.

Summary and Conclusions

The Roles of the Manager and the Employee Relations Specialist

Good employee relations involve providing fair and consistent treatment to all employees so that they will be committed to the organization. The backbone of an effective employee relations program is the manager, who is expected to evaluate, reward, and discipline employees in line with the company's employee relations philosophy. Employee relations representatives from the HR department ensure that employment policies are being fairly and consistently administered within the company. They often consult with both supervisors and employees on specific employee relations problems.

Developing Employee Communications

To develop effective employee relations, a company needs communication channels to move information up, down, and across the organization. Effective communications in an organization involve (1) a sender who encodes the message, (2) a communication channel that transmits the message, (3) a receiver who decodes the message, and (4) provisions for feedback because noise in the environment may distort the message's true meaning.

Facilitating Effective Communications

Working with supervisors and managers, employee relations representatives can facilitate effective communications by developing provisions for (1) information dissemination, (2) employee feedback, and (3) employee assistance programs.

Information dissemination involves making information available to decision makers, wherever they are located. Employee handbooks, written communications (memos, financial statements, newsletters, and bulletin boards), audiovisual communications, electronic communications (voice mail, e-mail, and multimedia applications), meetings, retreats, and informal communications are some of the choices available for disseminating information to employees.

Employee feedback programs are designed to improve communications by giving employees a voice in decision making and policy formulation and making sure they receive due process on any complaints they lodge against managers. Two programs that the HR department can establish to solicit employee feedback are (1) employee attitude surveys and (2) appeals procedures.

Employee assistance programs are designed to help employees whose emotional or psychological troubles are affecting their work performance. The employee is given the opportunity and resources to resolve the problem. Successful resolution of personal problems benefits both the employer and the employee.

Employee Recognition Programs

Employee recognition programs can enhance communications and employee relations by recognizing and rewarding employees who make important contributions to the organization's success. Recognition programs often use suggestion systems and recognition awards. The rewards given to individuals or teams may be monetary or nonmonetary.

Key Terms

appeals procedure, 451
downward communication, 439
electronic mail (e-mail), 445
employee assistance program (EAP), 452
employee attitude survey, 450
employee feedback program, 449
employee recognition program, 455
employee relations policy, 436
employee relations representative, 436
informal communications, 449
information dissemination, 440
knowledge worker, 440

management by walking around (MBWA), 449
multimedia technology, 447
nepotism, 440
teleconferencing, 443
upward communication, 439
voice mail, 444

Discussion Questions

1. List three ways the HR department can contribute to positive employee relations in a company.
2. Employee privacy has been called "today's most important workplace issue." What kinds of dilemmas have the new technologies created regarding employee privacy? What other kinds of problems have the new technologies created in employee relations and communications, and how might managers deal with them?
3. Bob Allenby's company handbook states that employees will be fired only if they violate the company's listed reasons for termination. Bob is fired, yet his conduct did not match any of the reasons outlined in the handbook. He has decided to file a lawsuit against his company for wrongful dismissal. Can an employee handbook be considered an employment contract, and if so, is Bob's company liable in this case? What can HR specialists do to protect a company against such lawsuits?
4. What are the advantages and disadvantages of telecommuting employees from the company's perspective?
5. Why do employees not take suggestion systems seriously in some companies? What can management do to improve the credibility of its employee suggestion system?
6. Shelly Wexler tells her supervisor, Rob Levine, that having to care for her aging mother is forcing her to leave work early and is making her feel increasingly "stressed out." While Rob refers her to the company's EAP, he also tries to convince her to put her mother in a home for the aged and even gives her some information about nursing homes in the area. Do you think Rob is just showing ordinary concern for his employee, or do you think he is overstepping managerial boundaries? Discuss the supervisor's role in implementing an EAP. Should a supervisor try to diagnose an employee's personal problem? Why or why not?
7. Do you think most employees have reservations about using an appeals procedure such as an open-door policy? What can managers do to convince employees that the available procedures are fair and effective?
8. Some communication experts claim that men and women have different styles of communication that create barriers to decoding messages from a sender of the opposite sex. What do you think are the important differences between the way men and women communicate with each other in a work environment? What are the implications of these sex differences in communication from the perspective of effective employee relations?
9. Many managers receive over 100 e-mail messages each day from diverse senders such as the employees who are their subordinates, customers, managers who are peers, top executives at higher ranks, and various other parties. Be able to list at least three effective practices for managers to deal with this large flow of information. Are there ways to prioritize the importance of these messages so that the senders receive the information they are seeking? How can a manager reduce the number of e-mail messages that are received each day to a more manageable number?
10. A minority of employees are actually demotivated by being given public recognition in front of their coworkers. What might be a reason why some employees feel uncomfortable being recognized in a public ceremony? Do you think that this could be an issue related to diversity in the workplace? Assuming that you are a manager and you are aware that one of your employees does not respond well to public recognition, what can you do to recognize this employee's good performance as an individual or part of a team?

There is a variety of additional material available on the Web site that accompanies this text. You can access this information by visiting the Web site at **www.prenhall.com/gomez.**

YOU MANAGE IT!

Emerging Trends Case 13.1

Coping with the 24-Hour Service Economy at Wal-Mart

A growing trend in the service economy is the recent appearance of the retail store that is open 24 hours per day and seven days per week. Wal-Mart has adopted this 24/7 service schedule to provide greater convenience to its customers. Some 1,400 Wal-Mart stores are now open 24 hours a day in 2002, up from no more than 300 six years earlier. Careful managers, with the aid of computer tracking, make sure that at any hour of the day a Wal-Mart has no more staff than is absolutely needed. Daytime shifts run from 7 A.M. to 4 P.M., which are the most desirable ones, and are allocated on the basis of employee seniority. The third shift is the nighttime one and most new employees start to work at Wal-Mart on the third shift or the second shift, which runs through the late afternoon and evening. The night work schedule has slightly higher pay than the day schedule, but it has all the disadvantages of nighttime work. These drawbacks include the difficulty of learning to sleep during the day and being out of phase with the lifestyles of family and friends so that it is more difficult to spend time together. Moreover, new Wal-Mart employees assigned to an evening or night shift receive minimum contact with their supervisors and managers who usually work on a daytime schedule. Ironically it is the new employees who have the greatest need for feedback from supervisors as they learn how to do their jobs and how to fit into the Wal-Mart culture, which places a high priority on giving excellent service to customers.

Wal-Mart stores traditionally have been located in smaller, rural cities not very different from that of Bentonville, Arkansas, where Wal-Mart headquarters is found. The company's progressive human resource policies, such as its "open-door" policy (empowering employees to bring their concerns to managers at any level), profit-sharing bonuses, retirement benefits funded with Wal-Mart stock, and time and a half pay on Sundays, were greatly appreciated by employees in these rural areas. For these employees, night shift work was tolerated because of the scarcity of alternative employers that provided the same benefits that Wal-Mart could give.

However, as Wal-Mart expanded to new markets, many stores opened in larger cities and urban areas such as Las Vegas and Dallas. For example, in the Las Vegas, Nevada, stores Wal-Mart is experiencing challenges it never faced in its stores in rural America. Wal-Mart in Las Vegas competes with hotels and gambling casinos for service workers and the unionized casino pay is considerably more. Wal-Mart stores have suffered high turnover rates and have difficulty retaining employees who have attractive job alternatives not available to those who work in small town stores. Consequently, sometimes jobs remain unfilled in Las Vegas stores, making it difficult to provide the level of service expected by Wal-Mart customers. Furthermore, Wal-Mart has recently had to deal with union organizing drives in Las Vegas, which it never experienced in its rural markets. Wal-Mart management has always strived to avoid unions so that its special culture of informality and rural friendliness to the customers is preserved. Strikes and formal contracts, often associated with unions, pose a threat to this culture. This situation in Las Vegas and other urban stores is troubling to Wal-Mart managers because future planned expansion of the company is focused on serving other urban markets where the opportunities for growth reside.

Critical Thinking Questions

1. What impact does the Wal-Mart policy of keeping stores open 24 hours per day have on employee relations? Why is the effect of the 24-hour service policy on employee relations different in urban areas such as Las Vegas than it is in smaller towns in rural areas?
2. Some countries such as Germany actually have laws that restrict retail stores from being open on Sundays, and regulate the weekday evening hours a store can remain open. The idea behind these laws is to protect employees' time with their families so that employees do not neglect their families to work additional hours. Do you agree or disagree with the approach of Germany to regulate store hours to protect the quality of employees' family life? What is the basis of your agreement or disagreement?

Team Exercise

With a group of four or five other students assume you have been asked for advice by Wal-Mart management to recommend some changes in human resource policies for stores located in urban areas to achieve the following goals: (1) improve retention rates of Wal-Mart employees and (2) improve the employee relations climate in Wal-Mart stores. Assume that Wal-Mart wants to retain its 24-hour service policy in those stores. Be able to justify your recommendations. You may want to visit the Wal-Mart Web site at www.walmart.com for additional information about the culture, policies, and recent news about Wal-Mart.

Source: Adapted from Gimein, M. (2002, March 18). Sam Walton made us a promise. *Fortune*, 121–130.

Discussion Case 13.2

YOU MANAGE IT!

Employers That Give Holiday Parties for Employees Are Exposed to Risks

During the holiday season, it is often customary to toast the end of another year with an annual company party. Employers give the party to boost employee morale, celebrate company success, and show their appreciation to employees who have dedicated themselves to achieving company goals. When giving a party for employees, the company must be aware of certain risks and liabilities that, if ignored, could put a damper on the festivities. Here is a worst-case scenario that happened in one company.

A female employee at a company holiday party had too much to drink. She then became "overly friendly" with some of her male supervisors, and her tongue made its way into a few of the gentlemen's ears. She hung all over these people and, to their dismay and shock, anyone who tried to stop her was yelled at and groped. In short, she was out of control in public, and her behavior repulsed those who witnessed it. When a female representative from human resources came to escort her to the women's restroom, she became belligerent and physically pushed her away. The result? The employee was terminated the next day for inappropriate workplace conduct. Unfortunately, she couldn't remember what happened, but the HR representative was able to recount enough of the details to give her a pretty accurate picture. Her response, interestingly enough, was defensive: "Why should I be terminated for my behavior at a company-sponsored event? After all, I never would have acted that way in the office. Besides, you provided the alcohol. When there's an open bar, I sometimes get carried away. I'll apologize to the appropriate people for my behavior, but I want my job back." Unfortunately, bad behavior at a company-sponsored event, even if she is a stellar performer, is still likely to lead to her termination as it did in this company. This particular employee was a good performer, yet her behavior violated the company's policies for professional conduct.

As this worst-case scenario illustrates, once management becomes aware of the potential risks with holiday parties, it may decide to cancel the event. This reaction is happening with greater frequency. However, canceling the holiday party may be an overreaction. HR can help management by providing some guidelines for organizing the party so that risks are minimized. Here are some areas of concern that should be anticipated in advance when organizing a company holiday party for employees.

One of the most common concerns at holiday parties is whether to serve alcohol. A legal liability is incurred when employees drive under the influence of alcohol and cause an accident that injures themselves or others. Unrestricted serving of alcohol also fuels the potential for outrageous employee behavior at the event, because some employees have difficulty controlling their drinking or are overly sensitive to the effects of alcohol. Finally, employers may be exposed to a risk if minors are served alcohol and the minors are involved in an accident.

Another important concern is whether to permit religious symbols and decorations to have a role related to the holiday party. For example, calling the event the "Office Christmas Party" may offend employees who practice non-Christian religions or who are not religious. Putting religious decorations, such as an image of the three wise men adoring the baby Jesus, in common work areas in the company building can also offend persons of different religions whose religion is not represented in the decorations. However, forbidding employees to decorate their own offices with Christmas lights and other paraphernalia may also be viewed as a violation of an employee's right to religious expression. Employers generally need to find a way to be inclusive so it does not appear that one religion is favored over all the others.

A final concern is the issue of gift giving. Employees can become resentful or have their feelings hurt if they sense there is social pressure on them to exchange gifts with co-workers or their boss during the holiday season. Employees may also feel pressured into giving an overly expensive gift to a colleague so that an important working relationship is preserved. Furthermore, an employee may give an inappropriate gift to a co-worker at a company function that causes humiliation or a perception of sexual harassment.

Critical Thinking Questions

1. In dealing with the employer liability related to serving alcohol at holiday parties, do you think all alcoholic beverages should be forbidden? Is there a way to manage the distribution of alcoholic beverages so they are not abused? What factors should enter into this decision? Who should be involved in the decision?
2. Should an employer giving a holiday party permit religious symbols to be displayed at the holiday party or in personal or public work areas at the company? If so, what procedures should be used to permit employees to display religious symbols?
3. Should the employer permit or forbid the exchange of gifts among employees during the holidays? How can gifts be exchanged without causing some of the problems raised in this case?

Team Exercise

With a group of four or five students develop a policy for holiday parties that can be used at a company or organization that your group identifies. One possibility is to have a policy that discourages holiday parties. If this position is selected, have a well-thought-out reason for why this company should discourage the holiday party. If your group decides to have a policy that permits holiday parties, develop some general guidelines for dealing with some of the areas of risk discussed in the case, such as the serving of alcohol, the display of religious decorations, and the exchange of gifts between employees. You may be asked to present your holiday party policy to the class. Be prepared to answer questions they may have about your policy.

Sources: Adapted from Falcone, P. (2001, December). 'Tis the season. *HRMagazine*, 97–101; and Segal, J. (2001, December). The most wonderful time of the year. *HRMagazine*, 103–108.

YOU MANAGE IT!

Customer-Driven HR Case 13.3

Casual Dress at Digital Devices

Digital Devices designs and manufactures custom integrated circuits for electronic consumer products such as pocket pagers, electronic calculators, and cellular phones. Based on the results of an employee attitude survey, the company's top executives decided to implement a casual dress-code policy for Digital employees. Management announced the casual dress policy in the employee newsletter and in an e-mail message sent to all employees. The policy stated simply that employees are encouraged to come to work in casual clothes except on days when they have meetings with clients (on those days, appropriate business attire is required).

There are several advantages of casual dress for both the company and employees. Casual dress improves employee morale by reducing status barriers that tend to separate managers (who are likely to wear suits and ties) from nonmanagement personnel. There is likely to be better communication and collaboration throughout the organization when status barriers are reduced. Casual dress is a good recruiting tool for top technical people, who tend to be young engineering graduates who want to work in a progressive company with a "fun" atmosphere. Employees also like the fact that casual dress is more comfortable and saves them money—they do not have to buy more expensive business clothes or use dry cleaning services to maintain the clothing.

Six months after the casual dress policy was announced, Sharon Greene, Digital's manager of human resources, noticed that the casual dress policy was a mixed blessing. Several unanticipated problems cropped up with employees' misuse of the policy, including the following:

- Some employees try to test the limits of casual dress. Computer programmers have come to work in T-shirts displaying their favorite musicians; such as the Grateful Dead, which may have references to drug use or sexual innuendoes that may offend other employees or clients.
- Employees' behavior has become more casual, and in phone conversations with clients they often refer to customers or prospects as "buddies." This casual attitude has resulted in some complaints to the sales manager.
- The HR department is now referred to as the "fashion police" because it is expected to uphold dress standards when employees wear inappropriate dress (tank tops, bicycle shorts, jeans with holes in them, and so on). This new role has undermined some of HR's credibility.

Greene is now contemplating ways to improve the casual dress policy at Digital Devices.

Critical Thinking Questions

1. Do you think Digital Devices should abandon its casual dress policy? Why or why not?
2. Suppose that Digital decides to revise its casual dress policy. Should the revised policy list approved types of clothing and unacceptable types of clothing so that employees know exactly what they can and cannot wear to work? Are there any potential problems with this approach?
3. How should the company communicate the revised casual dress policy to its employees?

Team Exercise

The class divides into groups of four or five students each. Each group develops a new casual dress code policy for Digital Devices. One representative of each group presents the group's recommended policy to the class. Other students and the instructor may ask questions or comment on the features of each group's policy.

Discussion Case 13.4

YOU MANAGE IT!

Improving Coaching and Feedback Skills

Managers must learn how to coach and provide feedback to subordinates in a way that motivates them to apply the feedback to improve performance. To provide useful feedback, a manager should first try to understand the job from the employee's point of view and the possible reasons why the employee is not achieving the expected levels of performance. Face-to-face communication and the ability to listen are tools that managers should be able to use to counsel employees so they are motivated to improve their performance. HR specialists provide resources for managers who may have difficulty communicating effectively with their subordinates to achieve harmonious employee relations. Read the following scenario between a manager and a subordinate and be prepared to find ways to improve the manager's process of giving feedback and coaching.

Feedback Session at Parker Manufacturing

Ron Davis, the relatively new general manager of the machine tooling group at Parker Manufacturing, was visiting one of the company's plants. He scheduled a meeting with Mike Leonard, a plant manager who reported to him.

Ron: Mike, I've scheduled this meeting with you because I've been reviewing performance data, and I wanted to give you some feedback. I know we haven't talked face-to-face before, but I think it's time we review how you're doing. I'm afraid that some of the things I have to say are not very favorable.

Mike: Since you're the new boss, I guess I'll have to listen. I've had meetings like this before with new people who come in my plant and think they know what's going on.

Ron: Look, Mike, I want this to be a two-way interchange. I'm not here to read a verdict to you, and I'm not here to tell you how to do your job. There are just some areas for improvement I want to review.

Mike: OK, sure. I've heard that before. But you called the meeting. Go ahead and lower the boom.

Ron: Well, Mike. I don't think this is lowering the boom. But there are several things you need to hear. One is what I noticed during the plant tour. I think you're too chummy with some of your female personnel. You know, one of them might take offense and level a sexual harassment suit against you.

Mike: Oh, come on. You haven't been around this plant before, and you don't know the informal, friendly relationships we have. The office staff and the women on the floor are flattered by a little attention now and then.

Ron: That may be so, but you need to be more careful. You may not be sensitive to what's really going on with them. But that raises another thing I noticed—the appearance of your shop. You know how important it is in Parker to have a neat and clean shop. As I walked through this morning, I noticed that it wasn't as orderly and neat as I would like to see it. Having things in disarray reflects poorly on you, Mike.

Mike: I'll stack my plant up against any in Parker for neatness. You may have seen a few tools out of place because someone was just using them, but we take a lot of pride in our neatness. I don't see how you can say that things are in disarray. You've got no experience around here, so who are you to judge?

Ron: Well, I'm glad you're sensitive to the neatness issue. I just think you need to pay attention to it, that's all. But regarding neatness, I notice that you don't dress like a plant manager. I think you're creating a substandard impression by not wearing a tie, for example. Casualness in dress can be used as an excuse for workers to come to work in really grubby attire. That may not be safe.

Mike: Look, I don't agree with making a big separation between the managers and the employees. By dressing like people out on the shop floor, I think we eliminate a lot of barriers. Besides, I don't have the money to buy clothes that might get oil on them every day. That seems pretty picky to me.

Ron: I don't want to seem picky, Mike. But I do feel strongly about the issues I've mentioned. There are some other things, though, that need to get corrected. One is the appearance of the reports you send into division headquarters. There are often mistakes, misspellings, and I suspect, some wrong numbers. I wonder if you are paying attention to these reports. You seem to be reviewing them superficially.

Mike: If there is one thing we have too much of, it's reports. I could spend three-quarters of my time filling out report forms and generating data for some bean counter in headquarters. We have reports coming out our ears. Why don't you give us a chance to get our work done and eliminate all this paperwork?

Ron: You know as well as I do, Mike, that we need to carefully monitor our productivity, quality, and costs. You just need to get more serious about taking care of that part of your responsibility.

Mike: OK. I'm not going to fight about that. It's a losing battle for me. No one at headquarters will ever decrease their demand for reports. But, listen, Ron, I also have one question for you.

Ron: OK. What's that?

Mike: Why don't you go find somebody else to pick on? I need to get back to work.

Critical Thinking Questions

1. What are some of the barriers to communication that are keeping Ron and Mike from understanding each other?
2. What do you think was the content of the message that Ron was trying to send to Mike?
3. What could Ron, as the manager, have done differently to get his intended message across to Mike?
4. Why did Mike respond defensively to the feedback that Ron was trying to give him?
5. Examine each of the statements made by Ron and Mike. Find a better way to make each statement so that the real content of the message can be decoded and understood by the intended target of communication.

Team Exercise

In a group of three or four students develop a plan for Ron to organize a follow-up meeting with Mike. Assume that in the intervening period, Ron has learned to improve his communication skills. Describe how Ron should conduct the meeting with Mike so that he can motivate Mike to improve in the areas that need improvement, instead of resisting the feedback and focusing on defending himself from criticism.

Source: Whetten, D. A., and Cameron, K. S. (1998). *Developing management skills* (4th ed.), 216–217. Upper Saddle River, NJ: Prentice Hall.

Respecting Employee Rights and Managing Discipline

Challenges

After reading this chapter, you should be able to deal more effectively with the following challenges:

1. **Understand** the origins and the scope of employee rights and management rights.
2. **Explain** why the HR department must balance management's rights and employees' rights when designing employment policies.
3. **Describe** the employment-at-will doctrine.
4. **Distinguish** between progressive discipline procedures and positive discipline procedures.
5. **Apply** fair standards to a case of employee misconduct and justify the use of discipline.
6. **Manage** difficult people who challenge their supervisors with such problems as poor attendance, low performance, insubordination, and substance abuse.
7. **Avoid** disciplinary actions by taking a proactive and strategic approach to HRM.

All employees have rights that are based on laws, company employment policies, and traditions. Employers also have rights that support their authority and what they can expect from their employees. Sometimes these two sets of rights conflict. Consider the following situations:

- An American Management Association study in 2001 revealed that 62 percent of companies monitored their employees' Internet use. Discipline for misuse of electronic communications is increasing in frequency and severity. The New York Times Company in 1999 discharged 23 employees in its Norfolk, Virginia, processing center for disseminating sexually explicit pictures through its e-mail system. The Xerox Corporation in 2000 discharged 40 employees for spending excessive time visiting non-work-related or sexually oriented sites. Are employees' privacy rights being violated by employers who monitor their use of the Internet and e-mail communications?[1]

- A few months after the attack on the World Trade Center in 2001 security officials at the FedEx sorting center at Newark Airport became concerned when they noticed that a contract mechanic, Egyptian-born Osama Sweilan, had been periodically disappearing into the company's flight simulator room. During his interrogation, Sweilan nervously stated he went into the room to make quick calls to his wife and sometimes even pray. His interrogators pressed him about his political beliefs and Osama bin Laden, the leader responsible for the attack. Afterward, Sweilan's ID was confiscated and his outsourcing firm was told he was no longer wanted in his 16-month-old job. After the terrorist attacks on the United States, employers and security personnel singled out males of Arab descent for personal interviews with security experts but did not apply this policy consistently to other employees. Employers justified these interrogations in order to protect the security of employees and customers. Don't employees with Arab backgrounds have the same rights to privacy that other employees are entitled to have?[2]
- Like many other companies, the Turner Broadcasting Company has a "no-smoker" policy that forbids its employees to smoke either on or off the job. Managers justify strict no-smoking policies because smokers raise the cost of health benefits for all employees. Employees have lost their jobs for violating a no-smoker policy. Do no-smoker policies infringe on an employee's right to engage in legal behavior (smoking) during nonwork hours?[3]

THE MANAGERIAL PERSPECTIVE

The three examples in the chapter opener suggest that the rights of both employees and employers should be clearly spelled out in every employment relationship. The HR department can help in several ways, such as:

- Developing and enforcing policies that inform employees of their rights and responsibilities.
- Making managers aware of employees' rights and managers' obligations to employees.
- Acting as an employee advocate, especially in cases where a supervisor misunderstands or disregards discipline policy.

But it is the manager who can make a tremendous difference here. Managers who respect employees' rights are more likely to have employees with high levels of morale and job satisfaction than managers who ignore these rights. Respecting employees' rights also lessens the likelihood of a costly grievance procedure or lawsuit. As a result, managers need to learn what their employees' rights are, conduct thorough investigations on behalf of employees with a complaint, and learn to administer discipline as a way to correct a behavior or habit that is nonproductive—rather than as a form of punishment.

In this chapter, we examine employee rights and employee discipline. These two issues are closely related to the quality of employee relations (discussed in the preceding chapter). Organizations with effective employee relations ensure that their managers respect employees' rights and use fair and consistent discipline procedures.

First, we examine the concepts of employee rights, management rights, and the employment-at-will doctrine that governs many nonunion employers. Second, we explore some challenges that managers encounter in balancing employee rights with the rights of management. Next, we discuss employee discipline and offer some suggestions for managing difficult employees. We conclude by examining how the HR department can support managers with proactive policies that minimize the need for disciplinary procedures.

Employee Rights

A **right** is the ability to engage in conduct that is protected by law or social sanction, free from interference by another party (such as an employer). For example, employees have the legal right to form a union. It is illegal for an employer to discourage employees from exercising their right to form a union by withholding pay increases from those who support the union.

Right
The ability to engage in conduct that is protected by law or social sanction, free from interference by another party.

The scope of *employee rights* has broadened in the last 35 years as the federal and state governments have enacted laws giving employees specific protections. Additionally, in the last decade courts have been more willing to protect employees from wrongful discharge than they were in the past. Many believe that the courts have been more proactive in protecting employees' rights because of the shrinking proportion of the labor force that is protected by union contracts.

Figure 14.1 shows the three different categories of employee rights that managers must consider: (1) statutory rights, (2) contractual rights, and (3) other rights.

Statutory Rights

Employees' **statutory rights** are protected by specific laws enacted by government. Employees' key statutory right is protection from discrimination based on race, sex, religion, national origin, age, handicap, or other protected status under Title VII of the Civil Rights Act of 1964 and other equal employment opportunity laws (see Chapter 3). The *Equal Employment Opportunity Commission (EEOC)* regulates employer conduct to ensure that employees are not discriminated against.

Statutory right
A right protected by specific laws.

Another important employee statutory right is protection from unsafe or unhealthy working conditions. The Occupational Safety and Health Act (OSHA) requires employers to provide safe working conditions for workers and has established the *Occupational Safety and Health Administration* to regulate health and safety practices at companies (see Chapter 16).

Employees also have the legal right to form unions and participate in union activities (see Chapter 15). The *National Labor Relations Board (NLRB)* regulates employer and employee conduct to ensure fair labor practices.

Contractual Rights

Contractual rights are based on the law of contracts. A **contract** is a legally binding promise between two or more competent parties.[4] A breach of contract, in which one of the parties does not perform his or her promised duty to the other party, is subject to legal remedy.

Contractual rights
A right based on the law of contracts.

Contract
A legally binding promise between two or more competent parties.

Both employers and employees have rights and obligations to each other when they enter into a contract. An **employment contract** spells out explicitly the terms of the employment relationship for both employee and employer. In general, such contracts state that the employee is expected to work competently over a stipulated period of time and that the employer is expected to provide a mutually agreed upon amount of pay, as well as specific working conditions, over this time period.[5] Employees covered by employment contracts include nonunionized public school teachers, college football coaches, actors in film and television, top-level executives, and middle management.[6] Only a very small percentage of the labor force works under employment contracts.

Employment contract
A contract that spells out explicitly the terms of the employment relationship for both employee and employer.

Figure 14.1

Statutory Rights	Contractual Rights	Other Rights
■ Protection from discrimination	■ Employment contract	■ Ethical treatment
■ Safe working conditions	■ Union contract	■ Privacy (limited)
■ Right to form unions	■ Implied contracts/employment policies	■ Free speech (limited)

Categories of Employee Rights

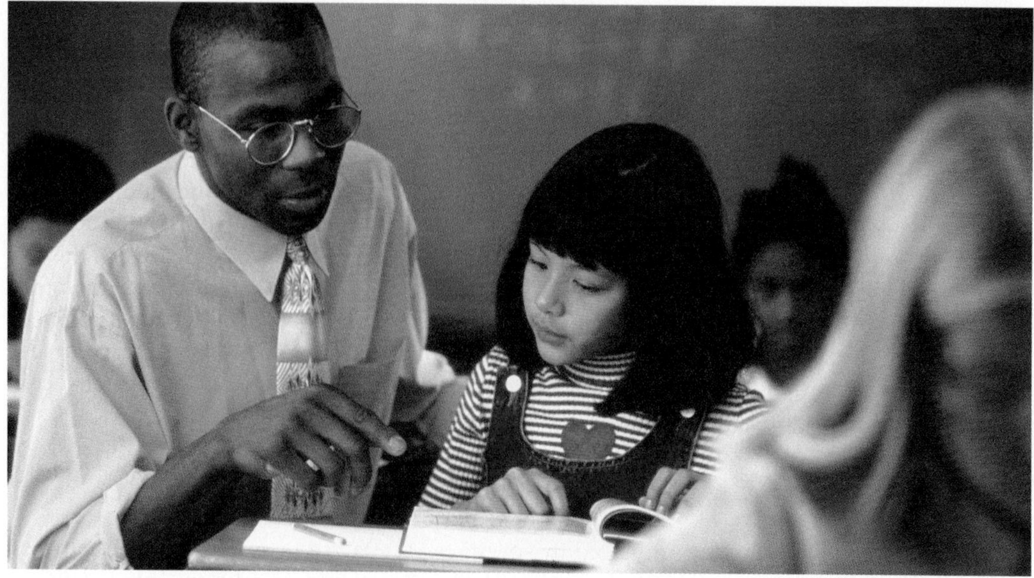

Many nonunion public school teachers have one-year contracts that follow a standard pattern, rather than being negotiated individually.

The provisions of the employment contract give the employee job security and are, at least theoretically, negotiated individually. We say "theoretically" because there are cases in which contracts are so similar as to be standard. For instance, many public school teachers not covered by union contracts are hired on a year-to-year basis by the school district. In theory, each teacher negotiates his or her own contract. In practice, because of the volume of contracts that must be written, the vast majority of these contracts follow a standard pattern.

Some industries have standard contract provisions to protect their interests more fully. For instance, employers in competitive technology and service industries often have several employment contract provisions that forbid employees to (1) disclose trade secret information during or after their employment, (2) solicit business from former customers, or (3) attempt to hire former coworkers after leaving the company.[7] For some high-profile jobs, such as top-level executives, the contract will not follow the standard pattern and will, in fact, be negotiated individually.[8] An employee under contract may be fired for reasons other than nonperformance, but he or she is then entitled to compensation for the life of the contract.

A significant percentage of employees in the U.S. labor force (around 14 percent) are covered by *union contracts*, which protect groups of unionized workers. Union contracts do not provide as much job security as individually negotiated employment contracts do, but they do provide some job security through seniority and union grievance procedures. Seniority provisions protect the jobs of the most senior workers through the "last in, first out" layoff criterion that is commonly written into the union contract (see Chapter 6), Union grievance procedures subject all disciplinary actions (including discharge) to **due process,** which requires a fair investigation and a showing of just cause to discipline employees who have not performed according to expectations. An arbitrator who is empowered to decide discipline and rights cases can restore the job rights and back pay of an employee who has been wrongfully discharged. (**Wrongful discharge** is discharge for reasons that are either illegal or inappropriate, such as age or the refusal to engage in illegal activities.)

Due process
Equal and fair application of a policy or law.

Wrongful discharge
Termination of an employee for reasons that are either illegal or inappropriate.

Sometimes employers and employees enter into a contract even though no formal contract exists. In this case, the employer and the employee are said to have entered into an *implied contract*. Certain employment policies and practices may unintentionally create an implied contract. The courts have interpreted statements made by an interviewer or manager such as "You will always have a job as long as you do your work" as a promise of job security.[9] Employees who lost their jobs because of layoffs have successfully obtained legal remedies when such promises were made.

Employee handbooks can be another source of implied employment contracts if they offer job security. Some courts have interpreted statements like "Employees will be dismissed only for just cause" as placing the burden of proof on the company for a termination decision.[10] In addition, when an employee handbook or employment policy makes a distinction between "probationary" and "permanent" employees, the courts have held that employers are promising continued employment to workers who successfully complete the probationary period and become permanent employees. To date, at least 30 state supreme courts have ruled that employee handbooks can be interpreted as enforceable contracts.[11]

Other Rights

Employees often expect certain other rights in addition to statutory and contract rights. These include a right to ethical treatment and limited rights to free speech and privacy. These rights differ from the first two categories of rights in an important way: Although employees may expect these rights, they may have no legal recourse if they feel that these rights have been violated. Even though the law does not require employers to extend these other rights to employees, doing so is likely to result in more satisfied workers who are willing to go the extra mile for the organization.

Right to Ethical Treatment

Employees expect to be treated fairly and ethically in return for providing their employer with a fair and reasonable amount of work. This expectation is called the *psychological contract*.[12] Employers who uphold the psychological contract generally have more productive employees. In contrast, those who violate the psychological contract may cause employees to quit or to form a union. Because employee turnover is costly and unionization results in some loss of control over the business, managers should be aware of the importance of the psychological contract to employees.[13] One way of sealing the psychological contract is to develop and publicize a code of ethics.[14] HR can contribute to maintaining an ethical environment by integrating the code of ethics into employment policies, orientations for new employees, and formal training programs.[15] The excerpt from Starbucks' mission statement, which includes ethical standards, gives an example of how a company can publicize its ethical values.

Managers and supervisors can influence their companies' climate of fairness and ethical behavior by the tone they set for employees in their work units.[16] Specifically, managers and supervisors should:

- Take actions that develop trust, such as sharing useful information and making good on commitments.
- Act consistently so that employees are not surprised by unexpected management actions or decisions.
- Be truthful and avoid white lies and actions designed to manipulate others by giving a certain (false) impression.
- Demonstrate integrity by keeping confidences and showing concern for others.
- Meet with employees to discuss and define what is expected of them.
- Ensure that employees are treated equitably, giving equivalent rewards for similar performance and avoiding actual or apparent special treatment of favorites.
- Adhere to clear standards that are seen as just and reasonable—for example, neither praising accomplishments nor imposing penalties disproportionately.
- Demonstrate respect toward employees, showing openly that they care about employees and recognize their strengths and contributions.[17]

Limited Right to Privacy

The right to privacy protects people from unreasonable or unwarranted intrusions into their personal affairs. Although this right is not explicitly stated in the U.S. Constitution, the Supreme Court found in a 1965 ruling that it is implicit in the Constitution. For instance, the Constitution does explicitly prohibit unreasonable searches and seizures, and this prohibition is consistent with a more general right to privacy.

There are two additional legal bases for privacy rights. First, several state constitutions (including those of Arizona and California) contain an explicitly stated right to privacy. Second, several federal laws protect specific aspects of an employee's privacy. For instance, the Crime Control and Safe Streets Act of 1968 has a provision that prevents employers from viewing or listening to an employee's private communications without obtaining prior consent.

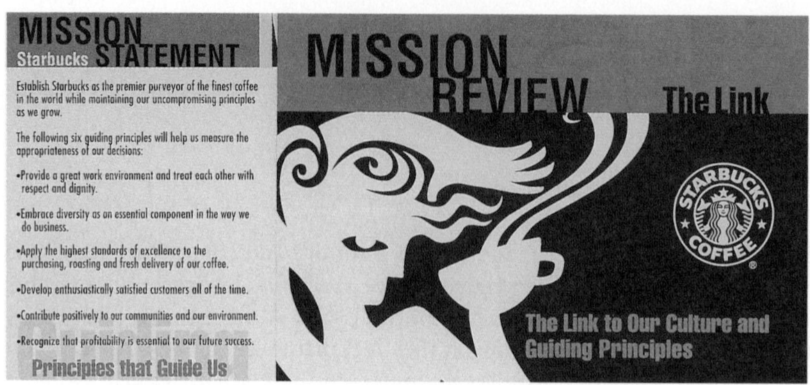

Starbucks' mission statement includes ethical values, such as respect for others and for the environment.

Because the U.S. and state constitutions limit the powers of the government, federal and state employees' privacy rights are protected, although not absolutely. For instance, under a program mandated by Congress, employees whose jobs in U.S. aviation are directly related to safety must undergo periodic blood alcohol testing.[18] However, the same constitutional protections do not apply to private employee arrangements. For instance, government employers are typically prohibited from searching their employees' personal work space (desks, lockers, etc.) unless they have reasonable cause, but private employers typically are not prohibited from this kind of activity. Still, because employees expect certain privacy rights, it is almost always good policy for an employer to respect employee privacy.

Personnel file
A file maintained for each employee, containing the documentation of critical HR-related information, such as performance appraisals, salary history, disciplinary actions, and career milestones.

A sensitive issue involving employee privacy rights is the maintenance of personnel files. Each worker's **personnel file** contains the documentation of critical information, such as performance appraisals, salary history, disciplinary actions, and career milestones. Access to the personnel file should be denied to all people except managers who have a job-related "need to know" certain information. Employees should be able to review the information in their personnel file periodically to ensure its accuracy. If personnel files are stored in a human resource information system (HRIS), access to this sensitive information should be controlled by the use of passwords or special codes to protect employees' privacy rights.

Privacy Act of 1974
Guarantees the privacy of personnel files for employees of the U.S. federal government.

Employees of the U.S. federal government have the privacy of their personnel files protected under the **Privacy Act of 1974.** The act requires federal agencies to permit employees to examine, copy, correct, or amend employee information in their personnel file. The act also includes provisions for an appeal procedure if there is a dispute over the accuracy of the information or what is to be included in the file.[19]

Limited Right to Free Speech

The First Amendment to the U.S. Constitution guarantees all U.S. citizens the right to free speech. This right is therefore more explicit than the right to privacy. However, it too is limited.[20] Again, government employees are more fully protected than those who work for private employers. For instance, an IRS agent who disagrees with the current president's tax policies is perfectly free to say so publicly without fear of official retribution. However, if a Sears store manager publicly disagrees with corporate pricing strategy, Sears is free to discipline or terminate that manager. Thus, managers in the private sector can legally discipline employees who say something damaging to the company or its reputation. Similarly, a company can and should discipline an employee for using demeaning language that insults a person based on his or her race or gender. Texaco did not discipline the managers who insulted African American employees on the basis of race, which resulted in an expensive discrimination lawsuit.[21] There are important exceptions to this situation, however. When employees reveal management misconduct to outsiders, they are engaging in whistleblowing, which is a legal right under federal and some state laws. We discuss whistleblowing in detail later in this chapter.

A Question of Ethics

A computer programming manager suspects that one of her programmers is sharing programming information with a competitor through electronic mail. Is it appropriate for the manager to examine her employee's e-mail files without the suspected programmer's permission?

As with the right to privacy, managers should interfere as little as possible with employees' free speech because this right is so deeply ingrained in U.S. culture. Managers need to balance the costs and benefits of extending versus not extending privacy and speech rights. For instance, we saw in Chapter 13 that e-mail is becoming a very popular method of communication. Should companies establish a policy allowing managers to read all their employees' electronic communications? For example, an employer could have employees sign a consent form acknowledging the company's right to access e-mail messages.[22] Employees who know that managers are looking at their communications are likely to "censor" them to some degree, and the loss of candor may lead to less-than-optimal decisions. In addition, such a policy would injure the trust relationship between employees and their employer. Thus, any theoretical benefit a company might gain from such a policy—like guarding against criminal activity—would almost certainly be offset by work-related and psychological costs.

Management Rights

The rights of the employer, usually called **management rights,** can be summed up as the rights to run the business and to retain any profits that result. In the United States, management rights are supported by property laws, common law (a body of traditional legal principles, most of which originated in England), and the values of a capitalistic society that accepts the concepts of private enterprise and the profit motive.[23] The stockholders and owners who control a firm through their property rights delegate the authority to run the business to managers.

Management rights
Management's rights to run the business and retain any profits that result.

Management rights include the right to manage the workforce and the rights to hire, promote, assign, discipline, and discharge employees. Management's right to direct the workforce is moderated by the right of employees (at least those who have not signed an employment contract) to quit their jobs at any time. Thus, it is in management's interest to treat employees fairly.

Management rights are influenced by the rights of groups who have an interest in decisions made in the workplace. For example, managers have the right to hire the employees they wish to hire, but this right is affected by EEOC laws that prevent the employer from discriminating on the basis of certain applicant characteristics (age, race, sex, and so on). Furthermore, managers have the right to set pay levels for their employees, but the presence of a union labor contract with a pay provision requires managers to pay employees according to the contract's terms.

Management rights are often termed *residual rights* because they pertain to the remaining rights that are not affected by contracts or laws that represent the interests of employees or other parties (such as a union).[24] According to the residual rights perspective, managers have the right to make decisions that affect the business and the workforce except where limited by laws or contract provisions.

One of the most important employer rights is employment at will.

Employment at Will

Employers have long used **employment at will,** a common-law rule, to assert their right to end their employment relationship with an employee at any time for any cause. U.S. courts adopted the rule in the nineteenth century to promote flexibility in the labor market by acknowledging the existence of a symmetrical relationship between employer and employee. Because workers were free to terminate their relationship with their employer for any reason, the courts deemed it fair for employers to be able to end their relationship with employees whenever they see fit to do so. Employment at will can be a particularly important management right in small business, where a low-performing employee can make the difference between a healthy profit and an unhealthy loss.

Employment at will
A common-law rule used by employers to assert their right to end an employment relationship with an employee at any time for any cause.

Although the courts originally assumed that employment at will would give both parties equal footing in the employment relationship, it is apparent that employment at will has stacked the deck in favor of employers. Because of the employment-at-will doctrine, many employees who are wrongfully discharged each year have no legal remedies.[25] One labor relations expert has estimated that approximately 150,000 employees are wrongfully discharged by their employers each year.[26] Virtually all of these wrongful discharges occur in the 70 percent of the U.S. labor force that is not protected by either a union contract or *civil service rules*, which guarantee government employees the right of due process in termination procedures. Employment at will is not accepted in other parts of the world, including Japan and the nations of the European Union. These countries have enacted laws that make it difficult for employers to discharge a worker without good cause. In France, Belgium, and the United Kingdom, the only grounds for immediate dismissal are criminal behavior.[27]

Legal Limitations to Employment at Will

For the past 15 years or so, state courts have been ruling that employment at will is limited in certain situations. Because these are state rather than federal cases, they have varied widely. In general, however, employment-at-will limitations can be grouped into three categories: public policy exceptions, implied contracts, and lack of good faith and fair dealing. In some states plaintiffs have received sizable settlements for punitive damages as well as back pay. Juries gave a median award of $205,000 to plaintiffs in wrongful discharge cases in 1996.[28]

Public Policy Exceptions. The courts have ruled that an employee may not be discharged for engaging in activities that are protected by law. Examples are:

- Filing a legitimate workers' compensation claim
- Exercising a legal duty, such as jury duty
- Refusing to violate a professional code of ethics
- Refusing to lobby for a political candidate favored by the employer[29]

Implied Contracts. As we saw on page 468, the courts have determined that an implied contract may exist when an employer makes oral or written promises of job security. For instance, an implied contract may exist when an employee handbook promises job security for good performance, or when a manager who is unaware of this doctrine makes promises during the selection interview, such as "good performers will always have opportunities at our company." To prevent implied contract lawsuits, employers should carefully rewrite employee handbooks to eliminate any language that could be interpreted as an implied contract. In addition, employers must train managers to refrain from implying promises of job security in conversations with new and current workers.

Lack of Good Faith and Fair Dealing

Courts in some jurisdictions expect each party in the employment relationship to treat the other in good faith. If one party acts with malice or bad faith, the courts may be willing to provide a remedy to the injured party. For example, the courts may reason that firing a worker shortly before he or she becomes eligible for a retirement plan indicates bad faith. In this situation, the burden of proof may be on the employer to show that the discharge was for just cause.

The following case makes it plain how costly it can be for an employer to act in bad faith in discharging employees:

> In 1987 two employees of a New Jersey real estate management firm took maternity leave. One was dismissed after she returned to work; the other was fired seven weeks before her planned return. Both women sued, and in 1992 a jury awarded them $210,000 and $225,000, respectively, in compensatory damages. They were awarded another $250,000 each in punitive damages, and on top of that the judge added another $374,000 in interest and legal fees. Total cost to the employer: $1.3 million.[30]

To minimize the risk of wrongful discharge lawsuits based on an implied contract, many employers have drawn up employment-at-will statements that all new employees must sign, acknowledging their understanding that the employer can terminate their employment at any time for any reason.[31]

A Question of Ethics

Is it ethical to require all employees to sign an employment-at-will statement acknowledging that they understand that the employer can terminate their employment at any time for any reason?

Employee Rights Challenges: A Balancing Act

Four workplace issues are particularly challenging to HR professionals and managers because they require walking a thin line between the rights of employees and those of management: (1) random drug testing, (2) electronic monitoring, (3) whistleblowing, and (4) office romance.

Random Drug Testing

The practice of random drug testing pits management's duty to protect the safety of its employees and customers against an employee's right to privacy. *Random drug testing* screens employees for the use of drugs randomly, without suspicion or cause. The test usually involves the analysis of a urine specimen provided by the employee.

Many employees consider random drug testing an unreasonable and illegal invasion of their privacy.[32] Although random drug testing is required by law for specific occupations where safety is critical, such as airline pilots and military personnel, it has been challenged in cases where the employer has other methods available to ensure a drug-free work environment. For example, the International Association of Fire Fighters will permit clauses in its labor contracts that allow drug testing based on "probable cause," but will not agree to random drug testing. Numerous employers also use preemployment drug testing as a condition of employment.[33]

Because no employee groups have succeeded in stopping drug testing under the U.S. Constitution, the legal battle between employee privacy and employer-mandated drug testing is being played out at the state level.[34] Not only do state constitutions vary widely in their protections of employee privacy—for example, New Jersey and California have added employee privacy provisions to their state constitutions, whereas Utah and Texas have not,[35] but the courts' interpretation of these protections has veered from one side to the other as well. For instance, the California Supreme Court dealt what was considered a death blow to random drug testing in that state when it ruled in 1990 that an employer must have a "compelling interest" to require employees not in safety-sensitive positions to submit to random drug tests.[36] Pro-employee groups cheered the ruling, but four years later the California Supreme Court allowed the National Collegiate Athletic Association to conduct random drug testing of student athletes. The court said that the private sector, like the government, must abide by the state constitution's right of privacy, but that the private sector can invade privacy for "legitimate" interests.[37]

Designing a random drug-testing policy poses numerous challenges. The HR staff can be helpful in counseling management on how to deal with some of the following issues:

- How should employees who have positive drug test results be treated? Should the manager discharge them or attempt to rehabilitate them?
- Sometimes drug-testing procedures generate a false-positive outcome. If an employee has a positive test for a legitimate reason, such as using a prescription drug or eating a poppy seed bagel (poppy seeds are the source of opium), how can the employer ensure that the employee is not charged with using illegal drugs? How can an employer protect employees from false-positive results in general?
- What can managers do to maintain security over urine specimens provided for the drug test so that they are free from adulteration designed to alter the results? Should managers require that employees be monitored while providing the urine sample to ensure its authenticity? Or does such monitoring violate the employee's privacy rights?

Motorola's random drug-testing policy was designed specifically to deal with these issues. It is administered by the company's HR department and is described in detail in the Issues and Applications feature, titled "How Motorola's Random Drug-Testing Policy Works." Motorola decided to implement random drug testing after it estimated the cost of employees' drug use in terms of lost time, reduced productivity, and health-care and workers' compensation claims at $190 million annually. This amounted to 40 percent of the company's net profits.[38]

The jury is still out on whether the benefits of random drug testing outweigh the resentment and mistrust this policy often generates. A survey of workers at one of the nation's largest railroads found that only 57 out of 174 respondents expressed support for periodic drug testing—and all stipulated that it was justifiable only for safety reasons. Many commented that drug testing undermined their loyalty to the company. One worker wrote:

> I am a faithful and loyal employee. I felt like a common criminal, and I didn't even do anything wrong. . . . I happen to have bashful kidneys. The first time I took a drug test it took me almost three hours of drinking water and coffee before I could give a sample. Needless to say I was upset, angry, humiliated, defensive, etc. . . .[39]

Employees' anger and humiliation about random drug testing is compounded by the evidence that it does not help deter accidents: In 1991 a Federal Railroad Administration report found that only 3.2 percent of workers involved in railroad accidents tested positive for drugs.[40]

In order to avoid some of the disadvantages related to having employees submit to random drug-testing procedures, management in firms that are not involved with transportation or safety-sensitive jobs may decide to use either a preemployment drug test or a probable cause drug test.[41] A *preemployment drug test* is given to each job applicant as part of the hiring process. For example, the preemployment drug test may be taken as part of a physical examination that a job candidate must take before being given a job offer. Those who fail the test are not hired.[42] A *probable cause drug test* is given to employees who have accidents, engage in unsafe job behavior, or show behavioral signs of drug use, which may include having impaired judgment or slurred speech. Notice that neither the preemployment drug test nor the probable cause drug test is given on a random basis but instead is given either at a predetermined time (such as the time an employee is hired) or for a predetermined reason, such as having an accident or being reprimanded for unsafe conduct in the workplace. In a survey taken in 2001 by the American Management Association, 67 percent of U.S. firms reported using some form of drug testing.

Moreover, there is an alternative to drug testing that does not invade employee privacy and that is much more reliable for determining an employee's fitness for work: the performance test. For example, there are computer-based performance tests that test workers' hand–eye coordination to measure their ability to do their jobs. Every morning at Silicon Valley's Ion Implant Services, Inc., delivery drivers line up in front of a computer console to "play" a short video game. Unless the machine spits out a receipt confirming they have passed the test, they cannot climb behind the wheel of their trucks. What happens to workers who fail their performance tests? Some companies refer them to a supervisor, others to an employee assistance program. Besides being both more reliable and less invasive of employees' privacy, performance testing has another advantage over random drug testing: It is cheaper. Performance tests cost from $0.60 to $1 per employee compared with the $10 per employee that the cheapest drug test costs.[43]

Issues and Applications

How Motorola's Random Drug-Testing Policy Works

Companies that wish to implement a random drug-screening process face many challenges. The following is a description of Motorola's drug-testing policy.[a]

Motorola's drug policy is stated simply. "No use of illegal drugs, no use of legal drugs illegally." To enforce the policy, the Illinois-based electronics manufacturer instituted a universal drug-testing program that HR administers. Here is how it works.

Every employee's name—including that of the chairperson and the contractors who remain on company premises for longer than 30 days—becomes part of a database. A specially designed computer program selects from each Motorola site employee names to be tested each day. The computer program ensures that every employee is selected at least once in three years for a drug test. It is possible, however, for some employees to be selected more than once during that period. This process is designed to prevent an employee's feeling safe from testing after taking one test. When the computer selects names of workers who are sick, on vacation, or away from the job site for any other legitimate reason, those names are put into a pool to be selected again randomly within 90 days.

After selecting the names of individuals to be tested on a particular day, an HR staff member informs the employees' supervisors, who are responsible for relaying the information to the employees. This serves two purposes. Not only does it get the information to the employees who will be tested, but it also allows the supervisors to prepare for those employees' brief absences. The employees whose names are selected must report at their designated times. Failure to do so results in disciplinary action.

The collection area prepares split samples for the Motorola employees, allowing for analyses from two different labs if the employees request it. If an employee's test results are positive, the company's medical review officer is contacted. The medical review officer discusses the situation with the employee to determine if there is a legitimate reason—such as a prescription drug that the employee forgot to mention—for a positive result. Except in security-sensitive positions, it is up to the employee to decide whether his or her supervisor should be notified of the results.

If it is determined that a drug abuse problem exists, the next step for the employee is to report to HR to set a meeting with an EAP adviser and plan a rehabilitation method. The company pays for the employee's rehabilitation. "We're trying to do as much as we can on the rehabilitation side, as opposed to the discipline or punitive side," says Motorola's assistant corporate director of employee relations.

All employees, except some in safety-sensitive or security clearance positions, continue working in their jobs during rehabilitation. (An exception is when the rehabilitation requires an extended stay at an in-patient treatment center.) The government requires that the organization report any positive tests of individuals who work in clearance-type operations. If the government deems it appropriate to suspend the employee's safety clearance, Motorola must remove the employee from that position. The company will try to place that employee in another position temporarily.

Similarly, if an employee who has positive test results works in a safety sensitive position, the organization will place the employee in another job during rehabilitation, if recommended by the EAP. Removal from the position is contingent on circumstances.

After employees complete their rehabilitation program, their names go into a special random pool. Motorola tests these employees once every 120 days for a one-year period.

If during this one-year period an employee again has a positive test, the organization terminates him or her. If, however, all test results following rehabilitation are negative, the employee's name goes back into the three-year pool, and he or she begins the testing process again.

Although Motorola gives an employee who has a positive test an automatic chance for rehabilitation, other companies take a different approach.[b] Toyota Manufacturing of Kentucky uses a peer review committee for its hourly production workers who have positive drug tests. After a review of the employee's work record and listening to his or her side of the story, the committee votes on the employee's fate. In 60 percent of the cases the employee is discharged and 40 percent of the time is asked to return to work. Managers are not given a peer review and are automatically discharged for a positive drug test because they are held to a higher standard of performance.[c]

Sources: [a]Gunsch, D. (1993, May). Training prepares workers for drug testing. *Personnel Journal*, 54. Copyright May 1993. Reprinted with the permission of *Personnel Journal*, ACC Communications Inc., Costa Mesa, CA: all rights reserved. [b]Gemignani, J. (1999, June). Substance abusers: Terminate or treat? *Business of Health*, 32–38. [c]*Ibid.*

Issues and Applications

Can an Employer Deny Jobs to People Who Smoke?

In one of the first court cases dealing with off-the-job smoking as part of the screening and selection process, the U.S. Supreme Court refused to hear the appeals of job applicants who were rejected from consideration for employment with the City of North Miami, Florida, because they are smokers. The denied appeal leaves in place an earlier Florida Supreme Court decision in favor of a city regulation requiring that all job applicants sign an affidavit stating that they have not used any tobacco products for one year before seeking a job with the city.[a]

Arlene Kurtz, a cigarette smoker who applied for a job as a clerk-typist, filed suit, claiming that the city's action interfered with her privacy rights to smoke during her time away from the job. Kurtz offered to comply with any reasonable on-the-job smoking restrictions, but indicated that she had smoked for 30 years and had tried to quit smoking without success. The city argued that it established the policy because employees who use tobacco cost as much as $4,611 per year more than nonsmokers. The court noted that the regulation was the least intrusive way to accomplish the city's interest because it does not affect current employees, only job applicants.[b]

Other companies have taken a more moderate approach to controlling smoking behavior. They have enacted nonsmoking policies that restrict on-the-job smoking due to safety concerns and to protect nonsmoking employees from secondary smoke exposure. For example, FedEx has a nonsmoking policy that prohibits the use of tobacco products in all company buildings, facilities, vehicles, and aircraft, but does not try to regulate employee's off-duty smoking behavior.[c]

Outside of Florida, a number of other states have recently enacted laws that protect employees' legal off-duty activities such as smoking or skiing (a high-risk leisure activity that an employer might also object to because of higher insurance costs). These state laws prohibit employers from using an applicant's off-the-job smoking as a basis for hiring or continuing the employment relationship.[d]

Sources: [a]Barlow, W., Hatch, D., and Murphy, B. (1996, April). Employer denies jobs to smoker applicants. *Personnel Journal*, 142. [b]Ibid. [c]Grensing-Pophal, L. (1999, May). Smokin' in the workplace. *Workforce*, 58–66. [d]Barlow et al., 1996.

Many employers justify random drug testing on the grounds that drug use is illegal. In recent years, however, some companies have also begun testing employees who engage in *legal* activities, such as smoking. The Issues and Applications feature titled "Can an Employer Deny Jobs to People Who Smoke?" examines the controversy surrounding employer policies that reject all applicants who smoke on or off the job.

Electronic Monitoring

Experts estimate that employee theft costs U.S. business over $400 billion a year.[44] "Theft" includes theft of merchandise, embezzlement, industrial espionage, computer crime, acts of sabotage, and misuse of time on the job. While the average annual loss a bank suffers from embezzlement is $42,000, the average computer crime costs around $400,000.[45] A retail store loses an average of $213 in a shoplifting incident (i.e., when a store customer steals merchandise) but loses an average of $10,587 for an employee theft incident.[46] Industrial spies who steal competitive trade secrets, such as software codes or plans for a microprocessor chip, may take property so valuable that its theft threatens the very existence of the business. Employees' theft of time from employers can also be costly. Employees steal time when they take long lunches, use the telephone for private conversations, misuse sick leave for extra vacation time, or moonlight for another employer on their principal employer's time.

Companies are attempting to fight these various forms of theft by using electronic surveillance devices to monitor employees.[47] In industries like telecommunications, banking, and insurance, as many as 80 percent of employees are subject to some form of electronic monitoring.[48] To eavesdrop on employees, companies use hidden microphones and transmitters attached to telephones and tiny fish-eye video lenses installed behind pinholes in walls and ceilings. In a survey published by *Macworld* magazine, more than 21 percent of respondents said they have "engaged in searches of employee computer files, voice mail, electronic mail or other networking communications." Most said they were monitoring work flow or investigating thefts or espionage.[49]

The increased sophistication of computer and telephone technology now makes it possible for employers to track employees' job performance electronically—for example, to count the number of keystrokes an employee makes on a computer terminal or determine how many reservations a travel agent books in a given time period.[50] This use of electronic monitoring has raised concerns not only about employee privacy but also about the dehumanizing effect such relentless monitoring can have on employees. Many employees whose work is tracked electronically feel that monitoring takes the human element out of their work and causes too much stress. One study comparing monitored and nonmonitored clerical workers showed that 50 percent of monitored workers felt stressed, compared with 33 percent of nonmonitored workers; and that 34 percent of monitored workers lost work time because of stress-induced illness, compared with 20 percent of nonmonitored workers.[51] Some research suggests that there is a higher incidence of headaches, backaches, and wrist pains among monitored employees.[52]

Employees are most likely to see electronic monitoring as legitimate when management uses it to control theft. But even in this area some managers have exceeded reasonable standards. For example, experts estimated that in the year 2000 thirty million U.S. workers were subjected to secret electronic monitoring.[53] In one case, the nurses at Holy Cross Hospital in Silver Spring, Maryland, became quite upset after discovering that a silver box hanging on the locker room wall was a video camera monitored by the hospital security chief—who was a man.[54]

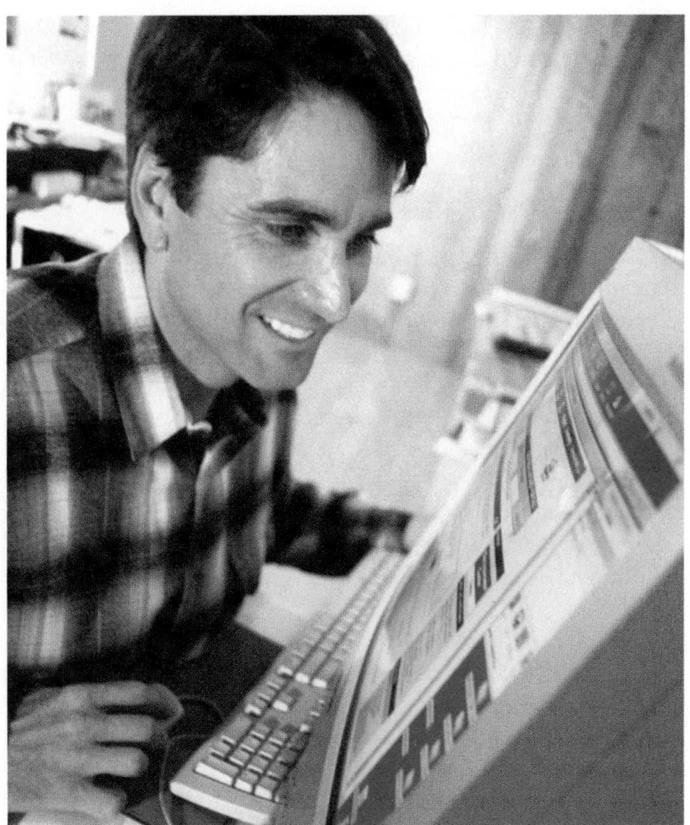

Electronic surveillance of employees' computer use is becoming more common, but it can cause friction between employees and employers. To maintain stronger employee relations, managers should notify employees of any surveillance in the workplace.

Some employers use electronic monitoring devices to control employee theft of time when they are on the company payroll. This wasted time is sometimes spent playing video games or visiting pornographic Web sites. Employers monitor to eliminate such wastage. For example, Turner Broadcast Systems, a unit of Time Warner Inc., is planning to use software that can monitor every Web page a worker visits and help pinpoint anyone wasting company time online. The company started monitoring online activity when it noticed substantial increases in overtime pay expenditures because some employees were wasting time browsing Web sites with their computer. Turner will not pay overtime to employees who are caught surfing the Web on company time.[55]

To use electronic monitoring devices to control theft while not intimidating or invading the privacy of honest employees (who make up the majority of the workforce), managers should:

- Make employees aware of any electronic surveillance devices that are being used to monitor their behavior. Secret monitoring should be avoided, except with specific individuals whom managers have reason to believe are stealing from the company. In those cases, management should obtain a court order to perform the secret surveillance.
- If the company decides to monitor employees' e-mail and Internet use, then management should provide guidelines to employees for exchanging e-mail messages and accessing Web sites. For example, the guidelines could suggest that inappropriate e-mail messages would be ones that contain racist and sexist language. The guidelines may also state that employees should not access Web sites that are related to gambling, chat rooms, online game playing, or sites with violent or sexually explicit images.[56]
- Find positive uses for electronic monitoring devices that are beneficial to employees as well as to the employer. Avis Rent A Car, for example, has used monitoring devices to provide feedback on employee performance. This practice has been accepted as a valuable training tool.
- Develop a systematic antitheft policy and publicize it throughout the company. Also establish other practices to discourage theft, such as reference checks, pencil-and-paper honesty or integrity tests that screen out employees who are likely to behave dishonestly, and internal

controls that control the use of cash (accounting controls), merchandise (inventory controls), computers and databases (computer security controls), and company trade secrets (security badges and clearance procedures).

Whistleblowing

Whistleblowing
Employee disclosure of an employer's illegal, immoral, or illegitimate practices to persons or organizations that may be able to take corrective action.

Whistleblowing occurs when an employee discloses an employer's illegal, immoral, or illegitimate practices to persons or organizations that may be able to take corrective action.[57] Whistleblowing can result in effective solutions, but it can also disrupt the organization's operations.

Whistleblowing is risky because managers and other employees sometimes deal harshly with the whistleblower.[58] Although whistleblowers often have altruistic motives, they may be shunned, harassed, and even fired for their efforts. For example:

- James Bingham, an assistant treasurer at Xerox, who was fired in 2000 when he complained about the accounting tricks that the copier company was using to boost its flagging earnings, found his subsequent battle with Xerox so all consuming that he was unable to work and earn a living.[59]
- The CEO of a New Jersey bank suspected that several of the members of the bank's board of directors were making deposits as a way to launder Panamanian drug money, so he reported the transactions to the New Jersey Banking Commissioner. When board members discovered he had blown the whistle on their activities, they ordered his subordinates not to talk to him, began criticizing his decisions, told major customers he was on his way out, and later fired him.[60]
- Mark Whitacre, an executive at Archer Daniels & Midland (ADM), a U.S. agribusiness firm, spent three years helping an FBI probe into alleged price fixing conducted by the company's top executives. When ADM discovered Whitacre's connection to the FBI, it accused him of stealing $2.5 million and fired him.[61]

A Question of Ethics

You discover that your supervisor has been billing the company for business trips that he never took. When you ask him about it, he says this is common practice throughout the company, the other department heads do the same thing, and corporate headquarters has set reimbursement rates so low that employees have to pad their expense accounts to be fairly reimbursed. What should you do?

Dealing with whistleblowing involves balancing employees' right to free speech with the employer's right to prevent employees from disregarding managers' authority or disclosing sensitive information to outsiders. Although whistleblowers who work for the federal government and some state and local governments have certain legal protections, there is far less protection for private-sector employees, except in states that have enacted whistleblower laws. Many times the whistleblower is subject to the employment-at-will rule and may be discharged in retaliation for going public about an illegal or unethical company activity. As Figure 14.2 indicates, a potential whistleblower should have good documentation of the evidence of wrongdoing before disclosing it to others. The whistleblower should also be prepared to deal with employer retaliation and have a contingency plan, which may include lining up another job in case the worst happens.

Despite all these risks, many employees have used whistleblowing to call their employers to account. For example, in 2001 Enron executive Sherron Watkins wrote a blunt memo to Enron CEO Kenneth Lay warning him that the company might "implode in a wave of accounting scandals." Instead of thanking her, management factions tried to squelch the bad news and intimidate her for not being a team player. After the financial scandal broke and became a media event, Watkins was adulated for her courage to confront a CEO about Enron's controversial off-the-books partnerships and shaky finances and became a positive role model for whistleblowers.[62] For this reason many companies have realized that it is in their best interests to establish a whistleblowing policy that encourages people to reveal misconduct internally instead of exposing it externally. This way the company can avoid negative publicity and all the investigative, administrative, and legal actions associated with it.[63] Figure 14.3 lists some of the most important elements of an effective whistleblowing policy. Probably the most important is support by top management, including the CEO. Other important elements of a whistleblowing policy are provisions for the whistleblower to remain anonymous initially and to be protected from retribution. Some companies that have effective whistleblowing policies are Bank of America, Pacific Gas & Electric, McDonald's, and General Electric.[64]

Figure 14.2

DO make sure your allegation is correct. Something may look fishy but be allowable under a technicality you don't understand.
DO keep careful records. Document what you've observed—and your attempt to rectify the problem or alert a supervisor. Keep copies outside the office.
DO research on whether or not your state provides protection for whistleblowers. It may require that you follow special procedures.
DO be realistic about your future. Talk to your family and make sure you're prepared for a worst-case scenario, which can include a loss of job, severe financial burdens, and blacklisting in your field. Even if you're not fired, you may be treated with suspicion by colleagues and management.
DON'T assume a federal or state law will protect you. Legal protection for private-sector workers is often inadequate and varies widely from state to state. Most federal protections cover only government workers.
DON'T run to the media. You may be giving up certain rights or risking a defamation suit. Check with an attorney before contacting any reporters.
DON'T expect a windfall if you're fired. Although some states allow punitive damages, you may be eligible only for back pay and reinstatement—in a place you probably don't want to work anyway.

Source: Reprinted from June 3, 1991 issue of *BusinessWeek* by special permission, © 1991 by The McGraw-Hill Companies, Inc.

Dos and Don'ts for Whistleblowers

Restrictions on Office Romance

The office is an inviting place for romance. People fall in love at work because that is where they spend much of their time and meet people with similar interests. Some controversial high-profile office romances such as the affair between President Clinton and Monica Lewinsky, a young White House intern, has influenced many companies to view an office romance with a

Figure 14.3

1. Get input from top management as you develop the policy and obtain approval of the final version.
2. Develop a written policy that is communicated to employees through multiple media, such as the employee handbook, e-mail and the company intranet site, and at department meetings and training sessions. Communicating the written policy signals the company's commitment to exposing misconduct.
3. Make it possible for employees to submit their initial complaint anonymously.
4. Develop a streamlined process that makes it easy for employees to report misconduct. Designate a special representative to hear initial employee complaints so that employees do not have to report to their supervisor first.
5. Safeguard employees who report suspected misconduct in good faith against reprisals.
6. Develop a formal investigative process and communicate to employees exactly how their reports will be handled. Use this process consistently in all cases.
7. If the investigation reveals that the employee's allegations are accurate, take prompt action to correct the wrongdoing. Whatever the outcome of the investigation, communicate it quickly to the whistleblower.
8. Establish an appeals process for employees dissatisfied with the outcome of the initial investigation. Provide an advocate (probably from the HR department) to assist the employee who wishes to appeal an unfavorable outcome.
9. To ensure the success of the whistleblowing policy, the organization—from top management on down—must be committed to creating an ethical work environment.

Sources: Adapted from Dworkin, T., and Baucus, M. (1998). Internal vs. external whistleblowers: A comparison of whistleblowing processes. *Journal of Business Ethics, 17*, 1281–1298; and Barrett, T., and Cochran, D. (1991). Making room for the whistleblower. *HRMagazine, 36*(1), 59. Reprinted with permission of *HRMagazine* (formerly *Personnel Administrator*) published by the Society for Human Resource Management, Alexandria, VA.

Developing an Effective Whistleblowing Policy

critical eye. The challenge of dealing with an office romance forces management to balance the need to protect the company from its liability for preventing sexual harassment with the need to protect the privacy of employees during their off-duty hours so they feel free to develop romantic relationships with people of their choosing. The biggest danger occurs when a person in authority dates a subordinate. If the romance goes sour, the subordinate may claim that the boss forced the relationship, which opens the door for a sexual harassment case.[65] A recent survey conducted by the Society for Human Resource Management (SHRM) found that 24 percent of employer respondents reported having had a sexual harassment claim filed against them as a result of a workplace romance.[66]

How organizations deal with office romance depends on the goals and culture of the organization. The U.S. military restricts personal relationships between officers and enlisted personnel when the relationship compromises the chain of command. In the military the need for a highly disciplined, strongly bonded group of individuals is critical to a combat unit's success. A minority of companies has enacted *no-dating policies* that attempt to eliminate the presence of romantic relationships at the workplace between employees. Enforcing no-dating policies can be difficult. Recently, a senior executive at Staples, an office supply company that instituted a no-dating policy, was forced to resign when it was revealed he was having a consensual affair with his secretary. Staples lost a valued officer, and the manager forfeited his lucrative job for violating company rules, even though he committed no illegal act.[67]

Other companies view office romance more positively by recognizing the beneficial effect it may have on employee morale due to the fact that many office romances lead to marriage. For example, Microsoft CEO Bill Gates met his wife, Melinda French, at the company when she was a marketing executive. Representative of companies that do not interfere with office romance is Delta Airlines, which does not have any rule against dating between employees. Delta expects its employees to maintain a professional and businesslike approach to work, which includes all work-related relationships. The only exception it makes is that the company does not allow a spouse or romantic partner to supervise the other. If that were to happen, one of the partners would be transferred to another work unit.[68] The employment trend of longer work hours in U.S. firms suggests that more employees will be tempted to develop a romantic relationship with a colleague at the workplace. Management can be expected to look for guidance on how to deal with office romance from HR representatives as they struggle with balancing the privacy rights of employees with the company's liability to prevent sexual harassment.

Disciplining Employees

Managers have traditionally recognized the need to control and change employees' behavior when it does not meet their expectations. *Employee discipline* is a tool that managers rely on to communicate to employees that they need to change a behavior. For example, some employees are habitually late to work, ignore safety procedures, neglect the details required for their job, act rude to customers, or engage in unprofessional conduct with coworkers. Employee discipline entails communicating the unacceptability of such behavior along with a warning that specific actions will follow if the employee does not change the behavior.[69]

Employee discipline is usually performed by supervisors, but in self-managed work teams employee discipline may be a team responsibility. For instance, at Hannaford Bros., a food distribution center outside Albany, New York, the 120 warehouse employees are divided into five teams, each of which has a serious conduct committee. The committee handles employee discipline and makes recommendations to management, including counseling and even termination. Management usually adopts these recommendations. The committees generally come up with creative solutions for handling discipline problems. In fact, it has rarely proved necessary to terminate an employee.[70]

Employee and employer rights may come into conflict over the issue of employee discipline. Sometimes employees believe they are being disciplined unfairly. In such situations, a company's HR staff may help sort out disputed rights. This HR contribution is particularly valuable because it can enable the employee and the supervisor to maintain an effective working relationship.

Two different approaches to employee discipline are widely used: (1) progressive discipline and (2) positive discipline. In both these approaches, supervisors must discuss the behavior in question with their employees. Managers almost invariably find it difficult to confront an employee for disciplinary purposes. Reasons for their discomfort range from not wanting to be the bearer of bad news, to not knowing how to start the discussion, to a fear that the discussion will get out of control. The Manager's Notebook titled "Five Steps for Effective Disciplinary Sessions" offers some guidelines that should make it easier for managers to handle an admittedly distasteful task.

MANAGER'S NOTEBOOK

Five Steps for Effective Disciplinary Sessions

1. Determine whether discipline is called for. Is the problem an isolated infraction or part of a pattern? Consult with HR experts and get some feedback before making a disciplinary decision.[a]
2. Have clear goals for the discussion that you outline in your opening remarks. Be specific. Do not rely on indirect communication or beat around the bush. At the end of the discussion, the employee should have a clear idea of your expectations for improvement.[b]
3. Ensure two-way communication. The most helpful disciplinary meeting is a discussion, not a lecture. The objective of the meeting, after all, is to devise a workable solution, not to berate the employee.[c]
4. Establish a follow-up plan. The agreement to a follow-up plan is crucial in both the progressive and positive disciplinary procedures. It is particularly important to establish the time frame in which the employee's behavior is to improve.[d]
5. End on a positive note. You may want to emphasize the employee's strengths so that he or she can leave the meeting believing that you—and the company—want the employee to succeed.[e]

Sources: [a]Higgins, L. (1998, March). Six pointers for addressing employee performance concerns. *Nursing Management*, 56. [b]Ibid. [c]Day, D. (1993, May). Training 101. Help for discipline dodgers. *Training & Development*, 19–22. [d]Ibid. [e]Ibid.

Progressive Discipline

The most commonly used form of discipline, progressive discipline, consists of a series of management interventions that gives employees opportunities to correct their behavior before being discharged. **Progressive discipline** procedures are warning steps, each of which involves a punishment that increases in severity the longer the undesirable behaviors persist.[71] If the employee fails to respond to these progressive warnings, the employer is justified in discharging the individual.

Progressive discipline
A series of management interventions that gives employees opportunities to correct undesirable behaviors before being discharged.

Progressive discipline systems usually have three to five steps, although a four-step system is the most common, as shown in Figure 14.4 on page 482. Minor violations of company policy involve using all the steps in the progressive discipline procedure. Serious violations, sometimes referred to as *gross misconduct*, can result in the elimination of several steps and sometimes even begin at the last step, which is discharge. Examples of gross misconduct are assaulting a supervisor and falsifying employment records. However, most applications of discipline involve minor rule infractions like violating a dress code, smoking at an inappropriate time or place, or being habitually late. Figure 14.5 (page 482) shows more examples of minor and serious violations.

A four-step progressive discipline procedure includes the following steps:[72]

1. Verbal Warning

An employee who commits a minor violation receives a verbal warning from the supervisor and is told that if this problem continues within a specific time period, harsher punishment will follow. The supervisor provides clear expectations for improvement.

Figure 14.4

1. Verbal Warning	2. Written Warning	3. Suspension	4. Discharge
The employee has an unexcused absence from work. He or she receives a verbal warning from the supervisor and is told that if he or she takes another unexcused absence within the next month, harsher punishment will follow.	Two weeks after the verbal warning from his or her supervisor, the employee takes another unexcused absence. He or she now receives a written warning that if he or she fails to correct the absenteeism problem within the next two months, more severe treatment will follow. This warning goes into the employee's personnel file.	Six weeks later the employee fails to show up for work for two consecutive days. This time he or she is suspended from work without pay for one week. He or she also receives a final warning from his or her supervisor that if there is another unexcused absence within three months after returning from suspension, he or she will be terminated.	Two weeks after his or her return from suspension, the employee does not show up for work. Upon his or her return to work the following day, he or she is discharged.

Four Steps in a Progressive Discipline Procedure

2. Written Warning
   The employee violates the same rule within the specified time period and now receives a written warning from the supervisor. This warning goes into the employee's records. The employee is told that failure to correct the violation within a certain time period will result in more severe treatment.
3. Suspension
   The employee still fails to respond to warnings and again violates the work rule. The employee is now suspended from employment without pay for a specific amount of time. He or she receives a final warning from the supervisor, indicating that discharge will follow upon violating the rule within a specified time period.
4. Discharge
   The employee violates the rule one more time within the specified time period and is discharged.

Figure 14.4 illustrates how an employer would use progressive discipline with an employee who has a pattern of unexcused absences from work.

Categories of Employee Misconduct

Figure 14.5

Minor Violations	Serious Violations
■ Absenteeism	■ Drug use at work
■ Dress code violation	■ Theft
■ Smoking rule violation	■ Dishonesty
■ Incompetence	■ Physical assault upon a supervisor
■ Safety rule violation	■ Sabotage of company operations
■ Sleeping on the job	
■ Horseplay	
■ Tardiness	

For infractions that fall between the categories of minor violation and serious violation, one or two steps in the procedure are skipped. These infractions are usually handled by supervisors, who give the employees an opportunity to correct the behavior before discharging them. For example, two employees get into a fistfight at work, but there are mitigating circumstances (one employee verbally attacked the other). In this situation, both employees may be suspended without pay and warned that another such violation will result in discharge.

Positive Discipline

In many situations punishment does not motivate an employee to change a behavior. Rather, it only teaches the person to fear or resent the allocator of punishment—that is, the supervisor. This emphasis on punishment in progressive discipline may encourage employees to deceive their supervisor rather than correct their actions. To avoid this outcome, some companies have replaced progressive discipline with **positive discipline,** which encourages employees to monitor their own behaviors and assume responsibility for their actions.

Positive discipline
A discipline procedure that encourages employees to monitor their own behaviors and assume responsibility for their actions.

Positive discipline is similar to progressive discipline in that it too uses a series of steps that increase in urgency and severity until the last step, which is discharge. However, positive discipline replaces the punishment used in progressive discipline with counseling sessions between employee and supervisor. These sessions focus on getting the employee to learn from past mistakes and initiate a plan to make a positive change in behavior. Rather than depending on threats and punishments, the supervisor uses counseling skills to motivate the employee to change. Rather than placing blame on the employee, the supervisor emphasizes collaborative problem solving. In short, positive discipline alters the supervisor's role from adversary to counselor.

To ensure that supervisors are adequately prepared to counsel employees, companies that use positive discipline must see that they receive appropriate training either from the company's own HR department or from outside professional trainers. At Union Carbide, which began using positive discipline in the late 1970s, managers attend a two-day training program to gain familiarity with positive discipline policies and practices. Because Union Carbide had long used a progressive discipline approach, a key element of the training is helping managers abandon their tendency to respond to performance problems in a punitive way. Managers also receive training in documenting their discussions specifically, factually, and defensibly.[73]

A four-step positive discipline procedure starts with a first counseling session between employee and supervisor that ends with a verbal solution that is acceptable to both parties. If this solution does not work, the supervisor and employee meet again to discuss why it failed and to develop a new plan and timetable to solve the problem. At this second step, the new agreed-upon solution to the problem is written down.

If there is still no improvement in performance, the third step is a final warning that the employee is at risk of being discharged. Rather than suspend the employee without pay (as would happen under progressive discipline), this third step gives the employee some time to evaluate his or her situation and come up with a new solution. In doing so, the employee is encouraged to examine why earlier attempts to improve performance did not work. Some companies even give the employee a "decision-making day off" with pay to develop a plan for improved performance.[74]

Managers often resist this aspect of positive discipline because they feel that it rewards employees for poor performance. Some suspect that employees intentionally misbehave to get a free day off. According to the employee relations director of Union Carbide, which uses a paid decision-making day off as part of its disciplinary procedure, this is not so. The company believes a paid day off is more effective than the unpaid suspension used in progressive discipline procedures because (1) workers returning from an unpaid suspension often feel anger or apathy, which may lead to either reduced effectiveness on the job or subtle sabotage; (2) paying the employee for the decision-making day off avoids making the employee a martyr in the eyes of coworkers; and (3) paying for the decision-making day off underscores management's "good faith" toward the employee and probably reduces the chances that the employee will win a wrongful discharge suit if he or she is eventually terminated.[75]

Failure to improve performance after the final warning results in discharge, the fourth step of the positive discipline procedure. Incidents of gross misconduct (such as theft) are treated no differently under a positive discipline procedure than under a progressive discipline procedure. In both systems, theft will most likely result in immediate discharge.

In addition to the costs of training managers and supervisors in appropriate counseling skills and approaches, positive discipline has another drawback. Counseling sessions require a lot of time to be effective, and this is time that both the supervisor and employee are not working on other tasks. Nonetheless, positive discipline offers considerable benefits to both employees and managers. Employees prefer it because they like being treated with respect by their supervisors. Counseling generally results in a greater willingness to change undesirable behaviors than discipline does. Supervisors prefer it because it does not demand that they assume the role of disciplinarian. Counseling makes for better-quality working relationships with subordinates than discipline does. In addition, under a system of positive discipline, managers are much more likely to intervene early to correct a problem.

Finally, positive discipline can have positive effects on a company's bottom line, as evidenced at Union Carbide. Studies in five of the company's facilities have shown an average decline in absenteeism of 5.5 percent since the company switched from punitive to positive discipline procedures. Moreover, in one unionized facility at the company, disciplinary grievances went down from 36 in one year to 8 in the next. Since Union Carbide executives estimate that taking an employee complaint through all steps of the grievance procedure (short of arbitration) costs approximately $400 at this facility, the switch in discipline procedures saved the company over $11,000 per year.[76] Pennzoil, General Electric, and Procter & Gamble also have adopted the positive discipline procedure and have reported successful outcomes with it.[77] In addition, many city police forces and some universities use positive discipline. For example, one university used positive discipline with a professor who would yell at, criticize, and belittle students when they volunteered the wrong answers to his questions or avoided class participation. The department chair and the professor worked together to develop a plan to control his temper in the classroom. The department chair saw a positive change in the professor's classroom behavior that would not have occurred had the chair used a more confrontational form of discipline, such as the progressive discipline procedure.

Administering and Managing Discipline

Managers must ensure that employees who are disciplined receive due process. In the context of discipline, *due process* means fair and consistent treatment. If an employee challenges a disciplinary action under the EEO laws or a union grievance procedure, the employer must prove that the employee engaged in misconduct and was disciplined appropriately for it. Thus, supervisors should be properly trained in how to administer discipline.[78] Two important elements of due process that managers need to consider in this area are (1) the standards of discipline used to determine if the employee was treated fairly and (2) whether or not the employee has a right to appeal a disciplinary action.

Basic Standards of Discipline

Some basic standards of discipline should apply to all rule violations, whether major or minor. All disciplinary actions should include the following procedures at a minimum:

- **Communication of rules and performance criteria** Employees should be aware of the company's rules and standards and the consequences of violating them. Every employee and supervisor should understand the company's disciplinary policies and procedures fully. Employees who violate a rule or do not meet performance criteria should be given the opportunity to correct their behavior.
- **Documentation of the facts** Managers should gather a convincing amount of evidence to justify the discipline. This evidence should be carefully documented so that it is difficult to dispute. For example, time cards could be used to document tardiness; videotapes could document a case of employee theft; the written testimony of a witness could substantiate a charge

of insubordination. Employees should have the opportunity to refute this evidence and provide documentation in self-defense.

- **Consistent response to rule violations** It is important for employees to believe that discipline is administered consistently, predictably, and without discrimination or favoritism. If they perceive otherwise, they will be more likely to challenge discipline decisions. This does not mean that every violation should be treated exactly the same. For example, an employee with many years of seniority and an excellent work record who breaks a rule may be punished less harshly than a recently hired employee who breaks the same rule. However, two recently hired employees who break the same rule should receive the same punishment.

The **hot-stove rule** provides a model of how a disciplinary action should be administered. The rule suggests that the disciplinary process is similar to touching a hot stove: (1) Touching a hot stove results in an immediate consequence, which is a burn. Discipline should also be an immediate consequence that follows a rule infraction. (2) The hot stove provides a warning that one will get burned if one touches it. Disciplinary rules should inform employees of the consequences of breaking the rules as well. (3) A hot stove is consistent in administering pain to anyone who touches it. Disciplinary rules should be consistently applied to all.[79]

Hot-stove rule
A model of disciplinary action: Discipline should be immediate, provide ample warning, and be consistently applied to all.

The Just Cause Standard of Discipline

In cases of wrongful discharge that involve statutory rights or exceptions to employment at will, U.S. courts require the employer to prove that an employee was discharged for *just cause*. This exacting standard, which is written into union contracts and into some nonunion companies' employment policies and employee handbooks, consists of seven questions that must be answered in the affirmative for just cause to exist.[80] Failure to answer "yes" to one or more of these questions suggests that the discipline may have been arbitrary or unwarranted.

1. Notification
   Was the employee forewarned of the disciplinary consequences of his or her conduct? Unless the misconduct is very obvious (for example, theft or assault), the employer should make the employee aware, either verbally or in writing, that he or she has violated a rule.
2. Reasonable Rule
   Was the rule the employee violated reasonably related to safe and efficient operations? The rule should not jeopardize an employee's safety or integrity in any way.
3. Investigation Before the Discipline
   Did managers conduct an investigation into the misconduct before administering discipline? If immediate action is required, the employee may be suspended pending the outcome of the investigation. If the investigation reveals no misconduct, all of the employee's rights should be restored.
4. Fair Investigation
   Was the investigation fair and impartial? Fair investigations allow the employee to defend himself or herself. An employee who is being interviewed as part of a disciplinary investigation has a right based on federal law to have another employee present to be his or her advocate, or to have someone to consult with, or simply to be a witness.[81]
5. Proof of Guilt
   Did the investigation provide substantial evidence or proof of guilt? Management may need a "preponderance of evidence" to prove serious charges of gross misconduct, and a less stringent (but still substantial) amount of evidence to prove minor violations.
6. Absence of Discrimination
   Were the rules, orders, and penalties of the disciplinary action applied evenhandedly and without discrimination? It is not acceptable for managers to go from lax enforcement of a rule to sudden rigorous enforcement of that rule without notifying employees that they intend to do so.
7. Reasonable Penalty
   Was the disciplinary penalty reasonably related to the seriousness of the rule violation? The employer should consider related facts, such as the employee's work record, when deter-

mining the severity of punishment. There might be a range of penalties for a given rule infraction that depend on the length and quality of the employee's service record.

Because the just cause standard is fairly stringent and can prove unwieldy in cases of minor infractions that require immediate supervisory attention, nonunion employers who believe that their employees work under employment at will may choose a less demanding discipline standard.[82]

The Right to Appeal Discipline

Sometimes employees believe they have been disciplined unfairly, either because their supervisors have abused their power or because their supervisors are biased in dealing with individuals whom they like or dislike. For a disciplinary system to be effective, employees must have access to an appeals procedure in which others (who are perceived to be free from bias) can examine the facts. As we discussed in Chapter 13, good employee relations requires establishing appeals procedures that employees can use to voice their disagreement with managers' actions. For challenging disciplinary actions, two of the most useful appeals procedures are the open-door policy and the use of employee relations representatives. These two methods are attractive because of their flexibility and their ability to reach quick resolutions. The Manager's Notebook titled "Mistakes to Avoid When Administering Discipline" lists some common pitfalls that can occur when disciplining employees and ways to avoid them.

Managing Difficult Employees

So far we've focused on the challenges of administering discipline. We now turn to some common problems that managers are likely to encounter. All of the problems we discuss here—poor attendance, poor performance, insubordination, and substance abuse—often lead to disciplinary actions. Managing the discipline of difficult employees requires good judgment and common sense.

Poor Attendance

The problem of poor attendance includes absenteeism and/or tardiness. Poor attendance can become a serious problem that leads to discharge for just cause. If poor attendance is not managed properly, employee productivity can decline and group morale can suffer as those with good attendance are forced to increase their efforts to compensate for people who shirk their responsibilities.

MANAGER'S NOTEBOOK

Mistakes to Avoid When Administering Discipline

1. **Losing your temper.** When you lose control of your temper you may say things that damage your relationship with the employee and that you may later regret. Your loss of self-control may also encourage the employee to lose control and yell right back at you. It is preferable to step back and take a deep breath before you begin to speak to the employee who is misbehaving, no matter how angry you are feeling. Once you are calm you can have a more constructive conversation with the employee.
2. **Avoiding disciplinary action entirely.** Many supervisors avoid disciplinary action entirely because they associate it with punishment and fear harming the relationship with an employee. A supervisor needs to understand that the purpose of discipline is to correct behav-

ior, not necessarily to punish an individual. Avoiding disciplinary action may actually harm an employee who is deprived of the chance to learn how to correct his or her behavior.

3. **Playing therapist.** Trying to get to the root causes and motives for a behavior may send the wrong message to an employee. Unless a supervisor is trained as a therapist, the employee may misinterpret the supervisor's personal questions as being nosy or overly analytical, which is unlikely to achieve the desired change in behavior. Employees respond more positively to a supervisor who is more decisive and points out the inappropriate behavior and communicates clearly what kind of performance is expected in its place.
4. **Making excuses for an employee.** It is common for employees to make excuses that explain their mistakes. Some employees become adept at creating sympathy for themselves by telling tales of woe involving their family or personal hardships. By falling for these excuses, supervisors deprive employees the chance to accept responsibility for their mistakes and instead enable them to continue rationalizing their performance deficiencies. If an employee truly has a serious personal problem that is affecting work performance, he or she should seek help with the EAP.

Sources: Adapted from Bielous, G. A. (1998, August). Five worst disciplinary mistakes (and how to avoid them). *Supervision*, 11–13; and Lisoski, E. (1998, October). Nine common mistakes made when disciplining employees. *Supervision*, 12–14.

Sometimes employees are absent or tardy for legitimate reasons—for example, sickness, child-care problems, inclement weather, or religious beliefs. Managers should identify those employees who have legitimate reasons and treat them differently than they treat those who are chronically absent or tardy.

When disciplining an employee for poor attendance, managers need to consider several factors:

- **Is the attendance rule reasonable?** Attendance rules should be flexible enough to allow for the emergencies or unforeseen circumstances that most employees experience from time to time, including religious or cultural holidays celebrated by a diverse workforce. Most companies deal with this issue by showing leniency when an employee gives notice that he or she is sick or experiencing an emergency.
- **Has the employee been warned of the consequences of poor attendance?** This could be particularly important when an employee is unaware of how much time flexibility is possible in reporting to the job.
- **Are there any mitigating circumstances that should be taken into consideration?** Sometimes special circumstances need to be considered. These circumstances include work history, length of service, reason for absence, and likelihood of improved attendance.[83]

Managers should be aware of patterns of poor attendance within a work unit. Systemic absenteeism or tardiness may be a symptom of job avoidance. Employees may dread coming to work because coworkers are unpleasant, the job has become unchallenging, they are experiencing conflicting demands from job and family, or supervision is poor. A disciplinary approach is not the best way to deal with this type of absenteeism. It would be better for the manager or company to look for ways to change the work environment. Possible solutions to job avoidance are redesigning jobs or, when the problem is widespread, restructuring the organization.

For employees whose absences are due to overwhelming family demands, flexible work schedules or permission to work at home (telecommuting) may be desirable. Flexible work schedules are gaining popularity at companies both large and small. Ten months into Xerox Corporation's experiment with flexible work schedules, absences had fallen by one-third, teamwork had improved, and worker surveys showed that morale had risen.[84]

Poor Performance

Every manager must deal with employees who perform poorly and who do not respond to coaching or feedback. In most cases, the performance appraisal (see Chapter 7) can be used to turn around poor performers by helping them develop an action plan for improvement. Sometimes, however, the poor performance is so serious that it requires immediate intervention. Consider the following situations:

- A restaurant manager receives daily complaints from angry customers about the quality of one waitress's service.
- A partner's poor interpersonal skills affect his working relationships with the other two partners in his firm. The firm is now failing to meet its goals because of the severe conflicts and disruptions instigated by this one person.

These examples suggest a glaring need for progressive or positive discipline procedures. If these employees failed to improve their performance after receiving some warnings or counseling, dismissal would be justified.

Companies and managers should follow three guidelines when applying discipline for poor performance:

1. The company's performance standards should be reasonable and communicated to all employees. Job descriptions can be used for this purpose.
2. Poor performance should be documented and poor performers should be told how they are not meeting the expected standards. One source of documented evidence can be the pattern of the employee's performance appraisals over a period of time.
3. Managers should make a good-faith attempt to give employees an opportunity to improve their performance before disciplining them.

Sometimes poor performance is the result of factors beyond the employee's control. In these cases, managers should avoid using discipline except as a last resort. For example, an employee may be unable to perform at expected standards because of incompetence. An *incompetent employee* (one who is lacking in ability, not effort) may be given remedial training (see Chapter 8) or transferred to a less demanding job rather than be dismissed. An incompetent employee's poor performance may be the result of a flaw in the organization's selection system that caused a poor match between the employee's skills and the job requirements.

Some organizations use a *probationary employment period* (a period of time that allows the employer to discharge any employee at will) to weed out incompetent employees early. Probationary employment periods typically last one to three months. In Europe, where permanent employment is the norm, many companies insist on a six-month trial period as part of the employment contract. However, this policy can present a problem when recruiting executives, who understandably want to be guaranteed a permanent position before leaving their current job.

It is not only inappropriate but also illegal to use discipline to correct poor performance when an employee has a physical or mental disability.[85] The Americans with Disabilities Act (ADA, see Chapter 3) requires employers to make reasonable accommodation for disabled employees who cannot perform the job as it is structured. Accommodation may include redesigning the job or modifying policies and procedures. For example, an employee who is diagnosed with a terminal illness may request a change from a full-time job to a part-time job or one with a more flexible work schedule. The EEOC, which regulates how employers respond to the needs of employees with disabilities, would probably consider this a reasonable request, so failure to make such an accommodation could lead to government sanctions.

Unfortunately, many myths hinder firms' compliance with the ADA. One myth is that reasonable accommodation always involves prohibitive expense. Actually, accommodation is not necessarily costly, and more often than not, the money spent to accommodate a disabled individual is minor compared with the cost of litigation. Samsonite Corporation, a luggage company located in Denver, has employed deaf production workers for years. The only accommodation necessary—beyond an accommodating attitude and the willingness of many employees to learn some sign language—has been the use of lights in the production area in addition to the standard beepers alerting employees to the presence of forklifts.[86]

Insubordination

The willingness of employees to carry out managers' directives is essential to a business's effective operations. For example, consider the case of a sales representative who refuses to submit the weekly activity reports requested by his manager.[87] How should the sales manager react to the sales representative's behavior?

Insubordination, which involves an employee's refusal to obey a direct order from a supervisor, is a direct challenge of management's right to run the company. Insubordination also occurs when an employee is verbally abusive to a supervisor. The discipline for insubordination usually varies according to the seriousness of the insubordination and the presence or absence of mitigating factors. Mitigating factors include the employee's work history and length of service and whether or not the employee was provoked by a supervisor's verbal abuse.

Insubordination
Either refusal to obey a direct order from a supervisor or verbal abuse of a supervisor.

To justify disciplining an employee for insubordination, managers should document the following: (1) The supervisor gave a direct order to a subordinate, either in writing or orally; and (2) the employee refused to obey the order, either by indicating so verbally or by not doing what was asked. The discipline for a first insubordination offense ranges from applying the first step of the progressive discipline procedure to immediate suspension or discharge.

Two exceptions allow an employee to disobey a direct order: illegal activities and safety considerations. For instance, a California court found that an employer had violated public policy when it fired an employee who refused to commit perjury. Other illegal orders that employees can refuse with legal protection are participation in price-fixing and improper bookkeeping.[88] The whistleblowing laws passed in some states provide further protection to employees who can prove they were discharged for refusing to break the law. The Occupational Safety and Health Administration protects the rights of employees who refuse to expose themselves to serious jeopardy. For insubordination to be acceptable, the employee should have "reasonable cause" to fear for his or her safety—for example, knowing that a truck the worker is ordered to drive has defective brakes.

Because the penalties for insubordination are severe, companies should create internal systems and cultures (open-door policies, appeal systems) that allow employees to appeal charges of insubordinate behavior. The legal and monetary penalties to companies for refusing to hear an employee's reasons for insubordination can be severe. Managers should be sure that insubordination charges are not being used to protect their own illegal or unethical behavior. For instance, a supervisor who charges an employee with insubordination may be attempting to force out someone who objects to the supervisor's illegal behavior. Companies that ignore such signs of trouble may find that a small problem has escalated into a very difficult and/or expensive situation.

Alcohol-Related Misconduct

Employees' use of alcohol presents two separate challenges to managers. First, there is the challenge of managing an employee who is an alcoholic. Second, there is the challenge of managing an employee who uses alcohol or is intoxicated on the job. Each of these employees should be disciplined differently.

Alcoholic employees are generally viewed sympathetically because alcoholism is an illness and medical treatment is the generally accepted remedy for it. However, as we mentioned in Chapter 13, some alcoholic employees have a strong denial mechanism that prevents them from admitting that they are alcoholics: Others may not view them as alcoholics either because alcoholism is often masked by behavioral symptoms such as poor attendance. Thus, a supervisor may perceive an alcoholic employee as someone who has an attendance or performance problem rather than an alcohol problem and discipline the employee accordingly. Organizations with EAPs give employees with performance problems the opportunity to visit a counselor as the last step in progressive discipline before discharge. This is where the alcoholism may finally be discovered and the employee referred to an alcohol rehabilitation facility.

Sometimes employees claim to be alcoholic to cover up their misconduct. If the EAP counselor determines that the individual is not an alcoholic, the discipline procedure is the appropriate managerial response to the problem.

Using alcohol on the job and coming to work intoxicated are both considered serious misconduct and can lead to harsh discipline. Organizations that have job-related reasons to restrict alcohol use at work or working "under the influence" should have clearly stated and reasonable policies. For example, it is reasonable to restrict the alcohol use, on or off the job, of heavy equipment operators at a construction site. It is more difficult to forbid a sales representative to drink alcohol when entertaining a prospective client at a lunch.

The best way to prove that an employee has come to work intoxicated is to administer a blood alcohol content test. A supervisor can ask an employee to submit to this test if there is a reasonable suspicion that the worker is intoxicated. Supervisors may suspect an individual is intoxicated if he or she engages in unusual behavior (talking particularly loud or using profanity), has slurred speech, or has alcohol on the breath.

A first intoxication offense may result in suspension or discharge because of the potential for damage that an alcohol-impaired employee can create. An extreme example of an alcohol-impaired employee's cost to an organization is the accident in which the Exxon *Valdez* oil tanker spilled oil off the coast of Alaska in March 1989. A blood alcohol test revealed that the ship's captain was intoxicated at the time of the oil spill, which cost Exxon over $1 billion to clean up.

Illegal Drug Use and Abuse

Drug use and abuse by employees also presents a serious challenge to managers. "Illegal drug use" refers to any use of prohibited substances such as marijuana, heroin, and cocaine as well as the illegal use of prescription drugs such as Valium. The problems associated with drug use are very similar to those associated with the use of alcohol. The key difference is that the use of illegal drugs is socially unacceptable, whereas the use of alcohol in moderation is socially acceptable.

We examined the specifics of drug-use detection systems earlier in this chapter, and we will address the health aspects of drug use in Chapter 16. Here we note only that illegal drug use is often masked by symptoms such as inattention and unexplained absences. Managers who suspect that drug use or addiction is the source of a performance problem should refer the employee to EAP counseling if the organization has such a program. Simultaneously, they should document performance problems and begin disciplinary procedures. These will prove valuable should it be necessary to terminate the employee because of failure to overcome the

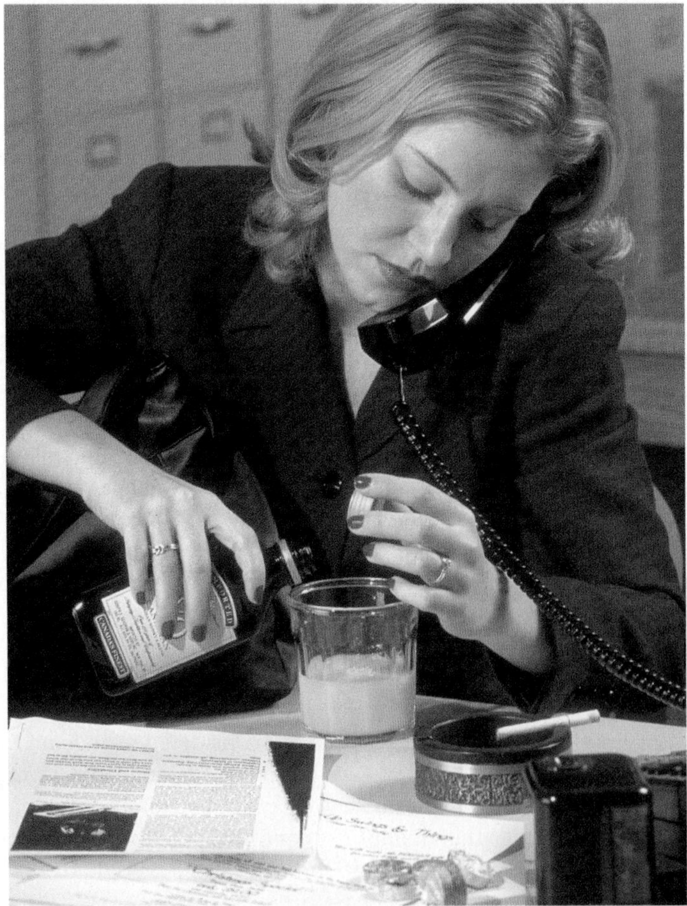

Managers need to be trained to recognize the symptoms of a troubled employee, such as those with alcohol-related problems.

substance abuse problem after counseling and treatment. Managers who refer employees to an EAP program for problems that are not strictly related to performance may create some risk for the company, as we see in Chapter 16.

Preventing the Need for Discipline with Human Resource Management

By taking a strategic and proactive approach to the design of HRM systems, managers can eliminate the need for a substantial amount of employee discipline. HR programs designed to use employees' talents and skills effectively, reduce the need to resort to discipline to shape employee behavior. In this section we briefly revisit some of the functional areas of HR we discussed in earlier chapters to show how each can be designed to prevent problem employees.[89]

Recruitment and Selection

By spending more time and resources on recruiting and selection, managers can make better matches between individuals and the organization.

- Workers can be selected for fit in the organization as well as the job. Choosing applicants who have career potential in the company decreases the likelihood that employees will exhibit performance problems later.
- Checking references and gathering background information on applicants' work habits and character are useful preliminaries to making a job offer.
- Multiple interviews that involve diverse groups in the company can reduce biases that lead to poor hiring decisions. When women, minorities, peers, and subordinates, as well as senior people, are involved in the interviewing process, companies stand a better chance of obtaining an accurate portrait of the applicant.

Training and Development

Investing in employees' training and development now saves a company from having to deal with incompetents or workers whose skills are obsolete down the road.

- An effective orientation program communicates to new employees the values important to the organization. It also teaches employees what is expected from them as members of the organization. These insights into the company can help employees manage their own behavior better. FedEx, for instance, has an extensive orientation program to communicate company values to employees.[90]
- Training programs for new employees can reduce skill gaps and improve competencies.
- Retraining programs can be used for continuing employees whose skills have become obsolete. For example, employees may need periodic retraining on word processing software as the technology changes and more powerful programs become available.
- Training supervisors to coach and provide feedback to their subordinates encourages supervisors to intervene early in problem situations with counseling rather than discipline.
- Career ladders can be developed to give employees incentives to develop a long-term commitment to the organization's goals. When employees know that the organization has a long-term use for their contributions, they are more likely to engage in acts of good citizenship with their coworkers and customers.

Human Resource Planning

Jobs, job families, and organizational units can be designed to motivate and challenge employees. Highly motivated workers seldom need to be disciplined for inadequate performance.

- Jobs should be designed to use the best talents of each employee. It may be necessary to build some flexibility into job designs to put an employee's strengths to best use. One way companies are creating greater job flexibility is through *job banding*. Discussed in Chapter 10, this system replaces traditional narrowly defined job descriptions with broader categories, or bands, of related jobs. By putting greater variety into jobs, job banding makes it less likely that employees will feel so underchallenged or bored that they start avoiding work through absences or tardiness. Job banding has been implemented successfully by companies such as Aetna, General Electric, and Harley Davidson.[91]

- Job descriptions and work plans should be developed to communicate effectively to employees the performance standards to which they will be held accountable.

Performance Appraisal

Many performance problems can be avoided by designing effective performance appraisal systems. An effective performance appraisal system lets people know what is expected of them, how well they are meeting those expectations, and what they can do to improve on their weaknesses.

- The performance appraisal criteria should set reasonable standards that employees understand and have some control over.
- Supervisors should be encouraged to provide continuous feedback to subordinates. Many problems can be avoided with early interventions.
- Performance evaluations for supervisors should place strong emphasis on their effectiveness at providing feedback and developing their subordinates.
- Employee appraisals should be documented properly to protect employers against wrongful discharge or discrimination suits.

Compensation

Employees who believe that rewards are allocated unfairly (perhaps on the basis of favoritism) are likely to lose respect for the organization. Worse, employees who believe that pay policies do not recognize the value of their contributions are more likely to withhold future contributions.

- Pay policies should be perceived as fair by all employees. Employees deserve rewards for their contributions. It is important to explain to them the procedures used to establish their compensation level.
- An appeal mechanism that gives employees the right to challenge a pay decision should be established. Employees who can voice their frustration with a pay decision through a legitimate channel are less likely to engage in angry exchanges with supervisors, co-workers, or customers.

Summary and Conclusions

Employee Rights

In the employment relationship, both employees and employers have rights. Employee rights fall into three categories: statutory rights (protection from discrimination, safe work conditions, the right to form unions), contractual rights (as provided by employment contracts, union contracts, and employment policies), and other rights (the rights to ethical treatment, privacy, and free speech).

Management Rights

Employers have the right to run their business and make a profit. These rights are supported by property laws, common law, and the values of a society that accepts the concepts of private enterprise and the profit motive. Management rights include the right to manage the workforce and to hire, promote, assign, discipline, and discharge employees. Another important management right is employment at will, which allows an employer to dismiss an employee at any time for any cause. There are three key exceptions to the employment-at-will doctrine: public policy exceptions, implied contracts, and lack of good faith and fair dealing.

Employee Rights Challenges: A Balancing Act

Sometimes the rights of the employer and employees are in conflict. For example, a random drug-testing policy can create a conflict between an employer's responsibility to provide a safe workplace and employees' rights to privacy. HR professionals need to balance the rights of the employee with those of the employer when designing policies that address workplace issues like random drug testing, electronic monitoring of employees, whistleblowing, and office romance.

Disciplining Employees

Managers rely on discipline procedures to communicate to employees the need to change a behavior. There are two approaches to discipline. The progressive discipline procedure relies on increasing levels of punishment leading to discharge. The positive discipline procedure uses counseling sessions between supervisor and subordinate to encourage the employee to monitor his or her own behavior. Both procedures are designed to deal with forms of misconduct that are correctable.

Administering and Managing Discipline

To avoid conflict and lawsuits, managers must administer discipline properly. This entails ensuring that disciplined employees receive due process. Managers need to be aware of the standards used to determine if an employee was treated fairly and whether or not the employee has a right to appeal disciplinary action. For a disciplinary system to be effective, an appeal mechanism must be in place.

Managing Difficult Employees

It is often necessary to discipline employees who exhibit poor attendance, poor performance, insubordination, or substance abuse. Managing the discipline process in these situations requires a balance of good judgment and common sense. Discipline may not be the best solution in all cases.

Preventing the Need for Discipline with Human Resource Management

The need for discipline can often be avoided by a strategic and proactive approach to HRM. A company can avoid discipline by recruiting and selecting the right employees for current positions as well as future opportunities, by training and developing workers, by designing jobs and career paths that best utilize people's talents, by designing effective performance appraisal systems, and by compensating employees for their contributions.

Key Terms

contract, 467
contractual rights, 467
due process, 468
employment at will, 471
employment contract, 467
hot-stove rule, 485
insubordination, 489
management rights, 471
personnel file, 470
positive discipline, 483
Privacy Act of 1974, 470
progressive discipline, 481
right, 467
statutory right, 467
whistleblowing, 478
wrongful discharge, 468

Discussion Questions

1. Why have managers needed to place greater emphasis on employee rights in recent years?
2. Do employers have rights? If so, what are these rights?
3. In a highly publicized court case in 1988, *Foley v. Interactive Data Corp.*, the plaintiff was fired two months after he told a company vice president that his supervisor, a recent hire, was under investigation by the FBI for embezzlement from his previous employer. (The supervisor pleaded guilty in court six months after Foley was fired.) In his more than six years of employment at Interactive Data, Foley had received a steady stream of raises, promotions, and superior performance reviews. Based on his performance reviews and the company's written termination policy (which prescribed a seven-step termination procedure), Foley believed that Interactive Data could not dismiss him. He sued the company on the basis of three theories, or causes, of action. What do you think these three causes of action were? Could any of these be considered exceptions to employment at will?
4. National Medical Enterprises, Inc., a $4 billion operator of hospitals and psychiatric treatment centers, faced criminal probes for practices such as widespread overbilling and fraudulent diagnoses to extend patients' hospital stays. Investigators found that NME's top management urged hospital administrators to adopt "intake" goals designed to lure patients into hospitals for lengthy and unnecessary treatments. Hospital staffers were also urged to admit fully half of all patients who came in for an evaluation. Suppose a hospital staffer at NME refused to admit patients for whom she felt treatment was unnecessary. Could her refusal be considered insubordination? If the same staffer considered exposing fraudulent diagnoses to an outside agency, what whistleblowing precautions would she be wise to consider before going public with her case?

5. Compare and contrast the progressive and positive discipline procedures.
6. Total Recall Corporation of Spring Valley, New York, has developed a camouflaged video surveillance system called Babywatch, designed for parents who are concerned about the quality of child care they are receiving from their babysitters. The small, inconspicuous device operates under low light and is capable of recording up to five hours of video and audio material. Do you think that parents using this system secretly would be invading the babysitter's privacy, or do you think they have a legitimate reason for monitoring the babysitter?
7. What are the advantages and disadvantages of letting the team administer discipline to a team member?
8. What alternatives to electronic monitoring could an employer use to effectively control employee theft?
9. What role should HR specialists play in ensuring that employees follow a company's code of ethics?
10. The administration of discipline usually occurs between a manager and a subordinate employee. How can HR staff contribute to the fairness of the administration of discipline? How can HR staff contribute to the reduction of the need to administer discipline to employees within a company?
11. Can you think of a job-related reason why a company would decide to restrict dating between employees and enforce a no-dating policy? Do you think employers have a right to restrict any or all of the following off-duty conduct of their employees: (1) smoking cigarettes, (2) engaging in high-risk leisure activities such as skiing, motocross racing, rock climbing, or sky diving, (3) actively supporting a radical political candidate in an election, (4) having a romantic affair outside of the marriage relationship, and (5) joining a religious cult that preaches hatred against minorities? Justify your answer.

There is a variety of additional material available on the Web site that accompanies this text. You can access this information by visiting the Web site at **www.prenhall.com/gomez.**

YOU MANAGE IT!

Emerging Trends Case 14.1

Do Religion and Business Mix?

The EEOC laws in the United States request that employers make accommodations for employees for religious observances outside the workplace. For example, an employer could reasonably accommodate an employee who seeks to take a few hours off work on Saturday morning to teach a Bible study class. However, technology, global competition, downsizing, and reengineering have created a workforce of employees seeking value, support, and meaning in their lives that finds expression not only at home but also on the job. This search for religious and spiritual meaning in the workplace is a departure from the more traditional business mentality. People who bring their religious practices to the workplace can create challenges for employers or other employees who want to maintain a secular business environment. When does an employee's right to practice a religion infringe on an employer's right to manage an enterprise? When does an employer's religious practice interfere with an employee's right to have a secular environment at the workplace? Consider the following situations and then answer the questions that follow.

- Numerous employee groups meet regularly for religious study in restaurants, conference rooms, or in an employee's residence. About 10,000 small companies participate in ongoing Bible study and other religious activities. The Pittsburgh Experiment is a Christian workplace ministry with about 40 affiliated groups, some of which meet weekly at Christian prework breakfasts in prayer and support gatherings. In a Manhattan business community, a Jewish Theological Seminary rabbi discusses confronting life's daily ethical dilemmas with a monthly Old Testament Bible study group of 20 business leaders.
- Corporate training courses are offered to employees on such topics as miracles, shamanic journeying, and yoga. Companies such as Xerox and Motorola offer workshops on meditation in order to let employees develop their spirituality.
- Courts have held that the rights of nonreligious employees should be protected from discrimination. For example, the seniority rights that determine employee work schedules under a union contract should override the need to make a religious accommodation to an employee. Thus, a nonreligious employee with the greatest amount of seniority has the right to bid on a preferred work schedule over that of a religious employee with less seniority, even if the latter employee's claim on the work schedule is based on a religious accommodation.

- A company attempted to control the customer greetings of employees with guidelines after customer complaints that food service employees greeted them with such phrases as "God bless you," and "Praise the Lord." The religious employees took their case to court, which settled in favor of letting the employees express themselves spontaneously. It reasoned that a brief greeting with a spiritual overtone does not mean the employees were trying to proselytize or impose their beliefs on customers, and there was no evidence of business lost as a result of employees' practices. Consequently, the employer did not have proof of undue hardship and the employees' religious freedom prevailed.

Critical Thinking Questions

1. Suppose that a religious Moslem employee in a U.S. company refuses to cooperate with a female supervisor because it violates his religion to take orders from a female boss. Should the employer at this company make a religious accommodation for the religious employee? Justify your answer. How should this situation be handled?
2. Several female tellers at a bank wear large and prominent Christian crucifixes that hang from a necklace. These tellers are born-again Christians and meet regularly to discuss the Bible. Some customers have complained to management that religious ornaments such as the large crucifix are not appropriate at the bank and have threatened to take their business elsewhere. Bank management does not want to lose these customers. Is there an accommodation that can be made to balance the employees' religious rights and the bank's need to serve customers efficiently?

Team Exercise

With a group of four or five students discuss the implications to employee rights when the CEO of a company is a devoutly religious person who brings his or her religious beliefs to the workplace. What are the advantages of having a devoutly religious CEO? What are the disadvantages? Would it make any difference if the CEO was a Christian, a Moslem, or a Jew? Would it make a difference when a CEO practices his or her religion at the workplace compared to the situation when any ordinary employee behaves in a similar fashion? Be prepared to share your ideas with other members of the class.

Sources: Adapted from Cash, K., and Gray, G. (2000, August). A framework for accommodating religion and spirituality in the workplace. *Academy of Management Executive*, 124–134; and Gunther, M. (2001, July 9). God & business. *Fortune*, 59–80.

Discussion Case 14.2

YOU MANAGE IT!

Welcome to the World of a Whistleblower

Randy Robarge, a nuclear power plant supervisor, never intended to be a whistleblower. To Robarge, raising concerns about the improper storage of radioactive material at Commonwealth Edison's Zion power plant on Lake Michigan was just part of doing a good job. The 20-year veteran was so respected when it came to safety issues that Commonwealth Edison used him to narrate the company's training video on safety, which is still used throughout the industry. So he never expected that speaking up would end his career.

At first the harassment was subtle. He says he was routinely denied days off and asked to cover for employees who were out. Co-workers kept their distance, and supervisors began criticizing his work. Three months later Robarge was out of a job. Over the next two years a federal investigation would prove that Zion's radiation containment procedures—the ones Robarge had complained about—were lax, and the plant was eventually shut down.

The Department of Labor also ordered the company to pay Robarge a small settlement for his improper treatment. In the eyes of the court, Robarge was vindicated. But six years after speaking up and hundreds of job applications later, Robarge still can't get a job in his industry. "It's a living hell," says Robarge, 49, who supports himself with savings and odd jobs. "This is my livelihood, what I love to do. But I'm off limits. No one wants to touch me. I was labeled as a whistleblower."

Unfortunately, Robarge is not alone. About half of all whistleblowers get fired, half of those fired will lose their homes, and most of those will then lose their families too, says C. Fred Alford, author of *Whistleblowers: Broken Lives and Organizational Power*. For every Sherron Watkins, who became a hero after she blew the whistle on Enron's shady financial deal making, there are about 200 whistleblowers that people never hear about who fare poorly. Overall, 90 percent of whistleblowers can expect some kind of reprisal—public humiliation, isolation, career freezing, firing, blacklisting—from their company.

Since co-workers and even friends rarely rally behind whistleblowers, feelings of isolation and betrayal run high. "It is lonely," says Michael Lissack, the former Smith Barney banker who became a whistleblower celebrity after exposing a municipal finance scam on Wall Street. "My wife said, 'Thank you for ruining both our lives,' and walked out the door." There is even an annual retreat for whistleblowers headed by a psychologist, to help them deal with the stress and repercussions of speaking up.

Critical Thinking Questions

1. What motivates an employee to become a whistleblower if the consequences to one's professional and personal life are so severe? Do you agree or disagree that more employees should be encouraged to become whistleblowers? State your reasons. What can management do to encourage an employee to blow the whistle on illegal or unethical activities committed within the company?
2. What could Robarge have done in preparation for blowing the whistle on the company that could have reduced the painful consequences he experienced? For example, do you think Robarge should have first found another job with a different employer before blowing the whistle on his former employer? Explain. Do you think Robarge should have sought out an experienced counselor to discuss his intention to blow the whistle? Explain. What other ways could Robarge prepare for whistleblowing?

Team Exercise

With a group of four or five students examine Figure 14.2 ("Dos and Don'ts for Whistleblowers") and Figure 14.3 ("Developing an Effective Whistleblowing Policy") with respect to Randy Robarge's experience with whistleblowing. Was Randy somewhat naïve when he blew the whistle on his company? What mistakes do you think he made? Was the company partially at fault for the way Randy was treated? What could the company have done differently with respect to protecting the rights of whistleblowers? What conclusions can you draw from Randy's experience with blowing the whistle on his company?

Source: Adapted from Daniels, C. (2002, April 15). It's a living hell: Whistleblowing makes for great TV. But the aftereffects can be brutal. *Fortune*, 367–368.

YOU MANAGE IT!

Emerging Trends Case 14.3

Stealing a Smoke, Losing a Job

Health Unlimited is a store in Jacksonville, Florida, that sells health foods to the general public. It offers organically grown produce, meat that is raised without chemical additives, vitamins, and a health food restaurant with a salad and sandwich bar. As a condition of employment, each employee is required to sign a statement that he or she is a nonsmoker and will not smoke either at work or away from work. Smoking at any time is considered a violation of this no-smoker policy and is enforced with immediate discharge. The company justifies this policy by saying that smokers are generally less healthy than nonsmokers and raise the health insurance rates it must pay for all employees. Many of the store's customers and employees are as adamantly opposed to smoking as the company is.

Lisa DeMarco is the produce manager of Health Unlimited. She was an ex-smoker at the time of her initial employment. In recent months, though, because she is experiencing stress over her separation from her husband, Lisa has started smoking again. She restricts her smoking to off-duty hours away from the market. However, one of Lisa's co-workers spotted her smoking in a local bar and informed the store's manager, Ellen Guidry.

The next day Ellen Guidry confronted Lisa, who admitted to smoking and explained her situation. Ellen said she was sorry, but the no-smoker policy had to be enforced. She had no recourse but to discharge Lisa immediately. Lisa felt that her discharge was not fair because she was honest with her boss and had a good work record. She also believed she deserved some consideration for the difficulties she was going through in her personal life.

Critical Thinking Questions

1. Is it legal for a business to institute a no-smoking policy that restricts smoking during off-duty hours as well as at work? If legal, is such a policy ethical?
2. Do you think Ellen treated Lisa fairly by discharging her for violating the no-smoker policy? Should the mitigating circumstances Lisa cited have entered into Ellen's decision? How would you have handled this case?

Team Exercise

In a small group, discuss why it is difficult to discipline employee off-duty conduct. Develop some general guidelines that managers should use to decide when and how to discipline employees' off-duty conduct.

Discussion Case 14.4

YOU MANAGE IT!

Applying "Employment at Will" to an Involuntary Separation

When an employee serves under employment at will, managers have more flexibility to discharge an employee who is not meeting performance expectations. It is important that managers understand the types of situations where their rights under employment at will can be sustained, and other situations when an employee's rights will preclude the application of employment at will. To gain a deeper understanding of employment at will, read the following situation carefully before answering the questions that follow:

An Involuntary Separation at Watkinsville Nursing Home

Betty Brewer was fired from her position as a nurse's helper at Watkinsville Nursing Home (WNH) in Birmingham, Alabama. Betty believed that the employee handbook that had been given to her when she was hired constituted a contract of employment. Not only did she feel she was wrongly discharged, but she also felt that her termination constituted extreme and outrageous conduct that intentionally or recklessly caused her severe emotional distress.

Betty maintained that she was being dismissed for a reason not specifically listed in the employee handbook. Further, she felt that the choice WNH had given her of resigning or being fired caused her severe emotional strain.

In defending its position, the nursing home pointed out that the general common law rule is that an employee may be terminated at will. It also stated that under Alabama law an employment contract may be terminated by either party for good reason, a wrong reason, or no reason at all. As for the handbook, WNH presented several excerpts. First, on the inside cover of the handbook was the following statement:

> This handbook and the policies contained herein do not in any way constitute, and should not be construed as, a contract of employment between the employer and the employee, or a promise of employment.

WNH went on to argue that there was no evidence anywhere that Betty had been told that she could be terminated only for the reasons listed on page 20 of the handbook. It stated that this must have been Betty's assumption. WNH pointed out that page 20 of the handbook clearly stated that the reasons for dismissal "include, but are not limited to, the following . . ." (a list of reasons followed). The company further added, and Betty agreed, that there had been no agreement as to the length or duration of employment and that therefore the term of employment was indefinite.

Critical Thinking Questions

1. Do you think that Betty was wrongly discharged or that she was legitimately dismissed under the notion of employment at will?
2. Do you think, based on the evidence presented, that the company did enough to clearly establish that an employee could be fired for reasons not listed in the employee handbook?
3. In your opinion, did the fact that the nursing home gave Betty the option of resigning or being fired constitute outrageous conduct that intentionally or recklessly caused her severe emotional distress? Why do you think WNH gave Betty this choice?
4. What should WNH do? Should it maintain its position with respect to the dismissal of Betty or should it rethink its position? What implications does this case have for the relationship between employer and employee at WNH?

Team Exercise

Work with a small group of four or five students to design an employment-at-will policy for WNH. Establish a procedure that ensures that each employee knows that they serve under the terms of employment at will. How will you know that an employee is aware and understands the implications of employment at will at WNH? Do you think it makes sense to put the three legal exceptions to employment at will into the policy?

Source: Adapted from Carroll, A. (1996). *Business & Society* (3rd ed.), 763. Cincinnati, OH: South-Western.

Working with Organized Labor

Challenges

After reading this chapter, you should be able to deal more effectively with the following challenges:

1. **Understand** why employees join unions.
2. **Understand** the National Labor Relations (Wagner) Act and how the National Labor Relations Board regulates labor practices and union elections.
3. **Describe** labor relations in the United States and other parts of the world.
4. **Identify** labor relations strategies and describe how they affect operational and tactical labor relations decisions.
5. **Describe** the three phases of the labor relations process: union organizing, collective bargaining, and contract administration.
6. **Explain** how the union grievance procedure works and why the supervisor's role is critical in achieving sound labor relations with a union.
7. **Identify** the ways in which a union can affect a company's entire pattern of human resource management, including its staffing, employee development, compensation, and employee relations policies.

Few institutions illustrate the power of people banding together for a common cause more effectively than labor unions. Unions can change the policies and practices of management profoundly. Consider the following two situations.

The UPS Strike

In one of the most significant labor relations events that occurred during the 1990s, a two-week strike took place in August 1997 between the Teamsters Union and the United Parcel Service (UPS). The opponents could not agree whether UPS would provide more full-time jobs for its workforce of 300,000 employees, 60 percent of whom are part-time workers. UPS settled the strike with the Teamsters after it cost the company about $700 million in lost revenues plus a decline in market share to rivals FedEx and the U.S. Postal Service.[1]

UPS agreed to create 10,000 new full-time jobs over a five-year period. Current part-time employees are eligible to apply for those jobs.[2] Some part-time employees had been working at UPS for as long as 10 years while waiting for the scarce full-time jobs that would become available. UPS full-time employees earned around $20 per hour, whereas part-time employees earned about $11 per hour. The benefits package (health insurance, pension, vacation days, and so on) is similar for both full- and part-time employees.[3]

In the aftermath of the strike, both union and management worked to improve their relationship. In 2002 UPS and the Teamsters Union successfully negotiated their next labor contract without a strike. The agreement included a wage increase of 22 percent over a six-year term. Health and retirement fund contributions were also improved. The labor contract was the result of negotiations that began six months earlier with an exchange of proposals over regularly held negotiating sessions that culminated in an agreement. Both the Teamsters Union and UPS management were more cooperative during the most recent bargaining sessions because they both wanted to avoid the losses they experienced during the 1997 strike.[4]

Doctors Unionize

Many doctors are turning to unions to battle fee cuts and controls over treatment decisions that are championed by health maintenance organizations (HMOs). As of 1999, the ranks of unionized doctors had swelled to 40,000.[5] In fact, a union succeeded for the first time in organizing U.S. doctors at a for-profit managed-care company. The Federation of Physicians and Dentists organized the doctors at Thomas-Davis Medical Centers, one of the oldest and most prestigious clinics in Tucson, Arizona. Many more doctors are considering forming unions to protect their ability to practice medicine as they see fit, rather than letting managed care organizations dictate how they treat patients. Doctors hope unions will make the following improvements to current managed-care practices:

- **Reduce patient loads** HMOs have increased doctors' patient loads, which reduces the amount of time a doctor can spend with each patient.
- **Reduce referral restrictions** HMOs enforce complicated procedures for approving referrals to other physicians, which take a doctor's valuable time. Doctors also complain about the overall quality of the approved list of specialists to which patients can be referred.
- **Regain control of patient care decisions** Doctors have to justify more of their professional decisions regarding patients, such as prescribing medication or types of treatment. Many HMOs require substantial paperwork to defend medical decisions and can override a doctor's decision.

Doctors hope that as union ranks grow, the balance of power in the medical field will shift away from health insurers back toward members of their profession.[6]

THE MANAGERIAL PERSPECTIVE

The relationship between managers and their employees changes in a unionized organization. The law requires managers to meet and confer with elected union representatives when making decisions that affect pay, hours of employment, or working conditions. When unionized employees are dissatisfied with pay or other job factors, the company faces the possibility of a strike or other form of collective action designed to pressure the firm to respond to employees' preferences. Managers, then, need to understand the basics of labor relations and labor law to handle day-to-day labor-management relations effectively.

The presence of a union increases managers' need for HR services. HR specialists in labor relations can help managers develop tactics and strategies to work constructively with the union and its representatives in areas such as negotiating the terms of new labor contracts, interpreting a labor contract, or responding to an employee grievance. Managers that grasp the basics of labor relations will know when to turn to HR specialists and what questions to ask.

In this chapter we explore the labor-management relationship between companies and unions. We begin by examining why employees join unions and why some employers prefer the workplace not to be unionized. Second, we outline the major U.S. legislation that governs labor issues and describe the current labor-relations climate in the United States and in some other countries. Third, we investigate different labor relations strategies and explore the rules and procedures that govern union activities. Finally, we address the impact of unions on a variety of HR practices.

Why Do Employees Join Unions?

Union
An organization that represents employees' interests to management on such issues as wages, work hours, and working conditions.

A **union** is an organization that represents employees' interests to management on issues such as wages, work hours, and working conditions. Employees participate in administering the union and support its activities with *union dues*, fees they pay for the union's services. The law protects employees' rights to join and participate in unions. The law also requires employers to bargain and confer with the union over certain employment issues that affect unionized employees.

Employees join unions for different reasons. For example, in Israel, employees join unions because many believe in the social justice the union represents.[7] Employees in the United States seek union representation when they (1) are dissatisfied with certain aspects of their job, (2) feel that they lack influence with management to make the needed changes, and (3) see unionization as a solution to their problems.[8] The union's best ally is bad management. If managers listen to employees, give them some say in the policies that affect their jobs, and treat them fairly, employees usually will not feel the need to organize. Managers who ignore their workers' interests and treat them inconsistently often end up having to deal with a union.

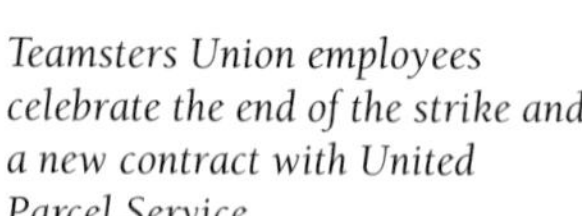

Teamsters Union employees celebrate the end of the strike and a new contract with United Parcel Service.

Companies usually prefer a nonunion workforce. The primary reason is that wages are typically higher for union employees, which puts unionized companies at a competitive disadvantage if their competitors are not unionized. In addition, unions constrain what managers can and cannot do with a particular employee. For instance, a unionized employee who is doing a particularly good job usually cannot be given a merit raise or promoted over someone who has greater seniority. And many labor agreements spell out the specific work responsibilities of certain employees, which reduces flexibility in work assignments. Of course, many unionized companies flourish, and unions have some very positive social benefits. For example, a study reported that unions boosted productivity at hospitals by 16 percent compared to nonunion hospitals.[9] But given the choice, most managers would prefer a nonunion environment.

The Origins of U.S. Labor Unions

Unions, as we think of them today, were largely unprotected by law in the United States until 1935. Certainly there were labor organizations before that time that attempted, with varying degrees of success, to influence and control the terms and conditions of their members' employment. The approach of the U.S. government to unions prior to 1935 was simple: In a free market economy the employment relationship is essentially a private one, and both employee and employer are free to accept or reject this relationship if they find it unsatisfactory. (See the discussion of employment at will in Chapter 14.)

This thinking regards the employer and the employee as in similar positions of power: Employees who find their compensation unfair or working conditions unreasonable are free to find another job; employers who are unhappy with an employee's performance can fire that employee. In practice, of course, employers have considerably more power than individual employees. A large steel manufacturer does not miss one employee who quits because there is usually a ready supply of applicants to replace that person. However, a large employer can so dominate a neighborhood, city, or region that there are few or no other employment alternatives. The large steel mills in Pittsburgh, the auto manufacturers in Detroit, the coal mine operators in Appalachia, and the tire companies in Akron are examples of employers and industries that have dominated their respective regions.

Early in the twentieth century, some of these large industrial employers created horrendous working conditions. Many of their employees were recent immigrants to the United States who had few skills, limited English, and no financial resources to cushion an employment interruption. Others were rural Americans who were part of the huge population shift from rural to urban areas. They, too, had few skills and financial resources. Employers were free to exploit both sets of workers because there was a ready supply of replacements. For instance, steel workers in Pittsburgh worked just inches away from molten iron and razor-sharp, fast-moving ribbons of steel.

In the Great Depression of the 1930s millions of workers lost their jobs as employers came under tremendous pressure to cut production costs. These cutbacks put even more pressure on the working class. It was in this environment that union activity as we know it was legalized by the Wagner Act (1935), which attempted to equalize the power of employers and employees. In fact, this goal explains much of the governmental and societal response to union activity during the Depression and in the years following World War II. Unions were widely supported because of the public perception that working people had little power.

Toward the end of the twentieth century, however, public perception had changed. When President Reagan ordered the firing of striking air traffic controllers on August 5, 1981, two days after they began an illegal strike, the terminated employees received little sympathy from society at large, probably because unions were widely perceived to have become too powerful. This action took place in the middle of a period of dramatic decline in strikes in the United States: From a peak of 424 in 1974, strikes decreased to 29 in 2001.[10] However, as we saw in the opening vignette, unions are growing in some fields such as medicine. Furthermore, the public had a relatively positive perception of the UPS strikers in the fight to make more part-time employees full-time workers. As unions tackle new issues and represent workers in new professions, public perception of union activities is likely to change.

The Role of the Manager in Labor Relations

Labor relations specialist
Someone, often a member of the HR department, who is knowledgeable about labor relations and can represent management's interests to a union.

The manager is on the front line in all labor–management relations. However, when a union represents a group of employees in a company, the company needs a staff of specialists who can represent management's interests to the union. These **labor relations specialists,** who are often members of the HR department, help resolve grievances, negotiate with the union over changes in the labor contract, and provide advice to top management on a labor relations strategy.

Still, it is managers who bear the major responsibility for day-to-day labor–management relations. Thus, it is important that they understand the workplace issues associated with unions. First, as we noted earlier, unions generally take hold only in firms where employees are dissatisfied with their jobs, and managers greatly influence how employees perceive their work environment. Second, where there is a union, managers are responsible for the day-to-day implementation of the terms of the labor agreement. The more effectively they carry out this responsibility, the less time the company will spend resolving labor conflicts. Third, managers need to have a basic understanding of labor law so that they do not unintentionally create a legal liability for the company. Finally, individual managers are often asked to serve on committees to hear grievances brought by union members against the company. A manager who understands general labor issues will be better prepared to hear and decide such cases.

Because the nature and function of unions are so dependent on legislation, we look at the specifics of that legislation next.

Labor Relations and the Legal Environment

The key labor relations legislation in the United States consists of three laws enacted between the 1930s and 1950s: the Wagner Act (1935), the Taft-Hartley Act (1947), and the Landrum-Griffin Act (1959). These laws regulate labor relations in the private sector. Public-sector labor relations are covered by federal or state laws that are patterned after these laws.

The history of labor relations law in the United States can be described as a balancing act. The government has tried to balance (1) employers' rights to operate their businesses free from unnecessary interference, (2) unions' rights to organize and bargain for their members, and (3) individual employees' right to choose their representatives or to decide that they do not want or need union representation. Balancing these three sets of rights has been an extremely complex task. Before 1935, employer rights were essentially unchecked by federal legislation. After passage of the Wagner Act, however, many felt that union rights were too strongly protected, relative to both employer and individual employee rights. This sentiment led Congress to pass two laws—the Taft-Hartley Act and the Landrum-Griffin Act—in an attempt to achieve balance. Commentators differ as to the effectiveness of these laws in achieving the correct balance of employer, union, and employee rights.[11]

The Wagner Act

Wagner Act/National Labor Relations Act (1935)
A federal law designed to protect employees' rights to form and join unions and to engage in such activities as strikes, picketing, and collective bargaining.

National Labor Relations Board (NLRB)
The independent federal agency created by the Wagner Act to administer U.S. labor law.

The **Wagner Act,** also known as the **National Labor Relations Act,** was passed during the Great Depression in 1935. It was designed to protect employees' rights to form and join unions and to engage in activities such as strikes, picketing, and collective bargaining. The Wagner Act created the **National Labor Relations Board (NLRB),** an independent federal agency charged with administering U.S. labor law.

The NLRB's primary functions are (1) to administer *certification elections*, secret ballot elections that determine whether employees want to be represented by a union and (2) to prevent and remedy unlawful acts called *unfair labor practices*. The NLRB remedies an unfair labor practice by issuing a *cease and desist order*, which requires the guilty party to stop engaging in the unlawful labor practice. The Wagner Act established five illegal labor practices that can be remedied by the National Labor Relations Board:

1. Interfering with, restraining, or coercing employees to keep them from exercising their rights to form unions, bargain collectively, or engage in concerted activities for mutual protection.

2. Dominating or interfering with the formation or administration of a union or providing financial support for it.
3. Discriminating against an employee to discourage union membership. Discrimination can include not hiring a union supporter, or not promoting, firing, or denying a pay raise to an employee who is a union member or who favors union representation.
4. Discharging or otherwise discriminating against an employee who has filed charges or given testimony under the act's provisions.
5. Refusing to bargain collectively with the union that employees chose to represent them.

The Taft-Hartley Act

The **Taft-Hartley Act,** enacted in 1947 shortly after the end of World War II, was designed to limit some of the power that unions acquired under the Wagner Act and to protect the rights of management and employees. Although the Taft-Hartley Act was basically favorable to management's interests, its goals were to adjust the regulation of labor–management relations to ensure a level playing field for both parties.

Taft-Hartley Act (1947)
A federal law designed to limit some of the power acquired by unions under the Wagner Act by adjusting the regulation of labor–management relations to ensure a level playing field for both parties.

Taft-Hartley included remedies from the National Labor Relations Board for six unfair union labor practices:

1. Restraining or coercing employees in the exercise of their rights guaranteed under the act, and/or coercing an employer's choice of a representative in collective bargaining.
2. Causing or attempting to cause an employer to discriminate against an employee who is not a member of a labor union for any reason other than failure to pay the union dues and initiation fees uniformly required as a condition of acquiring or retaining membership in the union.
3. Refusing to bargain in good faith with an employer after a majority of the employees in a unit have elected the union as their representative.
4. Asking or requiring its members to boycott products made by a firm engaged in a labor dispute with another union *(secondary boycott)*. However, a union can call a boycott of products produced by its own firm *(primary boycott)*.
5. Charging employees excessive or discriminatory union dues as a condition of membership in a union under a union shop clause. (A **union shop clause** requires employees to join the union 30 to 60 days after their date of hire.)
6. Causing an employer to pay for services that are not performed. This practice, often called *featherbedding*, is technically illegal, but the definition of unnecessary or unperformed work is often murky. For example, railroad unions continued to require the presence of firemen on engines long after their main duty (taking care of the fire on a steam engine) was eliminated by the advent of diesel engines.

Union shop clause
A union arrangement that requires new employees to join the union 30 to 60 days after their date of hire.

Twelve years later, the Landrum-Griffin Act added a seventh unfair union labor practice: It is illegal for a union to picket an employer for the purpose of union recognition (a practice known as *recognitional picketing*).

Perhaps the most controversial provision of the Taft-Hartley Act is Section 14b, which gives permission to the states to enact right-to-work laws. A state **right-to-work law** makes it illegal within that state for a union to include a union shop clause in its contract. Unions negotiate union shop clauses into their contracts to provide greater security to union employees and prevent nonunion employees from receiving union services without paying union dues. A less restrictive arrangement called the *agency shop clause* requires employees to pay a union service fee (about equal to union dues) but does not require them to join the union. Currently, 21 states have right-to-work laws, which make it more difficult to organize and sustain unions in those states.[12] Most of these states are located in the southern or western United States, away from major industrial centers.

Right-to-work law
A state law that makes it illegal within that state for a union to include a union shop clause in its contract.

Several other provisions of Taft-Hartley are noteworthy. First, the act made *closed shops*, which require an employee to be a union member as a condition of being hired, illegal. This provision was modified 12 years later by the Landrum-Griffin Act to allow a closed shop in the construction industry as the only exception. Second, Taft-Hartley allowed employees to get rid of a union they no longer want through a *decertification election* and charged the NLRB with regulating decertification elections. Finally, Taft-Hartley created a new agency, the *Federal Mediation and Conciliation Service*, to help mediate labor disputes so that economic disruptions due to strikes and other labor disturbances would be fewer and shorter.

The Landrum-Griffin Act

Landrum-Griffin Act (1959)
A law designed to protect union members and their participation in union affairs.

The **Landrum-Griffin Act** was enacted in 1959 to protect union members and their participation in union affairs. To protect this right, Landrum-Griffin allows the government, through the Department of Labor, to regulate union activities. Landrum-Griffin was enacted because a few unions experienced problems with corrupt leadership and the misuse of funds for illegal activities.

The Landrum-Griffin Act includes the following key provisions:

1. Each union must have a bill of rights for union members to ensure minimum standards of internal union democracy.
2. Each union must adopt a constitution and provide copies of it to the Department of Labor.
3. Each union must report its financial activities and the financial interests of its leaders to the Department of Labor.
4. Union elections are regulated by the government, and union members have the right to participate in secret ballot elections.
5. Union leaders have a fiduciary responsibility to use union money and property for the benefit of the membership and not for their own personal gain. Members can sue and recover damages from union leaders who fail to exercise their fiduciary responsibilities.

Railway Labor Act
A law designed to regulate labor relations in the transportation industry.

Other laws that affect labor relations include the Railway Labor Act (1926, last amended in 1970), the Norris-LaGuardia Act (1932), and the Byrnes Antistrikebreaking Act (1938). Of course, the equal employment opportunity laws discussed in Chapter 3 also apply to unionized workers. Most noteworthy of these other labor laws is the **Railway Labor Act**, which regulates labor relations in the transportation industry. This law covers the railway, airlines, and trucking industries that are critical to sustain commerce. It provides dispute settlement procedures if the parties are unable to achieve a labor agreement. The Railway Labor Act has provisions for congressional and presidential intervention in a labor dispute that could be disruptive to interstate commerce. For example, the president intervened in a labor dispute in the airline industry when one of the major airlines forced the union to go on strike because of a breakdown in negotiations.[13]

Although much of U.S. labor relations law is more than four decades old, it would be a mistake to assume that nothing new is happening in this area. As this text was being written, Congress was considering the Teamwork for Employees and Management Act, which would amend the Wagner Act to ensure that employers are permitted to establish and maintain employee involvement programs.[14] Another set of amendments under consideration would eliminate an employer's right to use permanent replacements during an economic strike or work stoppage.[15] In Canada, several provinces have recently enacted laws that restrict employers from using replacement workers during strikes.[16] Clearly, the struggle to find the correct balance of employer, union, and employee rights is ongoing.

We now turn to a description of the current state of labor relations in the United States.

Labor Relations in the United States

Labor relations in the United States evolved from the philosophy of the U.S. labor movement, which accepted the country's capitalist economic structure and wanted to operate within it.[17] U.S. unions have avoided a permanent affiliation with a political party and have focused on improving their members' welfare through dealing directly with the companies that employ their members. The key factors that characterize labor relations in the United States are (1) business unionism, (2) unions structured by type of job, (3) a focus on collective bargaining,

(4) labor contracts, (5) the adversarial nature of labor–management relations and shrinking union membership, and (6) the growth of unions in the public sector.

Business Unionism

U.S. unions put a high priority on improving the economic welfare of their members. **Business unionism** is unionism that focuses on "bread-and-butter" issues (such as wages, benefits, and job security) so that workers get a larger slice of the economic pie. U.S. unions, which practice business unionism, have traditionally avoided trying to influence the running of the company, and they provide little input to management on strategic decisions such as how to market a product or what types of new business to enter. It is rare to see U.S. union members on a company's board of directors.[18] The key concerns of U.S. unions are shop-floor issues that relate directly to workers. U.S. labor laws reinforce this tendency by making wages, hours, and working conditions mandatory topics for bargaining. This means that management is obligated to bargain on these issues in good faith. Other issues, such as how to run the business, are not mandatory bargaining topics.

Business unionism
A form of unionism that focuses on improving workers' economic well-being.

Unions Structured by Type of Job

In contrast to unions in some other countries, U.S. unions tend to be organized by type of job. For instance, truck drivers are often members of the Teamsters Union, many public school teachers are members of the National Education Association, and most auto workers belong to the United Auto Workers no matter which auto manufacturer employs them. Because most unions represent employees from multiple employers, they are typically arranged into *locals* governed by a national body. Each local consists of the union members in a particular geographical location. The local has its own officers and is generally concerned with day-to-day labor practices and disputes. The national organization ties these locals together, governs how locals are organized and operated, and, most importantly, establishes policy for contract negotiations.

The *AFL-CIO*, formed by the merger of the old American Federation of Labor and the Congress of Industrial Organizations, is a confederation of many different unions. Because it represents so many workers (approximately 13 million), the AFL-CIO has a tremendous influence on federal labor policies. It also provides support to individual national unions and mobilizes support for laws that are beneficial to working people. Finally, the AFL-CIO resolves disputes between national unions.[19]

Focus on Collective Bargaining

Unions and management are the dominant players in the U.S. labor relations system. Generally, the U.S. government takes a neutral role, allowing the players to make the rules that govern their particular workplace. The mechanism of choice for developing these rules is collective bargaining. Under a **collective bargaining** system, unions and management negotiate with each other to develop the work rules under which union members will work for a stipulated period of time, usually two or three years. **Work rules** include any terms or conditions of employment, including pay, work breaks and lunch periods, vacation, work assignments, and grievance procedures.

Unions that are legally elected by workers in the United States act as the sole representative of those workers' concerns to management. Although unions may compete for recognition, once one is recognized, individual employees cannot choose to be represented by another union.

Collective bargaining
A system in which unions and management negotiate with each other to develop the work rules under which union members will work for a stipulated period of time.

Work rules
Any terms or conditions of employment, including pay, work breaks and lunch periods, vacation, work assignments, and grievance procedures.

Labor Contracts

The product of collective bargaining is a **labor contract** that spells out the conditions of employment and work rules that affect employees in the unit represented by the union. Because both parties enter into the contract voluntarily, one party can use the legal system to enforce the terms of the contract if the other party does not fulfill its responsibilities.

Labor contracts are an important feature of the U.S. labor relations system. In many other countries, such as Germany and Sweden, working conditions and employee benefits are codified into labor laws, but in the United States labor and management have historically established workers' economic benefits without government interference. Increasingly, however, the United States is following the lead of other countries in this respect. The most recent example is the

Labor contract
A union contract that spells out the conditions of employment and work rules that affect employees in the unit represented by the union.

Family and Medical Leave Act of 1993 (see Chapter 3), which grants employees many protections that had previously been available only to employees covered by a union contract. Current health reform proposals also seek to mandate certain health insurance benefits that until now have been the subject of labor–management negotiation.

The Adversarial Nature of Labor–Management Relations and Shrinking Union Membership

U.S. labor laws view labor and management as natural adversaries who will disagree over the distribution of the firm's profits. For this reason, rules have been put in place so that the pie is distributed peacefully.

In a sense, the U.S. labor relations system is modeled on the U.S. court system. In a court, "justice" may be considered the result of the clash of adversaries, with the district attorney representing the plaintiff's interests and the defense attorney representing the defendant's interests. Similarly, "economic justice" may be considered the result of negotiations between the union (the advocate of the employees) and management (the advocate of the firm's owners). While this adversarial model worked well for many years in the United States, it has recently become an obstacle to union–management cooperation, which has grown in importance as both labor markets and product markets have become more globally competitive.

As Figure 15.1 shows, 14 percent of the U.S. labor force is unionized.[20] This is down from a peak of about 35 percent in 1945. There are several reasons for this decline: the shrinking base of blue-collar industrial jobs (the traditional area of unionization) due to automation and foreign competition; the increase in employment legislation that provides workers with remedies that address their needs; and the aggressively hostile labor relations strategies of many companies, which have made it difficult for unions to organize workers. Other possible reasons for declining union membership are an increasingly educated workforce, as well as the highly publicized legal problems of some union leaders.

Figure 15.1

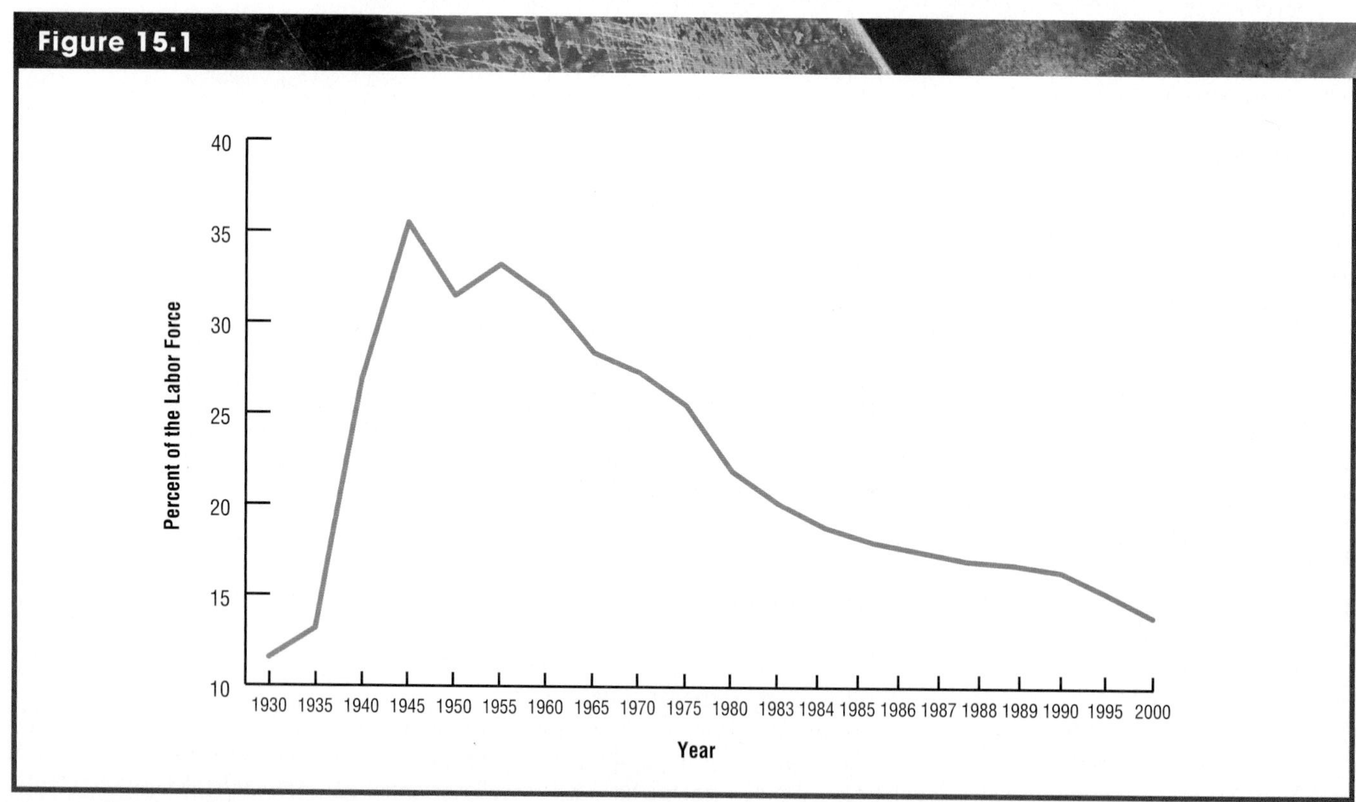

Union Membership in the United States, 1930–2000

Source: Bureau of Labor Statistics, Department of Labor.

Despite shrinking union membership, unions continue to be an important part of the U.S. labor relations system because they establish wage and benefit patterns that influence nonunion employers. In this way, unions indirectly affect about 40 to 50 percent of the U.S. labor force. In fact, many employees of nonunion firms benefit from the upward adjustments in their wages and benefits that their employers make to prevent a union from organizing their workers. Unions have also pioneered worker safety measures and antidiscriminatory labor practices. Unless the underlying causes that gave birth to unions are abolished—low wages, unsafe working conditions, health hazards, arbitrary firings, and layoffs—it is a safe bet that unions will not disappear.

The Growth of Unions in the Public Sector

As the percentage of unionized workers in the private sector has declined, the percentage of unionized workers in the public sector has increased substantially. This increase is due in part to the expansion of local government in the 1980s and in part to organizing efforts that have targeted both public-sector and service-sector employees.[21]

Unions in the public sector are in many ways a special case of labor relations because although public-sector employees are more likely to be organized than private-sector employees, public-sector workers tend to have less bargaining power. There are two main reasons for this difference.

First, governmental power is diffuse. The typical private-sector firm is hierarchically organized so that there is one individual at the top who is in charge. However, governmental bodies in the United States have been intentionally structured so that power is divided among the legislative, executive, and judicial branches. This makes it more difficult for public-sector unions to negotiate and bargain collectively because the employer's representative often has only limited authority. For instance, a city employees' union may bargain with the mayor's office for higher pay, but the money for the higher salaries has to be appropriated by the city council, which may not concur with the mayor.

The second reason public-sector unions have less power is that many governmental entities severely restrict their employees' right to strike. The reasoning is that the government is a monopoly provider of essential services like police protection, garbage collection, and highway maintenance. If its employees were to go on strike, there would be no one else to provide these essential services. States differ in restrictiveness on this issue. For instance, Colorado forbids strikes by any state employees, including teachers. In contrast, New York, Michigan, Wisconsin, and some other states give some of their employees the right to strike in certain circumstances.

Because their right to strike is limited, public-sector unions have taken the lead in devising and experimenting with new ways to negotiate, including mandated arbitration and mediation. Their limited economic power has also made public-sector unions less likely than private-sector unions to put pay issues at the top of their agendas. For instance, teachers' unions often focus on such issues as class size, job security, and academic freedom rather than straight salary issues.

Although having government as an employer can present difficulties to unionized workers, it also brings certain advantages. One is that union members, by virtue of the fact that they are also voters, have some political power over their employer. Because voter participation in nonfederal elections is often low in the United States, a well-organized public-sector union can be a powerful force in local politics. In fact, even national candidates court public-sector union support. A second advantage stems from the very diffusion of power we discussed earlier. This makes it possible for the union to play one branch of government against the other in certain circumstances. For instance, a union may be able to achieve a bargaining victory because it has the support of a city council member whose vote the mayor needs on some unrelated issue.

Labor Relations in Other Countries

Labor relations systems vary from country to country because unions mean different things in different countries. In the United States labor relations involves collective bargaining and labor contracts, but in Sweden and Denmark it involves national wage setting, in Japan it involves enterprise unions that cooperate with company management, in Great Britain it involves union affiliation with the Labor Party, and in Germany it involves union representation on the company's board of directors.[22] Moreover, the shrinking percentage of private-sector employees represented by unions in the United States is not a world trend. Unions not only represent a large portion of the labor force in most other industrialized countries but are also important factors in the labor relations systems of many of those countries.

Figure 15.2 compares union membership as a percentage of the labor force in 12 industrialized countries, including the United States. Union membership as a percentage of the labor force is higher in most European countries, with Italy and Sweden having, respectively, 32 percent and 87 percent of their workers represented by unions in 1995. Although unionism declined in Great Britain in the 1980s, British unions still represented 32 percent of the workforce in 1995, double the percentage of U.S. workers. Even in Japan, whose firms seek to avoid unions when they locate factories in the United States, 24 percent of workers are unionized. This is significantly higher than the U.S. percentage.[23]

How Unions Differ Internationally

One analysis of unionism around the globe suggests that unions in different countries have different priorities.[24] Unions in different nations can be classified according to whether they emphasize economic issues, political issues, neither, or both. As we have seen, U.S. unions place a very strong emphasis on economic issues, particularly pay, benefits, and job security. For example, in recent years outsourcing has become a major concern of U.S. unions because the first jobs to be subcontracted tend to be blue-collar jobs, the union's mainstay.[25] Compared to unions in other countries, U.S. unions place much less emphasis on political issues. True, some U.S. unions and union leaders are involved in political life, but their involvement tends to be less ideological than pragmatic. That is, political involvement is just another means to address economic concerns.

At the other end of the spectrum, unions in France tend to be much more politically involved and less concerned with economic issues. The two largest labor confederations in France have clear political orientations, and one is even religiously oriented. Strikes in France tend to focus on political change as the primary means of protecting or improving conditions for union members. Unions in Spain, like France, also use political tactics to carry out their goals. For example, in 2002 Spanish unions collaborated to organize a one-day general strike to convince the political leaders to reject the government proposal to lower the level of unemployment

Figure 15.2

Percent of Total Civilian Wage and Salary Employees

Year	United States	Canada	Austria	Australia	Japan	Denmark	France	Germany	Italy	Netherlands	Sweden	Switzerland	United Kingdom
1955	33	31	64	—	36	59	21	44	57	41	62	32	46
1960	31	30	61	—	33	63	20	40	34	42	62	33	45
1965	28	28	46	—	36	63	20	38	33	40	68	32	45
1970	30	31	43	—	35	64	22	37	43	38	75	31	50
1975	29	34	48	—	35	72	23	39	56	42	83	35	53
1980	25	35	47	—	31	86	19	40	62	41	88	35	56
1985	17	36	47	—	29	92	17	40	61	34	95	32	51
1990	16	36	43	34	25	88	—	—	—	28	95	31	46
1995	14	37	39	35	24	78	9	26	32	23	87	23	32

Sources: International Labor Organization (1997); and Chang, C., and Sorrentino, C. (1991, December). Union membership statistics in 12 countries. *Monthly Labor Review*, 48.

Union Membership in Selected Countries, 1955–1995

benefits for Spanish workers. A *general strike* is a work stoppage of all organized labor over a brief, predetermined time period that is designed to influence the government to support a particular political goal representing the interests of workers.[26]

In China, unions are low in both economic and political involvement, because of the pervasive control of the Chinese Communist Party over both political and economic affairs. A secondary reason is that the large majority of Chinese employees work for very small firms, which are notoriously difficult to organize.

Finally, Swedish unions tend to have a high degree of economic and political involvement. Swedish trade unions are often represented on governmental commissions in addition to actively representing their workers in economic affairs.[27]

We now turn our attention to two labor relations systems that have achieved high productivity and cooperation between unions and management: those of Germany and Japan.

Labor Relations in Germany

German law requires that all corporations involve workers in decisions at both the plant and the corporate level. This system is sometimes called *industrial democracy*. As practiced in Germany, industrial democracy means workers are represented at the plant level in works councils and at the corporate level through codetermination.

Works councils are committees composed of both worker representatives and managers who have responsibility for governing the workplace. They are involved in operational decisions, such as the allocation of overtime, the discipline and discharge of workers, the hiring of new workers, and training.[28] At the plant level, works councils make many decisions on which unions would bargain with management in the United States. German unions focus on bargaining across industries on such issues as wages, rather than on bargaining within an industry, as is typical in the United States. However, the unification of Germany's high-wage West and lower-wage East means that unions and employers need more wage flexibility in labor contracts. Currently, more wage agreements are occurring at the company level in Germany.[29] Works councils are also used in several other countries in addition to Germany. Austria, France, Belgium, the Netherlands, and Sweden have enacted laws that require that large companies organize works councils to represent the interests of employees.[30]

Works councils
A committee composed of both worker representatives and managers who have responsibility for governing the workplace; used in Germany.

Codetermination involves worker representation on a corporation's board of directors. German workers are well represented on boards of directors because it is assumed that labor and capital should form a partnership in governing the enterprise. With one-third to one-half of their boards of directors representing workers, German companies are likely to give employees' needs a high priority.[31] (The other board members represent the shareholders.) Not surprisingly, codetermination has fostered a spirit of cooperation between workers and managers. For the German economy, the results have been fewer strikes and higher productivity. For workers, the results have been both greater responsibility and greater security. For example, IG Metall, Germany's largest union, has taken the lead on a number of important issues instead of merely reacting to company proposals. The union's group-work policies, the product of nearly two decades of research and activism, are designed to protect workers from layoff or transfer to lower-paying jobs.

Codetermination
The representation of workers on a corporation's board of directors; used in Germany.

Labor Relations in Japan

Japan has developed a successful labor relations system characterized by a high degree of cooperation between unions and management. A key factor in this success has been the Japanese enterprise union. The **enterprise union,** which represents Japanese workers in large corporations such as Toyota, Toshiba, and Hitachi, organizes the workers in only one company. This practice ensures that the union's loyalty will not be divided among different companies. The enterprise union negotiates with management with an eye on the company's long-term prosperity. This labor relations system was long reinforced by large Japanese corporations' offer of lifelong employment, which allowed Japanese workers to feel secure and unthreatened by changes in technology or job characteristics.[32]

Enterprise union
A labor union that represents workers in only one large company rather than in a particular industry; used in Japan.

The traditional lifelong employment policy has encouraged cooperation between the enterprise unions and management. Many Japanese executives started their careers as union members

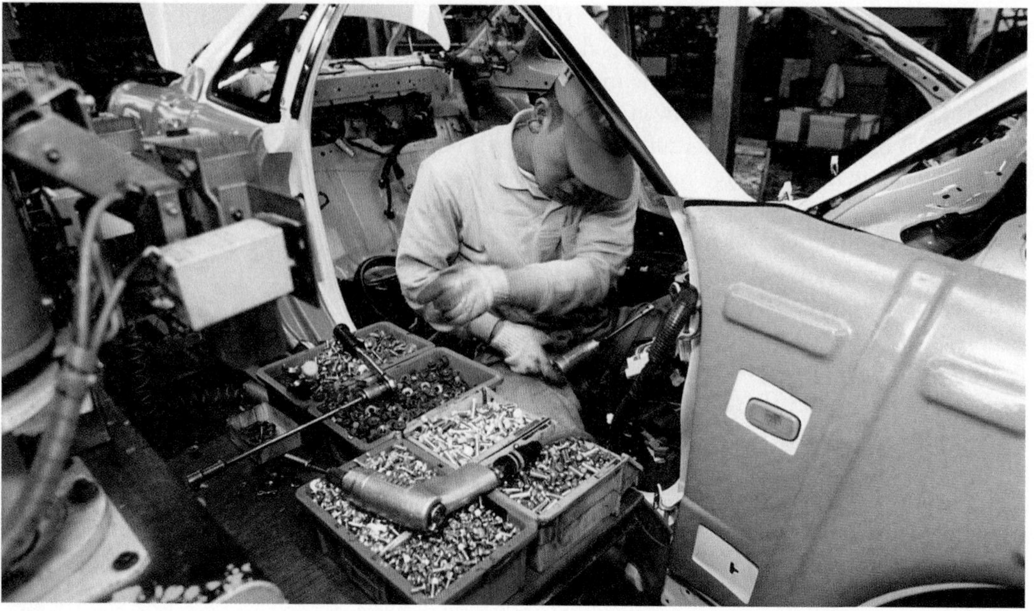

Several of Japan's corporations have had to lay off thousands of employees to compete globally, including automaker Nissan. Such actions are eroding Japan's lifelong employment policy, which has encouraged cooperation between unions and management.

right out of school, advanced to a leadership position in the union, and then got promoted into management, all within the same company. This type of labor relations system leads to close personal relationships among managers, union leaders, and workers that would be impossible under the more adversarial U.S. labor relations system. Because the enterprise union's legitimacy is unchallenged by management, there is a degree of trust and respect between the union and management in Japan that would be unthinkable in the United States. This fact helps to explain the behavior of Japanese executives who cooperate with a union in Japan but try at all costs to avoid unionization in their U.S. plants.

Unfortunately, there are signs that the labor relations systems in both Germany and Japan are in danger. In Germany, high labor costs for the average factory worker ($28 per hour versus $18 per hour in the United States in 1999) and the economic costs of unification with East Germany are forcing companies to drive a harder bargain with unions. Competition in global markets has led to downsizings in some of Germany's largest companies and has strained labor relations. For example, Daimler-Benz (now called Daimler-Chrysler), Germany's largest industrial company, reduced its work force by 70,000 jobs and announced expansion of a new automobile plant in Alabama, where labor costs are much lower than in Germany.[33] And in Japan, a closer look at lifelong employment policies shows that they have always been restricted to the largest companies, applied only to men, and end at age 55. Moreover, downsizing in Japan has made it difficult to sustain lifelong employment policies. NTT, Japan's giant telecommunications company, reduced its workforce by 45,000 jobs, a quarter of its total number of employees. Nissan, the auto maker, from 1999 to 2002 laid off 21,000 of its workers and closed five of its auto assembly plants.[34]

Labor Relations Strategy

Labor relations strategy
A company's overall plan for dealing with labor unions.

A company's **labor relations strategy** is its management's overall plan for dealing with unions. As Figure 15.3 shows, a company's labor relations strategy sets a tone that can range from open conflict with the union to labor–management cooperation.

The most important choice affecting a company's labor relations strategy is management's decision to accept or to avoid unions.[35]

Union Acceptance Strategy

Under a **union acceptance strategy,** management chooses to view the union as its employees' legitimate representative and accepts collective bargaining as an appropriate mechanism for establishing workplace rules. Management tries to obtain the best possible labor contract with the union, and then governs employees according to the contract's terms. The labor relations policy shown in Figure 15.4 is an example of a union acceptance strategy.

A union acceptance strategy is likely to result in labor relations characterized by labor–management cooperation or working harmony. The relationship between General Motors and the United Auto Workers (UAW) union at the Saturn auto plant in Tennessee is an example of such a strategy. The union negotiated a very flexible contract with management at this plant in exchange for union recognition and job security for its workers. Management can redesign jobs, change technology, and streamline work rules—a degree of flexibility unknown in other unionized General Motors auto plants.[36] In turn, labor is involved in decision making to a degree that is rare in unionized companies. Groups of 5 to 15 workers perform managerial tasks such as hiring. They also elect representatives to higher-level teams that make joint decisions with management on every aspect of the business from car design to marketing to sticker price.[37] Another tactic used to create a climate of union–management cooperation is the establishment of a joint committee composed of union and management representatives who work to solve long-term problems in the workplace that have a high potential for conflict. At Xerox, management and representatives of the Amalgamated Clothing Workers Union formed joint committees and workplace teams whose collaborative efforts resulted in improved plant safety, work flow and production, reduced grievance rates, and the preservation of jobs that otherwise would have been eliminated.[38]

Unfortunately, the road to union–management cooperation can be rocky. Even at Saturn, which is often held up as a model of cooperative labor relations, there are signs of trouble: Recent hires are frequently less committed to the employee participation idea than those who have been at the plant from the beginning, and some distrust the union's close ties with management. In fact, worker distrust of union–management cooperation threatens to derail teamwork initiatives at an increasing number of companies, especially since the NLRB ruled that management-led employee teams can violate the Wagner Act.[39] For management guidelines in this area, see the Manager's Notebook titled "When Is a Team Not a Team?"

Labor relations scholars have found that cooperative labor relations occur more often in industries with patterns of labor contract agreements that foster union–management collaboration. Industries with contract provisions that encourage labor–management cooperation include the automobile, telecommunications, steel, and construction industries.[40] An example of such a contract provision is one that establishes joint labor–management committees that meet on a regular basis and develop agreements over issues of mutual benefit such as (1) a drug-free work-

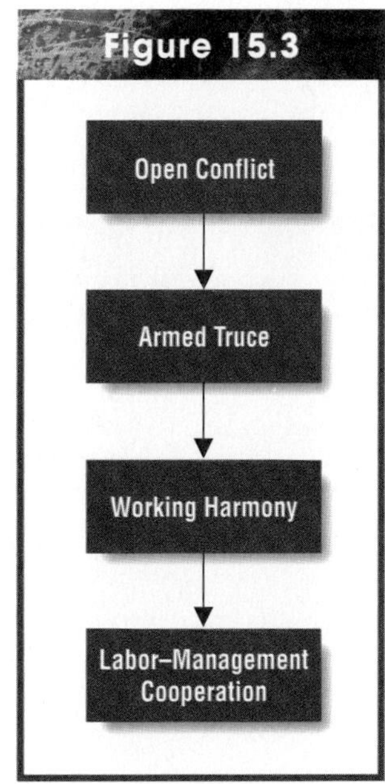

Types of Labor–Management Relations

Source: Mills, D. O. (1989). *Labor-management relations* (4th ed.), 222. New York: McGraw-Hill.

Union acceptance strategy
A labor relations strategy in which management chooses to view the union as its employees' legitimate representative and accepts collective bargaining as an appropriate mechanism for establishing workplace rules.

Figure 15.4

Our objective is to establish a labor policy that is consistent and fair. The purpose is to develop an agreeable working relationship with the union while retaining our full management rights. The rationale behind our labor relations policy is consistency, credibility, and fairness to union representatives and the workers who are in the union. In order to make our policy effective, the Company will:

- Accept union representation of employees in good faith, provided the union represents the majority of our employees;
- Maintain the right of management to manage;
- Adopt procedures by which top management continuously supports the positions of its representatives in implementing the firm's policies and practices in the area of industrial relations;
- Enforce disciplinary policies in a fair, firm, and consistent manner;
- See to it that union representatives follow all Company rules except those from which they are exempted under specific provisions of the labor contract;
- Handle all employee complaints fairly, firmly, and without discrimination;
- See that every representative of management exercises a maximum effort to follow Company policies fairly and consistently; and
- See to it that all decisions and agreements pertaining to the present contract are documented in writing.

Source: *The company policy manual* (1990), 332. New York Harper Business Division of HarperCollins Publishers.

Labor Relations Policy: Union Acceptance Strategy

place, (2) occupational safety rules, (3) gain-sharing plans, (4) equal opportunity for employees with disabilities, and (5) policies that prohibit any type of workplace harassment.[41]

MANAGER'S NOTEBOOK

When Is a Team Not a Team? Guidelines for Employee Involvement Committees

Two conditions determine whether a company's employee involvement (EI) group violates the Wagner Act. A group is illegal if it can be proved to be *both* "employer dominated" and a "labor organization" under the law. Although it is often unclear which category a specific condition or action falls under, here are some general guidelines to help managers steer clear of illegalities:

- Determine whether the issues addressed by an EI team clearly constitute "conditions of employment." Until legal developments shed new light on the situation, experts say EI groups should be limited to addressing production, quality, and safety matters.[a]
- Employer domination can be construed if any group of employees is perceived as constituting a "select" group empowered to speak to management on behalf of all employees. Managers can guard against such a charge by periodically rotating employee participants on EI teams.[b]
- Grievance committees, especially in a nonunion setting, can easily come under fire. Managers must make sure that any such group functions in a way that is strictly independent of management influence. If disputes are settled by means of a negotiation process between employer and employee, employer dominance is often readily established. But if management delegates the authority to resolve grievances to the group and the group resolves such problems on its own, the group is likely to be seen as benign, despite the fact that management played a key role in establishing and encouraging it.[c]
- In a unionized setting, getting union participation in EI committees is virtually a surefire way to avoid litigation.[d]
- If the company is nonunion, the situation can be trickier. Managers must be sure to get visible employee input and make the venture a cooperative and voluntary one.[e] An alternative would be to let peers nominate employees to participate rather than have management select them.[f]
- *Never* start up an EI group during a union organizing compaign. Such activity can readily be seen as union busting.[g]

Sources: [a]Adapted by permission of the publisher, from *Management Review Forum*, February 1994, © 1994. American Management Association, New York. All rights reserved. [b]Ibid. [c]Ibid. [d]Ibid. [e]Ibid. [f]LeRoy, M. H. (1999) Are employers constrained in the use of employee participation groups by Section 8(a)(2) of the NLRA? *Journal of Labor Research* 22(1), 63–71. [g]*Management Review Forum*, 1994.

For smaller companies in particular, the adversarial model of management-labor relations has been slow to give way to a cooperative model. Although many small business owners do work closely with their workers, they tend to regard such concepts as worker–management teams as a big company's game. "For the smallest firms, you start talking about things like that and they die laughing," says a research fellow at the National Federation of Independent Business, a small business lobbying group. According to the NLRB, two-thirds of unfair labor practice complaints are filed against employers with fewer than 100 workers. Since the great majority of small businesses are nonunionized, this record has encouraged unions to target small firms for membership expansion. In 1998 unions won certification at firms with fewer than 50 workers at twice their rate of success at companies employing more than 500 workers.[42] To avoid the loss of management control caused by unionization, many small companies have chosen to pursue a union avoidance strategy.

Union Avoidance Strategy

Management selects a **union avoidance strategy** when it fears the union will have a disruptive influence on its employees or fears losing control of its workers to a union. Companies that choose a union avoidance strategy are likely to be, at best, in an armed truce with unions and, at worst, in open conflict with them (see Figure 15.3).

Union avoidance strategy
A labor relations strategy in which management tries to prevent its employees from joining a union, either by removing the incentive to unionize or by using hardball tactics.

There are two different approaches to union avoidance: union substitution and union suppression.[43] Which approach a company pursues usually depends on the values of top management.

Union Substitution

In the **union substitution** approach, also known as the **proactive human resource management approach,** management becomes so responsive to employees' needs that it removes the incentive for unionization. Using this approach, IBM, Hewlett-Packard, Eli Lilly, Eastman Kodak, and Wal-Mart avoided unionization and simultaneously developed a reputation as good places to work. All these companies have instituted a number of policies that lead to employees' feeling generally satisfied with their jobs and their ability to participate in management decisions. Some of the policies used by companies that take the union substitution approach are:

Union substitution/proactive human resource management
A union avoidance strategy in which management becomes so responsive to employees' needs that it removes the incentives for unionization.

- Job security policies that protect the jobs of full-time workers. Among these is a policy that subcontracted, temporary, and part-time workers must be discharged before permanent employees can be laid off.
- Promoting-from-within policies that encourage the training and development of employees.
- Profit-sharing and employee stock ownership plans (see Chapter 11) that share the company's success with its employees.
- High-involvement management practices that solicit employee input into decisions.
- Open-door policies and grievance procedures that try to give workers the same sense of empowerment that they would have under a union contract.[44]

Union Suppression

Management uses the **union suppression** approach when it wants to avoid unionization at all costs and does not make any pretense of trying "to do the right thing" for its employees. Under this approach, management employs hardball tactics, which may be legal or illegal, to get rid of a union or to prevent the union from organizing its workers.[45]

Union suppression
A union avoidance strategy in which management uses hardball tactics to prevent a union from organizing its workers or to get rid of a union.

For example, in the mid-1980s, Continental Airlines' CEO Frank Lorenzo used the U.S. bankruptcy courts to reorganize Continental and escape the company's obligations to employees under its labor contracts with its unions. When the airline emerged from bankruptcy, it had a nonunion workforce with pay levels about 40 percent lower than had prevailed under the union contracts. In another case at about the same time, the *Chicago Tribune* bargained aggressively with its production unions and, when the union workers went out on strike, substituted permanent replacement workers. The result was a completely nonunionized workforce at the newspaper. More recently, in 2000 Wal-Mart used union suppression tactics to reduce its susceptibility to work with a union after the United Food & Commercial Workers union (UCFW) attempted to organize its meat cutters. Wal-Mart's response was to reorganize its supply chain and buy prepackaged meat for its U.S. stores and eliminate most of its meat counter jobs around the country.[46]

Sometimes the union suppression approach backfires and management reaps nothing but an angry union, bitter employees, and the worst kind of public relations. In 1990, management at the New York *Daily News*, which was then owned by the Chicago Tribune Company, tried to use replacement workers to intimidate its striking unions, but lost the battle because the media and the public sympathized with the union cause. J. P. Stevens, a textile manufacturer with plants in the southern United States, illegally tried to intimidate its workers by firing union organizers before a union certification election. The NLRB intervened on behalf of the union and ordered J. P. Stevens to recognize and bargain with the union.

In general, the union suppression approach is a higher-risk strategy than the union substitution approach and for this reason is used less frequently. Hardball tactics not only entail legal risks but can also come back to haunt management. Frank Lorenzo's use of the bankruptcy courts to break the company's unions looked like a great success at the time. However, in 1994 Lorenzo's bid to start a new low-fare airline was rejected by the Department of Transportation because of safety and regulatory compliance problems during Lorenzo's stewardship of Eastern and Continental Airlines. The DOT said that both of these airlines "experienced operational, maintenance, and labor-related problems that were among the most serious in the history of aviation."[47]

Managing the Labor Relations Process

Now that you have some grounding in the history of labor–management relations and relevant law, as well as a sense of the current state of labor relations and corporate strategies in this area, we can examine the specific components of the labor relations process. As Figure 15.5 shows, three phases of labor relations that managers and labor relations specialists must deal with are (1) union organizing, in which employees exercise their right to form a union; (2) collective bargaining, in which union and management representatives negotiate a labor contract; and (3) contract administration, in which the labor contract is applied to specific work situations on a daily basis.

Figure 15.5

Union Organizing → Collective Bargaining → Contract Administration

The Three Phases of the Labor Relations Process

Union Organizing

Union organizing takes place when employees work with a union to form themselves into a cohesive group. The key issues that managers confront in a union organizing campaign are union solicitation, preelection conduct, and the certification election.

Union Solicitation

Before it will order a union certification election, the NLRB requires a union to show that there is significant interest in unionization among a company's employees. To meet this requirement, a minimum of 30 percent of the employees in the relevant work unit must sign an authorization card indicating that they want to be represented by a specific union for collective bargaining purposes. A sample union authorization card is shown in Figure 15.6.

Unions often conduct the early stages of their solicitation effort in private homes or public facilities so that management will not be aware of the organizing drive until the required percentage of workers has signed authorization cards. However, sometimes the union finds it necessary to solicit on company property, which alerts management and gives it the opportunity to respond.

More than half of all unions have Web sites where they can communicate with current and potential members.[48] In a drive to organize IBM employees in Colorado, the Communication Workers of America (CWA) alerted employees to a special Web site designed to teach them how to form a union at IBM.[49] The AFL-CIO site (www.aflcio.org) discusses union organizing and other issues, such as the pay of the top executives in U.S. public corporations compared to average employee pay and work/family concerns. The Web site gives interested employees a way to turn to unions affiliated with the AFL-CIO to attain social and economic justice.

A Question of Ethics

One strategy for suppressing union activity is to ask certain workers to report to management any union-organizing activities that are taking place at the company. Is this strategy legal? Is it ethical? If you answered yes to both questions, do you think it is a good management practice? Why or why not?

Management's choice of labor relations strategy guides a company's response to union solicitation. Companies with a union avoidance strategy usually have a "no-solicitation" policy that restricts all solicitations to nonwork areas (for example, solicitation may take place in lunch or break rooms, but not in offices) and nonwork times. A no-solicitation policy makes it more difficult for the union to influence workers' attitudes toward the union and persuade them to sign authorization cards. However, companies that have a no-solicitation policy must be careful to enforce it consistently so that *all* solicitations (including those for charitable causes) are restricted. Singling out union-organizing activities for restriction is an unfair labor practice that can result in an NLRB order to cease and desist the discriminatory policy.

Consistent enforcement of a no-solicitation policy was one of the key factors that led the Supreme Court to rule in favor of Lechmere, Inc., a Newington, Connecticut, store that had banned unions from its premises. The court found that Lechmere did not violate the Wagner Act largely because it had consistently enforced its no-solicitation policy against all organizations,

Figure 15.6

Sample Union Authorization Card

Source: Office & Professional Employees Union, New York, NY.

Date .... 20 ....

STRICTLY CONFIDENTIAL

Office & Professional Employees International Union, Local 153, AFL-CIO
265 West 14th Street, New York, NY 10011 741-8282

I hereby authorize Office & Professional Employees International Union, Local 153, AFL-CIO, to represent me and to petition the National Labor Relations Board to conduct a secret ballot election among the staff.

Name...Tel. No. ....
(Please print)

Address...
(Zip Code)

Present Employer...

Present Employer's Address...

Position...Dept. ....

Signature...

CONFIDENTIAL

including the Girl Scouts and the Salvation Army. The court also found that the store's 200 workers were otherwise accessible to the union's nonemployee organizers.[50]

Preelection Conduct

If the union can show sufficient employee interest in forming a union, the NLRB will schedule a certification election. During the period before the election, management and union leaders

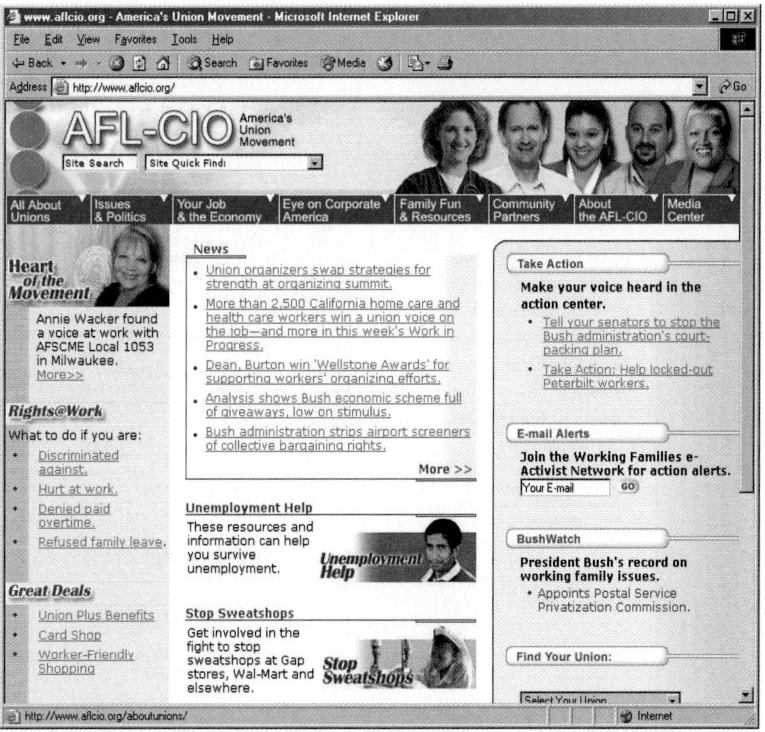

More than half of all unions have Web sites. The sites, such as this one, give employees who want to unionize the information they need quickly and efficiently.

should allow employees to freely exercise their right to vote for or against representation. It is the NLRB's policy to provide an environment in which employees can make an uncoerced choice in their selection of a bargaining agent—or, alternatively, an uncoerced choice not to be represented by any union.

During the preelection period, managers must avoid treating employees in a manner that could be interpreted as using their position to influence the outcome of the election. The NLRB "Notice to Employees" shown in Figure 15.7 indicates some types of conduct that are unacceptable before an election. Managers are prohibited from threatening employees with the loss of

Figure 15.7

NLRB Representation Election Notice to Employees

Source: National Labor Relations Board.

NOTICE TO EMPLOYEES

FROM THE

National Labor Relations Board

A PETITION has been filed with this Federal agency seeking an election to determine whether certain employees want to be represented by a union.

The case is being investigated and NO DETERMINATION HAS BEEN MADE AT THIS TIME by the National Labor Relations Board. IF an election is held Notices of Election will be posted giving complete details for voting.

It was suggested that your employer post this notice so the National Labor Relations Board could inform you of your basic rights under the National Labor Relations Act.

YOU HAVE THE RIGHT under Federal Law

- **To self-organization**
- **To form, join, or assist labor organizations**
- **To bargain collectively through representatives of your own choosing**
- **To act together for the purposes of collective bargaining or other mutual aid or protection**
- **To refuse to do any or all of these things unless the union and employer, in a state where such agreements are permitted, enter into a lawful union-security agreement requiring employees to pay periodic dues and initiation fees. Nonmembers who inform the union that they object to the use of their payments for nonrepresentational purposes may be required to pay only their share of the union's costs of representational activities *(such as collective bargaining, contract administration, and grievance adjustments).***

It is possible that some of you will be voting in an employee representation election as a result of the request for an election having been filed. While NO DETERMINATION HAS BEEN MADE AT THIS TIME, in the event an election is held, the NATIONAL LABOR RELATIONS BOARD wants all eligible voters to be familiar with their rights under the law IF it holds an election.

The Board applies rules that are intended to keep its elections fair and honest and that result in a free choice. If agents of either unions or employers act in such a way as to interfere with your right to a free election, the election can be set aside by the Board. Where appropriate the Board provides other remedies, such as reinstatement for employees fired for exercising their rights, including backpay from the party responsible for their discharge.

NOTE:

The following are examples of conduct that interfere with the rights of employees and may result in the setting aside of the election.

- **Threatening loss of jobs or benefits by an employer or a union**
- **Promising or granting promotions, pay raises, or other benefits to influence an employee's vote by a party capable of carrying out such promises**
- **An employer firing employees to discourage or encourage union activity or a union causing them to be fired to encourage union activity**
- **Making campaign speeches to assembled groups of employees on company time within the 24-hour period before the election**
- **Incitement by either an employer or a union of racial or religious prejudice by inflammatory appeals**
- **Threatening physical force or violence to employees by a union or an employer to influence their votes**

Please be assured that IF AN ELECTION IS HELD every effort will be made to protect your right to a free choice under the law. Improper conduct will not be permitted. All parties are expected to cooperate fully with this Agency in maintaining basic principles of a fair election as required by law. The National Labor Relations Board, as an agency of the United States Government, does not endorse any choice in the election.

NATIONAL LABOR RELATIONS BOARD
an agency of the
UNITED STATES GOVERNMENT

THIS IS AN OFFICIAL GOVERNMENT NOTICE AND MUST NOT BE DEFACED BY ANYONE

FORM NLRB-666 (5-90) ★U.S. GOVERNMENT PRINTING OFFICE: 1991-312-471/51356

their jobs or benefits if they vote for the union. They must also avoid promising employees benefits (such as pay raises or promotions) if they vote against the union. On their side, unions must avoid threatening workers with harm if they do not vote for unionization. Although the NLRB's rules for permissible conduct during a union election campaign are exceedingly complex and constantly changing, the Manager's Notebook titled "Quick TIPS for Preelection Conduct" provides some general guidelines for managers.

MANAGER'S NOTEBOOK

Quick TIPS for Preelection Conduct

The acronym TIPS is a quick way to remember the following guidelines developed by labor lawyers and consultants to guide managers' preelection conduct.

Threats. It is unlawful to threaten employees with theoretical dire consequences should the union win the election.

Intimidation. Employers by law cannot intimidate or coerce employees to vote against the union.

Promises. Management cannot promise employees benefits or rewards if they vote against the union.

Surveillance. It is unlawful to secretly or overtly spy on organizing meetings.

Adapted from Spognardi, M. A. (1998). Conducting a successful union-free campaign. A primer (Part II). *Employee Relations Law Journal, 24*(3), 31–53.

It *is* permissible for managers to try to persuade employees before a representation election that they would be better off without a union. Some of the methods that managers can legally use to do this are:[51]

- Making speeches to groups of employees emphasizing why they do not need a union (legal up to 24 hours before the election).
- Employing a labor relations consultant to assist with the antiunion strategy.
- Sending a personal letter to employees.
- Showing movies that view unions in an unfavorable light.
- Writing memos to employees that summarize all the good things that the employer has provided for them.

Firms in the United States seeking to stop organizing drives of unions are likely to hire consultants who specialize in helping management maintain a nonunion workforce. One study estimated that employers spent an average of $500 per employee on consultants in union election campaigns.[52]

Certification Election

The NLRB supervises the certification election, determining who is eligible to vote and counting the ballots. The voting is done by secret ballot, and the outcome is determined by the participating voters.

If the union receives a majority of the votes, it becomes the certified bargaining agent for all of the unit's employees. This means that it becomes the exclusive agent for both union and nonunion employees in collective bargaining with the employer. The *bargaining unit* consists of all the employees who are represented by a union that engages in collective bargaining with the employer.

If the majority of voters vote against the union, NLRB policy states that no other representation election may be held for a 12-month period. In recent years unions have been losing more than half of the representation elections held in the United States.[53] Because of this trend, unions have begun to devote more resources to organizing activities.[54] The Issues and Applications feature titled "Organizing Campaigns: A New Priority" gives some examples of successful attempts by U.S. unions to organize diverse groups of employees.

Collective Bargaining

If union organizing results in certification, the next step in the labor relations process is collective bargaining that results in a labor contract. Most labor contracts last for two to three years, after which they are subject to renegotiation.

Four of the most important issues related to collective bargaining are bargaining behavior, bargaining power, bargaining topics, and impasses in bargaining. In all of these areas, managers must monitor their behavior carefully.

Issues and Applications

Organizing Campaigns: A New Priority

In recent years, many unions have started to pour significant resources into their organizing campaigns. Here are some examples of recent successful union-organization activities:

- At Case Foods, Inc., a poultry plant in Morgantown, North Carolina, workers were required to pay for gloves and hairnets and had to ask permission to use the restroom. The workers were paid only $6.15 per hour. After three men were denied permission to use the restroom, the workers (most of whom spoke Spanish as their native language) walked off their jobs in protest. After the walkout, Spanish speaking organizers from the Laborers Union successfully organized the company.[a]
- Graduate students work long hours teaching courses, grading papers, and doing laboratory experiments and other important activities at universities for low salaries that average between $11,000 and $15,000 per year. At New York University graduate students attempted to form a union that was challenged in the courts by the administration. University administration argued that collective bargaining between the students and the university would be an infringement of academic freedom and justified the low wages paid to students by claiming that the graduate assistant work was part of their educational experience. The National Labor Relations Board disagreed with the administration's reasoning and decided to allow the graduate students to form a union organized by the United Auto Workers. Following in the footsteps of the graduate students at New York University, graduate students have begun union organizing drives at Columbia, Brandeis, and University of Pennsylvania.[b]
- Winning the biggest unionization drive in more than half a century the Service Employees International Union gained the right to represent 74,000 Los Angeles County home-care workers who feed, bathe, and clean the elderly and disabled. Many said they voted to join a union because they wanted to fight to raise their wages of $5.75 per hour and to obtain two benefits long denied them: health insurance and paid vacations.[c]

Sources: [a]Levinson, M. (1996, July 8). It's hip to be union. *Newsweek*, 44–45. [b]Greenhouse, S. (2001, May 15). Graduate students push for union membership. *New York Times*, A19. [c]Greenhouse, S. (1999, February 26). In biggest drive since 1937, union gains a victory, *New York Times*, A1, A15.

Bargaining Behavior

Once the NLRB certifies a union as the bargaining agent for a unit of employees, both management and the union have a duty to bargain with each other in "good faith." Refusing to bargain in good faith can result in an NLRB cease-and-desist order that is enforced in the courts. The parties are showing good faith in collective bargaining when:

- Both parties are willing to meet and confer with each other at a reasonable time and place.
- Both parties are willing to negotiate over wages, hours, and conditions of employment (the mandatory bargaining topics).

- The parties sign a written contract that formalizes their agreement and binds them to it.
- Each party gives the other a 60-day notice of termination or modification of the labor agreement before it expires.

In general, *good-faith bargaining* means treating the other party reasonably even when disagreements arise. To show good faith, management should develop different proposals and suggestions for negotiating with the union instead of simply rejecting all union proposals. For example, in the early 1960s a negotiator for General Electric made a single proposal to the union on a take-it-or-leave-it basis, and then refused to negotiate on any of the union's counteroffers. The NLRB interpreted this inflexible approach to bargaining as an unfair labor practice that did not show good faith.

A Question of Ethics

Suppose at a prebargaining meeting between the company's negotiating team and top management it is decided that the company will give up to a 4 percent raise. When negotiations start, however, the lead management negotiator states that the company cannot afford more than a 2 percent raise, and will go no higher. Is this ethical behavior? What if the situation were reversed and it was the union negotiator who stated an absolute minimum demand, knowing that the union leadership will accept less? Would that be ethical?

Bargaining Power

In collective bargaining sessions, both parties are likely to take opening positions that favor their goals but leave them some room to negotiate. For example, on the topic of pay raises, the union may initially ask for 8 percent but be willing to go as low as 5 percent. Management may initially offer the union 2 percent but be willing to go as high as 6 percent.

At which point will the parties reach agreement, 5 percent or 6 percent? The party that understands how to use its bargaining power will probably be able to achieve settlement closer to its initial bargaining position. *Bargaining power* is one party's ability to get the other party to agree to its terms. If management has greater bargaining power than the union, it is likely to get the union to agree to a 5 percent pay increase.

An important aspect of a party's bargaining power is how it is perceived by the other party. Each party can engage in behaviors that shape the other party's perceptions. Management that acts in a powerful and intimidating manner may influence the union to make additional concessions. However, aggressive posturing by management may backfire and cause union negotiators to make fewer concessions.

Parties in negotiations have several tactical alternatives. Two bargaining tactics are often used to increase bargaining power: distributive bargaining and integrative bargaining.[55]

Distributive Bargaining. **Distributive bargaining** focuses on convincing your counterpart in negotiations that the cost of disagreeing with your terms would be very high. In collective bargaining the cost of disagreement is often a strike. Strikes usually occur in the United States when a labor contract expires without both sides reaching a new agreement. Distributive bargaining tactics tend to be used when the two sides are competing for very limited resources.

Distributive bargaining
Bargaining that focuses on convincing the other party that the cost of disagreeing with the proposed terms would be very high.

Labor uses distributive bargaining when it attempts to convince management that it is willing and able to sustain a long strike that will severely damage the company's profits and weaken the company's position against its competitors. For example, in its 1993 negotiations with United Parcel Service, the Teamsters Union presented the company with several key bargaining demands, including substantial pay and benefit increases, improved job security, conversion of part-time jobs to full-time jobs, and less stringent productivity standards. When UPS, after intense contract talks and contract extensions, presented the Teamsters with a contract that did not come close to meeting the union's demands, the Teamsters suspended negotiations and set a strike date. A national strike against United Parcel Service could have crippled the company at a time when it was facing stiff competition from nonunion rivals, like FedEx and Roadway Package Services. Before this happened, however, Ron Carey, the Teamsters' reformist president, hammered out a contract that provided a good economic package and an end to some of the stringent work rules that had long irked union members.[56] Distributive bargaining tactics do not always avoid strikes. As the opening vignette shows, UPS and the Teamsters were not able to avoid a strike four years later when bargaining over terms of a new contract failed to reach a settlement before the old contract expired.

Management uses distributive bargaining when it tries to convince the union that it can sustain a long strike much better than union members, who will have to survive without their paychecks. For example, in 1975 management at the *Washington Post* tried to persuade the newspaper's unions that it could sustain a strike and still get the paper out because it had cross-trained managers to do the jobs of union workers. In this instance, management was able to pull it off.

Union leaders may also adopt distributive bargaining tactics when they believe union members are willing to accept the cost of a long strike that is likely to cause a vulnerable company severe economic damage. This situation occurred in 1998 when the UAW struck General Motors over the issue of preventing union jobs from being given to outsourcing firms. GM's motivation for outsourcing was to reduce its labor costs. A two-month strike ensued when there was a strong demand for but a short supply of new General Motors car models. The timing of the strike helped convince management to make concessions to the union after the strike cost GM $2.2 billion in losses.[57]

Integrative bargaining
Bargaining that focuses on convincing the other party that the benefits of agreeing with the proposed terms would be very high.

Integrative Bargaining. **Integrative bargaining** focuses on convincing your counterpart in negotiations that the benefits of agreeing with your terms would be very high. Integrative bargaining is similar to a problem-solving session in which both parties are seeking mutually beneficial alternatives. U.S. West and the Communication Workers of America (CWA) negotiated an agreement that illustrates the benefits of integrative bargaining. Because of technological changes in the telecommunications industry, U.S. West needed to reduce the size of its unionized work force. In exchange for the union's agreement to eliminate some jobs, the company offered to pay for retraining the affected union employees. Realizing that it was in both parties' best interests to keep the company competitive in its industry, the union accepted the company's terms. The Manager's Notebook titled "Guidelines for Integrative Bargaining" shows what both parties need to do to achieve integrative bargaining.

MANAGER'S NOTEBOOK

Guidelines for Integrative Bargaining

Integrative bargaining is the process of identifying a common, shared, or joint goal and developing a process to achieve it. An emphasis on integrative bargaining can lead to cooperation between union and management and the possibility of mutual gains for both. To achieve integrative bargaining, both parties should:

- **Attempt to understand the other negotiator's real needs and objectives.** To this end, the parties should engage in a dialogue in which both sides disclose preferences and priorities, rather than disguise or manipulate them.[a]
- **Create a free flow of information.** Negotiators must be willing to listen to the other negotiator carefully, and to accept a joint solution that incorporates both parties' needs.[b]
- **Emphasize the commonalities, and minimize the differences, between the parties.** Specific goals should be reframed to be considered part of a larger, collaborative goal. For example, a safe workplace may be a goal on which both the union and management agree, although they may differ on a specific approach to achieve this goal.[c]
- **Search for solutions that meet both parties' goals and objectives.** When parties are combative or competitive, they are more likely to focus only on their own objectives and ignore those of the other party. Integrative bargaining is successful only when both parties' needs are met.[d]
- **Develop flexible responses to the other negotiator's proposals.** Each negotiator should try to accommodate and adapt to the needs of the other party by modifying his or her proposals. Avoid getting stuck in one intractable position that does not provide room to make tactical trade-offs. By behaving flexibly, a negotiator can encourage the other party to reciprocate in a similar fashion and move toward a settlement with mutual gains.[e]

Sources: [a]Lewicki, R., and Litterer, J. (1985). *Negotiation.* Homewood, IL: Irwin. [b]Ibid. [c]Ibid. [d]Ibid. [e]Das, T. K., and Teng, B. (1998). Between trust and control: Developing confidence in partner cooperation and alliances. *Academy of Management Review,* 23, 491–512.

It is not unusual in collective bargaining for both sides to use both distributive and integrative bargaining tactics. However, the firm's overall labor relations strategy generally determines what type of bargaining it adopts.[58] Firms with a union acceptance strategy are more likely to mix integrative and distributive bargaining, while those with a union avoidance strategy are more likely to focus solely on distributive bargaining. In addition, the strategies selected by the union will influence a firm's bargaining strategies and tactics because collective bargaining is a dynamic process.

Bargaining Topics

The NLRB and courts classify bargaining topics into three categories: mandatory, permissive, and illegal.

As mentioned earlier, *mandatory bargaining topics* are wages, hours, and employment conditions. These are the topics that both union and management consider fundamental to the organization's labor relations. Some examples of each of these mandatory topics are shown in Figure 15.8.

The NLRB and courts have interpreted wages, hours, and employment conditions fairly broadly. "Wages" can mean any type of compensation, including base pay rates, pay incentives, health insurance, and retirement benefits. "Hours" can mean anything to do with work scheduling, including the allocation of overtime and the amount of vacation time granted. "Employment conditions" can mean almost any work rule that affects the employees represented by the union. These include grievance procedures, safety rules, job descriptions, and the bases for promotions.

Permissive bargaining topics may be discussed during collective bargaining if both parties agree to do so, but neither party is obligated to bargain on these topics. Some permissive bargaining topics are provisions for union members to serve on the company's board of directors and benefits for retired union members. In the recessionary economy of the early 1990s, some unions swapped wage concessions for equity in the company and a stronger voice in how it is run. Management–labor agreements in the airline industry have incorporated some novel approaches to rescue faltering airlines and thousands of jobs. For instance:

- Financially beleaguered Northwest Airlines and its three major unions—the Machinists, the Air Line Pilots Association, and the International Brotherhood of Teamsters—reached an agreement in 1993 on contract concessions to keep the carrier flying. The unions consented to more than $700 million worth of concessions in return for 30 percent of Northwest's preferred stock, three seats on the company's 15-member board, enhanced job security, and a significant voice in company operations.[59]
- At United Airlines, the unions that represent pilots and machinists traded 15 percent in pay cuts for 55 percent of the company stock and three of 12 board seats in 1994. By 1996 United's stock price had more than doubled and the employee-owned airline was outperforming most of its rivals.[60] However, United Airlines stock plunged in 2001 after the terrorist attack on the United States when United grounded 31 percent of its flights and furloughed 20,000 of its employees. This reversal of company fortunes put a damper on the

Figure 15.8 Mandatory Bargaining Topics

Wages	Hours	Employment Conditions
Base pay rates	Overtime	Layoffs
Overtime pay rates	Holidays	Promotions
Retirement benefits	Vacation	Seniority provisions
Health benefits	Shifts	Safety rules
Travel pay	Flextime	Work rules
Pay incentives	Parental leave	Grievance procedures
		Union shop
		Job descriptions

union's interest in taking additional pay cuts to help the company overcome its latest financial crisis.[61]

Illegal bargaining topics may not be discussed in collective bargaining. Examples of illegal topics are closed shop agreements, featherbedding, and discriminatory employment practices. The NLRB considers the discussion of illegal bargaining topics an unfair labor practice.

Impasses in Bargaining

A labor contract cannot be finalized until the bargaining representatives on both sides go back to their organizations and obtain approval of the contract. Union negotiators typically ask the members to vote on the contract. Most unions require a majority of union members to approve the contract. Management's negotiating team may need approval from the company's top executives. If the parties cannot agree on one or more mandatory issues, they have reached an *impasse* in bargaining. A party that insists on bargaining over a permissive topic to the point of impasse engages in an unfair labor practice.

If the impasse persists because the parties have taken rigid positions, a strike may result. Before a strike is called, either party may ask a mediator to help resolve the impasse. Mediators are trained in conflict resolution techniques and are sometimes able to improve communication so that the impasse is resolved. The Federal Mediation and Conciliation Service (FMCS), established by the Taft-Hartley Act, monitors labor disputes and (under certain circumstances) mediates disputes. In addition, the FMCS maintains a list of impartial mediators and arbitrators who are qualified to assist with contract disputes.

If the contract's expiration date approaches, and the parties are still at an impasse, the union may ask its members to vote on a strike. If members approve, the strike will start the day after the current labor contract expires. Striking union members withhold their labor from the employer and often publicize their dispute by picketing in front of the employer's buildings. A strike imposes costs on both parties. Striking union members receive no wages or benefits until they return to work, although they may draw some money from the union's strike fund, which is set up to give a small allowance to cover the striking members' basic expenses. However, a long strike may exhaust the strike fund, putting pressure on the union to make concessions in order to get its members back to work.

Workers on strike also face the risk of losing their jobs to permanent replacement workers. Caterpillar, Inc., the world's largest manufacturer of construction equipment, used the threat of hiring permanent replacement workers to win a heated dispute with the United Auto Workers. The company set a deadline and told striking workers, "Go back to work or lose your job." The strikers were scared off the picket line and returned to work on management's terms.[62] The use of permanent replacement workers is very controversial, and organized labor is trying to get Congress to pass legislation restricting it.[63] See the Issues and Applications feature titled "Permanent Replacement Workers: A Strike Against Labor or an Economic Necessity?" for more on this issue.

Sometimes unions are legally bound by their contracts to honor another union's picket line, which makes it more difficult for the company to hire replacement workers. For example, during a strike by the screenwriters at the three major U.S. television networks, all the other television production workers left their jobs in a *sympathy strike*. The solidarity of the unions forced the television studios to abandon all production work until they could reach a settlement with the screenwriters.

Issues and Applications

Permanent Replacement Workers: A Strike Against Labor or an Economic Necessity?

When over 6,300 drivers abandoned Greyhound buses during a bitter strike in 1989, the company had 700 new recruits on hand to drive the fleet and 900 more in training. And after the strike ended, most of the new hires remained on the job. Replacement workers also remained on the job after bitter protracted strikes at International Paper and Eastern and Continental Airlines.

Replacing striking workers has been a legal employer option for about 60 years, but it was not until 1981, when President Ronald Reagan fired striking air traffic controllers and kept the air traffic system going with replacements, that employers began using this tactic regularly.

To organized labor, the hiring of permanent replacement workers undermines the bargaining power granted to unions under the Wagner Act's guaranteed right to strike. Once the unions' trump card, the strike has become a card many unions are afraid to play in an era when strikers fear losing their jobs. Labor advocates argue that permanent replacement is the same as firing striking workers, which is illegal.

The current law on replacement workers derives from a 1938 case, *NLRB v. Mackay Radio & Telegraph Co.*, in which the court declared that while the company in this case (Mackay) was guilty of firing strikers, in other cases where management has committed no illegal practices, the company is not bound to discharge replacement workers and hire back strikers when they wish to return to work. Labor advocates insist that "not hired back" equals "fired." On their side, employers argue that the ability to hire permanent replacements is necessary to ensure the survival of companies. Jack Schwartz, the labor counsel for National Tea, a New Orleans–based company, echoed the views of many employers when he said that legislation banning permanent replacement workers will encourage companies to relocate to "Mexico or another country where they don't have to worry about that risk."

Sources: Singh, P., and Harish, J. (2001). Striker replacements in the United States and Mexico: A review of the law and empirical research. *Industrial Relations, 40*, 22–53; Budd, J. (1996). Canadian strike replacement legislation and collective bargaining: Lessons for the United States. *Industrial Relations, 3b*, 245–260. *BNA's Employee Relations Weekly*. (1994, January 24). Negotiators for management and labor gauge impact of striker replacements, *12*(4), 87–88. Bernstein, A. (1991, August 5). You can't bargain with a striker whose job is no more. *BusinessWeek*, 27, and Kliborn, P. T. (1990, March 13). Replacement workers. Management's big gun. *New York Times*. A24.

Management also faces significant strike costs. A strike can force a company to shut down operations and lose customers. In a highly competitive market such actions may plunge the company into bankruptcy. This is exactly what happened at Eastern Airlines when the International Association of Machinists and Aerospace Workers (IAM) struck the air carrier in a contract dispute in 1989. A strike also poses a threat to a company from a loss of market share to its rivals in highly competitive industries. This is what happened to Boeing in 2000 in the competitive commercial aircraft industry when it sustained a six-week strike of 18,000 engineers and technicians of the Society of Professional Engineering Employees in Aerospace (SPEEA) in the largest white-collar strike occurring in the United States. Eventually the company settled with a contract favorable to the union's demands. The union demanded and obtained in its contract provisions for the company to continue paying for all of the employees' health insurance benefits and to give employees a 5 percent annual pay increase over a three-year period.[64]

Despite the negative outcomes sometimes associated with strikes, they are an important feature of the collective bargaining process. The pressure of an impending strike deadline forces both union and management negotiators to make concessions and resolve their differences. In the United States less than 0.2 percent of total working time lost is lost because of strikes. Put another way, less working time is lost because of strikes than because of the common cold.[65] Without the potential for strikes, there would undoubtedly be more unresolved impasses in collective bargaining.

There are several different kinds of strikes. The type of strike we have been discussing thus far, which takes place when an agreement is not reached during collective bargaining, is called an **economic strike.** Another type of strike, called the **wildcat strike,** is a spontaneous work stoppage that happens under a valid contract and is usually not supported by union leadership. Wildcat strikes generally occur when workers are angered by a disciplinary action taken by management against one of their colleagues. This type of strike is designed to draw management's attention to an issue that the strikers want settled. Some contracts forbid wildcat strikes and penalize workers who participate in them, sometimes by termination. The preferred method of resolving disputes between unionized workers and management is the grievance procedure. One tool that employers can use against workers is the lockout. A **lockout** occurs when the employer shuts down its operation before or during a labor dispute. Employers may use a lockout during

Economic strike
A strike that takes place when an agreement is not reached during collective bargaining.

Wildcat strike
A spontaneous work stoppage that happens under a valid contract and is usually not supported by union leadership.

Lockout
Occurs when an employer shuts down its operations before or during a labor dispute.

a bargaining impasse to protect themselves from unusual economic hardship when the timing of a strike may ruin critical materials. For example, a brewer must bottle beer by a certain date or the entire batch can be ruined. Because employers have other alternatives to influence the union to make concessions, such as the use of replacement workers, lockouts are rarely used.

Contract Administration

The last phase of labor relations is contract administration, which involves application and enforcement of the labor contract in the workplace. Disputes occasionally arise between labor and management over such issues as who should be promoted or whether an employee has abused sick leave privileges. The steps taken to resolve such disputes are spelled out in the labor contract.

The mechanism preferred by most unions and managements to settle disputes is the grievance procedure.[66] A **grievance procedure** is a systematic, step-by-step procedure designed to settle disputes regarding the interpretation of the labor contract.

Grievance procedure
A systematic step-by-step process designed to settle disputes regarding the interpretation of a labor contract.

Although employees may attempt to settle their grievances through such alternatives as an open-door policy or a meeting with an employee relations representative in the HR department (see Chapter 13), grievance procedures under union contracts have two significant advantages for employees that no other HRM program can provide:

1. The grievance procedure provides the employee with an advocate dedicated to representing the employee's case to management. This representative is called the **union steward.** Under any other system used to handle grievances, the employee is represented by someone who is either a manager or an agent of management. Such people obviously cannot be entirely dedicated to the employee's position.
2. The last step in the grievance procedure is **arbitration,** a quasi-judicial process that is binding on both parties. The arbitrator is a neutral person selected from outside the firm and compensated by both the union and management (who split the fee). Unlike grievance panels, which are composed of people on the company payroll, the arbitrator has no personal stake in the outcome and can make a tough decision without worrying about how it will affect his or her career.[67]

Union steward
An advocate dedicated to representing an employee's case to management in a grievance procedure.

Arbitration
The last step in a grievance procedure. The decision of the arbitrator, who is a neutral individual selected from outside the firm, is binding on both parties.

Steps in the Grievance Procedure

Most union grievance procedures have three or four steps leading up to arbitration, the final step. Figure 15.9 illustrates a four-step union grievance procedure. Usually a time limit is set for resolution of the grievance at each step. Later steps in the procedure require more time than earlier steps, and the degree of formality increases with each step. Because the grievance procedure is time consuming and distracts several people from their regular job duties, it is generally advantageous for the company to resolve disputes as early as possible.

The key to an effective grievance procedure is training supervisors to understand the labor contract and to work with union stewards to settle grievances at the first step. The labor relations staff in the HR department can make an important contribution here by training and consulting with supervisors.

The first step of the grievance procedure is taken when an employee tells the union steward about his or her grievance. In our example in Figure 15.9, the employee must make the dispute known to the steward and/or the supervisor within five working days of its occurrence. The steward refers to the labor contract to determine if the grievance is valid and, if it is, tries to work with the employee's supervisor to settle it. The grievance may or may not be put in writing. Most grievances (about 75 percent) are settled at this first step.

If the dispute cannot be resolved at this first step, the grievance is put into writing, and, in our example, the department or plant manager and a union official (such as the union's business representative) have an additional five working days to resolve the issue. At this second step, a formal meeting is usually held to discuss the grievance.

If the second step is unsuccessful at resolving the grievance, the parties move on to the third step. This step usually involves both a corporate manager (for example, the company's director of labor relations) and a local and national union representative. In our example, the labor agree-

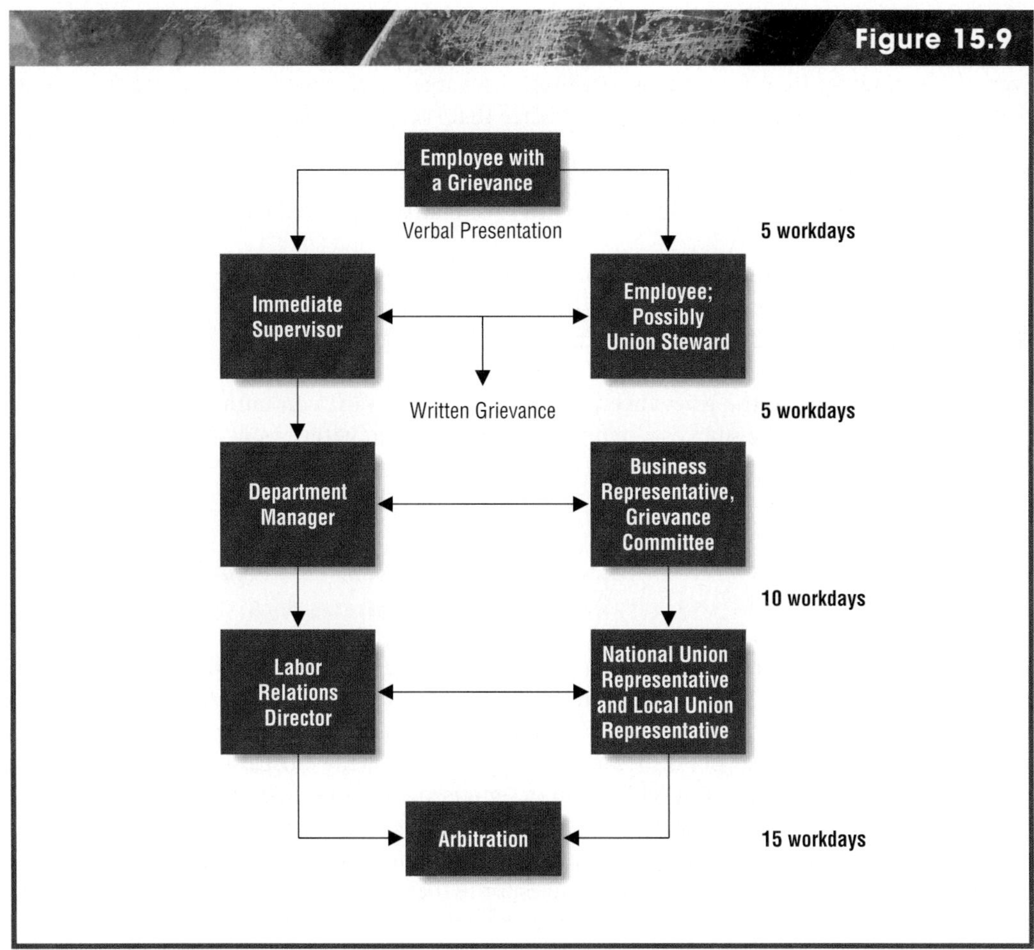

A Union Grievance Procedure

Source: Adapted from Allen, R., and Keavany, T. (1988). *Contemporary labor solutions* (2nd ed.), 530. Reading, MA: Addison-Wesley. Reprinted by permission of Robert Allen.

ment gives these people 10 days to respond to and resolve the grievance. Grievances that have the potential to set precedents affecting employment policy may get "kicked up" to this level because it is inappropriate for plant supervisors or managers to settle them. For example, a grievance concerning production standards may have widespread implications for all workers if a corporatewide labor contract is in effect. Because the third step is the last step before arbitration, it is management's final opportunity to negotiate a settlement with the union. It is common for management to try to "cut a deal" with the union at this step.

The final step of the grievance procedure is arbitration. Only about 1 percent of grievances get as far as arbitration; the rest are settled at the earlier steps. Both parties select the arbitrator, before whom the union and management advocates present their case and evidence at a hearing with a quasi-judicial format. The arbitrator then examines the evidence and makes a ruling. Most arbitrators also write an opinion outlining their reasoning and the sections of the labor contract that influenced their decision. This opinion can serve as a guideline for dealing with similar disputes in the future. The arbitrator's decision is final and binding on both parties.

Types of Grievances

Employees initiate two types of grievances. The first is a *contract interpretation grievance* based on union members' rights under the labor contract. If the contract's language is ambiguous, this type of grievance may go to arbitration for clarification. For example, suppose that a labor contract allows workers two 10-minute coffee breaks per day. If management decides it would be more efficient to get rid of coffee breaks, employees may file a contract interpretation grievance to get this privilege restored.

The second type of grievance involves employee discipline. In such cases, the grievance procedure examines whether the employee in question was disciplined for just cause, and management has the burden of proof. An important aspect of these cases is determining whether the disciplined employee received due process. For minor infractions, management is expected to give employees the opportunity to correct their behavior via the progressive discipline procedure (verbal warning, written warning, suspension, discharge). For more serious charges (such as theft), management must provide strong evidence that the discipline was warranted.

Benefits of Union Grievance Procedures

Union grievance procedures provide benefits to both management and employees. Specifically:

- The grievance procedure protects union employees from arbitrary management decisions; it is the mechanism for organizational justice.
- The grievance procedure helps management quickly and efficiently settle conflicts that could otherwise end up in the courts or result in work stoppages.
- Management can use the grievance procedure as an upward communications channel to monitor and correct the sources of employee dissatisfaction with jobs or company policies.

The Impact of Unions on Human Resource Management

A union can significantly alter a company's HRM policies because of its bargaining power, which is supported by labor law. In the absence of a union, management is more likely to develop HRM policies based on the principle of efficiency. For example, a nonunion company is more likely to adopt a meet-the-market pay policy because the market wage is the most efficient way to allocate labor costs (see Chapter 10). But when a union enters the picture, management must develop policies that reflect the preferences of the majority of workers who are represented by the union.[68] In this case, management is more likely to adopt an above-the-market pay policy because union members have strong preferences for higher wages. In this section, we look at the changes in staffing, employee development, compensation, and employee relations practices that are likely under unionization.

Staffing

Seniority
The length of time a person works for an employer.

Under a labor contract, job opportunities are allocated to people on the basis of seniority. **Seniority** is the length of time a person works for an employer. In a unionized company, promotions, job assignments, and shift preferences are given to the employee with the most seniority in the unit.[69] Layoffs in unionized firms are also governed according to the last in, first out rule (see Chapter 6).[70]

Work rules tend to be less flexible in a unionized workplace because they are likely to be formalized in the labor agreement. When labor relations are adversarial, labor contracts are more likely to have inflexible work rules written into them. When labor relations are more cooperative, work rule specifications may purposely be left out of the contract. In certain industries, this gives management the flexibility to adjust to the rapidly changing technological requirements of producing a product or service. For instance, under the terms of the 1999 contract between DaimlerChrysler and the UAW, the company agreed to give the union a rich economic pay package with a $1350 signing bonus and a 3 percent pay increase in addition to pay adjustments for inflation. In return, DaimlerChrysler got the union to agree to allow the company to reduce the size of the workforce through attrition (that is, the company does not have to fill jobs vacated through quits and retirements). The reduction of the workforce gives the company the opportunity to decrease costs through increased productivity.[71]

In the absence of a union, the employer is more likely to allocate job opportunities to employees on the basis of merit.[72] In most cases, merit is determined by a supervisor's judgment of the employee's performance. Supervisors in a nonunion workplace have more power and influence because of their authority to reward employees' efforts with promotions, attractive job assignments, and preferred work schedules. Layoff decisions in nonunion firms are more likely to take both merit and seniority into consideration. Finally, work rules are often more flexible in a nonunion firm because the employer is not tied to a contract and is, therefore, not required to

DaimlerChrysler workers bargained for pay increases. In exchange, the company can reduce the workforce through attrition, giving it the flexibility it needs to compete.

justify to employees any changes made in the way work is done. In nonunion firms it is management alone that determines the most efficient way to produce a product or service and deliver it to the customer.

Employee Development

In unionized companies, the uses of performance appraisal are very limited because the appraisal data usually come from the supervisor, a source that many unions find problematic. Unions tend to balk at using performance appraisal as the basis for making pay and staffing decisions. If performance appraisal is done at all for union employees, it is used simply to provide some feedback on their performance. In a nonunion workplace, however, the performance appraisal is likely to have a broad set of uses for HR decisions. It is used to determine pay raises, promotions, job assignments, career planning, training needs, and layoff or discharge.[73]

Unionized firms tend to retain their employees longer than nonunion firms do.[74] There are a few reasons for the lower quit rates in unionized firms. First, unionized employees are more likely to express their dissatisfaction through the grievance procedure, so this channel may become an alternative to quitting. Second, unionized firms on average pay their employees a higher wage, which may make it more difficult for them to find an equally high-paying job if they leave. The higher employee retention rates at unionized companies provide an incentive for those companies to make greater investments in training because they can expect a longer payback on their training investment.[75]

Unions themselves have become far more interested in worker training and development in recent years. The 1990 contract between General Motors and the UAW, for instance, specified that the company will create Skills Centers (adult educational facilities) for union workers. So far, 36 GM plants in the United States have set up these centers. As unions have stepped up their organizing efforts (see the Issues and Applications feature on page 522), many have offered to fund worker training programs. In New York City, for instance, locals of the Amalgamated Labor and Textile Workers Unions, the International Ladies Garment Workers Union, and other major unions work with a Center for Worker Education to provide English as a second language and high school equivalency classes for their members and for worker groups they are trying to organize.[76]

Compensation

A company experiences an increase in total compensation costs when a union organizes its employees. On average, union employees earn 10 percent to 20 percent higher wages than comparable nonunionized employees.[77]

Cost-of-living adjustment (COLA)
Pay raises, usually made across the board, that are tied to such inflation indicators as the consumer price index.

The presence of a union also affects the company's policy on pay raises. Unionized firms avoid using merit pay plans and are likely to give across-the-board pay raises to employees based on market considerations.[78] Across-the-board pay plans are often based on **cost-of-living adjustments (COLAs)** that are tied to inflation indicators such as the consumer price index. About 16 percent of U.S. workers received COLAs in 1995, down from 60 percent in 1983.[79] Unions prefer across-the-board pay raises to merit pay plans because they see the latter as undermining union solidarity by encouraging employees to compete against one another to win higher pay increases. Furthermore, unions are often skeptical of the fairness of merit pay increases because of the potential for favoritism on the part of supervisors (see Chapter 7). Unions apply this same logic to the use of individual pay incentives such as lump-sum bonuses. In contrast, nonunion firms tend to use merit pay and bonuses to encourage competition and recognize their top performers.

Unions are less likely to object to group pay incentives because group plans (such as gainsharing or profit sharing) tend to reinforce group cohesion. Each of the Big Three automakers in the United States has negotiated a profit-sharing plan with the UAW. It is not unusual to find gainsharing plans in both union and nonunion companies.[80] However, nonunion firms generally have more flexibility to use both individual and group pay incentives to reward different types of work outcomes.

Unions have generally influenced employers to offer a more valuable benefits package to each employee.[81] Through collective bargaining, they have been able to negotiate packages with a broader array of benefits than nonunion workers receive.

In unionized firms the employer pays for most benefits, while in nonunion firms employer and employee share the costs.[82] The result is better health benefits for unionized employees than for their nonunion counterparts. As U.S. health-care costs have soared over the last decade, nonunionized companies have begun asking their employees to pay a greater share of these costs through both higher monthly premiums and higher deductibles. Although unionized employers face the same rising health-care costs, unions have used collective bargaining to persuade many employers to pursue alternative cost-saving methods such as managed health care, second opinions, and audits.[83]

In terms of retirement benefits, unions have been able to provide more security for employees by influencing employers to adopt a defined benefit plan, which provides a fixed amount of income to employees upon retirement. Nonunion employers are more likely to adopt a defined contribution plan, which requires only that the employer set aside a fixed portion of the employee's income each month in a plan that meets the ERISA (Employee Retirement Income Security Act) standards for these plans. Under a defined contribution plan, employees do not know how much total income will be available for their retirement until they actually retire (see Chapter 12).

Unions can play an important role in monitoring and enforcing legally required benefits such as workers' compensation and unemployment insurance.[84] In a unionized firm, employees are more likely to receive workers' compensation and unemployment insurance benefits because union representatives give workers information on how to use them. Furthermore, unionized workers are less likely to be discouraged from filing claims for fear of being penalized or challenged by their employer.[85] In contrast, management in a nonunion firm is not as likely to make employees aware of their right to use these government-mandated benefits because a firm's payroll taxes to fund the benefit increase in proportion to the number of employees using the benefit (see Chapter 12).

Employee Relations

The union is an empowerment mechanism that gives employees a voice in the development of work rules that affect their jobs. The labor contract gives employees specific rights. Nonperformance by the employer of an employee right guaranteed in the contract can be remedied under the grievance procedure. For example, an employee overlooked for promotion may file a grievance and be reconsidered for the promotion if the contract stipulates that the employee has a right to that promotion.

Nonunion employers tend to document their employees' basic rights in an employee handbook (see Chapter 13). However, employee handbooks provide fewer employee rights than labor contracts do. In fact, many of them contain only general guidelines and specifically state that supervisors may need to make exceptions to the written policy from time to time. For example, employees may have the right to bid on a promotion posted on a job board, but the handbook usually states that management reserves the right to determine which employee will ultimately get the job.

The appeals mechanism that a nonunion employer is most likely to use is the open-door policy.[86] Unlike the grievance procedure, which is administered by both the union and management, the open-door policy is controlled by management. It gives management the opportunity to resolve an employee's complaint while balancing both parties' interests. The only recourse open to employees who are unhappy with the resolution of a complaint under the open-door policy is to find legal counsel and go to court to obtain justice—an option more employees are pursuing every year. Under the union grievance procedure, it is much less likely that an employee will take a case to court because judges are usually unwilling to challenge the results of arbitration.

When an employer is investigating a union employee for the purposes of imposing discipline, the employee has a right to have a union representative present during questioning. The right to have a union representative present during a disciplinary investigation is called a *Weingarten right* based on a 1975 Supreme Court case, *NLRB v. Weingarten*, which established this right from an interpretation of the National Labor Relations Act.[87] The union representative in the investigation is likely to be a union steward who is trained in conflict resolution methods and understands employee rights under the labor contract. In 2000 the National Labor Relations Board ruled that nonunion employees are also entitled to *Weingarten rights*, which permits them to have a co-worker present when undergoing an investigatory interview that could lead to a disciplinary action. However, the co-worker selected as an employee representative in the nonunion setting is likely to have fewer skills at resolving grievances or defusing conflict than a trained union steward.[88]

Summary and Conclusions

Why Do Employees Join Unions?

U.S. employees generally seek representation from a union because they (1) are dissatisfied with certain aspects of their job, (2) lack influence with management to make the needed changes, and (3) see the union as a solution to their problems.

Labor unions were largely unprotected by law in the United States until 1935. Economic conditions during the Great Depression led Congress to try to equalize the power of employers and employees. After several decades of widespread support, unions are today widely perceived as too powerful.

Managers strongly affect how employees perceive the work environment and thus whether they will be susceptible to unionization. Managers must possess enough knowledge of basic labor law to (1) avoid creating a legal liability for the company, (2) implement the terms of labor agreements fairly and impartially, and (3) hear and resolve employee grievances.

Labor Relations and the Legal Environment

The most important laws governing labor relations in the United States are the Wagner Act (1935), the Taft-Hartley Act (1947), and the Landrum-Griffin Act (1959). The Wagner Act created the National Labor Relations Board, which administers union certification elections and prevents and remedies unfair labor practices.

Labor Relations in the United States

Labor relations in the United States are characterized by (1) business unionism, (2) unions structured by type of job, (3) a focus on collective bargaining, (4) the use of labor contracts, (5) the adversarial nature of labor–management relations and shrinking union membership, and (6) the growth of unions in the public sector.

Labor Relations in Other Countries

The labor relations systems of two key global competitors of the United States, Germany and Japan, have achieved a greater degree of cooperation between unions and management than the U.S. system has. The German system uses works councils and codetermination to involve workers in decisions at all levels of the organization. In Japan, enterprise unions have worked closely with companies for the mutual benefit of both parties. Some believe that economic pressures are straining labor–management relations in these countries today.

Labor Relations Strategy

A labor relations strategy is a company's overall plan for dealing with unions. Companies that choose a union acceptance strategy view unions as their employees' legitimate representatives and accept collective bargaining as an appropriate mechanism for establishing workplace rules. Companies that choose a union avoidance strategy use either union substitution or union suppression to keep unions out of the workplace.

Managing the Labor Relations Process

The labor relations process has three phases: (1) union organizing, (2) collective bargaining, and (3) contract administration. In the union organizing phase, management must confront the issues involved with union solicitation, preelection conduct, and the certification election. In the collective bargaining phase, union and management representatives negotiate workplace rules that are formalized in a labor contract. The contract administration phase starts after the labor contract is settled and deals with day-to-day administration of the workplace. A key feature of the contract administration phase is the grievance procedure, a step-by-step process for settling employee disputes about contract interpretations or disciplinary actions.

The Impact of Unions on Human Resource Management

The impact of a union on the way a company manages its human resources is significant. Management can expect that the union will affect virtually every major area of HRM. In a unionized workplace, staffing decisions will be heavily influenced by seniority rather than by merit. Individually focused performance appraisals are severely curtailed, while training programs are emphasized. Unionized employees tend to receive larger compensation and benefit packages. Finally, employee relations processes in a union shop are by definition highly structured.

Key Terms

arbitration, 524
business unionism, 505
codetermination, 509
collective bargaining, 505
cost-of-living adjustment (COLA), 528
distributive bargaining, 519
economic strike, 523
enterprise union, 509
grievance procedure, 524
integrative bargaining, 520
labor contract, 505
labor relations specialist, 502
labor relations strategy, 510
Landrum-Griffin Act (1959), 504
lockout, 523
National Labor Relations Board (NLRB), 502
Railway Labor Act, 504
right-to-work law, 503
seniority, 526
Taft-Hartley Act (1947), 503
union, 500
union acceptance strategy, 511
union avoidance strategy, 513
union shop clause, 503
union steward, 524
union substitution/proactive human resource management, 513
union suppression, 513
Wagner Act/National Labor Relations Act (1935), 502
wildcat strike, 523
works councils, 509
work rules, 505

Discussion Questions

1. Why have labor and management tended to treat each other as adversaries in the U.S. labor relations system?
2. What factors are encouraging unions and management in the United States to adopt more cooperative strategies today?
3. What factors explain why unions in the United States have been losing more than 50 percent of all certification elections?
4. Suppose a goal of management is to reduce the number of grievances filed by union employees each year. What are some ways that the HRM staff can contribute to this goal?
5. How can management's collective bargaining tactics be influenced by the company's labor relations strategy? Provide examples.
6. What are some advantages and disadvantages of a strike from management's perspective? From the union's perspective?
7. What, in your opinion, is the most significant impact of a union on the management of human resources? Explain.
8. It is often said that "good pay and good management" are the keys to successful union avoidance. Spell out the kind of policies and practices companies should develop if they want to keep their workers from unionizing. Do you think the employee relations practices you've mentioned are less costly or more costly than working with unionized labor?
9. The Teamsters strike with the United Parcel Service in 1997 (see opening vignette) has been considered by labor relations experts to be one of the most important strikes in the United States in recent times. Do you agree or disagree with this assessment? What do you think were the issues that made this conflict between labor and management at UPS so noteworthy?

10. Some experts in the field of labor relations believe that when a union can pose a credible threat of a strike to management in the collective bargaining process, both parties—union and management—are motivated to move in the direction of a settlement and reach a labor agreement. They also claim that without a credible strike threat, the two parties are less likely to arrive at a joint agreement. What is the basis for this justification for giving the union the privilege of exercising its right to strike? Do you agree or disagree with this argument? Explain your reasoning.
11. Individuals who are sympathetic to unions claim that currently in the United States it is very difficult for unions to win certification elections, which is why union membership is in a period of decline. To remedy this situation, some experts propose changing the labor relations law governing elections, making it easier for the union to win an election. One way this could be done is to allow a union that receives a majority of employee signatures on the authorization cards during the preelection period to be recognized as the certified bargaining agent for the work unit of employees. The labor law in Canada already allows unions to win certification elections this way. Do you agree or disagree that the U.S. labor law needs to be changed to be more favorable to unions? Explain your position.

There is a variety of additional material available on the Web site that accompanies this text. You can access this information by visiting the Web site at **www.prenhall.com/gomez.**

Emerging Trends Case 15.1

YOU MANAGE IT!

Organized Labor Leads the Charge for Corporate Governance Reform

Labor unions have started throwing their considerable weight around in lobbying and shareholder fights to reform corporate governance practices that affect executive pay, independence of auditors, the accountability of board directors, and incorporations in remote off-shore locations such as Bermuda. For example, the Teamsters Union put forth a successful shareholder resolution to let Bank of America shareholders vote on executive severance deals such as golden parachutes, which would give top executives large sums of cash and stock when they are asked to leave after a merger or acquisition. Furthermore, the Machinists Union helped to block a management plan for the Stanley Works to relocate to Bermuda.

John J. Sweeney, president of labor federation A.F.L.-C.I.O., announced the labor movement's support of several proposals, among them recording stock options as expenses and prohibiting top corporate officials from selling company stock options while in office.

Noting that financial scandals at Enron, WorldCom, and Arthur Andersen had cost 28,500 workers their jobs, Mr. Sweeney called on the Securities and Exchange Commission and the three main stock exchanges to agree to a single higher standard for publicly traded corporations. Mr. Sweeney justified union involvement in these matters by saying "when corporate criminals invade our workplaces and our markets to steal our jobs and our savings, we must react every bit as decisively as when thieves enter our homes and try to bring harm to our loved ones."

Labor unions have already played a role in moving accounting reforms through Congress and in several successive shareholder battles that have brought about changes, among them persuading Walt Disney Company to stop using the same firm to audit its books and to do consulting work for it. Mr. Sweeney indicated that labor will increase these efforts by meeting with executives, putting pressure on corporate boards, having demonstrations, and lobbying and e-mail campaigns. He promises that the A.F.L.-C.I.O., a federation of 66 unions representing 13 million workers, will work for reforms, company by company, starting with Standard & Poor's 100. He says unions will use more than $5 trillion in union pension funds to pressure corporate managers to be more responsive and responsible. Mr. Sweeney also called for changes to give pension funds more power to choose directors who do not rubber-stamp the decisions of company executives.

Although unions represent only a fraction of workers at companies hit by corporate scandal, labor leaders say this is an opportune time to rein in executive compensation and align the interests of executives more closely with those of investors and workers.

Critical Thinking Questions

1. Why are U.S. unions putting pressure on Congress to change accounting practices and putting pressure on cor-

porate boards to reform the basis for the allocation of executive pay? How will union membership benefit when these changes are made?

2. How does control over union pension funds give unions the power to influence corporate boards to make decisions that are favorable to the interests of union members?

Team Exercise

With a group of four or five students discuss the implications of having unions use the financial leverage of their pension funds to achieve other union goals that are important to the membership beyond the corporate reforms that were mentioned in this case. Here are some examples: provide higher wages, improved working conditions, and shorter hours of employment; protect jobs of union workers from being outsourced to low-wage countries; construct on-site child-care centers for worker's children; and support a resolution to encourage unions to organize groups of employees within the company who remain nonunion. Do unions have alternative means for achieving any or all of these goals? What other tactics could be used?

Sources: Adapted from Borrus, A. (2002, July 15). Getting the boss to behave. *BusinessWeek*, 110; and Greenhouse, S. (2002, July 30). Labor to press for changes in corporate governance. *New York Times*, C7.

YOU MANAGE IT! Emerging Trends Case 15.2

High-Technology Employees Still Do Not March to the Union Beat—Yet!

As the labor movement sets its sights on the booming high-technology world, employees like Matt Shea, a 24-year-old software developer, seem ripe for the picking. He often clocks 70-hour weeks, his managers sometimes push him to work past midnight, and he never receives overtime pay. But ask Matt whether he wants a union at his workplace, a thriving Internet start-up called Go2Net, and his response is a puzzled expression that says: "Does not compute."

"As far as me personally, and for everyone else here, unions have never come up," said Shea, who says he loves his job, notwithstanding the sweatshop hours. "Everything I want is offered to me here."

The American labor movement has belatedly recognized that if it is to reverse the decades-long slide in the percentage of workers belonging to unions, it must make some headway in high technology, the economy's fastest-growing sector. To increase its numbers and its influence in politics and at the bargaining table, unions cannot afford to be shut out of the glamorous and powerful high-technology industry, which accounts for an ever-larger share of the workforce. Persuading technology workers to join unions will not be easy, though, because of all that is lavished on people like Mr. Shea. His job gives him valuable stock options, flexible hours, an excellent medical plan, a sense of family and, perhaps most important, the thrill of building something.

Labor leaders acknowledge that they face an uphill battle—only a small fraction of the nation's 2 million computer and software developers, programmers, and engineers belongs to labor unions. But organizers are far from packing their bags in Silicon Valley, convinced that many high-technology employees will eventually warm to labor's message that workers need a collective voice to stand up to management.

Although there are many contented high-tech workers such as Mr. Shea, there are also many discontented have-nots. Most have-nots come from the sea of long-term temporary employees who work at Microsoft and other high-tech companies. They often complain of being second-class citizens who receive bare-bones benefits and have no job security or stock options. Microsoft employs 20,500 regular workers domestically and 6,000 temps, who call themselves perma-temps because they work anywhere from six months to three years at the company, testing software, writing manuals, designing Web pages, and developing CD-ROMs. Industry experts estimate that at many companies, including Compaq Computer, Hewlett-Packard, and Intel, more than 10 percent of the workers are temps.

Critical Thinking Questions

1. Why do you think it is difficult to organize high-technology employees into unions?
2. Suppose you were trying to organize a union at a high-tech company such as Microsoft, which has a large group of disgruntled temporary employees who do not share in the success of the company with the full-time workers. How would you try to organize these employees into a union? What difficulties should you be prepared to overcome?
3. What possible threats do you think a union would pose for the management of a high-tech firm such as Microsoft?

Team Exercise

With a group of four or five students, assume that you have been hired as consultants to assist a union that wants to market its services to a group of high-technology employees in a large technology company similar to Microsoft or IBM. Work together to develop a list of five or six "selling points" that you could use to convince this group of high-technology employees that they could greatly benefit from union representation in their company. What objections might these employees have to one or more of your selling points? Be prepared to post your list of selling points on the blackboard or on an overhead transparency and be ready to explain your points to other members of the class.

Source: Adapted from Greenhouse, S. (1999, July 26). Unions need not apply: High-technology sector still unmoved by labor's song. *New York Times*, C1, C14.

Customer-Driven HR Case 15.3

YOU MANAGE IT!

When Is a Team a Union?

Amalgamated Tool, a nonunion manufacturer of auto parts in Michigan, suffered such significant financial losses in 2003 that it froze the pay of all its employees to conserve cash. The company also asked its employees to pay a larger share of their health insurance costs. The employees were extremely upset by these actions, and both morale and productivity declined.

To improve morale, Amalgamated's management decided to form several problem-solving employee teams. After meeting to discuss the problems at Amalgamated, the teams presented management with suggestions on how to provide pay raises and health insurance to employees fairly and efficiently. Each problem-solving team had a leader elected by the other team members to present the team's suggestions, but only about 20 percent of Amalgamated's employees were asked to serve on a team. The teams' suggestions were largely adopted by management, and morale and efficiency went up the next year.

On behalf of some dissatisfied Amalgamated employees, a local union filed an unfair labor practice claim stating that management had illegally used the problem-solving teams to form a management-dominated union, in violation of a provision of the Wagner Act that states: "It is an unfair labor practice for an employer to dominate or interfere with the formation of any labor organization or contribute financial support to it."

The National Labor Relations Board sustained the union's position and ordered Amalgamated to cease and desist using its problem-solving teams.

Critical Thinking Questions

1. Why did the local union object to the way Amalgamated's management used problem-solving teams?
2. What is the difference between a team and a union?
3. To avoid the NLRB's cease-and-desist order, what should Amalgamated's management have done differently in using problem-solving teams?

Team Exercise

Students form into groups of four to six members and role-play National Labor Relations Board members. Each group discusses whether or not Amalgamated violated the Wagner Act's prohibition of a company "dominating a union or providing financial support to it." Compare conclusions and arguments across groups.

Discussion Case 15.4

YOU MANAGE IT!

Recognizing and Avoiding Unfair Labor Practices

Managers who supervise employees need to be able to recognize situations that could be considered to be an unfair labor practice and avoid them. If an alleged unfair labor practice is committed, the Department of Labor may order an investigation to determine if a penalty or other sanction is warranted. The purpose of this exercise is to develop skills for recognizing and avoiding unfair labor practices and finding ways to manage the workplace without violating government labor policy. Before starting this exercise, review the five unfair management labor practices listed under the Wagner Act that we discussed in this chapter. Now read the next three scenarios and answer the questions that follow.

Scenario 1

You are finishing up some paperwork at the end of a hard day. As the HR manager, you have been involved in the company's negotiations with the union regarding the truck drivers' new contract with your firm. The negotiations have not been going well, and all indications are that a strike will be called in a matter of days. As you are preparing to leave your office, three long-time truck drivers ask to have a word with you in private. They inform you that they are not happy with their union and that a number of the other drivers feel the same way. They ask you to help them "get rid of the union." Should you act on this request?

Scenario 2

You are the store manager for a regional supermarket chain. Your store is nonunion. When a local union attempts to organize your employees, you receive orders from headquarters to discharge the employees from your store who have signed union authorization cards. Your regional manager also orders you to prepare termination slips for each of the fired employees detailing false reasons for their termination. How should you proceed?

Scenario 3

The negotiations between your company and the union representing the 110 production workers in your firm have reached a dead end. Union members have already voted to go on strike. At a meeting of the key managers involved in running the company, the production manager suggests using the remaining clerical, accounting, and managerial staff as replacements to keep the plant running. She also suggests contacting a temporary employment agency to help fill any remaining critical positions while the union members are on strike. As the HR manager, how would you respond to this suggestion?

Critical Thinking Questions

1. For each of the three scenarios you need to determine whether you think an unfair labor practice would be committed if you as a manager act on the request that is being given to you by management or employees. Which unfair labor practice(s) could be violated? In some situations, more than one unfair labor practice could occur.
2. Place yourself in the position of the manager in each of the scenarios and respond to each of the requests. If you decide to reject or accept the request, indicate the reason for your decision. Then develop a suggested plan of action that will deal with the issue that has been brought to your attention.

Team Exercise

With a group of four or five students, discuss and compare each of your responses to the three scenarios in the previous questions. Try to arrive at a consensus on how to handle these three cases. Then develop a policy or procedure to guide other managers for each case so that the company has a consistent approach to dealing with the union if these circumstances ever arise in the future.

Source: Adapted from Nkomo, S. M., Fottler, M. D., and McAfee, R. B. (2000). *Applications in human resource management* (4th ed.), 278–279. Cincinnati, OH: South-Western.

YOU MANAGE IT! Video Shorts Case 15.5

Labor Relations and Employee Security

Welcome once again to *SPOTLIGHT Inside HR*. This week you'll be going behind the scenes at Hot Jobs.com where the question of unions has come up. Later on in the show guest Martin Buckingham, associate director of human resources at Hot Jobs.com, and host Meg Allen will be joined via satellite by George Morgan, managing director at Morgan Incorporated.

Watch as HR professional Daryl Hulme deals with the sensitive situation of putting a young woman just starting out in her career at ease. Sara Lancaster has just accepted a position in Hot Jobs' computer programming department as a full-time programmer. Her prior work experience was at Microsoft, where she was a temp programmer and a card-carrying member of a trade union.

This is Sara's first week at Hot Jobs. She has come to HR, feeling a bit nervous, to ask whether she has the option of joining a union there. Sara has been given an employee orientation including a full benefits package, so Daryl may wonder why Sara is still unclear about the open-door policy at Hot Jobs. Do you think that Daryl is surprised by her question? Sara's experience at Microsoft led her to expect that there would be a union at Hot Jobs as well. When Daryl tells her there just isn't one, she seems incredulous. Do you think it was commendable of Sara to go to HR for help? You might ask yourself why it is important that Daryl establish a rapport with Sara.

Sara explains that she had a lot of benefits from union membership. She felt the union was looking out for her interests as an employee rather than for the interests of the company. Daryl does her best to assure Sara that Hot Jobs treats its employees fairly. She tells her that Hot Jobs' philosophy is to encourage direct communication between employees and management at all times, alleviating any need for a union. When that doesn't seem to satisfy Sara, Daryl glosses over the history of trade unions, stressing that unionization is rare in the Internet industry. Finally, she asks Sara to give Hot Jobs a chance to address whatever it is that Sara feels she is missing. Sara listens as Daryl points out that it is in the best interests of Hot Jobs to keep talented employees like herself, but does she really *hear*? As Martin Buckingham at Hot Jobs HR says during the discussion segment, "Employee satisfaction is key to corporate goals." Hot Jobs has obviously hired Sara in good faith. What do you think Daryl is feeling right now? As the tape stops rolling, Sara doesn't look any more relaxed than when she walked into Daryl's office. Consider why it might take some time for Sara to adjust to the corporate culture at Hot Jobs.

During the discussion portion of the show, Martin Buckingham points out that in the dot-com sector it is important to differentiate your company from the competition by attracting the best talent available. One of the most valuable enticements a company can offer a prospective employee is a superior benefits package. Hot Jobs is committed to its employees and grievances are dealt with on a case-by-case basis, so there has never been a need for a union. However, as Meg Allen's guest George Morgan points out, norms vary from industry to industry. In corporations that depend on a large labor force, often working in isolation (trucking), management may benefit from union presence. He says that in such cases, workers need to "have their voices heard." By belonging to a union workers are assured of better conditions, financial support, and access to health care and educational opportunities that a company may not provide. This, in turn, gives management a stable, productive workforce contributing toward building a more profitable business. In some ways things haven't really changed that much since the beginning of the American union movement.

Once again, Human Resource Management is called on to address the human need to be treated well in the workplace.

Critical Thinking Questions

1. Do you think Daryl has alleviated Sara's concerns that her interests as an employee might be better served by belonging to a union? Why or why not?
2. After the surveillance tape comes to a close, you heard Martin Buckingham say to Meg Allen, "A lot of people don't like to talk about unions." What do you suppose he means and why might that be true?
3. As an HR manager at Hot Jobs, how would you educate your supervisors in order to prevent unionization?
4. What measures might you take as a member of the Hot Jobs HR team to ensure that your employees have a work environment that is as healthy and safe as possible? Be sure to address issues that apply directly to the technology industry in your answer.
5. Do you agree with George Morgan that unions may serve management well in industries in which there is a large labor force composed of people working in isolated situations? Why? In making your argument, choose a specific industry to serve as your example.
6. (Optional) Imagine what lies ahead for Sara in the next six months at Hot Jobs. Will she succeed at Hot Jobs? What factors will be critical to her success or failure there?

Managing Workplace Safety and Health

Challenges

After reading this chapter, you should be able to deal more effectively with the following challenges:

1. **Describe** the extent of the employer's responsibility to maintain a safe and healthy work environment.
2. **Explain** the reasons for safety and health laws and the costs and obligations they impose on employers.
3. **Identify** the basic provisions of workers' compensation laws and the Occupational Safety and Health Act.
4. **Develop** an awareness of contemporary health and safety issues, including AIDS, workplace violence, smoking in the workplace, cumulative trauma disorders, fetal protection, hazardous chemicals, and genetic testing.
5. **Describe** the features of safety programs and understand the reasons for and the effects of programs designed to enhance employee well-being.

On May 11, 1996, ValuJet Flight 592 crashed into the Everglades about 10 minutes after takeoff from Miami, Florida. The flight was hit with a raging fire, and the flaming nose-dive crash took the lives of all 110 people aboard. Although the crash occurred years ago, its affects are still unfolding.

National Transportation Safety Board investigators concluded that the tragedy was the result of supervisory failures "all up and down the line, from federal regulators to airline executives in the board room to workers on the shop room floor."[1] The board found that the probable immediate or direct cause of the accident was hazardous oxygen containers that employees of SabreTech (a contractor for ValuJet) placed in the flight's cargo hold. However, safety board investigators found 34 violations by the airline, including delayed maintenance and failure to report jammed landing gear, within a month after the crash.[2] It also found that ValuJet knew of some problems for months but had not taken corrective action.

The crash had far-reaching effects. Some outcomes of the wake of the crash include

1. Replacement of the top leaders of the Federal Aviation Authority and the Department of Transportation
2. The addition of hundreds of inspectors to the Federal Aviation authority
3. ValuJet's struggle to rebuild its business (newly named American TransAir), which floundered after the crash

In July 1999 the state of Florida brought charges of 110 counts of third degree murder against SabreTech, and a federal grand jury also indicted the company, two of its mechanics, and a maintenance director on charges of conspiring to cover up problems that led to the accident. More specifically, the federal grand jury charged that the maintenance director at SabreTech pressured employees to skip prescribed work steps and falsely sign paperwork to confirm the work had been done. The grand jury also charged SabreTech with failing to train personnel in proper handling of the hazardous oxygen canisters.[3]

Leading up to these charges, the safety board concluded that someone at SabreTech had loaded more than 100 armed oxygen generators into the cargo hold of Flight 592. Furthermore, these canisters had been mislabeled "empty" and did not have attached protective caps that could have prevented accidental discharge and a 500° chemical reaction.

Murder indictments against a company are rare in the United States, and this marked the first time in U.S. history that criminal charges were filed in the case of an airline crash. Although the jury acquitted the SabreTech employees, it found the company guilty of nine hazardous materials violations, including the failure to train its workers properly.[4]

THE MANAGERIAL PERSPECTIVE

The crash of ValuJet Flight 592 and its aftermath dramatically illustrate the devastating consequences of paying insufficient attention to safety concerns and social responsibility. Ensuring a safe working environment is legally mandated. More important, it is an obligation for any socially responsible manager. As a manager, safety and health must be a priority in all that you do.

An organizational culture that places a greater value on speed or saving money than on safety can result in workplace accidents—some that involve the loss of human life. To disregard safety and health issues can cause more than legal difficulty for an organization. It can sever the trust between workers and management, irretrievably damage employee commitment and performance, and ruin an organization's reputation. Managers, then, must understand safety and health issues and take steps to maintain a safe work environment with the help of HR staff.

In this chapter we consider the contemporary context of the safety and health issue and how managers build and develop safe and healthy working conditions. First, we deal with the legal issues of workplace safety and health by exploring management's legal obligations to fund a workers' compensation system and to provide a safe and healthy workplace. Next we examine a variety of contemporary safety and health issues, including AIDS, violence in the workplace, cumulative trauma disorders, fetal protection, dangerous chemicals, and the use of genetic testing on employees. Finally, we describe and evaluate programs designed to maintain employee safety and health.

Workplace Safety and the Law

The most recent data from the Bureau of Labor statistics indicate that in 2000 more than 5.6 million people in the United States were injured on the job and 5,344 were killed.[5] Currently, the national average is 2.8 workplace injuries or illnesses per 100 workers that are serious enough to result in lost workdays.[6] Disabling injuries, those resulting in five or more days away from the job, have been found to have direct costs to employers of over $40 billion per year. Direct costs of accidents and injuries include payments made to injured workers and their medical care providers. When indirect costs, mainly lost productivity and overtime, are included, the estimated annual costs of injuries are $120 billion to $240 billion.[7]

To address this problem, all levels of government have passed numerous laws to regulate workplace safety. Many of these laws include detailed regulations dealing with work hazards in specific industries such as coal mining and railroads. However, there are two basic sets of workplace safety laws that affect most workers: the various workers' compensation laws at the state level and the Occupational Safety and Health Act of 1970 (OSHA) at the federal level. The objectives, policies, and operations of these two sets of laws are very different.

Each state has its own workers' compensation law, so the provisions for funding and enforcing the law differ by state. As we discussed in Chapter 12, the main goal of the workers' compensation system is to provide compensation to workers who suffer job-related injuries or illnesses. Workers' compensation laws have no safety regulations or mandates, but they do require employers to pay for workers' compensation insurance. Because insurance costs are higher for employers with more workplace accidents and injuries, employers have a financial incentive to create and maintain a safe work environment.

In contrast, OSHA is a federal law designed to make the workplace safer by ensuring that the work environment is free from hazards. The act mandates numerous safety standards and enforces these standards through a system of inspections, citations, and fines. Unlike the workers' compensation laws, however, OSHA does not provide for the compensation of accident victims.[8]

Workers' Compensation

In the early 1800s, people injured on the job went without medical care unless they could afford to pay for it themselves and rarely received any income until they could return to work. Employees who sued their employers for negligence had little hope of winning, because under U.S. common law the courts habitually ruled that employees assumed the usual risks of a job in return for their pay. In addition, under the *doctrine of contributory negligence* employers were not liable for an employee's injuries when that employee's own negligence contributed to or caused the injury. And under the *fellow-servant rule*, employers were not responsible for an employee's injury when the negligence of another employee contributed to or caused the injury.

In the early years of the twentieth century—after a host of workplace disasters including a 1911 fire in a New York shirt factory that killed more than 100 women—public opinion pressured several state legislatures to enact *workers' compensation* laws. The workers' compensation concept is based on the theory that work-related accidents and illnesses are costs of doing business that the employer should pay for and pass on to the consumer.[9] Since 1948, all states have had workers' compensation programs, although workers' compensation is mandatory in only 47 states. These state-administered and employer-funded programs are designed to provide financial and medical assistance to employees injured on the job.

The stated goals of the workers' compensation laws are:[10]

- Providing prompt, sure, and reasonable medical care to victims and income to both victims and their dependents.
- Providing a "no-fault" system in which injured workers can get quick relief without undertaking expensive litigation and suffering court delays.
- Encouraging employers to invest in safety.
- Promoting research on workplace safety.

To be eligible to receive an award from the workers' compensation system, an employee's injury must have occurred in the course of his or her employment. Sometimes serious accidents, even death, can occur in the workplace, but the accident may not be directly due to the performance of the job. Is the employer still liable for this unfortunate outcome? In many of today's workplaces, job descriptions are more ambiguous and broader than ever before. What is really inside or outside of someone's job responsibilities is often not clear. This breadth and ambiguity can encourage flexibility and broad commitment in the workplace, but it may also have the unintended consequence of increasing an employer's exposure to liability for accidents that may occur. The Manager's Notebook: Emerging Trend, "Greater Ambiguity—Increased Liability" provides an example of an unfortunate death that occurred at work. The example illustrates the importance of defining job duties to limit liability for accidental injury or death. This lesson is worth having in your manager's notebook.

The Benefits of Workers' Compensation

Workers' compensation benefits compensate employees for injuries or illnesses occurring on the job. These benefits are:[11]

- **Total disability benefits** Partial replacement of income lost as the result of a work-related total disability.
- **Impairment benefits** Benefits for temporary or permanent partial disability, based on the degree and duration of the impairment. Injuries are classified as scheduled or nonscheduled. Scheduled injuries are those in which a body part (such as an eye or a finger) is lost; there is a specific schedule of payments for these injuries. Unscheduled injuries are all other injuries (such as back injuries); these are dealt with on a case-by-case basis.
- **Survivor benefits** In cases of work-related deaths, the worker's survivors receive a burial allowance and income benefits.
- **Medical expense benefits** Workers' compensation provides medical coverage, normally without dollar or time limitations.
- **Rehabilitation benefits** All states provide medical rehabilitation for injured workers, and many states provide vocational training for employees who can no longer work at their previous occupation as the result of a job-related injury or illness.

Emerging Trends

MANAGER'S NOTEBOOK

Greater Ambiguity—Increased Liability

Keith Marshall was a lifeguard at an aquatic center. His job duties included performing general pool maintenance and supervising swimmers. Keith told his boss that he was trying to increase the distance he could swim under water. A few weeks later, Keith was found dead—he had drowned in the swimming pool. There were no witnesses and the autopsy concluded that the cause of death was drowning. Keith's mother sought workers' compensation benefits on behalf of Keith's child. A critical question in this unfortunate case is whether Keith Marshall died during his employment. If so, his child would be entitled to a workers' compensation award. A Virginia court concluded that the death occurred while at work and this decision was upheld by an appeals court.

We will never know exactly what led to Keith's death, but his statement about working on underwater endurance may be the best clue we have to go on. Although we can't be sure in this case, accidental drowning, particularly of an experienced swimmer working on increasing underwater distance, is most likely due to a phenomenon called shallow water blackout. This phenomenon can overcome victims without them ever realizing they are drowning. Shallow water blackout is most often associated with free diving, but it has also claimed victims in swimming pools.

Was underwater swimming endurance part of Keith's job? It certainly could be argued to at least be relevant to performance of the job of lifeguard. Even more pertinent to the question of workers' compensation benefits is that Keith's boss knew of the endurance training and didn't disallow it. His boss did not specify to Keith that his job was to be a lifeguard, not to be an underwater swimming champion. He did not tell Keith that the pool was not to be used for his personal goals. Key to the court awarding the compensation benefits was that the employer had knowledge of the endurance training (what would be conjectured to be the probable cause of the drowning) and didn't prohibit it.

Here are the lessons to be learned from this story.

First, given that part of your goal as manager is to limit liability and workers' compensation insurance costs, you need to clearly and immediately tell employees to stop if you encounter employees engaging in risky behavior outside of their normal job duties.

Second, courts rely on job descriptions to help make determinations of what is within the scope of employees' job duties. Ambiguity in these descriptions can lead to costly legal battles. Prohibited employee activities could be added to these job descriptions and posted in the workplace, resulting in decreased ambiguity and liability. Of course, you risk being labeled a spoilsport or worse. However, it's your choice as to whether you manage rationally and safely and risk being called spoilsport or risk liability for accidental injuries and possibly death.

And, third, on a personal note, if you or anyone you know swims, learn about shallow water blackout. It is a little-known phenomenon, but there is information about it that is readily available on the Internet. One of us (Bob Cardy) has a daughter (Lara) who had an episode of shallow water blackout while doing underwater endurance during a synchronized swimming practice. Luckily, it looks like Lara is going to be fine, but the phenomenon has claimed many lives. As the saying goes, knowledge is power. Learn about this risk and protect yourself and others.

Source: Marshall, A. (2002). Some employee "heroics" need to be saved for off the job. *Hotel & Motel Management*, 27, 10.

The Costs of Workers' Compensation

The cost to employers of workers' compensation insurance is directly affected by accidents with premiums that can increase dramatically and stay high for years as a result of a single injury.[12] Workers' compensation insurance is based on payroll, but premiums paid are modified by an organization's safety record. Workers' compensation insurers reported an average loss per claim of $6,189 in 1998.[13] The industry average is 27 weeks before a claimant is back to work. In addition to these direct costs, when the costs to employers of replacing the absent worker are considered, the costs of workers' compensation claims grow even larger. Losses to the workers' compensation insurance system due to the September 11, 2001, terrorist attacks have been estimated to be between $1.3 billion and $2 billion. Another terrorist disaster could drive workers' compensation insurers into insolvency and threaten the survival of the system.[14] Furthermore, fraudulent claims drive up the costs of workers' compensation.[15] To keep workers' compensation rates under control, companies are becoming more aware of fraud and many are contesting claims they believe to be fraudulent (see The Manager's Notebook: Emerging Trend, "Managing Fraud in Workers' Compensation Claims").

In another attempt to control and reduce workers' compensation costs, some employers are using on-site occupational health centers that provide immediate evaluation and treatment of injured workers. These on-site centers offer faster treatment of occupational injuries and can produce cost savings for employers.[16]

Other attempts to control costs focus on the causes of injuries and on their treatment. Liberty Mutual, an insurance company, charts the 10 most prevalent causes of workplace injuries.[17] Injuries resulting from these 10 leading causes account for 86 percent of direct workers' compensation costs. Perhaps surprisingly, the number-one cause of workplace injury, accounting for $10.5 billion in annual direct costs, is overexertion. Injuries associated with excessive lifting, pushing, pulling, carrying, or throwing an object cost employers more than any other cause of injury. However, many organizations perceive that repetitive-motion injuries are the most important source of workplace injury (actually they rank in sixth place and account for $2.7 billion in costs) and, therefore, that is where companies are expending their safety resources.[18] Although there are differences across organizations and industries, the data indicate that, on average, the most important source of injury and, thus, the area with the highest potential return on investment of safety resources is overexertion. Although a mundane cause of injury, smart organizations will recognize that the largest payoff in terms of lowered injury rates and workers' compensation costs will result from first attacking the major cause of the problem.

In terms of treatment, the Hartford Financial Services Group has reported that 67 percent of increased workers' compensation costs can be attributed to the use of more costly drugs. For example, pain medications for back, knee, and shoulder problems are common for workers' compensation patients, but there has been a shift toward use of more costly medications for these problems. The use of, for instance, a time-release version of a medication may cost $3.00 per dose while a traditional pain-relieving medication may cost $1.50 per dose.[19] The Hartford analysis found that higher-priced drugs were often prescribed for conditions that could be treated with lower-priced drugs. Hartford recommends managing workers' compensation costs by providing information to workers and physicians about alternative medications and recommending generic drug substitutions whenever possible.

The Occupational Safety and Health Act (OSHA)

Changing political and social values during the 1960s added considerable momentum to the movement to regulate workplace safety. In 1969, the death of 78 coal miners in a mine explosion galvanized public opinion and led to the passage of the Coal Mine Health and Safety Act to regulate mine health and safety.[20] While no single event is responsible for the passage of the **Occupational Safety and Health Act of 1970 (OSHA),** the dramatic increase in reported injury rates and workplace deaths during the 1960s (reflecting the inability of workers' compensation laws to give employers adequate incentives to maintain a safe work environment) was probably the major impetus.[21] During the latter part of that decade, the federal government reported that job-related accidents killed more than 14,000 workers and disabled nearly 2.5 million workers annually. In addition, an estimated 300,000 new cases of occupational diseases were being reported every year. OSHA was passed to address the staggering economic and human costs of workplace accidents and health hazards.[22]

Occupational Safety and Health Act of 1970 (OSHA)
A federal law that requires employers to provide a safe and healthy work environment, comply with specific occupational safety and health standards, and keep records of occupational injuries and illnesses.

OSHA's Provisions

OSHA is fairly straightforward. It imposes three major obligations on employers:

- **To provide a safe and healthy work environment** Each employer has a general duty to provide a place of employment free from recognized hazards that are likely to cause death or serious physical harm. This *general duty provision* recognizes that not all workplace hazards can be covered by a set of specific standards. The employer is obligated to identify and deal with safety and health hazards not covered by specific regulations.[23]
- **To comply with specific occupational safety and health standards** Each employer must become familiar with and comply with specific occupational standards (OSHA's rules deal with specific occupations rather than with industries), and must make certain that employees comply as well.
- **To keep records of occupational injuries and illnesses** Under OSHA, employers must record and report work-related accidents and injuries. Organizations with eight or more employees must keep records of any occupational injury or illness resulting in death, lost work time, or medical treatment and retain these records for five years. The injuries and illnesses must be recorded on OSHA forms and posted annually on an employee bulletin board for all to see. The records must also be made available to OSHA compliance officers, and annual summaries must be prepared.[24] Because record-keeping requirements have been unclear on some points, OSHA issued revised record-keeping standards that are meant to be more flexible and easier to follow.[25] Revised record-keeping rules for inquiries and illnesses went into effect in 2002 and new provisions for hearing loss and musculoskeletal disorders are scheduled to go into effect in 2003. The change in record-keeping standards is part of an outreach program to employers that includes online brochures, fact sheets, PowerPoint training programs, and record-keeping forms and instructions.[26] You can view current online materials by visiting the record-keeping page on OSHA's Web site at www.osha.gov. You will also find there a Spanish version of the Web site, designed for Spanish-speaking employers and employees. The Spanish version is part of the outreach program and is also prompted by year 2000 statistics, which are the most recent data currently available, revealing that the fatality rate for Hispanic employees rose by 11 percent while deaths in all other groups declined.[27] The information in Spanish is meant to overcome the language barrier and inform the OSHA-estimated 10 million U.S. employers and employees of their safety rights, responsibilities, and resources. The effort is intended to improve safety statistics for Hispanics.

MANAGER'S NOTEBOOK

Emerging Trends

Managing Fraud in Workers' Compensation Claims

Fraudulent workers' compensation claims add to the costs of doing business and need to be controlled. Here are suggestions for reducing abuse of the workers' compensation system and indicators for spotting potential fraud.

Managing to Limit Abuse of the Workers' Compensation System

- *Make the work environment as safe and risk free as possible.* Job-specific safety training can reduce on-the-job injuries and help to develop a culture of safety in the organization.
- *Institute postoffer screening for job-related physical capacity.* For jobs that require physical work, consider screening applicants for job-related physical capacity. A screening program must comply with the Americans with Disabilities Act; the screening should be given only after an offer of employment has been made and it should be based on a job analysis. A preemployment screening can lower accident rates by assuring that each worker has the capacity to perform the tasks. Furthermore, the screening can provide a baseline measure that could help guide rehabilitation efforts if an accident did occur.
- *Educate employees about the workers' compensation system.* False injury claims can be lessened when workers understand the workers' compensation system, why it exists, and how it works. Most important, false claims can be reduced when workers realize that, following a claim, their ability to perform the functions of the job will be objectively examined.
- *Offer temporary modified duty.* The goal is to get injured employees back to work as soon as they are medically able. However, the longer an employee is away from work, the greater the chances are that he or she will never return to work. An early-return-to-work program can ease workers back into the workplace by temporarily modifying their job functions to a nature and level that the employees are capable of performing. Modifying tasks to provide for an early return to work can result in a reduction in lost workdays and an increase in productivity in the organization.

Indicators of Potential Fraud

- Vague accident details.
- No witnesses.
- Minor accident but a major injury.
- Extended length of time between occurrence of an accident and filing of a report.
- Documentation by treating physician that doesn't support the type of injury claimed by the employee.
- A pattern of "doctor hopping" in which an employee frequently changes physicians, perhaps looking for a health-care provider who is sympathetic to his or her claims.
- A history of discipline or job dissatisfaction. Filing a workers' compensation claim can be a means for a worker to balance the scales of workplace justice.

Source: Adapted from Sanna, M. (2002). Sick and wrong: An expert offers advice about how to spot fraudulent injuries and maintain a healthy bottom line. *Walls & Ceilings, 65*, 60(3); and *Payroll Manager's Report*. (2002). Beware: Down markets breed false workers' compensation claims. January Newsletter of the Institute of Management and Administration, 7–8.

Under the new standard, failure to keep either written or electronic records can result in fines and citations. Falsifying records can result in a $110,000 fine and a six-month prison sentence. The revised standard also makes it clear that an accident that *could* have caused injury—not just one that *did* cause injury—should be recorded. In other words, close calls count under the OSHA standard.

In addition, the standard clarifies who is an employee under OSHA. For example, a temporary worker from an employment agency doing clerical work for an organization is considered an employee of that organization. However, an independent contractor is an employee only if the business hires and supervises the person. Thus, the Perfect Lawn landscaping crew is not likely to be considered a law firm's employees, but a software specialist the firm hires from an employment agency probably is. This distinction is important because an employer is responsible for keeping records on its employees.

Employees also have responsibilities under OSHA. Although they cannot be cited for violations, they must comply with the relevant safety and health standards. They should also report all hazardous conditions, injuries, or work-related illnesses to their employer. Employee rights under OSHA include the right to file safety or health grievances and complaints to the government, participate in OSHA inspections, and request information on safety and health hazards without fear of discrimination or retaliation by their employer.[28]

Under both OSHA and state *right-to-know regulations*, employers must provide employees with information about hazardous substances in the workplace.[29] OSHA's hazardous substance regulation, known as the *Hazard Communication Standard*, is explained in the pamphlet excerpt reproduced in Figure 16.1. In addition, the U.S. Supreme Court has upheld an employee's right to refuse to work under conditions where the employee reasonably believes there is an immediate risk of injury or death.[30] If the hazard is of a chemical nature, another federal agency may also be relevant. The Chemical Safety and Hazard Investigation Board, funded by Congress in 1997, is charged with promoting safety and preventing incidents of chemical release.[31] The board works closely with OSHA and the Environmental Protection Agency. A hazard in the form of a chemical spill would result in an accident investigation by the Board. The focus of the board is to then make recommendations to companies and government agencies regarding changes in process or equipment that would prevent similar accidents.

Figure 16.1

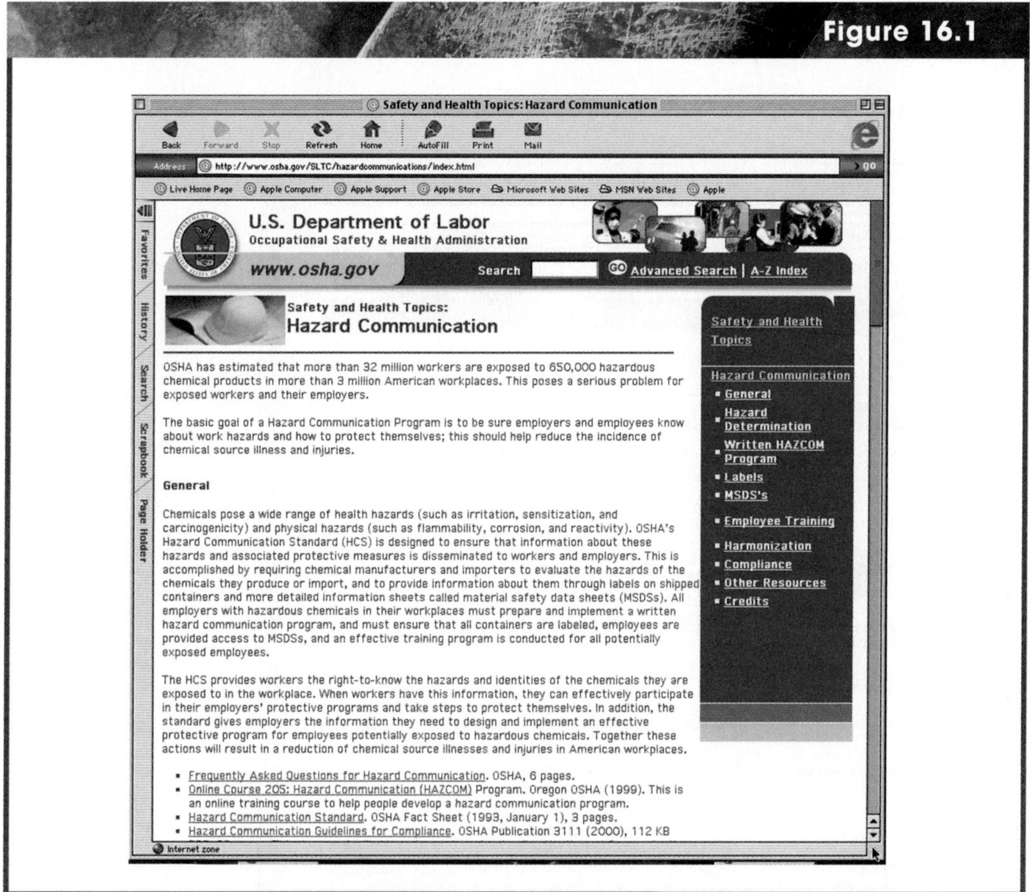

OSHA's Hazard Communication Standard

This excerpt from the OSHA Web site explains that employers must tell their employees how OSHA's hazardous communication standard is being put into effect in their workplace.

Three agencies administer and enforce OSHA: the *Occupational Safety and Health Administration* (the OSH Administration, also known by the acronym *OSHA*), the *Occupational Safety and Health Review Commission (OSHRC)*, and the *National Institute for Occupational Safety and Health (NIOSH)*. States with federally approved safety plans have their own regulatory apparatus.

The Occupational Safety and Health Administration

The Occupational Safety and Health Administration has the primary responsibility for enforcing OSHA. It develops occupational standards, grants variances to employers, conducts workplace inspections, and issues citations and penalties.

- **Occupational standards** Occupational standards, which cover hazards ranging from tools and machinery safety to microscopic airborne matter, can be exceedingly complex and detailed. While many standards are clearly reasonable and appropriate, OSHA has frequently been criticized for adopting infeasible standards or standards whose costs exceed their benefits. The courts, however, generally do not require OSHA to balance the costs and benefits of particular standards, only to demonstrate their feasibility.[32]

  The development of occupational standards can begin with OSHA, NIOSH, state and local governments, or a variety of other sources, including industry groups and labor organizations. Proposed new standards are published in the *Federal Register*, the official legal news publication of the U.S. government. Comments from interested parties are sought, and hearings regarding the standards may be held. The full text of any adopted standard and the implementation date are then reported in the *Federal Register*.[33]

  A current example of the development of standards is OSHA's proposed national ergonomics standard.[34] The National Institute for Occupational Safety and Health reported in 1997 that musculoskeletal disorders related to the neck, shoulders, elbow, hand, wrist, and back generated at least $13 billion a year in workers' compensation costs. Further, the Bureau of Labor Statistics reported that the incidence rate for cumulative trauma disorders per 10,000 full-time workers jumped from 6.3 in 1985 to 335 in 1996.

The OSHA Web site has information on ergonomics and the recently, released ergonomics program.

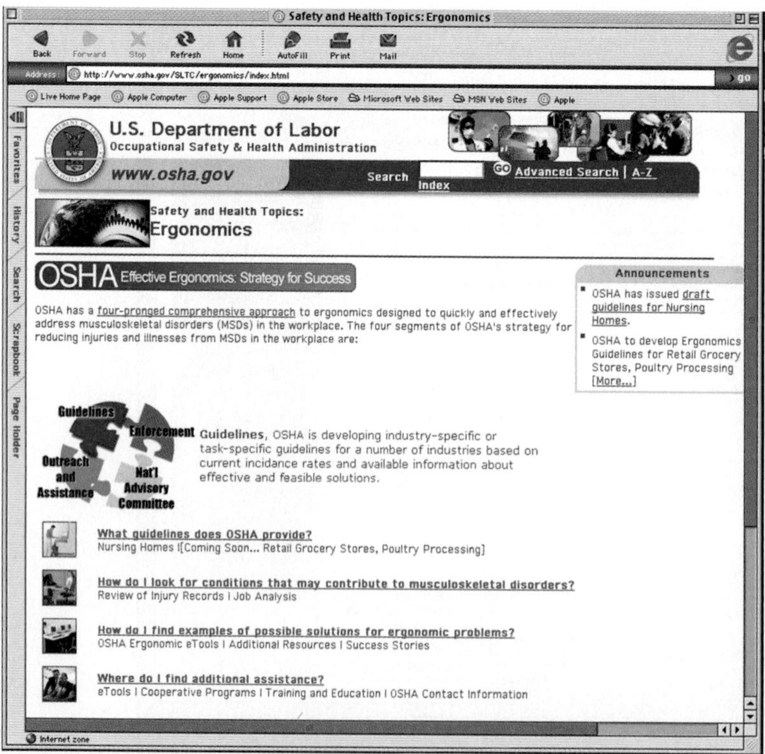

Based on these and other findings, OSHA began looking seriously at developing an ergonomics standard. (Ergonomics is the science of adapting working conditions to employee safety and comfort needs.) However, employer and industry groups voiced strong opposition to such a standard. More important, Congress opposed additional regulations on business during the 1990s, even going so far as to threaten to withhold funding for OSHA if the agency proposed an ergonomic standard. OSHA finally released a draft ergonomics standard, but it was repealed by Congress and President Bush in March 2001.

OSHA released its second ergonomics program on April 5, 2002. The new plan emphasizes the development of guidelines and best practices. OSHA will also conduct targeted inspections, offer training, and find ergonomics research.[35] At this point, business leaders are cautiously optimistic about the new ergonomics program and are positive about the program's focus on education and training rather than on new regulations and requirements. However, labor groups have criticized the new ergonomics program for not going far enough to protect workers from ergonomics hazards. James P. Hoffa, International Brotherhood of Teamsters president, considers the guidelines an insult to workers crippled by ergonomics hazards. He states, "There is no reason to think that businesses would voluntarily follow 'guidelines' that they have spent a decade trying to scuttle."[36]

- **Variances** Employers may ask OSHA for a temporary (up to one year) variance from a standard when they cannot comply with a new standard by its effective date. The OSH Administration may grant a permanent variance from a particular standard when an employer can demonstrate that it has in place alternatives that protect employees as effectively as compliance with the standard would.[37]
- **Workplace inspections** OSHA has the power to conduct workplace inspections to make sure that organizations are complying with OSHA standards. Because it would be impossible to inspect each of the hundreds of thousands of affected workplaces each year, OSHA has established an inspection priority system that calls for inspections to be made in the following order:[38] (1) situations involving "imminent danger" in the workplace, (2) incidents resulting in fatalities or hospitalization of five or more employees, (3) follow-up of employee complaints of unsafe or unhealthful working conditions, and (4) "high-hazard" industries and occupations (for example, mining, farming, construction, and transport).

  OSHA inspectors have the right to enter an establishment without notice to examine work environment, materials, and equipment, and to question both employers and employees. However, this right conflicts with the employer's constitutional protection from warrantless searches. In a 1978 case involving a company's refusal to allow an OSHA inspection until the agency could produce a search warrant, the Supreme Court ruled that the employer does have a right to demand a search warrant before OSHA can make an inspection. Although OSHA can generally obtain a search warrant based on an employee complaint or on the agency's own inspection priority system, some argue that forfeiting the element of surprise makes inspection less effective because it gives employers leeway to alter unsafe conditions or practices (for example, erratically using safety equipment) until the inspection is complete.[39]
- **Citations and penalties** OSHA may issue citations and impose penalties for any violations of OSHA standards. The exact penalty varies with the employer's good faith attempts to comply with OSHA regulations, its history of previous violations, the seriousness of the infraction, and the size of the business. These penalties may include criminal penalties as well as substantial fines. In fact, executives of firms that recklessly endanger workers are becoming increasingly likely to spend time in jail.[40] In 1987 five senior executives of Chicago Magnet Wire Company were prosecuted for causing workers' illnesses by allowing them to be exposed to hazardous chemicals. In 1989 a supervisor at Jackson Enterprises in Michigan was convicted of involuntary manslaughter in an employee's work-related death.[41]

Fines for violations of OSHA standards may range from no fine for minor violations to megafines of several million dollars for companies guilty of numerous, repeated, and willful infractions. A 1994 study of OSHA fines found the mean (average) fine to be $875,000 but the median fine to be greater than $3 million.[42] Thus, there are more fines of relatively smaller amounts, but the fines seem to be of substantial size nonetheless. A study of OSHA citations associated with musculoskeletal disorders during 1985 to 1994 found mean and median fine levels of $47,707 and $3,600, respectively.[43]

An important question is whether these fines have any meaningful impact on organizations. One approach to answering this question is to see if the announcement of fines levied by the OSHA has any impact on the value of the firm's stock. If there is no such impact, top executives have little incentive to improve safety and health conditions and avoid future fines. Research suggests that the announcement of OSHA penalties does have a significant negative impact on the firm's stock.[44] However, the downturn in stock prices is a short-term effect that occurs only in the day or two after the announcement of the penalties. Furthermore, it appears that it is simply the announcement of a violation, not the amount of the fine, that has the impact on the company's stock price. Figure 16.2 defines the various types of violations and their associated penalties.

OSHA funds a free consultation service that works with businesses to help them identify potential workplace hazards and improve safety management systems. This service is especially useful for small businesses. It provides for a confidential inspection, completely separate from OSHA's inspection program, that does not result in penalties or fines. However, the employer is obligated to correct serious safety and health hazards found in the inspection.

The procedure works as follow:[45]

1. The employer must contact the OSHA consultant to get things started.
2. An opening conference is scheduled at the work site to discuss the consultant's role and the employer's obligations under the service.
3. Employer and consultant examine workplace conditions together. The consultant may talk to employees, discuss OSHA standards with them, and point out safety problems.
4. In a closing conference the consultant reviews the findings of the inspection with the employer, detailing both what the employer is doing right and where improvement is needed.
5. After the closing conference, the consultant provides a written report explaining the findings and confirming proposed times within which the employer is to remedy hazards found in the inspection. (These are known as *abatement periods.*)

The Occupational Safety and Health Review Commission (OSHRC)

OSHRC operates independently of OSHA, and reviews its citations. An employer can appeal an OSHA citation, an abatement period, or a penalty to OSHRC. Rulings made by this commission can be appealed only through the federal court system.[46]

Figure 16.2

Violation	Description	Penalty
Other than serious violation	No direct relationship to job safety or health; probably not capable of causing death or serious physical harm.	Discretionary fine of up to $1,000 for each violation.
Serious violation	Serious probability of death or serious injury could result and employer knew, or should have known, of the hazard.	Mandatory $1,000 penalty for each violation.
Willful violation	Intentionally or knowingly committing a violation.	Fine of up to $70,000 per violation. Possible criminal penalties.
Repeated violation	Reinspection reveals a substantially similar violation.	Fine of up to $70,000 per violation.
Failure to correct prior violation	Failure to correct a violation for which the company was previously cited.	Fine of up to $1,000 for every day the violation continues.

Sources: U.S. Department of Labor. Occupational Safety and Health Administration. (1985). *All about OSHA* (rev. ed.). Washington, DC: U.S. Government Printing Office; and Roughton, J. E. (1995). The OSHA man cometh. *Security Management, 39*, 41–47.

Penalties for Violations of OSHA Standards

The National Institute for Occupational Safety and Health (NIOSH)

NIOSH exists mainly to research safety and health problems and to assist the OSHA in the creation of new health and safety standards. Like OSHA, NIOSH may inspect the workplace and gather information from employers and employees about hazardous materials. In addition, NIOSH trains inspectors and others associated with the enforcement of OSHA.[47]

State Programs

OSHA permits states to create their own occupational safety and health programs, and almost half of the states have chosen to do so. OSHA will approve a state plan if the state shows that it is able to set and enforce standards, provide and train competent enforcement personnel, and give educational and technical assistance to business. Upon approval of a state program, OSHA funds 50 percent of that program's operating costs and passes primary enforcement responsibility to the state. OSHA continually monitors and evaluates state programs and may withdraw approval if it determines that a state is failing to maintain an effective program.[48]

A Question of Ethics

Opponents of "Big Government" claim that excessive regulation of workplace safety hurts productivity and increases costs. They argue that in a free market, employees should be responsible for their own health and safety—that they should be free to choose between taking a wage premium for hazardous work and accepting lower pay for safer work. Would such a policy be ethical? What are its pros and cons?

The Effectiveness of OSHA

Has OSHA been an effective tool for creating a safer and healthier workplace? OSHA's critics suggest that its detailed and expansive regulations produce costs that exceed their benefits. However, many other people feel that while the OSHA-related costs borne by employers are direct and easy to measure, the benefits of an accident-free workplace are not. They point out that it is accident victims—employees—who bear the costs of an absence of health and safety regulations, not the employer.

Indeed, the costs of accidents and illness can be immense. For example, workplace accidents and injuries cost an estimated $171 billion each year.[49] The good news is that there is evidence that the regulations, penalties, and increased awareness brought about by OSHA have significantly reduced workplace accidents. For example, between 1912 and 1994, deaths in the workplace per 100,000 people decreased from 21 to 2.[50] In 1912 there were between 18,000 and 21,000 workplace deaths, while in 1994, with a workforce more than three times the size and producing 12 times the goods and services, there were only 5,000 deaths. Nonetheless, some occupations remain dangerous. Figure 16.3 shows the death rate for the deadliest industries in the United States. In addition, there may be reason to think that fines for the most egregious outcome of unsafe workplaces—death—is inadequate. The fines for safety violations that led to death are surprisingly small and at the low end of the distribution of fines, as highlighted in the Issues and Applications feature titled "Do Not Die on the Job in Arizona!"

Figure 16.3

Trucking	12.1
Logging	9.0
Fuel Dealers	5.6
Petroleum Products	5.2
Crop Production	4.2

*Rates are annual deaths per 100,000 workers.

Sources: Adapted from *Washington Post* (1998, August 4). Vital statistics: On the road on the job, 25.

Death Rates* for the Deadliest Industries

Issues and Applications

Do Not Die on the Job in Arizona!

Arizona ranks as the worst state in the United States in terms of the amount of workers' compensation given to spouses of people who die at work. As of 1998, Arizona widows and widowers received a maximum of $183.75 a week in compensation. If the workers had lived and worked in lowa, the state providing the highest level of support, the weekly maximum compensation would be $817. The amount of OSHA lines levied against Arizona companies for safety-related deaths seems to be just as small as the amount of support provided to surviving spouses.

An analysis of OSHA records found 134 worker death investigations between 1992 and 1997. Of these, 79 resulted in citations for serious safety violations. However, only 12 fines amounted to more than $10,000. The highest fine levied against an Arizona company for a safety violation contributing to the death of a worker was $103,000 during this period. The average fine was approximately $3,000. The relatively low amount of fines paid by Arizona companies can be due in part to the common practice of significantly reducing fines when a company appeals. The low fine levels for companies may also be a result of the independent nature of the Arizona culture. Whatever the reasons, the amount of the fines can hardly be seen as a deterrent to companies that may choose to cut safety corners and put employees at risk.

The case of Cory Powell is a tragic but real example of the outcome of death on the job in Arizona. Thirty-five-year-old Cory was driving a garbage truck in the city of Mesa on June 16,

1994. He stopped to fix a problem with the ram, a large bladed device that compacts garbage. He climbed into a pit behind the ram and worked on a switch. Unfortunately, the ram began to operate and his helper, his first day on the job; pushed the emergency stop button but to no avail. Powell was killed.

OSHA investigators found that there were mechanical problems with the truck. They also found that the sanitation company kept no maintenance records, had no formal drivers' training, and did not inspect its trucks. Finally, it found that the emergency stop button on Powell's truck did not work properly. The OSHA penalty for the safety violations resulting in Cory Powell's death? $7,500.

Judy Powell, Cory's wife, receives $530.79 a month through workers' compensation surviving spouse benefit. She lost her house after losing her husband.

Sources: Adapted from Muller, B. (1998, September 20). If you die on the job, your company may be fined. But how much is a life worth? You won't like the answer. Despite OSHA, there is little recourse for families left behind. *Arizona Republic*, A1; and Muller, B. (1998, September 20). Switch could have saved life. *Arizona Republic*, A20.

Managing Contemporary Safety, Health, and Behavioral Issues

Effectively managing workplace safety and health requires far more than reducing the numbers of job-related accidents and injuries. In practice, managers must deal with a variety of practical, legal, and ethical issues, many of which involve a careful balancing of individual rights (particularly the right to privacy) with the needs of the organization (see Chapter 14). Because these issues often give rise to legal questions, HR professionals are frequently called upon to develop and implement policies to deal with them. Among the weightiest issues facing employers today are dealing with AIDS in the workplace, workplace violence, smoking in the workplace, cumulative trauma disorders, hearing impairment, fetal protection, hazardous chemicals, and genetic testing.

It is important to recognize that, in addition to these direct challenges, there is also the challenge of employee commitment to safety and health programs. Many organizations face the problem of employees ignoring and even being hostile to safety and health measures. The reason: Employees often view safety and health measures as intrusive and inefficient.

Top managers can generate commitment to safety and health programs by explaining to supervisors and others the rationale for the relevant safety and health practices. For example, it is important that everyone understand the cost of accidents to the organization. Furthermore, the costs (such as fines) for violating safety and health standards should be clearly explained to employees at all levels. Once people understand the linkage between safety measures and the business's bottom line, resistance to safety programs should largely disappear. Of course, removing human resistance to any kind of program can be a difficult and delicate process that requires time and commitment.

Recent research supports the potential of taking a participative approach to the improvement of safety and empowering workers to manage and solve their own safety programs.[51] The research focused on cleaners at a 600-bed hospital. Consultative safety teams consisting of employees, supervisors, and safety experts were formed. The employees were trained in the basics, such as hazard identification and control, and were charged with identifying and reducing safety risks. Some of the solutions identified and implemented by these teams included changing purchasing procedures so that floors would be easier to clean, purchasing safer equipment, and more frequent job rotation to minimize repetitive strain. After implementation of the safety teams, workers' compensation claim rates fell by 67 percent, claim costs by 73 percent, and injury duration by 43 percent. An empowered approach to safety would appear to be an effective means to improve safety.

AIDS

Dealing effectively with workplace concerns that arise when an employee contracts acquired immunodeficiency syndrome (AIDS) will be one of the most important workplace health challenges of the next decade. In the early 1980s AIDS was scarcely known, but by 1996, the Centers for Disease Control and Prevention reported that two-thirds of organizations with more than 2,500 employees had already experienced an employee with this disease or HIV (the human immunodeficiency virus that leads to AIDS).[52]

The number of reported cases of HIV infection in the United States has risen in recent years.[53] For example, from June 1996 through July 1997 there were 13,111 new cases of HIV infection reported. The total number of cases of AIDS reported through June 1997 was 612,078, and the infection rate appears to be increasing. Today, approximately 1 million people in North America are infected with HIV. This number corresponds to 1 in every 290 people.[54] Among people of prime working age (25 to 44 years), HIV infection is now the leading cause of death.[55] Given these numbers, organizations in the United States and across the world are being increasingly forced to deal with AIDS in the workplace.

Although some U.S. companies (such as Digital Equipment Corporation, Levi Strauss, and Wells Fargo Bank) have corporate policies regarding the treatment of employees with AIDS that reflect a strong sense of social responsibility, other companies have been reluctant even to acknowledge the issue.[56] The overwhelming majority of U.S. organizations have not actively addressed the topic of HIV infection in the workplace.[57] In light of the public attention AIDS has received, the unwillingness of so many companies to formulate a formal AIDS policy is surprising. As the manager of Digital Equipment's HIV/AIDS program, Paul A. Ross, has stated, "Waiting for the first case of AIDS before starting an education program is like waiting to create a fire evacuation program until you smell smoke."[58]

Some companies are reluctant to come to grips with the AIDS issue because of the fear and anxiety it provokes. Failure to deal with the issue proactively, however, is a prescription for crisis because AIDS carries high economic and morale costs. The estimated treatment cost of a single patient with HIV infection from diagnosis to death ranges from $90,000 to $120,000; annual productivity losses from all AIDS patients could be more than $50 billion per year.[59] AIDS can also have indirect costs in the form of disruption of the workplace. When an employee of an Atlanta Toys "R" Us store died of AIDS in 1992, misinformed employees refused to use water fountains and restrooms, and morale and performance suffered dramatically.[60] Fear may lead some employees to refuse to work with infected coworkers, even though the law gives them no protection for such a refusal and they can be disciplined or discharged.[61] Others may come to resent an infected co-worker during the advanced stages of AIDS if the productivity of that co-worker suffers and they have to pick up the slack.[62]

It is clear that AIDS contagion is a primary health concern of U.S. workers. A Centers for Disease Control and Prevention survey of 2,000 adults found that 67 percent would have "some misgivings" about working near someone with AIDS, and 26 percent would feel "uncomfortable." And although 90 percent of the respondents said that HIV-positive employees should be treated like any other employee, this result was tempered by the fact that more than half of the respondents said their companies have no written policy to do so.[63]

Although companies may prefer to sweep the topic of AIDS under the rug, there are federal guidelines regarding AIDS that require organizational compliance. The major sources of these guidelines are OSHA and the Americans with Disabilities Act (ADA).

OSHA

In 1992 OSHA issued the Bloodborne Pathogens Standards, which must be followed in all workplaces where employees can reasonably be expected to come in contact with blood or other body fluids. For example, people who are in the environmental health, safety, or emergency response professions, among others, fall under this standard. Since AIDS became a recognized diagnosis in the early 1980s, 52 instances of HIV infection in health-care workers have been documented as work related.[64] At least another 114 instances of HIV infections in health-care workers are suspected of being work related. OSHA requires all workers who may come into contact with infectious bodily fluids to be educated about bloodborne pathogens and trained in how to reduce the risks of infection. This preparation should help workers reduce their risks and employers' health-care costs. Figure 16.4 summarizes the key points of the OSHA standards.

ADA and the Manager's Role

According to ADA guidelines, having HIV infection or AIDS would not prevent people from performing the essential functions of most jobs.[65] Thus, organizations must make reasonable accommodations for infected employees. Reasonable accommodation might include adjustments to work schedules or workstation modifications. For example, one company gave a manager with AIDS a chair that converted into a sleeping recliner and allowed a 90-minute break in the afternoon.[66] The chair allowed the manager to deal with the drop in his energy level in the afternoon. The manager scheduled all meetings in the morning and came into work extra hours on evenings and weekends, if needed. This arrangement was reasonable and provided an important accommodation for the manager at minimal cost.

ADA guidelines also affect the hiring process. Employers cannot ask job candidates about their HIV or AIDS status or require job candidates to take an HIV test before making a job offer. Testing *can* be done and questions posed after a job offer is made. However, test results must be kept confidential. The job offer cannot be withdrawn on the basis of a positive HIV test unless the employer can demonstrate that the person would pose a direct threat to co-workers or customers and that this threat could not be eliminated through reasonable accommodation. Such demonstration would be all but impossible in most jobs.

In addition to simply complying with the guidelines issued by federal agencies, organizations should proactively address the AIDS issue by developing an AIDS policy. Figure 16.5 outlines some of the issues that employers must consider when developing an AIDS policy. In addition to development and implementation issues, the content of the policy should address all terms and conditions of employment, from hiring and job assignments to compensation and termination.[67] Such a policy sends a clear signal of the importance the company places on its human resources and the support it provides to AIDS victims.

An effective AIDS policy should not only outline the procedures to be followed when an employee contracts HIV infection, but also educate the workforce. Many employees fear that they can contract the disease by working alongside someone who has AIDS. Educational programs can eliminate these fears by providing accurate information about the disease and how it is transmitted.

What is the role of managers and supervisors in dealing with AIDS in the workplace? Managers should be able to answer employee questions about AIDS and effectively deal with any AIDS-related issues that arise. For this reason, the educational effort should involve familiarizing supervisors and managers with the organization's AIDS policy and training them in how to deal with AIDS issues.[68] An open approach to educating and discussing AIDS in the workplace

Key Components of OSHA's Bloodborne Pathogens Standards

Figure 16.4

- **Exposure Control Plan** Outline the procedures to identify workers at risk and specify methods for complying with standards.
- **Universal Precautions** Follow the Centers for Disease Control and Prevention's recommendations for handling all blood and body fluid as though they are contaminated.
- **Personal Protective Equipment** Provide all necessary personal protection equipment, such as gloves and masks.
- **Cleaning Protocols** Identify the methods of decontamination and the procedures for handling waste.
- **Hazard Communication** Use warning labels and signs to identify restricted areas.
- **Information and Training** Educate employees regarding AIDS and the OSHA standards.
- **Recordkeeping** Document efforts relating to the standards and keep the medical records of employees exposed to risk for the duration of their employment plus 30 years.

Source: Adapted from Oswald, E. M. (1996). No employer is immune: AIDS exposure in the workplace. *Risk Management, 43*, 18–21; and Hunter, S. (1998). Your infection control program. *Occupational Health and Safety, 67*, 76–80.

Figure 16.5

Issues in the Development and Implementation of an AIDS Policy

- Who is responsible for development and implementation of the policy?
- What are the objectives of the AIDS policy?
- What is covered under the AIDS policy?
- What rights will covered employees have, particularly in terms of workplace accommodation and confidentiality?
- What benefits will victims receive?
- Who is in charge of administering the policy?
- What kind of training should supervisors and managers have, particularly to prepare them to manage co-workers' concerns and fears?
- How does the company deal with job restructuring issues, accommodation, and requests for transfers by AIDS victims and co-workers?
- How should the AIDS policy be communicated to employees?
- How should organizations deal with affected workers' productivity problems?
- How can organizations help victims cope by providing support and referral services?

Sources: Fremgen, B., and Whitty, M. (1992, December). How to avoid a costly AIDS crisis in the organization. *Labor Law Journal*, 751–758; Smith, J. M. (1993, March). How to develop and implement an AIDS workplace policy. *HR Focus*, 15; and Stodghill, R. (1993, February). Why AIDS policy must be a special policy. *BusinessWeek*, *3303*, 53–54.

is recommended. However, there are boundaries to discussion of AIDS-related issues. Specifically, the Americans with Disabilities Act (ADA) includes strict confidentiality provisions in regard to employee medical information. Confidential medical information can be disclosed to supervisory personnel only if they need to know for purposes of providing reasonable accommodation or to safety personnel who might be required to provide emergency medical services to the employee.[69] An employer who discloses an employee's medical condition, such as AIDS, risks violating the employee's right of privacy and the right to work without discrimination as provided by the ADA. Open discussion of the issue of AIDS in the workplace can help create a positive and productive environment, but disclosure of an employee's AIDS status is legally prohibited.

Violence in the Workplace

On January 28, 1993, a man in a business suit entered the cafeteria of Fireman's Fund Insurance Company in Tampa, Florida, then walked up to a table where managers, supervisors, and executives were seated. He pulled a gun from beneath his suit jacket and opened fire. Three men were killed in the attack and two women were injured.

The gunman was a former employee named Paul Calden who had been discharged about eight months earlier. Witnesses later recalled hearing him say, "This is what you get for firing me!" Police said that Calden had a longstanding and very bitter grudge against Fireman's Fund managers, and he appeared to have plotted his revenge for several weeks. Two hours after the shootings, Calden was found dead from a self-inflicted gunshot wound.[70]

Statistics show that homicides at work are declining, but scenarios of workplace homicide are still too common.[71] Based on the past decade of data, on average 900 workplace homicides occur per year,[72] but the rate of workplace homicides has decreased 37 percent from 1994 to 2000.[73] Robbery-related homicides in restaurants and stores declined from 530 in 1994 to 286 in 1998, a drop of 46 percent. The decline is being attributed to a combination of factors, including a growing economy and improved security measures, such as the use of security cameras. Although the declines are positive, homicide is second only to highway fatalities in causing death at work, with workplace murders accounting for one of every six deaths at work.[74] During the past decade, women accounted for only 7 percent of work-related fatalities but made up 19 percent of the work-related homicides.[75]

Violent death, particularly due to a rampage by a former employee or from a terrorist attack, seems to receive the most media attention and concern. These deplorable events are actually quite rare and the risk of dying on the job from this type of catastrophe is small. However, workplace violence can take a variety of forms, such as harassment, threats, assaults, and sabotage, and these noncatastrophic occurrences are commonplace events. OSHA estimates that over 2 million instances of workplace violence occur each year, including 1.5 million instances of simple assault, 396,000 cases of aggravated assault, 51,000 rapes and sexual assaults, and 84,000 robberies.[76]

Figure 16.6 presents the entry page for OSHA's recommendations for preventing violence in late-night retail establishments. You can view OSHA's recommendations on its Web site at www.osha.gov/SLTC/workplaceviolence/latenight/index.html.

Reducing Assaults and Threats

Organizations are now more aware of the possibility of workplace violence, and some are being proactive in trying to reduce it.[77] Many of these efforts are targeted at decreasing the numbers of assaults and threats. For example, American Express has given victims of domestic violence cell phones and parking spaces close to front doors. The Limited, a clothing retailer, trains supervisors to look for bruised employees as a sign of domestic abuse. The Limited also posts hot line numbers and has seen dozens of employees come forward and ask for help with their domestic abuse problems in the year since the program began. Previously, such employee requests were virtually nonexistent. The rationale for programs such as those at American Express and The Limited is that abuse can follow a worker into the workplace. The facts bear this out: It is estimated by the U.S. Department of Justice that husbands and boyfriends commit 13,000 acts of violence against women in the workplace each year.[78] The workplace relevance of domestic violence is further underscored by the finding that approximately 37 percent of women who were victims of domestic violence reported that the abuse negatively impacted their work performance. Organizations such as American Express and The Limited provide positive but uncommon examples of proactive programs regarding domestic violence. A Liz Claiborne survey found that 86 percent of corporate executives believe they have responsibility for the well-being of

OSHA Workplace Violence Prevention Web Page

Figure 16.6

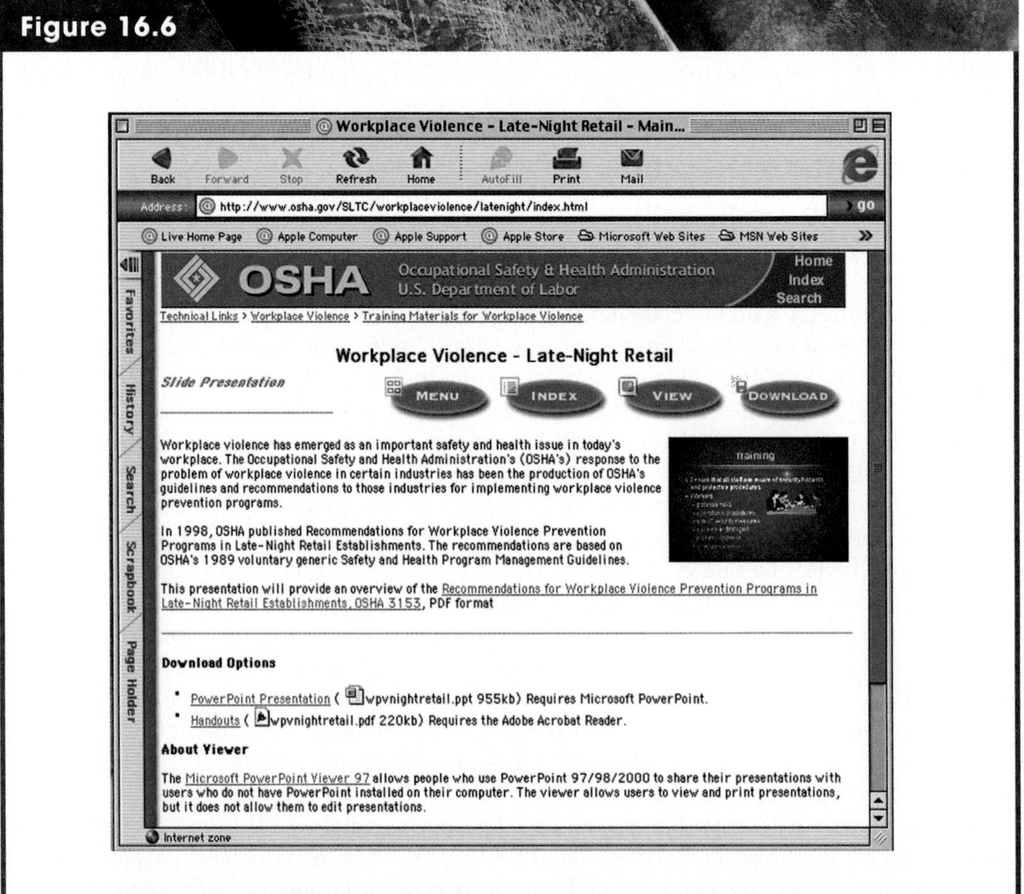

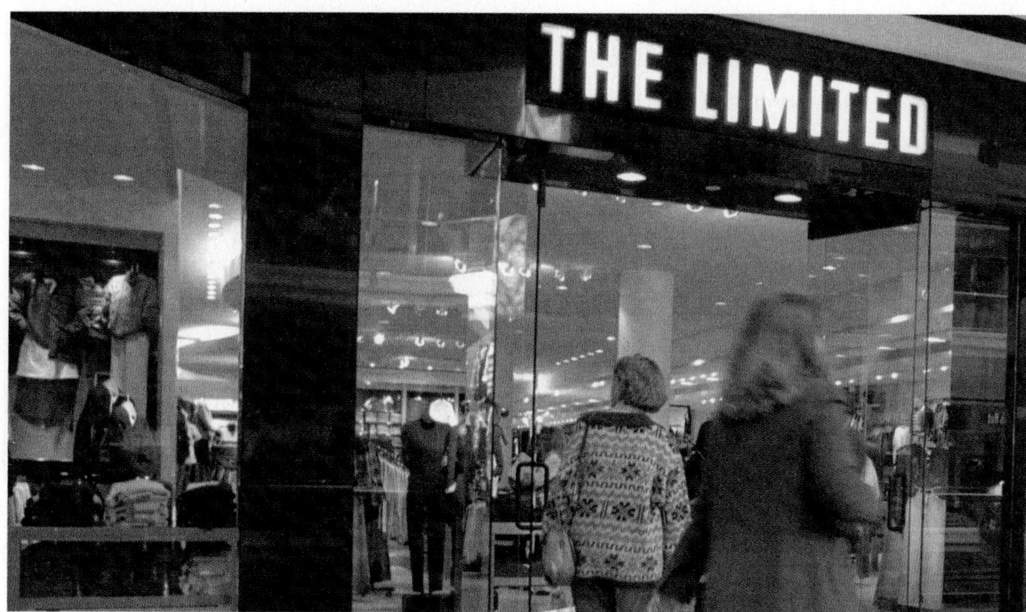

The Limited has started a training and hot line program to prevent domestic abuse from spilling over into the workplace.

their employees, but 95 percent reported that they do not have proactive domestic violence programs.[79]

In addition, there is ample potential for violence being inflicted by co-workers. A recent survey found that one of six employees were so angered by a co-worker that they wanted to hit the person.[80] Organizations also need to deal with the potential threat from within.

Reducing Threats from Sabotage

Another form of workplace violence is sabotage. Sabotage is not physical violence but is a violent act just the same. Acts of sabotage can be directed either at a person, such as attempts to damage someone's career, or at an organization, such as attempts to damage equipment or reputation. Most sabotage involves an aspect or motive of revenge. Angry and bitter employees have done everything from putting rodents into food products to needles in baby food and starting company fires and wiping out computer databases.[81]

Currently, no organizations keep track of acts of sabotage, so the frequency and prevalence of the problem is difficult to assess. However, experts suggest that sabotage is increasingly a problem for organizations. Many saboteurs are disgruntled former employees who, as the victims of downsizing or termination, feel underappreciated and unfairly treated by their former employers. Disgruntled employees who retaliate through damage to a computer system pose a major concern in organizations.

Although the frequency of sabotage is difficult to estimate, sabotage costs organizations dearly in the form of property damage and work stoppage. For example, a survey of computer sabotage found that 163 organizations reported a loss of $123 million as a result of violence. Experts estimate that losses from employee fraud and other forms of sabotage cost organizations $400 billion per year. Figure 16.7 on page 554 offers tips on how to prevent sabotage.

Whatever form workplace violence may take, it is the legal and social responsibility of managers to deal with workplace violence proactively. Under **negligent hiring** laws, employers can be held responsible for their employees' violent acts on the job, particularly when the employer knows, or should know, that an employee has a history of violent behavior (see Chapter 5). In one California case, for example, a temporary help agency employed a man who subsequently stabbed a woman co-worker to death. The man was a paroled murderer with a five-year gap in his résumé that the agency failed to investigate. A state court ordered the temporary agency to pay the dead woman's relatives $5.5 million. Negligence is not limited to hiring. In 1999 a North Carolina jury awarded $7.9 million to two families in a case of two men killed on the job in 1995 by a violent former worker who had been terminated.[82] The jury found that the company's management was negligent in failing to protect the workers. These types of cases are still uncommon, but their numbers appear to be increasing.[83]

Negligent hiring
Hiring an employee with a history of violent or illegal behavior without conducting background checks or taking proper precautions.

Managing the Threat of Sabotage

Figure 16.7

Here are some tips managers can take to prevent sabotage:

- Make it explicit in organizational policy statements that acts of sabotage will not be tolerated and the expense of any damage to organizational property due to an employee's negligence or fault will be the responsibility of the employee.
- Hire the best people for the jobs and treat them well. Sabotage is more likely to occur when a worker is frustrated and feels unfairly treated. Making sure that there is a good fit between the person and the job and that organizational treatment is fair can prevent sabotage.
- Offer employees training in conflict management and ways to appropriately vent anger.
- Consider offering a third party hotline for employees to report incidents of workplace sabotage.

Source: Adapted from Laabs, J. (1999). Employee sabotage: Don't be a target. *Workforce, 78*, 32–38.

Managers need to take responsibility for reducing or eliminating violence in the workplace. To this end, they must be sensitive to the causes of workplace violence. Many people feel pressured in their jobs and fear layoffs. Add to this stress level workplace events such as negative performance appraisals, personality conflicts with co-workers or managers, or personal problems such as a divorce, and a potentially dangerous person may emerge.

Certainly, managers cannot eliminate all these pressures, which are realities of everyday life in modern organizations. However, they can make sure that employees are treated fairly. Treating employees as though they are expendable will not create commitment to the company and could be enough to trigger a violent reaction. Managers should deal with performance problems by focusing on the behavior and future improvement, rather than condemning the person for past performance problems (see Chapter 7 on performance appraisal). Managers should never discipline employees in front of co-workers; doing so can humiliate the person and incite a violent reaction.[84]

Managers should also take steps to reduce the possibility of hiring workers who might be prone to violence. For example, interviewers might ask job candidates to describe how they reacted to a past management decision they did not agree with and why.[85] The responses to this question and follow-up questions could be quite revealing. Also, interviewers should check for evidence of substance abuse or emotional problems, which might be indicated by careless driving or DWI (driving while intoxicated) entries on driving records. Unexplained gaps in a person's employment history should be carefully examined. The Manager's Notebook titled "Profile of People Prone to Workplace Violence and Warning Signs" presents a profile of the characteristics of those who commit violence and a list of some warning signs.

Smoking in the Workplace

In 1994 Melvin Simon and Associates, owners of 85 large shopping malls throughout the United States, announced that smoking would no longer be allowed in any of its facilities. This announcement closely followed decisions by two major fast-food chains, McDonald's and Arby's, to eliminate smoking in their restaurants.[86] Since these actions, many organizations have enacted smoking elimination policies.

The push to restrict workplace smoking has come largely in the last decade. As far back as 1964, the U.S. Surgeon General published the initial government report on the health consequences of smoking. By 1981, however, a Bureau of National Affairs survey revealed that only 8 percent of U.S. companies restricted smoking. In the mid-1980s a report from Surgeon General C. Everett Koop asserted that smokers create health risks for nonsmoking co-workers and customers.[87] By 1986, 36 percent of all organizations restricted smoking in the workplace.[88] A 1998 survey of 80,000 employees found that 65 percent were employed in workplaces wherein smoking is not allowed.[89] Smoke-free workplaces are rapidly becoming the norm in the United States. As shown in Figure 16.8, the trend is more than a U.S. phenomenon.

Figure 16.8

Japanese companies are taking steps to reduce smoking in the workplace. It is now common for Japanese companies to separate smokers from nonsmokers to protect nonsmokers from secondhand smoke. Japanese companies are taking other steps to reduce or eliminate smoking. For example:

- K.K. Ashisuto, a Tokyo-based software company requires potential hires to be or become nonsmokers.
- Sato Corporation, a Tokyo-based manufacturer, provides a $15 monthly bonus to each nonsmoking employee.
- Taisho Pharmaceutical company banned smoking in all offices and factories nationwide in 1999 after an employee died of lung cancer.
- In 1999 the Japan Highway Public Corporation banned smoking in 688 public restrooms on Japan's expressways.

Source: Adapted from *Japan Times*. (1999, June 1–June 15). Health worries prompt firms to boot ashtrays from office, *39*, 15.

Workplace Smoking Being Banned in Japan

Profile of People Prone to Workplace Violence and Warning Signs

Profile of Characteristics:

- White men between 30 and 40 years of age
- Socially isolated—a "loner," who may avoid socializing during breaks or work functions
- Experiencing stress in personal life, such as divorce or death in the family
- Low self-esteem with no healthy outlet for anger
- Work is the person's primary, or sole, activity and it provides him with the opportunity to be "somebody"
- Difficulty dealing with criticism or frustration
- Difficulty dealing with authority
- Fascinated with weapons and the military
- Temper-control problems
- May abuse alcohol or drugs
- History of conflict with others

Warning Signs:

- May blame others for problems
- A behavioral change, such as becoming withdrawn, depressed, or irritable
- May hold a grudge over a termination, lost promotion, performance feedback, or some other outcome
- May make threats and intimidate other workers
- May exhibit paranoia and believe that management or other employees are out to get him
- May test the limits of policies

Sources: Adapted from Missouri Capitol Police (1996). Violence in the workplace. www.dps.state.mo.us.DPS/MCP/STUDY/WKVIOLNC.HTM, June 7, 1996, 1–6; and Bensimon, H. F. (1994). Crisis and disaster management. Violence in the workplace. *Training & Development*, *48*, 27–32.

Many cities and states have enacted regulations regarding smoking.[90] The state of New York has one of the most comprehensive laws protecting the rights of nonsmoking employees in the workplace. It requires each employer to adopt a written smoking policy, post the policy prominently in the workplace, and supply written copies to employees upon request. Requirements include:[91]

- A smoke-free work area for nonsmoking employees.
- A work area set aside for smoking if all working in the area agree.
- Contiguous nonsmoking areas in cafeterias and break rooms.
- A prohibition against smoking in auditoriums, gymnasiums, restrooms, elevators, hallways, and other common areas.
- A prohibition against smoking in company vehicles and meeting rooms unless all present agree that smoking be permitted.

Bans on smoking in the workplace and the refusal of some employers to hire smokers can be controversial. Telling employees they cannot do something that does not seem to affect job performance can seem overly intrusive. However, a growing number of employers do not view smoking prohibitions as off-limits because smoking affects business and the bottom line. How? Smoking poses a recognized cancer risk, increases the likelihood of death from heart disease, and causes other health-related problems. As a result, smokers increase employer health-care costs. Public health reports estimate the costs related to smoking in the United States total $72 billion annually.[92] In addition to increased health-care costs, recent evidence does link smoking to more absences from work and poorer productivity.[93]

Health costs aside, you may be surprised at the other costs of tobacco use in the workplace. Experts estimate that the cost of property fires caused by smoking is more than $500 million per year. The approximate cost of extra cleaning and maintenance due to tobacco use is a whopping $4 billion annually. Businesses consider these costs of smoking a legitimate concern. Currently, no laws prohibit discrimination against smokers in hiring. However, unless there is a legitimate business need, most organizations would be best served by avoiding the smoking issue when making hiring decisions.[94] A company cannot be faulted for focusing on performance issues.

A growing number of states have enacted legislation that restricts employers from discriminating against individuals for off-the-job use of lawful products, particularly tobacco. The laws vary considerably in terms of exemptions and penalties. Many exempt specific organizations (for example, hospitals and religious organizations) allow exceptions where not smoking is shown to be a bona fide occupational qualification (for example, working for an organization, such as the American Cancer Society, whose goal is to promote health), and require smokers to conform to on-the-job smoking rules. Many of these state laws, however, do allow employers to charge employees who smoke higher health insurance rates.[95]

Although OSHA does not as yet have specific workplace standards regarding smoking, the act's general duty clause does require a work environment free from recognized hazards.[96] In a 1976 case involving New Jersey Bell Telephone, the court applied the general duty provision by recognizing that secondhand smoke is a preventable recognized hazard and ordering a smoking ban in working areas in response to an employee's suit.

Another complication for employers could be the application of the ADA to the workplace smoking issue. It is clear that employees sensitive to smoke are qualified disabled employees under the ADA and must be accommodated. However, a reasonable accommodation for these employees need not mean a smoke-free workplace; other types of accommodation, such as fans, ventilation, and separate work areas, might suffice. Finally, while some employees have tried to claim that habitual smoking is a disability under the ADA and have asked for accommodation, this type of claim generally has not been very successful.

Managers need to understand and abide by any local or state regulations regarding smoking and ensure that employees do the same. Because smoking regulations can be controversial, managers should approach any problems in this area fairly and quickly, ensuring that all parties abide by legal and company regulations.

Cumulative Trauma Disorders

Cumulative trauma disorders (CTDs) are also called repetitive stress (or motion or strain) injuries (or illnesses or syndromes). CTDs do not refer to one disorder but rather to a wide array of maladies from *carpal tunnel syndrome (CTS)*, which often affects the wrists of computer keyboard users, to tennis elbow and forearm and shoulder complaints.[97] The number of workers with CTDs has risen dramatically in recent years. In 1983 there were fewer than 50,000 U.S. workers in whom CTDs were diagnosed. By 1993, that number had reached 302,000. The Bureau of Labor Statistics estimates that these injuries have increased 770 percent in the past decade.[98] In addition to prevalence, the costs associated with CTDs are impressive. The General Accounting Office stated that CTDs cost private employers more than $60 billion annually.

Cumulative trauma disorder (CTD)
An occupational injury that occurs from repetitive physical movements, such as assembly-line work or data entry.

As discussed previously (see the section on OSHA), OSHA has generated ergonomic workplace guidelines as a means of reducing CTDs. **Ergonomics** is a young science that focuses on adapting working conditions to employee safety and comfort needs. The guidelines from OSHA have generated some controversy over the extent to which they will actually lead to ergonomic improvement in workplaces. The prevalence of CTDs is itself a controversial issue. There has been much debate over the accuracy of statistics about CTDs. Labor advocates contend that the numbers underrepresent the true extent of the problem because the condition is misdiagnosed in many workers or they continue working as best they can. Business lobbyists contend that the problem is overstated, partially as a result of media hype. Interestingly, there is similar controversy in the medical community. For example, one medical doctor who has treated more than 900 workers complaining of CTDs claims that only about 20 percent of these patients have symptoms of a neuromuscular disorder. He contends that the other 80 percent may have the symptoms but the cause is not the physical workplace.[99] Likewise, a hand surgeon has stated that many workers complaining of a CTD are not model employees and that a precipitating event, such as a reprimand or negative performance feedback, often precedes the medical complaint. It is also interesting to note that numerous suits have been filed against computer keyboard makers, but that no plaintiff had won a judgment until 1996.[100]

Ergonomics
The science of adapting working conditions to employee safety and comfort needs.

Despite the absence of definitive OSHA standards to regulate workplace ergonomics, there may be substantial cost savings for organizations that work to prevent CTDs. Consider, for example, the approach taken by the U.S. Automobile Association (USAA), an insurance company based in San Antonio.[101] Since 1992 more than 20,000 USAA workers were given ergonomics training and 7,200 received individual ergonomics counseling. The company also provides employees with adjustable furniture and ergonomic keyboards. In 1998 the company received an award for outstanding office ergonomics. More importantly, payments for musculoskeletal disorders shrank from 66 percent to 48 percent of the company's workers' compensation payments.

Although legal compliance may not be an issue right now, socially responsible organizations should be aware of CTDs and their likely causes. Managers should take steps to reduce CTDs by educating workers and altering the physical arrangement of the workplace if necessary. Figure 16.9 presents a set of do's and don'ts to help workers avoid CTDs. Managers should also remember that posting these tips prominently can decrease the likelihood that workers will develop a CTD.

Hearing Impairment

It is widely recognized that loud noise can lead to loss of hearing. However, consistent exposure to loud noise of 95 decibels has also been found to be related to elevated blood pressure, various digestive, respiratory, allergenic, and musculoskeletal disorders. Exposure to loud noise has also been found to lead to disorientation and reduction of eye focus, possibly leading to an increase in the rate of accidents and injuries.[102] Evidence regarding the potential negative health effects of loud noise led OSHA to develop the Occupational Noise Exposure standard. This standard requires organizations to provide hearing protectors free to employees who are exposed to an average of 85 decibels of noise or greater. Regardless of this standard, research findings indicate that, on average, less than 50 percent of employees who should wear hearing protectors actually wear them.[103] Furthermore, many employees who wear hearing protectors don't wear them correctly. Part of the problem in dealing with the prevention of hearing loss is getting employees to

Avoiding CTDs: The Do's and Don'ts

Figure 16.9

Do:

- Take breaks (every 20 minutes).
- Stretch and relax at your work area (once per hour).
- Maintain and build your physical fitness.
- Maintain good posture when working at a computer/terminal:
  - Sit erect.
  - Feet flat on floor.
  - Bend elbows at a comfortable angle.
  - Sit about 18–28 inches from the screen.
  - Place documents at the same height and angle as the monitor.

Don't:

- Engage in a lot of repetitive motion with your hands and arms.
- Bend your wrists continuously.
- Grasp or pinch objects continuously.
- Work in an awkward position.
- Exert a lot of force with your arms and hands.

Source: Adapted from Worsnop, R. L. (1995). Repetitive stress injuries. *CQ Researcher, 5*, 537–560.

recognize and take seriously the threat that noise can pose to hearing acuity. The Manager's Notebook: Customer-Driven HR, "Say What? Management Steps to the Prevention of Hearing Loss" offers steps that can be taken to motivate employees to protect their hearing. Efforts to prevent hearing loss should not be limited to getting employees to protect their hearing. Reducing the amount of noise in the work environment is a direct and primary way of preventing hearing loss. Although noise reduction isn't always possible, many organizations are finding that new machinery often offers the advantage of quieter operation.[104] Efforts to prevent hearing loss need to be broad-based and include consideration of both system (e.g., machinery) and person (employee) factors.

Fetal Protection, Hazardous Chemicals, and Genetic Testing

During the 1970s and 1980s, a handful of large U.S. firms developed workplace policies designed to prevent pregnant employees from exposure to hazardous chemicals that might damage the fetus. These policies were controversial because they tended to restrict women's access to some of industry's better-paying jobs. For example, in 1978 several women working for American Cyanamid underwent sterilization rather than risk losing highly paid jobs.

MANAGER'S NOTEBOOK

Customer-Driven HR

Say What? Management Steps to the Prevention of Hearing Loss

Motivating workers to take seriously threats to their hearing can be difficult. Hearing loss is something that can't be seen and isn't immediately perceived by the victim. Furthermore, wearing hearing protection can be viewed as cumbersome. Here are some suggestions to help bring employees on board with a hearing loss prevention effort.

- *Show workers what hearing loss is like.* Knowing what it is like to have hearing loss can be an effective motivational technique. Demonstrations of hearing loss can be found at www.aero.com/html/industrial/tech01.asp#audiodemo.

- *Offer testimonials.* A former employee or someone in the industry who suffered work-related hearing loss can offer an effective and motivating presentation to employees. A testimonial can make the issue real to employees and make clear that it could happen to them.
- *Have them do their own demonstration.* If you have workers who resist wearing ear protection, even though it is needed, have them try this test: When arriving for work, turn down the car stereo so that it can barely be heard. Leaving it set at that volume, go to work. Returning to the car after a day's work, turn on the radio with the volume still as set in the morning. Can you hear the radio?
- *Offer incentives.* Offer incentives to supervisors or teams based on the percentage of workers who wear hearing protection devices.

Source: Adapted from Safety Director's Report (2002). Hearing protection strategies for any safety department budget. May Newsletter of the Institute of Management and Administration.

The fetal protection controversy came to national attention in 1982 when Johnson Controls, a battery manufacturer, prevented women of childbearing age from working in jobs involving contact with lead. The union sued Johnson Controls for sex discrimination because the company's policy restricted only female employees. The Supreme Court ruled against the company, finding it guilty of illegal sex bias.[105]

This decision caused great concern among companies like General Motors, DuPont, Olin, Monsanto, and others with fetal protection policies. These companies argue that their only alternative is to reduce the use of certain substances greatly. But reducing the use of these compounds, they claim, would be both difficult and costly. Critics counter that these companies should do more to protect *all* workers, not simply remove some from the workplace.[106]

Reproductive health concerns are an important workplace issue with the potential to affect thousands of employers and millions of workers. For example, one study of 1,600 pregnant women showed that those who use video display terminals (VDTs) heavily have a miscarriage rate double that of women who do not use monitors. A study of pregnant women at a Digital Equipment plant in Houston reached a similar conclusion. Clearly, the implications of this type of problem are substantial when one considers the number of VDTs currently in use.[107] The fetal health issue is compounded by the fact that only a handful of companies have comprehensive fetal health policies, and research about the effects of many industrial compounds on reproductive health is inconclusive or incomplete. Although some substances (for example, lead) represent clear health threats to fetuses, exposure to many other compounds may not cause problems. These compounds may also present significant reproductive hazards to *both* sexes, not just women.

Hazardous Chemicals

Many thousands of workplace accidents and injuries reported each year have been attributed to exposure to toxic chemicals. In the past, workers were often required to handle chemicals without being fully informed of the hazards involved. In 1983, however, OSHA's hazard communication standard gave employees the right to know about hazardous chemicals in the workplace (see Figure 16.1). The current standard requires manufacturers and users of hazardous chemicals to identify the chemicals, provide employees with information about them, and train employees in the dangers and handling of them.[108]

The Hazard Communications Standard is far-reaching, covering more than 35 million workers exposed to hazardous chemicals at more than 3.5 million sites.[109] Each year, companies receive thousands of dollars in fines for failing to make Material Safety Data Sheets (MSDS) available to employees. Part of the problem is the cumbersome paper-based MSDS system, which is difficult to keep up to date. To remedy the problem, many companies are putting MSDS information online to provide better access to information and easier compliance with the Hazard Communication Standard.

Genetic testing
A form of biological testing that identifies employees who are genetically susceptible to specific occupational substances.

Genetic Testing

A new and controversial tool used to deal with exposure to workplace substances is **genetic testing,** which identifies employees who are genetically susceptible to specific occupational substances. The goal is to avoid placing at-risk employees in dangerous jobs. Very few organizations use genetic testing at present (1 percent or fewer), but advances in genetic research may make this screening device more attractive in years to come. Critics question the predictive ability of genetic screening and criticize it from both legal and ethical perspectives because it has significant potential to discriminate. Indeed, heavy use of genetic screening may conflict with both Title VII of the Civil Rights Act and the ADA. In 1999 a U.S. Court of Appeals ruled that genetic tests conducted by a federal laboratory on its employees without the employees' permission may have violated the workers' civil rights and invaded their privacy.[110] An additional argument against genetic screening is similar to that raised against fetal protection policies: It is the work environment that is the problem, not the worker, and organizations should remove the hazard, not the person.[111]

The Burlington Northern Santa Fe Railroad began using genetic testing in March 2000. The company required employees who claimed a work-related CTD to provide blood samples as part of routine medical examinations used to evaluate employee injury claims. The blood samples were used to test for the presence of a genetic trait that might predispose someone to musculoskeletal disorders. The testing was brought to light when employees made complaints to their labor unions. The EEOC filed a lawsuit in February 2002 contending that the genetic testing violated the ADA. This is the first time that the EEOC challenged testing. In a mediated settlement reached in May 2002, the railroad agreed to pay 36 workers $2.2 million to resolve allegations that it conducted genetic testing without employee knowledge or consent.[112] The railroad contended that the genetic tests weren't used to screen out employees. However, the EEOC contends that the mere gathering of genetic information may violate the ADA. Currently, 22 states have banned the use of genetic screening for employment purposes.[113]

Managers have the obligation to stay informed and to help the HR department develop policies that balance employees' rights with the organization's needs. Because they are on the front line, managers are responsible for directly communicating information about hazards to employees in a clear and timely manner. In addition, they should make sure the employees understand the risks involved in working with hazardous substances and take all appropriate precautions. They should also inform employees of their rights, responsibilities, and alternatives, handling each situation with respect and fairness.

Safety and Health Programs

We have devoted most of the chapter thus far to discussing physical hazards in the workplace and their impact on both workers and the organization. However, there are other hazards that have major effects on workers, including stress, unsafe behaviors, and poor health habits. To cope with both types of hazards, companies often design comprehensive safety and health programs.

Safety Programs

A safe working environment does not just happen; it has to be created. The organizations with the best reputations for safety have developed well-planned, thorough safety programs. Concern for safety should begin at the highest level within the organization, and managers and supervisors at all levels should be charged with demonstrating safety awareness, held responsible for safety training, and rewarded for maintaining a safe workplace. Typically, however, the safety director and most safety programs are part of the HR function. HR managers are often responsible for designing and implementing safety programs, as well as for training supervisors and managers in the administration of workplace safety rules and policies.

Effective safety programs share the following features:

- They include the formation of a safety committee and participation by all departments within the company. Employees participate in safety decisions and management carefully considers employee suggestions for improving safety.

- They communicate safety with a multimedia approach that includes safety lectures, films, posters, pamphlets, and computer presentations.
- They instruct supervisors in how to communicate, demonstrate, and require safety, and they train employees in the safe use of equipment.
- They use incentives, rewards, and positive reinforcement to encourage safe behavior. They reward employee complaints or suggestions about safety. They may also provide rewards (such as safe driving awards given to truck drivers) to employees with exceptional safety records.
- They communicate safety rules and enforce them. They know that OSHA obligates employees to adhere to safety rules, and they are willing to use the disciplinary system to penalize unsafe work behavior.
- They use safety directors and/or the safety committee to engage in regular self-inspection and accident research to identify potentially dangerous situations, and to understand why accidents occur and how to correct them.

Companies with comprehensive safety programs are likely to be rewarded with fewer accidents, fewer workers' compensation claims and lawsuits, and lower accident-related costs. Keep in mind that OSHA considers employee involvement a key feature of a successful safety program. Organizations often involve employees by establishing a safety committee. Although the specific details may vary, the overall purpose of a safety committee is to have employees and managers collaborate to promote workplace safety and health.[114] Safety committees typically evaluate the adequacy of safety procedures; monitor findings and trends; review accidents, illnesses, and safety suggestions; and recommend and evaluate hazard solutions. However, experts recommend that safety committees do not enforce the policies and risk being viewed as the "safety police." Instead, the committees should make recommendations that management should implement and enforce.

Do's and Don'ts for Effective Safety Committees

Do:

- Train committee members on skills they will need to be effective contributors
- Give the committee the authority it needs to meet its responsibilities
- Have goals and objectives and use them to assess progress
- Encourage involvement and help to create an atmosphere of trust and partnership
- Be patient in expecting results
- Reward progress, participation, and leadership
- Have a mixture of experience levels in committees

Don't:

- Allow the safety committee to operate as "safety cops"
- Rotate members too quickly
- Let one member dominate the committee
- Let only problems be raised in committee—solutions need to be generated, too
- Let the committee become a scapegoat
- Blame workers for safety problems—explore causes

Source: Adapted from Cullen, L. (1999) Safety committees: A smart business decision. *Occupational Hazards, 61*, 99–104

Involving employees on safety committees has been effective. Pennsylvania, for example, has found such a return on investment that it offers a five percent discount for five years on workers' compensation insurance premiums as an incentive for organizations to establish safety committees.[115] State level OSHAs in Oregon, Nevada, and Washington have such a positive assessment of the effectiveness of safety committees that they are required in most workplaces. The Manager's Notebook titled "Do's and Don'ts for Effective Safety Committees" offers general guidelines for safety committee development and operation. Following these pointers can help you establish a participative component for your comprehensive safety program.

Employee Assistance Programs (EAPs)

As we saw in Chapter 13, *employee assistance programs (EAPs)* are programs designed to help employees whose job performance is suffering because of physical, mental, or emotional problems. EAPs address a variety of employee problems ranging from drug abuse to marital problems. Recent surveys indicate that EAPs are generally quite prevalent, but tend to be more common in larger organizations. For example, 45 percent of full-time employees have an EAP available to them, but EAPs are available to more than 70 percent of employees in organizations employing between 1,000 to 5,000 workers.[116]

Many organizations create EAPs because they recognize their ethical and legal obligations to protect not only their workers' physical health but their mental health as well. The ethical obligation stems from the fact that the causes of organizational stress—climate, change, rules, work pace, management style, work group characteristics, and so forth—are also frequently the causes of behavioral, psychological, and physiological problems for employees.[117] Ethical obligation becomes legal obligation when employees sue the company or file workers' compensation claims for stress-related illnesses. In fact, much of the heightened concern about dealing with the consequences of workplace stress stems from the increasing incidence and severity of stress-related workers' compensation claims and their associated costs.[118] In Japan work-related stress (*karoshi*) has come to be seen as a deadly national problem. Interestingly, a United Nations study released in September 1999 found Americans now work the longest hours in the industrialized world—surpassing even the Japanese.[119]

Burnout
A stress syndrome characterized by emotional exhaustion, depersonalization, and reduced personal accomplishment.

Stress often results in **burnout,** a syndrome characterized by emotional exhaustion, depersonalization, and reduced personal accomplishment.[120] People who experience burnout may dread returning to work for another day, treat co-workers and clients callously, withdraw from the organization, and feel less competent in their jobs. Some of the factors that may lead to burnout include ambiguity and conflict regarding how to deal with various job-related issues and problems.[121] A lack of social support can aggravate these effects.

Burnout can lead to serious negative consequences for the individual and for the organization and can have a negative impact on mental and physical health.[122] Mental health problems resulting from burnout can include depression, irritability, lowered self-esteem, and anxiety. Physical problems can include fatigue, headaches, insomnia, gastrointestinal disturbances, and chest pains. Organizational outcomes associated with burnout include turnover, absenteeism, and a decrease in job performance.[123] In addition, sometimes burnout leads to increased drug and alcohol use.[124]

Depression is another topic that merits consideration in any discussion of EAP issues. Clinical depression is a serious mental illness that is a bigger problem in the workplace than many people realize. Dr. Ronald Kessler, a health-care policy professor at Harvard Medical School, states that depressed workers report "having problems with time and motion, lifting things, and having accidents on the job."[125] Research studies are consistent with this observation and suggest that depressed workers may be more prone to accidents due to lack of concentration, fatigue, memory difficulties, and slower reaction time. In addition to possible accident proneness, depression has been linked to decreased productivity. It is estimated that as many as 15 to 20 million adult Americans experience depression each year, resulting in 200 million lost workdays and a total annual cost to the U.S. economy of $43.7 billion.[126] Because of the pervasiveness of depression, mental health experts contend that managers have an obligation to learn about depression, to recognize its warning signs, and to become aware of sources of help. The Manager's Notebook: Customer-Driven HR, "Warning Signs of Depression," presents symptoms of depression to be on the lookout for. However, keep in mind that you should not play armchair psychiatrist. As a manager, you are there to focus on performance and discuss observable job-relevant behaviors, not to discuss medical problems. There are numerous causes of depression, including genetic, situational, biological, and cognitive. Depression is treatable and can respond positively to counseling and medication, but you should leave this treatment to professionals by referral to your EAP or other source for help.

Many organizations perceive EAPs as being cost-effective solutions to performance, stress, and burnout problems. In fact, although U.S. businesses spend as much as $750 million per year on EAPs, many see this as an investment rather than a cost. EAP professionals claim that for every dollar invested in EAP programs, employers recover three to five dollars.[127] The savings come from lower insurance costs, reduced sick time, and better job performance.

Despite these benefits a manager should refer an employee to an EAP solely on the basis of a performance problem and no other. The case of a manager at Lucky Stores grocery store illustrates this point.[128] The manager had been a star performer but employees started complaining about his abusive and hostile manner. Company representatives asked if he were having "problems" and offered him assistance. He denied having problems and a transfer to another store did not improve the situation. He was then offered a leave of absence if he contacted the company's EAP. The EAP staff determined he was suffering from stress and diagnosed a mental illness. He was fired after six months of leave.

The store manager brought suit against the company and the court found that although he was not disabled, the company may have perceived him to be disabled. Therefore, the former manager may have a claim under the ADA. The company and former manager reached an out-of-court settlement. The message of this and some similar cases is that referral to an EAP should be based on work-related performance issues, rather than on inferences or conclusions about the worker's mental or emotional well-being.

Customer-Driven HR

MANAGER'S NOTEBOOK

Warning Signs of Depression

The following are signs that might be observed in the workplace if an employee is suffering from depression. However, these signs should not be considered symptomatic if they occur in isolation or only temporarily. For example, one absence does not mean that someone is suffering from depression.

- Decreased productivity
- Morale problems
- Lack of cooperation
- Taking safety risks
- Absenteeism
- Frequent statements about being fatigued
- Alcohol and drug abuse

If this pattern fits an employee, it is recommended that you focus on the performance issues and not offer a conclusion that you think the person is suffering from depression. You can tell the person that if personal issues are affecting his or her work you would recommend a confidential session with an employee assistance counselor.

Source: Adapted from Nighswonger, T. (2002). Depression: The unseen safety risk. *Occupation Hazards, 64*, 38(3).

Wellness Programs

As health-care costs have skyrocketed over the last two decades, organizations have become more interested in preventive programs. Recognizing that they can have an effect on their

Staying Healthy, Staying Happy. American Airlines offers a variety of activities designed to help employees stay happy, healthy, and productive. Here, food-service workers take a lunchtime aerobics class.

employees' behavior and lifestyle off the job, companies are encouraging employees to lead more healthy lives. They are also attempting to reduce health-care costs through formal employee wellness programs. Whereas EAPs focus on *treating* troubled employees, **wellness programs** focus on *preventing* health problems. A recent survey of employer coalitions found that 75 percent sponsored wellness programs.[129]

Wellness program
A company-sponsored program that focuses on preventing health problems in employees.

A complete wellness program has three components:

- It helps employees identify potential health risks through screening and testing.
- It educates employees about health risks such as high blood pressure, smoking, poor diet, and stress.
- It encourages employees to change their lifestyles through exercise, good nutrition, and health monitoring.

Wellness programs may be as simple and inexpensive as providing information about stop-smoking clinics and weight-loss programs or as comprehensive and expensive as providing professional health screening and multimillion-dollar fitness facilities.

A Question of Ethics

Some feel that wellness and employee assistance programs should be evaluated on a cost-benefit basis and discontinued if these programs' benefits do not exceed their costs. Others feel that since companies create many of the stressful conditions that contribute to employee health problems, they are ethically bound to continue providing these types of programs. What do you think?

The Rewards of Good Health Habits

Many organizations find that the employees who are involved in the company wellness plans are people who already are health conscious and have healthy habits. How can you get other employees, many of whom may benefit the most, involved in the wellness program? Some companies are finding that nothing motivates like incentives. Between 1992 and 1998, the number of employers offering incentives to workers to adopt healthier habits increased from 14 percent to 39 percent.[130]

For example, Providence Health Systems in Everett, Washington, has a Wellness Challenge program that rewards workers who meet its health and lifestyle criteria. Criteria are based on health risk factors and employee behavior that relates to health-care costs. They include standards such as checking blood pressure, obtaining exercise points, and completing a health risk assessment. Employers receive monetary rewards ($250 in year 1, $275 in year two, and $325 in year three) if they meet 8 of the 10 standards.

Monthly medical claims at Providence average 27 percent lower than the claims made at similar hospitals in the area. In addition, Providence found that participants in the Wellness Challenge program used 15 fewer hours in sick time per year than did nonparticipants.

Note, however, that punishing employees for unhealthy behavior may be illegal.[131] Penalties are disallowed according to guidelines associated with the 1997 Health Insurance Portability and

Accountability Act. For example, excluding certain employers from health insurance coverage or charging them more for health benefits would be discriminatory. Offering rewards is fine, but penalties relating to health insurance coverage or cost are not legally acceptable.

Wellness programs, if implemented effectively, can make a positive contribution to the bottom line in an organization. Although there are costs to starting and maintaining a wellness program, the return in terms of reduced health-care costs and absenteeism can greatly offset the investment. Consider the comprehensive wellness program at Eastman Chemical.[132] The program includes services such as exercise classes, health improvement programs, and personal exercise guidelines. The company projects a five-year savings of $12 million due to both reduced health-care costs and absenteeism, an impressive return on its investment.

Summary and Conclusions

Workplace Safety and the Law

There are two sets of workplace safety laws: (1) workers' compensation, an employer-funded insurance system that operates at the state level, and (2) the Occupational Safety and Health Act (OSHA), a federal law that mandates safety standards in the workplace.

Workers' compensation—which consists of total disability, impairment, survivor, medical expense, and rehabilitation benefits—is intended to ensure prompt and reasonable medical care to employees injured on the job, as well as income for them and their dependents or survivors. It also encourages employers to invest in workplace safety by requiring higher insurance premiums from employers with numerous workplace accidents and injuries.

OSHA compels employers to provide a safe and healthy work environment, to comply with specific occupational safety and health standards, and to keep records of occupational injuries and illnesses. Its safety standards are enforced through a system of inspections, citations, fines, and criminal penalties.

Managing Contemporary Safety, Health, and Behavioral Issues

The most significant safety, health, and behavioral issues for employers are AIDS, violence in the workplace, cumulative trauma disorders, fetal protection, hazardous chemicals, and genetic testing. In all of these areas line managers must deal with a variety of practical, legal, and ethical questions that often demand a careful balancing of individual rights (especially privacy rights) with the needs of the organization.

Safety and Health Programs

Comprehensive safety programs are well-planned efforts in which management (1) involves employees and carefully considers their suggestions, (2) communicates safety rules to employees and enforces them, (3) invests in training supervisors to demonstrate and communicate safety on the job, (4) uses incentives to encourage safe behaviors and discipline to penalize unsafe behaviors, and (5) engages in regular self-inspection and accident research to identify and correct potentially dangerous situations.

Employee assistance programs (EAPs) are designed to help employees cope with physical, mental, or emotional problems (including stress) that are undermining their job performance.

Wellness programs are preventive efforts designed to help employees identify potential health risks and deal with them before they become problems.

Key Terms

burnout, 562
cumulative trauma disorder (CTD), 557
ergonomics, 557
genetic testing, 559
negligent hiring, 553
Occupational Safety and Health Act of 1970 (OSHA), 541
wellness program, 564

Discussion Questions

1. What is the difference between the objectives of workers' compensation and the objectives of OSHA?
2. What kind of policies do you think would work best to prevent workplace violence?
3. Do you think the approach taken by OSHA to improve ergonomic safety will be effective? Why or why not?
4. If a job is potentially hazardous to the fetus of a pregnant employee, should it be legal for the company to restrict the job to men?
5. How could genetic testing be used to discriminate?
6. How can managers use the organization's reward system to encourage workplace safety?
7. *Karoshi*, a term coined by the Japanese, means "death from overwork." *Karoshi* is now the second leading cause of death, after cancer, among Japanese workers. Put yourself in the place of a Japanese manager. What could you do to reduce the risk of *karoshi* in your workers? Do you think *karoshi* will become a problem in the United States? Explain your answer.
8. It was argued in this chapter that an empowerment approach to improving safety could yield positive results. The operation of consultative safety teams including cleaning workers was used as an example. However, a participative approach to safety improvement means employee time away from other duties and decreased productivity. Do you think the trade-off may be worth it? Why or why not?

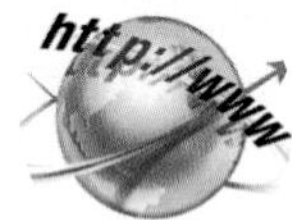

There is a variety of additional material available on the Web site that accompanies this text. You can access this information by visiting the Web site at **www.prenhall.com/gomez.**

YOU MANAGE IT!

Discussion Case 16.1

Back to School

Martin Marietta Energy Systems, Inc. employs approximately 20,000 people in the south central United States. For years the company consistently experienced annual costs of nearly $1 million as a result of employees' lower back injuries. In response, the company started an on-site physical therapy program. The program, which includes a staff of physical therapists, physicians, nurses, laboratory technicians, and an x-ray technician, is called the Back School and is taught as part of general employee training. The Back School staff also offers programs on fitness, stretching, flexibility, posture, and lifting. When all costs are considered, Martin Marietta's management estimates that the program has saved the company more than $800,000 per year—a whopping 9:1 benefit-to-cost ratio.[a]

Back pain is second only to the common cold as the nation's most common health problem. Some of the factors that contribute to this problem include stress, sedentary lifestyles, overweight workers, and improper lifting methods. The OSH Administration has lifting guidelines that are meant to reduce the chances of back injury. For example, the load should be held close to the body, knees should be bent, feet should be separated, and twisting while carrying a heavy load should be avoided.[b]

Critical Thinking Questions

1. Statistics indicate that lower back problems are a serious workplace issue but, like CTDs, are not directly observable and often defy diagnosis of specific physical cause. How could you convince your organization to establish a "Back School" program similar to Martin Marietta's, particularly when the costs are certain and benefits may not be so visible or immediate?
2. How might managers help workers prevent back injuries while keeping costs to a minimum?

Sources: [a]Anspaugh, D. J., Hunter, S., and Mosley, J. (1995). The economic impact of corporate wellness programs. *AAOHN Journal, 43*, 203–210. [b]Krucoff, C. (1999, June 15). Fit bits: Experts on lifting offer tips to give your back a break. *Washington Post*, 222.

Discussion Case 16.2

YOU MANAGE IT!

On-Site Occupational Health Centers: A Proactive Approach to Reducing Safety and Health Costs

On-the-job injuries can be costly for both employees and employers. For an employee, an injury may mean missing time from work and a reduction in income. The decrease in income can cause difficulty for the employee and his or her family. For the employer, an injury can mean treatment expenses, loss of productivity, and the cost of temporarily replacing an injured worker. Some employers are establishing on-site occupational health centers as a way of controlling and reducing some of these costs.

An on-site occupational health center (OHC) is a place where workers injured on the job can be evaluated and treated on the premises instead of seeing a doctor at an outside medical center. It can offer a number of advantages over the traditional approach of seeking outside treatment. Perhaps most evident, an injured worker can usually be treated right away because the facility provides service only to employees. The immediacy of attention is not only a convenience for employees, but it can also be good for his or her health and well-being. However, a serious injury will lead to a referral to a hospital because an OHC is usually staffed by a nurse or nurse practitioner. The staff can treat minor injuries and can also follow up and assist in the recovery program for employees who are more seriously injured and receive initial treatment at a hospital.

For employers, an on-site OHC can cut costs by providing quick treatment and assistance in managing recovery. Workers can be back on the job more quickly with the assistance of an OHC. As an example of the cost-saving possibility, a manufacturer distributor in Florida opened up three on-site OHCs in 1997. The organization employs 2,400 people and it invested $276,000 in OHC start-ups. The major cost items included staff, equipment, and supplies. The cost savings attributed to the operation of the OHCs in 1998 exceeded $1 million.

Critical Thinking Questions

1. Do you think an on-site OHC is a good idea? In answering this question, address the following issues:
   a. Is an on-site OHC a good thing for an employer? Explain.
   b. Is an on-site OHC a good thing for employees? Could the use of an on-site and employer-owned facility be a negative factor for the well-being of employees?
2. The most visible function of an on-site OHC is to provide treatment *after* an injury. How could you use an on-site OHC to increase safety and reduce the occurrence of accidents? Consider, for example, the Florida company mentioned above. Its OHCs reduced recordable injuries by 24 percent. How could you use a postaccident treatment facility as a preventive tool?
3. If the culture of the organization is such that labor distrusts management, how do you think workers would react to management's plans to establish an on-site OHC? How would you reduce this problem? Specifically, what steps would you take to implement an OHC to maximize its acceptance and effectiveness?

Source: Adapted from Wilkerson, M. (1999). Healthy savings. *Strategic Finance, 80*, 42–46.

Emerging Trends Case 16.3

YOU MANAGE IT!

Saving Lives and Liability

In January 1998 Jim Young stepped off a treadmill at the Michelin North America wellness center. He immediately collapsed. Fortunately for Mr. Young, Michelin had just added a defibrillator to the workplace. A security guard received a call about Mr. Young, grabbed the defibrillator, and was at the wellness center within one minute. The guard ripped open Mr. Young's shirt and applied the pads. He turned on the power for the defibrillator, and the machine's analysis concluded that Jim Young was in ventricular fibrillation. The machine indicated that a shock should be given and a button push later, Jim Young was brought back to life.

The condition of ventricular fibrillation occurs when the heartbeat degrades into a chaotic flutter. A fibrillating heart cannot pump blood, and brain damage and death can occur quickly. Experts estimated that chances of survival decrease 10 percent with each minute. An electric shock can restore the heartbeat, but it must be administered quickly.

Defibrillators are devices that deliver a shock and they have become highly automated and easy to use. A growing number of companies, such as Michelin North America, Raytheon, and State Farm Insurance, among others, now have these defibrillators available. Although supplying defibrillators seems like a humane idea, it may increase risk exposure. For example, if a minimally trained person panics and bungles the defibrillation process, could the company or person using the defibrillator be held liable?

Currently, automated defibrillators require some training for ideal use, but they are equipped with drawings that show proper placement of the paddles and voice prompts provide further instructions. The machine's analysis mode determines whether a shock should be administered. However, if this determination is ignored, and a shock is given to someone who is not in ventricular fibrillation, the error could cause death.

The cost of automated defibrillators is less than $5,000. They can save lives—just ask Jim Young. Waiting six minutes or more for paramedics to arrive could prove to be a fatal delay.

Critical Thinking Questions

1. Do you think the potential benefit of an on-site defibrillator offsets the potential liability cost? Explain.
2. What steps could be taken to reduce the liability problem?

Team Exercises

With your partner or team, develop an implementation plan for introducing defibrillators.

Based on your plan in response to item 3, estimate the costs associated with the implementation.

Consider with your partner or team the issue of who should be able to use the defibrillator(s). Should only selected personnel be allowed access to the equipment? Why and who? Come to a consensus and report your judgments to the rest of the class.

Source: Adapted from Chase, M. (1998, September 21). More workplaces make defibrillators part of first-aid kit. *Wall Street Journal*, B1.

YOU MANAGE IT!

Discussion Case 16.4

Refusing to Perform a Hazardous Task at Whirlpool

At the Whirlpool appliance plant in Marion, Ohio, overhead conveyors were used to transport appliance components from one area of the plant to another. To prevent workers from being harmed by falling parts, the company had installed a horizontal wire mesh screen secured to angle iron frames beneath the conveyor belts. The mesh was about 20 feet above the plant floor.

Part of regular maintenance at the plant included spending several hours each week removing parts from the screen and replacing paper used to catch grease that dropped from the conveyor. Maintenance employees had to stand on the angle frames, or on the mesh itself to perform the work.

In 1973 the company began to replace the mesh with a heavier mesh because of safety concerns. Several employees had fallen partway through the mesh, and one had even fallen to the floor below but had survived. When employees brought complaints about the unsafe conditions to the foreman, they were instructed to walk on the iron beams only, not the mesh.

In June 1974, a maintenance employee fell through the old mesh to his death. The next week two maintenance employees, Virgil Deemer and Thomas Cornwell, again complained about safety issues. Two days later, they asked the plant safety director to provide them with a phone number of the area OSH Administration office. They were told to think about what they were doing, but were given the number. They subsequently called an OSH Administration inspector.

The next day, the foreman instructed Deemer and Cornwell to walk on the mesh screen to perform regular maintenance. They refused to comply with the foreman's order, claiming that the work was unsafe. Both employees were told to go to the personnel office. They were then instructed to punch out for the remainder of the day and were subsequently given a written reprimand for insubordination.

This case eventually made its way to the U.S. Supreme Court. The Court upheld the rights of workers under the Occupational Safety and Health Act to choose not to perform their assigned task because of a reasonable apprehension of death or serious injury, when no other alternative is available to them.

Critical Thinking Questions

1. Was the refusal by Deemer and Cornwell to perform their assigned tasks justified by a reasonable apprehension of death or injury?
2. The HR manager has the responsibility to protect employees, but at the same time does not want to be perceived as undermining a supervisor's authority. Why is this balancing act so difficult in the type of situation discussed in this case?
3. What unanticipated and damaging results could an organization suffer if it forces workers to do what they perceive as dangerous work?

4. Place yourself in the position of safety director at Whirlpool. What would you say and/or do when the employees come to you asking about how to contact OSHA? Outline your plans.
5. Describe how you would approach safety so that the accident at Whirlpool might have been prevented. Design the type of system or policies that you think should be in place to maximize safety in that type of environment.

Team Exercises

Students form into groups of four or five. Each group should develop criteria for "reasonableness" by which to judge refusal to perform job tasks perceived as dangerous. The leader of each group should then present its set of criteria to the class.

Identify people in the class who have worked on dangerous jobs and ask them how dangerous tasks are assigned. Has anyone ever refused to perform, or been in a situation where they have seen others refuse to perform, dangerous work? If so, what was the result of the refusal?

Students form into groups of three or four to discuss the effects on individuals of asking them to choose between their livelihood (their job) and their safety. Each group should elect a leader to present its conclusions to the class.

Source: *Whirlpool Corp v. Marshall*, 100 S.Ct. 883 [1980].

Customer-Driven HR Case 16.5

YOU MANAGE IT!

Desk Rage: Safe Office Environment or Explosive Reactions Waiting to Happen?

Costas worked long hours in cramped quarters at an Internet company in New York. He continually had to deal with rushed deadlines, but he kept a check on his frustration over the work demands and his work environment. One day his boss pushed him one time too many and Costas unloaded with an obscenity-laden tirade. He quit his job one week later commenting "sometimes you just snap."

Two engineers at an aerospace company in Connecticut had a disagreement over the proper procedure for filing paperwork regarding a faulty computer chip. The disagreement quickly escalated and the engineers had to be physically separated.

These two real-life workplace examples illustrate the explosion of tempers that can occur in the workplace. Such incidents led the *Wall Street Journal* to label the phenomenon "desk rage." The occurrence of desk rage is thought to be a function of various sources of stress. For example, lost tempers, shouting matches, and fistfights can be induced by overwork and crowding. As pointed out by Victor Scarano, director of occupational and forensic psychiatry at Baylor College of Medicine in Houston, "You can't run an engine at full throttle for 10 years and not expect it to crack." In addition to high work demands, many workers are finding themselves more cramped for space than ever before. Perhaps due to cost-containment efforts and the price of commercial real estate, the average number of employees per square foot is at a peak level in many office spaces. In addition, many employees commute long distances and by the time they reach their demanding and cramped work environments, they are already frustrated, if not irate, from battling traffic congestion. The problem of stress appears to be more of an issue in larger organizations with approximately a third of employees in organizations with more than 1,000 people reporting that they are "at least somewhat" stressed whereas 16 percent of employees in organizations with fewer than 100 people report this level of stress.

Although many organizations ignore the desk rage issue, there are some companies that have taken steps to manage the problem. General Motors Corporation, for example, offers meditation and tai chi at its workout facilities. At its tax center in Indianapolis, Ernst & Young has included golfing areas, fish tanks, and a recreation room where workers can nap.

Critical Thinking Questions

1. Do you think desk rage is a problem that should be dealt with in organizations? Why or why not?
2. What do you think should be done when people lose their tempers in the workplace? What disciplinary actions should be taken for episodes such as yelling and using obscenities, physical engagement, and hitting? Does one episode merit disciplinary action or would you wait for a pattern to develop? Why?
3. Given your judgments in response to item 2, construct a matrix made up of desk rage examples along one axis and possible disciplinary actions along the other. (You may want to consult Chapter 14 and consider including positive discipline as an option in the array of possible management actions.) Make checks in the cells of the matrix when each type of disciplinary action is appropriate for the various forms of desk rage. Explain your rationale for the discipline choices.

Team Exercise

The management of desk rage, if it occurs, seems to focus on relaxing people and helping them to deal with stress. However, this approach can be viewed as addressing the symptom, not the causes. If desk rage is a problem, it would seem worthwhile to try to solve the problem rather than alleviate the symptom. In other words, a cure would seem more advisable than temporary improvement.

As a team, address two fundamental issues:

1. Is desk rage a problem?
2. What should be done about it?

Divide your team in half so that the two issues can be separately but simultaneously addressed. For the first issue, generate measures you think would indicate the extent to which desk rage may be a problem. For example, questionnaire items measuring the stress employees experience could be an important indicator. Also consider using measures that ask people about their intention or likelihood to, for example, throw items or yell at others in the workplace. You may also want to include measures of the occurrence of rage, asking, for example, if employees have observed or experienced someone acting out various forms of desk rage in the workplace. Finalize your set of measures.

The second issue of what to do to manage the problem leads to a consideration of causes. Specifically, what might be the major causes of desk rage? You might begin to structure sets of possible causes by categorizing causes as either person or system causes. Person causes would be factors that reside inside a worker, such as someone naturally being "hotheaded" or having little impulse control. Situational causes would be factors outside of the person that the employee experiences as stress. For each cause, identify whether it fits in the person or system category and brainstorm what, if anything, could be done to eliminate, reduce, or somehow improve the causal factor.

As one team, put together your measures with your model of causes and management actions. Are there causes that aren't being addressed in the measures of the extent to which desk rage is a problem? If so, can you add or refine the measures to include these causes? Finally, how could you determine the effectiveness of actions you might take to manage the causes of desk rage?

Place yourself in the role of a consultant team. You have an assessment tool and a model of possible solutions if you find a problem. Sell your products and process to the rest of the class. What can you offer? Does every organization need to take action to manage desk rage? How will you know what to do and how can you tell if it will be effective? In sum, what will the rest of the class as a fictitious organization, get if it invests in your consulting team?

Source: Adapted from Costello, D. (2001). Desk rage incidents erupt in more offices . . . Long hours produce some short fuses. *Asian Wall Street Journal*, January 18, N1.

YOU MANAGE IT! Customer-Driven HR Case 16.6

The Guy's a Nut: Managing Irrationality in the Workplace

The environment was a central concern to maintenance carpenter grade II, John Drummond. Drummond was described by others as an environmentalist—actually, as an environmental nut case. He was disturbed over carbon monoxide emissions, lax standards for chemicals in drinking water, global warming, deforestation, smokestack emissions, and many other environmental issues. He felt his own company was not concerned enough with the potential impact of its operations on the environment. He would rant and rave to anyone who would listen. He circulated proenvironment petitions. He verbally accosted a worker spraying insecticide on the front lawn of the plant.

Drummond reached the opinion that discharges from the plant were polluting a nearby stream. He wrote a letter to the company president complaining about it. The president asked Tony Gennara, a manager at the plant, to explain to Drummond that environmental experts had approved the discharge as being within EPA standards and to do his job and stay out of management business. Gennara warned Drummond that he had gone too far and that there was no basis for his concern that the stream was contaminating the environment. Drummond wasn't deterred and the next day an OSHA inspector showed up at the plant in response to a complaint he had lodged. It took over an hour out of a busy day for Gennara to convince the inspector that the plant was in compliance.

After the inspector left, the frustrated and angry Gennara crafted a dismissal notice and sent it to the plant's general manager for approval.

Critical Thinking Questions

1. Do you think there is basis for the dismissal of Drummond? Explain.
2. Drummond is inordinately concerned with environmental issues. His colleagues at work consider him irrational. Do you think he is a safety risk?
3. What if a worker had the same level of inordinate focus as Drummond, but it was focused on weapons and the possible infringement of U.S. citizens' rights to own and use weapons? Would you consider such an employee a safety risk?

Team Exercise

Divide your team in half with one side taking the position of favoring the termination of Drummond and the other side supporting his referral to professional help, such as an employee assistance program. Debate which action is appropriate and why. In addition to the facts you already have about the case, although Drummond may have had some irrational concerns and beliefs, his performance as a carpenter was not an issue.

Following debate of this issue, as an entire team, draft a policy for managing irrational employees. What actions should be taken? Who and how should irrationality be determined? Are there various forms or gradations of irrationality that should be dealt with differently? What if a worker's irrational behaviors endanger others or somehow cause safety concerns? Should such situations be managed differently than others that don't seem to pose such a hazard? After you have the basics of your policy, share it with the rest of the class, including rationale for your guidelines.

Source: Adapted with permission from Dreyfack, R. (2002). Emotionally disturbed employee? Be practical, firm, and compassionate. *Plant Engineering, 56*, 18(2).

Emerging Trends Case 16.7

YOU MANAGE IT!

Getting Fit Online

Most people know what they should be doing to improve their health. The problem with leading a healthier lifestyle doesn't usually seem to be lack of knowledge. There seems to be, however, two areas of difficulty when it comes to overcoming health problems and improving wellness. One is the reluctance to deal with health issues in a public domain. For example, someone with high cholesterol might avoid going to a health fair that offers cholesterol testing because of the public nature of the event. The person may not want others to find out about his or her high cholesterol level. Although this may, at first, not seem a rational concern, such health information can be viewed by people as private and they may be embarrassed if it were made public. Furthermore, and staying with the example of a high cholesterol level, the person may fear that others might view the high level as a sign of weakness, as evidence that the person isn't taking care of himself or herself properly. They may not want the attention and concern from others that publicly dealing with a health issue may bring. Even if outcomes aren't publicly seen or overheard, just being seen by others at a health function could be a worry for some people that it will lead to unwanted questions and concern.

A second problem with getting people to improve their health is motivation. People often know, for example, that they need to exercise, but getting to it is the issue. Numerous excuses might arise, such as competing demands, timing, the cost of a membership at a gym, and so on. The central problem, though, boils down to motivation. Changing behavior isn't easy and external prompting is often needed to push someone to make the change and to stick with it.

A growing number of organizations are attacking the problem of improving health and wellness with online services. The Web-based approach can reach everyone in an organization, not just people who are at headquarters, where the fitness facility and health fairs are located. In addition, an online health care system allows people to keep their privacy and maintain confidentiality concerning their health issues. According to the CEO of WellMed, an online health service used by Ford Motor Company, Chevron Corporation, and Microsoft Corporation, the anonymity of the Internet approach fosters higher participation rates. He also contends that the online service can be delivered for a much lower cost (around \$5 to \$15 per employee per year) than the traditional face-to-face wellness approach that relies on on-site health fairs and supplemental materials (around \$25 to \$50 per employee or more).

In addition to those benefits, there is at least one online health service that is promoting its ability to motivate employees to improve their health. Life Practice (www.life practice.com) focuses on changing behavior in the four key areas—exercise, nutrition, sleep and stress, and life balance. Other specific areas can be added by an employee by adding them as personal goals. The online service consists of a daily questionnaire that asks employees about how much food and water were consumed, how much exercise and sleep, and so on. The program then computes a score that employees can use to gauge how well they are doing in the program. In addition, the service includes an online "coach" that sends a daily e-mail either praising employees for progress toward their health goals or admonishing them to try harder if they are not making progress.

The Life Practice program is currently in use or being tested by organizations. A senior vice president at Vytra Health Plans in Melville, New York, liked the approach and gave it a six-month trial that ended in the summer of 2002. Other companies piloting the program report that the daily e-mails seem to help people stay on track. The idea is that the online "coach" motivates people to stay with their program for negligible administrative burden or cost.

Critical Thinking Questions

1. The online approach to improving health and fitness shifts responsibility from the employer to the employees. The approach is one of self-service in which it is up to the

workers to use the online tool to manage and improve their own fitness. Do you agree with this approach of shifting responsibility for health to the employees? What responsibility, if any, should the employer have in regard to employee health? Is offering the online service sufficient?

2. The self-service nature of the online approach fits with the general trend in organizations toward empowerment. However, some people seem to need a more directive approach when it comes to health improvement. For example, personal trainers are an expense that some people claim is necessary if they are to improve and maintain their fitness levels. These people need the direction, social interaction, and expectations that a face-to-face approach provides. Do you think an online approach will work for people who think they need this face-to-face directive approach? If not, should the employer be concerned and offer an alternative? Are there certain types of people for whom an online system would be effective? Do you think measurement of this characteristic should be part of the selection process?
3. A possible downside of online tracking of progress, such as the approach used by Life Practice, is falsification of data. An employee could easily enter data indicating activities and other progress toward a health goal that never occurred. How much of a problem do you think this might be? Would there seem to be more of a chance of this problem occurring with an online approach than with the traditional face-to-face approach to wellness?

Team Exercise

Online health programs offer lower costs and rationale can be generated that supports the potential effectiveness of the approach (e.g., anonymity and electronic motivation). However, return on investment (ROI) only occurs if a program is used and develops the intended results. Simply placing a program online and reducing costs does not mean that there will be a positive return on the investment.

a. As a team, identify measures that would serve as criteria for effectiveness of a health improvement program. Use the levels (reaction, behavior, results, ROI) framework presented in the training chapter (Chapter 8) to structure and guide your measures.
b. What level of evidence would you want before making a long-term commitment to an online approach to health improvement?
c. Consider the potential costs and benefits of an online approach, traditional approach, and a blended approach to health improvement. A blended approach could offer the advantage of online assessment and tracking along with the social motivation of, for example, the routine and bond developed when engaging in fitness activities with a group of colleagues. Which approach would your team estimate as providing the best cost/benefit ratio? Are there ways to shift costs in the traditional or blended approach to employees who prefer these approaches? Should these costs be shifted, and would it be a fair policy? Summarize your conclusions and provide your recommendations to the rest of the class.

Sources: Adapted from Prince, M. (2002). Altering lifestyles through Internet fitness monitoring. *Business Insurance, 36*, T6; and Purdum, T. (2002). Healthy, wealthy, wise and Web based: Online wellness programs can keep employees healthy while lowering health-care costs. *Industry Week, 251*, 52(1).

YOU MANAGE IT!

Emerging Trends Case 16.8

The Bioterrorism Threat: Managing for Safety

The introduction of anthrax into the mail system following the September 11, 2001, attack on the World Trade Center made real the possibility of bioterrorism. The resulting illnesses and deaths due to anthrax made clear that the mail may be a source of hazard. The presence of mail centers and the distribution of mail in workplaces make the mail a safety issue for organizations. Although small, an envelope can be an effective means for delivering bioterrorism weapons. The flaps of an envelope aren't always tight and bacterial spores can be squeezed out by machines or carriers and can be bellowed out by the weight of other parcels. A contaminated letter can leak its contents and expose a chain of handlers and the workplace to fatal infection.

In response to the bioterrorism threat, the U.S. Postal Service (USPS) has taken multiple steps to make the mail safe. For example, the USPS appointed a security task force to review all its procedures regarding mail security and the handling of hazardous materials. Employee training on safe mail handling has been stepped up. Facilities and employees have been tested for the presence of infection. Irradiation equipment has been put in place in some postal locations.

The threat of bioterrorism as well as more conventional terrorism, such as explosives, is a real concern in the mail system. However, given the amount of mail, the risk, over all, remains small. However, the risk is not equal across all organizations, with some being at a much higher risk for attack through the mail system than others. The following factors can help to identify the extent of an organization's vulnerability to a mail-based threat.

- *Foreign involvement*—the extent to which the organization has a presence in areas where there is instability and political unrest.
- *Type of business*—extent to which the organization is "high profile" and generates public attention or controversy.
- *Defense supplier*—extent to which the organization is perceived to support the U.S. military.
- *Politics*—extent to which the organization might be a target for hate groups.

Organizations, particularly those most at risk, need to be proactive and take steps to manage the possibility of a mail-based attack. The risk of a mail-based attack can be lessened and fear and anxiety can be reduced by developing a plan to manage this threat to safety. An emerging response plan would be a good place to start. Depending on the size of the organization and the degree to which it is judged to be at risk, it may be advisable to assign the duty of security coordinator of the mail center to an individual. Screening procedures for incoming mail need to be developed, including steps to follow to segregate and isolate suspicious packages.

Critical Thinking Questions

1. Do you think organizations need to be concerned with the possibility of a mail-based attack as part of their safety program? Why or why not?
2. Estimates of ROI often drive business decisions. However, safety issues can sometimes be difficult to fit into this framework. What dollar value, for instance, should be placed on an arm, a leg, or a life? How would you argue for the time and cost of implementing a risk management system in regard to the mail receipt and distribution function in an organization? What might be the major costs? What benefits might be associated with the risk management effort?
3. The possibility of a mail-based threat is analogous to the possibility of a customer receiving a defective product, but in this case the "defect" can be fatal. Much management attention has been directed to the prevention and elimination of defects in the production or service process. The quality approach has championed the idea that it is better to eliminate the occurrence or cause of errors rather than try to detect them. One reason for this assertion is that no screening system can be 100 percent effective—sometime, somewhere, a defect will get through to the customer.

Can you apply the quality approach to the issue of a mail-based threat? What do you think could be done from a quality management perspective?

Team Exercise

As a team, benchmark selected organizations in terms of their efforts in dealing with mail-based threats. What kind of screening do they do? Do they have an emergency response plan? Do they have a mail screening system? Do they have training related to mail handling and mail security? How much of their efforts were put in place after the September terrorist attacks and the anthrax scare? These are some of the issues you may want to address.

Include in your benchmarking efforts an assessment of the degree of risk experienced by each organization. Make this assessment by using the vulnerability factors just identified. Use these factors to form rating scales or interview questions and use them in your benchmarking study. Does your estimate of the degree of vulnerability seem to correspond with the extent of the risk management effort in the organizations?

Summarize your findings and conclusions. Share them with the rest of the class.

Source: Adapted from *Mail Center Management Report*. (2001). Mail center security checklist: How safe is your facility and its staff? December Newsletter of the Institute of Management and Administration, *1*, 12–14; *Mail Center Management Report*. (2001). U.S. Postal Service pulls out all the stops to make the mail safe. December Newsletter of the Institute of Management and Administration, *1*, 2–3.

International HRM Challenge

Challenges

After reading this chapter, you should be able to deal more effectively with the following challenges:

1. **Specify** the HRM strategies that are most appropriate for firms at different stages of internationalization.
2. **Identify** the best mix of hostcountry and expatriate employees given the conditions facing a firm.
3. **Explain** why international assignments often fail and the steps a firm can take to ensure success in this area.
4. **Reintegrate** returning employees into the firm after they complete an international assignment.
5. **Develop** HRM policies and procedures that match the needs and values of different cultures.

How to distinguish foreign firms from domestic firms becomes less clear as globalization continues to increase. You saw in Chapter 4 that an increasing percentage of the workforce in the industrialized world consists of people who have immigrated from someplace else. Since moving to the United States 15 years ago, Nicaraguan-born Roberto Castillo has had a series of jobs at car dealerships—first Ford, then Pontiac, and eventually Hyundai. But two years ago he landed the job he really wanted: selling Toyotas. "Everyone knows the reputation (of Toyotas)," he says, "so you never have to sell (people) on the benefits." Nowadays, Castillo works at Longo Toyota in the Los Angeles suburb of El Monte. Last year he piled up commissions worth more than $80,000. "You can make good money with Toyota," he says. Toyota is the world's third largest automaker.

From headquarters in Toyota City, 62 miles east of Nozoya, Japan, Toyota Chief Executive Fujio Cho has given Toyota's top executives this simply stated goal: "We must Americanize!"

That goal and its results are being achieved. Consider the following facts, including some statistics that scare Toyota's rivals in Detroit:

- Toyota sells more vehicles in the United States (1.74 million) than in Japan (1.71 million). Analysts figure that almost two-thirds of Toyota's operating profit comes from the United States. Some Toyota executives think it won't be long before Toyota displaces DaimlerChrysler's third place in the Big Three.
- Toyota's U.S. factories and dealerships employ 123,000 Americans—that's more employees than the number working for Coca-Cola, Microsoft, and Oracle combined.
- Toyota's top U.S. executives are increasingly U.S. hires. Ford Motor Company veteran Gary Convis was recently appointed manager of Toyota's key Georgetown, Kentucky, plant, which makes the Camry. James Press, chief operating officer of Toyota Motor Sales USA Inc. in Torrance, California, says "Thirty years ago, we were more dependent on Japan." Now, Press says, "there's not much Japanese influence on a day-to-day basis."

Toyota executives in Japan are reluctant to stray from the Toyota Way, a philosophy set forth by the company's legendary founder Kiichiro Toyoda, a zealot for consensus-style decision making, merciless cost cutting, and fanatical devotion to quality and customer satisfaction. So, to ensure that it doesn't lose what makes it great, Toyota in 2002 opened the Toyota Institute, an internal, M.B.A.-style program near Toyota City whose faculty is comprised of Toyota executives and visiting professors from the University of Pennsylvania's Wharton School.

THE MANAGERIAL PERSPECTIVE

As firms such as Toyota begin to dominate international markets, HRM practices must have a global perspective to give the company a competitive advantage. There are at least 53,000 multinational companies with 45,000 affiliates worldwide.[1] Managers must find ways to select, retain, promote, reward, and train employees to help them meet this global challenge. Even small firms trying to export their products or services via the Internet must learn to cope with the challenges of international business. For the growing number of companies operating in various countries, it is imperative that the HRM system and practices can be successfully adapted to a variety of cultural, socioeconomic, and legal conditions.

Virtually every U.S. company now faces competition from abroad, and the fortunes of most U.S. firms, large and small, are inextricably bound to the global economy.[2] In this chapter we demonstrate how managers can use HRM practices to enhance their firms' competitiveness in an era of international opportunities and challenges. First, we cover the stages of international involvement, the challenges of expatriate job assignments, and ways to make those assignments more effective. We then discuss the development of HRM policies in a global context and the specific HR concerns of exporting firms.

The Stages of International Involvement

As Figure 17.1 shows, firms progress through five stages as they internationalize their operations.[3] The higher the stage, the more HR practices must be adapted to diverse cultural, economic, political, and legal environments.

- In *Stage 1*, the firm's market is exclusively domestic. Prior to World War II, most U.S. firms fell into this category. One firm at this stage today is Boulder Beer, which produces its ales in the Boulder, Colorado, area and seldom sells them outside the Mountain States region. Many other U.S. firms are still at this stage, but their number is diminishing, particularly in manu-

Figure 17.1

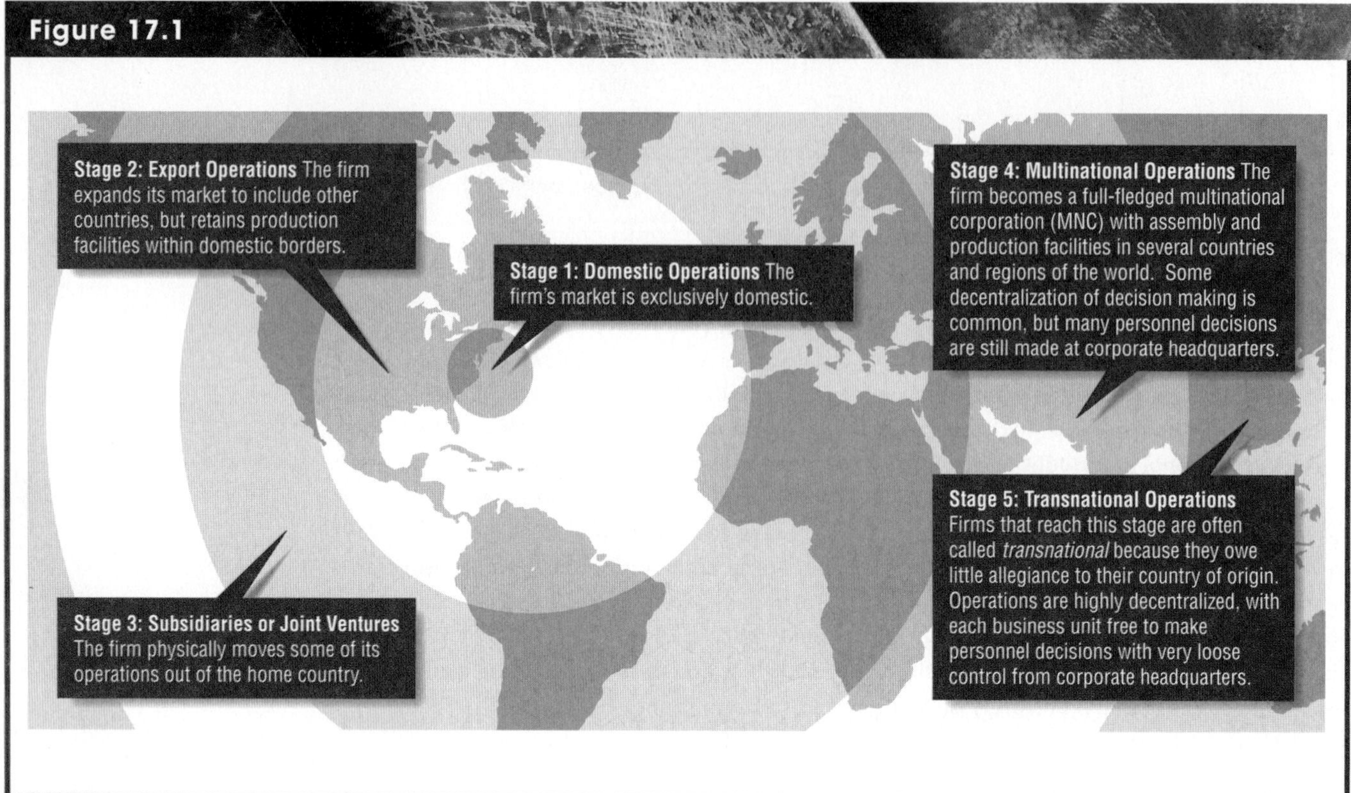
Stage 2: Export Operations The firm expands its market to include other countries, but retains production facilities within domestic borders.
Stage 1: Domestic Operations The firm's market is exclusively domestic.
Stage 4: Multinational Operations The firm becomes a full-fledged multinational corporation (MNC) with assembly and production facilities in several countries and regions of the world. Some decentralization of decision making is common, but many personnel decisions are still made at corporate headquarters.
Stage 5: Transnational Operations Firms that reach this stage are often called *transnational* because they owe little allegiance to their country of origin. Operations are highly decentralized, with each business unit free to make personnel decisions with very loose control from corporate headquarters.
Stage 3: Subsidiaries or Joint Ventures The firm physically moves some of its operations out of the home country.

The Stages of Internationalization

facturing. Staffing, training, and compensation for firms at Stage I are dictated primarily by local and/or national forces. The only sites considered for plant locations are in the United States, and only the national or regional market is considered in strategic business decisions about production and marketing issues.

- In *Stage 2*, the firm expands its market to include foreign countries but retains its production facilities within domestic borders. HRM practices at this stage should facilitate exporting of the firm's products through managerial incentives, appropriate training, and staffing strategies that focus on the demands of international customers.[4]

Bosch supports its international business practices with international training. For instance, Bosch uses its German training system to teach workers in other countries. Here Harmon Jones is learning his job in Charleston, South Carolina, with the help of a German training system.

An example of a Stage 2 firm is Turbo-Tek Enterprises, Inc., located in Los Angeles. It generates $50 million a year in revenues, 38 percent of which comes from overseas sales. The firm's single product is Turbo Wash, a water-spraying attachment for common household hoses. Turbo-Tek's entire manufacturing, packaging, and distribution system is designed with international markets in mind, and the firm's HRM practices play a crucial role in this system. Turbo Wash is produced in Los Angeles, but the product is repackaged in the Netherlands for European markets. Managerial bonuses are substantially based on foreign sales. Turbo-Tek rewards its employees for developing innovative ideas to increase exports. For instance, the firm's marketing department translated user instructions into 11 languages; production made changes to meet local tastes and needs, such as including a special adapter to fit English hoses; and research and development ensured that the exact chemical composition of the shampoo included with Turbo Wash would comply with strict governmental regulations in Finland, France, and other European countries.

Falling trade barriers are greatly increasing the number of U.S. firms that fall into Stage 2.[5] Approximately 40 percent of companies with fewer than 500 employees exported products and services in 2003—more than three times the number of companies that did so in 1992. For instance, Jeff A. Victor, who is general manager of $6 million Treatment Products Ltd., credits NAFTA (the North American Free Trade Agreement) for his firm's surging export volume. The company, which makes car cleaners and waxes, had been trying to expand its small presence in Mexico since 1990. But stiff Mexican tariffs made that impossible. After NAFTA went into effect in January 1993, Victor landed contracts with almost every major retail chain in Mexico. His shipments to Mexico have tripled to roughly $300,000, about 20 percent of the company's total current exports.[6]

- In *Stage 3,* the firm physically moves some of its operations out of the home country. These facilities are primarily used for parts assembly, although some limited manufacturing may take place. For instance, many U.S. apparel manufacturers have opened facilities throughout the Caribbean to assemble a wide variety of garments. The foreign branches or subsidiaries tend to be under close control of corporate headquarters at this stage, and a high proportion of top managers are **expatriates** (employees who are citizens of the corporation's home country). HRM practices at Stage 3 need to focus on the selection, training, and compensation of expatriates, as well as on the development of personnel policies for local employees where the foreign facilities are located.

Expatriate
A citizen of one country living and working in another country.

- In *Stage 4,* the firm becomes a full-fledged **multinational corporation (MNC),** with assembly and production facilities in several countries and regions of the world. Strategic alliances between domestic and foreign firms, such as that between Ford Motor Company and Mazda Motor Corporation to build trucks in Thailand, are very common.[7] While there is usually some decentralization of decision making for firms at Stage 4, many personnel decisions affecting foreign branches are still made at corporate headquarters, typically by an international personnel department. In addition, foreign operations are still managed by expatriates. Amoco, IBM, Rockwell, General Motors, General Electric, and Xerox are all at Stage 4. HRM practices at these companies are quite complex because they must deal with large numbers of expatriates and their families in overseas assignments, and diverse ethnic and cultural groups in multiple countries. They must also facilitate the control of overseas subsidiaries from corporate headquarters. Many of these firms merging with one another across national boundaries (such as the merger of Daimler from Germany and Chrysler from the United States) introduces another layer of complexity as firms try to integrate their new units and manage the culture clashes that may be inherent in cross-border deals.[8]

Multinational corporation (MNC)
A firm with assembly and production facilities in several countries and regions of the world.

- In *Stage 5,* the most advanced stage of internationalization, firms are often called **transnational corporations** because they owe little allegiance to their country of origin and have weak ties to any given country. Operations are highly decentralized; each business unit is free to make personnel decisions with very loose control from corporate headquarters. The board of directors is often composed of people of different nationalities, and the firm tries hard to develop managers who see themselves as citizens of the world. These firms freely hire employees from any country. For example, Olivetti, the large Italian-based conglomerate, has an extensive "no frontiers" recruitment program to hire managers and professionals from around the world.

Transnational corporation
A firm with operations in many countries and highly decentralized operations. The firm owes little allegiance to its country of origin and has weak ties to any given country.

HRM practices at Stage 5 companies are designed to blend individuals from diverse backgrounds to create a shared corporate (rather than national) identity and a common vision.

A Question of Ethics

U.S. law does not prohibit selection decisions based on marital status, as long as they are applied equally to men and women. Why might a company have such a policy? Is it ethical? Is it in the best long-term interests of the company?

For instance, Gillette (which develops and manufactures personal care products) has developed an extensive program in which local personnel offices in 48 countries search for the best young university graduates who are single and fluent in English. The individuals selected are given six months of training in the home country, and those who come through this probationary period successfully travel to Gillette's headquarters in Boston to begin 18 months of management: training. They are then sent on one- to three-year assignments overseas to gain greater international exposure. In the words of Gillette's international personnel director, "The person we are looking for is someone who says, 'Today, it's Manila. Tomorrow, it's the U.S. Four years from now, it's Peru or Pakistan.' . . . We really work hard at finding people who aren't parochial and who want international careers."[9]

Determining the Mix of Host-Country and Expatriate Employees

Wholly owned subsidiary
In international business, a foreign branch owned fully by the home office.

Joint venture
In international business, a foreign branch owned partly by the home office and partly by an entity in the host country (a company, a consortium of firms, an individual, or the government).

Once a firm passes from the exporting stage (Stage 2) to the stage in which it opens a foreign branch (Stage 3)—either a **wholly owned subsidiary** (the foreign branch is fully owned by the home office) or a **joint venture** (part of the foreign branch is owned by a host-country entity: another company, a consortium of firms, an individual, or the government)—it must decide who will be responsible for managing the unit. This decision is important because in most cases the investment required for plant and equipment is enormous, and the success of the foreign venture (like that of any other business) depends largely on who is in charge. A survey of 151 executives representing 138 large companies identified the choice of management for overseas units as one of their most crucial business decisions.[10]

There are three approaches to managing an international subsidiary: ethnocentric, polycentric, and geocentric.[11]

Ethnocentric approach
An approach to managing international operations in which top management and other key positions are filled by people from the home country.

- In the **ethnocentric approach** to managing international operations, top management and other key positions are filled by people from the home country. For instance, Fluor Daniel, Inc., has 50 engineering and sales offices on five continents and concurrent construction projects in as many as 80 countries at any given time. The firm uses a large group of expatriate managers, including 500 international HRM professionals who are involved in recruitment, development, and compensation worldwide and who report directly to a corporate vice president. The vice president himself is a roving expatriate who spends at least two months a year abroad supervising international operations.

Polycentric approach
An approach to managing international operations in which subsidiaries are managed and staffed by personnel from the host country.

- In the **polycentric approach,** international subsidiaries are managed and staffed by personnel from the host country. For instance, General Electric's Tungsram subsidiary in Hungary runs eight factories and employs 8,000 people, almost all of whom are Hungarian nationals.[12] Coca-Cola, which has been global for most of its 100-year history, currently operates in 160 countries, employing about half a million workers worldwide.[13]

  Some countries are trying to attract multinational firms by preparing local executives to work in the local factories and offices of these firms. For example, executive M.B.A. programs are being launched across China. In 2003, there were 21 degree programs run jointly by Chinese and foreign universities, plus about 40 more degree programs by Chinese universities alone. For the joint ventures, foreign institutions—including Harvard and Fordham universities—and the European Union provide much of the curriculum and faculty. Chinese universities supply the rest.[14] In addition, a flurry of online business skills courses are being designed for use in China.[15]

Geocentric approach
An approach to managing international operations in which nationality is downplayed and the firm actively searches on a worldwide or regional basis for the best people to fill key positions.

- In the **geocentric approach,** nationality is deliberately downplayed and the firm actively searches on a worldwide or regional basis for the best people to fill key positions.[16] Transnational firms (those in Stage 5) tend to follow this approach. For example, Electrolux (the vacuum cleaner company) has for many years attempted to recruit and develop a group of international managers from diverse countries. These people constitute a mobile pool of managers who are used in a variety of facilities as the need arises. Rather than representing a particular country, they represent the organization wherever they are. Most important to Electrolux is the development of a common culture and an international perspective, and the expansion of its international networks.[17] Similarly, a German autoparts supplier, Bosch hires managers from all over the world and brings together researchers from different nationalities to work on common projects.[18]

As Figure 17.2 shows, there are both advantages and disadvantages to using local nationals and expatriates in foreign subsidiaries. Most firms use expatriates only for key positions such as senior managers, high-level professionals, and technical specialists. Because expatriates tend to be very costly (approximately $88,000 to $253,000 per person per year, with some expatriates in Tokyo costing $473,396 a year), it makes little financial sense to hire expatriates for positions that can be competently filled by foreign nationals. It has been estimated that an expatriate costs 2000 to 4000 percent more than a local employee.[19] For instance, most firms pay private school tuition, which can be very expensive, for expatriate's children. Just the annual fees of the International High School in Geneva, Switzerland, range from $18,000 to $20,000 per student.[20] In addition, many countries require that a certain percentage of the workforce be local citizens, with exceptions usually made for upper management. In general, reliance on expatriates increases when:[21]

- **Sufficient local talent is not available** This is most likely to occur in firms operating in developing countries. For instance, top managers of Falcombridge and Alcoa (both mining companies operating in Latin America and Africa) are almost always expatriates.

Figure 17.2

Locals

Advantages	Disadvantages
■ Lowers labor costs ■ Demonstrates trust in local citizenry ■ Increases acceptance of the company by the local community ■ Maximizes the number of options available in the local environment ■ Leads to recognition of the company as a legitimate participant in the local economy ■ Effectively represents local considerations and constraints in the decision-making process ■ Greater understanding of local conditions	■ Makes it difficult to balance local demands and global priorities ■ Leads to postponement of difficult local decisions (such as layoffs) until they are unavoidable, when they are more difficult, costly, and painful than they would have been if implemented earlier ■ May make it difficult to recruit qualified personnel ■ May reduce the amount of control exercised by headquarters

Expatriates

Advantages	Disadvantages
■ Cultural similarity with parent company ensures transfer of business/management practices ■ Permits closer control and coordination of international subsidiaries ■ Gives employees a multinational orientation through experience at parent company ■ Establishes a pool of internationally experienced executives ■ Local talent may not yet be able to deliver as much value as expatriates can ■ Provides broader global perspective	■ Creates problems of adaptability to foreign environment and culture ■ Increases the "foreignness" of the subsidiary ■ May involve high transfer, salary, and other costs ■ May result in personal and family problems ■ Has disincentive effect on local-management morale and motivation ■ May be subject to local government restrictions

Sources: Adapted from Hamil, J. (1989). Expatriate policies in British MNNs. *Journal of General Management, 14*(4), 20; Sheridan, W. R., and Hansen, P. T. (1996, Spring). Linking international business and expatriate compensation strategies. *ACA Journal*, 66–78; Hill, C. W. (2000). *International Business*. Chicago: Irwin; and Wilson, M. L. (1999, July 16). She got the last laugh when colleagues bet she would fail in Japan. *Wall Street Journal*, B-1.

Advantages and Disadvantages of Using Local and Expatriate Employees to Staff International Subsidiaries

- **An important part of the firm's overall business strategy is the creation of a corporatewide global vision** Some firms prefer to make subsidiaries part of an international network with a shared corporate identity. When this is the case, expatriates are used to link the organization's international subsidiaries. (Locals are generally more concerned with their own unit than with the organization as a whole.) For example, Whirlpool Corporation, the world's largest home appliance manufacturer, has operations in 40 countries and is deeply committed to the notion of one global company with one global vision. The company has a worldwide leadership program involving extensive use of expatriates, conferences that bring together top executives from different subsidiaries around the world, and global project teams that tackle common problems and facilitate a total international integration process.[22]
- **International units and domestic operations are highly interdependent** In some cases, the production process requires that all divisions of a corporation, both international and domestic, work closely with one another. This is particularly necessary when the output of one business unit is needed as an input by another business unit of the same corporation. For example, IBM, Hewlett-Packard, and Xerox have specialized manufacturing facilities in different parts of the United States and the world. The outputs of these different facilities (computer chips, software) must be closely monitored and integrated to produce highly sophisticated products such as computers, medical equipment, and photocopying machines. Linking production processes generally calls for greater reliance on expatriate managers and specialists, who can bridge the gaps and tie the units of the organization together.

  This policy is not necessary in corporations with primarily stand-alone operations with low interdependence across units. For instance, McDonald's Corporation operates in more than 50 countries; approximately 3,000 of its 12,000 restaurants are located overseas. The primary involvement of corporation headquarters in Oak Brook, Illinois, is to train restaurant managers from all over the world in McDonald's Hamburger University. The company also has five international personnel directors who serve as internal consultants. Thus, although McDonald's demands strict product quality standards across countries, expatriates play a minor role in this process because each restaurant functions as a highly autonomous unit.

  Technology has dramatically reduced the need for expatriates to link the international units of the firm to the home office. For instance, a Wal-Mart outpost opens every week somewhere outside the United States, managed primarily by local employees. Wal-Mart can rely on local employees because it has 1,000 full-time information technology developers in the United States who develop systems that allow close monitoring of the stores from corporate headquarters in Bentonville, Arkansas.

  The monitoring process works this way: At a Wal-Mart store in another country, an employee leans over a freezer full of boneless, skinless chicken breasts. He swipes a handheld computer over a bar code near the freezer. Within seconds, computers in the home office download a pile of statistics—how much the store makes selling chicken breasts, how many packages it has on hand, how many are on their way to the store, and how many are sitting in freezers within a 150-mile radius.

  Wal-Mart's computers track everything there is to know about all the products the company sells. They know how much an item costs, the time a checkout person needs to scan it at the register, other items customers tend to buy along with it, and how many more the supplier has on hand. And Wal-Mart's executives know exactly how to use those data to keep the company's merchandisers in sync with its stores, its stores in sync with its distribution centers, and its distribution centers in sync with its suppliers.[23]
- **The political situation is unstable** Corporations tend to rely on expatriates for top management positions when the risk of government intervention in the business is high, when actual or potential turmoil within the country is serious, when the threat of terrorism exists, and when there has been a recent history of social upheaval in the country. Although expatriate top managers may increase tensions between nationalistic groups and a foreign firm, they do provide some assurance to the home office that its interests are well represented locally. Expatriates are also less susceptible to the demands of local political forces.

  Most Western ventures in the new republics of Eastern Europe and the former Soviet Union are run by expatriates. The same is true in the few remaining communist countries, where political instability remains potentially high.[24]

- **There are significant cultural differences between the host country and the home country** The more dissimilar the culture where the subsidiary is located to that of the home office (in terms of language, religion, customs, and so forth), the more important it is to appoint expatriates who can serve as interpreters or go-betweens for the two cultures. Since this boundary-spanning role demands much cross-cultural sensitivity, the MNC needs to select and carefully train individuals suitable for these positions. This may require considerable career planning.[25]

  Researchers have identified nations and world regions where dissimilarities with U.S. culture are great and the expatriate needs exceptional skills to be successful. Cultural barriers are lowest in European countries, Canada, Australia, and New Zealand; midrange in most of Latin America; and greatest in India/Pakistan, Southeast Asia, the Middle East, North Africa, East Africa, and Liberia.[26] A recent study indicates that among countries with the largest percentage of U.S. expatriates, the countries that present the greatest assignment challenges include (in order of ranking) China, Brazil, Russia, India, and Japan.[27] Economic hardship can complicate cultural adjustments in less-developed countries.[28]

The Challenges of Expatriate Assignments

One of the most challenging tasks for any international firm is to manage its expatriate workforce effectively. The statistics, unfortunately, are not encouraging. The failure of U.S. expatriates—that is, the percentage who return prematurely, without completing their assignment—is estimated to be in the 20 to 40 percent range. This failure rate is three to four times higher than the failure rates experienced by European and Asian companies. Perhaps this accounts for the fact that more and more U.S. firms prefer to send Europeans or Asians to foreign assignments, which usually last from one to three years.[29] One reason for the high U.S. failure rate: Two generations of economic dominance and a strong domestic market have contributed to the creation of a colonial mentality in many U.S. companies.[30]

Failures can be very expensive. Premature returnees cost $100,000 to $300,000 each in 2003, which translates into $3.9 billion per year in direct costs to U.S. firms. The more intangible costs of failure include business disruptions, lost opportunities, and negative impact on the firm's reputation and leadership and are probably many times greater. In addition, the personal hardship on the people involved and their families, including diminished self-image, marital strife, uprooted children, lost income, and tarnished career reputation, can be substantial.[31]

Why International Assignments End in Failure

It is important to understand the reasons behind expatriates' high failure rates so that preventive measures can be taken. Six factors account for most failures, although their relative importance varies by firm.[32] These are career blockage, culture shock, lack of cross-cultural training, an overemphasis on technical qualifications, a tendency to use international assignments as a way to get rid of problem employees, and family problems.

Career Blockage

Initially, many employees see the opportunity to work and travel abroad as exciting. But once the initial rush wears off, many feel that the home office has forgotten them and that their career has been sidetracked while their counterparts at home are climbing the corporate ladder. One survey conducted about 10 years ago indicates that less than one-half of 1 percent of U.S. expatriates view international assignments as a career route to the top.[33] In fact, although U.S. companies give themselves high marks for career planning for their expatriate employees, most of their employees do not, according to another survey by the Society for Human Resources Management (SHRM) conducted in 1993. Only 14 percent of the 209 expatriate managers who completed the society's questionnaire said their firm's career planning for them was sufficient.[34] Fortunately, this situation may be changing for the better, although there is still a long way to go. A recent survey in which the SHRM also participated indicates that in comparing the careers of expatriates against employees with no international experience, 41 percent of respondents report that expatriates obtain new positions in the company more easily; 39 percent said that expatriates are promoted faster; and 27 percent say that the expatriate assignment helped them get a better job at another company.[35]

Culture Shock

Culture shock
The inability to adjust to a different cultural environment.

Many people who take international assignments cannot adjust to a different cultural environment, a phenomenon called **culture shock.** Instead of learning to work within the new culture, the expatriate tries to impose the home office's or home country's values on the host country's employees. This practice may trigger cultural clashes and misunderstandings that escalate until the expatriate decides to return home to more familiar surroundings—perhaps leaving a mess behind.

In his book *Going International*, coauthor and consultant Lewis Griggs recounts the culture shock of a female vice president of a U.S. company doing business in Saudi Arabia. She was invited to dinner at the home of a Saudi businessman, and, on entering the home, was escorted to a room set aside for women. Feeling that she was not being accorded proper respect, she joined the men in their dining room. Dinner and business discussion ended abruptly.

Firms can help employees avoid culture shock by using selection tools to choose the employees with the highest degree of cultural sensitivity. However, research indicates that few companies are doing so. For example, only 18 percent of the companies in a mid-1990's survey used structured interviews, only 12 percent used candidate/spouse self-assessment, only 6 percent used psychological and cognitive testing, and only 2 percent used a formal assessment center.[36]

Lack of Predeparture Cross-Cultural Training

Surprisingly, only about one-third of MNCs provide *any* cross-cultural training to expatriates, and those that do tend to offer rather cursory programs.[37] Often the expatriate and his or her family literally pack their bags and travel to their destination with only a U.S. passport and whatever information they could cull from magazines, tourist brochures, and the library. This is a recipe for trouble, as the following example illustrates:

> I once attended a business meeting in Tokyo with a senior U.S. executive. The Japanese go through a very elaborate ritual when exchanging business cards, and the American didn't have a clue. She just tossed some of her business cards across the table at the stunned Japanese executives. One of them turned his back on her and walked out. Needless to say, the deal never went through.[38]

Overemphasis on Technical Qualifications

The person chosen to go abroad may have impressive credentials and an excellent reputation in the home office for getting things done. He or she may seem like the natural choice to start a new international facility, to manage a subsidiary that needs tightening up, or to act as a troubleshooter when technical difficulties arise. Unfortunately, the same traits that led to success at home can be disastrous in another country. Consider the experience of one executive from a large U.S. electronics firm who spent only three months of what was supposed to be a two-year assignment in Mexico:

> I just could not accept the fact that my staff meetings would always start at least a half hour late and that schedules were treated as flexible guidelines with much room to spare. Nobody seemed to care but me! I also could not understand how many of the first-line supervisors would hire their friends and relatives, regardless of competence. What I viewed as nepotism of the worst kind was seen by them as an honorable obligation to their extended families, and this included many adopted relatives or compadres who were not even related by blood.[39]

In a recent survey, 96 percent of respondents rated the technical requirements of a job as the most important selection criteria for international assignments, largely ignoring cultural sensitivity.[40] This outlook is a recipe for failure. In more enlightened companies, such as Prudential Relocation (an arm of Prudential Insurance), nearly 35 percent of managers cite "cultural adaptability" as the most important trait for overseas success. Only 22 percent of Prudential managers cite technical skills as the most important.[41]

Getting Rid of a Troublesome Employee

International assignments may seem to be a convenient way of dealing with managers who are having problems in the home office. By sending these managers abroad, the organization is able to resolve difficult interpersonal situations or political conflicts at the home office, but at a significant cost to its international operations. Although the number of people in this category is difficult to assess, the "let's find an out-of-the-way place for So-and-So" syndrome is not unusual. The following true story was told to one of the authors:

> Joe and Paul were both competing for promotion to divisional manager. The corporate vice president responsible for making the selection decision felt that Joe should get the promotion but also believed that Paul would never be able to accept the decision and would actively try to undermine Joe's authority. Paul also had much support from some of the old-timers, so the only way to avoid the dilemma was to find a different spot for Paul where he could not cause any trouble. The vice president came up with the idea of promoting Joe to divisional manager while appointing Paul as a senior executive at the Venezuelan subsidiary. Paul (who had seldom been out of the country and who had taken introductory Spanish in high school 20 years earlier) took the job. It soon became obvious that the appointment was a mistake. Two months after being assigned to the Venezuelan post there was a major wildcat strike attributed to Paul's heavy-handed style in dealing with the labor unions, and he had to be replaced.

Family Problems

The inability or unwillingness of the expatriate's spouse and children to adapt to life in another country is one of the most important reasons for failure. In fact, more than half of all early returns can be attributed to family problems.[42] Given the stress the employee usually experiences in trying to function in unfamiliar surroundings, trouble at home can easily become the proverbial straw that breaks the camel's back.

It is surprising that most firms do not anticipate these problems and develop programs to prevent them from happening. Indeed, few companies consider the feelings of the spouses of those they have selected for international assignments.[43] One expatriate's wife comments:

> A husband who is racked by guilt over dragging his wife halfway around the world, or distracted because she is ill-equipped to handle a foreign assignment, is not a happy or productive employee. . . . Most women actually start out all right. The excitement quickly fades for a traveling wife, though, when her husband abandons her for a regional tour immediately upon arrival and she's left behind with the moving boxes and the responsibility of finding good schools. Or when she is left to hire servants to set up a household without knowing the language . . . [Often] they are asked to jump off their own career paths and abandon healthy salaries . . . just so that they can watch their self-esteem vanish somewhere over the international date line.[44]

The expectations of dual-career couples are another cause of failure in expatriate assignments. MNCs are increasingly confronted with couples who expect to work in the same foreign location—at no sacrifice to either's career. Yet one spouse usually has to sacrifice, and this often leads to dissatisfaction. When 10-year AT&T veteran Eric Phillips was asked to move to Brussels, his wife, Angelinà, had to give up her well-paying job as a market researcher. Although the move represented a terrific career opportunity for Phillips, his wife recalls finding it very difficult to adjust.[45]

Difficulties on Return

Although the failure of expatriates abroad has received the most attention in research journals, a number of studies suggest that expatriates' return home may also be fraught with difficulties. It is estimated that 20 to 40 percent of returning expatriates (called *repatriates*) leave the organization shortly after returning home.[46] Some employers report that nearly half of employees leave the company within two years.[47] Four common problems confronting returning expatriates are their company's lack of respect for the skills they acquired while abroad, loss of status, poor planning for the expatriate's return, and reverse culture shock.[48] The Manager's Notebook, titled "Communicate to Repatriate," summarizes some of the practices companies can use to counter these problems. We discuss these practices in greater detail later in this chapter.

MANAGER'S NOTEBOOK

Communicate to Repatriate

Companies that have relatively low repatriation failure rates attribute their success to intensive interactions with the individual and his or her family before, during, and after the international assignment. Here are some of the practices and programs that have been found to increase organizational commitment among expatriate employees:

- ***Advance career planning helps expatriates know what to expect when they return to the United States.*** Management needs to sit down with HR professionals and the employee to lay out a potential career path before the employee goes abroad.
- ***Mentors can make expatriates feel they are vital members of the organization.*** At Nashville-based Northern Telecom, Inc., for instance, senior managers and vice presidents correspond regularly with expatriate employees and meet with them periodically either at the home office or on location. The reentry process is much easier for employees who do not feel they were forgotten while they were away.
- ***Opening global communication channels keeps expatriates up-to-date on organizational developments.*** Some companies do this through newsletters and briefings. And, of course, telecommunications technology enables expatriates to stay in constant touch with the home office through faxes and e-mail.
- ***Recognizing the contributions of repatriated employees eases their reentry.*** Repatriated employees whose accomplishments abroad are acknowledged are more likely to stay with the company.

Source: Adapted from Shilling, M. (1993, September). How to win at repatriation. *Personnel Journal*, 40.

Lack of Respect for Acquired Skills

Most U.S. firms are still heavily oriented toward the domestic market. This is true even of those that have a long history of operating internationally. As a result, international experience is not highly valued. The expatriate who has gathered a wealth of information and valuable skills on a foreign assignment may be frustrated by the lack of appreciation shown by peers and supervisors at corporate headquarters. Some in the organization even see the expatriate as out of touch, particularly if the international assignment lasted several years. According to recent data, only 12 percent of expatriates felt that their overseas assignment had enhanced their career development, and almost two-thirds reported that their firm did not take advantage of what they had learned overseas.[49]

Loss of Status

Returning expatriates often experience a substantial loss of prestige, power, independence, and authority. This *status reversal* affects as many as three-fourths of repatriated employees.[50] A recent survey shows that disappointment upon return is so profound that 77 percent of returning expatriates would prefer to accept an international position with another employer than a domestic position with their current company.[51] It is common to respond to this situation with bitterness, as the following example illustrates:

> When I was in Chile, I had occasions to meet various ministers in the government and other high-ranking industry officials. Basically my word was the final one. I had a lot of latitude because the home office didn't really want to be bothered with what was happening in Chile and therefore was uninformed anyway. I made decisions in Chile that only our CEO would make for the domestic operation. When I returned, I felt as though all the training and experience I had gotten in Chile was totally useless. The position I had seemed about six levels down as far as I was concerned. I had to get approval for hiring. I had to get my boss's signature for purchases worth one-tenth of the values of ones I approved in Chile. To say I felt a letdown would be a significant understatement.[52]

Poor Planning for Return Position

Often management repatriates an employee with no idea of what position this person should hold in the home office. Uncertainties regarding their new career assignment may provoke much anxiety in returning employees. One survey suggests that more than half of expatriates were unaware of what job awaited them at home.[53] The following story is typical of returning expatriates:

> I received a letter from the home office three months prior to the expiration of my assignment in Hungary (where I was responsible for a team of engineers developing a computerized system for handling inventories in four new joint ventures). I was told that I would be assuming the position of Supervisor of Technical Services in corporate headquarters. It sounded impressive enough. I was astonished to find out upon return, however, that I was given the honorary title of supervisor with nobody under my command. It smelled like a dead rat to me so I jumped ship as soon as I could.[54]

Reverse Culture Shock

Most firms assume the returning expatriate will be happy to be back home. But this is not always true, particularly for those returning from extended international assignments. Living and working in another culture for a long time changes a person, especially if he or she has internalized some of the foreign country's norms and customs. Because much of this internalization occurs subconsciously, expatriates are usually unaware of how much psychological change they have undergone until they return home. It has been reported that as many as 80 percent of returning expatriates experience *reverse culture shock,* which sometimes leads to alienation, a sense of uprootedness, and even disciplinary problems.[55] One expatriate who had worked in Spain notes:

> I began to take for granted the intense camaraderie at work and after hours among male friends. Upon returning to the U.S. I realized for the first time in my life how American males are expected to maintain a high psychological distance from each other, and their extremely competitive nature in a work environment. My friendly overtures were often misperceived as underhanded maneuvers for personal gain.[56]

Despite all these difficulties, many managers today are lining up for international assignments as companies gradually realize that employees with international experience can be a valuable asset. One recent survey showed that a majority of companies have increased their expatriate populations since 1989 and expect to increase or maintain that volume.[57] The "out of sight—out of mind" mentality that has long governed international assignments is being replaced in some companies by the notion that these assignments should be structured to enhance the firm's global efforts. For instance, Gerber Products, which is busily building markets in Latin America and Central and Eastern Europe, has announced that from now on, international assignments will be emphasized as part of normal career development for company executives. As a result, Gerber's country manager in Poland feels he has an edge over many of his colleagues. "My overseas experience sets me apart from the rest of the M.B.A. bunch," he says. "I'm not just one of hundreds of thousands."[58]

Effectively Managing Expatriate Assignments with HRM Policies and Practices

Although expatriate assignments will probably always be more problematic than domestic transfers, companies can minimize the chances of failure by creating a sensible set of HRM policies and practices that get to the root of the problems we have discussed. In this section we look at how selection, training, career development, and compensation policies can help companies avoid these problems.

Selection

The choice of an employee for an international assignment is a critical decision. Because most expatriates work under minimal supervision in a distant location, mistakes in selection are likely to go unnoticed until it is too late. To choose the best employee for the job, management should:

- **Emphasize cultural sensitivity as a selection criterion** The firm should assess the candidate's ability to relate to people from different backgrounds. For instance, one large electronics manufacturing firm conducts in-depth interviews with the candidate's supervisors, peers, and subordinates, particularly those whose gender, race, and ethnic origin are different from the candidate's. Personal interviews with the candidate and written tests that measure social adjustment and adaptability should also be part of the selection process.
- **Establish a selection board of expatriates** Some HRM specialists strongly recommend that all international assignments be approved by a selection board consisting of managers who have worked as expatriates for a minimum of three to five years.[59] This kind of board should be better able to detect potential problems than managers with no international background. For instance, an employee may express the desire to work in South America where "maids are cheap." This kind of remark may be regarded as inconsequential or humorous by the HR director, but would probably raise a red flag among managers with international experience.
- **Require previous international experience** Although not always feasible, it is highly desirable to choose candidates who have already spent some time in a different country. The major reason the state of Utah is in the forefront of international business is its large Mormon population, whose church requires them to spend a minimum of two years as missionaries in another country. Some schools (such as the American Graduate School of International Management in Phoenix, Arizona) and some MNCs offer overseas internships. In this way, candidates acquire some knowledge of a country's language and customs before taking on a full-blown expatriate assignment.
- **Explore the possibility of hiring foreign-born employees who can serve as "expatriates" at a future date** Japanese companies have been quite successful at hiring young foreign-born (non-Japanese) employees straight out of college to work in the home office in Japan. These recruits enter the firm with little experience and exposure to work in their host country and, thus, are blank slates on which the Japanese MNC can write its own philosophy and values.[60] Some U.S. companies, such as Coca-Cola, have been following a similar practice for years.

As the labor market becomes more global, firms actively search all over the world for talent to meet their needs. For instance, the Internet is fueling worldwide hiring. An increasing number of prestigious universities around the world are offering business and professional programs where the best students from many countries learn from each other and establish lifelong relationships. These programs are an excellent recruitment source for MNCs.[61]

Businesses such as Citi-group, McKinsey & Co., and several Silicon Valley firms actively recruit students from the Indian Institutes of Technology. IIT has produced several star CEOs, including Sun Microsystems cofounder Vinod Khosla and US Airways CEO Rakesh Gangwal.

- **Screen candidates' spouses and families** Because the unhappiness of expatriates' family members plays such a large role in the failure of international assignments, some companies are screening candidates' spouses. For instance, Ford formally assesses spouses on qualities such as flexibility, patience, and adaptability, asking questions such as: "How do you feel about this assignment? Do you feel you can adjust?" Exxon, too, meets with spouses and children during the selection process.[62]

Emerging Trends

MANAGER'S NOTEBOOK

The Internet Is Removing Barriers to Labor in Service Sector

Antiglobalization protesters are often in the front-page news in such cities as Seattle, Naples, Washington, Buenos Aires, and Mexico City. These protestors worry about sweatshop labor in the Third World. But Western firms increasingly hire skilled service employees abroad, paying them higher wages relative to the wages in their local labor market (although the wages paid to Third World workers are a fraction of the wages the firm would have to pay to workers in its own country). Largely unnoticed by the protesters is a fundamental shift that has occurred in globalization. Microsoft Office and the Internet are as useful in Madrid or Kingston (Jamaica) as in Minneapolis—the service sector has gone mobile. Poor countries are sewing sneakers. They are also exporting billions of dollars in services, from answering 1–800 numbers to producing software coding and doing mathematical risk-modeling work.

The implications are immense. Consider:

- General Electric hired 6,000 people in India last year, bringing its head-count there to 10,000 to handle accounting, claims processing, customer service, and credit evaluation and research for GE around the world. This year it expects to hire roughly 1,000 scientists in India.
- More than 2,000 Moroccans are speaking to Spanish and French consumers from call centers near Rabat and Tangiers built by outsourcers and a unit of Spain's phone giant, Telefonica. India, the Philippines, Jamaica, Estonia, Hungary, and the Czech Republic also are establishing themselves as low-cost call center sites. Ireland used to be a call center favorite, but wages there now are on par with the rest of Europe.
- When Tony Blair went to India in 2002, he didn't visit the Taj Mahal; he visited the lavish corporate campus of Inform, one of the most successful players in the $12 billion market for offshore software coding and maintenance. The Nasdaq-listed company earned $131 million last year on $413 million in revenues. And, of course, success has many imitators: In India, the Philippines, Belorussia, and even in Ghana software coders and data-entry workers hope business will increase after new undersea fiber lines boost Africa-to-Europe bandwidth.
- Hong Kong Shanghai Bank Corp, which has 6,000 people in India handling back-office work, last fall announced it would triple its workers hired in India. HSBC joins companies such as British Airways (accounting), American Express (finance and customer service), America Online (customer service), and McKinsey & Co. (research) that already are enjoying savings of up to 60 percent in low-wage markets.

What's enabling all of this change? The Internet explosion and Moore's Law (whereby computer power grows exponentially each year without a corresponding increase in costs) have played a spectacular part—transforming fields such as logistics, design, marketing, engineering, and law into computer inputs and outputs. Thus, Eastern Europe, China, and India, with their immense labor forces and sophisticated schools, are opening up to the world economy. And there is a technological leapfrog effect. Thanks to powerful fiber optics, businesses that could hardly get a dial tone a decade ago can now link into the world.

Source: Adapted with permission from Lavin, D. (2002, February 1), Globalization goes upscale. *Wall Street Journal*, A-3.

Training

The assumption that people everywhere respond in similar fashion to the same images, symbols, and slogans has hurt U.S. companies offering their products in international markets. Consider the following examples:

- An international division of a U.S. airline translated its slogan, "Travel on leather," for the Latin American market. Unfortunately, the literal translation, *viaje en cuero*, means "travel naked." The advertisements had to be pulled.
- Choice Hotels now makes sure the suitcase it depicts in the German version of its international commercial is the hard-sided kind after discovering that, for Germans, a cloth suitcase conjures up images of job-seeking immigrants rather than upscale travelers.
- John P. Woolley, general manager of PC Industries, shipped a $10,000 replacement computer component to a French customer and was stunned when he was billed $2,500 for value-added tax. The company had to absorb the unexpected bill.[63]

If these companies had given their expatriate executives appropriate cross-cultural training before their departure, these blunders would never have been committed. Cross-cultural training sensitizes candidates for international assignment to the local culture, customs, language, tax laws, and government.[64] Ideally, the training process should begin nine to twelve months in advance of the international assignment.[65]

Because insensitivity to the local culture can have severe financial consequences, cross-cultural training seminars are increasing in global-minded companies. Although these seminars cost $1,000 and upward per manager, many companies feel the expense is minor compared to the huge cost of failed expatriate stints. For instance, despite massive cost-cutting moves at General Motors, the auto giant still spends nearly $500,000 a year on cross-cultural training for about 150 Americans and their families headed abroad. GM's general director of international personnel attributes the very low (less than 1 percent) premature return rate of GM expatriates to this training. The experience of a Cortland, Ohio, family transferred to Kenya by GM is typical. The family members underwent three days of cross-cultural training that consisted of a crash course in African political history, business practices, social customs, and nonverbal gestures. The family's two teenagers, who were miserable about moving to Africa, sampled Indian food (popular in Kenya) and learned how to ride Nairobi public buses, speak a little Swahili, and even how to juggle.[66]

Another type of cross-cultural training is designed not to address the cultural and political realities of a particular country but rather to give executives the skills to deal with a wide range of people with different values. For instance, Motorola has opened a special center for cultural training at its headquarters in Schaumburg, Illinois, with the goal of making Motorola managers "transculturally competent."[67]

Although all employees embarking on an international assignment would benefit from extensive training, economic sense dictates that the more rigorous and lengthy training be reserved for expatriates whose stay abroad will exceed one year and whose job assignment requires a good deal of knowledge of the local culture. A recent survey indicates that 57 percent of companies provide one day's worth of cross-cultural preparation; 32 percent provide it for the expatriate employee's entire family; and 22 percent for only the expatriate employee and spouse. Surprisingly, only 41 percent of firms mandated participation in cross-cultural preparation.[68] Figure 17.3 shows three approaches to cross-cultural training. The least expensive type, the *information-giving approach*, lasts less than a week and merely provides indispensable briefings and a little language training. The *affective approach* (one to four weeks) focuses on providing the psychological and managerial skills the expatriate will need to perform effectively during a moderate-length assignment. The most extensive training, the *impression approach* (one to two months), prepares the manager for a long assignment with greater authority and responsibility by providing, for instance, field experiences and extended language training. Ideally, at least a portion of these training programs should be targeted to the expatriate's family. Although Figure 17.3 is concerned with predeparture training, it is also possible (indeed desirable) to use similar "decompression" training programs for returning expatriates to help them cope with reverse culture shock.

Figure 17.3

Three Approaches to Cross-Cultural Training

Length of Stay	Length and Level of Training	Cross-Cultural Training Approach
1–3 years	1–2 months + High	**Impression Approach** Assessment center Field experiences Simulations Sensitivity training Extensive language training
2–12 months	1–4 weeks Moderate	**Affective Approach** Language training Role-playing Critical incidents Cases Stress-reduction training Moderate language training
1 month or less	Less than a week Low	**Information-Giving Approach** Area briefings Cultural briefings Films/books Use of interpreters "Survival-level" language training

Source: Adapted from Mendenhall, M., and Oddou, G. (1986). Acculturation profiles of expatriate managers: Implications for cross-cultural training. *Columbia Journal of World Business*, 78. Copyright 1986. *Columbia Journal of World Business*. Reprinted with permission.

Career Development

The expatriate's motivation to perform well on an international assignment, to remain in the post for the duration of the assignment, and to be a high performer upon returning to the home office will depend to a large extent on the career development opportunities offered by the employer. At a minimum, successful career planning for expatriates requires the firm to do two things:

- **Position the international assignment as a step toward advancement within the firm** The firm should explicitly define the job, the length of the assignment, and the expatriate's reentry position, level, and career track on return. Companies with successful expatriate programs, such as Dow Chemical and Arthur Andersen, have practiced this policy for years. At Whirlpool, a person's career may be planned for up to 25 years into the future through positioning in critical international locations that are clearly marked as posts along a career path leading to top management.
- **Provide support for expatriates** To prevent expatriates from feeling isolated and disconnected, the home office should stay in regular touch with them. Maintaining contact can be accomplished in a number of ways.[69] A popular method is the buddy system, in which a manager or mentor at the home office is appointed to keep in touch with the expatriate and to provide assistance wherever necessary. Another approach has the expatriate employee coming back to the home office occasionally to foster a sense of belonging to the organization and to reduce reentry shock. A third approach offers mini-sabbaticals in the home office at specified intervals (for example, for two weeks every six months) to keep the expatriate tuned in to current happenings and future plans at the corporate base. Some firms will pay for the expatriate's family to return home with him or her during this time.

- **Provide career support for spouse** The dislocated expatriate employee's partner is no longer considered the stereotypical "trailing spouse." In fact, if the partner is going to give up his or her job to move, giving it up would result in a reduction of family income averaging 28 percent.[70] Conducted by Merrill Lynch, 569 respondents to its survey indicated that most expatriates now expect the company to provide dual career support. For a company that does not meet that expectation, the expatriate assignment is likely to be disappointing.[71]

MANAGER'S NOTEBOOK

Emerging Trends

Supporting the Dual-Career Expatriate Couple

Most companies now realize that an expatriate's failure is often due to the unhappiness of the spouse whose career was thwarted as a "trailing partner." Surveys have shown that spousal career issues are among the main reasons why a domestic worker or manager turns down the opportunity to go on an expatriate assignment. To attract internationally mobile staff, employers need to reassure expatriate candidates that their spouses may be able to work in the host country. As companies strive for more diversity in their expatriate population, the issue has become more visible and requires a proactive effort to remove this barrier to mobility. Shell is a good example of how a multinational firm deals with this issue.

Shell International has established a Shell Spouse Expatriate Center in response to an employee attitude survey about expatriation. The survey highlighted the need for expatriates' spouses to continue to follow their own career paths. Many accompanying spouses and partners felt they would feel better about relocating if they had effective assistance in finding new employment in the host location.

Consequently, the Shell Spouse Expatriate Center attempts to help expatriate spouses and partners by providing:

- Up-to-date, useful information on job prospects, opportunities, and constraints in the host country.
- A series of workshops focusing on "managing your career for a life on the move," and covering self-assessment, portable skills, making a curriculum vitae/résumé, active job search in a new area, and job interview skills.
- Career options that present alternative paths—employment, self-employment, further education and training, volunteer work, and so forth—with consideration of short-term and long-term plans.
- A network comprising contacts with companies and organizations and an internal database of more than 1,000 Shell spouses worldwide.
- Resources including reference books and publications on careers, networking, curriculum vitae/résumés, self-employment, and job search; employment and education Web sites accessible via the Internet; distance learning opportunities worldwide; brochures on useful external services; job vacancy publications; and general information on companies and organizations.
- Financial assistance, funded by host companies, to help meet the costs incurred in transferring employment skills from one country to another, including reintegration into the home country (eligibility is not confined to spouses employed prior to expatriation); assistance typically covers job search and career counseling, continuing education and professional courses, business start-up advice, mandatory professional accreditation, and tuition for intensive language learning.
- Support from one posting to the next, helping the individual fulfill long-term career aspirations.

Source: Welk-Carton, K. V. (2001). The push to get work permits for expatriate spouses. *Innovations in International Careers. HR*, 27(4), 7–9.

Customer-Driven HR

MANAGER'S NOTEBOOK

Identifying and Developing Potential International Assignees

Companies usually turn to skills assessment resources for help in evaluating which employees might be suitable for international assignment, as well as for help in educating and preparing those employees to work and live successfully in the international location. Tools such as Prudential's Overseas Assignment Inventory (OAI) can help measure the attitudes and attributes that are important to cross-cultural adjustment. A standard instrument such as the OAI enables potential candidates to increase their understanding and awareness of the cultural factors that could affect their success or failure in an international assignment. This type of tool also provides the employee and spouse with the opportunity to study individual attitudes based on objective, relevant information, rather than subjective impressions.

Prudential's Overseas Assignment Inventory

The Overseas Assignment Inventory (OAI), Prudential Relocation International's assessment and development resource, evaluates potential candidates according to 14 distinct attributes considered vital to successful international adaptability:

- Expectations
- Open-mindedness
- Respect for others' beliefs
- Trust in people
- Discomfort tolerance
- Personal control
- Flexibility
- Patience
- Social adaptability
- Initiative
- Risk taking
- Sense of humor
- Interpersonal interest
- Spouse communication

Of these dimensions, more than several stand out as both critical and usually misunderstood:

Open-mindedness—the degree to which expatriate employees feel strongly about their own country's values, ideas, products, and ways of doing things; and the degree to which they are receptive to and nonjudgmental of the ideas and ways of other countries, cultures, and ethnic groups.

Flexibility—the ability and willingness to consider and accept viewpoints and action plans different from those you would normally adopt.

Personal control—the belief that your actions and abilities play a direct role in the process and outcome of the events in your life.

Patience—the ability to be patient in the face of unanticipated delays or frustrating situations.

Sense of humor—the ability to use humor to cope with difficult, tense, or confusing situations, and to face challenges with spontaneity and ease.

Discomfort tolerance—the willingness and ability to adapt to physical surroundings and circumstances that are different or less comfortable than your usual living conditions.

Source: Adapted from Hauser, J. A. (2000). Filling the candidate pool and developing qualities in potential international assignees. *Wordatwork Journal*, 9(2), 1–7.

Compensation

Firms can use compensation packages to enhance the effectiveness of expatriate assignments. However, compensation policies can create conflict if locals compare their pay packages to the expatriate's and conclude that they are being treated unfairly.

Planning compensation for expatriates requires management to follow three important guidelines:

- **Provide the expatriate with a disposable income that is equivalent to what he or she would receive at home** This usually requires granting expatriate employees an allowance for price differences in housing, food, and other consumer goods. Allowances for children's schooling and the whole family's medical treatment may also be necessary. The best-known cost-of-living index for world locations is published by Corporate Resources Group, a Geneva-based consulting firm that surveys 97 cities worldwide twice a year.

  The U.S. State Department also maintains a current cost-of-living index for most major cities around the world. Some of the most expensive locations around the world—including Tokyo, Osaka, London, and most Scandinavian cities—cost at least 50 percent more to live in than New York City.

  For short-term stays, the Runzheimer Guide provides per diem costs for 1,000 international cities. This index is used by hundreds of organizations to approve, benchmark, and budget travel expenses.[72]

  Maintaining income equality with the home office is not an exact science (for example, finding housing in Japan comparable to that available in U.S. suburbs is nearly impossible), but as a general rule, it is better to err on the side of generosity. See Figure 17.4 for a comparison of living costs in various cities around the world.
- **Provide an explicit "add-on" incentive for accepting an international assignment** This incentive may take several forms. The company may provide a sign-on bonus before departure. Or it may offer the employee a percentage increase over his or her home base salary; the standard increase is 15 percent of the base salary.[73] Or it may provide a lump-sum payment upon successful completion of the foreign assignment. Some firms offer a combination of these incentives. Generally, the greatest incentives are reserved for the least desirable locations. For instance, MNCs hoping to lure Western managers to Eastern Europe, where poor air quality, political instability, and a shortage of quality housing make assignments unattractive, often offer packages that include company-paid housing, subsidized shipment of scarce consumer goods, up to four trips home a year, and weekend getaways to Western Europe.[74] Oil companies operating in Colombia amid a 38-year-old civil war face a constant threat of terrorism. Expatriates have been kidnapped and murdered. Occidental Petroleum alone has seen its pipeline bombed by rebels about 170 times a year.[75] In this situation, most expatriates receive hardship pay three to five times greater than the pay they would earn at home.
- **Avoid having expatriates fill the same jobs held by locals or lower-ranking jobs** This is to prevent perceptions of inequity. Local employees tend to compare their pay and living standards to those of expatriates, and feelings of unfairness are more likely to surface if an expatriate at the same or lower rank than the local is receiving greater pay. Unfortunately, it may be impossible to prevent those feelings of inequity, particularly if a U.S. firm sends one of its top executives overseas. Compared to Western European countries, for instance, U.S. executives may earn as much as 20 times what a similar executive makes locally. These differences are greatly magnified in Eastern Europe, Asia, and less developed countries. Unless there are compelling reasons to do otherwise, the multinational firm should attempt to place locals in managerial positions.

Figure 17.4

Cost-of-Living Index 2001*

Seoul	147.0
Tokyo	138.8
Moscow	113.4
New York	100.0
Singapore	96.3
London	95.1
Beijing	84.0
Mexico City	77.6
Paris	65.4
Rio de Janeiro	64.9
Rome	60.3
Sydney	56.6
Bombay	55.5
Toronto	51.3

*For three-person U.S. family at $100,000 income level

Source: Koretz, G. (2001). Where expats spend the most. *BusinessWeek*, 30.

Living Costs Around the Globe

Calculating compensation packages for expatriate employees is one of the most difficult tasks facing MNCs.[76] Compensation used to be a relatively simple issue: Low-level local hires got paid in the local currency, while expatriate managers' pay was pegged to U.S. salaries. However, in an era of dramatic corporate restructuring to cut costs, expatriate packages based on U.S. salaries are increasingly being considered too expensive. Moreover, as companies move into the later stages of internationalization, they work with a team of international employees operating out of the home office rather than just expatriates. As it has become more costly to maintain salary equity between these two groups of employees, more U.S. companies have been devising pay packages like the one created by Oklahoma-based Phillips Petroleum Company. When a British geophysicist first went abroad to work for Phillips in the mid-1970s, he was paid in dollars and his salary was equivalent to that of someone in the United States doing a similar job. Today, under Phillips' third-party nationals program, he gets the same housing allowance, home leave, and educational assistance for his children. However, his salary is now pegged to the more modest level at which he would be paid in his home country rather than to the U.S. salary for that job.[77]

Still, some companies continue to compensate their expatriates generously. To avoid potential pay inequities when employees are transferred from one international post to another, 3M compares net salaries in both the old and the new country and provides the transferred employee with whichever pay package is higher.[78] And Seagram Spirits and Wine Group has come up with an "international cadre policy" for those expatriates who work abroad permanently (as opposed to expatriates who will return to the United States in the future). The package features a standardized cost-of-living adjustment and a global standard employee housing contribution that is the same regardless of location. For temporary U.S. expatriates, Seagram maintains what it terms a "pure expatriate" package that keeps people up to par with U.S. compensation standards.[79] One thing that makes these pay comparisons easier today is the availability of international pay and benefit surveys on the Web. For instance, Personnel Systems Associates offers a directory of 1,500 such surveys covering hundreds of job titles. The user can access a Microsoft Word file that works with the Internet browser to automatically connect to the survey sites.[80]

Role of HR Department

A recent survey asked expatriates, "What advice would you have for HR departments about handling expatriates?" According to Professor Joyce Osland, who conducted the study in 2002, "What they want most from the HR department is to have unnecessary uncertainty eliminated. There is enough ambiguity overseas—they don't need any more from the HR department. Expatriates want HR to remove obstacles." According to one survey respondent, "The first thing that HR needs to do is to make sure it knows how to handle the logistics such as getting the furniture moved. Because you have all of these little . . . [problems] that take up all of your time when you are trying to deal with other things . . . many people pull their hair out and scream, and all of a sudden get the mind-set, 'I hate you!' [toward HR]." Another respondent remarked, "A lot of the expatriates I met when I was over there were real unhappy with their jobs because . . . the company just had some slot and said, 'Good, let's have Harry do it in Belgium for three years,' with no real reason to have Harry there."[81] Whether or not HR deserves it, the HR department is sometimes a lightning rod for expatriates as the safest place to vent their frustrations.

Another recent survey by Polak International Consultants, an international human resources consulting firm, confirms that most expatriates are unhappy with the services provided by their HR departments; the survey respondents considered the HR department unprepared to meet the requirements of a global workforce. This suggests that a priority in coming years is for multinational corporations' HR departments to be more aware and sensitive to the needs of an international workplace.[82] To achieve this requires not only better service to expatriates but also keeping track of HR trends overseas. For instance, basic pay laws may be quite different overseas and may change often.[83] By offering strong logistic support (e.g., transportation, paperwork for visa application, work permits), providing accurate information (e.g., concerning schools, housing, clothing needs) about the foreign site, and developing clear job definitions with specific objectives, the HR department can help decrease the expatriate's perceived uncertainty of the foreign assignment.

Women and International Assignments

Although in 2003 women represented 49 percent of all managers in the United States, only 13 percent of American managers sent abroad are women. According to a recent study by Catalyst, an international consulting firm, the meager representation of women among expatriates is due to the following three misconceptions or erroneous assumptions about women's ability and will-

Figure 17.5

Strategies	HR Tool, Method, or Intervention	Possible Problems/ Strategies for Implementation
1. Select female expatriates who demonstrate the technical or managerial skills for the position. Don't send tokens.	Selection based on demonstrated competencies. Additional technical or managerial training prior to departure, if needed.	It may be difficult to find a person with every necessary credential who is willing to accept the assignment. The organization should identify every skill needed for a given global assignment.
2. Select female expatriates who possess a greater perceptual orientation (e.g., openness).	Select expatriates based on personality characteristics, such as openness and flexibility. Consider using the SAGE (Self-Assessment for Global Endeavors) or a similar instrument.	It may be difficult to find someone with the requisite personality characteristics who is willing to accept the assignment.
3. Train female expatriates on the norms, values, and traditions the host nationals possess regarding women.	Offer predeparture plus on-site, culture-specific training for female expatriates.	All of the difficult situations cannot possibly be anticipated.
4. To dispel the "token" image, MNCs should actively promote expatriate women as their "best-qualified" candidate.	Letters of introduction. In-person introduction by a senior executive. A statement of qualification. Any other culturally appropriate method for establishing credibility.	Some of these initiatives could be misinterpreted, depending on the cultural context. The intervention should be culture specific.
5. Provide female expatriates with an in-country support network or mentor.	Have a mentor back home and a method for communication. Have an in-country mentor.	Communication is more difficult from a great distance. Provide specific communication media (e.g., videoconferencing, e-mail) plus training on their use and protocol.
6. Offer mechanisms to improve the likelihood the spouses of female expatriates will adjust well cross-culturally.	Cross-cultural training for spouses. Male-oriented social networks. Language classes.	There is always a chance that the spouse's needs will not match what is being offered. The spouse may choose not to use the services.

Strategies for Maximizing the Effectiveness of Women on Global Assignments

ingness to handle international assignments: (1) Companies assume that women are not as internationally mobile as men, yet 80 percent of women have never turned down an expatriate assignment offered to them, whereas only 71 percent of men have never turned down expatriate assignments. (2) Companies assume that women encounter more work/life conflict working on a global schedule. However, nearly half of *both* women *and* men report they find work/life balance difficult. (3) Most companies believe clients outside the United States are not as comfortable doing business with women as they are with men. In fact, 76 percent of expatriate women said being a woman had a positive or neutral impact on their effectiveness overseas.[84]

Figure 17.5 addresses some of the ways women can overcome key barriers to getting selected for the global business arena.

Strategies	HR Tool, Method, or Intervention	Possible Problems/ Strategies for Implementation
	Reemployment assistance. Money for professional or personal development.	The options may not be available in a given location. To promote usage, try to match these services to the spouses' needs.
7. Offer mechanisms to improve the likelihood that the children of female expatriates will adjust well cross-culturally.	Day care. Educational assistance. Language classes. Cross-cultural training.	Some services may not be available for expatriate children in a given location. Find the necessary services for expatriate children.
8. Western female expatriates should not attempt to "blend in" with host national women.	Train women on how to cope with being "different" from the host national women. Train women on the behaviors that could be required (e.g., serving tea in Japan).	It may be difficult for the female expatriate to balance perceptions (i.e., not appear too masculine). Provide role models from which expatriate women can learn appropriate (and professional) behaviors.
9. Give host nationals greater exposure to successful women in the organization.	Have more professional women take short business trips to the host country to increase interactions between Western females and host nationals. Have host nationals take business trips to headquarters for the same purpose.	Provide pretrip training to professional women.
10. Offer training to the host nationals who are going to be interacting with female expatriates.	Offer training to host nationals before the female expatriate arrives on location.	The host nationals may not participate in the training; and if they do, they may not change their behaviors toward women as a result of the training.
11. Ensure that female expatriates fill jobs with high position power.	Succession planning into high-level expatriate positions for women.	Can be a risky strategy if the person in the position did not have the competence for the job.

Source: Adapted with permission from Caliguiri, P., and Cascio, W. F. (2002). Sending women on global assignments. Challenges, myths, and solutions. *Worldatwork Journal*, *9*(2), 1–8.

Figure 17.5 continued

Developing HRM Policies in a Global Context

Firms operating in multiple countries need to worry not just about meeting the special needs of expatriate employees but also about the design and implementation of HRM programs in diverse cross-cultural settings. One company that is widely viewed as exceptional in its achievement of a unified global HRM program—even with two-thirds of its employees working overseas—is Coca-Cola.

In many countries reliance on U.S., or Western, managerial practices is likely to clash with deeply ingrained norms and values.[85] For instance, the open-door style of management, which works well in a culture that readily accepts questioning of authority, will probably not work in countries where such behavior is considered unacceptable—for example, China.[86] Effectively meeting the multinational challenge requires a sophisticated HRM system that can be adapted to a variety of cultural conditions. In other words, rather than simply transferring abroad HRM practices that are based on the home country's social and cultural standards, managers should mold these practices to the cultural environment in which a particular facility is located.[87] If there is too much inconsistency between a nation's culture and a company's HRM practices, the company is likely to face noncompliance at best, and acts of open hostility at worst.

National Culture, Organizational Characteristics, and HRM Practices

"Culture is important to HRM practices." This statement may seem obvious, but its relevance may be lost in a country like the United States, where many of the best-known theories of management practice are firmly rooted in Western culture. Geert Hofstede, a Dutch professor, has spent the better part of his professional life studying the similarities and differences among cultures. He has concluded that there are five major dimensions to culture:

1. **Power distance** Extent to which individuals expect a hierarchical structure that emphasizes status differences between subordinates and superiors.
2. **Individualism** Degree to which a society values personal goals, autonomy, and privacy over group loyalty, commitment to group norms, involvement in collective activities, social cohesiveness, and intense socialization.
3. **Uncertainty avoidance** Extent to which a society places a high value on reducing risk and instability.
4. **Masculinity/femininity** Degree to which a society views assertive or "masculine" behavior as important to success and encourages rigidly stereotyped gender roles.
5. **Long-term/short-term orientation** Extent to which values are oriented toward the future (saving, persistence) as opposed to the past or present (respect for tradition, fulfilling social obligations).[88]

Although Hofstede's research has been criticized for being based largely on the experiences of employees working for only one company (IBM) and for downplaying the importance of cultural differences within countries, other evidence suggests that the five dimensions are a fair summary of cultural differences.[89] These dimensions have proved useful for examining how cultural factors affect organizations. Most important, they provide clues regarding the general configuration of HRM strategies that are most likely to mesh with a particular culture's values. Figure 17.6 (pages 597–601) outlines the characteristics of cultures ranking high or low on each of Hofstede's dimensions, lists sample countries falling at each end of the spectrum, and summarizes the organizational features and HRM practices that work best at each end of the scale.

The information in Figure 17.6 has enormous implications for international firms. As businesses move out of their home countries and employ people with potentially very different cultural values, it is essential that corporations consider the inevitable clash between their "exported" HRM practices and the national culture.

As a general principle, *the more an HRM practice contradicts the prevailing societal norms, the more likely it will fail.*[90] For instance, Hofstede describes management by objectives (MBO) as "perhaps the single most popular management technique 'made in the U.S.A.'"[91] because it assumes (1) negotiation between the boss and employee, or a not-too-large power distance, (2) a willingness on the part of both parties to take risks, or weak uncertainty avoidance, and (3) that both supervisors and subordinates see performance and its associated rewards as important. Because all three assumptions are prominent features of U.S. culture, MBO "fits" the United States. But in other countries—France, for example—MBO has generally run into problems because of cultural incompatibility:

> The high power distance to which the French are accustomed from childhood ultimately has thwarted the successful utilization of MBO as a truly participative process. . . . The problem is not necessarily

Figure 17.6

Power Distance: Organizational Characteristics and Selected HR Practices

Dominant Values	Sample Countries	Organizational Features	Reward Practices	Staffing/Appraisal Practices
		Power Distance		
High				
■ Top-down communications ■ Class divisions seen as natural ■ Authoritarianism ■ High dependence on superiors ■ Power symbols ■ White-collar jobs valued more than blue-collar jobs	■ Malaysia ■ Philippines ■ Mexico ■ Arab nations ■ Venezuela ■ Spain	■ Centralization and tall organizational structures ■ Traditional line of command	■ Hierarchical compensation system ■ Difference in pay and benefits reflect job and status differences; large differential between higher and lower-level jobs ■ Visible rewards that project power, such as a large office or company car	■ Limited search methods in recruitment; emphasis on connections and "whom you know" ■ Few formal mechanisms of selection ■ Superior makes selection choice for his or her sphere of influence ■ Personal loyalty to superior is crucial trait for advancement ■ Social class and extended family may play a role in personnel decisions ■ Nepotism may be commonly practiced ■ Formal appraisals lacking; more "verbal" or "psychological contracts" between supervisor and subordinate
Low				
■ Egalitarianism ■ Status based on achievement ■ Joint decision making ■ High value placed on participation ■ Low dependence on superiors ■ Disdain for power symbols ■ Hard work valued even if manual in nature	■ The Netherlands ■ Australia ■ Switzerland ■ Sweden	■ Flatter organizational structures ■ Decentralized control ■ Great degree of worker involvement	■ Egalitarian-based compensation systems ■ Small differences in pay and benefits between higher- and lower-level jobs ■ Participatory pay strategies (such as gainsharing) more prevalent	■ Multiple search methods; extensive advertisement ■ Formalized selection methods "to give everyone a fair chance" ■ Superior constrained in making selection choices ■ Selection based on merit; loyalty to superiors deemphasized ■ Contextual non-job-related factors (such as social class) ignored ■ Nepotism viewed as conflict of interest and even unethical ■ Formal appraisals based on nation of joint planning, two-way feedback, and performance documentation

(continued)

Cultural Characteristics and Dominant Values

Individualism: Organizational Characteristics and Selected HR Practices

Dominant Values	Sample Countries	Organizational Features	Reward Practices	Staffing/Appraisal Practices
		Individualism		
High				
■ Personal accomplishment ■ Selfishness ■ Independence ■ Belief in individual control and responsibility ■ Belief in creating one's own destiny ■ Business relationship between employer and employee	■ United States ■ Great Britain ■ Canada ■ New Zealand	■ Organizations not compelled to care for employees total well-being ■ Employees look after their own individual interests ■ Explicit systems of control necessary to ensure compliance and prevent wide deviation from organizational norms	■ Performance-based pay ■ Individual achievement rewarded ■ External equity emphasized ■ Extrinsic rewards are important indicators of personal success ■ Attempts made to isolate individual contributions (i.e., who did what) ■ Emphasis on short-term objectives	■ Emphasis on credentials and visible performance outcomes attributed to individual ■ High turnover; commitment to organization for career reasons ■ Performance rather than seniority as criterion for advancement ■ "Fitting in" deemphasized; belief in performance as independent of personal likes and dislikes ■ Attempts of ascertaining individual strengths and weaknesses and providing frequent feedback to employee
Low				
■ Team accomplishment ■ Sacrifice for others ■ Dependence on social unit ■ Belief in group control and responsibility ■ Belief in the hand of fate ■ Moral relationship between employer and employee	■ Singapore ■ South Korea ■ Indonesia ■ Japan ■ Taiwan	■ Organizations committed to high-level involvement in workers' personal lives ■ Loyalty to the firm is critical ■ Normative, rather than formal, systems of control to ensure compliance	■ Group-based performance is important criterion for rewards ■ Seniority-based pay utilized ■ Intrinsic rewards essential ■ Internal equity guides pay policies ■ Personal needs (such as number of children) affect pay received	■ Value of credentials and visible performance outcomes depends on perceived contributions to team efforts ■ Low turnover; commitment to organization as "family" ■ Seniority plays an important role in personnel decisions ■ "Fitting in" with work group crucial: belief that interpersonal relations are important performance dimension ■ Limited or no performance feedback to individual to prevent conflict and defensive reactions

Figure 17.6 continued

with MBO per se but the French managers . . . who are unaware that they are trying to exert control through the implementation of the objectives of MBO almost by flat.[92]

EEO in the International Context

As you well know by now, employee selection in the United States is highly regulated by federal and state equal employment opportunity (EEO) legislation. The globalization of industry raises numerous EEO issues, some of which the U.S. courts have addressed and others of which they

Uncertainty Avoidance: Organizational Characteristics and Selected HR Practices

Dominant Values	Sample Countries	Organizational Features	Reward Practices	Staffing/Appraisal Practices
		Uncertainty Avoidance		
High				
■ Fear of random events and the unknown ■ High value placed on stability and routine ■ Low tolerance for ambiguity ■ Low risk propensity ■ Comfort in security, lack of tension, and lack of contradictions	■ Greece ■ Portugal ■ Italy	■ Mechanistic structures ■ Written rules and policies guide the firm ■ Organizations strive to be predictable ■ Management avoids making risky decisions ■ Careful delineations of responsibilities and work flows	■ Bureaucratic pay policies utilized ■ Compensation programs tend to be centralized ■ Fixed pay more important than variable pay ■ Little discretion given to supervisor in dispensing pay	■ Bureaucratic rules/procedures to govern hiring and promotion ■ Seniority an important factor in hiring and promotions ■ Government/union regulations limit employer discretion in recruitment, promotion, and terminations ■ Limited external hires ■ Limited use of appraisals requiring judgment
Low				
■ Unexpected viewed as challenging and exciting ■ Stability and routine seen as boring ■ Ambiguity seen as providing opportunities ■ High risk propensity ■ Tensions and contradictions spur innovation, discovery, and mastery of change	■ Singapore ■ Denmark ■ Sweden ■ Hong Kong	■ Less-structured activities ■ Fewer written rules to cope with changing environmental forces ■ Managers are more adaptable and tend to make riskier decisions	■ Variable pay a key component in pay programs ■ External equity emphasized ■ Decentralized pay program is the norm ■ Much discretion given to supervisors and business units in pay allocation	■ Fewer rules/procedures to govern hiring and promotions ■ Seniority deemphasized in personal decisions ■ Employer provided much latitude in recruitment, promotion, and terminations ■ External hiring at all levels ■ Extensive use of appraisals requiring judgment

Figure 17.6 continued

have not. Several texts devoted solely to employment law do not deal explicitly with international issues, indicating that this is not a well-developed area of employment law.[93] However, the following principles seem clear:

- U.S. companies are prohibited from basing employment decisions on employee characteristics such as race, sex, and age. This prohibition applies to international assignments, with the single exception that companies are not required to violate a host nation law. Thus, if a nation prohibits women from working in a specific business context, a U.S. company doing business in that nation is free to offer the particular international assignment covered by this host country law only to men. However, it should be noted that most countries that openly dis-

Masculinity/Femininity: Organizational Characteristics and Selected HR Practices

Dominant Values	Sample Countries	Organizational Features	Reward Practices	Staffing/Appraisal Practices
		Masculinity		
High ■ Material possessions important ■ Men given higher power and status than women ■ Rigid gender stereotypes ■ Gender inequities in pay accepted as a given	■ Austria ■ Mexico ■ Germany ■ United States	■ Some occupations labeled as "male," others as "female" ■ Fewer women in higher-level positions	■ Differential pay policies that allow for gender inequities ■ Tradition on acceptable basis for pay decisions ■ "Male" traits rewarded in promotions and other personnel decisions ■ Paternalistic benefits for women (such as paid maternity leave, day care, special work hours)	■ De facto preferential treatment for men in hiring/promotion decisions into higher-level jobs (even if it is illegal) ■ "Glass ceiling" for women ■ Occupational segregation ■ Only small proportion of men supervised by women ■ "Male" traits (such as aggressiveness, initiative, leadership) highly valued in appraisals
Low ■ Quality of life valued more than material gain ■ Men not believed to be inherently superior ■ Minimal gender sterotyping ■ Strong belief in equal pay for jobs of equal value, regardless of workers' gender	■ The Netherlands ■ Norway ■ Sweden ■ Finland ■ Denmark	■ More flexibility in career choice for men and women ■ More women in higher-level jobs	■ Jobs evaluated without regard for gender of job holders ■ Focus on work content rather than tradition to assess value of different jobs ■ Well-developed "equity goals" for pay determination ■ "Masculine" traits carry no special value for promotions and other personnel decisions ■ Few perks based on genders	■ Gender deemphasized in hiring/promotion decisions for any job ■ More women in upper-level positions ■ Occupational integration between the sexes ■ Little stigma for men to be supervised by women ■ Appraisals not biased in favor of male-oriented characteristics

Figure 17.6 continued

criminate against their own female citizens are quite flexible in dealing with U.S. companies' female employees. Therefore, companies should not make exclusions automatically.

- Foreign national employees of U.S. companies working in their own country or in some other foreign country are not covered by U.S. employment law. For instance, the U.S. Supreme Court ruled that a Saudi Arabian citizen working for an American oil company in Saudi Arabia could not sue his employer under Title VII.[94]
- Under the Immigration Control and Reform Act of 1986, people who are not U.S. citizens but who are living and have legal work status in the United States may not be discriminated against.

Important Caveats

The effectiveness of an HRM practice depends on how well it matches a culture's value system. Even so, managers need to keep several caveats in mind.

- **"National culture" may be an elusive concept** For this reason, managers should be careful not to be guided by stereotypes that hold some truth but may not apply to very many people

Long-Term/Short-Term Orientation: Organizational Characteristics and Selected HR Practices

Dominant Values	Sample Countries	Organizational Features	Reward Practices	Staffing/Appraisal Practices
		Long-Term/Short-Term Orientation		
High				
■ Future-oriented ■ Delayed gratification ■ Persistence ■ Long-term goals	■ Japan ■ Hong Kong ■ China	■ Stable organizations ■ Low employee turnover ■ Strong company culture	■ Long-term rewards ■ Seniority as basis for pay ■ Managers rewarded for multiyear accomplishments ■ Reliance on qualitative measures to distribute rewards ■ No expectation of frequent pay adjustments	■ Slow promotions ■ Promotions from within ■ High employment security ■ Minimal feedback ■ High emphasis on saving employees' face ■ High emphasis on coaching versus evaluation ■ High investment in training and employee development
Low				
■ Past- or present-oriented ■ Immediate gratification ■ Change course of action as necessary ■ Short-term goals	■ United States ■ Indonesia ■ Weak company culture	■ Changing organization ■ High employee turnover	■ Short-term rewards ■ Recent performance as a basis for pay ■ Managers rewarded for annual accomplishments ■ Reliance on quantitative measures to distribute rewards ■ High expectation of frequent pay adjustments	■ Fast promotions ■ Internal and external hires ■ Low employment security ■ High appraisal feedback ■ Low emphasis on saving employees' face ■ High emphasis on evaluation versus coaching ■ Low investment in training and employee development

Source: This is an updated and expanded version of an earlier chart appearing in Gómez-Mejía, L. R., and Welbourne, T. (1991). Compensation strategies in a global context. *Human Resource Planning, 14*(1), 38.

Figure 17.6 continued

in a culture. Stereotyping is a great danger in large, heterogeneous countries such as the United States, where cultural differences are often huge, but it can also cause problems even in relatively homogeneous nations. For instance, Western German firms hiring Eastern German workers frequently found that the latter reacted negatively to incentive systems that had been used successfully with their Western German counterparts—despite the fact that the two groups shared the same language, ethnicity, and cultural background. The Eastern Germans distrusted such incentive schemes, reported they felt manipulated by management, and shunned those workers who outproduced others.[95]

- **Corporate headquarters sometimes blame international personnel problems on cultural factors without careful study** Often personnel problems have little to do with cultural values and much to do with poor management. For example, a U.S. company introduced individual incentives for R&D employees at its English subsidiary. This policy created intense conflict, lack of cooperation, and declining performance. Top managers blamed the strong role of labor unions in England for these disappointing results. In fact, a large amount of evidence indicates that individual-based incentives are counterproductive when the nature of the task requires extensive teamwork (as is the case in R&D). The outcome in this case had nothing to do with national culture.[96]
- **Hard data on the success or failure of different HRM practices as a function of national culture are practically nonexistent** This means that judgment calls, gut feeling, and some trial

A Question of Ethics

In some areas of the world business practices that are contrary to Western values—such as child labor, payment of bribes to government officials, and sex or race discrimination in hiring and promotion—are common. Should U.S. corporations and their expatriate representatives refuse to engage in such practices even if doing so would put the firm at a competitive disadvantage?

and error based on a fine-tuned cultural sensitivity and open-mindedness are mandatory in international HRM.

- **Different cultures often have very different notions of right and wrong** In many cases, corporate headquarters may have to impose its own value system across multiple nations with conflicting value structures. For example, child labor is common in many Asian and African countries. The corporation may choose to avoid such practices on ethical grounds, but it must recognize that doing so can put it at a competitive disadvantage because local firms that have no qualms about using child labor will have lower labor costs. And, although members of the World Trade Organization and the United Nations have agreed to a set of "core labor standards" prohibiting employment discrimination, exploitative forms of child labor, and the use of forced labor such as prison labor, violations still occur in many countries, with at least 13 million children working in export industries, such as textiles.[97]
- **The business laws of other countries often force companies to change their practices** In some cases, if the firm wants to do business in another country, it must accept local regulations and practices even if these differ significantly from those in the home country.[98] In Spain, Nike established a joint venture with a local Spanish firm. The joint venture dissolved because management could not get along. The local firm sued Nike for a right to continue selling the sports apparel in Spain and other Latin American countries under the Nike label. The Spanish court agreed with the local firm saying that it had used the label Nike about 30 years earlier and that it is a mythological term for a God in Greek literature that should not be patented. The court decided that the Nike company may use the swoosh as a trademark in Spain but not the Nike label.
- Multinationals must find the right balance between tailor-made HR policies to fit particular cultures and the need to integrate global consistency with local adaptability. The current trend in establishing international HR policies appears to be to strive toward integration rather than segmentation of HR policies. The reason for this trend toward integration, according to a recent survey, is that 85 percent of global companies are trying to establish a corporate culture in all locations consistent with the organization's goals and vision. However, 88 percent report that local culture and customs have a "moderate to great" influence on the way they conduct business in particular locations.[99] This requires that organizations try to balance the need for local adaptation with the trend toward global consistency of HR policies.

  For instance, the appliance manufacturer, Whirlpool, has implemented Protégé, a comprehensive, culturally sensitive, global leadership development program that incorporates intensive mentoring by senior executives. The process, which also includes 360-degree assessment surveys, day-in-the-life behavioral simulations, and multiple personality and business skills-focused inventories, is built around competencies that have been identified as crucial for global leadership success. As another example, Sonoco Products, a major industrial and consumer-packaging supplier employing 16,500 people at 275 locations in 32 countries, implemented a performance management program for its executives located around the world. The aim of this program is for employees, regardless of their location, to understand the link between individual performance and organizational goals, while remaining sensitive to local conditions.[100]

Although the discussion in this chapter has focused mainly on differences in HRM practices across different countries, global forces are exerting a great deal of influence to make them more similar. Financial investors and the stock market in general appear to favor certain organizational practices (such as pay for performance, promotion based on merit, and restructuring), regardless of nationality, and firms all over the world appear to be responding accordingly, as we see in the Issues and Applications feature titled "HRM Practices Becoming More Alike Around the Globe."

Human Resource Management and Exporting Firms

Our discussion so far has focused on larger firms with international facilities (that is, those in Stages 3 to 5 of internationalization). However, the practices we have discussed are also relevant to smaller firms that are interested solely in exporting their products. It is estimated that only about 20 percent of U.S. firms with fewer than 500 employees have ever been active exporters, a percentage that lags way behind that found in most industrialized nations. At least 30,000 small firms in the United States have the potential to export competitively but do not do so.[101]

A number of studies have shown that the key impediments to exporting are (1) lack of knowledge of international markets, business practices, and competition and (2) lack of management commitment to generating international sales.[102] These impediments can be largely attributed to poor utilization of human resources within U.S. firms rather than to external factors. There is some evidence that a company that clearly reinforces international activities in its HRM practices is more likely to fare better in its export attempts.[103] Reinforcing international activities in HRM practices requires a company to:

- Explicitly consider international experience when making promotion and recruitment decisions, particularly to the senior management ranks.
- Provide developmental activities designed to equip employees with the skills and knowledge necessary to carry out their jobs in an international context. Developmental activities that enhance a firm's ability to compete globally include (1) programs designed to provide specific job skills and competencies in international business, (2) opportunities for development and growth in the international field, and (3) the use of appraisal processes that explicitly consider international activities as part of performance reviews.
- Create career ladders that take into account short- and long-term international strategies.
- Design a reward structure that motivates key organizational players to take full advantage of the company's export potential. Reinforcing desired export-related behaviors is likely to increase commitment to foreign sales as managers devote greater attention to skill development, information gathering, and scanning the environment for international opportunities.

Issues and Applications

HRM Practices Becoming More Alike Around the Globe

Expectations for higher returns from the stock market and investment funds irrespective of national boundaries are forcing firms all over the world to adopt HRM practices that until recently were seen as American. These include low job security, performance-based pay, flatter organizations, frequent performance appraisals, promotions based on merit, global hiring, "scientific" selection programs, and teaming up with firms across frontiers in part to have access to a broader employee base and expertise. For example:

- When Sony Corp. announced plans to cut 17,000 jobs—10 percent of its workforce—in a sweeping restructuring during 2000–2004, long-suffering investors finally had something to feel good about. Sony's American depository receipts (ADRs) promptly soared by more than one-third, to $104.
- Many European firms such as Nokia, Shell, DaimlerChrysler, Volkswagen, and Hoechst are now compensating employees with stocks, a practice almost unheard of a few years earlier.
- Firms such as Toshiba and NEC review employee performance on a regular basis, and employees who do not meet certain objectives are put on probation or terminated. Traditionally, such firms would find makeshift jobs for low performers and keep them on payroll.
- In Mexico two large firms have instituted HR practices to become more efficient. For instance, Grupo Televisa, the world's largest Spanish-language media company, and Empresas ICA, the country's biggest construction outfit, use batteries of selection devices to hire employees and avoid the traditional "amigismo" practices (hiring your friends) used by many Latin American firms.
- Sweden has become a less attractive place to live and work. As a result, talented employees are leaving the country in record numbers. For instance, 800 engineers left in a single year. Swedish firms have traditionally operated under a system of interlocking, closely held companies and a generous welfare state that governs many terms of employment. But this has come at a price. Personal tax rates of close to 60 percent make it nearly impossible for Swedish companies to recruit top-level managers. Swedish firms have responded to the challenge by engaging

in a sweeping program of joint venture, strategic alliances, and mergers and acquisitions with foreign firms, often moving operations out of their homeland to satisfy investor demands for better returns. Some of these include, for instance, a 50–50 joint venture between SAAB and General Motors, the car division of Volvo being sold to General Motors, and Ericksson moving its European headquarters from Sweden to England.

- European conglomerates ranging from Germany's Veba to France's Lagardère Group are bringing in hot new talent from all over the world, a radical practice for European firms.

The decision to export will require CEOs and senior marketing personnel to spend a significant time away from the office attending trade shows and developing relationships with distributors and companies abroad. Particularly in small companies, this means that the staff back home must be empowered to make decisions regarding the running of the business, with the traveling CEOs and executives keeping in touch via phone, fax, or e-mail.

The process of making the right export connections and establishing relationships used to be slow and painstaking, but the Web is changing all that, opening exports to firms of any size. For instance, net sales of clothing and accessories overseas by U.S. firms through the Internet are projected to soar to $30 billion by 2004, from $330 million in 1998. In the first year of its operation New York-based Girlshop.com, for example, exported 2 million dollars worth of avant-garde merchandise and made $250,000 in operating profit.[104]

To succeed internationally on the Web, however, firms must provide HR practices such as selection and training programs. These services can help firms surmount language barriers, use cutting-edge technology to mix and match products to diverse customer needs, adapt products to different cultural tastes and preferences, engender customer trust, and the like. Although many of these issues also apply to the domestic market, they become more challenging overseas where the market is far more heterogeneous and segmented.[105]

Summary and Conclusions

The Stages of International Involvement

Firms progress through five stages as they internationalize their operations: (1) domestic operations, (2) export operations, (3) subsidiaries or joint ventures, (4) multinational operations, and (5) transnational operations. The higher the stage, the more HR practices need to be adapted to diverse cultural, economic, political, and legal environments.

Determining the Mix of Host-Country and Expatriate Employees

In managing its overseas subsidiaries, a firm can choose an ethnocentric, polycentric, or geocentric approach. Firms tend to rely on expatriates more when sufficient local talent is unavailable, the firm is trying to create a corporatewide global vision, international and domestic units are highly interdependent, the political situation is unstable, and there are significant cultural differences between the host country and the home country.

The Challenges of Expatriate Assignments

All important part of international HRM is managing expatriate employees, both during their international assignments and when they return home. International assignments fail because of career blockage, culture shock, lack of predeparture cross-cultural training, an overemphasis on technical qualifications, the use of such assignments to get rid of troublesome employees, and family problems. Upon returning, expatriates may meet with a lack of respect for their acquired skills, a loss of status, poorly planned jobs, and reverse culture shock.

Enhancing the Effectiveness of Expatriate Assignments

To avoid problems in the international arena, a sensible set of HR policies should be put in place. In selecting people for international assignments, employers should emphasize cultural sensitivity, establish a selection board of expatriates, require previous international experience when possible, explore the possibility of hiring the foreign-born who can later serve as "expatriates," and screen candidates' spouses and families. Cross-cultural training programs of various lengths and levels of rigor can be implemented to prepare employees for their assignments. In terms of career development for expatriates, companies should position international assignments as a step toward advancement within the firm and provide support for expatriates. To avoid problems in the compensation area, companies should provide expatriates with enough disposable income and incentive bonuses and avoid having expatriates fill the same or lower-ranking jobs than locals hold in the international operation.

Developing HRM Policies in a Global Context

Managers should not simply transfer abroad HRM practices based on the home country's social and cultural standards. Rather, they should mold these practices to the cultural environments in which the international facilities are located. In general, the more an HRM practice contradicts prevailing societal norms, the more likely it will fail.

Human Resource Management and Exporting Firms

Many firms have the potential to export profitably. A company is more likely to fare better in its export attempts when it clearly reinforces international activities by (1) explicitly considering international experience in hiring decisions, (2) providing developmental activities to equip employees with international skills, (3) creating career ladders for internationally experienced employees, and (4) designing a reward structure that motivates employees to begin export activities.

Key Terms

culture shock, 582
ethnocentric approach, 578
expatriate, 577
geocentric approach, 578
joint venture, 578
multinational corporation (MNC), 577
polycentric approach, 578
transnational corporation, 577
wholly owned subsidiary, 578

Discussion Questions

1. According to a recent news story in *BusinessWeek*, "For years, American multinationals have been pilloried for shipping U.S. jobs overseas. Now, they're exporting something else: layoffs. Among the giants going abroad with their axes: Motorola, Goodyear, Procter & Gamble, Compaq Computer, JDS Uniphase, and Delphia Automotive. Each is cutting at least 2,500 overseas jobs. Sara Lee is cutting 1,300 jobs—not one in the U.S. All are at its Hanes clothing plants in Central and South America. Those were on top of 7,000 European layoffs at Hanes plants."[106] Many people abroad are shocked at how easily U.S. firms can throw long-term employees out of work, particularly when it is very difficult to find another job in a labor market where layoffs are uncommon. Do you think that U.S. companies should be more compassionate with employees when local conditions in a foreign country make it very difficult for laid-off workers to find alternative employment opportunities?
2. How might an international firm trying to adapt HRM practices to the local culture produce worse results than it would produce by "exporting" HRM practices from the home office?
3. Under what specific conditions would you recommend an ethnocentric, a polycentric, and a geocentric approach to international staffing?
4. U.S. MNCs experience a much higher rate of early returns with their expatriate employees than European and Japanese MNCs do. What explains this difference? What HRM policies and procedures would you develop to reduce this problem?
5. Expatriates frequently complain that when they accept an international assignment they put their career on hold while their peers in the home office continue to climb the corporate ladder. To what would you attribute this perception? What recommendations would you make to change it?
6. Some people believe that U.S. MNCs should serve as vehicles for cultural change in developing countries by introducing modern U.S. HRM practices and instilling values (such as punctuality and efficiency) in the workforce that are necessary for industrialization. Do you agree with this assertion? Explain your position.
7. Despite the growth of airfreight, ships transport 90 percent of world trade. According to a recent report by the International Shipping Commission, "For thousands of today's international seafarers, life at sea is modern slavery and their workplace is a slave ship."[107] There are probably 1 million workers in the shipping industry; the Philippines alone supplies 180,000 entry-level sailors each year. Two separate United Nations agencies have rules regarding fair pay, adequate food, and decent housing for sailors. But neither group has enforcement powers over individual ship owners, and in terms of applicable labor laws many of these people live in a "no-man's" land. A ship can be registered in Liberia, owned in Greece, chartered to a Chinese company, and crewed by men from the Philippines.[108] Do you think manufacturers and retailers should take greater responsibility for the conditions of workers aboard the vessels that ferry their products? Explain.

8. Some people believe that the Internet is rewriting the rules of how to attract, motivate, and retain talent internationally. Consider Planet-Intra.com Ltd., a software company that is nominally based in Mountain View, California. Alan J. McMillan, the 37-year-old founder and CEO, is a Canadian who had been working in Hong Kong. A software team in Croatia wrote the company's product. The vice president for technology is Russian, while the vice president of international sales is a German living in Tokyo. They use the Internet—in fact, their own product—to collaborate across borders. "We live and breathe the Internet," says McMillan.[109] In what ways do you foresee that the Internet will change HR practices in the future?

There is a variety of additional material available on the Web site that accompanies this text. You can access this information by visiting the Web site at **www.prenhall.com/gomez.**

YOU MANAGE IT!

Emerging Trends Case 17.1

Globalization: Good or Evil?

Globalization may be good or not so good, depending on who you are and where it is perceived. Many see globalization as the key to world prosperity, particularly to prosperity in the United States where firms have benefited immensely from having access to a larger market of inputs (such as cheaper labor and raw material) and a larger market of outputs (the United States is the leading producer and exporter of products and services). Yet, an increasing number of people see globalization as a threat to their standard of living. Japan is one of those countries that for decades saw its growth tied to increased globalization; but many in Japan are now thinking increased globalization is the reason for its problems.

Japan has been suffering a decade of economic decline. The previous growth that made it possible for Japanese firms to have bought Rockerfeller Center and Pebble Beach golf courses has been displaced by a growing economic malaise. Joblessness, bankruptcy, crime, and suicide, once rare in Japan, now do make the headlines. In the recession-ravaged, hot-springs resort town of Yufuin, citizens are hedging their futures by resorting to barter trade. Taxi rides, sake, and hospital bills can be paid for with a local scrip called the yufu. What backs it? Locals do odd jobs in return for yufu. "Our wealth is slipping away," moans Eisuke Sakakibara, a former vice minister in the once powerful Ministry of Finance.

In Tokyo's parks, permanent communities of homeless live under tents. Real estate values have declined to 1982 levels, which means it's not unusual for houses now to be worth less than their remaining mortgage balances.

In Japan, employment was once guaranteed for life; now no job is secure. In a recent Kyodo News survey, 70 of 100 Japanese business leaders said they plan to cut wages this year. Wide-eyed, unshaven men walk the subways begging for money. Signs around their necks read, "Help Me"—Japan's euphemism for "fired." "We hope this is the bottom, but really, who knows?" sighs Masyuki Watanabe, 48, a meat wholesaler who closed his business in 2002 when rumors of mad cow disease chased away so many customers that it wasn't worth battling the steady increase in local taxes and other expenses.

Most of Japan's manufacturing jobs these days are migrating to China, where quality is high and labor is cheap. Sony makes all its first-generation PlayStations there—about 7 million of them. Nearly half of Toshiba's 45 plants are now in China, cranking out air conditioners, mobile phones, and TVs, and prepared to produce whatever the next hot product is likely to be. In an astonishing twist, Japanese engineers and factory managers are lining up at employment agencies in search of jobs in China. "They need experienced people," explains Tomko Hata, a manager at PaHuma, a private employment agency that finds jobs in Asia for unemployed Japanese. "People here will take a job there even though the pay is half what they were making. They're desperate."

Critical Thinking Questions

1. About 10 years ago business writers and academics attributed Japan's spectacular economic success after World War II to the way it managed its human resources: a guaranteed job for life, progression through a career ladder within the company, a paternalistic approach to benefits (such as generous retirement, scholarships for employees' children, and housing allowance), lack of individual-based appraisals (which presumably avoids competition among workers for scarce merit dollars), use of teams to organize work, and the like. Some of these practices were preached to U.S. managers in executive education courses around the country until the mid-1990s as a way to make U.S. companies more competitive. Why do you think the situation has changed so much in recent years? Do you believe that such practices as permanent employment and

lifelong company training are partly responsible for Japan's current problems? Explain.

2. Tough-minded economists agree that the only way countries such as Japan can move ahead is to drastically change their "entitlement organizational culture." That means recognizing top performers, terminating low performers, hiring talented people at all levels within the firm, attracting skilled foreign workers, and generating internal competition through individual/team-based rewards linked to the achievement of organizational goals. Do you agree? Justify your answer.
3. Some people attribute the United States' recent economic success to the fact that it has been willing to let its manufacturing industry move out of the country (to such places as Mexico, Singapore, and China) while concentrating on the knowledge economy (such as computers, electronics, and pharmaceutical) and service sectors (such as education and financial) where it enjoys a competitive advantage. Although this has hurt many blue-collar workers, it has increased economic well-being over all. Do you agree with this view? Why do you think countries such as Japan may be reluctant to follow this path? Explain.

Team Exercise

The U.S. government fears that Japan's woes will ripple through the rest of the world, triggering a major financial crisis. Students divide up into groups of five to role-play a situation in which a group of HR experts provides advice to Japanese conglomerates as to what kinds of HR practices may help reduce some of those problems.

Source: Adapted with permission from Gibney, F. (2002, February 18). Time for hardball. *Time*, 42–44.

Discussion Case 17.2

YOU MANAGE IT!

Managing Human Resources in a European Context

Jerome Wirth and his business partner, Frederic Herbinet, launched the Internet start-up Beweb in 1997. Today, Beweb is a $2.5 million-a-year business providing software and services to e-commerce companies. It has operations in France and Britain and plans to expand across Europe.

But Beweb is saying "au revoir" to its Paris operations and moving them to London, where payroll taxes will be less than one-fourth of the 45 percent that the company pays in Paris. The coup de grace for Beweb, though, was a French law cutting the maximum workweek from 39 to 35 hours. Introduced in 2000 for major employers, it was extended in 2002 to businesses with under 20 workers (although in 2003 the law changed again to allow for more flexibility). Hiring extra staff to make up the lost work hours is impractical for Beweb, which has 15 employees. "It's impossible," says Wirth, who is 33 years old. "I love France, but I am very pessimistic for my country."

To the 76 million tourists who visit each year, France looks as desirable as ever. The Centre Pompidou and the Paris Opéra boast expensive face-lifts. On spring afternoons, parks and cafés are filled with people, thanks to the 35-hour workweek. That's because the country's corporations are laying off and aren't hiring. To avoid rigid antilayoff laws, big companies such as tire maker Michelin and building materials giant St. Gobain are moving manufacturing abroad. Others, such as carmakers Renault and PSA Peugeot Citroën, have relied on improved productivity to limit hiring. For most young people, the best places to get a job are with small businesses, which accounted for nearly 90 percent of the jobs created in France during the past decade. But taxes and rules are making it ever harder for these businesses to compete.

France also is failing to integrate some 1.5 million North African immigrants and their French-born children. (At least 7 percent of the population of France is foreign born, mostly from the French ex-colonies.) Housing projects, hidden from tourists' view outside big cities, teem with young people who feel locked out of society. "Even if you have a diploma, you can't find a job because you're a 'foreigner,'" says Yams, 19, one of a group of unemployed young men loitering outside a dilapidated high-rise in the Paris suburb of La Courneuve. Yams and his friends, who wouldn't give their last names, all were born in France to Algerian immigrants but say they don't feel French.

At the same time, an alarming number of France's brightest young people are leaving the country. Since 1995, the number of French citizens living outside the country has risen 30 percent, to nearly 2 million, including 240,000 in Silicon Valley. Almost all are in their twenties and thirties. An additional 200,000 or so have fled to Britain. Even worse, young people living in France are about to get socked with the pension bill for the baby boomers. France has the most generous retirement system in Europe, allowing workers to leave their jobs at age 60 with full benefits. In the meantime joblessness for those under 25 is around 21 percent.

Critical Thinking Questions

1. According to Gary Becker, Nobel laureate in economics, "The European pattern of high unemployment rates, long average duration of unemployment, early retirement of older workers, and very slow growth in employment . . . are the result of high social security and other labor taxes,

laws that make it difficult to lay off employees, generous payments to the unemployed, and, in France, high minimum-wage laws. I advocate easing the cost to companies when they hire and fire workers, lowering labor taxes, lowering minimum wages, and raising retirement ages." Do you agree? Explain.

2. Many Europeans view HR practices in the United States as harsh: high employee risk bearing with their pay and jobs; long work hours; pay-as-you-go health benefits; little buffer between personal life and work life; lack of commitment from the business to the employee and vice versa; and constant turnover. According to a European commentator, "HR practices in the U.S. often reflect the inhumane, cutthroat capitalism underlying American society." Europeans boast about their superior quality of life and how they avoid the stress of the U.S. work environment. Americans see European HR practices as too inflexible, paternalistic, with government-mandated regulations (such as the 35-hour workweek) as too inhospitable to productivity, competition, and entrepreneurship. What is your assessment of these two starkly different views? Explain.
3. In Spain, as in many other European countries, traditionally it has been difficult, time consuming, and expensive to terminate an employee. For this reason, many companies just keep low performers on their payrolls rather than attempt to fire them. However, many say the high unemployment rate in Spain (from 10 percent to 24 percent during the last 10 years) is because companies are reluctant to hire new people since they would have little choice but to make a long-term commitment to the new hire. To get around its restrictive labor laws, in 2002 Spain significantly extended the percentage of workers who could be on temporary contracts. In 2003 at least one third of Spanish workers have temporary contracts. In the United States approximately 40 percent of employees work under such contracts, meaning they are hired for a fixed time and at the end of that time the company decides whether or not to renew the contract for another specified time. Do you think that this is a good policy and that more companies should use it? Justify your answer.

Team Exercise

A U.S. automobile company is trying to decide whether or not to expand its operations in France. One consideration in this decision is whether the HR practices in France would make it cumbersome for the company to manage its workers. Students divide up into groups of five to role-play a situation in which they provide advice to top management as to what decision to make.

Source: Adapted with permission from Matlack, C. and Rossant, J. (2002, April 22). France: Who speaks for youth? *BusinessWeek*, 48–50.

YOU MANAGE IT! Discussion Case 17.3

Two Sides to Every Story

Four years ago Pressman Company, a U.S.-based firm, entered into a joint venture with a Polish firm to manufacture a variety of plumbing supplies, both for the internal Polish market and for export to neighboring countries. Last week Pressman received the resignation of Jonathan Smith, an expatriate from the home office who nine months ago was appointed general manager of the Polish subsidiary for a four-year term. In the previous 39 months, two other expatriate general managers had also decided to call it quits long before their foreign assignments expired. In addition, 13 of the 28 U.S. technicians sent to work in the Polish facility returned home early. George Stevens, a senior vice president in corporate headquarters, estimates that these expatriates' resignations and early returns have cost the company at least $4 million in direct expenses and probably three times as much in lost production and delayed schedules.

When he heard rumors of widespread discontent in the workforce and a threatened strike, Stevens decided to travel to the Polish facility to find out what was happening. In the course of interviewing five local supervisors and 10 workers with the help of a translator, he repeatedly heard three complaints: first, the American managers and technicians thought they "knew it all" and treated their Polish counterparts with contempt; second, the American employees had unrealistic expectations of what could be accomplished within the stipulated deadlines established at corporate headquarters; and third, American employees were making three times more money than their Polish counterparts and enjoyed looking down their noses at locals by driving fancy cars, living in expensive homes, and hiring an army of maids and helpers.

When he arrived back in the States, Stevens also interviewed Jonathan Smith and five of the technicians who returned early. Some common reasons for their early resignations emerged from these interviews. First, they described their Polish colleagues as "lazy" and "just doing the minimum to get by while keeping a close eye on the clock for breaks, lunches, and go-home time." Pushing them to work harder only provoked anger. Second, they indicated that the Polish workers and managers had a sense of entitlement with little intrinsic motivation and initiative. Third, they complained of loneliness and their inability to communicate in Polish. Finally, most reported that their spouses and children were homesick and longing to return to the States after the first month or so. As he sits in his office, George Stevens is staring blankly out the window, trying to decide what to do.

Critical Thinking Questions

1. Based on what you have learned in this chapter, what do you think are the underlying problems in the Polish subsidiary of Pressman Company?
2. How would you account for the sharp differences in the perceptions of the Polish locals and U.S. expatriates?
3. If you were hired as a consultant by Pressman Company, what steps would you recommend that Stevens take?

Team Exercise

Students form pairs. One student plays Stevens, the other an HRM consultant. Role-play the initial meeting between these two, with Stevens explaining the problems at the Polish plant and the consultant identifying the additional information that will be needed to get to the root of the difficulties, and how this information might be collected.

Students form into groups of four or five. Each group's task is to make suggestions for the content of a training program for the next group of employees to be sent to Pressman's Polish plant. Besides information from this chapter, use principles you learned from Chapters 4 "Managing Diversity" and 8 "Training the Workforce" to develop these programs. When the task is finished (approximately 20 minutes), a member from each group should present the group's recommendations to the class. How similar or dissimilar are the groups' recommendations? Why? Which recommendations are likely to be most effective?

Discussion Case 17.4

YOU MANAGE IT!

Are Culture-Specific HR Policies a Good Idea?

Over the past 10 years, East Computer Company has grown from a domestic producer of IBM clones in Boston to a multinational company with assembly plants in four foreign locations. The company's personnel policies were developed five years ago, before East Computer's international expansion, by a task force headed by the vice president for HRM in Boston. The company's CEO has just appointed a new task force to examine the extent to which current domestic personnel policies can be "exported" to East's new international locations. The essential elements of these policies are the following:

1. All job openings are posted to allow any employee to apply for a position.
2. Selection is based on merit. Appropriate selection devices (for example, tests, structured interviews, and the like) are used to ensure proper implementation of this policy.
3. Nepotism is expressly forbidden.
4. Promotion from within is the norm whenever feasible.
5. Equal employment opportunities are available to all, regardless of sex, race, national origin, or religion.
6. Pay for various positions is established through a rational process that includes both job evaluation and market survey data.
7. There is equal pay for equal work, regardless of sex, race, national origin, or religion.
8. Goals are jointly set by supervisor and subordinate, with an annual formal appraisal session at which both parties have the chance to discuss progress toward goal achievement. The appraisal is used both to provide performance feedback to the employee and as a basis for merit pay decisions.

As a first step in evaluating these policies, the vice president for HRM classified the countries where East's facilities are located according to Hofstede's dimensions. She came up with the following matrix.

Cultural Dimensions

Facility Location	Power Distance	Individualism	Uncertainty Avoidance	Masculinity	Long-Term Orientation
Australia	Low	High	Medium	Medium	Low
Mexico	High	Low	High	High	Medium
England	Low	High	Low	High	Low
Norway	Low	Medium	Medium	Low	High

You have been hired by East Computer Company to help management develop personnel policies for each of the four international facilities. Ideally, management would prefer to use the same policies that it uses in the United States to maintain consistency and reduce administrative problems. However, the vice president for HRM has made a strong case for "tailor-made" personnel policies that are suitable to each facility's cultural environment.

Critical Thinking Questions

1. Given East Computer Company's present personnel policies, what problems is the company likely to face in each facility if it transports its domestic policies abroad?
2. How would you change or adapt each of the company's current personnel policies to better fit the cultural environment of each international facility?
3. What set of management recommendations would you provide for keeping, changing, or adapting East Computer Company's HR policies for the United States, Australia, Mexico, England, and Norway? In your recommendations, be sure to mention any risks associated with implementing your recommendations.

Team Exercises

Students break into groups of five. One student role-plays a consultant who is conducting an exercise to uncover possible problems in uniform application of the company's current policy. Each of the other four students takes the role of advocate for one of the four international locations. Each advocate should make an argument for or against keeping specific parts of East's existing HR policies.

Students form groups of four students, with each group acting as the advocate for one of the four international locations. After deciding which policies to keep and which to change, a representative from each group presents the group's recommendations to the class. After these brief presentations, the class discusses the costs and benefits of culture-specific HR policies.

YOU MANAGE IT!

Video Shorts Case 17.5

Global Human Resource Management

In this final segment of *SPOTLIGHT inside HR*, host Meg Allen takes you behind closed doors at Focus Pointe for a revealing look at some of the problems the company encountered recently in relocating an employee abroad. Meg will be joined later on in the show by guests Cheryl Brie, director of recruitment at Focus Pointe, and Paul Fiolek, vice president of human resources at Bertelsman, BMG.

One of the greatest challenges faced by HR professionals today is selecting and successfully relocating international managers. As you revisit the HR offices of Focus Pointe, provider of qualitative research services and facilities, HR professional Chona Castillo and Cheryl Brie, director of recruitment at Focus Pointe, are trying to assess why the relocation of Samuel Lafayette, facility director, turned out to be a huge mistake. Samuel had worked at the New York offices of Focus Pointe for nine years, building and managing a strong team of employees. When Focus Pointe decided to enter the European market, Samuel, eager to take on the challenge of starting up a new operation, volunteered for the position of facility director in Paris. With his enthusiasm, ambition, and excellent managerial skills, he seemed like a natural fit. His wife, a novelist, was excited about sharing the experience with their two young children.

After a disheartening few months, during which Samuel's wife felt isolated and abandoned by her workaholic husband, the family is back home in New York City. Watch as *SPOTLIGHT*'s surveillance tape reveals a tense and tired Samuel. He has just returned from his ordeal in France feeling, as he puts it, "hugely disappointed." Now he is trying to place the blame for his failure on the HR department. He complains that his wife found the French people to be extremely closed to foreigners and that HR had failed to inform him that he had options aside from the neighborhood school for his children. Samuel explains to Chona and Cheryl that his family did not participate in the employee relocation program, as Samuel reasoned that it was *he* who would be taking on the actual job. Do you think there might have been a crucial lapse in communication at this juncture?

Samuel's overseas venture has proved to be a costly error for the company, as well as a letdown for Samuel. Consider how devastating this is to corporate plans for globalization. He has spoken with his manager, who has referred him to the HR department. Focus Pointe HR has graciously agreed to let him out of his three-year contract and brought him home, along with his family, two and one-half years early! Now that he is back, he faces the twofold dilemma of having sold his home and seemingly fallen off the career track at Focus Pointe. Think about what programs might be put into place to prevent employees from loosing a foothold at the home office. Cheryl offers him a lesser position at his current salary, which he flatly refuses. He makes it clear that relocating to the company's Chicago or Los Angeles offices for a higher-level post is not an option. He's not likely to want to uproot his family again so soon! You might notice that while Samuel is obviously quite agitated, both Chona and Sheryl remain calm and businesslike. Despite their efforts to reassure him that he is still a highly valued employee, no solution seems forthcoming. We leave the scene with the two parties unable to reach a mutually acceptable solution.

Guests Cheryl Brie, director of recruitment at Focus Pointe, and Paul Fiolek, vice president of human resources at Bertelsman, BMG, differ in their responses to this problem. During the discussion segment, Paul Fiolek suggests the use of an outside relocation company. This may be worth exploring because it saves HR personnel time and gives employees a central source for all their relocation needs. It is, of course, an additional expense that Focus Pointe would have to absorb. Cheryl feels the problem might have been ameliorated by providing more frequent visits home for the Lafayettes, who were obviously homesick. You will notice that both executives are trying to be sympathetic to Samuel's personal plight, even though they feel that he is at least somewhat responsible. Paul and Cheryl concur that this crisis might have been avoided altogether through better communication. Would you agree that communication is the central issue?

This concludes the *SPOTLIGHT Inside HR* series. By now you have learned a great deal about addressing human needs in the workplace in order to get results and the strategic importance of flexibility. Hopefully, you will be able to put this knowledge to use in your own management career, whether it be in human resources or in another managerial capacity.

Critical Thinking Questions

1. What are some of the evaluation selection steps you would take at Focus Pointe to ensure a successful relocation? Consider how Samuel Lafayette would rate as an international assignee according to your assessment.
2. Do you think that Samuel is unfair in portraying the company as largely responsible for his failure? Using psychology to understand Samuel's personal "crisis," explain your viewpoint.
3. Is Samuel's predicament unusual? What can be done about it?
4. How could an executive development training program to staff international offices improve Focus Pointe's relocation process?
5. How do the approaches of Cheryl Brie and Paul Fiolek toward international staffing differ? Do you think that Fiolek's suggested use of a relocation company might be helpful to Focus Pointe in the future? Why or why not? As you answer this question, consider that Focus Pointe employs a total of about 200 employees in its five U.S. locations. Bertelsman, BMG, by contrast, has a staff of over 11,000 in its 200 branches worldwide.
6. (optional) As this segment of *SPOTLIGHT* was being filmed, America was at war in Afghanistan and anti-American sentiment abroad was high. Using what you have learned about the importance of competing in a global marketplace, what effect do you think this might have on HR practices regarding expansion abroad at Focus Pointe?

Appendix A

HRM and Business Periodicals

The following is an annotated listing of general business publications and specialized HRM publications. Many of these resources may prove helpful to you, not only in your study of HRM but also in your own career development. As we noted in the text, more and more companies are shifting career development responsibilities onto their employees, while providing them with tools for career planning. These tools can be the first in your career-planning toolkit.

General Business Periodicals

Across the Board. Conference Board. 845 Third Avenue, New York, NY 10022. Provides articles that present business topics in nontechnical terms. Articles range from discussions of general business issues to examinations of specific companies and industries.

Black Enterprise. Earl G. Graves Publishing Co. 130 Fifth Avenue, New York, NY 10011. Black Enterprise focuses on business, jobs, career potential, and financial opportunities as they relate to African, Caribbean, and African-American consciousness. Its annual list of the nation's top black businesses and financial institutions is considered an invaluable accounting of African-American business enterprises.

Business Week. McGraw-Hill, Inc. 1221 Avenue of the Americas, New York, NY 10020. The leading general business magazine, Business Week offers comprehensive coverage of the news and developments affecting the business world. It includes information on computers, finance, labor, industry, marketing, science, and technology.

Fast Company. P.O. Box 52760, Boulder, CO 80321-2760. Fairly new on the scene, Fast Company focuses on a wide variety of business topics and is geared toward giving companies an edge in a very competitive marketplace. The magazine's subtitle is "How smart business works."

Forbes. Forbes, Inc. 60 Fifth Avenue, New York, NY 10011. A general business magazine that celebrates capitalism. Short articles report on company activities, industry developments, economic trends, and investment tips.

Fortune. Time, Inc. Time & Life Building, Rockefeller Center, New York, NY 10020. Fortune reports on companies and industries, developments and trends. Its articles tend to be longer than those in other business magazines, and its frequent use of sidebars allows readers to learn more about corollary issues.

Harvard Business Review. Graduate School of Business Administration, Harvard University. Boston, MA 02163. This well-known product of Harvard Business School publishes articles in the areas of business and management. Topics include planning, manufacturing, and innovation. Each issue includes a case study.

Hispanic Business. P.O. Box 469038, Escondido, CA 92046-9038. A general business magazine focusing on a variety of business issues (including career opportunities, entrepreneurial ventures, and legislation) as they relate to Latino workers and Latino-owned businesses in the United States.

Inc.: The Magazine for Growing Companies. Goldhirsch Group, Inc. 38 Commercial Wharf, Boston, MA 02110. Inc. is targeted to the person involved in managing new, small, or growing companies. Articles focus on entrepreneurial ventures, general business topics, and profiles of successful managers.

Journal of Business Ethics. Kluwar Academic Publishers. 101 Philip Dr., Norwell, MA 02061. This journal publishes scholarly articles dealing with the ethical issues confronted in business. It is clearly written, free of technical jargon, and contains articles on such topics as ethics and business schools, competitor intelligence, corporate executives, and disasters.

Management Review. American Management Association. 135 West 50th St., New York, NY 10020. This monthly publication describes management trends, techniques, and issues for middle- and upper-level managers in the corporate and public sector.

Nation's Business: U.S. Chamber of Commerce. 1615 H St. N.W., Washington, DC 20062. *Nation's Business* reports on current business activities and topics such as quality, entrepreneurship, and going public. It is directed mainly to entrepreneurs and small business owners and managers. Each issue contains a feature on issues affecting family businesses.

Small Business Reports. American Management Association. 135 West 50th St., New York, NY 10020. Articles in this monthly magazine tend to offer practical advice for small business owners and managers. However, topics are of interest to all business managers.

The Wall Street Journal. Dow Jones & Co., Inc. 200 Liberty St., New York, NY 10281. With a greater circulation than either The New York Times or USA Today, this comprehensive national newspaper offers in-depth coverage of national and international finance and business. A must for anyone interested in the business of business.

Working Woman. Working Woman, Inc. 230 Park Avenue, New York, NY 10169. Geared toward the white-collar career woman interested in advancing in her field. Articles focus on career advancement, management, communicaiton skills, money management, and investment information. Features items on new technology, changing demographics, and profiles of successful businesswomen. Of special interest is the annual "Hottest Careers" issue featuring listings of up-and-coming occupations.

HRM Periodicals

Workspan. WorldatWork Association, 14040 N. Northsight Blvd., Scottsdale, AZ 58260. Published monthly, this newsletter includes articles of interest to HR practitioners. It also reports on the resources available to practitioners, as well as positions available in the field.

Academy of Management Executive. Pace University, P.O. Box 3020, Briarcliff Manor, NY 10510. Published quarterly and geared toward executives and students of business, this journal presents straightforward practical articles, many of them written by leading management scholars.

WorldatWork Journal. WorldatWork Association, 14040 N. Northsight Blvd., Scottsdale, AZ 85260. The *ACA Journal* is a specialized publication of the WorldatWork Association. Issues appear quarterly and feature six to eight articles on such compensation-related topics as pay for performance, compensation strategy, tax considerations, executive pay, and benefits.

Compensation & Benefits Review. American Management Association. 135 West 50th St., New York, NY 10020. A specialized publication of the American Management Association, this journal contains four to six articles in each issue, covering compensation management and strategy and such diverse topics as job evaluation as a barrier to excellence and compensating overseas executives. One invaluable feature is its condensations of noteworthy articles appearing in other business publications.

CompFlash. WorldatWork Association, 14040 N. Northsight Blvd., Scottsdale, AZ 58260. Published monthly, this newsletter includes short articles and information on the latest trends/statistics useful for compensation management, including the most recent surveys.

Employee Relations Law Journal. Executive Enterprises, Inc. 22 West 21st St., New York, NY 10010. While geared toward attorneys specializing in employment law, in-house counsel, and HR executives, this journal contains practical advice that is not highly technical. Articles deal with such topics as personnel management techniques, legal compliance, and court cases, and such issues as sex discrimination, privacy in the workplace, and drug testing. Features up-to-date coverage of federal regulatory agency actions.

Employee Relations Weekly. Bureau of National Affairs. 1231 25th Street, N.W. Washington, DC 20037. This government publication covers such workplace issues as EEO developments, health and safety, pay and benefits, and policy and practices. Recent articles have touched on employee committees, domestic partner benefits, and sexual harassment. Useful for discussions of court cases relevant to employee relations.

HRMagazine. Society for Human Resource Management. 606 N. Washington St., Alexandria, VA 22314. Formerly called Personnel Administrator, this magazine offers in-depth coverage of all areas of HRM.

International Journal of Human Resource Management. Routledge Journals, 11 New Fetter Lane, London EC4P 4EE. Published monthly, this journal covers research on international HRM issues and trends.

Labor Notes. Labor and Education Research Project. 7435 Michigan Avenue, Detroit, MI 48210. This workers' magazine is as critical of big labor as it is of management. It features nationwide coverage of such issues as contracts, ongoing negotiation, boycotts, working conditions, and problems confronting women and minority workers. Useful for its "shop-floor" view and as counterbalance to the management perspective.

Monthly Labor Review. Bureau of Labor Statistics. U.S. Department of Labor, Washington, DC 20402. The source for U.S. labor statistics. Each issue carries four in-depth articles on labor-related topics.

Organizational Dynamics. American Management Association. 135 West 50th St., New York, NY 10020. Articles deal with appraisal systems and management systems in general, as well as with other relevant aspects of systems administration.

Personnel Journal. 245 Fischer Ave. B-2, Costa Mesa, CA 92626. *Personnel Journal* covers the full range of issues in human resources. There is extensive coverage of current HR policies and practices at actual companies, and each article contains company vital statistics. Personnel Journal also sponsors the annual Optimas Awards, which spotlight companies with excellent HR initiatives in a variety of categories.

Public Personnel Management. Personnel Management Association. 1617 Duke St., Alexandria, VA 22314. Research articles useful to personnel administrators in public-sector personnel management. Typical subjects are recruiting, interviewing, training, sick leave, and home-based employment.

Supervisory Management. American Management Association, 135 West 50th St., New York, NY 10020. Within its concise 12-page format, this magazine contains numerous brief articles offering practical advice on such topics as building quality awareness, handling problem employees, and conducting effective meetings.

Training & Development. American Society for Training & Development. 1640 King St., Alexandria, VA 22313. The official magazine of ASTD, *Training & Development* is directed toward HR professionals and other managers. It covers both practical issues and trends in training and development, including such topics as how to make a training video, how to train workers to write more clearly, and the ins and outs of successful diversity training.

Notes

Chapter 1

1. Tergesen, A. (2000, January 17). Dealing with risk. *BusinessWeek*, 104.
2. Levering, R., and Moskowitz, M. (2002, February 4). The best in the worst of times. *Fortune*, 60–68.
3. Cooper, J. C., Marigan, K., and Miller, R. (2002 February 11). What recession? *BusinessWeek*, 32–33.
4. Mandel, M. (2002, April 1). Restating the 90s. *BusinessWeek*, 55–58.
5. Cooper, J. C., Madigan, K., and Miller, R. (2002 February 11). What recession? *BusinessWeek*, 32–33.
6. Coy, P. (2002, February 11). Enron. How good an energy trader? *BusinessWeek*, 42–44.
7. Butler, J. E., Ferris, G. R., and Napier, N. K. (1991). *Strategy and human resources management*. Cincinnati, OH: South-Western; and McDonald, D. (2002). Radical change: Breaking ground for e-HR implementation. *Workspan, 45*(2), 5–10.
8. Golden, K., and Ramanujan, V. (1985). Between a dream and a nightmare: On the integration of the human resource function and the strategic business planning process. *Human Resource Management, 24*, 429–451; and Gagne, K. (2002). One day at a time: Using performance management to translate strategy into results. *Workspan, 45*(2), 20–26. See also Huselid, M.A. (1995). The impact of human resource management on turnover, productivity, and corporate financial performance. *Academy of Management Journal, 38*, 635–672.
9. Zingheim, P., and Schuster, J. (2002, February 12). Creating a workplace business brand. *HR.com*, www4.hr.com/hrcom.
10. Gunther, M. (2000, January 10). Publish or perish? *Fortune*, 141–160.
11. Ante, S. E., and Sager, I. (2002, February 11). IBM's new boss. *BusinessWeek*, 66–72.
12. Cited in Useem, J. (2000, January 10). Welcome to the new company. *Fortune*, 63.
13. Id.
14. Tejada, C. (2002, March 5). Home office: Millions don't leave work at home. *Wall Street Journal*, A-1.
15. *BusinessWeek* (1999, November 29). Tough love for techie souls, 164.
16. Id.
17. See, for instance, stories appearing in Port, O. (2002, March 4). Web. *BusinessWeek*, 97; Green, H., and Hof, R. D. (2002, April 22). Lessons from the cyber survivors. *BusinessWeek*, 42; Nusbaum, A. (2000, January 5). Web cuts an entire order of middlemen. *Financial Times*, 14; Bulkeley, W. M. (2000, January 6). Virtual utilities peddle power over the Web. *Wall Street Journal*, B-1; Aeppel, T. (2000, January 5). A Web auctioneer soils the rust belt. *Wall Street Journal*, B-1; and Ramstad, E. (2000, January 5). Hot e-products from small fry jolt tech giants. *Wall Street Journal*, B-1.
18. Dreazen, Y. J. (2002, February 4). U.S. says Web use has risen to 54% of the population. *Wall Street Journal*, B-4.
19. Anders, G. (1999, November 22). Better, faster, prettier. *Wall Street Journal*, 6.
20. Dreazen, Y. J. (2002, February 4). U.S. says Web use has risen to 54% of the population. *Wall Street Journal*, B-4; *Newsline* (2001, July 18). U.S. corporations losing millions through poor e-mail control. Available from http://resourcepro.worldatwork.org.
21. *Business 2.0* (2000, January). Who uses the Internet, 36.
22. *BusinessWeek* (2000, January 17). The top technological blunders of the century, 8.
23. Wartzman, R. (1999, October 20). One adviser's mission: Creating Hispanic investors. *Wall Street Journal*, C-1.
24. Weinstein, E. (2002, January 10). Help! I'm drowning in e-mail. *Wall Street Journal*, B-1.
25. *Newsline* (2001, June 14).
26. *Newsline* (2001, July 19). E-mail not a time saver. resourcepro.worldatwork.org.
27. Wysocki, B. (1999, November 9). Corporate America confronts the measuring of a "core" business. *Wall Street Journal*, A-1.
28. *BusinessWeek* (2000, January 10). The best managers: What it takes, 158.
29. Lublin, J. (1999a, October 26). To find CEOs, Web firms rev-up search engines. *Wall Street Journal*, B-1; and Lublin, J. S. (1999b, November 9). An e-company CEO is also the recruitment chief. *Wall Street Journal*, B-1.
30. McWilliams, G. (1999, December 6). The best way to find a job. *Wall Street Journal*, R-16; and Dodge, S. (2002, February 12). Recruitment. *HR.com*. www4.hr.com/hrcom, 2.
31. Cited in *Wall Street Journal* (1999, November 15). The outlook: Worker capitalists of the world, unite. A-1.
32. Levering, R., and Moskowitz, M. (2000, January 10). The best 100 companies to work for. *Fortune*, 81–110; and Sager, I. (2000, January 10). Compaq's long road back. *BusinessWeek*, 52.
33. Id.
34. Symonds, W. C. (2000, January 10). Log on for company training. *BusinessWeek*, 138–139.
35. Symonds, W. C. (2002, December 3). Giving it the old online try. *BusinessWeek*, 76–80.
36. Richards, B. (1999, November 15). Automating human-resources operations used to be a luxury only big companies could afford. Not any longer. *Wall Street Journal*, R-18; and McDonald, D. (2002). Radical change: Breaking ground for e-HR implementation. *Workspan, 45*(2), 5–10.
37. Cited in Id.
38. Flanery, P. (2000, January 2). Racial, ethnic shifts transform region. *Arizona Republic*, A-1.
39. Lundstrom, M. (1999, December 20). "Mommy, do you love your company more than me?" *BusinessWeek*, 175.
40. National Bureau of Economic Research study by David Card, John Dinardo, and Eugena Estes, summarized in Koretz, G. (2000, January 17). Hazardous to your career. *BusinessWeek*, 26.
41. Wartzman, R. (1999, October 20). One adviser's mission: Creating Hispanic investors. *Wall Street Journal*, C-1.

42. *Las Vegas Review Journal* (2000, January 1). Who are the managers? Percent of U.S. minorities who are in managerial and professional jobs, 1998, B-1; and Cose, E. (2002, January 28). Rethinking black leadership. *Newsweek*, 42–48.
43. Roberts, J. L. (2002, January 28). The race to the top. *Newsweek*, 44–49.
44. Zachary, P. G. (2000, January 1). A mixed future. *Wall Street Journal*, R-41.
45. Id.
46. Conlin, M., and Zellner, W. (1999, November 22). The CEO still wears wingtips. *BusinessWeek*, 83; and *BusinessWeek* (2000, January 10). The best managers: What it takes, 158.
47. Millman, J. (2002, January 23). Mexico attracts U.S. aerospace industry. *Wall Street Journal*, A-17; Mandel, M. J. (1999, December 13). Global growing pains. *BusinessWeek*, 40–45; Mitchener, B. (1999, November 22). Border crossings. *Wall Street Journal*, R-41; and Smith, G. (1999, December 20). Breaking the curse. *BusinessWeek*, 61–62.
48. Smith, G. (2002). The decline of the maquiladora. *BusinessWeek*, 59.
49. Id.; and Borden, T. (2002). Recovery is sluggish at U.S. plants in Mexico. *Arizona Republic*, A-6.
50. Hagerty, B. (1993, June 14). Trainers help expatriate employees. *Wall Street Journal*, B1, B3.
51. Dodge, S. (2002, February 12). Using? on recruitment. *HR.com*. www4.hr.com/hrcom, 2.
52. Walker, J. (1992). *Human resource strategy*. New York: McGraw-Hill.
53. Newman, B. (1999, December 9). In Canada, the point of immigration is still unsentimental. *Wall Street Journal*, A-1.
54. Conlin, M., Coy, P., Palmer, A., and Saveri, G. (1999, December 6). The wild new workforce. *BusinessWeek*, 35–46; and Tejada, C. (2002, March 5). Home office: Millions don't leave work at home. *Wall Street Journal*, A-1.
55. Flynn, J. (1999, October 25). E-mail, cellphones, and frequent-flier miles let virtual expats work abroad but live at home. *Wall Street Journal*, A-26.
56. Gómez-Mejía, L. R. (1994). *Fostering a strategic partnership between operations and human resources*. Scarsdale, NY: Work in America Institute.
57. Ledvinka, J., and Scarpello, V. G. (1991). *Federal regulation of personnel and human resource management*. Boston: Kent.
58. Machalaba, M. (2000, January 3). E-commerce's newest portals: Truck drivers. *Wall Street Journal*, A-11; and Weinstein, E. (2002, January 10). Help! I'm drowning in e-mail. *Wall Street Journal*, B-1.
59. Barrett, P. M. (2000, January 4). Why Americans look to the courts to cure the nation's social ills. *Wall Street Journal*, A-1.
60. *Wall Street Journal* (1993, June 21). Work and family, R5.
61. Levering, R., and Moskowitz, M. (2002, February 4). The best in the worst of times. *Fortune*, 60–68.
62. www.runzeimer.com (2003, February 13).
63. Shellenbarger, S. (1993b, August 10). More women become partners in accounting. *Wall Street Journal*, B1.
64. Reinberg, J. (2002). It is about time: PTOs gain popularity. *Workspan*, *45*(2), 27–32.
65. Bureau of Labor Statistics Web page (2002). www.stats.bls.gov/empind/htm.
66. Perry, N. (1988, November 7). Saving the schools: How business can help. *Fortune*, 42–52.
67. Nussbaum, B. (1988, September 19). Needed: Human capital. *BusinessWeek*, 100–103.
68. Miller, W. H. (1988, July 4). Employers wrestle with "dumb" kids. *Industry Week*, 4.
69. Salwen, K. G., and Thomas, P. (1993, December 16). Job programs flunk at training but keep Washington at work. *Wall Street Journal*, A1.
70. Denney, W. (2002, February 12). Ford takes a wrong turn and ends up in a ditch. *HR.com*. www4.hr.com/hrcom, 2.
71. Muller, J., and Kerwin, K. (September 3). Cruising for quality. *BusinessWeek*, 74–76.
72. Doeringer, P. B., and Piore, M. J. (1971). Theories of low-wage labor workers. In L. G. Reynolds, S. H. Masters, and C. H. Moser (Eds.), *Readings in labor economics and labor relations*, 15–31. Upper Saddle River, NJ: Prentice Hall; and Pinfield, L. T., and Berner, M. F. (1994). Employment systems: Toward a coherent conceptualization of internal labor markets. In G. Ferris (Ed.), *Research in Personnel and Human Resources Management, 12*, 50–81.
73. Gumbel, P., and Wartzman, R. (2000, January 5). E-covery. *Wall Street Journal*, A-1; and Dreazen, Y. J. (2002, February 4). U.S. says Web use has risen to 54% of the population. *Wall Street Journal*, B-4.
74. Lublin, J. S. (1994b, February 9). Before you take that great job, get it in writing. *Wall Street Journal*, B1; and Nussbaum, B. (2002, January 28). Can you trust anybody anymore? *BusinessWeek*, 31–35.
75. Landers, P. (2002, March 1). Japan's Sony, Hitachi slash work forces. *Wall Street Journal*, A-3.
76. Matlock, C. (2001, November 5). The high cost of France's aversion to layoffs. *BusinessWeek*, 58; Lavelle, L. (2002, February 11). Swing that ax with care. *BusinessWeek*, 78; Colvin, G. (2002, February 4). You are on your own. *Fortune*, 42; and Fairlamb, D. (2002, January 21). Wiggle room for euro bosses. *BusinessWeek*, 20.
77. See, for example, De Meuse, K. P., and Tornow, W. W. (1990). The tie that binds has become very, very frayed. *Human Resource Planning, 13*(3), 203–213; Shellenbarger, S. (2002, February 20). Along with benefits and pay, employers seek friends on the job. *Wall Street Journal*, B-1; and Colvin, G. (2002, February 4). You are on your own. *Fortune*, 42.
78. Salwen, K. G. (1994, February 8). Decades of downsizing eases stigma of layoffs. *Wall Street Journal*, B1; Upfront Section (2001, September 10). Job hopping. *BusinessWeek*, 16; and Lavelle, L. (2002, February 11). Swing that ax with care. *BusinessWeek*, 78.
79. Upfront Section (2001, September 10). Job hopping. *BusinessWeek*, 16.
80. *USA Today* (2002, February 13). Some companies reassuring employees of no layoffs. www.usatoday.com.
81. Conlin, M. (2001, October 8). Where layoffs are the last resort. *BusinessWeek*, 42.
82. Levering, R., and Moskowitz, M. (2002, February 4). The best in the worst of times. *Fortune*, 60–68.
83. Ireland, D. R., and Hitt, M. A. (1999, February). Achieving and maintaining strategic competitiveness in the 21st century. *Academy of Management Executive, 13*(1), 43–57; and Deogun, N., and Lipin, S. (1999, December 8). Some hot mergers come undone for a variety of reasons. *Wall Street Journal*, C-1.
84. Manz, C. C. (1992). *Mastering self-leadership: Empowering yourself for personal excellence*. Upper Saddle River, NJ: Prentice Hall.
85. Manz, C. C., and Sims, H. P., Jr. (1993). *Business without bosses: How self-managing teams are building high performance companies*. New York: Wiley.
86. Id.
87. Id.
88. U.S. Small Business Administration. (n.d.). SBA Loan Programs. Washington, DC: U.S. Small Business Administration.
89. Fry, F. L. (1993). *Entrepreneurship: A planning approach*. St. Paul, MN: West.
90. Gómez-Mejía, L. R., Larraza, M., and Makri, M. (2003). Determinants of executive compensation in family owned firms. *Academy of Management Journal*, vol. 42, 2, 130–141.

91. Id.
92. Adapted from Schein, E. H. (1986). *Organizational culture and leadership*. San Francisco, CA: Jossey Bass.
93. Adapted from Id.
94. Drucker, P. F. (1993, October 21). The five deadly business sins. *Wall Street Journal*, A1.
95. Khermouch, G. (2002, January 21). There goes the creative juices. *BusinessWeek*, 52.
96. Odom, M. (1994, February 23). Management guru preaches to choir. *Arizona Republic*, E2.
97. Doeringer, P. B. (1991). *Turbulence in the American workplace*. New York: Oxford University Press.
98. Stewart, T. (2000, January 10). How Teledyne solved the innovator's dilemma. *Fortune*, 188–189.
99. Stepanek, M. (1999, December 13). Using the net for brainstorming, *BusinessWeek*, EB 55–58.
100. www.telecommute.org (2002, February 13).
101. Simpson, G. R. (2000, January 6). E-commerce firms start to rethink opposition to privacy regulation as abuses, anger rise. *Wall Street Journal*, A-24.
102. *Harper's Magazine* (2000, January 1). Special issue on the Internet, 57.
103. Rothfeder, J. (1994, January). Dangerous things strangers know about you. *McCall's*, 88–94.
104. McCarthy, M. J. (1999a, October 21). Now the boss knows where you are clicking. *Wall Street Journal*, B-1.
105. Id.
106. Greenberger, R. S. (1999, November 10). Privacy battle over databases at high court. *Wall Street Journal*, B-1; Dreazen, Y. (2000, January 1). It's great being all connected, until, that is, something goes wrong. *Wall Street Journal*, 38; and Simpson, G. R. (2000, January 6). E-commerce firms start to rethink opposition to privacy regulation as abuses, anger rise. *Wall Street Journal*, A-24.
107. Wilke, J. R. (1993, December 9). Computer links erode hierarchical nature of workplace culture. *Wall Street Journal*, A10.
108. Id.
109. Lavelle, L. (2002, January 14). First, kill the consultants. *BusinessWeek*, 122.
110. Davis, A. (2002, February 6). Companies want the FBI to screen employees for suspected terrorists. *Wall Street Journal*, B-1.
111. Conlin, M., and Salkever, A. (2001, July 30). Revenge of the downsized nerds. *BusinessWeek*, 40.
112. Green, H. (2001, April 23). Your right to privacy going, going . . . *BusinessWeek*, 32–33.
113. Armour, S. (2002b, June 19). Security checks worry workers. *USA Today*, A-1.
114. Lancaster, H. (1995, September 12). Saving your career when your position has been outsourced. *Wall Street Journal*, B-1
115. Berstein, A., and Zellner, A. (1995, July 17). Outsourced—and out of luck. *BusinessWeek*, 61.
116. Id.
117. Tejada, C. (2002, March 5). Home office: Millions don't leave work at home. *Wall Street Journal*, A-1.
118. Melcher, R. A. (1996, January 8). Who says you can't find good help? *BusinessWeek*, 107.
119. Gupta, A. K., and Govindarajan, V. (1984). Business unit strategy, managerial characteristics, and business unit effectiveness at strategy implementation. *Academy of Management Journal 27*, 25–41.
120. Balkin, D. B., and Gómez-Mejía, L.R. (1985). Compensation practices in high tech industries. *Personnel Administrator, 30*(6), 111–123.
121. Hymowitz, C. (2002, February 19). Managers must respond to employee concerns about honest business. *Wall Street Journal*, A-1; Eisenberg, D. (2002, February 11). Ignorant and poor? *Time*, 32–38; Kadlec, D. (2002, January 21). Who is accountable? *Time*, 31–34; Pulliam, S., and Smith, R. (2002, February 15). Enron's actions before news event may have had multimillion payoff. *Wall Street Journal*, C-1; and Dreazen, Y. J. (2002, February 15). WorldCom suspends executives in scandal over order booking. *Wall Street Journal*, A-3.
122. Hamburger, T., and Brown, K. (2002, January 17). Andersen knew of Enron woes a year ago. *Wall Street Journal*, A-3
123. *USA Today* (2001, December 3). Snapshots, B-1.
124. Armour, S. (2002a, February 4). Employees' motto: Trust no one. *USA Today*, 5-A.
125. Pastin, M. (1986). *The hard problems of management: Giving the ethics edge*. San Francisco: Jossey Bass.
126. Noe, R., Hollenbeck, J. R. Gerhart, G., and Wright, P. M. (1994). *Human resource management: Gaining a competitive advantage*. Homewood, IL: Austen.
127. Brown, K. (2002a February 21). Creative accounting: How to buff a company. *Wall Street Journal*, C-1.
128. Brown, K. (2002b, March 7). Accounting industry fights calls for "audit only" rules. *Wall Street Journal*, C-1.
129. Mathieu, J. E., and Zajac, D. M. (1990). A review and meta-analysis of the antecedents, correlates, and consequences of organizational commitment. *Psychological Bulletin, 108*, 171–194.
130. McCarthy, M. J. (1999b, October 21). How one firm tracks ethics electronically. *Wall Street Journal*, B-1.
131. Berstein, A. (2001, February 26). Low skilled jobs: Do they have to move? *BusinessWeek*, 94–96.
132. White, J. B. (2000, January 1). Corporation aren't going to disappear but they are going to look a lot different. *Wall Street Journal*, R-36
133. Kelly, L. (2000, January 2). Preparation by applicant key to successful interview. *Arizona Republic*, C-1.
134. Hom, P., and Griffeth, R.(1994). *Employee turnover*. Cincinnati, OH: South-Western.
135. Campion, M. A., and McClelland, C. L. (1991). Interdisciplinary examination of the costs and benefits of enlarged jobs. *Journal of Applied Psychology, 76*, 186–198.
136. Cited in Hymowitz, C. (2000, January 4). How can a manager encourage employees to take bold risks? *Wall Street Journal*, B-1.
137. Id.
138. Petzinger, T. (2000, January 1). There is a new economy out there. *Wall Street Journal*, R-31; and White, J. B. (2000, January 1). Corporations aren't going to disappear but they are going to look a lot different. *Wall Street Journal*, R-36.
139. Shirouzu, N. (2000, January 5). Leaner and meaner. *Wall Street Journal*, A-1.
140. Conlin, M., and Salkever, A. (2001, July 30). Revenge of the downsized nerds. *BusinessWeek*, 40.
141. Dempsey, J., and Siebenhaar, M. (2002). Bankruptcy blues: retaining key employees during a financial crisis. *Workspan*, vol. 45, 2, 1–5.
142. Arndt, M. (2002, January 21). 3M: A lab for growth? *BusinessWeek*, 50–52.
143. Id., 51.
144. Drucker, P. (1993, October 21). The five deadly business sins. *Wall Street Journal*, R2.
145. Arndt, M. (2002, January 21). 3M: A lab for growth? *BusinessWeek*, 50–52.
146. Butler, J. E., Ferris, G. R., and Napier, N. K. (1991). *Strategy and human resources management*. Cincinnati, OH: South-Western.
147. Mintzberg, H. (1990). The design school: Reconsidering the basic premises of strategic management. *Strategic Management Journal, 11*, 171–196; and Walker, J. (1992). *Human resource management strategy*, Chapter 1. New York: McGraw-Hill.

148. Id.
149. Brockner, J. (1992). The escalation of commitment to a failing course of action: Toward theoretical progress. *Academy of Management Review, 17*(1), 39–61; and Staw, B. (1976). Knee-deep in Big Muddy: A study of escalating commitment to a chosen course of action. *Organizational Behavior and Human Performance, 16*, 27–44.
150. See the following reviews: Dyer, L., and Holder, G. W. (1988). A strategic perspective of human resource management. In L. Dyer (Ed.), *Human resource management: Evolving roles and responsibilities*. Washington, DC: Bureau of National Affairs; and Gómez-Mejía, L. R., and Balkin, D. B. (1992). *Compensation, organizational strategy, and firm performance*. Cincinnati, OH: South-Western.
151. Bulkeley, W. M. (2000, January 6). Virtual utilities peddle power over the Web. *Wall Street Journal*, B-1.
152. Warren, S. (2002, February 5). DuPont cajoles independent units to talk to one another. *Wall Street Journal*, B-4.
153. Kerr, J. (1985). Diversification strategies and managerial rewards: An empirical study. *Academy of Management Journal, 28*, 155–179; Leontiades, M. (1980). Strategies for diversification and change. Boston: Little, Brown; and Pitts, R. A. (1974, May). Incentive compensation and organization design. *Personnel Journal, 20*(5), 338–344.
154. Gómez-Mejía, L. R. (1992). Structure and process of diversification, compensation strategy, and firm performance. *Strategic Management Journal, 13*, 381–397; and Kerr, J. (1985). Diversification strategies and managerial rewards: An empirical study. *Academy of Management Journal, 28*, 155–179.
155. Farnam, A. (1994, February 7). Corporate reputations. *Fortune*, 50–54.
156. Porter, M. E. (1980). *Competitive strategy*. New York: Free Press; Porter, M. E. (1985). *Competitive advantage*. New York: Free Press; and Porter, M. E. (1990). *The competitive advantage of nations*. Boston: Free Press.
157. Miles, R. E., and Snow, C. C. (1978). *Organizational strategy, structure, and process*. New York: McGrawHill; and Miles, R. E., and Snow, C. C. (1984). Designing strategic human resources systems. *Organizational Dynamics, 13*(1), 36–52.
158. Montemayor, E. F. (1994). Pay policies that fit organizational strategy: Evidence from high-performing firms. Unpublished paper. East Lansing, MI: School of Industrial and Labor Relations, Michigan State University.
159. Porter, M. E. (1980). *Competitive strategy*. New York: Free Press.
160. Id.
161. Byrne, H. S. (1992, November 16). Illinois Tool Works: Satisfying customers . . . and investors. *Barron's*, 51–52.
162. Miles, R. E., and Snow, C. C. (1978). *Organizational strategy, structure, and process*. New York: McGraw-Hill; and Miles, R. E., and Snow, C. C. (1984). Designing strategic human resources systems. *Organizational Dynamics, 13*(1), 36–52.
163. Miles, R. E., Snow, C. C., Meyer, A. D., and Coleman, H. J. (1978). Organizational strategy, structure, and process. *Academy of Management Review, 3*, 546–562.
164. Gómez-Mejía, L. R., and Balkin, D. B. (1992). *Compensation, organizational strategy, and firm performance*, 125. Cincinnati, OH: South-Western; and Gagne, K. (2002). One day at a time: Using performance management to translate strategy into results. *Workspan, 45*(2), 20–26.
165. For another example, see Corden, R., Elmer, M., Knudsen, J., Mountain, R., Rider, M., and Ross, W. (1994, March–April). When a new pay plan fails: The case of Beta Corporation. *Compensation & Benefits Review*, 26–32.
166. Jones, G., and Wright, P. (1992). An economic approach to conceptualizing the utility of human resource management practices. *Research in Personnel/Human Resources, 10*, 271–299; and Kearns, P. (2002, February 12). The case against HR benchmarks. *HR.com*, www4.hr.com/hrcom.
167. Gómez-Mejía, L. R. (1994). *Fostering a strategic partnership between operations and human resources*. Scarsdale, NY: Work in America Institute; Cadorette, S. (2002, February 12). Where exactly is your HR career headed? *HR.com*, www4.hr.com/hrcom; and Stoskopt, G. A. (2002). Taking performance management to the next level. *Workspan, 45*(2), 15–22.
168. Zingheim, P., and Schuster, J. (2002, February 12). Creating a workplace business brand. *HR.com*, www4.hr.com/hrcom; and McDonald, D. (2001). HR—earning its place at the table. *Worldatwork Journal, 10*(1), 1–6.
169. For more information, see Wiley, C. (1992, August). The certified HR professional. *HRMagazine, 37*(8), 77–79, 82–84; and Wiley, C., and Goff, E. F. (1994). *Trends, strategies, objectives, linkages, and professionalism. Compensation guide*. New York: Warren Gorham and Lamont.
170. *Newsline* (2001, May 18); *Newsline* (2002, January 8); and *Newsline* (2001, June 26).
171. Cooper, Marigan, and Miller (2002), 33.
172. Armour, S. (2002a, February 4). Employees' motto: Trust no one. *USA Today*, 5-A.
173. Haddad, C. (2002, March 4). When auditors also consult. *BusinessWeek*, 12.
174. Quoted in Conlin, M., Coy, P., Palmer, A., and Saveri, G. (1999, December 6). The wild new workforce. *BusinessWeek*, 35–46.
175. Armour, S. (2002b, June 19). Security checks worry workers. *USA Today*, A–1.

Chapter 2

1. Waler, K. (1997, June). Proceed with care, Southwest Airlines reaches strategic development crossroads. *Airline Business, 6*(13), 70.
2. Keenan, F., and Ante, S. (2002, February 18). The new teamwork. *BusinessWeek e.biz*, 12–16.
3. Ante, S. (2001, August 27). Simultaneous software. *BusinessWeek*, 146–147.
4. Thompson, A., and Strickland, A. (1993). *Strategic management* (7th ed.). Homewood, IL: Irwin.
5. Smart, T. (1996, October 28). Jack Welch's encore. *BusinessWeek*, 155–160.
6. Hammer, M., and Champy, J. (1993). *Reengineering the corporation*. New York: HarperCollins.
7. Lawler, E. (1992). *The ultimate advantage*. San francisco, CA: Jossey-Bass.
8. Hof, R. D. (1999, January 18). Is the center of the computing universe shifting? Sun power. *BusinessWeek*, 64–72; and Sager, I., and Yang, C. (1998, December 7). A new cyber order. *BusinessWeek*, 27–31.
9. Hammer, M., and Champy, J. (1994, April). Avoiding the hottest new management cure. *Inc.*, 25–26.
10. Hammer, M., and Champy, J. (1993). *Reengineering the corporation*. New York: HarperCollins.
11. Ibid.
12. Greengard, S. (1993, December). Reengineering: Out of the rubble. *Personnel Journal*, 48B–48O; and Verity, J. (1993, June 21). Getting work to go with the flow. *BusinessWeek*, 156–161.
13. Hammer, M., and Champy, J. (1993). *Reengineering the corporation*. New York: HarperCollins.
14. Ibid.
15. Hammer, M. (1995, May 15). Beating the risks of reengineering. *Fortune*, 105–114.
16. *The Economist*. (1994, July 2). Re-engineering reviewed, 66.

17. Katzenback, J., and Smith, D. (1993, March–April). The discipline of teams. *Harvard Business Review*, 111–120.
18. Orsburn, J., Moran, L., Musselwhite, E., and Zenger, J. (1990). *Self-directed work teams*. Homewood, IL: Business One Irwin.
19. Katzenback, J., and Smith, D. (1993, March–April). The discipline of teams. *Harvard Business Review*, 111–120.
20. Jassawalla, A. R., and Sashittal, H. C. (1999). Building collaborative cross-functional new product teams. *Academy of Management Executive, 13*(3), 50–63.
21. Hoerr, J. (1989, July 10). The payoff from teamwork. *BusinessWeek*, 56–62.
22. Caudron, S. (1993, December). Are self-directed teams right for your company? *Personnel Journal*, 76–84.
23. Bassin, M. (1996, January). From team to partnerships. *HRMagazine*, 86–92.
24. Balkin, D., and Montemayor, E. (2000). Explaining team-based pay: A contingency perspective based on the organizational life cycle, team design, and organizational learning literatures. *Human Resource Management Review, 10*, 249–269.
25. Kirsner, S. (1998, April). Four lessons on teamwork from SEI investments. *Fast Company*, 132.
26. Orsburn, J., Moran, L., Musselwhite, E., and Zenger, J. (1990). *Self-directed work teams*. Homewood, IL: Business One Irwin.
27. Ibid.
28. Dumaine, B. (1994, September 5). The trouble with teams. *Fortune*, 86–92.
29. Caramanica, L., Ferris, S., and Little, J. (2001, December). Self-directed teams: Use with caution. *Nursing Management*, 77.
30. Orsburn, J., Moran, L., Musselwhite, E., and Zenger, J. (1990). *Self-directed work teams*. Homewood, IL: Business One Irwin.
31. Chatman, J., and Flynn, F. (2001). The influence of dempgraphic hetereogeneity on the emergence and consequences of cooperative norms in work teams. *Academy of Management Journal, 44*, 956–974.
32. Hoerr, J. (1989, July 10). The payoff from teamwork. *BusinessWeek*, 56–62.
33. Lawler, E. (1992). *The ultimate advantage*. San Francisco, CA: Jossey-Bass.
34. Keenan, F., and Ante, S. (2002, February 18). The new teamwork. *BusinessWeek e.biz*, 12–16.
35. Kostner, J. (2001, October). Bionic eTeamwork. *Executive Excellence*, 78.
36. Steers, R. (1984). *Introduction to organizational behavior* (2nd ed.). Glenview, IL: Scott, Foresman.
37. Herzberg, F. (1968, January–February). One more time: How do you motivate employees? *Harvard Business Review*, 52–62.
38. Lofquist, L., and Dawis, R. (1969). *Adjustment to work: A psychological view of man's problems in a work-oriented society*. Upper Saddle River, NJ: Prentice Hall.
39. Locke, E. (1968). Toward a theory of task motives and incentives. *Organizational Behavior and Human Performance, 3*, 157–189.
40. Pinder, C. (1984). *Work motivation*. Glenview, IL: Scott, Foresman.
41. Hackman, J., and Oldham, G. (1976). Motivation through the design of work: Test of a theory. *Organizational Behavior and Human Performance, 16*, 250–279.
42. Nadler, D. A., Hackman, J. R., and Lawler, E. E. (1979). *Managing organizational behavior*. Boston: Little, Brown.
43. Ibid.
44. Behson, S., Eddy, E., and Lorenzet, S., (2000). The importance of critical psychological states in the job characteristics model: A meta-analytic and structural equations modeling examination. *Current Research in Social Psychology, 5*(12), 170–189.
45. Hackman, J. (1976). Work design. In Hackman, J., and Suttle, J. (Eds.). *Improving life at work*, 96–162. Santa Monica, CA: Goodyear.
46. Denton, D. K. (1992, August). Redesigning a job by simplifying every task and responsibility. *Industrial Engineering*, 46–48.
47. Szilagyi, A., and Wallace, M. (1980). *Organizational behavior and performance* (2nd ed.). Santa Monica, CA: Goodyear.
48. Lawler, E. (1986). *High involvement management*. San Francisco, CA: Jossey-Bass.
49. Ibid.
50. Steers, R. (1984). *Introduction to organizational behavior* (2nd ed.). Glenview, IL: Scott, Foresman.
51. Lawler, E. (1986). *High involvement management*. San Francisco, CA: Jossey-Bass.
52. Campion, M. A., and Higgs, A. C. (1995, October). Design work teams to increase productivity and satisfaction. *HRMagazine*, 101–107.
53. Lawler, E. (1992). *The ultimate advantage*. San Francisco, CA: Jossey-Bass.
54. Geber, B. (1992, June). Saturn's grand experiment. *Training*, 27–35.
55. Drauden, G. M. (1988). Task inventory analysis in industry and the public sector. In S. Gael (Ed.), *The job analysis handbook for business, industry, and government*, 105–171. New York: Wiley and Sons.
56. Flanagan, J. C. (1954). The critical incident technique. *Psychological Bulletin, 51*, 327–358.
57. McCormick, E., and Jeannerette, R. (1988). The position analysis questionnaire. In S. Gael (Ed.), *The job analysis handbook for business, industry, and government*, 880–901. New York: John Wiley and Sons.
58. Fine, S. A. (1992). *Functional job analysis: A desk aid*. Milwaukee, WI: Sidney A. Fine.
59. Harvey, R. (2002). Functional job analysis. *Personnel Psychology, 55*, 202–205.
60. U.S. Department of Labor. (1991). *Dictionary of occupational titles* (4th ed.). Washington, DC: U.S. Government Printing Office.
61. Chatman, J. A. (1989). Improving interaction organizational research: A model of person–organization fit. *Academy of Management Review, 14*, 333–349.
62. Cardy, R. L., and Dobbins, G. H. (1994). *Performance appraisal: Alternative perspectives*. Cincinnati, OH: South-Western.
63. Leonard, S. (2000, August). The demise of the job description. *HRMagazine*, 184.
64. Johnson, C. (2001, January). Refocusing job descriptions. *HRMagazine*, 66–72.
65. Cardy, R. L. and Dobbins, G. H. (2000, January). Jobs disappear when work becomes more important. *Workforce*, 30–32.
66. Cardy, R., and Dobbins, G. (1992, Fall). Job analysis in a dynamic environment. *Human Resources Division News*, 4–6.
67. Ibid.
68. Jones, M. (1984, May). Job descriptions made easy. *Personnel Journal*, 31–34.
69. Fierman, J. (1994, January 24). The contingent work force. *Fortune*, 30–36.
70. Hershey, R. D. (1995, August 19). Survey finds 6 million, fewer than thought, in impermanent jobs. *New York Times*, 1, 17; and Melcher, R. A. (1996, June 10). Manpower upgrades its résumé. *BusinessWeek*, 81+.
71. Stewart, T. A. (1995, March 20). World without managers. *Fortune*, 72.
72. Uchitelle, L., and Kleinfield, N. R. (1996, March 3). The downsizing of America. *New York Times*, special report.
73. Flynn, G. (1999, September). Temp staffing carries legal risk. *Workforce*, 56–62; and Bernstein A. (1999, May 31). Now temp workers are a full-time headache. *BusinessWeek*, 46.
74. *The Economist*. (2000, June 10). Western Europe's job-seekers limber up, 53–54.

75. Rogers, B. (1992, May). Companies develop benefits for part timers. *HRMagazine*, 89–90.
76. Sunoo, B. P., and Laabs, J. J. (1994, March). Winning strategies for outsourcing contracts. *Personnel Journal*, 69–78.
77. *The Economist*. (1995, October 25). The outing of outsourcing, 57–58.
78. Klaas, B., McClendon, K., and Gainey, T. (2001, Summer). Outsourcing HR: The impact of organizational characteristics. *Human Resource Management*, 125–138.
79. Bates, S. (2002, April). Fishing bigger: HR outsourcing firms are forming partnerships and acquiring resource in a bid to get contracts from big business. *HRMagazine*, 38–42.
80. James, G. (1997, November). Tipping the scales your way. *Datamation*, 48–53.
81. Sunoo, B. P., and Laabs, J. J. (1994, March). Winning strategies for outsourcing contracts. *Personnel Journal*, 69–78.
82. *The Economist*. (1994, April 23). Benetton: The next era, 68.
83. For information on a new twist on outsourcing, see Semler, R. (1993). *Maverick*. New York: Warner Books.
84. Pearce, J. (1993). Toward an organizational behavior of contract laborers: Their psychological involvement and effects on employee co-workers. *Academy of Management Journal, 36*, 1082–1096.
85. Albrecht, D. G. (1998, April). New heights: Today's contract workers are highly promotable. *Workforce*, 43–48.
86. Sheppard, E. M., Clifton, T. J., and Kruse, D. (1996). Flexible work hours and productivity: Some evidence from the pharmaceutical industry. *Industrial Relations, 35*, 123–129.
87. Denton, D. (1993, January–February). Using flextime to create a competitive workplace. *Industrial Management*, 29–31.
88. Ibid.
89. Pierce, J., and Dunham, R. (1992). The 12-hour work day: A 48-hour, eight-day week. *Academy of Management Journal*, 1086–1098.
90. Sunoo, B. P. (1996, January). How to manage compressed workweeks. *Personnel Journal*, 110.
91. *Forbes ASAP*. (1995, August 28). Their private Idaho, 20–25.
92. Garvey, C. (2001, August). Teleworking HR. *HRMagazine*, 56–60.
93. Kavanaugh, M., Gueutal, H., and Tannenbaum, S. (1990). *Human resource information systems: Development and application*. Boston, MA: PWS-Kent.
94. Dzamba, A. (2001, January). What are your peers doing to boost HRIS performance? *HR Focus*, 56.
95. Leonard, B. (1991, July). Open and shut HRIS. *Personnel Journal*, 59–62.
96. Ibid.

Chapter 3

1. Zellner, W. (2002, March 18). A Texas-size case of discrimination? *BusinessWeek*, 14.
2. Long, S. (1999, April). Quick reactions by employer prevents sexual harassment liability. *HR Focus*, 3.
3. Bernstein, A. (2001, July 30). Racism in the workplace. *BusinessWeek*, 35–37.
4. Adapted from Commerce Clearing House. (1992). *Equal employment opportunity manual for managers and supervisors* (2nd ed.). Chicago, IL.
5. Hall, F. S., and Hall, E. L. (1994). The ADA: Going beyond the law. *Academy of Management Executive, 8*, 17–26.
6. Coie, P. (2001, December). Ninth circuit affirms $1.03 million jury verdict in race discrimination suit. *Washington Employment Law Letter*, 1.
7. *AIDS Litigation Reporter*. (2001, September 10). California court clarifies continuing violation doctrine in disability bias case, 7.
8. Faircloth, A. (1998, August 3). Guess who's coming to Denny's? *Fortune*, 108–110.
9. Ibid., 110.
10. Labich, K. (1999, September 6). No more crude at Texaco, *Fortune*, 205–212.
11. *Griggs v. Duke Power Co.*, 401 U.S. 424 (1971).
12. *Wards Cove v. Antonio*, 109 S.Ct. 2115, 49 FEP CASES 1523 (1989).
13. Hall, F. S., and Hall, E. L. (1994). The ADA: Going beyond the law. *Academy of Management Executive, 8*, 17–26.
14. Greenlaw, P. S., and Kohl, J. P. (1995). The equal pay act: Responsibilities and rights. *Employee Responsibilities and Rights Journal, 8*, 295–307.
15. Adams, M. (1999, May). Fair and square. *HRMagazine*, 38–44.
16. Strout, E. (2001, July). Tough sell. *Sales & Marketing Management*, 50–55.
17. Ledvinka, J., and Scarpello, V. G. (1991). *Federal regulation of personnel and human resource management* (2nd ed.). Boston: PWS-Kent; and Twomey, D. P. (1990). *Equal employment opportunity* (2nd ed.). Cincinnati, OH: South-Western.
18. *BNA's Employee Relations Weekly*. (1993, September 13). EEOC meets new, higher burden of proof in race bias case in California court. *11*, 1991.
19. *Griggs v. Duke Power Co.*, 401 U.S. 424 (1971).
20. *HR News*. (1994, February). No beard rule found to have disparate impact, 17.
21. *Albemarle Paper Co. v. Moody*, 422 U.S. 405 (1975).
22. *McDonnell Douglas Corp. v. Green*, 411 U.S. 792 (1973).
23. Equal Employment Opportunity Commission. (1978). *Uniform Guidelines on Employee Selection Procedures*, 29 Code of Federal Regulations, Part 1607, Sec. 6.A.
24. Uheling, A. (2002, April 29). Pregnancy Discrimination Act set clear management limits. *Federal Human Resources Week*, 1.
25. Ibid.
26. *Employment Law Report*. (2002, March). $230K punitive award found not excessive in pregnancy bias case, 1.
27. *HR Reporter*. (2001, June 4). City settles discrimination charge by pregnant police officer, 1.
28. Fitzgerald, L. F., Drasgow, F., Hulin, C., Gelfond, M., and Magley, V. J. (1997). Antecedents and consequences of sexual harassment in organizations: A test of an integrated model. *Journal of Applied Psychology, 82*, 578–589.
29. Gruber, J. E. (1998). The impact of male work environments and organizational policies on women's experiences of sexual harassment. *Gender & Society, 12*, 301–321.
30. Hendrix, W. H. (1998). Sexual harassment and gender differences. *Journal of Social Behavior and Personality, 13*, 135–253.
31. *BNA's Employee Relations Weekly*. (1994, January 31). Medical center employee awarded $1 million in Massachusetts suit, *12*, 111–112.
32. Shepela, S. T., and Levesque, L. L. (1998). Poisoned waters: Sexual harassment and the college climate. *Sex Roles, 8*, 589–611; and Shelton, N. J., and Chavous, T. M. (1999). Black and white college women's perceptions of sexual harassment. *Sex Roles, 40*, 593–615.
33. *Harris v. Forklift Systems, Inc.* 114 S. Ct. 367 (1993).
34. Cole, J. (1999, March). Sexual harassment: New rules, new behavior. *HR Focus*, 1–15.
35. Muller, J. (1999, November 15). Ford: The high cost of harassment. *BusinessWeek*, 94–96.
36. Aronson, P. (2002, April 29). Mitsubushi comes back from disaster of 1998. *National Law Review*, A23.

37. Lewis, N. A. (1999, July 30). New penalty of Clinton in Jones case. *New York Times*, A15.
38. Rospenda, K. M., Richman, J. A., and Nawyn, S. J. (1998). Doing power: The influence of gender, race, and class in contrapower sexual harassment. *Gender & Society, 12*, 40–61.
39. *Human Resource Management Ideas and Trends*. (1996, February 14). Sexual harassment complaints no longer limited to women, 30.
40. *The Economist*. (1998, July 4). Men, women, work and law, 21–22.
41. *BNA's Employee Relations Weekly*. (1994, April 4). Survey finds 31 percent of women report having been harassed at work, *12*, 367.
42. Luthar, H., and Pastille, C. (2000). Modeling subordinate perceptions of sexual harassment: The role of superior–subordinate social-sexual interaction. *Human Resource Management Review, 10*, 211–244.
43. Flynn, G. (1999, May). Sexual harassment interpretations give cause for new concerns. *Workforce*, 105–106; and Garland, S. B. (1998, July 13). Finally, a corporate tip sheet on sexual harassment *BusinessWeek*, 39.
44. O'Leary-Kelly, A., and Bowes-Sperry, L. (2001). Sexual harassment as unethical behavior: The role of moral intensity. *Human Resource Management Review, 11*, 73–92.
45. Slade, M. (1998, July 19). A hint of clarity in harassment case law. *New York Times*, www.nytimes.com.
46. *Wards Cove Packing Co. v. Antonio*, 409 U.S. 642 (1989).
47. Bureau of National Affairs. (1991, November 11). Civil rights act of 1991. *Employee Relations Weekly* (special supplement).
48. Carson, K. P. (1991, November 22). New civil rights law shoots itself in the foot. *Wall Street Journal*, A10.
49. Geyelin, M. (1993, December 17). Age-bias cases found to bring big jury awards. *Wall Street Journal*, B1.
50. Harper, L. (1994, April 5). Labor letter. *Wall Street Journal*, A1.
51. Milkovich, G. T., and Newman, J. M. (1996). *Compensation* (5th ed.). Chicago: Irwin.
52. Sharpe, R. (1994, April 19). Labor letter. *Wall Street Journal*, A1.
53. EEOC. (1992, January). *A technical assistance manual on the employment provisions of the Americans with Disabilities Act*.
54. Stevens, M. (2002, April 29). "Toyota" may be seen as a reasonable balancing act. *The National Law Journal*, A34.
55. Hall, J. E., and Hatch, D. D. (1999, August). Supreme Court decisions require ADA revision. *Workforce*, 60–67.
56. Petesch, P. J. (1999, June). Are the newest ADA guidelines "reasonable"? *HRMagazine*, 54–58.
57. *The Economist*. (1998, April 18). The halt, the blind, the dyslexic, 25–26.
58. Martinez, M. N. (1990, November). Creative ways to employ people with disabilities. *HRMagazine*, 40–44, 101.
59. EEOC. (1992, January). *A technical assistance manual on the employment provisions of the Americans with Disabilities Act*.
60. Wells, S. (2001, April). Is the ADA working? *HRMagazine*, 38–46.
61. Ledvinka, J., and Scarpello, V. G. (1991). *Federal regulation of personnel and human resource management* (2nd ed.). Boston: PWS-Kent.
62. Evans, S. (1994, March). Doing mediation to avoid litigation. *HRMagazine*, 48–51.
63. The U.S. Equal Employment Opportunity Commission. (2002, February 22). EEOC issues fiscal 2001 enforcement data. www.eeoc.gov/press.
64. *Johnson v. Santa Clara County, Transportation Agency, Santa Clara County*, 107 S.Ct. 1442, 43 FEP Cases 411 (1987); Nazario, S. L. (1989, June 27). Many minorities feel torn by experience of affirmative action. *Wall Street Journal*, A1; and Roberts, S. V. (1995, February 13). Affirmative action on the edge. *U.S. News & World Report*, 32–38.
65. *Regents of the University of California v. Bakke*, 438 U.S. 265 (1978).
66. *The Economist*. (1995, April 15). A question of colour, 13–14.
67. Wynter, L. (1996, February 7). Business and race. *Wall Street Journal*, B1.
68. Sovereign, K. L. (1994). *Personnel Law* (2nd ed.). Upper Saddle River, NJ: Prentice Hall.
69. Ledvinka, J., and Scarpello, V. G. (1991). *Federal regulation of personnel and human resource management* (2nd ed.). Boston: PWS-Kent.
70. *BNA's Employee Relations Weekly*. (1994, March 28). Testing programs deter abuse, are cost effective, report says, *12*, 349.
71. *HR News*. (1994, March). Washington scorecard, *13*, 4.
72. Hall, F. S., and Hall, E. L. (1994). The ADA: Going beyond the law. *Academy of Management Executive, 8*, 17–26.
73. *HR News*. (1994, March). Legal report, 18.
74. Miclat, C. (2000, January). Recognition policies protect from potential discrimination. *Workforce*, 72–73.

Chapter 4

1. Edwards, A. (1991, January). The enlightened manager. *Working Woman*, 45–51.
2. Allport, G. W., and Odbert, H. S. (1933). Trait-names: A psycholexical study. *Psychological Monographs, 47*, 171–220.
3. Loden, M., and Rosener, J. B. (1991). *Workforce America, 18*. Homewood, IL: Irwin; and Society for Human Resource Management (SHRM). (2002c, February 13). What are employee networks and should they be a part of our diversity initiative? www.shrm.org/diversity.
4. Hymowitz, C. (1995, April 24). How a dedicated mentor gave momentum to a woman's career. *Wall Street Journal*, B1; Fellows, D. S. (2001). Striking gold in a silver mine: Leveraging senior workers as knowledge champions. *Worldatwork Journal, 10*(4), 112; and Lynnes, K. S. (2002). Finding the key to the executive suite: Challenges for women and people of color. In R. Sitzer (Ed.). *The 21st Century Executive*, 229–274. San Francisco: Jossey-Bass.
5. Rosen, R. H. (2000). *Global literacies*. New York: Simon & Schuster, and Lynnes, K. S. (2002). Finding the key to the executive suite: Challenges for women and people of color. In R. Sitzer (Ed.). *The 21st Century Executive*, 229–274. San Francisco: Jossey-Bass.
6. *Fortune* (2003). Best companies for Asian, Black, and Hispanic employees. www.fortune.com.
7. Ibid.
8. Society for Human Resource Management (SHRM). (2002a, February 13). Diversity training. www.shrm.org/diversity.
9. Dass, P., and Parker, B. (1999). Strategies for managing human resource diversity: From resistance to learning. *The Academy of Management Executive, 13*(2), 68–80, White, J. E. (1999, August 23). Affirmative actions Alamo. *Time*, 48; and Society for Human Resource Management (SHRM). (2002f, February 13). How is a diversity initiative different from my organization's affirmative action plan? www.shrm.org/diversity.
10. Society for Human Resource Management (SHRM). (2002d, February 13). Where HR meets the world: How should my organization define diversity? www.shrm.org/diversity.
11. Merritt, J. (2002, March 11). Guess who's pushing a bold plan for diversity? Big business. *BusinessWeek*, 56–58; Amendariz, Y. (2002a, March 16). Many want more contracts with minority, female firms. *Arizona Republic*, D-1; and Amendariz, Y. (2002b, March 16). Minority groups looking for increased accountability. *Arizona Republic*, D-1.

12. Bureau of Labor Statistics, Economic Surveys (2002). Data and reports. www.lib.gsu.edu.
13. Johnson, R. S. (1998, August 3). The 50 best companies for blacks and Hispanics. *Fortune*, 94–112.
14. Moore, S. (1999). Study results cited in Shaffer, M. (1999, September 3). Importing poverty. *Arizona Republic*, A-1. See also Amendariz, Y. (2002a, March 16). Many want more contracts with minority, female firms. *Arizona Republic*, D-1; and Amendariz, Y. (2002b, March 16). Minority groups looking for increased accountability. *Arizona Republic*, D-1.
15. Kannan, J., and Rosenberg, H. (2002, February 7). Survey looks at residents with foreign roots. *Arizona Republic*, A-8.
16. *Fortune* (2003).
17. Weaver, V. (2001, September 10). Winning with diversity. *BusinessWeek*, special section.
18. Dass, P., and Parker, B. (1999). Strategies for managing human resource diversity: From resistance to learning. *The Academy of Management Executive, 13*(2), 68–80; and Society for Human Resource Management (SHRM). (2002e, February 13). How can the results of our initiative be measured? www.shrm.org/diversity.
19. Kanter, R. M. (1983). *The change masters, 52*. New York: Simon & Schuster.
20. Author's files.
21. Sheppard, C. R. (1964). *Small groups, 118*. San Francisco: Chandler; and Gómez-Mejía, L. R., and Balkin, D. B. (2002). *Management*. New York: Irwin/McGraw-Hill.
22. Roberts, E. (1999, July 19). The trickle-up effect. *Fortune,* 64.
23. *Fortune*. (1999, April 26). The bus company that stopped pretending it was an airline, 48.
24. Crockett, R. O. (1999, May 24). African-Americans get the investing bug. *BusinessWeek*, 39; and Koretz, G. (2001, September 3). Giant strides for U.S. blacks. *BusinessWeek*, 28.
25. Coker, S., and Weaver, V. J. (2001, September 10). Embracing the future Verizon addresses its Hispanic market opportunities. *BusinessWeek,* special section.
26. Duke, L. (1991, January 1). Cultural shifts bring anxiety for white men: Growing diversity imposing new dynamic in work force. *Washington Post,* A1; and Society for Human Resource Management (SHRM). (2002c, February 13). What are employee networks and should they be part of our diversity initiative? www.shrm.org/diversity.
27. Edwards, A. (1991, January). The enlightened manager. *Working Woman*, 46.
28. Dass, P., and Parker, B. (1999). Strategies for managing human resource diversity: From resistance to learning. *The Academy of Management Executive, 13*(2), 68–80; and Society for Human Resource Management (SHRM). (2002f, February 13). How is a diversity initiative different from my organization's affirmative action plan? www.shrm.org/diversity.
29. Author's files.
30. Study results reported in McDonough, D. C. (1999, April 26). A fair workplace? Not everywhere. *BusinessWeek*, 6.
31. Fine, M. C., Johnson, P. L., and Regan, S. M. (1990). Cultural diversity in the workplace. *Public Personnel Management, 19*(3), 305–319 (p. 307). See also Society for Human Resource Management (SHRM). (2002f, February 13). How is a diversity initiative different from my organization's affirmative action plan? www.shrm.org/diversity.
32. Harrison, D. A., Price, K. H., and Bell, M. P. (1998). Beyond relational demography: Time and the effects of surface- and deep-level diversity on work group cohesion. *Academy of Management Journal, 41*(1), 96–107.
33. Loden, M., and Rosener, J. B. (1991). *Workforce America, 18*. Homewood, IL.
34. Fine, M. C., Johnson, P. L., and Regan, S. M. (1990). Cultural diversity in the workplace. *Public Personnel Management, 19*(3), 305–319 (p. 307).
35. Pinkerton, J. P. (1995, November 23). Why affirmative action won't die. *Fortune,* 191–198; and Merritt, J. (2002, March 11). Guess who's pushing a bold plan for diversity? Big business. *BusinessWeek*, 56–58.
36. Merritt, J. (2002, March 11). Guess who's pushing a bold plan for diversity? Big business. *BusinessWeek*, 56–58.
37. Morris, K. (1998, November 23). You've come a short way, baby. *BusinessWeek*, 82–86; and *The Economist*. (2002, March 2). Women in suits, 60–61.
38. Dwyer, P., and Cuneo, A. (1991, July 8). The "other minorities" demand their due. *BusinessWeek*, 60; and Pimentel, R. O. (2002, January 1). For Latinos, 2001 played tag with issues, emotions. *Arizona Republic*, A-18.
39. Kasindorf, M. (1999, September 10). Hispanics and blacks find their futures entangled. *USA Today*, 21-A; Pimentel, R. O. (2002, February 19). Latino assimilation: A median point or a melting pot? *Arizona Republic*, B-1; and Pimentel, R. O. (2002, February 26). Latino question insults Latino politicians. *Arizona Republic*, B-7.
40. Smith, R. S. (2002, April 15). Hooray Halle!. *US News and World Reports*, 22–26.
41. Gleckman, H., Smart, T., Dwyer, P., Segal, T., and Weber, J. (1991, July 8). Race in the workplace, *BusinessWeek*, 50–63.
42. Paltrow, S. J. (2002, January 9). Life of Georgia nears settlement over race bias. *Wall Street Journal*, C-1.
43. Berstein, A. (2002, February 25). The time bomb in the workforce: Illiteracy. *BusinessWeek,* 122.
44. *Wall Street Journal*. (2002a, April 8). The good news on race, A-26; and Koretz, G. (2001, September 3). Giant strides for U.S. blacks. *BusinessWeek,* 28.
45. Society for Human Resource Management (SHRM). (2002f, February 13). How is a diversity initiative different from my organization's affirmative action plan? www.shrm.org/diversity.
46. Marosi, R. (2002, March 11). Study finds deadly spike in racial violence against Asian Americans. *Arizona Republic*, A-18.
47. Loden, M., and Rosener, J. B. (1991). *Workforce America, 18*. Homewood, IL; and Lynnes, K. S. (2002). Finding the key to the executive suite: Challenges for women and people of color. In R. Sitzer (Ed.). *The 21st Century Executive*, 229–274. San Francisco: Jossey-Bass.
48. L H Research national phone poll. (1994, March 4). *Chattanooga Times*, 1.
49. Colvin, J. (1999, July 19). The 50 best companies for Asians, blacks, and Hispanics. *Fortune*, 53–57.
50. Wong, J. (1996, February 9). Asian women migrant workers suffering abuse. *Wall Street Journal*, A-7.
51. Marosi, R. (2002, March 11). Study finds deadly spike in racial violence against Asian Americans. *Arizona Republic,* A-18.
52. Weber, J. (1988, June 6). Social issues: The disabled. *BusinessWeek*, 140; and Savage, D. G. (2002, March). Wordaday rulings. *ABA Journal*, 34–35.
53. Koss-Feder, L. (1999, January 25). Able to work. *Time,* 25–30; and Savage, D. G. (2002, March). Wordaday rulings. *ABA Journal*, 34–35.
54. Weber, J. (1988, June 6). Social issues: The disabled. *BusinessWeek*, 140.
55. Perry, N. J. (1991, June 10). The workers of the future. *Fortune,* 51–58; and Pimentel, R. O. (2002, January 3). Untold story: Hispanic middle class blazing new trails. *Arizona Republic,* B-9.
56. Briefs. (1993, February 22). *Workforce Strategies, 4*(2), WS-12; and Society for Human Resource Management (SHRM). (2002e, February 13). How can the results of our initiative be measured? www.shrm.org/diversity.

57. Koss-Feder, L. (1999, January 25). Able to work. *Time,* 25–30.
58. Ibid.
59. Savage, D. G. (2002, March). Wordaday rulings. *ABA Journal,* 34–35.
60. *Wall Street Journal.* (2002, February 13). Economic focus: Immigrants, B-13.
61. Moore, S. (1999). Study results cited in Shaffer, M. (1999, September 3). Importing poverty. *Arizona Republic,* A-1; *Time.* (2002, January 7). Immigration: The home front, 130; Merritt (2002); Kannan and Rosenberg (2002).
62. Golden, D. (2002, April 2). Some community colleges fudge facts to attract foreign students. *Wall Street Journal,* B-1.
63. *Time.* (2002, January 7). Immigration: The home front, 130.
64. *Wall Street Journal.* (2002b, April 18). RICOing immigrants, A-12.
65. Yang, C. (1995, May 29). Immigration: You can't test for drive and ambition. *BusinessWeek,* 35–36; *Wall Street Journal.* (2002, February 13). Economic focus: Immigrants, B-13; and *Wall Street Journal.* (2002b, April 18). RICOing immigrants, A-12.
66. Rose, F. (1995, April 22). Muddled masses. *Wall Street Journal,* A1; and *Wall Street Journal.* (2002b, April 18). RICOing immigrants, A-12.
67. Kannan, J., and Rosenberg, H. (2002, February 7). Survey looks at residents with foreign roots. *Arizona Republic,* A-8.
68. Doyle, R. (2002, February). Assembling the future. *Scientific American,* 30.
69. Baker, S., Cappel, K. and Carlisle, K. (2002, March 18). Crime and politics. *BusinessWeek,* 50–53.
70. Ibid.
71. For a critical discussion of the higher figure, see Muir, J. G. (1993, March 31). Homosexuals and the 10% fallacy. *Wall Street Journal,* A13.
72. Portes, A., and Truelove, L. (1987). Making sense of diversity: Recent research on Hispanic minorities in the U.S. *American Review of Sociology, 13,* 359–385 (p. 360); and Pimentel, R. O. (2002, February 19). Latino assimilation: A median point or a melting pot? *Arizona Republic,* B-1.
73. Wynter, L. (1996, February 7). Business and race. *Wall Street Journal,* B1; and Pimentel (2002). Latino question insults Latino politicians.
74. Porter, E. (2002a, April 19). Hispanic targeted advertising outpaces overall ad growth. *Wall Street Journal,* A-17.
75. Porter, E. (2002b, February 13). Quirky English course evolves into a fixture of Latino pop culture. *Wall Street Journal,* A-1.
76. Romero, C. L. (2002, January 19). Hard time for Hispanics. *Arizona Republic,* D-1; and Porter, E. (2002b, February 13). Quirky English course evolves into a fixture of Latino pop culture. *Wall Street Journal,* A-1.
77. Doyle, R. (2002, February). Assembling the future. *Scientific American,* 30; and Society for Human Resource Management (SHRM). (2002f, February 13). How is a diversity initiative different from my organization's affirmative action plan? www.shrm.org/diversity.
78. Russel, J. (1995, September). Trading with the world. *Hispanic Business,* 26–27; and Porter, E. (2002a, April 19). Hispanic targeted advertising outpaces overall ad growth. *Wall Street Journal,* A-17.
79. Kaufman, J. (2002, January 10). Whites and Hispanics fall out over quest for suburban dream. *Wall Street Journal,* A-1; Pimentel, R. O. (2002, January 1). For Latinos, 2001 played tag with issues, emotions. *Arizona Republic,* A-18; Pimentel, R. O. (2002, January 3). Untold story: Hispanic middle class blazing new trails. *Arizona Republic,* B-9; and Pimentel, R. O. (2002, February 19). Latino assimilation: A median point or a melting pot? *Arizona Republic,* B-1.
80. Munk, N. (1999, February 1). Finished at forty. *Fortune,* 50–64; and Goldberg B. (2000). *Age works.* New York: The Free Press.
81. Chen, K. (2002, February 25). Age discrimination complaints rose 8.7% in 2001 amid overall increase in claims. *Wall Street Journal,* B-13.
82. Loden, M., and Rosener, J. B. (1991). *Workforce America, 18.* Homewood, IL, 65.
83. Levin, D. P. (1994, February 20). The graying factory. *New York Times,* 3, 1, 6; and Trilch, T. (2002, Winter). Young or old are about equally dedicated to their jobs. *Gallup Management Journal,* 32.
84. Bureau of Labor Statistics; Employment and Earnings. (1999, January). Tables 44 and 45.
85. Trilch, T. (2002, Winter). Young or old are about equally dedicated to their jobs. *Gallup Management Journal,* 32.
86. Fellows, D. S. (2001). Striking gold in a silver mine: Leveraging senior workers as knowledge champions. *Worldatwork Journal, 10*(4), 112.
87. McNamee, M. (1998, August 17). First hired, first fired? *BusinessWeek,* 22; and Society for Human Resource Management (SHRM). (2002e, February 13). How can the results of our initiative be measured? www.shrm.org/diversity.
88. Reingold, J., and Brody, D. (1999, September 20). Brain drain. *BusinessWeek,* 113–122.
89. Levin, D. P. (1994, February 20). The graying factory. *New York Times,* 3, 1, 6.
90. Bureau of Labor Statistics, stats.bls.gov.
91. Highlights of Women's Earnings. (2002). Bureau of Labor Statistics, stats.bls.gov.
92. Morris, K. (1998, November 23). You've come a short way, baby. *BusinessWeek,* 82–86; and *The Economist.* (2002, March 2). Women in suits, 60–61.
93. Greenfeld, K. T. (1999, August 2). What glass ceiling? *Time,* 72; and Lynnes, K. S. (2002). Finding the key to the executive suite: Challenges for women and people of color. In R. Sitzer (Ed.). *The 21st Century Executive,* 229–274. San Francisco: Jossey-Bass.
94. *BusinessWeek.* (2002, January 14). The top 25 managers of the year, 52–71; Berman, D. K. (2002, January 7). Lucent veteran Russo to return as CEO. *Wall Street Journal,* A-3.
95. Shellenbarger, S. (1995, May 11). Women indicate satisfaction with role of breadwinner. *Wall Street Journal,* B6–B7; Conlin, M. (2003, January 27). Look who is bringing home the bacon. *BusinessWeek,* 85.
96. Dwyer, P. (1996, April 15). Out of the typing pool, into career limbo. *BusinessWeek,* 92–94; and Lynnes, K. S. (2002). Finding the key to the executive suite: Challenges for women and people of color. In R. Sitzer (Ed.). *The 21st Century Executive,* 229–274. San Francisco: Jossey-Bass.
97. Blass, F. D. (1998, March). The well-being of American women: 1970–1995. *Journal of Economic Literature, 36*(1), 112–165; and Lynnes, K. S. (2002). Finding the key to the executive suite: Challenges for women and people of color. In R. Sitzer (Ed.). *The 21st Century Executive,* 229–274. San Francisco: Jossey-Bass.
98. Lynnes, K. S. (2002). Finding the key to the executive suite: Challenges for women and people of color. In R. Sitzer (Ed.). *The 21st Century Executive,* 229–274. San Francisco: Jossey-Bass.
99. Baird, J. E., Jr., and Bradley, P. H. (1979, June). Styles of management and communication: A comparative study of men and women. *Communication Monographs, 46,* 101–110.
100. DePalma, A. (1991, November 12). Women can be hindered by lack of "boys" network. *Boulder Daily Camera,* Business Plus Section, 9; and Society for Human Resource Management (SHRM). (2002c, February 13). What are employee networks and should they be a part of our diversity initiative? www.shrm.org/diversity.
101. Castro, L. L. (1992, January 2). More firms "gender train" to bridge the chasms that still divide the sexes. *Wall Street Journal,* 7–11.
102. Crockett, R. O. (2003, January 23). Memo to the supreme court: Diversity is good business. *BusinessWeek,* 96.
103. *The Economist.* (2002, March 2). Women in suits, 60–61; and Carlson, M. (1999, September 20). Sexual harassment, Chapter 999. *BusinessWeek,* 94–95; see also Morris, B., (1999, May 10). Addicted to sex. *Fortune,* 65–70.

104. Conlin, M., and Zellner, W. (2001, July 16). Is Wal-Mart hostile to women? *BusinessWeek*, 58–60.
105. *The Economist*. (2002, March 2). Women in suits, 60–61.
106. Ibid.
107. NiCarthy, G., Gottlieb, N., and Coffman, S. (1993). *You don't have to take it! A woman's guide to confronting emotional abuse at work*. Seattle: Seal Press; and *The Economist*. (2002, March 2). Women in suits, 60–61.
108. Weaver, V. (2001, September 10). Winning with diversity. *BusinessWeek*, special section.
109. Society for Human Resource Management (SHRM). (2002b, February 13). What if your diversity training is successful? www.shrm.org/diversity.
110. Wynter, L. (1996, February 7). Business and race. *Wall Street Journal*, B1.
111. Wheeler, M. L. (1998, December 14).
112. Stewart, T. A. (1991, December 10). Gay in corporate America. *Fortune*, 42–50 (p. 43).
113. Thomas, R. F (1990, March–April). From affirmative action to affirming diversity. *Harvard Business Review*, 107–119; and Society for Human Resource Management (SHRM). (2002d, February 13). Where HR meets the world: How should my organization define diversity? www.shrm.org/diversity.
114. Wynter, L. (1996, February 7). Business and race. *Wall Street Journal*, B1.
115. Ibid.
116. Society for Human Resource Management (SHRM). (2002a, February 13). Diversity training. www.shrm.org/diversity.
117. Society for Human Resource Management (SHRM). (2002b, February 13). What if your diversity training is successful? www.shrm.org/diversity.
118. Ibid.
119. Society for Human Resource Management (SHRM). (2002c, February 13). What are employee networks and should they be part of our diversity initiative? www.shrm.org/diversity.
120. *Comp/flash*. (1994, January). Benefits flash. *American Management Association*, 5.
121. Ashton, A. (2002, February). Around-the-clock child care. *Working Woman*, 14.
122. Conlin, M. (1999, September 20). 9 to 5 isn't working anymore. *BusinessWeek*, 94–95.
123. Newman, A. M. (2002, February). Fair shares. *Working Woman*, 64–71.
124. Goodstein, J. D. (1994). Institutional pressures and strategic responsiveness: Employer involvement in work–family issues. *Academy of Management Journal*, *37*(2), 350–383; and Society for Human Resource Management (SHRM). (2002e, February 13). How can the results of our initiative be measured? www.shrm.org/diversity.
125. Kantrowitz, B., and Wingert, P. (1993, February). Being smart about the mommy track. *Working Woman*, 49–51, 80–81; and Horowitz, J. M. Rawe, J., and Song, S. (2002, April 15). Making time for a baby. *Time*, 49–58.
126. Horowitz et al. (2002).
127. Shellenbarger, S. (1995, May 11). Women indicate satisfaction with role of breadwinner. *Wall Street Journal*, B6–B7.
128. Fisher, A. (1998, October 12). Women need at least one mentor and one pantsuit. *Fortune*, 208.
129. Hymowitz, C. (1995, April 24). How a dedicated mentor gave momentum to a woman's career. *Wall Street Journal*, B1.
130. Crockett, R. (1998, October 5). Invisible—and loving it. *BusinessWeek*, 124–125.
131. Branigin, W. (1998, August 7). Patent office looks like U.S. future: Agency celebrates multicultural mix. *Washington Post*, A-23.
132. Microsoft Diversity. (2002, April 29). Equal access. www.microsoft.com/diversity.
133. Society for Human Resource Management (SHRM). (2002e, February 13). How can the results of our initiative be measured? www.shrm.org/diversity.
134. Wartzman, R. (1992, May 4). A Whirlpool factory raises productivity and pay of workers. *Wall Street Journal*, A1.
135. Scott, R. S. (2002, April 15). Hooray Halle! *U.S. News & World Report*, 8–12; Pimentel, R. O. (2002, February 26). Latino question insults Latino politicians. *Arizona Republic*, B-7; and *Time*. (2002, January 7). Immigration: The home front, 130.
136. Zellner, W. (2002, March 18). A Texas-size case of discrimination. *BusinessWeek*, 14.
137. Ibid.
138. *The Economist*. (2002, March 2). Women in suits, 60–61.

Chapter 5

1. Hand, T. (2002). Choosing the right recruiter. *Network World*, *19*, 41.
2. *The Controller's Report*. (2002, March). Working alternatives to job cuts: The latest strategies for preserving human capital.
3. *Managing HR Information Systems*. (2002). Three companies reveal how they use employ! to cut hiring paperwork. January Newsletter, *1*, 12–14.
4. *Managing HR Information Systems*. (2001). Automating recruitment: How to select and implement the best new recruiting app. December Newsletter, *1*, 11–14.
5. See, for example, Rothwell, W. J., and Kazanis, H. C. (1988). *Strategic human resources planning and management*. Upper Saddle River, NJ: Prentice Hall; Bartholomew, D. J., and Forbes, A. F. (1979). *Statistical techniques for manpower planning*. Chichester, England: Wiley-Interscience; Heneman, H. G., III, and Sandver, M. G. (1977). Markov analysis in human resource administration: Applications and limitations. *Academy of Management Review*, *2*(4), 535–542; and Burack, E. H., and Mathys, N. J. (1987). *Human resource planning: A pragmatic approach to manpower staffing and development*. Lake Forest, IL: Brace-Park.
6. Cardy, R. L., and Carson, K. P. (1996). Total quality and the abandonment of performance appraisal: Taking a good thing too far? *Journal of Quality Management*, *1*, 193–206.
7. Piper, G. (1999). Under inspection. *Credit Union Management*, *22*, 48–51.
8. Wah, L. (1998). The perfect match. *Management Review*, *87*, 50.
9. O'Reilly, C. A., and Chatman, J. (1994). Working smarter and harder: A longitudinal study of managerial success. *Administrative Science Quarterly*, *39*, 603–627.
10. Semler, R. (1993). *Maverick*, 169–177. New York: Warner Books.
11. Rynes, S. L. (1991). Recruitment, job choice, and posthire consequences: A call for new research directions. In M. D. Dunnette and L. M. Hough (Eds.), *Handbook of industrial and organizational psychology* (2nd ed.), Vol. 2, 399–444. Palo Alto, CA: Consulting Psychologists.
12. Ibid.
13. Kaplan, K. (2002). Help (still) wanted: No hiring? It doesn't matter. Even managers wielding the layoff ax should keep their eyes open for tomorrow's superstars. Here's how to recruit in any economy. *Sales & Marketing Management*, *154*, 38(6).
14. *Human Resource Department Management Report*. (2002). What's your department's policy on rehiring laid-off employees? Institute of Management and Administration February Newsletter, *1*, 13–14.
15. Komando, K. (1999, April 26). Job hunt made easier by variety of online sites. *Arizona Republic*, E2.
16. Monster.com (2002, April 16). See www.monster.com.
17. Leonard, B. (1999). Staffing firms struggle to meet labor demand. *HRMagazine*, *44*, 23–24.

18. Kever, J. (2002, January 27). Life as a temp. *Houston Chronicle*, Texas Magazine section, 6.
19. Ibid.
20. Wellner, A. S. (2002). Tapping a silver mine: Older workers represent a wealth of talent—but may require increased flexibility from HR. *HRMagazine, 47*, 26(7).
21. Wiscombe, J. (2002). Creative hiring on the green. *Workforce, 81*, 21(1).
22. Perry, P. (2002). Battle for the best: What works today in recruiting top technical talent. *Research Technology Management, 45*, 17(5).
23. Yamamoto, T. (1993, October). Recruiting system badly designed, badly run, unlikely to change. *Tokyo Business Today*, 52–54.
24. Posner, B. G. (1990). Putting customers to work. *Inc., 12*, 111–112.
25. Kanter, R. M. (2002). Strategy as improvisational theater: Companies that want to outpace the competition throw out the script and improvise their way to new strategies. *MIT Sloan Management Review, 43*, 76(6).
26. Owen, T. (1998). Finding and keeping good employees. *Specialty Coffee Retailer, 5*, 30–40.
27. Klein, E. (1993, January–February). Heroes for hire. *D&B Reports*, 26–28.
28. Sackett, P. R., and Arvey, R. D. (1993). Selection in small settings. In N. Schmitt, W. C. Borman (Eds.). *Personnel selection in organizations*. San Francisco: Jossey-Bass.
29. Wanous, J. P. (1992). *Organizational entry* (2nd ed.). Reading, MA: Addison-Wesley.
30. Wiscombe, J. (2002). Creative hiring on the green. *Workforce, 81*, 21(1).
31. Andrews, J. (2001). Labor intensive. *Materials Management in Health Care, 10*, 20–30.
32. Leonhardt, D., and Cohn, L. (1999, April 26). Business takes up the challenge of training its rawest recruits. *BusinessWeek*, 30.
33. Overman, S. (1999). Put overlooked labor pools on your recruiting list. *HRMagazine, 44*, 86–90.
34. Kageyama, Y. (1998, December 1). Jobs disappearing at alarming rate for Japan teens. *Arizona Republic*, E10.
35. Ibid.
36. O'Donnell, A. (2001). Reaching out for diversity. *Insurance and Technology, 26*, 65.
37. Laab, J. J. (1991, May). Affirmative outreach. *Personnel Journal*, 86–93.
38. Brooks, S. (2001). Kaleidscope eyes: These days, diversity is becoming more diverse than ever before. Smart marketers are beginning to see this, and here's what they're up to. *Restaurant Business, 101*, 28(6).
39. Walker, J. W. (1990, December). Human resource planning, 1990s style. *Human Resource Planning*, 229–230.
40. Hunter, J. E., and Hunter, R. F. (1984). Validity and utility of alternative predictors of job performance. *Psychological Bulletin, 96*, 72–98; Hunter, J. E., and Schmidt, F. L. (1982). The economic benefits of personnel selection using psychological ability tests. *Industrial Relations, 21*, 293–308; and Schmidt, F. L., and Hunter, J. E. (1983). Individual differences in productivity: An empirical test of the estimate derived from studies of selection procedure utility. *Journal of Applied Psychology, 68*, 407–414.
41. Hunter, J. E., and Hunter, R. F. (1984). Validity and utility of alternative predictors of job performance. *Psychological Bulletin, 96*, 72–98.
42. Gilbertson, D. (1999, August 22). Résumé fraud growing: Companies are often lax in checking. *Arizona Republic*, A1, A18.
43. Heneman, H. G., III, Heneman, R. L., and Judge, T. A. (1997). *Staffing organizations*. Middleton, WI: Mendota House/Irwin.
44. Kleiman, L. S., and Faley, R. H. (1985). The implications of professional and legal guidelines for court decisions involving criterion-related validity: A review and analysis. *Personnel Psychology, 38*, 803–833.
45. Heneman et al., 1997.
46. Ibid.
47. Muchinsky, P. M. (1979). The use of reference reports in personnel selection: A review and evaluation. *Journal of Occupational Psychology, 52*, 287–297.
48. Aamodt, M. G., Bryan, D. A., and Whitcomb, A. J. (1993). Predicting performance with letters of recommendation. *Public Personnel Management, 22*, 81–90.
49. Peres, S. H., and Garcia, J. R. (1962). Validity and dimensions of descriptive adjectives used in reference letters for engineering applicants. *Personnel Psychology, 15*, 279–296.
50. Taylor, P. (1999). Providing structure to interviews and reference checks. *Workforce Tools* (supplement to *Workforce*), 7, 10.
51. Russell, C. J., Mattson, J., Devlin, S. F., and Atwater, D. (1990). Predictive validity of biodata items generated from retrospective life experience essays. *Journal of Applied Psychology, 75*, 569–580.
52. Hunter, J. E. (1986). Cognitive ability, cognitive aptitudes, job knowledge, and job performance. *Journal of Vocational Behavior, 29*, 340–362.
53. Bounds, G. M., Dobbins, G. H., and Fowler, O. S. (1995). *Management: A total quality perspective*. Cincinnati, OH: South-Western.
54. Harville, D. L. (1996). Ability test equity in predicting job performance work samples. *Educational and Psychological Measurement, 56*, 344–348.
55. Hogan, J., and Quigley, A. (1994). Effects of preparing for physical ability tests. *Public Personnel Management, 23*, 85–104.
56. Guion, R. M., and Gottier, R. F. (1965). Validity of personality measures in personnel selection. *Personnel Psychology, 18*, 135–163.
57. Bernardin, H. J., and Beatty, R. W. (1984). *Performance appraisal: Assessing human behavior at work*. Boston: Kent.
58. Landy, F. J. (1989). *The psychology of work behavior* (4th ed.). Pacific Grove, CA: Brooks/Cole.
59. Guion, R. M., and Gottier, R. F. (1965). Validity of personality measures in personnel selection. *Personnel Psychology, 18*, 135–163.
60. Kleiman, L. S., and Faley, R. H. (1985). The implications of professional and legal guidelines for court decisions involving criterion-related validity: A review and analysis. *Personnel Psychology, 38*, 803–833.
61. Funder, D. C., and Dobroth, J. M. (1987). Difference between traits: Properties associated with inter-judge agreement. *Journal of Personality and Social Psychology, 52*, 409–418.
62. Digman, J. M. (1990). Personality structure: Emergence of the five-factor model. *Annual Review of Psychology, 41*, 417–440; and Goldberg, L. R. (1993). The structure of phenotypic personality traits. *American Psychologist, 48*, 26–34.
63. Barrick, M. R., and Mount, M. K. (1991). The big five personality dimensions and job performance: A meta analysis. *Personnel Psychology, 41*, 1–26; Digman, J. M. (1990). Personality structure: Emergence of the five-factor model. *Annual Review of Psychology, 41*, 417–440; and Hogan, R. (1991). Personality and personality measurement. In M. D. Dunnette and L. M. Hough (Eds.), *Handbook of industrial and organizational psychology* (2nd ed.), Vol. I. Palo Alto, CA: Consulting Psychologists.
64. Barrick, M. R., and Mount, M. K. (1991). The big five personality dimensions and job performance: A meta analysis. *Personnel Psychology, 41*, 1–26.
65. House, R. J., Shane, S. A., and Herold, D. M. (1996). Rumors of the death of dispositional research are vastly exaggerated. *Academy of Management Review, 21*, 203–224.
66. Dunn, W., Mount, M. K., Barrick, M. R., and Ones, D. S. (1995). Relative importance of personality and general mental ability in managers' judgments of applicant qualifications. *Journal of Applied Psychology, 80*, 500–509.

67. Wolfe, R. N., and Johnson, S. D. (1995). Personality as a predictor of college performance. *Educational and Psychological Measurement, 55,* 177–185.
68. Lublin, S. (1992, February 13). Trying to increase worker productivity, more employers alter management style. *Wall Street Journal,* B1, B3.
69. Martin, S. I., and Lehnen, L. P. (1992, June). Select the right employees through testing. *Personnel Journal,* 46–51.
70. *Preventing Business Fraud.* (2002). Industry focus: What can retailers do now to curtail employee theft? Institute of Management and Administration February Newsletter, 5–8.
71. Arnold, D. W., and Jones, J. W. (2002). Who the devil's applying now? Companies can use tests to screen out dangerous job candidates. *Security Management, 46,* 85.
72. Terris, W., and Jones, J. W. (1982). Psychological factors elating to employees' theft in the convenience store industry. *Psychological Reports, 51,* 1219–1238.
73. Bernardin, H. J., and Cooke, D. K. (1993). Validity of an honesty test in predicting theft among convenience store employees. *Academy of Management Journal, 36,* 1097–1108.
74. Arnold, D. W., and Jones, J. W. (2002). Who the devil's applying now? Companies can use tests to screen out dangerous job candidates. *Security Management, 46,* 85.
75. Budman, M. (1993, November–December). The honesty business. *Across the Board,* 34–37.
76. Arvey, R. D., and Campion, J. E. (1982). The employment interview: A summary and review of recent research. *Personnel Psychology, 35,* 281–322; and Harris, M. M. (1989). Reconsidering the employment interview: A review of recent literature and suggestions for future research. *Personnel Psychology, 42,* 691–726.
77. Springbett, B. M. (1958). Factors affecting the final decision in the employment interview. *Canadian Journal of Psychology, 12,* 13–22.
78. Buckley, M. R., and Eder, R. W. (1988). B. M. Springbett and the notion of the "snap decision" in the interview. *Journal of Management, 14,* 59–67.
79. Campion, M. A., Pursell, F. D., and Brown, B. K. (1988). Structured interviewing: Raising the psychometric properties of the employment interview. *Personnel Psychology, 41,* 252.
80. Pursell, E. D., Campion, M. A., and Gaylord, S. R. (1980). Structured interviewing: Avoiding selection problems. *Personnel Journal, 59,* 907–912.
81. Wright, P. M., Licthenfels, P. A., and Pursell, E. D. (1989). The structured interview: Additional studies and a meta-analysis. *Journal of Occupational Psychology, 62,* 191–199.
82. See Pulakos, E. D., and Schmitt, N. (1995). Experience-based and situational interview questions: Studies of validity. *Personnel Psychology, 48,* 289–308.
83. Hunter, J. E., and Hunter, R. F. (1984). Validity and utility of alternative predictors of job performance. *Psychological Bulletin, 96,* 72–98.
84. Warmke, D. L., and Weston, D. J. (1992, April). Success dispels myths about panel interviewing. *Personnel Journal,* 120–126.
85. Harris, M. M. (1989). Reconsidering the employment interview: A review of recent literature and suggestions for future research. *Personnel Psychology, 42,* 691–726.
86. Kerr, J. (1982). Assigning managers on the basis of the life cycle. *Journal of Business Strategy, 2,* 58–65; Olian, J. D., and Rynes, S. L. (1984). Organizational staffing: Integrating practice with strategy. *Industrial Relations, 23,* 170–183; and Rynes, S., and Gerhart, B. (1990). Interviewer assessments of applicant "fit": An exploratory investigation. *Personnel Psychology, 43,* 13–35.
87. Chatman, J. A. (1989). Improving interaction organizational research: A model of person–organization fit. *Academy of Management Review, 14,* 333–349.
88. Ibid.
89. Pouliot, J. S. (1992, July). Topics to avoid with applicants. *Nation's Business,* 57–59.
90. Corning, B. (1999). Seek and you may find. *Accountancy, 123,* 46–47.
91. Boyle, S., Fullerton, J., and Yapp, M. (1993). The rise of the assessment centre: A survey of AC usage in the UK. *Selection and Development Review, 9,* 14.
92. McEvoy, G. M., and Beatty, R. W. (1989). Assessment centers and subordinate appraisals of managers: A seven-year study of predictive validity. *Personnel Psychology, 42,* 37–52.
93. Coulton, G. F., and Feild, H. S. (1995). Using assessment centers in selecting entry-level police officers: Extravagance or justified expense? *Public Personnel Management, 24,* 223–254.
94. Argetsinger, A. (1998, May 21). Principles for principals: Written exam replaces role-playing for applicants. *Washington Post,* M1.
95. Bender, J. M. (1973). What is "typical" of assessment centers? *Personnel, 50,* 50–57; and Carrick, P., and Williams, R. (1999). Development centres—A review of assumptions. *Human Resource Management Journal, 9,* 77–92.
96. Lopez, J. A. (1993, October 6). Firms force job seekers to jump through hoops. *Wall Street Journal,* B1, B6.
97. Thatcher, M. (Ed.). (1993, November). "Front-line" staff selected by assessment centre. *Personnel Management,* 83.
98. Cowan, T. R. (1987). Drugs and the workplace: to drug test or not to test? *Public Personnel Management, 16,* 313–322.
99. Wessel, D. (1989, September 7). Evidence is skimpy that drug testing works, but employers embrace practice. *Wall Street Journal,* B1, B9.
100. Brown, M. (1991, December). Reference checking: The law is on your side. *Human Resource Measurements* (a supplement to *Personnel Journal*), 4–5.
101. Hernan, P. (2002). Looking for trouble: Employee's backgrounds face closer scrutiny in the wake of September 11. *Industry Week, 251,* 15(3).
102. Steen, M. (2002, March 25). Under security. *San Jose Mercury News,* E1.
103. Fowler, A. (1991). An even-handed approach to graphology. *Personnel Management, 23,* 40–43.
104. Rafaeli, A., and Klimoski, R. J. (1983). Predicting sales success through handwriting analysis: An evaluation of the effects of training and handwriting sample content. *Journal of Applied Psychology, 68,* 212–217.
105. Cox, A., and Tapsell, J. (1991). Graphology and its validity in personnel assessment. Paper presented at the British Psychological Society.
106. Bianchi, A. (1996, February). The character-revealing handwriting analysis. *Inc.,* 77–79.
107. Kleinmutz, B. (1990). Why we still use our heads instead of formulas: Toward an integrative approach. *Psychological Bulletin, 107,* 296–310.
108. For a review, see Gatewood, R. D., and Feild, H. S. (1994). *Human resource selection.* Orlando, FL: Harcourt, Brace.
109. Cardy, R. L., and Stewart, G. (1998). Quality and teams: Implications for HRM theory and research. In S. Ghosh and D. B. Fedor (Eds.), *Advances in the management of organization quality,* Vol. 3, Greenwich, CT: JAI Press.
110. Kristof, A. L. (1996). Person–organization fit: An integrative review of the conceptualizations, measurement, and implications. *Personnel Psychology, 49,* 1–49; and Barrett, R. S. (1995). Employee selection with the performance priority survey. *Personnel Psychology, 48,* 653–662.
111. Rynes, S. L. (1991). Recruitment, job choice, and posthire consequences: A call for new research directions. In M. D. Dunnette and L. M. Hough (Eds.), *Handbook of industrial and organizational psychology* (2nd ed.), Vol. 2, 399–444. Palo Alto, CA: Consulting Psychologists.

112. Macan, T. H., Avedon, M. J., Paese, M., and Smith, D. (1994). The effects of applicants' reactions to cognitive ability tests and an assessment center. *Personnel Psychology, 47*, 715–738.
113. Heneman, H. G., Huett, D. L., Lavigna, R. J., and Oston, D. (1995). Assessing managers' satisfaction with staffing service. *Personnel Psychology, 48*, 163–172.
114. Cook, S. H. (1988, November). Playing it safe: How to avoid liability for negligent hiring. *Personnel*, 32–36.
115. Ibid.

Chapter 6

1. Polsky, D. (1999). Changing consequences of job separation in the United States. *Industrial and Labor Relations Review, 52*, 565–580.
2. Cascio, W. F. (1991). *Costing human resources: The financial impact of behavior in organizations*. Boston: PWS-Kent.
3. Gerencher, K. (1999, May 3). How to say "farewell." *InfoWorld*, 83–84.
4. DeMers, A. (2002). Solutions and strategies for IT recruitment and retention: A manager's guide. *Public Personnel Management, 31*, 27.
5. Abrams, M. (2002). Back to basics: Employee retention and turnover. *Health Forum*, 55.
6. Schiesel, S. (1998, February 8). AT&T: A leaner company without a crash diet. *New York Times*. www.nytimes.com/library/financial/Sunday/archive/.
7. Retention management and metrics. (2002). Available at www.nobscot.com/sales/retention.cfm.
8. Bliss, W. G. (2002). Fair treatment in firings avoids suits. *National Underwriter Property & Casualty, 106*, 20(3).
9. Alexander, S. (1999, March 3). No cure in sight. *Computerworld*. www.computerworld.com/home/print.nsf/all/9903299EA.
10. *Report on Salary Surveys*. (2002). How companies now structure severance and separation benefits. April Newsletter of the Institute of Management and Administration.
11. Taylor, J. (1999, April). Avoid avoidable turnover. *Workforce*, 6.
12. Mobley, W. H. (1982). *Employee turnover: Causes, consequences, and control*. Reading, MA: Addison-Wesley.
13. Quint, M. (1995, December 15). Company buyout: Was it that good? *New York Times*, C1, C2.
14. *The Economist*. (1999, September 4). Aging workers: A full life, 65–68.
15. Munk, N. (1999, February 1). Finished at forty. *Fortune*, 50–54.
16. Richards, D. (1999, July 5). Petrochemical manufacturers lay off thousands. *Chemical Market Reporter, 5*, 40.
17. Rimer, S. (1996, March 6). The downsizing of America (part 4 of a 7-part series). *New York Times*, A1, A8–A10.
18. Plety, J., and Plohetski, T. (2002, February 18). Job cuts forever changed Dell Computer, workers, Austin, Texas, are firm. *Austin American-Statesman*, $$$
19. Ibid.
20. *The Economist*. (1999, October 23). Restructuring Nissan: O-hayo gozaimasu, mon ami, 70–71.
21. Robbins, D. K., and Pearce, J. A. (1992). Turnaround: Retrenchment and recovery. *Strategic Management Journal, 13*, 287–309.
22. Laabs, J. (1999, April). Has downsizing missed its mark? *Workforce*, 30–38.
23. Kuczynski, S. (1999, June). Help! I shrunk the company. *HRMagazine*, 40–45.
24. Messmer, M. (1991, October). Right-sizing reshapes staffing strategies. *HRMagazine*, 60–62.
25. Balkin, D. B. (1992). Managing employee separations with the reward system. *Academy of Management Executive, 6*(4), 64–71.
26. Byrne, J. (1994, May 9). The pain of downsizing. *BusinessWeek*, 60–68.
27. Hill, R. E., and Dwyer, P. C. (1990, September). Grooming workers for early retirement. *HRMagazine*, 59–63.
28. Grant, P. B. (1991). The "open window"—Special early retirement plans in transition. *Employee Benefits Journal, 16*(1), 10–16.
29. Lopez, J. A. (1993, October 25). Out in the cold: Many early retirees find the good deals not so good after all. *Wall Street Journal*, B1.
30. Tomasko, R. (1991). Downsizing: Layoffs and alternatives to layoffs. *Compensation and Benefits Review, 23*(4), 19–32.
31. Grant, P. B. (1991). The "open window"—Special early retirement plans in transition. *Employee Benefits Journal, 16*(1), 10–16.
32. Beck, M. (1991, December 9). Old enough to get fired. *Newsweek*, 64.
33. Johnson, P. B. (2002, February 24). FedEx finds ways to fight tough times in High Point, NC, area. *High Point Enterprise*.
34. *HR Focus*. (2002, February). How employers are handling layoffs and their aftermath, *79*, 8; and *HR Focus*. (2002, January). If you must lay off workers: Consider the long-term consequences, *79*, 8.
35. Greenhouse, S. (1999, September 23). In the U.A.W. deal, something for almost everyone? *New York Times*. www.nytimes.com/library/financial.
36. McGarvey, R. (2002). Solving the personnel puzzle: Finding the right number of employees is only part of the staffing picture—the pieces also need to fit together. *Electronic Business, 28*, 62(5).
37. Saccomano, A. (2002). The times, they are a-changin': a just-in-time workforce for a just-in-time economy. *World Trade, 15*,20–22.
38. Bernstein, A. (1996, March 18). United we own. *BusinessWeek*, 96–102.
39. Ehrenberg, R. G., and Jakubson, G. H. (1989). Advance notification of plant closing: Does it matter? *Industrial Relations, 28*, 60–71.
40. Brockner, J., Grover, S., Reed, T. F., and DeWitt, R. L. (1992). Layoffs, job insecurity, and survivors' work effort: Evidence of an inverted-U relationship. *Academy of Management Journal, 35*, 413–425.
41. Ehrenberg, R. G., and Jakubson, G. H. (1988). *Advance notice provisions in plant closing legislation*. Kalamazoo, MI: W.E. Upjohn Institute for Employment Research.
42. Reingold J. (1999, September 20). Brain drain. *BusinessWeek*, 112–126.
43. Eisman, R. (1992, May). Remaking a corporate giant. *Incentive*, 57–63.
44. Bayer, R. (2000, January). Firing: Letting people go with dignity is good for business. *HR Focus*, 10.
45. Bunning, R. L. (1990). The dynamics of downsizing. *Personnel Journal, 69*(9), 69–75.
46. Thibodeau, P. (1998, February 19). Computer security woes come from outside as well as within. *Computerworld*. www.computerworld.com/home/onine9697.nsf/all/980218computer1CEBA; and Fabis, P. (1998, June 15). Safe exits. *CIO*, Sect. 1, 32.
47. Brockner, J. (1992). Managing the effects of layoffs on survivors. *California Management Review, 34*(2), 9–28.
48. *Inside Business*. (2002). By the numbers, *4*, 12.
49. Reibstein, L. (1988, December 5). Survivors of layoffs receive help to lift morale and reinstate trust. *Wall Street Journal*, 31.
50. O'Neil, H. M., and Lenn, D. J. (1995). Voices of survivors: Words that downsizing CEOs should hear. *Academy of Management Executive, 9*(4), 23–34.
51. Noer, David M. (1993). *Healing the wounds: Overcoming the trauma of layoffs and revitalizing downsized organizations*. San Francisco: Jossey-Bass.
52. *Pay for Performance Report*. (2002, March). One key to success after layoffs.

53. Enright, E. (2002). After the fall: How to cope in a downsized workplace. *Meetings & Conventions, 37*, 47.
54. Ibid.
55. Sweet, D. H. (1989). Outplacement. In W. Cascio (Ed.), *Human resource planning, employment and placement*. Washington, DC: Bureau of National Affairs.
56. Newman, L. (1988). Goodbye is not enough. *Personnel Administrator, 33*(2), 84–86.
57. Naumann, S. E., Bennett, N., Bies, R. J., and Martin, C. L. (1999). Laid off, but still loyal: The influence of perceived justice and organizational support. *International Journal of Conflict Management, 9*, 356–368.
58. Sweet, D. H. (1989). Outplacement. In W. Cascio (Ed.), *Human resource planning, employment and placement*. Washington, DC: Bureau of National Affairs.
59. Gibson, V. M. (1991). The ins and outs of outplacement. *Management Review, 80*(10), 59–61.
60. Burdett, J. O. (1988). Easing the way out. *Personnel Administrator, 33*(6), 157–166.
61. Crofts, P. (1991). Helping people face up to redundancy. *Personnel Management, 23*(12), 24–27.
62. Rudolph, B. (1986, December 8). The sun also sets. *BusinessWeek*, 60–61.

Chapter 7

1. Carroll, S. J., and Schneir, C. E. (1982). *Performance appraisal and review systems: The identification, measurement, and development of performance in organizations*. Glenview, IL: Scott, Foresman.
2. Banks, C. G., and Roberson, L. (1985). Performance appraisers as test developers. *Academy of Management Review, 10*, 128–142.
3. Cleveland, J. N., Murphy, K. R., and Williams, R. E. (1989). Multiple uses of performance appraisals: Prevalence and correlates. *Journal of Applied Psychology, 74*, 130–135.
4. *Report on Salary Surveys*. (2002). Annual reviews are standard at most companies. April Newsletter of the Institute of Management and Administration.
5. Landy, F. J., and Farr, J. L. (1980). Performance ratings. *Psychological Bulletin, 87*, 72–107.
6. Haunstein, N. M. H. (1998). Training raters to increase the accuracy of appraisals and the usefulness of feedback. In J. W. Smither (Ed). *Performance appraisal: State of the art in practice*. San Francisco: Jossey-Bass.
7. Bernardin, H. J., Hagen, C. M., Kane, J. S., and Villanova, P. (1998). Effective performance management: A focus on precision, customers, and situational constraints. In J. W. Smither (Ed.), *Performance appraisal: State of the art in practice*. San Francisco: Jossey-Bass.
8. Lancaster, H. (1998, December 1). Performance reviews: Some bosses try a fresh approach. *Wall Street Journal*, B1.
9. Kennett, M. (2001, December). First class coach. *Management Today*, 84.
10. Scholtes, P. R. (1999). Review of performance appraisal: State of the art in practice. *Personnel Psychology, 52*, 177–181.
11. Gray, G. (2002). Performance appraisals don't work. *Industrial Management, 44*, 15.
12. Heffes, E. M. (2002). Measure like you mean it: Q&A with Michael Hammer. *Financial Executive, 18*, 46(3).
13. Gillespie, G. (2002). Do employees make the grade? *Health Data Management, 10*, 60.
14. Nunnally, J. C. (1978). *Psychometric theory*. New York: McGraw-Hill.
15. Bernardin, H. J., and Beatty, R. W. (1984). *Performance appraisal: Assessing human behavior at work*. Boston, MA: Kent; Latham, G. P., and Wexley, K. N. (1981). *Increasing productivity through performance appraisal*. Reading, MA: Addison-Wesley; and Miner, J. B. (1988). Development and application of the rated ranking technique in performance appraisal. *Journal of Occupational Psychology, 6*, 291–305.
16. Miner, J. B. (1988). Development and application of the rated ranking technique in performance appraisal. *Journal of Occupational Psychology, 6*, 291–305.
17. Bernardin, H. J., Kane, J. S., Ross, S., Spina, J. D., and Johnson, D. L. (1995). Performance appraisal design, development, and implementation. In G. R. Ferris, S. D. Rosen, and D. T. Barnum (Eds.), *Handbook of human resources management*. Cambridge, MA: Blackwell.
18. Cardy, R. L., and Sutton, C. L. (1993). *Accounting for halo-accuracy paradox: Individual differences*. Paper presented at the Annual Conference of the Society for Industrial and Organizational Psychology, 1993, San Francisco.
19. Bernardin, H. J., and Beatty, R. W. (1984). *Performance appraisal: Assessing human behavior at work*. Boston, MA: Kent.
20. Ibid.
21. Latham, G. P., and Wexley, K. N. (1981). *Increasing productivity through performance appraisal*. Reading, MA: Addison-Wesley.
22. Blood, M. R. (1973). Spin-offs from behavioral expectation scale procedures. *Journal of Applied Psychology, 59*, 513–515.
23. Harris, C. (1988). A comparison of employee attitudes toward two performance appraisal systems. *Public Personnel Management, 17*, 443–456.
24. Drucker, P. F. (1954). *The practice of management*. New York: Harper.
25. Gillespie, G. (2002). Do employees make the grade? *Health Data Management, 10*, 60.
26. Cardy, R. L., and Krzystofiak, F. J. (1991). Interfacing high technology operations with blue collar workers: Selection and appraisal in a computerized manufacturing setting. *Journal of High Technology Management Research, 2*, 193–210.
27. Bernardin, H. J., and Beatty, R. W. (1984). *Performance appraisal: Assessing human behavior at work*. Boston, MA: Kent.
28. See, for example, Smith, R. W. (1992, Fall). Moving managers to a higher plane of performance. *Business Forum, 17*, 5–6.
29. Cardy, R. L., and Dobbins, G. H. (1994a). *Performance appraisal: Alternative perspectives*. Cincinnati, OH: South-Western.
30. Borman, W. C. (1979). Individual difference correlates of rating accuracy using behavior scales. *Applied Psychological Measurement, 3*, 103–115.
31. Cardy, R. L., and Kehoe, J. F. (1984). Rater selective attention ability and appraisal effectiveness: The effect of a cognitive style on the accuracy of differentiation among ratees. *Journal of Applied Psychology, 69*, 589–594.
32. Thorndike, E. L. (1920). A constant error in psychological ratings. *Journal of Applied Psychology, 4*, 25–29.
33. Cooper, W. H. (1981). Ubiquitous halo. *Psychological Bulletin, 90*, 218–244.
34. Haunstein, N. M. H. (1998). Training raters to increase the accuracy of appraisals and the usefulness of feedback. In J. W. Smither (Ed). *Performance appraisal: State of the art in practice*. San Francisco: Jossey-Bass.
35. Rosen, D. I. (1992, November). Appraisals can make—or break—your court case. *Personnel Journal*, 113–116.
36. Edwards, M. R., Wolfe, M. E., and Sproull, J. R. (1983). Improving comparability in performance appraisal. *Business Horizons, 26*, 75–83.
37. Bernardin, H. J., and Buckley, M. R. (1981). Strategies in rater training. *Academy of Management Review, 6*, 205–212.
38. Haunstein, N. M. H. (1998). Training raters to increase the accuracy of appraisals and the usefulness of feedback. In J. W.

Smither (Ed). *Performance appraisal: State of the art in practice*. San Francisco: Jossey-Bass.

39. Bernardin, H. J., and Pence, E. C. (1980). Rater training: Creating new response sets and decreasing accuracy. *Journal of Applied Psychology, 65*, 60–66; and Cardy, R. L., and Keefe, T. J. (1994). Observational purpose and valuative articulation in frame-of-reference training: The effects of alternative processing models on rating accuracy. *Organizational Behavior and Human Decision Processes, 57*, 338–357.
40. Zajonc, R. B. (1980). Feeling and thinking: Preferences need no inferences. *American Psychologist, 35*, 151–175.
41. Cardy, R. L., and Dobbins, G. H. (1994b). Performance appraisal: The influence of liking on cognition. *Advances in Managerial Cognition and Organizational Information Processing, 5*, 115–140.
42. Antonioni, D., and Park, H. (2001). The relationship between rater affect and three sources of 360-degree feedback ratings. *Journal of Management, 27*, 479–495
43. Cardy, R. L., and Dobbins, G. H. (1994a). *Performance appraisal: Alternative perspectives*. Cincinnati, OH: South-Western.
44. Cardy, R. L., and Dobbins, G. H. (1986). Affect and appraisal: Liking as an integral dimension in evaluating performance. *Journal of Applied Psychology, 71*, 672–678.
45. Cardy, R. L., and Dobbins, G. H. (1994a). *Performance appraisal: Alternative perspectives*. Cincinnati, OH: South-Western.
46. Bernardin, H. J., and Walter, C. S. (1977). Effects of rater training and diary keeping on psychometric error in ratings. *Journal of Applied Psychology, 62*, 64–69; and Flanagan, J. C. (1954). The critical incident technique. *Psychological Bulletin, 51*, 327–358.
47. Painter, C. N. (1999). Ten steps for improved appraisals. *Supervision, 60*, 11–13.
48. Flanagan, J. C., and Burns, R. K. (1955, September–October). The employee performance record: A new appraisal and development tool. *Harvard Business Review*, 95–102.
49. Bookman, R. (1999). Tools for cultivating constructive feedback. *Association Management, 51*, 73–79.
50. Jacobs, H. (1993, October). The rating game. *Small Business Reports*, 21–25.
51. Ferris, G. R., and Judge, T. A. (1991). Personnel/human resources management: A political influence perspective. *Journal of Management, 17*, 1–42.
52. Murphy, K. R., and Cleveland, J. N. (1991). *Performance appraisal: An organizational perspective*. Boston: Allyn & Bacon.
53. Adapted from C. O. Longenecker, H. P. Sims, Jr., and D. A. Gioia. Behind the mask: The politics of employee appraisal. Copyright © by the Academy of Management. Reprinted by permission of the publisher. *Academy of Management Executive, 1*(3), August 1987, 183–193.
54. Ferris, G. R., and Judge, T. A. (1991). Personnel/human resources management: A political influence perspective. *Journal of Management, 17*, 1–42; and Ferris, G. R., Judge, T. A., Rowland, K. M., and Fitzgibbons, D. E. (1993). Subordinate influence and the performance evaluation process: Test of a model. *Organizational Behavior and Human Decision Processes, 58*, 101–135.
55. Kozlowski, S. W., Chao, G. T., and Morrison, R. F. (1998). Games raters play: Politics, strategies, and impression management in performance appraisal. In J. W. Smither (Ed.), *Performance appraisal: State of the art in practice*. San Francisco: Jossey-Bass.
56. Banks, C. G., and Roberson, L. (1985). Performance appraisers as test developers. *Academy of Management Review, 10*, 128–142.
57. Cardy, R. L., and Dobbins, G. H. (1994a). *Performance appraisal: Alternative perspectives*. Cincinnati, OH: South-Western.
58. Ibid.
59. Reilly, R. R., and McGourty, J. (1998). Performance appraisal in team settings. In J. W. Smither (Ed.), *Performance appraisal: State of the art in practice*. San Francisco: Jossey-Bass.
60. Dominick, P. G., Reilly, R. R., and McGourty, J. W. (1997). The effects of peer feedback on team member behavior. *Group and Organization Management, 22*, 508–520.
61. Reilly, R. R., and McGourty, J. (1998). Performance appraisal in team settings. In J. W. Smither (Ed.), *Performance appraisal: State of the art in practice*. San Francisco: Jossey-Bass.
62. Denton, K. D. (2001). Better decisions with less information. *Industrial Management, 43*, 21.
63. Cardy, R. L., and Stewart, G. L. (1997). Quality and teams: Implications for HRM theory and research. In D.B. Fedor (Ed.), *Advances in the management of organization quality*, Vol. 2, Greenwich, CT: JAI Press.
64. Ibid.
65. Barrett, G. V., and Kernan, M. C. (1987). Performance appraisal and terminations: A review of court decisions since *Brito v. Zia* with implications for personnel practices. *Personnel Psychology, 40*, 489–503.
66. Werner, J. M., and Bolino, M. C. (1997). Explaining U.S. courts of appeals decisions involving performance appraisal: Accuracy, fairness, and validation. *Personnel Psychology, 50*, 1–24.
67. Meyer, H. H., Kay, E., and French, J. R. P., Jr. (1965, March). Split roles in performance appraisal. *Harvard Business Review*, 9–10.
68. Prince, J. B., and Lawler, E. E. (1986). Does salary discussion hurt the development appraisal? *Organizational Behavior and Human Decision Processes, 37*, 357–375.
69. *Report on Salary Surveys*. (2002). Annual reviews are standard at most companies. April Newsletter of the Institute of Management and Administration.
70. Bernardin, H. J., and Beatty, R. W. (1984). *Performance appraisal: Assessing human behavior at work*. Boston, MA: Kent.
71. Dobbins, G. H., Cardy, R. L., and Carson, K. P. (1991). Perspectives on human resource management: A contrast of person and system approaches. In G. R. Ferris and K. M. Rowland (Eds.), *Research in personnel and human resources management*, Vol. 9. Greenwich, CT: JAI Press; and Ilgen, D. R., Fisher, C. D., and Taylor, S. M. (1979). Consequences of individual feedback on behavior in organizations. *Journal of Applied Psychology, 64*, 347–371.
72. Carson, K. P., Cardy, R. L., and Dobbins, G. H. (1991). Performance appraisal as effective management or deadly management disease: Two initial empirical investigations. *Group and Organization Studies, 16*, 143–159.
73. Kelly, H. H. (1973). The processes of causal attribution. *American Psychologist, 28*, 107–128.
74. Cascio, W. F. (1998). *Applied psychology in human resource management* (5th ed.). Upper Saddle River, NJ: Prentice Hall.
75. Blumberg, M., and Pringle, C. D. (1982). The missing opportunity in organizational research: Some implications for a theory of work performance. *Academy of Management Review, 7*, 560–569; Carson, K. P., Cardy, R. L., and Dobbins, G. H. (1991). Performance appraisal as effective management or deadly management disease: Two initial empirical investigations. *Group and Organization Studies, 16*, 143–159; and Schermerhorn, J. R., Jr., Gardner, W. L., and Martin, T. N. (1990). Management dialogues: Turning on the marginal performers. *Organizational Dynamics, 18*, 47–59.
76. Blumberg, M., and Pringle, C. D. (1982). The missing opportunity in organizational research: Some implications for a theory of work performance. *Academy of Management Review, 7*, 560–569; and Rummler, G. A. (1972). Human performance problems and their solutions. *Human Resource Management, 19*, 2–10.
77. Bernardin, H. J., Hagan, C. M., Kane, J. S., and Villanova, P. (1998). Effective performance management: A focus on precision customers, and situational constraints. In J. W. Smither (Ed.), *Performance appraisal: State of the art in practice*. San Francisco: Jossey-Bass.

78. Cardy, R. L., and Dobbins, G. H. (1994a). *Performance appraisal: Alternative perspectives*. Cincinnati, OH: South-Western.
79. *Small Business Reports*. (1993, July). A twist on performance reviews, 27–28.
80. Jarman, M. (1998, April 19). Complete turnaround 360-degree evaluations gaining favor with workers, management. *Arizona Republic*, D1.
81. Marshall, S. (1999, July 30). Executive action: Scrutinized from every angle—360-degree appraisals: Managers are graded on an unfamiliar curve. *Asian Wall Street Journal*, P3.
82. *Pay for Performance Report*. (2002). Which HR/comp. practices have the biggest impact on the bottom line? April Newsletter of the Institute of Management and Administration.
83. Edwards, M., and Ewen, A. (1996, March). Automating 360 degree feedback. *HR Focus, 70*, 3.
84. Rummler, G. A. (1972). Human performance problems and their solutions. *Human Resource Management, 19*, 2–10.
85. Evered, R. D., and Selman, J. C. (1989). Coaching and the art of management. *Organizational Dynamics, 18*, 16–33.
86. Schermerhorn, J. R., Jr., Gardner, W. L., and Martin, T. N. (1990). Management dialogues: Turning on the marginal performers. *Organizational Dynamics, 18*, 47–59.
87. Cardy, R. L. (1997). Process and outcomes: A performance-management paradox? *News: Human Resources Division, 21*, 12–14.

Chapter 8

1. Fitzgerald, W. (1992). Training versus development. *Training & Development, 46*, 81–84.
2. Bartz, D. E., Schwandt, D. R., and Hillman, L. W. (1989). Differences between "T" and "D." *Personnel Administrator, 34*, 164–170.
3. Sullivan, J. (1998, July 20). Why training doesn't work . . . and what operators better do about it. *Nation's Restaurant News, 32*, 54, 138.
4. Bernardin, H. J., Hagan, C. M., Kane, J. S., and Villanova, P. (1998). Effective performance management: A focus on precision, customers, and situational constraints. In J. W. Smither (Ed.), *Performance appraisal: State of the art in practice*. San Francisco: Jossey-Bass.
5. Calvacca, L. (1999). The value of employee training. *Folio: The Magazine for Magazine Management, 27*, 186–187.
6. Ibid.
7. Galvin, T. (2001). The money. *Training, 38*, 42–47.
8. Leibs, S. (2002). Class struggle: E-learning technology may be poised to go mainstream. *CFO: The Magazine for Senior Executives, 18*, 31(2).
9. *HR Focus*. (2002). Training investments climb despite recession and layoffs. May Newsletter of the Institute of Management and Administration.
10. Galligano, M. L. (2002, April 12). Employer's failure to train managers is "extraordinary mistake." Warrants double damages in age discrimination case. *Monday Business Briefing*, Report of Mondag Ltd.
11. Salopek (2002). Think of the economic turndown as a pit stop: The race will still run. *T&D, 56*, 68–71.
12. Ibid.
13. Galvin, T. (2002). The 2002 Training Top 100. *Training, 39*, 20(6).
14. Pfeffer, J. (1999). Seven practices of successful organizations: Part 2. *Health Forum Journal, 42*, 55–57.
15. Goldstein, I. L. (1986). *Training in organizations: Needs assessment, development, and evaluation* (2nd ed.). Monterey, CA: Brooks-Cole.
16. Mirabile, R. J. (1991). Pinpointing development needs: A simple approach to skills assessment. *Training & Development, 45*, 19–25.
17. Mager, R. F., and Pipe, P. (1984). *Analyzing performance problems: Or, you really oughta wanna*. Belmont, CA: Lake and Rummler, 1972.
18. Meyers C. (1999). Mars and Venus: In the meeting room. *Successful Meetings, 48*, 46–50.
19. Nowack, K. M. (1991). A true training needs analysis. *Training & Development, 45*, 69–73; and Phillips, J. J. (1983, May). Training programs: A results-oriented model for managing the development of human resources. *Personnel*, 11–18.
20. Galvin, T. (2002). The 2002 Training Top 100. *Training, 39*, 20(6).
21. Nowack, K. M. (1991). A true training needs analysis. *Training & Development, 45*, 69–73; and Phillips, J. J. (1983, May). Training programs: A results-oriented model for managing the development of human resources. *Personnel*, 11–18.
22. McKenna, J. F. (1992, January 20). Apprenticeships: Something old, something new, something needed. *Industry Week*, 14–20.
23. *Wood Technology*. (1999). Industry asked to help create skills standards, *126*, 16.
24. Ibid.
25. Gupta, U. (1996, January 3). TV seminars and CD-ROMs train workers. *Wall Street Journal*, B1, B8.
26. Sickler, N. G. (1993). Synchronized videotape teletraining: Efficient, effective and timely. *Tech Trends, 38*, 23–24.
27. Goodridge, E. (2001, November 12). Slowing economy sparks boom in e-learning. *Information Week*, 100–104.
28. Leibs, S. (2002). Class struggle: E-learning technology may be poised to go mainstream. *CFO: The Magazine for Senior Executives, 18*, 31(2).
29. Goodridge, E. (2001, November 12). Slowing economy sparks boom in e-learning. *Information Week*, 100–104.
30. *Managing HR Information Systems*. (2002). Lessons learned: How one company's plan for e-learning fizzled. May Newsletter of the Institute of Management and Administration.
31. Goodridge, E. (2002, May 13). E-learning struggles to make the grade—Users say online training isn't living up to its potential. *Information Week*, 64.
32. Leibs, S. (2002). Class struggle: E-learning technology may be poised to go mainstream. *CFO: The Magazine for Senior Executives, 18*, 31(2).
33. For more on CD-ROM training, see Murphy, K. (1996, May 6). Pitfalls vs. promise in training by CD-ROM. *New York Times*, D3.
34. Agry, B. W. (1999). Class is out. *US Banker, 109*, 52–55.
35. Major, M. (2002). E-learning becomes essential: New and enhanced computer-based training programs have become a high priority for aggressive retailers. *Progressive Grocer, 81*, 35(2).
36. Henderson, J., and Crawford, G. (2002). 10 ways to wire sales training: How AT&T used a Web-enabled process to improve sales skills and connect them to the bottom line. *T + D, 56*, 48(8).
37. Geber, B. (1990). Simulating reality. *Training, 27*, 41–46.
38. Scheier, R. L. (1999, May 31). Virtual control tower tests new flight patterns. *Computerworld, 33*, 63.
39. Ginsberg, S. (1998, July 6). This shot won't hurt you at all: On-screen CathSim does the prepping. *Washington Post*, F5.
40. Ibid.
41. Geber, B. (1990). Simulating reality. *Training, 27*, 41–46.
42. *Wall Street Journal*. (1999, August 18). Army to award USC a $45 million contract for better simulation, B9.
43. Haitsuka, A. (1997, July 31). Virtual-reality training idea puts Mesa firm in demand. *Arizona Republic*, E1.
44. Orenstein, D. (1999). Virtual reality saves on training. *Computerworld, 33*, 44.
45. Psotka, J. (1995). Immersive training systems: Virtual reality and education and training. *Instructional Science, 23*, 405–431.

46. Agry, B. W. (1999). Class is out. *US Banker, 109*, 52–55.
47. Estabrooke, R. M., and Foy, N. F. (1992). Answering the call of "tailored training." *Training, 29*, 85–88.
48. Patterson, P. A. (1991). Job aids: Quick and effective training. *Personnel, 68*, 13.
49. Overman, S. (1993, October). Retraining our work force. *HRMagazine*, 40–44.
50. Simmons, D. L. (1995). Retraining dislocated workers in the community college: Identifying factors for persistence. *Community College Review, 23*, 47–58.
51. Nilson, C. (1990). How to use peer training. *Supervisory Management, 35*, 8.
52. Messmer, M. (1992). Cross-discipline training: A strategic method to do more with less. *Management Review, 81*, 26–28.
53. Fyock, C. D. (1991). Teaching older workers new tricks. *Training & Development, 45*, 21–24.
54. Ludeman, K. (1995). Motorola's HR learns the value of teams firsthand. *Personnel Journal, 74*, 117–123.
55. Burns, G. (1995). The secrets of team facilitation. *Training & Development, 49*, 46–52.
56. Phillips, S. N. (1996). Team training puts fizz in Coke plant's future. *Personnel Journal, 75*, 87–92.
57. Goldstein, I. L. (1993). *Training in organizations* (3rd ed.). Pacific Grove, CA: Brooks-Cole.
58. Hequet, M. (1992, February). Creativity training gets creative. *Training*, 41–46.
59. *Training*. (1995b). Vital statistics, *32*, 55–66.
60. Wise, R. (1991). The boom in creativity training. *Across the Board, 28*, 38–42.
61. Solomon, C. M. (1990). Creativity training. *Personnel Journal, 69*, 65–71.
62. Hequet, M. (1992, February). Creativity training gets creative. *Training*, 41–46.
63. Shane, C. (1999). The fine arts of corporate management. *Across the Board, 36*, 7–8.
64. Wise, R. (1991). The boom in creativity training. *Across the Board, 28*, 38–42.
65. Koretz, G. (1996, May 20). A crash course in the 3R's? *BusinessWeek*, 26; and Educational Testing Service (1990). *From school to work*. Princeton, NJ: Educational Testing Service.
66. Rosow, J. M., and Zager, R. (1992). *Job-linked literacy: Innovative strategies at work. Part II. Meeting the challenges of change: Basic skills for a competitive workforce*. Scottsdale, NY: Work in America Institute.
67. Hays, S. (1999). Basic skills training 101. *Workforce, 78*, 76–82.
68. Anfuso, D. (1998). I would like to go as far as I can go. *Workforce, 77*, 112.
69. Lund, L., and McGuire, E. P. (1990). *Literacy in the work force*. New York: The Conference Board.
70. Gillian, F. (1999). White males see diversity's other side. *Workforce, 78*, 52–55.
71. *Managing Training and Development*. (2001). 5 hours of diversity training has a positive bottom-line impact. July Newsletter of the Institute of Management and Administration, 10–12.
72. Nelms, D. W. (1993). Managing the crisis. *Air Transport World, 30*, 62–65.
73. Bensimon, H. F. (1994). Crisis and disaster management: Violence in the workplace. *Training & Development, 48*, 27–32.
74. Berta, D. (2002). Operators strive to include all in the family: Claim progress toward diversity amid new rash of bias suits. *Nation's Restaurant News, 36*, 1(4).
75. Densford, L. E. (1999, February). Motorola University: The next 20 years. *Corporate University Review*.
76. Edwards, M. R. (1999, February). Measurement as a catalyst for learning. *HR Focus*, S9–S10.
77. Wanous, J. P., Reichers, A. E., and Matik, S. D. (1984). Organizational socialization and group development: Toward an integrative perspective. *Academy of Management Review, 9*, 670–683.
78. Breaugh, J. A. (1983). Realistic job previews: A critical appraisal and future research directions. *Academy of Management Review, 8*, 612–623.
79. Philips, J. M. (1998). Effects of realistic job previews on multiple organizational outcomes: A meta-analysis. *Academy of Management Journal, 41*, 673–690.
80. Bragg, A. (1989, September). Is a mentor program in your future? *Sales & Marketing Management*, 54–63.
81. Little, P. J. (1998). Selection of the fittest. *Management Review*, July/August, 43–47.
82. Winkler, K., and Janger, I. (1998). You're hired! *Across the Board, 35*, 16–23.
83. Ibid.

Chapter 9

1. Leibowitz, Z. B. (1987). Designing career development systems: Principles and practices. *Human Resource Planning, 10*, 195–207.
2. Gutteridge, T. G., Leibowitz, Z. B., and Shore, J. E. (1993). *Organizational career development: Benchmarks for building a world-class workforce*. San Francisco: Jossey-Bass; and London, M., Larsen, H. H., and Thisted, L. N. (1999). Relationships between feedback and self development. *Group and Organization Management, 24*, 5–27.
3. Murphy, D. (1999, July 18). New attitude for employees: "Emergent" workers think job, not career. *Arizona Republic*, AZ11.
4. Weber, P. F. (1998). Getting a grip on employee growth. *Training & Development, 53*, 87–91.
5. Morgan, D. C. (1977). Career development programs. *Personnel, 54*, 23–27.
6. Gutteridge, T., and Otte, F. (1983). Organizational career development: What's going on out there? *Training & Development, 37*, 22–26; Hall, D. T. (1986). An overview of current career development, theory, research, and practice. In D. T. Hall et al. (Eds.), *Career development in organizations*, 1–20, San Francisco: Jossey-Bass; and Leibowitz, Z. B., and Schlossberg, N. K. (1981). Designing career development programs in organizations: A systems approach. In D. H. Montross and C. J. Shinkman (Eds.), *Career development in the 1980s*, 277–291, Springfield, IL: Charles C Thomas.
7. Russell, J. E. A. (1991). Career development interventions in organizations. *Journal of Vocational Behavior, 38*, 237–287.
8. Koonce, R. (1991, January–February). Management development: An investment in people. *Credit Magazine*, 16–19.
9. Steele, B., Bratkovich, J. R., and Rollins, T. (1990). Implementing strategic redirection through the career management system. *Human Resource Planning, 13*, 241–263.
10. Feldman, D. C., and Weitz, B. A. (1991). From the invisible hand to the gladhand: Understanding a careerist orientation to work. *Human Resource Management, 30*, 237–257.
11. Aryee, S., Wyatt, T., and Stone, R. (1996). Early career outcomes of graduate employees: The effect of mentoring and ingratiation. *Journal of Management Studies, 33*, 95–118.
12. Kalish, B. B. (1992, March). Dismantling the glass ceiling. *Management Review*, 64; and Hawkins, B. (1991, September 8). Career-limiting bias found at low job levels. *Los Angeles Times Magazine*, 33.
13. Galvin, K. (1999, January 7). Texaco settlement with female staff to cost $3 million. *Arizona Republic*, D1.

14. Swoboda, F. (1998, December 3). US Airways settles "glass ceiling" case. *Washington Post*, E2.
15. *Arizona Republic*. (1999, February 7). Glass ceiling at universities, A24.
16. Deogun, N. (1999, May 20). Coca-Cola report addressed race in '95. *Wall Street Journal*, Brussels, A5.
17. Mazier, E. E. (2002). Insurance women still hit "glass ceiling." *National Underwriter Property & Casualty, 106*, 23.
18. Jackson, M. (1998, February 25). Women hit glass ceiling, open businesses: Study respondents say corporations don't value them. *Arizona Republic*, E2.
19. Mattern, H. (1999, July 22). Women making headway push "glass ceiling" as federal workers. *Arizona Republic*, D1.
20. Jones, D. (1999, July 20). What glass ceiling? *USA Today*, B1, B2.
21. Applebaum, S. (2002). A real operator. *Multichannel News, 23*, 8.
22. Kelly, J. (2002). Does health care still have a glass ceiling? *H & HN, 76*, 30.
23. Jones, D. (1999, July 20). What glass ceiling? *USA Today*, B1, B2.
24. Kelly, J. (2002). Does health care still have a glass ceiling? *H & HN, 76*, 30.
25. Barnett, R. C., and Rivers, C. (1999, May 10). Family values go to work. *Washington Post, A23*.
26. *LIMRA's Market Facts*. (1998). Outlook on essential benefits and trends, *17*, 6.
27. Bourne, K. (1992). Companies offer career management for couples. *Journal of Compensation and Benefits, 7*, 32–36.
28. Ibid.
29. Harvey, M., and Wiese, D. (1998). Global dual-career couple mentoring: A phase model approach. *Human Resource Planning, 21*, 33–48.
30. Frazee, V. (1999). Expert help for dual-career spouses. *Workforce, 4*, 18–20.
31. Bures, A. L., Henderson, D., Mayfield, J., Mayfield, M., and Worley, J. (1995). The effects of spousal support and gender on workers' stress and job satisfaction: A cross national investigation of dual career couples. *Journal of Applied Business Research, 12*, 52–58.
32. Barnett, R. C., and Rivers, C. (1999, May 10). Family values go to work. *Washington Post*, A23.
33. Gordon, J. (1998). The new paternalism. *Forbes, 162*, 68–70.
34. Scarpello, V. G., and Ledvinka, J. (1988). *Personnel/human resource management: Environment and functions*. Boston: PWS-Kent; and Russell, 1991.
35. Haskell, J. R. (1993, February). Getting employees to take charge of their careers. *Training & Development*, 51–54.
36. Anastasi, A. (1976). *Psychological testing* (4th ed.). New York: Macmillan.
37. Burn, A. (1998, November/December). Testing times. *British Journal of Administrative Management*, 16–17.
38. Engelbrecht, A. S., and Fischer, A. H. (1995). The managerial performance implications of a developmental assessment center process. *Human Relations, 48*, 387–404.
39. Scarpello, V. G., and Ledvinka, J. (1988). *Personnel/human resource management: Environment and functions*. Boston: PWS-Kent; and Russell, 1991.
40. Morgan, M. A., Hall, D. T., and Martier, A. (1979). Career development strategies in industry—Where are we and where should we be? *Personnel, 56*, 13–30.
41. Rocco, J. (1991, August). Computers track high-potential managers. *HRMagazine*, 66–68.
42. Villeneure, K. (1999). Thought about succession? You should. *Discount Store News, 38*, 16.
43. Howard, A. (1986). College experiences and managerial performance. *Journal of Applied Psychology, 71*, 530–552.
44. Judge, T. A., Cable, D. M., Boudreau, J. W., and Bretz, R. D. (1995). An empirical investigation of the predictors of executive career success. *Personnel Psychology, 48*, 485–519.
45. Baehr, M. E., and Orban, J. A. (1989). The role of intellectual abilities and personality characteristics in determining success in higher-level positions. *Journal of Vocational Behavior, 35*, 270–287.
46. Seibert, S. E., and Kraimer, M. L. (1999). The five-factor model of personality and its relationship with career success. Paper presented at the Annual Meeting of the Academy of Management, Chicago.
47. Garrett, E. M. (1994, April). Going the distance. *Small Business Reports*, 22–30.
48. Ibid.
49. Weber, P. F. (1998). Getting a grip on employee growth. *Training & Development, 53*, 87–91.
50. Russell, J. E. A. (1991). Career development interventions in organizations. *Journal of Vocational Behavior, 38*, 237–287.
51. Gutteridge, T. (1986). Organizational career development systems: The state of the practice. In D. T. Hall et al., *Career development in organizations*, 50–94. San Francisco: Jossey-Bass.
52. Smith, S. (2002). Content at your service: Online content has to become more service oriented, offering content packages and even direct service that help users complete specific tasks. *Econtent, 25*, 44(2).
53. Gutteridge, T. G., Leibowitz, Z. B., and Shore, J. E. (1993). *Organizational career development: Benchmarks for building a world-class workforce*. San Francisco: Jossey-Bass.
54. Gutteridge, T. (1986). Organizational career development systems: The state of the practice. In D. T. Hall et al., *Career development in organizations*, 50–94. San Francisco: Jossey-Bass.
55. Russell, J. E. A. (1991). Career development interventions in organizations. *Journal of Vocational Behavior, 38*, 237–287.
56. Noe, R. A. (1988). An investigation of the determinants of successful assigned mentoring relationships. *Personnel Psychology, 41*, 457–479.
57. Hill, S. K., and Bahniuk, M. H. (1998). Promoting career success through mentoring. *Review of Business, 19*, 4–7.
58. Starcevich, M., and Friend, F. (1999, July). Effective mentoring relationships from the mentee's perspective. *Workforce*, Extra Supplement, 2–3.
59. *Association Management*. (1993, May). Mentor program promotes opportunity for all, 166.
60. Barbian, J. (2002). The road best traveled. *Training, 39*, 38(4).
61. Dansky, K. H. (1996). The effect of group mentoring on career outcomes. *Group & Organization Management, 21*, 5–21.
62. Kaye, B. (1993, December). Career development—Anytime, anyplace. *Training & Development*, 46–49.
63. Ibid.
64. Lesly, E. (1993, November 29). Sticking it out at Xerox by sticking together. *BusinessWeek*, 77.
65. Stephenson, S. (2002). And wind up better off: Join the team! *Food Service Director, 15*, 80.
66. Morrisey, G. L. (1992, November). Your personal mission statement: A foundation for your future. *Training & Development*, 71–74.
67. Matejka, K., and Dunsing, R. (1993). Enhancing your advancement in the 1990s. *Management Decision, 31*, 52–54.

Chapter 10

1. Milkovich, G. T., and Newman, J. M. (2002). *Compensation* (5th ed.). Homewood, IL: McGraw-Hill/Irwin.
2. Brenan, J. (1999). Group legal insurance: An effective recruitment and retaining tool. *Compensation and Benefits Review, 31*(3), 46–53; and *HR Focus b*. (2002, February).
3. Gómez-Mejía, L. R., and Balkin, D. B. (1992a). The determinants of faculty pay: An agency theory perspective. *Academy of*

Management Journal, 35(5), 921–955; and Lee, J. (2002, April). Finding the sweet spots: Optimal executive compensation. *Workspan*, 40–46.

4. Melcher, R. A., Cohn, L., and Symonds, W. C. (1999, July 19). You can go home again—with a raise. *BusinessWeek*, 44–45; Gorman, C. (1999, February 8). Black days for doctors. *Time*, 53; and *HR Focus a*. (2002).
5. Delves, D. (1999). Practical lessons for designing an economic value incentive plan. *Compensation and Benefits Review, 31*(2), 61–70; Ray, H. H., and Altmansberger, H. N. (1999). Introducing goal sharing in a public sector organization. *Compensation and Benefits Review, 31*(3), 40–45; and Jaross, J., Byrnes, R., and Mercer, W. (2002, April). Mastering the share plan circus. *Workspan*, 55–64.
6. Heneman, R. L., and Dixon, K. E. (2001, November–December). Reward and organizational systems alignment: An expert system. *Compensation and Benefits Review*, 18–27; Ledeler, J., and Weinberg, L. R. (1999). Setting executive compensation: Does the industry you are in really matter? *Compensation and Benefits Review, 31*(1), 13–24; and Bloom, M. (1999). The art and context of the deal: A balanced view of executive incentives. *Compensation and Benefits Review, 31*(1), 25–31.
7. Milkovich, G. T., and Newman, J. M. (2002). *Compensation* (5th ed.). Homewood, IL: McGraw-Hill/Irwin.
8. Zingheim, P. K., and Schuster, J. (2001, November–December). Creating a powerful customized workplace reward brand. *Compensation and Benefits Review, 33*(6), 30–34; and Wolf, M. G. (2000). Compensation: An overview. In Berger, L. A., and Berger, D. R. (Eds.), *The compensation handbook* (4th ed.). New York: McGraw-Hill.
9. Gómez-Mejía, L. R., and Balkin, D. B. (1992a). The determinants of faculty pay: An agency theory perspective. *Academy of Management Journal, 35*(5), 921–955.
10. Balkin, D. B., and Gómez-Mejía, L. R. (2000). Is CEO pay related to innovation in high-technology firms? *Academy of Management Journal, 43*(6), 30–41.
11. Gómez-Mejía, L. R., and Welbourne, T. M. (1988). Compensation strategy: An overview and future steps. *Human Resource Planning, 11*(3), 173–189; and Heneman, R. L., and Dixon, K. E. (2001, November–December). Reward and organizational systems alignment: An expert system. *Compensation and Benefits Review*, 18–27.
12. *Workspan*. (2002a, February). Hiring down, but retention still an issue, 13.
13. Dunham, K. J. (2002, February 5). The jungle: Focus on recruitment, pay, and getting ahead. *Wall Street Journal*, B-8.
14. *Arizona Republic*. (2002, February 19). Retention bonuses under fire, D-15.
15. Conlin, M., and Berner, R. (2002, February 18). A little less in the envelope. *BusinessWeek*, 64–66.
16. Desmond, E. W. (1996, April 22). The failed miracle. *Time*, 61–64; Longnecker, B. M., Petersen, B., and Hitt, R. (1999). Long-term incentives: How private companies can compete with public companies. *Compensation and Benefits Review, 31*(1), 44–53.
17. Gilles, P. L. (1999). A fresh look at incentive plans. *Compensation and Benefits Review, 31*(1), 61–72; Saura, M. D., and Gómez-Mejía, L. R. (1997). The effectiveness of organization-wide compensation strategies in technology intensive firms. *Journal of High Technology Management Research, 8*(2), 301–317.
18. Lancaster, H. (1996, January 27). Chasing start ups may not always lead to a pot of gold. *Wall Street Journal*, B-1; and Milkovich, G. T., Gerhart, B., and Hannon, J. (1991). The effects of research and development intensity on managerial compensation in large organizations. *Journal of High Technology Management Research, 2*(1), 133–150.
19. Berner, R. (2002, March 18). Keeping a lid on unemployment: No bonus may mean fewer layoffs. *BusinessWeek*, 18.
20. Stewart, T. A. (2002, February). Doing more with less. *Fortune*, 41–46.
21. Blumestien, R., Solomon, D., and Chen, K. (2002, February 21). As global crossing crashed, executives got loan relief pension payouts. *Wall Street Journal*, B-1; Schultz, E. E. (2002, January 16). "Lockdowns" of 401(k) plans draw scrutiny. *Wall Street Journal*, C-1; and Schultz, E. E., and Francis, T. (2002, January 23). Enron pensions had more room at the top. *Wall Street Journal*, A-4.
22. *Workspan*. (2002b, February). Financial awards produce better results, 12; and Swinford, D. N. (1999). Don't pay for executive failure. *Compensation and Benefits Review, 31*(1), 54–60.
23. Lehr, L. W. (1986, Winter). The care and flourishing of entrepreneurs at 3M. *Directors and Boards*, 18–20.
24. Bylinsky, G. (1990, July 2). Turning R&D into real products. *Fortune*, 72.
25. Worldatwork. (2002a, February 13). Topic briefing: Skill-based pay. See customerrelations@worldatwork.org.
26. Milkovich, G. T., and Newman, J. M. (2002). *Compensation* (5th ed.). Homewood, IL: McGraw-Hill/Irwin.
27. Tosi, H., and Tosi, L. (1986). What managers need to know about knowledge-based pay. *Organizational Dynamics, 14*(3), 52–64; and Ledford, G. E., and Heneman, R. L. (2000). Pay for skills, knowledge, and competencies. In Berger, L. A., and Berger, D. R. (Eds.), *The compensation handbook* (4th ed.). New York: McGraw-Hill.
28. Ledford, G. E., and Heneman, R. L. (2000). Pay for skills, knowledge, and competencies. In Berger, L. A., and Berger, D. R. (Eds.), *The compensation handbook* (4th ed.). New York: McGraw-Hill; and Brown, D. (2000). Relating competencies to pay: A desirable or dangerous practice. In Berger, L. A., and Berger, D. R. (Eds.), *The compensation handbook* (4th ed.). New York: McGraw-Hill.
29. Gómez-Mejía, L. R., and Balkin, D. B. (1992b). *Compensation, organizational strategy, and firm performance*. Cincinnati, OH: South-Western; and Milkovich, G. T., and Newman, J. M. (2002). *Compensation* (5th ed.). Homewood, IL: McGraw-Hill/Irwin.
30. Caudron, S. (1993, June). Master the compensation maze. *Personnel Journal*, 64B–64O.
31. Gilles, P. L. (1999). A fresh look at incentive plans. *Compensation and Benefits Review, 31*(1), 61–72.
32. *Fortune*. (2002). The 100 best companies to work for in America. www.fortune.com/lists/bestcompanies/snap502.html.
33. Eisenberg, D. (1999, August 16). We are for hire, just click. *Time*, 46–50.
34. Gómez-Mejía, L. R., Balkin, D. B., and Milkovich, G. T. (1990). Rethinking your rewards for technical employees. *Organizational Dynamics, 1*(1), 107–118; and Lawler, E. E., III. (1990). *Strategic pay*. San Francisco: Jossey-Bass.
35. *Fortune*. (2002). The 100 best companies to work for in America. www.fortune.com/lists/bestcompanies/snap502.html.
36. Handel, J. (2002, February). Capital view: IASB takes on controversial stock option accounting. *Workspan, 45*(2), 1–4.
37. Milkovich, G. T., and Newman, J. M. (2002). *Compensation* (5th ed.). Homewood, IL: McGraw-Hill/Irwin; and Ingster, B. (2000). Methods of job evaluation. In Berger, L. A., and Berger, D. R. (Eds.), *The compensation handbook* (4th ed.). New York: McGraw-Hill.
38. *Fortune*. (2002). The 100 best companies to work for in America. www.fortune.com/lists/bestcompanies/snap502.html.
39. Lavelle, L. (2002, March 4). The danger of deferred compensation. *BusinessWeek*, 110; McNamee, M. (2002, February 18). 401(k)s: Workers need education, not handcuffs. *BusinessWeek*, 30; and Conlin and Berner (2002).

40. Bureau of Labor Statistics (2002). *Business Economics and Financial Statistics*. www.lib.gsu.edu/collections/govdocs/stats.htm; and Jarrel, S. B., and Staley, T. D. (1990). A meta-analysis of the union–nonunion wage gap. *Industrial and Labor Relations Review, 44*(1), 54–67.
41. Hambrick, D. C., and Snow, C. C. (1989). Strategic reward systems. In C. C. Snow (Ed.), *Strategy, organization design, and human resources management*. Greenwich. CT: JAI Press; Gilles, P. L. (1999). A fresh look at incentive plans. *Compensation and Benefits Review, 31*(1), 61–72; and Heneman, R. L., and Dixon, K. E. (2001, November–December). Reward and organizational systems alignment: An expert system. *Compensation and Benefits Review*, 18–27.
42. Associated Press. (1991, April 4). What matters to Americans, *Arizona Republic*, AZ.
43. Bloom, M. (1999). The art and context of the deal: A balanced view of executive incentives. *Compensation and Benefits Review, 31*(1), 25; and Thompson, M. A., and Cook, F. W. (2002, February). Forget white tablecloths: Executives like cafeteria plans too. *Workspan*, 34–40.
44. Seidman, W. L., and Skancke, S. L. (1989). *Competitiveness: The executive's guide to success*. New York: M.E. Sharpe.
45. *Fortune*. (2002). The 100 best companies to work for in America. www.fortune.com/lists/bestcompanies/snap502.html.
46. Lewin, R., and Regine, B. (2000). *The soul at work*. Boston: The Free Press, Simon and Schuster.
47. Stewart, T. A. (1998, June 8). Can even heroes get paid too much? *Fortune*, 289–290; and Poster, C. Z. (2002, January–February). Retaining key people in troubled companies. *Compensation and Benefits Review, 34*(1), 7–12.
48. Lawler, E. E., III. (1990). *Strategic pay*. San Francisco: Jossey-Bass.
49. Gómez-Mejía, L. R., and Balkin, D. B. (1992a). The determinants of faculty pay: An agency theory perspective. *Academy of Management Journal, 35*(5), 921–955; and Milkovich, G. T., and Newman, J. M. (2002). *Compensation* (5th ed.). Homewood, IL: McGraw-Hill/Irwin.
50. Balkin, D. B., and Gómez-Mejía, L. R. (1990). Matching compensation and organizational strategies. *Strategic Management Journal, 11*, 153–169; Heneman, R. L., and Dixon, K. E. (2001, November–December). Reward and organizational systems alignment: An expert system. *Compensation and Benefits Review*, 18–27; and Lee, J. (2002, April). Finding the sweet spots: Optimal executive compensation. *Workspan*, 40–46.
51. Cantoni, C. J. (1995, May 15). A waste of human resources. *Wall Street Journal*, B-1; and Berstein, A. (1999, June 14). Stock options bite back. *BusinessWeek*, 50–51.
52. Milkovich, G. T., and Newman, J. M. (2002). *Compensation* (5th ed.). Homewood, IL: McGraw-Hill/Irwin.
53. Ibid.
54. Ibid.
55. Ibid.
56. Additional information on the criteria, contentions, interpretation, and application of the MAA (NMTA) plan can be obtained by contacting the nearest MAA association office: AAIM Management Association, St. Louis, MO; AAIM, The Management Association, North Haven, CT; American Society of Employers, Southfield, MI; Capital Associated Industries, Inc., Raleigh, NC; CMEA The Employers Association, Worcester, MA; Employers Association, Inc., Minneapolis, MN; Employers Association of Western Massachusetts, Inc., Ludlow, MA; TEA-The Employers Association, Inc., Braintree, MA; The Employers Association, Lincoln, RI; Employers Resource Council, Seven Hills, OH; IMA Management Association, Inc., Clifton, NJ; IMC-Industrial Management Council, Rochester, NY; The Management Association of Illinois, Broadview, IL; MidAtlantic Employers' Association, Valley Forge, PA; MRA-The Management Association, Inc., Brookfield, WI.
57. Gómez-Mejía, L. R., Page, R. C., and Tornow, W. (1987). Computerized job evaluation systems. In D. B. Balkin and L. R. Gómez-Mejía (Eds.), *New perspectives on compensation*. Upper Saddle River, NJ: Prentice Hall.
58. NMTA Associates. (1992). National position evaluation plan, 3. Clifton, NJ.
59. Werner, S., Konopaske, R., and Touchey, C. (1999). Ten questions to ask yourself about compensation surveys. *Compensation and Benefits Review, 31*(3), 54–59.
60. Dunlop, J. T. (1957). The task of contemporary wage theory. In G. W. Taylor and F. C. Pierson (Eds.), *New concepts in wage determination*. New York: McGraw-Hill; Gerhart, B., and Milkovich, G. T. (1993). Employee compensation: Research and practice. In M. D. Dunnette and L. M. Hough (Eds.), *Handbook of industrial and organizational psychology*, Vol. 3. Palo Alto, CA: Consulting Psychologists Press; Treiman, D. J., and Hartmann, H. I. (Eds.). (1981). *Women, work, and wages: Equal pay for jobs of equal value*. Washington, DC: National Academy Press; and Berstein, A. (1999, June 14). Stock options bite back. *BusinessWeek*, 50–51.
61. HR.com (2002, February 12). Salarysource. www.salarysource.com: Creelman, D. (2002, February). Basics of job match salary surveys. In HR.com at www4.hr.com/hrcom/index.cfm; Werner, S., Konopaske, R., and Touchey, C. (1999). Ten questions to ask yourself about compensation surveys. *Compensation and Benefits Review, 31*(3), 54–59; Lichty, D. T. (2000). Compensation surveys. In Berger, L. A., and Berger, D. R. (Eds.), *The compensation handbook* (4th ed.). New York: McGraw-Hill; and Spiegel, B. I., and Slobodziam, T. (2000). Developing competitive compensation programs. In Berger, L. A., and Berger, D. R. (Eds.), *The compensation handbook* (4th ed.). New York: McGraw-Hill.
62. Risher, H. (2003, March). Making managers responsible for handling pay. *Workspan*, 8–12.
63. LeBlanc, P. V., and Ellis, G. M. (1995, Winter). The many faces of banding. *ACA Journal*, 52–62; *ACA Journal*. (1995, Autumn). Clark refining and marketing broadbands: Annual pay rates, 57.
64. Haslett, S. (1995, November/December). Broadbanding: A strategic tool for organizational change. *Compensation and Benefits Review*, 40–43; and Worldatwork. (2002b, February 12). Topic briefings: Broadbanding. Customerrelations@worldatwork.org/topicbriefings.
65. Ledford, G. E., and Heneman, R. L. (2000). Pay for skills, knowledge, and competencies. In Berger, L. A., and Berger, D. R. (Eds.), *The compensation handbook* (4th ed.). New York: McGraw-Hill; and Worldatwork. (2002a, February 13). Topic briefing: Skill-based pay. See customerrelations@worldatwork.org.
66. Workspan (2003, March). The work experience, 16.
67. Barton, P. (1996, February). Team-based pay. *ACA Journal, 5*(1), 15–30; Watson Wyatt Data Services (1996). The 1995–1996 ECS surveys of middle management and office personnel compensation. Rochelle Park, NJ; Gross, S. E. (2000). Team based pay. In Berger, L. A., and Berger, D. R. (Eds.), *The compensation handbook* (4th ed.). New York: McGraw-Hill; and Welbourne, T., and Gómez-Mejía, L. R. (2000). Optimizing team based incentives. In Berger, L. A., and Berger, D. R. (Eds.), *The compensation handbook* (4th ed.). New York: McGraw-Hill.
68. Gupta, N., Ledford, G. E., Jenkins, G. D., and Doty, D. (1992). Survey-based prescriptions for skill-based pay. *American Compensation Association Journal, 1*(1), 48–59; Ledford, G. E., and Heneman, R. L. (2000). Pay for skills, knowledge, and competencies. In Berger, L. A., and Berger, D. R. (Eds.), *The compensation handbook* (4th ed.). New York: McGraw-Hill; and Tosi, H., and Tosi, L. (1986). What managers need to know about knowledge-based pay. *Organizational Dynamics, 14*(3), 52–64.

69. Barton, P. (1996, February). Team-based pay. *ACA Journal, 5*(1), 15–30; Watson Wyatt Data Services (1996). The 1995–1996 ECS surveys of middle management and office personnel compensation. Rochelle Park, NJ.
70. Aaron, H. J., and Lougy, C. M. (1986). *The comparable worth controversy*, 3–4. Washington, DC: The Brookings Institution; Rhoads, S. E. (1993, July–August). Pay equity won't go away. *Across the Board*, 37–41; and Stillson, C. A., and Mohler, K. M. (2001). History still in the making—the continuing struggle for equal pay. *Worldatwork Journal, 10*(1), 1–8.
71. Werner, S., Konopaske, R., and Touchey, C. (1999). Ten questions to ask yourself about compensation surveys. *Compensation and Benefits Review, 31*(3), 54–59.
74. Ibid.

Chapter 11

1. *HR Focus*. (2001, April). Incentive pay plans: Which ones work . . . and why, 3–5; Poster, C. Z. (2002, January–February). Retaining key people in troubled companies. *Compensation and Benefits Review, 34*(1), 7–12; and Gilles, P. L. (1999). A fresh look at incentive plans for privately held companies. *Compensation and Benefits Review, 31*(1), 61–72.
2. Branch, S. (1999, January 11). The 100 best companies to work for in America. *Fortune*, 118.
3. Newsline. (2002). Companies understand need to recognize outstanding performance. www.worldatwork.org/newslinenews.
4. Poster, C. Z. (2002, January–February). Retaining key people in troubled companies. *Compensation and Benefits Review, 34*(1), 7–12.
5. Merrick, A. (2002, April 17). Kmart officers got big loans before it filed for bankruptcy. *Wall Street Journal*, B-1.
6. Milkovich, G. T., and Newman, J. (2002). *Compensation* (7th ed.). New York: McGraw-Hill.
7. Ray, H. H., and Altmansberger, H. N. (1999, May/June). Introducing goalsharing in a public sector organization. *Compensation and Benefits Review, 31*(3), 40–45; and Gómez-Mejía, L. R., Welbourne, T., and Wiseman, R. (2000). Gainsharing and employee risk takings. *Academy of Management Review, 25*(3), 492–509.
8. Bloom, M. (1999). The art and context of the deal: A balanced view of executive incentives. *Compensation and Benefits Review, 31*(1), 25–31; Tully, S. (1999, April 26). The earnings illusion. *Fortune*, 206–210; Byrne, J. A. (2002, April 15). Pay related wealth: Winners and losers. *BusinessWeek*, 83; and Makri, M., and Gómez-Mejía, L. R. (2002). Rewarding executives. In R. Silzer (Ed.), *The 21st Century Executive* (pp. 200–228). San Francisco: Jossey-Bass.
9. *Boston Globe*. (1992, October 16). Teaching to the test shortchanges pupils. *Arizona Republic*, A4; and Symonds, W. C. (2001, March 19). How to fix American schools. *BusinessWeek*, 68–73.
10. Spiro, L. N., and Schoeder, M. (1995, February 20). Can you trust? *BusinessWeek*, 70–76; Byrnes, N., McNamee, M., Grover, L., Muller, J., and Park, A. (2002, April 8). Auditing here, consulting over there. *BusinessWeek*, 34–36; and Kahn, J. (2002, April 29).
11. Byrnes, N., McNamee, M., Grover, L., Muller, J., and Park, A. (2002, April 8). Auditing here, consulting over there. *BusinessWeek*, 34–36; and Kahn, J. (2002, April 29). Deloitte restates its case. *Fortune*, 64–74.
12. Elmstrom, P. (2002, April 22). A case of conflicts at Qwest. *BusinessWeek*, 37.
13. Saura, M. D. and Gómez-Mejía, L. R. (1997). The effectiveness of organization-wide compensation strategies in technology intensive firms. *Journal of High Technology Management Research, 8*(2), 301–317; Nofsinger, G. A. (2000). Performance measures: An overview. In L. Berger and D. R. Berger (Eds.) *The compensation handbook*. New York: McGraw-Hill; and Rich, J. T. (2002, February). The solution to employee performance mismanagement. *Workspan, 45*(2), 1–6.
14. Gómez-Mejía, L. R., and Balkin, D. B. (2002). *Management*. New York: Irwin/McGraw-Hill.
15. Gorman, C. (1999, February 8). Bleak days for doctors. *Time*, 53.
16. Ibid.
17. Bloom, M. (1999). The art and context of the deal: A balanced view of executive incentives. *Compensation and Benefits Review, 31*(1), 25–31; Edwards, M., and Ewen, A. J. (1995, Winter). Moving multisource assessment beyond development. *ACA Journal, 5*(1), 82–87; Bors, K. K., Clark, A. W., Power, V., Seltz, J. C., Schwartz, R. B., and Turbidy, G. S. (1996, Spring). Multiple perspectives: Essays on implementing performance measures. *ACA Journal, 5*(1), 40–45; and Milkovich, G. T., and Newman, J. M. (2002). *Compensation* (7th ed.), New York: McGraw-Hill.
18. Lawler, E. E., III, and Cohen, S. G. (1992). Designing a pay system for teams. *American Compensation Association Journal, 1*(1), 6–19.
19. Heneman, R. L., and Dixon, K. E. (2001, November–December). Reward and organizational systems alignment: An expert system. *Compensation and Benefits Review*, 18–27.
20. Hills, F. S., Scott, D. K., Markham, S. E., and Vest, M. J. (1987). Merit pay: Just or unjust desserts? *Personnel Administrator, 32*(9), 53–64; Hughes, C. L. (1986). The demerit of merit. *Personnel Administrator, 31*(6), 40; and Berstein, A. (1999, June 14). Stock options bite back. *BusinessWeek*, 50–51.
21. Rich, J. T. (2002, February). The solution to employee performance mismanagement. *Workspan, 45*(2), 1–6.
22. Symonds, W. C. (2001, March 19). How to fix American schools. *BusinessWeek*, 68–73.
23. *BusinessWeek*. (1992, July 6), 38.
24. Walters, S. (1999, September 19). Fury over Blunkett's huge wage rises for teachers. *The Mail on Sunday*, 5; Symonds, W. C. (2001, March 19). How to fix American schools. *BusinessWeek*, 68–73; and Pollock, R. L. (2001, August 20). The truth about the teacher "shortage." *Wall Street Journal*, A-5.
25. Rich, J. T. (2002, February). The solution to employee performance mismanagement. *Workspan, 45*(2) 1–6.
26. Schwab, D. P. (1974). Conflicting impacts of pay on employee motivation and satisfaction. *Personnel Journal, 53*(3), 190–206.
27. Makri, M., and Gómez-Mejía, L. R. (2002). Rewarding executives. In R. Silzer (Ed.), *The 21st Century Executive* (pp. 200–228). San Francisco: Jossey-Bass.
28. Deci, E. L. (1972). The effects of contingent and non-contingent rewards and controls on intrinsic motivation. *Organizational Behavior and Human Performance, 8*, 15–31. See related discussion in Bloom, M. (1999). The art and context of the deal: A balanced view of executive incentives. *Compensation and Benefits Review, 31*(1), 25–31; and Kohn, A. (1993, September–October). Why incentive plans cannot work. *Harvard Business Review*, 54–63.
29. *Fortune* (2002). Fortune's best companies to work for. www.fortune.com/lists/bestcompanies/snap_502.html.
30. *Academy of Management Review*. (1998, August). Special issue on trust.
31. *Profit-Building Strategies for Business Owners*. (1992, December), *22*(12), 23–24.
32. Newsline. (2002). Companies understand need to recognize outstanding performance. www.worldatwork.org/newslinenews.
33. Rich, J. T. (2002, February). The solution to employee performance mismanagement. *Workspan, 45*(2), 1–6; Parks, T. (2002). Uphill battle: Motivating a sales force in tough times.

Workspan, 4(2), 65–67; and *HR Focus*. (2001, April). Incentive pay plans: Which ones work . . . and why, 3–5.

34. Gómez-Mejía, L. R., and Balkin, D. B. (1992). *Compensation, organizational strategy, and firm performance*. Cincinnati, OH: South-Western.
35. *Work in America Institute*. (1991, October). AT&T credit: Continuous improvement as a way of life, *16*(10), 2.
36. Gómez-Mejía, L. R., Page, R. C., and Tornow, W. (1982). A comparison of the practical utility of traditional, statistical, and hybrid job evaluation approaches. *Academy of Management Journal, 25*, 790–809; Stiller (2001).
37. Rich, J. T. (2002, February). The solution to employee performance mismanagement. *Workspan, 45*(2), 1–6; *Workspan* (2002b).
38. Masternak, R. L., and Ross, T. L. (1992, January–February). A bonus for employee involvement. *Compensation and Benefits Review*, 46–54.
39. Greenberg, J. (1990). Looking fair vs. being fair: Managing impressions of organizational justice. In L. Cummings and B. M. Staw (Eds.), *Research in organizational behavior*, Vol. 2. Greenwich, CT: JAI Press.
40. Federico, R. E., and Goldsmith, H. B. (1998). Linking work/life benefits to performance. *Compensation and Benefits Review, 30*(4), 66–70; Schwartz, N. D. (1999, February 15). The tech boom will keep on rocking. *Fortune*, 64–69; Lewin, R., and Regime, B. (2000). *The soul at work*. Boston, MA: The Free Press, Simon and Schuster; and Newsline. (2002). Companies understand need to recognize outstanding performance. www.worldatwork.org/news linenews.
41. *Fortune* (2002). Fortune's best companies to work for. www.fortune.com/lists/bestcompanies/snap_502.html.
42. Milkovich, G. T., and Newman, J. M. (2002). *Compensation* (7th ed.), Plano, TX: B.P.I.
43. Gómez-Mejía, L. R., and Balkin, D. B. (1989). Effectiveness of individual and aggregate compensation strategies. *Industrial Relations, 28*, 431–445; and Balkin, D. B., and Gómez-Mejía, L. R. (2000). Is CEO pay related to innovation in high technology firms? *Academy of Management Journal, 43*(6), 30–41.
44. *HR Focus*. (2001, April). Incentive pay plans: Which ones work . . . and why, 3–5.
45. Weiss, T. B. (2000). Performance management. In L. Berger and D. R. Berger (Eds.), *The compensation handbook*. New York: McGraw-Hill; and Miller, J. S., Wiseman, R. M., and Gómez-Mejía, L. R. (2002). The fit between CEO compensation design and firm risk. *Academy of Management Journal, 45*(5), 90–99.
46. Locke, E. A., Shaw, K., Saari, L. M., and Latham, G. P. (1981). Goal setting and task performance: 1969–1980. *Psychological Bulletin, 90*, 125–152.
47. Fuchsberg, G. (1990, April 18). Culture shock. *Wall Street Journal*, R5:1.
48. Larimer, T., and Dickerson, J. F. (2002, February 18). Time for hardball. *Time*, 42–44.
49. Rich, J. T. (2002, February). The solution to employee performance mismanagement. *Workspan, 45*(2), 1–6.
50. Gómez-Mejía, L. R., and Balkin, D. B. (1992). *Compensation, organizational strategy, and firm performance*. Cincinnati, OH: South-Western; and Makri, M., and Gómez-Mejía, L. R. (2002). Rewarding executives. In R. Silzer (Ed.), *The 21st Century Executive* (pp. 200–228). San Francisco: Jossey-Bass.
51. Leaky, C. (1999, September 19). Motorists face a huge increase in speed cameras. *The Mail on Sunday*, 22.
52. Hewitt Associates, Lincolnshire, IL, reported in *Wall Street Journal* (1995, November 28), A1.
53. Welbourne, T. M., and Gómez-Mejía, L. R. (2000). Team incentives in the workplace. In L. Berger (Ed.), Handbook of wage and salary administration (2nd ed., pp. 240–245). New York: McGraw-Hill; and *HR Focus*. (2001, April). Incentive pay plans: Which ones work . . . and why, 3–5.
54. Bassim, M. (1988). Teamwork at General Foods: New and improved. *Personnel Journal, 67*(5), 62–70.
55. Welbourne, T. M., and Gómez-Mejía, L. R. (2000). Team incentives in the workplace. In L. Berger (Ed.), *Handbook of wage and salary administration* (2nd ed., pp. 240–245). New York: McGraw-Hill.
56. Gross, S., and Blair, J. (1995, September/October). Reinforcing team effectiveness through pay. *Compensation and Benefits Review*, 34–36; Zigon, J. (1996). How to measure the results of work teams. Zigon Performance Group, Media, PA; and Welbourne, T. M., and Gómez-Mejía, L. R. (2000). Team incentives in the workplace. In L. Berger (Ed.), *Handbook of wage and salary administration* (2nd ed., pp. 240–245). New York: McGraw-Hill.
57. Liden, R. C., and Mitchell, T. R. (1983). The effects of group interdependence on supervisor performance evaluations. *Personnel Psychology, 36*, 289–299.
58. *HR Focus*. (2001, April). Incentive pay plans: Which ones work . . . and why, 3–5.
59. Butler, M. J. (2001, 2nd Quarter). Worldwide growth of employee ownership phenomena. *Worldatwork Journal, 10*(2), 1–5.
60. Heneman, F., and Von Hippel, C. Interview appearing in *Wall Street Journal* (1995, November 28), A1.
61. Albanese, R., and VanFleet, D. D. (1985). Rational behavior in groups: The free-riding tendency. *Academy of Management Review, 10*, 244–255.
62. Heneman, F., and Von Hippel, C. Interview appearing in *Wall Street Journal* (1995, November 28), A1.
63. Gordon, D. M., Edwards, R., and Reich, M. (1982). *Segmented work, divided workers: The historical transformation of labor in the United States*. London: Cambridge University Press.
64. Mohrman, A. M., Mohrman, S. A., and Lawler, E. E. (1992). *Performance measurement, evaluation and incentives*. Boston: Harvard Business School.
65. Milkovich, G. T., and Newman, J. M. (2002). *Compensation* (7th ed.), New York: McGraw-Hill.
66. Miller, J. S., Wiseman, R. M., and Gómez-Mejía, L. R. (2002). The fit between CEO compensation design and firm risk. *Academy of Management Journal, 45*(5), 90–99; and Makri, M., and Gómez-Mejía, L. R. (2002). Rewarding executives. In R. Silzer (Ed.), *The 21st Century Executive* (pp. 200–228). San Francisco: Jossey-Bass.
67. Pinchot, G. (1985). *Intrapreneuring*. New York: Harper & Row.
68. Selz, M. (1994, January 11). Testing self-managed teams, entrepreneur hopes to lose job. *Wall Street Journal*, B1-B2.
69. McGregor, D. (1960). *The human side of enterprise*. New York: McGraw-Hill.
70. Gómez-Mejía, L. R., Welbourne, T., and Wiseman, R. (2000). Gainsharing and employee risk takings. *Academy of Management Review, 25*(3), 492–509.
71. Ross, T. L., Hatcher, L., and Ross, R. A. (1989, May). The incentive switch: From piecework to companywide gainsharing. *Management Review*, 22–26; and *HR Focus*. (2001, April). Incentive pay plans: Which ones work . . . and why, 3–5.
72. Gómez-Mejía, L. R., Welbourne, T., and Wiseman, R. (2000). Gainsharing and employee risk takings. *Academy of Management Review, 25*(3), 492–509.
73. Welbourne, T., and Gómez-Mejía, L. R. (1995). Gainsharing: A critical review. *Journal of Management, 21*(3), 559–609; Welbourne, T., Balkin, D., and Gómez-Mejía, L. R. (1995). Gainsharing and mutual monitoring. *Academy of Management Journal, 38*(3), 818–834; and Gómez-Mejía, L. R., Welbourne, T., and Wiseman, R. (2000). Gainsharing and employee risk takings. *Academy of Management Review, 25*(3), 492–509.

74. Florkowski, G. W. (1987). The organizational impact of profit sharing. *Academy of Management Review, 12*, 622–636; and Berner, R. (2002, March 18). Keeping a lid on unemployment: No bonus may mean fewer layoffs. *BusinessWeek*, 18.
75. *Time*. (1988, February 1), 13.
76. Jaross, J., Byrnes, R., and Mercer, W. (2002, April). Mastering the share plan circus. *Workspan*, 55–64; and Lee, J. (2002, April). Finding the sweet spots: Optimal executive compensation. *Workspan*, 40–46.
77. Kaplan, J., and Granados, L. (2002, April). Tax law changes affect ESOPs. *Workspan*, 46–50.
78. Branch, S. (1999, January 11). The 100 best companies to work for in America. *Fortune*, 118.
79. Landstrom, B. G., and Hoeffner, S. J. (2002, April). Taking a closer look at Enron from a retirement benefits perspective. *Workspan*, 26–31; Healy, A. (2002, April). Walking on eggshells: What's next for the 401(k) plan? *Workspan*, 18–26; Handel, J. (2002, April). Worldatwork 401(k) survey. Big corporations likely to put all employees' eggs in one basket. *Workspan*, 32–34; and Kaplan, J., and Granados, L. (2002, April). Tax law changes affect ESOPs. *Workspan*, 46–50.
80. Newsline. (2002). Companies understand need to recognize outstanding performance. www.worldatwork.org/newslinenews.
81. Butler, M. J. (2001, 2nd Quarter). Worldwide growth of employee ownership phenomena. *Worldatwork Journal, 10*(2), 1–5.
82. Burmeister, E. D. (2001). The top mistakes in implementing a global stock plan. *Worldatwork Journal, 10*(2), 3.
83. Ibid., 1–5.
84. *HR Focus*. (2001, April). Incentive pay plans: Which ones work . . . and why, 3–5; Conlin, M., and Berner, R. (2002, February 18). A little less in the envelope. *BusinessWeek*, 64–66; and Lavelle, L. (2002, March 4). The danger of deferred compensation. *BusinessWeek*, 110.
85. Handel, J. (2002, April). Worldatwork 401(k) survey. Big corporations likely to put all employees' eggs in one basket. *Workspan*, 32–34.
86. Gómez-Mejía, L. R., and Balkin, D. B. (2002). *Management*. New York: Irwin/McGraw-Hill.
87. Cheadle, A. (1989). Explaining patterns of profit sharing activity. *Industrial Relations, 28*, 387–401.
88. Lublin, J. (2002a, April 11). Executive pay under radar. *Wall Street Journal*, B-7; Lublin, J. (2002b, April 11). The hot seat. *Wall Street Journal*, B-10; Lublin, J. (2002c, March 5). CEOs' pay last year was lowest since 1989. *Wall Street Journal*, A-6; and Lavelle, L. (2002, March 25). Even CEOs get the blues sort of. *BusinessWeek*, 37.
89. Byrne, J. P. (2002, April 22). Extra helpings on the gravy train. *BusinessWeek*, 39; and Saposito, B. (2002, April 1). When one stock is enough. *Time*, 176.
90. Saposito, B. (2002, April 1). When one stock is enough. *Time*, 176.
91. Stewart, T. A. (1998, June 8). Can even heroes get paid too much? *Fortune*, 289–300; and Poster, C. Z. (2002, January–February). Retaining key people in troubled companies. *Compensation and Benefits Review, 34*(1), 7–12.
92. Lublin, J. (2002a, April 11). Executive pay under radar. *Wall Street Journal*, B-7; and Lublin, J. (2002b, April 11). The hot seat. *Wall Street Journal*, B-10.
93. *BusinessWeek*, (2002, April 15), Round UP, 15.
94. Rundell, A. G., and Gómez-Mejía, L. R. (2002). Power as a determinant of exective pay. *Human Resource Management Review, 12*(3), 3–23.
95. Thompson, M. A. (2001). Managing stock options in down market conditions. *Worldatwork Journal, 10*(2), 1–6; Bryniski, T., and Harsen, B. (2002, January–February). The cancel and regrant: A roadmap for addressing underwater options. *Compensation and Benefits Review, 34*(1), 28–33; and Fox, R. D., and Hauder, E. A. (2001). Sending out an SOS—Methods for companies to resuscitate underwater stock options. *Worldatwork Journal, 10*(2), 7–12.
96. Kahn, J. (2002, January 7). When 401(k)s are KO'd. *Fortune*, 104; Hymowitz, C. (2003, February 24). How to fix a broken system. *Wall Street Journal*, R–1.
97. *Wall Street Journal*. (2002, April 11). The boss's pay, B-15–B-19.
98. Hyman, J. S. (2000). Long-term incentives. In L. Berger and D. R. Berger (Eds.), *The compensation handbook*. New York: McGraw-Hill; Gómez-Mejía, L. R., and Wiseman, R. (1997). Reframing executive compensation: An assessment and outlook. *Journal of Management, 23*(3), 291–374; Mazer, M. A. and Larre, E. C. (2000). Executive compensation strategy. In L. Berger and D. R. Berger (Eds.), *The compensation handbook*. New York: McGraw-Hill; Lublin, J. (2002a, April 11). Executive pay under radar. *Wall Street Journal*, B-7; and Lublin, J. (2002b, April 11). The hot seat. *Wall Street Journal*, B-10.
99. Tosi, H., Katz, J., Werner, S., and Gómez-Mejía, L. R. (2000). A meta-analysis of executive compensation studies. *Journal of Management, 26*(2), 1–39.
100. Lublin, J. (2002a, April 11). Executive pay under radar. *Wall Street Journal*, B-7.
101. *Wall Street Journal*. (2002, April 11). The boss's pay, B-15–B-19.
102. *Wall Street Journal News Roundup*. (1995, March 7). In a cost-cutting era, many CEOs enjoy imperial perks, B-1.
103. Lublin, J. (2002a, April 11). Executive pay under radar. *Wall Street Journal*, B-7.
104. Ibid.
105. Ibid.
106. Gómez-Mejía, L. R., and Wiseman, R. (1997). Reframing executive compensation: An assessment and outlook. *Journal of Management, 23*(3), 291–374; and Wiseman, R., and Gómez-Mejía, L. R. (1998). A behavioral agency model. *Academy of Management Review, 23*(1), 150–196.
107. Dalton, D. R., and Daily, C. M. (1999). Directors and shareholders as equity partners? *Compensation and Benefits Review, 31*(1), 73–79.
108. Ibid.
109. Creswell, J. (1999, April 4). More companies are linking directors' pay to performance. *Wall Street Journal*, R6; and McNamee, M. (2002, April 22). Turn up the heat on board cronyism. *BusinessWeek*, 36.
110. Makri, M., and Gómez-Mejía, L. R. (2002). Rewarding executives. In R. Silzer (Ed.), *The 21st Century Executive* (pp. 200–228). San Francisco: Jossey-Bass; Johnson, A. M. (2000). Designing and implementing total executive compensation programs. In L. Berger and D. R. Berger (Eds.), *The compensation handbook*. New York: McGraw-Hill; and Parks, T. (2002). Uphill battle: Motivating a sales force in tough times. *Workspan, 4*(2), 65–67.
111. Ibid.; Watson Wyatt Data Services, (1996). *The 1995–1996 sales and marketing personnel report*. New York, New York.
112. Parks, T. (2002). Uphill battle: Motivating a sales force in tough times. *Workspan, 4*(2), 65–67.
113. *HR Focus*. (2001, April). Incentive pay plans: Which ones work . . . and why, 3–5.
114. Sager, I., McWilliams, G., and Hof, D. (1994, February 7). IBM leans on its salesforce. *BusinessWeek*, 110.
115. *Forbes*. (1994, February 28), 15–20.
116. Rich, J. T. (2002, February). The solution to employee performance mismanagement. *Workspan, 45*(2), 1–6.
117. Mullaney, T. J., and Darnell, L. (2002, April 22). Ford: Europe has a better idea. *BusinessWeek*, 86–88.
118. *BusinessWeek*. (2002, January 14). The fallen, 77–79.
119. Edmonson, G. (1999, August 9). France: A CEO's pay secret shouldn't be a secret. *BusinessWeek*, 47.
120. Kohn, A. (1993, September–October). Why incentive plans cannot work. *Harvard Business Review*, 54–63.

Chapter 12

1. McNamee, M. (1999, October 4). Good pensions, bad sales pitch. *BusinessWeek*, 44.
2. Sager, I. (1999, October 11). Look for the union label—at IBM. *BusinessWeek*, 46.
3. Kerwin, K. (2000, February 21). Employee benefits: Workers of the world, log on. *BusinessWeek*, 52.
4. DeYoung, P. (2000, October). High-tech talent perks are ripe for the picking. *Workspan*, 28–33.
5. U.S. Bureau of Labor Statistics. (2001, June). *Employer costs for employee compensation*, 1–4.
6. Lieb, J. (1990, March 19). Day-care demand creates new perk. *Denver Post*, 1C, 5C.
7. Gómez-Mejía, L. R., and Balkin, D. B. (1992). *Compensation, organizational strategy and firm performance*. Cincinnati, OH: South-Western.
8. Jusko, J. (2002, April). Benefits costs below average. *Industry Week*, 18.
9. McCaffery, R. M. (1992). *Employee benefit programs: A total compensation perspective* (2nd ed.). Boston: PWS-Kent.
10. McCaffery, R. M. (1989). Employee benefits and services. In L. R. Gómez-Mejía (Ed.), *Compensation and benefits*. Washington, DC: The Bureau of National Affairs.
11. Lawler, E. E. III. (1990). *Strategic pay*. San Francisco: Jossey-Bass.
12. Levering, R., Moskowitz, M., and Katz, M. (1984). *The 100 best companies to work for in America*. Reading, MA: Addison-Wesley.
13. U.S. Chamber of Commerce. (1991). *Employee benefits 1990*. Washington, DC: U.S. Chamber of Commerce.
14. Hansen, F. (1999, May/June). Workers' compensation: Hard times ahead. *Compensation and Benefits Review*, 15–20.
15. Thompson, R. (1990, March). Fighting the high cost of workers' compensation. *Nation's Business*, 20–29.
16. Light, L. (1992, October 5). When injured employees act anything but. *BusinessWeek*, 120.
17. Lorenz, C. (1995, May–June). Nine practical suggestions for streamlining workers' compensation costs. *Compensation and Benefits Review*, 40–44.
18. *Occupational Safety Hazards*. (2002, February). A checklist for managing workers' comp claims, 24.
19. Fefer, M. D. (1994, October 3). Taking control of your workers' comp costs. *Fortune*, 131–136.
20. Milkovich, G. T., and Newman, J. M. (2002). *Compensation* (7th ed.). Homewood, IL: Irwin, McGraw-Hill.
21. Richman, L. S. (1995, April 17). Getting past economic insecurity. *Fortune*, 161–168.
22. Preston, H. (2002, March 16). Walking papers: How to make the best of losing a job. *International Herald Tribune*, 13.
23. Snarr, B. (1993, May–June). The Family and Medical Leave Act of 1993. *Compensation and Benefits Review*, 6–9.
24. Crampton, S. M., and Mishra, J. M. (1995). Family and medical leave legislation: Organizational policies and strategies. *Public Personnel Management, 24*(3), 271–289.
25. Gunsch, D. (1993, September). The Family Leave Act: A financial burden? *Personnel Journal*, 48–57.
26. Paltell, E. (1999, September). FMLA: After six years, a bit more clarity. *HRMagazine*, 144–150.
27. McNamee, M. (1993, August 9). Sure, "unpaid leave" sounds simple, but. . . . *BusinessWeek*, 32–33.
28. Hansen, F. (2001, March/April). Seven years after the FMLA. *Compensation and Benefits Review*, 22–30; *HR Focus*. (2001, March). What's wrong with the FMLA? Two views from SHRM and the DOL, 3–4.
29. *The Economist*. (1999, October 16). Health care: The right to sue, 30–31.
30. Sunoo, B. P. (1998, November). Carrying the weight of the HIPAA-potamus. *Workforce*, 58–64.
31. Weber, J. (2002, January 28). The new power play in health care. *BusinessWeek*, 90–91.
32. Ibid.
33. Kendall, J. (2001, February 19). Patients' rights for all patients? *BusinessWeek*, 90–92.
34. Weber, J. (2002, January 28). The new power play in health care. *BusinessWeek*, 90–91.
35. Jefferson, D. J. (1994, March 8). Family matters: Gay employees win benefits for partners at more corporations. *Wall Street Journal*, A1, A6: and Jenner, L. (1994, January), Domestic partner update: Awareness and resistance. *HR Focus*, 10.
36. Newton, C. (2002, February). Branching out with self-funded health care. *Workspan*, 45–47.
37. Bernstein, A. (1991, August 19). Playing "Pin the insurance on the other guy." *BusinessWeek*, 104–105.
38. Reese, A. (1999, August). Setting the pace. *Business & Health*, 17–18.
39. Bunch, D. K. (1992, March). Coors Wellness Center—Helping the bottom line. *Employee Benefits Journal*, 14–18.
40. Wiley, J. L. (1993, August). Preretirement education: Benefits outweigh liability. *HR Focus*, 11.
41. Johnson, R. (1998, Autumn). Dispelling the fables of ERISA. *ACA Journal*, 19–27.
42. *Money*. (1993, May). The best benefits, 130–131.
43. Murray, K. A. (1993, July). For some companies, portable pensions aren't practical. *Personnel Journal*, 38–39.
44. Milkovich, G. T., and Newman, J. M. (2002). *Compensation* (7th ed.). Homewood, IL: Irwin, McGraw-Hill.
45. Rotello, P., and Cornwell, R. (1994, February). Is it time to rethink your retirement program? *HR Focus*, 4–5.
46. Dimeo, J. (1992, October). Women receive the short end when it comes to their retirement pension incomes. *Pension World*, 28, 30.
47. Poterba, J. M., Venti, S. F., and Wise, D. A. (1998). 401(k) plans and future patterns of retirement saving. *American Economic Review, 88*, 179–184.
48. Hogan, M. C. (1992, December). Educating the 401(k) investor. *Employee Benefits Journal*, 18–22.
49. Cropper, C. (2002, January 28). The ins and outs of the new tax law: The golden years get more golden. *BusinessWeek*, 110–111.
50. Ibid.
51. *The Economist*. (2001, December 15). American company pensions: When labor and capital don't mix, 60.
52. Quinn, J. (2002, January 21). 401(k)s and the Enron mess. *Newsweek*, 25.
53. Foran, N., and Bryant, J. (1999, September). Roth IRA regs. offer clarity and guidance. *Tax Advisor*, 654–663.
54. McNamee, M. (1999, October 4). Good pensions, bad sales pitch. *BusinessWeek*, 44.
55. Murray, K. A. (1993, July). How HR is making pensions portable. *Personnel Journal*, 36–46; Tobin, V. M. (1992). Beyond defined contribution or defined benefit pension plans. In *The Conference Board report 1004: Controlling the costs of employee benefits*. New York: The Conference Board; and Snell, N. W. (1992). Pension plan modifications. In *The Conference Board report 1004: Controlling the costs of employee benefits*. New York: The Conference Board.
56. DeCenzo, D. A., and Holoviak, S. J. (1990). *Employee benefits*. Upper Saddle River, NJ: Prentice Hall.
57. *Money*. (1993, May). The best benefits, 130–131.
58. U.S. Chamber of Commerce. (1991). *Employee benefits 1990*. Washington, DC: U.S. Chamber of Commerce.
59. Eckhouse, J. (1993, March 24). Retired exec at HP received $937,225 for unused sick leave. *San Francisco Chronicle*, C1, C40.

60. Tully, S. (1995, June 12). America's healthiest companies. *Fortune*, 98–106.
61. Reinberg, J. (2002, February). It's about time: PTOs gain popularity. *Workspan*, 53–55.
62. Matthes, K. (1992, May). In pursuit of leisure: Employees want more time off. *HR Focus*, 1.
63. Gómez-Mejía, L. R., Balkin, D. B., and Milkovich, G. T. (1990). Rethinking your rewards for technical employees. *Organizational Dynamics, 1*(1), 62–75.
64. *Inc.* (1996, July). Severance policies, 92.
65. DeCenzo, D., and Robbins, S. (2002). *Human resource management* (7th ed.). New York: John Wiley & Sons.
66. Fuchsberg, G. (1992, April 22). What is pay, anyway? *Wall Street Journal*, R3.
67. Huang, A. (1999, July). Concierge services free employees from distractions. *HR Focus*, 6.
68. BNA. (1994, January 31). Self-defense classes for employees becoming popular. *Workforce Strategies* (published with *BNA's Employee Relations Weekly*), 5, 3.
69. Symonds, W. (2002, June 10). Providing the killer perk: Companies say on-site day care pays off in higher productivity and reduced turnover. *BusinessWeek*, 101.
70. Dex, S., and Schneibel, F. (1999, Summer). Business performance and family-friendly policies. *Journal of General Management*, 22–37.
71. *The Conference Board.* (1995). Child care services, 5(4), 3–12.
72. Henderson, R. (1989). *Compensation management* (5th ed.). Upper Saddle River, NJ: Prentice Hall.
73. Barringer, M. W., and Milkovich, G. T. (1998). A theoretical exploration of the adoption and design of flexible benefit plans: A case of human resource innovation. *Academy of Management Review, 23*, 305–324.
74. Alderman, L., and Kim S. (1996, January). Get the most from your company benefits. *Money*, 102–106.
75. DeCenzo, D. A., and Holoviak, S. J. (1990). *Employee benefits.* Upper Saddle River, NJ: Prentice Hall.
76. McCaffery, R. M. (1992). *Employee benefit programs: A total compensation perspective* (2nd ed.). Boston: PWS-Kent.
77. Wilson, M., Northcraft, G. R., and Neale, M. A. (1985). The perceived value of fringe benefits. *Personnel Psychology, 38*, 309–320.
78. Cohen, A., and Cohen, S. (1998, November/December). Benefits Websites: Controlling costs while enhancing communication. *Journal of Compensation and Benefits*, 11–18.
79. Shalowitz, D. (1992, October 12). Cracking the case of the confusing retirement plan. *Business Insurance*, 22.

Chapter 13

1. Roberts, K. (2002, May). Honest communications. *Executive Excellence*, 20.
2. Noer, D. M. (1993). *Healing the wounds: Overcoming the trauma of layoffs and revitalizing downsized organizations*, 103–104. San Francisco: Jossey-Bass.
3. Johnson, P. R., and Gardner, S. (1989). Legal pitfalls of employee handbooks. *SAM Advanced Management Journal, 54*(2), 42–46.
4. Hesser, R. G. (1991, July). Watch your language. *Small Business Reports*, 45–49.
5. Farr, J. (1999, January). Put your rules in writing. *Restaurant Hospitality*, 38.
6. Sosnin, B. (2001, July). Package your policies: To be effective, employee handbooks must be well-structured, carefully drafted in plain language and reflective of your practices and culture. *HRMagazine*, 67–72.
7. Brady, T. (1993, June). Employee handbooks: Contracts or empty promises? *Management Review*, 33–35.
8. Aronoff, C. E., and Ward, J. L. (1993, January). Rules for nepotism. *Nation's Business*, 64–65.
9. Prasad, A. (2002, January). Digging deep for meaning: A critical hermeneutic analysis of CEO letters to shareholders in the oil industry. *The Journal of Business Communication*, 92–116.
10. Sosnin, B. (1996, June). Corporate newsletters improve employee morale. *HRMagazine*, 106–110.
11. Flanagan, P. (1994, February). Videoconferencing changes the corporate meeting. *Management Review*, 7; and Bhargava, S. W., and Coy, P. (1991, November 12). Video-screen meetings: Still out of sight. *BusinessWeek*, 162E.
12. *Information Management Forum.* (1993, January). Voice mail or voice pony express, insert into *Management Review*, 3.
13. Weeks, D. (1995, February). Voice mail: Blessing or curse? *World Traveler*, 51–54.
14. Leonard, A. (1999, September 20). We've got mail—always. *Newsweek*, 58–61.
15. Pearl, J. A. (1993, July). The e-mail quandary. *Management Review*, 48–51.
16. Ibid.
17. France, M. (1999, April 2). A site for soreheads. *BusinessWeek*, 86–90.
18. Brady, R. (1995, October). Electronic mail: Drafting a policy. *HR Focus*, 19; Daniel, T. (1995, Summer). Electronic and voice mail monitoring of employees: A practical approach. *Employee Relations Today*, 1–10; and Weiss, B. (1996, January). Four black holes in cyberspace. *Management Review*, 30–32.
19. *Information Management Journal.* (2002, January/February). Company e-mail: To monitor or not to monitor, 8.
20. *Information Management Forum.* (1993, July). Who's reading your e-mail? An insert into *Management Review*, 1, 4; and Casarez, N. B. (1993, Summer), Electronic mail and employee relations: Why privacy must be considered. *Public Relations Quarterly*, 37–39.
21. Baig, E., Stepnek, M., and Gross, N. (1999, April 5). Privacy: The Internet wants your personal information. *BusinessWeek*, 84–90; and McGrath, P. (1999, March 29). Knowing you too well. *Newsweek*, 48–50.
22. *The Economist.* (1996, April 20). Textbooks on CD-ROM, 11.
23. *HR Focus.* (2002, May). Time to take another look at telecommuting, 6–7.
24. Kugelmass, J. (1995). *Telecommuting.* New York: Lexington Books.
25. Falcone, P. (1998, October). Communication breakdown. *HR Focus*, 8.
26. Mintzberg, H. (1975, July–August). The manager's job: Folklore or fact. *Harvard Business Review, 53*, 69–71.
27. Michaels, E. A. (1989, February). Business meetings. *Small Business Reports*, 82–88.
28. Interview of Deborah Tannen by L. A. Lusardi (1990, July). Power talk. *Working Woman*, 92–94.
29. Elashmawi, F. (1991, November). Multicultural business meetings and presentations. *Tokyo Business Today, 59*(11), 66–68.
30. Montgomery, E. (1993, October). A family affair. *Small Business Reports*, 10–14; and Jaffe, D. T. (1992, June). How to create a family council. *Nation's Business*, 54–55. For more on succession planning, see *Inc.* (1996, July). Three ways to plan ahead, 96.
31. McCune, J. C. (1998, July/August). That elusive thing called trust. *Management Review*, 10–16.
32. *Business 2.0.* (2002, May). eePulse Inc. helps hospital save thousands and improve productivity. www.business2.com.
33. Mandel, M. J. (1996, June 24). Satisfaction at work. *BusinessWeek*, 28.
34. Gómez-Mejía, L. R., and Balkin, D. B. (1992). *Compensation, organizational strategy, and firm performance.* Cincinnati, OH: South-Western.

35. Aram, J. D., and Salipante, P. F., Jr. (1981). An evaluation of organizational due process in the resolution of employee/employer conflict. *Academy of Management Review, 16*, 197–204.
36. Kirrane, D. (1990). EAPs: Dawning of a new age. *HRMagazine, 35*(1), 30–34.
37. Filipowicz, C. A. (1979). The troubled employee: Whose responsibility? *Personnel Administrator, 24*(6), 5–10.
38. Bahls, J. (1999, March). Handle with care. *HRMagazine*, 60–66.
39. Lee, K. (2000). Bringing home benefits. *Employee Benefit News, 13*(4), 1–3.
40. Carson, K. D., and Balkin, D. B. (1992). An employee assistance model of health care management for employees with alcohol-related problems. *Journal of Employment Counseling, 29*, 146–156.
41. Wise, D. (1993, April). Employee assistance programs expand to fit companies' needs. *Business & Health*, 40–45.
42. Feldman, S. (1991, February). Today's EAPs make the grade. *Personnel*, 3.
43. Fisher, C., Schoenfeldt, L., and Shaw, J. (1996). *Human resource management* (3rd ed.). Boston, MA: Houghton Mifflin.
44. Cascio, W. F. (1991). *Costing human resources: The financial impact of behavior in organizations*, Vol. 6 (3rd ed.). Boston: PWS-Kent.
45. Luthans, F., and Waldersee, R. (1989). What do we really know about EAPs? *Human Resource Management, 28*, 385–401.
46. *Risk Management*. (1999, May). Working assistance, 8.
47. Deal, T. E., and Key, M. K. (1998). *Corporate celebration*. San Francisco: Barrett-Koehler.
48. Meyers, D. W. (1986). *Human resources management*. Chicago: Commerce Clearing House.
49. Nelson, B. (1994). *1001 ways to reward employees*. New York: Workman Publishing.
50. Arthur, J., and Aiman-Smith, L. (2001). Gainsharing and organizational learning: An analysis of employee suggestions over time. *Academy of Management Journal, 44*, 737–754.
51. Trunko, M. E. (1993). Open to suggestions. *HRMagazine, 38*(2), 85–89.
52. Oldering, S. R. (1998, May/June). Mitsubishi and Honda on competition and quality circles. *Journal for Quality & Participation*, 55–59.
53. Knouse, S. (1995). *The reward and recognition process*. Milwaukee, WI: ASQC Quality Press.
54. Orsburn, J. D., Moran, L., Musselwhite, E., and Zenger, J. H. (1990). *Self-directed work teams*. Homewood, IL: Business One Irwin.
55. Flynn, G. (1998, July). Is your recognition program understood? *Workforce*, 30–35.
56. Ruffalo, N. (2000, January). HR 101: Recognition. *Workforce*, 62–63.
57. Wiscombe, J. (2002, April). Rewards get results. *Workforce*, 42–48.

Chapter 14

1. Lewis, J. (2002, January). I know what you e-mailed last summer. *Security Management*, 93–99; and Zimmerman, E. (2002, February). HR must know when employee surveillance crosses the line. *Workforce*, 38–45.
2. Conlin, M. (2001, December 3). Taking precautions—or harassing workers? Arab Americans say employers are violating their rights. *BusinessWeek*, 84.
3. Miller, J. L., Balkin, D. B., and Allen, R. (1993). Employer restrictions on employees' legal off-duty conduct. *Labor Law Journal, 44*(4), 208–219.
4. Cheeseman, H. (1997). *Contemporary business law* (2nd ed.). Upper Saddle River, NJ: Prentice Hall.
5. Egler, T. (1996, May). A manager's guide to employment contracts. *HRMagazine*, 28–33.
6. Flynn, G. (1999, February). Employment contracts gain ground in corporate America. *Workforce*, 99–101.
7. Ibid.
8. LaVan, H. (2000). A logit model to predict the enforceability of noncompete agreements. *Employee Responsibilities and Rights Journal, 12*, 219–235.
9. Gullett, C. R., and Greenwade, G. D. (1988). Employment at will: The no fault alternative. *Labor Law Journal, 39*(6), 372–378.
10. Ibid.
11. McWhirter, D. (1989). *Your rights at work*. New York: Wiley.
12. Brett, J. M. (1980, Spring). Why employees want unions. *Organizational Dynamics, 8*, 316–332.
13. Rousseau, D. (1995). *Psychological contracts in organizations*. Thousand Oaks, CA: Sage.
14. Weaver, G. R., Trevino, L. K., and Cochran, P. L. (1999). Corporate ethics programs as control systems: Influence of executive commitment and environmental factors. *Academy of Management Journal, 42*, 41–57.
15. Weaver, G., and Trevino, L. (2001). The role of human resources in ethics/compliance management: A fairness perspective. *Human Resource Management Review, 11*, 113–134.
16. Driscoll, D. (1998, March). Business ethics and compliance: What management is doing and why. *Business and Society Review*, 33–51.
17. Sashkin, M., and Kiser, K. J. (1993). *Putting total quality management to work*. San Francisco: Berrett-Koehler.
18. Otto, J. (1993, January 11). Random alcohol test proposed. *Aviation Week & Space Technology, 138*(2), 33.
19. Sovereign, K. (1994). *Personnel law* (3rd ed.). Upper Saddle River, NJ: Prentice Hall.
20. Hays, S. (1999, September). Censured! "Free" speech at work. *Workforce*, 34–37.
21. Labich, K. (1999, September 6). No more crude at Texaco. *Fortune*, 205–212.
22. Anton, G., and Ward, J. (1998, March). Every breath you take: Employee privacy rights in the workplace—An Orwellian prophecy come true? *Labor Law Journal*, 897–911.
23. Holley, W. H., and Jennings, K. M. (1991). *The labor relations process* (4th ed.). Chicago, IL: Dryden.
24. Elkouri, F., and Elkouri, E. A. (1973). *How arbitration works* (3rd ed.). Washington, DC: Bureau of National Affairs.
25. Brown, D. R., and Gray, G. R. (1988, Summer). A positive alternative to employment at will. *SAM Advanced Management Journal, 53*, 13–16.
26. Maltby, L. L. (1990). The decline of employment at will—a quantitative analysis. *Labor Law Journal, 41*(1), 51–54.
27. Utroska, D. R. (1992, November). Management in Europe. *Management Review*, 21–24.
28. Jones, D. (1998, April 2). Fired workers fight back . . . and win. *USA Today*, IB.
29. Buckley, M. R., and Weitzel, W. (1988). Employing at will. *Personnel Administrator, 33*(8), 78–80.
30. Bordwin, M. (1993, November). Timing is everything. *Small Business Reports*, 43–51.
31. Flynn, G. (2000, July). How do you treat the at-will employment relationship? *Workforce*, 178–179.
32. Rosse, J., Miller, J., and Ringer, R. (1996, Summer). The deterrent value of drug and integrity testing. *Journal of Business and Psychology, 10*, 477–485.
33. Flynn, G. (1999, January). How to prescribe drug testing. *Workforce*, 107–109.
34. Zigarelli, M. (1995). Drug testing litigation: Trends and outcomes. *Human Resource Management Review, 5*, 245–265; and Flynn, G. (1996, April). Will drug testing pass or fail in court? *Personnel Journal*, 141–144.

35. Green, W. E. (1989, November 21). Drug testing becomes corporate mine field. *Wall Street Journal*, B1, B8.
36. Verespoj, M. A. (1990, July 2). Death blow for random testing. *Industry Week*, 47–48.
37. *Wall Street Journal*. (1994, February 8). Drug testing gets big boost from the California Supreme Court, A1.
38. Gunsch, D. (1993, May). Training prepares workers for drug testing. *Personnel Journal*, 52–59.
39. Hanson, A. (1990, July). What employees say about drug testing. *Personnel*, 32–36.
40. Maltby, L. (1990, July). Put performance to the test. *Personnel*, 30–31.
41. Griffin, S., Keller, A., and Cohn, A. (2001, Winter). Developing a drug testing policy at a public university: Participant perspectives. *Public Personnel Management*, 467–481.
42. Nadell, B. (2001, August). Is your corporate culture on drugs? *Occupational Health & Safety*, 28–31.
43. Hamilton, J. O. (1991, June 3). A video game that tells if employees are fit for work. *BusinessWeek*, 36; and Maltby, L. (1990, July). Put performance to the test. *Personnel*, 30–31.
44. Eisenberg, B., and Johnson, L. (2001, December). Being honest about being dishonest. Society for Human Resources Management. www.shrm.org/whitepapers/.
45. Willis, R. (1986, January). White collar crime. *Management Review, 75*, 22–30.
46. Payne, M. (2001, April 8). Sticky fingers. *Boulder Daily Camera*, 6F.
47. Vaught, B., Taylor, R., and Vaught, S. (2000, January). The attitudes of managers regarding the electronic monitoring of employee behavior: Procedural and ethical considerations. *American Business Review, 18*, 107–114.
48. DeTienne, K., and Flint, R. (1996, Spring). The boss's eyes and ears: A case study of electronic monitoring and the privacy for consumers and workers act. *Labor Lawyer*, 93–115.
49. *USA Today*. (1993, May 24). Bosses peak at e-mail, B1:2.
50. *BusinessWeek*. (1990, January 15). Is your boss spying on you? 74–75.
51. See Garson, B. (1988). *The electronic sweatshop: How computers are transforming the office of the future into the factory of the past*. New York: Penguin Books; and Piturro, M. (1989, May). Employee performance monitoring . . . or meddling? *Management Review*, 31–33.
52. DeTienne, K., and Flint, R. (1996, Spring). The boss's eyes and ears: A case study of electronic monitoring and the privacy for consumers and workers act. *Labor Lawyer*, 93–115.
53. Bates, R., and Holton, E. (1995). Computerized performance monitoring: A review of human resource issues. *Human Resource Management Review, 5*, 267–288.
54. *BusinessWeek*. (1990, January 15). Is your boss spying on you? 74–75.
55. McCarthy, M. J. (1999, October 21). Now the boss knows when you're clicking. *Wall Street Journal*, B1.
56. Zimmerman, E. (2002, February). HR must know when employee surveillance crosses the line. *Workforce*, 38–45.
57. Near, J., and Miceli, M. (1985). Organizational dissidence: The case of whistleblowing. *Journal of Business Ethics, 4*, 1–16.
58. Near, J., and Miceli, M. (1995). Effective whistle-blowing. *Academy of Management Review, 20*, 679–708.
59. *The Economist*. (2002, January 12). Peep and weep: As companies cut costs they cut corners too. Time to blow the whistle? 55–56.
60. Dworkin, T. M., and Baucas, M. S. (1998). Internal vs. external whistleblowers: A comparison of whistleblower processes. *Journal of Business Ethics, 17*, 1281–1298.
61. *The Economist*. (1995, August 19). The uncommon good, 55–56.
62. Wiscombe, J. (2002, July). Don't fear whistleblowers. *Workforce*, 26–32; and Zellner, W. (2002, January 28). A hero—and a smoking gun letter. *BusinessWeek*, 34–35.
63. Boyle, R. D. (1990). A review of whistle-blower protection and suggestions for change. *Labor Law Journal, 41*(12), 821–828.
64. Miceli, M., and Near, J. (1994). Whistle-blowing: Reaping the benefits. *Academy of Management Executive, 8*(3), 65–72.
65. Overman, S. (1998, November). Relationships: When labor leads to love. *HR Focus, 1*, 14.
66. Greenwald, J. (2000, February 14). Office romances may court trouble. *Business Insurance*, 3–4.
67. Stanton, M. (1998, October). Courting disaster: The perils of office romance. *Government Executive*, 35–39.
68. Overman, S. (1998, November). Relationships: When labor leads to love. *HR Focus*, 1, 14.
69. Trevino, L. (1992). The social effects of punishment in organizations: A justice perspective. *Academy of Management Review, 17*, 647–676.
70. Weinstein, S. (1992, September). Teams without managers. *Progressive Grocer*, 101–104.
71. Redeker, J. R. (1989). *Employee discipline*. Washington, DC: Bureau of National Affairs.
72. Ramsey, R. D. (1998, February). Guidelines for the progressive discipline of employees. *Supervision*, 10–12.
73. Osigweh, C., Yg, A. B., and Hutchison, W. R. (1989, Fall). Positive discipline. *Human Resource Management, 28*(3), 367–383.
74. Grote, D. (2001, September/October). Discipline without punishment. *Across the Board*, 52–57.
75. Osigweh, C., Yg, A. B., and Hutchison, W. R. (1989, Fall). Positive discipline. *Human Resource Management, 28*(3), 367–383.
76. Ibid.
77. Harvey, E. L. (1987, March). Discipline vs. punishment. *Management Review, 76*, 25–29.
78. Falcone, P. (1998, November). Adopt a formal approach to progressive discipline. *HRMagazine*, 55–59.
79. Sherman, C. V. (1987). *From losers to winners*. New York: American Management Association.
80. Bureau of National Affairs. (1987). *Grievance guide* (7th ed.). Washington, DC: Bureau of National Affairs.
81. Flynn, G. (2000, September). Does a new right make a wrong? *Workforce*, 122–123.
82. Hindera, J. L., and Josephson, J. L. (1998). Reinventing the public employer–employee relationship. The just cause standard. *Public Administration Quarterly, 22*, 98–113.
83. Redeker, J. R. (1989). *Employee discipline*. Washington, DC: Bureau of National Affairs.
84. Shellenbarger, S. (1994, January 13). More companies experiment with workers' schedules. *Wall Street Journal*, B1-3.
85. Segal, J. (1997, July). Looking for trouble? When it comes to the Americans with Disabilities Act, what you know about your employees can hurt you. *HRMagazine*, 76–83.
86. Breuer, N. L. (1993, September). Resources can relieve ADA fears. *Personnel Journal*, 131–142.
87. Mamis, R. (1995, January). Employees from hell. *Inc.*, 50–57.
88. Sculnick, M. W. (1990, Spring). Key court cases. *Employee Relations Today, 17*(1), 53–59.
89. Sherman, C. V. (1987). *From losers to winners*. New York: American Management Association.
90. Denton, D. K. (1992, Summer). Keeping employees: The Federal Express approach. *SAM Advanced Management Journal, 57*(3), 10–13.
91. Leblanc, P. V., and McInerney, M. (1994, January). Need a change? Jump on the banding wagon. *Personnel Journal*, 72–78.

Chapter 15

1. Harris, N. (1997, October 27). UPS puts its back into it. *BusinessWeek*, 50.
2. Rocks, D. (1999, November 15). UPS: Will this IPO deliver? *BusinessWeek*, 41.
3. Bernstein, A. (1997, August 25). This package is a heavy one for the Teamsters. *BusinessWeek*, 40–41.
4. Blake, N. (2002, July 16). UPS, Teamsters reach agreement on new six-year contract. www.pressroom.ups.com.
5. Bernstein, A. (1999, June 28). The Amalgamated Doctors of America? *BusinessWeek*, 36.
6. Adelson, A. (1997, April 5). Physician, unionize thyself. *New York Times*, A21–A22.
7. Haberfeld, Y. (1995). Why do workers join unions? The case of Israel. *Industrial and Labor Relations Review, 48*, 656–670.
8. Brett, J. M. (1980). Why employees want unions. *Organizational Dynamics, 9*, 316–332.
9. Bernstein, A. (1994, May 23). Why America needs unions. *BusinessWeek*, 70–82.
10. U.S. Bureau of Labor Statistics. (2002, July 25). Work stoppage data. data.bls.gov/cgi-bin/surveymost.
11. Kaufman, B. E., and Lewis, D. (1998, September). Is the NLRA still relevant to today's economy and workplace? *Labor Law Journal*, 113–126.
12. Delaney, J. T. (1998). Redefining the right-to-work debate: Unions and the dilemma of free choice. *Journal of Labor Research, 19*, 425–443.
13. Moorman, R. (2000, March). Throwing down the gauntlet. *Air Transport World*, 49–51.
14. Flynn, G. (1996, February). TEAM Act: What it is and what it can do for you. *Personnel Journal*, 85–87.
15. *HR News*. (1994, February). Washington scorecard. *13*(2), 5.
16. Budd, J. (1996). Canadian strike replacement legislation and collective bargaining: Lessons for the United States. *Industrial Relations, 35*, 245–260.
17. Holley, W. H., and Jennings, K. M. (1991). *The labor relations process*. Chicago: Dryden.
18. Hunter, L. W. (1998). Can strategic participation be institutionalized? Union representation on American corporate boards. *Industrial and Labor Relations Review, 51*, 557–578.
19. Fossum, J. (1995). *Labor relations* (6th ed.). Chicago: Irwin.
20. Greenhouse, S. (2000, January 20). Growth in union membership in 1999 was the best in two decades. *New York Times*, A10.
21. Overman, S. (1991, December). The union pitch has changed. *HRMagazine*, 44–46.
22. Freeman, R. B. (1989). The changing status of unionism around the world. In W. C. Huang (Ed.), *Organized labor at the crossroads*. Kalamazoo, MI: W. E. Upjohn Institute for Employee Research.
23. International Labor Organization (1997); and Chang, C., and Sorrentino, C. (1991, December). Union membership statistics in 12 countries. *Monthly Labor Review*, 46–53.
24. Ofori-Dankwa, J. (1993). Murray and Reshef revisited: Toward a typology/theory of paradigms of national trade union movements. *Academy of Management Review, 18*, 269–292.
25. Husain, I. (1995, January). Fresh start: Laid off workers need somewhere to turn. *Entrepreneur*, 306.
26. *The Economist*. (2002, May 25). Europe: A general strike looms; Spanish labor law, 50.
27. Ofori-Dankwa, J. (1993). Murray and Reshef revisited: Toward a typology/theory of paradigms of national trade union movements. *Academy of Management Review, 18*, 269–292.
28. Mills, D. Q. (1989). *Labor–management relations*. New York: McGraw-Hill.
29. *The Economist*. (1999, June 5). Germany's economy: The sick man of the euro, 21–23.
30. *The Economist*. (2001, April 14). You're fired, 45–46.
31. Wilpert, B. (1975). Research in industrial democracy and the German case. *Industrial Relations Journal, 6*(1), 53–64.
32. Marsland, S. E., and Beer, M. (1985). Note on Japanese management and employment systems. In M. Beer and B. Spector (Eds.), *Readings in human resource management*. New York: The Free Press.
33. *The Economist*. (1996, February 10). Stakeholder capitalism: Unhappy families, 23–25.
34. Thornton, E. (1999, November 15). Remaking Nissan. *BusinessWeek*, 70–76.
35. Delaney, J. T. (1991). Unions and human resource policies. In K. Rowland and G. Ferris (Eds.), *Research in personnel and human resources management*. Greenwich, CT: JAI Press.
36. Lawler and Mohrman, 1987. Lawler, E. E, and Mohrman, S. A. unions and the new management. *Academy of Management Executive*, 1, 293–300.
37. Bernstein, A. (1993, January 25). Making teamwork work—and appeasing Uncle Sam. *BusinessWeek*, 101.
38. Lewin, D. (2001, Winter). IR and HR perspectives on workplace conflict: What can they learn from each other? *Human Resource Management Review*, 453–485.
39. Woodruff, D. (1993, February 8). Saturn: Labor's love lost? *BusinessWeek*, 122, 124.
40. McHugh, P. P., and Yim, S. G. (1999, Fall). Developments in labor–management cooperation: The codification of cooperative mechanisms. *Labor Law Journal*, 230–236.
41. Gray, G. R., Meyers, D. W., and Meyers, P. S. (1999, January). Cooperative provisions in labor agreements: A new paradigm? *Monthly Labor Review*, 29–45.
42. Farber, H. (2001, January). Union success in representation elections: Why does unit size matter? *Industrial and Labor Relations Review*, 329–348.
43. Kochan, T. A., and Katz, H. C. (1988). *Collective bargaining and industrial relations*. Homewood, IL: Irwin.
44. *The Economist*. (1999, October 2). Wal-Mart wins again, 33.
45. Bernstein, A. (1999, July 19). All's not fair in labor wars. *BusinessWeek*, 43.
46. Zellner, W. (2000, March 13). Up against the Wal-Mart. *BusinessWeek*, 76–78.
47. Bryant, A. (1994, April 6). Lorenzo plan for airline rejected. *New York Times*, D53.
48. Olafson, C. (1999, May). Cyber unions. *The Futurist*, 70.
49. Romero, C. L. (1999, November 11). Union makes pitch to local IBMers. *Boulder Daily Camera*, 3A.
50. *Small Business Reports*. (1933, March). Unions vs. private property, 25.
51. Spognardi, M. A. (1998). Conducting a successful union-free campaign: A primer (Part II). *Employee Relations Law Journal, 24*(3), 31–53.
52. Kleiner, M. (2001, Summer). Intensity of management resistance: Understanding the decline of unionization in the private sector. *Journal of Labor Research*, 519–540.
53. Rose, J., and Chaison, G. (1996). Linking union density and union effectiveness: The North American experience. *Industrial Relations, 35*, 78–105.
54. Bernstein, A. (1997, February). Sweeney's bitz. *BusinessWeek*, 56–62.
55. Walton, B., and McKersie, R. (1965). *A behavioral theory of labor negotiations*. New York: McGraw-Hill.
56. Cimini, M. H., Behrmann, S. L., and Johnson, E. M. (1994, January). Labor–management bargaining in 1993. *Monthly Labor Review*, 20–35.

57. McGinn, D. (1998, August 10). GM still has miles to go: The settlement doesn't fix its deep problems. *Newsweek*, 46.
58. Voos, P. (2001, Winter). As IR perspective on collective bargaining. *Human Resource Management Review*, 487–503.
59. Ibid.; and Kelly, K. (1993, August 2). Labor deals that offer a break from "us vs. them." *BusinessWeek*, 30.
60. Bernstein, A. (1995, March 18). United we own. *BusinessWeek*, 96–102.
61. Arndt, M. (2001, November 12). To-do list for United's Mr. Fix-It. *BusinessWeek*, 62.
62. Cook, M. (Ed.). (1993). *The human resources yearbook: 1993/1994 edition*, 162. Upper Saddle River, NJ: Prentice Hall.
63. BLS Reports. (1994, February 14). Record low number of strikes continues into 1993. *BNA's Employee Relations Weekly, 12*(7), 167.
64. Greenhouse, S. (2000, March 21). Unions predict gain from Boeing strike. *New York Times*, A11; and *The Economist*. (2000, March 18). The slow death of Boeing man, 29–30.
65. Freeman, R. B., and Medoff, J. L. (1984). *What do unions do?* New York: Basic Books.
66. Lewin, D. (2001, Winter). IR and HR perspectives on workplace conflict: What can they learn from each other? *Human Resource Management Review*, 453–485.
67. Holley, W., and Jennings, K. (1994). *The labor relations process* (5th ed.). Fort Worth, TX: The Dryden Press; and Fossum, J. (1995). *Labor relations* (6th ed.). Chicago: Irwin.
68. Freeman, R. B., and Medoff, J. L. (1979). The two faces of unionism. *The Public Interest, 57*, 69–93.
69. Abraham, K. G., and Medoff, J. L. (1985). Length of service and promotions in union and nonunion work groups. *Industrial and Labor Relations Review, 38*, 408–420.
70. Abraham, K. G., and Medoff, J. L. (1984). Length of service and layoffs in union and nonunion work groups. *Industrial and Labor Relations Review, 38*, 87–97.
71. Greenhouse, S. (1999, September 23). In the UAW deal, something for almost everyone? *New York Times*, retrieved online at www.nytimes.com/library/financial, and Meredith, R. (1999, September 17). DaimlerChrysler and the UAW reach tentative pack, *New York Times*, retrieved online at www.nytimes.com/html.
72. Foulkes, F. (1980). *Personnel policies in large nonunion companies*. Upper Saddle River, NJ: Prentice Hall.
73. Bernardin, J., and Beatty, R. (1984). *Performance appraisal: Assessing human behavior at work*. Boston: Kent.
74. Abraham, K. G., and Farber, H. S. (1988). Returns to seniority in union and nonunion jobs: A new look at evidence. *Industrial and Labor Relations Review, 42*, 3–19; and Freeman, R. B., and Medoff, J. L. (1984). *What do unions do?* New York: Basic Books.
75. Bartel, A. P. (1989). *Formal employee training programs and their impact on labor productivity: Evidence from a human resources survey*. National Bureau of Economic Research Working Paper No. 3026.
76. Gunsch, D. (1993, March). On-site schools are required by a UAW contract. *Personnel Journal*, 43.
77. Stevens, C. (1995). The social cost of rent seeking by labor unions in the United States. *Industrial Relations, 34*, 190–202; Jarrel, S., and Stanley, T. (1990). A meta-analysis of the union-nonunion wage gap. *Industrial and Labor Relations Review, 44*, 54–67; and Freeman, R. B. (1982). Union wage practices and wage dispersion within establishments. *Industrial and Labor Relations Review, 36*, 3–21.
78. Freeman, R. B. (1982). Union wage practices and wage dispersion within establishments. *Industrial and Labor Relations Review, 36*, 3–21.
79. Wasilewski, E. (1996, January). Bargaining outlook for 1996. *Monthly Labor Review*, 10–24.
80. Driscoll, J. W. (1979). Working creatively with a union: Lessons from the Scanlon plan. *Organizational Dynamics, 8*, 61–80.
81. Freeman, R. B. (1981). The effect of unionism on fringe benefits. *Industrial and Labor Relations Review, 34*, 489–509.
82. Fosu, A. G. (1984). Unions and fringe benefits: Additional evidence. *Journal of Labor Research, 5*, 247, 254.
83. Gómez-Mejía, L. R., and Balkin, D. B. (1992). *Compensation, organizational strategy and firm performance*. Cincinnati: South-Western.
84. Budd, J. W., and McCall, B. P. (1997). The effect of unions on the receipt of unemployment insurance benefits. *Industrial and Labor Relations Review, 50*, 478–492.
85. Hirsch, B. T., MacPherson, D. A., and Dumond, M. (1997). Workers' compensation recipiency in union and nonunion workplaces. *Industrial and Labor Relations Review, 50*, 213–236.
86. Foulkes, F. (1980). *Personnel policies in large nonunion companies*. Upper Saddle River, NJ: Prentice Hall.
87. Flynn, G. (2000, September). Does a new right make a wrong? *Workforce*, 122–123.
88. Morgan, J., Owens, J., and Gomes, G. (2002, Winter). Union rules in nonunion settings: The NLRB and workplace investigations. *SAM Advanced Management Journal*, 22–32; and Hodges, A., Coke, C., and Trumble, R. (2002, Summer). *Weingarten* in the nonunion workplace: Looking in the funhouse mirror. *Labor Law Journal*, 89–97.

Chapter 16

1. Anonymous (1997, August 21). ValuJet: The alarming truth. *Washington Post*, 18.
2. Schmid, R. E. (1997, August 18). Planes still have no cargo fire detectors, extinguishers might have averted '96 ValuJet crash, safety official says. *Arizona Republic*, A2.
3. Phillips, D. (1999, July 14). Murder charged in ValuJet crash: Rare indictment names repair firm. *Washington Post*, A1.
4. ABC News. (1999, December 7). ValuJet verdict: No conspiracy. ABCNEWS.com, retrieved online at more.abcnews.go.con/sections/us/dailynews/valujetverdict 991207.html.
5. Bureau of Labor Statistics. (2002, June 15). Injuries, illnesses, and fatalities. stats.bls.gov/iif/home.htm#News.
6. Bureau of Labor Statistics. (2002, June 15). News release: Workplace injuries and illnesses in 2000. stats.bls.gov/iif/oshwc/osh/os/osshr0013.txt.
7. Roberts, S. (2002). Employer priorities don't match costly worker injuries. *Business Insurance, 36*, 3.
8. Ledvinka, J., and Scarpello, V. G. (1991). *Federal regulation of personnel and human resource management* (2nd ed.), 209. Boston: PWS-Kent.
9. Sherman, A. W., and Bohlander, G. W. (1996). *Managing human resources* (10th ed.). Cincinnati, OH: South-Western.
10. McCaffery, R. M. (1992). *Employee benefit programs: A total compensation perspective*, 57–58. Boston: PWS-Kent.
11. Ibid., 59–60.
12. Bauer, T. F. (2002). Safety: A profit opportunity? Companies that consider safety more than a nuisance might profit from it. *C & D Recycler, 4*, 26(3).
13. Goch, L. (1999). Working toward a speedy recovery. *Best's Review Property/Casualty, 100*, 73–74.
14. Hays, D. (2002). Second terrorism hit could "ruin" WC. *National Underwriter Property & Casualty, 106*, 6(1).
15. Colburn, L. E. (1995). Defending against workers' compensation fraud. *Industrial Management, 37*, 1–2.

16. Wilkerson, M. (1999). Healthy savings. *Strategic Finance, 80*, 42–46.
17. Gunsauley, C. (2002, June 1). Workers' comp costs to $40 billion annually. *Employee Benefit News.*
18. Roberts, S. (2002). Employer priorities don't match costly worker injuries. *Business Insurance, 36*, 3.
19. Hays, D. (2002). Costly prescription drugs are jacking up WC bills. *National Underwriter Life & Health, 106*, 36(2).
20. French, W. L. (1994). *Human resources management* (3rd ed.), 529. Boston: Houghton Mifflin.
21. Ashford, N. A. (1976). *Crisis in the workplace: Occupational disease and injury*, 3, Cambridge, MA: MIT Press.
22. U.S. Department of Labor, Occupational Safety and Health Administration. (1985). *All about OSHA* (rev. ed.), 1. Washington, DC: U.S. Government Printing Office.
23. Ledvinka, J., and Scarpello, V. G. (1991). *Federal regulation of personnel and human resource management* (2nd ed.), 215. Boston: PWS-Kent.
24. Anthony, W. P., Perrewe, P. L., and Kacmar, K. M. (1993). *Strategic human resource management*, 514. Fort Worth, TX: Dryden; and Cascio, W. F. (1989). *Managing human resources: Productivity, quality of work life, profits* (2nd ed.), 554–556. New York: McGraw-Hill.
25. *HR Focus*. (2002). OSHA delays enforcing revised record-keeping rules until late April, *79*, 2.
26. *Professional Safety*. (2001). OSHA launches outreach on new recordkeeping rule, *46*, 6.
27. *Environs*. (2002). OSHA designs Web page for Spanish-speaking employers and employees. April Newsletter of the PMA Environmental Activities Department.
28. U.S. Department of Labor, Occupational Safety and Health Administration. (1985). *All about OSHA* (rev. ed.), 43–46. Washington, DC: U.S. Government Printing Office.
29. May, B. D. (1986, August). Hazardous substances: OSHA mandates the right to know. *Personnel Journal, 65*, 128.
30. See *Whirlpool Corporation v. Marshall*, 445 U.S. 1, 10–12 (1980).
31. Ellis, T. (1999). The governments' new response. *Occupational Health and Safety, 68*, 77–79.
32. Ledvinka, J., and Scarpello, V. G. (1991). *Federal regulation of personnel and human resource management* (2nd ed.), 221–224. Boston: PWS-Kent.
33. U.S. Department of Labor, Occupational Safety and Health Administration. (1985). *All about OSHA* (rev. ed.), 8. Washington, DC: U.S. Government Printing Office.
34. Atkinson, W. (1999). OSHA takes another shot at standardizing ergonomics. *Bobbin, 40*, 36–38.
35. Edwards, T. (2002, April 22). United States: OSHA's new ergonomics program. *Monday Business Briefing.*
36. *Logistics Management & Distribution Report*. (2002). OSHA issues new ergonomics plan, *41*, 22.
37. U.S. Department of Labor, Occupational Safety and Health Administration. (1985). *All about OSHA* (rev. ed.), 10. Washington, DC: U.S. Government Printing Office.
38. Ibid., 19–22.
39. Ledvinka, J., and Scarpello, V. G. (1991). *Federal regulation of personnel and human resource management* (2nd ed.), 224. Boston: PWS-Kent; and *Marshall v. Barlow's, Inc.*, 436 U.S. 307 (1978).
40. Garland, S. B. (1989, February 20). This safety ruling could be hazardous to employer's health. *BusinessWeek*, 34.
41. Ibid.; and Bureau of National Affairs. (1989, July 24). Michigan Supreme Court rules OSH Act does not preempt state proceedings. *BNA's Employee Relations Weekly*, 945.
42. Davidson, W. N., Worrell, D., and Cheng, L. T. W. (1994). The effectiveness of OSHA penalties: A stock-market–based test. *Industrial Relations, 33*, 283–296.
43. Courntey, T. K., and Clancy, E. A. (1998). A descriptive study of U.S. OSHA penalties and inspection frequency for musculoskeletal disorders in the workplace. *American Industrial Hygiene Association Journal, 59*, 563–571.
44. Ibid.
45. U.S. Department of Labor. (1989). *Fact sheet no. OSHA 89–04.* Washington, DC: U.S. Government Printing Office.
46. U.S. Department of Labor, Occupational Safety and Health Administration. (1985). *All about OSHA* (rev. ed.), 31–32. Washington, DC: U.S. Government Printing Office.
47. Ibid., 8; and Ledvinka, J., and Scarpello, V. G. (1991). *Federal regulation of personnel and human resource management* (2nd ed.), 220. Boston: PWS-Kent.
48. U.S. Department of Labor, Occupational Safety and Health Administration. (1985). *All about OSHA* (rev. ed.), 33–34. Washington, DC: U.S. Government Printing Office.
49. Caldwell, B. (1998). Work-at-home trend may redefine traditional workers' compensation concepts. *Employee Benefit Plan Review, 53*, 6–7.
50. National Safety Council, 1995. *Accident facts, 1995 edition*, Itasca, IL; National Safety Council.
51. Safety Director's Report. (2002). Hearing protection strategies for any safety department budget. May Newsletter of the Institute of Management and Administration.
52. Oswald, E. M. (1996). No employer is immune: AIDS in the workplace. *Risk Management, 43*, 18–21.
53. Hunter, S. (1998). Your infection control program. *Occupational Health and Safety, 67*, 76–80.
54. Ibid.; and Oswald, E. M. (1996). No employer is immune: AIDS in the workplace. *Risk Management, 43*, 18–21.
55. Mello, J. A. (1999). Ethics in employment law: The Americans with Disabilities Act and the employee with HIV. *Journal of Business Ethics, 20*, 67–83.
56. Fremgen, B., and Whitty, M. (1992, December). How to avoid a costly AIDS crisis in the organization. *Labor Law Journal*, 751–758; and Stodghill R., II. (1993a, February 1). Managing AIDS: How one boss struggled to cope. *BusinessWeek, 3303*, 48.
57. Ibid.
58. Woolsey, C. (1993, February 1). Ensuring proper AIDS treatment: Employer drafts standards for HMOs. *Business Insurance*, 17.
59. Ibid., 17; and Harris (1987, November). AIDS: We'll all pay. *Money*, 109–134.
60. Stodghill R., II. (1993b, February 1). Why AIDS policy must be a special policy. *BusinessWeek, 3303*, 33.
61. Berger, R. S., and Lewis, G. L. (1992). AIDS and employment: Judicial and arbitral responses. *Labor Law Journal, 43*, 259–280.
62. Stodghill R., II. (1993a, February 1). Managing AIDS: How one boss struggled to cope. *BusinessWeek, 3303*, 48–52.
63. Bureau of National Affairs. (1993, April 5). AIDS ranks as chief health concern of half of U.S. workers, survey says. *BNA Employee Relations Weekly, 11*, 4.
64. Hunter, S. (1998). Your infection control program. *Occupational Health and Safety, 67*, 76–80.
65. Oswald, E. M. (1996). No employer is immune: AIDS in the workplace. *Risk Management, 43*, 18–21.
66. Ibid.
67. Mello, J. A. (1999). Ethics in employment law: The Americans with Disabilities Act and the employee with HIV. *Journal of Business Ethics, 20*, 67–83.
68. Oswald, E. M. (1996). No employer is immune: AIDS in the workplace. *Risk Management, 43*, 18–21.
69. Bee, L., and Maatman, G. L. (2002). Workers with AIDS have legal rights. *National Underwriter Property & Casualty, 106*, 32(3).
70. Associated Press. (1993, January 28). Ex-employee opens fire on former bosses, kills 3. *Arizona Republic*, A2; and Associated Press.

(1993, January 29). Firings, stress fuel workplace violence. *Arizona Republic*, A2.
71. Jackson, M. (1999, August 2). No ignoring workplace violence. *Arizona Republic*, A1.
72. Stussie, G. (2002). The real terror at work. *Risk Management, 49*, 30(5).
73. Bureau of Labor Statistics. (2002b). Injuries, illnesses, and fatalities. Available at stats.bls.gov/iif/peoplebox.htm#fagb.
74. *Wall Street Journal*. (1998, July 27). Workplace violence study finds police, guards, cab drivers most likely targets.
75. Stussie, G. (2002). The real terror at work. *Risk Management, 49*, 30(5).
76. Ibid.
77. Jackson, M. (1999, August 2). No ignoring workplace violence. *Arizona Republic*, A1.
78. Security Director's Report. (2001b). Domestic violence costs much more than you think. November Newsletter of the Institute of Management and Administration.
79. Ibid.
80. *Arizona Republic*. (1999, September 6). Poll: 1 in 6 workers want to hit someone, A11.
81. Laabs, J. (1999). Employee sabotage: Don't be a target. *Workforce, 78*, 32–38.
82. Jackson, M. (1999, August 2). No ignoring workplace violence. *Arizona Republic*, A1.
83. Bureau of National Affairs. (1993, April 26). Preventing workplace violence: Legal imperatives can clash. *Employee Relations Weekly, 11*(17), 451–452.
84. Missouri Capitol Police. (1996, June 6). Violence in the workplace . . . , 1–6. www.dps.state.mo.us/DPS/MCP/STUDY/WKVIOLNC.HTM.
85. Ibid.
86. Boddenhausen, K. G. (1994, March 3). It's . . . becoming a fact of life. *Springfield News-Leader*, B3.
87. Rudolph, B. (1987, May 18). Thou shalt not smoke. *Time, 129*, 58–59.
88. Prewitt, E. (1986, September 15). The drive to kick smoking at work. *Fortune, 114*, 42–43.
89. Joyce, A. (1998, November 15). Smoke-free workplaces spreading like wildfire: Sharp rise in number of employers that ban cigarettes is good news for advocates, and a burden for those who enjoy a puff. *Washington Post*, H4.
90. Litvan, L. M. (1994). A smoke-free workplace? *Nation's Business, 82*, 65.
91. New York Public Health Law, Section 1399 (Consol. 1993).
92. Grensing, P. L. (1999). Smokin' in the workplace. *HRMagazine, 44*, 58–66.
93. *HR Focus*. (2001). Latest data on how smoking affects workplace productivity, *78*, 9.
94. Ibid.
95. Drake, J. (1994). The dynamics of the rights and privileges of smoking and non-smoking employees. Unpublished master's thesis, Southwest Missouri State University.
96. Davenport, F. C. (1989, May-June). The legal aspects of a smoking policy in the workplace. *Industrial Management, 31*(3), 25–32.
97. Worsnop, R. L. (1995). Repetitive stress injuries. *CQ Researcher, 5*, 539–556.
98. Hartelt, C. (1999). Ouch! *Credit Union Management, 22*, 18–21.
99. Voiss, D. V. (1995). What a little brain work can do: Rethinking workers' compensation problems. *Compensation & Benefits Review, 27*, 30–32.
100. Worsnop, R. L. (1995). Repetitive stress injuries. *CQ Researcher, 5*, 539–556.
101. Hartelt, C. (1999). Ouch! *Credit Union Management, 22*, 18–21.
102. Whalen, J. (2001). Silence is golden. *Warehousing Management, 8*, 29.
103. Safety Director's Report. (2002). Hearing protection strategies for any safety department budget. May Newsletter of the Institute of Management and Administration.
104. Whalen, J. (2001). Silence is golden. *Warehousing Management, 8*, 29.
105. Wermiel, S. (1991, March 21). Justices bar "fetal protection" policies. *Wall Street Journal*, B1, B5.
106. Trost, C. (1990, October 8). Business and women anxiously watch suit on "fetal protection." *Wall Street Journal*, 1.
107. Altman, L. E. (1988, June 5). Pregnant women's use of VDT's is scrutinized. *New York Times*, 22; and Meier, B. (1987, February 5). Companies wrestle with threats to reproductive health. *Wall Street Journal*, 23.
108. Jacob, S. L. (1988, November 22). Small business slowly wakes to OSHA hazard rule. *Wall Street Journal*, B2; and Myers, D. W. (1992). *Human resource management* (2nd ed.), 717. Chicago: Commerce Clearing House.
109. Pirtle, L. (1999). Chemical safety goes online. *Occupational Hazards, 61*, 59–60.
110. *Employee Benefit Plan Review*. (1999). Genetic testing: "Minefield" of potential legal liability for employers, *53*, 41–42.
111. Bureau of National Affairs (1991, November 18). Value of genetic testing said minimal for gauging workplace risks. *BNA's Employee Relations Weekly*, 1235; Draper, E. (1991). *Risky business: Genetic testing and exclusionary practices in the hazardous workplace*. Cambridge, England: Cambridge University Press; Olian, J. D. (1984). Genetic screening for employment purposes. *Personnel Psychology, 37*, 423–438; and Schuler, R. S., and Huber, V. L. (1993). *Personnel and human resource management* (5th ed.), 251. Minneapolis: West.
112. *Medicine & Health*. (2002). Government, railroad settle genetic testing case, *56*, 5.
113. *Occupational Hazards*. (2001). Railroad halts genetic testing, *63*, 34.
114. Cullen, L. (1999). Safety committees: A smart business decision. *Occupational Hazards, 61*, 99–104.
115. Ibid.
116. Johnson, A. T. (1995). Employee assistance programs and employee downsizing. *Employee Assistance Quarterly, 10*, 13–27.
117. Fisher, C. C., Schoenfeldt, L. F., and Shaw, J. B. (1996). *Human resource management* (3rd ed.). Boston: Houghton Mifflin; and Schuler, R. S., and Huber, V. L. (1993). *Personnel and human resource management* (5th ed.), 667–669. Minneapolis: West.
118. Thompson, R. (1990). Fighting the high cost of workers' comp. *Nation's Business, 78*(3), 28.
119. Moulson, G. (1999, September 6). The longest workday: It's in the U.S. *Arizona Republic*, A1.
120. Maslach, C., and Jackson, S. E. (1981). The measurement of experienced burnout. *Journal of Occupational Behavior, 2*, 99–113.
121. Cordes, C. L., and Dougherty, T. W. (1993). A review and integration of research on job burnout. *Academy of Management Review, 18*, 621–656.
122. Kahill, S. (1988). Symptoms of professional burnout: A review of the empirical evidence. *Canadian Psychology, 29*, 284–297.
123. Cordes, C. L., and Dougherty, T. W. (1993). A review and integration of research on job burnout. *Academy of Management Review, 18*, 621–656.
124. Jackson, S. E., and Maslach, C. (1982). After effects of job-related stress: Families as victims. *Journal of Occupational Behavior, 3*, 63–77.
125. Nighswonger, T. (2002). Depression: The unseen safety risk. *Occupational Hazards, 64*, 38(3).
126. Ibid.
127. Kirrane, D. (1990, January). EAPs: Dawning of a new age. *HRMagazine*, 34.

128. Bahls, J. E. (1999). Handle with care. *HRMagazine, 44*, 60–66.
129. Helmer, D. C., Dunn, L. M., Eaton, K., Macedonio, C., and Lubritz, L. (1995). Implementing corporate wellness programs. *AAOHN Journal, 43*, 558–563.
130. Brotherton, P. (1998). Paybacks are healthy. *HRMagazine, 43*, F2–F6.
131. Ibid.
132. Bourne, R. W. (1999). Square deal. *Executive Excellence, 16*, 11–12.

Chapter 17

1. Wellins, R., and Rioux, S. (2001, February). Solving the global HR puzzle. *Workspan, 44*(2), 1–14.
2. Kahn, J. (1999, June 7). Wal-Mart goes shopping in Europe. *Fortune*, 105–110; Guyon, J. (1999, February 15). Europe's new capitalists. *Fortune*, 104–110; Oyama, D. I. (1999, June 1). World watch. *Wall Street Journal*, A-16; and Mandel, M. J. (2002, March 6). How companies can marry well. *BusinessWeek*, 28.
3. Wild, J. J., Wild, K. L., and Han, J. C. Y. (2003). *International business*. Upper Saddle River, NJ: Prentice Hall.
4. Collins, S. M. (1998). *Export, imports, and the American worker*. Washington, DC: Brooking Institute.
5. World Trade Organization, International Trade Trends and Statistics, 2003; and Dickson, M. (1998, October 16). All those expectations aside, many firms are finding the Internet invaluable in pursuing international trade. *Los Angeles Times*, 10; Millman, J. (2002a, January 23). Mexico attracts U.S. aerospace industry. *Wall Street Journal*, A-1; and Millman, J. (2002b, February 13). Visions of sugar plums south of the border. *Wall Street Journal*, A-15.
6. Mandel, M. J. (2002, March 6). How companies can marry well. *BusinessWeek*, 28; Cooper, J. C., and Madigan, K. C. (1999, October 4). So much for that safety valve. *BusinessWeek*, 31–32; and Smith, G., and Malkin, E. (1998, December 21). Mexican makeover. *BusinessWeek*, 50–52.
7. Millman, J. (2002a, January 23). Mexico attracts U.S. aerospace industry. *Wall Street Journal*, A-1; Millman, J. (2002b, February 13). Visions of sugar plums south of the border. *Wall Street Journal*, A-15; Khanna, T., Gulati, R., and Nohria, N. (1998). The dynamics of learning alliances: Competition, cooperation, and relative scope. *Strategic Management Journal, 19*, 193–210; and Vitzhum, C. (1999, July 20). Global strategy powers Endesa's power moves. *Wall Street Journal Europe*, 4–6.
8. Mandel, M. J. (2002, March 6). How companies can marry well. *BusinessWeek*, 28.
9. Prasso, S. (2002, April 22). To get an MNA is glorious. *BusinessWeek*, 14; Oster, P. (1993, November 1). The fast track leads overseas. *BusinessWeek*, 64–68; and Murray, S. (1999, June 22). Europe's MBA programs attract Americans—Demand for global view gets students across Atlantic. *Wall Street Journal Europe*, 4–5.
10. *ACA News*. (1996, June). International, 32.
11. Heher, E. C. (2001). Helping expatriates get ready for a healthy assignment. *Innovations in International HR, 27*(3), 5–10; Schindler, K. P. (2001). Strategies for compensating married assignees. *Innovations in International HR, 27*(3), 11–20; and Withercup, M. B. (2001). Location evaluation reports: An overview of troubled spots. *Innovations in International HR, 27*(3), 1–12.
12. Beck, E. (1995, May 1). Foreign companies in Hungary concerned about wage increase. *Wall Street Journal*, B13(1).
13. *Fortune*. (2002). American's most admired companies. www.fortune.com.
14. Prasso, S. (2002, April 22). To get an MNA is glorious. *BusinessWeek*, 14.
15. *Newsline*. (2002, January 17). Skillsoft breaking into China market. Available at www.nashuatelegraph.com.
16. Perkins, S. J. (2002). The people dimension: A European perspective on globalization. *Workspan, 43*(10), 15–25.
17. Carrico-Kahn, J., and Brahy, S. (2000). A meeting of minds: The importance of culture awareness in cross-border virtual teams. *Innovations in International HR, 26*(3), 1–11.
18. Siekman, P. (1999, January 11). Bosch wants to build more of your car. *Fortune*, 143–147.
19. De La Torre, J., Doz, Y., and Devinney T. (2000). *Managing the global corporation*. New York: Irwin/McGraw-Hill; Sheridan, W. R., and Hansen, P. T. (1996, Spring). Linking international business and expatriate compensation strategies. *ACA Journal*, 66–78; Greenburg, L. (2001). Long distance care giving: Providing for elderly parents while living abroad. *Expatriate Observer, 24*(2), 9–11; and Rogers, M. J. (2001). Effective tax rates: How much do you really pay? *Expatriate Observer, 24*(2), 1–3.
20. Cafaro, D. (2001, February). A passport to productivity in the new global economy. *Workspan, 44*(2), 1–8.
21. Boyacigiller, N. (1990). Role of expatriates in the management of interdependence, complexity, and risk of MNNs. *Journal of International Business Studies*, 3rd quarter, 357–378; and Hill, C. W. (2003). *International business*. Chicago: Irwin.
22. Dunn, E. (1991, January). Global outlook; Whirlpool Corporation. *Personnel Journal*, 52.
23. *Fortune*. (2002). American's most admired companies. www.fortune.com.
24. Chang, L. (1999, May 7). A dream project turned nightmare. *Wall Street Journal Europe*, 10; McGeary, J. (1999, September 27). Russia's ruble shakedown. *BusinessWeek*, 54–57; and Polak International Consultants. (2002). International HR practices lay behind workplace trends. www.polak.net.
25. Palich, L. E., and Gómez-Mejía, L. R. (1999). A theory of global strategy and firm efficiencies: Considering the effects of cultural diversity. *Journal of Management, 25*(4), 587–606.
26. Mendenhall, M., and Oddou, G. (1985). Dimensions of expatriate acculturation. *Academy of Management Review, 10*(1), 39–47; Tanski, A. (2001). Going home again: A checklist for easy repatriation. *Expatriate Observer, 24*(1), 1–3; and Kittell, A. J. (2001). Globally mobile children. *Expatriate Observer, 24*(1), 5–9.
27. *Newsline*. (2002, February 14). Expatriate activity expands but at a slower rate than expected. Available at www.windhamworld.com.
28. Allen, J. L. (1999). *Student atlas of economic growth*, 50. Guilford, CT: Dushkin/McGraw-Hill.
29. Runzheimer Report on Relocation. (2002). U.S. companies impact high level employees. Available at www.runzheimer.com.
30. *Fortune*. (1995, October 16). From the front, 225.
31. Wilson, M. L. (1999, July 16). She got the last laugh when colleagues bet she would fail in Japan. *Wall Street Journal*, B-1; and Frisbie, P. E. (2000). Expatriate policy and practices: Heading into the 21st century. *International HR, 26*(2), 1–11.
32. Gómez-Mejía, L. R., and Balkin, D. B. (1987). The determinants of managerial satisfaction with the expatriation and repatriation process. *Journal of Management Development, 6*, 7–18; Cigna Corporation. (2002). Employers missing ROI when expatriating employees. Available at www.cigna.com; and Osland, J. (2002). What do expatriates want from HR departments? *HR.com*. Available at www.hr.com.
33. Follett, L. N. (2000). Why ORC links certain locations. *Innovations in International HR, 26*(4), 1–11.
34. Rowland, M. (1993, December 5). Thriving in a foreign environment. *New York Times*, Sect. 3, 17; and Ossorio, S. (2002). Misconceptions about women in international area limit numbers. Available at www.catlystwomen.org.

35. *Newsline*. (2002, February 14). Expatriate activity expands but at a slower rate than expected. Available at www.windhamworld.com.
36. Swaak, R. (1995, November–December). Expatriate failures: Too many, too much cost, too little planning. *Compensation and Benefits Review*, 47–75.
37. De La Torre, J., Doz, Y., and Devinney T. (2000). *Managing the global corporation*. New York: Irwin/McGraw-Hill; Wild, J. J., Wild, K. L., and Han, J. C. Y. (2003). *International business*. Upper Saddle River, NJ: Prentice Hall; and Austin, J. W. (2001). Miscommunication: The most challenging issue for expatriate managers. *Expatriate Observer, 24*(2), 1–10.
38. *Fortune*, 1995.
39. Personal interview conducted by authors.
40. Swaak, R. (1995, November–December). Expatriate failures: Too many, too much cost, too little planning. *Compensation and Benefits Review*, 47–75.
41. Dallas, S. (1995, May 15). Working overseas: Rule no. 1: Don't diss the locals. *BusinessWeek*, 8.
42. Tung, R. (1988). *The new expatriates: Managing human resources abroad*. Cambridge, MA: Bellinger.
43. Swaak, R. (1995, November–December). Expatriate failures: Too many, too much cost, too little planning. *Compensation and Benefits Review*, 47–75.
44. Pascoe, R. (1992, March 2). Employers ignore expatriate wives at their own peril. *Wall Street Journal*, A10; and Osland, J. (2002). What do expatriates want from HR departments? *HR.com*. Available at www.hr.com.
45. Oster, P. (1993, November 1). The fast track leads overseas. *BusinessWeek*, 64–68; and *Newsline*. (2002, February 14). Expatriate activity expands but at a slower rate than expected. Available at www.windhamworld.com.
46. Oddou, G. R., and Mendenhall, M. E. (1991, January–February). Succession planning for the 21st century: How well are we grooming our future business leaders? *Business Horizons*, 26–35; and Fulkerson, J. R. (2002). Growing global executives. In R. Silzer (Ed.), *The 21st Century Executive*, 300–335.
47. Cigna Corporation. (2002). Employers missing ROI when expatriating employees. Available at www.cigna.com.
48. Grant, L. (1997, April 14). That overseas job could derail your career. *Fortune*, 166; and Fulkerson, J. R. (2002). Growing global executives. In R. Silzer (Ed.), *The 21st Century Executive*, 300–335.
49. Oddou, G. R., and Mendenhall, M. E. (1991, January–February). Succession planning for the 21st century: How well are we grooming our future business leaders? *Business Horizons*, 26–35.
50. Gómez-Mejía, L. R., and Balkin, D. B. (1987). The determinants of managerial satisfaction with the expatriation and repatriation process. *Journal of Management Development, 6*, 7–18; and Tanski, A. (2001). Going home again: A checklist for easy repatriation. *Expatriate Observer, 24*(1), 1–3.
51. Handel, J. (2001). Out of sight, out of mind—opinions differ on assignment success. *Workspan, 44*(6), 1–8.
52. Oddou, G. R., and Mendenhall, M. E. (1991, January–February). Succession planning for the 21st century: How well are we grooming our future business leaders? *Business Horizons*, 29.
53. Gómez-Mejía, L. R., and Balkin, D. B. (1987). The determinants of managerial satisfaction with the expatriation and repatriation process. *Journal of Management Development, 6*, 7–18; and Wellins, R., and Rioux, S. (2001, February). Solving the global HR puzzle. *Workspan, 44*(2), 1–14.
54. Personal interview conducted by authors.
55. Gómez-Mejía, L. R., and Balkin, D. B. (1987). The determinants of managerial satisfaction with the expatriation and repatriation process. *Journal of Management Development, 6*, 7–18; and Wellins, R., and Rioux, S. (2001, February). Solving the global HR puzzle. *Workspan, 44*(2), 1–14.
56. Personal interview conducted by authors.
57. *Newsline*. (2002, February 14). Expatriate activity expands but at a slower rate than expected. Available at www.windhamworld.com.
58. Oster, P. (1993, November 1). The fast track leads overseas. *BusinessWeek*, 64–68.
59. Hixon, A. L. (1986, March). Why corporations make haphazard overseas staffing decisions. *Personnel Administrator*, 91–94.
60. Bird, A., and Makuda, M. (1989). Expatriates in their own home: A new twist in the human resource management strategies of Japanese MNCs. *Human Resource Management, 28*(4), 437–453.
61. Murray, S. (1999, June 22). Europe's MBA programs attract Americans—Demand for global view gets students across Atlantic. *Wall Street Journal Europe*, 4–5; Oster, P. (1993, November 1). The fast track leads overseas. *BusinessWeek*, 64–68; Byrne, J. (1999, October 4). The search of the young and gifted. *BusinessWeek*, 108–119; Kripalani, M., Engardio, P., and Nathans, L. (1998, December 7). Whiz kids. *BusinessWeek*, 116–120.
62. Shellenbarger, S. (1991, September 6). Spouses must pass test before global transfers. *Wall Street Journal*, B1.
63. Barrett, A. (1995, April 17). It is a small business world. *BusinessWeek*, 96–97.
64. Hill, C. W. (2003). *International business*. Chicago: Irwin; Wild, J. J., Wild, K. L., and Han, J. C. Y. (2003). *International business*. Upper Saddle River, NJ: Prentice Hall; and De La Torre, J., Doz, Y., and Devinney T. (2000). *Managing the global corporation*. New York: Irwin/McGraw-Hill.
65. Osland, J. (2002). What do expatriates want from HR departments? *HR.com*. Available at www.hr.com.
66. Lublin, J. S. (1992, August 4). Companies use cross-cultural training to help their employees adjust abroad. *Wall Street Journal*, B1, B3.
67. Hagerty, B. (1993a, June 14). Trainers help expatriate employees build bridges to different cultures. *Wall Street Journal*, B1, B3.
68. *Newsline*. (2002, February 14). Expatriate activity expands but at a slower rate than expected. Available at www.windhamworld.com.
69. Grant, L. (1997, April 14). That overseas job could derail your career. *Fortune*, 166; and Handel, J. (2001). Out of sight, out of mind—opinions differ on assignment success. *Workspan, 44*(6), 1–8.
70. Runzheimer Report on Relocation. (2000). Circle of chaos often develops during family relocation process. Available at www.runzheimer.com.
71. Cafaro, D. (2001, February). A passport to productivity in the new global economy. *Workspan, 44*(2), 1–8.
72. Ibid.
73. Fuchsberg, G. (1992, January 9). As costs of overseas assignments climb, firms select expatriates more carefully. *Wall Street Journal*, B1.
74. Lublin, J. S. (1993, March 12). Jobs in Eastern Europe demand more goodies. *Wall Street Journal*, B1.
75. Barrionuevo, A., and Herrick, T. (2002, February 7). Wages of terror: For oil companies defense abroad is the order of the day. *Wall Street Journal*, A-1.
76. Herod, R. (2001). The cardinal sins of expatriate policies. *International HR, 27*(4), 1–5.
77. Bennett, A. (1993, April 21). What's an expatriate? *Wall Street Journal*, R5.
78. Ibid.
79. Cook, M. (Ed.). (1993). *The human resources yearbook, 1993–1994 edition*, 3.14–3.16.
80. Survey Sources for U.S. and International Pay and Benefits Survey. (2002, February 14). Available at resource.worldatwork.org.
81. Osland, J. (2002). What do expatriates want from HR departments? *HR.com*. Available at www.hr.com.

82. Polak International Consultants. (2002). International HR practices lay behind workplace trends. www.polak.net.
83. Sassalos, S. (2002, February 1). Basic pay laws outside the U.S. resourcepro.worldatwork.org.
84. Ossorio, S. (2002). Misconceptions about women in international area limit numbers. Available at www.catlystwomen.org.
85. *BusinessWeek*. (1990, May 14). The stateless corporation, 98–105.
86. Chang, L. (1999, May 7). A dream project turned nightmare. *Wall Street Journal Europe*, 10.
87. Burg, J. H., Siscovick, I., and Brock, D. (2000). Aligning performance and reward practices in multinational subsidiaries. *Worldatwork Journal, 9*(3), 10–20; and Bhagat, R. S., Kedia, B. L. Harveston, P. D., and Triandis, H. C. (2002). Cultural variations in the cross-border transfer of organizational knowledge. *Academy of Management Review, 27*(2), 204–222.
88. Hofstede, G. (1980). *Culture's consequences*. Beverly Hills, CA: Sage; and *Academy of Management Executive*. (1993). Cultural constraints in management theories, 7, 81–94.
89. Jaeger, A. (1986). Organization development and national culture: Where's the fit? *Academy of Management Review, 11*(1), 178–190; and Bhagat, R. S., Kedia, B. L. Harveston, P. D., and Triandis, H. C. (2002). Cultural variations in the cross-border transfer of organizational knowledge. *Academy of Management Review, 27*(2), 204–222.
90. Palich, L. E., and Gómez-Mejía, L. R. (1999). A theory of global strategy and firm efficiencies: Considering the effects of cultural diversity. *Journal of Management, 25*(4), 587–606.
91. Hofstede, G. (1980). *Culture's consequences*. Beverly Hills, CA: Sage; and *Academy of Management Executive*. (1993). Cultural constraints in management theories, 7, 58.
92. Jaeger, A. (1986). Organization development and national culture: Where's the fit? *Academy of Management Review, 11*(1), 180.
93. Player, M. A. (1991). *Federal law of employment discrimination*. St. Paul, MN: West Publishing; Twomey, D. P. (1994). *Equal employment opportunity* (3rd ed.). Cincinnati, OH: South-Western; and Ledvinka, J., and Scarpello, V. G. (1991). *Federal regulation of personnel and human resource management* (2nd ed.). Boston: PWS-Kent.
94. Player, M. A. (1991). *Federal law of employment discrimination*, 28. St. Paul, MN: West Publishing.
95. Gómez-Mejía, L. R., and Welbourne, T. (1991). Compensation strategies in a global context. *Human Resource Planning, 14*(1), 38; and Woodruff, D., and Widman, M. (1996, June 17). East Germany is still a mess—$580 billion later. *BusinessWeek*, 58.
96. Gómez-Mejía, L. R., and Welbourne, T. (1991). Compensation strategies in a global context. *Human Resource Planning, 14*(1), 38.
97. Bureau of National Affairs. (2001). Economic report calls for regulation of core labor standards. Available at www.bna.com.
98. Landsburg, S. (2002, February 11). Highway robbery. *Wall Street Journal*, B-2; and Tran, K. T. L., and Johnson, K. (1999, September 30). Nike barred by Spanish court from use of name on sports apparel sold there. *Wall Street Journal*, B-24.
99. Wellins, R., and Rioux, S. (2001, February). Solving the global HR puzzle. *Workspan, 44*(2), 1–14.
100. Ibid.
101. Barrett, A. (1995, April 17). It is a small business world. *BusinessWeek*, 96–97.
102. Cavusgil, T. S. (1984). Organizational characteristics associated with export activity. *Journal of Management Studies, 24*(1), 3–21; and Hill, C. W. (2003). *International business*. Chicago: Irwin.
103. Gómez-Mejía, L. R. (1988). The role of human resources strategy in export performance: A longitudinal study. *Strategic Management Journal, 9*(3), 493–505.
104. Echikson, W. (1999, October 11). Designers climb onto the virtual catwalk. *BusinessWeek*, 164–165.
105. Ibid.
106. Prasso, S. (2002, April 22). To get an MNA is glorious. *BusinessWeek*, 10.
107. Day, P. (2002, February 12). Some shipping concerns skirt worker-rights rules. *Wall Street Journal*, A-14.
108. Ibid.
109. Byrne, J. (1999, October 4). The search of the young and gifted. *BusinessWeek*, 108–119; and Millman, J. (2002b, February 13). Visions of sugar plums south of the border. *Wall Street Journal*, A-15.

Concise Dictionary of HR Terminology

Ability Competence in performing a job. (19)

Absolute judgment An appraisal format that asks supervisors to make judgments about an employee's performance based solely on performance standards. (226)

Adverse impact Discrimination that occurs when the equal application of an employment standard has an unequal effect on one or more protected classes. Also called *disparate impact*. (91)

Affirmative action A strategy intended to achieve fair employment by urging employers to hire certain groups of people who were discriminated against in the past. (89)

Age Discrimination in Employment Act (1967) The law prohibiting discrimination against people who are 40 or older. (100)

Americans with Disabilities Act (1990) The law forbidding employment discrimination against people with disabilities who are able to perform the essential functions of the job with or without reasonable accommodation. (100)

Appeals procedure A procedure that allows employees to voice their reactions to management practices and to challenge management decisions. (451)

Apprenticeship A program in which promising prospective employees are groomed before they are actually hired on a permanent basis. (144)

Arbitration The last step in a grievance procedure. The decision of the arbitrator, who is a neutral individual selected from outside the firm, is binding on both parties. (524)

Assessment center A set of simulated tasks or exercises that candidates (usually for managerial positions) are asked to perform. (182)

Attrition An employment policy designed to reduce the company's workforce by not refilling job vacancies that are created by turnover. (207)

Award A one-time reward usually given in the form of a tangible prize. (372)

Base compensation The fixed pay an employee receives on a regular basis, either in the form of a salary or as an hourly wage. (329)

Behavioral appraisal instrument An appraisal tool that asks managers to assess a worker's behaviors. (229)

Benchmark or key jobs A job that is similar or comparable in content across firms. (348)

Benefits mix The complete package of benefits that a company offers its employees. (404)

Bona fide occupational qualification (BFOQ) A characteristic that must be present in all employees for a particular job. (93)

Bonus program or lump-sum payment A financial incentive that is given on a one-time basis and does not raise the employee's base pay permanently. (371)

Boundaryless organizational structure An organizational structure that enables an organization to form relationships with customers, suppliers, and/or competitors, either to pool organizational resources for mutual benefit or to encourage cooperation in an uncertain environment. (52)

Brain drain The loss of high-talent key personnel to competitors or start-up ventures. (20)

Brainstorming A creativity training technique in which participants are given the opportunity to generate ideas openly, without fear of judgment. (280)

Bureaucratic organizational structure A pyramid-shaped organizational structure that consists of hierarchies with many levels of management. (49)

Burnout A stress syndrome characterized by emotional exhaustion, depersonalization, and reduced personal accomplishment. (562)

Business process reengineering (BPR) A fundamental rethinking and radical redesign of business processes to achieve dramatic improvements in cost, quality, service, and speed. (53)

Business unionism A form of unionism that focuses on improving workers' economic well-being. (505)

Business unit strategy The formulation and implementation of strategies by a firm that is relatively autonomous, even if it is part of a larger corporation. (28)

Career development An ongoing and formalized effort that focuses on developing enriched and more capable workers. (297)

Career path A chart showing the possible directions and career opportunities available in an organization; it presents the steps in a possible career and a plausible timetable for accomplishing them. (311)

Career resource center A collection of career development materials such as workbooks, tapes, and texts. (312)

Codetermination The representation of workers on a corporation's board of directors; used in Germany. (509)

Coinsurance Payments made to cover health-care expenses that are split between the employer's insurance company and the insured employee. (401)

Collective bargaining A system in which unions and management negotiate with each other to develop the work rules under which union members will work for a stipulated period of time. (505)

Comparability In performance ratings, the degree to which the performance ratings given by various supervisors in an organization are similar. (233)

Comparable worth A pay concept or doctrine that calls for comparable pay for jobs that require comparable skills, effort, and responsibility and have comparable working conditions, even if the job content is different. (355)

Compensable factors Work-related criteria that an organization considers most important in assessing the relative value of different jobs. (345)

Compensatory damages Fines awarded to a plaintiff to compensate for the financial or psychological harm the plaintiff has suffered. (99)

Conciliation An attempt to reach a negotiated settlement between the employer and an employee or applicant in an EEO case. (104)

Consolidated Omnibus Budget Reconciliation Act of 1985 (COBRA) Legislation that gives employees the right to continue their health insurance coverage for 18 to 36 months after their employment has terminated. (412)

Contingent workers Workers hired to deal with temporary increases in an organization's workload or to do work that is not part of its core set of capabilities. (71)

Contract A legally binding promise between two or more competent parties. (467)

Contractual rights A right based on the law of contracts. (467)

Contributions Payments made for benefits coverage. Contributions for a specific benefit may come from the employer, employee, or both. (401)

Copayment A small payment made by the employee for each office visit to a physician under a health plan. The health plan pays for additional medical expenses that exceed the copayment at no cost to the employee. (401)

Core time Time when all employees are expected to be at work. Part of a flexible work hours arrangement. (75)

Core workers An organization's full-time employees. (71)

Corporate strategy The mix of businesses a corporation decides to hold and the flow of resources among those businesses. (28)

Cost-of-living adjustment (COLA) Pay raises, usually made across the board, that are tied to such inflation indicators as the consumer price index. (528)

Cross-functional training Training employees to perform operations in areas other than their assigned job. (278)

Cultural determinism The idea that one can successfully infer an individual's motivations, interests, values, and behavioral traits based on that individual's group memberships. (148)

Cultural relativity concept of management The management concept holding that management practices should be molded to the different sets of values, beliefs, attitudes, and behaviors exhibited by a diverse workforce. (128)

Culture shock The inability to adjust to a different cultural environment. (582)

Cumulative trauma disorder (CTD) An occupational injury that occurs from repetitive physical movements, such as assembly-line work or data entry. (557)

Decentralization Transferring responsibility and decision-making authority from a central office to people and locations closer to the situation that demands attention. (11)

Deductible An annual out-of-pocket expenditure that an insurance policyholder must make before the insurance plan makes any reimbursements. (401)

Defined benefit plan or pension A retirement plan that promises to pay a fixed dollar amount of retirement income based on a formula that takes into account the average of the employee's last three to five years' earnings prior to retirement. (417)

Defined contribution plan A retirement plan in which the employer promises to contribute a specific amount of funds into the plan for each participant. The final value of each participant's retirement income depends on the success of the plan's investments. (418)

Development An effort to provide employees with the abilities the organization will need in the future. (260)

Dimension An aspect of performance that determines effective job performance. (224)

Discrimination The making of distinctions. In HR context, the making of distinctions among people. (91)

Disparate treatment Discrimination that occurs when individuals are treated differently because of their membership in a protected class. (91)

Distinctive competencies The characteristics that give a firm a competitive edge. (36)

Distributive bargaining Bargaining that focuses on convincing the other party that the cost of disagreeing with the proposed terms would be very high. (519)

Diversity Human characteristics that make people different from one another. (121)

Diversity audit A review of the effectiveness of an organization's diversity management program. (145)

Diversity training programs Programs that provide diversity awareness training and educate employees on specific cultural and sex differences and how to respond to these in the workplace. (140)

Downsizing A company strategy to reduce the scale (size) and scope of its business in order to improve the company's financial performance. (202)

Downsizing A reduction in a company's workforce to improve its bottom line. (11)

Downward communication Communication that allows managers to implement their decisions and to influence employees lower in the organizational hierarchy. (439)

Dual-career couple A couple whose members both have occupational responsibilities and career issues at stake. (303)

Due process Equal and fair application of a policy or law. (468)

Economic strike A strike that takes place when an agreement is not reached during collective bargaining. (523)

Egalitarian pay system A pay plan in which most employees are part of the same compensation system. (335)

Electronic mail (e-mail) A form of electronic communication that allows employees to communicate with each other via electronic messages sent through personal computer terminals linked by a network. (445)

Elitist pay system A pay plan in which different compensation systems are established for employees or groups at different organizational levels. (335)

Employee assistance program (EAP) A company-sponsored program that helps employees cope with personal problems that are interfering with their job performance. (452)

Employee attitude survey A formal anonymous survey designed to measure employee likes and dislikes of various aspects of their jobs. (450)

Employee benefits or indirect compensation Group membership rewards that provide security for employees and their family members. (399)

Employee feedback program A program designed to improve employee communications by giving employees a voice in policy formulation and making sure that they receive due process on any complaints they lodge against managers. (449)

Employee recognition program A program that rewards employees for their ideas and contributions. (455)

Employee relations policy A policy designed to communicate management's thinking and practices concerning employee-related matters and prevent problems in the workplace from becoming serious. (436)

Employee relations representative A member of the HR department who ensures that company policies are followed and consults with both supervisors and employees on specific employee relations problems. (436)

Employee Retirement Income Security Act (ERISA) A federal law established in 1974 to protect employees' retirement benefits from mismanagement. (417)

Employee separation The termination of an employee's membership in an organization. (195)

Employee stock ownership plan (ESOP) A corporatewide pay-for-performance plan that rewards employees with company stocks, either as an outright grant or at a favorable price that may be below market value. (380)

Employment at will A common-law rule used by employers to assert their right to end an employment relationship with an employee at any time for any cause. (471)

Employment contract A contract that spells out explicitly the terms of the employment relationship for both employee and employer. (467)

Empowerment Providing workers with the skills and authority to make decisions that would traditionally be made by managers. (19)

Enterprise union A labor union that represents workers in only one large company rather than in a particular industry; used in Japan. (509)

Environmental challenges Forces external to a firm that affect the firm's performance but are beyond the control of management. (3)

Equal Employment Opportunity Commission (EEOC) The federal agency responsible for enforcing EEO laws. (104)

Equal Pay Act (1963) The law that requires the same pay for men and women who do the same job in the same organization. (90)

Ergonomics The science of adapting working conditions to employee safety and comfort needs. (557)

Essential functions Job duties that each person in a certain position must do or must be able to do to be an effective employee. (101)

Ethnocentric approach An approach to managing international operations in which top management and other key positions are filled by people from the home country. (578)

Executive order A presidential directive that has the force of law. In HR context, a policy with which all federal agencies and organizations doing business with the federal government must comply. (99)

Exempt employee An employee who is not covered by the provisions of the Fair Labor Standards Act. Most professional, administrative, executive, and outside sales jobs fall into this category. (354)

Exit interview An employee's final interview following separation. The purpose of the interview is to find out the reasons why the employee is leaving (if the separation is voluntary) or to provide counseling and/or assistance in finding a new job. (197)

Expatriate A citizen of one country living and working in another country. (577)

Expectancy theory A theory of behavior holding that people tend to do those things that are rewarded. (372)

Extended leave A benefit that allows an employee to take a long-term leave from the office, while retaining benefits and the guarantee of a comparable job on return. (143)

External equity The perceived fairness in pay relative to what other employers are paying for the same type of labor. (329)

Fair employment The goal of EEO legislation and regulation: a situation in which employment decisions are not affected by illegal discrimination. (89)

Fair Labor Standards Act (FLSA) The fundamental compensation law in the United States. Requires employers to record earnings and hours worked by all covered employees and to report this information to the U.S. Department of Labor. Defines two categories of employees: exemp and nonexempt. (353)

Family and Medical Leave Act of 1993 (FMLA) A federal law that requires employers to provide up to 12 weeks' unpaid leave to eligible employees for the birth or adoption of a child; to care for a sick parent, child, or spouse; or to take care of health problems that interfere with job performance. (409)

Flat organizational structure An organizational structure that has only a few levels of management and emphasizes decentralization. (50)

Flexible or cafeteria benefits program A benefits program that allows employees to select the benefits they need most from a menu of choices. (401)

Flexible work hours A work arrangement that gives employees control over the starting and ending times of their daily work schedules. (75)

Flextime Time during which employees can choose not to be at work. Part of a flexible work hours arrangement. (75)

Four-fifths rule An EEOC provision for establishing a prima facie case that an HR practice is discriminatory and has an adverse impact. A practice has an adverse impact if the hiring rate of a protected class is less than four-fifths the hiring rate of a majority group. (93)

Frame-of-reference (FOR) training A type of training that presents supervisors with fictitious examples of worker performance (either in writing or on videotape), asks the supervisors to evaluate the workers in the examples, and then tells them what their ratings should have been. (233)

Gainsharing A plantwide pay-for-performance plan in which a portion of the company's cost savings is returned to workers, usually in the form of a lump-sum bonus. (378)

Genetic testing A form of biological testing that identifies employees who are genetically susceptible to specific occupational substances. (559)

Geocentric approach An approach to managing international operations in which nationality is downplayed and the firm actively searches on a worldwide or regional basis for the best people to fill key positions. (578)

Glass ceiling The intangible barrier in an organization that prevents female and minority employees from rising to positions above a certain level. (129)

Grievance procedure A systematic step-by-step process designed to settle disputes regarding the interpretation of a labor contract. (524)

Health Insurance Portability and Accountability Act (HIPAA) A federal law that protects an employee's ability to transfer between health insurance plans without a gap in coverage due to a preexisting condition. (412)

Health maintenance organization (HMO) A health-care plan that provides comprehensive medical services for employees and their families at a flat annual fee. (414)

Hiring freeze An employment policy designed to reduce the company's workforce by not hiring any new employees into the company. (207)

Hostile work environment sexual harassment Harassment that occurs when the behavior of anyone in the work setting is sexual in nature and is perceived by an employee as offensive and undesirable. (95)

Hot-stove rule A model of disciplinary action: Discipline should be immediate, provide ample warning, and be consistently applied to all. (485)

HR audit A periodic review of the effectiveness with which a company uses its human resources. Frequently includes an evaluation of the HR department itself. (39)

Human resource information system (HRIS) A system used to collect, record, store, analyze, and retrieve data concerning an organization's human resources. (76)

Human resource planning (HRP) The process an organization uses to ensure that it has the right amount and the right kind of people to deliver a particular level of output or services in the future. (156)

Human resource strategy A firm's deliberate use of human resources to help it gain or maintain an edge against its competitors in the marketplace. The grand plan or general approach an organization adopts to ensure that it effectively uses its people to accomplish its mission. (2)

Human resources (HR) People who work in an organization. Also called *personnel*. (2)

Human resource tactic A particular HR policy or program that helps to advance a firm's strategic goal. (2)

Individual challenges Human resource issues that address the decisions most pertinent to individual employees. (17)

Individual equity The perceived fairness of individual pay decisions. (350)

Individuals with disabilities Persons who have a physical or mental impairment that substantially affects one or more major life activities. (100)

Informal communications Also called "the grapevine." Information exchanges without a planned agenda that occur informally among employees. (449)

Information dissemination The process of making information available to decision makers, wherever they are located. (440)

Insubordination Either refusal to obey a direct order from a supervisor or verbal abuse of a supervisor. (489)

Integrative bargaining Bargaining that focuses on convincing the other party that the benefits of agreeing with the proposed terms would be very high. (520)

Internal equity The perceived fairness of the pay structure within a firm. (329)

Internal Revenue Code (IRC) The code of tax laws that affects how much of their earnings employees can keep and how benefits are treated for tax purposes. (356)

Involuntary separation A separation that occurs when an employer decides to terminate its relationship with an employee due to (1) economic necessity or (2) a poor fit between the employee and the organization. (199)

Job aids External sources of information, such as pamphlets and reference guides, that workers can access quickly when they need help in making a decision or performing a specific task. (277)

Job analysis The systematic process of collecting information used to make decisions about jobs. Job analysis identifies the tasks, duties, and responsibilities of a particular job. (61)

Job banding The practice of replacing narrowly defined job descriptions with broader categories (bands) of related jobs. (351)

Job description A written document that identifies, describes, and defines a job in terms of its duties, responsibilities, working conditions, and specifications. (68)

Job design The process of organizing work into the tasks required to perform a specific job. (59)

Job enlargement The process of expanding a job's duties. (60)

Job enrichment The process of putting specialized tasks back together so that one person is responsible for producing a whole product or an entire service. (60)

Job evaluation The process of evaluating the relative value or contribution of different jobs to an organization. (342)

Job hierarchy A listing of jobs in order of their importance to the organization, from highest to lowest. (346)

Job rotation The process of rotating workers among different narrowly defined tasks without disrupting the flow of work. (60)

Job sharing A work arrangement in which two or more employees divide a job's responsibilities, hours, and benefits among themselves. (73)

Job specifications The worker characteristics needed to perform a job successfully. (71)

Job-posting system A system in which an organization announces job openings to all employees on a bulletin board, in a company newsletter, or through a phone recording or computer system. (311)

Joint venture In international business, a foreign branch owned partly by the home office and partly by an entity in the host country (a company, a consortium of firms, an individual, or the government). (578)

Knowledge worker A worker who transforms information into a product or service. (440)

Knowledge, skills, and abilities (KSAs) The knowledge, skills, and abilities needed to perform a job successfully. (63)

Knowledge-based pay or skill-based pay A pay system in which employees are paid on the basis of the jobs they can do or talents they have that can be successfully applied to a variety of tasks and situations. (334)

Labor contract A union contract that spells out the conditions of employment and work rules that affect employees in the unit represented by the union. (505)

Labor demand How many workers the organization will need in the future. (156)

Labor relations specialist Someone, often a member of the HR department, who is knowledgeable about labor relations and can represent management's interests to a union. (502)

Labor relations strategy A company's overall plan for dealing with labor unions. (510)

Labor supply The availability of workers with the required skills to meet the firm's labor demand. (155)

Landrum-Griffin Act (1959) A law designed to protect union members and their participation in union affairs. (504)

Line employee An employee involved directly in producing the company's good(s) or delivering the service(s). (3)

Literacy The mastery of basic skills (reading, writing, arithmetic, and their uses in problem solving). (281)

Lockout Occurs when an employer shuts down its operations before or during a labor dispute. (523)

Management by objectives (MBO) A goal-directed approach to performance appraisal in which workers and their supervisors set goals together for the upcoming evaluation period. (230)

Management by walking around (MBWA) A technique in which managers walk around and talk to employees informally to monitor informal communications, listen to employee grievances and suggestions, and build rapport and morale. (449)

Management of diversity The set of activities involved in integrating nontraditional employees (women and minorities) into the workforce and using their diversity to the firm's competitive advantage. (123)

Management rights Management's rights to run the business and retain any profits that result. (471)

Manager A person who is in charge of others and is responsible for the timely and correct execution of actions that promote his or her unit's success. (3)

Medicare A part of the Social Security program that provides health insurance coverage for people aged 65 and over. (406)

Mentoring A developmentally oriented relationship between senior and junior colleagues or peers that involves advising, role modeling, sharing contacts, and giving general support. (314)

Merit pay An increase in base pay, normally given once a year. (370)

Motivation A person's desire to do the best possible job or to exert the maximum effort to perform assigned tasks. (19)

Motivation That which energizes, directs, and sustains human behavior. In HRM, a person's desire to do the best possible job or to exert the maximum effort to perform assigned tasks. (57)

Multimedia technology A form of electronic communication that integrates voice, video, and text, all of which can be encoded digitally and transported on fiber optic networks. (447)

Multinational corporation (MNC) A firm with assembly and production facilities in several countries and regions of the world. (577)

National Labor Relations Board (NLRB) The independent federal agency created by the Wagner Act to administer U.S. labor law. (502)

Negligent hiring Hiring an employee with a history of violent or illegal behavior without conducting background checks or taking proper precautions. (553)

Nepotism The practice of favoring relatives over others in the workplace. (440)

Nonexempt employee An employee who is covered by the provisions of the Fair Labor Standards Act. (354)

Occupational Safety and Health Act of 1970 (OSHA) A federal law that requires employers to provide a safe and healthy work environment, comply with specific occupational safety and health standards, and keep records of occupational injuries and illnesses. (541)

Office of Federal Contract Compliance Programs (OFCCP) The federal agency responsible for monitoring and enforcing the laws and executive orders that apply to the federal government and its contractors. (105)

Old boys' network An informal social and business network of high-level male executives that typically excludes women and minorities. Access to the old boys' network is often an important factor in career advancement. (137)

Organizational challenges Concerns or problems internal to a firm; often a by-product of environmental forces. (10)

Organizational culture The basic assumptions and beliefs shared by members of an organization. These beliefs operate unconsciously and define in a basic taken-for-granted fashion an organization's view of itself and its environment. (13)

Organizational structure The formal or informal relationships between people in an organization. (48)

Orientation The process of informing new employees about what is expected of them in the job and helping them cope with the stresses of transition. (286)

Outcome appraisal instrument An appraisal tool that asks managers to assess the results achieved by workers. (230)

Outplacement assistance A program in which companies help their departing employees find jobs more rapidly by providing them with training in job-search skills. (197)

Outsourcing Subcontracting work to an outside company that specializes in and is more efficient at doing that kind of work. (16)

Pay grades Groups of jobs that are paid within the same pay range. (341)

Pay incentive A program designed to reward employees for good performance. (329)

Pay policy A firm's decision to pay above, below, or at the market rate for its jobs. (349)

Pay-for-performance system or incentive system A system that rewards employees on the assumptions that (1) individual employees and work teams differ in how much they contribute to the firm; (2) the firm's overall performance depends to a large degree on the performance of individuals and groups within the firm; and (3) to attract, retain, and motivate high performers and to be fair to all employees, the firm needs to reward employees on the basis of their relative performance. (364)

Peer review A performance appraisal system in which workers at the same level in the organization rate one another. (243)

Peer trainers High-performing workers who double as internal on-the-job trainers. (278)

Pension Benefit Guaranty Corporation (PBGC) The government agency that provides plan termination insurance to employers with defined benefit retirement programs. (417)

Performance appraisal The identification, measurement, and management of human performance in organizations. (222)

Perquisites ("perks") Noncash incentives given to a firm's executives. (387)

Personnel file A file maintained for each employee, containing the documentation of critical HR-related information, such as performance appraisals, salary history, disciplinary actions, and career milestones. (470)

Piece-rate system A compensation system in which employees are paid per unit produced. (368)

Polycentric approach An approach to managing international operations in which subsidiaries are managed and staffed by personnel from the host country. (578)

Portable benefits Employee benefits, usually retirement funds, that stay with the employee as he or she moves from one company to another. (417)

Positive discipline A discipline procedure that encourages employees to monitor their own behaviors and assume responsibility for their actions. (483)

Preexisting condition A medical condition treated while an employee was covered under a former employer's health plan and requires treatment under a new employer's different health plan. (412)

Preferred provider organization (PPO) A health-care plan in which an employer or insurance company establishes a network of doctors and hospitals to provide a broad set of medical services for a flat fee per participant. In return for the lower fee, the doctors and hospitals who join the PPO network expect to receive a larger volume of patients. (414)

Premium The money paid to an insurance company for coverage. (413)

Privacy Act of 1974 Guarantees the privacy of personnel files for employees of the U.S. federal government. (470)

Problem-solving team A team consisting of volunteers from a unit or department who meet one or two hours per week to discuss quality improvement, cost reduction, or improvement in the work environment. (55)

Productivity A measure of how much value individual employees add to the goods or services that the organization produces. (18)

Profit sharing A corporatewide pay-for-performance plan that uses a formula to allocate a portion of declared profits to employees. Typically, profit distributions under a profit-sharing plan are used to fund employees' retirement plans. (380)

Progressive discipline A series of management interventions that gives employees opportunities to correct undesirable behaviors before being discharged. (481)

Promotability forecast A career development activity in which managers make decisions regarding the advancement potential of subordinates. (307)

Protected class A group of people who suffered discrimination in the past and who are given special protection by the judicial system. (91)

Punitive damages Fines awarded to a plaintiff in order to punish the defendant. (99)

Quality of work life A measure of how safe and satisfied employees feel with their jobs. (19)

Quid pro quo sexual harassment Harassment that occurs when sexual activity is required in return for getting or keeping a job or job-related benefit. (95)

Quotas Employer adjustments of hiring decisions to ensure that a certain number of people from a certain protected class are hired. (99)

Railway Labor Act A law designed to regulate labor relations in the transportation industry. (504)

Rater error An error in performance appraisals that reflects consistent biases on the part of the rater. (232)

Realistic job preview (RJP) Realistic information about the demands of the job, the organization's expectations of the job holder, and the work environment. (286)

Reasonable accommodation An action taken to accommodate the known disabilities of applicants or employees so that disabled persons enjoy equal employment opportunity. (101)

Recruitment The process of generating a pool of qualified candidates for a particular job; the first step in the hiring process. (159)

Relative judgment An appraisal format that asks supervisors to compare an employee's performance to the performance of other employees doing the same job. (225)

Reliability Consistency of measurement, usually across time but also across judges. (172)

Reverse discrimination Discrimination against a nonprotected-class member resulting from attempts to recruit and hire members of protected classes. (106)

Right The ability to engage in conduct that is protected by law or social sanction, free from interference by another party. (467)

Right-to-work law A state law that makes it illegal within that state for a union to include a union shop clause in its contract. (503)

Rightsizing The process of reorganizing a company's employees to improve their efficiency. (203)

Selection The process of making a "hire" or "no hire" decision regarding each applicant for a job; the second step in the hiring process. (160)

Self-managed team (SMT) A team responsible for producing an entire product, a component, or an ongoing service. (54)

Self-review A performance appraisal system in which workers rate themselves. (243)

Senior mentoring program A support program in which senior managers identify promising women and minority employees and play an important role in nurturing their career progress. (144)

Seniority The length of time a person works for an employer. (526)

Simulation A device or situation that replicates job demands at an off-the-job site. (272)

Situational factors or system factors A wide array of organizational characteristics that can positively or negatively influence performance. (242)

Skills inventory A company-maintained record of employees' abilities, skills, knowledge, and education. (311)

Social Security A government program that provides income for retirees, the disabled, and survivors of deceased workers, and health care for the aged through the Medicare program. (405)

Socialization The process of orienting new employees to the organization or the unit in which they will be working; the third step in the hiring process. (160)

Special-purpose team A team or task force consisting of workers who span functional or organizational boundaries and whose purpose is to examine complex issues. (55)

Staff employee An employee who supports line employees. (3)

Statutory right A right protected by specific laws. (467)

Strategic HR choices The options available to a firm in designing its human resources system. (24)

Strategic human resource (HR) planning The process of formulating HR strategies and establishing programs or tactics to implement them. (20)

Structured interview Job interview based on a thorough job analysis, applying job-related questions with predetermined answers consistently across all interviews for a job. (178)

Subordinate review A performance appraisal system in which workers review their supervisors. (243)

Succession planning A career development activity that focuses on preparing people to fill executive positions. (307)

Supplemental unemployment benefits (SUB) Benefits given by a company to laid-off employees over and above state unemployment benefits. (409)

Support group A group established by an employer to provide a nurturing climate for employees who would otherwise feel isolated or alienated. (141)

Taft-Hartley Act (1947) A federal law designed to limit some of the power acquired by unions under the Wagner Act by adjusting the regulation of labor–management relations to ensure a level playing field for both parties. (503)

Team A small number of people with complementary skills who work toward common goals for which they hold themselves mutually accountable. (54)

Telecommuting A work arrangement that allows employees to work in their homes full-time, maintaining their connection to the office through phone, fax, and computer. (75)

Teleconferencing The use of audio and video equipment to allow people to participate in meetings even when they are a great distance away from the conference location or one another. (443)

360° feedback The combination of peer, subordinate, and self-review. (244)

Title VII Section of the Civil Rights Act of 1964 that applies to employment decisions; mandates that employment decisions not be based on race, color, religion, sex, or national origin. (90)

Total compensation The package of quantifiable rewards an employee receives for his or her labors. Includes three components: base compensation, pay incentives, and indirect compensation/benefits. (329)

Total quality management (TQM) An organizationwide approach to improving the quality of all the processes that lead to a final product or service. (10)

Training The process of providing employees with specific skills or helping them correct deficiencies in their performance. (260)

Trait appraisal instrument An appraisal tool that asks a supervisor to make judgments about worker characteristics that tend to be consistent and enduring. (228)

Transnational corporation A firm with operations in many countries and highly decentralized operations. The firm owes little allegiance to its country of origin and has weak ties to any given country. (577)

Turnover rate The rate of employee separations in an organization. (195)

Unemployment insurance A program established by the Social Security Act of 1935 to provide temporary income for people during periods of involuntary unemployment. (408)

Union An organization that represents employees' interests to management on such issues as wages, work hours, and working conditions. (500)

Union acceptance strategy A labor relations strategy in which management chooses to view the union as its employees' legitimate representative and accepts collective bargaining as an appropriate mechanism for establishing workplace rules. (511)

Union avoidance strategy A labor relations strategy in which management tries to prevent its employees from joining a union, either by removing the incentive to unionize or by using hardball tactics. (513)

Union shop clause A union arrangement that requires new employees to join the union 30 to 60 days after their date of hire. (503)

Union steward An advocate dedicated to representing an employee's case to management in a grievance procedure. (524)

Union substitution/proactive human resource management A union avoidance strategy in which management becomes so responsive to employees' needs that it removes the incentives for unionization. (513)

Union suppression A union avoidance strategy in which management uses hardball tactics to prevent a union from organizing its workers or to get rid of a union. (513)

Universal concept of management The management concept holding that all management practices should be standardized. (128)

Upward communication Communication that allows employees at lower levels to communicate their ideas and feelings to higher-level decision makers. (439)

Validity The extent to which the technique measures the intended knowledge, skill, or ability. In the selection context, it is the extent to which scores on a test or interview correspond to actual job performance. (172)

Vesting A guarantee that accrued retirement benefits will be given to retirement plan participants when they retire or leave the employer. (417)

Virtual reality (VR) The use of a number of technologies to replicate the entire real-life working environment in real time. (273)

Virtual team A team that relies on interactive technology to work together when separated by physical distance. (56)

Voice mail A form of electronic communication that allows the sender to leave a detailed voice message for a receiver. (444)

Voluntary separation A separation that occurs when an employee decides, for personal or professional reasons, to end the relationship with the employer. (198)

Wagner Act/National Labor Relations Act (1935) A federal law designed to protect employees' rights to form and join unions and to engage in such activities as strikes, picketing, and collective bargaining. (502)

Wellness program A company-sponsored program that focuses on preventing health problems in employees. (564)

Whistleblowing Employee disclosure of an employer's illegal, immoral, or illegitimate practices to persons or organizations that may be able to take corrective action. (478)

Wholly owned subsidiary In international business, a foreign branch owned fully by the home office. (578))

Wildcat strike A spontaneous work stoppage that happens under a valid contract and is usually not supported by union leadership. (523)

Work flow The way work is organized to meet the organization's production or service goals. (48)

Work flow analysis The process of examining how work creates or adds value to the ongoing processes in a business. (52)

Work rules Any terms or conditions of employment, including pay, work breaks and lunch periods, vacation, work assignments, and grievance procedures. (505)

Worker Adjustment and Retraining Notification Act (WARN) of 1988 A federal law requiring U.S. employers with 100 or more employees to give 60 days' advance notice to employees who will be laid off as a result of a plant closing or a mass separation of 50 or more workers. (209)

Workers' compensation A legally required benefit that provides medical care, income continuation, and rehabilitation expenses for people who sustain job-related injuries or sickness. Also provides income to the survivors of an employee whose death is job related. (406)

Works councils A committee composed of both worker representatives and managers who have responsibility for governing the workplace; used in Germany. (509)

Wrongful discharge Termination of an employee for reasons that are either illegal or inappropriate. (468)

Photo Credits

Chapter 1
3 Goodman Architects, Kansas City, Missouri/Robert Wright Photography; 13 Gregory Foster Photography

Chapter 2
51 Michael Newman/PhotoEdit;
62 Copyright © 1999 Saturn Corp./All Rights Reserved; 76 John W. Clark

Chapter 3
87 Wyatt McSpadden Photography; 94 Bob Daemmrich Photography, Inc.; 97 Todd Buchanan; 103 Alan Levenson.com

Chapter 4
124 Jean Christian Bourcart/Getty Images, Inc - Liaison; 127 Brian Coats Photography; 132 Index Stock Imagery, Inc.; 146 Rex Rystedt/Rex Rystedt Photography

Chapter 5
168 Chris Usher Photography; 179 Walter Bibikow/Index Stock Imagery, Inc.

Chapter 6
202 Wyatt McSpadden Photography; 205 Roger Mastroianni

Chapter 7
235 Mark Richards; 244 Matthew Borkoski/Stock Boston

Chapter 8
264 Men's Wearhouse; 269 Bruce Hands/Stock Boston; 273 Russ Carmack/AP/Wide World Photos; 274 IMMERSION MEDICAL

Chapter 9
302 Jeff Christensen/AFP/CORBIS; 308 Jay Dickman

Chapter 10
354 Andy Sacks/Getty Images Inc. - Stone Allstock; Gregory Foster Photography

Chapter 11
364 Kingston Technology Company/Co-Founders John Tu & David Sun; 375 James Schnepf/Getty Images, Inc - Liaison

Chapter 12
401 J. Nordell/The Image Works; 410 Jeff Greenberg/The Image Works

Chapter 13
444 Gabe Palmer/Mug Shots/Corbis/Stock Market; 448 Will & Deni McIntyre; 457 Michael Cogliantry/Getty Images Inc. - Image Bank

Chapter 14
468 Jim Cummins/Getty Images, Inc. - Taxi; 477 Roger Allyn/SuperStock, Inc.; 490 Bob Daemmrich/The Image Works

Chapter 15
500 Ron Haviv/Corbis/SABA Press Photos, Inc.; 510 Stuart Isset/Corbis/Sygma; 527 Greg Rannells/New York Times Pictures

Chapter 16
553 Chris Kasson/AP/Wide World Photos; 564 The Dallas Morning News/Kim Ritzenthaller of Michael Kay

Chapter 17
576 Gregory Foster Photography; 586 Pablo Bartholomew/Getty Images, Inc - Liaison

Company, Name, and Product Index

Subject Index

S